ROTHMANS RUGBY UNION YEARBOOK 1989-90

Editor: Stephen Jones
Statistician: John Griffiths

ROTHMANS
Queen Anne Press

A *Queen Anne Press* BOOK

© **Rothmans Publications Ltd 1989**

First published in Great Britain in 1989 by

Queen Anne Press, a division of
Macdonald & Co (Publishers) Ltd
66-73 Shoe Lane
London
EC4P 4AP

A member of Maxwell Pergamon Publishing Corporation plc

Cover photographs: The 1989 International Championship. Andy Robinson powers over the line for England's second try in their 11-0 defeat of France at Twickenham (front). Scotland's Gary Armstrong is tackled by Nigel Davies in the match against Wales at Murrayfield, which Scotland won 23-7 (back).

All photographs by Colin Elsey/Andrew Cowie of Colorsport

British Library Cataloguing in Publication Data

Rothmans rugby union yearbook—1989-90
  1. Rugby football—Periodicals
796.33'3'05   GV944.8

ISBN 0-356-17862-5

Photoset by Cylinder Typesetting Limited, London

Printed and bound in Great Britain by BPCC Hazell Books Ltd, Aylesbury, Bucks

CONTENTS

Foreword   4
Editorial Preface   5
Review of the Season   6

FEATURES
Rothmans Team of the Decade   10
The Romantic Realist
    by Bob Donahue   14
The Unexpected and the Unthinkable
    by Michael Austin   17

Tours 1988-89   21
The International Championship 1989   46
Results of International Matches   59
Other International Matches 1988-89   88
FIRA Championship 1988-89   91
Other International Tournaments   94
B Internationals 1988-89   96
National Trial Matches 1988-89   98
Cathay Pacific–Hong Kong Bank Sevens
  1988   99
The 1988-89 Season in England   101
English International Players   105
English International Records   115
Toshiba Divisional Championship
  1988   117
Pilkington Cup 1988-89   120
Courage Leagues   125
Toshiba County Championship
  1988-89   140
The Barbarians 1988-89   147
The Varsity Match 1988   151
Varsity Match Results   154
Oxford and Cambridge Blues   155
UAU Championship 1988-89   163
British Polytechnics Cup 1988-89   166
Hospitals' Challenge Cup 1989   167
Inter-Services Tournament 1988-89   168

Middlesex Sevens 1989   171
Schools Rugby 1988-89   174
Colts and Youth Rugby 1988-89   182
The 1988-89 Season in Scotland   186
Scottish International Players   193
Scottish International Records   202
The 1988-89 Season in Ireland   204
Irish International Players   208
Irish International Records   217
The 1988-89 Season in Wales   219
Schweppes/WRU Challenge Cup
  1988-89   223
Welsh International Players   226
Welsh International Records   234
The 1988-89 Season in France   236
French International Players   239
French International Records   247
The 1988 Season in South Africa   250
South African International Players   252
South African International Records   257
The 1988 Season in New Zealand   259
New Zealand International Players   261
New Zealand International Records   267
The 1988 Season in Australia   269
Australian International Players   271
Australian International Records   278
Leading Cap-Winners   280
International Referees 1988-89   286
International Referees   287
International Match Appearances for
  British Isles Teams   292
Results of British Isles Matches   295
British Isles Records   297
World International Records   299
International Tours   302
Top 50 Scorers 1988-89   349
Clubs Section   351
Fixtures 1989-90   385

3

FOREWORD
FROM ROTHMANS PUBLICATIONS LTD

We are proud to welcome this, the 18th edition of *Rothmans Rugby Union Yearbook*, and in this issue there is some evidence, at last, that the enormous gap in standards between the Northern and Southern Hemispheres may be closing.

Our panel of international contributors has once again provided the kind of comprehensive coverage that has made the Yearbook the most esteemed and reliable record of the game worldwide and as ever we hope that all followers of rugby, not to mention players and media, will find it indispensable.

Above all, this edition chronicles the growing pains of the sport. Can rugby fend off the lure of professionalism and solve the problem of the ever-increasing demands on players? Happily, at this stage, the answer on both counts is a resounding 'yes'.

EDITORIAL PREFACE

This is the 18th annual Yearbook and once again the scope has been considerably expanded to keep pace with the massive increase in major rugby all over the world. The chief feature this year, however, is the Rothmans Team of the Decade, a selection by an illustrious panel of the World XV of the 1980s. The result of the deliberations of panel chairman Gareth Edwards and his colleagues can be found on page 10.

Among the special articles are portraits of two of the greatest entertainers the game has ever seen. There is a profile of Serge Blanco, the brilliant Frenchman, by Bob Donahue, a regular contributor to the Yearbook whose pieces for the *International Herald Tribune* in Paris are among the most perceptive rugby writing you will find. In addition Michael Austin pays tribute to Les Cusworth, the Leicester and England fly-half who is still making magic in the first-class game.

Perhaps the most important innovation is the Other International Tournaments section. This will report on the major tournaments around the globe and this year contains details of the South Pacific Championship and the Asian tournament. Full coverage of the Scottish inter-district championship and of the Irish inter-provincial tournament appear and in the clubs section stage one of a complete revision has already been completed.

In the record sections the pace of improvement and refinement continues and we can justly claim that this Yearbook contains the most complete and painstakingly compiled statistics you will find anywhere. John Griffiths, our statistician, has extended the refereeing records this year so that for the first time they now extend back to the 1870s.

Finally, we would like to thank our contributors most sincerely for their wonderful service and the many readers who have written in with suggestions.

Please Note: **the statistical sections for the Yearbook, as usual, go up to 30 April 1989. Full coverage of the British Lions tour of Australia will appear in the next issue.**

STEPHEN JONES *Editor*

A VIVID PROGRAMME – BUT WAS IT ART?

REVIEW OF THE 1988-89 SEASON

The Editor

If the strength of the army is determined by the state of the generals then rugby was on the retreat in 1988-89. All over the world the foot soldiers – the players – continued rugby's boom and, in Britain especially, more and more people turned up to watch. Nearly half a million people watched rugby at Twickenham alone during the season. It was another packed, vivid period topped by the British Lions tour of Australia, just outside the scope of this year's Yearbook. The season threw the well-meaning fumblings of the International Rugby Board into the sharpest relief. This body, whether it likes it or not, is the governing body of rugby. If it does not like it then it should disband.

The standard of leadership it gave in so many areas during the year, its ponderous, even static nature and its secretive refusal to share its debate and decisions with the 107 or so rugby-playing countries amounted to dereliction of duty. Furthermore, at least two of the eight member unions now feel cut off from the Board, and that the Board is now almost renegade and lacks accountability. Those nations not in full membership, those scores of countries desperate for a lead, some encouragement, remain utterly bewildered. The tiny Hawaiian Union, for example, which has no formal connection with the Board, was reprimanded because under its auspices Stu Wilson, the former All Black who is now professionalised, took part in a gentle fun match.

The pompous high-handedness of this, from a Board which has failed lamentably to stop far more serious infringements among its members, angered American rugby and rightly so. It recalled the victimisation of the Fijians after a rebel tour of South Africa organised wholly by South Africa. Is it any wonder that so many of the smaller unions are flocking to FIRA, the European rugby federation which is more in tune, more dynamic. More power to FIRA.

What of other issues – the preparations for the World Cup, the South African question, the installation of referees into the law-making procedure? You name it, the Board failed. The public relations profile of the Board is miniscule and, occasionally, downright insulting to the media (the messengers for the millions of rugby players and followers in the world). Even then, all news was bad news. The tide of opinion against contact with South Africa receded somewhat with the growing realisation that the commendable efforts of sportsmen in the country goes far beyond those of their politicians in liberalising their own sphere. Cries of tokenism cannot always be tolerated because, especially in the sports of cricket and rugby, the authorities have made genuine efforts to take sport into the townships.

Men like Dr Danie Craven have proven their convictions and courage time and again, often in the face of ferocious and distasteful opposition from the right wing in their own country. Of course, any resumption of full international sports schedules is still impossible and would in any case do untold harm to the image of rugby, which needs to co-operate with governments and local authorities. As we went to press the South African Board were trying to assemble a powerful team from the world of rugby to go to South Africa to celebrate the SARB Centenary. Some of those rugby people against large scale resumption of contact would not begrudge the South Africans some sport.

In one sense all these arguments passed over the heads of the world's rugby players. The massive increase in pressure matches, in high-octane rugby and the huge commitment now needed left no time for contemplation. And yet again, every single major union in the world let down its players in some respect in rugby's central bargain – that if the players are to be asked for more and more, week by week, and are still not to be paid, then they must be treated wonderfully well. Could every union put its hand on its heart and say it did everything possible within the by-laws for its leading players and their families? And the players gave us so much. New Zealand, beyond doubt, remained at the top of the tree – belligerent and committed on the field and booming and calculating off it. They beat Australia in Australia and, if they never quite avoided the fall into arrogance and gracelessness, and that is the trap for all outstanding teams, then so be it.

In fact, the Australians provided a fascinating contrast. On their tour to England and Scotland in the pre-Christmas period they began slowly, but eventually showed all the grit and rough edge of their sporting

Rugby's family is seen thriving at the Hong Kong Sevens as Bahrain and Tunisia fight out a tie. The Sevens is comfortably the best and the biggest forum for world rugby.

David Campese, whose unique brilliance illuminated rugby in several parts of the world, gets the ball away in the tackle playing for Australia against England B.

history. Yet the party was probably the most charming and well-liked ever to tour here. While the All Blacks carried on in their joyless, unsmiling, earnest way the Australians toured with a smile and with the realisation that a tour is not just a head-down succession of matches.

Elsewhere the second rank nations enjoyed themselves. Argentina, now in the post-Hugo Porta era, took a Test from the French on their home soil; America, tantalisingly close to a breakthrough but not close enough as yet, won the annual Can-Am match, breaking Canada's grip on the series. Significantly, the Eagles boldly marched on Moscow for a four-team tournament involving the Romanians and the Soviet and Soviet B teams. Unfortunately, the Eagles lost their first-ever meeting with the Soviet team in a rough match, but regular contact between the teams of the superpowers can do wonders for them and for rugby. Typically, the IRB missed the chance to galvanise the 1991 World Cup by excluding the Soviet Union on what amounted to technical grounds. There will be a return match in America in 1990.

Apart from Campese, who signed off the Australian tour with a wondrous individual try against the Barbarians and was cheered all the way back to halfway by the Cardiff crowd, the biggest names of the home season were probably Jonathan Davies and Dusty Hare. Davies, seriously underrated by his own countrymen until the last, moved to Widnes Rugby League club. He balanced his dear wish to remain in

West Wales and in the Welsh and British Lions team with the promise of long-term financial security for his family. This prompted a mini-exodus of Welsh players to League. Suddenly, without Davies, both Wales and the Lions were bereft of a genius.

Hare was another matter. As his world goal-kicking record steadily climbed above 7,000 points and his general play and essential goodness as a team-mate and as a man continued to shine, there was a brief illusion that Hare would go on forever. Instead he retired, and Leicester paid him the compliment of fighting tooth and nail and reaching the Pilkington final: they could not, quite, give Dusty the Cup – that went to Bath on a packed and emotional Twickenham afternoon. But, we hope, this retirement will be merely the first of several for Hare!

Bath, proud, aggressive and thoroughly deserving, took the Cup to add to the Courage Division 1 title, which they won at a gallop. It was a tribute to the sheer togetherness of the team and also to Stuart Barnes, the captain, and Jack Rowell, the coach. The only failure was the stadium – the Recreation Ground is too small to take Bath's legions.

In Wales there was a similar story of club excellence: Neath may be an attractive side only to their own supporters but they had a storming season, beating Llanelli in the Schweppes-WRU final before a packed house at Cardiff and continuing their efforts to build an image of New Zealand down at the Gnoll. It was a shame that Mark Jones, their outstanding No 8, should have soured the final by stamping on the head of Delaney of Llanelli and a shame that Les Peard, the referee, did not send him off completely – Jones received ten minutes in the sin-bin. Elsewhere in Wales the season was a shambles. Predictably and wrongly, the win over England banished the sad memories – the defeat by a desperately limited Romanian team in Cardiff; three convincing defeats in the Championship and bickering throughout the game where there should have been unity in order to rebuild in the aftermath of the New Zealand disasters.

In the International Championship there was biting tension and some juddering contests. There was a disturbing lack of subtlety and charm as well. France growled their way to the title; England failed because in the end they were only bludgeoners and even the bludgeon failed in the graveyard of Cardiff. Ireland made no real progress in the long search for talent in depth and Scotland, despite providing the Lions captain and unearthing two promising new half-backs in Craig Chalmers and Gary Armstrong, were not exactly an irresistible force. None of this stopped the massive interest in the tournament, however. Tickets were as scarce as sweeping movements. This was a shame because at the start of the season England, inspired by a London Division win over Australia engineered by the coaching of Richard Best, ran Australia off their feet in the Test at Twickenham. It was another compelling season but whether in the corridors of power or on the pitch, the pace was not always lung-bursting.

ROTHMANS TEAM OF THE DECADE

FULL-BACK
Serge Blanco (France)
RIGHT WING
John Kirwan (New Zealand)
CENTRE
Philippe Sella (France)
CENTRE
Danie Gerber (South Africa)
LEFT WING
David Campese (Australia)
FLY-HALF
Hugo Porta (Argentina)
SCRUM-HALF
Dave Loveridge (New Zealand)
PROP
Robert Paparemborde (France)

HOOKER
Colin Deans (Scotland)
PROP
Graham Price (Wales)
LOCK
Steve Cutler (Australia)
LOCK
Andy Haden (New Zealand)
FLANKER
Michael Jones (New Zealand)
NO 8
Morne Du Plessis (South Africa)
FLANKER
Graham Mourie (New Zealand)
(*captain*)

REPLACEMENTS:
Backs: Stu Wilson (New Zealand), Terry Holmes (Wales), Jonathan Davies (Wales);
Forwards: Sean Fitzpatrick (New Zealand), Alan Whetton (New Zealand), Steve McDowell (New Zealand).
Coach: Brian Lochore (New Zealand)

To mark the end of a decade of international rugby, we present the Rothmans Team of the Decade, chosen by our panel from the cream of the world's leading players. The criterion for selection was that the players must have played international rugby in the 1980s. Each player considered must have played for his country between 1 January 1980 and 29 March 1989 and each was judged on his ability at his peak. The best individual in each position was selected – team blend was the lesser consideration.

The panel consisted of: Gareth Edwards (chairman); Jean-Pierre Rives, the former French captain who provided the Gallic expertise; Ian Robertson, the former Scottish fly-half who provided the commentator's view; David Kirk, who led New Zealand to their World Cup triumph. Their choice is bound to lead to arguments. What is beyond question is that the result of their deliberations, the Rothmans Team of the Decade, would take an awful lot of beating! To complete the exercise, the panel chose six replacements and their ideal coach – who turned out, not surprisingly, to be a New Zealander – Brian Lochore.

To students of front row play, the choice of two tight-head props might be puzzling. However, after animated discussion, the panel decided that since Graham Price and Robert Paparemborde, tight-heads both, are certainly among the greatest forwards the world has seen they should both be chosen, with Paparemborde moving across to the loose-head, where he had considerable experience.

The pack looks unbeatable. Surely, no other combination could have fielded a line-out capability such as that provided by Steve Cutler, Andy Haden and Morne Du Plessis, while the pace of the back row, containing team captain Graham Mourie and the brilliant All Black Michael Jones, not to mention Colin Deans, the Scottish hooker, would ensure possession in the loose.

The backs are a mouth-watering combination. Imagine Serge Blanco coming up from full-back to set up wings of the calibre of David Campese and John Kirwan; or the options presented by the midfield of Hugo Porta, Philippe Sella and Danie Gerber. 'The team has such a depth of talent,' says panel chairman Gareth Edwards, 'that apart from being unbeatable, they would dictate any kind of game against any opposition and at whatever pace they chose. The selection process was straightforward for a couple of positions but for the majority there were at least half a dozen players under consideration. Beyond any question, we have left out so many favourites. It was a shame that we could fit only 15 into the team.'

In the replacements, the recent power of the New Zealand pack is aptly reflected – all three replacement forwards are current All Blacks; while the Welsh half-back factory has a look-in with Jonathan Davies and Terry Holmes. Surprisingly, perhaps, not a single Englishman makes our squad. Better luck in 1999.

To mark his selection in the Rothmans Team of the Decade, each player will receive a special commemorative Rothmans cap.

Serge Blanco (France)

John Kirwan (New Zealand)

Danie Gerber (South Africa)

Philippe Sella (France)

David Campese (Australia)

Hugo Porta (Argentina)

Dave Loveridge (New Zealand)

Morne Du Plessis (South Africa)

Graham Mourie (New Zealand)

Michael Jones (New Zealand)

Steve Cutler (Australia)

Andy Haden (New Zealand)

Graham Price (Wales)

Colin Deans (Scotland)

Robert Paparemborde (France)

Brian Lochore (coach) (New Zealand)

BLANCO: THE ROMANTIC REALIST

Serge Blanco towered over European rugby during the 1980s. *Bob Donahue* **of the** *International Herald Tribune* **examines the foundation stones of Blanco's greatness.**

'I'm a realist'. Surprising words from rugby's paramount wizard? No, not if you watch him closely. Never does Serge Blanco's gaze lack a veil of caution: reined anger, controlled irony, deliberate clowning, even cautious jubilation. Pierre Villepreux got it right: 'What I like best about Blanco is the mastered audacity'. He possesses an uncommon gift harnessed by common sense – in a word, realism.

I was in Dublin when France completed their second Grand Slam. That night, no one gave a thought to what was happening back in northern France, where a youth international took place between France and England, under lights at Lille. The French full-back was an unknown 18-year-old from Biarritz. The bigger English boys were favoured but the news from Dublin inspired the French youngsters, the pack performed and they won 33-6. Blanco – a six-footer standing five inches taller than his centres, Didier Codorniou and Pierre Berbizier – scored one of the team's seven tries and made at least two of the others. He kicked a conversion and a penalty goal.

The following Monday *Midi Olympique* compared the boy to Villepreux. 'His deftness under the high ball was remarkable. His defence let no one past. His line-kicking kept the pack going forward. But it was mostly in attack that he excited the crowd. His participation in attack was decisive. His strength, pace and acceleration were precious assets for France and caused the young Englishmen serious problems.'

Three weeks later in the Netherlands, France won the FIRA youth tournament with a 32-3 defeat of Italy. Don Rutherford, in his 1983 book *International Rugby*, said: 'Although Welsh supporters would rightly point to the exploits of their legendary full-back J P R Williams, who for years was their best attacking threequarter, not even he matched the running lines of a French youth full-back I saw taking part in a FIRA competition in Hilversum . . . Blanco took a running line that allowed him to penetrate the opposing defence and either continue on inwards where he usually found forward support, or sweep outwards to link up with his right wing. His execution was devastating!'

In 1989, talking to John Mason of the *Daily Telegraph*, Dusty Hare added this neat flourish: 'The defence think they have him well in their sights and suddenly they haven't – a little shuffle, a stretch of the legs and he's away'. But the essential framework had already been sketched years before by Rutherford and *Midi Olympique's* Jacques Galy. It was simply a matter for Blanco of colouring in the fulfilment: a great career.

He played in the autumn of 1977 against England Under-23 and the

Blanco shadowed by Sean Lineen, the Scottish centre, when France and Scotland met in Paris

touring New Zealanders; then in 1978-79 against Wales B, Spain and England Under-23 again. He toured with the senior squad to Fiji and New Zealand in 1979, but did not win a cap; Jean-Michel Aguirre held his position in the Tests. Blanco appeared against Tunisia, Yugoslavia, Italy, Canada, Wales B and the USSR (twice) before finally winning his first senior caps, aged 22, at full-back against South Africa and Romania in November 1980. Blanco's next 12 caps were earned on the wing, Serge Gabernet or Marc Sallefranque being preferred at full-back. Patiently, he imposed his gift at No 15 from the start of the 1982-83 season. And there he remains, despite periodic threats (genuine or feigned) by Fouroux to move him to the wing, to centre or even to fly-half. Fouroux wants the kicks to find touch, which demands sustained concentration. Blanco, whose concentration occasionally short-circuits, never complains in public. His relationship with Fouroux includes heart-to-heart encounters behind closed doors but is good nonetheless.

With 68 caps in March 1989, he was poised to surpass – and quite possibly by a long way – the world record of 69 caps shared by Mike Gibson of Ireland and Roland Bertranne of France. His string of 34 consecutive Championship appearances is already longer than Gibson's 33 and Bertranne's 32. He has never been dropped, though he has missed six matches through illness or minor injury. Otherwise he has played in every cap-earning French international since November 1980. That means playing in an average of eight Tests a year, with never a serious injury. 'He is still improving', Villepreux thinks. 'His reading of the game, and therefore his anticipation in attack and defence, is

15

better than ever'.

To the boring but mandatory question, Blanco responds that no, he hasn't decided when to retire. Or he says: 'My plan is to carry on until my son Sébastien replaces me'. (The first-born is aged seven. His little brother Stéphan is two.) But seriously: 'When you pass 30, you know it can't last forever. Maybe that's why I'm keener to play than ever. I want to get the most out of every match. I don't chase records; there will be time for leafing through record books after retirement. Right now I only want to think about the game'. In March 1989, his international records already included the most tries by a French player (27) and the most tries from full-back by a player of any country (23). 'A one-man revolution in full-back play', Frank Keating exclaimed in the *Guardian*.

Blanco points out that, of course, no one scores a try all by himself. And Villepreux, who ought to know, traces the change in full-back play back to the 1960s. The statistics are striking: there were only seven international tries by full-backs representing the eight current International Board countries in all the years from 1871 to 1959; then 13 such tries in the 1960s, 31 in the 1970s and 76 in the 1980s by the end of the World Cup, with more to come. Today, full-back and wings play as a unit – three full-backs, as it were. Villepreux expects the trend towards 'total rugby' to continue. The fact remains that full-back Blanco, with four, was the leading try-scorer in the 1989 Championship. It took French full-backs 75 years, from 1906 to 1981, to total 11 international tries between them, but Blanco recorded his 11th in less than four years. Villepreux himself – like Aguirre, Droitecourt or Gabernet – scored just two international tries. Within the general evolution of full-back play, Blanco has himself been a revolution.

But is he a star? Another silly question. 'I like it', he naturally says about the chanting of his name at the Parc des Princes. Who wouldn't? But then he returns to his family, closes the door of their house outside Biarritz and is 'content'. The rest is nobody's business. Except that his public relations functions, three days a week, do require him to behave like a star more often than not. He brings it off nicely. He seems especially effective among children, and he knows that many a youngster idolises him, so he doesn't smoke in public. On 1 April 1989, All Fools Day, he convincingly told the French television public that he had reluctantly signed with an Australian club to play Rugby League. The stunt was not his idea, but he showed he can be a star, if necessary.

The real Blanco, remember, is a romantic realist. Fatherless from the age of two, deeply conscious of the sacrifices his mother made to raise him, grateful to the men in Biarritz who launched him in rugby, proud that the town is proud of him, aware that athletic prowess is a passing thing – in all this, Blanco the man makes sense. Patrice Lagisquet has said of him: 'Serge doesn't touch the ground. If there were snow, he would leave no tracks'. True enough, but the fact that in reality his feet are also firmly on the ground can only add to our pleasure.

THE UNEXPECTED AND THE UNTHINKABLE

Les Cusworth has never received due recognition as an international fly-half. However, he has consistently been one of the most popular, innovative and influential players in the game, revered by the faithful at Welford Road, Leicester. *Michael Austin* has followed Cusworth throughout his career and provides an appreciation of a great entertainer.

If Jacques Fouroux was *le petit général* of France, then Les Cusworth, another of the game's Lilliputians with a big heart and talent to match, qualifies for the title of the little dictator, imposing himself on those around him as well as on the opposition. Cusworth has done his impression of the Artful Dodger for 15 years, playing fly-half for Wakefield, Moseley and Leicester, showing the sleight of hand and foot which has transcended the passing of time.

A balding head, a pale complexion and a slight frame offer no suggestion that Cusworth would win a place in any list of sporting heroes, but skill, like beauty, is more than skin deep. His sharp, innovative mind has enabled him to attempt both the unexpected and the unthinkable – such as passes between his legs and behind his back. Cusworth plays the game with a smile on his face and tricks up his sleeve, but England recognised him intermittently, awarding him only 12 caps over the past decade.

On 24 November 1979 Les became England's 11th fly-half of the 1970s for the game against New Zealand at Twickenham; at 5 feet 6¼ inches and 11 stone 4 pounds he was also the smallest. However, it was an inauspicious debut and he was immediately dropped and did not return to the side until 1982. 'It was a humbling experience', says Cusworth. 'One day I was on cloud nine and the next I felt sadly let down, because I thought that the selectors had not been fair'. He had been selected to play the punting game which Alan Old had implemented so successfully for the North in their victory over the All Blacks at Otley the previous week. However, the tactic was totally alien to Les and contradicted his extrovert style of relying on instincts and not playing to a stodgy game plan. It also devalued his strengths in distribution and making breaks. England lost a dour game 10-9 and he was out.

Arriving on the international scene fulfilled an ambition Cusworth had cherished from his schooldays under the rugby tutorship of Alan

Jubb, a former Harlequin and master in charge at Normanton Grammar School in Cusworth's home town in Yorkshire. 'Alan used to drive the Normanton sevens team all over England and Wales in a battered VW Caravanette and he showed what is now an old-fashioned and disappearing commitment to school teams. This fostered my interest in sevens, which, if you are fit and athletic, shows rugby at its very best', reflects Cusworth, who has won a worldwide reputation as a sevens player. The pinnacle of his achievements in sevens came when he scored the winning try for the Barbarians against Australia in the Hong Kong final of 1981 and then returned as their captain the next year. He is still a fixture at the tournament and in 1989 he represented the Irish Wolfhounds.

Cusworth, a miner's son, acknowledges that his success is due in part to his father, Cec, his school coach Alan Jubb, and Chalkie White, his former mentor at Leicester. 'My father was twice the man I shall ever be', says Cusworth. 'He swore that his three boys would not have to go down the pit as he did and he spent everything on sending us to college. He was a keen greyhound breeder but encouraged us to play rugby. Both my brothers were centres. Roy played for Yorkshire Schools and Ian for Yorkshire Colts'.

Cusworth's striking personal quality is his honesty: 'Looking back on my schooldays, far better players than me did not go on to play for England, because of family circumstances or the financial need to turn professional. I have been fortunate that Marcia, my wife, has been and is a great supporter of my rugby, as well as being my biggest critic. It has always been my philosophy to balance enjoyment with striving for success. To me, rugby is a mirror of life. If you never make a decision, you never make a mistake. I decided to run the ball in the first minute of a cup semi-final when playing for Wakefield against Rosslyn Park. They promptly scored and we lost 12-6'.

Many of Cusworth's views have been shaped by White, whose coaching acumen helped Leicester to win the John Player Special Cup in three consecutive seasons between 1979 and 1981 in a feast of open rugby. White encouraged Cusworth to reconsider lines of running, the angle and timing of passes and ways of committing the opposing back row. 'I was part of a back division that was second to none in England. It included Paul Dodge, Clive Woodward, Dusty Hare and Steve Kenney and we were helped by a well-drilled and motivated pack', he says.

Cusworth regards his move from Moseley to Leicester in the autumn of 1978, as successor to Bleddyn Jones, as a vital stage in his development. Although he had qualified as a physical education teacher at West Midlands College of Education in Walsall, gained a Bachelor of Education degree at Birmingham University and helped North Midlands to win the County Championship, his rugby education was only just beginning when the presence of an international fly-half,

Cusworth, watched anxiously by his forwards, unleashes a kick in a league match against Wasps in September 1988 when Leicester were the reigning champions.

Martin Cooper, at Moseley forced him to change clubs. Cooper declined to play out of position on the wing and Cusworth found his own selection at full-back unacceptable.

At the last count, Cusworth has played in 17 countries and won matches and friends with his visionary style and his art of dropping goals in tight matches. He smiles at the irony of scoring four dropped goals in a Pilkington Cup match against Liverpool St Helens in January 1989, almost a year to the day after he missed four on his penultimate appearance for England against France in Paris, when he returned to the international arena after a four-year gap, his second long exile from England's team.

In 1974-75 Cusworth dropped 25 goals for Wakefield, then a world record in any season, to overtake Keith James' 22 for Newport. He asserts that many people believe he played his best rugby during his two seasons with Wakefield when place-kicking featured strongly in his repertoire. But the presence of Dusty Hare, the world record points-scorer in the same Leicester side, has prevented him from becoming a master of the art. He scored 30 points in a match against Harlequins in March 1980, then a Leicester record, and reminded everyone of his accuracy in 1983, when Hare missed the start of the season after the British Lions tour of New Zealand. Cusworth amassed 77 points in five games, including six penalty goals in the 18-15 win over Bath, and he would probably have achieved the rare feat of scoring 100 points in September, had not Hare returned as place-kicker for the last two matches of that month.

Cusworth has come a long way in more than one sense since his schooldays: he is now a director of an insurance broking company and plans to take two years off rugby after retiring at the end of season 1989-90 to enjoy family life with his wife and daughters Hannah, aged six, and Sarah, aged one. When he returns to rugby, probably in a coaching capacity, he expects to see more differences in a rapidly changing game since the onset of leagues, a revolutionary step of which he approves. 'It has become more difficult to break down defences. Backs are becoming better organised at tackling and so much depends on the quick ball. The best fly-half I have played against is Jonathan Davies – not in terms of tactical expertise but in sheer natural ability.' Davies, formerly of Neath, Llanelli and Wales, has joined Widnes Rugby League Club but Cusworth hurries on towards 350 appearances for Leicester with the challenge of his final season offering rich appeal. As he says, with a sharp intake of breath, you are a long time retired.

The finest tribute to Cusworth when he reaches for his armchair and slippers would be that if a World XV of the past decade were selected with a balance of skill and ambassadorial qualities for the game, then his name would be among the first on the teamsheet.

TOURS 1988-89
AUSTRALIA TO ENGLAND
AND SCOTLAND 1988

This was the tour of the proverbial two halves. After the match against England at Twickenham, the tourists had lost four and won only three of their first seven games. However, the last six matches, including those against Scotland and the Barbarians, were won by such convincing margins that the early problems were almost forgotten. The tourists scored 211 points in those last six games, including 34 tries, which spoke volumes for their character. Furthermore, this was possibly the most gracious and likeable party ever to tour here.

Initially, the Wallabies foundered against the English Divisional teams, and were then well beaten by England at Twickenham. Three of the four Divisional teams – London (21-10), North (15-9), South-West (26-10) – achieved exciting victories that bore the hallmark of discipline, good coaching and homework. Only the Midlands (18-25) came unstuck. When England won 28-19, it seemed that the tour was washed up.

The arrival on tour of Michael Lynagh after several injuries to key players was a significant factor together with the consistent brilliance of David Campese. Eight of the 1984 team still had crucial roles to play, and the younger element – especially Scott Gourley, who had not taken up rugby until 1985; the Fijian international Niuqila; and the ACT centres Cornish and Girvan – made enormous progress. The team was exceedingly well led by Farr-Jones, while the splendid Campese, and the evergreen forwards Tom Lawton, Cutler and Tuynman were key men. Coaches Bob Dwyer and Bob Templeton brought the tour round as it reached Scotland.

In their 32-13 victory at Murrayfield Australia were only six points away from equalling the record 1984 score against Scotland, while the Barbarian match served as a dazzling epitaph to the tour. A solo try by Campese towards the end earned the Australian wing a prolonged standing ovation.

MATCH DETAILS

1988	OPPONENTS	VENUE	RESULT
15 Oct	London	Twickenham	L 10-21
19 Oct	Northern Division	Otley	L 9-15
22 Oct	England B	Sale	W 37-9
26 Oct	South-West Division	Bristol	L 10-26
29 Oct	Midland Division	Leicester	W 25-18
1 Nov	England Students	Cambridge	W 36-13
5 Nov	ENGLAND	Twickenham	L 19-28
9 Nov	Edinburgh	Myreside	W 25-19
12 Nov	South of Scotland	Hawick	W 29-4
15 Nov	North and Midlands (of Scotland)	Dundee	W 37-17
19 Nov	SCOTLAND	Murrayfield	W 32-13
22 Nov	Combined Services	Aldershot	W 48-7
26 Nov	Barbarians	Cardiff	W 40-22

Scorers: 65 – *Campese (12T 4C 3PG);* 61 – *Lynagh (1T 15C 9PG);* 54 – *Knox (4T 10C 6PG);* 37 – *Leeds (2T 4C 7PG);* 20 – *Grant (5T);* 16 – *Carozza (4T), Niuqila (4T);* 12 – *Gourley (3T);* 8 – *Burke (2T), Farr-Jones (2T), Gardner (2T), Girvan (2T), T Lawton (2T), Tuynman (2T);* 4 – *Carter (1T), Gavin (1T), James (1T), McBain (1T), Miller (1T), Tombs (1T), Walker (1T)*

Appearances: 9 – *Campese;* 8 – *T Lawton, Leeds, Walker;* 7 – *Burke (inc 1 as replacement), Cook (inc 1 as replacement), Cutler, Farr-Jones, Frawley, Gourley, Hartill (inc 1 as replacement), R Lawton, McIntyre, Miller, Niuqila, Tuynman;* 6 – *Campbell, Carozza (inc 1 as replacement), Carter, Gardner, Gavin, Girvan, Grant, McBain (inc 1 as replacement), McCall, McKenzie;* 5 – *James, Lynagh, Tombs;* 4 – *Cornish, Knox*

THE TOURING PARTY

Captain N C Farr-Jones   **Manager** A J Conway
Assistant Manager-Coach R S F Dwyer   **Assistant Coach** R I Templeton
Doctor J E Moulton   **Physiotherapist** G S Craig

FULL-BACKS

D J Knox (Randwick/NSW)
A J S Leeds (Paramatta/NSW)

THREEQUARTERS

D I Campese (Randwick/NSW)
P V Carozza (Wests/Queensland)
M T Cook (University/Queensland)
P Cornish (Royals/ACT)
B Girvan (Norths/ACT)
J C Grant (Orange City/NSW)
A S Niuqila (Randwick/NSW)
R C Tombs (Souths/Queensland)

HALF-BACKS

B T Burke (Randwick/NSW)
N C Farr-Jones (Sydney University/NSW)
S L James (Western Suburbs/NSW)
***M P Lynagh** (Brisbane/Queensland)
L F Walker (Randwick/NSW)
* *replacement during tour*

FORWARDS

W A Campbell (Wests/Queensland)
D G Carter (Quirindi/NSW)
S A G Cutler (Gordon/NSW)
D Frawley (Sydney University/NSW)
J M Gardner (Wests/Queensland)
T B Gavin (Eastern Suburbs/NSW)
S R Gourley (Eastwood/NSW)
M N Hartill (Gordon/NSW)
R Lawton (Souths/Queensland)
T A Lawton (Souths/Queensland)
M I McBain (Brothers/Queensland)
R J McCall (Brothers/Queensland)
A J McIntyre (University/Queensland)
E J A McKenzie (Randwick/NSW)
J S Miller (University/Queensland)
S N Tuynman (Eastwood/NSW)

TOUR RECORD

All matches   Played 13   Won 9   Lost 4   Points for 357   Against 212
International matches   Played 2   Won 1   Lost 1   Points for 51   Against 41

SCORING DETAILS

All matches

For: 54T 33C 25PG   357 Pts
Against: 26T 15C 24PG   2DG 212 Pts

International matches

For: 8T 5C 3PG   51 Pts
Against: 6T 4C 3PG   41 Pts

MATCH 1   15 October, Twickenham

London 21 (3G 1PG)   **Australian XV 10** (2PG 1T)
London: S E Thresher (Harlequins); A T Harriman (Harlequins), F J Clough (Wasps), R A P Lozowski (Wasps), M D Bailey (Wasps); A L Thompson (Harlequins), S M Bates (Wasps); P A G Rendall (Wasps), C J Olver (Harlequins), J A Probyn (Wasps), N G B Edwards (Harlequins), P J Ackford (Harlequins), M G Skinner (Harlequins), D Ryan (Saracens), D J Pegler (Wasps) *(capt)*
Scorers *Tries:* Bailey, Pegler, Harriman   *Conversions:* Thresher (3)
Penalty Goal: Thresher
Australian XV: Leeds; Campese, Grant, Tombs, Carozza; Walker, Farr-Jones *(capt)*; R Lawton, McBain, McIntyre, Cutler, Frawley, Gourley, Gavin, Gardner

Replacement Hartill for Lawton
Scorers *Try:* Farr-Jones   *Penalty Goals:* Leeds (2)
Referee J M Fleming (Scotland)

MATCH 2   19 October, Otley

Northern Division 15 (1G 2PG 1DG)   **Australian XV 9** (1G 1PG)
Northern Division: S Langford (Orrell); S Burnhill (Sale), W D C Carling (Harlequins), J R D Buckton (Saracens), R Underwood (Leicester); C R Andrew (Wasps), C D Morris (Liverpool St Helens); M Whitcombe (Sale), M Fenwick (Durham City), P Huntsman (Headingley), J Howe (Sale), W A Dooley (Preston Grasshoppers), S Hodgson (Vale of Lune), A McFarlane (Sale) (*capt*), P Buckton (Liverpool St Helens)
Scorers *Try:* Morris   *Conversion:* Andrew   *Penalty Goals:* Andrew (2)
Dropped Goal: Andrew
Australian XV: Knox; Campese, Girvan, Cook, Niuqila; James, Burke; Hartill, T Lawton, McKenzie, Campbell (*capt*), McCall, Carter, Tuynman, Gourley *Replacement* McBain for Lawton
Scorer *Try:* Campese   *Conversion:* Campese   *Penalty Goal:* Campese
Referee O E Doyle (Ireland)

MATCH 3   22 October, Sale

England B 9 (2PG 1DG)   **Australian XV 37** (4G 3PG 1T)
England B: S E Thresher (Harlequins); S Hackney (Nottingham), J C Guscott (Bath), J Buckton (Saracens), M D Bailey (Wasps) (*capt*); D Pears (Sale), C D Morris (Liverpool St Helens); L Johnson (Nottingham), K Dunn (Gloucester), A Mullins (Harlequins), R Kimmins (Orrell), D Cusani (Liverpool St Helens), S Hodgson (Vale of Lune), D Ryan (Saracens), P Thornley (Leicester) *Replacement* D J Pegler for Hodgson
Scorers *Penalty Goals:* Thresher (2)   *Dropped Goal:* Pears
Australian XV: Leeds; Campese, Girvan, Cornish, Grant; Walker, Farr-Jones (*capt*); Hartill, T Lawton, McIntyre, Cutler, Frawley, Miller, Tuynman, Gardner *Replacement* Cook for Cornish
Scorers *Tries:* Campese (3), Leeds, Grant   *Conversions:* Leeds (4) *Penalty Goals:* Leeds (3)
Referee J-C Doulcet (France)

MATCH 4   26 October, Bristol

South-West Division 26 (1G 4PG 2T)   **Australian XV 10** (2PG 1T)
South-West Division: J M Webb (Bristol); J Carr (Bristol), S J Halliday (Bath) (*capt*), J C Guscott (Bath), R Knibbs (Bristol); S Barnes (Bath), R M Harding (Bristol); M Preedy (Gloucester), K Dunn (Gloucester), R Pascall (Gloucester), N C Redman (Bath), J Morrison (Bath), J Hall (Bath), D Egerton (Bath), R A Robinson (Bath) *Replacement* A J Buzza (Cambridge U) for Halliday
Scorers *Tries:* Halliday, Preedy, Barnes   *Conversion:* Barnes   *Penalty Goals:* Barnes (4)
Australian XV: Leeds; Niuqila, Tombs, Walker, Carozza; James, Burke; R Lawton, McBain, McKenzie, Campbell (*capt*), McCall, Miller, Gavin, Carter
Scorers *Try:* Carozza   *Penalty Goals:* Leeds (2)
Referee R J Megson (Scotland)

MATCH 5   29 October, Leicester

Midland Division 18 (1G 4PG)   **Australian XV 25** (2G 3PG 1T)
Midland Division: S Hodgkinson (Nottingham); B Evans (Leicester), G J Hartley (Nottingham), P W Dodge (Leicester), S Hackney (Nottingham); L Cusworth (Leicester) (*capt*), S Thomas (Coventry); L Johnson (Nottingham), B C Moore (Nottingham), G Mosses (Nottingham), P W Cook (Nottingham), M Bayfield (Met Police), J Wells (Leicester), D Richards (Leicester), P Thornley (Leicester) *Replacement* C Jones (Nottingham) for Hackney
Scorers *Try:* Richards   *Conversion:* Hodgkinson   *Penalty Goals:* Hodgkinson (4)
Australian XV: Leeds; Grant, Girvan, Cook, Campese; Lynagh, Farr-Jones (*capt*);

Hartill, T Lawton, McIntyre, Campbell, Cutler, Miller, Tuynman, Gardner
Scorers *Tries:* Farr-Jones, Grant, Girvan   *Conversions:* Lynagh (2)
Penalty Goals: Lynagh (3)
Referee L J Peard (Wales)

MATCH 6   1 November, Cambridge

England Students 13 (1G 1PG 1T)   **Australian XV 36** (3G 2PG 3T)
England Students: A Lumsden (Bath U); P Hopley (St Thomas's Hospital),
P de Glanville (Durham U), K G Simms (St Mary's Hospital), T Underwood (Leicester
U); A J Buzza (Cambridge U), R H Q B Moon (Polytechnic of Wales); V Obugu (Oxford
U), J Locke (University of Wales), A Mullins (City U) *(capt)*, T Swan (Liverpool U),
S T O'Leary (St Mary's Hospital), J Green (South Glam Inst), C Vyvyan (Cambridge U),
A Bick (St Paul and St Mary, Cheltenham) *Replacement* A Hobbs (St Thomas's Hospital)
for Simms
Scorers *Tries:* Moon, Hopley   *Conversion:* Buzza   *Penalty Goal:* Buzza
Australian XV: Campese *(capt)*; Niuqila, Tombs, Walker, Carozza; James, Burke; R Lawton,
McBain, McKenzie, McCall, Frawley, Gourley, Gavin, Carter
Scorers *Tries:* Campese (2), McBain, Carozza, Niuqila, Carter
Conversions: Campese (3)   *Penalty Goals:* Campese (2)
Referee G Simmonds (Wales)

MATCH 7   5 November, Twickenham   First Test

ENGLAND 28 (3G 2PG 1T)   AUSTRALIA 19 (2G 1PG 1T)

England displayed a wholly refreshing boldness in this match and erased
memories of sad defeats in Australia the previous summer with a
convincing victory in a magnificent game at Twickenham. The style was
shaped by the success of the Divisional teams and England, with a new
captain in Carling, and three new caps – Ackford, Harriman and Morris –
responded well.

Australia led twice, once after Leeds scored a try to which Lynagh added
a penalty and conversion; and again after Campese intercepted a Webb
pass destined for Halliday and sprinted 60 yards for a try early in the
second half to bring the score to 13-9. Morris had the great pleasure of a try
on his debut: it came just before half-time and Webb converted. From 9-13
England took control. Underwood scored twice within six minutes, the
first try created by Andrew, the second courtesy of the deft handling of
four England forwards, who outflanked the Australian defence. It was the
sixth successive international in which Underwood had crossed for a try.
Webb's conversion and a penalty goal moved England away at 22-13.

Girvan was then allowed to escape for a well-taken try which, with a
Leeds conversion, narrowed the margin alarmingly. But a slightly
concussed Carling then put the match beyond doubt with a break and a
pass for Halliday to score at the posts, and for Webb to convert. In a
memorable team effort there were outstanding performances from
England's numbers 7, 8 and 9 – Robinson, Richards and Morris.

ENGLAND: J M Webb (Bristol); A T Harriman (Harlequins), W D C Carling (Harlequins)
(capt), S J Halliday (Bath), R Underwood (Leicester); C R Andrew (Wasps), C D Morris
(Liverpool St Helens); P A G Rendall (Wasps), B C Moore (Nottingham), J A Probyn
(Wasps), W A Dooley (Preston Grasshoppers), P J Ackford (Harlequins), D W Egerton
(Bath), D Richards (Leicester), R A Robinson (Bath) *Replacement* J R D Buckton (Saracens)
for Carling

Scorers *Tries:* Underwood (2), Morris, Halliday   *Conversions:* Webb (3)
Penalty Goals: Webb (2)
AUSTRALIA: Leeds; Grant, Girvan, Cook, Campese; Lynagh, Farr-Jones (*capt*); Hartill,
T Lawton, McIntyre, Cutler, Campbell, Miller, Tuynman, Gardner
Scorers *Tries:* Leeds, Campese, Grant   *Conversions:* Lynagh (2)
Penalty Goal: Lynagh
Referee D J Bishop (New Zealand)

MATCH 8   9 November, Edinburgh Myreside

Edinburgh 19 (5PG 1T)   **Australian XV 25** (2G 3PG 1T)
Edinburgh: C Spence (Stewart's-Melville FP); P D Steven (Heriot's FP), S Hastings
(Watsonians), S R P Lineen (Boroughmuir), M Debusk (Boroughmuir); D S Wyllie
(Stewart's-Melville FP), J Scott (Stewart's-Melville FP); D M B Sole (Edinburgh Acads),
K S Milne (Heriot's FP), I G Milne (Heriot's FP) (*capt*), J Richardson (Edinburgh
Acads), E Simpson (Stewart's-Melville FP), J H Calder (Stewart's-Melville FP), J Price
(Boroughmuir), K Rafferty (Heriot's FP) *Replacement* A Adamson (Edinburgh Acads)
for Rafferty
Scorers *Try:* Debusk   *Penalty Goals:* Spence (5)
Australian XV: Knox; Niuqila, Tombs, Cornish, Carozza; Walker, Burke; R Lawton,
T Lawton, McKenzie, McCall, Frawley, Gourley, Gavin, Carter
Scorers *Tries:* Knox, Niuqila, Carozza   *Conversions:* Knox (2)
Penalty Goals: Knox (3)
Referee J A F Trigg (England)

MATCH 9   12 November, Hawick

South of Scotland 4 (1T)   **Australian XV 29** (3G 1PG 2T)
South of Scotland: P W Dods (Gala); D Robeson (Kelso), G R T Baird (Kelso),
K W Robertson (Melrose), I Tukalo (Selkirk); A B M Ker (Kelso), G Armstrong
(Jedforest); T McLeish (Melrose), G J Callander (Kelso) (*capt*), K Sudlow (Melrose),
A J Campbell (Hawick), D B White (Gala), J Jeffrey (Kelso), I A M Paxton (Selkirk),
G R Marshall (Selkirk)
Scorer *Try:* Robeson
Australian XV: Leeds; Niuqila, Cook, Walker, Campese; Lynagh, Farr-Jones (*capt*);
R Lawton, McBain, McKenzie, Cutler, Frawley, Miller, Tuynman, Gourley
Scorers *Tries:* Niuqila (2), Gourley (2), Campese *Conversions:* Lynagh (3)
Penalty Goal: Lynagh
Referee S R Hilditch (Ireland)

MATCH 10   15 November, Dundee

North & Midlands of Scotland 17 (1G 1PG 2T)   **Australian XV 37** (2G 3PG 4T)
North & Midlands of Scotland: H Murray (Heriot's FP); C Macartney (Boroughmuir),
B Edwards (Boroughmuir), J N Thompson (Kirkcaldy), M Cross (Dunfermline);
C MacGregor (Gordonians), M Allingham (Heriot's FP); G Mackenzie (Highland),
M Scott (Dunfermline), J Scobie (Glasgow Acads), I Rankin (Howe of Fife), B Bell
(Highland), H Edwards (Boroughmuir), N Harris (Glasgow Acads), D McIvor
(Edinburgh Acads) *Replacement* D Love (Gordonians) for McIvor
Scorers *Tries:* Scobie, Edwards, penalty try   *Conversion:* MacGregor
Penalty Goal: MacGregor
Australian XV: Knox; Grant, Girvan, Cornish, Carozza; James, Burke; Hartill,
T Lawton, McIntyre, Campbell (*capt*), McCall, Carter, Gavin, Gardner
Scorers *Tries:* Gardner (2), Knox, James, Gavin, Burke   *Conversions:* Knox (2)
Penalty Goals: Knox (3)
Referee I M Bullerwell (England)

MATCH 11   19 November, Murrayfield   Second Test

SCOTLAND 13 (1G 1PG 1T)   AUSTRALIA 32 (3G 2PG 2T)

Australia, revelling in possession which they used superbly, beat Scotland almost as convincingly as they did in their 37-12 victory at Murrayfield in 1984. Forward domination gave Lynagh the platform to atone for a somewhat rusty display against England. His lack of match fitness on that day had been replaced by a controlled display of tactical genius and a tally of 12 points.

Australia were without Tuynman, who injured his back getting out of bed, and they capped the immensely promising Gourley for the first time. Gourley was a revelation. He was involved in the early move which saw Campese go over for a try, Lynagh converted. Lynagh immediately kicked a penalty, then Gavin Hastings responded with a penalty for Scotland. Tom Lawton, the massive hooker, scored the first of his two tries, for Lynagh to convert, and shortly after half-time Campese scored his second, set up by Niuqila, with Lynagh again converting. Australia led 21-3 with 38 minutes remaining.

There was a brief Scottish revival when a sidestep by Robertson created room for him to score a try, but soon Niuqila and Leeds set up a

David Campese, the outstanding figure on the 1988 Australian tour, closes in on the loose ball after a tackle by Michael Cook on Matt Duncan of Scotland.

try for Gourley, who brushed through three tackles. Another Lynagh penalty and a try and conversion by Gavin Hastings were a prelude to Lawton's second effort from a driving ruck.

Gavin, who came in for Tuynman, Gourley and Miller, who had his nose broken, were an excellent loose trio, while Frawley gave his best international performance. However, the outstanding Australian forward was hooker Tom Lawton, who even at 17 stones, can outsprint backs.

SCOTLAND: A G Hastings (London Scottish); M D F Duncan (West of Scotland), S Hastings (Watsonians), K W Robertson (Melrose), I Tukalo (Selkirk); R I Cramb (Harlequins), G Armstrong (Jedforest); D M B Sole (Edinburgh Acads), G J Callander (Kelso) *(capt)*, I G Milne (Heriot's FP), A J Campbell (Hawick), D F Cronin (Bath), D B White (Gala), I A M Paxton (Selkirk), J Jeffrey (Kelso) *Replacement* G R Marshall (Selkirk) for White
Scorers: *Tries:* A G Hastings, Robertson *Conversion:* A G Hastings
Penalty Goal: A G Hastings
AUSTRALIA: Leeds; Niuqila, Cook, Walker, Campese; Lynagh, Farr-Jones *(capt)*; R Lawton, T Lawton, McIntyre, Cutler, Frawley, Miller, Gavin, Gourley
Replacement Burke for Farr-Jones
Scorers *Tries:* T Lawton (2), Campese (2), Gourley *Conversions:* Lynagh (3)
Penalty Goals: Lynagh (2)
Referee D J Bishop (New Zealand)

MATCH 12   22 November, Aldershot

Combined Services 7 (1PG 1T)   **Australian XV 48** (6G 3T)
Combined Services: Lt C Allcock (Royal Navy and Camborne); POPT R Penfold (Royal Navy and Plymouth Albion), Sgt C Spowart (Army and Newbridge), SAC P Hull (RAF and Bristol), FO R Underwood (RAF and Leicester); Lt J Steele (Army and Northampton) *(capt)*, S/Sgt G Morgan (Army and Cambridge C); L/Cpl G Graham (Army and Sterling), WO2 R Matthews (Army and Rushmoor), SAC A Billett (RAF and Neath), Cpl C Hall (Army and Coventry), Sgt B Richardson (RAF and Boroughmuir), Sgt M Reece (Royal Marines and Taunton), Cpl D Parsonage (RAF and Nottingham), 2nd Lt R Wainwright (Army and Cambridge U) *Replacement* S/Sgt S Peacock (Army) for Parsonage
Scorers *Try:* Wainwright *Penalty Goal:* Hull
Australian XV: Knox; Grant, Tombs, Cornish, Girvan; James, Burke; Hartill, McBain, McKenzie, Campbell, McCall, Gardner, Tuynman, Carter *Replacement* Carozza for Girvan
Scorers *Tries:* Knox (2), Grant (2), Girvan, Tuynman, Tombs, Burke, Carozza
Conversions: Knox (6)
Referee R Yemen (Wales)

MATCH 13   26 November, Cardiff

Barbarians 22 (3G 1T)   **Australian XV 40** (5G 2PG 1T)
Barbarians: A G Hastings (London Scottish & Scotland); M D F Duncan (West of Scotland & Scotland), C Laity (Neath), M G Ring (Cardiff & Wales), R Underwood (Leicester & England); J Davies (Llanelli & Wales), R N Jones (Swansea & Wales); D M B Sole (Edinburgh Acads & Scotland), S J Smith (Ballymena & Ireland), D Young (Cardiff & Wales), W A Dooley (Preston Grasshoppers & England), R L Norster (Cardiff & Wales), P M Matthews (Wanderers & Ireland) *(capt)*, I A M Paxton (Selkirk & Scotland), R A Robinson (Bath & England)
Scorers *Tries:* Duncan, Hastings, Robinson, Laity *Conversions:* Hastings (3)
Australian XV: Leeds; Niuqila, Cook, Walker, Campese; Lynagh, Farr-Jones *(capt)*; R Lawton, T Lawton, McIntyre, Cutler, Frawley, Miller, Tuynman, Gourley
Scorers *Tries:* Campese (2), Miller, Lynagh, Walker, Tuynman *Conversions:* Lynagh (5) *Penalty Goals:* Lynagh (2)
Referee G Maurette (France)

AUSTRALIA TO ITALY 1988

MATCH 1   30 November, Prato

ITALY B 18 (3G)   **AUSTRALIANS 26** (3G 2T)
ITALY B *Tries:* Pesce, Ravanelli, Brunello   *Conversions:* Capitani (3)
AUSTRALIANS *Tries:* Knox, Grant (3), Gavin   *Conversions:* Knox (3)

MATCH 2   3 December, Rome

ITALY 6 (2PG)   **AUSTRALIA 55** (8G 1PG 1T)
ITALY: L Troiani (L'Aquila); E Venturi (Rovigo), R Ambrosio (San Dona), S Barba (Roma), C De Biase (Roma); S Bettarello (Treviso), F Pietrosani (L'Aquila); G Rossi (Treviso), M Trevisol (Treviso), T Lupini (Rovigo), R Favero (Treviso), F Berni (Amatori Milan), P Reale (Rovigo), M Innocenti (Padova) (*capt*), C Covi (Padova)
Replacements S Appiani (Calvi) for Berni (63 mins); D Tebaldi (Noceto) for Ambrosio (51 mins)
Scorer *Penalty Goals:* Bettarello (2)
AUSTRALIA: Leeds; Niuqila, Cook, Walker, Campese; Lynagh, Farr-Jones (*capt*); McIntyre, T Lawton, Hartill, Frawley, Cutler, Miller, Gourley, Tuynman
Replacement Gavin for Frawley (41 mins)
Scorers *Tries:* Campese (3), Niuqila (3), Leeds, Gourley, Lynagh
Conversions: Lynagh (8)   *Penalty Goal:* Lynagh
Referee M Robin (France)

NEW ZEALAND TO AUSTRALIA 1988

Greg Campbell *The Australian*

The All Blacks arrived in Australia only a week after they had demolished Wales in New Zealand. And, seven weeks later, they headed home in triumph having convincingly beaten Australia in the Test series, widely acclaimed as the finest All Black team ever to cross the Tasman Sea. It was always acknowledged that Australia would provide stubborn resistance but at no stage did the Kiwis falter, although they only managed a draw, 19-19, in the second Test. This mighty All Black team, so superbly prepared physically, mentally and tactically, swept aside all comers with a devastating playing style based on strength, speed, skill and teamwork in the forwards combined with the flamboyant adventurousness, pace and confidence of a most efficient backline unit.

The tourists scored an impressive 476 points in 13 matches at an average of 36.6 per match and crossed for 77 tries at an average of 5.9 a match. The All Blacks' defence was also brilliant: in 12 Tests and in 10 tour matches since 1986 they have never conceded more than two tries in any single game. And, working in perfect unison with these winning factors, fly-half Grant Fox was a deadly accurate goal-kicker. He scored a record 119 points in his 10 tour appearances and surpassed the previous New Zealand points-scoring record of Don Clarke (207 points) in the third and final Test, and he has to date scored 214 points in only 13 Tests.

Often the All Blacks were matched in the set pieces, but it was in the second phase that the tourists were in total command. Wayne Shelford, the explosive No 8, led the pack in dynamic fashion and he was superbly supported by Alan Whetton, Michael Jones and Mike Brewer. Brewer played the first international, held on a Sunday, because Jones' religious beliefs prevented him from taking the field. Bruce Deans, a busy and lively scrum-half, capably filled the position vacated by David Kirk, while Joe Stanley played possibly the best rugby of his career in the centre. Stanley's centre partner, John Schuster, who had previously played for his native Western Samoa, was in splendid form for the All Blacks after Warwick Taylor's tour was curtailed because of injury. The most lethal attacking players, as shown by their try-scoring tallies, were full-back John Gallagher and winger John Kirwan, who registered a try in every Test match.

Despite the All Blacks' awesome recent record, Australia were confident of matching the New Zealanders as they knew their players well, thanks to regular playing contact in the South Pacific Championship series and other annual Test clashes. Although the All Blacks didn't play as smoothly as coach Alex Wyllie would have wished in the opening four matches, they were still superior and exploded into a points-scoring frenzy in the second half of the tour.

Australia attempted with determination to hold the All Black forwards and win enough adequate possession to allow the back-line speed of David Campese and Ian Williams to take charge. But the forwards were unable to supply a regular stream of quality possession and the close, flat passing game the Australians were trying to perfect came unstuck, the attack becoming sitting targets for the punishing All Black defence.

THE TOURING PARTY

Captain W T Shelford   **Manager** J Sturgeon   **Assistant manager/coach** A J Wyllie
Assistant coach L Penn   **Hon medical officer** Dr J Mayhew
Physiotherapist D Abercrombie

FULL-BACKS
J A Gallagher (Wellington)
*S Philpott (Canterbury)

THREEQUARTERS
J J Kirwan (Auckland)
T J Wright (Auckland)
J Goldsmith (Waikato)
J T Stanley (Auckland)
W T Taylor (Canterbury)
J Schuster (Wellington)
*B J McCahill (Auckland)

HALF-BACKS
G J Fox (Auckland)
F M Botica (North Harbour)
B Deans (Canterbury)
G Bachop (Canterbury)

FORWARDS
R W Loe (Canterbury)
R Williams (North Harbour)
S C McDowell (Auckland)
K G Boroevich (North Harbour)
S B T Fitzpatrick (Auckland)
W Gatland (Waikato)
G W Whetton (Auckland)
M J Pierce (Wellington)
A Anderson (Canterbury)
A T Earl (Canterbury)
A J Whetton (Auckland)
M N Jones (Auckland)
M R Brewer (Otago)
M Z Brooke (Auckland)
W T Shelford (North Harbour)
replacement during tour

TOUR RECORD

All matches Played 13 Won 12 Drew 1 Points for 476 Against 96
International matches Played 3 Won 2 Drew 1 Points for 81 Against 35

SCORING DETAILS

All matches
For: 77T 45C 25PG 1DG 476 Pts
Against: 10T 4C 16PG 96 Pts

International matches
For: 11T 8C 7PG 81 Pts
Against: 4T 2C 5PG 35 Pts

MATCH DETAILS

1988	OPPONENTS	VENUE	RESULT
19 June	Western Australia	Perth	W 60-3
22 June	Randwick	Sydney	W 25-9
26 June	Australia B	Brisbane	W 28-4
29 June	NSW Country	Singleton	W 29-4
3 July	AUSTRALIA	Sydney	W 32-7
6 July	Australia Capital Territory	Canberra	W 16-3
10 July	Queensland	Brisbane	W 27-12
13 July	Queensland B	Townsville	W 39-3
16 July	AUSTRALIA	Brisbane	D 19-19
20 July	New South Wales B	Gosford	W 45-9
23 July	New South Wales	Sydney	W 42-6
26 July	Victoria Invitation XV	Melbourne	W 84-8
30 July	AUSTRALIA	Sydney	W 30-9

Scorers: 119 – Fox (22PG 1DG 25C); 84 – Gallagher (12T 2PG 15C); 44 – Kirwan (11T); 33 – Botica (5T 1PG 5C); 28 – Bachop (7T); 24 – Wright (6T); 20 – Schuster (5T), Shelford (5T), Brooke (5T), Goldsmith (5T); 16 – Earl (4T); 8 – Brewer (2T), A Whetton (2T), Philpott (2T); 4 – Stanley (1T), Jones (1T), Deans (1T), McDowell (1T), Gatland (1T), Taylor (1T)

Appearances: 11 – Gallagher; 10 – Fox (inc 1 as replacement), Kirwan, Schuster (inc 2 as replacement), Shelford (inc 2 as replacement); 9 – Stanley (inc 1 as replacement); 8 – Botica (inc 1 as replacement), Brooke (inc 1 as replacement), Earl (inc 1 as replacement), Goldsmith, Brewer, Pierce, G Whetton; 7 – Loe, Fitzpatrick, McDowell, Deans, Jones, A Whetton; 6 – Boroevich, Williams, Anderson, Gatland, Bachop; 3 – McCahill, Taylor; 2 – Philpott

MATCH 1 19 June, Perry Lakes Stadium, Perth

Western Australia 3 (1PG) **New Zealand XV 60** (7G 2PG 3T)
Western Australia: T Fearn; G Wagstaff, H Sutherland, G Birmingham, P Earsman; M Allan, G Holmes; C Hennings, R Walter, D Galbraith, M McDonagh, P Tuoro, N Edwards, L Tinny, W Tepania
Scorer *Penalty Goal:* Earsman
New Zealand XV: Gallagher; Kirwan, Botica, Taylor, Goldsmith; Fox, Bachop; Loe, Gatland, Williams, Anderson, Earl, Brewer, Brooke, Shelford (*capt*)
Scorers *Tries:* Kirwan (3), Goldsmith (2), Gallagher (2), Brewer, Brooke, Shelford
Conversions: Fox (7) *Penalty Goals:* Fox (2)
Referee F van der Westhuizen (Sydney)

MATCH 2 22 June, Coogee Oval, Sydney

Randwick 9 (1G 1PG) **New Zealand XV 25** (1G 4PG 1DG 1T)
Randwick: D Knox; A Niuqila, Gary Ella, R Carmont, D Campese; L Walker, B Burke; M Murray, E Jones, E McKenzie, T Kava (*capt*), G Logan, S Poidevin, G Boneham, M Cheika *Replacement* M Clift for Poidevin
Scorers *Try:* Walker *Conversion:* Knox *Penalty Goal:* Knox
New Zealand XV: Gallagher; Kirwan, Stanley, Schuster, Wright; Fox, Deans;

McDowell, Fitzpatrick, Boroevich, Pierce, G Whetton, A Whetton, Jones, Shelford (*capt*)
Scorers *Tries:* Shelford, A Whetton *Conversion:* Fox *Penalty Goals:* Fox (4)
Dropped Goal: Fox
Referee B Kinsey (Sydney)

MATCH 3 26 June, Ballymore, Brisbane

Australia B 4 (1T) **New Zealand XV 28** (3G 2PG 1T)
Australia B: G Martin; A Niuqila, A Herbert, L Walker, J Grant; S James, B Burke (*capt*); M Hartill, M McBain, E McKenzie, P FitzSimons, R McCall, J Gardner, S Lidbury, T Gavin *Replacement* B Nasser for Lidbury
Scorer *Try:* Niuqila
New Zealand XV: Gallagher; Goldsmith, Stanley, Taylor, Kirwan; Botica, Deans; McDowell, Fitzpatrick, Loe, G Whetton, Pierce, A Whetton, Brewer, Shelford (*capt*)
Replacement Fox for Taylor
Scorers *Tries:* Kirwan, Taylor, Gallagher, Goldsmith *Conversions:* Gallagher (3)
Penalty Goals: Gallagher (2)
Referee K V J Fitzgerald (Brisbane)

MATCH 4 29 June, Rugby Park, Singleton

New South Wales Country 4 (1T) **New Zealand XV 29** (1G 1PG 5T)
New South Wales Country: D Vignes; G White, A Parkes, C Callow, J Grant; P Tonkin, R Long (*capt*); G Bucknell, D Grant, M Prior, P Challender, J Perrignon, J Sampson, R Clarke, A Model *Replacement* M Hamling for Grant
Scorer *Try:* Model
New Zealand XV: Goldsmith; Wright, Botica, Schuster, McCahill; Fox, Bachop; Boroevich, Gatland, Williams, Earl, Anderson (*capt*), Brewer, Jones, Brooke
Replacements Stanley for Schuster; A Whetton for Brewer
Scorers *Tries:* Schuster (2), Wright (2), Brooke, Bachop *Conversion:* Fox
Penalty Goal: Fox
Referee Dr M Edye (Sydney)

MATCH 5 3 July, Concord Oval, Sydney   First Test

AUSTRALIA 7 (1PG 1T) NEW ZEALAND 32 (3G 2PG 2T)

Australia entered this first international with high hopes following their 2–0 series win over England. Furthermore, in their opening four tour matches, the All Blacks hadn't shown the awesome form that had crushed Wales in New Zealand a month earlier. The vigorous and tireless Simon Poidevin was enticed out of his short retirement to wear Australia's battle dress again and the chosen pack appeared to have the high degree of experience, size and toughness to engage in trench warfare. However, the All Blacks scored 14 points in the first 12 minutes, trampling Australia's hopes of winning deep into the turf and confirming to Nick Farr-Jones' men that New Zealand still reigned supreme. If it had been a boxing match, New Zealand would have been awarded an early KO decision.

The match was only two minutes old when McDowell scored after gratefully gathering a high kick spilt by Leeds under pressure from Schuster. Then John Kirwan demonstrated his class to deliver knock-out blows with tries in the 8th and 12th minutes, overhauling Stu Wilson's record as New Zealand's most prolific try-scorer in Test

31

matches. Australia, desperately clinging to the ropes, rallied and were only 14–4 behind at half-time thanks to a fine, opportunistic try by Williams. The margin could have been further reduced had Poidevin not dropped the ball over the line and if Williams had been awarded a try that was disallowed by English referee Fred Howard.

Australia moved to within seven points of the All Blacks after half-time when Lynagh landed a penalty goal, but then the All Blacks exploded again. A glaring defensive lapse at the Australian scrum base was exposed when Alan Whetton raced over to score. Fox then added two penalty goals to put the match beyond Australia's reach and Schuster, making his debut for the All Blacks, completed the rout when backing up a movement down the right by Kirwan and Stanley.

This was Australia's heaviest defeat by New Zealand since 1972 and the final score would have been even worse had not Farr-Jones effected many desperate, last-ditch tackles. While admitting that the All Blacks were worthy and convincing winners, Australian coach Bob Dwyer launched a vicious verbal tirade on referee Mr Howard describing him as a 'novice' and his performance as an 'abomination'. Contrastingly, his performance was praised by the All Black camp.

AUSTRALIA: A J Leeds (New South Wales); I M Williams (New South Wales), Gary Ella (New South Wales), M T Cook (Queensland), D I Campese (New South Wales); M P Lynagh (Queensland), N C Farr-Jones (New South Wales) (*capt*); M N Hartill (New South Wales), T A Lawton (Queensland), A J McIntyre (Queensland), S A G Cutler (New South Wales), D Frawley (New South Wales), J M Gardner (Queensland), S P Poidevin (New South Wales), D G Carter (New South Wales)
Scorers *Try:* Williams *Penalty Goal:* Lynagh
NEW ZEALAND: Gallagher; Kirwan, Stanley, Schuster, Wright; Fox, Deans; McDowell, Fitzpatrick, Loe, G Whetton, Pierce, A Whetton, Brewer, Shelford (*capt*)
Scorers *Tries:* Kirwan (2), Schuster, A Whetton, McDowell *Conversions:* Fox (3) *Penalty Goals:* Fox (2)
Referee F Howard (England)

MATCH 6   6 July, Seiffert Oval, Queanbeyan

Australian Capital Territory 3 (1PG)   **New Zealand XV 16** (4T)
Australian Capital Territory: A Friend; C Morton, B Girvan, P Cornish, P Alchin; M Apps, P Doyle; L Donnellan (*capt*), J Taylor, G Didier, M Sinderberry, H Kasprzak, G Scott, F Lopilato, M McInnes
Scorer *Penalty Goal:* Friend
New Zealand XV: Gallagher; Goldsmith, McCahill, Schuster, Kirwan; Botica, Bachop; Boroevich, Gatland, Williams, G Whetton (*capt*), Pierce, Brooke, Jones, Earl
Scorers *Tries:* Brooke (2), Goldsmith, Bachop
Referee D Reordan (United States)

MATCH 7   10 July, Ballymore, Brisbane

Queensland 12 (4PG)   **New Zealand XV 27** (3G 3PG)
Queensland: G Martin; P Grigg, A Herbert, M Cook, A Knox; M Lynagh (*capt*), P Slattery; R Lawton, T Lawton, A McIntyre, R McCall, I Savai, J Miller, J Gardner, B Nasser *Replacement* M Palm for Lynagh
Scorers *Penalty Goals:* Lynagh (2), Palm (2)

New Zealand XV: Gallagher; Goldsmith, Stanley, Schuster, Kirwan; Fox, Deans; McDowell, Fitzpatrick, Loe, G Whetton, Anderson, Brooke, Brewer, Shelford (*capt*)
Replacement Earl for Brewer
Scorers *Tries:* Gallagher (2), Stanley *Conversions:* Fox (3) *Penalty Goals:* Fox (3)
Referee R Fordham (Sydney)

MATCH 8   13 July, Townsville

Queensland B 3 (1PG)   **New Zealand XV 39** (3G 3PG 3T)
Queensland B: A King; P Carozza, P Mills, D Maguire, R McCartney; M Palm, S Tait; W Abrams, M McBain (*capt*), D Crowley, D Cooper, S Nightingale, G Hassall, D Williams, T Dodson
Scorer *Penalty Goal:* Palm
New Zealand XV: Gallagher; Wright, Botica, McCahill, Goldsmith; Fox, Bachop; Boroevich, Gatland, Williams, Earl, Anderson (*capt*), Brewer, Jones, Brooke
Replacements Schuster for McCahill; Shelford for Jones
Scorers *Tries:* Bachop (2), Shelford (2), Botica, Gatland *Conversions:* Fox (3)
Penalty Goals: Fox (3)
Referee A MacNeill (Newcastle)

MATCH 9   16 July, Ballymore, Brisbane   Second Test

AUSTRALIA 19 (1G 3PG 1T)   **NEW ZEALAND 19** (2G 1PG 1T)
Following the All Blacks' superb performance in the first Test, there was a great deal of apprehension about Australia's chances in the second international. This concern deepened when David Campese was chosen at full-back ahead of the reliable Andrew Leeds. But, after Michael Lynagh was forced to withdraw because of a badly bruised thigh, Leeds was recalled because of his goal-kicking ability and the backline was re-shuffled with new cap Lloyd Walker playing at fly-half instead of inside centre. The selectors chose three different players in all: James Grant, Jeff Miller and Walker. A further late change was required when Julian Gardner withdrew because of injury and Tim Gavin was named at No 8 in his debut Test.

This time it was Australia that began with a hurricane start, opening up with tries by Grant and Williams, one of which was converted by Leeds, who also added two penalty goals. At half-time Australia led 16–6 following a controversial try by All Black flanker Jones. Many believed that Jones had made a double movement, but Scottish referee Brian Anderson disagreed and the score stood. The key to Australia's revival after the first Test was the domination of Steve Cutler in the line-out. Although no team can relax against a side as good as the All Blacks, had a 60-metre movement before half-time initiated by Williams been converted instead of being knocked on at the All Black line, victory would surely have been guaranteed.

But the All Blacks came storming back to level the scores at 19–19 with tries through Terry Wright and Kirwan and a penalty goal by Fox. If Fox had converted Kirwan's try, New Zealand would have taken the lead, the match and the series. Typical of Australia's unstinting effort was Cutler's match-saving cover tackle at the corner flag when Kirwan appeared certain to score a try. It was undoubtedly the finest match in

Cutler's career. Australia's performance was even more meritorious as Cook left the field after only 21 minutes because of a groin strain, which necessitated further reshuffling in the back line, and Mark Hartill snapped a knee ligament and was replaced by Rob Lawton.

Australia viewed the match as the one that got away while the All Blacks, despite having recaptured the Bledisloe Cup, believed in their hearts that they had lost, whatever the scoreboard said.

AUSTRALIA: A J Leeds (New South Wales); I M Williams (New South Wales), J C Grant (New South Wales), M T Cook (Queensland), D I Campese (New South Wales); L F Walker (New South Wales), N C Farr-Jones (New South Wales) (*capt*); M N Hartill (New South Wales), T A Lawton (Queensland), A J McIntyre (Queensland), S A G Cutler (New South Wales), D Frawley (New South Wales), S P Poidevin (New South Wales), J S Miller (Queensland), T B Gavin (New South Wales)
Replacements S L James (New South Wales) for Cook; R Lawton (Queensland) for Hartill
Scorers *Tries:* Grant, Williams *Conversion:* Leeds *Penalty Goals:* Leeds (3)
NEW ZEALAND: Gallagher; Wright, Stanley, Schuster, Kirwan; Fox, Deans; McDowell, Fitzpatrick, Loe, Pierce, G Whetton, A Whetton, Jones, Shelford (*capt*)
Scorers *Tries:* Jones, Kirwan, Wright *Conversions:* Fox (2) *Penalty Goal:* Fox
Referee J B Anderson (Scotland)

MATCH 10 20 July, Graham Park, Gosford

New South Wales B 9 (1G 1PG) **New Zealand XV 45** (5G 1PG 3T)
New South Wales B: M Roebuck; G White, A Parkes, I Vest, P Meehan; P Tonkin, B Burke (*capt*); G Bucknell; S Kowalick, A Blades, J Fewtrell, T Kava, G Boneham, D Reen, C Douglas *Replacement* G Palmer for Fewtrell
Scorers *Try:* White *Conversion:* Roebuck *Penalty Goal:* Roebuck
New Zealand XV: Philpott; Goldsmith, Stanley, Taylor, Wright; Botica, Bachop; Boroevich, Gatland, Williams, Pierce, Anderson (*capt*), Brooke, Brewer, Earl
Replacement Schuster for Taylor
Scorers *Tries:* Schuster (2), Philpott (2), Earl, Brooke, Bachop, Botica *Conversions:* Botica (5) *Penalty Goal:* Botica
Referee P McPhillips (Canberra)

MATCH 11 23 July, Concord Oval, Sydney

New South Wales 6 (2PG) **New Zealand XV 42** (4G 2PG 3T)
New South Wales: A Leeds; M Roebuck, J Grant, G Ella, D Campese; S James, N Farr-Jones; M Murray, E Jones, E McKenzie, P FitzSimons, D Frawley, D Carter, S Poidevin (*capt*), C Douglas *Replacement* T Kava for Frawley
Scorer *Penalty Goals:* Leeds (2)
New Zealand XV: Gallagher; Kirwan, Stanley, Schuster, Wright; Fox, Deans; McDowell, Fitzpatrick, Loe, G Whetton, Earl, Brewer, Jones, Shelford (*capt*)
Replacements Botica for Fox; Brooke for Jones
Scorers *Tries:* Gallagher (2), Wright (2), Botica, Shelford, Brewer *Conversions:* Fox (2), Gallagher (2) *Penalty Goals:* Fox (2)
Referee C Waldon (Brisbane)

MATCH 12 26 July, Olympic Park, Melbourne

Victorian Invitation XV 8 (2T) **New Zealand XV 84** (10G 6T)
Victorian Invitation XV: D Knox; C MacGregor, R Tombs, J McArthur, L Strauss; P Cornish, R Ah Kuoi; N Raikuna, N Carter (*capt*), D Wellings, P FitzSimons, N Farnan, W Oliver, D Thyns, M McInnes
Scorers *Tries:* McArthur, Cornish
New Zealand XV: Gallagher; Wright, Goldsmith, Philpott, Kirwan; Botica, Bachop; Boroevich, Gatland, Williams, Anderson (*capt*), Pierce, A Whetton, Brooke, Earl
Replacement Shelford for Brooke

Scorers *Tries:* Gallagher (4), Kirwan (3), Earl (3), Bachop (2), Botica (2), Wright, Goldsmith *Conversions:* Botica (10)
Referee B Feinberg (Queensland)

MATCH 13   30 July, Concord Oval, Sydney   Third Test
AUSTRALIA 9 (1G 1PG)   NEW ZEALAND 30 (3G 4PG)

Before the third Test, the All Blacks were a brooding outfit. Their pride was hurt by the second Test draw and they were angered by allegations of rough-house play against New South Wales. They were hellbent on ending the tour on a decisive note.

The match was only two minutes old when Bruce Deans took the ball from the back of a maul and was awarded a try, although there was a deep suspicion of a knock-on. Grant Fox landed the angled conversion and followed it with a penalty goal four minutes later and a second in the 15th minute, giving the Kiwis a commanding 12–0 lead. No All Black team, especially this one, can be afforded the luxury of such a healthy early lead as it is virtually impossible for any opposing team to catch them up. The New Zealand line-out was winning adequate possession while Australia had no answer to the power and support of the All Black forwards in the loose. However, Leeds did lift Australia's spirits by half-time with a penalty goal.

After the break the All Blacks' pressure gradually took its toll on the Australians. Fox converted two further penalty goals to pass Don Clarke's New Zealand points-scoring record and extend the score to 18–3. John Gallagher, who was a continual threat at full-back, sliced through to score in the corner before Deans engineered Kirwan's final try. Australia's courage was unrelenting until the final moment, when Walker dummied his way over the line for Australia's only try.

AUSTRALIA: A J Leeds (New South Wales); I M Williams (New South Wales), J C Grant (New South Wales), M T Cook (Queensland), D I Campese (New South Wales); L F Walker (New South Wales), N C Farr-Jones (New South Wales) *(capt)*; R Lawton (Queensland), T A Lawton (Queensland), A J McIntyre (Queensland), S A G Cutler (New South Wales), D Frawley (New South Wales), S P Poidevin (New South Wales), J S Miller (Queensland), T B Gavin (New South Wales)
Replacement M P Lynagh (Queensland) for Leeds
Scorers *Try:* Walker *Conversion:* Lynagh *Penalty Goal:* Leeds
NEW ZEALAND: Gallagher; Wright, Stanley, Schuster, Kirwan; Fox, Deans; McDowell, Fitzpatrick, Loe, Pierce, G Whetton, A Whetton, Jones, Shelford *(capt)*
Scorers *Tries:* Gallagher, Kirwan, Deans *Conversions:* Fox (3) *Penalty Goals:* Fox (4)
Referee J B Anderson (Scotland)

WESTERN SAMOA TO WALES AND IRELAND 1988

Western Samoa are keen to participate in the 1991 World Cup after they were unluckily omitted from the 1987 event. So, having won the Pacific Championship against Tonga and Fiji in 1987, they undertook this tour to Wales and Ireland, in which they won four and lost six of their ten matches, as a learning and public relations exercise. Displaying the usual Pacific gifts for uninhibited running, passing and backing-up, they scored a full quota of spectacular tries, but on the debit side showed loose defence and a lack of discipline when behind.

They were not without formidable players: the wing and captain Koko, the full-back Aiolupo, the hard-tackling centre Sio and forwards Toomalatai, Fatialofa, Williams and Lemamea were all of genuine class. Their best performance was a narrow win over Welsh Cup semi-finalists Newbridge. They also succeeded in making Wales and Ireland, especially the former, look a little insecure under pressure.

THE TOURING PARTY

Captain L Koko   **Coach** R Cook
Manager F Satini   **Assistant Coach** P Schuster

FULL-BACKS

A Aiolupo (Mota'a)
T Faamasino (Vaiamoso)
T Salesa (Mota'a)

THREEQUARTERS

L Koko (Tuamasaga)
K Sio (Scoba)
J Ah Kuoi (Marist)
T Ugapo (Vaiamoso)
L Foai (Marist)
P Young (Apia)

HALF-BACKS

F Saena (Mota'a)
P Petaia (Apia)
V Fepuleai (Marist)
M Moke (Vailele)

FORWARDS

F Aimaasu (Mota'a)
V Alalatoa (Apia)
O Crichton (Apia)
V Faasua (Mota'a)
P Fatialofa (Tuamasaga)
M Iupeli (Vaiamoso)
S Lemamea (Lefaga)
L Mano (Marist)
R Rimoni (Mota'a)
L Sasi (Iavai)
T Sefo (Mota'a)
S Toomalatai (Vaiala)
S Tupuola (Iavai)
D Williams (Apia)

TOUR RECORD

All matches   Played 10   Won 4   Lost 6   Points for 171   Against 254
International matches   Played 2   Lost 2   Points for 28   Against 73

SCORING DETAILS

All matches				International matches				
For:	29T 11C 11PG		171 Pts	For:	5T	4C		28 Pts
Against:	34T 17C 27PG	1DG	254 Pts	Against:	12T	8C	2PG 1DG	73 Pts

MATCH DETAILS

1988	OPPONENTS	VENUE	RESULT
11 Oct	Welsh Counties Under-23	Llanelli	W 19-18
15 Oct	Newbridge	Newbridge	W 16-15
19 Oct	North Wales	Wrexham	W 24-12
22 Oct	Bridgend	Bridgend	L 17-21
26 Oct	Aberavon	Aberavon	L 11-21
29 Oct	IRELAND	Lansdowne Road	L 22-49
2 Nov	Ulster	Ravenhill	L 15-47
5 Nov	Connacht	Galway	L 18-25
8 Nov	Pontypridd	Pontypridd	W 23-22
12 Nov	WALES	Cardiff	L 6-24

Scorers: 26 – Aiolupo (1T 5C 4PG); 24 – Salesa (1T 4C 4PG); 16 – Koko (4T), Sio (4T); 12 – Iupeli (3T), Ugapo (3T), Young (3T); 11 – Faamasino (2T 1PG); 8 – Ah Kuoi (2T), Petaia (1C 2PG); 4 – Alalatoa (1T), Fepuleai (1T), Foai (1T), Lemamea (1T), Mano (1T), Toomalatai (1T); 2 – Crichton (1C)

Appearances: 10 – Fatialofa; 9 – Sio (inc 1 as replacement), Ugapo (inc 1 as replacement), Williams; 8 – Ah Kuoi, Iupeli, Koko, Mano (inc 1 as replacement), Toomalatai; 7 – Alalatoa (inc 1 as replacement), Faasua (inc 1 as replacement), Lemamea; 6 – Aiolupo (inc 1 as replacement), Faamasino, Fepuleai, Saena, Tupuola; 5 – Sefo, Young (inc 1 as replacement); 4 – Foai; 3 – Aimaasu, Crichton, Petaia, Rimoni (inc 2 as replacement), Salesa; 2 – Sasi; 1 – Moke

MATCH 1   11 October, Llanelli

Welsh Counties Under-23 18 (2PG 3T)   **Western Samoa XV 19** (1PG 4T)
Welsh Counties Under-23 *(Glamorgan unless stated)*: J Callard (Mon); R Subbiani (Pembroke), T Michael, S Davies (Carmarthen), A Griffiths (Mon) *(capt)*, A Booth; F Hillman (Mon), K Gregory (Mon), R Buckley (Mon), A Allen (Mon), J Wakeford, G Williams, E Lewis (Carmarthen), I Hemburrow
Scorers *Tries:* Subbiani, Wakeford, Gregory   *Penalty Goals:* Evans (2)
Western Samoa XV: Aiolupo; Koko *(capt)*, Sio, Ah Kuoi, Ugapo; Saena, Fepuleai; Alalatoa, Toomalatai, Fatialofa, Sefo, Williams, Tupuola, Faasua, Iupeli
Replacement Rimoni for Sefo
Scorers *Tries:* Sio, Alalatoa, Koko, Toomalatai   *Penalty Goals:* Aiolupo
Referee R C Quittenton (England)

MATCH 2   15 October, Newbridge

Newbridge 15 (1G 3PG)   **Western Samoa XV 16** (1G 2PG 1T)
Newbridge: D Rees; S Hill, C Manley, D Hussey, C Phillips; P Turner, R Lewis; J Rowlands, K Waters, N Hitchman, T Shaw, A Sutton, S Griffiths *(capt)*, R Smith, P Jones *Replacement* Harries for Hussey
Scorers *Try:* Jones   *Conversion:* Turner   *Penalty Goals:* Turner (3)
Western Samoa XV: Aiolupo; Koko *(capt)*, Sio, Ah Kuoi, Ugapo; Saena, Fepuleai; Sasi, Toomalatai, Fatialofa, Faasua, Lemamea, Williams, Iupeli, Tupuola
Replacement Alalatoa for Sasi
Scorers *Tries:* Ah Kuoi, Ugapo   *Conversion:* Aiolupo   *Penalty Goals:* Aiolupo (2)
Referee R McDowell (Ireland)

MATCH 3   19 October, Wrexham

North Wales 12 (1G 2PG)   **Western Samoa XV 24** (1G 2PG 3T)
North Wales: P Martin (Pwllheli); D Jones (Wrexham), N Holifield (Wrexham), M Ferguson (Mold), I ap Daffyd (Orrell); A Williams (Polytechnic of Wales), G Williams (Pwllheli) *(capt)*; I Buckett (Pwllheli), I Studt (Pwllheli), A Edwards (Liverpool St Helens), S Roy (Cardiff), W Pugh (Liverpool St Helens), D Cooke (Cardiff Medicals), T Davies (Wrexham), I Jones (Llanelli)   *Replacement* G James (Wrexham) for Jones
Scorers *Try:* ap Dafydd   *Conversion:* Williams   *Penalty Goals:* Williams (2)
Western Samoa XV: Faamasino; Foai, Sio, Young, Koko *(capt)*; Petaia, Fepuleai; Alalatoa, Toomalatai, Fatialofa, Mano, Rimoni, Williams, Tupuola, Sefo
Replacements Ugapo for Faamasino; Aiolupo for Sio
Scorers *Tries:* Fepuleai, Koko, Sio, Aiolupo   *Conversion:* Petaia
Penalty Goals: Petaia (2)
Referee S Griffiths (England)

MATCH 4   22 October, Bridgend

Bridgend 21 (2G 3PG)   **Western Samoa XV 17** (1G 1PG 2T)
Bridgend: A Parry; G Webbe, J Apsee, S Pritchard, R Diplock; A Williams, B Roach; M Griffiths, W Hall, P Edwards, P Kawulok, M Langley, P Yardley, O Williams, J Morgan *(capt)*
Scorers *Tries:* Apsee, Webbe   *Conversions:* Parry (2)   *Penalty Goals:* Parry (3)

Western Samoa XV: Aiolupo; Koko (*capt*), Sio, Ah Kuoi, Ugapo; Saena, Fepuleai; Fatialofa, Toomalatai, Alalatoa, Sefo, Tupuola, Williams, Iupeli, Faasua
Replacements Young for Fepuleai; Mano for Iupeli
Scorers *Tries:* Iupeli, Mano, Ugapo   *Conversion:* Aiolupo   *Penalty Goal:* Aiolupo
Referee D Templeton (Ireland)

MATCH 5   26 October, Aberavon

Aberavon 21 (1G 1PG 3T)   **Western Samoa XV 11** (1PG 2T)
Aberavon: L Lewis; J Hopkins, G Matthews (*capt*), A John, J Spender; A Jones, M Roberts; A Thomas, P Morgan, K Yates, T Jarrams, A Twomey, P Hamley, A Varney, P Middleton   *Replacements* N Forester for John; J Jardine for Spender
Scorers *Tries:* Hopkins, Middleton, Forester, Jones   *Conversion:* Lewis
Penalty Goal: Lewis
Western Samoa XV: Faamasino; Foai, Koko (*capt*), Saena, Ugapo; Petaia, Moke; Fatialofa, Crichton, Aimaasu, Sasi, Lemamea, Tupuola, Mano, Faasua *Replacement* Rimoni for Tupuola
Scorers *Tries:* Foai, Koko   *Penalty Goal:* Faamasino
Referee C Norling (Wales)

MATCH 6   29 October, Lansdowne Road

IRELAND 49 (4G 2PG 1DG 4T)   **WESTERN SAMOA 22** (3G 1T)
Twelve tries were scored in this match in which Ireland led 21-6 at half-time and 37-6 only ten minutes into the second half before the Western Samoans conjured up three late tries.

Koko opened the scoring with a try which Aiolupo converted, but the Samoan lead was soon overhauled by tries from Matthews, Mullin and Francis, all converted by Kiernan who had begun the Irish reply with a penalty goal. Crossan scored two tries and McBride added another directly after half-time, one of which was converted by Kiernan, in a rush of Irish scoring. From then on a carnival atmosphere prevailed: Young (2) and Ah Kuoi scored tries for Western Samoa, two of which were converted by Aiolupo and Crichton. Sexton added a try and a dropped goal for Ireland, and Kiernan – roundly booed for his successful second-half penalty by a crowd wanting to see running action – chalked up 18 points when he crossed the line and so surpassed Ollie Campbell's Irish record of 217 points.

IRELAND: P P Danaher (Garryowen); J F Sexton (Lansdowne), B J Mullin (London Irish), M J Kiernan (Dolphin), K D Crossan (Instonians); P M Dean (St Mary's Coll), L F P Aherne (Lansdowne); T P J Clancy (Lansdowne), S J Smith (Ballymena), J J McCoy (Bangor), D G Lenihan (Cork Const); N P T Francis (London Irish), P M Matthews (Wanderers) (*capt*), N P Mannion (Corinthians), W D McBride (Malone)
Replacement P T J O'Hara (Sunday's Well) for Matthews (75 mins)
Scorers *Tries:* Crossan (2), Kiernan, Matthews, Mullin, Francis, McBride, Sexton
Conversions: Kiernan (4)   *Penalty Goals:* Kiernan (2)   *Dropped Goal:* Sexton
WESTERN SAMOA: Aiolupo; Koko (*capt*), Sio, Ah Kuoi, Ugapo; Saena, Young; Fatialofa, Toomalatai, Alalatoa, Williams, Lemamea, Mano, Iupeli, Sefo   *Replacement* Crichton for Koko
Scorers *Tries:* Young (2), Koko, Ah Kuoi   *Conversions:* Aiopulo (2), Crichton
Referee W D Bevan (Wales)

MATCH 7   2 November, Ravenhill

Ulster 47 (4G 1PG 5T)   **Western Samoa XV 15** (2G 1PG)
Ulster (*Malone unless stated*): C Wilkinson; T M Ringland (Ballymena), D G Irwin

(Instonians) (*capt*), J Hewitt (London Irish), K D Crossan (Instonians); P Russell (Instonians), R Brady (Ballymena); J J McCoy (Bangor), J P McDonald, M Reynolds, J Rodgers (Bangor), C Morrison, D Whittle (London Irish), D McBride, W A Anderson (Dungannon)
Scorers *Tries:* Crossan (3), Rodgers (2), Ringland, Anderson, Hewitt, McBride *Conversions:* Russell (4) *Penalty Goal:* Russell
Western Samoa XV: Faamasino; Koko (*capt*), Sio, Ah Kuoi, Salesa; Petaia, Young; Fatialofa, Crichton, Aimaasu, Williams, Lemamea, Mano, Iupeli, Sefo
Scorers *Tries:* Young, Sio *Conversions:* Salesa (2) *Penalty Goal:* Salesa
Referee G Black (Leinster)

MATCH 8   5 November, Galway

Connacht 25 (7PG 1T)   **Western Samoa XV 18** (1G 3T)
Connacht: J Staples (London Irish); F O'Flynn (Corinthians), R Hernan (St Mary's Coll), M Cosgrove (Wanderers), E Guerin (Galwegians); C Cruess-Callaghan (O Belvedere), S O'Beirne (St Mary's Coll); T P J Clancy (Lansdowne) (*capt*), J O'Riordan (UC Galway), D Henshaw (Athlone), A Higgins (UC Galway), M M F Moylett (Shannon), M Fitzgibbon (Shannon), J O'Driscoll (Liverpool St Helens), N P Mannion (Corinthians)   *Replacement* C Donne (Blackrock Coll) for Guerin
Scorers *Try:* Henshaw   *Penalty Goals:* O'Beirne (7)
Western Samoa XV: Faamasino; Foai, Sio, Ah Kuoi, Ugapo; Salesa, Young; Fatialofa, Toomalatai, Alalatoa, Lemamea, Williams, Mano, Faasua, Iupeli (*capt*)
Scorers *Tries:* Ugapo, Iupeli, Sio, Faamasino   *Conversion:* Salesa
Referee A Mason (England)

MATCH 9   8 November, Pontypridd

Pontypridd 22 (6PG 1T)   **Western Samoa XV 23** (1G 3PG 2T)
Pontypridd: J Mason; G Loxton, C Jones (*capt*), S Lewis, E Ford; A Phillips, K Lee; G Davies, P John, P Knight, A Owen, G Davies, N Saunders, A Carpenter, M Butts *Replacements* C Gupwell for Lewis; H Evans for Lee
Scorers *Try:* Ford   *Penalty Goals:* Phillips (6)
Western Samoa XV: Salesa; Foai, Faamasino, Saena, Ugapo; Ah Kuoi, Fepuleai; Fatialofa, Toomalatai, Aimaasu, Mano, Lemamea, Williams, Iupeli (*capt*), Faasua *Replacement* Sio for Saena
Scorers *Tries:* Salesa, Iupeli, Faamasino   *Conversion:* Salesa   *Penalty Goals:* Salesa (3)
Referee D Leslie (Scotland)

MATCH 10   12 November, Cardiff

WALES 24 (4G)   WESTERN SAMOA 6 (1G)

Although Wales scored four tries, they played with little real authority and gave no indication that the scars from their mauling in New Zealand during the previous summer had healed. The scoreline did less than justice to the Western Samoans, who with a little more luck and steadiness should have scored three more tries. Unexpectedly, the visitors won the line-out battle against Bob Norster and company.

Carwyn Davies opened the scoring for Wales with a try on his debut and Jonathan Davies scored the second, both of which were converted by Thorburn to give Wales an early 12-point lead and what should have been a secure platform for a runaway victory. Instead, Faamasino created a splendid try for Lemamea, converted by Aiolupo. In a second half when tactical awareness went from bad to worse for Wales, two tries by Nigel Davies, both converted by Thorburn, were the only comfort. So, although Thorburn passed Phil Bennett's Welsh record of 166 points in his 19th international, it did nothing to relieve their anxiety.

WALES: P H Thorburn (Neath); M R Hall (Cambridge U & Bridgend), N G Davies (Llanelli), B Bowen (Swansea), C Davies (Llanelli); J Davies (Llanelli) (*capt*), R N Jones (Swansea); M Griffiths (Bridgend), W H Hall (Bridgend), D Young (Cardiff), J D M Wakeford (S Wales Police), R L Norster (Cardiff), R Phillips (Neath), D J Bryant (Bridgend), P T Davies (Llanelli) *Replacements* R V Wintle (London Welsh) for C Davies (50 mins); A Clement (Swansea) for Thorburn (76 mins)
Scorers *Tries:* N Davies (2), J Davies, C Davies *Conversions:* Thorburn (4)
WESTERN SAMOA: Aiolupo; Koko (*capt*), Sio, Faamasino, Ugapo; Ah Kuoi, Fepuleai; Alalatoa, Toomalatai, Fatialofa, Mano, Lemamea, Williams, Iupeli, Tupuola *Replacement* Faasua for Iupeli (74 mins)
Scorers *Try:* Lemamea *Conversion:* Aiolupo
Referee O E Doyle (Ireland)

FRANCE TO ARGENTINA 1988

This 1988 French trip to Argentina resulted in the almost traditional 1-1 draw in the Test series. Argentina have now beaten France in Buenos Aires in 1985, 1986 and 1988. France toured under new captain Pierre Berbizier, who was being groomed by coach Jacques Fouroux for the home season.

France were held 18-18 against Tucuman, the provincial champions, although they scored the only try of the game, but San Isidro, the club champions, were beaten. There was yet another claimant for the world record international rugby score when the French moved to Paraguay and won 106-12. This equalled New Zealand's score against Japan in 1987, but Japan, unlike Paraguay, had played in the World Cup and their status therefore had more credence.

THE TOURING PARTY
Manager Y Noé **Coach** J Fouroux
Captain P Berbizier

FULL-BACKS	FORWARDS
J-B Lafond (Racing Club)	**L Rodriguez** (Dax)
S Blanco (Biarritz)	**C Deslandes** (Montferrand)
THREEQUARTERS	**J Gratton** (Agen)
	E Champ (Toulon)
P Bérot (Agen)	**M Cecillon** (Bourgoin)
B Lacombe (Agen)	**A Carminati** (Béziers)
P Lagisquet (Bayonne)	**A Lorieux** (Aix les Bains)
F Velo (Grenoble)	**D Erbani** (Agen)
P Sella (Agen)	**J Condom** (Biarritz)
D Charvet (Toulouse)	**P Beraud** (Dax)
M Andrieu (Nîmes)	**D Dubroca** (Agen)
	P Dintrans (Tarbes)
HALF-BACKS	**P Ondarts** (Biarritz)
	P Marocco (Montferrand)
F Mesnel (Racing Club)	**J-P Garuet** (Lourdes)
J-P Trille (Tarbes)	**L Armary** (Lourdes)
D Camberabero (Béziers)	
M Hondagne (Tarbes)	
P Berbizier (Agen)	

TOUR RECORD

All matches Played 8   Won 6   Drawn 1   Lost 1   Points for 337   Against 107
International matches   Played 2   Won 1   Lost 1   Points for 24   Against 33

SCORING DETAILS

All matches

For: 57T 35C 12PG 1DG 337 Pts
Against: 6T   4C 24PG 1DG 107 Pts

International matches

For: 1T 1C 6PG   24 Pts
Against: 1T 1C 8PG 1DG 33 Pts

MATCH DETAILS

1988	OPPONENTS	VENUE	SCORE
4 June	San Isidro Club	Buenos Aires	W 29-16
7 June	Tucuman	Tucuman	D 18-18
11 June	Buenos Aires XV	Buenos Aires	W 82-0
15 June	Select XV	Posodas	W 36-19
18 June	ARGENTINA	Buenos Aires	W 18-15
21 June	Rosario Union	Cordoba	W 42-9
25 June	ARGENTINA	Buenos Aires	L 6-18
27 June	Paraguay XV	Asunción	W 106-12

MATCH 1   4 June, Buenos Aires

San Isidro Club 16 (1G 2PG 1T)   **French XV 29** (1G 1DG 5T)
San Isidro *Tries:* Chevallier-Boutell, Ramallo   *Conversion:* Madero
Penalty Goals: Madero (2)
French XV *Tries:* Camberabero (2), Blanco, Rodriguez, Lagisquet, Charvet
Conversion: Camberabero   *Dropped Goal:* Mesnel

MATCH 2   7 June, Tucuman

Tucuman 18 (6PG)   **French XV 18** (1G 4PG)
Tucuman *Penalty Goals:* Meson (6)
French XV *Try:* Deslandes   *Conversion:* Bérot   *Penalty Goals:* Bérot (4)

MATCH 3   11 June, Buenos Aires

Buenos Aires XV 0   **French XV 82** (9G 7T)
French XV *Tries:* Lagisquet (5), Blanco (4), Sella (3), Cecillon (2), Mesnel, Dintrans
Conversions: Bérot (9)

MATCH 4   15 June, Posodas

Select XV 19 (5PG 1T)   **French XV 36** (4G 3T)
Select XV *Try:* Teran   *Penalty Goals:* Meson (5)
French XV *Tries:* Carminati (3), Andrieu (2), Lafond, Marocco   *Conversions:* Bérot (4)

MATCH 5   18 June, Velez, Buenos Aires   First Test

ARGENTINA 15 (1G 2PG 1DG)   FRANCE 18 (1G 4PG)

Argentina were playing without Hugo Porta for only the second time
since 1973 but they only narrowly failed to share the spoils in a bruising
Test. France won thanks to a 63rd-minute try from Philippe Dintrans.
Bérot, who converted and kicked all four of his penalties in the first 26
minutes, had earlier given the tourists a 12-9 lead.

Argentina had gone ahead through a try by their hooker, Angelillo,
converted by Baetti. They also fought back to lead 15-12 at the interval
following two penalties by Baetti and a 22nd-minute dropped goal from
Turnes. Dintrans' converted try was the only score of a tight second
half, but it was sufficient to edge France home.

41

ARGENTINA: A Scolni (Alumni); G Teran (Tucuman), D Cuesta Silva (San Isidro Club), M Loffreda (San Isidro Club), C Mendy (Los Tilos); F Turnes (Banco Nación), D Baetti (Rosario); S Dengra (San Martin), J Angelillo (San Isidro Club), D M Cash (San Isidro Club), E N Branca (CA San Isidro), A Iachetti (Hindu), J Allen (CA San Isidro) (*capt*), P Garreton (Tucuman), G E Milano (Rosario) *Replacement* D Gonzalez (San Luis) for Angelillo (78 mins)
Scorers *Try:* Angelillo   *Conversion:* Baetti   *Penalty Goals:* Baetti (2)
Dropped Goal: Turnes
FRANCE: Blanco; Bérot, Sella, Andrieu, Lagisquet; Mesnel, Berbizier (*capt*); Ondarts, Dintrans, Garuet, Lorieux, Condom, Champ, Carminati, Rodriguez
Scorers *Try:* Dintrans   *Conversion:* Bérot   *Penalty Goals:* Bérot (4)
Referee O E Doyle (Ireland)

MATCH 6   18 June, Rosario

Rosario Union 9 (1G 1PG)   **French XV 42** (4G 2PG 3T)
Rosario Union *Try:* Musi   *Conversion:* Dominquez   *Penalty Goal:* Dominquez
French XV *Tries:* Camberabero (3), Lacombe (2), Lagisquet (2)
Conversions: Camberabero (3), Trille   *Penalty Goal:* Camberabero

MATCH 7   18 June, Velez, Buenos Aires   Second Test

ARGENTINA 18 (6PG)   **FRANCE 6** (2PG)
Argentina's third Test win in successive tours by France was deserved but the match will live in the memory only for the score and for its violence. This was a bitter battle. French captain Berbizier broke his arm five minutes from time, then two minutes later Lorieux was sent off for a vengeful retaliation. The Pumas hero was Daniel Baetti, a 33-year-old doctor from Rosario, who punished French indiscipline with six penalty goals – three in each half.
ARGENTINA: A Scolni (Alumni); D Cuesta Silva (San Isidro Club), M Loffreda (San Isidro Club), F Turnes (Banco Nación), C Mendy (Los Tilos); R Madero (San Isidro Club), D Baetti (Rosario); S Dengra (San Martin), A Courreges (CA San Isidro), D M Cash (San Isidro Club), E N Branca (CA San Isidro), A Iachetti (Hindu), J Allen (CA San Isidro) (*capt*), P Garreton (Tucuman), G E Milano (Rosario)
Scorer *Penalty Goals:* Baetti (6)
FRANCE: Blanco; Bérot, Sella, Andrieu, Lagisquet; Mesnel, Berbizier (*capt*); Ondarts, Dintrans, Garuet, Lorieux, Condom, Cecillon, Carminati, Rodriguez
Replacement Hondagne for Berbizier (75 mins)
Scorer *Penalty Goals:* Bérot (2)
Referee O E Doyle (Ireland)

MATCH 8   27 June, Ascunción

Paraguay XV 12 (1G 2PG)   **French XV 106** (15G 4T)
Paraguay XV *Try:* Cabrera   *Conversion:* Baez   *Penalty Goals:* Baez (2)
French XV *Tries:* Lagisquet (7), Charvet (4), Sella (3), Bérot, Mesnel, Champ, Velo, Trille   *Conversions:* Bérot (10), Trille (4), Charvet

ARGENTINA TO FRANCE 1988

Argentina are usually a tough proposition on their own grounds but still find it far more difficult to make an impression in other parts of the world. In an eight-match tour to France in October and November 1988, the Pumas lost both Test matches, conceding nine tries without scoring one in reply, and three of the six regional matches – this after sharing the series with France 1-1 some four months earlier on home soil.

The inspiration of the side since 1973, Hugo Porta, did not tour and so, although the Pumas still kicked their penalties, they lacked flair and generalship without him.

The tour, which ran concurrently with the Maoris' visit to France, found the opposition regional XVs in unusually good shape for early in the season. But the failure to create try-scoring opportunities were matters that disappointed the French crowds and the Argentine management alike. The Pumas played bravely in the two Tests, but found the French far too powerful and committed.

THE TOURING PARTY

Captain J Allen   **Manager** H Vidou
Coach R O'Reilly   **Assistant Coach** R Sanz

FULL-BACKS	FORWARDS
A Scolni (Alumni)	D M Cash (San Isidro Club)
S Salvat (Alumni)	S Dengra (San Martin)
	M Urbano (Buenos Aires)
THREEQUARTERS	J Angelillo (San Isidro Club)
J Soler (Tucuman Lawn Tennis)	A Courreges (CA San Isidro)
G Teran (Tucuman)	A Iachetti (Hindu)
C Mendy (Los Tilos)	M Valesani (Rosario Ath)
D Cuesta Silva (San Isidro Club)	E N Branca (CA San Isidro)
F Turnes (Banco Nación)	P Buabse (Los Tarcos, Tucuman)
P Garzon (El Taba, Cordoba)	J Allen (CA San Isidro)
M Loffreda (San Isidro Club)	D Gonzalez (San Luis)
S Meson (Tucuman)	M Bertranou (Los Tordos)
HALF-BACKS	F Conti (San Isidro Club)
R Madero (San Isidro Club)	P Garreton (Tucuman U)
D Dominguez (La Tablada, Cordoba)	G E Milano (Rosario Jockey Club)
D Baetti (Rosario Ath)	M Carreras (Olivos)
F Silvestre (Mendoza)	*replacement during tour*
*A Soares Gache (San Isidro Club)	

TOUR RECORD

All matches   Played 8   Won 3   Lost 5   Points for 158   Against 169
International matches   Played 2   Lost 2   Points for 27   Against 57

SCORING DETAILS

All matches
For: 14T   6C   29PG   1DG   158 Pts
Against: 19T   12C   22PG   1DG   169 Pts

International matches
For: 8PG   1DG   27 Pts
Against: 9T   6C   3PG   57 Pts

MATCH DETAILS

1988	OPPONENTS	VENUE	RESULT
18 Oct	Bourgogne	Dijon	L 15-18
22 Oct	Auvergne	Clermont-Ferrand	L 19-23
25 Oct	Roussillon	Perpignan	W 24-15
29 Oct	Select XV	Marmande	W 16-10
1 Nov	Atlantique	Niort	L 22-31
5 Nov	FRANCE	Nantes	L 9-29
8 Nov	Armed Forces	Melun	W 35-15
11 Nov	FRANCE	Lille	L 18-28

Leading points-scorers: Turnes 36 (12PG), Dominquez 29 (4C 7PG) and Baetti 26 (1C 8PG). Cuesta Silva, Carreras, Meson and Teran each scored two tries. In the internationals Turnes scored 24 points (8PG) and Madero scored a dropped goal.

MATCH 1   18 October, Dijon

Bourgogne 18 (6PG)   **Argentinians 15** (5PG)
Bourgogne *Penalty Goals:* Ponnel (3), Lafond (3)
Argentinians *Penalty Goals:* Baetti (5)

MATCH 2   22 October, Clermont-Ferrand

Auvergne 23 (1G 3PG 2T)   **Argentinians 19** (1G 3PG 1T)
Auvergne *Tries:* Blanc, Garcia, Nicol   *Conversion:* Trille   *Penalty Goals:* Trille (3)
Argentinians *Tries:* Cuesta Silva, Carreras   *Conversion:* Baetti   *Penalty Goals:* Baetti (3)

MATCH 3   25 October, Perpignan

Roussillon 15 (1G 3PG)   **Argentinians 24** (1G 2PG 3T)
Roussillon *Try:* Bey   *Conversion:* Almaric   *Penalty Goals:* Almaric (3)
Argentinians *Tries:* Cuesta Silva, Conti, Meson, Madero   *Conversion:* Meson
Penalty Goals: Meson, Loffreda

MATCH 4   29 October, Marmande

Select XV 10 (2PG 1T)   **Argentinians 16** (4PG 1T)
Select XV *Try:* Carbonel   *Penalty Goals:* Bérot (2)
Argentinians *Try:* Mendy   *Penalty Goals:* Turnes (4)

MATCH 5   1 November, Niort

Atlantique 31 (2G 4PG 1DG 1T)   **Argentinians 22** (1G 4PG 1T)
Atlantique *Tries:* Courtoils, Peytavin, Lespinasse   *Conversions:* Lafond (2)
Penalty Goals: Lafond (3), Le Bourhis   *Dropped Goal:* Barboteau
Argentinians *Tries:* Meson, Dominquez   *Conversion:* Dominquez
Penalty Goals: Dominquez (4)

MATCH 6   5 November, Beaujoire Stadium, Nantes   First Test

FRANCE 29 (3G 1PG 2T)   ARGENTINA 9 (3PG)

The French had an overwhelming amount of possession which could
have been more constructively used, even if they did score five tries.
They were inspired by outstanding performances from Blanco and
Rodriguez and plentiful line-out possession from Bourguignon. After
Blanco had scored an early try from a Rodriguez charge, the French
were always in control. He then added his second try under the posts,
which Bérot converted to give the home side a 10-0 lead after 37
minutes. Turnes' penalty in injury time in the first half was the first of
his three successful kicks.

Rodriguez set up the third French try, scored by Cecillon after 52
minutes, which Bérot converted, to add to his penalty goal four minutes
earlier. After two more penalties from Turnes, Lagisquet scored a try
in the corner after 72 minutes and, fittingly, Rodriguez scored the final
try in a typical burst from the 22 to the posts, leaving Bérot the
formality of a conversion. France, dominant at the line-out (26-13) and
in the rucks (29-10) spoiled much good work by poor passing and by
conceding too many penalties.

FRANCE: S Blanco (Biarritz); P Bérot (Agen), P Sella (Agen), M Andrieu (Nîmes),
P Lagisquet (Bayonne); F Mesnel (Racing Club), H Sanz (Narbonne); L Armary

(Lourdes), P Dintrans (Tarbes) (*capt*), P Ondarts (Biarritz), G Bourguignon (Narbonne), J Condom (Biarritz), E Champ (Toulon), M Cecillon (Bourgoin), L Rodriguez (Dax)
Scorers *Tries:* Blanco (2), Cecillon, Lagisquet, Rodriguez   *Conversions:* Bérot (3)
Penalty Goal: Bérot
ARGENTINA: Scolni; Cuesta Silva, Loffreda, Turnes, Mendy; Madero, Silvestre; Dengra, Angelillo, Cash, Branca, Iachetti, Conti, Garreton, Allen (*capt*)
Scorer *Penalty Goals:* Turnes (3)
Referee M O'Neill (Australia)

MATCH 7   8 November, Melun

Armed Forces 15 (2G 1PG)   **Argentinians 35** (3G 3PG 2T)
Armed Forces: *Tries:* Nivet, penalty try   *Penalty Goal:* Farenq
Argentinians: *Tries:* Loffreda, Teran (2), Buabse, Carreras   *Conversions:* Dominquez (3)
Penalty Goals: Dominquez (3)

MATCH 8   11 November, Stade Grimomporez-Jooris, Lille
Second Test

FRANCE 28 (3G 2PG 1T)   ARGENTINA 18 (5PG 1DG)

Argentina kept almost in touch throughout this game due to the boot of Fabien Turnes, and also because France were again guilty of not making the most of their chances and of conceding too many penalties. Turnes kicked well after being thrown into the role following Baetti's injury in the third game of the tour. France scored tries at regular intervals: Sanz (6 minutes), Cecillon (30 minutes), Andrieu (55 minutes) and Sella at the death. However, thanks to Madero's dropped goal and Turnes' five penalties, the 10-point margin appeared only in injury time after another fierce encounter.

FRANCE: S Blanco (Biarritz); P Bérot (Agen), P Sella (Agen), M Andrieu (Nîmes), P Lagisquet (Bayonne); F Mesnel (Racing Club), H Sanz (Narbonne); L Armary (Lourdes), P Marocco (Montferrand), P Ondarts (Biarritz), A Lorieux (Aix-les-Bains), J Condom (Biarritz), E Champ (Toulon), M Cecillon (Bourgoin), L Rodriguez (Dax) (*capt*)
Replacement P Arthapignet (Tarbes) for Marocco (6 mins)
Scorers *Tries:* Sanz, Cecillon, Andrieu, Sella   *Conversions:* Bérot (3)
Penalty Goals: Bérot (2)
ARGENTINA: Scolni; Cuesta Silva, Loffreda, Turnes, Mendy; Madero, Soares Gache; Dengra, Angelillo, Cash, Branca, Iachetti, Allen (*capt*), Garreton, Milano
Replacements Salvat for Cuesta Silva (21 mins); Gonzalez for Angelillo (42 mins)
Scorers *Penalty Goals:* Turnes (5)   *Dropped Goal:* Madero
Referee M O'Neill (Australia)

FRANCE WIN THE BATTLES AND THE WAR

The International Championship 1989

As the demand for tickets for the ten Championship games continues to spiral and as the preparations for the five competing teams become ever more scientific and time-consuming, the question has to be asked, is the whole thing not becoming *too* important? There was an all-pervading air of tension and sometimes bitterness about the proceedings in 1989. Certainly, almost every game was compelling as a contest but only two games – Ireland against France in Dublin and Scotland against Ireland in Edinburgh – really broke free from that tension and added real spectacle to the harshness of the contest.

France won the title with three wins but were denied a Grand Slam by their emphatic defeat at Twickenham, where the England pack had a storming day aided, it must be said, by a baffling lack of pride and passion in the French performance, especially in the front five of the scrum. Yet France, with the peerless Blanco and with Berbizier and Sella again outstanding, were unquestionably the best side in the competition. They did have to go some to overhaul Ireland when the Irish, memorably, led by 15-0 and 21-7, but they were never remotely in bother against either Scotland or Wales in Paris.

England provided two of the players of the Championship in Wade Dooley and Paul Ackford, who in all but the final match against Wales played with real athleticism to go with their ball-winning capabilities. Yet, sadly, England never kept up the momentum of their early season win against Australia: they failed to maintain the pace and spectacle of that game because they could not clear the ball from the base of the scrum, and anyway they lacked the inclination. But above all, the 1989 Championship was certainly not the environment for spreading the ball wide. England's running sore remains their failure to win at Cardiff since the early 1960s and even though they came ostensibly full of confidence to Cardiff in March 1989, even though they were in for at least a share of the Championship if they won and even though they faced the most limited and self-doubting Welsh team for years, they did not even come close. Admittedly, the scoring was close but for the second half of the match they were locked, in increasing desperation, into their own territory.

Ireland briefly threatened France; they beat Wales at Cardiff and they took a full part in the sweeping magnificence of the Murrayfield encounter against Scotland, when they proved they could make inroads behind the scrum with the best of them. Still, they were lacking. They had a platform of sorts because McCoy, Smith and Clancy in the front row played well all season and Mullin returned to form in the centre.

But they lacked direction; too often they played without the old fire and they were below true international class in too many areas, notably at full-back.

There was a brave attempt at imitating the New Zealand style of play from Scotland and the wonderful bonus of the form of Craig Chalmers and Gary Armstrong, the new half-backs. Once again, their back row were prominent when going forward and perhaps their player of the season was the least-heralded of the trio, Derek White, who won a richly-deserved place on the Lions tour. Again, the quality did not extend throughout the team but Scotland are still building. They are well led, expertly coached and, unlike England, are making the most of what they have.

The single Welsh victory certainly did not blind their followers to the deficiencies in the squad. At last there are signs of a new generation of potential international players – notably in Stephens and Iwan Jones of Llanelli; Damien Griffiths, the Newport wing and Llewelyn, the Neath lock. Norster and Robert Jones played as well as ever and Mark Jones emerged as a No 8 of class. But the team never recovered from the loss of the multi-talented and supremely confident Jonathan Davies. For the first three matches the team was drained of confidence and conviction – there were some strange selections, apparently with loyalty to some players being misplaced. The New Zealand lessons have not been learned as the overall pace and footballing ability of the side was still low.

The fact remains that with the Championship in its present form the side with most power and most desire will be far more likely to win than the team with more all-round rugby talents. The annual rugby festival now provides heads-down rugby. It is the responsibility of every team, if they can, to rein back on adrenalin a little and to give the artists of the game a look-in.

The final table was:

	P	W	D	L	F	A	Pts
France	4	3	0	1	76	47	6
England	4	2	1	1	48	27	5
Scotland	4	2	1	1	75	59	5
Ireland	4	1	0	3	64	92	2
Wales	4	1	0	3	44	82	2

21 January, Murrayfield
SCOTLAND 23 (1G 2PG 1DG 2T)   WALES 7 (1PG 1T)

(Sponsored by the Royal Bank)

The Welsh challenge for the Championship had an uneasy background. Jonathan Davies had departed for Widnes and Rugby League, Wales had lost their pre-Christmas match against Romania and at half-time in this match they trailed by a thumping 19-0. Although they did recover with a long period of pressure in the second half there was simply no denying the driving excellence of the Scots.

The highlight for the Scots was undoubtedly the confidence shown by Chalmers and Armstrong, their new half-back combination from the Borders. No doubt everyone in Scotland feared it would take two or three years to bed down a half-back partnership to succeed that of the departed Rutherford and Laidlaw, but here were two young men controlling the tactics and kicking splendidly. It was fitting that the final Scottish try, which killed off the Welsh revival in the second half, should have been touched down by Chalmers.

Two imposing performances in the loose play by Sole and White of Scotland practically shut Wales out in the first half and the visitors were desperately lacking in experience and composure. Even when they won a stream of possession in the second half they could manufacture only one try and the only unqualified good news from the day was the return to the side of Mark Jones at No 8, who played with fire and pace. Sadly for Wales, Griffiths at scrum-half had a poor game.

Scotland's two tries in the first half provided a contrast. The first came after Sole had drawn in the Welsh defence with a fierce drive and Lineen was given the ball with an overlap outside. For some reason he turned back inside but Chalmers doubled outside to carry on the move and Armstrong scored in the corner. White scored the second try merely by driving through some thin Welsh defence close to the scrum. A calm drop by Chalmers and the boot of Dods made it 19-0 at half-time. Wales came back with a superb try engineered from the back of a scrum and finished brilliantly by Hall on the wing, but Chalmers' late try re-established Scotland with a vengeance.

SCOTLAND: P W Dods (Gala); M D F Duncan (West of Scotland), S Hastings (Watsonians), S R P Lineen (Boroughmuir), I Tukalo (Selkirk); C M Chalmers (Melrose), G Armstrong (Jedforest); D M B Sole (Edinburgh Acads), K S Milne (Heriot's FP), I G Milne (Heriot's FP), C A Gray (Nottingham), D F Cronin (Bath), J Jeffrey (Kelso), D B White (Gala), F Calder (Stewart's-Melville FP) *(capt)*
Scorers *Tries:* Armstrong, White, Chalmers   *Conversion:* Dods
Penalty Goals: Dods (2)   *Dropped Goal:* Chalmers
WALES: P H Thorburn (Neath) *(capt)*; M R Hall (Cambridge U & Bridgend), N G Davies (Llanelli), J A Devereux (Bridgend), C Davies (Llanelli); B Bowen (Swansea), J L Griffiths (Llanelli); M Griffiths (Bridgend), I J Watkins (Ebbw Vale), D Young (Cardiff), K Moseley (Pontypool), P T Davies (Llanelli), R Phillips (Neath), M A Jones (Neath), D J Bryant (Bridgend)
Replacement H Williams-Jones (South Wales Police) for Young
Scorers *Try:* Hall   *Penalty Goal:* Bowen
Referee J-C Doulcet (France)

21 January, Lansdowne Road
IRELAND 21 (1G 5PG)   **FRANCE 26** (2G 2PG 2T)

(Sponsored by Digital)

At one stage of this extraordinary match, France trailed by 15 points and a score by Ireland at that stage would most certainly have killed them off. However, France came storming back with a mixture of hard-nosed forward effort and some sweeping brilliance from their gifted backs. Leading the charge for France was Blanco. It was his 65th match for France and certainly one of his best.

The intensity of Ireland's initial challenge certainly took France by surprise. They scored an early try when Dean put up a high kick into the sun and Lafond moved in front of Blanco as the French full-back was lining up the catch. The ball duly went loose and Mullin seized it to run on and score. Kiernan put over a conversion and had added three penalties by half-time for a 15-0 lead, and another two afterwards to extend it to 21-7. In the first half, Anderson and Lenihan and Ireland's line-out provided a steady source of possession and French plans to impose a bulldozer-like scrum on European rugby were strangled at source because Clancy and McCoy and the Irish scrum refused to be budged. For a time it was only Blanco's endless excellence in defence and his raking clearances that kept France going.

By the start of the second half, however, the flow of the game had been reversed. In a fury of attack and counter-attack the French scored four memorable tries; two from Lagisquet, a clinical finisher on the wing, and one each by Blanco and Lafond. Yet it was Blanco who lit the blue touch-paper. He appeared three times in a superb movement that ended in a try for himself. His kick out of defence had been charged down and the Irish briefly threatened to score. However, Mesnel broke clean out of defence and, 13 passes later, Blanco launched himself over for the try. Ireland led until the last six minutes but as both coaches admitted afterwards, the writing had been on the wall for some time before that. Nevertheless, it did show how the sheer ferocity of exchanges in the Championship can close the gap in class between teams. It was a thrilling match to set off the first day of the international season.

IRELAND: P P Danaher (Garryowen); J F Sexton (Lansdowne), B J Mullin (London Irish), D G Irwin (Instonians), M J Kiernan (Dolphin); P M Dean (St Mary's Coll), L F P Aherne (Lansdowne); T P J Clancy (Lansdowne), S J Smith (Ballymena), J J McCoy (Bangor), D G Lenihan (Cork Const), W A Anderson (Dungannon), P M Matthews (Wanderers) *(capt)*, N P Mannion (Corinthians), P T J O'Hara (Sunday's Well)
Scorers *Try:* Mullin *Conversion:* Kiernan *Penalty Goals:* Kiernan (5)
FRANCE: S Blanco (Biarritz); J-B Lafond (Racing Club de France), P Sella (Agen), M Andrieu (Nîmes), P Lagisquet (Bayonne); F Mesnel (Racing Club de France), P Berbizier (Agen) *(capt)*; P Ondarts (Biarritz), P Marocco (Montferrand), C Portolan (Toulouse), G Bourguignon (Narbonne), J Condom (Biarritz), M Cecillon (Bourgoin), L Rodriguez (Dax), A Carminati (Béziers) *Replacement* D Erbani (Agen) for Bourguignon
Scorers *Tries:* Lagisquet (2), Blanco, Lafond *Conversions:* Lafond (2)
Penalty Goals: Lafond (2)
Referee J B Anderson (Scotland)

4 February, Cardiff Arms Park
WALES 13 (3PG 1T)   IRELAND 19 (1G 3PG 1T)

(Sponsored by British Gas)

Wales had not lost their first two Championship matches for more than 20 years. In this gloomy, low-standard affair they were certainly hard done by, but in the final analysis their own failings condemned them as much as anything. Ireland were a limited team trying to cash in on mistakes rather than creating scores themselves. Yet it was another deeply satisfying Irish raid on Cardiff for all that, and the highlight was a heroic charge for a try by Mannion, the No 8, who ran nearly 70 yards into a place in Irish folklore. Not much else will go down in history, unless it is the error of Mr Quittenton in allowing play to proceed after a blatant Irish knock-on – the decisive Irish try was the result.

The two most impressive individual performances came from the two scrum-halves, Aherne of Ireland and Jones of Wales. Their sharpness and competitive edge illuminated the contest. However, the Welsh attack was fitful and short of ideas; their lack of poise often gave Ireland the scraps of loose ball on which they feed hungrily. Yet Wales still carved out enough chances, which lack of experience and steadiness as the line approached managed to waste. The only Welsh try came after Hall, moving to the centre after the departure of Devereux, carved through the centre. Ieuan Evans could not quite get in at the corner but immediately afterwards Mark Jones rumbled over the line to score.

The two fateful Irish tries turned the game late on. Mannion's charge began when he caught an attempted chip ahead by Bowen and outpaced the Welsh cover in a thrilling chase to the corner. Near the end, Wales won a defensive scrum but Irwin of Ireland came up and knocked Jones' pass down and clearly forward. There was no whistle, so Dean picked up the ball and scored. Wales laid siege to Ireland's line in the closing stage, running a whole barrage of penalties. Each time, however, they tried to smash their way over in the forward wedge when the backs should have been given another chance. It was an apt comment on Wales in the post-Jonathan Davies era that they could manufacture not a single score from such a long period of unbroken pressure.

WALES: P H Thorburn (Neath) *(capt)*; I C Evans (Llanelli), J A Devereux (Bridgend), N G Davies (Llanelli), M R Hall (Cambridge U); B Bowen (Swansea), R N Jones (Swansea); M Griffiths (Bridgend), I J Watkins (Ebbw Vale), L Delaney (Llanelli), P T Davies (Llanelli), K Moseley (Pontypool), R Phillips (Neath), M A Jones (Neath), D J Bryant (Bridgend)
Scorers *Try:* M Jones   *Penalty Goals:* Thorburn (3)
IRELAND: F J Dunlea (Lansdowne); M J Kiernan (Dolphin), B J Mullin (London Irish), D G Irwin (Instonians), K D Crossan (Instonians); P M Dean (St Mary's Coll), L F P Aherne (Lansdowne); T P J Clancy (Lansdowne), S J Smith (Ballymena), J J McCoy (Bangor), D G Lenihan (Cork Const), W A Anderson (Dungannon), P M Matthews (Wanderers) *(capt)*, N P Mannion (Corinthians), P T J O'Hara (Sunday's Well)
Scorers *Tries:* Mannion, Dean   *Conversion:* Kiernan   *Penalty Goals:* Kiernan (3)
Referee R C Quittenton (England)

4 February, Twickenham
ENGLAND 12 (4PG)   SCOTLAND 12 (1G 2PG)

(Sponsored by Save & Prosper)

It took just one match for the high optimism of the England season so far to evaporate – this was a match which England desperately wanted to win to maintain momentum following their 28-19 defeat of Australia in November. However, it descended into a morass of tension, mistakes and bitterness. England missed seven kicks at goal as both Andrew and Webb misfired. They also meandered tactically and became sucked in as Scotland tried to stem the England flow.

It was an excellent result for the Scots, especially in the absence of Milne, the giant cornerstone of their side. Burnell, his stand-in, filled the gap expertly and the Scots showed fierce commitment – fuelled, as they stated afterwards, by the eulogies directed at England's promising team. The Scots were accused of killing the game in the loose and the referee did award any number of penalties at the bottom of the rucks. However, it was England's own fault that they let the Scots escape with a draw.

The Scots led by 9-6 at half-time. Andrew had flattered to deceive by putting over two early penalties with confidence and Dods pegged England back with a penalty and a conversion of the game's only try, scored by Jeffrey. Chalmers, who once again performed with composure, put up a high kick and Webb, under pressure from the onrushing Tukalo, dropped it. Jeffrey hacked the ball on and won the race for the touchdown deep in the in-goal area.

Dods extended Scotland's lead to 12-6 when England killed a ruck after a storming Scottish attack, and another Scots score at that stage would probably have killed England off. In fact, England came back strongly. Webb did manage to level the scores with his only two successful kicks at goal and a powerful run by Oti lifted their hopes further. However, Andrew consolidated England's frustration by hooking a penalty kick wide in the last act of the game.

ENGLAND: J M Webb (Bristol); R Underwood (Leicester & RAF), W D C Carling (Harlequins) *(capt)*, S J Halliday (Bath), C Oti (Wasps); C R Andrew (Wasps), C D Morris (Liverpool St Helens); P A G Rendall (Wasps), B C Moore (Nottingham), J A Probyn (Wasps), W A Dooley (Preston Grasshoppers), P J Ackford (Harlequins), M C Teague (Gloucester), D Richards (Leicester), R A Robinson (Bath)
Scorers *Penalty Goals:* Andrew (2), Webb (2)
SCOTLAND: P W Dods (Gala); K W Robertson (Melrose), S Hastings (Watsonians), S R P Lineen (Boroughmuir), I Tukalo (Selkirk); C M Chalmers (Melrose), G Armstrong (Jedforest); D M B Sole (Edinburgh Acads), K S Milne (Heriot's FP), A P Burnell (London Scottish), C A Gray (Nottingham), D F Cronin (Bath), J Jeffrey (Kelso), D B White (Gala), F Calder (Stewart's-Melville FP) *(capt)*
Scorers *Try:* Jeffrey   *Conversion:* Dods   *Penalty Goals:* Dods (2)
Referee G Maurette (France)

18 February, Parc des Princes
FRANCE 31 (3G 2PG 1DG 1T)   WALES 12 (4PG)

This was a record defeat for Wales, but such were the tribulations suffered by the team in the weeks and months prior to the match that the feeling afterwards was one of relief that the damage was not greater – a stark reflection of changing fortunes since the days, not long ago, when Wales and France dominated the Championship every year. Wales rarely looked like shaking the French grip and there was an almost complete lack of penetration and flair in their team; all they had to show was a certain courage in adversity.

France certainly did not fire on all cylinders and they were profligate with their chances. Furthermore, the Welsh front five gave them a stern test, with Griffiths in the loose head position scrummaging with conspicuous effect against Ondarts; and Norster, back in the side, had a superb day in the line-out. For all that, France had power in reserve. It was lucky for Wales that the French had chosen such a large and ponderous back row, because Bryant of Wales, despite suffering heavy punishment for his pains from the cynical French forwards, was often able to reach the loose ball first. Carminati threw a ridiculous punch at a Welsh forward at the very start of an explosive move, which meant that a brilliant French 'try' by Lafond was disallowed.

Serge Blanco scored the 25th and 26th tries of his international career, far and away a record for a full-back. The second came when he controlled a high pass effortlessly on his fingertips, above his head, and brought the ball down to score. Blanco also gave the pass that set up Berbizier for a try and there was a typical bulldozing touchdown by Dintrans, the French hooker, who was prominent in the ceaseless driving by the French pack. Mesnel scored a dropped goal and the boot of Lafond added a further 12 points. The result left Wales facing their first-ever whitewash in the full Championship programme.

FRANCE: S Blanco (Biarritz); J-B Lafond (Racing Club de France), P Sella (Agen), M Andrieu (Nîmes), P Lagisquet (Bayonne); F Mesnel (Racing Club de France), P Berbizier (Agen) (*capt*); L Armary (Lourdes), P Dintrans (Tarbes), P Ondarts (Biarritz), A Lorieux (Aix-les-Bains), J Condom (Biarritz), E Champ (Toulon), A Carminati (Béziers), D Erbani (Agen)
Scorers *Tries:* Blanco (2), Berbizier, Dintrans   *Conversions:* Lafond (3)
Penalty Goals: Lafond (2)   *Dropped Goal:* Mesnel
WALES: P H Thorburn (Neath) (*capt*); I C Evans (Llanelli), D W Evans (Oxford U & Cardiff), M R Hall (Cambridge U & Bridgend), C Davies (Llanelli); P Turner (Newbridge), R N Jones (Swansea); M Griffiths (Bridgend), I J Watkins (Ebbw Vale), L Delaney (Llanelli), P T Davies (Llanelli), R L Norster (Cardiff), G Jones (Llanelli), M A Jones (Neath), D J Bryant (Bridgend)
Scorer *Penalty Goals:* Thorburn (4)
Referee J M Fleming (Scotland)

18 February, Lansdowne Road
IRELAND 3 (1PG)　ENGLAND 16 (1G 2PG 1T)

(Sponsored by Digital)

This was a performance of character by England. They knew that their season would be in ruins if they failed against an Ireland side which played with a consuming drive. It was never a classic match, but it was a fearsome confrontation and, unfortunately, some of the harshness in the relationship between the two teams showed on the field.

Ireland's great hope was that they could pressurise the England defence with high kicks and work up an unstoppable momentum. However, the England pack, especially through Dooley and Ackford in the line-out, held a grip that rarely slackened. Meanwhile, Richards and Teague swept up the pieces around the fringes and ensured that Ireland had nothing to feed off.

Aherne, the Irish scrum-half, was endlessly resourceful at the base of the scrum, while Clancy and McCoy tried desperately to initiate charges in the loose. Ireland trailed by just 6-0 at half-time, thanks to two penalties for England by Andrew. However, it was Andrew's lack of confidence in kicking which led directly to England's first try. In the second half, they were awarded a penalty in kickable range but Carling, the captain, demanded that his side take a tap penalty. Rendall set up the maul and both Morris and Moore prised the ball away and dived over for the try. Following considerable discussion after the match, Moore was eventually credited with the score.

There was no doubt, however, about the try that sealed the match for England. Oti made a run through a crowd of Irishmen before Moore and Morris launched the unmistakable figure of Richards over the line from a typically unstoppable charge through the remnants of the cover defence. Ireland's only score was a penalty by Kiernan and, despite a barrage of attacks in the final quarter, they never really looked like scoring a try. After such a physically punishing encounter the English bruises were deep – but so was their satisfaction.

ENGLAND: J M Webb (Bristol); R Underwood (Leicester & RAF), W D C Carling (Harlequins) *(capt)*, S J Halliday (Bath), C Oti (Wasps); C R Andrew (Wasps), C D Morris (Liverpool St Helens); P A G Rendall (Wasps), B C Moore (Nottingham), J A Probyn (Wasps), W A Dooley (Preston Grasshoppers), P J Ackford (Harlequins), M C Teague (Gloucester), D Richards (Leicester), R A Robinson (Bath) *Replacement* G J Chilcott (Bath) for Probyn
Scorers *Tries:* Moore, Richards　*Conversion:* Andrew　*Penalty Goals:* Andrew (2)
IRELAND: F J Dunlea (Lansdowne); M J Kiernan (Dolphin), B J Mullin (London Irish), D G Irwin (Instonians), K D Crossan (Instonians); P M Dean (St Mary's Coll), L F P Aherne (Lansdowne); T P J Clancy (Lansdowne), S J Smith (Ballymena), J J McCoy (Bangor), D G Lenihan (Cork Const), W A Anderson (Dungannon), P M Matthews (Wanderers) *(capt)*, N P Mannion (Corinthians), P T J O'Hara (Sunday's Well) *Replacement* B J Spillane (Bohemians) for O'Hara
Scorer *Penalty Goal:* Kiernan
Referee L J Peard (Wales)

4 March, Twickenham
ENGLAND 11 (2T 1PG)   FRANCE 0

(Sponsored by Save & Prosper)

This was unquestionably an outstanding result for England, because it confirmed their rise from the basement of European rugby and put them on top of the table. It was a performance of real character and commitment in which Dean Richards, Andy Robinson and both locks, Wade Dooley and Paul Ackford, were outstanding. The discipline of the side was impressive too – Roger Uttley, the coach, had been critical of the team in this department earlier in the season, but when it counted England never retaliated.

Although England performed well, they were greatly helped by a very poor performance from France. At the very stage at which Jacques Fouroux's team should have peaked they showed weaknesses and, even more surprisingly, lack of heart. They rarely threatened a try and, for a team including Blanco and Sella, that was an indictment. Only Dintrans and Berbizier played with sustained energy and the lack of a fast openside flanker and a genuine line-out jumper cost France dear. In contrast, the England forwards carried the team on their own because, once again, the link at half-back was shaky – Dewi Morris was a real force with his charging runs at France's ponderous back row, but his service was either patchy or non-existent.

In fact, England's first try came from humble beginnings when a rare passing movement across the England backs was executed so poorly that Chris Oti mistimed a diagonal run to take a scissors pass from Carling. When Carling realised that Oti was well marked he held on to the ball and, as Oti had drawn the French defence, he ran on to score in space. Andrew's kicking was off target again, but he did extend England's lead with a straightforward penalty in the second half and, after a series of tap penalties, Morris and Richards made a try for Robinson at the end of the match. The result gave England vast encouragement and caused France to wonder if they were still facing in the right direction. However, after the match, coach Fouroux held that their defence was 'heroic'.

ENGLAND: J M Webb (Bristol); R Underwood (Leicester & RAF), W D C Carling (Harlequins), S J Halliday (Bath), C Oti (Wasps); C R Andrew (Wasps), C D Morris (Liverpool St Helens); P A G Rendall (Wasps), B C Moore (Nottingham), G J Chilcott (Bath), W A Dooley (Preston Grasshoppers), P J Ackford (Harlequins), M C Teague (Gloucester), D Richards (Leicester), R A Robinson (Bath)
Scorers *Tries:* Carling, Robinson   *Penalty Goal:* Andrew
FRANCE: S Blanco (Biarritz); J-B Lafond (Racing Club de France), P Sella (Agen), M Andrieu (Nîmes), P Lagisquet (Bayonne); F Mesnel (Racing Club de France), P Berbizier (Agen) *(capt)*; P Ondarts (Biarritz), P Dintrans (Tarbes), C Portolan (Toulouse), G Bourguignon (Narbonne), J Condom (Biarritz), M Cecillon (Bourgoin), L Rodriguez (Dax), D Erbani (Agen) *Replacements* J-P Garuet (Lourdes) for Portolan; D Charvet (Toulouse) for Lagisquet
Referee S R Hilditch (Ireland)

4 March, Murrayfield
SCOTLAND 37 (4G 3PG 1T)   **IRELAND 21** (3G 1PG)

(Sponsored by the Royal Bank)

This was one of the most memorable matches in the recent history of the Championship, produced by two teams that had attracted some criticism for negative rugby earlier in the season. Six of the eight tries came in the last 25 minutes of the first half when Scotland developed a commanding 19-6 lead which was rapidly eroded and, amazingly, they trailed 19-21 at half-time. However, Scotland always played with authority and they re-established themselves with courage, pace and skill. Iwan Tukalo, the left wing, ended with a hat-trick. Peter Dods and Craig Chalmers were the Scottish stars behind the scrum, while the hard-rucking Scots pack, with Derek White and David Sole to the fore, were on brilliant form. It confirmed Sole's world-class status as a mobile and intelligent prop forward.

Ireland did superbly well to recover from their early shocks and, with Brendan Mullin at his sharpest in the centre, they played expansively too. But, despite major line-out effort from Neil Francis, Ireland never wielded the same power or the same craft as the Scottish scrum. Two tries by Tukalo and one by John Jeffrey all featured the pace of the strong-running Scots back row, while clever work by Lineen in the centre helped Tukalo on his way to his second.

Ireland's storming comeback gave them three tries by half-time, all scored from set pieces – two by Mullin and another by Dunlea – thanks to much-improved Irish back play. Cronin, the Scots lock, sprinted over to finish off a Scotland forward drive in the second half and this calmed Scottish nerves as Peter Dods continued to fire over the conversions for Scotland and also kicked three penalties. Scotland pulled clear when a break by Hastings, carried on by Dods, sent Tukalo over for his hat-trick. It set up the Scots for a chance of the Championship, since they were level on points with England at the end of a memorable afternoon. This was a wonderful achievement considering that the Scots were still rebuilding their team.

SCOTLAND: P W Dods (Gala); K W Robertson (Melrose), S Hastings (Watsonians), S R P Lineen (Boroughmuir), I Tukalo (Selkirk); C M Chalmers (Melrose), G Armstrong (Jedforest); D M B Sole (Edinburgh Acads), K S Milne (Heriot's FP), A P Burnell (London Scottish), C A Gray (Nottingham), D F Cronin (Bath), J Jeffrey (Kelso), D B White (London Scottish), F Calder (Stewart's-Melville FP)
Scorers *Tries:* Tukalo (3), Jeffrey, Cronin   *Conversions:* Dods (4)
Penalty Goals: Dods (3)
IRELAND: F J Dunlea (Lansdowne); M J Kiernan (Dolphin), B J Mullin (London Irish), D G Irwin (Instonians), K D Crossan (Instonians); P M Dean (St Mary's Coll), L F P Aherne (Lansdowne); T P J Clancy (Lansdowne), S J Smith (Ballymena), J J McCoy (Bangor), D G Lenihan (Cork Const), N P T Francis (London Irish), P M Matthews (Wanderers) (*capt*), N P Mannion (Corinthians), W D McBride (Malone)
Scorers *Tries:* Mullin (2), Dunlea   *Conversions:* Kiernan (3)   *Penalty Goal:* Kiernan
Referee K V J Fitzgerald (Australia)

Above: *Brendan Mullin carves his way past Damien Cronin (No 5) during the thrilling Scotland-Ireland game at Murrayfield. Mullin had a superb game in defeat.* Below: *Action from France's victory over Scotland in Paris which saw the French take the Championship outright. The Scots back row of Jeffrey, White and Calder (No 7) secure possession.*

18 March, Parc des Princes
FRANCE 19 (2G 1PG 1T)   SCOTLAND 3 (1PG)

France won the Championship outright with this thumping victory over Scotland and because England failed in Cardiff on the same day. Not even the most fervent French supporter would pretend that this was the complete team but their title was deserved and their only hiccup was the curiously passionless effort at Twickenham. At least the French went off for the summer tour to New Zealand in good heart.

Berbizier, the French scrum-half and captain, was the major figure in the match. His tactical direction ensured that the ferocity of the French forward effort would not go to waste and he also scored a brilliant try to give France a half-time lead. The driving of the French pack, so muted at Twickenham, was back to full power, with Dintrans usually at the apex, so even though France won a low return from the line-out they had enough pace and muscle in the loose to take them forward.

The Scots, as they themselves admitted afterwards, were well and truly hammered and could not have complained had the margin been considerably greater. They did have a good spell in the first quarter, and White and Calder in the back row were outstanding in the resistance movement throughout. But Chalmers and Armstrong were unhappy under the severe pressure and Scotland rarely looked like adding to the early penalty goal by Dods, the full-back.

Berbizier scored with an arrow-like burst after he had been fed after a scrum by Rodriguez, his No 8, and it would be difficult to over-estimate the importance of the score, because it banished memories of Scotland's early effort and indicated that France had found themselves and would surge away in the second half. They did so. Berbizier was again involved in the second try when he put in a clever kick ahead from which Blanco touched off a second-half burst of scoring. This was Blanco's fourth try of the Championship. A garryowen by Mesnel, expertly re-gathered by Sella, was the springboard for the third French try. Sella and Blanco moved the ball on and Lagisquet finished off the move. Bérot kicked a penalty and two conversions.

FRANCE: S Blanco (Biarritz); J-B Lafond (Racing Club de France), P Sella (Agen), M Andrieu (Nîmes), P Lagisquet (Bayonne); F Mesnel (Racing Club de France), P Berbizier (Agen) (*capt*); L Armary (Tarbes), P Dintrans (Tarbes), J-P Garuet (Lourdes), D Erbani (Agen), J Condom (Biarritz), E Champ (Toulon), L Rodriguez (Dax), A Carminati (Béziers)
Scorers *Tries:* Berbizier, Blanco, Lagisquet   *Conversions:* Bérot (2)   *Penalty Goal:* Bérot
SCOTLAND: P W Dods (Gala); K W Robertson (Melrose), S Hastings (Watsonians), S R P Lineen (Boroughmuir), I Tukalo (Selkirk); C M Chalmers (Melrose), G Armstrong (Jedforest); D M B Sole (Edinburgh Acads), K S Milne (Heriot's FP), A P Burnell (London Scottish), C A Gray (Nottingham), D F Cronin (Bath), J Jeffrey (Kelso), D B White (Gala), F Calder (Stewart's-Melville FP) (*capt*)
Scorer *Penalty Goal:* Dods
Referee O E Doyle (Ireland)

18 March, Cardiff Arms Park
WALES 12 (1G 2PG) **ENGLAND 9** (2PG 1DG)

(Sponsored by British Gas)

The catalogue of England failures at Cardiff continued when Wales, in their best performance of the season, exerted fearsome pressure on the scrum and line-out, eventually squeezing the life and confidence out of the opposition. Yet it was a gloomy and dull day and much of the play matched the weather. There was a protracted punch-up in the second half involving most of the forwards and in particular Richards of England and Griffiths of Wales. It was a game choking with tension. The Welsh front five scrummaged powerfully, Griffiths having a conspicuous game and, yet again, Norster was a dominating figure in the line-out. Considering the difficult conditions his succession of two-handed catches in the line-out was one of the features of the whole Championship. Behind him, Robert Jones put up a succession of high kicks which plainly unnerved the England defence.

England never found the urgency which had seen them through the season to date unbeaten. Andrew and Morris desperately tried to make something of the trickle of possession they received but their execution was poor. The loss of Teague in the opening passage of the match was a cruel blow for them. Andrew did put over two penalties and a dropped goal in the first half and England led 9-6 at half-time – Thorburn, who played immaculately all day at full-back for Wales, replied with two penalty goals.

The match turned early in the second half with a Welsh try and for the rest of the match England were locked in their own territory as Wales pounded away. The fateful try came when Turner put up a high kick in the direction of Underwood on the England right. Underwood eventually gathered the ball but fired a pass which missed Webb, his full-back. Emyr of Wales hacked on the loose ball and Hall came up for the try. Later, television replays suggested that Hall did not ground the ball properly but Bryant, following up, dived to make sure. England made some sporadic attempts to run the ball out of defence but their nerves were shattered and these often ended in disaster.

WALES: P H Thorburn (Neath) *(capt)*; I C Evans (Llanelli), D W Evans (Oxford U & Cardiff), M R Hall (Cambridge U & Bridgend), A Emyr (Swansea); P Turner (Newbridge), R N Jones (Swansea); M Griffiths (Bridgend), I J Watkins (Ebbw Vale), L Delaney (Llanelli), P T Davies (Llanelli), R L Norster (Cardiff), G Jones (Llanelli), M A Jones (Neath), D J Bryant (Bridgend)
Scorers *Try:* Hall *Conversion:* Thorburn *Penalty Goals:* Thorburn (2)
ENGLAND: J M Webb (Bristol); R Underwood (Leicester & RAF), W D C Carling (Harlequins) *(capt)*, S J Halliday (Bath), C Oti (Wasps); C R Andrew (Wasps), C D Morris (Liverpool St Helens); P A G Rendall (Wasps), B C Moore (Nottingham), G J Chilcott (Bath), W A Dooley (Preston Grasshoppers), P J Ackford (Harlequins), M C Teague (Gloucester), D Richards (Leicester), R A Robinson (Bath) *Replacement* G W Rees (Nottingham) for Teague
Scorer *Penalty Goals:* Andrew (2) *Dropped Goal:* Andrew
Referee K V J Fitzgerald (Australia)

RESULTS OF INTERNATIONAL MATCHES *(up to 30 April 1989)*

Years for Five Nations' matches are for the second half of the season: eg 1972 means season 1971-72. Years for matches against touring teams from the Southern Hemisphere refer to the actual year of the match.

Points-scoring was first introduced in 1886, when an International Board was formed by Scotland, Ireland and Wales. Points-values varied between countries until 1890, when England agreed to join the Board, and uniform values were adopted. The table below shows points-values from the 1890-91 season onwards.

Northern Hemisphere seasons	Try	Conversion	Penalty goal	Dropped goal	Goal from mark
1890-91	1	2	2	3	3
1891-92 to 1892-93	2	3	3	4	4
1893-94 to 1904-05	3	2	3	4	4
1905-06 to 1947-48	3	2	3	4	3
1948-49 to 1970-71	3	2	3	3	3
1971-72 onwards	4	2	3	3	3*

★The goal from mark ceased to exist when free kick clause was introduced, 1977-78.
WC indicates a fixture played during the Rugby World Cup.

ENGLAND v SCOTLAND
Played 105   England won 50, Scotland won 38, Drawn 17

1871 Raeburn Place (Edinburgh)
Scotland 1G 1T to 1T

1872 The Oval (London)
England 1G 1DG 2T to 1DG

1873 Glasgow
Drawn no score

1874 The Oval
England 1DG to 1T

1875 Raeburn Place
Drawn no score

1876 The Oval
England 1G 1T to 0

1877 Raeburn Place
Scotland 1DG to 0

1878 The Oval
Drawn no score

1879 Raeburn Place
Drawn Scotland 1DG England 1G

1880 Manchester
England 2G 3T to 1G

1881 Raeburn Place
Drawn Scotland 1G 1T England 1DG 1T

1882 Manchester
Scotland 2T to 0

1883 Raeburn Place
England 2T to 1T

1884 Blackheath (London)
England 1G to 1T

1885 No Match

1886 Raeburn Place
Drawn no score

1887 Manchester
Drawn 1T each

1888 No Match

1889 No Match

1890 Raeburn Place
England 1G 1T to 0

1891 Richmond (London)
Scotland 2G 1DG (9) to 1G (3)

1892 Raeburn Place
England 1G (5) to 0

1893 Leeds
Scotland 2DG (8) to 0

1894 Raeburn Place
Scotland 2T (6) to 0

1895 Richmond
Scotland 1PG 1T (6) to 1PG (3)

1896 Glasgow
Scotland 1G 2T (11) to 0

1897 Manchester
England 1G 1DG 1T (12) to 1T (3)

1898 Powderhall (Edinburgh)
Drawn 1T (3) each

1899 Blackheath
Scotland 1G (5) to 0

1900 Inverleith (Edinburgh)
Drawn no score

1901 Blackheath
Scotland 3G 1T (18) to 1T (3)

1902 Inverleith
England 2T (6) to 1T (3)

1903 Richmond
Scotland 1DG 2T (10) to 2T (6)

1904 Inverleith
Scotland 2T (6) to 1T (3)

1905 Richmond
Scotland 1G 1T (8) to 0

1906 Inverleith
England 3T (9) to 1T (3)

1907 Blackheath
Scotland 1G 1T (8) to 1T (3)

1908 Inverleith
Scotland 1G 2DG 1T (16) to 2 G (10)

1909 Richmond
Scotland 3G 1T (18) to 1G 1T (8)

1910 Inverleith
England 1G 3T (14) to 1G (5)

1911 Twickenham
England 2G 1T (13) to 1G 1T (8)

1912 Inverleith
Scotland 1G 1T (8) to 1T (3)

1913 Twickenham
England 1T (3) to 0

1914 Inverleith
England 2G 2T (16) to 1G 1DG 2T (15)

1920 Twickenham
England 2G 1T (13) to 1DG (4)

1921 Inverleith
England 3G 1T (18) to 0

1922 Twickenham
England 1G 2T (11) to 1G (5)

1923 Inverleith
England 1G 1T (8) to 2T (6)

1924 Twickenham
England 3G 1DG (19) to 0

1925 Murrayfield
Scotland 2G 1DG (14)
to 1G 1PG 1T (11)

1926 Twickenham
Scotland 2G 1DG 1T (17) to 3T (9)

1927 Murrayfield
Scotland 1G 1DG 4T (21)
to 2G 1PG (13)

1928 Twickenham
England 2T (6) to 0

1929 Murrayfield
Scotland 4T (12) to 2T (6)

1930 Twickenham
Drawn no score

1931 Murrayfield
Scotland 5G 1T (28) to 2G 1PG 2T (19)

1932 Twickenham
England 2G 2T (16) to 1T (3)

1933 Murrayfield
Scotland 1T (3) to 0

1934 Twickenham
England 2T (6) to 1T (3)

1935 Murrayfield
Scotland 2G (10) to 1DG 1T (7)

1936 Twickenham
England 3T (9) to 1G 1PG (8)

1937 Murrayfield
England 2T (6) to 1PG (3)

1938 Twickenham
Scotland 2PG 5T (21)
to 1DG 3PG 1T (16)

1939 Murrayfield
England 3PG (9) to 2T (6)

1947 Twickenham
England 4G 1DG (24) to 1G (5)

1948 Murrayfield
Scotland 2T (6) to 1PG (3)

1949 Twickenham
England 2G 3T (19) to 1PG (3)

1950 Murrayfield
Scotland 2G 1T (13) to 1G 1PG 1T (11)

1951 Twickenham
England 1G (5) to 1T (3)

1952 Murrayfield
England 2G 1DG 2T (19) to 1T (3)

1953 Twickenham
England 4G 2T (26) to 1G 1T (8)

1954 Murrayfield
England 2G 1T (13) to 1T (3)

1955 Twickenham
England 1PG 2T (9) to 1PG 1T (6)

1956 Murrayfield
England 1G 2PG (11) to 1PG 1T (6)

1957 Twickenham
England 2G 1PG 1T (16) to 1PG (3)

1958 Murrayfield
Drawn 1PG (3) each

1959 Twickenham
Drawn 1PG (3) each

1960 Murrayfield
England 3G 1PG 1DG (21)
to 3PG 1T (12)

1961 Twickenham
England 1PG 1T (6) to 0

1962 Murrayfield
Drawn 1PG (3) each

1963 Twickenham
England 2G (10) to 1G 1DG (8)

1964 Murrayfield
Scotland 3G (15) to 1PG 1T (6)

1965 Twickenham
Drawn England 1T (3) Scotland 1DG (3)

1966 Murrayfield
Scotland 1PG 1T (6) to 1DG (3)

1967 Twickenham
England 3G 2PG 1DG 1T (27)
to 1G 2PG 1T (14)

1968 Murrayfield
England 1G 1PG (8) to 1PG 1DG (6)

1969 Twickenham
England 1G 1T (8) to 1PG (3)

1970 Murrayfield
Scotland 1G 2PG 1T (14) to 1G (5)

1971 Twickenham
Scotland 2G 1DG 1T (16) to 3PG 2T (15)

*1971 Murrayfield
Scotland 4G 1PG 1T (26) to 1PG 1DG (6)
* *Special Centenary match – non-championship*

1972 Murrayfield
Scotland 4PG 1DG 2T (23) to 3PG (9)

1973 Twickenham
England 2G 2T (20) to 1G 1PG 1T (13)

1974 Murrayfield
Scotland 1G 2PG 1T (16)
to 1PG 1DG 2T (14)

1975 Twickenham
England 1PG 1T (7) to 2PG (6)

1976 Murrayfield
Scotland 2G 2PG 1T (22)
to 1G 2PG (12)

1977 Twickenham
England 2G 2PG 2T (26) to 2PG (6)

1978 Murrayfield
England 2G 1PG (15) to 0

1979 Twickenham
Drawn 1PG 1T (7) each

1980 Murrayfield
England 2G 2PG 3T (30)
to 2G 2PG (18)

1981 Twickenham
England 1G 3PG 2T (23)
to 1G 1PG 2T (17)

1982 Murrayfield
Drawn Scotland 2PG 1DG (9)
England 3PG (9)

1983 Twickenham
Scotland 1G 3PG 1DG 1T (22)
to 3PG 1DG (12)

1984 Murrayfield
Scotland 2G 2PG (18) to 2PG (6)

1985 Twickenham
England 2PG 1T (10) to 1PG 1T (7)

1986 Murrayfield
Scotland 3G 5PG (33) to 2PG (6)

1987 Twickenham
England 2G* 3PG (21) to 1G 2PG (12)
includes one penalty try

1988 Murrayfield
England 2PG 1DG (9) to 2PG (6)

1989 Twickenham
Drawn England 4PG (12)
Scotland 1G 2PG (12)

ENGLAND v IRELAND
Played 102   England won 58, Ireland won 36, Drawn 8

1875 The Oval (London)
England 1G 1DG 1T to 0

1876 Dublin
England 1G 1T to 0

1877 The Oval
England 2G 2T to 0

1878 Dublin
England 2G 1T to 0

1879 The Oval
England 2G 1DG 2T to 0

1880 Dublin
England 1G 1T to 1T

1881 Manchester
England 2G 2T to 0

1882 Dublin
Drawn 2T each

1883 Manchester
England 1G 3T to 1T

1884 Dublin
England 1G to 0

1885 Manchester
England 2T to 1T

1886 Dublin
England 1T to 0

1887 Dublin
Ireland 2G to 0

1888 No Match

1889 No Match

1890 Blackheath (London)
England 3T to 0

1891 Dublin
England 2G 3T (9) to 0

1892 Manchester
England 1G 1T (7) to 0

1893 Dublin
England 2T (4) to 0

1894 Blackheath
Ireland 1DG 1T (7) to 1G (5)

1895 Dublin
England 2T (6) to 1T (3)

1896 Leeds
Ireland 2G (10) to 1DG (4)

1897 Dublin
Ireland 1GM 3T (13) to 2PG 1T (9)

1898 Richmond (London)
Ireland 1PG 2T (9) to 1PG 1T (6)

1899 Dublin
Ireland 1PG 1T (6) to 0

1900 Richmond
England 1G 1DG 2T (15) to 1DG (4)

1901 Dublin
Ireland 2G (10) to 1PG 1T (6)

1902 Leicester
England 2T (6) to 1T (3)

1903 Dublin
Ireland 1PG 1T (6) to 0

1904 Blackheath
England 2G 3T (19) to 0

1905 Cork
Ireland 1G 4T (17) to 1T (3)

1906 Leicester
Ireland 2G 2T (16) to 2T (6)

1907 Dublin
Ireland 1G 1GM 3T (17) to 1PG 2T (9)

1908 Richmond
England 2G 1T (13) to 1PG (3)

1909 Dublin
England 1G 2T (11) to 1G (5)

1910 Twickenham
Drawn no score

1911 Dublin
Ireland 1T (3) to 0

1912 Twickenham
England 5T (15) to 0

1913 Dublin
England 1PG 4T (15) to 1DG (4)

1914 Twickenham
England 1G 4T (17) to 1G 1DG 1T (12)

1920 Dublin
England 1G 3T (14) to 1G 1PG 1T (11)

1921 Twickenham
England 1G 1DG 2T (15) to 0

1922 Dublin
England 4T (12) to 1T (3)

1923 Leicester
England 2G 1DG 3T (23) to 1G (5)

1924 Belfast
England 1G 3T (14) to 1T (3)

1925 Twickenham
Drawn 2T (6) each

1926 Dublin
Ireland 2G 1PG 2T (19) to 3G (15)

1927 Twickenham
England 1G 1T (8) to 1PG 1T (6)

1928 Dublin
England 1DG 1T (7) to 2T (6)

1929 Twickenham
Ireland 2T (6) to 1G (5)

1930 Dublin
Ireland 1DG (4) to 1T (3)

1931 Twickenham
Ireland 1PG 1T (6) to 1G (5)

1932 Dublin
England 1G 2PG (11) to 1G 1PG (8)

1933 Twickenham
England 1G 4T (17) to 1PG 1T (6)

1934 Dublin
England 2G 1T (13) to 1T (3)

1935 Twickenham
England 1G 3PG (14) to 1T (3)

1936 Dublin
Ireland 2T (6) to 1T (3)

1937 Twickenham
England 1PG 2T (9) to 1G 1T (8)

1938 Dublin
England 6G 1PG 1T (36) to 1G 3T (14)

1939 Twickenham
Ireland 1G (5) to 0

1947 Dublin
Ireland 2G 1PG 3T (22) to 0

1948 Twickenham
Ireland 1G 2T (11) to 2G (10)

1949 Dublin
Ireland 1G 2PG 1T (14) to 1G (5)

1950 Twickenham
England 1T (3) to 0

1951 Dublin
Ireland 1PG (3) to 0

1952 Twickenham
England 1T (3) to 0

1953 Dublin
Drawn 2PG 1T (9) each

1954 Twickenham
England 1G 1PG 2T (14) to 1PG (3)

1955 Dublin
Drawn Ireland 1PG 1T (6)
England 2T (6)

1956 Twickenham
England 1G 3PG 2T (20) to 0

1957 Dublin
England 1PG 1T (6) to 0

1958 Twickenham
England 1PG 1T (6) to 0

1959 Dublin
England 1PG (3) to 0

1960 Twickenham
England 1G 1DG (8) to 1G (5)

1961 Dublin
Ireland 1G 2PG (11) to 1G 1T (8)

1962 Twickenham
England 2G 1PG 1T (16) to 0

1963 Dublin
Drawn no score

1964 Twickenham
Ireland 3G 1T (18) to 1G (5)

1965 Dublin
Ireland 1G (5) to 0

1966 Twickenham
Drawn 1PG 1T (6) each

1967 Dublin
England 1G 1PG (8) to 1PG (3)

1968 Twickenham
Drawn England 2PG 1DG (9)
Ireland 3PG (9)

1969 Dublin
Ireland 1G 2PG 1DG 1T (17)
to 4PG 1T (15)

1970 Twickenham
England 2DG 1T (9) to 1PG (3)

1971 Dublin
England 3PG (9) to 2T (6)

1972 Twickenham
Ireland 1G 1PG 1DG 1T (16)
to 1G 2PG (12)

1973 Dublin
Ireland 2G 1PG 1DG (18) to 1G 1PG (9)

1974 Twickenham
Ireland 2G 1PG 1DG 2T (26)
to 1G 5PG (21)

1975 Dublin
Ireland 2G (12) to 1G 1DG (9)

1976 Twickenham
Ireland 2PG 1DG 1T (13) to 4PG (12)

1977 Dublin
England 1T (4) to 0

1978 Twickenham
England 2G 1PG (15) to 2PG 1DG (9)

1979 Dublin
Ireland 1G 1PG 1DG (12) to 1PG 1T (7)

1980 Twickenham
England 3G 2PG (24) to 3PG (9)

1981 Dublin
England 1G 1T (10) to 2 DG (6)

1982 Twickenham
Ireland 1G 2PG 1T (16) to 1G 3PG (15)

1983 Dublin
Ireland 1G 5PG 1T (25) to 5PG (15)

1984 Twickenham
England 3PG 1DG (12) to 3PG (9)

1985 Dublin
Ireland 2PG 1DG 1T (13) to 2PG 1T (10)

1986 Twickenham
England * 3G 1PG 1T (25)
to 1G 2PG 2T (20)
* *includes one penalty try*

1987 Dublin
Ireland 1G 1PG 2T (17) to 0

1988 Twickenham
England 4G 1PG 2T (35) to 1DG (3)

*1988 Dublin
England 2G 3PG (21) to 1G 1T (10)
Non-championship match

1989 Dublin
England 1G 2PG 1T (16) to 1 PG (3)

ENGLAND v WALES
Played 95   England won 36, Wales won 47, Drawn 12

1881 Blackheath (London)
England 7G 1DG 6T to 0

1882 No Match

1883 Swansea
England 2G 4T to 0

1884 Leeds
England 1G 2T to 1G

1885 Swansea
England 1G 4T to 1G 1T

1886 Blackheath
England 1GM 2T to 1G

1887 Llanelli
Drawn no score

1888 No Match

1889 No Match

1890 Dewsbury
Wales 1T to 0

1891 Newport
England 2G 1T (7) to 1G (3)

1892 Blackheath
England 3G 1T (17) to 0

1893 Cardiff
Wales 1G 1PG 2T (12) to 1G 3T (11)

1894 Birkenhead
England 4G 1GM (24) to 1T (3)

1895 Swansea
England 1G 3T (14) to 2T (6)

1896 Blackheath
England 2G 5T (25) to 0

1897 Newport
Wales 1G 2T (11) to 0

1898 Blackheath
England 1G 3T (14) to 1DG 1T (7)

1899 Swansea
Wales 4G 2T (26) to 1T (3)

1900 Gloucester
Wales 2G 1PG (13) to 1T (3)

1901 Cardiff
Wales 2G 1T (13) to 0

1902 Blackheath
Wales 1PG 2T (9) to 1G 1T (8)

1903 Swansea
Wales 3G 2T (21) to 1G (5)

1904 Leicester
Drawn England 1G 1PG 2T (14)
Wales 2G 1GM (14)

1905 Cardiff
Wales 2G 5T (25) to 0

1906 Richmond (London)
Wales 2G 2T (16) to 1T (3)

1907 Swansea
Wales 2G 4T (22) to 0

1908 Bristol
Wales 3G 1PG 1DG 2T (28)
to 3G 1T (18)

1909 Cardiff
Wales 1G 1T (8) to 0

1910 Twickenham
England 1G 1PG 1T (11) to 2T (6)

1911 Swansea
Wales 1PG 4T (15) to 1G 2T (11)

1912 Twickenham
England 1G 1T (8) to 0

1913 Cardiff
England 1G 1DG 1T (12) to 0

1914 Twickenham
England 2G (10) to 1G 1DG (9)

1920 Swansea
Wales 1G 1PG 2DG 1T (19) to 1G (5)

1921 Twickenham
England 1G 1DG 3T (18) to 1T (3)

1922 Cardiff
Wales 2G 6T (28) to 2T (6)

1923 Twickenham
England 1DG 1T (7) to 1T (3)

1924 Swansea
England 1G 4T (17) to 3T (9)

1925 Twickenham
England 1PG 3T (12) to 2T (6)

1926 Cardiff
Drawn 1T (3) each

1927 Twickenham
England 1G 1PG 1GM (11)
to 1PG 2T (9)

1928 Swansea
England 2G (10) to 1G 1T (8)

1929 Twickenham
England 1G 1T (8) to 1T (3)

1930 Cardiff
England 1G 1PG 1T (11) to 1T (3)

1931 Twickenham
Drawn England 1G 2PG (11)
Wales 1G 1GM 1T (11)

1932 Swansea
Wales 1G 1PG 1DG (12) to 1G (5)

1933 Twickenham
Wales 1DG 1T (7) to 1T (3)

1934 Cardiff
England 3T (9) to 0

1935 Twickenham
Drawn England 1PG (3) Wales 1T (3)

1936 Swansea
Drawn no score

1937 Twickenham
England 1DG (4) to 1T (3)

1938 Cardiff
Wales 1G 2PG 1T (14) to 1G 1T (8)

1939 Twickenham
England 1T (3) to 0

1947 Cardiff
England 1G 1DG (9) to 2T (6)

1948 Twickenham
Drawn England 1PG (3) Wales 1T (3)

1949 Cardiff
Wales 3T (9) to 1DG (3)

1950 Twickenham
Wales 1G 1PG 1T (11) to 1G (5)

1951 Swansea
Wales 4G 1T (23) to 1G (5)

1952 Twickenham
Wales 1G 1T (8) to 2T (6)

1953 Cardiff
England 1G 1PG (8) to 1PG (3)

1954 Twickenham
England 3T (9) to 1PG 1T (6)

1955 Cardiff
Wales 1PG (3) to 0

1956 Twickenham
Wales 1G 1T (8) to 1PG (3)

1957 Cardiff
England 1PG (3) to 0

1958 Twickenham
Drawn England 1T (3) Wales 1PG (3)

1959 Cardiff
Wales 1G (5) to 0

1960 Twickenham
England 1G 2PG 1T (14) to 2PG (6)

1961 Cardiff
Wales 2T (6) to 1T (3)

1962 Twickenham
Drawn no score

1963 Cardiff
England 2G 1DG (13) to 1PG 1T (6)

1964 Twickenham
Drawn 2T (6) each

1965 Cardiff
Wales 1G 1DG 2T (14) to 1PG (3)

1966 Twickenham
Wales 1G 2PG (11) to 1PG 1T (6)

1967 Cardiff
Wales 5G 2PG 1DG (34) to 4PG 3T (21)

1968 Twickenham
Drawn England 1G 1PG 1T (11)
Wales 1G 1DG 1T (11)

1969 Cardiff
Wales 3G 2PG 1DG 2T (30) to 3PG (9)

1970 Twickenham
Wales 1G 1DG 3T (17) to 2G 1PG (13)

1971 Cardiff
Wales 2G 1PG 2DG 1T (22)
to 1PG 1T (6)

1972 Twickenham
Wales 1G 2PG (12) to 1PG (3)

1973 Cardiff
Wales 1G 1PG 4T (25) to 2PG 1DG (9)

1974 Twickenham
England 1G 2PG 1T (16)
to 1G 2PG (12)

1975 Cardiff
Wales 1G 2PG 2T (20) to 1T (4)

1976 Twickenham
Wales 3G 1PG (21) to 3PG (9)

1977 Cardiff
Wales 2PG 2T (14) to 3PG (9)

1978 Twickenham
Wales 3PG (9) to 2PG (6)

1979 Cardiff
Wales 2G 1DG 3T (27) to 1PG (3)

1980 Twickenham
England 3PG (9) to 2T (8)

1981 Cardiff
Wales 1G 4PG 1DG (21) to 5PG 1T (19)

1982 Twickenham
England 3PG 2T (17) to 1DG 1T (7)

1983 Cardiff
Drawn 2PG 1DG 1T (13) each

1984 Twickenham
Wales 1G 4PG 2DG (24) to 5PG (15)

1985 Cardiff
Wales 2G 3PG 1DG (24)
to 1G 2PG 1DG (15)

1986 Twickenham
England 6PG 1DG (21)
to 1G 3PG 1DG (18)

1987 Cardiff
Wales 5PG 1T (19) to 4PG (12)

1987 Brisbane *WC*
Wales 2G 1T (16) to 1PG (3)

1988 Twickenham
Wales 1DG 2T (11) to 1PG (3)

1989 Cardiff
Wales 1G 2PG (12) to 2PG 1DG (9)

ENGLAND v FRANCE

Played 64   England won 33, France won 24, Drawn 7

1906 Paris
England 4G 5T (35) to 1G 1T (8)

1907 Richmond (London)
England 5G 1DG 4T (41)
to 2G 1PG (13)

1908 Paris
England 2G 3T (19) to 0

1909 Leicester
England 2G 4T (22) to 0

1910 Paris
England 1G 2T (11) to 1T (3)

1911 Twickenham
England 5G 2PG 2T (37) to 0

1912 Paris
England 1G 1DG 3T (18) to 1G 1T (8)

1913 Twickenham
England 1G 5T (20) to 0

1914 Paris
England 6G 3T (39) to 2G 1T (13)

1920 Twickenham
England 1G 1PG (8) to 1T (3)

1921 Paris
England 2G (10) to 2PG (6)

1922 Twickenham
Drawn England 1G 2PG (11)
France 1G 2T (11)

1923 Paris
England 1G 1DG 1T (12) to 1PG (3)

1924 Twickenham
England 2G 3T (19) to 1DG 1T (7)

1925 Paris
England 2G 1GM (13) to 1G 2T (11)

1926 Twickenham
England 1G 2T (11) to 0

1927 Paris
France 1T (3) to 0

1928 Twickenham
England 3G 1T (18) to 1G 1T (8)

1929 Paris
England 2G 2T (16) to 2T (6)

1930 Twickenham
England 1G 2T (11) to 1G (5)

1931 Paris
France 2DG 2T (14) to 2G 1T (13)

1947 Twickenham
England 2T (6) to 1PG (3)

1948 Paris
France 1G 1DG 2T (15) to 0

1949 Twickenham
England 1G 1DG (8) to 1DG (3)

1950 Paris
France 2T (6) to 1T (3)

65

1951 Twickenham
France 1G 1DG 1T (11) to 1T (3)

1952 Paris
England 2PG (6) to 1T (3)

1953 Twickenham
England 1G 2T (11) to 0

1954 Paris
France 1G 1DG 1T (11) to 1T (3)

1955 Twickenham
France 2G 2DG (16) to 2PG 1T (9)

1956 Paris
France 1G 2PG 1T (14) to 2PG 1T (9)

1957 Twickenham
England 3T (9) to 1G (5)

1958 Paris
England 1G 1PG 2T (14) to 0

1959 Twickenham
Drawn 1PG (3) each

1960 Paris
Drawn France 1PG (3) England 1T (3)

1961 Twickenham
Drawn 1G (5) each

1962 Paris
France 2G 1T (13) to 0

1963 Twickenham
England 2PG (6) to 1G (5)

1964 Paris
England 1PG 1T (6) to 1T (3)

1965 Twickenham
England 2PG 1T (9) to 1PG 1T (6)

1966 Paris
France 2G 1T (13) to 0

1967 Twickenham
France 2G 1PG 1DG (16)
to 3PG 1DG (12)

1968 Paris
France 1G 1PG 2DG (14)
to 2PG 1DG (9)

1969 Twickenham
England 2G 3PG 1T (22)
to 1G 1DG (8)

1970 Paris
France 4G 1PG 2DG 2T (35)
to 2G 1PG (13)

1971 Twickenham
Drawn England 1G 3PG (14)
France 1G 1PG 1DG 1T (14)

1972 Paris
France 5G 1PG 1T (37) to 1G 2PG (12)

1973 Twickenham
England 2PG 2T (14) to 1G (6)

1974 Paris
Drawn 1G 1PG 1DG (12) each

1975 Twickenham
France 4G 1PG (27) to 4PG 2T (20)

1976 Paris
France 3G 3T (30) to 1G 1PG (9)

1977 Twickenham
France 1T (4) to 1PG (3)

1978 Paris
France 2G 1PG (15) to 2DG (6)

1979 Twickenham
England 1PG 1T (7) to 1G (6)

1980 Paris
England 1PG 2DG 2T (17)
to 1G 1PG 1T (13)

1981 Twickenham
France 1G 2DG 1T (16) to 4 PG (12)

1982 Paris
England 2G 5PG (27) to
1G 2PG 1DG (15)

1983 Twickenham
France 2G 1PG 1T (19)
to 4PG 1DG (15)

1984 Paris
France 3G 1PG 1DG 2T (32)
to 2G 2PG (18)

1985 Twickenham
Drawn England 2PG 1DG (9)
France 3DG (9)

1986 Paris
France* 2G 3PG 2T (29)
to 2PG 1T (10)
* *includes one penalty try*

1987 Twickenham
France 1G 1PG 2DG 1T (19)
to 4PG 1DG (15)

1988 Paris
France 2PG 1T (10) to 2PG 1DG (9)

1989 Twickenham
England 1PG 2T (11) to 0

ENGLAND v NEW ZEALAND

Played 15   England won 3, New Zealand won 12, Drawn 0

1905 Crystal Palace (London)
New Zealand 5T (15) to 0

1925 Twickenham
New Zealand 1G 1PG 3T (17)
to 1G 1PG 1T (11)

1936 Twickenham
England 1DG 3T (13) to 0

1954 Twickenham
New Zealand 1G (5) to 0

1963 *1* Auckland
New Zealand 3G 1PG 1DG (21)
to 1G 2PG (11)

2 Christchurch
New Zealand 1GM 2T (9)
to 1PG 1T (6)
New Zealand won series 2-0

1964 Twickenham
New Zealand 1G 2PG 1T (14) to 0

1967 Twickenham
New Zealand 4G 1T (23)
to 1G 1PG 1T (11)

1973 Twickenham
New Zealand 1G 1DG (9) to 0

1973 Auckland
England 2G 1T (16) to 1G 1T (10)

1978 Twickenham
New Zealand 1G 2PG 1T (16)
to 1PG 1DG (6)

1979 Twickenham
New Zealand 2PG 1T (10) to 3PG (9)

1983 Twickenham
England 1G 3PG (15) to 1G 1PG (9)

1985 *1* Christchurch
New Zealand 6PG (18) to 1G 1PG 1T (13)

2 Wellington
New Zealand 3G 3PG 1DG 3T (42)
to 2G 1DG (15)
New Zealand won series 2-0

ENGLAND v SOUTH AFRICA
Played 9   England won 2, South Africa won 6, Drawn 1

1906 Crystal Palace (London)
Drawn 1T (3) each

1913 Twickenham
South Africa 2PG 1T (9) to 1T (3)

1932 Twickenham
South Africa 1DG 1T (7) to 0

1952 Twickenham
South Africa 1G 1PG (8) to 1T (3)

1961 Twickenham
South Africa 1G (5) to 0

1969 Twickenham
England 1G 1PG 1T (11) to 1G 1PG (8)

1972 Johannesburg
England 1G 4PG (18) to 3PG (9)

1984 *1* Port Elizabeth
South Africa 3G 5PG (33)
to 4PG 1DG (15)

2 Johannesburg
South Africa 4G 1PG 2T (35) to 3PG (9)
South Africa won series 2-0

ENGLAND v AUSTRALIA
Played 16   England won 6, Australia won 10, Drawn 0

1909 Blackheath (London)
Australia 3T (9) to 1T (3)

1928 Twickenham
England 3G 1T (18) to 1G 2T (11)

1948 Twickenham
Australia 1G 2T (11) to 0

1958 Twickenham
England 1PG 2T (9) to 1PG 1DG (6)

1963 Sydney
Australia 3G 1T (18) to 3T (9)

1967 Twickenham
Australia 1G 2PG 3DG 1T (23)
to 1G 2PG (11)

1973 Twickenham
England 1G 2PG 2T (20) to 1PG (3)

1975 *1* Sydney
Australia 2PG 2DG 1T (16)
to 1G 1PG (9)

2 Brisbane
Australia 2G 2PG 3T (30)
to 2G 3PG (21)
Australia won series 2-0

1976 Twickenham
England 1G 3PG 2T (23) to 2PG (6)

1982 Twickenham
England 1G 3PG (15) to 1PG 2T (11)

1984 Twickenham
Australia 2G 1PG 1T (19) to 1PG (3)

1987 Sydney *WC*
Australia 1G 3PG 1T (19) to 1G (6)

1988 *1* Brisbane
Australia 6PG 1T (22) to 1G 2PG 1T (16)

2 Sydney
Australia 3G 2PG 1T (28) to 2T (8)
Australia won series 2-0

1988 Twickenham
England 3G 2PG 1T (28) to
2G 1PG 1T (19)

SCOTLAND v IRELAND

Played 100   Scotland won 50, Ireland won 45, Drawn 4, Abandoned 1

1877 Belfast
Scotland 4G 2DG 2T to 0

1878 No Match

1879 Belfast
Scotland 1G 1DG 1T to 0

1880 Glasgow
Scotland 1G 2DG 2T to 0

1881 Belfast
Ireland 1DG to 1T

1882 Glasgow
Scotland 2T to 0

1883 Belfast
Scotland 1G 1T to 0

1884 Raeburn Place (Edinburgh)
Scotland 2G 2T to 1T

1885 Belfast
Abandoned Ireland 0 Scotland 1T

1885 Raeburn Place
Scotland 1G 2T to 0

1886 Raeburn Place
Scotland 3G 1DG 2T to 0

1887 Belfast
Scotland 1G 1GM 2T to 0

1888 Raeburn Place
Scotland 1G to 0

1889 Belfast
Scotland 1DG to 0

1890 Raeburn Place
Scotland 1DG 1T to 0

1891 Belfast
Scotland 3G 1DG 2T (14) to 0

1892 Raeburn Place
Scotland 1T (2) to 0

1893 Belfast
Drawn no score

1894 Dublin
Ireland 1G (5) to 0

1895 Raeburn Place
Scotland 2T (6) to 0

1896 Dublin
Drawn no score

1897 Powderhall (Edinburgh)
Scotland 1G 1PG (8) to 1T (3)

1898 Belfast
Scotland 1G 1T (8) to 0

1899 Inverleith (Edinburgh)
Ireland 3T (9) to 1PG (3)

1900 Dublin
Drawn no score

1901 Inverleith
Scotland 3T (9) to 1G (5)

1902 Belfast
Ireland 1G (5) to 0

1903 Inverleith
Scotland 1T (3) to 0

1904 Dublin
Scotland 2G 3T (19) to 1T (3)

1905 Inverleith
Ireland 1G 2T (11) to 1G (5)

1906 Dublin
Scotland 2G 1GM (13) to 2T (6)

1907 Inverleith
Scotland 3G (15) to 1PG (3)

1908 Dublin
Ireland 2G 2T (16) to 1G 1PG 1T (11)

1909 Inverleith
Scotland 3T (9) to 1PG (3)

1910 Belfast
Scotland 1G 3T (14) to 0

1911 Inverleith
Ireland 2G 2T (16) to 1DG 2T (10)

1912 Dublin
Ireland 1PG 1DG 1T (10) to 1G 1T (8)

1913 Inverleith
Scotland 4G 3T (29) to 2G 1DG (14)

1914 Dublin
Ireland 2T (6) to 0

1920 Inverleith
Scotland 2G 1PG 2T (19) to 0

1921 Dublin
Ireland 3T (9) to 1G 1T (8)

1922 Inverleith
Scotland 2T (6) to 1T (3)

1923 Dublin
Scotland 2G 1T (13) to 1T (3)

1924 Inverleith
Scotland 2G 1T (13) to 1G 1T (8)

1925 Dublin
Scotland 2G 1DG (14) to 1G 1PG (8)

1926 Murrayfield
Ireland 1T (3) to 0

1927 Dublin
Ireland 2T (6) to 0

1928 Murrayfield
Ireland 2G 1T (13) to 1G (5)

1929 Dublin
Scotland 2G 2T (16) to 1DG 1T (7)

1930 Murrayfield
Ireland 1G 3T (14) to 1G 2T (11)

1931 Dublin
Ireland 1G 1T (8) to 1G (5)

1932 Murrayfield
Ireland 4G (20) to 1G 1T (8)

1933 Dublin
Scotland 2DG (8) to 2T (6)

1934 Murrayfield
Scotland 2G 1PG 1T (16) to 3T (9)

1935 Dublin
Ireland 4T (12) to 1G (5)

1936 Murrayfield
Ireland 1DG 2T (10) to 1DG (4)

1937 Dublin
Ireland 1G 2T (11) to 1DG (4)

1938 Murrayfield
Scotland 2G 1PG 1DG 2T (23)
to 1G 3T (14)

1939 Dublin
Ireland 1PG 1GM 2T (12) to 1T (3)

1947 Murrayfield
Ireland 1T (3) to 0

1948 Dublin
Ireland 2T (6) to 0

1949 Murrayfield
Ireland 2G 1PG (13) to 1PG (3)

1950 Dublin
Ireland 3G 2PG (21) to 0

1951 Murrayfield
Ireland 1DG 1T (6) to 1G (5)

1952 Dublin
Ireland 1PG 3T (12) to 1G 1PG (8)

1953 Murrayfield
Ireland 4G 2T (26) to 1G 1PG (8)

1954 Belfast
Ireland 2T (6) to 0

1955 Murrayfield
Scotland 2PG 1DG 1T (12) to 1PG (3)

1956 Dublin
Ireland 1G 3T (14) to 2G (10)

1957 Murrayfield
Ireland 1G (5) to 1PG (3)

1958 Dublin
Ireland 2PG 2T (12) to 2T (6)

1959 Murrayfield
Ireland 1G 1PG (8) to 1PG (3)

1960 Dublin
Scotland 1DG 1T (6) to 1G (5)

1961 Murrayfield
Scotland 2G 1PG 1T (16) to 1G 1T (8)

1962 Dublin
Scotland 1G 2PG 1DG 2T (20)
to 1PG 1T (6)

1963 Murrayfield
Scotland 1PG (3) to 0

1964 Dublin
Scotland 2PG (6) to 1PG (3)

1965 Murrayfield
Ireland 2G 1DG 1T (16) to 1PG 1DG (6)

1966 Dublin
Scotland 1G 2T (11) to 1PG (3)

1967 Murrayfield
Ireland 1G (5) to 1PG (3)

1968 Dublin
Ireland 1G 1PG 2T (14) to 2PG (6)

1969 Murrayfield
Ireland 2G 2T (16) to 0

1970 Dublin
Ireland 2G 2T (16) to 1G 1DG 1T (11)

1971 Murrayfield
Ireland 1G 2PG 2T (17) to 1G (5)

1972 No Match

1973 Murrayfield
Scotland 2PG 3DG 1T (19)
to 2PG 2T (14)

1974 Dublin
Ireland 1G 1PG (9) to 2PG (6)

1975 Murrayfield
Scotland 2PG 2DG 2T (20)
to 1G 1PG 1T (13)

1976 Dublin
Scotland 4PG 1DG (15) to 2PG (6)

1977 Murrayfield
Scotland 2PG 1DG 3T (21)
to 1G 3PG 1DG (18)

1978 Dublin
Ireland 1G 2PG (12) to 3PG (9)

1979 Murrayfield
Drawn 1PG 2T (11) each

1980 Dublin
Ireland 1G 3PG 1DG 1T (22)
to 2G 1PG (15)

1981 Murrayfield
Scotland 1PG 1DG 1T (10)
to 1G 1PG (9)

1982 Dublin
Ireland 6PG 1DG (21) to 1G 2PG (12)

1983 Murrayfield
Ireland 1G 3PG (15)
to 2PG 1DG 1T (13)

1984 Dublin
Scotland *3G 2PG 2T (32) to 1G 1PG (9)
includes one penalty try

1985 Murrayfield
Ireland 2G 1PG 1DG (18)
to 4PG 1DG (15)

1986 Dublin
Scotland 2PG 1T (10) to 1G 1PG (9)

1987 Murrayfield
Scotland 1G 2DG 1T (16)
to 1G 1PG 1DG (12)

1988 Dublin
Ireland 2G 1PG 1DG 1T (22)
to 2G 2PG (18)

1989 Murrayfield
Scotland 4G 3PG 1T (37) to 3G 1PG (21)

SCOTLAND v WALES
Played 93   Scotland won 39, Wales won 52, Drawn 2

1883 Raeburn Place (Edinburgh)
Scotland 3G to 1G

1884 Newport
Scotland 1DG 1T to 0

1885 Glasgow
Drawn no score

1886 Cardiff
Scotland 2G 1T to 0

1887 Raeburn Place
Scotland 4G 8T to 0

1888 Newport
Wales 1T to 0

1889 Raeburn Place
Scotland 2T to 0

1890 Cardiff
Scotland 1G 2T to 1T

1891 Raeburn Place
Scotland 1G 2DG 6T (15) to 0

1892 Swansea
Scotland 1G 1T (7) to 1T (2)

1893 Raeburn Place
Wales 1PG 3T (9) to 0

1894 Newport
Wales 1DG 1T (7) to 0

1895 Raeburn Place
Scotland 1G (5) to 1GM (4)

1896 Cardiff
Wales 2T (6) to 0

1897 No Match

1898 No Match

1899 Inverleith (Edinburgh)
Scotland 1GM 2DG 3T (21) to 2G (10)

1900 Swansea
Wales 4T (12) to 1T (3)

1901 Inverleith
Scotland 3G 1T (18) to 1G 1T (8)

1902 Cardiff
Wales 1G 3T (14) to 1G (5)

1903 Inverleith
Scotland 1PG 1T (6) to 0

1904 Swansea
Wales 3G 1PG 1T (21) to 1T (3)

1905 Inverleith
Wales 2T (6) to 1T (3)

1906 Cardiff
Wales 3T (9) to 1PG (3)

1907 Inverleith
Scotland 2T (6) to 1PG (3)

1908 Swansea
Wales 2T (6) to 1G (5)

1909 Inverleith
Wales 1G (5) to 1PG (3)

1910 Cardiff
Wales 1G 3T (14) to 0

1911 Inverleith
Wales 2G 1DG 6T (32)
to 1DG 2T (10)

1912 Swansea
Wales 2G 2DG 1T (21) to 2T (6)

1913 Inverleith
Wales 1G 1T (8) to 0

1914 Cardiff
Wales 2G 1PG 2DG 1T (24) to 1G (5)

1920 Inverleith
Scotland 2PG 1T (9) to 1G (5)

1921 Swansea
Scotland 1G 1PG 2T (14) to 2DG (8)

1922 Inverleith
Drawn Scotland 1PG 2T (9)
Wales 1G 1DG (9)

1923 Cardiff
Scotland 1G 2T (11) to 1G 1PG (8)

1924 Inverleith
Scotland 4G 1PG 4T (35) to 2G (10)

1925 Swansea
Scotland 1G 1DG 5T (24)
to 1G 1PG 2T (14)

1926 Murrayfield
Scotland 1G 1PG (8) to 1G (5)

1927 Cardiff
Scotland 1G (5) to 0

1928 Murrayfield
Wales 2G 1T (13) to 0

1929 Swansea
Wales 1G 3T (14) to 1PG 1DG (7)

1930 Murrayfield
Scotland 1G 1DG 1T (12)
to 1G 1DG (9)

1931 Cardiff
Wales 2G 1T (13) to 1G 1T (8)

1932 Murrayfield
Wales 1PG 1T (6) to 0

1933 Swansea
Scotland 1G 1PG 1T (11) to 1T (3)

1934 Murrayfield
Wales 2G 1T (13) to 1PG 1T (6)

1935 Cardiff
Wales 1DG 2T (10) to 2T (6)

1936 Murrayfield
Wales 2G 1T (13) to 1T (3)

1937 Swansea
Scotland 2G 1T (13) to 2T (6)

1938 Murrayfield
Scotland 1G 1PG (8) to 2T (6)

1939 Cardiff
Wales 1G 1PG 1T (11) to 1PG (3)

1947 Murrayfield
Wales 2G 1PG 3T (22) to 1G 1PG (8)

1948 Cardiff
Wales 1G 1PG 2T (14) to 0

1949 Murrayfield
Scotland 2T (6) to 1G (5)

1950 Swansea
Wales 1PG 1DG 2T (12) to 0

1951 Murrayfield
Scotland 2G 1PG 1DG 1T (19) to 0

1952 Cardiff
Wales 1G 2PG (11) to 0

1953 Murrayfield
Wales 1PG 3T (12) to 0

1954 Swansea
Wales 1PG 4T (15) to 1T (3)

1955 Murrayfield
Scotland 1G 1PG 1DG 1T (14)
to 1G 1T (8)

1956 Cardiff
Wales 3T (9) to 1PG (3)

1957 Murrayfield
Scotland 1PG 1DG 1T (9)
to 1PG 1T (6)

1958 Cardiff
Wales 1G 1T (8) to 1PG (3)

1959 Murrayfield
Scotland 1PG 1T (6) to 1G (5)

1960 Cardiff
Wales 1G 1PG (8) to 0

1961 Murrayfield
Scotland 1T (3) to 0

1962 Cardiff
Scotland 1G 1T (8) to 1DG (3)

1963 Murrayfield
Wales 1PG 1DG (6) to 0

1964 Cardiff
Wales 1G 1PG 1T (11) to 1T (3)

1965 Murrayfield
Wales 1G 2PG 1T (14) to 2PG 2DG (12)

1966 Cardiff
Wales 1G 1T (8) to 1PG (3)

1967 Murrayfield
Scotland 1G 1DG 1T (11) to 1G (5)

1968 Cardiff
Wales 1G (5) to 0

1969 Murrayfield
Wales 1G 2PG 2T (17) to 1PG (3)

1970 Cardiff
Wales 3G 1T (18) to 1PG 1DG 1T (9)

1971 Murrayfield
Wales 2G 1PG 2T (19) to 4PG 2T (18)

1972 Cardiff
Wales 3G 3PG 2T (35) to 1G 2PG (12)

1973 Murrayfield
Scotland 1G 1T (10) to 3PG (9)

1974 Cardiff
Wales 1G (6) to 0

1975 Murrayfield
Scotland 3PG 1DG (12) to 2PG 1T (10)

1976 Cardiff
Wales 2G 3PG 1DG 1T (28) to 1G (6)

1977 Murrayfield
Wales 2G 2PG (18) to 1G 1DG (9)

1978 Cardiff
Wales 1PG 1DG 4T (22) to 2PG 2T (14)

1979 Murrayfield
Wales 1G 3PG 1T (19) to 3PG 1T (13)

1980 Cardiff
Wales 1G 1PG 2T (17) to 1G (6)

1981 Murrayfield
Scotland *2G 1PG (15) to 2PG (6)
includes one penalty try

1982 Cardiff
Scotland 4G 2DG 1T (34)
to 1G 4PG (18)

1983 Murrayfield
Wales 1G 3PG 1T (19) to 1G 3PG (15)

1984 Cardiff
Scotland 2G 1PG (15) to 1G 1PG (9)

1985 Murrayfield
Wales 1G 4PG 1DG 1T (25) to 2G 1PG
2DG (21)

1986 Cardiff
Wales 5PG 1DG 1T (22) to 1PG 3T (15)

1987 Murrayfield
Scotland 2G 2PG 1DG (21)
to 1G 2PG 1DG (15)

1988 Cardiff
Wales 2G 1PG 2DG 1T (25)
to 4PG 2T (20)

1989 Murrayfield
Scotland 1G 2PG 1DG 2T (23)
to 1PG 1T (7)

SCOTLAND v FRANCE
Played 60   Scotland won 28, France won 29, Drawn 3

1910 Inverleith (Edinburgh)
Scotland 3G 4T (27) to 0

1911 Paris
France 2G 2T (16) to 1G 1DG 2T (15)

1912 Inverleith
Scotland 5G 1PG 1T (31) to 1T (3)

1913 Paris
Scotland 3G 2T (21) to 1T (3)

71

1914 No Match

1920 Paris
Scotland 1G (5) to 0

1921 Inverleith
France 1T (3) to 0

1922 Paris
Drawn 1T (3) each

1923 Inverleith
Scotland 2G 2T (16) to 1GM (3)

1924 Paris
France 4T (12) to 1PG 1DG 1T (10)

1925 Inverleith
Scotland 2G 5T (25) to 1DG (4)

1926 Paris
Scotland 1G 1PG 4T (20) to 1PG 1T (6)

1927 Murrayfield
Scotland 4G 1PG (23) to 2T (6)

1928 Paris
Scotland 5T (15) to 2T (6)

1929 Murrayfield
Scotland 1PG 1T (6) to 1T (3)

1930 Paris
France 1DG 1T (7) to 1T (3)

1931 Murrayfield
Scotland 2PG (6) to 1DG (4)

1947 Paris
France 1G 1T (8) to 1PG (3)

1948 Murrayfield
Scotland 2PG 1T (9) to 1G 1PG (8)

1949 Paris
Scotland 1G 1T (8) to 0

1950 Murrayfield
Scotland 1G 1T (8) to 1G (5)

1951 Paris
France 1G 2PG 1T (14) to 2PG 2T (12)

1952 Murrayfield
France 2G 1PG (13) to 1G 2PG (11)

1953 Paris
France 1G 1PG 1DG (11) to 1G (5)

1954 Murrayfield
France 1T (3) to 0

1955 Paris
France 1PG 4T (15) to 0

1956 Murrayfield
Scotland 2PG 2T (12) to 0

1957 Paris
Scotland 1PG 1DG (6) to 0

1958 Murrayfield
Scotland 1G 1PG 1T (11) to 2PG 1T (9)

1959 Paris
France 2DG 1T (9) to 0

1960 Murrayfield
France 2G 1T (13) to 1G 1PG 1T (11)

1961 Paris
France 1G 1PG 1DG (11) to 0

1962 Murrayfield
France 1G 2PG (11) to 1PG (3)

1963 Paris
Scotland 1G 1PG 1DG (11)
to 1PG 1DG (6)

1964 Murrayfield
Scotland 2G (10) to 0

1965 Paris
France 2G 2T (16) to 1G 1T (8)

1966 Murrayfield
Drawn Scotland 1T (3) France 1PG (3)

1967 Paris
Scotland 2PG 1DG (9) to 1G 1T (8)

1968 Murrayfield
France 1G 1T (8) to 1PG 1T (6)

1969 Paris
Scotland 1PG 1T (6) to 1PG (3)

1970 Murrayfield
France 1G 1DG 1T (11) to 2PG 1T (9)

1971 Paris
France 2G 1PG (13) to 1G 1PG (8)

1972 Murrayfield
Scotland 1G 1PG 1DG 2T (20)
to 1G 1PG (9)

1973 Paris
France 3PG 1DG 1T (16)
to 2PG 1DG 1T (13)

1974 Murrayfield
Scotland 1G 3PG 1T (19) to 1PG 1DG (6)

1975 Paris
France 1PG 1DG 1T (10) to 3PG (9)

1976 Murrayfield
France 3PG 1T (13) to 1PG 1DG (6)

1977 Paris
France 2G 1PG 2T (23) to 1PG (3)

1978 Murrayfield
France 1G 3PG 1T (19)
to 1G 1PG 1DG 1T (16)

1979 Paris
France 2PG 1DG 3T (21)
to 1G 1PG 2T (17)

1980 Murrayfield
Scotland 2G 2PG 1T (22)
to 1PG 1DG 2T (14)

1981 Paris
France 1G 2PG 1T (16)
to 1G 1PG (9)

1982 Murrayfield
Scotland 3PG 1DG 1T (16)
to 1PG 1T (7)

1983 Paris
France 1G 1T 3PG (19)
to 1G 1PG 2DG (15)

1984 Murrayfield
Scotland 1G 5PG (21)
to 1G 1PG 1DG (12)

1985 Paris
France 1PG 2T (11) to 1PG (3)

1986 Murrayfield
Scotland 6PG (18) to 2PG 1DG 2T (17)

1987 Paris
France 3PG 1DG 4T (28)
to 1G 4PG 1T (22)

1987 Christchurch *WC*
Drawn Scotland 4PG 2T (20)
France 1G 2PG 2T (20)

1988 Murrayfield
Scotland 4PG 1DG 2T (23)
to 1G 1PG 1DG (12)

1989 Paris
France 2G 1PG 1T (19) to 1PG (3)

SCOTLAND v NEW ZEALAND

Played 13   Scotland won 0, New Zealand won 11, Drawn 2

1905 Inverleith (Edinburgh)
New Zealand 4T (12) to 1DG 1T (7)

1935 Murrayfield
New Zealand 3G 1T (18) to 1G 1T (8)

1954 Murrayfield
New Zealand 1PG (3) to 0

1964 Murrayfield
Drawn no score

1967 Murrayfield
New Zealand 1G 2PG 1T (14)
to 1DG (3)

1972 Murrayfield
New Zealand 1G 2T (14) to 2PG 1DG (9)

1975 Auckland
New Zealand 4G (24) to 0

1978 Murrayfield
New Zealand 2G 2PG (18) to 1G
1DG (9)

1979 Murrayfield
New Zealand 2G 2T (20) to 2PG (6)

1981 *1* Dunedin
New Zealand 1PG 2T (11) to 1T (4)

2 Auckland
New Zealand 6G 1T (40) to 1G 2PG
1DG (15)
*New Zealand won series 2-0

1983 Murrayfield
Drawn Scotland 5PG 2DG 1T (25)
New Zealand 2G 3PG 1T (25)

1987 Christchurch *WC*
New Zealand 2G 6PG (30) to 1PG (3)

SCOTLAND v SOUTH AFRICA

Played 8   Scotland won 3, South Africa won 5, Drawn 0

1906 Glasgow
Scotland 2T (6) to 0

1912 Inverleith
South Africa 2G 2T (16) to 0

1932 Murrayfield
South Africa 2T (6) to 1T (3)

1951 Murrayfield
South Africa 7G 1DG 2T (44) to 0

1960 Port Elizabeth
South Africa 3G 1T (18) to 2G (10)

1961 Murrayfield
South Africa 2PG 2T (12) to 1G (5)

1965 Murrayfield
Scotland 1G 1DG (8) to 1G (5)

1969 Murrayfield
Scotland 1PG 1T (6) to 1PG (3)

SCOTLAND v AUSTRALIA

Played 12   Scotland won 7, Australia won 5, Drawn 0

1927 Murrayfield
Scotland 2G (10) to 1G 1T (8)

1947 Murrayfield
Australia 2G 2T (16) to 1PG 1DG (7)

1958 Murrayfield
Scotland 2PG 2T (12) to 1G 1T (8)

1966 Murrayfield
Scotland 1G 1PG 1T (11) to 1G (5)

1968 Murrayfield
Scotland 2PG 1T (9) to 1PG (3)

1970 Sydney
Australia 1G 1PG 5T (23) to 1PG (3)

1975 Murrayfield
Scotland 1G 1T (10) to 1PG (3)

1981 Murrayfield
Scotland 1G 5PG 1DG (24)
to 1PG 3T (15)

1982 *1* Brisbane
Scotland 1G 1PG 1DG (12) to 1PG 1T (7)

2 Sydney
Australia 3G 5PG (33) to 3PG (9)
Series drawn 1-1

1984 Murrayfield
Australia 3G 5PG 1T (37) to 4PG (12)

1988 Murrayfield
Australia 3G 2PG 2T (32)
to 1G 1PG 1T (13)

IRELAND v WALES

Played 92   Ireland won 31, Wales won 56, Drawn 5

1882 Dublin
Wales 2G 2T to 0

1883 No Match

1884 Cardiff
Wales 1DG 2T to 0

1885 No Match

1886 No Match

1887 Birkenhead
Wales 1DG 1T to 3T

1888 Dublin
Ireland 1G 1DG 1T to 0

1889 Swansea
Ireland 2T to 0

1890 Dublin
Drawn 1G each

1891 Llanelli
Wales 1G 1DG (6) to 1DG 1T (4)

1892 Dublin
Ireland 1G 2T (9) to 0

1893 Llanelli
Wales 1T (2) to 0

1894 Belfast
Ireland 1PG (3) to 0

1895 Cardiff
Wales 1G (5) to 1T (3)

1896 Dublin
Ireland 1G 1T (8) to 1DG (4)

1897 No Match

1898 Limerick
Wales 1G 1PG 1T (11) to 1PG (3)

1899 Cardiff
Ireland 1T (3) to 0

1900 Belfast
Wales 1T (3) to 0

1901 Swansea
Wales 2G (10) to 3T (9)

1902 Dublin
Wales 1G 1DG 2T (15) to 0

1903 Cardiff
Wales 6T (18) to 0

1904 Belfast
Ireland 1G 3T (14) to 4T (12)

1905 Swansea
Wales 2G (10) to 1T (3)

1906 Belfast
Ireland 1G 2T (11) to 2T (6)

1907 Cardiff
Wales 2G 1PG 1DG 4T (29) to 0

1908 Belfast
Wales 1G 2T (11) to 1G (5)

1909 Swansea
Wales 3G 1T (18) to 1G (5)

1910 Dublin
Wales 1DG 5T (19) to 1T (3)

1911 Cardiff
Wales 2G 1PG 1T (16) to 0

1912 Belfast
Ireland 1G 1DG 1T (12) to 1G (5)

1913 Swansea
Wales 2G 1PG 1T (16) to 2G 1PG (13)

1914 Belfast
Wales 1G 2T (11) to 1T (3)

1920 Cardiff
Wales 3G 1DG 3T (28) to 1DG (4)

1921 Belfast
Wales 1PG 1T (6) to 0

1922 Swansea
Wales 1G 2T (11) to 1G (5)

1923 Dublin
Ireland 1G (5) to 1DG (4)

1924 Cardiff
Ireland 2G 1T (13) to 1DG 2T (10)

1925 Belfast
Ireland 2G 1PG 2T (19) to 1T (3)

1926 Swansea
Wales 1G 2T (11) to 1G 1PG (8)

1927 Dublin
Ireland 2G 1PG 2T (19) to 1G 1DG (9)

1928 Cardiff
Ireland 2G 1T (13) to 2G (10)

1929 Belfast
Drawn 1G (5) each

1930 Swansea
Wales 1PG 3T (12) to 1PG 1DG (7)

1931 Belfast
Wales 1G 1DG 2T (15) to 1T (3)

1932 Cardiff
Ireland 4T (12) to 1DG 2T (10)

1933 Belfast
Ireland 1PG 1DG 1T (10) to 1G (5)

1934 Swansea
Wales 2G 1T (13) to 0

1935 Belfast
Ireland 2PG 1T (9) to 1PG (3)

1936 Cardiff
Wales 1PG (3) to 0

1937 Belfast
Ireland 1G (5) to 1PG (3)

1938 Swansea
Wales 1G 1PG 1T (11) to 1G (5)

1939 Belfast
Wales 1DG 1T (7) to 0

1947 Swansea
Wales 1PG 1T (6) to 0

1948 Belfast
Ireland 2T (6) to 1T (3)

1949 Swansea
Ireland 1G (5) to 0

1950 Belfast
Wales 2T (6) to 1PG (3)

1951 Cardiff
Drawn Wales 1PG (3) to Ireland 1T (3)

1952 Dublin
Wales 1G 1PG 2T (14) to 1PG (3)

1953 Swansea
Wales 1G (5) to 1T (3)

1954 Dublin
Wales 3PG 1DG (12) to 2PG 1T (9)

1955 Cardiff
Wales 3G 1PG 1T (21) to 1PG (3)

1956 Dublin
Ireland 1G 1PG 1DG (11) to 1PG (3)

1957 Cardiff
Wales 2PG (6) to 1G (5)

1958 Dublin
Wales 3T (9) to 1PG 1T (6)

1959 Cardiff
Wales 1G 1T (8) to 1PG 1T (6)

1960 Dublin
Wales 2G (10) to 2PG 1T (9)

1961 Cardiff
Wales 2PG 1T (9) to 0

1962 Dublin
Drawn Ireland 1DG (3) Wales 1PG (3)

1963 Cardiff
Ireland 1G 2PG 1DG (14)
to 1DG 1T (6)

1964 Dublin
Wales 3G (15) to 2PG (6)

1965 Cardiff
Wales 1G 1PG 1DG 1T (14)
to 1G 1PG (8)

1966 Dublin
Ireland 1PG 1DG 1T (9) to 1PG 1T (6)

1967 Cardiff
Ireland 1T (3) to 0

1968 Dublin
Ireland 1PG 1DG 1T (9) to 1PG 1DG (6)

1969 Cardiff
Wales 3G 1PG 1DG 1T (24)
to 1G 2PG (11)

1970 Dublin
Ireland 1G 1PG 1DG 1T (14) to 0

1971 Cardiff
Wales 1G 2PG 1DG 3T (23) to 3PG (9)

1972 No Match

1973 Cardiff
Wales 1G 2PG 1T (16) to 1G 2PG (12)

1974 Dublin
Drawn Ireland 3PG (9)
Wales 1G 1PG (9)

1975 Cardiff
Wales 3G 2PG 2T (32) to 1T (4)

1976 Dublin
Wales 3G 4PG 1T (34) to 3PG (9)

1977 Cardiff
Wales 2G 2PG 1DG 1T (25) to 3PG (9)

1978 Dublin
Wales 4PG 2T (20) to 3PG 1DG 1T (16)

1979 Cardiff
Wales 2G 4PG (24) to 2G 3PG (21)

1980 Dublin
Ireland 3G 1PG (21) to 1PG 1T (7)

1981 Cardiff
Wales 2PG 1DG (9) to 2T (8)

1982 Dublin
Ireland 1G 2PG 2T (20)
to 1G 1PG 1DG (12)

1983 Cardiff
Wales 1G 3PG 2T (23) to 3PG (9)

1984 Dublin
Wales 1G 4PG (18) to 3PG (9)

1985 Cardiff
Ireland 2G 3PG (21) to 1G 1DG (9)

1986 Dublin
Wales 1G 3PG 1T (19) to 1G 2PG (12)

1987 Cardiff
Ireland 2G 1PG (15) to 1PG 2T (11)

1987 Wellington *WC*
Wales 1PG 2DG 1T (13) to 2PG (6)

1988 Dublin
Wales 1G 1PG 1DG (12) to 1G 1PG (9)

1989 Cardiff
Ireland 1G 3PG 1T (19) to 3PG 1T (13)

IRELAND v FRANCE

Played 62   Ireland won 25, France won 32, Drawn 5

1909 Dublin
Ireland 2G 1PG 2T (19) to 1G 1T (8)

1910 Paris
Ireland 1G 1T (8) to 1T (3)

1911 Cork
Ireland 3G 1DG 2T (25) to 1G (5)

1912 Paris
Ireland 1G 2T (11) to 2T (6)

1913 Cork
Ireland 3G 3T (24) to 0

1914 Paris
Ireland 1G 1T (8) to 2T (6)

1920 Dublin
France 5T (15) to 1DG 1T (7)

1921 Paris
France 4G (20) to 2G (10)

1922 Dublin
Ireland 1G 1PG (8) to 1T (3)

1923 Paris
France 1G 3T (14) to 1G 1T (8)

1924 Dublin
Ireland 2T (6) to 0

1925 Paris
Ireland 1PG 2T (9) to 1T (3)

1926 Belfast
Ireland 1G 1PG 1T (11) to 0

1927 Paris
Ireland 1G 1PG (8) to 1T (3)

1928 Belfast
Ireland 4T (12) to 1G 1T (8)

1929 Paris
Ireland 2T (6) to 0

1930 Belfast
France 1G (5) to 0

1931 Paris
France 1T (3) to 0

1947 Dublin
France 4T (12) to 1G 1PG (8)

1948 Paris
Ireland 2G 1T (13) to 2T (6)

1949 Dublin
France 2G 2PG (16) to 3PG (9)

1950 Paris
Drawn France 1DG (3) Ireland 1PG (3)

1951 Dublin
Ireland 1PG 2T (9) to 1G 1T (8)

1952 Paris
Ireland 1G 1PG 1T (11) to 1G 1PG (8)

1953 Belfast
Ireland 2G 2T (16) to 1DG (3)

1954 Paris
France 1G 1T (8) to 0

1955 Dublin
France 1G (5) to 1PG (3)

1956 Paris
France 1G 2DG 1T (14) to 1G 1PG (8)

1957 Dublin
Ireland 1G 1PG 1T (11) to 2PG (6)

1958 Paris
France 1G 1PG 1DG (11) to 2PG (6)

1959 Dublin
Ireland 1PG 1DG 1T (9) to 1G (5)

1960 Paris
France 1G 3DG 3T (23) to 2T (6)

1961 Dublin
France 2PG 2DG 1T (15) to 1PG (3)

1962 Paris
France 1G 2T (11) to 0

1963 Dublin
France 3G 2DG 1T (24) to 1G (5)

1964 Paris
France 3G 1DG 3T (27) to 1DG 1T (6)

1965 Dublin
Drawn 1T (3) each

1966 Paris
France 1G 1PG 1T (11) to 1PG 1DG (6)

1967 Dublin
France 1G 2DG (11) to 1PG 1T (6)

1968 Paris
France 2G 1PG 1DG (16) to 2PG (6)

1969 Dublin
Ireland 1G 3PG 1DG (17) to 2PG 1T (9)

1970 Paris
France 1G 1DG (8) to 0

1971 Dublin
Drawn Ireland 2PG 1T (9)
France 2PG 1DG (9)

1972 Paris
Ireland 2PG 2T (14) to 1G 1PG (9)

*1972 Dublin
Ireland 3G 2PG (24) to 1G 2T (14)
* *Non-championship match*

1973 Dublin
Ireland 2PG (6) to 1T (4)

1974 Paris
France 1G 1PG (9) to 2PG (6)

1975 Dublin
Ireland 2G 1PG 2DG 1T (25)
to 1PG 1DG (6)

1976 Paris
France 2G 2PG 2T (26) to 1PG (3)

1977 Dublin
France 1G 3PG (15) to 2PG (6)

1978 Paris
France 2PG 1T (10) to 3PG (9)

1979 Dublin
Drawn Ireland 3PG (9)
France 1G 1PG (9)

1980 Paris
France 1G 2PG 1DG 1T (19)
to 1G 3PG 1DG (18)

1981 Dublin
France 3PG 2DG 1T (19)
to 3PG 1T (13)

1982 Paris
France 1G 4PG 1T (22) to 3PG (9)

1983 Dublin
Ireland 1G 4PG 1T (22)
to 1G 2PG 1T (16)

1984 Paris
France 1G 4PG 1DG 1T (25) to 4PG (12)

1985 Dublin
Drawn Ireland 5PG (15)
France 2G 1PG (15)

1986 Paris
France 1G 4PG 1DG 2T (29) to 3PG (9)

1987 Dublin
France 1G 3PG 1T (19)
to 1G 1PG 1T (13)

1988 Paris
France 1G 1PG 4T (25) to 2PG (6)

1989 Dublin
France 2G 2PG 2T (26) to 1G 5PG (21)

IRELAND v NEW ZEALAND

Played 9   Ireland won 0, New Zealand won 8, Drawn 1

1905 Dublin
New Zealand 3G (15) to 0

1924 Dublin
New Zealand 1PG 1T (6) to 0

1935 Dublin
New Zealand 1G 2PG 2T (17)
to 2PG 1T (9)

1954 Dublin
New Zealand 1G 1PG 1DG 1T (14)
to 1PG (3)

1963 Dublin
New Zealand 1PG 1T (6) to 1G (5)

1973 Dublin
Drawn Ireland 2PG 1T (10)
New Zealand 1G 1T (10)

1974 Dublin
New Zealand 1G 3PG (15) to 2PG (6)

1976 Wellington
New Zealand 1PG 2T (11) to 1PG (3)

1978 Dublin
New Zealand 2DG 1T (10) to 2PG (6)

IRELAND v SOUTH AFRICA

Played 10   Ireland won 1, South Africa won 8, Drawn 1

1906 Belfast
South Africa 1PG 4T (15)
to 1PG 3T (12)

1912 Dublin
South Africa 4G 6T (38) to 0

1931 Dublin
South Africa 1G 1T (8) to 1PG (3)

1951 Dublin
South Africa 1G 1DG 3T (17) to 1G (5)

1960 Dublin
South Africa 1G 1T (8) to 1PG (3)

1961 Cape Town
South Africa 3G 1PG 2T (24)
to 1G 1PG (8)

1965 Dublin
Ireland 2PG 1T (9) to 1PG 1T (6)

1970 Dublin
Drawn 1G 1PG (8) each

1981 *1* Cape Town
South Africa 1G 3PG 2T (23)
to 2G 1PG (15)

2 Durban
South Africa 1PG 3DG (12)
to 2PG 1T (10)
South Africa won series 2-0

IRELAND v AUSTRALIA

Played 12   Ireland won 6, Australia won 6, Drawn 0

1927 Dublin
Australia 1G (5) to 1PG (3)

1947 Dublin
Australia 2G 2T (16) to 1PG (3)

1958 Dublin
Ireland 1PG 2T (9) to 2T (6)

1967 Dublin
Ireland 1PG 2DG 2T (15) to 1G 1DG (8)

1967 Sydney
Ireland 1G 1DG 1T (11) to 1G (5)

1968 Dublin
Ireland 2G (10) to 1T (3)

1976 Dublin
Australia 1G 2PG 2T (20)
to 2PG 1T (10)

1979 *1* Brisbane
Ireland 2G 4PG 1DG (27)
to 1G 2PG (12)

2 Sydney
Ireland 1PG 2DG (9) to 1PG (3)
Ireland won series 2-0

1981 Dublin
Australia 3PG 1DG 1T (16) to 4PG (12)

1984 Dublin
Australia 1PG 3DG 1T (16) to 3PG (9)

1987 Sydney *WC*
Australia 4G 3PG (33) to 2G 1PG (15)

WALES v FRANCE

Played 62   Wales won 36, France won 23, Drawn 3

1908 Cardiff
Wales 3G 1PG 6T (36) to 1DG (4)

1909 Paris
Wales 7G 4T (47) to 1G (5)

1910 Swansea
Wales 8G 1PG 2T (49)
to 1G 2PG 1T (14)

1911 Paris
Wales 3G (15) to 0

1912 Newport
Wales 1G 3T (14) to 1G 1T (8)

1913 Paris
Wales 1G 2T (11) to 1G 1T (8)

1914 Swansea
Wales 5G 2T (31) to 0

1920 Paris
Wales 2T (6) to 1G (5)

1921 Cardiff
Wales 2PG 2T (12) to 1DG (4)

1922 Paris
Wales 1G 2T (11) to 1T (3)

1923 Swansea
Wales 2G 1PG 1T (16) to 1G 1T (8)

1924 Paris
Wales 1DG 2T (10) to 2T (6)

1925 Cardiff
Wales 1G 2T (11) to 1G (5)

1926 Paris
Wales 1DG 1T (7) to 1G (5)

1927 Swansea
Wales 2G 5T (25) to 1DG 1T (7)

1928 Paris
France 1G 1T (8) to 1T (3)

1929 Cardiff
Wales 1G 1T (8) to 1T (3)

1930 Paris
Wales 2DG 1T (11) to 0

1931 Swansea
Wales 5G 1DG 2T (35) to 1T (3)

1947 Paris
Wales 1PG (3) to 0

1948 Swansea
France 1G 2T (11) to 1PG (3)

1949 Paris
France 1G (5) to 1T (3)

1950 Cardiff
Wales 3G 1PG 1T (21) to 0

1951 Paris
France 1G 1PG (8) to 1T (3)

1952 Swansea
Wales 2PG 1DG (9) to 1G (5)

1953 Paris
Wales 2T (6) to 1PG (3)

1954 Cardiff
Wales 2G 3PG (19) to 2G 1PG (13)

1955 Paris
Wales 2G 2PG (16) to 1G 1PG 1DG (11)

1956 Cardiff
Wales 1G (5) to 1T (3)

1957 Paris
Wales 2G 1PG 2T (19) to 2G 1T (13)

1958 Cardiff
France 2G 2DG (16) to 1PG 1T (6)

1959 Paris
France 1G 1PG 1T (11) to 1PG (3)

1960 Cardiff
France 2G 2T (16) to 1G 1PG (8)

1961 Paris
France 1G 1T (8) to 2T (6)

1962 Cardiff
Wales 1PG (3) to 0

1963 Paris
France 1G (5) to 1PG (3)

1964 Cardiff
Drawn 1G 2PG (11) each

1965 Paris
France 2G 1PG 1DG 2T (22)
to 2G 1T (13)

1966 Cardiff
Wales 2PG 1T (9) to 1G 1T (8)

1967 Paris
France 1G 1PG 2DG 2T (20)
to 1G 2PG 1DG (14)

1968 Cardiff
France 1G 1PG 1DG 1T (14)
to 2PG 1T (9)

1969 Paris
Drawn France 1G 1PG (8)
Wales 1G 1T (8)

1970 Cardiff
Wales 1G 2PG (11) to 2T (6)

1971 Paris
Wales 1PG 2T (9) to 1G (5)

1972 Cardiff
Wales 4PG 2T (20) to 2PG (6)

1973 Paris
France 3PG 1DG (12) to 1DG (3)

1974 Cardiff
Drawn 3PG 1DG 1T (16) each

1975 Paris
Wales 1G 1PG 4T (25) to 2PG 1T (10)

1976 Cardiff
Wales 5PG 1T (19) to 1G 1PG 1T (13)

1977 Paris
France 1G 2PG 1T (16) to 3PG (9)

1978 Cardiff
Wales 1G 2DG 1T (16) to 1DG 1T (7)

1979 Paris
France 2PG 2T (14) to 3PG 1T (13)

1980 Cardiff
Wales 1G 3T (18) to 1G 1DG (9)

1981 Paris
France 5PG 1T (19) to 1G 3PG (15)

1982 Cardiff
Wales 6PG 1T (22) to 1G 2PG (12)

1983 Paris
France 3PG 1DG 1T (16) to 1G 1PG (9)

1984 Cardiff
France 1G 4PG 1DG (21)
to 1G 2PG 1T (16)

1985 Paris
France 2PG 2T (14) to 1PG (3)

1986 Cardiff
France 2G 1DG 2T (23) to 5PG (15)

1987 Paris
France 1G 2PG 1T (16) to 3PG (9)

1988 Cardiff
France 2PG 1T (10) to 1G 1PG (9)

1989 Paris
France 3G 2PG 1DG 1T (31) to 4PG (12)

WALES v NEW ZEALAND

Played 14   Wales won 3, New Zealand won 11, Drawn 0

1905 Cardiff
Wales 1T (3) to 0

1924 Swansea
New Zealand 2G 1PG 2T (19) to 0

1935 Cardiff
Wales 2G 1T (13) to 1G 1DG 1T (12)

1953 Cardiff
Wales 2G 1PG (13) to 1G 1PG (8)

1963 Cardiff
New Zealand 1PG 1DG (6) to 0

1967 Cardiff
New Zealand 2G 1PG (13)
to 1PG 1DG (6)

1969 *1* Christchurch
New Zealand 2G 1PG 2T (19) to 0

      2 Auckland
New Zealand 3G 5PG 1DG (33)
to 2PG 2T (12)
New Zealand won series 2-0

1972 Cardiff
New Zealand 5PG 1T (19)
to 4PG 1T (16)

1978 Cardiff
New Zealand 3PG 1T (13) to 4PG (12)

1980 Cardiff
New Zealand 2G 1PG 2T (23)
to 1PG (3)

1987 Brisbane *WC*
New Zealand 7G 1PG 1T (49) to 1G (6)

1988 *1* Christchurch
New Zealand 6G 4T (52) to 1PG (3)

      2 Auckland
New Zealand 8G 2PG (54) to 1G 1PG (9)
New Zealand won series 2-0

WALES v SOUTH AFRICA

Played 7   Wales won 0, South Africa won 6, Drawn 1

1906 Swansea
South Africa 1G 2T (11) to 0

1912 Cardiff
South Africa 1PG (3) to 0

1931 Swansea
South Africa 1G 1T (8) to 1T (3)

1951 Cardiff
South Africa 1DG 1T (6) to 1T (3)

1960 Cardiff
South Africa 1PG (3) to 0

1964 Durban
South Africa 3G 2PG 1DG (24) to 1PG (3)

1970 Cardiff
Drawn 1PG 1T (6) each

WALES v AUSTRALIA
Played 13   Wales won 8, Australia won 5, Drawn 0

1908 Cardiff
Wales 1PG 2T (9) to 2T (6)

1927 Cardiff
Australia 3G 1T (18) to 1G 1T (8)

1947 Cardiff
Wales 2PG (6) to 0

1958 Cardiff
Wales 1PG 1DG 1T (9) to 1T (3)

1966 Cardiff
Australia 1G 1PG 1DG 1T (14) to 1G 1PG 1T (11)

1969 Sydney
Wales 2G 2PG 1T (19) to 2G 2PG (16)

1973 Cardiff
Wales 4PG 3T (24) to 0

1975 Cardiff
Wales 3G 1PG 1DG 1T (28) to 1PG (3)

1978 *1* Brisbane
Australia 1G 4PG (18) to 2T (8)

2 Sydney
Australia 3PG 2DG 1T (19) to 2PG 1DG 2T (17)
Australia won series 2-0

1981 Cardiff
Wales 1G 3PG 1DG (18) to 1G 1PG 1T (13)

1984 Cardiff
Australia 3G 2PG 1T (28) to 1G 1PG (9)

1987 Rotorua *WC*
Wales 2G 2PG 1T (22) to 2G 2PG 1DG (21)

FRANCE v NEW ZEALAND
Played 24   France won 5, New Zealand won 19, Drawn 0

1906 Paris
New Zealand 4G 6T (38) to 1G 1T (8)

1925 Toulouse
New Zealand 3G 5T (30) to 2T (6)

1954 Paris
France 1T (3) to 0

1961 *1* Auckland
New Zealand 2G 1DG (13) to 2DG (6)

2 Wellington
New Zealand 1G (5) to 1T (3)

3 Christchurch
New Zealand 4G 3PG 1T (32) to 1T (3)
New Zealand won series 3-0

1964 Paris
New Zealand 1PG 1DG 2T (12) to 1PG (3)

1967 Paris
New Zealand 3G 1PG 1T (21) to 3PG 1DG 1T (15)

1968 *1* Christchurch
New Zealand 3PG 1T (12) to 2PG 1DG (9)

2 Wellington
New Zealand 3PG (9) to 1PG (3)

3 Auckland
New Zealand 2G 2PG 1DG (19) to 1DG 3T (12)
New Zealand won series 3-0

1973 Paris
France 1G 1PG 1T (13) to 2PG (6)

1977 *1* Toulouse
France 1G 3PG 1DG (18) to 2PG 1DG 1T (13)

2 Paris
New Zealand 1G 2PG 1DG (15) to 1PG (3)
Series drawn 1-1

1979 *1* Christchurch
New Zealand 1G 3PG 2T (23) to 1G 1DG (9)

2 Auckland
France 1G 1PG 1DG 3T (24) to 1G 3PG 1T (19)
Series drawn 1-1

1981 *1* Toulouse
New Zealand 2PG 1DG 1T (13) to 2PG 1DG (9)

2 Paris
New Zealand *2G 2PG (18) to 2PG (6)
indicates a penalty try
New Zealand won series 2-0

1984 *1* Christchurch
New Zealand 2PG 1T (10) to 1G 1DG (9)

2 Auckland
New Zealand 2G 5PG 1T (31)
to 2PG 3T (18)
New Zealand won series 2-0

1986 Christchurch
New Zealand 1G 1PG 3DG (18)
to 3DG (9)

1986 *1* Toulouse
New Zealand 3PG 2DG 1T (19)
to 1PG 1T (7)

2 Nantes
France 1G 2PG 1T (16) to 1PG (3)
Series drawn 1-1

1987 Auckland *WC*
New Zealand 1G 4PG 1DG 2T (29)
to 1G 1PG (9)

FRANCE v SOUTH AFRICA

Played 19   France won 3, South Africa won 12, Drawn 4

1913 Bordeaux
South Africa 4G 1PG 5T (38) to 1G (5)

1952 Paris
South Africa 2G 1PG 4T (25)
to 1DG (3)

1958 *1* Cape Town
Drawn South Africa 1T (3)
France 1DG (3)

2 Johannesburg
France 1PG 2DG (9) to 1G (5)
France won series 1-0, with 1 draw

1961 Paris
Drawn no score

1964 Springs (SA)
France 1G 1PG (8) to 1PG 1T (6)

1967 *1* Durban
South Africa 4G 1PG 1T (26) to 1T (3)

2 Bloemfontein
South Africa 2G 1PG 1T (16) to 1PG (3)

3 Johannesburg
France 2G 1PG 2DG (19)
to 1G 2PG 1T (14)

4 Cape Town
Drawn South Africa 1PG 1DG (6)
France 1PG 1T (6)
South Africa won series 2-1, with 1 draw

1968 *1* Bordeaux
South Africa 4PG (12) to 3T (9)

2 Paris
South Africa 2G 1PG 1T (16)
to 1G 2DG (11)
South Africa won series 2-0

1971 *1* Bloemfontein
South Africa 2G 3PG 1DG (22)
to 2PG 1T (9)

2 Durban
Drawn 1G 1DG (8) each
South Africa won series 1-0, with 1 draw

1974 *1* Toulouse
South Africa 3PG 1T (13) to 1T (4)

2 Paris
South Africa 2PG 1T (10) to 2T (8)
South Africa won series 2-0

1975 *1* Bloemfontein
South Africa 3G 4PG 2T (38)
to 3G 1PG 1T (25)

2 Pretoria
South Africa 2G 7PG (33)
to 1G 3PG 1DG (18)
South Africa won series 2-0

1980 Pretoria
South Africa 4G 3PG 1T (37)
to 1G 3PG (15)

FRANCE v AUSTRALIA

Played 18   France won 10, Australia won 6, Drawn 2

1928 Paris
Australia 1G 2T (11) to 1G 1T (8)

1948 Paris
France 2G 1T (13) to 2PG (6)

1958 Paris
France 2G 2DG 1T (19) to 0

1961 Sydney
France 2DG 3T (15) to 1G 1PG (8)

1967 Paris
France 1G 4PG 1DG (20)
to 1G 1PG 1DG 1T (14)

1968 Sydney
Australia 1G 1PG 1DG (11) to 2G (10)

1971 *1* Toulouse
Australia 1G 1PG 1T (13) to 1PG 2T (11)

81

2 Paris
France 1G 4PG (18) to 3PG (9)
Series drawn 1-1

1972 *1* Sydney
Drawn Australia 2PG 2T (14)
France 1G 2T (14)

2 Brisbane
France 2G 1T (16) to 5PG (15)
France won series 1-0, with 1 draw

1976 *1* Bordeaux
France 3G (18) to 4PG 1DG (15)

2 Paris
France 2G 1PG 1DG 4T (34) to 2PG (6)
France won series 2-0

1981 *1* Brisbane
Australia 1G 1PG 2T (17)
to 1G 2PG 1DG (15)

2 Sydney
Australia 2G 4PG (24) to 2DG 2T (14)
Australia won series 2-0

1983 *1* Clermont-Ferrand
Drawn France 3PG 2DG (15)
Australia 1G 1PG 2DG (15)

2 Paris
France 1G 3PG (15) to 1PG 1DG (6)
France won series 1-0, with 1 draw

1986 Sydney
Australia 1G 6PG 1DG (27) to 1G 2T (14)

1987 Sydney *WC*
France 4G 2PG (30) to 2G 3PG 1DG (24)

NEW ZEALAND v SOUTH AFRICA

Played 37   New Zealand won 15, South Africa won 20, Drawn 2

1921 *1* Dunedin
New Zealand 2G 1T (13) to 1G (5)

2 Auckland
South Africa 1G 1DG (9) to 1G (5)

3 Wellington
Drawn no score
Series drawn 1-1, with 1 draw

1928 *1* Durban
South Africa 2PG 2DG 1T (17) to 0

2 Johannesburg
New Zealand 1PG 1DG (7)
to 1PG 1GM (6)

3 Port Elizabeth
South Africa 1G 2T (11) to 2T (6)

4 Cape Town
New Zealand 2PG 1DG 1T (13)
to 1G (5)
Series drawn 2-2

1937 *1* Wellington
New Zealand 2PG 1DG 1T (13)
to 1DG 1T (7)

2 Christchurch
South Africa 2G 1PG (13) to 2T (6)

3 Auckland
South Africa 1G 4T (17) to 2PG (6)
South Africa won series 2-1

1949 *1* Cape Town
South Africa 5PG (15)
to 1G 1PG 1DG (11)

2 Johannesburg
South Africa 1PG 1DG 2T (12)
to 1PG 1DG (6)

3 Durban
South Africa 3PG (9) to 1T (3)

4 Port Elizabeth
South Africa 1G 1PG 1DG (11)
to 1G 1T (8)
South Africa won series 4-0

1956 *1* Dunedin
New Zealand 2G (10) to 1PG 1T (6)

2 Wellington
South Africa 1G 1T (8) to 1T (3)

3 Christchurch
New Zealand 1G 2PG 2T (17)
to 2G (10)

4 Auckland
New Zealand 1G 2PG (11) to 1G (5)
New Zealand won series 3-1

1960 *1* Johannesburg
South Africa 2G 1PG (13) to 0

2 Cape Town
New Zealand 1G 1PG 1DG (11)
to 1T (3)

3 Bloemfontein
Drawn 1G 2PG (11) each

4 Port Elizabeth
South Africa 1G 1PG (8) to 1PG (3)
South Africa won series 2-1, with 1 draw

1965 *1* Wellington
New Zealand 2T (6) to 1DG (3)

2 Dunedin
New Zealand 2G 1T (13) to 0

3 Christchurch
South Africa 2G 1PG 2T (19)
to 2G 1PG 1T (16)

4 Auckland
New Zealand 1G 1DG 4T (20)
to 1PG (3)
New Zealand won series 3-1

1970 *1* Pretoria
South Africa 1G 2PG 1DG 1T (17)
to 1PG 1T (6)

2 Cape Town
New Zealand 1PG 2T (9) to 1G 1PG (8)

3 Port Elizabeth
South Africa 1G 2PG 1T (14) to 1PG (3)

4 Johannesburg
South Africa 1G 4PG 1T (20)
to 1G 4PG (17)
South Africa won series 3-1

1976 *1* Durban
South Africa 1G 1PG 1DG 1T (16)
to 1PG 1T (7)

2 Bloemfontein
New Zealand 1G 2PG 1DG (15)
to 3PG (9)

3 Cape Town
South Africa 1G 2PG 1DG (15)
to 2PG 1T (10)

4 Johannesburg
South Africa 1G 2PG 1DG (15)
to 1PG 1DG 2T (14)
South Africa won series 3-1

1981 *1* Christchurch
New Zealand 1G 2T (14) to 1G 1DG (9)

2 Wellington
South Africa 1G 5PG 1DG (24)
to 4PG (12)

3 Auckland
New Zealand 1G 4PG 1DG 1T (25)
to 2G 2PG 1T (22)
New Zealand won series 2-1

NEW ZEALAND v AUSTRALIA
Played 86   New Zealand won 60, Australia won 21, Drawn 5

1903 Sydney
New Zealand 1G 1PG 2GM 2T (22)
to 1PG (3)

1905 Dunedin
New Zealand 1G 3T (14) to 1T (3)

1907 *1* Sydney
New Zealand 4G 2T (26)
to 1PG 1GM (6)

2 Brisbane
New Zealand 1G 3T (14) to 1G (5)

3 Sydney
Drawn 1G (5) each
New Zealand won series 2-0, with 1 draw

1910 *1* Sydney
New Zealand 2T (6) to 0

2 Sydney
Australia 1G 2T (11) to 0

3 Sydney
New Zealand 2G 6T (28) to 2G 1PG (13)
New Zealand won series 2-1

1913 *1* Wellington
New Zealand 3G 5T (30) to 1G (5)

2 Dunedin
New Zealand 3G 1DG 2T (25)
to 2G 1T (13)

3 Christchurch
Australia 2G 2T (16) to 1G (5)
New Zealand won series 2-1

1914 *1* Sydney
New Zealand 1G (5) to 0

2 Brisbane
New Zealand 1G 4T (17) to 0

3 Sydney
New Zealand 2G 4T (22) to 1DG 1T (7)
New Zealand won series 3-0

1929 *1* Sydney
Australia 2PG 1T (9) to 1G 1PG (8)

2 Brisbane
Australia 1G 2PG 2T (17) to 1PG 2T (9)

3 Sydney
Australia 3PG 2T (15) to 2G 1T (13)
Australia won series 3-0

1931 Auckland
New Zealand 1G 4PG 1T (20)
to 2G 1T (13)

1932 *1* Sydney
Australia 2G 2PG 2T (22)
to 2G 1DG 1T (17)

2 Brisbane
New Zealand 1G 1PG 1DG 3T (21)
to 1T (3)

3 Sydney
New Zealand 3G 2T (21) to 2G 1T (13)
New Zealand won series 2-1

1934 *1* Sydney
Australia 2G 3PG 2T (25) to 1G 2T (11)

2 Sydney
Drawn 1T (3) each
Australia won series 1-0, with 1 draw

1936 *1* Wellington
New Zealand 1G 2T (11) to 1PG 1T (6)

2 Dunedin
New Zealand 4G 1PG 5T (38)
to 2G 1PG (13)
New Zealand won series 2-0

1938 *1* Sydney
New Zealand 3G 2PG 1T (24) to 3PG (9)

2 Brisbane
New Zealand 2G 1DG 2T (20)
to 1G 1PG 2T (14)

3 Sydney
New Zealand 1G 2PG 1T (14)
to 1PG 1T (6)
New Zealand won series 3-0

1946 *1* Dunedin
New Zealand 5G 2T (31) to 1G 1T (8)

2 Auckland
New Zealand 1G 3PG (14) to 2G (10)
New Zealand won series 2-0

1947 *1* Brisbane
New Zealand *2G 1T (13) to 1G (5)
includes one penalty try

2 Sydney
New Zealand 3G 4PG (27)
to 1G 3PG (14)
New Zealand won series 2-0

1949 *1* Wellington
Australia 1G 2T (11) to 1PG 1T (6)

2 Auckland
Australia 2G 1PG 1T (16)
to 1PG 1DG 1T (9)
Australia won series 2-0

1951 *1* Sydney
New Zealand 1G 1PG (8) to 0

2 Sydney
New Zealand 1G 1DG 3T (17)
to 1G 1PG 1T (11)

3 Brisbane
New Zealand 2G 2T (16) to 2PG (6)
New Zealand won series 3-0

1952 *1* Christchurch
Australia 1G 1DG 2T (14) to 1PG 2T (9)

2 Wellington
New Zealand 2PG 1DG 2T (15)
to 1G 1PG (8)
Series drawn 1-1

1955 *1* Wellington
New Zealand 2G 1PG 1T (16)
to 1G 1PG (8)

2 Dunedin
New Zealand 1G 1DG (8) to 0

3 Auckland
Australia 1G 1T (8) to 1T (3)
New Zealand won series 2-1

1957 *1* Sydney
New Zealand 2G 3PG 2T (25)
to 1G 2PG (11)

2 Brisbane
New Zealand 2G 1DG 1GM 2T (22)
to 2PG 1T (9)
New Zealand won series 2-0

1958 *1* Wellington
New Zealand 2G 5T (25) to 1T (3)

2 Christchurch
Australia 1PG 1T (6) to 1T (3)

3 Auckland
New Zealand 1G 4PG (17)
to 1G 1PG (8)
New Zealand won series 2-1

1962 *1* Brisbane
New Zealand 1G 1PG 1DG 3T (20)
to 2PG (6)

2 Sydney
New Zealand 1G 2PG 1T (14) to 1G (5)
New Zealand won series 2-0

1962 *1* Wellington
Drawn New Zealand 2PG 1T (9)
Australia 3PG (9)

2 Dunedin
New Zealand 1PG (3) to 0

3 Auckland
New Zealand 2G 1DG 1T (16)
to 1G 1PG (8)
New Zealand won series 2-0, with 1 draw

1964 *1* Dunedin
New Zealand 1G 2PG 1DG (14)
to 2PG 1T (9)

2 Christchurch
New Zealand 3G 1T (18) to 1T (3)

3 Wellington
Australia 1G 3PG 1DG 1T (20) to 1G (5)
New Zealand won series 2-1

1967 Wellington
New Zealand 4G 2PG 1DG (29)
to 1PG 2T (9)

1968 *1* Sydney
New Zealand 3G 1PG 3T (27)
to 1G 2PG (11)

2 Brisbane
New Zealand *2G 2PG 1T (19)
to 5PG 1T (18)
includes one penalty try
New Zealand won series 2-0

1972 *1* Wellington
New Zealand 3G 1DG 2T (29)
to 2PG (6)

2 Christchurch
New Zealand 2G 2PG 3T (30)
to 1G 1DG 2T (17)

3 Auckland
New Zealand 4G 2PG 2T (38)
to 1PG (3)
New Zealand won series 3-0

1974 *1* Sydney
New Zealand 1PG 2T (11) to 1G (6)

2 Brisbane
Drawn 1G 2PG 1T (16) each

3 Sydney
New Zealand 2G 1T (16) to 2PG (6)
New Zealand won series 2-0, with 1 draw

1978 *1* Wellington
New Zealand 3PG 1T (13)
to 1G 2PG (12)

2 Christchurch
New Zealand 2G 1PG 1DG 1T (22)
to 1PG 1DG (6)

3 Auckland
Australia 2G 1PG 1DG 3T (30)
to 1G 2PG 1T (16)
New Zealand won series 2-1

1979 Sydney
Australia 3PG 1DG (12)
to 1PG 1DG (6)

1980 *1* Sydney
Australia 1G 1DG 1T (13) to 3PG (9)

2 Brisbane
New Zealand 1G 2PG (12)
to 1G 1PG (9)

3 Sydney
Australia 2G 1PG 1DG 2T (26)
to 2PG 1T (10)
Australia won series 2-1

1982 *1* Christchurch
New Zealand 2G 1PG 2T (23)
to 1G 2PG 1T (16)

2 Wellington
Australia 1G 3PG 1T (19)
to 1G 2PG 1T (16)

3 Auckland
New Zealand 2G 5PG 2DG (33)
to 1G 3PG 1DG (18)
New Zealand won series 2-1

1983 Sydney
New Zealand 1G 4PG (18) to 2T (8)

1984 *1* Sydney
Australia 1G 1PG 1DG 1T (16)
to 2PG 1DG (9)

2 Brisbane
New Zealand 5PG 1T (19) to 1G 3PG (15)

3 Sydney
New Zealand 1G 5PG 1T (25)
to 1G 6PG (24)
New Zealand won series 2-1

1985 Auckland
New Zealand 2PG 1T (10) to 1G 1PG (9)

1986 *1* Wellington
Australia 1G 1PG 1T (13) to 1G 2PG (12)

2 Dunedin
New Zealand 2PG 1DG 1T (13) to 3PG
1DG (12)

3 Auckland
Australia 1G 4PG 1T (22) to 3PG (9)
Australia won series 2-1

1987 Sydney
New Zealand 1G 3PG 1DG 3T (30)
to 3PG 1DG 1T (16)

1988 *1* Sydney
New Zealand 3G 2PG 2T (32)
to 1PG 1T (7)

2 Brisbane
Drawn Australia 1G 3PG 1T (19)
New Zealand 2G 1PG 1T (19)

3 Sydney
New Zealand 3G 4PG (30) to 1G 1PG (9)
New Zealand won series 2-0, with 1 draw

SOUTH AFRICA v AUSTRALIA

Played 28   South Africa won 21, Australia won 7, Drawn 0

1933 *1* Cape Town
South Africa 1G 1PG 3T (17) to 1PG (3)

2 Durban
Australia 3G 1PG 1T (21) to 1PG 1T (6)

3 Johannesburg
South Africa 1G 1DG 1T (12) to 1T (3)

4 Port Elizabeth
South Africa 1G 1PG 1T (11) to 0

5 Bloemfontein
Australia 1G 1DG 2T (15) to 1DG (4)
South Africa won series 3-2

1937 *1* Sydney
South Africa 1PG 2T (9) to 1G (5)

2 Sydney
South Africa 4G 2T (26)
to 1G 2PG 2T (17)
South Africa won series 2-0

1953 *1* Johannesburg
South Africa 2G 2PG 3T (25) to 1PG (3)

2 Cape Town
Australia 3G 1T (18) to 1G 3T (14)

3 Durban
South Africa 3G 1T (18) to 1G 1PG (8)

4 Port Elizabeth
South Africa 2G 2PG 2DG (22)
to 2PG 1T (9)
South Africa won series 3-1

1956 *1* Sydney
South Africa 1PG 2T (9) to 0

2 Brisbane
South Africa 1DG 2T (9) to 0
South Africa won series 2-0

1961 *1* Johannesburg
South Africa 2G 6T (28) to 1PG (3)

2 Port Elizabeth
South Africa 1G 3PG 1DG 2T (23)
to 1G 2PG (11)
South Africa won series 2-0

1963 *1* Pretoria
South Africa 1G 2PG 1T (14) to 1T (3)

2 Cape Town
Australia 1PG 1DG 1T (9) to 1G (5)

3 Johannesburg
Australia 1G 1PG 1DG (11) to 3PG (9)

4 Port Elizabeth
South Africa 2G 3PG 1T (22)
to 1PG 1DG (6)
Series drawn 2-2

1965 *1* Sydney
Australia 4PG 2T (18) to 1G 1PG 1T (11)

2 Brisbane
Australia 4PG (12) to 1G 1T (8)
Australia won series 2-0

1969 *1* Johannesburg
South Africa 3G 3PG 2T (30)
to 1G 2PG (11)

2 Durban
South Africa 2G 1PG 1T (16) to 3PG (9)

3 Cape Town
South Africa 1G 1PG 1T (11) to 1PG (3)

4 Bloemfontein
South Africa 2G 2PG 1T (19)
to 1G 1PG (8)
South Africa won series 4-0

1971 *1* Sydney
South Africa 2G 1PG 1DG 1T (19)
to 1G 2PG (11)

2 Brisbane
South Africa 1G 1PG 2T (14)
to 1PG 1DG (6)

3 Sydney
South Africa 3G 1PG (18) to 1PG 1T (6)
South Africa won series 3-0

Dewi Morris of England gets his pass away in the gloom of Cardiff, as Robert Jones of Wales and Andy Robinson of England follow anxiously. Wales now lead 47-36 in the series between the two countries, with 12 drawn matches.

RESULTS OF INTERNATIONAL MATCHES

WORLD CUP WINNERS
New Zealand Once 1987

GRAND SLAM WINNERS
Wales 8 times: 1908, 1909, 1911, 1950, 1952, 1971, 1976, 1978.
England 8 times: 1913, 1914, 1921, 1923, 1924, 1928, 1957, 1980.
France 4 times: 1968, 1977, 1981, 1987. **Scotland** twice: 1925, 1984. **Ireland** once: 1948.

TRIPLE CROWN WINNERS
Wales 17 times: 1893, 1900, 1902, 1905, 1908, 1909, 1911, 1950, 1952, 1965, 1969, 1971, 1976, 1977, 1978, 1979, 1988. **England** 15 times: 1883, 1884, 1892, 1913, 1914, 1921, 1923, 1924, 1928, 1934, 1937, 1954, 1957, 1960, 1980. **Scotland** 9 times: 1891, 1895, 1901, 1903, 1907, 1925, 1933, 1938, 1984. **Ireland** 6 times: 1894, 1899, 1948, 1949, 1982, 1985.

INTERNATIONAL CHAMPIONSHIP WINNERS

1883 England	1910 England	1938 Scotland	1966 Wales
1884 England	1911 Wales	1939 { England / Wales / Ireland	1967 France
1885* ———	1912 { England / Ireland		1968 France
1886 { England / Scotland	1913 England	1947 { Wales / England	1969 Wales
1887 Scotland	1914 England	1948 Ireland	1970 { France / Wales
1888* ———	1920 { England / Scotland / Wales	1949 Ireland	1971 Wales
1889* ———	1921 England	1950 Wales	1972* ———
1890 { England / Scotland	1922 Wales	1951 Ireland	1973 Quintuple tie
1891 Scotland	1923 England	1952 Wales	1974 Ireland
1892 England	1924 England	1953 England	1975 Wales
1893 Wales	1925 Scotland	1954 { England / France / Wales	1976 Wales
1894 Ireland	1926 { Scotland / Ireland		1977 France
1895 Scotland	1927 { Scotland / Ireland	1955 { France / Wales	1978 Wales
1896 Ireland	1928 England	1956 Wales	1979 Wales
1897* ———	1929 Scotland	1957 England	1980 England
1898* ———	1930 England	1958 England	1981 France
1899 Ireland	1931 Wales	1959 France	1982 Ireland
1900 Wales	1932 { England / Wales / Ireland	1960 { France / England	1983 { France / Ireland
1901 Scotland	1933 Scotland	1961 France	1984 Scotland
1902 Wales	1934 England	1962 France	1985 Ireland
1903 Scotland	1935 Ireland	1963 England	1986 { France / Scotland
1904 Scotland	1936 Wales	1964 { Scotland / Wales	1987 France
1905 Wales	1937 England	1965 Wales	1988 { Wales / France
1906 { Ireland / Wales			1989 France
1907 Scotland			
1908 Wales			
1909 Wales			

* *Matches not completed, for various reasons*

Wales have won the title outright most times, 21; England have won it 18 times, Scotland 12, Ireland 10, and France 9.

87

OTHER INTERNATIONAL MATCHES 1988-89

11 June 1988, Saranac Lake
USA 28 (3G 2PG 1T)   CANADA 16 (1G 1PG 1DG 1T)

The United States Eagles won the 13th Can-Am encounter, ending Canada's four-game winning streak in the series. After Mark Williams and Wyatt had exchanged early penalties, O'Brien converted his own try to give USA the lead after 21 minutes. O'Brien then kicked another penalty before Barry Williams' try on half-time gave the home side an 18-3 advantage. Wyatt kicked another penalty soon after the interval, but any revival was halted by US hooker Pat Johnson's try after 20 minutes of the second half. Pat Palmer's try eight minutes later, with Tynan's conversion, brought the score to 22-12. Three minutes from time Gary Lambert scored unopposed, with O'Brien adding the conversion. Ron Vandenbrink finished the scoring with a try in injury time for Canada.

USA: A Montgomery (Mystic River); M Smith (Old Blues), M Williams (Santa Monica), K Higgins (OMBAC), B Williams (Los Angeles); C O'Brien (Hawaii Harlequins), M Saunders (OMBAC) (*capt*); T Whelan (Life Chiropractic Coll), P Johnson (Louisville), F Paoli (Denver Barbarians), T Ridnell (Old Puget Sound Beach), K Swords (Beacon Hill), G Lambert (Life Chiropractic Coll), S Lipman (Santa Monica), B Vizard (OMBAC)
Scorers *Tries:* O'Brien, B Williams, Johnson, Lambert   *Conversions:* O'Brien (3) *Penalty Goals:* M Williams, O'Brien
CANADA: M Wyatt (Velox Valhallians); A Heaman (U of Victoria), T Woods (James Bay), I Stuart (Vancouver Rowing Club), P Palmer (UBC OB); I Hyde-Lay (Cowichan), C Tynan (Vancouver Meralomas); S Creagh (St Anne de Bellevue), D Spiers (Velox Valhallians), T Arthurs (Velox Valhallians), C Fowler (Vancouver Meralomas), R Vandenbrink (Vancouver Kats), G McKinnon (Pocomo), R Radu (U of British Colombia) (*capt*), G Ennis (Vancouver Kats)
Scorers *Tries:* Palmer, Vandenbrink   *Conversion:* Tynan   *Penalty Goal:* Wyatt *Dropped Goal:* Wyatt
Referee A MacNeill (Australia)

10 December 1988, Cardiff Arms Park
WALES 9 (1G 1PG)   ROMANIA 15 (1G 3PG)

This was probably the worst defeat Wales have ever suffered. At least in the debacle in New Zealand during the previous summer they were up against a magnificent team, but Romania never remotely aspired to those heights. Indeed, they were desperately limited and without a shadow of real class. When they celebrated their first win in one of the four Home Countries, they were probably disbelieving as well as exultant. The crowd slow handclapped Wales towards the end of the game.

Perhaps the worst aspect of the match from the Welsh point of view was that they dominated possession and were awarded 18 penalties against six to Romania – yet still they could only manufacture one try. For Romania, long kicks by Ignat from fly-half were their only attacking plan, but Murariu and his pack were better foragers in the loose. Ion, Romania's hooker, was their try-scorer. He finished off a churning movement from the back of a line-out initiated by Neaga, Radulescu and Murariu, and Ignat kicked the conversion. He also kicked a penalty before Thorburn opened the Welsh account with a penalty to make it 9-3 at half-time. Although the hard-working Devereux scored a converted try to even the score in the second half, two more penalties from Ignat settled the match.

Traian Oroian comes away from the scrum with the ball, despite the efforts of Robert Jones, during Romania's famous victory over Wales at Cardiff Arms Park.

WALES: A Clement (Swansea); G M C Webbe (Bridgend), M R Hall (Cambridge U & Bridgend), J A Devereux (Bridgend), R Diplock (Bridgend); J Davies(Llanelli) (*capt*), R N Jones (Swansea); M Griffiths (Bridgend), I J Watkins (Ebbw Vale), D Young (Cardiff), J D M Wakeford (S Wales Police), K Moseley (Pontypool), R G Collins (Cardiff), P T Davies (Llanelli), D J Bryant (Bridgend) *Replacement* P H Thorburn (Neath) for Webbe
Scorers *Try:* Devereux   *Conversion:* Thorburn   *Penalty Goal:* Thorburn
ROMANIA: M Toader; N Racean, N Fulina, A Lungu, D Boldor; G Ignat, D Neaga; G Leonte, V Ion, G Dumitrescu, S Ciorascu, H Dumitras, F Murariu (*capt*), I Doja, A Radulescu *Replacement* T Oroian for Dumitras
Scorers *Try:* Ion   *Conversion:* Ignat   *Penalty Goals:* Ignat (3)
Referee I M Bullerwell (England)

13 May 1989, 23 August Stadium, Bucharest
ROMANIA 3 (1PG)   ENGLAND 58 (8G 1PG 1DG 1T)

On the surface this was a dangerous visit for England. Romanian rugby had been boosted by their earlier win over Wales and on the day the temperature in the bowl of the 23 August Stadium was in the 90s. As it turned out, England put on a memorable display of attacking rugby, inspired by Simon Halliday and Jeremy Guscott in the centre – the latter scored a hat-trick on a marvellous debut – and expertly finished by Chris Oti, who scored four tries.

It was a shattering day for Romania, but perhaps the start of something for England. In the 1989 Championship they lacked calm footballers but, with the arrival of Guscott, replacing the injured Carling, and of Simon Hodgkinson at full-back, England's back play seemed galvanised. The sharp service from Steve Bates, another debutant, at scrum-half was another blessing. Hodgkinson missed just one kick all day – a conversion attempt.

Romania's resistance was increasingly sporadic and only Neaga at scrum-half and Ion at hooker really distinguished themselves. Even in the heat the big England forwards, especially Rendall and Dooley, made magnificent efforts in the loose so that every last escape route for the home side was slammed shut. It was a splendid way to mark Rob Andrew's first match as captain of his country.

ROMANIA: M Toader; N Racean, N Fulina, A Lungu, D Boldor; G Ignat, D Neaga; G Leonte, V Ion, G Dumitrescu, S Ciorascu, G Caragea, F Murariu (*capt*), H Dumitras, A Radulescu *Replacements* C Raducanu for Caragea; T Oroian for Radulescu
Scorer *Penalty Goal:* Ignat
ENGLAND: S D Hodgkinson (Nottingham); R Underwood (RAF & Leicester), J C Guscott (Bath), S J Halliday (Bath), C Oti (Wasps); C R Andrew (Wasps) (*capt*), S M Bates (Wasps); P A G Rendall (Wasps), B C Moore (Nottingham), G J Chilcott(Bath), W A Dooley (Preston Grasshoppers), P J Ackford (Harlequins), M C Teague (Gloucester), D Richards (Leicester), P J Winterbottom (Harlequins) *Replacements* J A Probyn (Wasps) for Chilcott; G W Rees (Nottingham) for Richards
Scorers *Tries:* Oti (4), Guscott (3), Probyn, Richards   *Conversions:* Hodgkinson (8)   *Penalty Goal:* Hodgkinson   *Dropped Goal:* Andrew
Referee J B Anderson (Scotland)

FRANCE JUST SCRAPE HOME

THE FIRA CHAMPIONSHIPS 1988-89

Chris Rhys

France retained the FIRA Championship – held over the past two seasons – but only after a desperately close 18-16 victory against the Soviet Union in what turned out to be the Championship decider at Valence. Traditionally France tend to field their full national side against Romania, and a 'B' side against the other nations. However, with places available for the tour to New Zealand, the team that played the Soviets assumed greater importance than usual: the line-up featured the likes of Lafond, the Camberaberos, Andrieu and Carminati.

For all the tactical naïvety of the Soviets on the world stage, their enthusiasm and fitness make them now, in anyone's language, redoubtable opponents. They were 10-3 up at half-time against the French with a first-minute try by prop Moltchanov, a penalty and a dropped goal from Mironov to a Camberabero penalty. The six-feet-six Dax flanker Roumat scored a try for France after 50 minutes, which was converted by Lafond, who added a penalty to give France a 12-10 lead. A further penalty from Dzaganidze and another dropped goal by Mironov appeared to have given the Soviets the title for the first time, but penalty goals after 66 and 71 minutes from Lafond saved France from having the double completed against them.

Romania finished third after a season of stark contrasts. Initially they were almost overrun by the Soviets, but then they performed heroics with a new team to almost check France. The side went on to their historic win in Cardiff. The second half of the season began with a useful win over Italy, who find life without Bettarello's boot somewhat difficult. A last-minute converted try enabled Romania to beat Spain, who will be relegated and replaced by the winners of the B Group play-offs.

The season was notable for a record of a different kind: the first win at international level for tiny Luxembourg. Their 10-8 victory – admittedly over Andorra – is a further manifestation of the popularity of Rugby Union, now the fourth most popular team sport in the world.

MATCH 11   **23 October, Alma Ata**

Soviet Union 23 (1G 3PG 2T)   **Romania 9** (3PG)
Soviet Union *Tries:* Demidov, Tikhonov, Moltchanov   *Conversion:* Organidze
Penalty Goals: Organidze (3)
Romania *Penalty Goals:* Alexandru (3)

MATCH 12   6 November, Treviso

Italy 12 (4PG)   **Soviet Union 18** (1G 2PG 2DG)
Italy *Penalty Goals:* Bettarello (4)
Soviet Union *Try:* Mironov   *Conversion:* Dzagnidze   *Penalty Goals:* Dzagnidze (2)
Dropped Goals: Mironov (2)

MATCH 13   20 November, Madrid

Spain 9 (2PG 1DG)   **Soviet Union 21** (2G 3PG)
Soviet Union *Tries:* Kharyulin, Netchanov   *Conversions:* Mironov (2)
Penalty Goals: Mironov (2), Dzagnidze
Spain *Penalty Goals:* Blanco (2)   *Dropped Goal:* Diaz

MATCH 14   26 November, Bucharest

Romania 12 (1G 2PG)   **France 16** (1G 2PG 1T)
France *Tries:* Blanco, Lagisquet   *Conversion:* Bérot   *Penalty Goals:* Bérot (2)
Romania *Try:* Neaga   *Conversion:* Ignat   *Penalty Goals:* Ignat (2)

MATCH 15   19 February, Brescia

Italy 12 (3PG 1DG)   **France 40** (3G 2PG 4T)
Italy *Penalty Goals:* Capitani (3)   *Dropped Goal:* Tebaldi
France *Tries:* Lecomte (2), Sallaber (2), Trille, Hondagne, Tremouille
Conversions: Bérot (3)   *Penalty Goals:* Bérot (2)

MATCH 16   23 March, Hendaye

France 57 (7G 1PG 3T)   **Spain 7** (1DG 1T)
France *Tries:* Hontas (5), Preux, Dalmaso, Theron, Labat, Frentzel
Conversions: Gosse (6), Velo   *Penalty Goal:* Gosse
Spain *Try:* Rivero   *Dropped Goal:* Diaz

MATCH 17   16 April, Bucharest

Romania 28 (3G 1PG 1DG 1T)   **Italy 4** (1T)
Romania *Tries:* Boldor, Ignat, Coman, Murariu   *Conversions:* Ignat (3)
Penalty Goal: Ignat   *Dropped Goal:* Ignat
Italy *Try:* Ceselin

MATCH 18   20 May, Valence

France 18 (1G 4PG)   **Soviet Union 16** (2PG 2DG 1T)
France *Try:* Roumat   *Conversion:* Lafond   *Penalty Goals:* Lafond (3), Camberabero
Soviet Union *Try:* Moltchanov   *Penalty Goals:* Mironov, Dzagnidze
Dropped Goals: Mironov (2)

MATCH 19   21 May, Valencia

Spain 16 (4PG 1T)   **Romania 19** (1G 3PG 1T)
Spain *Try:* Guttierez   *Penalty Goals:* Diaz (4)
Romania *Tries:* Chirila, Dimitrescu   *Conversion:* Ignat   *Penalty Goals:* Ignat (3)

MATCH 20   2 June, L'Aquila

Italy 33 (2G 3PG 3T)   **Spain 19** (1G 3PG 1T)
Italy *Tries:* Venturi, Pietrosanti, Pivetta, Saetti, Covi   *Conversions:* Troiani (2)
Penalty Goals: Troiani (3)
Spain *Tries:* Puertas, Malo   *Conversion:* Diaz   *Penalty Goals:* Tejada (3)

FINAL TABLE

	P	W	D	L	F	A	Pts
France	8	7	0	1	241	92	22
Soviet Union	8	6	0	2	129	92	20
Romania	8	5	0	3	117	128	18
Italy	8	2	0	6	95	148	12
Spain	8	0	0	8	81	203	8

GROUP B1 RESULTS

Tunisia	9	Poland	30
Morocco	6	Tunisia	6
Morocco	6	Czechoslovakia	6
Czechoslovakia	12	Poland	26
Tunisia	26	Czechoslovakia	16
Morocco	7	Poland	13

FINAL TABLE

	P	W	D	L	F	A	Pts
Poland	6	6	0	0	126	49	18
Czechoslovakia	6	2	1	3	76	85	11
Morocco	6	1	2	3	36	64	10
Tunisia	6	1	1	4	62	102	9

GROUP B2 RESULTS

Belgium	27	Holland	9
Yugoslavia	9	Belgium	31
West Germany	29	Yugoslavia	6

Yugoslavia	6	Holland	0
Belgium	7	West Germany	16
Holland	21	West Germany	13
West Germany	30	Portugal	15
Belgium	15	Portugal	15
Holland	23	Portugal	17
Portugal	13	Yugoslavia	9

FINAL TABLE

	P	W	D	L	F	A	Pts
Belgium	8	6	1	1	155	98	21
West Germany	8	5	0	3	139	95	18
Portugal	8	4	1	3	118	117	17
Holland	8	3	0	5	111	115	14
Yugoslavia	8	1	0	7	61	159	9

GROUP C RESULTS

Bulgaria	13	Luxembourg	4
Andorra	7	Bulgaria	21
Luxembourg	10	Andorra	8

FINAL TABLE

	P	W	D	L	F	A	Pts
Bulgaria	4	4	0	0	78	21	12
Andorra	4	1	0	3	43	64	6
Luxembourg	4	1	0	3	21	57	6

Season	Winners	Runners Up	Third
1973-74	**France**	Romania	Spain
1974-75	**Romania**	France	Italy
1975-76	**France**	Italy	Romania
1976-77	**Romania**	France	Italy
1977-78	**France**	Romania	Spain
1978-79	**France**	Romania	Soviet Union
1979-80	**France**	Romania	Italy
1980-81	**Romania**	France	Soviet Union
1981-82	**France**	Italy	Romania
1982-83	**Romania**	Italy	Soviet Union
1983-84	**France**	Romania	Italy
1984-85	**France**	Romania	Soviet Union
1985-86	**France**	Soviet Union	Italy
1986-87	**France**	Soviet Union	Romania
1987-88	**France**	Soviet Union	Romania
1988-89	**France**	Soviet Union	Romania

OTHER INTERNATIONAL TOURNAMENTS

ASIAN TOURNAMENT 1988

Austin Daniel

The Asian Rugby Football tournament, which takes place every two years, was won by Korea in a hard-fought match against Japan in the Government Stadium, Hong Kong in November 1988. The tournament began in 1969 and eight of the 11 tournaments held since, including every one of the first seven, were won by Japan. Yet this win by Korea, their second, was another indication of the decline of the Japanese influence in the region. 'While Japan is running out of ideas, the Koreans and the Taiwanese are mastering our style and even improving on it', said Shiggy Konno, the Japanese secretary-general of the Asian RFU since 1968.

The tournament contained some explosive matches, especially when the unbalanced contests of the first few days of competition were over. There was considerable added importance because the last two teams in the competition qualified for the next World Cup. Korea and Japan therefore advance to join the 'big brothers' of the rugby family in the United Kingdom in 1991. The final itself, which was watched by IRB secretary Keith Rowlands, was a magnificent contest. Korea won by 17-13 and scored three tries to two. The final group matches were equally exciting: in the first, Japan had to withstand a terrific onslaught from Chinese Taipei (Taiwan), who led until deep in the last quarter only to lose eventually by a single point; Hong Kong played bravely against the Koreans before going down 39-19. They were inspired by Bruce Vogel, their captain, who tragically died of a heart attack during a match two months later.

12 November Korea 102 (11G 9T), Malaysia 0; Hong Kong 45 (5G 1PG 3T), Sri Lanka 3 (1PG)
13 November Japan 82 (7G 10T), Singapore 0; Chinese Taipei 32 (4G 2T), Thailand 9 (3PG)
14 November Korea 39 (5G 3PG), Hong Kong 19 (2G 1PG 1T); Sri Lanka 12 (3T), Malaysia 6 (2PG)
15 November Japan 108 (16G 3T), Thailand 7 (1PG 1T); Chinese Taipei 86 (11G 5T), Singapore 3 (1PG)
16 November Korea 68 (10G 2T), Sri Lanka 6 (1G); Hong Kong 50 (3G 8T), Malaysia 0
17 November Japan 20 (4PG 2T), Chinese Taipei 19 (2G 1PG 1T); Thailand 17 (3PG 2T), Singapore 3 (1PG)
Final Standings
Group A: 1 Korea 2 Hong Kong 3 Sri Lanka 4 Malaysia
Group B: 1 Japan 2 Chinese Taipei 3 Thailand 4 Singapore

Korea 17 (1G 1PG 2T)   **Japan 13** (1G 1PG 1T)   **Final**

Korea: Yong-Duk Cho; Jin-Hwan Cho, Cheon-Oh Seo, Yeon-Ki Kim, Jin-Hwan Yoo; Chang-Kyu Shin, Yun-Pil Yung; Dong-Chung Yu, Ji-Dong Kim, Hang-Mook Choi, Jae-Hyeong Shon, Sang-Ho Ma, Dong-In Woo, Young-Chun Kim, Hyeon Kim (*capt*)
Scorers *Tries:* Jin-Hwan Yoo, Yeon-Ki Kim, Cheon-Oh Seo
Conversion: Chan-Kyu Shin   *Penalty Goal:* Chan-Kyu Shin
Japan: Yamamoto; Taumoefolau, Imakoma, Hirao, Yoshida; Matsuo, Horikoshi; Aizawa (*capt*), Hirose, Nagai, Sakuraba, Oyagi, Koda, Miyamoto, Taione
Scorers *Tries:* Imakoma, Yoshida   *Conversion:* Matsuo   *Penalty Goal:* Matsuo
Referee I Scott (Hong Kong)
Japan have won the title seven times; Korea twice

THE SOUTH PACIFIC CHAMPIONSHIP 1989

New South Wales 32, Fiji 7; Queensland 16, Canterbury 6; Auckland 51, Wellington 3; New South Wales 25, Canterbury 24; Auckland 24, Queensland 15; Fiji 18, Wellington 9; Canterbury 19, Fiji 23; Wellington 32, Queensland 18; New South Wales 16, Auckland 11; Auckland 72, Fiji 9; Queensland 31, New South Wales 3; Wellington 31, Canterbury 28; New South Wales 23, Wellington 19; Queensland 39, Fiji 13; Auckland 33, Canterbury 15.

Final Table

	P	W	D	L	F	A	Pts
Auckland	5	4	0	1	191	58	17★
New South Wales	5	4	0	1	99	92	16
Queensland	5	3	0	2	119	78	12
Wellington	5	2	0	3	94	139	9★
Fiji	5	2	0	3	70	171	8
Canterbury	5	0	0	5	92	128	3★★

The rules of the competition allow one point for any team defeated by a margin of six points or less.
★ One point added for a defeat of six points or less
★★ Three points added for three defeats of six points or less

B INTERNATIONALS 1988-89
(for details of the England B match against Australia, see tours section)

29 October 1988, Brecon
Wales B 12 (1G 1PG 1DG)   France B 18 (2G 2PG)

Wales B: D Rees (Newbridge); R V Wintle (Bridgend), C Laity (Neath), S Davies (Llanelli), C Davies (Llanelli); A Clement (Swansea), J L Griffiths (Llanelli) *(capt)*; M Griffiths (Bridgend), W H Hall (Bridgend), P Edwards (Bridgend), P Kawulok (Bridgend), K Moseley (Pontypool), H Stone (Cardiff), M A Jones (Neath), M Budd (Bridgend)
Scorers *Try:* J Griffiths   *Conversion:* Rees   *Penalty Goal:* Rees
Dropped Goal: Clement
France B: J Bianchi (Toulon); B Lacombe (Agen), E Blanc (Racing Club de France) *(capt)*, P Tremouille (Toulon), D Faugeron (Brive); T Lacroix (Dax), A Hueber (Lourdes); H Chabowski (Bourgoin), P Berbizier (Agen), L Seigne (Agen), Y Roux (Toulon), T Devergie (Nîmes), L Cabannes (Racing Club de France), O Roumat (Dax), P Benetton (Agen)
Scorers *Tries:* Lacombe, Tremouille   *Conversions:* Lacroix (2)
Penalty Goals: Lacroix (2)
Referee K McCartney (Scotland)

4 December 1988, L'Aquila
Italy B 3 (1PG)   Scotland B 26 (2G 2PG 2T)

Italy B: M Brunello (Rovigo); P Sturaro (Rovigo), M Molina (L'Aquila), M Morelli (L'Aquila), L Salvati (Cus Roma); L Capitani (Parma), U Casellato (Treviso); G Baratelli (Rovigo), M de Stafani (Rovigo), A Piazza (San Dona), G P Vezzoli (Calvisano), R Dell'Uomo (Padova), S Bordon (Rovigo), F Siciliano (Cus Roma), V Pesce (Treviso) *(capt) Replacement* A Paolone (Amatori Catania) for Vezzoli (35 mins)
Scorer *Penalty Goal:* Capitani
Scotland B: M Wright (Kelso); W L Renwick (London Scottish) *(capt)*, A C McGuffie (Ayr), B Edwards (Boroughmuir), D A Stark (Ayr); C M Chalmers (Melrose), G T MacGregor (Glasgow Acads); G Graham (Stirling County & Army), K S Milne (Heriot's FP), A P Burnell (London Scottish), C A Gray (Nottingham), J F Richardson (Edinburgh Acads), K P Rafferty (Heriot's FP), R I Wainwright (Cambridge U), C B S Richardson (London Scottish)
Scorers *Tries:* Stark, Wright, Chalmers, Burnell   *Conversions:* Chalmers (2)
Penalty Goals: Chalmers (2)
Referee J-C Debat (France)

18 February 1989, The Greenyards, Melrose
Scotland B 14 (2PG 2T)   France B 12 (4PG)

Scotland B: M Wright (Kelso); D A Stark (Ayr), B Edwards (Boroughmuir), R R W Maclean (Gloucester), W L Renwick (London Scottish); D K Shiel (Jedforest), J M Scott (Stewart's-Melville FP); D F Milne (Heriot's FP), J A Hay (Hawick), P H Wright (Boroughmuir), D S Munro (Glasgow High/Kelvinside), J F Richardson (Edinburgh Acads), G A E Buchanan-Smith (London Scottish), K P Rafferty (Heriot's FP), C B S Richardson (London Scottish) *(capt) Replacement* M Walker (Boroughmuir) for Edwards
Scorers *Tries:* Renwick, Buchanan-Smith   *Penalty Goals:* Shiel (2)
France B: J Dupuy (Toulouse); B Lacombe (Agen), A Salse (Graulhet), E Blanc (Racing Club de France) *(capt)*, D Faugeron (Brive); T Lacroix (Dax), A Hueber (Lourdes); J-M Puginier (Graulhet), M Dalmaso (Mont-de-Marsan), L Seigne (Agen), H Chaffardon (Grenoble), J Cadieu (Toulouse), T Mazet (Toulouse), P Benetton (Agen), O Roumat (Dax)

Scorer *Penalty Goals:* Lacroix (4)
Referee B W Stirling (Ireland)

3 March 1989, Welford Road, Leicester
England B 16 (2G 1T)   France B 35 (4G 1PG 2T)

England B: S Thresher (Harlequins); A Lumsden (Bath), J Guscott (Bath), K G Simms (Wasps), A Underwood (Leicester); D Pears (Sale), R M Harding (Bristol) (*capt*); M Whitcombe (Sale), K Dunn (Gloucester), R Pascall (Gloucester), R Kimmins (Orrell), S O'Leary (Wasps), S Hodgson (Vale of Lune), D W Egerton (Bath), D Pegler (Wasps)
Scorers *Tries:* Harding, Lumsden, Dunn *Conversions:* Thresher (2)
France B: P Bérot (Agen); B Lacombe (Agen), A Salse (Graulhet), E Blanc (Racing Club de France) (*capt*), P Saint André (Montferrand); F Velo (Grenoble), D Mazille (Grenoble); H Chabowski (Bourgoin), J-P Cantin (Grenoble), L Seigne (Agen), J-M Cadieu (Toulouse), Y Theron (Bourgoin), P Benetton (Agen), C Deslandes (Grenoble), H Leconte (Toulon)
Scorers *Tries:* Saint André (2), Lacombe, Salse, Deslandes, Cantin
Conversions: Bérot (4) *Penalty Goal:* Bérot
Referee J Groves (Wales)

19 March 1989, Galleana Stadium, Piacenza
Italy B 0   England B 44 (5G 2PG 2T)

Italy B: L Capitani (Parma); M Bimbati (Camarillo Brillo), S Parladori (Petrarca), G Ravanelli (Colli Euganie Rovigo), M Brunello (Colli Euganie Rovigo); D Tebaldi (Casone Noceto), S Boccazzi (Brescia); C Dioli (Bilboa Athletico, Lyons), C Pratichetti (Cus Romana), F Properzi (Mediolanum Milano), P Pedroni (Mediolanum Amatori), G Croci (Colli Euganie Rovigo), M Giovanelli (Casone Noceto), O Longo (Petraca), V Pesce (Benetton) (*capt*) *Replacement* M Visentin (Colli Euganie Rovigo) for Boccazzi
England B: S D Hodgkinson (Nottingham); B J Evans (Leicester), G H Hartley (Nottingham), J C Guscott (Bath), T Underwood (Leicester); D Pears (Sale), G Doggart (Aspatria); P Curtis (Harlequins), K Dunn (Gloucester), G S Pearce (Northampton), R Kimmins (Orrell), J Etheridge (Gloucester), D Pegler (Wasps) (*capt*), D Ryan (Saracens), M G Skinner (Harlequins) *Replacement* P de Glanville (Durham U) for Evans
Scorers *Tries:* Ryan, Dunn, Underwood, Hodgkinson, penalty try, Pears, Kimmins *Conversions:* Hodgkinson (5) *Penalty Goals:* Hodgkinson (2)
Referee D Neyrat (France)

14 May 1989, Madrid
Spain 9 (1G 1PG)   England B 31 (2G 1PG 4T)

Spain: F Puertos (Canoe); J Moreno (Arquitectura), J Azcargorta (Guecho), S Torres (Santboyana) (*capt*), I Oller (Santboyana); F Tejada (Oviedo), J Diaz (Guecho); J Moral (Valladolid), J Aguiar (Liceo Frances), A Antuna (Hernani), J Marcos (Ciencias Sevilla), H Morsorri (Santboyana), A Malo (Santboyana), J Gutiérrez (Arquitectura), J A Egido (Canoe)
Scorers *Try:* Puertos *Conversion:* Diaz *Penalty Goal:* Tejada
England B: J Callard (Bath); S Hackney (Nottingham), R Lozowski (Wasps), G Ainscough (Orrell), N Heslop (Orrell); M Hamlin (Gloucester), G Doggart (Aspatria); A Sharp (Bristol), N Hitchen (Orrell), A Mullins (Harlequins), J Morrison (Bath), R Kimmins (Orrell), J Wells (Leicester), D Pegler (Wasps) (*capt*), D Thresher (Harlequins) *Replacements* S Irving (Headingley) for Ainscough; M Linnett (Moseley) for Sharp
Scorers *Tries:* Pegler, Doggart, Morrison, Linnett, Callard, Hackney
Conversions: Callard (2) *Penalty Goal:* Hamlin
Referee M Lamoulie (France)

NATIONAL TRIAL MATCHES 1988-89

IRELAND

17 December 1988, Lansdowne Road

Irish XV 27 (3G 3PG)   **Combined Provinces 23** (2G 1PG 2T)
Irish XV: M J Kiernan (Dolphins); J Sexton (Lansdowne), D G Irwin (Instonians),
B J Mullin (London Irish), K D Crossan (Instonians); P M Dean (St Mary's Coll),
L F P Aherne (Lansdowne); K P J Clancy (Lansdowne), S J Smith (Ballymena),
J J McCoy (Bangor), D G Lenihan (Cork Const), N P T Francis (London Irish),
P M Matthews (Wanderers) (*capt*), N P Mannion (Corinthians), W D McBride (Malone)
Scorers *Tries:* Crossan, Aherne, Sexton   *Conversions:* Kiernan (2), Danaher
Penalty Goals: Kiernan, Danaher
Combined Provinces: P P A Danaher (Lansdowne); K Hooks (Ards),
V J G Cunningham (St Mary's Coll), J Hewitt (London Irish), P P Haycock (Terenure
Coll); R P Keyes (Cork Const), R Brady (Ballymena); N Popplewell (Greystones),
J McDonald (Malone), D Fitzgerald (Lansdowne), B Rigney (Bective Rangers),
W A Anderson (Dungannon) (*capt*), P T J O'Hara (Sunday's Well), B J Spillane (London
Irish), P Kenny (Wanderers)
Scorers *Tries:* Hooks, Cunningham, Haycock, Dunlea *Conversions:* Keyes (2)
Penalty Goal: Keyes
Referee S R Hilditch

SCOTLAND

7 January 1989, Murrayfield
Blues 24 (2G 4PG)   Reds 23 (1G 3PG 2T)

Blues: P W Dods (Gala); M D F Duncan (West of Scotland), S Hastings (Watsonians),
S R P Lineen (Boroughmuir), D A Stark (Ayr); D S Wyllie (Stewart's-Melville FP),
G H Oliver (Hawick); D M B Sole (Bath), K S Milne (Heriot's FP), I G Milne (Heriot's
FP) (*capt*), A J Campbell (Hawick), J F Richardson (Edinburgh Acads), K P Rafferty
(Heriot's FP), F Calder (Stewart's-Melville FP), D B White (Gala)
Scorers *Tries:* Dods, Hastings   *Conversions:* Dods (2)   *Penalty Goals:* Dods (4)
Reds: M Wright (Kelso); I Tukalo (Selkirk), K W Robertson (Melrose), R R W Maclean
(Gloucester), M R DeBusk (Boroughmuir); C M Chalmers (Melrose), G Armstrong
(Jedforest); A K Brewster (Stewart's-Melville FP), G J Callander (Kelso) (*capt*),
A P Burnell (London Scottish), C A Gray (Nottingham), D F Cronin (Bath),
G A E Buchanan-Smith (London Scottish), G R Marshall (Selkirk), I A M Paxton
(Selkirk) *Replacement* J A Hay (Hawick) for Callander (47 mins)
Scorers *Tries* Tukalo, Chalmers, Gray   *Conversion:* Chalmers
Penalty Goals: Chalmers (3)
Referee J B Anderson (Currie)

TIME TO FLY THE BRITISH FLAG
The 1989 Cathay Pacific – Hong Kong Bank Sevens

Nick Cain *Rugby World & Post*

'As we are the oldest and largest Union and anxious to re-establish ourselves in the forefront of world rugby, we should try to be represented at high profile events like the Hong Kong Sevens. With the vast playing resources we have, we should be capable of fielding a decent representative seven, despite an admittedly congested fixture list. If New Zealand can find the time, we ought to try to match them on every occasion. We should be flying the flag for English rugby'.

Let's hope that the words of Geoff Cooke, the England manager, don't fall on stony ground and that the RFU, which has of late taken such a progressive stance on parochial issues, heeds his views and takes the long overdue step of despatching a representative side to the next Hong Kong Sevens. It would certainly add a new dynamic to this great rugby fiesta which currently has only one potential drawback – that it could always be dominated by the Kiwis and the Wallabies.

This is sad for British sevens, not least because from being the best exponents of the shortened code our standards have dropped significantly since the Scottish Centenary Sevens at Murrayfield in 1973. It was mooted then that an international sevens competition should be promoted as an annual event – but nobody did anything until the Hong Kong Sevens was launched in 1976. One can only surmise that the dog-in-a-manger attitude with which the tournament has been received by the British Unions stems from resentment that the HKRFU decided to plough its own furrow and launch the event rather than cogitate over 101 reasons why it shouldn't.

The subsequent phenomenal success of the HKRFU's bold venture – this year a sell-out 28,000 crowd watched finals day with only a couple of thousand less for the first day's pool matches – is unlikely to have helped to heal the rift. The upshot is that the Home Unions have consistently refused requests to send national sevens to the tournament using overcrowded domestic itineraries as a pretext. The same criticism cannot be levelled at their New Zealand and Australian counterparts, even allowing for the convenient overlapping of the Sevens with their early season preparations. The Australians, who started sending their national seven in 1977, have won the Cup five times, while the New Zealanders have won it three times.

So, while British administrators played ostrich and forfeited crucial playing experience to aspiring internationals, the New Zealanders assessed the All Black potential of another set of backs and back-row forwards. On the evidence of the way they brushed aside holders Australia – Campese, Lynagh, Tuynman *et al* – in the final (22-10) to take pole position and avenge last year's narrow defeat, they should be well equipped for some years to come. New Zealand produced a combination of power, pace and co-ordination, underpinned by supreme fitness, that could not be matched.

But it's a sure indicator of the high standards on show at Soo Kun Poo that the Kiwis were pushed to the limit by Fiji in the semi-final. They recovered from a 10-0 half-time deficit to win 12-10, the turning point being a superlative tackle by John Gallagher which halted young Waisale Serevi – a wonderfully balanced runner later voted Best and Fairest Player – inches from the Kiwi line. The other semi-final provided an intriguing Wallabies v Lions taster, with the men from Down Under staving off a magnificent Barbarians fight-back to stop Finlay Calder's outfit making the final (12-10).

The two other tiers of the tournament, the Plate and the Bowl, also produced some magic moments. In the Plate the Tunisians, making their Hong Kong debut, made a tremendous impression in testing the Tongans far more thoroughly than the disappointing Japanese seven they overran in the final (32-14). But this year the Plate, and indeed the Cup, had to give pride of place to the Bowl, or third-place competition, as the real drama unfolded around the Dutchmen and the man who provided them with the will to snatch victory – Marcel Bierman.

Bierman, who was tragically paralysed when making a tackle in last year's Sevens, yelled his friends to glory from the touch-line as they clawed their way back in the final against Spain from a 16-4 deficit. Sheer guts and determination fired them as tries from Dinkla and a last-ditch effort by the powerful Verhofstad brought them level. In extra time Andre Marcker, the skipper and one of four brothers in the Dutch side, glided past the hapless Spaniards to score the winning try. When Bierman wheeled himself onto the pitch to congratulate his countrymen, they told him: 'We did it for you, Marcel'. Such are the bonds of fellowship that set rugby apart.

Pool A: Australia 52 Brunei 0; Japan 20 Brunei 4; Australia 32 Japan 4 **Pool B:** Irish Wolfhounds 36 Singapore 0; South Korea 38 Singapore 0; Irish Wolfhounds 18 South Korea 4 **Pool C:** Canada 22 Sri Lanka 10; Taipei 22 Sri Lanka 12; Canada 22 Taipei 12 **Pool D:** Barbarians 26 Papua New Guinea 0; Papua New Guinea 12 Spain 8; Barbarians 24 Spain 4 **Pool E:** Fiji 16 Thailand 0; Thailand 28 Italy 16; Fiji 42 Italy 6 **Pool F:** American Eagles 24 Netherlands 4; Hong Kong 16 Netherlands 14; Hong Kong 16 American Eagles 6 **Pool G:** Western Samoa 34 Malaysia 6; Tonga 22 Malaysia 0; Western Samoa 16 Tonga 6 **Pool H:** New Zealand 54 Bahrain 0; Tunisia 34 Bahrain 0; New Zealand 38 Tunisia 0.

Cup: Quarter-finals: Australia 22 Irish Wolfhounds 8; Barbarians 24 Canada 12; Fiji 26 Hong Kong 0; New Zealand 22 Western Samoa 6 **Semi-finals:** Australia 12 Barbarians 10; New Zealand 12 Fiji 10 **Final:** NEW ZEALAND 22 AUSTRALIA 10

Plate: Quarter-finals: Japan 12 South Korea 10; Papua New Guinea 12 Taipei 6; American Eagles 28 Thailand 0; Tonga 8 Tunisia 7 **Semi-finals:** Japan 20 Papua New Guinea 12; Tonga 19 American Eagles 6 **Final:** Tonga 32 Japan 14

Bowl: Quarter-finals: Brunei 16 Singapore 4; Spain 14 Sri Lanka 12; Netherlands 8 Italy 3; Bahrain 22 Malaysia 6 **Semi-finals:** Spain 36 Brunei 0; Netherlands 24 Bahrain 4 **Final:** Netherlands 20 Spain 16 (*aet*)

MIXED FORTUNE FOR A YOUNG LEADER

THE 1988-89 SEASON IN ENGLAND

David Hands *The Times*

Given that the national side returned from the 1988 summer tour to Australia and Fiji well beaten by the Wallabies and with a hardly-contested win against the islanders to their credit, to finish joint second in the International Championship may be regarded as a considerable advance. But, in a sense, the English scene at international level was dominated by one match – the 'return' against Australia in November. With hindsight the extravagant 28-19 victory over the touring Australians stands alone, having no relationship to the internationals which followed in the New Year. Yet the expectations of the press and public were set at that stage, with no allowance made for the claustrophobic atmosphere which notoriously pervades the Championship. It was a campaign for which England received the help of Pierre Villepreux, the Toulouse coach, during a squad weekend in Portugal, which did not go down well with the French federation.

Some bold decision-making had preceded Australia's tour of England and Scotland: a year earlier the Rugby Football Union had decided the time was right to appoint a team manager, Geoff Cooke, to the national side. In October 1988 he decided that the captaincy of England was also a long-term job and invited Will Carling to lead the side against Australia. At 22 Carling was the youngest England captain for 57 years, as well as being the youngest player in the team, and he was embarking on only his second international season. 'We have had a succession of short-term captaincies and the feeling was that we had to establish an England captain who, though it is early for him, would take us through the next three seasons and into the 1991 World Cup', Cooke said. Carling, who had earlier in the year bought his way out of the Army, was an inspired choice. His play at centre had already gained him many admirers and, even though his tactical grasp on the field lacked security (which was scarcely surprising), his responsible approach and detailed preparation off the field belied his years. It was a misfortune that a damaged shin forced him out of England's concluding international of 1988-89, against Romania, and out of the British Lions' tour to Australia.

The Lions squad was indication enough of England's improved status – they had 10 representatives, even after Carling's withdrawal which brought the then uncapped Jeremy Guscott of Bath a place. The rugby they produced in the Championship was limited, however. Against Australia, they were able to play a loose game which their visitors, not yet in any great state of readiness, could not match. The gamble of selecting Dewi Morris, in his first season of senior club rugby, at scrum-half came off, but there remained the possibility that

The England team before the match against Scotland: L-R, back row: S M Bates (replacement), A L Thompson (replacement), R A Robinson, C Oti, W A Dooley, D Richards, P J Ackford, M C Teague, P A G Rendall, J A Probyn, M D Bailey (replacement), G W Rees (replacement); front row: G J Chilcott (replacement), C R Andrew, S J Halliday, R Underwood, W D C Carling (capt), B C Moore, J M Webb, C D Morris, J Olver (replacement).

more knowledgeable opponents would disrupt England.

They did. Scotland came to Twickenham, preyed on English uncertainty at half-back and went home with a draw after Jonathan Webb and Rob Andrew between them failed to kick enough of the many penalty awards they received. England's positive response was to nominate the same XV against Ireland and they received the reward such loyalty deserved by winning in Dublin. It was there, though, that Jeff Probyn's season came to grief: the Wasps prop had to leave the field with a head injury which was diagnosed as concussion. He was replaced by Bath's Gareth Chilcott for the next two matches and probably lost his chance to tour with the Lions as a consequence. That was the only change England made in the Championship and their next match, against France at Twickenham, was their finest hour. An exceptional forward platform permitted Morris to plague the life out of the French, Andrew kicked shrewdly and Andy Robinson, later nominated player of the year, scored the try which concluded an 11-0 victory.

Even if Scotland had doused hopes of a Triple Crown, the Championship remained within reach, provided that England beat Wales in Cardiff, where they had not won since 1963. Given Wales' downcast season, England were expected to do that. But it was not to be. On a gloomy, wet day they lost Mike Teague, the Gloucester flanker who had fought his way back into the side, in the opening minute and could not match Wales' tactical approach or opportunism. The back division, hailed as potentially the best in Europe remained just that – potential. The raw strength of Morris was not a match for the experienced Robert Jones and he was dropped for the game against Romania.

It was, perhaps, a case of too much hope being piled on too slim a base, but there remained positive elements about England's international season: it was as fit a side as the country have yet fielded, Paul Ackford was a revelation at lock and their discipline was good. However, two incidents in the games against Ireland and Wales remained at the back of the memory to show how self-control can break down: Wade Dooley might have been penalised more heavily than he was for stamping in Dublin and Dean Richards, England's pack leader, could have been dismissed along with Mike Griffiths, the Welsh prop, had not Kerry Fitzgerald, the Australian referee, decided their fisticuffs were untypical of the game in Cardiff as a whole – which they were.

But the season demonstrated once more what has long been true of English sides in the 1980s, that they could be too easily knocked out of their stride and were slow to adapt to changing match circumstances. Andrew became England's most-capped fly-half during the Championship, and Rory Underwood the country's most-capped wing, but there were too many occasions when both struggled for the consistency that such long experience suggests should be automatic. That is to take only two players at random. What is more serious is that, in representative games at other levels, there is every indication that the skill levels

103

of English backs are declining. For many years one took for granted such skills because of the healthy teaching of rugby in schools; now that is no longer the case, many youngsters win caps in schools or youth rugby without, apparently, the ability to perform many of the basics. The unit skills of the forwards remain generally good and are more easily coached; behind the scrum it is a different tale and one to which the Rugby Football Union have paid attention with their policy of appointing development officers in as many areas as funds permit.

Basic skills, though, carried Bath forward on an irresistible flood tide. They did not lose a game until February, they had won the Courage Clubs Championship by March and the Pilkington Cup was gained in April. Along the road they had many critics (born of jealousy?) – they were said to be arrogant and self-seeking. That they were prepared to share their approach and attitudes to the game at an RFU seminar was apparently overlooked, as was the fact that they scored over 1,200 points, matched the talents of Toulouse and had two of their backs among the country's leading try-scorers for most of the season.

The two Pilkington Cup finalists, Bath and Leicester, have probably put more thought into their preparations than most other clubs in the country. Others are scurrying to catch up, after the second season of league rugby which saw some famous names decline sadly. London Welsh and London Scottish were relegated to Division 3, their places taken by Plymouth Albion and Rugby. Plymouth, unbeaten in Division 3, should form an apt focal point for West Countrymen who do not feel inclined to go so far as Bath or Bristol for their rugby and it is a pity that the North does not have a similar outpost. While London boasts four Division 1 clubs in 1989-90 (the well-organised Saracens won promotion), like the Midlands, the North has only one survivor, Orrell. In an area where so much rugby is played that is a cruel disappointment and could lead to more amalgamations as with Liverpool St Helens.

London, under the tutelage of Harlequins coach Dick Best, offered great enthusiasm against the Australians, a game which lifted Steven Bates, the Wasps scrum-half, out of the common run, onto the England bench and ultimately to a full cap against Romania. Wasps, too, had the satisfaction of supplying three England captains at the season's end: Andrew took over from Carling against Romania, David Pegler's success with London carried him into the England B team and Steve Pilgrim, the full-back, led the first national Under-21 XV against the Romanians.

Approaching the 1990s, it is hard to ignore the feeling that while quantity exists, quality in English rugby remains limited. That feeling was confirmed in 1989 by the retirement of three outstanding players – Dusty Hare, Leicester's world-record points-scorer, John Palmer of Bath and Jamie Salmon, the Harlequins centre who played for both New Zealand and England. All three brought genuine vision, individual genius and hard-learned skills to the game – they would be hard to beat as role models for the next generation.

ENGLISH INTERNATIONAL PLAYERS
(up to 30 April 1989)

ABBREVIATIONS

A – Australia; *Arg* – Argentina; *F* — France; *Fj*– Fiji; *I* – Ireland; *J* – Japan; *M* – Maoris; *NSW* – New South Wales; *NZ* – New Zealand; *R* – Romania; *S* – Scotland; *SA* – South Africa; *US* – United States; *W* – Wales; (C) – Centenary match v Scotland at Murrayfield, 1971 (non-championship); P – England v President's Overseas XV at Twickenham in RFU's Centenary season, 1970-71; (R) – Replacement. Entries in square brackets [ ] indicate appearances in the World Cup.

Note: Years given for Five Nations' matches are for second half of season; eg 1972 means season 1971-72. Years for all other matches refer to the actual year of the match. When a series has taken place, figures have been used to denote the particular matches in which players have featured. Thus 1984 *SA* 2 indicates that a player appeared in the second Test of the series.

Aarvold, C D (Cambridge U, W Hartlepool, Headingley, Blackheath) 1928 *NSW, W, I, F, S,* 1929 *W, I, F,* 1931 *W, S, F,* 1932 *SA, W, I, S,* 1933 *W*
Ackford, P J (Harlequins) 1988 *A,* 1989 *S, I, F, W*
Adams, A A (London Hospital) 1910 *F*
Adams, F R (Richmond) 1875 *I, S,* 1876 *S,* 1877 *I,* 1878 *S,* 1879 *S, I*
Adey, G J (Leicester) 1976 *I, F*
Adkins, S J (Coventry) 1950 *I, F, S,* 1953 *W, I, F, S*
Agar, A E (Harlequins) 1952 *SA, W, S, I, F,* 1953 *W, I*
Alcock, A (Guy's Hospital) 1906 *SA*
Alderson, F H R (Hartlepool R) 1891 *W, I, S,* 1892 *W, S,* 1893 *W*
Alexander, H (Richmond) 1900 *I, S,* 1901 *W, I, S,* 1902 *W, I*
Alexander, W (Northern) 1927 *F*
Allison, D F (Coventry) 1956 *W, I, S, F,* 1957 *W,* 1958 *W, S*
Allport, A (Blackheath) 1892 *W,* 1893 *I,* 1894 *W, I, S*
Anderson, S (Rockcliff) 1899 *I*
Anderson, W F (Orrell) 1973 *NZ*
Anderton, C (Manchester FW) 1889 *M*
Andrew, C R (Cambridge U, Nottingham, Wasps) 1985 *R, F, S, I, W,* 1986 *W, S, I, F,* 1987 *I, F, W,* [*J*(R), *US*], 1988 *S, I* 1,2, *A*1,2, *Fj, A,* 1989 *S, I, F, W*
Archer, H (Bridgwater A) 1909 *W, F, I*
Armstrong, R (Northern) 1925 *W*
Arthur, T G (Wasps) 1966 *W, I*
Ashby, R C (Wasps) 1966 *I, F,* 1967 *A*
Ashcroft, A (Waterloo) 1956 *W, I, S, F,* 1957 *W, I, F, S,* 1958 *W, A, I, F, S,* 1959 *I, F, S*
Ashcroft, A H (Birkenhead Park) 1909 *A*
Ashford, W (Richmond) 1897 *W, I,* 1898 *S, W*
Ashworth, A (Oldham) 1892 *I*
Askew, J G (Cambridge U) 1930 *W, I, F*
Aslett, A R (Richmond) 1926 *W, I, F, S,* 1929 *S, F*
Assinder, E W (O Edwardians) 1909 *A, W*
Aston, R L (Blackheath) 1890 *S, I*
Auty, J R (Headingley) 1935 *S*

Bailey, M D (Cambridge U, Wasps) 1984 *SA* 1,2, 1987 [*US*]
Bainbridge, S (Gosforth, Fylde) 1982 *F, W,* 1983 *F, W, S, I, NZ,* 1984 *S, I, F, W,* 1985 *NZ* 1,2, 1987 *F, W, S,* [*J, US*]
Baker, D G S (OMTs) 1955 *W, I, F, S*
Baker, E M (Moseley) 1895 *W, I, S,* 1896 *W, I, S,* 1897 *W*
Baker, H C (Clifton) 1887 *W*
Bance, J F (Bedford) 1954 *S*
Barley, B (Wakefield) 1984 *I, F, W, A,* 1988 *A*1,2, *Fj*
Barnes, S (Bristol, Bath) 1984 *A,* 1985 *R* (R), *NZ* 1,2, 1986 *S* (R), *F* (R), 1987 *I* (R), 1988 *Fj*
Barr, R J (Leicester) 1932 *SA, W, I*
Barrett, E I M (Lennox) 1903 *S*
Barrington, T J M (Bristol) 1931 *W, I*
Barrington-Ward, L E (Edinburgh U) 1910 *W, I, F, S*
Barron, J H (Bingley) 1896 *S,* 1897 *W, I*
Bartlett, J T (Waterloo) 1951 *W*
Bartlett, R M (Harlequins) 1957 *W, I, F, S,* 1958 *I, F, S*
Barton, J (Coventry) 1967 *I, F, W,* 1972 *F*
Batchelor, T B (Oxford U) 1907 *F*

Bateson, A H (Otley) 1930 *W, I, F, S*
Bateson, H D (Liverpool) 1879 *I*
Batson, T (Blackheath) 1872 *S,* 1874 *S,* 1875 *I*
Batten, J M (Cambridge U) 1874 *S*
Baume, J L (Northern) 1950 *S*
Baxter, J (Birkenhead Park) 1900 *W, I, S*
Bazley, R C (Waterloo) 1952 *I, F,* 1953 *W, I, F, S,* 1955 *W, I, F, S*
Beaumont, W B (Fylde) 1975 *I, A* 1(R),2, 1976 *A, W, S, I, F,* 1977 *S, I, F, W,* 1978 *F, W, S, I, NZ,* 1979 *S, I, F, W, NZ,* 1980 *I, F, W, S,* 1981 *W, S, I, F, Arg* 1,2, 1982 *A, S*
Bedford, H (Morley) 1889 *M,* 1890 *S, I*
Bedford, L L (Headingley) 1931 *W, I*
Beer, I D S (Harlequins) 1955 *F, S*
Beese, M C (Liverpool) 1972 *W, I, F*
Bell, F J (Northern) 1900 *W*
Bell, H (New Brighton) 1884 *I*
Bell, J L (Darlington) 1878 *I*
Bell, P J (Blackheath) 1968 *W, I, F, S*
Bell, R W (Northern) 1900 *W, I, S*
Bendon, G J (Wasps) 1959 *W, I, F, S*
Bennett, N O (St Mary's Hospital, Waterloo) 1947 *W, S, F,* 1948 *A, W, I, S*
Bennett, W N (Bedford, London Welsh) 1975 *S, A* 1, 1976 *S* (R), 1979 *S, I, F, W*
Bennetts, B B (Penzance) 1909 *A, W*
Bentley, J (Sale) 1988 *I* 2, *A* 1
Bentley, J E (Gipsies) 1871 *S,* 1872 *S*
Berridge, M J (Northampton) 1949 *W, I*
Berry, H (Gloucester) 1910 *I, F, S*
Berry, J (Tyldesley) 1891 *W, I, S*
Berry, J T W (Leicester) 1939 *W, I, S*
Beswick, E (Swinton) 1882 *I, S*
Biggs, J M (UCH) 1878 *S,* 1879 *I*
Birkett, J G G (Harlequins) 1906 *S, F, SA,* 1907 *F, W, S,* 1908 *F, W, I, S,* 1910 *W, I, S,* 1911 *W, F, I, S,* 1912 *W, I, S, F*
Birkett, L (Clapham R) 1875 *S,* 1877 *I, S*
Birkett, R H (Clapham R) 1871 *S,* 1875 *S,* 1876 *S,* 1877 *I*
Bishop, C C (Blackheath) 1927 *F*
Black, B H (Blackheath) 1930 *W, I, F, S,* 1931 *W, I, S, F,* 1932 *S,* 1933 *W*
Blacklock, J H (Aspatria) 1898 *I,* 1899 *I*
Blakeway, P J (Gloucester) 1980 *I, F, W, S,* 1981 *W, S, I, F,* 1982 *I, F, W,* 1984 *I, F, W, SA* 1, 1985 *R, F, S, I*
Blakiston, A F (Northampton) 1920 *S,* 1921 *W, I, S, F,* 1922 *W,* 1923 *S, F,* 1924 *W, I, F, S,* 1925 *NZ, W, I, S, F*
Blatherwick, T (Manchester) 1878 *I*
Body, J A (Gipsies) 1872 *S,* 1873 *S*
Bolton, C A (United Services) 1909 *F*
Bolton, R (Harlequins) 1933 *W,* 1936 *S,* 1937 *S,* 1938 *W, I*
Bolton, W N (Blackheath) 1882 *I, S,* 1883 *W, I, S,* 1884 *W, I, S,* 1885 *I,* 1887 *I, S*
Bonaventura, M S (Blackheath) 1931 *W*
Bond, A M (Sale) 1978 *NZ,* 1979 *S, I, NZ,* 1980 *I,* 1982 *I*
Bonham-Carter, E (Oxford U) 1891 *S*
Bonsor, F (Bradford) 1886 *W, I, S,* 1887 *W, S,* 1889 *M*

Boobbyer, B (Rosslyn Park) 1950 *W, I, F, S,* 1951 *W, F,* 1952 *S, I, F*
Booth, L A (Headingley) 1933 *W, I, S,* 1934 *S,* 1935 *W, I, S*
Botting, I J (Oxford U) 1950 *W, I*
Boughton, H J (Gloucester) 1935 *W, I, S*
Boyle, C W (Oxford U) 1873 *S*
Boyle, S B (Gloucester) 1983 *W, S, I*
Boylen, F (Hartlepool R) 1908 *F, W, I, S*
Bradby, M S (United Services) 1922 *I, F*
Bradley, R (W Hartlepool) 1903 *W*
Bradshaw, H (Bramley) 1892 *S,* 1893 *W, I, S,* 1894 *W, I, S*
Brain, S E (Coventry) 1984 *SA* 2, *A* (R), 1985 *R, F, S, I, W, NZ* 1,2, 1986 *W, S, I, F*
Braithwaite, J (Leicester) 1905 *NZ*
Braithwaite-Exley, B (Headingley) 1949 *W*
Brettargh, A T (Liverpool OB) 1900 *W,* 1903 *I, S,* 1904 *W, I, S,* 1905 *I, S*
Brewer, J (Gipsies) 1876 *I*
Briggs, A (Bradford) 1892 *W, I, S*
Brinn, A (Gloucester) 1972 *W, I, S*
Broadley, T (Bingley) 1893 *W, S,* 1894 *W, I, S,* 1896 *S,* 1893 *W, I, S,* 1895 *W, I, S,* 1896 *I*
Bromet, W E (Richmond) 1891 *W, I,* 1892 *W, I, S,* 1893 *W, I, S,* 1895 *W, I, S,* 1896 *I*
Brook, P W P (Harlequins) 1930 *S,* 1931 *F,* 1936 *S*
Brooke, T J (Richmond) 1968 *F, S*
Brooks, F G (Bedford) 1906 *SA*
Brooks, M J (Oxford U) 1874 *S*
Brophy, T J (Liverpool) 1964 *I, F, S,* 1965 *W, I,* 1966 *W, I, F*
Brough, J W (Silloth) 1925 *NZ, W*
Brougham, H (Harlequins) 1912 *W, I, S, F*
Brown, A A (Exeter) 1938 *S*
Brown, L G (Oxford U, Blackheath) 1911 *W, F, I, S,* 1913 *SA, W, F, I, S,* 1914 *W, I, S, F,* 1921 *W, I, S, F,* 1922 *W*
Brown, T W (Bristol) 1928 *S,* 1929 *W, I, S, F,* 1932 *S,* 1933 *W, I, S*
Brunton, J (N Durham) 1914 *W, I, S*
Brutton, E B (Cambridge U) 1886 *S*
Bryden, C C (Clapham R) 1876 *I,* 1877 *S*
Bryden, H A (Clapham R) 1874 *S*
Buckingham, R A (Leicester) 1927 *F*
Bucknall, A L (Richmond) 1969 *SA,* 1970 *I, W, S, F,* 1971 *W, I, F, S* (2[1C])
Buckton, J R D (Saracens) 1988 *A* (R)
Budd, A (Blackheath) 1878 *I,* 1879 *S, I,* 1881 *W, S*
Budworth, R T D (Blackheath) 1890 *W,* 1891 *W, S*
Bull, A G (Northampton) 1914 *W*
Bullough, E (Wigan) 1892 *W, I, S*
Bulpitt, M P (Blackheath) 1970 *S*
Bulteel, A J (Manchester) 1876 *I*
Bunting, W L (Moseley) 1897 *I, S,* 1898 *I, S, W,* 1899 *S,* 1900 *S,* 1901 *I, S*
Burland, D W (Bristol) 1931 *W, I, F,* 1932 *I, S,* 1933 *W, I, S*
Burns, B H (Blackheath) 1871 *S*
Burton, G W (Blackheath) 1879 *S, I,* 1880 *S,* 1881 *I, W, S*
Burton, H C (Richmond) 1926 *W*
Burton, M A (Gloucester) 1972 *W, I, F, S, SA,* 1974 *F, W,* 1975 *S, A* 1,2, 1976 *A, W, S, I, F,* 1978 *F, W*
Bush, J A (Clifton) 1872 *S,* 1873 *S,* 1875 *S,* 1876 *I, S*
Butcher, C J S (Harlequins) 1984 *SA* 1,2, *A*
Butcher, W V (Streatham) 1903 *S,* 1904 *W, I, S,* 1905 *W, I, S*
Butler, A G (Harlequins) 1937 *W, I*
Butler, P E (Gloucester) 1975 *A* 1, 1976 *F*
Butterfield, J (Northampton) 1953 *F, S,* 1954 *W, NZ, I, S, F,* 1955 *W, I, F, S,* 1956 *W, I, S, F,* 1957 *W, I, F, S,* 1958 *W, A, I, F, S,* 1959 *W, I, F, S*
Byrne, F A (Moseley) 1897 *W*
Byrne, J F (Moseley) 1894 *W, I, S,* 1895 *I, S,* 1896 *I,* 1897 *W, I, S,* 1898 *I, S, W,* 1899 *I*

Cain, J J (Waterloo) 1950 *W*
Campbell, D A (Cambridge U) 1937 *W, I*
Candler, P L (St Bart's Hospital) 1935 *W,* 1936 *NZ, W, I, S,* 1937 *W, I, S,* 1938 *W, S*
Cannell, L B (Oxford U, St Mary's Hospital) 1948 *F,* 1949 *W, I, F, S,* 1950 *W, I, F, S,* 1952 *SA, W,* 1953 *W, I, F,* 1956 *I, S, F,* 1957 *W, I*

Caplan, D W N (Headingley) 1978 *S, I*
Cardus, R M (Roundhay) 1979 *F, W*
Carey, G M (Blackheath) 1895 *W, I, S,* 1896 *W, I*
Carleton, J (Orrell) 1979 *NZ,* 1980 *I, F, W, S,* 1981 *W, S, I, F, Arg* 1,2, 1982 *A, S, I, F, W,* 1983 *F, W, S, I, NZ,* 1984 *S, I, F, W, A*
Carling, W D C (Durham U, Harlequins) 1988 *F, W, S, I* 1,2, *A2, Fj, A,* 1989 *S, I, F, W*
Carpenter, A D (Gloucester) 1932 *SA*
Carr, R S L (Manchester) 1939 *W, I, S*
Cartwright, V H (Nottingham) 1903 *W, I, S,* 1904 *W, S,* 1905 *W, I, S, NZ,* 1906 *W, I, S, F, SA*
Catcheside, H C (Percy Park) 1924 *W, I, F, S,* 1926 *W, I,* 1927 *I, S*
Cattell, R H B (Blackheath) 1895 *W, I, S,* 1896 *W, I, S,* 1900 *W*
Cave, J W (Richmond) 1889 *M*
Cave, W T C (Blackheath) 1905 *W*
Challis, R (Bristol) 1957 *I, F, S*
Chambers, E L (Bedford) 1908 *F,* 1910 *W, I*
Chantrill, B S (Bristol) 1924 *W, I, F, S*
Chapman, C E (Cambridge U) 1884 *W*
Chapman, F E (Hartlepool) 1910 *W, I, F, S,* 1912 *W,* 1914 *W, I*
Cheesman, W I (OMTs) 1913 *SA, W, F, I*
Cheston, E C (Richmond) 1873 *S,* 1874 *S,* 1875 *I, S,* 1876 *S*
Chilcott, G J (Bath) 1984 *A,* 1986 *I, F,* 1987 *F* (R), *W,* [*J, US, W*(R)], 1988 *I* 2(R), *Fj,* 1989 *I* (R), *F, W*
Christopherson, P (Blackheath) 1891 *W, S*
Clark, C W H (Liverpool) 1876 *I*
Clarke, A J (Coventry) 1935 *W, I, S,* 1936 *NZ, W, I*
Clarke, S J S (Cambridge U, Blackheath) 1963 *W, I, F, S, NZ* 1,2, *A,* 1964 *NZ, W, I,* 1965 *I, F, S*
Clayton, J H (Liverpool) 1871 *S*
Clements, J W (O Cranleighans) 1959 *I, F, S*
Cleveland, C R (Blackheath) 1887 *W, S*
Clibborn, W G (Richmond) 1886 *W, I, S,* 1887 *W, I, S*
Clough, F J (Cambridge U, Orrell) 1986 *I, F,* 1987 [*J*(R), *US*]
Coates, C H (Yorkshire W) 1880 *S,* 1881 *S,* 1882 *S*
Coates, V H M (Bath) 1913 *SA, W, F, I, S*
Cobby, W (Hull) 1900 *W*
Cockerham, A (Bradford Olicana) 1900 *W*
Colclough, M J (Angoulême, Wasps, Swansea) 1978 *S, I,* 1979 *NZ,* 1980 *F, W, S,* 1981 *W, S, I, F,* 1982 *A, S, I, F, W,* 1983 *F, NZ,* 1984 *S, I, F, W,* 1986 *W, S, I, F*
Coley, E (Northampton) 1929 *F,* 1932 *W*
Collins, P J (Camborne S of M) 1952 *S, I, F*
Collins, W E (O Cheltonians) 1874 *S,* 1875 *I, S,* 1876 *I, S*
Considine, S G U (Bath) 1925 *F*
Conway, G S (Cambridge U, Rugby, Manchester) 1920 *F, I, S,* 1921 *F,* 1922 *W, I, F, S,* 1923 *W, I, S, F,* 1924 *W, I, F, S,* 1925 *NZ,* 1927 *W*
Cook, J G (Bedford) 1937 *S*
Cook, P W (Richmond) 1965 *I, F*
Cooke, D A (Harlequins) 1976 *W, S, I, F*
Cooke, D H (Harlequins) 1981 *W, S, I, F,* 1984 *I,* 1985 *R, F, S, I, W, NZ* 1,2
Cooke, P (Richmond) 1939 *W, I*
Coop, T (Leigh) 1892 *S*
Cooper, J G (Moseley) 1909 *A, W*
Cooper, M J (Moseley) 1973 *F, S, NZ* (R), 1975 *F, W,* 1976 *A, W,* 1977 *S, I, F, W*
Coopper, S F (Blackheath) 1900 *W,* 1902 *W, I,* 1905 *W, I, S,* 1907 *W*
Corbett, L J (Bristol) 1921 *F,* 1923 *W, I,* 1924 *W, I, F, S,* 1925 *NZ, W, I, S, F,* 1927 *W, I, S, F*
Corless, B J (Coventry, Moseley) 1976 *A, I* (R), 1977 *S, I, F, W,* 1978 *F, W, S, I*
Cotton, F E (Loughborough Colls, Coventry, Sale) 1971 *S* (2[1C]), *P,* 1973 *W, I, F, S, NZ, A,* 1974 *S, I,* 1975 *I, F, W,* 1976 *A, W, S, I, F,* 1977 *S, I, F, W,* 1978 *S, I,* 1979 *NZ,* 1980 *I, F, W, S,* 1981 *W*
Coulman, M J (Moseley) 1967 *A, I, F, S, W,* 1968 *W, I, F, S*
Coulson, T J (Coventry) 1927 *W,* 1928 *NSW, W*
Court, E D (Blackheath) 1885 *W*
Coverdale, H (Blackheath) 1910 *F,* 1912 *I, F,* 1920 *W, I, S, F,* 1924 *W, I, S, F,* 1925 *NZ, W, I, S,* 1927 *W, I, S, F,* 1928 *NSW, W, I, F, S,* 1929 *W, I*
Cove-Smith, R (OMTs) 1921 *S, F,* 1922 *I, F, S,* 1923 *W, I, S, F,* 1924 *W, I, S, F,* 1925 *NZ, W, I, S,* 1927 *W, I, S, F,* 1928 *NSW, W, I, F, S,* 1929 *W, I*

Cowling, R J (Leicester) 1977 *S, I, F, W*, 1978 *F, NZ*, 1979 *S, I*
Cowman, A R (Loughborough Colls, Coventry) 1971 *S* (2[1C]), *P*, 1973 *W, I*
Cox, N S (Sunderland) 1901 *S*
Cranmer, P (Richmond, Moseley) 1934 *W, I, S*, 1935 *W, I, S*, 1936 *NZ, W, I, S*, 1937 *W, I, S*, 1938 *W, I, S*
Creed, R N (Coventry) 1971 *P*
Cridlan, A G (Blackheath) 1935 *W, I, S*
Crompton, C A (Blackheath) 1871 *S*
Crosse, C W (Oxford U) 1874 *S*, 1875 *I*
Cumberlege, B S (Blackheath) 1920 *W, I, S*, 1921 *W, I, S, F*, 1922 *W*
Cumming, D C (Blackheath) 1925 *S, F*
Cunliffe, F L (RMA) 1874 *S*
Currey, F I (Marlborough N) 1872 *S*
Currie, J D (Oxford U, Harlequins, Bristol) 1956 *W, I, S, F*, 1957 *W, I, F, S*, 1958 *W, A, I, F, S*, 1959 *W, I, F, S*, 1960 *W, I, F, S*, 1961 *SA*, 1962 *W, I, F*
Cusani, D A (Orrell) 1987 *I*
Cusworth, L (Leicester) 1979 *NZ*, 1982 *F, W*, 1983 *F, W, NZ*, 1984 *S, I, F, W*, 1988 *F, W*

D'Aguilar, F B G (Royal Engineers) 1872 *S*
Dalton, T J (Coventry) 1969 *S* (R)
Danby, T (Harlequins) 1949 *W*
Daniell, J (Richmond) 1899 *W*, 1900 *I, S*, 1902 *I, S*, 1904 *I, S*
Darby, A J L (Birkenhead Park) 1899 *I*
Davenport, A (Ravenscourt Park) 1871 *S*
Davey, J (Redruth) 1908 *S*, 1909 *W*
Davey, R F (Teignmouth) 1931 *W*
Davidson, Jas (Aspatria) 1897 *S*, 1898 *S, W*, 1899 *I, S*
Davidson, Jos (Aspatria) 1899 *W, S*
Davies, G H (Cambridge U, Coventry, Wasps) 1981 *S, I, F, Arg* 1,2, 1982 *A, S, I*, 1983 *F, W, S*, 1984 *S, SA* 1,2, 1985 *R* (R), *NZ* 1,2, 1986 *W, S, I, F*
Davies, P H (Sale) 1927 *I*
Davies, V G (Harlequins) 1922 *W*, 1925 *NZ*
Davies, W J A (United Services, RN) 1913 *SA, W, F, I, S*, 1914 *I, S, F*, 1920 *F, I, S*, 1921 *W, I, S, F*, 1922 *I, F, S*, 1923 *W, I, S, F*
Davies, W P C (Harlequins) 1953 *S*, 1954 *NZ, I*, 1955 *W, I, F, S*, 1956 *W*, 1957 *F, S*, 1958 *W*
Davis, A M (Harlequins) 1963 *W, I, S, NZ* 1,2, 1964 *NZ, W, I, F, S*, 1966 *W, I*, 1967 *A*, 1969 *SA*, 1970 *I, W, S*
Dawe, R G R (Bath) 1987 *I, F, W, [US]*
Dawson, E F (RIEC) 1878 *I*
Day, H L V (Leicester) 1920 *W*, 1922 *W, F*, 1926 *S*
Dean, G J (Harlequins) 1931 *P*
Dee, J M (Hartlepool R) 1962 *S*, 1963 *NZ* 1
Devitt, Sir T G (Blackheath) 1926 *I, F*, 1928 *NSW, W*
Dewhurst, J H (Richmond) 1887 *W, I, S*, 1890 *W*
De Winton, R F C (Marlborough N) 1893 *W*
Dibble, R (Bridgwater A) 1906 *S, F, SA*, 1908 *F, W, I, S*, 1909 *A, W, F, I, S*, 1910 *S*, 1911 *W, F, S*, 1912 *W, I, S*
Dicks, J (Northampton) 1934 *W, I, S*, 1935 *W, I, S*, 1936 *S*, 1937 *I*
Dillon, E W (Blackheath) 1904 *W, I, S*, 1905 *W*
Dingle, A J (Hartlepool R) 1913 *I*, 1914 *S, F*
Dixon, P J (Harlequins, Gosforth) 1971 *P*, 1972 *W, I, F, S*, 1973 *I, F, S*, 1974 *S, I, F, W*, 1975 *I*, 1976 *F*, 1977 *S, I, F, W*, 1978 *F, S, I, NZ*
Dobbs, G E B (Devonport A) 1906 *W, I*
Doble, S A (Moseley) 1972 *SA*, 1973 *NZ, W*
Dobson, D D (Newton Abbot) 1902 *W, I, S*, 1903 *W, I, S*
Dobson, T H (Bradford) 1895 *S*
Dodge, P W (Leicester) 1978 *W, S, I, NZ*, 1979 *S, I, F, W*, 1980 *W, S*, 1981 *W, S, I, F, Arg* 1,2, 1982 *A, S, F, W*, 1983 *F, W, S, I, NZ*, 1985 *R, F, S, I, W, NZ* 1,2
Donnelly, M P (Oxford U) 1947 *I*
Dooley, W A (Preston Grasshoppers, Fylde) 1985 *R, F, S, I, W, NZ* 2 (R), 1986 *W, S, I, F*, 1987 *F, W, [A, US, W]*, 1988 *F, W, S, I* 1,2, *A* 1,2, *Fj, A*, 1989 *S, I, F, W*
Dovey, B A (Rosslyn Park) 1963 *W, I*
Down, P J (Bristol) 1909 *A*
Dowson, A O (Moseley) 1899 *S*
Drake-Lee, N J (Cambridge U, Leicester) 1963 *W, I, F, S*, 1964 *NZ, W, I*, 1965 *W*
Duckett, H (Bradford) 1893 *I, S*

Duckham, D J (Coventry) 1969 *I, F, S, W, SA*, 1970 *I, W, S, F*, 1971 *W, I, F, S* (2[1C]), *P*, 1972 *W, I, F, S*, 1973 *NZ, W, I, F, S, NZ, A*, 1974 *S, I, F, W*, 1975 *I, F, W*, 1976 *A, W, S*
Dudgeon, H W (Richmond) 1897 *S*, 1898 *I, S, W*, 1899 *W, I, S*
Dugdale, J M (Ravenscourt Park) 1871 *S*
Dun, A F (Wasps) 1984 *W*
Duncan, R F H (Guy's Hospital) 1922 *I, F, S*
Dunkley, P E (Harlequins) 1931 *I, S*, 1936 *NZ, W, I, S*
Duthie, J (W Hartlepool) 1903 *W*
Dyson, J W (Huddersfield) 1890 *S*, 1892 *S*, 1893 *I, S*

Ebdon, P J (Wellington) 1897 *W, I*
Eddison, J H (Headingley) 1912 *W, I, S, F*
Edgar, C S (Birkenhead Park) 1901 *S*
Edwards, R (Newport) 1921 *W, I, S, F*, 1922 *W, F*, 1923 *W*, 1924 *W, F, S*, 1925 *NZ*
Egerton, D W (Bath) 1988 *I* 2, *A* 1, *Fj* (R), *A*
Elliot, C H (Sunderland) 1886 *W*
Elliot, E W (Sunderland) 1901 *W, I, S*, 1904 *W*
Elliot, W (United Services, RN) 1932 *I, S*, 1933 *W, I, S*, 1934 *W, I*
Elliott, A E (St Thomas's Hospital) 1894 *S*
Ellis, J (Wakefield) 1939 *S*
Ellis, S S (Queen's House) 1880 *I*
Emmott, C (Bradford) 1892 *W*
Enthoven, H J (Richmond) 1878 *I*
Estcourt, N S D (Blackheath) 1955 *S*
Evans, B J (Leicester) 1988 *A* 2, *Fj*
Evans, E (Sale) 1948 *A*, 1950 *W*, 1951 *I, F, S*, 1952 *SA, W, S, I, F*, 1953 *I, F, S*, 1954 *W, NZ, I, F*, 1956 *W, I, S, F*, 1957 *W, I, F, S*, 1958 *W, A, I, F, S*
Evans, G W (Coventry) 1972 *S*, 1973 *W* (R), *F, S, NZ*, 1974 *S, I, F, W*
Evans, N L (RNEC) 1932 *W, I, S*, 1933 *W, I*
Evanson, A M (Richmond) 1883 *W, I, S*, 1884 *S*
Evanson, W A D (Richmond) 1875 *S*, 1877 *S*, 1878 *S*, 1879 *S, I*
Evershed, F (Blackheath) 1889 *M*, 1890 *W, S, I*, 1892 *W, I, S*, 1893 *W, I, S*
Eyres, W C T (Richmond) 1927 *I*

Fagan, A R St L (Richmond) 1887 *I*
Fairbrother, K E (Coventry) 1969 *I, F, S, W, SA*, 1970 *I, W, S, F*, 1971 *W, I, F*
Faithfull, C K T (Harlequins) 1924 *I*, 1926 *F, S*
Fallas, H (Wakefield T) 1884 *I*
Fegan, J H C (Blackheath) 1895 *W, I, S*
Fernandes, C W L (Leeds) 1881 *I, W, S*
Fidler, J H (Gloucester) 1981 *Arg* 1,2, 1984 *SA* 1,2
Field, E (Middlesex W) 1893 *W, I*
Fielding, K J (Moseley, Loughborough Colls) 1969 *I, F, S, SA*, 1970 *I, F*, 1972 *W, I, F, S*
Finch, R T (Cambridge U) 1880 *S*
Finlan, J F (Moseley) 1967 *I, F, S, W, NZ*, 1968 *W, I*, 1969 *I, F, S, W*, 1970 *F*, 1973 *NZ*
Finlinson, H W (Blackheath) 1895 *W, I, S*
Finney, S (RIE Coll) 1872 *S*, 1873 *S*
Firth, F (Halifax) 1894 *W, I, S*
Fletcher, N C (OMTs) 1901 *W, I, S*, 1903 *S*
Fletcher, T (Seaton) 1897 *W*
Fletcher, W R B (Marlborough N) 1873 *S*, 1875 *S*
Fookes, E F (Sowerby Bridge) 1896 *W, I, S*, 1897 *W, I, S*, 1898 *I, W*, 1899 *I, S*
Ford, P J (Gloucester) 1964 *W, I, F, S*
Forrest, J W (United Services, RN) 1930 *W, I, F, S*, 1931 *W, I, S, F*, 1934 *I, S*
Forrest, R (Wellington) 1899 *W*, 1900 *S*, 1902 *I, S*, 1903 *I, S*
Foulds, R T (Waterloo) 1929 *W, I*
Fowler, F D (Manchester) 1878 *S*, 1879 *S*
Fowler, H (Oxford U) 1878 *S*, 1881 *W, S*
Fowler, R H (Leeds) 1877 *I*
Fox, F H (Wellington) 1890 *W, S*
Francis, T E S (Cambridge U) 1926 *W, I, F, S*
Frankcom, G P (Cambridge U, Bedford) 1965 *W, I, F, S*
Fraser, E C (Blackheath) 1875 *I*
Fraser, G (Richmond) 1902 *W, I, S*, 1903 *W, I*
Freakes, H D (Oxford U) 1938 *W*, 1939 *W, I*
Freeman, H (Marlborough N) 1872 *S*, 1873 *S*, 1874 *S*
French, R J (St Helens) 1961 *W, I, F, S*

Fry, H A (Liverpool) 1934 *W, I, S*
Fry, T W (Queen's House) 1880 *I, S*, 1881 *W*
Fuller, H G (Bath) 1882 *I, S*, 1883 *W, I, S*, 1884 *W*

Gadney, B C (Leicester, Headingley) 1932 *I, S*, 1933 *I, S*, 1934 *W, I, S*, 1935 *S*, 1936 *NZ, W, I, S*, 1937 *S*, 1938 *W*
Gamlin, H T (Blackheath) 1899 *W, S*, 1900 *W, I, S*, 1901 *S*, 1902 *W, I, S*, 1903 *W, I, S*, 1904 *W, I, S*
Gardner, E R (Devonport Services) 1921 *W, I, S*, 1922 *W, I, F*, 1923 *W, I, S, F*
Gardner, H P (Richmond) 1878 *I*
Garnett, H W T (Bradford) 1877 *S*
Gavins, M N (Leicester) 1961 *W*
Gay, D J (Bath) 1968 *W, I, F, S*
Gent, D R (Gloucester) 1905 *NZ*, 1906 *W, I*, 1910 *W, I*
Genth, J S M (Manchester) 1874 *S*, 1875 *S*
George, J T (Falmouth) 1947 *S, F*, 1949 *I*
Gerrard, R A (Bath) 1932 *SA, W, I, S*, 1933 *W, I, S*, 1934 *W, I, S*, 1936 *NZ, W, I, S*
Gibbs, G A (Bristol) 1947 *F*, 1948 *I*
Gibbs, J C (Harlequins) 1925 *NZ, W*, 1926 *F*, 1927 *W, I, S, F*
Gibbs, N (Harlequins) 1954 *S, F*
Giblin, L F (Blackheath) 1896 *W, I*, 1897 *S*
Gibson, A S (Manchester) 1871 *S*
Gibson, C O P (Northern) 1901 *W*
Gibson, G R (Northern) 1899 *W*, 1901 *S*
Gibson, T A (Northern) 1905 *W, S*
Gilbert, F G (Devonport Services) 1923 *W, I*
Gilbert, R (Devonport A) 1908 *W, I, S*
Giles, J L (Coventry) 1935 *W, I*, 1937 *W, I*, 1938 *I, S*
Gittings, W J (Coventry) 1967 *NZ*
Glover, P B (Bath) 1967 *A*, 1971 *F, P*
Godfray, R E (Richmond) 1905 *NZ*
Godwin, H O (Coventry) 1959 *F, S*, 1963 *S, NZ* 1,2, *A*, 1964 *NZ, I, F, S*, 1967 *NZ*
Gordon-Smith, G W (Blackheath) 1900 *W, I, S*
Gotley, A L H (Oxford U) 1910 *F, S*, 1911 *W, F, I, S*
Graham, D (Aspatria) 1901 *W*
Graham, H J (Wimbledon H) 1875 *I, S*, 1876 *I, S*
Graham, J D G (Wimbledon H) 1876 *I*
Gray, A (Otley) 1947 *W, I, S*
Green, J (Skipton) 1905 *I*, 1906 *S, F, SA*, 1907 *F, W, I, S*
Green, J F (West Kent) 1871 *S*
Greenwell, J H (Rockcliff) 1893 *W, I*
Greenwood, J E (Cambridge U, Leicester) 1912 *F*, 1913 *SA, W, F, I, S*, 1914 *W, S, F*, 1920 *W, F, I, S*
Greenwood, J R H (Waterloo) 1966 *I, F, S*, 1967 *A*, 1969 *I*
Greg, W (Manchester) 1876 *I, S*
Gregory, G G (Bristol) 1931 *I, S, F*, 1932 *SA, W, I, S*, 1933 *W, I, S*, 1934 *I, S*
Gregory, J A (Blackheath) 1949 *W*
Grylls, W M (Redruth) 1905 *I*
Guest, R H (Waterloo) 1939 *W, I, S*, 1947 *W, I, S, F*, 1948 *A, W, I, S*, 1949 *F, S*
Guillemard, A G (West Kent) 1871 *S*, 1872 *S*
Gummer, C H A (Plymouth A) 1929 *F*
Gunner, C R (Marlborough N) 1876 *I*
Gurdon, C (Richmond) 1880 *I, S*, 1881 *I, W, S*, 1882 *I, S*, 1883 *S*, 1884 *W, S*, 1885 *I*, 1886 *W, I, S*
Gurdon, E T (Richmond) 1878 *S*, 1879 *I*, 1880 *S*, 1881 *I, W, S*, 1882 *S*, 1883 *W, I, S*, 1884 *W, I, S*, 1885 *W, I*, 1886 *S*

Haigh, L (Manchester) 1910 *W, I, S*, 1911 *W, F, I, S*
Hale, P M (Moseley) 1969 *SA*, 1970 *I, W*
Hall, C (Gloucester) 1901 *I, S*
Hall, J (N Durham) 1894 *W, I, S*
Hall, J P (Bath) 1984 *S* (R), *I, F, SA* 1,2, *A*, 1985 *R, F, S, I, W, NZ* 1,2, 1986 *W, S*, 1987 *I, F, W, S*
Hall, N M (Richmond) 1947 *W, I, S, F*, 1949 *W, I*, 1952 *SA, W, S, I, F*, 1953 *W, I, F, S*, 1955 *W, I*
Halliday, S J (Bath) 1986 *W, S*, 1987 *S*, 1988 *S, I* 1,2, *A* 1, *A*, 1989 *S, I, F, W*
Hamersley, A St G (Marlborough N) 1871 *S*, 1872 *S*, 1873 *S*, 1874 *S*
Hamilton-Hill, E A (Harlequins) 1936 *NZ, W, I*
Hamilton-Wickes, R H (Cambridge U) 1924 *I*, 1925 *NZ, W, I, S, F*, 1926 *W, I, S*, 1927 *W*

Hammett, E D G (Newport) 1920 *W, F, S*, 1921 *W, I, S, F*, 1922 *W*
Hammond, C E L (Harlequins) 1905 *S, NZ*, 1906 *W, I, S, F*, 1908 *W, I*
Hancock, A W (Northampton) 1965 *F, S*, 1966 *F*
Hancock, G E (Birkenhead Park) 1939 *W, I, S*
Hancock, J H (Newport) 1955 *W, I*
Hancock, P F (Blackheath) 1886 *W, I*, 1890 *W*
Hancock, P S (Richmond) 1904 *W, I, S*
Handford, F G (Manchester) 1909 *W, F, I, S*
Hands, R H M (Blackheath) 1910 *F, S*
Hanley, J (Plymouth A) 1927 *W, S, F*, 1928 *W, I, F, S*
Hannaford, R C (Bristol) 1971 *W, I, F*
Hanvey, R J (Aspatria) 1926 *W, I, F, S*
Harding, E H (Devonport Services) 1931 *I*
Harding, R M (Bristol) 1985 *R, F, S*, 1987 *S*, [*A, J, W*], 1988 *I* 1(R),2, *A* 1,2, *Fj*
Harding, V S J (Saracens) 1961 *F, S*, 1962 *W, I, F, S*
Hardwick, P F (Percy Park) 1902 *I, S*, 1903 *W, I, S*, 1904 *W, I, S*
Hardy, E M P (Blackheath) 1951 *I, F, S*
Hare, W H (Nottingham, Leicester) 1974 *W*, 1978 *F, NZ*, 1979 *NZ*, 1980 *I, F, W, S*, 1981 *W, S, Arg* 1,2, 1982 *F, W*, 1983 *F, W, S, I, NZ*, 1984 *S, I, F, W, SA* 1,2,
Harper, C H (Exeter) 1899 *W*
Harriman, A T (Harlequins) 1988 *A*
Harris, S W (Blackheath) 1920 *I, S*
Harris, T W (Northampton) 1929 *S*, 1932 *I*
Harrison, A C (Hartlepool R) 1931 *I, S*
Harrison, A L (United Services, RN) 1914 *I, F*
Harrison, G (Hull) 1877 *I, S*, 1879 *S, I*, 1880 *S*, 1885 *W, I*
Harrison, H C (United Services, RN) 1909 *S*, 1914 *I, S, F*
Harrison, M E (Wakefield) 1985 *NZ* 1,2, 1986 *S, I, F*, 1987 *I, F, W, S*, [*A, J, US, W*], 1988 *F, W*
Hartley, B C (Blackheath) 1901 *S*, 1902 *S*
Haslett, L W (Birkenhead Park) 1926 *I, F*
Hastings, G W D (Gloucester) 1955 *W, I, F, S*, 1957 *W, I, F, S*, 1958 *W, A, I, F, S*
Havelock, H (Hartlepool R) 1908 *F, W, I*
Hawcridge, J J (Bradford) 1885 *W, I*
Hayward, L W (Cheltenham) 1910 *I*
Hazell, D St G (Leicester) 1955 *W, I, F, S*
Hearn, R D (Bedford) 1966 *F, S*, 1967 *I, F, S, W*
Heath, A H (Oxford U) 1876 *S*
Heaton, J (Waterloo) 1935 *W, I, S*, 1939 *W, I, S*, 1947 *I, S, F*
Henderson, A P (Edinburgh Wands) 1947 *W, I, S, F*, 1948 *I, S, F*, 1949 *W, I*
Henderson, R S F (Blackheath) 1883 *W, S*, 1884 *W, S*, 1885 *W*
Heppell, W G (Devonport A) 1903 *I*
Herbert, A J (Wasps) 1958 *F, S*, 1959 *W, I, F, S*
Hesford, R (Bristol) 1981 *S* (R), 1982 *A, S, F* (R), 1983 *F* (R), 1985 *R, F, S, I, W*
Hetherington, J G G (Northampton) 1958 *A, I*, 1959 *W, I, F, S*
Hewitt, E N (Coventry) 1951 *W, I, F*
Hewitt, W W (Queen's House) 1881 *I, W, S*, 1882 *I*
Hickson, J L (Bradford) 1887 *W, I, S*, 1890 *W, S, I*
Higgins, R (Liverpool) 1954 *W, NZ, I, S*, 1955 *W, I, F, S*, 1957 *W, I, F, S*, 1959 *W*
Hignell, A J (Cambridge U, Bristol) 1975 *A* 2, 1976 *A, W, S, I*, 1977 *S, I, F, W*, 1978 *W, I, F, W*, 1979 *S, I, F, W*
Hill, B A (Blackheath) 1903 *I, S*, 1904 *W, I*, 1905 *W, NZ*, 1906 *SA*, 1907 *F, W*
Hill, R J (Bath) 1984 *SA* 1,2, 1985 *I* (R), *NZ* 2 (R), 1986 *F* (R), 1987 *I, F, W*, [*US*]
Hillard, R J (Oxford U) 1925 *NZ*
Hiller, R (Harlequins) 1968 *W, I, F, S*, 1969 *I, F, S, W, SA*, 1970 *I, W, S*, 1971 *F, S, W* (2[1C]), *P*, 1972 *W, I*
Hind, A E (Leicester) 1905 *NZ*, 1906 *W*
Hind, G R (Blackheath) 1910 *S*, 1911 *I*
Hobbs, R F A (Blackheath) 1899 *S*, 1903 *W*
Hobbs, R G S (Richmond) 1932 *SA, W, I, S*
Hodges, H A (Nottingham) 1906 *W, I*
Hodgson, J Mc D (Northern) 1932 *SA, W, I, S*, 1934 *W, I*, 1936 *I*
Hodgson, S A M (Durham City) 1960 *W, I, F, S*, 1961 *SA, W*, 1962 *W, I, F, S*, 1964 *W*
Hofmeyr, M B (Oxford U) 1950 *W, F, S*

108

Hogarth, T B (Hartlepool R) 1906 *F*
Holford, G (Gloucester) 1920 *W, F*
Holland, D (Devonport A) 1912 *W, I, S*
Holliday, T E (Aspatria) 1923 *S, F*, 1925 *I, S, F*, 1926 *F, S*
Holmes, C B (Manchester) 1947 *S*, 1948 *I, F*
Holmes, E (Manningham) 1890 *S, I*
Holmes, W A (Nuneaton) 1950 *W, I, F, S*, 1951 *W, I, F, S*, 1952 *SA, S, I, F*, 1953 *W, I, F, S*
Holmes, W B (Cambridge U) 1949 *W, I, F, S*
Hook, W G (Gloucester) 1951 *S*, 1952 *SA, W*
Hooper, C A (Middlesex W) 1894 *W, I, S*
Hopley, F J V (Blackheath) 1907 *F, W*, 1908 *I*
Hordern, P C (Gloucester) 1931 *I, S, F*, 1934 *W*
Horley, C H (Swinton) 1885 *I*
Hornby, A N (Manchester) 1877 *I, S*, 1878 *S, I*, 1880 *I*, 1881 *I, S*, 1882 *I, S*
Horrocks-Taylor, J P (Cambridge U, Leicester, Middlesbrough) 1958 *W, A*, 1961 *S*, 1962 *S*, 1963 *NZ 1,2, A*, 1964 *NZ, W*
Horsfall, E L (Harlequins) 1949 *W*
Horton, A L (Blackheath) 1965 *W, I, F, S*, 1966 *F, S*, 1967 *NZ*
Horton, J P (Bath) 1978 *W, S, I, NZ*, 1980 *I, F, W, S*, 1981 *W*, 1983 *S, I*, 1984 *SA 1,2*
Horton, N E (Moseley, Toulouse) 1969 *I, F, S, W*, 1971 *I, F, S*, 1974 *S*, 1975 *W*, 1977 *S, I, F, W*, 1978 *F, W*, 1979 *S, I, F, W*, 1980 *F*
Hosen, R W (Bristol, Northampton) 1963 *NZ 1,2, A*, 1964 *F, S*, 1967 *A, I, F, S, W*
Hosking, G R d'A (Devonport Services) 1949 *W, I, F, S*, 1950 *W*
Houghton, S (Runcorn) 1892 *I*, 1896 *W*
Howard, P D (O Millhillians) 1930 *W, I, F, S*, 1931 *W, I, S, F*
Hubbard, G C (Blackheath) 1892 *W, I*
Hubbard, J C (Harlequins) 1930 *S*
Hudson, A (Gloucester) 1906 *W, I, F*, 1908 *F, W, I, S*, 1910 *F*
Hughes, G E (Barrow) 1896 *S*
Hulme, F C (Birkenhead Park) 1903 *W, I*, 1905 *W, I*
Hunt, J T (Manchester) 1882 *I, S*, 1884 *W*
Hunt, R (Manchester) 1880 *I*, 1881 *W, S*, 1882 *I*
Hunt, W H (Manchester) 1876 *S*, 1877 *I, S*, 1878 *I*
Huntsman, R P (Headingley) 1985 *NZ 1,2*
Hurst, A C B (Wasps) 1962 *S*
Huskisson, T F (OMTs) 1937 *W, I, S*, 1938 *W, I*, 1939 *W, I, S*
Hutchinson, F (Headingley) 1909 *F, I, S*
Hutchinson, J E (Durham City) 1906 *I*
Hutchinson, W C (RIE Coll) 1876 *S*, 1877 *I*
Hutchinson, W H H (Hull) 1875 *I*, 1876 *I*
Huth, H (Huddersfield) 1879 *S*
Hyde, J P (Northampton) 1950 *F, S*
Hynes, W B (United Services, RN) 1912 *F*

Ibbitson, E D (Headingley) 1909 *W, F, I, S*
Imrie, H M (Durham City) 1906 *NZ*, 1907 *I*
Inglis, R E (Blackheath) 1886 *W, I, S*
Irvin, S H (Devonport A) 1905 *W*
Isherwood, F W (Ravenscourt Park) 1872 *S*

Jackett, E J (Leicester, Falmouth) 1905 *NZ*, 1906 *W, I, S, F, SA*, 1907 *W, I, S*, 1909 *W, F, I, S*
Jackson, A H (Blackheath) 1878 *I*, 1880 *I*
Jackson, B S (Broughton Park) 1970 *S* (R), *F*
Jackson, P B (Coventry) 1956 *W, I, F*, 1957 *W, I, F, S*, 1958 *W, A, F, S*, 1959 *W, I, F, S*, 1961 *S*, 1963 *W, I, F, S*
Jackson, W J (Halifax) 1894 *S*
Jacob, F (Cambridge U) 1897 *W, I, S*, 1898 *I, S, W*, 1899 *W, I*
Jacob, H P (Blackheath) 1924 *W, I, F, S*, 1930 *F*
Jacob, P G (Blackheath) 1898 *I*
Jacobs, C R (Northampton) 1956 *W, I, S, F*, 1957 *W, I, F, S*, 1958 *W, A, I, F, S*, 1960 *W, I, F, S*, 1961 *SA, W, I, F, S*, 1963 *NZ 1,2, A*, 1964 *W, I, F, S*
Jago, R A (Devonport A) 1906 *W, I, SA*, 1907 *W, I*
Janion, J P A G (Bedford) 1971 *W, I, F, S* (2[1C]), *P*, 1972 *W, S, SA*, 1973 *A*, 1975 *A 1,2*
Jarman, J W (Bristol) 1900 *W*
Jeavons, N C (Moseley) 1981 *S, I, F, Arg 1,2*, 1982 *A, S, I, F, W*, 1983 *F, W, S, I*

Jeeps, R E G (Northampton) 1956 *W*, 1957 *W, I, F, S*, 1958 *W, A, I, F, S*, 1959 *I*, 1960 *W, I, F, S*, 1961 *SA, W, I, F, S*, 1962 *W, I, F, S*
Jeffery, G L (Blackheath) 1886 *W, I, S*, 1887 *W, I, S*
Jennins, C R (Waterloo) 1967 *A, I, F*
Jewitt, J (Hartlepool R) 1902 *W*
Johns, W A (Gloucester) 1909 *W, F, I, S*, 1910 *W, I, F*
Johnston, W R (Bristol) 1910 *W, I, S*, 1912 *W, I, S, F*, 1913 *SA, W, F, I, S*, 1914 *W, I, S, F*
Jones, F P (N Brighton) 1893 *S*
Jones, H A (Barnstaple) 1950 *W, I, F*
Jorden, A M (Cambridge U, Blackheath, Bedford) 1970 *F*, 1973 *I, F, S*, 1974 *F*, 1975 *W, S*
Jowett, D (Heckmondwike) 1889 *M*, 1890 *S, I*, 1891 *W, I, S*
Judd, P E (Coventry) 1962 *W, I, F, S*, 1963 *S, NZ 1,2, A*, 1964 *NZ*, 1965 *I, F, S*, 1966 *W, I, F, S*, 1967 *A, I, F, S, W, NZ*

Kayll, H E (Sunderland) 1878 *S*
Keeling, J H (Guy's Hospital) 1948 *A, W*
Keen, B W (Newcastle U) 1968 *W, I, F, S*
Keeton, G H (Leicester) 1904 *W, I, S*
Kelly, G A (Bedford) 1947 *W, I, S*, 1948 *W*
Kelly, T S (London Devonians) 1906 *W, I, S, F, SA*, 1907 *F, W, I, S*, 1908 *F, I, S*
Kemble, A T (Liverpool) 1885 *W, I*, 1887 *I*
Kemp, D T (Blackheath) 1935 *W*
Kemp, T A (Richmond) 1937 *W, I*, 1939 *S*, 1948 *A, W*
Kendall, P D (Birkenhead Park) 1901 *S*, 1902 *W*, 1903 *S*
Kendall-Carpenter, J MacG K (Oxford U, Bath) 1949 *I, F, S*, 1950 *W, I, F, S*, 1951 *I, F, S*, 1952 *SA, W, S, I, F*, 1953 *W, I, F, S*, 1954 *W, NZ, I, F*
Kendrew, D A (Leicester) 1930 *W, I*, 1933 *I, S*, 1934 *S*, 1935 *W, I*, 1936 *NZ, W, I*
Kennedy, R D (Camborne S of M) 1949 *I, F, S*
Kent, C P (Rosslyn Park) 1977 *S, I, F, W*, 1978 *F* (R)
Kent, T (Salford) 1891 *W, I, S*, 1892 *W, I, S*
Kershaw, C A (United Services, RN) 1920 *W, F, I, S*, 1921 *W, I, S, F*, 1922 *W, I, F, S*, 1923 *W, I, S, F*, 1924 *W, I, S*
Kewley, E (Liverpool) 1874 *S*, 1875 *S*, 1876 *I, S*, 1877 *I, S*, 1878 *S*
Kewney, A L (Leicester) 1906 *W, I, S, F*, 1909 *A, W, F, I, S*, 1911 *W, F, I, S*, 1912 *I, S*, 1913 *SA*
Key, A (O Cranleighans) 1930 *I*, 1933 *W*
Keyworth, M (Swansea) 1976 *A, W, S, I*
Kilner, B (Wakefield T) 1880 *I*
Kindersley, R S (Exeter) 1883 *W*, 1884 *S*, 1885 *W*
King, I (Harrogate) 1954 *W, NZ, I*
King, J A (Headingley) 1911 *W, F, I, S*, 1912 *W, I, S*, 1913 *SA, W, F, I, S*
King, Q E M A (Army) 1921 *S*
Kingston, P (Gloucester) 1975 *A 1,2*, 1979 *I, F, W*
Kitching, A E (Blackheath) 1913 *I*
Kittermaster, H J (Harlequins) 1925 *NZ, W, I*, 1926 *W, I, F, S*
Knight, F (Plymouth) 1909 *A*
Knight, P M (Bristol) 1972 *F, S, SA*
Knowles, E (Millom) 1896 *S*, 1897 *S*
Knowles, T C (Birkenhead Park) 1931 *S*
Krige, J A (Guy's Hospital) 1920 *W*

Labuschagne, N A (Harlequins, Guy's Hospital) 1953 *W*, 1955 *W, I, F, S*
Lagden, R O (Richmond) 1911 *S*
Laird, H C C (Harlequins) 1927 *W, I, S*, 1928 *NSW, W, I, F, S*, 1929 *W, I*
Lambert, D (Harlequins) 1907 *F*, 1908 *F, W, S*, 1911 *W, F, I*
Lampkowski, M S (Headingley) 1976 *A, W, S, I*
Lapage, W N (United Services, RN) 1908 *F, W, I, S*
Larter, P J (Northampton, RAF) 1967 *A, NZ*, 1968 *W, I, F, S*, 1969 *I, F, S, W, SA*, 1970 *I, W, F, S*, 1971 *W, I, F, S* (2[1C]), *P*, 1972 *SA*, 1973 *NZ, W*
Law, A F (Richmond) 1877 *S*
Law, D E (Birkenhead Park) 1927 *I*
Lawrence, Hon H A (Richmond) 1873 *S*, 1874 *S*, 1875 *I, S*
Lawrie, P W (Leicester) 1910 *S*, 1911 *S*
Lawson, R G (Workington) 1925 *I*
Lawson, T M (Workington) 1928 *NSW, W*
Leadbetter, M M (Broughton Park) 1970 *F*

Leadbetter, V H (Edinburgh Wands) 1954 *S, F*
Leake, W R M (Harlequins) 1891 *W, I, S*
Leather, G (Liverpool) 1907 *I*
Lee, F H (Marlborough N) 1876 *S*, 1877 *I*
Lee, H (Blackheath) 1907 *F*
Le Fleming, J (Blackheath) 1887 *W*
Leslie-Jones, F A (Richmond) 1895 *W, I*
Lewis, A O (Bath) 1952 *SA, W, S, I, F*, 1953 *W, I, F, S*, 1954 *F*
Leyland, R (Waterloo) 1935 *W, I, S*
Livesay, R O'H (Blackheath) 1898 *W*, 1899 *W*
Lloyd, R H (Harlequins) 1967 *NZ*, 1968 *W, I, F, S*
Locke, H M (Birkenhead Park) 1923 *S, F*, 1924 *W, F, S*, 1925 *W, I, S, F*, 1927 *W, I, S*
Lockwood, R E (Heckmondwike) 1887 *W, I, S*, 1889 *M*, 1891 *W, I, S*, 1892 *W, I, S*, 1893 *W, I*, 1894 *W, I*
Login, S H M (RN Coll) 1876 *I*
Lohden, F C (Blackheath) 1893 *W*
Longland, R J (Northampton) 1932 *S*, 1933 *W, S*, 1934 *W, I, S*, 1935 *W, I, S*, 1936 *NZ, W, I, S*, 1937 *W, I, S*, 1938 *W, I, S*
Lowe, C N (Cambridge U, Blackheath) 1913 *SA, W, F, I, S*, 1914 *W, I, S, F*, 1920 *W, F, I, S*, 1921 *W, I, S, F*, 1922 *W, I, F, S*, 1923 *W, I, S, F*
Lowrie, F (Wakefield T) 1889 *M*, 1890 *W*
Lowry, W M (Birkenhead Park) 1920 *F*
Lozowski R A P (Wasps) 1984 *A*
Luddington, W G E (Devonport Services) 1923 *W, I, S, F*, 1924 *W, I, F, S*, 1925 *W, I, S, F*, 1926 *W*
Luscombe, F (Gipsies) 1872 *S*, 1873 *S*, 1875 *I, S*, 1876 *I, S*
Luscombe, J H (Gipsies) 1871 *S*
Luxmoore, A F C C (Richmond) 1900 *S*, 1901 *W*
Luya, H F (Waterloo, Headingley) 1948 *W, I, S, F*, 1949 *W*
Lyon, A (Liverpool) 1871 *S*
Lyon, G H d'O (United Services, RN) 1908 *S*, 1909 *A*

McCanlis, M A (Gloucester) 1931 *W, I*
McFadyean, C W (Moseley) 1966 *I, F, S*, 1967 *A, I, F, S, W, NZ*, 1968 *W, I*
MacIlwaine, A H (United Services, Hull & E Riding) 1912 *W, I, S, F*, 1920 *I*
Mackie, O G (Wakefield T, Cambridge U) 1897 *S*, 1898 *I*
Mackinlay, J E H (St George's Hospital) 1872 *S*, 1873 *S*, 1875 *I*
MacLaren, W (Manchester) 1871 *S*
MacLennan, R R F (OMTs) 1925 *I, S, F*
McLeod, N F (RIE Coll) 1879 *S, I*
Madge, R J P (Exeter) 1948 *A, W, I, S*
Malir, F W S (Otley) 1930 *W, I, S*
Mangles, R H (Richmond) 1897 *W, I*
Manley, D C (Exeter) 1963 *W, I, F, S*
Mann, W E (United Services, Army) 1911 *W, F, I*
Mantell, N D (Rosslyn Park) 1975 *A* 1
Markendale, E T (Manchester R) 1880 *I*
Marques, R W D (Cambridge U, Harlequins) 1956 *W, I, S, F*, 1957 *W, I, F, S*, 1958 *W, A, I, F, S*, 1959 *W, I, F, S*, 1960 *W, I, F, S*, 1961 *SA, W*
Marquis, J C (Birkenhead Park) 1900 *I, S*
Marriott, C J B (Blackheath) 1884 *W, I, S*, 1886 *W, I, S*, 1887 *I*
Marriott, E E (Manchester) 1876 *I*
Marriott, V R (Harlequins) 1963 *NZ* 1,2, *A*, 1964 *NZ*
Marsden, G H (Morley) 1900 *W, I, S*
Marsh, H (RIE Coll) 1873 *S*
Marsh, J (Swinton) 1892 *I*
Marshall, H (Blackheath) 1893 *W*
Marshall, M W (Blackheath) 1873 *S*, 1874 *S*, 1875 *I, S*, 1876 *I, S*, 1877 *I, S*, 1878 *S, I*
Marshall, R M (Oxford U) 1938 *I, S*, 1939 *W, I, S*
Martin, C R (Bath) 1985 *F, S, I, W*
Martin, N O (Harlequins) 1972 *F* (R)
Martindale, S A (Kendal) 1929 *F*
Massey, E J (Leicester) 1925 *W, I, S*
Mathias, J L (Bristol) 1905 *W, I, S, NZ*
Matters, J C (RNE Coll) 1899 *S*
Matthews, J R C (Harlequins) 1949 *F, S*, 1950 *I, F, S*, 1952 *SA, W, S, I, F*
Maud, P (Blackheath) 1893 *W, I*
Maxwell, A W (New Brighton, Headingley) 1975 *A* 1, 1976 *A, W, S, I, F*, 1978 *F*

Maxwell-Hyslop, J E (Oxford U) 1922 *I, F, S*
Maynard, A F (Cambridge U) 1914 *W, I, S*
Meikle, G W C (Waterloo) 1934 *W, I, S*
Meikle, S S C (Waterloo) 1929 *S*
Mellish, F W (Blackheath) 1920 *W, F, I, S*, 1921 *W, I*
Melville, N D (Wasps) 1984 *A*, 1985 *I, W, NZ* 1,2, 1986 *W, S, I, F*, 1988 *F, W, S, I* 1
Merriam, L P B (Blackheath) 1920 *W, F*
Michell, A T (Oxford U) 1875 *I, S*, 1876 *I*
Middleton, B B (Birkenhead Park) 1882 *I*, 1883 *I*
Middleton, J A (Richmond) 1922 *S*
Miles, J H (Leicester) 1903 *W*
Millett, H (Richmond) 1920 *F*
Mills, F W (Marlborough N) 1872 *S*, 1873 *S*
Mills, S G F (Gloucester) 1981 *Arg* 1,2, 1983 *W*, 1984 *SA* 1, *A*
Mills, W A (Devonport A) 1906 *W, I, S, F, SA*, 1907 *F, W, I, S*, 1908 *F, W*
Milman, D L K (Bedford) 1937 *W*, 1938 *W, I, S*
Milton, C H (Camborne S of M) 1906 *I*
Milton, J G (Camborne S of M) 1904 *W, I, S*, 1905 *S*, 1907 *I*
Milton, W H (Marlborough N) 1874 *S*, 1875 *I*
Mitchell, F (Blackheath) 1895 *W, I, S*, 1896 *W, I, S*
Mitchell, W G (Richmond) 1890 *W, S, I*, 1891 *W, I, S*, 1893 *S*
Mobbs, E R (Northampton) 1909 *A, W, F, I, S*, 1910 *I, F*
Moberly, W O (Ravenscourt Park) 1872 *S*
Moore, B C (Nottingham) 1987 *S*, [*A, J, W*], 1988 *F, W, S, I* 1,2, *A* 1,2, *Fj, A*, 1989 *S, I, F, W*
Moore, E J (Blackheath) 1883 *I, S*
Moore, N J N H (Bristol) 1904 *W, I, S*
Moore, P B C (Blackheath) 1951 *W*
Moore, W K T (Leicester) 1947 *W, I*, 1949 *F, S*, 1950 *I, F, S*
Mordell, R J (Rosslyn Park) 1978 *W*
Morfitt, S (W Hartlepool) 1894 *W, I, S*, 1896 *W, I, S*
Morgan, J R (Hawick) 1920 *W*
Morgan, W G D (Medicals, Newcastle) 1960 *W, I, F, S*, 1961 *SA, W, I, F, S*
Morley, A J (Bristol) 1972 *SA*, 1973 *NZ, W, I*, 1975 *S, A* 1,2
Morris, A D W (United Services, RN) 1909 *A, W, F*
Morris, C D (Liverpool St Helens) 1988 *A*, 1989 *S, I, F, W*
Morrison, P H (Cambridge U) 1890 *W, S, I*, 1891 *I*
Morse, S (Marlborough N) 1873 *S*, 1874 *S*, 1875 *S*
Mortimer, W (Marlborough N) 1899 *W*
Morton, H J S (Blackheath) 1909 *I, S*, 1910 *W, I*
Moss, F (Broughton) 1885 *W, I*, 1886 *W*
Mycock, J (Sale) 1947 *W, I, S, F*, 1948 *A*
Myers, E (Bradford) 1920 *I, S*, 1921 *W, I*, 1922 *W, I, F, S*, 1923 *W, I, S, F*, 1924 *W, I, F, S*, 1925 *S, F*
Myers, H (Keighley) 1898 *I*

Nanson, W M B (Carlisle) 1907 *F, W*
Nash, E H (Richmond) 1875 *I*
Neale, B A (Rosslyn Park) 1951 *I, F, S*
Neale, M E (Blackheath) 1912 *F*
Neame, S (O Cheltonians) 1879 *S, I*, 1880 *I, S*
Neary, A (Broughton Park) 1971 *W, I, F, S* (2[1C]), *P*, 1972 *W, I, F, S, SA*, 1973 *NZ, W, I, F, S, NZ, A*, 1974 *S, I, F, W*, 1975 *I, F, S, A* 1, 1976 *A, W, S, I, F*, 1977 *I*, 1978 *F* (R), 1979 *S, I, F, W, NZ*, 1980 *I, F, W, S*
Nelmes, B G (Cardiff) 1975 *A* 1,2, 1978 *W, S, I, NZ*
Newbold, C J (Blackheath) 1904 *W, I, S*, 1905 *W, I, S*
Newman, S C (Oxford U) 1947 *F*, 1948 *A, W*
Newton, A W (Blackheath) 1907 *S*
Newton, P A (Blackheath) 1882 *S*
Newton-Thompson, J O (Oxford U) 1947 *S, F*
Nichol, W (Brighouse R) 1892 *W, S*
Nicholas, P L (Exeter) 1902 *W*
Nicholson, B E (Harlequins) 1938 *W, I*
Nicholson, E S (Leicester) 1935 *W, I, S*, 1936 *NZ, W*
Nicholson, E T (Birkenhead Park) 1900 *W, I*
Nicholson, T (Rockcliff) 1893 *I*
Ninnes, B F (Coventry) 1971 *W*
Norman, D J (Leicester) 1932 *SA, W*
North, E H G (Blackheath) 1891 *W, I, S*
Northmore, S (Millom) 1897 *I*
Novak, M J (Harlequins) 1970 *W, S, F*

Novis, A L (Blackheath) 1929 *S, F*, 1930 *W, I, F*, 1933 *I, S*

Oakeley, F E (United Services, RN) 1913 *S*, 1914 *I, S, F*
Oakes, R F (Hartlepool R) 1897 *W, I, S*, 1898 *I, S, W*, 1899 *W, S*
Oakley, L F L (Bedford) 1951 *W*
Obolensky, A (Oxford U) 1936 *NZ, W, I, S*
Old, A G B (Middlesbrough, Leicester, Sheffield) 1972 *W, I, F, S, SA*, 1973 *NZ, A*, 1974 *S, I, F, W*, 1975 *I, A 2*, 1976 *S, I*, 1978 *F*
Oldham, W L (Coventry) 1908 *S*, 1909 *A*
O'Neill, A (Teignmouth, Torquay A) 1901 *W, I, S*
Openshaw, W E (Manchester) 1879 *I*
Orwin, J (Gloucester, RAF, Bedford) 1985 *R, F, S, I, W, NZ* 1,2, 1988 *F, W, S, I* 1,2, *A* 1,2
Osborne, R R (Manchester) 1871 *S*
Osborne, S H (Oxford U) 1905 *S*
Oti, C (Cambridge U, Nottingham, Wasps) 1988 *S, I* 1, 1989 *S, I, F, W*
Oughtred, B (Hartlepool R) 1901 *S*, 1902 *W, I, S*, 1903 *W, I*
Owen, J E (Coventry) 1963 *W, I, F, S, A*, 1964 *NZ*, 1965 *W, I, F, S*, 1966 *I, F, S*, 1967 *NZ*
Owen-Smith, H G O (St Mary's Hospital) 1934 *W, I, S*, 1936 *NZ, W, I, S*, 1937 *W, I, S*

Page, J J (Bedford, Northampton) 1971 *W, I, F, S*, 1975 *S*
Pallant, J N (Notts) 1967 *I, F, S*
Palmer, A C (London Hospital) 1909 *I, S*
Palmer, F H (Richmond) 1905 *W*
Palmer, G V (Richmond) 1928 *I, F, S*
Palmer, J A (Bath) 1984 *SA* 1,2, 1986 *I* (R)
Pargetter, T A (Coventry) 1962 *S*, 1963 *F, NZ* 1
Parker, G W (Gloucester) 1938 *I, S*
Parker, Hon S (Liverpool) 1874 *S*, 1875 *S*
Parsons, E I (RAF) 1939 *S*
Parsons, M J (Northampton) 1968 *W, I, F, S*
Patterson, W M (Sale) 1961 *SA, S*
Pattisson, R M (Blackheath) 1883 *I, S*
Paul, J E (RIE Coll) 1875 *S*
Payne, A T (Bristol) 1935 *I, S*
Payne, C M (Harlequins) 1964 *I, F, S*, 1965 *I, F, S*, 1966 *W, I, F, S*
Payne, J H (Broughton) 1882 *S*, 1883 *W, I, S*, 1884 *I*, 1885 *W, I*
Pearce, G S (Northampton) 1979 *S, I, F, W*, 1981 *Arg* 1,2, 1982 *A, S*, 1983 *F, W, S, I, NZ*, 1984 *S, SA* 2, *A*, 1985 *R, F, S, I, W, NZ* 1,2, 1986 *W, S, I, F*, 1987 *I, F, W, S, [A, US, W]*, 1988 *Fj*
Pearson, A W (Blackheath) 1875 *I, S*, 1876 *I, S*, 1877 *S*, 1878 *S, I*
Peart, T G A H (Hartlepool R) 1964 *F, S*
Pease, F E (Hartlepool R) 1887 *I*
Penny, S H (Leicester) 1909 *A*
Penny, W J (United Hospitals) 1878 *I*, 1879 *S, I*
Percival, L J (Rugby) 1891 *I*, 1892 *I*, 1893 *S*
Periton, H G (Waterloo) 1925 *W*, 1926 *W, I, F, S*, 1927 *W, I, S, F*, 1928 *NSW, I, F, S*, 1929 *W, I, S, F*, 1930 *W, I, F, S*
Perrott, E S (O Cheltonians) 1875 *I*
Perry, D G (Bedford) 1963 *F, S, NZ* 1,2, *A*, 1964 *NZ, W, I*, 1965 *W, I, F, S*, 1966 *W, I, F*
Perry, S V (Cambridge U, Waterloo) 1947 *W, I*, 1948 *A, W, I, S, F*
Peters, J (Plymouth) 1906 *S, F*, 1907 *I, S*, 1908 *W*
Phillips, C (Birkenhead Park) 1880 *S*, 1881 *I, S*
Phillips, M S (Fylde) 1958 *A, I, F, S*, 1959 *W, I, F, S*, 1960 *W, I, F, S*, 1961 *W*, 1963 *W, I, F, S, NZ* 1,2, *A*, 1964 *NZ, W, I, F, S*
Pickering, A S (Harrogate) 1907 *I*
Pickering, R D A (Bradford) 1967 *I, F, S, W*, 1968 *F, S*
Pickles, R C W (Bristol) 1922 *I, F*
Pierce, R (Liverpool) 1898 *I*, 1903 *S*
Pilkington, W N (Cambridge U) 1898 *S*
Pillman, C H (Blackheath) 1910 *W, I, F, S*, 1911 *W, F, I, S*, 1912 *W, F*, 1913 *SA, W, F, I, S*, 1914 *W, I, S*
Pillman, R L (Blackheath) 1914 *F*
Pinch, J (Lancaster) 1896 *W, I*, 1897 *S*
Pinching, W W (Guy's Hospital) 1872 *S*
Pitman, I J (Oxford U) 1922 *S*

Plummer, K C (Bristol) 1969 *W*, 1976 *S, I, F*
Poole, F O (Oxford U) 1895 *W, I, S*
Poole, R W (Hartlepool R) 1896 *S*
Pope, E B (Blackheath) 1931 *W, S, F*
Portus, G V (Blackheath) 1908 *F, I*
Poulton, R W (later **Poulton Palmer**) (Oxford U, Harlequins, Liverpool) 1909 *F, I, S*, 1910 *W*, 1911 *S*, 1912 *W, I, S*, 1913 *SA, W, F, I, S*, 1914 *W, I, S, F*
Powell, D L (Northampton) 1966 *W, I*, 1969 *I, F, S, W*, 1971 *W, I, F, S* (2[1C])
Pratten, W E (Blackheath) 1927 *S, F*
Preece, I (Coventry) 1948 *I, S, F*, 1949 *F, S*, 1950 *W, I, F, S*, 1951 *W, I, F*
Preece, P S (Coventry) 1972 *SA*, 1973 *NZ, W, I, F, S, NZ*, 1975 *I, F, W, A* 2, 1976 *W* (R)
Preedy, M (Gloucester) 1984 *SA* 1
Prentice, F D (Leicester) 1928 *I, F, S*
Prescott, R E (Harlequins) 1937 *W, I*, 1938 *I*, 1939 *W, I, S*
Preston, N J (Richmond) 1979 *NZ*, 1980 *I, F*
Price, H L (Harlequins) 1922 *I, S*, 1923 *W, I*
Price, J (Coventry) 1961 *I*
Price, P L A (RIE Coll) 1877 *I, S*, 1878 *S*
Price, T W (Cheltenham) 1948 *S, F*, 1949 *W, I, F, S*
Probyn, J A (Wasps) 1988 *F, W, S, I* 1,2, *A* 1,2, *A*, 1989 *S, I*
Prout, D H (Northampton) 1968 *W, I*
Pullin, J V (Bristol) 1966 *W*, 1968 *W, I, F, S*, 1969 *I, F, S, W, SA*, 1970 *I, W, S, F*, 1971 *W, I, F, S,* (2[1C]), *P*, 1972 *W, I, F, S, SA*, 1973 *NZ, W, I, F, S, NZ, A*, 1974 *S, I, F, W*, 1975 *I, W*, (R), *S, A*, 1,2, 1976 *F*
Purdy, S J (Rugby) 1962 *S*
Pyke, J (St Helens Recreation) 1892 *W*
Pym, J A (Blackheath) 1912 *W, I, S, F*

Quinn, J P (New Brighton) 1954 *W, NZ, I, S, F*

Rafter, M (Bristol) 1977 *S, F, W*, 1978 *F, W, S, I, NZ*, 1979 *S, I, F, W, NZ*, 1980 *W* (R), 1981 *W, Arg* 1,2
Ralston, C W (Richmond) 1971 *S* (C), *P*, 1972 *W, I, F, S, SA*, 1973 *NZ, W, I, F, S, NZ, A*, 1974 *S, I, F, W*, 1975 *I, F, W, S*
Ramsden, H E (Bingley) 1898 *W, S*
Ranson, J M (Rosslyn Park) 1963 *NZ* 1,2, *A*, 1964 *W, I, F, S*
Raphael, J E (OMTs) 1902 *W, I, S*, 1905 *W, S, NZ*, 1906 *W, S, F*
Ravenscroft, J (Birkenhead Park) 1881 *I*
Rawlinson, W C W (Blackheath) 1876 *S*
Redfern, S (Leicester) 1984 *I* (R)
Redman, N C (Bath) 1984 *A*, 1986 *S* (R), 1987 *I, S, [A, J, W]*, 1988 *Fj*
Redmond, G F (Cambridge U) 1970 *F*
Redwood, B W (Bristol) 1968 *W, I*
Rees, G W (Nottingham) 1984 *SA* 2 (R), *A*, 1986 *I, F*, 1987 *F, W, S, [A, J, US, W]*, 1988 *S*(R), *I* 1,2, *A* 1,2, *Fj*, 1989 *W, F, S*
Reeve, J S R (Harlequins) 1929 *F*, 1930 *W, I, F, S*, 1931 *W, I, S*
Regan, M (Liverpool) 1953 *W, I, F, S*, 1954 *W, NZ, I, S, F*, 1956 *I, S, F*
Rendall, P A G (Wasps) 1984 *W, SA* 2, 1986 *W, S*, 1987 *I, F, S, [A, J, W]*, 1988 *F, W, S, I* 1,2, *A* 1,2, *A*, 1989 *S, I, F, W*
Rew, H (Blackheath) 1929 *S, F*, 1930 *F, S*, 1931 *W, S, F*, 1934 *W, I, S*
Reynolds, F J (O Cranleighans) 1937 *S*, 1938 *I, S*
Reynolds, S (Richmond) 1900 *W, I, S*, 1901 *I*
Rhodes, J (Castleford) 1896 *W, I, S*
Richards, D (Leicester) 1986 *I, F*, 1987 *S, [A, J, US, W]*, 1988 *F, W, S, I* 1, *A* 1,2, *Fj, A*, 1989 *S, I, F, W*
Richards, E E (Plymouth A) 1929 *S, F*
Richards, J (Bradford) 1891 *W, I, S*
Richards, S B (Richmond) 1965 *W, I, F, S*, 1967 *A, I, F, S, W*
Richardson, J V (Birkenhead Park) 1928 *NSW, W, I, F, S*
Richardson, W R (Manchester) 1881 *I*
Rickards, C H (Gipsies) 1873 *S*
Rimmer, G (Waterloo) 1949 *W, I*, 1950 *W*, 1951 *W, I, F*, 1952 *SA, W*, 1954 *W, NZ, I, S*
Rimmer, L I (Bath) 1961 *SA, W, I, F, S*
Ripley, A G (Rosslyn Park) 1972 *W, I, F, S, SA*, 1973

NZ, W, I, F, S, NZ, A, 1974 *S, I, F, W*, 1975 *I, F, S, A* 1,2, 1976 *A, W, S*
Risman, A B W (Loughborough Colls) 1959 *W, I, F, S*, 1961 *SA, W, I, F*
Ritson, J A S (Northern) 1910 *F, S*, 1912 *F*, 1913 *SA, W, F, I, S*
Rittson-Thomas, G C (Oxford U) 1951 *W, I, F*
Robbins, G L (Coventry) 1986 *W, S*
Robbins, P G D (Oxford U, Moseley, Coventry) 1956 *W, I, S, F*, 1957 *W, I, F, S*, 1958 *W, A, I, S*, 1960 *W, I, F, S*, 1961 *SA, W*, 1962 *S*
Roberts, A D (Northern) 1911 *W, F, I, S*, 1912 *I, S, F*, 1914 *I*
Roberts, E W (RNE Coll) 1901 *W, I*, 1905 *NZ*, 1906 *W, I*, 1907 *S*
Roberts, G D (Harlequins) 1907 *S*, 1908 *F, W*
Roberts, J (Sale) 1960 *W, I, F, S*, 1961 *SA, W, I, F, S*, 1962 *W, I, F, S*, 1963 *W, I, F, S*, 1964 *NZ*
Roberts, R S (Coventry) 1932 *I*
Roberts, S (Swinton) 1887 *W, I*
Roberts, V G (Penryn, Harlequins) 1947 *F*, 1949 *W, I, F, S*, 1950 *I, F, S*, 1951 *W, I, F, S*, 1956 *W, I, S, F*
Robertshaw, A R (Bradford) 1886 *W, I, S*, 1887 *W, S*
Robinson, A (Blackheath) 1889 *M*, 1890 *W, S, I*
Robinson, E F (Coventry) 1954 *S*, 1961 *I, F, S*
Robinson, G C (Percy Park) 1897 *I, S*, 1898 *I*, 1899 *W*, 1900 *I, S*, 1901 *I, S*
Robinson, J J (Headingley) 1893 *S*, 1902 *W, I, S*
Robinson, R A (Bath) 1988 *A* 2, *Fj, A*, 1989 *S, I, F, W*
Robson, A (Northern) 1924 *W, I, F, S*, 1926 *W*
Robson, M (Oxford U) 1930 *W, I, F, S*
Rogers, D P (Bedford) 1961 *I, F, S*, 1962 *W, I, F*, 1963 *W, I, F, S, NZ* 1,2, *A*, 1964 *NZ, W, I, F, S*, 1965 *W, I, F, S*, 1966 *W, I, F, S*, 1967 *A, S, W, NZ*, 1969 *I, F, S, W*
Rogers, J H (Moseley) 1890 *W, S, I*, 1891 *S*
Rogers, W L Y (Blackheath) 1905 *W, I*
Rollitt, D M (Bristol) 1967 *I, F, S, W*, 1969 *I, F, S, W*, 1975 *S, A* 1,2
Roncoroni, A D S (West Herts, Richmond) 1933 *W, I, S*
Rose, W M H (Cambridge U, Coventry, Harlequins) 1981 *I, F*, 1982 *A, S, I*, 1987 *I, F, W, S, S, [A]*
Rossborough, P A (Coventry) 1971 *W*, 1973 *NZ, A*, 1974 *S, I*, 1975 *I, F*
Rosser, D W A (Wasps) 1965 *W, I, F, S*, 1966 *W*
Rotherham, Alan (Richmond) 1883 *W, S*, 1884 *W, S*, 1885 *W, I*, 1886 *W, I, S*, 1887 *W, I, S*
Rotherham, Arthur (Richmond) 1898 *S, W*, 1899 *W, I, S*
Roughley, D (Liverpool) 1973 *A*, 1974 *S, I*
Rowell, R E (Leicester) 1964 *W*, 1965 *W*
Rowley, A J (Coventry) 1932 *SA*
Rowley, H C (Manchester) 1879 *S, I*, 1880 *I, S*, 1881 *I, W, S*, 1882 *I, S*
Royds, P M R (Blackheath) 1898 *S, W*, 1899 *W*
Royle, A V (Broughton R) 1889 *M*
Rudd, E L (Liverpool) 1965 *W, I, S*, 1966 *W, I, S*
Russell, R F (Leicester) 1905 *NZ*
Rutherford, D (Percy Park, Gloucester) 1960 *W, I, F, S*, 1961 *SA*, 1965 *W, I, F, S*, 1966 *W, I, F, S*, 1967 *NZ*
Ryalls H J (N Brighton) 1885 *W, I*
Ryan, P H (Richmond) 1955 *W, I*

Sadler, E H (Army) 1933 *I, S*
Sagar, J W (Cambridge U) 1901 *W, I*
Salmon, J L B (Harlequins) 1985 *NZ* 1,2, 1986 *W, S*, 1987 *I, F, S, W, S, [A, J, US, W]*
Sample, C H (Cambridge U) 1884 *I*, 1885 *I*, 1886 *S*
Sanders, D L (Harlequins) 1954 *W, NZ, I, S, F*, 1956 *W, I, S, F*
Sanders, F W (Plymouth A) 1923 *I, S, F*
Sandford, J R P (Marlborough N) 1906 *I*
Sangwin, R D (Hull and E Riding) 1964 *NZ, W*
Sargent, G A F (Gloucester) 1981 *I* (R)
Savage, K F (Northampton) 1966 *W, I, F, S*, 1967 *A, I, F, S, W, NZ*, 1968 *W, F, S*
Sawyer, C M (Broughton) 1880 *S*, 1881 *I*
Saxby, L E (Gloucester) 1932 *SA, W*
Schofield, J W (Manchester) 1880 *I*
Scholfield, J A (Preston Grasshoppers) 1911 *W*
Schwarz, R O (Richmond) 1899 *S*, 1901 *W, I*
Scorfield, E S (Percy Park) 1910 *F*

Scott, C T (Blackheath) 1900 *W, I*, 1901 *I, W*
Scott, E K (St Mary's Hospital, Redruth) 1947 *W*, 1948 *A, W, I, S*
Scott, F S (Bristol) 1907 *W*
Scott, H (Manchester) 1955 *F*
Scott, J P (Rosslyn Park, Cardiff) 1978 *F, W, S, I, NZ*, 1979 *S* (R), *I, F, W, NZ*, 1980 *I, F, W, S*, 1981 *W, S, I, F, Arg* 1,2, 1982 *I, F, W*, 1983 *F, W, S, I, NZ*, 1984 *S, I, F, W, SA* 1,2
Scott, J S M (Oxford U) 1958 *F*
Scott, M T (Cambridge U) 1887 *I*, 1890 *S, I*
Scott, W M (Cambridge U) 1889 *M*
Seddon, R L (Broughton R) 1887 *W, I, S*
Sellar, K A (United Services, RN) 1927 *W, I, S*, 1928 *NSW, W, I, F*
Sever, H S (Sale) 1936 *NZ, W, I, S*, 1937 *W, I, S*, 1938 *W, I, S*
Shackleton, I R (Cambridge U) 1969 *SA*, 1970 *I, W, S*
Sharp, R A W (Oxford U, Wasps, Redruth) 1960 *W, I, F, S*, 1961 *I, F*, 1962 *W, I, F*, 1963 *W, I, F, S*, 1967 *A*
Shaw, C H (Moseley) 1906 *S, SA*, 1907 *F, W, I, S*
Shaw, F (Cleckheaton) 1898 *I*
Shaw, J F (RNE Coll) 1898 *S, W*
Sheppard, A (Bristol) 1981 *W* (R), 1985 *W*
Sherrard, C W (Blackheath) 1871 *S*, 1872 *S*
Sherriff, G A (Saracens) 1966 *S*, 1967 *A, NZ*
Shewring, H E (Bristol) 1905 *I, NZ*, 1906 *W, S, F, SA*, 1907 *F, W, I, S*
Shooter, J H (Morley) 1899 *I, S*, 1900 *I, S*
Shuttleworth, D W (Headingley) 1951 *S*, 1953 *S*
Sibree, H J H (Harlequins) 1908 *F*, 1909 *I, S*
Silk, N (Harlequins) 1965 *W, I, F, S*
Simms, K G (Cambridge U, Liverpool, Wasps) 1985 *R, F, S, I, W*, 1986 *I, F*, 1987 *I, F, W, [A, J, W]*, 1988 *F, W*
Simpson, C P (Harlequins) 1965 *W*
Simpson, P D (Bath) 1983 *NZ*, 1984 *S*, 1987 *I*
Simpson, T (Rockcliff) 1902 *S*, 1903 *W, I, S*, 1904 *I, S*, 1905 *I, S*, 1906 *S, SA*, 1909 *F*
Skinner, M G (Harlequins) 1988 *F, W, S, I* 1,2
Sladen, G M (United Services, RN) 1929 *W, I, S*
Slemen, M A C (Liverpool) 1976 *I, F*, 1977 *S, I, F, W*, 1978 *F, W, S, I, NZ*, 1979 *S, I, F, W, NZ*, 1980 *I, F, W, S*, 1981 *W, S, I, F*, 1982 *A, S, I, F, W*, 1983 *NZ*, 1984 *S*
Slocock, L A N (Liverpool) 1907 *F, W, I, S*, 1908 *F, W, I, S*
Slow, C F (Leicester) 1934 *S*
Small, H D (Oxford U) 1950 *W, I, F, S*
Smallwood, A M (Leicester) 1920 *F, I*, 1921 *W, I, S, F*, 1922 *I, S*, 1923 *W, I, S, F*, 1925 *I, S*
Smart, C E (Newport) 1979 *F, W, NZ*, 1981 *S, I, F, Arg* 1,2, 1982 *A, S, I, F, W*, 1983 *F, W, S, I*
Smart, S E J (Gloucester) 1913 *SA, W, F, I, S*, 1914 *W, I, S, F*, 1920 *W, I, S*
Smeddle, R W (Cambridge U) 1929 *W, I, S*, 1931 *F*
Smith, C C (Gloucester) 1901 *W*
Smith, D F (Richmond) 1910 *W, I*
Smith, J V (Cambridge U, Rosslyn Park) 1950 *W, I, F, S*
Smith, K (Roundhay) 1974 *F, W*, 1975 *W, S*
Smith, M J K (Oxford U) 1956 *W*
Smith, S J (Sale) 1973 *I, F, S, A*, 1974 *I, F*, 1975 *W* (R), 1976 *F*, 1977 *F* (R), 1979 *NZ*, 1980 *I, F, W, S*, 1981 *W, S, I, F, Arg* 1,2, 1982 *A, S, I, F, W*, 1983 *F, W, S*
Smith, S R (Richmond) 1959 *W, F, S*, 1964 *F, S*
Smith, S T (Wasps) 1985 *R, F, S, I, W, NZ* 1,2, 1986 *W, S*
Smith, T A (Northampton) 1951 *W*
Soane, F (Bath) 1893 *S*, 1894 *W, I, S*
Sobey, W H (O Millhillians) 1930 *W, F, S*, 1932 *SA, W*
Solomon, B (Redruth) 1910 *W*
Sparks, R H W (Plymouth A) 1928 *I, F, S*, 1929 *W, I, S*, 1931 *I, S, F*
Speed, H (Castleford) 1894 *W, I, S*, 1896 *S*
Spence, F W (Birkenhead Park) 1890 *I*
Spencer, J (Harlequins) 1966 *W*
Spencer, J S (Cambridge U, Headingley) 1969 *I, F, S, W, SA*, 1970 *I, W, S, F*, 1971 *W, I, S* (2[1C]), *P*
Spong, R S (O Millhillians) 1929 *F*, 1930 *W, I, F, S*, 1931 *F*, 1932 *SA, W*

Spooner, R H (Liverpool) 1903 *W*
Springman, H H (Liverpool) 1879 *S*, 1887 *S*
Spurling, A (Blackheath) 1882 *I*
Spurling, N (Blackheath) 1886 *I, S*, 1887 *W*
Squires, P J (Harrogate) 1973 *F, S, NZ, A*, 1974 *S, I, F, W*, 1975 *I, F, W, S, A* 1,2, 1976 *A, W*, 1977 *S, I, F, W*, 1978 *F, W, S, I, NZ*, 1979 *S, I, F, W*
Stafford, R C (Bedford) 1912 *W, I, S, F*
Stafford, W F H (RE) 1874 *S*
Stanbury, E (Plymouth A) 1926 *W, I, S*, 1927 *W, I, S, F*, 1928 *NSW, W, I, F, S*, 1929 *W, I, S, F*
Standing, G (Blackheath) 1883 *W, I*
Stanger-Leathes, C F (Northern) 1905 *I*
Stark, K J (O Alleynians) 1927 *W, I, S, F*, 1928 *NSW, W, I, F, S*
Starks, A (Castleford) 1896 *W, I*
Starmer-Smith, N C (Harlequins) 1969 *SA*, 1970 *I, W, S, F*, 1971 *S* (C), *P*
Start, S P (United Services, RN) 1907 *S*
Steeds, J H (Saracens) 1949 *F, S*, 1950 *I, F, S*
Steele-Bodger, M R (Cambridge U) 1947 *W, I, S, F*, 1948 *A, W, I, S, F*
Steinthal, F E (Ilkley) 1913 *W, F*
Stevens, C B (Penzance-Newlyn, Harlequins) 1969 *SA*, 1970 *I, W, S*, 1971 *P*, 1972 *W, I, F, S, SA*, 1973 *NZ, W, I, F, S, NZ, A*, 1974 *S, I, F, W*, 1975 *I, F, W, S*
Still, E R (Oxford U, Ravenscourt P) 1873 *S*
Stirling, R V (Leicester, RAF, Wasps) 1951 *W, I, F, S*, 1952 *SA, W, S, I, F*, 1953 *W, I, F, S*, 1954 *W, NZ, I, S, F*
Stoddart, A E (Blackheath) 1885 *W, I*, 1886 *W, I, S*, 1889 *M*, 1890 *W, I*, 1893 *W, S*
Stoddart, W B (Liverpool) 1897 *W, I, S*
Stokes, F (Blackheath) 1871 *S*, 1872 *S*, 1873 *S*
Stokes, L (Blackheath) 1875 *I*, 1876 *S*, 1877 *I, S*, 1878 *S*, 1879 *S, I*, 1880 *I, S*, 1881 *I, W, S*
Stone, F le S (Blackheath) 1914 *F*
Stoop, A D (Harlequins) 1905 *S*, 1906 *S, F, SA*, 1907 *F, W*, 1910 *W, I, S*, 1911 *W, F, I, S*, 1912 *W, S*
Stoop, F M (Harlequins) 1910 *S*, 1911 *F, I*, 1913 *SA*
Stout, F M (Richmond) 1897 *W, I*, 1898 *I, S, W*, 1899 *I, S*, 1903 *S*, 1904 *W, I, S*, 1905 *W, I, S*
Stout, P W (Richmond) 1898 *S, W*, 1899 *W, I, S*
Stringer, N C (Wasps) 1982 *A* (R), 1983 *NZ* (R), 1984 *SA* 1 (R), *A*, 1985 *R*
Strong, E L (Oxford U) 1884 *W, I, S*
Summerscales, G E (Durham City) 1906 *NZ*
Sutcliffe, J W (Heckmondwike) 1889 *M*
Swarbrick, D W (Oxford U) 1947 *W, I, F*, 1948 *A, W*, 1949 *I*
Swayne, D H (Oxford U) 1931 *W*
Swayne, J W R (Bridgwater) 1929 *W*
Swift, A H (Swansea) 1981 *Arg* 1,2, 1983 *F, W, S*, 1984 *SA* 2
Syddall, J P (Waterloo) 1982 *I*, 1984 *A*
Sykes, A R V (Blackheath) 1914 *F*
Sykes, F D (Northampton) 1955 *F, S*, 1963 *NZ* 2, *A*
Sykes, P W (Wasps) 1948 *F*, 1952 *S, I, F*, 1953 *W, I, F*
Syrett, R E (Wasps) 1958 *W, A, I, F*, 1960 *W, I, F, S*, 1962 *W, I, F*

Tallent, J A (Cambridge U, Blackheath) 1931 *S, F*, 1932 *SA, W*, 1935 *I*
Tanner, C C (Cambridge U, Gloucester) 1930 *S*, 1932 *SA, W, I, S*
Tarr, F N (Leicester) 1909 *A, W, F*, 1913 *S*
Tatham, W M (Oxford U) 1882 *S*, 1883 *W, I, S*, 1884 *W, I, S*
Taylor, A S (Blackheath) 1883 *W, I*, 1886 *W, I*
Taylor, E W (Rockcliff) 1892 *I*, 1893 *I*, 1894 *W, I, S*, 1895 *W, I, S*, 1896 *W, I*, 1897 *W, I, S* 1899 *I*
Taylor, F (Leicester) 1920 *F, I*
Taylor, F M (Leicester) 1914 *W*
Taylor, H H (Blackheath) 1879 *S*, 1880 *S*, 1881 *I, W*, 1882 *S*
Taylor, J T (W Hartlepool) 1897 *I*, 1899 *I*, 1900 *I*, 1901 *W, I*, 1902 *W, I, S* 1903 *W, I*, 1905 *S*
Taylor, P J (Northampton) 1955 *W, I*, 1962 *W, I, F, S*
Taylor, R B (Northampton) 1966 *W*, 1967 *I, F, S, W, NZ*, 1969 *F, S, W, SA*, 1970 *I, W, S, F*, 1971 *S* (2[1C])
Taylor, W J (Blackheath) 1928 *NSW, W, I, F, S*
Teague, M C (Gloucester) 1985 *F* (R), *NZ* 1,2, 1989 *S, I, F, W*

Teden, D E (Richmond) 1939 *W, I, S*
Teggin, A (Broughton R) 1884 *I*, 1885 *W*, 1886 *I, S*, 1887 *I, S*
Tetley, T S (Bradford) 1876 *S*
Thomas, C (Barnstaple) 1895 *W, I, S*, 1899 *I*
Thompson, P H (Headingley, Waterloo) 1956 *W, I, S, F*, 1957 *W, I, F, S*, 1958 *W, A, I, F, S*, 1959 *W, I, F, S*
Thomson, G T (Halifax) 1878 *S*, 1882 *I, S*, 1883 *W, I, S*, 1884 *I, S*, 1885 *I*
Thomson, W B (Blackheath) 1892 *W*, 1895 *W, I, S*
Thorne, J D (Bristol) 1963 *W, I, F*
Tindall, V R (Liverpool U) 1951 *W, I, F, S*
Tobin, F (Liverpool) 1871 *S*
Todd, A F (Blackheath) 1900 *I, S*
Todd, R (Manchester) 1877 *S*
Toft, H B (Waterloo) 1936 *S*, 1937 *W, I, S*, 1938 *W, I, S*, 1939 *W, I, S*
Toothill, J T (Bradford) 1890 *S, I*, 1891 *W, I*, 1892 *W, I, S*, 1893 *W, I, S*, 1894 *W, I*
Tosswill, L R (Exeter) 1902 *W, I, S*
Touzel, C J C (Liverpool) 1877 *I, S*
Towell, A C (Bedford) 1948 *F*, 1951 *S*
Travers, B H (Harlequins) 1947 *W, I*, 1948 *A, W*, 1949 *F, S*
Treadwell, W T (Wasps) 1966 *I, F, S*
Trick, D M (Bath) 1983 *I*, 1984 *SA* 1
Tristram, H B (Oxford U) 1883 *S*, 1884 *W, S*, 1885 *W*, 1887 *S*
Troop, C L (Aldershot S) 1933 *I, S*
Tucker, J S (Bristol) 1922 *W*, 1925 *NZ, W, I, S, F*, 1926 *W, I, F, S*, 1927 *W, I, S, F*, 1928 *NSW, W, I, F, S*, 1929 *W, I, F*, 1930 *W, I, F, S*, 1931 *W*
Tucker, W E (Blackheath) 1894 *W, I*, 1895 *W, I, S*
Tucker, W E (Blackheath) 1926 *I*, 1930 *W, I, F*
Turner, D P (Richmond) 1871 *S*, 1872 *S*, 1873 *S*, 1874 *S*, 1875 *I, S*
Turner, E B (St George's Hospital) 1876 *I*, 1877 *I*, 1878 *I*
Turner, G R (St George's Hospital) 1876 *S*
Turner, H J C (Manchester) 1871 *S*
Turner, M F (Blackheath) 1948 *S, F*
Turquand-Young, D (Richmond) 1928 *NSW, W*, 1929 *I, S, F*
Twynam, H T (Richmond) 1879 *I*, 1880 *I*, 1881 *W*, 1882 *I*, 1883 *I*, 1884 *W, I, S*

Underwood, A M (Exeter) 1962 *W, I, F, S*, 1964 *I*
Underwood, R (Leicester, RAF) 1984 *I, F, W, A*, 1985 *R, F, S, I, W*, 1986 *W, I, F*, 1987 *I, F, W, S*, [A, J, W], 1988 *F, W, S, I* 1,2, *A* 1,2, *Fj, A*, 1989 *S, I, F, W*
Unwin, E J (Rosslyn Park, Army) 1937 *S*, 1938 *W, I, S*
Unwin, G T (Blackheath) 1898 *S*
Uren, R (Waterloo) 1948 *I, S, F*, 1950 *I*
Uttley, R M (Gosforth) 1973 *I, F, S, NZ, A*, 1974 *I, F, W*, 1975 *F, W, S, A* 1,2, 1977 *S, I, F, W*, 1978 *NZ*, 1979 *S*, 1980 *I, F, W, S*

Valentine, J (Swinton) 1890 *W*, 1896 *W, I, S*
Vanderspar, C H R (Richmond) 1873 *S*
Van Ryneveld, C B (Oxford U) 1949 *W, I, F, S*
Varley, H (Liversedge) 1892 *S*
Vassall, H (Blackheath) 1881 *W, S*, 1882 *I, S*, 1883 *W*
Vassall, H H (Blackheath) 1908 *I*
Vaughan, D B (Headingley) 1948 *A, W, I, S*, 1949 *I, F, S*, 1950 *W*
Vaughan-Jones, A (Army) 1932 *I, S*, 1933 *W*
Verelst, C L (Liverpool) 1876 *I*, 1878 *I*
Vernon, G F (Blackheath) 1878 *S, I*, 1880 *I, S*, 1881 *I*
Vickery, G (Aberavon) 1905 *I*
Vivyan, E J (Devonport A) 1901 *W*, 1904 *W, I, S*
Voyce, A T (Gloucester) 1920 *I, S*, 1921 *W, I, S, F*, 1922 *W, I, S*, 1923 *W, I, S, F*, 1924 *W, I, F, S*, 1925 *NZ, W, I, S, F*, 1926 *W, I, F, S*

Wackett, J A S (Rosslyn Park) 1959 *W, I*
Wade, C G (Richmond) 1883 *W, I, S*, 1884 *W, S*, 1885 *W*, 1886 *W, I*
Wade, M R (Cambridge U) 1962 *W, I, F*
Wakefield, W W (Harlequins) 1920 *W, F, I, S*, 1921 *W, I, S, F*, 1922 *W, I, F, S*, 1923 *W, I, S, F*, 1924 *W, I, S, F*, 1925 *NZ, W, I, F, S*, 1926 *W, I, F, S*, 1927 *S, F*
Walker, G A (Blackheath) 1939 *W, I*

Walker, H W (Coventry) 1947 *W, I, S, F*, 1948 *A, W, I, S, F*
Walker, R (Manchester) 1874 *S*, 1875 *I*, 1876 *S*, 1879 *S*, 1880 *S*
Wallens, J N S (Waterloo) 1927 *F*
Walton, E J (Castleford) 1901 *W, I*, 1902 *I, S*
Walton, W (Castleford) 1894 *S*
Ward, G (Leicester) 1913 *W, F, S*, 1914 *W, I, S*
Ward, H (Bradford) 1895 *W*
Ward, J I (Richmond) 1881 *I*, 1882 *I*
Ward, J W (Castleford) 1896 *W, I, S*
Wardlow, C S (Northampton) 1969 *SA* (R), 1971 *W, I, F, S* (2[1C])
Warfield, P J (Rosslyn Park, Durham U) 1973 *NZ, W, I*, 1975 *I, F, S*
Warr, A L (Oxford U) 1934 *W, I*
Watkins, J A (Gloucester) 1972 *SA*, 1973 *NZ, W, NZ, A*, 1975 *F, W*
Watkins, J K (United Services, RN) 1939 *W, I, S*
Watson, F B (United Services, RN) 1908 *S*, 1909 *S*
Watson, J H D (Blackheath) 1914 *W, S, F*
Watt, D E J (Bristol) 1967 *I, F, S, W*
Webb, C S H (Devonport Services, RN) 1932 *SA, W, I, S*, 1933 *W, I, S*, 1935 *S*, 1936 *NZ, W, I, S*
Webb, J M (Bristol) 1987 [*A*(R), *J, US, W*], 1988 *F, W, S, I* 1,2, *A* 1,2, *A*, 1989 *S, I, F, W*
Webb, J W G (Northampton) 1926 *F, S*, 1929 *S*
Webb, R E (Coventry) 1967 *S, W, NZ*, 1968 *I, F, S*, 1969 *I, F, S, W*, 1972 *I, F*
Webb, St L H (Bedford) 1959 *W, I, F, S*
Webster, J G (Moseley) 1972 *W, I, SA*, 1973 *NZ, W, NZ*, 1974 *S, W*, 1975 *I, F, W*
Wedge, T G (St Ives) 1907 *F*, 1909 *W*
Weighill, R H G (RAF, Harlequins) 1947 *S, F*, 1948 *S, F*
Wells, C M (Cambridge U, Harlequins) 1893 *S*, 1894 *W, S*, 1896 *S*, 1897 *W, S*
West, B R (Loughborough Colls, Northampton) 1968 *W, I, F, S*, 1969 *SA*, 1970 *I, W, S*
Weston, H T F (Northampton) 1901 *S*
Weston, L E (W of Scotland) 1972 *F, S*
Weston, M P (Richmond, Durham City) 1960 *W, I, F, S*, 1961 *SA, W, I, F, S*, 1962 *W, I, F*, 1963 *W, I, F, S*, *NZ* 1,2, *A*, 1964 *NZ, W, I, F, S*, 1965 *F, S*, 1966 *S*, 1968 *F, S*
Weston, W H (Northampton) 1933 *I, S*, 1934 *I, S*, 1935 *W, I, S* 1936 *NZ, W, S*, 1937 *W, I, S*, 1938 *W, I, S*
Wheatley, A A (Coventry) 1937 *W, I, S*, 1938 *W, S*
Wheatley, H F (Coventry) 1936 *I*, 1937 *S*, 1938 *W, S*, 1939 *W, I, S*
Wheeler, P J (Leicester) 1975 *F, W*, 1976 *A, W, S, I*, 1977 *S, I, F, W*, 1978 *F, W, S, I, NZ*, 1979 *S, I, F, W, NZ*, 1980 *I, F, W, S*, 1981 *W, S, I, F*, 1982 *A, S, I, F, W*, 1983 *F, S, I, NZ*, 1984 *S, I, F, W*
White, C (Gosforth) 1983 *NZ*, 1984 *S, I, F*
White, D F (Northampton) 1947 *W, I, S*, 1948 *I, F*, 1951 *S*, 1952 *SA, W, S, I, F*, 1953 *W, I, S*
Whiteley, E C P (O Alleynians) 1931 *S, F*
Whiteley, W (Bramley) 1896 *W*
Whitley, H (Northern) 1929 *W*
Wightman, B J (Moseley, Coventry) 1959 *W*, 1963 *W, I, NZ* 2, *A*
Wigglesworth, H J (Thornes) 1884 *I*
Wilkins, D T (United Services, RN, Roundhay) 1951 *W, I, F, S*, 1952 *SA, W, S, I, F*, 1953 *W, I, F, S*
Wilkinson, E (Bradford) 1886 *W, I, S*, 1887 *W, S*
Wilkinson, H (Halifax) 1929 *W, I, S*, 1930 *F*
Wilkinson, H J (Halifax) 1889 *M*
Wilkinson, P (Law Club) 1872 *S*
Wilkinson, R M (Bedford) 1975 *A* 2, 1976 *A, W, S, I, F*
Willcocks, T J (Plymouth) 1902 *W*
Willcox, J G (Oxford U, Harlequins) 1961 *I, F, S*, 1962 *W, I, F, S*, 1963 *W, I, F, S*, 1964 *NZ, W, I, F, S*
William-Powlett, P B R W (United Services, RN) 1922 *S*

Williams, C G (Gloucester, RAF) 1976 *F*
Williams, C S (Manchester) 1910 *F*
Williams, J E (O Millhillians and Sale) 1954 *F*, 1955 *W, I, F, S*, 1956 *I, S, F*, 1965 *W*
Williams, J M (Penzance-Newlyn) 1951 *I, S*
Williams, P N (Orrell) 1987 *S*, [*A, J, W*]
Williams, S G (Devonport A) 1902 *W, I, S*, 1903 *I, S*, 1907 *I, S*
Williams, S H (Newport) 1911 *W, F, I, S*
Williamson, R H (Oxford U) 1908 *W, I, S*, 1909 *A, F*
Wilson, A J (Camborne S of M) 1909 *I*
Wilson, C E (Blackheath) 1898 *I*
Wilson, C P (Cambridge U, Marlborough N) 1881 *W*
Wilson, D S (Met Police, Harlequins) 1953 *F*, 1954 *W, NZ, I, S, F*, 1955 *F, S*
Wilson, G S (Tyldesley) 1929 *W, I*
Wilson, K J (Gloucester) 1963 *F*
Wilson, R P (Liverpool OB) 1891 *W, I, S*
Wilson, W C (Richmond) 1907 *I, S*
Winn, C E (Rosslyn Park) 1952 *SA, W, S, I, F*, 1954 *W, S, F*
Winterbottom, P J (Headingley) 1982 *A, S, I, F, W*, 1983 *F, W, S, I, NZ*, 1984 *S, F, W, SA* 1,2, 1986 *W, S, I, F*, 1987 *I, F, W*, [*A, J, US, W*], 1988 *F, W, S*
Wintle, T C (Northampton) 1966 *S*, 1969 *I, F, S, W*
Wodehouse, N A (United Services, RN) 1910 *F*, 1911 *W, F, I, S*, 1912 *W, I, S, F*, 1913 *SA, W, F, I, S*
Wood, A (Halifax) 1884 *I*
Wood, A E (Gloucester, Cheltenham) 1908 *F, W, I*
Wood, G W (Leicester) 1914 *W*
Wood, R (Liversedge) 1894 *I*
Wood, R D (Liverpool OB) 1901 *I*, 1903 *W, I*
Woodgate, E E (Paignton) 1952 *W*
Woodhead, E (Huddersfield) 1880 *I*
Woodruff, C G (Harlequins) 1951 *W, I, F, S*
Woods, S M J (Cambridge U, Wellington) 1890 *W, S, I*, 1891 *W, I, S*, 1892 *I, S*, 1893 *W, I*, 1895 *W, I, S*
Woods, T (Bridgwater) 1908 *S*
Woods, T (United Services, RN) 1920 *S*, 1921 *W, I, S, F*
Woodward, C R (Leicester) 1980 *I* (R), *F, W, S*, 1981 *W, S, I, F, Arg* 1,2, 1982 *A, S, I, F, W*, 1983 *I, NZ*, 1984 *S, I, F, W*
Woodward, J E (Wasps) 1952 *SA, W, S*, 1953 *W, I, F, S*, 1954 *W, NZ, I, S, F*, 1955 *W, I*, 1956 *S*
Wooldridge, C S (Oxford U, Blackheath) 1883 *W, I, S*, 1884 *W, I, S*, 1885 *I*
Wordsworth, A J (Cambridge U) 1975 *A* 1 (R)
Worton, J R B (Harlequins, Army) 1926 *W*, 1927 *W*
Wrench, D F B (Harlequins) 1964 *F, S*
Wright, C C G (Cambridge U, Blackheath) 1909 *I, S*
Wright, F T (Edinburgh Acady, Manchester) 1881 *S*
Wright, I D (Northampton) 1971 *W, I, F, S*, (R)
Wright, J C (Met Police) 1934 *W*
Wright, J F (Bradford) 1890 *W*
Wright, T P (Blackheath) 1960 *W, I, F, S*, 1961 *SA, W, I, F, S*, 1962 *W, I, F, S*
Wright, W H G (Plymouth) 1920 *W, F*
Wyatt, D M (Bedford) 1976 *S* (R)

Yarranton, P G (RAF, Wasps) 1954 *W, NZ, I*, 1955 *F, S*
Yiend, W (Hartlepool R, Gloucester) 1889 *M*, 1892 *W, I, S*, 1893 *I, S*
Young, A T (Cambridge U, Blackheath, Army) 1924 *W, I, F, S*, 1925 *NZ, F*, 1926 *I, F, S*, 1927 *I, S, F*, 1928 *NSW, W, I, F, S*, 1929 *I*
Young, J R C (Oxford U, Harlequins) 1958 *I*, 1960 *W, I, F, S* 1961 *SA, W, I, F*
Young, M (Gosforth) 1977 *S, I, F, W*, 1978 *F, W, S, I, NZ*, 1979 *S*
Young, P D (Dublin Wands) 1954 *W, NZ, I, S, F*, 1955 *W, I, F, S*
Youngs, N G (Leicester) 1983 *I, NZ*, 1984 *S, I, F, W*

ENGLISH INTERNATIONAL RECORDS

Both team and individual records are for official England international matches up to 30 April 1989.

TEAM RECORDS

Highest score
60 v Japan (60-7) 1987 Sydney
v individual countries
19 v Argentina (19-19) 1981 Buenos Aires
28 v Australia (28-19) 1988 Twickenham
25 v Fiji (25-12) 1988 Suva
41 v France (41-13) 1907 Richmond
36 v Ireland (36-14) 1938 Dublin
60 v Japan (60-7) 1987 Sydney
16 v N Zealand (16-10) 1973 Auckland
22 v Romania (22-15) 1985 Twickenham
30 v Scotland (30-18) 1980 Murrayfield
18 v S Africa (18-9) 1972 Johannesburg
34 v United States (34-6) 1987 Sydney
25 v Wales (25-0) 1896 Blackheath
   (London)

Biggest winning points margin
53 v Japan (60-7) 1987 Sydney
v individual countries
  6 v Argentina (12-6) 1981 Buenos Aires
17 v Australia $\left\{\begin{array}{l}\text{(20-3) 1973 Twickenham}\\\text{(23-6) 1976 Twickenham}\end{array}\right.$
13 v Fiji (25-12) 1988 Suva
37 v France (37-0) 1911 Twickenham
32 v Ireland (35-3) 1988 Twickenham
53 v Japan (60-7) 1987 Sydney
13 v N Zealand (13-0) 1936 Twickenham
  7 v Romania (22-15) 1985 Twickenham
20 v Scotland (26-6) 1977 Twickenham
  9 v S Africa (18-9) 1972 Johannesburg
28 v United States (34-6) 1987 Sydney
25 v Wales (25-0) 1896 Blackheath

Highest score by opposing team
42 N Zealand (15-42) 1985 Wellington
by individual countries
19 Argentina (19-19) 1981 Buenos Aires
30 Australia (21-30) 1975 Brisbane
12 Fiji (25-12) 1988 Suva
37 France (12-37) 1972 Colombes
26 Ireland (21-26) 1974 Twickenham
  7 Japan (60-7) 1987 Sydney
42 N Zealand (15-42) 1985 Wellington
15 Romania (22-15) 1985 Twickenham
33 Scotland (6-33) 1986 Murrayfield

35 S Africa (9-35) 1984 Johannesburg
  6 United States (34-6) 1987 Sydney
34 Wales (21-34) 1967 Cardiff

Biggest losing points margin
27 v N Zealand (15-42) 1985 Wellington
27 v Scotland (6-33) 1986 Murrayfield
v individual countries
20 v Australia (8-28) 1988 Sydney
25 v France (12-37) 1972 Colombes
22 v Ireland (0-22) 1947 Dublin
27 v N Zealand (15-42) 1985 Wellington
27 v Scotland (6-33) 1986 Murrayfield
26 v S Africa (9-35) 1984 Johannesburg
25 v Wales (0-25) 1905 Cardiff
No defeats v Argentina, Fiji, Japan, Romania or United States

Most tries by England in an international
13 v Wales 1881 Blackheath

Most tries against England in an international
8 by Wales (6-28) 1922 Cardiff

Most points by England in International Championship in a season – 82
in season 1913-14

Most tries by England in International Championship in a season – 20
in season 1913-14

INDIVIDUAL RECORDS

Most capped player
A Neary   43   1971-80
in individual positions
Full-back
W H Hare   25   1974-84
Wing
R Underwood   32[1]   1984-89

Centre
P W Dodge   32[1]   1978-85
Fly-half
C R Andrew   24(25)[2]   1985-89
Scrum-half
S J Smith   28   1973-83
Prop
G S Pearce   35   1979-88
Hooker
J V Pullin   42   1966-76
Lock
W B Beaumont   34   1975-82
Flanker
A Neary   43   1971-80
No 8
J P Scott   31(34)[3]   1978-84

[1]*David Duckham, England's most capped back, played 14 times at centre and 22 times on the wing, making a total of 36 caps*
[2]*Andrew has also played once as a full-back*
[3]*Scott also played three times as a lock*

Longest international career
J Heaton 13 seasons 1935-47

Most internationals as captain
W B Beaumont 21 1978-82

Most points in internationals – 240
W H Hare (25 matches) 1974-84

Most points in International Championship in a season – 44
W H Hare (4 matches) 1983-84

Most points in an international – 22
D Lambert v France 1911 Twickenham

Most tries in internationals – 18
C N Lowe (25 matches) 1913-23

Most tries in International Championship in a season – 8
C N Lowe (4 matches) 1913-14

Most tries in an international – 5
D Lambert v France 1907 Richmond

Most conversions in internationals – 18
J M Webb (16 matches) 1987-89

Most conversions in International Championship in a season – 7
G S Conway (4 matches) 1923-24

Most conversions in an international – 7
J M Webb v Japan 1987 Sydney

Most dropped goals in internationals – 8
C R Andrew (25 matches) 1985-89

Most penalty goals in internationals – 67
W H Hare (25 matches) 1974-84

Most penalty goals in International Championship in a season – 14
W H Hare (4 matches) 1982-83

Most points on overseas tour – 48
W N Bennett (4 matches) Australia 1975
W H Hare scored 79 points on the N American tour of 1982, but this was not a major tour

Most points in a tour match – 36
W N Bennett v Western Australia 1975 Perth

Most tries in a tour match – 4
A J Morley v Western Australia 1975 Perth

P S Preece v New South Wales 1975 Sydney
R E Webb scored 4 tries v Canada in 1967, and J Carleton scored 4 against Mid-West at Cleveland in 1982, but these were not on major tours

TOSHIBA
DIVISIONAL CHAMPIONSHIP 1988

Chris Jones *The Standard*

The Australian tour and early warm-up games for all the divisions gave the Championship an added edge. But there was no consistency and on a hectic last day of fixtures each side was still capable of taking the title.

Thankfully, the complicated mathematical possibilities on that day were made simple by London's second win and yet another poor return from the South & South-West. Once again Bath and Gloucester had impressed in the early months of the season, only for the division to fail as a cohesive unit. They beat London but lost both away fixtures. The Midlands had terrible trouble putting out their first choice XV as injuries were a constant problem and early defeats at the hands of the USA and Australia revealed their paucity of players.

Wins over Munster and Australia convinced London that running the ball would make a big impact. It didn't at Gloucester against the South & South-West. However, they tore the North apart and then secured the Championship on points difference on the same Imber Court pitch against the Midlands. The North, without Rob Andrew for the entire Championship, had the boot of Will Carling to thank for their victory over the South & South-West. Simon Halliday of Bath was also ruled out by injury along with Wasps prop Paul Rendall. While London found an able deputy in Harlequins' Paul Curtis there was no substitute for Halliday in the South & South-West. The competition thus provided largely negative information for England's selectors.

Final Table

	P	W	D	L	F	A	Pts
London	3	2	0	1	76	30	4
Northern	3	2	0	1	45	57	4
South & South-West	3	1	0	2	46	43	2
Midlands	3	1	0	2	31	68	2

3 December, Otley RFC

Northern Division 27 (5PG 3T)   **Midlands Division 9** (1G 1PG)
Northern Division: S Langford (Orrell); S Burnhill (Sale), W D C Carling (Harlequins), J Buckton (Saracens), R Underwood (Leicester); D Pears (Sale), D Morris (Liverpool St Helens); M Whitcombe (Sale), M Fenwick (Durham City), P Huntsman (Headingley), W A Dooley (Preston Grasshoppers), R Kimmins (Orrell), S Hodgson (Vale of Lune), A McFarlane (Sale), P J Winterbottom (Harlequins) (*capt*)
Scorers *Tries:* Morris, Pears, Underwood   *Penalty Goals:* Pears (5)
Midlands Division: J Harris (Leicester); B Evans (Leicester), B Musto (Nottingham), G J Hartley (Nottingham), S Hackney (Nottingham); L Cusworth (Leicester) (*capt*), S Robson (Moseley); L Johnson (Nottingham), B C Moore (Nottingham), G S Pearce (Northampton), M Bayfield (Met Police), M Reid (Leicester), J Wells (Leicester), P Cook (Nottingham), G W Rees (Nottingham)
Scorers *Try:* Cook   *Conversion:* Harris   *Penalty Goal:* Harris
Referee J B Anderson (Scotland)

Nigel Redman leads the South & South-West pack on a drive during his team's only win in the Divisional Championship, against London at Gloucester.

3 December, Gloucester RFC

South & South-West Division 20 (2G 2T)   **London Division 13** (1G 1PG 1T)
South & South-West Division: J M Webb (Bristol); A W Swift (Bath), J Guscott (Bath), S Hogg (Bristol), R Knibbs (Bristol); S Barnes (Bath) (*capt*), R M Harding (Bristol); M Preedy (Gloucester), K Dunn (Gloucester), R Pascall (Gloucester), J Morrison (Bath), N C Redman (Bath), J Hall (Bath), M C Teague (Gloucester), A Robinson (Bath)
Scorers *Tries:* Swift (2), Barnes, Teague   *Conversions:* Barnes (2)
London Division: S Thresher (Harlequins); S Smith (Wasps), J L B Salmon (Harlequins), F Clough (Wasps), M D Bailey (Wasps); A Thompson (Harlequins), S M Bates (Wasps); P Curtis (Harlequins), J Olver (Harlequins), J A Probyn (Wasps), N Edwards (Harlequins), P Ackford (Harlequins), M G Skinner (Harlequins), J Ellison (Wasps), D Pegler (Wasps) (*capt*)
Scorers *Tries:* Bailey, Thresher   *Conversion:* Thresher   *Penalty Goal:* Thresher
Referee I M Bullerwell (East Midlands)

10 December, Nottingham RFC

Midlands Division 16 (3PG 1DG 1T)   **South & South-West Division 14** (1G 2T)
Midlands Division: S Hodgkinson (Nottingham); B Evans (Leicester), P W Dodge (Leicester), K Stiles (Nottingham), S Hackney (Nottingham); L Cusworth (Leicester) (*capt*), S Robson (Moseley); M Linnett (Moseley), B C Moore (Nottingham), G Mosses (Nottingham), M Reid (Leicester), M Bayfield (Met Police), J Wells (Leicester), P Cook (Nottingham), G W Rees (Nottingham)
Scorers *Try:* Mosses   *Penalty Goals:* Hodgkinson (3)   *Dropped Goal:* Hodgkinson
South & South-West Division: J M Webb (Bristol); A W Swift (Bath), R Knibbs (Bristol), J Guscott (Bath), A Lumsden (Bath); S Barnes (Bath) (*capt*), R Hill (Bath); M Preedy (Gloucester), R G R Dawe (Bath), R Pascall (Gloucester), J Morrison (Bath), N C Redman (Bath), J Hall (Bath), M C Teague (Gloucester), A Robinson (Bath)
Scorers *Tries:* Teague, Webb, Guscott   *Conversion:* Barnes
Referee C J High (Manchester)

10 December, Imber Court, Met Police RFC

London Division 36 (3G 2PG 3T)   **Northern Division 4** (1T)
London Division: S Thresher (Harlequins); A Harriman (Harlequins), J L B Salmon (Harlequins), F Clough (Wasps), M D Bailey (Wasps); A Thompson (Harlequins), S M Bates (Wasps); P Curtis (Harlequins), J Olver (Harlequins), J A Probyn (Wasps), N Edwards (Harlequins), P Ackford (Harlequins), M G Skinner (Harlequins), J Ellison (Wasps), D J Pegler (Wasps) (*capt*)
Replacements S Pilgrim (Wasps) for Harriman; A Mullins (Harlequins) for Probyn
Scorers *Tries:* Bailey (2), Clough, Salmon, Ellison, Edwards
Conversions: Thresher (3)   *Penalty Goals:* Thresher (2)
Northern Division: S Langford (Orrell); A Underwood (Leicester), J Buckton (Saracens), W D C Carling (Harlequins), R Underwood (Leicester); D Pears (Sale), D Morris (Liverpool St Helens); M Whitcombe (Sale), M Fenwick (Durham City), P Huntsman (Headingley), R Kimmins (Orrell), W A Dooley (Preston Grasshoppers), S Hodgson (Vale of Lune), A McFarlane (Sale), P J Winterbottom (Harlequins) (*capt*)
Scorer *Try:* A Underwood
Referee L Peard (Wales)

17 December, Imber Court, Met Police RFC

London Division 27 (1G 3PG 3T)   **Midlands Division 6** (1G)
London Division: S Thresher (Harlequins); S Smith (Wasps), J L B Salmon (Harlequins), F Clough (Wasps), M D Bailey (Wasps); A Thompson (Harlequins), S M Bates (Wasps); P Curtis (Harlequins), J Olver (Harlequins), J A Probyn (Wasps), N Edwards (Harlequins), P Ackford (Harlequins), M G Skinner (Harlequins), J Ellison (Wasps), D J Pegler (Wasps) (*capt*)
Scorers *Tries:* Bates, Pegler, Thresher, Ackford   *Conversion:* Thresher
Penalty Goals: Thresher (3)
Midlands Division: S Hodgkinson (Nottingham); B Evans (Leicester), P W Dodge (Leicester), G J Hartley (Nottingham), S Hackney (Nottingham); L Cusworth (Leicester) (*capt*), S Robson (Moseley); L Johnson (Nottingham), B C Moore (Nottingham), G Mosses (Nottingham), M Reid (Leicester), M Bayfield (Met Police), J Wells (Leicester), D Richards (Leicester), G W Rees (Nottingham) *Replacement* J Harris (Leicester) for Cusworth
Scorers *Try:* Hackney   *Conversion:* Hodgkinson
Referee O E Doyle (Ireland)

17 December, Orrell RFC

Northern Division 14 (2PG 2T)   **South & South-West Division 12** (1G 2PG)
Northern Division: M Lowther (Sale); A Underwood (Leicester), W D C Carling (Harlequins), B Barley (Wakefield), R Underwood (Leicester); S Townend (Wakefield), D Morris (Liverpool St Helens); M Whitcombe (Sale), N Hitchin (Orrell), D Southern (Orrell), R Kimmins (Orrell), W A Dooley (Preston Grasshoppers), S Hodgson (Vale of Lune), P Buckton (Liverpool St Helens), P J Winterbottom (Harlequins) (*capt*) *Replacements* J Buckton (Saracens) for A Underwood; G Doggart (Aspatria) for Lowther
Scorers *Tries:* Dooley, R Underwood   *Penalty Goals:* Carling (2)
South & South-West Division: A Buzza (Cambridge U); A W Swift (Bath), J Guscott (Bath), R Knibbs (Bristol), A Lumsden (Bath); S Barnes (Bath) (*capt*), R Hill (Bath); M Preedy (Gloucester), K Dunn (Gloucester), R Pascall (Gloucester), J Morrison (Bath), N C Redman (Bath), J Hall (Bath), M C Teague (Gloucester), A Robinson (Bath)
Replacement I Smith (Gloucester) for Morrison
Scorers *Try:* Swift   *Conversion:* Barnes   *Penalty Goals:* Barnes (2)
Referee R C Quittenton (London Society)

PILKINGTON CUP 1988-89

(RFU Club Competition)

Michael Austin

29 April, Twickenham
Bath 10 (2PG 1T)   **Leicester 6** (2PG)

Two superbly well-organised defences, the hallmark of seasoned finalists who had survived rumbustious challenges, ruled out a classic game but tension reigned until Barnes, Bath's captain, scored the solitary and match-winning try with two minutes remaining. Bath's triumph had been predictable throughout the season. It had long seemed simply a question of whom they would meet and Leicester, winners three times in consecutive seasons beginning in 1979 but absent from the final for six years, provided the answer.

As an expression of rugby's hard, competitive though pure elements, there has been no better final and the crowd of 59,300 was a world record for a club match. The execution of Bath's tactical plan was poor by their standards but their supremacy at the set pieces, notably Cronin's line-out catching and driving, imposed an inevitability on the result, which ended Palmer's career for the club on a high note and Hare's for Leicester with disappointment. Bath coach Jack Rowell correctly described his side as showing 'distinctive competence' but Hare, extending his record Cup points total to 537 and Cusworth, the competition's dropped goal expert with 30, another record, punted with such excellence that Bath looked unusually uncertain.

Leicester led until the 69th minute, when a second penalty goal, awarded in mysterious circumstances, by Barnes expunged Leicester's advantage gained from Hare's penalty goals after 26 and 37 minutes. Penalties awarded for off-side and then slipped binding by Bath's front row enabled Hare to put Leicester ahead, though he later missed three penalty attempts, none easy. Barnes landed his first goal after Richards was off-side and then a second when, as the front rows attempted to lock horns, Thacker, Leicester's hooker, was penalised by Fred Howard, officiating at his fourth consecutive final.

Two poor clearances by Hare and Underwood in quick succession offered Bath the match-winning opportunity. Leicester halted Simpson, a replacement for Egerton, from a five-metre scrum but Hall drove through and created a long-awaited try for Barnes. This left Leicester to rue their own missed chances before half-time. Wells failed to notice Evans outside him, then Kardooni's kick to the corner bounced cruelly for Sagoe, Bath's wing. Wells, Leicester's flanker, was first there but lost the ball. Dodge and Bates tackled admirably for Leicester and Ian Smith, an experienced flanker, rolled back the years. Richards, the England No 8, rivalled Cronin of Bath and Scotland as the game's outstanding forward.

Stuart Barnes, Bath's captain, scores the only try of the final which won the match for his side with only two minutes of the game remaining.

A match lacking in counter-attacks brought Bath their fifth Cup win, to add to their Courage League title, and they have yet to lose a final. Ironically, Kevin Andrews, Leicester's president and former lock, is the only player to have captained both clubs. Hare, aged 36, finished the season with 444 points, including six scored in what was, remarkably, his first Barbarians appearance for five years. The book apparently closed on his world career record of 7,191 points, including 4,507 for Leicester. Perhaps Hare's least-known distinction is his astonishing record of having scored in all the last 196 consecutive first-class matches in which he played for England, Barbarians, Midlands and Leicester. His most recent 'blank' was more than five years ago in a club game at Blackheath on 10 December 1983.

Bath: J A Palmer; A H Swift, S J Halliday, J C Guscott, F K Sagoe; S Barnes (*capt*), R J Hill; G J Chilcott, R G R Dawe, M R Lee, J S C Morrison, D F Cronin, R A Robinson, J P Hall, D W Egerton *Replacement* P D Simpson for Egerton (52 mins)
Scorer *Try:* Barnes   *Penalty Goals:* Barnes (2)
Leicester: W H Hare; B J Evans, P W Dodge (*capt*), I Bates, R Underwood; L Cusworth, A Kardooni; S Redfern, T Thacker, W P Richardson, M V Foulkes-Arnold, T Smith, J M Wells, I R Smith, D Richards
Scorer *Penalty Goals:* Hare (2)
Referee F A Howard (Liverpool Society)

In their advance to Twickenham, Bath and Leicester increased the total of successful away teams in semi-finals to an astonishing 25 – there have been only 11 home semi-final winners in the competition's history. Leicester's success was less predictable than that of Bath, who had been unbeaten in 37 club matches between April 1988 and the following February when they lost 18-12 at Gloucester. Bath revisited Kingsholm five weeks later for the semi-final and, watched by a crowd of 10,000, the biggest at the ground since the 1940s, they won a dour game 6-3, Barnes kicking two penalty goals to one by Tim Smith.

Harlequins, the holders, were marginal favourites to beat Leicester in the semi-final at The Stoop but lost 17-6 to a side prospering on the Cusworth-Hare connection. Cusworth's cross-kick to the left corner flag, intended for Rory Underwood, the England wing, instead found the galloping, 36-year-old Hare, who scored an important try. Hare had exceeded 500 Cup points in the third-round win over Liverpool St Helens at Moss Lane, where Cusworth's four dropped goals were another competition record.

Wasps' disappointments – they had been beaten in two finals and then in extra time of the semi-final in successive years – continued as they were narrowly eliminated in the quarter-final at Leicester. Leicester had knocked out Rosslyn Park for the third consecutive season, all the games being at Roehampton, and were also the first club to reach 1,000 competition points, in their 54th match.

Bath, granted three consecutive home ties, overwhelmed Oxford 82-9, scoring 16 tries including four each from Lumsden and Swift, together with Barnes' record nine conversions. In the fourth round, Hereford held Bath to 4-0 at half-time before losing by 48 points, Sagoe scoring four tries. On near-waterlogged pitch, Bath proceeded to eliminate Bristol 14-12 through Hill's try with three minutes remaining. The captains had disagreed about whether the game should go ahead and Andrew Mason, the London referee, had had the casting vote.

The competition had other quirks and controversies. Two third-round matches were played by the joint tenants of the Richmond Athletic Ground on the same pitch on the same day, which will not be repeated. Richmond's game against Northampton was contested in a mudbath an hour after London Scottish's meeting with Saracens. Both home sides won unexpectedly and without conceding a point. Several clubs standing three leagues lower than their opponents laid claim to join the ranks of the giant-killers but Aspatria, members of North 1, performed the major feat with a deserved 6-3 win over Moseley, who were four divisions higher, in National 1. Berry Hill repeated their previous season's victory over declining London Welsh and increased the margin while other meritorious performances were given by Wakefield, who became quarter-finalists for the second time having won at Headingley and Gosforth, and by Havant, who beat Exeter.

Nottingham and Orrell vied for the draw's tough luck story. Orrell lost a third-round tie at Bristol, having travelled and lost to Gloucester at the same stage the previous season. Without a home Cup match for three years, Nottingham increased their successive away ties to six, just two short of Leicester's unwanted record of eight between 1971-77.

The competition's welcome expansion from 60 clubs last season to 80 prompted 12 newcomers, bringing the total to 183 participants in 18 seasons. They were Barking, Brixham, Combe Down, Finchley, Medway, Okehampton, Old Juddian, Sandal, Stoneygate (in their Centenary season), West Park, Winnington Park and Wolverhampton.

As John Player's sponsorship terminated after 13 years, Pilkington signed an initial three-year agreement with an option to renew. The first season's prize-money amounted to £136,625, shared among 147 clubs, the sums given ranging from £3,750 for each of the finalists to £300 to the losing semi-finalists of the smaller county club competitions. This should help to ensure that the competition's status remains undiminished despite the introduction of leagues.

RESULTS

First Round
Barking 12, Ealing 7; Berry Hill 18, Askeans 7; Birkenhead Park 13, Bedworth 7; Brixham 38, Okehampton 9; Combe Down 19, Havant 24; Exeter 40, Sudbury 12; Finchley 10, Lydney 9; Fylde 17, Wolverhampton 6; Guildford and Godalming 12, Old Culverhaysians 20; Harrogate 10, West Hartlepool 22; Hereford 18, Leighton Buzzard 12; Marlow 15, Maidstone 37; Matlock 12, Aspatria 34; Medway 11, Old Mid-Whitgiftians 9; Metropolitan Police 13, Reading 11; Middlesbrough 30, West Park 21; Newark 6, Winnington Park 12; North Walsham 38, Old Juddian 6; Oxford 17, Tabard 6; Plymouth Albion 60, Stoke Old Boys 3; Redruth 21, Worthing 6; Rugby 27, Vale of Lune 6; Sandal 0, Durham City 3; Sheffield 3, Wakefield 16; Swindon 22, Ruislip 0; Stoneygate 9, Nuneaton 30; Tynedale 15, Stockwood Park 0; Widnes 16, Bromsgrove 13

Second Round
Bedford 16, Nuneaton 0; Berry Hill 24, London Welsh 9; Birkenhead Park 3, Tynedale 38; Coventry 7, Plymouth Albion 12; Durham City 19, Sale 10; Exeter 18, Redruth 3; Finchley 6,

Richmond 40; Gosforth 31, Fylde 10; Headingley 7, Wakefield 10; Hereford 28, Widnes 9; London Irish 25, Metropolitan Police 13; Maidstone 12, London Scottish 37; Medway 9, Havant 30; Middlesbrough 12, Aspatria 18; North Walsham 3, Saracens 31; Old Culverhaysians 3, Brixham 13; Oxford 28, Barking 0; Swindon 3, Blackheath 13; West Hartlepool 9, Rugby 30; Winnington Park 4, Northampton 37

Third Round
Aspatria 6, Moseley 3; Bath 82, Oxford 9; Bedford 3, Nottingham 6; Blackheath 6, Waterloo 13; Bristol 13, Orrell 7; Brixham 4, Gloucester 28; Gosforth 9, Wakefield 29; Havant 9, Exeter 3; Hereford 10, Tynedale 6; Liverpool St Helens 6, Leicester 37; London Irish 14, Berry Hill 3; London Scottish 16, Saracens 0; Richmond 6, Northampton 0; Rosslyn Park 18, Plymouth Albion 0; Rugby 3, Harlequins 25; Wasps 33, Durham City 3

Fourth Round
Bath 48, Hereford 0; Bristol 45, London Irish 16; Gloucester 19, Waterloo 16; Harlequins 22, London Scottish 6; Richmond 9, Nottingham 12; Rosslyn Park 9, Leicester 23; Wakefield 18, Havant 10; Wasps 39, Aspatria 7

Quarter-finals
Bath 14, Bristol 12; Harlequins 15,
Nottingham 9; Leicester 22, Wasps 18;
Wakefield 13, Gloucester 28

Semi-finals
Gloucester 3, Bath 6; Harlequins 7,
Leicester 16

Previous finals (*all at Twickenham*)
1972 Gloucester 17 Moseley 6
1973 Coventry 27 Bristol 15
1974 Coventry 26 London Scottish 6
1975 Bedford 28 Rosslyn Park 12

1976 Gosforth 23 Rosslyn Park 14
1977 Gosforth 27 Waterloo 11
1978 Gloucester 6 Leicester 3
1979 Leicester 15 Moseley 12
1980 Leicester 21 London Irish 9
1981 Leicester 22 Gosforth 15
1982 Gloucester 12 Moseley 12
     (Title shared)
1983 Bristol 28 Leicester 22
1984 Bath 10 Bristol 9
1985 Bath 24 London Welsh 15
1986 Bath 25 Wasps 17
1987 Bath 19 Wasps 12
1988 Harlequins 28 Bristol 22

COUNTY CUP WINNERS 1988-89

Berkshire	Reading	Lancashire	Orrell
Buckinghamshire	High Wycombe	Leicestershire	Vipers
Cheshire	Lymm	Middlesex	Ealing
Cornwall	Redruth	North Midlands	Dudley Kingswinford
Cumbria	Aspatria	Northumberland	Northern
Devon	Exeter	Notts, Lincs	
Dorset-Wilts	Swanage and Wareham	and Derbys	Mansfield
Durham	West Hartlepool	Oxfordshire	Oxford
Eastern Counties	North Walsham	Somerset	Taunton
East Midlands	Peterborough	Staffordshire	Stafford
Gloucestershire	Berry Hill	Surrey	Old Alleynians
Hampshire	Havant	Sussex	Worthing
Hertfordshire	Cheshunt	Warwickshire	Bedworth
Kent	Askeans	Yorkshire	Headingley

TITLE FOR UNSTOPPABLE BATH
THE COURAGE LEAGUES 1988-89

Perhaps the only drawback in the second year of the Courage Leagues, which once again galvanised the club season, was the predictable nature of the contest at the top. Bath had prepared for the league season assiduously and by the end of September they looked unstoppable. Stuart Barnes' team won the title with two matches to go having reeled off nine wins in nine matches.

In many ways, the other outstanding performance was that of Orrell. Unlike the other big clubs they have no large town from which to draw support and players. But for a long time they chased Bath from second place and eventually finished a creditable fifth. Unfortunately for rugby in the north, both Waterloo and Liverpool St Helens dropped into Division 2. It will be surprising if both clubs do not challenge for an immediate return to the top division.

Saracens dominated Division 2 and proudly marched on to a 100 per cent record. Bedford emerged to rise with them on the last day of the season when five teams still had a chance of promotion. London Irish were bitterly frustrated. At one stage on that final afternoon they led Blackheath by 19 points and a win would have put them in Division 1. Unaccountably they collapsed and lost, ending in only sixth place.

At the bottom of Division 2 Richmond saved themselves by winning their last match and thereby condemned London Scottish to Division 3. The Scottish suggested forcibly that they would return at the first attempt, however. They crushed Coventry, one of the pack of promotion hopefuls, on the same day. London Welsh had already sunk into Division 3 and face a hard fight to arrest the decline.

Plymouth dominated Division 3 and Rugby, recently on the verge of extinction, won a promotion duel against Wakefield on the last day of the league season. Roundhay move up from Area League North, reversing the trend of poor northern club performances, and Lydney join them in Division 3 next year as winners of Area League South.

NATIONAL DIVISION

National 1

	P	W	D	L	F	A	Pts
Bath	11	10	0	1	263	98	20
Gloucester	11	7	1	3	215	112	15
Wasps	11	7	1	3	206	138	15
Nottingham	11	6	1	4	142	122	13
Orrell	11	6	1	4	148	157	13
Leicester	11	6	1	4	189	199	13
Bristol	11	6	0	5	188	117	12
Harlequins	11	5	0	6	194	184	10
Rosslyn Park	11	5	0	6	172	208	10
Moseley	11	3	0	8	113	242	6
Waterloo	11	1	1	9	120	235	3
L'pool St Helens	11	1	0	10	116	254	2

National 2

	P	W	D	L	F	A	Pts
Saracens	11	11	0	0	288	80	22
Bedford	11	6	2	3	141	187	14
Northampton	11	6	1	4	165	131	13
Sale	11	5	2	4	195	152	12
Coventry	11	6	0	5	150	143	12
L Irish	11	5	2	4	194	222	12
Headingley	11	5	1	5	179	136	11
Blackheath	11	4	1	6	181	144	9
Richmond	11	4	1	6	112	216	9
Gosforth	11	4	0	7	176	246	8
L Scottish	11	3	1	7	146	160	7
L Welsh	11	1	1	9	125	235	3

National 3

	P	W	D	L	F	A	Pts
Plymouth A	11	11	0	0	311	89	22
Rugby	11	10	0	1	268	99	20
Wakefield	11	9	0	2	282	114	18
W Hartlepool	11	5	1	5	164	133	11
Nuneaton	11	5	0	6	178	214	10
Sheffield	11	4	1	6	170	182	9
Vale of Lune	11	4	1	6	120	145	9
Askeans	11	4	1	6	141	215	9
Exeter	11	4	0	7	142	180	8
Fylde	11	4	0	7	136	181	8
Met Police	11	4	0	7	130	275	8
Maidstone	11	0	0	11	74	289	0

Area League North

	P	W	D	L	F	A	Pts
Roundhay	10	8	1	1	235	81	17
Broughton Pk	10	8	0	2	179	92	16
Stourbridge	10	6	0	4	118	79	12
Northern	10	5	0	5	182	131	10
Winnington Pk	10	5	0	5	188	155	10
Preston G'h	10	5	0	5	161	141	10
Durham City	10	5	0	5	172	157	10
Morley	10	5	0	5	135	141	10
Lichfield	10	4	1	5	112	113	9
Stoke	10	3	0	7	88	138	6
Birmingham*	10	0	0	10	29	371	0

* Merging with Solihull

Area League South

	P	W	D	L	F	A	Pts
Lydney	10	8	1	1	240	98	17
Havant	10	8	1	1	177	92	17
Camborne	10	6	1	3	198	126	13
Redruth	10	6	1	3	136	81	13
Sudbury	10	5	1	4	141	89	11
Cheltenham	10	4	2	4	122	151	10
Salisbury	10	4	1	5	113	139	9
Southend	10	4	0	6	116	168	8
Ealing	10	3	0	7	144	188	6
Stroud	10	3	0	7	119	180	6
Sidcup	10	0	0	10	74	268	0

LONDON ZONE

London 1

	P	W	D	L	F	A	Pts
Basingstoke	10	8	1	1	240	98	17
Sutton	10	8	1	1	165	80	17
Ruislip	10	8	0	2	181	94	16
North Walsham	10	6	0	4	165	105	12
Lewes	10	6	0	4	167	116	12
Streath/Croy	10	5	0	5	139	137	10
Old Gaytonians	10	5	0	5	154	154	10
US Portsmouth	10	3	1	6	110	113	7
Ipswich	10	2	1	7	98	163	5
Guildfd/Godlmg	10	2	0	8	80	189	4
Dartfordians	10	0	0	10	30	280	0

London 2 North

	P	W	D	L	F	A	Pts
Cheshunt	10	8	1	1	243	110	17
Bishop's Stort	10	6	1	3	177	104	13
Norwich	10	6	1	3	182	120	13
O Albanians	10	6	0	4	121	91	12
*Barking	10	7	0	3	113	103	12
Grasshoppers	10	6	0	4	111	138	12
OMT	10	4	0	6	76	125	8
Thurrock	10	3	1	6	107	122	7
Woodford	10	3	0	7	143	162	6
Upper Clapton	10	3	0	7	89	134	6
Hertford	10	1	0	9	44	210	2

* 2 points deducted for ineligible player

London 2 South

	P	W	D	L	F	A	Pts
O Alleynians	10	9	0	1	224	64	18
Worthing	10	7	1	2	186	66	15
O Mid-Whitgift	10	6	1	3	121	109	13
Camberley	10	6	1	3	123	112	13
Gravesend	10	5	0	5	127	115	10
Tunbridge W	9	4	0	5	96	110	8
Esher	10	4	0	6	77	181	8
O Brockleians	10	3	1	6	84	157	7
Purley	9	3	0	6	93	118	6
O Reigatian	9	2	0	7	64	106	4
KCS Old Boys	9	1	2	6	82	139	4

London 3 North-East

	P	W	D	L	F	A	Pts
Eton Manor	10	10	0	0	369	55	20
Chingford	10	8	0	2	200	104	16
Cambridge	10	6	0	4	272	86	12
West Norfolk	10	6	0	4	215	138	12
O Westcliffians	10	6	0	4	167	98	12
Met Pol, Chig	10	5	0	5	168	131	10
O Cantabrigians	10	5	0	5	147	116	10
Brentwood	10	5	0	5	153	217	10
Colchester	10	3	0	7	190	125	6
Saffron Walden	10	1	0	9	65	375	2
Ipswich YMCA	10	0	0	10	24	525	0

London 3 North-West

	P	W	D	L	F	A	Pts
Finchley	10	8	0	2	156	40	16

	P	W	D	L	F	A	Pts
Tabard	10	8	0	2	162	88	16
Mill Hill	10	6	2	2	136	89	14
Kingsburians	10	7	0	3	122	81	14
St Mary's Hosp	10	6	1	3	130	110	13
Hemel Hemp	10	3	2	5	135	104	8
Bacavians	10	3	2	5	110	140	8
Fullerians	10	4	0	6	127	169	8
Letchworth	10	3	1	6	117	171	7
Hendon	10	3	0	7	84	128	6
Harrow	10	0	0	10	61	220	0

London 3 South-East

	P	W	D	L	F	A	Pts
O Colfeians	10	9	0	1	183	81	18
Westcombe Park	8	6	1	1	106	77	13
O Beccehamians	9	6	0	3	102	80	12
O Juddian	10	5	2	3	131	132	12
Charlton Park	10	6	0	4	116	130	12
Crawley	9	5	0	4	119	79	10
Beckenham	9	5	0	4	102	98	10
East Grinstead	10	2	1	7	92	154	5
Horsham	10	2	0	8	123	128	4
Bognor	9	2	0	7	94	105	4
O Dunstonian	10	2	0	8	64	168	4

London 3 South-West

	P	W	D	L	F	A	Pts
Alton	10	9	0	1	207	71	18
O Guildfordians	10	8	0	2	231	66	16
O Walcountians	10	6	0	4	152	102	12
O Emanuel	10	6	0	4	111	127	12
*Portsmouth	9	6	0	3	109	109	10
O Whitgiftians	10	5	0	5	85	166	10
Guy's Hospital	10	4	0	6	157	113	8
Gosport	10	3	0	7	118	142	6
Eastleigh	10	3	0	7	72	141	6
Winchester	10	3	0	7	69	178	6
Jersey	9	1	0	8	42	166	2

* 2 points deducted for ineligible player

Eastern Counties 1

	P	W	D	L	F	A	Pts
Harlow	10	9	0	1	247	55	18
Romfd/Gidea Pk	10	9	0	1	194	50	18
Canvey Island	10	7	0	3	314	61	14
Basildon	10	7	0	3	116	142	14
Shelford	10	6	0	4	150	113	12
Ely	10	5	0	5	106	131	10
Rochford	10	3	1	6	77	161	7
Crusaders	10	3	0	7	77	169	6
Redbridge	10	2	1	7	69	275	5
Bury St Ed	10	2	0	8	81	132	4
Lowestoft/Yar	10	1	0	9	85	227	2

Eastern Counties 2

	P	W	D	L	F	A	Pts
O Edwardians	10	9	1	0	274	65	19
Braintree	10	8	1	1	232	61	17
Diss	10	6	0	4	111	138	12
Wanstead	10	5	1	4	91	112	11
Chelmsford	10	5	0	5	125	80	10
Port of London	10	4	2	4	139	111	10
Upminster	10	5	0	5	119	168	10
Woodbridge	10	4	1	5	154	108	9
S Woodham F	10	4	1	5	72	121	9
East London	10	1	0	9	70	189	2
Thetford	10	0	1	9	65	299	1

Eastern Counties 3

	P	W	D	L	F	A	Pts
Campion	10	9	1	0	289	64	19
Maldon	10	8	1	1	201	88	17
O Bealonians	10	8	0	2	174	85	16
Wymondham	10	6	0	4	140	91	12
Beccles	10	5	0	5	138	108	10
Newmarket	10	5	0	5	125	102	10
Holt	10	5	0	5	123	119	10
Ilford Wands	10	5	0	5	89	119	10
H'wich/Doverct	10	2	0	8	111	201	4
Lakenm-Hewett	10	1	0	9	33	156	2
Wisbech	10	0	0	10	20	310	0

Eastern Counties 4

	P	W	D	L	F	A	Pts
Bancrofts	10	9	0	1	412	74	18
O Brentwoods	9	8	0	1	166	73	16
O Palmerians	10	8	0	2	190	121	16
Mayfield OB	10	6	0	4	171	135	12
Clacton	10	6	0	4	122	110	12
Felixstowe	10	6	0	4	153	160	12
Stowmarket	10	2	2	6	78	137	6
Fakenham	10	2	1	7	88	185	5
Southwold	10	2	1	7	111	253	5
Gothic	10	2	0	8	92	202	4
Chigwell	9	1	0	8	34	167	2

Eastern Counties 5

	P	W	D	L	F	A	Pts
London Hosp	8	7	0	1	282	60	14
Loughton	8	6	0	2	164	104	12
Dereham	8	6	0	2	132	93	12
March	8	5	0	3	97	89	10
Haverhill	8	4	0	4	138	109	8
Thurston	8	4	0	4	78	109	8
Swaffham	8	2	0	6	96	137	4
Norwich Union	8	2	0	6	83	157	4
Sawston	8	0	0	8	26	238	0

Eastern Counties 6

	P	W	D	L	F	A	Pts
Thames Sports	7	6	1	0	203	49	13
Ongar	7	6	0	1	206	26	12
Billericay	7	5	0	2	124	50	10
O Cooperians	7	4	0	3	78	52	8
Witham	7	2	2	3	59	72	6
Hadleigh	7	1	1	5	57	120	3
Brightlingsea	7	1	0	6	40	143	2
Orwell	7	1	0	6	28	283	2

Hampshire 1

	P	W	D	L	F	A	Pts
Southampton	9	8	1	0	225	71	17
Esso	10	8	0	2	191	87	16
Millbrook	10	6	0	4	219	92	12
Guernsey	9	6	0	3	188	89	12
Fareham Hthns	9	5	1	3	125	104	11
Sandown/Shank	10	4	3	3	121	108	11
Trojans	10	5	0	5	95	167	10
Isle of Wight	10	4	0	6	102	152	8
Rushmoor	9	2	1	6	89	152	5
Tottonians	10	1	0	9	76	156	2
Fordingbridge	10	1	0	9	52	305	2

Hampshire 2

	P	W	D	L	F	A	Pts
Petersfield	9	8	0	1	243	50	16
Andover	9	8	0	1	206	44	16
Romsey	8	7	0	1	106	48	14
New Milton	7	5	0	2	153	57	10
Jersey United B	8	4	0	4	84	98	8
Overton	9	3	1	5	90	111	7
Ellingham	9	2	2	5	72	168	6
Waterlooville	9	2	1	6	63	176	5
Ventnor	9	1	2	6	48	106	4
Nomads	9	0	0	9	38	245	0

Hertfordshire 1

	P	W	D	L	F	A	Pts
Welwyn	7	5	2	0	112	45	12
Barnet	7	5	0	2	99	43	10
Harpenden	7	4	1	2	105	31	9
O Verulamians	7	4	1	2	81*	55	9
Stevenage	7	3	1	3	73	79	7
O Elizabethans	7	2	1	4	44	34	5
O Ashmoleans	7	2	0	5	43	104	4
Royston	7	0	0	7	46	212	0

Hertfordshire 2

	P	W	D	L	F	A	Pts
Hitchin	5	5	0	0	86	30	10
Tring	5	3	0	2	72	46	6

St Albans	5	3	0	2	66	42	6
Datchworth	5	2	0	3	60	36	4
Watford	5	2	0	3	58	74	4
De Havilland	5	0	0	5	9	123	0

Kent 1

	P	W	D	L	F	A	Pts
Gillingham Anc	10	8	1	1	138	59	17
Betteshanger	10	8	0	2	121	84	16
Park House	10	7	1	2	143	83	15
Medway	10	6	0	4	165	105	12
Bromley	10	6	0	4	117	112	12
Snowdown CW	10	5	0	5	122	104	10
Thanet Wands	10	4	1	5	91	103	9
Erith	10	4	0	6	98	105	8
Canterbury	10	3	0	7	68	143	6
Tonbridge	10	1	1	8	43	117	3
O Elthamians	10	1	0	9	67	158	2

Kent 2

	P	W	D	L	F	A	Pts
Sevenoaks	10	10	0	0	261	56	20
Dover	10	7	0	3	164	62	14
New Ash Green	10	6	2	2	115	83	14
Folkestone	10	6	2	2	139	109	14
Linton	10	6	0	4	167	84	12
O Shootershill	10	5	1	4	111	100	11
Midland Bank	10	4	0	6	105	144	8
Nat West Bank	9	3	1	5	86	136	7
Ashford	10	2	0	8	95	142	4
Greenwich	9	1	0	8	52	156	2
Lloyds Bank	10	1	0	9	40	263	2

Kent 3

	P	W	D	L	F	A	Pts
Met Pol, Hayes	10	10	0	0	239	24	20
Sittingbourne	10	8	0	2	166	40	16
Vigo	10	7	0	3	164	68	14
Sheppey	10	5	1	4	155	130	11
O Williamson	10	5	0	5	148	132	10
Deal	10	4	1	5	155	124	9
Cranbrook	10	4	0	6	114	139	8
O Olavians	10	3	2	5	100	151	8
O Gravesend	10	3	1	6	101	178	7
Thames Poly	10	3	0	7	119	165	6
Orpington	10	0	1	9	33	343	1

Kent 4

	P	W	D	L	F	A	Pts
Citizens	8	7	1	0	247	47	15
Darenth Valley	8	6	1	1	144	64	13
STC Footscray	8	6	0	2	131	75	12
Edenbridge	7	3	2	2	85	48	8

Bexley	8	3	1	4	77	72	7
Whitstable	7	2	1	4	52	76	5
Univ of Kent	7	2	1	4	71	115	5
Lordswood	7	1	0	6	18	165	2
East Peckham	8	0	1	7	30	193	1

Middlesex 1

	P	W	D	L	F	A	Pts
Twickenham	10	9	1	0	186	79	19
London NZ	10	8	1	1	188	93	17
Uxbridge	10	5	2	3	150	98	12
Centaurs	10	5	2	3	136	118	12
Lensbury	10	5	1	4	120	101	11
Staines	10	3	4	3	93	88	10
Hampstead	10	4	2	4	138	144	10
Sudbury Court	10	3	0	7	110	125	6
O Haberdashers	10	2	2	6	67	176	6
O Paulines	10	1	2	7	83	162	4
O Abbotstonians	10	1	1	8	88	175	3

Middlesex 2

	P	W	D	L	F	A	Pts
O Millhillians	10	9	0	1	286	37	18
O Meadonians	10	7	0	3	130	80	14
Barclays Bank	10	6	0	4	114	137	12
Haringey	10	5	1	4	140	77	11
Hackney	10	5	1	4	145	101	11
Orleans FP	10	4	1	5	71	124	9
Civil Service	10	4	1	5	67	123	9
St Bart's Hosp	10	4	0	6	98	167	8
Richmd Thames	10	3	0	7	98	145	6
O Hamptonians	10	3	0	7	86	158	6
H'Smith/Flham	10	3	0	7	132	218	6

Middlesex 3

	P	W	D	L	F	A	Pts
O Grammarians	10	7	1	2	126	82	15
Osterley	10	6	2	2	176	82	14
Wembley	10	6	1	3	158	105	13
Quintin	10	6	1	3	102	64	13
L Cornish	9	6	0	3	126	88	12
Antlers	10	5	1	4	147	106	11
O Tottonians	10	3	2	5	108	118	8
O Isleworthians	10	4	0	6	71	100	8
Pinner/Gram	9	3	0	6	62	147	6
Northolt	10	2	0	8	63	143	4
Belsize Park	10	2	0	8	77	181	4

Middlesex 4

	P	W	D	L	F	A	Pts
Bank of England	9	8	0	1	182	70	16
Meadhurst	9	7	0	2	160	65	14
Enfield Ignat	9	6	1	2	137	43	13

Roxeth Man OB	8	5	0	3	106	63	10
O Actonians	9	4	1	4	90	100	9
L French	9	3	2	4	98	86	8
Feltham	9	4	0	5	105	104	8
UCS OB	9	2	2	5	85	106	6
Hayes	9	2	0	7	102	157	4
ST & C	8	0	0	8	19	290	0

Middlesex 5

	P	W	D	L	F	A	Pts
HAC	8	8	0	0	347	17	16
Royal Free Hosp	8	7	0	1	161	47	14
Brunel Univ	8	6	0	2	225	69	12
St Nicholas OB	7	4	0	3	119	121	8
Middlesex Hosp	7	3	1	3	132	113	7
British Airways	8	3	0	5	129	134	6
Kodak	8	2	0	6	71	233	4
Southall Tec C	8	1	1	6	114	272	3
GWR	8	0	0	8	19	311	0

* St Mary's Hosp readmitted next season

Surrey 1

	P	W	D	L	F	A	Pts
Dorking	10	9	1	0	149	73	19
O Blues	10	7	1	2	161	107	15
O Rutlishians	10	7	0	3	185	116	14
Cranleigh	10	6	2	2	121	74	14
Warlingham	10	5	1	4	120	89	11
O Cranleighans	10	5	0	5	111	122	10
O Tiffinians	10	4	1	5	145	134	9
O Wimbledon's	10	4	0	6	124	112	8
Merton	10	3	0	7	91	128	6
Effingham	10	1	0	9	84	161	2
O Surbitonians	10	1	0	9	66	241	2

Surrey 2 'A'

	P	W	D	L	F	A	Pts
Harrodians	10	9	0	1	261	80	18
Wimbledon	10	9	0	1	211	54	18
Univ Vandals	10	6	0	4	120	125	12
Raynes Park	10	5	0	5	141	116	10
Charing X/West	10	5	0	5	138	129	10
O Haileybury	10	5	0	5	140	136	10
O Reedonians	10	5	0	5	123	152	10
O Freemans	10	4	1	5	125	97	9
Kingston	10	3	0	7	95	183	6
Farnham	10	2	1	7	92	148	5
Chobham	10	1	0	9	81	307	2

Surrey 2 'B'

	P	W	D	L	F	A	Pts
John Fisher OB	10	9	0	1	296	50	18

O Wandsworth	10	9	0	1	185	59	18
Bec Old Boys	11	8	0	3	193	84	16
Mitcham	11	7	1	3	180	97	15
Law Society	10	7	1	2	151	91	15
O Johnians	10	5	0	5	121	161	10
O Pelhamians	11	4	0	7	134	97	8
Shirley Wands	11	4	0	7	100	144	8
Chipstead	11	3	1	7	69	139	7
King's Coll Hosp	11	2	1	8	69	239	5
O Suttonians	11	2	0	9	98	195	4
O Epsomians	11	2	0	9	55	295	4

Surrey 3

	P	W	D	L	F	A	Pts
Battersea Iron	9	8	0	1	204	46	16
O Caterhamians	9	7	0	2	178	68	14
Reigate/Redhill	9	6	1	2	182	60	13
Surrey Police	9	6	1	2	129	81	13
BBC	9	5	0	4	87	55	10
O Bevonians	9	5	0	4	95	91	10
O Croydonians	8	2	2	4	50	74	6
Shene G	9	1	1	7	76	194	3
L Fire Brigade	9	1	1	7	56	183	3
Haslemere	8	0	0	8	36	241	0

Surrey 4

	P	W	D	L	F	A	Pts
*Surrey Univ	11	11	0	0	303	60	22
*Royal Holloway	10	8	0	2	286	84	16
**Economicals	10	5	1	4	128	141	11
**Oxted	9	4	0	5	143	103	8
**Racal Decca	10	4	0	6	92	158	8
**Lightwater	11	3	1	7	86	203	7
**British Aero	11	0	0	11	30	319	0

* Remain in new Surrey 4 for next season
** Form new Surrey 5 for next season

Sussex 1

	P	W	D	L	F	A	Pts
Hove	9	7	1	1	233	103	15
Chichester	9	6	0	3	153	124	12
Burgess Hill	9	6	0	3	128	130	12
Crowborough	9	5	1	3	131	98	11
Haywards Heath	10	5	0	5	108	148	10
Uckfield	10	4	1	5	53	76	9
Brighton	9	4	0	5	115	102	8
Sussex Police	10	4	0	6	90	122	8
Seaford	10	4	0	6	118	155	8
Eastbourne	10	3	1	6	138	143	7
Hellingly	9	2	0	7	69	135	4

Sussex 2

	P	W	D	L	F	A	Pts
Heathfield	8	8	0	0	163	39	16
St Francis	8	7	0	1	113	46	14
Hastings/Bexhill	7	5	0	2	280	47	10
Plumpton	8	4	0	4	108	87	8
Pulborough	8	3	0	5	86	107	6
Sussex Univ	7	3	0	4	85	113	6
Brighton Poly	7	2	0	5	68	152	4
Midhurst	7	1	0	6	39	226	2
*Br Caledonian	6	0	0	6	14	139	0

* Renamed BA Wingspan for next season

Sussex 3

	P	W	D	L	F	A	Pts
O Brightonians	6	6	0	0	326	7	12
RMP Chichester	5	5	0	0	149	28	10
Ditchling	7	4	0	3	124	100	8
Newick	7	4	0	3	101	106	8
W Sussex Inst	5	3	0	2	137	105	6
Arun	7	1	1	5	37	250	3
Sunallon	6	1	0	5	52	123	2
Azurians	7	0	1	6	19	226	1

NORTH ZONE

North 1

	P	W	D	L	F	A	Pts
Kendal	10	8	0	2	188	88	16
Tynedale	10	7	1	2	215	123	15
Aspatria	10	7	1	2	190	100	15
Harrogate	10	7	1	2	204	120	15
Halifax	10	5	1	4	146	147	11
Otley	10	5	0	5	199	112	10
Wigton	10	4	1	5	105	120	9
Hull & ER	10	3	0	7	97	224	6
Hartlepool	10	2	1	7	112	197	5
Birkenhead Pk	10	2	0	8	106	188	4
West Park	10	2	0	8	119	262	4

North 2

	P	W	D	L	F	A	Pts
Bradford/Bing	10	9	0	1	204	95	18
Middlesbrough	10	8	0	2	133	71	16
Wharfedale	10	7	0	3	220	96	14
Sandal	10	6	0	4	128	113	12
Alnwick	10	6	0	4	104	109	12
Widnes	10	5	0	5	121	103	10
Lymm	10	5	0	5	137	132	10
Carlisle	10	3	1	6	68	115	7
Huddersfield	10	2	1	7	105	186	5
New Brighton	10	1	1	8	80	156	3
Davenport	10	1	1	8	35	159	3

North-West 1

	P	W	D	L	F	A	Pts
Wigan	10	9	0	1	223	75	18

Egremont	10	5	2	3	142	121	12
Sedgley Park	10	6	0	4	108	132	12
Mid-Cheshire	10	5	1	4	141	104	11
Sandbach	10	5	0	5	128	126	10
Wirral	10	5	0	5	92	150	10
Rochdale	10	4	1	5	80	87	9
Chester	10	4	1	5	93	121	9
Caldy	10	3	1	6	102	148	7
Manchester	10	3	0	7	115	128	6
Wilmslow	10	3	0	7	78	110	6

North-West 2

	P	W	D	L	F	A	Pts
Cockermouth	10	8	1	1	146	69	17
Macclesfield	10	7	1	2	200	96	15
O Aldwinians	10	7	0	3	182	87	14
Merseyside Pol	10	6	1	3	179	146	13
Penrith	10	5	1	4	108	108	11
Blackburn	10	5	1	4	131	138	11
Workington	10	3	2	5	117	165	8
Netherall	10	3	2	5	78	137	8
Southport	10	3	1	6	118	140	7
Leigh	10	1	2	7	86	146	4
Burnage	10	1	0	9	65	178	2

NW West 1

	P	W	D	L	F	A	Pts
Warrington	10	7	1	2	108	118	15
O Parkonians	10	7	0	3	116	57	14
St Edwards OB	10	6	1	3	173	117	13
Newton le W	10	6	1	3	128	95	13
Ormskirk	10	6	0	4	135	121	12
O Instonians	10	5	0	5	91	101	10
Liverpool COB	10	4	0	6	168	125	8
Ruskin Park	10	4	0	6	150	160	8
Douglas (IoM)	10	4	0	6	158	192	8
Aspull	10	3	0	7	165	146	6
Birchfield	10	1	1	8	49	209	3

NW West 2

	P	W	D	L	F	A	Pts
Oldershaw	9	8	1	0	164	65	17
S Liverpool	9	7	2	0	126	57	16
O Rockferrians	9	7	0	2	121	73	14
Eagle	9	4	1	4	102	127	9
Port Sunlight	9	4	0	5	106	87	8
Vulcan	9	3	0	6	97	113	6
O Anselmians	9	3	0	6	84	103	6
Sefton	9	3	0	6	102	137	6
Hightown	9	2	0	7	85	150	4
Halton	9	2	0	7	79	154	4

NW West 3

	P	W	D	L	F	A	Pts
Hoylake	11	10	0	1	280	32	20
Shell Stanlow	11	9	1	1	198	73	19
St Mary's OB	11	9	0	2	299	82	18
Mossley Hill	11	8	0	3	164	103	16
Helsby	11	6	1	4	148	107	13
Moore	11	6	1	4	97	167	13
Wallasey	11	6	0	5	111	102	12
Wigan CoT	11	3	0	8	153	174	6
Prescot Rnhill	11	3	0	8	101	241	6
Burtonwood	11	2	0	9	85	214	4
Shell Carr'ton	11	1	1	9	77	266	3
Lucas	11	1	0	10	93	245	2

NW E/North 1

	P	W	D	L	F	A	Pts
Moresby	10	9	0	1	219	74	18
Windermere	10	7	0	3	166	80	14
Furness	10	6	0	4	160	132	12
De La Salle	10	6	0	4	135	118	12
Oldham	10	6	0	4	107	115	12
Heaton Moor	10	4	0	6	115	139	8
Eccles	10	4	0	6	93	130	8
Fleetwood	10	4	0	6	66	117	8
Vickers	10	3	1	6	91	111	7
Toc H	10	3	0	7	103	163	6
Littleborough	10	2	1	7	58	134	5

NW East 1

	P	W	D	L	F	A	Pts
Ashton on M	10	10	0	0	195	32	20
O Salians	10	8	0	2	201	77	16
Kersal	10	8	0	2	174	75	16
Crewe/Nant'ch	10	6	0	4	100	67	12
Tyldesley	10	4	1	5	87	115	9
Metrovick	10	4	0	6	91	89	8
O Bedians	10	4	0	6	82	160	8
Colne/Nelson	10	3	1	6	84	154	7
Bolton	10	3	0	7	73	142	6
Calder Vale	10	3	0	7	47	136	6
Congleton	10	1	0	9	66	153	2

NW East 2

	P	W	D	L	F	A	Pts
Broughton	11	9	0	2	194	80	18
Gtr Man Fire S	11	8	0	3	174	69	16
Ashton-u-Lyne	11	8	0	3	147	90	16
Bury	11	6	3	2	124	81	15
Dukinfield	11	6	1	4	132	79	13
Chorley	11	6	1	4	124	92	13
N Manchester	11	5	1	5	86	146	11
Marple	11	4	1	6	77	165	9
Man YMCA	11	3	2	6	106	102	8

Agecroft	11	3	0	8	79	206	6
Bowden	11	1	2	8	100	146	4
Oldham Coll	11	1	1	9	38	121	3

NW North 1

	P	W	D	L	F	A	Pts
Kirkby Lons	9	8	1	0	220	41	17
Rossendale	9	7	1	1	157	65	15
Keswick	9	6	0	3	164	73	12
Thornton Cleve	9	6	0	3	112	92	12
St Benedicts	8	5	0	3	122	95	10
British Steel	9	3	0	6	108	129	6
Carnforth	9	3	0	6	99	140	6
Blackpool	8	2	1	5	37	128	5
Millom	9	1	1	7	42	143	3
Creighton	9	1	0	8	70	225	2

NW North 2

	P	W	D	L	F	A	Pts
Upper Eden	5	5	0	0	96	22	10
Whitehaven	5	4	0	1	74	32	8
Silloth	5	3	0	2	50	34	6
Smith Bros	5	2	0	3	136	33	4
Ambleside	5	0	1	4	22	125	1
Clitheroe	5	0	1	4	12	144	1

North-East 1

	P	W	D	L	F	A	Pts
Rotherham	10	10	0	0	273	54	20
Stockton	10	7	0	3	190	123	14
O Crossleyans	10	7	0	3	119	83	14
Gateshead Fell	10	7	0	3	138	105	14
Novocastrians	10	6	0	4	104	141	12
O Brodleians	10	5	0	5	131	141	10
Keighley	10	4	0	6	113	132	8
Morpeth	10	3	0	7	98	129	6
Thornensians	10	3	0	7	70	104	6
Blaydon	10	2	0	8	85	137	4
Westoe	10	1	0	9	72	244	2

North-East 2

	P	W	D	L	F	A	Pts
York	10	8	1	1	161	94	17
Selby	10	7	1	2	134	90	15
Roundhegians	10	6	2	2	150	72	14
Pontefract	10	5	1	4	142	112	11
Beverley	10	5	0	5	90	97	10
Newcastle Univ	10	5	0	5	129	154	10
Ripon	10	4	0	6	123	122	8
Blyth	10	3	1	6	113	144	7
O Hymerians	10	3	0	7	107	143	6
Ryton	10	3	0	7	95	152	6
Pocklington	10	3	0	7	75	139	6

Durham/Northumberland 1

	P	W	D	L	F	A	Pts
Rockcliff	10	8	0	2	140	83	16
Mowden Park	10	7	1	2	124	81	15
Seghill	10	6	3	1	106	83	15
Acklam	10	7	0	3	141	84	14
Horden	10	6	0	4	200	98	12
Ashington JW	10	5	0	5	124	129	10
Darlington	10	4	0	6	123	169	8
Ponteland	10	3	1	6	81	143	7
Redcar	10	3	0	7	132	116	6
Hartlepool	10	3	0	7	90	174	6
Winlaton Vul	10	0	1	9	78	179	1

Durham/Northumberland 2

	P	W	D	L	F	A	Pts
Whitby	10	10	0	0	255	65	20
Sunderland	10	8	0	2	251	77	16
Seaham	10	6	1	3	143	118	13
Percy Park	10	6	1	3	133	120	13
B'p Auckland	10	5	1	4	204	119	11
Consett	10	5	1	4	141	133	11
Medicals	10	3	3	4	122	114	9
North Durham	10	4	0	6	101	157	8
Wallsend	10	2	1	7	91	198	5
Billingham	10	2	0	8	96	191	4
Hartlep'l BBOB	10	0	0	10	76	321	0

Durham/Northumberland 3

	P	W	D	L	F	A	Pts
Darlington RA	9	6	2	1	154	63	14
North Shields	9	7	0	2	102	67	14
Wensleydale	9	6	1	2	168	74	13
Wearside	9	6	0	3	128	109	12
Chester-le-St	9	5	1	3	119	78	11
Guisborough	9	4	1	4	87	91	9
H'pool TDS OB	9	3	0	6	92	116	6
Prudhoe	9	2	1	6	66	131	5
Seaton Carew	9	2	1	6	78	168	5
Houghton	9	0	1	8	47	144	1

Durham/Northumberland 4

	P	W	D	L	F	A	Pts
Barnard Castle	9	9	0	0	181	52	18
S Tyneside Coll	9	7	0	2	228	87	14
Jarrovians	9	7	0	2	114	103	14
Richmondshire	9	5	0	4	182	96	10
Hartlepool Ath	9	5	0	4	94	84	10
N'ton Aycliffe	9	5	0	4	106	111	10
C Serv, Durham	9	2	1	6	108	138	5
Sedgefield	9	2	1	6	53	123	5

Shildon Town	9	1	0	8	48	148	2
Benton	9	1	0	8	64	236	2

Yorkshire 1

	P	W	D	L	F	A	Pts
Bramley	10	9	1	0	236	57	19

W Pk Bramhope	10	7	2	1	153	82	16
Hemsworth	10	6	1	3	125	103	13
Driffield	10	5	1	4	138	85	11
N Ribblesdale	10	5	1	4	102	108	11
Barnsley	10	5	0	5	97	114	10
Cleckheaton	10	4	1	5	106	146	9
H'field YMCA	10	3	1	6	90	116	7
Castleford	10	3	1	6	91	168	7

Goole	10	2	0	8	119	202	4
Moortown	10	1	1	8	55	131	3

Yorkshire 2

	P	W	D	L	F	A	Pts
Bridlington	10	9	0	1	243	60	18
Doncaster	10	8	1	1	230	75	17

York RI	10	7	1	2	224	88	15
Wath-on-Dearne	10	6	0	4	140	106	12
Sheffield Tigers	10	5	0	5	93	168	10
Ilkley	10	4	1	5	113	146	9
Malton/Norton	10	4	0	6	166	185	8
Wheatley Hills	10	3	1	6	134	140	7
Scarborough	10	3	0	7	65	164	6

Marist	10	3	0	7	91	215	6
Ionians	10	1	0	9	87	239	2

Yorkshire 3

	P	W	D	L	F	A	Pts
Yarnbury	10	8	2	0	171	53	18
O Otliensians	10	8	1	1	227	81	17

Leodiensians	10	7	0	3	136	94	14
Wibsey	10	5	2	3	152	113	12
Knottingley	10	5	0	5	134	133	10
O Modernians	10	4	1	5	139	109	9
Baildon	10	4	1	5	104	141	9
Airebronians	10	4	0	6	86	110	8
Rodillians	10	3	0	7	66	204	6

Leeds CSSA	10	2	1	7	70	148	5
Heath	10	1	0	9	78	213	2

Yorkshire 4

	P	W	D	L	F	A	Pts
Hessle	10	9	0	1	241	68	18
West Leeds	10	9	0	1	211	66	18

Northallerton	10	7	0	3	164	94	14
Bradford Salem	10	6	0	4	149	99	12
Halifax Vandals	10	6	0	4	105	130	12
Hullensians	10	5	0	5	128	133	10

Leeds YMCA	10	4	0	6	111	151	8
O Rishworthians	10	3	0	7	74	117	6
Dinnington	10	3	0	7	148	204	6

Yorkshire CW	10	2	0	8	56	242	4
Wetherby	10	1	0	9	97	180	2

Yorkshire 5

	P	W	D	L	F	A	Pts
Sheffield Oaks	10	10	0	0	236	53	20
Phoenix Park	10	9	0	1	174	61	18

Skipton	10	6	0	4	140	93	12
Burley	10	6	0	4	143	112	12
Yorkshire Main	10	5	0	5	119	125	10
Danum Phoenix	10	4	1	5	106	114	9
Rowntrees	10	4	0	6	87	129	8
BP Chemicals	10	4	0	6	72	150	8
Ossett	10	3	0	7	129	135	6

Leeds Corinth	10	2	1	7	57	115	5
Hornsea	10	1	0	9	65	241	2

Yorkshire 6

	P	W	D	L	F	A	Pts
De-la-Salle	10	8	0	2	143	55	16
Withernsea	10	8	0	2	143	79	16

Granville Coll	10	7	1	2	141	102	15
Adwick-le-Street	10	7	0	3	128	124	14
Mosborough	10	6	0	4	93	98	12
Knaresborough	10	5	1	4	75	93	11
Maltby OB	10	4	1	5	96	101	9
Stocksbridge	10	3	1	6	129	151	7
Armthorpe Mark	10	3	0	7	99	153	6
Sheff Medicals	10	1	0	9	78	130	2
Sheff Steels	10	0	0	10	36	75	0

WEST ZONE

South-West 1

	P	W	D	L	F	A	Pts
Clifton	10	9	0	1	237	76	18

High Wycombe	10	9	0	1	168	85	18
Berry Hill	10	8	0	2	214	100	16
Taunton	10	6	0	4	154	136	12
Reading	10	5	0	5	144	146	10
St Ives	10	5	0	5	110	139	10
Weston-s-Mare	10	4	0	6	188	183	8
Maidenhead	10	3	0	7	159	148	6
Oxford	10	3	0	7	141	211	6

Torquay	10	3	0	7	97	177	6
Bridgwater	10	0	0	10	53	264	0

South-West 2

	P	W	D	L	F	A	Pts
Matson	10	9	0	1	244	81	18
Brixham	10	8	0	2	250	74	16

Cinderford	10	7	0	3	156	97	14
Barnstaple	10	6	0	4	114	96	12
Henley	10	6	0	4	137	163	12
Abbey	10	4	1	5	150	158	9
Newbury	10	4	0	6	102	134	8
Redingensians	10	3	1	6	110	176	7
Bournemouth	10	3	0	7	60	177	6
Launceston	10	2	0	8	120	160	4
D & C Const	10	2	0	8	93	220	4

Western Counties

	P	W	D	L	F	A	Pts
Gordon League	10	10	0	0	218	80	20
Avonmouth OB	10	7	0	3	162	112	14
Cirencester	10	6	1	3	124	109	13
Clevedon	10	5	1	4	136	95	11
Okehampton	10	5	1	4	109	78	11
Tiverton	10	5	0	5	109	143	10
O Redcliffians	10	4	0	6	108	113	8
Truro	10	3	1	6	89	130	7
Newquay Hornet	10	3	1	6	101	152	7
Devonport Serv	10	3	0	7	139	198	6
Crediton	10	1	1	8	87	162	3

Southern Counties

	P	W	D	L	F	A	Pts
Banbury	10	8	1	1	242	92	17
Aylesbury	10	8	0	2	192	69	16
Swanage & W	10	7	0	3	146	79	14
Wimborne	10	7	0	3	145	98	14
Marlow	10	6	1	3	140	102	13
Swindon	10	5	1	4	152	127	11
Oxford OB	10	5	0	5	147	144	10
Windsor	10	3	0	7	108	154	6
Bletchley	10	3	0	7	73	188	6
Slough	10	1	1	8	119	189	3
Oxford Mara	10	0	0	10	42	264	0

Gloucestershire/Somerset

	P	W	D	L	F	A	Pts
O Culverhays	10	10	0	0	207	82	20
Combe Down	10	8	1	1	243	83	17
Mid'mer Norton	10	7	0	3	120	110	14
Spartans	10	6	1	3	178	84	13
Coney Hill	10	6	0	4	89	71	12
Avon & Som Pol	10	5	1	4	110	99	11
Keynsham	10	3	0	7	108	161	6
Whitehall	10	3	0	7	82	175	6
Cleve	10	2	1	7	76	94	5
Gordano	10	2	0	8	82	189	4
Minehead	10	1	0	9	84	231	2

Gloucestershire 1

	P	W	D	L	F	A	Pts
Drybrook	10	10	0	0	196	42	20
Dings Crusad	10	7	1	2	150	95	15
St Mary's OB	10	7	1	2	155	113	15
North Bristol	10	7	0	3	161	113	14
Widden OB	10	6	1	3	168	117	13
Longlevens	10	5	0	5	154	116	10
Saintbridge FP	10	3	2	5	109	122	8
O Patesians	10	3	0	7	133	140	6
Bream	10	3	0	7	116	166	6
Tredworth	10	1	1	8	75	192	3
O Colstonians	10	0	0	10	29	230	0

Gloucestershire 2

	P	W	D	L	F	A	Pts
Gloucester OB	10	10	0	0	252	63	20
Cheltenham N	10	9	0	1	188	75	18
O Bristolians	10	7	1	2	145	92	15
Ashley Down OB	10	6	1	3	136	121	13
Bristol Sara	10	5	0	5	115	148	10
Chelt'ham Sara	10	4	0	6	102	133	8
O Cryptians	10	3	0	7	101	146	6
Barton Hill	10	3	0	7	84	138	6
Brockworth	10	3	0	7	96	152	6
Cotham Park	10	3	0	7	115	181	6
Cheltenham CS	10	1	0	9	74	159	2

Gloucestershire 3

	P	W	D	L	F	A	Pts
Frampton Cott	10	10	0	0	281	63	20
Thornbury	10	9	0	1	296	66	18
Dursley	10	6	1	3	128	92	13
Chipping Sod	10	5	0	5	182	77	10
Tewkesbury	10	4	2	4	114	174	10
Painswick	10	3	2	5	90	128	8
O Elizabethans	10	4	0	6	94	180	8
Cainscross	10	4	0	6	76	183	8
Smiths Indust	10	3	0	7	83	228	6
Kingswood	10	2	1	7	86	182	5
Chosen Hill FP	10	2	0	8	79	136	4

Gloucestershire 4

	P	W	D	L	F	A	Pts
Bristol Tele	11	10	0	1	295	66	20
Hucclecote OB	11	10	0	1	270	70	20
Bishopston	11	7	1	3	242	90	15
Aretians	11	7	0	4	166	84	14
Newent	11	7	0	4	191	184	14
Bristol AC	11	6	0	5	174	142	12
Minchin'ton	11	5	1	5	201	160	11
Gloucester CS	11	5	0	6	149	131	10

Broad Plain	11	5	0	6	124	152	10
All Blues	11	2	0	9	123	263	4
O Cothamians	11	0	1	10	54	308	1
Dowty	11	0	1	10	76	415	1

Somerset 1

	P	W	D	L	F	A	Pts
Frome	10	9	1	0	266	69	19
Oldfield OB	10	9	0	1	299	93	18
St Bernadettes	10	6	1	3	178	140	13
O Sulians	10	5	1	4	172	78	11
Hornets	10	5	0	5	153	134	10
Bristol Harl	10	4	2	4	124	144	10
Yatton	10	4	1	5	113	148	9
Walcot OB	10	4	0	6	122	116	8
N Petherton	10	4	0	6	128	161	8
Burnham	10	2	0	8	94	202	4
St Brendans OB	10	0	0	10	61	425	0

Somerset 2

	P	W	D	L	F	A	Pts
Avonvale	11	10	0	1	181	107	20
Yeovil	11	9	1	1	170	110	19
Avon	11	7	1	3	185	142	15
Imperial	11	6	2	3	149	102	14
Bath	11	6	0	5	151	117	12
Stothert & Pitt	11	5	1	5	179	138	11
Crewkerne	11	5	1	5	115	132	11
Wells	11	5	0	6	144	120	10
Winscombe	11	5	0	6	130	148	10
Blagdon	11	4	0	7	127	157	8
Wellington	11	1	0	10	90	170	2
Westland	11	0	0	11	76	254	0

Somerset 3

	P	W	D	L	F	A	Pts
Wiveliscombe	11	11	0	0	459	50	22
Tor	11	10	0	1	236	57	20
Backwell	11	9	0	2	243	100	18
Chard	11	8	0	3	272	90	16
O Ashtonians	11	7	0	4	207	107	14
Bath Civil S	11	5	1	5	194	116	11
Cheddar	11	4	1	6	108	194	9
Aller	11	3	0	8	120	254	6
Castle Cary	11	3	0	8	88	175	6
Morganians	11	3	0	8	81	197	6
Chew Valley	11	2	0	9	90	335	4
Wincanton	11	0	0	11	47	470	0

Devon/Cornwall

	P	W	D	L	F	A	Pts
Penryn	10	9	0	1	261	64	18
Teignmouth	10	6	0	4	146	106	12
Falmouth	10	6	0	4	116	117	12
Sidmouth	10	6	0	4	104	123	12
Bideford	10	5	0	5	141	138	10
Illogan Park	10	5	0	5	84	105	10
Penzance & N'lyn	10	5	0	5	120	147	10
Exeter Saracens	10	5	0	5	81	123	10
Paignton	10	4	0	6	114	152	8
Exmouth	10	2	0	8	130	134	4
Hayle	10	2	0	8	108	196	4

Cornwall 1

	P	W	D	L	F	A	Pts
Wadebridge	10	8	1	1	198	75	17
St Austell	10	7	1	2	194	68	15
Liskeard & L	10	6	2	2	153	57	14
Saltash	10	6	0	4	118	81	12
Helston	10	5	1	4	170	78	11
Bude	10	4	2	4	147	82	10
Redruth Alb	10	4	2	4	82	174	10
Bodmin	10	4	0	6	128	143	8
Veor	10	3	1	6	90	104	7
Lankelly	10	2	0	8	55	349	4
St Agnes	10	0	2	8	87	211	2

Cornwall 2

	P	W	D	L	F	A	Pts
Stithians	10	9	0	1	177	26	18
St Just	10	8	0	2	164	55	16
Roseland	10	5	0	5	73	131	10
Redruth GSOB	10	4	0	6	113	70	8
Perranporth	10	2	0	8	34	131	4
RNAS Culdrose	10	2	0	8	41	186	4

Devon 1

	P	W	D	L	F	A	Pts
Plymouth CS	10	9	0	1	235	86	18
South Molton	10	8	0	2	263	119	16
Ivybridge	10	7	0	3	191	88	14
Cullompton	10	7	0	3	199	122	14
Newton Abbot	10	7	0	3	168	124	14
Totnes	10	6	0	4	159	113	12
O Technicians	10	3	0	7	106	93	6
Plymouth Arg	10	3	0	7	110	299	6
Honiton	10	2	1	7	114	194	5
Devonport HSOB	10	1	1	8	84	292	3
Kingsbridge	10	1	0	9	96	195	2

Devon 2 'A'

	P	W	D	L	F	A	Pts
Prince Rock	8	8	0	0	182	38	16
Jesters	8	7	0	1	89	62	14
Victoria	8	5	0	3	127	82	10
O Public Oaks	8	5	0	3	89	72	10
O Plymouth & M	8	4	0	4	100	86	8

Tamar Sara	8	3	0	5	80	148	6
St Columba	8	2	0	6	71	93	4
Plymouth YMCA	8	1	0	7	64	137	2
Plympton	8	1	0	7	32	116	2

Devon 2 'B'

	P	W	D	L	F	A	Pts
Topsham	6	5	0	1	154	50	10
Tavistock	6	4	1	1	113	36	9
Ilfracombe	6	4	1	1	74	48	9
Withycombe	6	3	0	3	94	53	6
North Tawton	6	2	0	4	75	86	4
Salcombe	6	2	0	4	40	134	4
Dartmouth	6	0	0	6	47	190	0

Berks/Dorset/Wilts 1

	P	W	D	L	F	A	Pts
Bracknell	10	10	0	0	222	59	20
Dorchester	10	9	0	1	256	64	18
Sherborne	10	7	0	3	350	71	14
Chippenham	10	6	0	4	157	126	12
Devizes	10	5	0	5	230	100	10
Wootton Bass	10	5	0	5	140	116	10
Weymouth	10	5	0	5	95	157	10
Corsham	10	4	0	6	89	148	8
REME Ar'fld	10	3	0	7	128	209	6
Aldermaston	10	1	0	9	65	327	2
Marlborough	10	0	0	10	68	423	0

Berks/Dorset/Wilts 2

	P	W	D	L	F	A	Pts
North Dorset	10	9	0	1	242	76	18
Puddletown	10	9	0	1	176	75	18
Trowbridge	10	7	0	3	247	86	14
Supermarine	10	5	1	4	96	76	11
Lytchet Min	10	5	1	4	127	121	11
Swindon Coll	10	4	0	6	76	148	8
Poole	10	4	0	6	99	171	8
Bradf'd-on-Avon	10	3	0	7	149	123	6
Hungerford	10	3	0	7	109	167	6
Oakmedians	10	3	0	7	83	259	6
Minety	10	2	0	8	29	131	4

Berks/Dorset/Wilts 3 East

	P	W	D	L	F	A	Pts
Melksham	6	5	1	0	221	30	11
Shire Hall	6	5	1	0	138	47	11
Colerne	6	3	1	2	84	48	7
Tadley	6	1	2	3	52	101	4
Thatcham	6	2	0	4	31	81	4
Amesbury	6	1	1	4	43	101	3
Calne	6	1	0	5	38	199	2

Berks/Dorset/Wilts 3 West

	P	W	D	L	F	A	Pts
Westbury	6	5	0	1	258	40	10
Warminster	6	5	0	1	135	67	10
Dorset Inst	6	5	0	1	93	40	10
Portcastrians	6	2	0	4	51	72	4
Bridport	6	2	0	4	69	187	4
Blandford	6	1	0	5	67	88	2
Plessey	6	1	0	5	48	227	2

Bucks/Oxon 1

	P	W	D	L	F	A	Pts
Chiltern	10	8	0	2	164	84	16
Littlemore	10	6	1	3	155	63	13
Pennanians	10	6	1	3	116	110	13
Beaconsfield	10	6	0	4	158	95	12
Chinnor	10	6	0	4	160	109	12
Bicester	10	6	0	4	158	133	12
Drifters	10	4	1	5	99	113	9
Grove	10	3	2	5	101	145	8
Milton Keynes	10	3	0	7	101	150	6
Witney	10	2	1	7	99	192	5
Buckingham	10	2	0	8	104	221	4

Bucks/Oxon 2

	P	W	D	L	F	A	Pts
Cholsey	9	9	0	0	178	40	18
Olney	9	8	0	1	285	57	16
Wheatley	9	6	0	3	129	55	12
Didcot	9	6	0	3	161	99	12
Abingdon	9	5	0	4	98	99	10
Gosford AB	9	4	0	5	116	104	8
Phoenix	9	4	0	5	111	132	8
Harwell	9	2	0	7	54	252	4
Chesham	9	0	1	8	71	178	1
Chipping Ntn	9	0	1	8	46	233	1

MIDLANDS ZONE

Midlands 1

	P	W	D	L	F	A	Pts
Walsall	10	10	0	0	210	71	20
Hereford	10	8	0	2	163	108	16
Newark	10	7	0	3	197	142	14
Derby	10	6	0	4	156	102	12
Paviors	10	5	0	5	128	119	10
Mansfield	10	5	0	5	130	154	10
Barker's Butts	10	4	1	5	174	169	9
Stockwood Pk	10	4	1	5	140	167	9
Solihull	10	3	0	7	107	156	6
Westleigh	10	1	0	9	102	205	2
Wolverhampton	10	1	0	9	83	197	2

Midlands 2 West

	P	W	D	L	F	A	Pts
S Coldfield	10	8	0	2	150	79	16
Bedworth	10	7	1	2	192	95	15
O Yardleians	10	6	1	3	114	116	13
Stafford	10	5	2	3	130	102	12
Dudley	10	5	1	4	120	99	11
Burton-on-T	10	5	0	5	100	128	10
Newbold	10	5	0	5	89	121	10
Bromsgrove	10	3	2	5	90	99	8
Dixonians	10	3	1	6	76	110	7
Tamworth	10	1	3	6	78	108	5
Worcester	10	1	1	8	83	165	3

Midlands 2 East

	P	W	D	L	F	A	Pts
Leighton Buzz	10	8	1	1	190	98	17
Syston	10	7	0	3	170	100	14
Moderns	10	6	2	2	131	88	14
Kettering	10	6	0	4	146	115	12
Vipers	10	6	0	4	159	140	12
Stewart & L	10	6	0	4	112	134	12
Lincoln	10	3	2	5	120	138	8
Matlock	10	3	1	6	100	153	7
Stoneygate	10	3	0	7	104	146	6
Peterborough	10	2	0	8	166	160	4
Hinckley	10	2	0	8	96	222	4

North Midlands 1

	P	W	D	L	F	A	Pts
Camp Hill	10	9	0	1	216	78	18
Kings Norton	10	7	1	2	153	52	15
Newport	10	7	1	2	124	78	15
Luctonians	10	5	2	3	100	97	12
Shrewsbury	10	4	2	4	117	105	10
Evesham	10	5	0	5	84	135	10
Whitchurch	10	4	1	5	119	120	9
Kidderminster	10	4	1	5	77	105	9
Bridgnorth	10	2	1	7	68	106	5
O Halesonians	10	1	2	7	75	168	4
Malvern	10	1	1	8	97	186	3

North Midlands 2

	P	W	D	L	F	A	Pts
Aston OE	10	10	0	0	258	66	20
Ludlow	10	8	0	2	169	75	16
Woodrush	10	8	0	2	159	81	16
Droitwich	10	6	0	4	147	123	12
Selly Oak	10	6	0	4	120	125	12
Telford	10	5	0	5	123	107	10
Pershore	10	4	0	6	83	130	8
Five Ways	10	4	0	6	84	144	8
Erdington	10	1	1	8	100	132	3
Bourneville	10	1	1	8	76	175	3
Edwardians	10	1	0	9	67	228	2

North Midlands 3

	P	W	D	L	F	A	Pts
W Midlands Pol	10	9	0	1	278	67	18
Veseyans	10	8	1	1	228	64	17
Redditch	10	7	0	3	139	93	14
O Centrals	10	5	0	5	121	129	10
O Griffinians	10	5	0	5	107	185	10
Birmingham City	10	4	1	5	222	125	9
Warley	10	4	0	6	96	125	8
O Saltleians	10	4	0	6	119	153	8
B'ham Welsh	10	3	1	6	122	181	7
Kynoch	10	2	1	7	89	216	5
Ledbury	10	2	0	8	47	230	4

North Midlands 4

	P	W	D	L	F	A	Pts
Tenbury	12	11	0	1	284	72	22
Birchfield	12	11	0	1	310	104	22
Oswestry	12	9	0	3	210	124	18
Market Dray	12	7	1	4	149	93	15
Yardley & Dist	12	7	0	5	202	111	14
Upton-on-Severn	12	7	0	5	158	152	14
Bromyard	12	7	0	5	122	210	14
O Moseleians	12	5	0	7	141	167	10
Birmingham CS	12	4	1	7	125	216	9
Ross-on-Wye	12	4	0	8	111	158	8
Witton	12	3	0	9	111	214	6
Thimblemill	12	1	0	11	76	162	2
Bewdley	12	1	0	11	80	296	2

Staffs/Warwicks

	P	W	D	L	F	A	Pts
Keresley	10	9	0	1	213	63	18
Leamington	10	7	0	3	178	88	14
O Leamington	10	7	0	3	144	132	14
Stratford	10	6	0	4	141	113	12
Nuneaton OE	10	5	0	5	132	121	10
Leek	10	4	0	6	149	87	8
Newcastle	10	4	0	6	104	115	8
O Longtonian	10	4	0	6	130	150	8
Willenhall	10	4	0	6	100	128	8
Stoke OB	10	3	0	7	90	148	6
Trentham	10	2	0	8	58	294	4

Warwickshire 1

	P	W	D	L	F	A	Pts
Coventry Welsh	10	10	0	0	274	82	20
Trinity Guild	10	6	1	3	172	106	13

	P	W	D	L	F	A	Pts
O Coventrians	10	6	0	4	130	96	12
Southam	10	6	0	4	132	183	12
Broadstreet	10	5	0	5	155	134	10
O Wheatlians	10	5	0	5	157	148	10
Kenilworth	10	3	2	5	150	147	8
Dunlop	10	4	0	6	116	159	8
Manor Park	10	4	0	6	120	167	8
GEC (Coventry)	10	3	1	6	112	149	7
R St Andrews	10	1	0	9	101	248	2

Warwickshire 2

	P	W	D	L	F	A	Pts
Coventry Sara	10	8	1	1	193	60	17
Spartans	10	8	0	2	226	91	16
Coventrians	10	8	0	2	196	96	16
O Laurentian	10	8	0	2	175	111	16
Harbury	10	5	0	5	123	113	10
Earlsdon	10	4	0	6	125	129	8
Silhillians	10	4	0	6	98	179	8
Atherstone	10	3	1	6	80	122	7
O Warwickians	10	3	0	7	88	178	6
Pinley	10	2	0	8	71	188	4
Standard	10	1	0	9	82	190	2

Warwickshire 3

	P	W	D	L	F	A	Pts
Lanchester Poly	8	8	0	0	160	42	16
Berks/Balsall	9	7	1	1	153	63	15
Rugby Welsh	9	7	0	2	191	36	14
Shipston	9	6	1	2	207	77	13
Warwick	9	5	0	4	142	83	10
Claverdon	8	4	0	4	105	65	8
Coventry PO	9	3	0	6	74	125	6
Shottery	9	2	0	7	62	142	4
Alcester	9	1	0	8	33	224	2
Coventry Tech	9	0	0	9	33	303	0

Staffordshire 1

	P	W	D	L	F	A	Pts
Handsworth	6	6	0	0	140	41	12
Rugeley	6	3	2	1	96	53	8
Uttoxeter	6	3	1	2	39	46	7
Burntwood	6	2	0	4	50	76	4
GEC	6	2	0	4	68	107	4
Cannock	6	2	0	4	44	86	4
Linley	6	1	1	4	52	80	3

Staffordshire 2

	P	W	D	L	F	A	Pts
Eccleshall	9	8	0	1	222	52	16
Wednesbury	9	7	0	2	134	38	14
Rubery Owen	9	6	0	3	141	79	12
Wheaton Aston	9	5	2	2	119	57	12
Michelin	9	5	1	3	87	105	11
Old Oaks	9	5	0	4	95	76	10
Wulfrun	9	4	0	5	99	86	8
St Matthews	9	2	0	7	74	256	4
St Georges	9	1	0	8	75	156	2
Cheadle	9	0	1	8	57	198	1

E Midlands/Leicester

	P	W	D	L	F	A	Pts
Towcestrians	10	10	0	0	191	50	20
Wellingborough	10	9	0	1	217	74	18
Aylestone St J	10	6	1	3	134	110	13
Long Buckby	10	6	0	4	147	113	12
Belgrave	10	4	2	4	165	163	10
Bedford Ath	10	4	1	5	123	126	9
Northampton T	10	4	0	6	133	143	8
Luton	10	4	0	6	107	124	8
Oadby-Wygg	10	3	0	7	100	180	6
Loughborough	10	2	0	8	79	182	4
Wigston	10	1	0	9	83	214	2

Leicestershire 1

	P	W	D	L	F	A	Pts
Lutterworth	9	9	0	0	198	19	18
Mkt Bosworth	9	8	0	1	234	39	16
O Bosworthians	9	7	0	2	169	94	14
Coalville	9	6	0	3	115	52	12
Melton M'bray	9	4	0	5	76	124	8
Kibworth	9	3	1	5	109	113	7
S Leicester	9	3	0	6	101	173	6
W Leicester	9	2	0	7	79	186	4
Aylestonians	9	1	1	7	58	183	3
New Parks OB	9	0	2	7	53	209	2

Leicestershire 2

	P	W	D	L	F	A	Pts
O Newtonians	7	7	0	0	211	38	14
Birstall Comm	7	6	0	1	160	58	12
O Ashbeians	7	5	0	2	157	56	10
Oakham	7	4	0	3	93	61	8
Anstey	7	2	1	4	86	90	5
Burbage	7	2	1	4	49	148	5
Braunston	7	1	0	6	57	160	2
Shepshed	7	0	0	7	34	236	0

East Midlands 1

	P	W	D	L	F	A	Pts
Biggleswade	10	9	0	1	213	76	18
Ampthill & D	10	7	1	2	192	104	15
N'hampton MO	10	6	1	3	142	111	13
N'hampton OS	10	6	0	4	121	116	12
Rushden & High	10	5	0	5	140	112	10

	P	W	D	L	F	A	Pts
O N'hampt'ians	10	5	0	5	128	131	10
Huntingdon	10	3	2	5	98	115	8
N'ton BBOB	10	3	1	6	110	141	7
Brackley	10	2	2	6	96	171	6
Daventry	10	2	2	6	113	221	6
St Neots	10	2	1	7	73	128	5

East Midlands 2

	P	W	D	L	F	A	Pts
Wellingboro OG	10	8	1	1	176	71	17
Corby	10	7	1	2	256	52	15
Dunstablians	10	7	1	2	181	78	15
N'ton Casuals	10	7	0	3	154	109	14
Westwood	10	5	1	4	113	121	11
Colworth House	10	5	0	5	126	133	10
Bedford Queens	10	5	0	5	140	152	10
Oundle	10	3	1	6	93	134	7
St Ives	10	2	1	7	72	162	5
Vauxhall	10	2	0	8	83	151	4
Cutler Hammer	10	1	0	9	37	268	2

East Midlands 3

	P	W	D	L	F	A	Pts
Bedford Swifts	5	5	0	0	147	36	10
Deepings	5	4	0	1	58	21	8
Bugbrooke	5	3	0	2	78	58	6
O Wellingburian	5	1	0	4	41	69	2
N'ton Heathens	5	1	0	4	35	85	2
Potton	5	1	0	4	42	132	2

Notts, Lincs & Derbys 1

	P	W	D	L	F	A	Pts
Scunthorpe	10	9	1	0	218	67	19
Southwell	10	7	0	3	173	87	14
Chesterfield	10	5	1	4	134	89	11
Amber Valley	10	5	1	4	121	107	11
Mellish	10	5	1	4	98	96	11
Kesteven	10	5	0	5	91	127	10
Stamford	10	4	0	6	89	114	8
Worksop	10	3	2	5	64	96	8
West Bridgford	10	4	0	6	99	147	8
East Retford	10	3	1	6	73	146	7
Glossop	10	1	1	8	60	144	3

Notts, Lincs & Derbys 2

	P	W	D	L	F	A	Pts
Sleaford	10	7	1	2	120	63	15
Spalding	10	6	1	3	148	96	13
Mkt Rasen & L	10	5	3	2	110	87	13
Ilkeston	10	6	0	4	103	111	12
Nottingham Cas	10	5	0	5	147	109	10
Nottinghamians	10	5	0	5	116	100	10

	P	W	D	L	F	A	Pts
*Long Eaton	9	4	1	4	88	130	10
Grimsby	10	4	1	5	116	124	9
*Keyworth	9	3	2	4	67	88	9
All Spartans	10	2	2	6	87	137	6
Boston	10	1	1	8	63	120	3

* 1 point for game when ground unfit.

Notts, Lincs & Derbys 3

	P	W	D	L	F	A	Pts
Dronfield	10	10	0	0	181	57	20
Nottingham Pol	10	8	0	2	178	78	16
Boots	10	6	1	3	114	76	13
Rolls Royce	10	6	0	4	136	115	12
Belper	10	5	1	4	130	78	11
Ashbourne	10	5	0	5	111	70	10
*Ashfield Swans	9	3	1	5	70	114	9
Barton & Dist	10	4	0	6	87	118	8
N Kesteven	10	3	0	7	86	128	6
Skegness	10	2	1	7	75	165	5
Gainsborough	9	0	0	9	57	226	0

* 2 points because opposition did not fulfil fixture.

Notts, Lincs & Derbys 4 East

	P	W	D	L	F	A	Pts
Cleethorpes	8	7	1	0	241	51	15
Bingham	8	7	0	1	124	40	14
Meden Vale	8	6	1	1	152	47	13
Ollerton & Bever	8	4	0	4	105	132	8
Yarborough Bees	8	3	0	5	76	94	6
Rainworth	8	3	0	5	103	139	6
Horncastle	8	2	0	6	56	256	4
Harworth Coll	8	1	1	6	113	121	3
Bourne	8	1	1	6	63	153	3

Notts, Lincs & Derbys 4 West

	P	W	D	L	F	A	Pts
Melbourne	7	6	0	1	189	63	12
Hope Valley	7	6	0	1	185	78	12
*Bakewell Mann	6	4	0	2	84	90	10
*Leesbrook	6	4	0	2	104	58	10
Buxton	7	2	0	5	101	95	4
Bolsover	6	2	0	4	39	127	4
Tupton	7	1	0	6	83	168	2
East Leake	6	1	0	5	52	158	2

* 2 points for cancelled game.

TOSHIBA COUNTY CHAMPIONSHIP 1988-89

1 April, Twickenham
Durham 13 (3PG 1T)   **Cornwall 9** (3PG)

Chris Jones   *The Standard*

This was the final that brought county rugby supporters out of the closet. They arrived at Twickenham in their thousands to extol the virtues of a competition that seems only to excite those who do not play for the top 36 clubs. The 27,000 who turned Twickenham into a part of Cornwall for much of the match and a little bit of Durham at the final whistle, lifted the county competition on to a higher plane and dominated the headlines in the run-up to the match. In the end they were the better story. Over 100 coaches and three special trains transported a 20,000-strong Trelawny's Army to London, while 4,000 came from one of the northern outposts of the union game.

It wasn't much of a final, with the verdict going to Durham following Haag's indecision when a high kick was aimed at the Cornish line. The ball bounced awkwardly and the winger Trevaskis was caught in possession. Fenwick, the Durham hooker, emerged from the mayhem with the ball and burrowed his way over for the only try of the match. Trevaskis accepted the blame, but Haag should have taken charge of the ball. All the other points came from the boot of Bland, the Durham skipper, and his Cornish opposite number, Champion, both of whom kicked three penalties.

Cornwall surprised many by nominating Cambridge University captain Buzza at fly-half, even though he had been unable to play in any of the games prior to the final. Chapman, who had shared the kicking duties in early games, was put on the replacements' bench. Buzza managed to shine as an individual but did not link effectively with his centres on the day.

Cooke, the Durham wing, provided some of the best moments with his considerable pace and his eye for the tortuous route. He seems to take the view that it is easier to run around a defence rather than through it, and the wide open spaces of Twickenham took him close to the try-line on a couple of occasions.

Durham made an early impact in the competition when they defeated Yorkshire 37-20 in the opening round of Northern Division games and they followed this up by knocking over holders Lancashire 24-6 away from home. Only Northumberland managed to defeat them (12-8), although Cumbria came close before losing 17-16. Durham met Kent in the semi-finals and beat them 10-6 in London. Kent had emerged as winners in the London Division after defeating Hertfordshire 35-15 in the play-off following a poor season for Surrey and Middlesex. Cornwall had to overcome Warwickshire 13-10 at Redruth to make it to the final. It was at this same venue that they had beaten arch rivals Gloucestershire 25-7 at the beginning of their campaign in October. Warwickshire had, as usual, triumphed in the Midlands, disposing of North Midlands 24-6 in the play-off, but they could not overcome Cornwall in the semi-final.

TEAMS IN THE FINAL

Durham: J Bland (Durham City) (*capt*); O Evans (West Hartlepool), P de Glanville (Durham U), M Boyd (West Hartlepool), D Cooke (West Hartlepool); J Stabler

Contrasting reactions from the crowd, which was dominated by Cornwall supporters, because, underneath the pile, Mark Fenwick of Durham has scored the try which won his county the Toshiba Trophy.

(West Hartlepool), S Havery (Gateshead Fell); G Naisbitt (Stockton), M Fenwick
(Durham City), M Douthwaite (Stockton), J Dixon (West Hartlepool), J Howe (Sale),
A Harle (Gosforth), B Dixon (Stockton), A Brown (Stockton)
Scorers *Try:* Fenwick   *Penalty Goals:* Bland (3)
Cornwall (*Camborne unless stated*): C Alcock; B Trevaskis (Bath), G Champion (Devon &
Cornwall Police & Truro) (*capt*), S Rogers, D Weeks; A J Buzza (Cambridge U &
Redruth), D Rule; J May (Redruth), G Dawe (Bath), R Keast (Redruth), A Reed,
A Cook, G Williams (Redruth), M Haag (Bath), A Bick (Bath)
Scorer *Penalty Goals:* Champion (3)
Referee F A Howard (Liverpool Society)

TEAMS IN THE SEMI-FINALS

21 January, Redruth RFC
Cornwall 13 (3PG 1T)   Warwickshire 10 (2PG 1T)

Cornwall (*Camborne unless stated*): C Alcock; B Trevaskis (Bath), G Champion (Truro)
(*capt*), S Rogers, D Weeks; D Chapman, D Rule; J May (Redruth), B Andrew, R Keast
(Redruth), A Reed, A Cook, G Williams (Redruth), M Haag (Bath), A Bick (Bath)
Scorers *Try:* Trevaskis   *Penalty Goals:* Champion (3)
Warwickshire (*Coventry unless stated*): S Hall (Barker's Butts); W Boffey (Nuneaton),
C Medford, J Graham, C Leake (Nuneaton); R Massey (Nuneaton) (*capt*), M Calverly
(Nuneaton); M Linnett (Moseley), A Farrington, T Revan (Rugby), A Gulliver,
P Bowman (Rugby), P Thomas, R Travers, K Hickey   *Replacement* D Garforth
(Nuneaton) for Revan
Scorers *Try:* Hickey   *Penalty Goals:* Hall (2)
Referee R C Quittenton (London Society)

21 January, Blackheath RFC
Kent 6 (2PG)   Durham 10 (2PG 1T)

Kent: P Ashworth (Old Alleynians); D Osborne (Rosslyn Park), M Scott (Blackheath),
G Hughes (Llanelli), H Corless (Askeans); J Field (Askeans), H Evans (Pontypridd);
P Essenhigh (Rosslyn Park), R Taylor (Nottingham) (*capt*), F Croxford (London Irish),
P Catt (Richmond), R Langhorn (Harlequins), M Skinner (Harlequins), D Thresher
(Harlequins), M Harris (Blackheath)
Scorer *Penalty Goals:* Field (2)
Durham: J Bland (Durham City) (*capt*); O Evans (West Hartlepool), P de Glanville
(Durham U), M Boyd (West Hartlepool), D Cooke (West Hartlepool); J Stabler
(West Hartlepool), S Havery (Gateshead Fell); G Naisbitt (Stockton), M Fenwick
(Durham City), M Douthwaite (Stockton), J Howe (Sale), J Dixon (West Hartlepool),
A Harle (Gosforth), A Brown (Stockton), B Dixon (Stockton)
Scorers *Try:* Dixon   *Penalty Goals:* Bland (2)
Referee I M Bullerwell (East Midlands)

DIVISIONAL ROUNDS

Northern Division

Cumbria	9	Cheshire	7
Durham	37	Yorkshire	20

Lancashire	23	Northumberland	15
Cheshire	10	Yorkshire	17
Cumbria	13	Lancashire	7
Northumberland	12	Durham	8
Cumbria	30	Yorkshire	22
Lancashire	6	Durham	24
Northumberland	19	Cheshire	9
Durham	17	Cumbria	16
Lancashire	14	Cheshire	0
Yorkshire	9	Northumberland	20
Cheshire	6	Durham	27
Northumberland	18	Cumbria	22
Yorkshire	27	Lancashire	18

	P	W	D	L	F	A	Pts
Durham	5	4	0	1	113	60	8
Cumbria	5	4	0	1	90	71	8
Northumberland	5	3	0	2	84	71	6
Lancashire	5	2	0	3	68	79	4
Yorkshire	5	2	0	3	95	115	4
Cheshire	5	0	0	5	32	86	0

Midlands Division (Group A)

Staffordshire	22	East Midlands	24
East Midlands	18	North Midlands	23
North Midlands	16	Staffordshire	9

	P	W	D	L	F	A	Pts
North Midlands	2	2	0	0	39	27	4
East Midlands	2	1	0	1	42	45	2
Staffordshire	2	0	0	2	31	40	0

Midlands Division (Group B)

Leicestershire	16	Notts, Lincs & Derbys	21
Notts, Lincs & Derbys	8	Warwickshire	29
Warwickshire	23	Leicestershire	4

	P	W	D	L	F	A	Pts
Warwickshire	2	2	0	0	52	12	4
Notts, Lincs & Derbys	2	1	0	1	29	45	2
Leicestershire	2	0	0	2	20	44	0

Play-off Matches

North Midlands	29	Notts, Lincs & Derbys	16
Warwickshire	53	East Midlands	19

Divisional Final

Warwickshire	24	North Midlands	6

London Division (Group A)

Middlesex	9	Hertfordshire	12
Hertfordshire	12	Surrey	12
Surrey	22	Middlesex	46

	P	W	D	L	F	A	Pts
Hertfordshire	2	1	1	0	24	21	3
Middlesex	2	1	0	1	55	34	2
Surrey	2	0	1	1	34	58	1

London Division (Group B)

Eastern Counties	13	Hampshire	7
Kent	19	Sussex	9
Hampshire	16	Kent	21
Sussex	7	Eastern Counties	22
Eastern Counties	6	Kent	35
Hampshire	45	Sussex	9

	P	W	D	L	F	A	Pts
Kent	3	3	0	0	75	31	6
Eastern Counties	3	2	0	1	41	49	4
Hampshire	3	1	0	2	68	43	2
Sussex	3	0	0	3	25	86	0

Play-off Match

| Kent | 35 | Hertfordshire | 15 |

Kent were promoted to Group A for the 1989-90 season, while Surrey were relegated to Group B.

South-Western Division
Division 1

Cornwall	25	Gloucestershire	7
Devon	0	Dorset & Wilts	15
Devon	3	Cornwall	33
Dorset & Wilts	15	Gloucestershire	14
Dorset & Wilts	26	Cornwall	36
Gloucestershire	26	Devon	3

	P	W	D	L	F	A	Pts
Cornwall	3	3	0	0	94	22	6
Dorset & Wilts	3	2	0	1	42	50	4
Gloucestershire	3	1	0	2	47	43	2
Devon	3	0	0	3	6	74	0

Division 2

Buckinghamshire	10	Berkshire	24
Somerset	17	Oxfordshire	6
Berkshire	27	Oxfordshire	13
Buckinghamshire	3	Somerset	31

Oxfordshire	18	Buckinghamshire	10
Somerset	10	Berkshire	29

	P	W	D	L	F	A	Pts
Berkshire	3	3	0	0	80	33	6
Somerset	3	2	0	1	58	38	4
Oxfordshire	3	1	0	2	37	54	2
Buckinghamshire	3	0	0	3	23	73	0

Berkshire were promoted to Division 1 for the 1989-90 season, while Devon were relegated to Division 2.

ENGLISH COUNTY CHAMPIONS 1889-1989

FIRST SYSTEM

1889 **Yorkshire,** undefeated, declared champions by RU (scored 18G 17T to 1G 3T)

1890 **Yorkshire,** undefeated, declared champions (scored 10G 16T to 2G 4T)

SECOND SYSTEM

1891	**Lancashire** champions.	Group Winners — Yorkshire, Surrey, Gloucestershire.
1892	**Yorkshire** champions.	Group winners — Lancashire, Kent, Midlands.
1893	**Yorkshire** champions.	Group Winners — Cumberland, Devon, Middlesex.
1894	**Yorkshire** champions.	Group Winners — Lancashire, Gloucestershire, Midlands.
1895	**Yorkshire** champions.	Group Winners — Cumberland, Devon, Midlands.

THIRD SYSTEM

	Champions	*Runners-up*	*Played at*
1896	**Yorkshire**	Surrey	Richmond
1897	**Kent**	Cumberland	Carlisle
1898	**Northumberland**	Midlands	Coventry
1899	**Devon**	Northumberland	Newcastle
1900	**Durham**	Devon	Exeter
1901	**Devon**	Durham	W Hartlepool
1902	**Durham**	Gloucestershire	Gloucester
1903	**Durham**	Kent	W Hartlepool
1904	**Kent**	Durham	Blackheath (2nd meeting)
1905	**Durham**	Middlesex	W Hartlepool
1906	**Devon**	Durham	Exeter
1907	**Devon** and **Durham** joint champions after drawn games at W Hartlepool and Exeter		
1908	**Cornwall**	Durham	Redruth
1909	**Durham**	Cornwall	W Hartlepool
1910	**Gloucestershire**	Yorkshire	Gloucester
1911	**Devon**	Yorkshire	Headingley
1912	**Devon**	Northumberland	Devonport
1913	**Gloucestershire**	Cumberland	Carlisle
1914	**Midlands**	Durham	Leicester
1920	**Gloucestershire**	Yorkshire	Bradford

FOURTH SYSTEM

	Champions	*Runners-up*	*Played at*
1921	**Gloucestershire (31)**	Leicestershire (4)	Gloucester
1922	**Gloucestershire (19)**	N Midlands (0)	Birmingham
1923	**Somerset (8)**	Leicester (6)	Bridgwater
1924	**Cumberland (14)**	Kent (3)	Carlisle
1925	**Leicestershire (14)**	Gloucestershire (6)	Bristol
1926	**Yorkshire (15)**	Hampshire (14)	Bradford
1927	**Kent (22)**	Leicestershire (12)	Blackheath
1928	**Yorkshire (12)**	Cornwall (8)	Bradford
1929	***Middlesex (9)**	Lancashire (8)	Blundellsands

1930	Gloucestershire (13)	Lancashire (7)	Blundellsands
1931	Gloucestershire (10)	Warwickshire (9)	Gloucester
1932	Gloucestershire (9)	Durham (3)	Blaydon
1933	Hampshire (18)	Lancashire (7)	Boscombe
1934	E Midlands (10)	Gloucestershire (0)	Northampton
1935	Lancashire (14)	Somerset (0)	Bath
1936	Hampshire (13)	Northumberland (6)	Gosforth
1937	Gloucestershire (5)	E Midlands (0)	Bristol
1938	Lancashire (24)	Surrey (12)	Blundellsands
1939	Warwickshire (8)	Somerset (3)	Weston
1947	†Lancashire (14)	Gloucestershire (3)	Gloucester
1948	Lancashire (5)	E Counties (0)	Cambridge
1949	Lancashire (9)	Gloucestershire (3)	Blundellsands
1950	Cheshire (5)	E Midlands (0)	Birkenhead Park
1951	E Midlands (10)	Middlesex (0)	Northampton
1952	Middlesex (9)	Lancashire (6)	Twickenham
1953	Yorkshire (11)	E Midlands (3)	Bradford
1954	Middlesex (24)	Lancashire (6)	Blundellsands
1955	Lancashire (14)	Middlesex (8)	Twickenham
1956	Middlesex (13)	Devon (9)	Twickenham
1957	Devon (12)	Yorkshire (3)	Plymouth
1958	Warwickshire (16)	Cornwall (8)	Coventry
1959	Warwickshire (14)	Gloucestershire (9)	Bristol
1960	Warwickshire (9)	Surrey (6)	Coventry
1961	oCheshire (5)	Devon (3)	Birkenhead Park
1962	Warwickshire (11)	Hampshire (6)	Twickenham
1963	Warwickshire (13)	Yorkshire (10)	Coventry
1964	Warwickshire (8)	Lancashire (6)	Coventry
1965	Warwickshire (15)	Durham (9)	Hartlepool
1966	Middlesex (6)	Lancashire (0)	Blundellsands
1967	*Surrey and Durham		
1968	Middlesex (9)	Warwickshire (6)	Twickenham
1969	Lancashire (11)	Cornwall (9)	Redruth
1970	Staffordshire (11)	Gloucestershire (9)	Burton-on-Trent
1971	Surrey (14)	Gloucestershire (3)	Gloucester
1972	Gloucestershire (11)	Warwickshire (6)	Coventry
1973	Lancashire (17)	Gloucestershire (12)	Bristol
1974	Gloucestershire (22)	Lancashire (12)	Blundellsands
1975	Gloucestershire (13)	E Counties (9)	Gloucester
1976	Gloucester (24)	Middlesex (9)	Richmond
1977	Lancashire (17)	Middlesex (6)	Blundellsands
1978	N Midlands (10)	Gloucestershire (7)	Moseley
1979	Middlesex (19)	Northumberland (6)	Twickenham
1980	Lancashire (21)	Gloucestershire (15)	Vale of Lune
1981	Northumberland (15)	Gloucestershire (6)	Gloucester
1982	Lancashire (7)	North Midlands (3)	Moseley

FIFTH SYSTEM

	Champions	Runners-up	Played at
1983	Gloucestershire (19)	Yorkshire (7)	Bristol
1984	Gloucestershire (36)	Somerset (18)	Twickenham
1985	Middlesex (12)	Notts, Lincs and Derbys (9)	Twickenham
1986	Warwickshire (16)	Kent (6)	Twickenham
1987	Yorkshire (22)	Middlesex (11)	Twickenham
1988	Lancashire (23)	Warwickshire (18)	Twickenham
1989	Durham (13)	Cornwall (9)	Twickenham

*After a draw at Twickenham. †After a draw, 8-8, at Blundellsands. oAfter a draw 0-0, at Plymouth.
**Surrey and Durham drew 14 each at Twickenham and no score at Hartlepool and thus became joint champions. Gloucestershire have won the title 15 times, Lancashire 13, Yorkshire 12, Warwickshire 8, Middlesex 8, Durham 8 (twice jointly), Devon 7 (once jointly), Kent 3 times, Hampshire, East Midlands, Cheshire and Northumberland twice each, Surrey twice (once jointly), and Cornwall, Midlands (3rd System), Somerset, Cumberland, Leicestershire, Staffordshire and North Midlands once each.

THE BARBARIANS 1988-89

Geoffrey Windsor-Lewis

The Barbarians committee feel that the next five years will be of vital importance to the club. The 1988-89 season brought a feast of high-scoring matches, the highlight being a memorable game against the touring Australians, the final match of the tour, at Cardiff Arms Park. So the club is in excellent health. A vivid end-of-season occasion was provided when the Barbarians went to the Hong Kong Sevens.

However, the Australian game was the centrepiece of the season, and Cardiff Arms Park was almost full for the occasion. The lasting memory will be the brilliance of David Campese. He scored two tries and rounded off the game with a sublime individual try, weaving his way over from almost halfway. The crowd stood and applauded Campese all the way back to halfway, as did his team. Two early tries by Australia meant that the Barbarians were always struggling to get into the match. They led 18-6 at half-time, and although the Barbarians later reduced a 31-12 deficit to 31-22 the Wallabies were never in serious danger of losing. The highlight for the Barbarians was a try by Laity. The move was begun by Jonathan Davies near his own line. Davies re-gathered his own clever kick ahead and Laity and Underwood exchanged passes for Laity to score.

The Barbarians' season had started in September with a match against Glasgow Academicals at New Anniesland, in memory of Herbert Waddell, who was president from 1974 and had been an integral part of the Barbarian club for over 60 years. Thirteen tries were scored in a match which the Baa-Baas won 42-22. Iain Paxton celebrated his selection with four tries from No 8 and had a splendid game, while Matt Duncan was always a threat to the Accies on the wing and scored a fine try. Jonathan Davies scored another try with a scintillating run down the blindside. Graeme MacGregor, the Accies scrum-half and captain, led his side magnificently, and his team's three tries in the last quarter were due largely to his efforts.

The visit to Newport, now firmly established in early October, brought another victory for the Baa-Baas, by 60-18. Mark Ring enjoyed himself, registering 20 points. A powerful pack, in which Philip Matthews and Andy Robinson were outstanding, enabled Ring, Simon Halliday and Carwyn Davies to exploit all their attacking abilities.

The annual festive season encounter at Leicester, before a capacity crowd of 17,000, brought another thrilling match, which the Baa-Baas won by 36-10. The Baa-Baas included Campese, flown in from Italy, plus Frenchmen Lafond and Mesnel in their side. Two tries from that afternoon stand out. The first came when, from deep in their own territory, Campese and Lafond fed Thresher. He made a long pass to Hall who, with a dummy and fast acceleration, ran to the corner to complete a fine movement. The last try inevitably came from Campese. Mesnel linked with the Australian, who was all by himself some 50 metres out. But it made little difference to this amazing man. He left the opposition for dead and finished underneath the Leicester posts.

The visit to Northampton for the Mobbs Memorial Match later in the season is always a great occasion. Chris Oti, who scored three tries in the 1988 match, repeated his hat-trick within 22 minutes of the start of play in 1989. Although the East Midlands fought well, the Baa-Baas had the last word, winning 34-22. A happy feature of this match was that the three Milne brothers, Iain, Kenneth and David, all played in the front row for the Barbarians, the first time in the history of the club that three brothers had played in the same team. It was also a fitting farewell to Dusty Hare, who was captain for the day on his last appearance for the club.

Easter Saturday and Cardiff are synonymous with Barbarian rugby, and in 1989 a huge crowd enjoyed a rousing match, which Cardiff won by 24-21. Cardiff scored first when a clearance did not find touch. Steve Ford sprinted all the way down the touch-line to score. Chalmers, Hartley and Rob Egerton, who had a most effective game at full-back, scored tries for the Baa-Baas; Chalmers converted them all and kicked a penalty goal. In the last quarter of the match, the Baa-Baas, who held the lead, lost Craig Chalmers and Cardiff took a couple of chances to clinch a narrow victory. A tribute should be paid to Alan Phillips, the Cardiff hooker, who has now retired after a long career in Welsh rugby. He is a fine Barbarian.

After two successive victories against Swansea, the trend was reversed by a 30-35 defeat. The home side had a flying start with the wind behind them and were leading by 22 points after only 20 minutes of play. It proved a decisive phase of the game: the Baa-Baas, trying to involve Egerton and Oti as much as possible, twice crept up to within two points at 26-24 and 32-30. But errors and a lack of cohesion at vital moments prevented them taking the lead. Bob Kimmins had one of his finest games of the season and impressed everyone with a powerful all-round display for the visitors.

The Barbarians may have been defeated in both their Easter tour matches, but their tradition was upheld at Cardiff and St Helens and the entertainment did not lack colour. The season produced 245 points from seven matches but, more importantly, 46 tries. An interesting point is that only one penalty goal was scored.

The Baa-Baas returned to the Hong Kong Sevens after a gap of seven years and thoroughly enjoyed taking part in this superb tournament. Finlay Calder led the team and was ably supported by his squad. After victories against Papua New Guinea and Spain in their group the team went on to beat Canada, just losing to Australia in the semi-final. The result was a disappointment since the Baa-Baas had been very much on top at the end of the match – but they had left it too late.

The two Barbarian locks, Wade Dooley and Bob Norster, join forces to win possession against Australia in the tour finale at Cardiff.

RESULTS 1988-89

Played 7   Won 4   Lost 3   Points for 245   (29G 1PG 17T)   **Points against 180**
(17G 6PG 15T)
1988

3 Sept	**Beat Glasgow Academicals** at New Anniesland (Herbert Waddell Memorial Match) 42 (5G 3T) to 22 (1G 4T)
4 Oct	**Beat Newport** at Newport 60 (8G 3T) to 18 (3G)
26 Nov	**Lost to Australia** at Cardiff Arms Park 22 (3G 1T) to 40 (5G 2PG 1T)
28 Dec	**Beat Leicester** at Leicester 36 (4G 3T) to 19 (1G 3PG 1T)
1989	
8 March	**Beat East Midlands** at Franklin Gardens, Northampton 34 (3G 4T) to 22 (1G 4T)
25 March	**Lost to Cardiff** at Cardiff Arms Park 21 (3G 1PG) to 24 (2G 3T)
27 March	**Lost to Swansea** at St Helens, Swansea 30 (3G 3T) to 35 (4G 1PG 2T)
	Cathay Pacific-Hong Kong Bank Invitation Sevens Pool D: Barbarians 26, Papua New Guinea 0; Barbarians 24, Spain 4

Quarter-final: Barbarians 24, Canada 12
Semi-final: Barbarians 10, Australia 12
Total Points: for 84; against 28

PLAYERS 1988-89
Abbreviations GA – Glasgow Academicals; N – Newport; A – Australia; L – Leicester; EM – East Midlands; SW1 – Cardiff; SW2 – Swansea; HK – Hong Kong Sevens; (R) – Replacement; * – New Barbarian

Full-backs: P H Thorburn (Neath & Wales) [GA]; A G Hastings (London Scottish & Scotland) [N, A]; R Giles (Cardiff & Wales) [N(R) replaced Hastings]; * S E Thresher (Harlequins) [L]; W H Hare (Leicester & England) [EM]; * R H Egerton (Oxford U) [SW1, SW2]

Threequarters: M D F Duncan (West of Scotland & Scotland) [GA, A, SW1, SW2]; C Laity (Neath) [GA, A]; R J Laidlaw (Jedforest & Scotland) [GA(R) replaced Laity]; W D C Carling (Harlequins & England) [GA]; * C Davies (Llanelli) [GA, N]; M D Bailey (Wasps & England) [N, SW1]; * S Davies (Llanelli) [N]; S J Halliday (Bath & England) [N]; M G Ring (Cardiff & Wales) [A]; R Underwood (Leicester, RAF & England) [A]; J-B Lafond (Racing Club de France & France) [L]; * M R Hall (Cambridge U & Wales) [L, EM, HK]; M H J Douglas (London Welsh & Wales) [L(R) replaced Hall]; * F Mesnel (Racing Club de France & France) [L]; * D I Campese (Milan & Australia) [L]; * A T Harriman (Harlequins) [EM]; S Hastings (Watsonians & Scotland) [EM, HK]; R H Q B Moon (Harlequins) [EM (R) replaced Hastings]; C Oti (Wasps & England) [EM, SW2]; * W L Renwick (London Scottish) [SW1, SW2]; G J Hartley (Nottingham) [SW1, SW2]; A Emyr (Swansea & Wales) [HK]

Half-backs: J Davies (Llanelli & Wales) [GA, A]; R N Jones (Swansea & Wales) [GA, A]; M G Ring (Cardiff & Wales) [N]; M H J Douglas (London Welsh & Wales) [N]; * P Turner (Newbridge) [L]; J L Griffiths (Llanelli & Wales) [L, HK]; S Barnes (Bath & England) [EM, HK]; * L F P Aherne (Lansdowne & Ireland) [EM]; * C M Chalmers (Melrose & Scotland) [SW1]; M E Hancock (Nottingham) [SW1(R) replaced Chalmers, SW2]; * S M Bates (Wasps) [SW1]; * D W Evans (Cardiff & Wales) [SW2]

Forwards: D C Fitzgerald (Lansdowne & Ireland) [GA]; I J Watkins (Ebbw Vale & Wales) [GA, L, SW1, SW2(R) replaced I Jones]; D Young (Swansea & Wales) [GA, A]; * N G B Edwards (Harlequins) [GA, EM, SW2, HK]; D G Lenihan (Cork & Ireland) [GA]; G W Rees (Nottingham & England) [GA, EM]; F Calder (Stewart's-Melville FP & Scotland) [GA, L, HK]; I A M Paxton (Selkirk & Scotland) [GA, A]; D M B Sole (Edinburgh Acads & Scotland) [N, A]; S J Smith (Ballymena & Ireland) [N, A]; J J McCoy (Bangor & Ireland) [N]; * A J Kembury (Neath) [N]; J Olver (Harlequins) [N(R) replaced Kembury, EM (R) replaced K Milne]; D F Cronin (Bath & Scotland) [N]; P M Matthews (Dublin Wanderers & Ireland) [N, A]; D B White (Gala & Scotland) [N]; * R A Robinson (Bath & England) [N, A]; W A Dooley (Preston Grasshoppers & England) [A]; R L Norster (Cardiff & Wales) [A]; * A K Brewster (Stewart's Melville FP & Scotland) [L]; * J A Probyn (Wasps & England) [L, SW1]; N C Redman (Bath & England) [L]; P J Ackford (Harlequins & England) [L]; A S Hodgson (Vale of Lune) [L, EM, SW2]; M C Teague (Gloucester & England) [L]; * D F Milne (Heriot's FP) [EM]; * K S Milne (Heriot's FP) [EM]; I G Milne (Heriot's FP & Scotland) [EM]; W A Anderson (Dungannon & Ireland) [EM]; W P Moriarty (Swansea & Wales) [EM]; P A G Rendall (Wasps & England) [SW1]; C A Gray (Nottingham & Scotland) [SW1]; * R Kimmins (Orrell) [SW1, SW2]; R I Wainwright (Cambridge U) [SW1, HK]; * I Jones (Llanelli) [SW1, SW2]; * D Ryan (Saracens) [SW1, SW2]; M Griffiths (Bridgend & Wales) [SW2]; * P John (Pontypridd) [SW2]; R Morgan (Newport) [SW2]; J Jeffrey (Kelso & Scotland) [HK]

TRIUMPHANT OXFORD'S ADVANTAGE
THE VARSITY MATCH 1988
(for the Bowring Bowl)

6 December, Twickenham
Oxford University 27 (2G 1DG 3T)
Cambridge University 7 (1DG 1T)

The revival of interest and excellence in the Varsity match reached new heights when, in front of 54,000 spectators, one of the biggest crowds ever seen at Twickenham outside internationals, Oxford won a magnificent victory. It was a thoroughbred performance and both Cambridge and Clive Norling, the referee, played a full part. Cambridge were nothing like so far behind the run of play as the score would suggest and Mr Norling gave a display of refereeing, especially in his use of the advantage law, that won widespread praise.

The mastery at half-back of Brian Smith and David Kirk, two antipodean internationals, was the basis of Oxford's authority, while the talents of Rob Egerton, the full-back, provided a cutting edge. Cambridge were badly wounded by the withdrawal of Andy Macdonald, their 6 feet 8-inch lock, and their lack of composure when the try-line beckoned was another drawback; but the class and ambition of both teams still left an unforgettable impression.

Adrian Davies, the Cambridge centre, opened the scoring with a dropped goal but then Egerton made Smith's first try with a startling run. However, a lovely pass from Alan Buzza made a try for Cameron Glasgow to put Cambridge back in front. After this, Oxford took over: Egerton scored a try with a chip-and-chase and after half-time Oxford hammered in the nails with three tries. David Evans cut through within three minutes of the restart for a try which Smith converted and shortly afterwards Evans dropped a goal. Smith scored his second try and converted it himself, thus securing the Bowring Bowl. Finally, David Cook, who was unlucky not to have started the match after playing so well for Oxford throughout the term, scored with his first touch after arriving as replacement for Ian Williams. Mark Hancock, Cambridge's captain, was asked afterwards if he was despondent. 'How could I be after a game like that?' he replied.

Oxford University: R H Egerton (Marist, Canberra & University); I M Williams (Epping HS, Sydney & St Catherine's), M E O Brown (Diocesan College, Cape Town & Worcester), D W Evans (Aberdare CS & St Anne's), S J R Vessey (Magdalen College School & Green) *(capt)*; B A Smith (Brisbane State HS & St Anne's), D E Kirk (Wanganui Collegiate School & Worcester); A D Williams (Fishguard CS & St Anne's), E R Norwitz (South African Collegiate & University), T G Willis (Wellington College & St Edmund Hall), W M C Stileman (Wellington College & Wycliffe), S C Wensley (Bishop of Llandaff HS & Wadham), T Coker (St Paul's, Brisbane & Lady Margaret Hall), M S Egan (Terenure College & St Anne's), A J Cameron (Knox GS, Sydney &

Rupert Vessey, the Oxford captain, flourishes the Bowring Bowl after his side's triumph.

University) *Replacements* S R Williams (Caldey Grange & Lincoln) for Willis; D J Cook (St John's Leatherhead & Christ Church) for I Williams
Scorers *Tries:* Smith (2), Egerton, Evans, Cook *Conversions:* Smith (2)
Dropped Goal: Evans
Cambridge University: A J Buzza (Redruth CS & Hughes Hall); I C Glasgow (Dollar Academy & Magdalene), M R Hall (Brynteg CS & Wolfson), A Davies (Pencoed CS & Robinson), G Davies (Pencoed CS & Magdalene); A J Sutton (Llanishen HS, Cardiff & Magdalene), M E Hancock (Heversham GS & Hughes Hall) (*capt*); J Foster (Magdalen College School & Robinson), J Ashworth (George Fox, Lancaster & Homerton), S A Wordley (Queen Mary's GS & Downing), M Vickerstaff (Bishop Veysey GS & Selwyn), J J Cake (Worthing VIth Form College & Corpus Christi), S S Bryant (Sherborne & Hughes Hall), C B Vyvyan (Downside & Wolfson), R I Wainwright (Glenalmond & Magdalene) *Replacement* A J Tunningley (Downing) for Buzza
Scorers *Try:* Glasgow *Dropped Goal:* A Davies
Referee C Norling (Wales)

Cambridge University LX Club 6 (2PG)
Oxford University Greyhounds 29 (2G 3PG 2T)

Cambridge University LX Club: M A Risman; S Bell, S Townsley, A J Tunningley, D David; D Shufflebotham, S James; A Jones, I Singleton (*capt*), D Meirion-Jones, J Kemshall, W Cozzens, S Ives, R Pool-Jones, J J Cake *Replacement* R Given for Pool-Jones
Scorer *Penalty Goals:* Townsley (2)
Oxford University Greyhounds: D J Cook; N Watson, D Polkinghorne, M Rees, S Dineen; E Egan, G Fell; A Orr, N Sharrock, S R Williams, D Wood, S Crawford, P Buckland, R Horrocks-Taylor, J Park (*capt*) *Replacement* D Wooller for Rees
Scorers *Tries:* Orr, Cook (2), Polkinghorne *Conversions:* Polkinghorne, Dineen
Penalty Goals: Polkinghorne (3)
Referee K Morgan (Eastern Counties)

Oxford University Whippets 25, Cambridge University LX Club II 24; Cambridge University 28, M R Steele-Bodger's XV 16; Oxford University 37, Major R V Stanley's XV 15

VARSITY MATCH RESULTS

107 Matches played   Oxford 46 wins   Cambridge 48 wins   13 Draws

Match played at Oxford 1871-72; Cambridge 1872-73; The Oval 1873-74 to 1879-80; Blackheath 1880-81 to 1886-87; Queen's Club 1887-88 to 1920-21; then Twickenham.   *At this date no match could be won unless a goal was scored.

Year	Winner	Score
1871-72	Oxford	1G 1T to 0
1872-73	Cambridge	1G 2T to 0
1873-74	Drawn	1T each
1874-75*	Drawn	Oxford 2T to 0
1875-76	Oxford	1T to 0
1876-77	Cambridge	1G 2T to 0
1877-78	Oxford	2T to 0
1878-79	Drawn	No score
1879-80	Cambridge	1G 1DG to 1DG
1880-81	Drawn	1T each
1881-82	Oxford	2G 1T to 1G
1882-83	Oxford	1T to 0
1883-84	Oxford	3G 4T to 1G
1884-85	Oxford	3G 1T to 1T
1885-86	Cambridge	2T to 0
1886-87	Cambridge	3T to 0
1887-88	Cambridge	1DG 2T to 0
1888-89	Cambridge	1G 2T to 0
1889-90	Oxford	1G 1T to 0
1890-91	Drawn	1G each
1891-92	Cambridge	2T to 0
1892-93	Drawn	No score
1893-94	Oxford	1T to 0
1894-95	Drawn	1G each
1895-96	Cambridge	1G to 0
1896-97	Oxford	1G 1DG to 1G 1T
1897-98	Oxford	2T to 0
1898-99	Cambridge	1G 2T to 0
1899-1900	Cambridge	2G 4T to 0
1900-01	Oxford	2G to 1G 1T
1901-02	Oxford	1G 1T to 0
1902-03	Drawn	1G 1T each
1903-04	Oxford	3G 1T to 2G 1T
1904-05	Cambridge	3G to 2G
1905-06	Cambridge	3G (15) to 2G 1T (13)
1906-07	Oxford	4T (12) to 1G 1T (8)
1907-08	Oxford	1G 4T (17) to 0
1908-09	Drawn	1G (5) each
1909-10	Oxford	4G 5T (35) to 1T (3)
1910-11	Oxford	4G 1T (23) to 3G 1T (18)
1911-12	Oxford	2G 3T (19) to 0
1912-13	Cambridge	2G (10) to 1T (3)
1913-14	Cambridge	1DG 3T (13) to 1T (3)
1914-18	*No matches*	
1919-20	Cambridge	1DG 1PG (7) to 1G (5)
1920-21	Oxford	1G 4T (17) to 1G 3T (14)
1921-22	Oxford	1G 2T (11) to 1G (5)
1922-23	Cambridge	3G 2T (21) to 1G 1T (8)
1923-24	Oxford	3G 2T (21) to 1G 1PG 2T (14)
1924-25	Oxford	1G 2T (11) to 2T (6)
1925-26	Cambridge	3G 6T (33) to 1T (3)
1926-27	Cambridge	3G 5T (30) to 1G (5)
1927-28	Cambridge	2G 2PG 2T (22) to 1G 3T (14)
1928-29	Cambridge	1G 3T (14) to 1DG 1PG 1T (10)
1929-30	Oxford	1G 1DG (9) to 0
1930-31	Drawn	Oxford 1PG (3) Cambridge 1T (3)
1931-32	Oxford	1DG 2T (10) to 1T (3)
1932-33	Oxford	1G 1T (8) to 1T (3)
1933-34	Oxford	1G (5) to 1T (3)
1934-35	Cambridge	2G 1DG 1PG 4T (29) to 1DG (4)
1935-36	Drawn	No score
1936-37	Cambridge	2T (6) to 1G (5)
1937-38	Oxford	1G 4T (17) to 1DG (4)
1938-39	Cambridge	1G 1PG (8) to 2PG (6)
1939-45	*War-time series*	
1945-46	Cambridge	1G 2T (11) to 1G 1PG (8)
1946-47	Oxford	1G 1DG 2T (15) to 1G (5)
1947-48	Cambridge	2PG (6) to 0
1948-49	Oxford	1G 1DG 2T (14) to 1G 1PG (8)
1949-50	Oxford	1T (3) to 0
1950-51	Oxford	1G 1PG (8) to 0
1951-52	Oxford	2G 1T (13) to 0
1952-53	Cambridge	1PG 1T (6) to 1G (5)
1953-54	Drawn	Oxford 1PG 1T (6) Cambridge 2PG (6)
1954-55	Cambridge	1PG (3) to 0
1955-56	Oxford	1PG 2T (9) to 1G (5)
1956-57	Cambridge	1G 1DG 1PG 1T (14) to 2PG 1T (9)
1957-58	Oxford	1T (3) to 0
1958-59	Cambridge	1G 1PG 3T (17) to 1PG 1T (6)
1959-60	Oxford	3PG (9) to 1PG (3)
1960-61	Cambridge	2G 1T (13) to 0
1961-62	Cambridge	1DG 2T (9) to 1DG (3)
1962-63	Cambridge	1G 1DG 1PG 1T (14) to 0
1963-64	Cambridge	2G 1PG 2T (19) to 0
1964-65	Oxford	2G 1PG 2T (19) to 1PG 1GM (6)
1965-66	Drawn	1G each
1966-67	Oxford	1G 1T (8) to 1DG 1T (6)
1967-68	Cambridge	1T 1PG (6) to 0
1968-69	Cambridge	1T 1PG 1DG (9) to 2T (6)
1969-70	Oxford	3PG (9) to 2PG (6)
1970-71	Oxford	1G 1DG 2T (14) to 1PG (3)
1971-72	Oxford	3PG 3T (21) to 1PG (3)
1972-73	Cambridge	1G 1PG 1DG 1T (16) to 2PG (6)
1973-74	Cambridge	1DG 1PG 2T (14) to 2PG (12)
1974-75	Cambridge	1G 2PG 1T (16) to 5PG (15)
1975-76	Cambridge	2G 5PG 1DG (34) to 3PG 1DG (12)
1976-77	Cambridge	1G 3PG (15) to 0
1977-78	Oxford	4PG 1T (16) to 2PG 1T (10)
1978-79	Cambridge	2G 3PG 1T (25) to 1PG 1T (7)
1979-80	Oxford	2PG 1DG (9) to 1PG (3)
1980-81	Cambridge	3PG 1T (13) to 3PG (9)
1981-82	Cambridge	3PG (9) to 2PG (6)
1982-83	Cambridge	3PG 1DG 2T (20) to 1G 1PG 1T (13)
1983-84	Cambridge	4PG 2T (20) to 3PG (9)
1984-85	Cambridge	4G 2T (32) to 2PG (6)
1985-86	Oxford	1PG 1T (7) to 2PG (6)
1986-87	Oxford	3PG 2DG (15) to 1PG 1DG 1T (10)
1987-88	Cambridge	1DG 3T (15) to 2PG 1T (10)
1988-89	Oxford	2G 3T 1DG (27) to 1DG 1T (7)

THE WAR-TIME MATCHES

Year	Winner	Score		Winner	Score
1939-40	Oxford	1G 1DG 2T (15) to 1T (3) (at Cambridge)		Cambridge	1G 3T (14) to 2G 1T (13) (at Oxford)
1940-41	Cambridge	1G 2T (11) to 1G 1DG (9) (at Oxford)		Cambridge	2G 2T (16) to 1T (3) (at Cambridge)
	Cambridge	2G 1T (13) to 0 (at Cambridge)	1943-44	Cambridge	2G 1T (13) to 1DG (4) (at Cambridge)
1941-42	Cambridge	1PG 2T (9) to 1PG 1T (6) (at Cambridge)		Oxford	2T (6) to 1G (5) (at Oxford)
	Cambridge	1G 2PG 2T (17) to 1G 1T (8) (at Oxford)	1944-45	Drawn	1T (3) each (at Oxford)
1942-43	Cambridge	1G 1DG (9) to 0 (at Oxford)		Cambridge	2G 2T (16) to DG (4) (at Cambridge)

OXFORD and CAMBRIDGE BLUES 1872-1988

(Each year indicates a separate appearance, and refers to the first half of the season. Thus 1879 refers to the match played in the 1879-80 season). (R) indicates an appearance as a Replacement.

OXFORD

Abbott, J S	1954-55	Bowers, J B	1932-34	Chislett, J	1986-87
Abell, G E B	1923-24-25-26	Boyce, A W	1952-53	Cholmondeley, F G	1871-73
Adamson, J A	1928-29-31	Boyd, A de H	1924	Christopherson, P	1886-87-88
Adcock, J R L	1961	Boyd, E F	1912	Clark, R B	1978-79
Aitken, G G	1922-24	Boyle, D S	1967-68-69	Clarke, E J D	1973
Aldridge, J E	1888	Brace, D O	1955-56	Clarke, I A	1913
Alexander, H	1897-98	Bradby, G F	1882-85	Clauss, P R	1889-90-91
Alexander, P C	1930	Bradford, C C	1887	Clements, B S	1975
Allaway, R C P	1953-54-55	Branfoot, E P	1878-79	Cleveland, C R	1885-86
Allen, C P	1881-82-83	Bray, C N	1979	Cochran, P C	1889-91
Allen, T	1909	Bremridge, H	1876-77	Cohen B A	1884
Allen, W C	1910	Brett, J A	1935-36-37	Coker, J B H	1965
Allison, M G	1955	Brett, P V	1978	Coker, T	1988
Almond, R G P	1937	Brewer, R J	1965	Cole, B W	1945
Ashby, C J	1973	Brewer, T J	1951	Coleman, D J	1982-83
Asher, A G G	1881-82-83-84	Bridge, D J W	1946-47-48	Coles, D G G	1937-38
Asquith, P R	1974	Brierley, H	1871	Coles, P	1884-85-86
Atkinson, C C	1876	Britton, R B	1963-64	Coles, S C	1954-56-57
		Bromet, W E	1889	Collingwood, J A	1961-62
Back, A	1878	Brooks, A W	1980-81-82	Colville, A H	1892-93
Badenoch, D F	1971	Brooks, M J	1873	Conway-Rees, J	1891-92-93
Baden-Powell, F S	1873	Brooks, W	1872	Cook, D J	1988 (R)
Baggaley, J C	1953-54	Broster, L R	1912	Cooke, J L	1968-69
Bain, D McL	1910-11-12-13	Broughton, R C	1965	Cooke, P	1936-37
Bainbrigge, J H	1874-76-77	Brown, L G	1910-11-12	Cooke, W R	1976
Baird, J S	1966-67	Brown, M E O	1988	Cookson, G H F	1891-92
Baiss, R S H	1894-95	Brunskill, R F	1873-74	Cooper, A H	1951
Baker, C D	1891-93	Bryan, T A	1975-76-77	Cooper, M McG	1934-35-36
Baker, D G S	1951-52	Bryer, L W	1953	Cooper, R A	1937
Baker, E M	1893-94-95-96	Buchanan, F G	1909-10	Cooper, R M	1946
Baker, P	1980 (R)	Bucknall, A L	1965-66	Cornish, W H	1876
Baker, R T	1968	Budge, K J	1977-78-79	Couper, T	1899-1900
Balfour, E R	1893-94-95	Budworth, R T D	1887-88-89	Court, E D	1882-83
Bannerman, J MacD	1927-28	Bullard, G L	1950-51	Cousins, F C	1885-86
Barker, A C	1966-67	Bullock, H	1910-11	Coutts, I D F	1951
Barnes, S	1981-82-83	Bulpett, C W L	1871	Coventry, R G T	1889-90-91
Barr, D C A	1980	Burnet, P J	1960	Cowen, T J	1938
Barry, C E	1897-98-99	Burrow, K C	1933	Cowlishaw, F I	1890-91
Barry, D M	1968-69-70	Burse, R M	1974	Cox, G V	1878
Barwick, W M	1880-81	Bush, A	1934	Cozens-Hardy, B	1904-05-06
Bass, R G	1961	Bussell, J G	1903-04	Crabbie, J E	1898-99-1900-01
Batchelor, T B	1906	Butcher, W M	1954	Craig, F J R	1963-64-65
Bateson, H D	1874-75-77	Butler, F E R	1959-60	Crane, C M	1985-86-87
Baxter, T J	1958-59	Button, E L	1936	Cranmer, P	1933-34
Beamish, S H	1971	Byers, R M	1926	Crawfurd, J W F A	1900
Beare, A	1982			Creese, N A H	1951
Bedford, T P	1965-66-67	Caccia, H A	1926	Cridlan, A G	1928-29-30
Behn, A R	1968-69	Cadell, P R	1890	Croker, J R	1966-67
Bell, D L	1970	Cairns, A G	1899-1900-01	Crole, G B	1913-19
Benson, E T	1928	Calcraft, W J	1986-87	Cronje, S N	1907-08
Bentley, P J	1960	Cameron, A J	1988	Crosse, C W	1874
Berkeley, W V	1924-25-26	Campbell, E	1919-20-21	Crowe, P J	1981-82-83
Berry, C W	1883-84	Campbell, W	1987	Crump, L M	1896
Bettington, R H B	1920-22	Cannell, L B	1948-49-50	Cuff, T W	1945
Bevan, J H	1946	Cardale, C F	1929-30	Cunningham, G	1907-08-09
Bibby, A J	1980-81	Carey, G M	1891-92-94	Currie, J D	1954-55-56-57
Binham, P A	1971	Carey, W J	1894-95-96-97	Curry, J A H	1961
Birrell, H B	1953	Carlyon, H B	1871	Curtis, A B	1949
Black, B M	1929	Carroll, B M	1970-71		
Blair, A S	1884	Carroll, P R	1968-69-70	Dalby, C	1923
Blencowe, L C	1907-08	Carter, C R	1885	Davey, P	1967
Bloxham, C T	1934-35-36-37	Cartwright, V H	1901-02-03-04	Davey, R A E	1972
Blyth, P H	1885-86	Cass, T	1961	David, A M	1921-22
Bolton, W H	1873-74-75	Castens, H H	1886-87	Davies, D B	1905-06-07
Bonham-Carter, E	1890-91	Cattell, R H B	1893	Davies, D E	1951
Boobbyer, B	1949-50-51	Cave, H W	1881	Davies, D M	1958-59-60
Booker, J L	1880	Cawkwell, G L	1946-47	Davies, J A B	1920
Booth, J L	1956	Chadwick, A J	1898-99	Davies, L L J	1927
Bos, F H ten	1958-59-60	Chambers, J C	1921	Davies, R	1969
Boswell, J D	1885-86-87	Champain, F H B	1897-98-99	Davies, R H	1955-56-57
Botfield, A S G	1871	Champneys, F W	1874-75-76	Davies S J T	1972-73
Botting, I J	1949-50	Charles, A E S	1932	Davies, W G	1977
Bourdillon, H	1873-74-75	Cheesman, W I	1910-11	Davis, R A	1974-75
Bourns, C	1903	Cheyne, H	1903-04	Davis, T M E	1978-79-80

Dawkins, P M	1959-60-61
Deacon, E A	1871-72
De Winton, R F C	1888-89-90
Dew, C J	1978
Diamond, A J	1957
Dickson, M R	1903
Dickson, W M	1912
Diggle, P R	1908-09
Dingemans, J M	1985
Dingle, A J	1911
Disney, P C W	1935
Dixon, P J	1967-68-69-70
Dobson, D D	1899-1900-01
Donald, D G	1911-12-13
Donaldson, C L	1895
Donaldson, D W	1893
Donaldson, W P	1892-93-94
Donnelly, M P	1946
Donovan, T J	1971
Douglas, A I	1970-71
Dorman, J M A	1964
Dowson, A O	1896
Druitt, W A H	1929-30-31
Dryburgh, D J W	1926
Drysdale, D	1925
Dunbar, I T	1970-71-73
Duncan, D D	1919-20
Dunn, L B	1897
Duthie, A L	1986-87
Eberle, G S J F	1901-02
Edgell, E M R	1871-73
Edmiston, J H F	1926-27
Edmonds, J N	1978
Egan, M S	1988
Egerton, R H	1987-88
Ellis, A W	1975
Elwes, A C	1892-93
Emms, D A	1949-50
Enevoldson, T P	1976-77-78-79-80
Evans, A H	1877-78
Evans, C D	1984
Evans, C H	1919-20
Evans, D P	1959
Evans, D W	1887-88
Evans, D W	1988
Evanson, A M	1880-81
Evers, C P	1897-98
Evers, R W	1909
Ewart, C B	1982
Ewing, M H O	1886
Faktor, S J	1977
Fallon, T J	1953-55
Farquharson, J C L	1903
Fearenside, E	1903
Fellows-Smith, J P	1953-54
Ferguson, S M	1986
Fergusson, E A J	1952-53
Field, H	1873
Filby, L L	1960
Fildes, D G	1922-25
Finch, C J	1978
Findlay, A C	1983
Fisher, C D C	1902
Fisher, S J	1976
Fleming, C J N	1887-88-89-90
Flemmer, W K	1906
Fletcher, K R	1871
Fletcher, W R B	1871-73-74
Forman, J	1875-76
Forsayth, H H	1920-21
Forster, F M McL	1937
Fowler, H	1877-78
Francis, C K	1871
Francis, D G	1919
Franklin, H W F	1923
Fraser, E C	1872-73-74-75
Freakes, H D	1936-37-38
Furnival, A G D	1987
Gabitass, J R	1965-66
Gaisford, R B	1876

Galbraith, J H	1947
Game, W H	1872-73-74
Gardner, C J	1905-06
Gardner, J W	1871
Gargan, M F	1980-82-83
Gedge, H T S	1893
Geen, W P	1910-11-12
Gent, G N	1949
German, G J	1922
Gibson, A G	1894-95
Gibson, C H	1927
Gill, R D	1947-48
Gilmour, A	1911
Gilray, C M	1908-09
Gilthorpe, C G	1946-47
Glover, J	1959-60
Glover, T R	1973-74
Glubb, J M	1887
Glynn, R I	1985
Gooding, W F	1872-73
Goold, A N	1927
Gordon, P F C	1970
Gotley, A L H	1909
Gould, E J H	1963-64-65-66
Grant, A D	1922
Grant, A H	1892
Green, R	1948-49-50
Greenhalgh, J E	1984
Gregson, R E S	1903
Grellet, R C	1899-1900-01-02
Grenfell, W T	1888
Grieve, C F	1934-35-36
Griffin, S J M	1985-86
Griffith, C J L	1950-51-52
Griffiths, D A	1969-70
Griffiths, R L	1969
Grischotti, W	1899
Gubb, T W	1926-27-28-29
Gush, E P	1963
Guy, J C	1934
Habergham, W D R	1980-82
Hadman, W G	1964-65-66
Hall, J D	1885-86
Halliday, S J	1979-80-81
Hamilton, C W	1872
Hammond, C E L	1899-1900
Hands, K C M	1912
Hands, P A M	1910
Hands, R H M	1908-09
Harcourt, A B	1945-46
Harding, R F	1935
Harper, C H	1897-98
Harrison, C F	1873-74-75
Hartley, J C	1894-95-96
Harvey, R C M	1886
Havard, W T	1919
Hawkesworth, C J	1970-71-72
Heal, M G	1971
Hearn, R D	1964
Heath, A H	1875-77-78-79
Hefer, W J	1949-50
Henderson, J H	1952
Henderson, N F	1886
Henley, W E	1929-30-31
Heppenstall, A F	1926-27
Herring, D G	1909
Herrod, N J	1981-82-83
Higham, J R S	1959
Hillard, R J	1923-24
Hiller, R	1965
Hines, G W	1961-62
Hirst, E T	1877-78-79
Hoadley, A A	1905-06
Hoare, A H M	1956-57
Hobart, A H	1981
Hockley, M	1975
Hodges, H A	1905-06-07-08
Hodgson, F W	1881
Hofmeyr, K de J	1927
Hofmeyr, M B	1948-49-50
Hofmeyr, S J	1928-29-30
Hofmeyr, S M	1979

Hollis, G	1938
Holroyd, C A	1966
Honey, R	1909-10
Hood, R K	1976
Hoolahan, R M C	1976-77-78
Hopkins, K M	1977
Hordern, P C	1928
Horne, E C	1975-76-77
Hoskin, W W	1904-05-06-07
Houston, K J	1964
Hovde, F L	1931
Howard, A	1907
Howard, P D	1929-30
Howe-Browne, N R F G	1905-06
Hoyer-Millar, G C	1952
Hughes, H M	1935-36
Hughes, R A	1978
Hugo-Hamman, C T	1981-82
Hume, J W G	1927-28
Humfrey, L C	1892-93
Humphrey, M W	1923
Hunt, R W	1890
Hunter, R S	1888-89
Hutchinson, J M	1972-73
Hutchison, R O	1902
Ilett, N L	1947
Inglis, R E	1883-84
Irwin, H	1880
Isherwood, F W	1871
Jackson, K L T	1932-33
Jackson, W M	1938
Jacob, G O	1878-79
Jacob, H P	1923-24-25
Jacot, B L	1920
James, A I	1934
James, J	1875-76-77
James, S	1970-71
James, S J B	1966
Jenkin, J M	1952
Jenkins, A	1971
Jenkins, O	1913-19
Jenkins, P	1980
Jenkins, V G J	1930-31-32
Jesson, D	1957-58-59
Johnson, A M	1985-86-87
Johnson, P M	1968-70
Johnson, T F	1875
Johnstone, P G	1952-53-54
Jones, D K	1963
Jones, D R R	1972
Jones, G S A	1896
Jones, I C	1962-63-64
Jones, K W J	1931-32
Jones, R O P	1969-70-71
Jones, T O	1898
Jones, T W	1978-79
Jones, V W	1954
Joyce, A L	1984
Jupp, H B	1873
Kay, A R	1889-90-91
Kay, D C	1972-73
Kelly, H M	1932
Kendall-Carpenter, J MacG K	1948-49-50
Kennedy, A P	1985
Kennedy, N	1901
Kennedy, W D	1904
Kent, C P	1972-73-74-75
Kent, P C	1970
Kershaw, F	1898-99-1900-01
Key, K J	1885-86
Kindersley, R S	1882-83
King, B B H	1963
King, P E	1975
King, T W	1929
Kininmonth, P W	1947-48
Kirk, D E	1987-88
Kitson, J A	1895
Kittermaster, H J	1922-24
Kitto, R C M	1884-85-86-87

Knight, R L	1879
Knott, F H	1910-11-12-13
Koe, A P	1886
Kyrke, G V	1902-03
Kyrke-Smith, P St L	1973-74-75 (R)
Lagden, R O	1909-10-11
Laidlaw, C R	1968-69
Lamb, R H	1962-63-64
Lamport, N K	1930-31-32
Landale, D F	1925-26
Lane, R O B	1887-88-89
Langley, P J	1949
Latham, H E	1907
Latter, A	1892
Law, A F	1875
Lawrence, W S	1954-56
Lawrie, A A	1903-05
Lawton, T	1921-22-23
Lee, F H	1874-75-76-77
Lee, J W	1973-74
Lee, R J	1972
Legge, D	1897
Lennox-Cook, J M	1945
Leslie, C F H	1880-81
Leslie, R E	1954
Leslie-Jones, F A	1894-95-96
Lewin, A J A	1962-63
Lewis, A K	1888
Lewis, D J	1950
Lewis, S M	1973
Light, B	1977
Lindsay, G C	1882-83-84-85
Littlechild, E J F	1972
Littlewood, R B	1893
Lloyd, E A	1964-65-66
Lloyd, J E	1872-74
Lloyd, R	1908
Lombard, L T	1956-57-58
Longdon, J S	1889
Lorraine, H D B	1932-33-34
Loudoun-Shand, E G	1913-19
Love, R D	1972
Low, R C S	1933
Luce, F M	1899-1900
Luddington, R S	1980-81-82
Lusty, W	1927
Luyt, R E	1938
Lyle, A M P	1902-04-05
McBain, N S	1986-87
McCanlis, M A	1926-27
McClure, R N	1973
Macdonald, C P	1985-86
Macdonald, D A	1975-76
Macdonald, D S M	1974-75-76
Macdonald, G E	1922
Macdonald, N L	1926
Macdonald, N W	1984-85
MacEwen, G L	1895
McFarland, P R E	1967
MacGibbon, R R	1930-31
McGlashan, J R C	1945
McGrath, N F	1934-35-36
MacGregor, A	1871
Mackenzie, A O M	1880-81
Mackenzie, D W	1974
Mackenzie, F J C	1882-83
Mackintosh, C E W C	1925
MacLachlan, L P	1953
Maclachlan, N	1879-80
Macmillan, M	1876
McNeill, A	1884
MacNeill, H P	1982-83-84
McPartlin, J J	1960-61-62
Macpherson, G P S	1922-23-24
Macpherson, N M S	1928
McQuaid, A S J	1983
McShane, J M S	1933-35
Maddock, W P	1972
Mallalieu, J P W	1927
Mallett, N V H	1979
Marshall, H P	1921
Marshall, R M	1936-37-38
Martin, H	1907-08-09
Marvin, T G R	1984-85
Mather, E G S	1933
Maxwell-Hyslop, J E	1920-21-22
Mayhew, P K	1937
Mead, B D	1972-73
Meadows, H J	1948
Merivale, G M	1874
Merriam, L P B	1913
Michell, A T	1871-72-73-74
Millerchip, C J	1981-82
Mills, D J	1983-84
Milton, N W	1905-06-07
Minns, P C	1930-31-32
Mitchell, M D	1977
Moberly, W O	1871-72-73
Moir, M J P	1977
Molohan, M J B	1928
Monteath, J G	1912
Montgomery, J R	1958
Moorcroft, E K	1966
Moore, E J	1882-83
Moore, H B	1912-13
Moore, H R	1956
Moore, P B C	1945-46
Moresby-White, J M	1913-19
Morgan, A K	1963-64
Morgan, D J	1979
Morgan, F	1888
Morgan, R de R	1983
Morris, E G	1904
Morrison, W E A	1979-80
Mortimer, L	1892
Moubray, J J	1876-77-78
Muller, H	1938
Mullin, B J	1986-87
Mullins, R C	1894
Mulvey, R S	1968
Munro, P	1903-04-05
Murray, G C	1959
Nash, E H	1874-75
Nelson, T A	1897-98
Nesbitt, J V	1904-05
Neser, V H	1919-20
Neville, T B	1971-72
Newman, A P	1973
Newman, S C	1946-47
Newton, H F	1895-96-97
Newton, P A	1879-80
Newton-Thompson, J O	1945-46
Nicholas, P L	1897-98-99
Nicholson, E S	1931-32-33-34
North, E G H	1888-89-90
Norwitz, E R	1988
Novis, A L	1927
Nunn, J A	1925-26
Obolensky, A	1935-37
O'Brien, T S	1983-84
O'Connor, A	1958
Odgers, W B	1901-02
Orpen, L J J	1898
Osborn, E C	1969
Osborne, S H	1900-01-02
Osler, S G	1931
Owen-Smith, H G O	1932-33
Page, H V	1884-85
Painter, J L	1967
Palmer, M S	1960
Parker, L	1905
Parker, T	1888
Parkin, W H	1890
Paterson, A M	1889-90
Patterson, A R	1879-80-81
Patterson, L R	1886-87
Payne, C M	1960
Peacock, M B	1880
Peacock, M F	1932-33
Peacock, N C	1987
Peake, H W	1871
Pearce, J K	1945
Pearson, S B	1983-84-85
Pearson, T S	1871
Peat, W H	1898
Peck, A Q	1981
Pennington, H H	1937-38
Percival, L J	1889-91
Percy, H R G	1936-38
Pether, S	1938
Phillips, C	1876-77-78-79
Phillips, E L	1933
Phillips, L R L	1984
Phillips, M S	1956-57-58-59
Phillips, P C	1938
Phillips, R H	1966-67-68
Pienaar, J H	1933-34-35
Pitman, I J	1921
Plant, W I	1958
Pleydell-Bouverie, Hon B	1923
Plumbridge, R A	1954-55-56
Podmore, G	1872
Pollard, D	1952
Poole, F O	1891-92-93-94
Poulton, R W	1909-10-11
Prescott, A E C	1928
Prescott, R E	1932
Preston, B W	1925
Price, H L	1920-21
Price, V R	1919-20-21
Pritchard, N S M	1985(R)
Prodger, J A	1955
Quinnen, P N	1974-75
Quist-Arcton, E A K	1978-79
Rahmatallah, F J	1976
Ramsay, A W	1952-53
Ramsden, J E	1945
Raphael, J E	1901-02-03-04
Rashleigh, W	1887-88
Ravenscroft, J	1877-78
Raymond, R L	1924
Rayner-Wood, A C	1895-96
Read, R F	1965
Reed, D K	1984
Reeler, I L	1955-56
Rees, H	1930
Rees, H J V	1913
Rees, P S	1974-75-78
Rees-Jones, G R	1933-34-35
Reid, C J	1896
Reid, G A	1935-36
Reid, N	1912-13
Renwick, W N	1936-37
Rice-Evans, W	1890
Richards, C A L	1932
Richards, S B	1962
Richardson, J V	1925
Richardson, W R	1881
Rigby, J P	1955-56
Rimmer, L I	1958
Risman, J M	1984-85-86
Rittson-Thomas, G C	1949-50
Robbins, P G D	1954-55-56-57
Roberts, G D	1907-08
Roberts, M G	1968
Roberts, N T	1979-80-81
Roberts, S N J	1985-86
Roberts, W	1928-29-30-31
Robertson, A M	1903
Robertson, J W	1921
Robertson, M A	1894-96
Robinson, D A B	1952-53
Robinson, R G	1976-77
Robson, M	1929
Rogers, W L Y	1898-1900
Rolfe, A J	1987
Roos, G D	1936
Rosier, J R H	1983
Ross, W S	1980
Rotherham, A	1882-83-84
Roughead, W N	1924-25-26

Name	Years	Name	Years	Name	Years
Rousseau, W P	1929	Stoneman, B M	1962	Walford, M M	1935-36-37
Row, A W L	1921	Stoop, A D	1902-03-04	Walker, A	1880
Rowley, J V D'A	1929	Strand-Jones, J	1899-1900-01	Walker, J C	1955
Rucker, R W	1874-76	Stratton, J W	1897	Walker, J G	1879-80-81
Rudd, E L	1963-64	Strong, E L	1881-83	Walker, M	1950-51
Russell, H	1872-73-74-75	Strong, W I N	1924-25	Wall, T W	1875-76-77
Russell, J H	1929	Stuart-Watson, J L	1935	Wallace, A C	1922-23-24-25
Russell-Roberts, F D	1931	Summerskill, W H J	1945	Walton, E J	1900-01
Rydon, R A	1985-86	Surtees, E A	1885	Ward, J M	1972
		Sutherland, I W	1938	Ware, M A	1961-62
Sachs, D M	1962	Sutherland, J G B	1885	Warr, A L	1933-34
Sampson, D H	1945	Sutton, M A	1945-46	Waterman, J S	1974
Sampson, H F	1910-11	Swan, M W	1957	Wates, C S	1961
Sanctuary, C F S	1879-80	Swanston, J F A	1897-98-99-1900	Watkins, L	1879
Sandford, J R P	1902-03	Swanzy, A J	1901-02	Watkinson, A F	1977-78
Saunders, C J	1951	Swarbrick, D W	1946-47-48	Watson, P W	1954-55
Sawtell, P R	1972	Swayne, D H	1930-31	Watt, K A	1976
Sayer, J	1871	Sweatman, E A	1927	Watts, I H	1937-38
Sayer, J B	1887			Watts, L D	1957-58
Scholefield, B G	1920-21	Taberer, H M	1892	Webster, J G M	1980-81
Scott, J S M	1957-58	Tahany, M P	1945	Webster, J P	1982-83
Searle, J P	1981-82	Tanner, T L	1931	Welsh, A R	1984
Seccombe, L S	1925	Tarr, F N	1907-08-09	Wensley, S C	1988
Selby, E	1891	Tatham, W M	1881-82-83	Wesche, V V G	1924
Sexton, C M	1976	Taylor, E G	1926-27-28	Weston, B A G	1957
Seymour, T M	1971-73	Taylor, J A	1974	Weston, J W	1871
Shacksnovis, A	1922-23	Terry, H F	1900-01	White, G L	1976-77
Sharp, H S	1910-11	Theron, T P	1923	White, N T	1905-06
Sharp, R A W	1959-60-61	Thomas, A C	1979	Whyte, A G D	1963
Sharp, R G	1919	Thomas, T R	1938	Whyte, D J	1963
Shaw, C	1974-75	Thomas, W E	1911-12	Wilcock, R M	1962
Shearman, M	1878-79	Thomas, W L	1893-94	Wilcock, S H	1957-58-59
Sheffield, R W	1873-74	Thomson, B E	1951-52	Wilkinson, J V S	1904
Sheil, A G R	1958	Thomson, C	1896	Wilkinson, W E	1891
Shillito, G V	1930	Thomson, F W	1912-13	Willcox, J G	1959-60-61-62
Sidgwick, A	1872	Thomson, J B	1983	Williams, A D	1988
Siepmann, C A	1921	Thomson, W J	1895-96	Williams, C D	1945
Silk, N	1961-62-63	Thorburn, C W	1964	Williams, I M	1988
Sim, A C	1876	Thorniley-Walker, M J	1967	Williams, J R	1969
Simmie, M S	1965-66	Tongue, P K	1975	Williams, S R	1988 (R)
Simonet, P M	1984	Torry, P J	1968-69	Williamson, A C	1913
Simpson, E P	1887	Travers, B H	1946-47	Williamson, R H	1906-07-08
Simpson, H B	1920	Tristram, H B	1882-83-84	Willis, D C	1975-76-77
Skipper, D J	1952	Troup, D S	1928	Willis, T G	1985-86-88
Slater, N T	1960	Tudor, H A	1878-79-80-81	Wilson, C T M	1948
Sloan, T	1908	Turcan, H H	1928	Wilson, D B	1874
Sloane, A D	1902	Turner, A B	1884	Wilson, G A	1946-48
Small, H D	1949-50	Turner, F H	1908-09-10	Wilson, J	1967-68
Smith, A R	1894-95-96-97			Wilson, J H G	1888-89-90
Smith, B A	1988	Ubogu, V E	1987	Wilson, N G C	1967
Smith, I S	1923	Unwin, G T	1894-95-96	Wilson, R W	1956
Smith, J A	1892-93			Wilson, S	1963-64
Smith, M J K	1954-55	Valentine, A C	1923-24-25	Wilson, S E	1890
Southee, E A	1913	Van Der Riet, E F	1920-21	Wilson, W G	1887
Speed, R R	1967-68-69	Van Ryneveld, A J	1946-47-48	Wimperis, E J	1951
Spence, K M	1951-52	Van Ryneveld, C B	1947-48-49	Winn, C E	1950
Spencer, B L	1960	Vassall, H	1879-80-81-82	Winn, R R	1953
Spragg, F F	1926	Vassall, H H	1906-07-08	Witney, N K J	1970-71
Springman, P	1877-78	Vecqueray, A H	1877-78	Wix, R S	1904-05-06-07
Squire, W H S	1882-83-84	Vecqueray, G C	1873	Wood, A E	1904
Stagg, P K	1961-62	Vessey, S J R	1984-85-86-87-88	Wood, D E	1952-53
Stafford, P M W	1961-62	Vidal, R W S	1872	Wood, G F	1919
Starmer-Smith, N C	1965-66	Vincent, A N	1948-49	Woodhead, P G	1974
Steel, J J	1953			Woodrow, D K	1978-79-80
Steinthal, F E	1906			Wooldridge, C S	1882
Stevens, D T	1959			Wordsworth, C R	1922-23-24
Stewart, A	1947-48	Wade, C G	1882-83-84	Wordsworth, C W	1902
Stewart, W B	1892	Waide, S L	1932	Wordsworth, J R	1885
Steyn, S S L	1911-12	Wake, H B L	1922	Wray, M O	1933-34
Stileman, W M C	1988	Wakefield, W H	1891-92	Wyatt, D M	1981
Still, E R	1871-73	Wakelin, W S	1964	Wydell, H A	1951
Stobie, A M	1945	Waldock, F A	1919	Wynter, E C C	1947
Stobie, W D K	1947	Waldock, H F	1919-20		
Stone, T	1897	Waldron, O C	1965-67	Young, J R C	1957-58

CAMBRIDGE

Name	Years	Name	Years	Name	Years
Aarvold, C D	1925-26-27-28	Agnew, C M	1875-76	Alderson, F H R	1887-88
Ackford, P J	1979	Agnew, G W	1871-72-73	Alexander, E P	1884-85-86
Adams, G C A	1929	Agnew, W L	1876-77-78	Alexander, J W	1905-06
Adams, H F S	1884-85	Albright, G S	1877	Allan, C J	1962

Allan, J L F 1956
Allchurch, T J 1980-81
Allen, A D 1925-26-27
Allen, D B 1975
Allen, J 1875-76
Anderson, W T 1931-32
Andrew, C R 1982-83-84
Anthony, A J 1967
Archer, G M D 1950-51
Arthur, T G 1962
Ashcroft, A H 1908-09
Ashford, C L 1929
Ashworth, J 1988
Askew, J G 1929-30-31
Asquith, J P K 1953
Aston, R L 1889-90
Atkinson, M L 1908-09
Attfield, S J W 1982-84

Back, F F 1871-72
Bailey, G H 1931
Bailey, M D 1982-83-84-85
Bailey, R C 1982-83
Balding, I A 1961
Balfour, A 1896-97
Bance, J F 1945
Barker, R E 1966
Barlow, C S 1923-24-25-26
Barlow, R M M 1925
Barrow, C 1950
Barter, A F 1954-55-56
Bartlett, R M 1951
Bateman-Champain, P J C 1937
Batten, J M 1871-72-73-74
Batty, P A 1919-20
Baxter, R 1871-72-73
Baxter, W H B 1912-13
Bealey, R J 1874
Beard, P L 1987
Bearne, K R F 1957-58-59
Beazley, T A G 1971
Bedell-Sivright, D R 1899-1900-01-02
Bedell-Sivright, J V 1900-01-02-03
Beer, I D S 1952-53-54
Bell, R W 1897-98-99
Bell, S P 1894-95-96
Bennett, G M 1897-98
Bennett, N J 1981
Benthall, E C 1912
Beringer, F R 1951-52
Beringer, G G 1975-76
Berman, J V 1966
Berry, S P 1971
Bevan, G A J 1951
Bevan, J A 1877-80
Bevan, W 1887
Biddell, C W 1980-81
Biggar, M A 1971
Bird, D R J 1958-59
Birdwood, C R B 1932
Bishop, C C 1925
Black, M A 1897-98
Blair, P C B 1910-11-12-13
Blake, W H 1875
Boggon, R P 1956
Bole, H 1945-46-47
Bonham-Carter, J 1873
Bordass, J H 1923-24
Borthwick, T J L 1985
Boughton-Leigh, C E W 1878
Boulding, P V 1975-76
Bowcott, H M 1927-28
Bowcott, J E 1933
Bowen, R W 1968
Bowhill, J W 1888-89
Bowman, J H 1933-34
Boyd, C W 1909
Boyd-Moss, R J 1980-81-82
Brandram, R A 1896
Brash, J C 1959-60-61
Brathwaite, G A 1934

Breakey, J N F 1974-75(R)-77
Bree-Frink, F C 1888-89-90
Briggs, P D 1962
Bromet, E 1887-88
Brook, P W P 1928-29-30-31
Brookstein, R 1969
Brooman, R J 1977-78
Browell, H H 1877-78
Brown, A C 1920-21
Brown, S L 1975-76
Browning, O C 1934
Bruce Lockhart, J H 1910
Bruce Lockhart, L 1945-46
Bruce Lockhart, R B 1937-38
Brutton, E B 1883-85-86
Bryant, S S 1988
Bryce, R D H 1965
Bull, H A 1874-75
Bunting, W L 1894-95
Burt-Marshall, J 1905
Burton, B C 1882-83
Bush, J D 1983
Bussey, W M 1960-61-62
Butler, E T 1976-77-78
Buzza, A J 1988

Cake, J J 1988
Campbell, D A 1936
Campbell, H H 1946
Campbell, J A 1897-98-99
Campbell, J D 1927
Campbell, J W 1973-74
Campbell, R C C 1907
Candler, P L 1934
Cangley, B T G 1946
Carey, G V 1907-08
Carpmael, W P 1885
Carris, H E 1929
Carter, C P 1965
Cave, J W 1887-88
Cave, W T C 1902-03-04
Chadwick, W O 1936-37-38
Chalmers, P S 1979
Chambers, E L 1904
Chapman, C E 1881-84
Chapman, E S 1879-80
Chapman, G M 1907-08-09
Chapman, J M 1873
Chilcott, E W 1883
Child, H H 1875-76
Clarke, B D F 1978
Clarke, S J S 1962-63
Clayton, H R 1876-77-78
Clayton, J R W 1971
Clements, J W 1953-54-55
Clifford, P H 1876-77-78
Clough, F J 1984-85-86-87
Coates, C H 1877-78-79
Coates, V H M 1907
Cobby, W 1900
Cock, T A 1899
Cocks, F W 1935
Coghlan, G B 1926-27-28
Cohen, A S 1922
Colbourne, G L 1883
Coley, M 1964
Collett, G F 1898
Collier, R B 1960-61
Collin, T 1871
Collins, W O H 1931
Collis, W R F 1919-20
Collison, L H 1930
Combe, P H 1984-85
Considine, W C D 1919
Conway, G S 1919-20-21
Cook, D D B 1920-21
Cook, S 1920-21
Cooke, S J 1981
Cooper, H S 1981
Cooper, P T 1927-28
Cope, W 1891
Corry, T M 1966
Cosh, N J 1966

Covell, G A B 1949
Cove-Smith, R 1919-20-21
Cox, F L 1879
Craig, H J 1891
Craigmile, H W C 1920
Crichton-Miller, D 1928
Crothers, G 1977(R)
Crow, W A M 1961-62
Cullen, J C 1980-81-82
Cumberlege, B S 1910-11-12-13
Cumberlege, R F 1897
Cumming, D C 1922-23-24
Currie, W C 1905
Cushing, A 1986

Dalgleish, K J 1951-52-53
Dalton, E R 1872-73-74
Dalton, W L T 1875-76
Daniell, J 1898-99-1900
Darby, A J L 1896-97-98
Darch, W J 1875
David, P W 1983
Davies, A 1988
Davies, G 1988
Davies, G 1948-49-50
Davies, G H 1980-81
Davies, H J 1958
Davies, J C 1949
Davies, J S 1977
Davies, P M 1952-53-54
Davies, T G R 1968-69-70
Davies, W G 1946-47
Deakin, J E 1871
Delafield, G E 1932
De Nobriga, A P 1948
De Villiers, D I 1913
Devitt, Sir T G 1923-24-25
Dewhurst, J H 1885-86
Dick, R C S 1933
Dickins, J P 1972-73
Dickson, J W 1881
Dinwiddy, H P 1934-35
Dixon, A M 1928
Dixon, C 1894
Dods, M 1938
Doherty, H D 1950
Doherty, W D 1913
Don Wauchope, A R 1880-81
Dorward, A F 1947-48-49
Douglas, E A 1882-83-84
Douglas, R N 1891
Douty, P S 1924
Dovey, B A 1960
Downes, K D 1936-37-38
Downey, W J 1954-55-56-57
Doyle, M G 1965
Drake-Lee, N J 1961-62-63
Drake, T R 1965
Druce, W G 1893-94
Drummond, N W 1971
Drysdale, T 1900-01
Dudgeon, R F 1871
Duncan, C 1966
Duncan, M M 1885-86-87
Dutson, C S 1963

Edlmann, S R R 1974-75
Edmonds, G A 1976
Edwards, E F 1971
Edwards, R J 1971-72
Elliott, A E 1891
Ellis, P R 1975
Ellison, J F 1983-84
Embleton, J J E 1928-29-30
Evans, A E 1906-07
Evans, D P 1922
Evans, E D 1903-04
Evans, M R M 1955
Evans, W R 1955
Ewbank, C F 1983

Fairbanks, W 1873-74
Fairgrieve, J 1945

Falcon, W 1894-95
Fasson, F H 1897-98-99
Fforde, A B 1891
Fiddian, J V 1908-09
Field, E 1892-93-94
Finch, R T 1876-77-78-79
Fitch, C E 1889
Fleming, R S 1964
Fletcher, N C 1897-98-99
Fogg-Elliott, J W 1887
Folker, E L A 1937
Folwell, A J S 1967-68
Forbes, A S 1873
Ford, J N 1977-78-79
Fordham, J G 1898
Forman, A 1904-05
Forrest, J G S 1936-37-38
Fosh, M K 1977-78
Foster, J 1988
Fowler, T G 1911-12
Fox, S 1945
Francis, T E S 1922-23-24-25
Frankcom, G P 1961-63-64
Fraser, R 1908-09-10
Freeman, J P 1987
French, N J 1973
French, R B 1969
Fuller, H G 1878-79-80-81-82-83
Fyfe, K C 1932-33-34-35

Gardiner, F A 1921-22-23
Gatford, H J H 1946
Geddes, K I 1938
Geoghegan, K F 1977
Gethin, D 1965-66
Gibbins, R B 1905-06
Gibbons, J F 1882
Gibbs, J D 1965
Giblin, L F 1894-95-96
Gibson, C M H 1963-64-65
Gibson, E 1925-26
Gibson, T A 1901-02
Gilchrist, B W 1986-87
Gill, S M 1980-81
Gilliland, W D 1979
Glanvill, S F 1977-79-80
Glasgow, I C 1988
Gloag, I S 1949-50-52
Gloag, L G 1948
Godby, T A 1906-07
Godson, A 1959-60
Golightly, C H 1879
Goodhue, F W J 1885-86
Gover, J J 1879
Gowans, J J 1892-93
Grant, A R 1975-76
Grant, J J H 1978
Green, M J 1965-66-67
Green, P A 1984-85
Greenlees, J R C 1898-99-1900-01
Greenwood, G M 1929-30
Greenwood, J E 1910-11-12-13-19
Greenwood, J R H 1962-63
Greg, A H 1893
Greig, I A 1977-78
Griffith, J M 1933
Griffith, R 1894-95
Griffiths, H B 1953
Gurdon, C 1877
Gurdon, E T 1874-75-76
Guthrie, G B 1883
Gwilliam, J A 1947-48

Hacking, A 1898-99
Hall, M R 1987-88
Hamilton, G A C 1925-26
Hamilton, H A 1871-73
Hamilton-Smythe, A F 1926
Hamilton-Wickes, R H 1920-21-22-23
Hammond, J 1881

Hampel, A K R 1982
Hamp-Ferguson, A J C 1964-65
Hancock, M E 1987-88
Hannaford, C 1967
Harding, R 1973-74
Harding, V S J 1958-59-60
Harding, W R 1924-25-26-27
Harper, A G R 1983
Harriman, A T 1985
Harris, B G 1904-05-06
Harrison, R B 1951
Hartley, B C 1900
Hartley, J J 1974
Harvey, M J 1957
Harvey, J R W 1963-64
Hastings, A G 1984-85
Hearfield, J 1901
Hearson, H F P 1904-06
Heath, F M N 1936-37
Heath, N R M 1977-78
Heginbotham, R C 1984
Henderson, A P 1945-46-47
Herbert, A J 1954-55-56
Herrod, N J 1985-86-87
Heslip, M R 1967
Hetherington, J G G 1955
Hewett, B J 1963
Heywood, F M 1928
Higham, C F W 1961-62
Hignell, A J 1974-75-76-77
Hill, D B 1892
Hind, A E 1900
Hinton, N P 1969-70
Hobbs, A R 1986-87
Hockey, J R 1957
Hodges, E C 1903-04-05
Hodgson, J T 1955
Hodgson, M E 1973
Holloway, B H 1907-09
Holmes, W B 1947-48
Hooper, C A 1890
Hopkins, A A 1874
Hopkins, W D B 1929
Hopper, L B 1897
Hornby, J J 1873-74-76
Horner, P J 1982
Horrocks-Taylor, J P 1956-57
Horsfall, J 1903-04
Horsley, S 1901-02-03
Howard, J M 1971-72
Howell, R G B 1924
Hughes, K 1968-69
Hull, F M 1871-72-73
Hunt, N 1986
Hunter, J M 1946

Illingworth, P H 1889-90
Inglis, F C 1959
Inglis, W M 1935-36
Irving, K G 1935
Isaac, T W D 1986

Jackson, A L 1889
Jackson, T L 1892
Jacob, F 1895-96
Jacob, P G 1894-95-96
Jagger, D 1954
James, A M 1948-49
James, J H H 1962-63-64
James, S R 1876-77-78
Jameson, A 1874
Jeffcock, C E 1877
Jeffery, G L 1884-85
Jenkins, J D 1964
Jenkins, J M 1949-51
Jenkins, W G 1948
Jessop, A W 1972
Johnson, J N 1981
Johnston, D 1897
Johnston, W G S 1932-33-34
Johnstone, H B L 1931
Jolliffe, R L K 1965
Jones, B M 1949

Jones, C W 1933-34-35
Jones, D G H 1951-52
Jones, E A A 1895
Jones, F H 1898-99-1900
Jones, J S 1908-09
Jones, R B 1931-32-33
Jones, S E 1878
Jones, T R K 1921
Jones, W I 1923-24-25
Jones, W W A 1968-69-70-72
Jorden, A M 1968-69
Juckes, R 1913
Juckes, T R 1938

Keeton, G H 1899-1900
Keith-Roach, P d'A 1969-70-71
Kelly, S R 1985-86-87
Kemp, T A 1936
Kennedy, C M 1877-78
Kennedy, R S 1907-09
Kershaw, M E 1955
Killick, S E 1978
Kimberley, H M 1945-46-47-48
King, R H 1950
Kingston, C J 1980-81-82
Kirby, T K M 1945
Kitchin, P A 1965
Kitching, A E 1910-11
Koop, G G 1905

Laborde, C D 1933-34-35-36
Laing, H 1893
Lambert, I C 1871
Langton, E C 1888-89
Lawry, S J 1894-95
Laxon, H 1903-04
Laycock, A M 1979
Leadbetter, V H 1951-52
Leake, W R M 1885-86-87
Leather, W H 1931-32
Leather, W J 1931-32-33-34
Lee, H 1904
Lees, J 1883
Le Fanu, V C 1884-85-86
Le Fleming, J 1884-85-86
Leishman, F J 1938
Lely, W G 1906-07-08
Leonard, R J N 1957
Lewis, A D 1975-76
Lewis, A R 1875
Lewis, A R 1964
Lewis, B R 1909-10-11
Lewis, G A 1872-73-74-75
Lewis, G G 1976
Lewis, G W 1956-57-58
Lewis, J M C 1913-19
Lewis, W H 1926-27
Lewthwaite, W 1872-73
Lillington, P M 1981-82
Lindsay, P A R 1937-38
Linnecar, R J D 1970
Lintott, T M R 1974
Lister, R C 1969
Lloyd-Davies, R H 1947
Lord, J R C 1933-34-35
Lord, M 1960
Lord, T M 1986
Loveday, B R 1956-57
Low, J D 1935-36-37
Lowden, G S 1945
Lowe, C N 1911-12-13
Lowry, R H W 1923
Loxdale, J W 1874
Lucas, P M 1882
Luscombe, R P 1871-72-73-74
Lushington, A J 1872
Luxmoore, A F C C 1896-97
Lyon, C E 1871
Lyon, D W 1967-68

McAfee, L A 1910
McClung, T 1954

160

McCosh, E — 1910
McCosh, R — 1905-06-07
MacDonald, A — 1871
MacDonald, J A — 1936-37
MacEwen, D L — 1887
MacEwen, R K G — 1953-54
McGahey, A M J — 1979-80-81
McGown, T M W — 1896
MacGregor, G — 1889-90
McIlwaine, G A — 1926-27-28
Mackenzie, W G B — 1922
McKenzie, M R — 1968
Mackie, O G — 1895-96-97
Macklin, A J — 1979-80-82
Maclay, J P — 1920
MacLeod, K G — 1905-06-07-08
MacLeod, L M — 1903-04-05
Macleod, W M — 1880-82
McMorris, L — 1963
MacMyn, D J — 1921-22-23-24
McNeill, A H — 1902-03
McRoberts, T S — 1946-47-48
MacSweeney, D A — 1957-58-59
Mainprice, H — 1902-03-04-05
Makin, R L — 1959
Malik, N A — 1975
Mann, F T — 1910
Marburg, C L H — 1909-10
Margerison, R — 1871-72-73
Marques, R W D — 1954-55-56-57
Marr, D M — 1929-30-31-32
Marr, T C K — 1945
Marriott, C J B — 1881-82-83
Marsden, E W — 1950
Marshall, T R — 1950
Martin, A W — 1983-84
Martin, N O — 1965-66-67
Martin, S A — 1961-62-63
Massey, D G — 1952
Massey, M J O — 1951-52-53
Maxwell, D M W — 1922
Mayfield, E — 1891
Maynard, A F — 1912-13
Mayne, W N — 1888
Mellor, J E — 1906
Melluish, R K — 1922
Metcalfe, I R — 1978-79
Methuen, A — 1886-87-88
Michaelson, R C B — 1960-61-62
Michell, W G — 1873-75-76
Middlemas, P — 1912
Miliffe, M J — 1964
Millard, D E S — 1956
Miller, J L H — 1920
Mills, D C — 1958
Mills, H H — 1947-48
Mills, P R — 1958-59
Milne, C J B — 1882-83-84
Mitchell, F — 1893-94-95
Mitchell, W G — 1886
Monahan, J D — 1967-68
Monro, A H — 1973
Monteith, H G — 1903-04-05
Montgomery, R — 1891
Moon, R H Q B — 1984
Moore, A W — 1874
Moore, P J de A — 1947-48
Morel, T E — 1920-22
Morgan, H P — 1952-53
Morgan, W G — 1926-27-28-29
Moriarty, S P — 1980
Morpeth, G — 1925
Morrison, B J — 1965
Morrison, I R — 1983-84
Morrison, P H — 1887-88-89-90
Morse, E St J — 1871
Mortimer, W — 1895-96
Morton, H J S — 1908
Moyes, J L — 1974-75
Mulligan, A A — 1955-56-57
Murray, R A — 1982
Murray, R O — 1933-34

Napier, Hon M F — 1871
Neild, W C — 1911-12
Neilson, H — 1884
Neilson, W — 1891-92-93
Nelson, W E — 1892
Newbold, C J — 1902-03
Newman, C H — 1882
Newton-Thompson, C L — 1937-38
Nicholl, C B — 1890-91-92-93
Nixon, P J L — 1976

O'Brien, T S — 1981-82
O'Callaghan, C — 1978
O'Callaghan, M W — 1974-75-76-77
O'Leary, S T — 1984-85
Odgers, F W — 1901
Ogilvy, F J L — 1887
Onyett, P S — 1966-67
Orr, J C S — 1891
Orr-Ewing, D — 1919
Oswald, G B R — 1945
Oti, C — 1986-87
Oulton, E V — 1901
Ovens, A B — 1910-11
Owen, A V — 1945
Owen, J E — 1961

Page, J J — 1968-69-70
Page, R S — 1972-73
Palmer, H R — 1899
Parker, G W — 1932-33-34-35
Parr, M F — 1978
Parry, T R — 1936-37-38
Parsons, J — 1938
Pater, S — 1880-81
Paterson, L R — 1886-87
Paterson-Brown, T — 1983
Patterson, H W T — 1890
Patterson, W M — 1956
Pattisson, R M — 1881-82
Payne, J H — 1879
Payne, O V — 1900
Pearce, D — 1873-74
Pearson, T C — 1952-53
Peck, I G — 1979
Pender, A R — 1963
Penny, W M — 1906
Perry, D G — 1958
Perry, S V — 1946-47
Phillips, G P — 1971-72
Phillips, J H L — 1930-32
Phillips, R J — 1964
Pienaar, L L — 1911
Pierce, D J — 1985(R)
Pilkington, L E — 1893-94
Pilkington, W N — 1896-97
Pinkham, C — 1910
Pitt, T G — 1905-06
Plews, W J — 1884
Pope, E B — 1932
Powell, R — 1900
Pratt, S R G — 1973-74
Price, P R — 1967
Pringle, A S — 1897-98
Pringle, J S — 1902
Prosser-Harries, A — 1957
Pumphrey, C E — 1902
Purves, W D C L — 1907-08-09
Pyman, F C — 1907-08

Rae, A J — 1901
Raffle, N C G — 1954-55
Raikes, W A — 1872-74
Raine, J B — 1947
Rainforth, J J — 1958-59
Ramsay, A R — 1930
Ransome, H F — 1882-83-84
Rawlence, J R — 1935-36
Raybould, W H — 1966
Redmond, G F — 1969-70-71
Reed, E D E — 1937
Rees, A M — 1933-34
Rees, B I — 1963-64-65-66

Rees, G — 1972-73
Rees, J I — 1931-32
Reeve, P B — 1950-51
Reid, J L P — 1932
Rendall, H D — 1892-93
Reynolds, E P — 1909
Rice, E — 1880-81
Richards, T B — 1955
Richardson, W P — 1883
Rigby, J C A — 1982
Riley, H — 1871-72-73
Risman, M A — 1987(R)
Ritchie, W T — 1903-04
Robbie, J C — 1977-78
Roberts, A F — 1901-02
Roberts, A J R — 1901-02
Roberts, J — 1952-53-54
Roberts, J — 1927-28
Roberts, S N J — 1983
Robertson, D D — 1892
Robertson, I — 1967
Robinson, A — 1886-87
Robinson, B F — 1891-92-93
Robinson, J J — 1892
Robinson, P J — 1962
Rocyn-Jones, D N — 1923
Roden, W H — 1936-37
Rodgers, A K — 1968-69-70
Roffey, D B — 1874-75
Rose, H — 1872
Rose, W M H — 1979-80-81
Rosser, D W A — 1962-63-64
Rosser, M F — 1972-73
Ross-Skinner, W M — 1924
Rotherham, A — 1890-91
Rottenburg, H — 1898
Rowell, W I — 1890
Ryan, C J — 1966
Ryan, P H — 1952-53
Ryder, D C D — 1921-23

Sagar, J W — 1899-1900
Salmon, W B — 1883
Sample, C H — 1882-83-84
Sample, H W — 1884
Sanderson, A B — 1901
Saunders-Jacobs, S M — 1929
Saville, C D — 1967-68-69-70
Sawyer, B T C — 1910
Saxon, K R J — 1919-21
Scholfield, J A — 1909-10
Schwarz, R O — 1893
Scotland, K J F — 1958-59-60
Scott, A W — 1945-48
Scott, C T — 1899
Scott, J M — 1927
Scott, M T — 1885-86-87
Scott, R R F — 1957
Scott, W B — 1923-24
Scott, W M — 1905-06
Scoular, J G — 1905-06
Seddon, E R H — 1921
Shackleton, I R — 1968-69-70
Shaw, P A V — 1977
Shepherd, J K — 1950
Sherrard, P — 1938
Shipsides, J — 1970
Shirer, J A — 1885
Silk, D R W — 1953-54
Sim, R G — 1966-67
Simms, K G — 1983-84-85
Simpson, C P — 1890
Simpson, F W — 1930-31
Sisson, J P — 1871
Skinner, R C O — 1970-71
Slater, K J P — 1964
Smallwood, A M — 1919
Smeddle, R W — 1928-29-30-31
Smith, A F — 1873-74
Smith, A R — 1954-55-56-57
Smith, H K P — 1920
Smith, H Y L — 1878-79-80-81
Smith, J — 1889

Name	Year	Name	Year	Name	Year
Smith, J J E	1926	Thomas, W H	1886-87	Watherston, J G	1931
Smith, J M	1972	Thompson, M J M	1950	Watson, C F K	1919-20
Smith, J V	1948-49-50	Thompson, R	1890	Watt, J R	1970
Smith, K P	1919	Thompson, R V	1948-49	Webb, G K M	1964-65
Smith, M A	1966-67	Thorman, W H	1890	Webster, A P	1971
Smith, P K	1970	Thorne, C	1911	Wells, C M	1891-92
Smith, S R	1958-59	Thornton, J F	1976-78-79	Wells, T U	1951
Smith, S T	1982-83	Threlfall, R	1881-83	Wetson, M T	1958-59-60
Sobey, W H	1925-26	Timmons, F J	1983	Wheeler, P J F	1951-52-53
Spencer, J S	1967-68-69	Todd, A F	1893-94-95	White, J B	1922
Spicer, N	1901-02	Todd, T	1888	White, W N	1947
Spray, K A N	1946-47	Topping, N P	1986-87	Whiteway, S E A	1893
Sprot, A	1871	Touzel, C J C	1874-75-76	Wiggins, C E M	1928
Staunton, H	1891	Tredwell, J R	1968	Wiggins, C M	1964
Stead, R J	1977	Trethewy, A	1888	Wilkinson, R M	1971-72-73
Steeds, J H	1938	Trubshaw, A R	1919	Will, J G	1911-12-13
Steel, D Q	1877	Tucker, W E	1892-93-94	Williams, A G	1926-27
Steele, H K	1970	Tucker, W E	1922-23-24-25	Williams, C C U	1950
Steele, J T	1879-80	Tudsbery, F C T	1907-08	Williams, C H	1930
Steele-Bodger, M R	1945-46	Tunningley, A J	1988 (R)	Williams, C R	1971-72-73
Stevenson, H J	1977(R)-79	Turnbull, B R	1924-25	Williams, D B	1973
Stevenson, L E	1884-85	Turner, J A	1956	Williams, E J H	1946
Steward, R	1875-76	Turner, J M P C	1985	Williams, H A	1876
Stewart, A A	1975-76	Turner, M F	1946	Williams, J M	1949
Stewart, J R	1935	Tyler, R H	1978-79-80	Williams, L T	1874-75
Stileman, W M C	1985			Williams, N E	1950
Stokes, R R	1921	Umbers, R H	1954	Williams, P T	1888-89
Stone, R J	1901	Ure, C McG	1911	Williamson, I S	1972
Storey, E	1878-79-80			Williamson, P R	1984
Storey, L H T	1909	Valentine, G E	1930	Willis, H	1949-50-51
Storey, T W P	1889-90-91-92	Van Schalkwijk, J	1906	Wilson, A H	1911-12-13
Stothard, N A	1979	Vaughan, G P	1949	Wilson, C P	1877-78-79-80
Style, H B	1921	Vaux, J G	1957	Wilton, C W	1936
Surtees, A A	1886	Vickerstaff, M	1988	Winthrop, W Y	1871
Sutherland, J F	1908	Vincent, C A	1913	Wintle, T C	1960-61
Sutton, A J	1987-88	Vivian, J M	1976	Withyman, T A	1985-86
Swanson, J C	1938	Vyvyan, C B	1987-88	Wood, G E	1974-75-76
Swayne, F G	1884-85-86			Wood, G E C	1919
Symington, A W	1911-12-13	Wace, H	1873-74	Woodall, B J C	1951
Synge, J S	1927	Waddell, G H	1958-60-61	Woodroffe, O P	1952
		Wade, M R	1958-59-60-61	Woods, S M J	1888-89-90
Tait, J G	1880-82	Wainwright, J F	1956	Wooller, W	1933-34-35
Talbot, S C	1900	Wainwright, M A	1980	Wordley, S A	1988
Tallent, J A	1929-30-31	Wainwright, R I	1986-87-88	Wordsworth, A J	1973-75
Tanner, C C	1930	Wakefield, W W	1921-22	Wotherspoon, W	1888-89
Tarsh, D N	1955	Walker, A W	1929-30	Wrench, D F B	1960
Taylor, A S	1879-80-81	Walker, D R	1980-81	Wright, C C G	1907-08
Taylor, D G	1982	Walker, E E	1899-1900	Wrigley, P T	1877-78-79-80
Taylor, H B J	1894-96	Walker, R M	1963	Wyles, K T	1985-86
Taylor, W J	1926	Walkey, J R	1902	Wynne, E H	1887
Templer, J L	1881-82	Wallace, W M	1912-13		
Thomas, B E	1960-61-62	Waller, G S	1932	Yetts, R M	1879-80-81
Thomas, D R	1972-73-74	Wallis, H T	1895-96	Young, A B S	1919-20
Thomas, H W	1912	Ward, R O C	1903	Young, A T	1922-23-24
Thomas, J	1945	Ware, C H	1882	Young, J S	1935
Thomas, M D C	1986-87	Warfield, P J	1974	Young, J V	1906
Thomas, N B	1966	Warlow, S	1972-74	Young, P D	1949
Thomas, R C C	1949	Waters, F H	1927-28-29	Young, S K	1974
Thomas, T J	1895-96	Waters, J B	1902-03-04	Young, W B	1935-36-37

VARSITY MATCH REFEREES

(From 1881, when referees first officiated at the match. Prior to this date, the match was controlled by a pair of umpires elected by the Universities.) Each year indicates a separate appearance, and refers to the first half of the season. Thus 1881 refers to the match played in the 1881-82 season.

Name	Year	Name	Year	Name	Year
Allan, M A	1933-34	Gadney, C H	1935-36-37-38-45-47	Norling, C	1977-78-81-88
Ashmore, H L	1891-92-93-95-96	Gillespie, J I	1905	Pattinson, K A	1974
Bean, A S	1948-49	Harnett, G H		Potter-Irwin, F C	1909-11-13-19
Bolton, W N	1882		1897-98-99-1900-01-02	Prideaux, L	1984
Boundy, L M	1958	Hill, G R	1883-84-86-87-88-89-90	Quittenton, R C	1985-87
Burnett, D I H	1980-82	Hosie, A M	1979	Sanson, N R	1976
Burrell, R P	1963	Howard, F A	1986	Sturrock, J C	1921
Clark, K H	1973	Jeffares, R W	1930	Taylor, H H	1881
Cooper, Dr P F	1951-53	John, K S	1956-67	Titcombe, M H	1969
Crawford, S H	1920	Johnson, R F	1972	Trigg, J A F	1983
Currey, F I	1885	Jones, T	1950	Vile, T H	1922-24-26-28
Dallas, J D	1910-12	Lamb, Air Cdre G C	1970	Walters, D G	
D'Arcy, D P	1968	Lambert, N H	1946		1957-60-61-62-64-65-66
David, I	1954-55	Lawrence, Capt H D	1894	Welsby, A	1975
Evans, G	1907	Lewis, R	1971	Williams, R C	1959
Findlay, J C	1904-08	Marsh, F W	1906	Williams, T	1903
Freethy, A E	1923-25-27-29-31-32	Murdoch, W C W	1952		

UAU CHAMPIONSHIP 1988-89

15 March, Twickenham
Loughborough Students 13 (2PG 1DG 1T)
Swansea University 10 (2PG 1T)

Swansea University kept their noses in front until 14 minutes from the end, but they could not keep their heads. So Loughborough were able to triumph for the second consecutive year, gaining their 22nd UAU title in the process. The Welsh students opted to play into a steady breeze, but still went into the lead after six minutes when Loughborough collapsed a maul. Evans kicked the resultant penalty from 20 metres. Although Swansea brought their backs into play at every opportunity, the Loughborough pack began to exert pressure in tight play and the equalising score came in the 13th minute when Tubb dropped a goal.

Swansea regained the lead nine minutes later. They moved the ball to the right, switched to the left and Jones looped with Mynott to score a brilliant try in the left corner. Loughborough showed their own skills when Tubb created an opening which swept 60 metres downfield before Wedderburn was halted near the line. Their efforts were still rewarded, for the ensuing scrum produced a pushover try by Hastings.

Twelve minutes into the second half, Swansea regained the lead once more when Evans kicked a penalty from the left-hand touch-line. Then in the space of eight minutes midway through the half, Swansea's habit of conceding penalties at rucks and mauls – they gave away 16 against only 6 by Loughborough – proved fatal. In the 18th minute, they went over the top at a maul and Rowan kicked a penalty to tie the match. In the 26th minute they committed the same offence, from a similar spot 30 metres out in front of the posts, and Rowan again made no mistake to give his side the lead for the first time. Even then, Swansea almost snatched victory. Two minutes from time, Mynott was narrowly beaten to the touchdown after a shrewd kick to the left corner by Evans. Then, with the final kick of the match, Evans just missed a penalty attempt from near the touch-line.

Loughborough Students: R Greed; M Wedderburn, D Spiller, R Rowan, C Nichols; S Tubb, M Newall; G Baldwin, C Atkins, R Wareham, A Swain, A Robertson (*capt*), A Millward, G Taylor, J Hastings
Scorers *Try:* Hastings   *Penalty Goals:* Rowan (2)   *Dropped Goal:* Tubb
Swansea University: R Jones; J Devonald, G Thomas, A Moore, R Mynott; L Evans (*capt*), A Booth; D Francis, R Tandy, M Donelan, J Presley, M Langley, J Lewis, M Bennett, J Kingdon
Scorers *Try:* Jones   *Penalty Goals:* Evans (2)
Referee J A F Trigg (London Society)
Loughborough have won the title 22 times, Durham 8, Liverpool and Swansea 7, Bristol 5, Manchester 4, Cardiff 3, Bangor and UWIST 2, Aberystwyth, Birmingham, Leeds and Newcastle once each.

Although the Championship was not marred by foul play, there were incidents in Twickenham in the aftermath of the final. The UAU

Executive Committee has already proposed that Swansea should forfeit its first two matches in the 1989-90 Championship – a proposal which will make it difficult, though not wholly impossible, to qualify for the later stages – and action is also being considered along similar lines against Loughborough. The complaints lie mainly against team supporters who misbehaved near the ground. But, if the measures seem harsh, the UAU should be congratulated for grasping this particular nettle. It has expelled clubs from the competition on two previous occasions and this extension of its view of club responsibility will surely enable the Championship to avoid the stigma earned by other student competitions.

On the representative front, the English Universities had an unexpectedly poor season for no easily discernible reason. However, they pulled themselves together for the annual fixture against British Polytechnics, although a breakdown in backroom administration did nothing to help the team management.

Representative matches: Scottish Universities 0, Welsh Universities 28 (Edinburgh); Welsh Universities 21, Irish Universities 27 (Cross Keys); English Universities 3, Scottish Universities 4 (Richmond); English Universities 3, Irish Universities 22 (Preston); Welsh Universities 21, English Universities 7 (Newbridge); UAU 10, British Polytechnics 3 (Northampton)

Jones, the Swansea full-back, steps inside Greed, his opposite number, on the way to a try in the UAU final.

DIVISIONAL RESULTS
Eastern Division
NORTH-EAST GROUP

	P	W	D	L	F	A	Pts
Durham	3	3	0	0	114	24	6
Newcastle	3	2	0	1	106	25	4
Leeds	3	1	0	2	42	80	2
Hull	3	0	0	3	22	155	0

EAST MIDLANDS GROUP

	P	W	D	L	F	A	Pts
Loughbor'gh	3	3	0	0	121	18	6
Nottingham	3	2	0	1	89	38	4
Sheffield	3	1	0	2	46	51	2
Bradford	3	0	0	3	16	165	0

Section winners qualify for Challenge Round. Runners-up and third-placed teams proceed to Qualifying Round.

Western Division
NORTH-WEST GROUP

	P	W	D	L	F	A	Pts
Salford	4	4	0	0	53	19	8
Manchester	4	3	0	1	72	35	6
Liverpool	4	2	0	2	40	37	4
Lancaster	4	1	0	3	42	92	2
UMIST	4	0	0	4	30	54	0

WEST MIDLANDS GROUP

	P	W	D	L	F	A	Pts
Warwick	4	3	0	1	113	47	6
Aston	4	3	0	1	60	22	6
Leicester	4	3	0	1	49	41	6
Birmingham	4	1	0	3	53	69	2
Keele	4	0	0	4	32	128	0

Section winners qualify for Challenge Round. Runners-up and third-placed teams proceed to Qualifying Round.

Southern Division
NORTH-THAMES GROUP

	P	W	D	L	F	A	Pts
Brunel	4	4	0	0	69	17	8
UC London	4	3	0	1	42	20	6
East Anglia	4	2	0	2	68	36	4
The City	4	1	0	3	15	33	2
Essex	4	0	0	4	16	104	0

SOUTH THAMES GROUP

	P	W	D	L	F	A	Pts
Imperial Coll	5	5	0	0	186	24	10
Surrey	5	4	0	1	134	40	8
Sussex	5	3	0	2	131	87	6
Ryl Holloway	5	1	0	4	49	119	2
Kent	5	1	0	4	23	128	2
LSE	5	1	0	4	40	165	2

SOUTH-WEST GROUP

	P	W	D	L	F	A	Pts
Exeter	4	3	0	1	102	43	6
Bath	4	3	0	1	27	71	6
Bristol	4	2	0	2	72	38	4
Southampton	4	1	0	3	28	43	2
Reading	4	1	0	3	29	63	2

Section winners qualify for Challenge Round. Runners-up and third-placed teams proceed to Qualifying Round.

Welsh Division

	P	W	D	L	F	A	Pts
Swansea	4	4	0	0	155	32	8
UWCM	4	3	0	1	112	67	6
Aberystwyth	4	2	0	2	55	56	4
UW Cardiff	4	1	0	3	85	79	2
Bangor	4	0	0	4	23	196	0

Qualifying Round: UWCM 23, Leicester 0; Aston 13, Aberystwyth 16; UC London 0, Bristol 28; Bath 46, Sussex 3; Surrey 18, East Anglia 0; Manchester 6, Sheffield 27; Newcastle 19, Liverpool 3; Nottingham 14, Leeds 10

Challenge Round: Loughborough 26, UWCM 3; Brunel 6, Aberystwyth 17; Warwick 8, Bristol 9; Salford 0, Bath 27; Swansea 61, Surrey 0; Durham 20, Sheffield 16; Imperial Coll 0, Newcastle 22; Exeter 15, Nottingham 18 (*aet*)

Quarter-finals: Loughborough 52, Aberystwyth 3; Bristol 18, Bath 21; Swansea 34, Durham 4; Newcastle 29, Nottingham 0

Semi-finals: Loughborough 22, Bath 0 (Stourbridge RFC); Swansea 26, Newcastle 10 (Northampton RFC)

BRITISH POLYTECHNICS CUP 1989

8 March, Saracens RFC
Wales Polytechnic 22 (1G 4PG 1T)
Bristol Polytechnic 3 (1PG)

This was not a happy day for either of the competing clubs, their supporters or Polytechnic rugby in general. There was a ridiculous amount of rough play on the field and the behaviour of some of the visiting supporters was equally bad. Even Mr Mike Iticombe, a lecturer at Bristol Poly, was moved to express disgust at the attitude of his own players. It all put in the shade the achievement of Wales Polytechnic in winning their ninth title. Kingston, with three titles, are the next most successful Poly in the Cup competition. There was heart-searching on the part of the competition organisers afterwards and action will be taken to avoid a repeat performance by the teams and their followers.

When the players left the brawling to concentrate on the rugby, Wales were clearly the better team and they were well marshalled by Gary Abraham, and by Aled Williams and Rupert Moon, two half-backs with vast experience of top-level rugby. Abraham kicked four goals and converted one of Wales Poly's two tries, scored by Hughes on the wing and Pearn, the Wales captain, on the flank.

Bristol have a magnificent record in the tournament in that they have reached as many finals as the Welsh team, yet they seem, perenially, to be runners-up. They have won the title just twice and throughout this match they were struggling. Wales had more experience and this was reflected in the frustration of the Bristol players. More self-control would have helped, while there was little chance of the Wales Poly pack, no saints themselves, being put off their game.

Wales Polytechnic: C Evans; P Hughes, A Porter, G Abraham, S Wood; A Williams, R Moon; T Hill, D Titcombe, N Jones, D Law, J Berrington, J Pearn (*capt*), T Warren, S Baston *Replacement* G Chalmers for Titcombe
Scorers *Tries:* Pearn, Hughes *Conversion:* Abraham *Penalty Goals:* Abraham (4)
Bristol Polytechnic: C Norton (*capt*); N Wakefield, D Cheng, P Shields, S Flint; A Hibbert, M de Maid; J Holmes, D Bronks, C Newth, D Phelps, M Espley, S Truelove, B Atkins, S Bishop *Replacement* D Finnear for Truelove
Scorer *Penalty Goal:* Hibbert
Referee P J Wakefield (London)

First round proper: Newcastle 7, Sheffield 16; Liverpool 16, Leicester 0; Wales 16, Portsmouth 0; Oxford 38, Central London 0; Leeds 30, Teesside 3; Wolves 22, Staffordshire 12; Kingston 0, Bristol 17; Thames 33, West London 7
Quarter-finals: Sheffield 21, Liverpool 10; Wales 40, Oxford 12; Leeds 25, Wolves 12; Bristol 18, Thames 6
Semi-finals: Sheffield 12, Wales 20; Leeds 6, Bristol 20
Wales (formerly Glamorgan Poly) have won the title nine times; Kingston three times; Bristol, Liverpool and Leeds twice each; Manchester and Middlesex once each.

HOSPITALS' CHALLENGE CUP 1989

Rupert Cherry

8 March, Old Deer Park
St Mary's Hospital 20 (1G 1PG 1DG 2T)
The London Hospital 9 (2PG 1DG)

St Mary's won the Hospitals' Cup for the third successive season. It was their 28th title, but they scarcely looked confident until the last few minutes of the final. It was certainly not a typical St Mary's side, although they fielded half of last year's team, and The London gave them a tremendous fright. Early in the last quarter, when they were only a point behind, The London forwards several times drove towards the St Mary's line, and on at least three occasions nearly scored a try.

It was a tense match with ceaseless kicking by the two fly-halves. Duncan McLaren of St Mary's began with a dropped goal, to which Angus MacLean of The London replied with a penalty goal from near touch. Amid the stalemate, St Mary's hopes were raised by winger Richard Robinson, who did well to score a try in the corner. McLaren then scored an easy penalty goal, but MacLean kept The London in contention with another penalty goal and a dropped goal. The London's revival petered out as St Mary's began to play much better. Paul Mitchell scored a try from a scrum near the line, and Richard Wintle added another in injury time, which McLaren converted.

St Mary's had scored 50 points in their two games leading to the final, but The London found it very difficult to overcome the Royal Free in their semi-final. It was the first time that the final had been played at the Old Deer Park and the students were asked not to have their usual 'rag'.

St Mary's: R Wintle; R Robinson, D Gillan, K G Simms, J Walters; D McLaren, I O'Connor; D Vaughan, S Stacey, A Ellery (*capt*), S O'Leary, P Tooze-Hobson, J Hartley, S Kelly, P Mitchell
Scorers *Tries:* Robinson, Mitchell, Wintle *Conversion:* McLaren
Penalty Goal: McLaren *Dropped Goal:* McLaren
The London: C Jones; N Payne, P Merrifield, I Hamilton, G Hall; A MacLean, H Thomas; R Baker (*capt*), C Mann, S Curry, P Barnes, T McPartlin, J Burch, A Martin, J McAllister *Replacement* P Farquhar-Smith for Merrifield (75 mins)
Scorer *Penalty Goals:* MacLean (2) *Dropped Goal:* MacLean
Referee R C Rees (London Society)

First Round: UCH/Middlesex 11, St Thomas's 0; Guy's 17, St George's 3
Second Round: St Mary's 29, UCH/Middlesex 6; The London 43, King's College 0; Guy's 10, Royal Free 22; Barts 9, Charing Cross/Westminster 19
Semi-finals: St Mary's 21, Charing Cross/Westminster 3; The London 9, Royal Free 6
Final: St Mary's 20, The London 9

Guy's have won the Cup 30 times, St Mary's 28, St Thomas's 17, The London 11, St Bartholomew's 9, St George's and Westminster 3 times each, and Middlesex once.

THE INTER-SERVICES TOURNAMENT 1989

Rupert Cherry

The Army beat their own points-scoring record for the tournament set in the 1988 competition when they piled up 62 points in the two matches. This time they increased the total to 64 and, of course, retained the Services Championship. On paper all three teams were weaker than in 1988, particularly the Army, which had lost England captain Will Carling and the outstanding forwards Willie Carr and Dean Ryan. Despite this, the Army scored four tries against the Navy and eight against the RAF.

The Army beat the RAF 43-10. It was one of the worst tournament defeats the airmen had ever had, and yet the margin could have been greater. The Army, obsessed with their back row, which was certainly a good one, tried to advance close to the scrum; a ploy which the RAF, like the Navy, were mostly able to control. However, when long passes were thrown to the wings, the RAF backs were nearly always beaten. Gordon-Lennox, who has developed into a fine, attacking full-back, exploited these opportunities admirably, as did the Army's wing, Atkins. He was the outstanding player in both matches, not only for his try-scoring, two in each game, but also for his truly magnificent defence.

The RAF learned their lesson and, when they met the Navy in the last match, made sure that they got the ball out to Rory Underwood on the left wing. He had not been available against the Army because he was playing for England, and in previous years the RAF had neglected him shamefully. This time he received three passes in the first ten minutes and scored a try each time. He scored a fourth try in the second half which was the most spectacular of them all. The move began on the RAF's own line and involved eight or nine men before Underwood finished it off. I cannot remember any other player in a Services tournament match scoring four tries.

11 March, Twickenham
Royal Navy 9 (3PG)   **Army 21** (1G 1DG 3T)
for the Willis Faber Trophy

Royal Navy: Lt C Alcock (HMS Dryad) (*capt*); PO E Over (HMS Collingwood), Lt R Bigland (HMS Seahawk), LWEM(R) D Oakley (HMS Alacrity), Lt S D Phillips RM (MoD DNR London); S/Lt B Nicholas RN (BRNC Dartmouth), Mne P Livingstone (40 Cdo RM); C/Sgt J Martin (FO Plymouth), POPT M Clay (HMS Raleigh), MEM(M) N Fox (HMS Seahawk), POAE P J Elliott (HMS Seahawk), Sgt D Hadlow (RM Poole), CWEA M Sheldon (HMS Nelson NCG), Lt M Sweett RM (CTCRM Lympstone), L/Cpl J Bryant (40 Cdo RM) *Replacement* WEA I Fletcher (HMS Manchester) for Over (46 mins)
Scorer *Penalty Goals:* Nicholas (3)
Army: Capt E Gordon-Lennox (Grenadier Gds); Sgt E Atkins (Royal Sigs),

Sgt Inst C Spowart (APTC), 2nd Lt S Hopkin (King's Own Bordrs), 2nd Lt L Drakeley (Para); Bdr S Commander (RHA), S/Sgt G Morgan (REME); Bdr D Coghlan (RHA), L/Bdr C Wood (RHA), Cpl C Campbell (RWF), Major B McCall (REME) (*capt*), Sgt C Turley (Cheshire Regt), 2nd Lt G Knight (DWR), 2nd Lt R Wainwright (RAMC), 2nd Lt T Rodber (Green Howards) *Replacements* 2nd Lt A Wheatley (DWR) for Drakeley (72 mins); Gnr A Howard (RA) for Commander (30 mins)
Scorers *Tries:* Drakeley, Atkins (2), Rodber   *Dropped Goal:* Spowart
Conversion: Gordon-Lennox
Referee M Bayliss (Gloucester Society)

18 March, Twickenham
Army 43 (4G 1PG 4T)   **Royal Air Force 10** (1G 1T)
for the Windsor Life Challenge Cup

Army: Capt E Gordon-Lennox (Grenadier Gds); 2nd Lt A Wheatley (DWR), 2nd Lt S Hopkin (King's Own Bordrs), Sgt Inst C Spowart (APTC), Sgt E Atkins (Royal Sigs); Capt J Steele (RA), S/Sgt G Morgan (REME); Bdr D Coghlan (RHA), L/Bdr C Wood (RHA), Cpl C Campbell (RWF), Major B McCall (REME) (*capt*), Sgt C Turley (Cheshire Regt), 2nd Lt G Knight (DWR), 2nd Lt R Wainwright (RAMC), 2nd Lt T Rodber (Green Howards) *Replacement* L/Bdr J Denwood (RHA) for Morgan (75 mins)
Scorers *Tries:* Knight, Gordon-Lennox (2), Atkins (2), Wood, Steele, Wainwright   *Conversions:* Steele (4)   *Penalty Goal:* Steele
RAF: Cpl S J Lazenby (Brize Norton); Cpl K M Holifield (Brize Norton), Jnr Tech S M Roke (St Athan), SAC P A Hull (Cosford), SAC S K Crossland (Finningley); SAC P J Bradley (St Athan), Sgt S Worrall (Finningley) (*capt*); F/O NDR Carter (Wroughton), F/O R L Miller (Chivenor), Cpl A Billett (St Athan), F/O R Burn (Benson), Sgt B R Richardson (Pitreavie Castle), Cpl C D Morgan (Newton), Cpl D R Milne (Marham), Cpl D A Parsonage (Finningley)   *Replacement* SAC R J Rees (Lyneham) for Morgan (79 mins)
Scorers *Tries:* Crossland (2)   *Conversion:* Hull
Referee G R Seddon (Manchester Society)

8 April, Twickenham
Royal Navy 23 (2G 1PG 2T)   **Royal Air Force 30** (2G 2PG 3T)
for the Windsor Life Trophy

Royal Navy: Lt C Alcock (HMS Heron) (*capt*); PO E Over (HMS Collingwood), Lt R Bigland (HMS Seahawk), LWEM(R) D Oakley (HMS Alacrity), Lt S D Phillips RM (MoD DNR London); S/Lt B Nicholas (BRNC Dartmouth), LPT I Torpey (HMS Newcastle); C/Sgt J Martin (FO Plymouth), POPT M Clay (HMS Raleigh), CPO M Brough (HMS Talent), L/Cpl S Trench (40 Cdo RM), Mne R Armstrong (42 Cdo RM), Sgt M Reece (MoD DNR London), POPT S Jones (HMS Minerva), LAEM D Philpott (HMS Osprey)   *Replacement* LWEM S Whitter (HMS Southampton) for Philpott (43 mins)
Scorers *Tries:* Oakley, Over, Bigland, Torpey   *Conversions:* Nicholas (2)   *Penalty Goal:* Nicholas
Royal Air Force: Cpl S J Lazenby (Brize Norton); SAC S K Crossland (Finningley), Jnr Tech S M Roke (St Athan), SAC P A Hull (Cosford), Flt Lt R Underwood (Wyton); SAC P J Bradley (St Athan), Sgt S Worrall (Finningley) (*capt*); F/O N D R Carter (Wroughton), F/O R L Miller (Chivenor), Cpl A Billett (St Athan), F/O R Burn (Benson), Sgt B R Richardson (Pitreavie Castle), Cpl C D Morgan (Newton), Cpl D R Milne (Marham), Cpl D A Parsonage (Finningley)
Replacement SAC I Thickpenny (St Athan) for Burn (76 mins)
Scorers *Tries:* Underwood (4), Crossland   *Conversions:* Bradley (2)
Penalty Goals: Worrall, Bradley
Referee E Morrison (Bristol Society)

Inter-Services Tournament Champions

The Army have won the Tournament outright 27 times, the Royal Navy 16 times, and the RAF 11 times.

1920	**Navy**	1947	**RAF**	1968	**Army**
1921	**Navy**	1948	Triple Tie	1969	**Army**
1922	**Navy**	1949	**Army** / **RAF**	1970	**Navy**
1923	**RAF**			1971	**RAF**
1924	Triple Tie	1950	**Army**	1972	**Army**
1925	**Army** / **RAF**	1951	**Navy**	1973	**Navy**
		1952	**Army**	1974	**Navy**
1926	**Army**	1953	**Army**	1975	Triple Tie
1927	**Navy**	1954	Triple Tie	1976	**Army**
1928	**Army**	1955	**RAF**	1977	**Navy**
1929	**Army**	1956	Triple Tie	1978	Triple Tie
1930	**Army**	1957	**Army**	1979	**RAF**
1931	**Navy**	1958	**RAF**	1980	**Army**
1932	**Army**	1959	**RAF**	1981	**Navy**
1933	**Army**	1960	**Army**	1982	**RAF**
1934	**Army**	1961	**Navy**	1983	**Army**
1935	Triple Tie	1962	**RAF**	1984	Triple Tie
1936	**Army**	1963	**Army**	1985	**RAF**
1937	**Army**	1964	**Army**	1986	**RAF**
1938	**Navy**	1965	**Army**	1987	**Navy**
1939	**Navy**	1966	**Navy**	1988	**Army**
1946	**Army**	1967	**Army**	1989	**Army**

Royal Navy v Army Royal Navy have won 31, Army 38, and 3 matches have been drawn
Royal Navy v RAF Royal Navy have won 36, RAF 24, and 4 matches have been drawn
Army v RAF Army have won 37, RAF 19, and 8 matches have been drawn

The victorious Army squad before the match against the Royal Navy at Twickenham.

Inter-Services Under-21 Tournament
27 January 1989 Army 4, RAF 13; **28 January** Royal Navy 4, RAF 25; **29 January** Royal Navy 4, Army 30

THE MIDDLESEX SEVENS 1989
(Sponsored by Save & Prosper)

Rupert Cherry

No matter what their problems there seems to be no stopping Harlequins when they come to play sevens. Again they triumphed at Twickenham. It was their fourth victory in succession, equalling their achievement at the beginning of the tournament 60 years ago in the days of Wavell Wakefield, J C Gibbs and Dick Hamilton-Wickes. In 1989, though, they needed no nucleus of international runners to gain their 12th victory in the competition, which is three more than any other club has achieved. None of their previous year's seven was available and, although they won the Wang Sevens at Richmond a fortnight before Twickenham, only half that side were available for the big Middlesex event. Still their coach, Dick Best, welded together a side which played almost perfect sevens.

Most of the other sides who got through to the finals played to a high standard, so that the matches were evenly fought and the 'Quins' final triumph bore great merit. London Scottish had found something of the form that earned them four successive victories in the 1960s, and they played a stupendous semi-final against the 'Quins, who just managed to win because their outstanding runner, Jon Eagle, raced from his own 25 to make a try for Chris Sheasby. Rosslyn Park, having beaten Bristol in extra time, opposed the 'Quins in the final, and kept the result in doubt until the last minute. However, Harlequins scored three tries to their two and were very worthy winners.

The event was all the more enjoyable because the Middlesex Sevens Committee had tightened up considerably on crowd control. The attendance was limited to 52,000, so that there was movement in comfort; there were no cushions to be thrown about; the 'Mexican Wave' was considerably subdued; and there was only one streaker – a great improvement.

RESULTS
Sixth Round: Bristol 6, London Irish 4; Richmond 6, Blackheath 26; Rosslyn Park I 16, Old Alleynians 0; Loughborough Students 16, Hawick 8; Rugby 6, London Scottish I 26; Rosslyn Park II 18, London Scottish II 12; Saracens 0, Wasps 22; W London Institute 10, Harlequins 24
Seventh Round: Bristol 20, Blackheath 18; Rosslyn Park I 14, Loughborough Students 12; London Scottish I 34, Rosslyn Park II 6; Wasps 10, Harlequins 16
Semi-finals: Bristol 16, Rosslyn Park I 20; London Scottish I 12, Harlequins 16
Final: Rosslyn Park I 12, Harlequins 18

Jon Eagle lifts high the Russell-Cargill Memorial Cup signalling another Harlequins triumph in the Middlesex Sevens after one of the most exciting tournaments for many years.

Teams in Final

Rosslyn Park I: T Hyde; D Barnett, A Dent, A Woodhouse, M Jermyn; S Hunter, K Wyles
Scorers *Tries:* Jermyn, Wyles *Conversions:* Jermyn, Woodhouse
Harlequins: C Sheasby; P Winterbottom, S Thresher, R Glenister, A Thompson; J Johnston, J Eagle
Scorers *Tries:* Sheasby, Glenister, Eagle *Conversions:* Thresher(3)
Referee: R C Quittenton (London)

WINNERS

1926	Harlequins	1958	Blackheath
1927	Harlequins	1959	Loughborough Colleges
1928	Harlequins	1960	London Scottish
1929	Harlequins	1961	London Scottish
1930	London Welsh	1962	London Scottish
1931	London Welsh	1963	London Scottish
1932	Blackheath	1964	Loughborough Colleges
1933	Harlequins	1965	London Scottish
1934	Barbarians	1966	Loughborough Colleges
1935	Harlequins	1967	Harlequins
1936	Sale	1968	London Welsh
1937	London Scottish	1969	St Luke's College
1938	Metropolitan Police	1970	Loughborough Colleges
1939	Cardiff	1971	London Welsh
1940	St Mary's Hospital	1972	London Welsh
1941	Cambridge University	1973	London Welsh
1942	St Mary's Hospital	1974	Richmond
1943	St Mary's Hospital	1975	Richmond
1944	St Mary's Hospital	1976	Loughborough Colleges
1945	Notts	1977	Richmond
1946	St Mary's Hospital	1978	Harlequins
1947	Rosslyn Park	1979	Richmond
1948	Wasps	1980	Richmond
1949	Heriot's FP	1981	Rosslyn Park
1950	Rosslyn Park	1982	Stewart's Melville FP
1951	Richmond II	1983	Richmond
1952	Wasps	1984	London Welsh
1953	Richmond	1985	Wasps
1954	Rosslyn Park	1986	Harlequins
1955	Richmond	1987	Harlequins
1956	London Welsh	1988	Harlequins
1957	St Luke's College	1989	Harlequins

Harlequins have won the title 12 times, Richmond 9 (including one by their second VII), London Welsh 8, London Scottish 6, St Mary's Hospital and Loughborough Colleges 5 each, Rosslyn Park 4, Wasps 3, Blackheath and St Luke's College (now Exeter University) twice, Barbarians, Sale, Met Police, Cardiff, Cambridge University, Notts (now Nottingham), Heriot's FP and Stewart's-Melville FP once each

ENGLAND DENIED IN CARDIFF – AGAIN!

SCHOOLS RUGBY 1988-89

George Abbott

England's 18 Group team were denied a record of unbroken triumph by a determined Welsh team at Cardiff. In a game played in mud and rain handling moves were rare and difficult and the only scoring in a 6-6 draw came from penalty goals. England had already defeated Ireland and France, both of whom had gained narrow victories over Wales, and three days after the Cardiff match they finished their season successfully by beating Scotland 15-6 at Doncaster. After an unbeaten season it may seem like petty criticism to draw attention to England's meagre tally of tries – in the four matches they managed only five, of which three were scored by the backs and two by the lively flanker, Adams. But the fact remains that the bulk of their scoring came from penalty goals, reflecting on the one hand insistent pressure by an efficient, workmanlike pack and on the other a surprising lack of penetration by the backs, despite the presence of a match-winner in Adebayo on the left wing.

Ireland had a ratio of tries to penalty goals (ten to four) which was more satisfying to traditionalists and their team included some players of high class, notably the half-backs Hogan and Malone and the big lock forward Costello. Although they lost to England in Cork, two away victories over Wales and Scotland, added to an earlier success against the touring Zimbabwe side, made a highly creditable record. The party from *Zimbabwe* played all four provinces in Ireland as well as the international side, losing to Leinster and Ulster, drawing with Munster and defeating Connacht.

Although *Wales* (Senior Group) managed only a single victory, against Scotland, all three of their other matches were very closely contested. Early in the season they also had a narrow win (13-10) over the Canadian Juniors. For this match the Welsh side was picked mainly from those members of the previous season's Senior Group squad who had not been absorbed into Youth teams.

At the lower age level *England's* international engagements in the 16 Group were confined to a short tour in Italy, where they beat Italy B 19-3, but lost the full international 10-9. *Wales,* whose Intermediate Group have the age limit of 15 at the beginning of the season, also played two matches in Italy, winning both against Italy B (41-0) and against Italy A (28-6). They also played Scotland at 15 Group (or Intermediate) level and won 18-6. In this Group Wales have won their last 14 internationals against Italy A, Italy B and Scotland, their last defeat being in 1984.

ENGLISH SCHOOLS (18 GROUP)
TOUR TO AUSTRALIA 1988

THE TOURING PARTY
Manager R Milner **Assistant Manager-Coach** I M Gibson
Assistant Coach R J Tilley **Physiotherapist** A Bell
Full-back: A P Challinor (RGS, Guildford)
Threequarters: A Adebayo (Kelly), P G Bingham (Ampleforth), P Hopkins
(Midhurst GS), D P Hopley (Harrow), P M Maynard (QEGS, Wakefield),
R J R Whitelaw (Ampleforth)
Half-backs: O Benkert (Wellington, Berkshire), T Ashworth (Sherborne), R D Booth
(Ampleforth), M A Corcoran (John Fisher), P D P Williams (John Fisher)
Forwards: D P Meirion-Jones (Marlborough) (*capt*), G E Adams (Batley GS),
J P Amery (Farnham College), A R Fields (Millfield), N R Griffiths (Oakham),
I St J F Hendry (Millfield), P C M Irons (Wellington, Berkshire), M O Johnson
(Robert Smyth Upper, Leics), J A H Mallett (Millfield), J N Mitchell (Bradford GS),
S O Ojomoh (West Buckland), M J Ord (Pemberton, Northants), J A Overall (Dulwich),
S J Reid (St Bees), M A Smith (St Cuthbert's HS, Newcastle), L Watt (Sevenoaks)
(*replacement after injury to Adams*)
TOUR RECORD
Played 12   Won 11   Lost 1   Points for 408   Against 67
RESULTS
v Western Australia W66-3; v South Australia Colts W34-6; v South Australia
Schools W58-0; v Victoria W50-6; v ACT W36-3; v NSW Country W31-0; v New South
Wales W11-8; v Queensland Sec Schools W37-0; v Queensland Country L19-21; v NEW
ZEALAND W15-8; v NSW Combined HS W38-12; v AUSTRALIA W13-0

SCOTTISH SCHOOLS (18 GROUP)
TOUR TO NEW ZEALAND 1988

THE TOURING PARTY
President J J Lobban **Administrator** A P Macintyre **Coach** R A Moffat
Assistant Coach P Gallagher **Hon Physician** Dr E I Adam
Full-back: D R D Pulfrey (Morrison's Academy)
Threequarters: D R W Adam (Dollar Academy), K D Boon (Strathallan), S A Nichol
(Selkirk HS), K E Squires (Dollar Academy), C N White (Merchiston Castle), B J Whyte
(Golspie HS)
Half-backs: R M Dickson (Berwickshire HS), A H R Hay (Merchiston Castle),
A D Nicol (Dundee HS), A G Shiel (Earlston HS), G Sisman (Dollar Academy)
Forwards: G M Kenhard (Harris Academy) (*capt*), G M Adam (Strathallan),
S A Aitken (Earlston HS), D J Archibald (Berwickshire HS), S J Brotherstone
(Earlston HS), K R Brown (Earlston HS), R J Gray (Galashiels Academy), J S Jowett
(Merchiston Castle), G D McGill (Dundee HS), A G Ness (Dollar Academy), S W Paul
(George Heriot's), L B A Thomson (Selkirk HS), G F Walsingham (Merchiston Castle),
G W Weir (Stewart's-Melville)
TOUR RECORD
Played 8   Won 5   Lost 3   Points for 112   Against 125
RESULTS
v Hannan Shield District L15-28; v Otago W32-14; v Horowhenua W22-11;
v Wellington W14-12; v Taranaki W8-7; v Waikato L7-14; v Thames Valley W4-3;
v NEW ZEALAND L10-36

School teams which achieved the distinction of an unbeaten season were *Ampleforth, Brighton, Merchiston Castle* in Scotland and *Methodist College, Belfast*. Near misses were recorded by *Aylesbury GS, Chislehurst & Sidcup GS, Gresham's, Judd, Monkton Combe, Rossall, Silcoates, Wellington* (Berkshire) and *Dundee HS*.

Ampleforth's accomplished team won all 12 school matches, remaining unbeaten for the third year running, and the supply of talented young players at the school shows no sign of drying up. Their hardest test came from *Stonyhurst*, whose final record (W11, D2, L5) does them less than justice, for three of their defeats came in the Lent Term, when three of their backs, all picked for England's 18 Group team, were not available. *Newcastle RGS* had a very successful season, playing 21 matches in all and winning 18 of them. Although *Durham* were outplayed by Ampleforth, they won 14 of their other 15 games, the second defeat coming from Ellesmere by a narrow margin.

Both Wakefield schools enjoyed a good deal of success. *QEGS*, although inexperienced, won 16 of their 21 fixtures, but lost narrowly to their neighbours, *Silcoates*, who went through until February before suffering their only setback, at the hands of Leeds GS, and won 16 games in all, drawing two. *Woodhouse Grove* drew with Silcoates and their figures (W14, D3, L3) were very creditable, especially as their three defeats were by only three points or less. *Bradford GS*, after two great seasons, had some rebuilding to do, but won 16 out of 26 games over two terms. *Leeds GS* lost heavily to Ampleforth early in the season, but scored nearly 500 points in winning 20 of their 24 engagements.

In a shorter fixture list forward strength saw *Rossall* through to 15 successes and they lost only to King's, Macclesfield. The best *Merchant Taylors', Crosby* team for some years settled down to play good rugby after two early reverses and lost only one more game, winning 17 in all. Playing in their traditional open style, *Cowley* scored more than 100 tries in 21 matches, of which they won 13. Most of the *King's, Macclesfield* team will be available again next season and their 1988-89 results were most encouraging – 22 wins and only two losses.

A lean period, with defeats outnumbering victories, was an unusual experience for *Sedbergh*, but they finished well by beating Loretto and *Ellesmere*, who had returned from a tour of Australia to win their first ten matches and 12 in all out of 15.

The benefit of the previous season's team-building was seen at *Nottingham HS* and the XV won 16 games and lost only three times. One of those defeats came from *Trent*, who used their resources well, moving the ball around behind a light pack with successful results (W11, L3). After losing five of their first six matches *Bromsgrove* improved dramatically to win eight and draw one of the remaining nine. Open rugby produced 12 successes for *Worcester RGS* and they lost only to Cheltenham and Christ, Brecon. Three reverses at the end of the term spoilt *King's, Worcester's* figures, but they were still very satisfactory

(W11, D1, L5). *Rugby* at their best could compare well with any school side and their record of nine wins, one draw and three losses against schools was regarded as somewhat disappointing.

Strength at forward and in midfield served *Marlborough* well and they won ten games out of 12. The only defeat on their regular circuit came from *Bryanston*, who recovered from a mauling by Sherborne to win 14 of their other 15 fixtures. Injuries hit *Sherborne* around mid-term and later results were mixed after a good start; the final figures were W8, D2, L3. A record of nine wins, one draw and two losses, *Cheltenham's* best for some years, was due to balanced strength. *Millfield* are never short of talent, but their 1988 team was not of vintage quality; they won five games, drew one and lost five.

The strength of the junior sides at *King's, Taunton* gives high hopes for the future, but the First XV were only just in credit, with six victories against five defeats. *Taunton* followed an unbeaten 1987 season with satisfactory figures (W7, L4). *Wellington* (Somerset), who won nine out of 13 matches and drew with King's, Taunton, attributed their successes largely to sound defence. After a comparatively lean spell *Downside* improved to record seven wins in all, drawing two games and losing three. One of those three defeats was inflicted by *Blundell's*, whose major points of strength were in the pack and on the wings and who won nine out of 12 fixtures on the demanding West Country circuit. *Monkton Combe* mastered all their regular opponents and won 15 games in all; their only setback came from Sevenoaks, who were on tour during the half-term break. They were one of only three teams to overcome *Colston's*, who had ten successes. *St Brendan's* (Bristol), in a long list of 29 fixtures against schools and club colts sides, won 25, drew one and lost only three. *Truro* were again supreme in the far west, providing seven of the Cornwall 18 Group team, winning 14 of their 15 matches and losing only to Plymouth.

One of the best ever seasons at *Bloxham* finished with the fine record of 12 wins and two losses and included the first success against Warwick for 25 years. *St Edward's, Oxford* ended a splendid term with three victories on tour in the north, bringing the figures to W16, L3. They had a narrow victory over *Radley*, who won six out of 11 fixtures in a tough circuit. *Wellington* (Berkshire), who had won every match in 1987, faced their final fixture in 1988 with a similar record, but went down this time to Marlborough by 13-6.

The *RGS, High Wycombe* and *Aylesbury GS* competed, as often before, for supremacy in Buckinghamshire. The RGS won that contest 12-10 and went on to win 18 of their 22 matches, but this was Aylesbury's only defeat. *Windsor* too had an exceptionally good season, losing only three times. After a difficult start *Oakham* won nine of their 13 school matches with a team which relied upon mobility and speed. One of the defeats came from *Oundle*, who were unbeaten after mid-October and who look forward keenly to the 1989-90 season, when an exceptionally talented age group will be reaching the top.

After taking 44 players on tour to Australia *Harrow* won seven of their 14 fixtures – a somewhat disappointing result, although there were some bright spots. *Brighton's* spirited and adaptable side went from strength to strength, overcoming all 12 school rivals and winning 15 games in all. An almost new *Tonbridge* side, built around an experienced pair of half-backs, proved to be one of the best in their strong group, winning eight matches and suffering only three narrow defeats. Their neighbours, *Judd*, were well equipped all round and their only defeat in 19 fixtures came as late as February from the useful *Wallington HS* team. Judd was the only school to master *Chislehurst & Sidcup GS*, whose pack played consistently well to win 18 games and draw one.

Dulwich, with one of the strongest fixture lists in the south-east, gained ten victories and lost only to Wellington and Tonbridge. They were one of three sides to defeat *Sevenoaks*, who had many spirited performances among their 13 successes. *Epsom* had a promising blend of players, but did not settle down as well as had been hoped and their results (W10, L5) were a little disappointing after recent successes. *KCS Wimbledon*, with 14 wins, two draws and two losses, had their best figures since 1977. *Emanuel* had 21 fixtures spread over two terms and won 17 of them. *Gresham's* proved themselves the strongest side in East Anglia with an unbroken run of 16 successes, including three on tour in France, but were finally outplayed by *Te Aute*, an exceptionally powerful touring team from New Zealand. Outside the main stream *Chichester HS* enjoyed their best season since starting rugby in 1945. They scored 545 points to 164, winning 21 out of 23 matches.

Merchiston Castle's achievements in Scotland were remarkable by any standards. They started by winning the Hull University 15-a-side Festival in September in the face of strong competition. Despite being hit severely by injuries they went on to play rugby of consistently high quality throughout the season, in which they won all 19 matches and scored more than 600 points. Among Merchiston's early results was a 17-0 defeat of *Dundee HS*. This turned out to be the only setback suffered by Dundee, who won their other 22 games in spite of being without their two international players, scrum-half A Nicol and flanker G McGill, for a while through injuries. Only 20 boys represented *Dollar Academy* during the season and they proved to be an honest, hard-working squad who well deserved their success (W16, L4). *Kelvinside Academy's* record of 24 wins from 27 matches was almost certainly their best ever. Their strength lay mainly in the pack, which was responsible for 30 pushover tries.

The *Llandovery* team was full of talent and gave some memorable displays, notably in beating Millfield 32-0 and in winning the 100th match of the series against Christ, Brecon by 19-0. *Christ, Brecon* too had some notable triumphs, winning ten and drawing one out of 14 games. Useful Welsh sides among the state schools included *Cwmtawe, Gowerton* (a name to note for next season) and *St Cyres* (Penarth), who had a victory over Llandovery to their credit.

In Northern Ireland *Methodist College, Belfast* brought a great season to a triumphant conclusion when they won the Ulster Schools Senior Cup for the 26th time, beating *Wallace HS*, Lisburn 26-12 in an excellent final which was a credit to schools' rugby.

The 'sevens' season of 1989 will be remembered as the year of *Ampleforth's* triumph in winning both Open and Festival Tournaments at Rosslyn Park's National Schools Sevens meeting. This was a monumental feat of endurance and character, spread over four days with four matches on each day, many of them in rain and mud which made the physical effort even more taxing. Few schools attempt to bring off the double and it had been done only once before, by Ampleforth in 1977. Their opponents in the 1989 finals were *King's, Worcester*, who were comprehensively defeated 38-0 in the Open, and *Cheltenham*, who took an early lead before going down 12-6 in the Festival. Ampleforth's victory in the Festival completed a hat-trick of successes in that event and a remarkable record for R D Booth and P G Bingham, who were members of the winning teams in all three years.

The popular Preston Grasshoppers Festival, in its 11th year, welcomed several newcomers among the 32 entrants. The weather once again was far from kind, but 95 of the scheduled 102 matches were completed, leaving *Ellesmere* and *Arnold* (Blackpool) to contest the final, Ellesmere winning 6-0 to add a fresh name to the list of winners.

The following players took part in the 18 Group international matches. (Countries played against are shown in square brackets.) Abbreviations: *E* – England, *F* – France, *I* – Ireland, *S* – Scotland, *W* – Wales, *Z* – Zimbabwe, (R) – Replacement.

ENGLAND
Full-back: T Allison (Gresham's) [*I, F, W, S*]
Threequarters: P Harries (Gaynes, Upminster) [*I*]; S C W Ravenscroft (Bradford GS) [*F, W, S*]; J P Flood (Stonyhurst) [*I, F, W, S*]; D L Clift (Merchant Taylors', Crosby) [*I, F, W, S*]; A Adebayo (Kelly) [*I, F, W, S*]
Half-backs: V Gradillas (Stonyhurst) [*I, F, W, S*]; M A Slavin (John Fisher) [*S* (R)]; K P P Bracken (Stonyhurst) [*I, F , W*]; A R Royer (Loughborough FE College) [*W* (R) *S*]
Forwards: I St J F Hendry (Millfield) [*I, W, S*]; C J Clark (Marlborough) [*F*]; P A Simmonds (Bedford Modern) [*I, F, W, S*]; G C Rowntree (John Cleveland, Hinckley) [*I, F, W, S*]; G K Bulstrode (Sherborne) [*I, F, W, S*]; R A Bramley (QEGS, Wakefield) [*S* (R)]; J G Barton (Kingsbridge) [*I, F, W, S*]; D G Walton (St Mary's & St Joseph's, Sidcup) [*I, F, W, S*]; G E Adams (Batley GS) [*I, F, W, S*]; C J Wilkins (Brentwood) [*I, F, W, S*]
Adams was captain in all four matches

IRELAND
Full-backs: J Dunn (Belvedere) [*Z*]; R Davidson (RS, Dungannon) [*E*]; R Kelleher (CBC, Cork) [*W, S*]

Threequarters: G McCluskey (Portadown) [Z]; G Anderson (Bangor GS) [E, W, S];
D Hernan (Cistercian, Roscrea) [Z, E, W(R), S]; G Lavin (St Mary's) [E, W, S];
M Ridge (Blackrock) [Z, E, W, S]; T Moran (St Munchin's) [Z, W]
Half-backs: P Allen (Dublin HS) [Z]; N Malone (Methodist, Belfast) [E, W, S];
K Hodgen (Campbell) [Z]; N Hogan (Terenure) [E, W, S]
Forwards: L Murphy (PBC, Cork) [Z, E, W, S]; C Twomey (CBC, Cork) [Z];
M Kernohan (Royal Belfast Acad Inst) [E, W, S]; A McDonald (CBC, Cork) [Z];
D Cole (Dublin HS) [E]; P Wallace (Crescent, Limerick) [W, S]; K Martin
(Methodist, Belfast) [S(R)]; S Kirkpatrick (Sullivan Upper) [Z, E, W, S]; V Costello
(Blackrock) [Z, E, W, S]; S Rooney (St Michael's) [Z, E, W, S]; S Liston
(St Munchin's) [Z]; J Callaghan (Wallace HS) [E, W, S]; D Widger (St Michael's)
[Z, E, W, S]
Widger was captain against Zimbabwe, Hogan against England, Wales and Scotland

SCOTLAND
Full-backs: G J Findlay (Dollar Academy) [F, W, E]; J R L Doran (St Aloysius) [I]
Threequarters: J W K Anderson (Merchiston Castle) [F, W, E]; G J Findlay
(Dollar Academy) [I]; K R Milligan (Stewart's-Melville) [I, E]; N G Douglas
(Edinburgh Academy) [F, W, E]; C N White (Merchiston Castle) [F, W, I, E];
K C Thomson (Glasgow Academy) [F, W]; M M Thomson (Stewart's-Melville) [I]
Half-backs: J R Newton (Dundee HS) [F, W]; G J E McIntosh (Stewart's-Melville)
[I, E]; A D Nicol (Dundee HS) [F, W, I, E]
Forwards: O Fowara (Edinburgh Academy) [F, W]; T Smith (Rannoch) [E];
F M Graham (Dunbar GS) [F, W, I, E]; G F Walsingham (Merchiston Castle) [F, W, I];
J K McKechnie (Dundee HS) [E]; A J Kittle (Ross HS) [I, E]; D A Barnett (Perth
Academy) [F, W, E]; P G Mauritzen (Stewart's-Melville) [I(R), E]; M J McVie
(Edinburgh Academy) [F, W, I]; S P Thompson (Morrison's Academy) [F, W, I, E];
G D McGill (Dundee HS) [F, W, I, E]; A G Ness (Dollar Academy) [F, W, I, E];
J C M van Beusekom (Strathallan) [W(R)]
Nicol was captain in all four matches

WALES
Full-back: L Evans (Llandovery) [S, F, I, E]
Threequarters: G Lewis (Glantaf) [S, F, I, E]; P Jones (Pencoed) [S, I, E]; I Jones
(Llandovery) [S, F, I, E]; A Palfrey (St Cyres) [F]; G Matthews (Brynteg) [S, F, I, E]
Half-backs: M Lewis (Llandovery) [S, F]; R Phillips (Llanharri) [I, E]; R Howley
(Brynteg) [S, F, I, E]
Forwards: M Davies (Pontypool) [S, F, I, E]; H Daniel (Gorseinon) [S, F, I, E];
D Lloyd (Ynysawdre) [S, F, I, E(R)]; D Othen (Pontypool) [E]; L Harvey (Maesteg)
[S, F, I, E]; D Jones (Ystalyfera) [S, F, I]; C Goodwin (Mold) [E]; O Lloyd
(Llandovery) [S, I]; S Jenkins (Amman Valley) [S]; A Price (Amman Valley) [S, F, E];
S Davies (Porth County) [F, I, E]; S Williams (Neath) [F, I, E]
Howley was captain in all four matches

MATCH DETAILS (18 Group)

20 December, Lansdowne Road

IRELAND 22 (3G 1T)   **ZIMBABWE 0**
IRELAND *Tries:* Moran, Costello, Dunn, penalty try   *Conversions:* Allen (3)
Referee M Clayton (Scotland)

---

22 December, Montauban

FRANCE 23 (2G 1PG 2T)   **SCOTLAND 6** (2PG)
FRANCE *Tries:* Vincent, Agrech, Bellot, Martin   *Conversions:* Lloberes, Bellot
Penalty Goal: Lloberes

SCOTLAND *Penalty Goals:* Newton (2)
Referee M Roelands (Belgium)

7 January, Melrose

SCOTLAND 6 (2PG)　**WALES 13** (1G 1PG 1T)
SCOTLAND *Penalty Goals:* Newton (2)
WALES *Tries:* Matthews, Howley　*Conversion:* Evans　*Penalty Goal:* Evans
Referee G H Black (Ireland)

25 March, Cork

IRELAND 10 (1G 1T)　**ENGLAND 19** (1G 3PG 1T)
IRELAND *Tries:* Lavin, Ridge　*Conversion:* Malone
ENGLAND *Tries:* Adebayo (2)　*Conversion:* Flood　*Penalty Goals:* Flood (3)
Referee D Herbert (Wales)

25 March, Bayonne

FRANCE 25 (1G 1PG 4T)　**WALES 24** (2G 4PG)
FRANCE *Tries:* Bellot, Gratien, Agrech, Berton (2)　*Conversion:* Viars
Penalty Goal: Viars
WALES *Tries:* S Davies, Howley　*Conversions:* Evans (2)　*Penalty Goals:* Evans (4)
Referee A L Mason (England)

28 March, Bristol

ENGLAND 12 (2G)　**FRANCE 7** (1PG 1T)
ENGLAND *Tries:* Adams, Allison　*Conversions:* Flood (2)
FRANCE *Try:* Berton　*Penalty Goal:* Viars
Referee D Reordan (USA)

1 April, Aberystwyth

WALES 6 (2PG)　**IRELAND 9** (1G 1PG)
WALES *Penalty Goals:* Evans (2)
IRELAND *Try:* Hernan　*Conversion:* Malone　*Penalty Goal:* Malone
Referee T Spreadbury (England)

5 April, Cardiff

WALES 6 (2PG)　**ENGLAND 6** (2PG)
WALES *Penalty Goals:* Evans (2)
ENGLAND *Penalty Goals:* Allison (2)
Referee H A Smith (Ireland)

5 April, Galashiels

SCOTLAND 12 (1G 2PG)　**IRELAND 27** (3G 3PG)
SCOTLAND *Try:* Findlay　*Conversion:* McIntosh　*Penalty Goals:* McIntosh (2)
IRELAND *Tries:* Hogan, Hernan (2)　*Conversions:* Malone (3)
Penalty Goals: Malone (3)
Referee P Robin (France)

8 April, Doncaster

ENGLAND 15 (1G 3PG)　**SCOTLAND 6** (1G)
ENGLAND *Try:* Adams　*Conversion:* Allison　*Penalty Goals:* Allison (3)
SCOTLAND *Try:* White　*Conversion:* McIntosh
Referee G Davies (Wales)

GOOD PROGRESS ON MOST FRONTS

COLTS AND YOUTH RUGBY 1988-89
Michael Stevenson

England Colts, although they stumbled at the final hurdle in France, enjoyed a goodish season and in their exciting No 8, Stephen Ojomoh, displayed one of the richest talents in British rugby. Following the normal Divisional trials, they met Italy at Wolverhampton and opened their international campaign with a good 38-3 win, scoring seven tries to nil, their fast wing, Wray, from West Park, Bramhope, contributing four of them. Another plus was that Winterton, of Aspatria, was a cool and capable goal-kicker. In England's victory over Wales Youth at Torquay in April, Ojomoh's work-rate was formidable and with the ball in his hands he looked like a high-class centre or wing. His perfectly-timed pass to his fly-half, Saverimutto, made a try under the posts that translated a 9-11 deficit into victory over Wales by a goal and three penalties to two tries and a penalty.

Wales regarded this as their most disappointing match. Wrong options were too often taken and the speed of their fine wings, Donovan and Jenkins, was too frequently unexploited. Wales, scoring two tries to one, regarded this as a game that they lost rather than one England won. Like Wales, England found French Juniors something of a handful. They visited Perpignan in mid-April and, despite scoring two good tries to three, England went down 8-20. The main problem was that France were appreciably the more powerful side.

Wales Youth had three good wins under their belt against Canadian Juniors (33-25); Italian Youth (18-3); and Welsh Schools (30-10) before they met France. They had predictably lost, 3-27, to Welsh Students (Under-20s) and must have fancied their chances of registering a rare win against France. But it was not to be and, despite a great showing by the Welsh pack, France's ability for turning opposition errors into points proved crucial. Wales Youth's best performance of the season was their 30-10 win over Welsh Schools in a resurrected fixture at Stradey Park, Llanelli. The match produced eight tries, both sides scoring from their own 22-metre line, and a penalty try was in no way typical of a clean, hard and enjoyable contest. Wales Youth's victory was based on their fine pack, in which Mayze, a flanker, well-supported by Lamerton and McKim, was outstanding. A number of WYRU President's matches were held throughout the season, all of which were won convincingly: the WYRU President's XV beat Blackwood Youth 90-0; Pencoed Youth 53-7; and Anglo Welsh Youth XV 27-0.

Scotland played three Youth matches, two at Under-18 level and an Under-19 match. One was a real mis-match against Sweden at Trelleborg, which Scotland won 6-85; the other was a creditable 21-12 victory over Italy at Ayr in April. The Under-19 match, against Italy, was won 29-13.

In domestic rugby, the powerful Warwickshire side was dominant in the Midlands, running up 193 points to 16 conceded and not losing a match until the County Championship final. David Ray, who has done so much for Rugby School over the years, helps with the coaching of Warwickshire Colts. Warwickshire had previously won the Championship for two consecutive years and, after a cracking 25-11 semi-final triumph over Yorkshire, they must have been very confident of winning a third time. However, Somerset, whom Warwickshire had badly mauled the previous year, turned the tables at Twickenham, winning the Championship 12-10.

Ray's view of the Colts scene is worth an airing. 'In many ways Colts is the most rewarding level to coach. They play some very entertaining football and are very receptive to ideas. The Colts level is increasingly crucial to bridge the gap between school and the adult game. As fewer schools play rugby, England will have to rely more and more on Colts rugby as a source of players. But the really important thing is that Colts play because they want to and not because it's expected of them. Also the link between Colts rugby and clubs is far stronger than that between schools and clubs.' He is disappointed in the lack of interest shown by the media: 'There was little or no coverage of our County Championship until the final and then only in *The Times*. Secretaries could do their bit by bombarding the media with information'.

A successful County Colts Sevens Tournament, under the sponsorship of Labatt's, was held in April at Wirral RFC. Nine counties and an Army team competed, and Yorkshire achieved a runaway victory in the final, where they met Cumbria. Yorkshire had beaten Notts, Lincs and Derbys 14-4 in one semi-final but romped home 42-6 in the final. Cumbria beat Lancashire 14-8 in the other semi-final.

A significant development for Colts rugby is the appointment of Youth Development Officers – Scotland were among the first to recognise this need. John Roxburgh is in charge of Youth Development at the Scottish Rugby Union and five YDOs have been appointed for the five Scottish Districts. Wales have followed suit and three Development Officers, appointed by the WRU, have taken up their posts, while England are in the process of appointing up to 100 YDOs.

The following players took part in the Colts/Youth international matches. (Countries played against are shown in square brackets.)
Abbreviations: *C* – Canada, *E* – England, *F* – France, *It* – Italy, *S* – Scotland, *Sw* – Sweden, *W* – Wales, (R) – Replacement

ENGLAND
Full-backs: J Cowling (Sudbury) [*It*, *W*(R), *F*]; L Corbett (Abbey) [*W*];
G Mitchell (Nuneaton) [*F*(R)]
Threequarters: N Winterton (Aspatria) [*It*, *W*]; G Evans (West Hartlepool) [*F*];

P Maynard (Wakefield) [*It, W, F*]; D Hopley (Wasps) [*It, W, F*]; J Wray
(West Park, Bramhope) [*It, W, F*]; G Allison (Rosslyn Park) [*W*(R)]
Half-backs: N Matthews (Gloucester) [*It*]; A Saverimutto (New Brighton)
[*It*(R), *W, F*]; J Austin (Wellington School) [*It, W, F*]
Forwards: N Griffiths (Leamington) [*It, W, F*]; A Fields (Winchester) [*It, W, F*];
J Mallett (Harlequins) [*It, W, F*]; P Bell (Askeans) [*It, W, F*]; M Johnson (Leicester)
[*It, W, F*]; M Ord (Northampton) [*It, W, F*]; S Ojomoh (Rosslyn Park) [*It, W, F*];
R Jenkins (Brixham) [*It, W, F*]
John Mallett was captain in all three matches

SCOTLAND
Under-18
Full-backs: A M Fraser (Highland) [*It*]; G Renwick (Hawick Wanderers) [*Sw*]
Threequarters: A Barton (Stirling County) [*It*]; A M Fraser (Highland) [*Sw*]; M Craig
(Haddington) [*It, Sw*]; R J S Shepherd (Edinburgh Acads) [*It, S*]; P J Stanger
(Hawick Wanderers) [*It, Sw*]
Half-backs: M McKenzie (Stirling County) [*It, Sw*]; B W Redpath (Melrose) [*It, Sw*]
Forwards: A N Pringle (Musselburgh) [*It, Sw*]; S J Brotherstone (Melrose) [*It, Sw*];
D J Armour (West of Scotland) [*It, Sw*]; C J Pow (Musselburgh) [*It, Sw*]; A Grahamslaw
(Berwick) [*It, Sw*]; J M Clinkenbeard (Currie) [*It, Sw*]; E Murchison (Rugby School)
[*It, Sw*]; L B A Thomson (Selkirk YC) [*It, Sw*]; D J Archibald (Melrose) [*It*(R)]; S
Guyan
(Kirkcaldy) [*It*(R)]; C M Stevenson (Cambuslang) [*It*(R)]
Euan Murchison was captain in both matches

Under-19 (*Against Italy*)
Full-back: A C Redpath (Melrose)
Threequarters: D R W Adam (Edinburgh Acads), A J Douglas (Jedforest), A G Shiel
(Melrose), D Macrae (Morpeth)
Half-backs: S A Nichol (Selkirk), R A R Gray (Edinburgh U), C T Simmers
(Edinburgh U) (R)
Forwards: J A Couper (Glasgow High/Kelvinside), G L Peterson
(Glasgow High/Kelvinside), G T MacKee (Glasgow High/Kelvinside), S W Paul
(Heriot's FP), G W Weir (Melrose), S J Reid (Vale of Lune), D T H Jackson (Wasps),
W S Lancaster (Wakefield)
G L Peterson was captain

WALES
Full-backs: S McCracken (Blackwood) [*C*]; M Silva (Llandaff) [*It, F, E*]
Threequarters: C Jenkins (Neath Colts) [*C, It, F, E*]; J Thomas (Pontyberem) [*C, It*],
I Scott-Gibbs (Pencoed) [*C, It, F, E*]; A Donovan (Llanharan) [*C, It, F, E*]; L Bishop
(Cardiff) [*F*]; G Bowden (Newport HSOB) [*E*]
Half-backs: J Howells (Carmarthen Quins) [*C, It, F*]; S Cheshire (Crumlin) [*E*];
D Williams (Pontypool Utd) [*C, It, F, E*]; R Evans (Pontarddulain) [*E*(R)]
Forwards: M Thomas (Neath Colts) [*C, E*]; A Orrell (Cardiff) [*It, F*]; A Lamerton
(Beddau) [*C, It, F, E*]; D Lloyd (Nantymoel) [*E*(R)]; R Shaw (Neath Colts)
[*C, It, F, E*]; C Doughty (Lampeter) [*C, It, F, E*]; P Johnson (Morriston) [*C, It, E*];
J Perry (Aberaman) [*F*]; J Mayze (Llanelli) [*C, It, F*]; I McKim (Newport) [*C, It, F, E*];
D Edwards (Tonmawr) [*C, It, F, E*]; B Shenton (Neath Colts) [*E*]
Darren Williams was captain in all four matches

MATCH DETAILS 1988-89

8 October 1988, Rodney Parade, Newport

Wales Youth 33 (2G 3PG 3T)   **Canada Juniors 25** (3G 1PG 1T)

Wales *Tries:* McCracken, Jenkins, Donovan, Williams, Lamerton
Conversions: Howells (2)   *Penalty Goals:* Howells (2), Donovan
Canada *Tries:* Macdonald (2), Schmid (2)   *Conversions:* Ross (3)   *Penalty Goal:* Ross
Referee A Mason (England)

12 February 1989, Stadio Angelini, Chieti

Italy Youth 3 (1PG)   **Wales Youth 18** (1G 3T)
Italy *Penalty Goal:* Zanutto
Wales *Tries:* Silva, Edwards, Thomas, McKim   *Conversion:* Donovan
Referee C J High (England)

11 March, Aldersley Stadium, Wolverhampton

England Colts 38 (5G 2T)   **Italy Youth 3** (1PG)
England *Tries:* Wray (4), Matthews, Fields, Ojomoh   *Conversions:* Winterton (5)
Italy *Penalty Goal:* Zanutto
Referee R Yeman (Wales)

11 March, Aberavon RFC, Port Talbot

Wales Youth 9 (1G 1PG)   **French Juniors 17** (1G 1PG 2T)
Wales *Try:* Donovan   *Conversion:* Howells   *Penalty Goal:* Silva
France *Tries:* N'Tamak, Marfaing, Berty   *Conversion:* Campan   *Penalty Goal:* Mazas
Referee J A F Trigg (England)

1 April, Torquay

England Colts 15 (1G 3PG)   **Wales Youth 11** (1PG 2T)
England *Try:* Saverimutto   *Conversion:* Hopley   *Penalty Goals:* Winterton (3)
Wales *Tries:* Scott-Gibbs, Donovan   *Penalty Goal:* Silva
Referee D Reardon (USA)

8 April, Millbrae, Ayr

Scotland Under-18 21 (2G 2PG 1DG)   **Italy Under-18 12** (1G 2PG)
Scotland *Tries:* Craig, Thomson   *Conversions:* Shepherd (2)
Penalty Goals: Shepherd (2)   *Dropped Goal:* Shepherd
Italy *Try:* penalty try   *Conversion:* Dolfin   *Penalty Goals:* Dolfin (2)
Referee S W Piercy (England)

8 April, Millbrae, Ayr

Scotland Under-19 29 (3PG 5T)   **Italy Under-19 13** (1G 1PG 1T)
Scotland *Tries:* Macrae (2), Douglas, Shiel, Reid   *Penalty Goals:* Shiel (3)
Italy *Tries:* Dotto, Mazzi   *Conversion:* Dotto   *Penalty Goal:* Dotto
Referee D W Matthews (England)

15 April, Stade Aime Giral, Perpignan

French Juniors 20 (1G 1PG 1DG 2T)   **England Colts 8** (2T)
France *Tries:* Campan, Bellot, Labrousse   *Conversion:* Bellot
Penalty Goal: Bellot   *Dropped Goal:* Bellot
England *Tries:* Wray, Austin
Referee R Clark (Scotland)

22 April, Trelleborg

Sweden Under-18 6   **Scotland Under-18 85** (11G 1PG 4T)
Scotland *Tries:* Renwick (2), Shepherd (2), Stanger (2), Thomson (2), Fraser, Craig,
McKenzie, Redpath, Pringle, Brotherstone, Grahamslaw
Conversions: Shepherd (11)   *Penalty Goal:* Shepherd

FORTUNE FAVOURS BOLD SELECTORS

THE 1988-89 SEASON IN SCOTLAND

Bill McMurtrie *Glasgow Herald*

When Australia won their Murrayfield international by 32-13 the portents certainly did not favour a good season in Scotland. The national selectors, however, were bold. The choice of Finlay Calder as captain was inspired and a new, young half-back partnership, Gary Armstrong and Craig Chalmers, emerged. The Championship season was better than could have been expected in November, and Scotland finished joint runners-up.

Scotland not only won their two Murrayfield internationals, but did so with style and by sizeable margins. They opened with a 23-7 victory, their biggest home win against Wales, and after a 12-12 draw at Twickenham the Scots defeated Ireland 37-21 at Murrayfield. It was Scotland's biggest score against any International Board country, although the Irish contributed much to the enjoyment. To finish the season Scotland had to visit Paris, where they had not won since 1969, but the French were not to be prevented from gaining their fourth successive Championship and won 19-3, though the Scots merited more.

Armstrong made his international debut against Australia. Scotland had simply turned from one Jedforest scrum-half, Roy Laidlaw, to another, and Chalmers, the Melrose fly-half, followed against Wales. The former was 22 years old, and the latter 20. Yet they fitted in like new models of the Laidlaw-Rutherford partnership. Three other new caps came in with Chalmers: Sean Lineen, Boroughmuir's New Zealand centre, who qualified through his Scottish grandfather, Nottingham's Chris Gray and Kenneth Milne, the Heriot's hooker.

Calder's previous captaincy had been limited to one game for Edinburgh after which he asked the district selectors to release him from that duty in favour of someone with more knowledge of leadership. But in the international arena Calder showed little sign of his lack of experience.

Scotland had to make only two changes throughout the Championship, although one of those was enforced by the potentially disastrous loss of Iain Milne after he had played only one international in the same side as his brother, Kenneth. Paul Burnell, however, adequately filled the gap for the three remaining games, making his debut against England, and Keith Robertson returned in that same match in place of the injured Matt Duncan on the right wing. Like Peter Dods, Robertson enjoyed a new lease of life in his final season of international rugby.

Edinburgh, though under new management, retained the McEwan's

The Scottish team which began the Championship with a win over Wales at Murrayfield. L-R, back row: G H Oliver, A K Brewster, G R Marshall, D S Wyllie, K W Robertson, G J Callander (all replacements); middle row: D M B Sole, J Jeffrey, D F Cronin, D B White, I G Milne, S Hastings; front row: I Tukalo, C A Gray, G Armstrong, S R P Lineen, F Calder (capt), K S Milne, C M Chalmers, M D F Duncan, P W Dods.

District Championship, scoring their third successive Grand Slam. Ian Barnes, the former international lock, took over from Douglas Morgan as coach, while Iain Milne followed Alex Brewster as captain.

Scotland won their two B internationals, beating Italy by 26-3 in L'Aquila and France by 14-12 at Melrose. The latter result was the Scots' fifth victory in the previous six matches against France. Scotland's Under-21 team lost again to the Welsh, going down 18-26 in Neath, but the younger boys did better. The Under-19 team beat Italy 29-13 at Ayr, and the Under-18 boys defeated Italy 21-12 and Sweden 85-6.

Kelso retained the McEwan's National League trophy, albeit with the unenviable distinction of being the first club to win the title with three defeats. They were beaten by both of their closest rivals, Boroughmuir and Hawick, but held on to the championship because of their superior points difference.

It was an unsatisfactory conclusion to a league season with fewer highs than lows. Boroughmuir's 26-6 win at Hawick was the undoubted peak. The visitors' performance in that game was almost complete. It was the heaviest league defeat Hawick had suffered on their own Mansfield Park in the competition's 16 seasons. Kelso had to wait a month before they were confirmed as champions as another re-arranged match allowed Edinburgh Academicals an outside chance of the title. Academicals had to beat West of Scotland by the unlikely margin of 132 points to edge Kelso out on points difference! In the end West won by 15-14.

In such a season the form of Melrose, who slipped to tenth, was especially disappointing. Jedforest, Division Two champions in 1987-88, came through to sixth place, their best ever league position. Watsonians suffered heavily from the loss of key personnel, notably Gavin Hastings, though his brother Scott remained as captain. His personal example, however, was not enough and the club dropped to Division Two for the first time accompanied by Glasgow Academicals. Stirling became the first club to climb through all seven divisions of the national league and they did so by winning all their league matches.

Two clubs were lost from the competition: Hillhead and Jordanhill amalgamated two weeks before the start of the league and Crieff dropped out of Division Seven as they were unable to fulfil their championship fixtures. To rationalise the league only one club was relegated from each of the divisions from the third downwards.

Kelso won the Melrose trophy in the most prodigious of the Border seven-a-side tournaments. Jedforest won the Hawick and Langholm tournaments, and Selkirk also received a double, winning their trophy and the Jedforest cup. Melrose won at Kelso, while the Saltires, breaking the Border monopoly, retained the Gala trophy.

The New Zealand *Rugby News* youth team toured, as did the USSR Students, the first national team from their country to visit the British Isles. The New Zealanders won their Under-21 international against

Scotland by 25-21 and also beat the North and Midlands, Edinburgh and the Anglo-Scots but they fell to Glasgow and the South. The Soviets lost their opening match 12-13 against their Scottish counterparts, a reversal of the result in the students' inaugural World Cup in France in 1988. However, after a 15-17 defeat against the Co-optimists, a Select XV including seven caps, the tourists ended with a 19-13 victory against a British Isles Students Select at Murrayfield.

McEWAN'S CLUB CHAMPIONSHIP

Division 1	P	W	D	L	F	A	Pts
Kelso	13	10	0	3	357	111	20
Boroughmuir	13	9	2	2	314	145	20
Hawick	13	10	0	3	280	161	20
Edinburgh Acs	13	8	2	3	242	127	18
Heriot's FP	13	9	0	4	301	196	18
Jedforest	13	8	1	4	270	164	17
Selkirk	13	7	1	5	175	153	15
W of Scotland	13	5	1	7	164	263	11
Stewart's-Mel	13	5	1	7	168	278	11
Melrose	12	5	0	7	208	162	10
Ayr	13	4	1	8	202	271	9
Glasgow H/K	13	3	1	9	144	258	7
Glasgow Acs	12	2	0	10	112	225	4
Watsonians	13	0	0	13	97	520	0

Previous champions: Hawick 10 times, 1973-74 to 1977-78, 1981-82, 1983-84 to 1986-87; Gala 3 times, 1979-80, 1980-81, 1982-83; Heriot's FP 1978-79; Kelso 1987-88

Division 2	P	W	D	L	F	A	Pts
Stirling County	13	13	0	0	391	103	26
Gala	13	11	0	2	376	107	22
Currie	13	9	0	4	277	151	18
Kilmarnock	13	8	0	5	172	186	16
Edinburgh W	13	7	1	5	231	172	15
Preston Lodge	13	7	0	6	184	139	14
Musselburgh	13	5	2	6	175	234	12
Hillhead/Jord	13	5	1	7	152	237	11
Corstorphine	13	4	2	7	165	225	10
Dalziel HSFP	12	5	0	7	163	257	10
Langholm	12	3	3	6	132	238	9
Dunfermline	13	4	0	9	144	250	8
Portobello FP	13	3	1	9	136	247	7
Howe of Fife	13	1	0	12	144	296	2

Division 3	P	W	D	L	F	A	Pts
Kirkcaldy	12	12	0	0	263	77	24
Gordonians	11	8	1	2	188	115	17
Trinity Acs	12	8	0	4	233	138	16
Dundee HSFP	11	7	0	4	173	121	14
Biggar	12	5	2	5	116	144	12
Haddington	11	6	0	5	159	188	12
Royal High	11	5	0	6	153	140	10
East Kilbride	11	5	0	6	119	140	10
Highland	12	4	1	7	159	185	9
Morgan FP	12	4	0	8	136	186	8
Aberdeen GSFP	12	4	0	8	132	185	8
Clarkston	11	4	0	7	126	188	8
Greenock W	12	1	0	11	85	235	2

Division 4	P	W	D	L	F	A	Pts
Wigtownshire	13	11	1	1	253	71	23
Grangemouth	13	11	1	1	207	89	23
Peebles	13	11	1	1	192	77	23
Linlithgow	13	8	0	5	205	113	16
Leith Acs	13	6	2	5	180	135	14
Edinburgh U	13	7	0	6	173	198	14
Cambuslang	12	6	0	6	164	154	12
Perthshire	13	5	2	6	162	209	12
Hutchesons'	13	5	0	8	123	212	10
Dumfries	13	4	1	8	135	154	9
Cartha QP	13	4	1	8	97	126	9
St Boswells	13	3	0	10	97	168	6
Alloa	13	3	0	10	102	283	6
Lenzie	12	1	1	10	93	194	3

Division 5	P	W	D	L	F	A	Pts
Paisley	13	12	0	1	292	92	24
Penicuik	13	12	0	1	209	79	24
Madras FP	13	9	0	4	177	109	18
Ardrossan Acs	12	8	1	3	164	107	17
Hillfoots	13	7	1	5	150	188	15
Dunbar	13	6	0	7	185	137	12
Livingston	13	6	0	7	134	172	12
Murrayfield	13	5	1	7	146	166	11
Lismore	12	3	4	5	126	165	10
Glenrothes	13	4	1	8	142	147	9
Aberdeen U	13	3	2	8	136	176	8
Broughton FP	13	3	2	8	140	190	8
Moray	13	3	2	8	107	172	8
Marr	13	1	2	10	59	267	4

Division 6	P	W	D	L	F	A	Pts
Aberdeenshire	13	10	2	1	255	55	22
Waysiders	12	9	1	2	222	62	19
Carnoustie FP	13	8	0	5	223	81	16
St Andrews U	12	8	0	4	172	97	16
Harris FP	13	5	3	5	145	138	13
Montrose	13	5	2	6	150	146	12
Earlston	13	6	0	7	146	181	12
Panmure	13	5	2	6	125	229	12
Old Aloysians	13	5	1	7	93	229	11
Stewartry	13	4	2	7	133	152	10
Drumpellier	13	4	2	7	105	173	10
Walkerburn	13	5	0	8	108	199	10
North Berwick	13	4	1	8	164	164	9
Dalkeith	13	4	0	9	102	237	8

Division 7	P	W	D	L	F	A	Pts
Clydebank	11	11	0	0	205	63	22
Cumbernauld	12	9	1	2	209	84	19
Falkirk	12	9	0	3	202	107	18
Duns	12	7	0	5	160	120	14
Cumnock	11	7	0	4	172	149	14
Lasswade	11	6	0	5	159	82	12
Stobswell FP	12	6	0	6	91	148	12
Forrester FP	12	5	0	7	133	165	10
Garioch	12	5	0	7	125	184	10
Rosyth & Dist	12	4	1	7	119	149	9
Garnock	12	3	1	8	90	146	7
Birkmyre	11	1	1	9	78	182	3
Strathclyde P	12	0	2	10	78	242	2

District League Champions (*promoted to Division 7*):
East: Ross High
Midlands: Strathmore
West: Irvine

BORDER LEAGUE

	P	W	D	L	F	A	Pts
Hawick	12	10	0	2	252	124	20
Kelso	11	7	0	4	255	142	14
Melrose	12	7	0	5	210	162	14
Selkirk	12	7	0	5	176	183	14
Jedforest	12	5	0	7	178	160	10
Gala	11	5	0	6	156	184	10
Langholm	12	0	0	12	74	346	0

McEWAN'S DISTRICT CHAMPIONSHIP

	P	W	D	L	F	A	Pts
Edinburgh	4	4	0	0	115	45	8
South	4	3	0	1	93	58	6
Anglo-Scots	4	2	0	2	89	79	4
Glasgow	4	1	0	3	56	117	2
North & Midlands	4	0	0	4	27	81	0

Edinburgh won the sponsor's tankards for scoring most tries, 17, in the competition, the South had 15, the Anglo-Scots 12, Glasgow and the North and Midlands 4.

McEWAN'S DISTRICT CHAMPIONSHIP 1988-89

8 November, Imber Court, London
Anglo-Scots 22 (2G 2PG 1T)   **North and Midlands 6** (1G)

Anglo-Scots: A G Hastings (Cambridge U); C Henderson (Durham U), D W Caskie (London Scottish), D Cummin (Gloucester), W L Renwick (London Scottish); R I Cramb (Harlequins), S Jardine (South Glamorgan Inst); D J D Butcher (London Scottish), B W Gilchrist (Rosslyn Park), A P Burnell (London Scottish), C A Gray (Nottingham), D F Cronin (Bath), G A E Buchanan-Smith (London Scottish), R I Wainwright (Cambridge U), C B S Richardson (London Scottish) (*capt*)   *Replacement* R Howe (London Scottish) for Buchanan-Smith
Scorers *Tries:* Wainwright (2), Caskie   *Conversions:* Hastings (2)   *Penalty Goals:* Hastings (2)
North and Midlands: H A Murray (Heriot's FP); C J Macartney (Boroughmuir), B Edwards (Boroughmuir), J W Thomson (Kirkcaldy), M Cross (Dunfermline); C G MacGregor (Gordonians), D J Kennedy (Aberdeen GSFP); A D G Mackenzie (Highland), M W Scott (Dunfermline), J L Scobbie (Glagow Acads), B H Bell (Highland) (*capt*), I T Rankin (Howe of Fife), H J Edwards (Boroughmuir), D M McIvor (Edinburgh Acads), N Harris (Glasgow Acads)   *Replacement* D Love (Gordonians) for H J Edwards
Scorers *Try:* Murray   *Conversion:* MacGregor
Referee G M Anderson (London)

3 December, Chris Anderson Stadium, Aberdeen
North and Midlands 3 (1PG)   **South 30** (2G 2PG 3T)

North and Midlands: H A Murray (Heriot's FP); D Tully (Dundee HSFP), M Cross (Dunfermline), J W Thomson (Kirkcaldy), B Ireland (Stirling County); C G MacGregor (Gordonians), M J de G Allingham (Heriot's FP); A D G Mackenzie (Highland), M W Scott (Dunfermline), J L Scobbie (Glasgow Acads), B H Bell (Highland) (*capt*), I T Rankin (Howe of Fife), H J Edwards (Boroughmuir), D M McIvor (Edinburgh Acads), N Harris (Glasgow Acads)
Scorer *Penalty Goal:* MacGregor

South: P W Dods (Gala); A G Stanger (Hawick), A C Redpath (Melrose), G R T Baird (Kelso), D R Robeson (Kelso); A B M Ker (Kelso), G H Oliver (Hawick); N A McIlroy (Jedforest), G J Callander (Kelso), C R Guntley (Selkirk), A J Campbell (Hawick), R S Graham (Hawick), J Jeffrey (Kelso) (*capt*), G R Marshall (Selkirk), I A M Paxton (Selkirk)
Scorers *Tries:* Robeson (2), Stanger, Jeffrey, Paxton   *Conversions:* Dods (2)   *Penalty Goals:* Dods (2)
Referee R S Clark (Stewart's-Melville FP)

10 December, Riverside Park, Jedburgh
South 30 (2G 2PG 3T)   **Anglo-Scots 16** (2G 1T)

South: P W Dods (Gala); A G Stanger (Hawick), A C Redpath (Melrose), G R T Baird (Kelso), D R Robeson (Kelso); C M Chalmers (Melrose), G H Oliver (Hawick); N A McIlroy (Jedforest), J A Hay (Hawick), K S Sudlow (Melrose), A J Campbell (Hawick), R S Graham (Hawick), J Jeffrey (Kelso) (*capt*), G R Marshall (Selkirk), I A M Paxton (Selkirk)
Scorers *Tries:* Jeffrey (2), Robeson, Chalmers, Marshall   *Conversions:* Dods (2)   *Penalty Goals:* Dods (2)
Anglo-Scots: A G Hastings (Cambridge U); I C Glasgow (Cambridge U), D Cummin (Gloucester), W L Renwick (London Scottish) (*capt*), N Grecian (London Scottish); R I Cramb (Harlequins), S Jardine (South Glamorgan Inst); D F Milne (Heriot's FP), B W Gilchrist (Rosslyn Park), A P Burnell (London Scottish), C A Gray (Nottingham), D F Cronin (Bath), R I Wainwright (Cambridge U), C I M Dixon (Royal Marines), A C Murray (Waterloo)
Replacement C Campbell (Sale) for Hastings
Scorers *Tries:* Glasgow, Jardine, Wainwright   *Conversions:* Hastings , Glasgow
Referee J B Anderson (Currie)

10 December, Goldenacre, Edinburgh
Edinburgh 48 (4G 4PG 3T)   **Glasgow 12** (2G)

Edinburgh: S B Douglas (Boroughmuir); P D Steven (Heriot's FP), S Hastings (Watsonians), S R P Lineen (Boroughmuir), M R DeBusk (Boroughmuir); D S Wyllie (Stewart's-Melville FP), D M B Sole (Edinburgh Acads), K S Milne (Heriot's FP), I G Milne (Heriot's FP) (*capt*), J D Price (Boroughmuir), J F Richardson (Edinburgh Acads), J H Calder (Stewart's-Melville FP), F Calder (Stewart's-Melville FP), K P Rafferty (Heriot's FP)   *Replacement* R C Hurst (Currie) for Scott
Scorers *Tries:* Steven (2), Hastings (2), DeBusk, Scott, Hurst   *Conversions:* Steven (4)
Penalty Goals: Steven (2), Stott (2)
Glasgow: R A Gilmour (Ayr); M D F Duncan (West of Scotland), A C McGuffie (Ayr), S W McAslan (Glasgow Acads), D A Stark (Ayr); D N Barrett (West of Scotland), G T MacGregor (Glasgow Acads) (*capt*); G Graham (Stirling County), R Cairney (Glasgow Acads), G B Robertson (Stirling County), D S Munro (Glasgow High/Kelvinside), R T Pirrie (Glasgow Acads), W H Malcolm (Glasgow Acads), K Young (Kilmarnock), H M Parker (Wigtownshire)
Scorers *Tries:* Stark (2)   *Conversions:* Barrett (2)
Referee W W Calder (Selkirk)

17 December, Myreside, Edinburgh
Edinburgh 22 (3G 1T)   **Anglo-Scots 19** (1G 2PG 1DG 1T)

Edinburgh: S B Douglas (Boroughmuir); P D Steven (Heriot's FP), D S Wyllie (Stewart's-Melville FP), S R P Lineen (Boroughmuir), M R DeBusk (Boroughmuir); J F Paton (Edinburgh Acads), J M Scott (Stewart's-Melville FP); D M B Sole (Edinburgh Acads), K S Milne (Heriot's FP), I G Milne (Heriot's FP) (*capt*), J D Price (Boroughmuir), J F Richardson (Edinburgh Acads), G J Drummond (Boroughmuir), K P Rafferty (Heriot's FP), D E W Leckie (Edinburgh Acads)
Scorers *Tries:* Steven, DeBusk, Scott, Rafferty   *Conversions:* Steven (3)
Anglo-Scots: I C Glasgow (Cambridge U); N Grecian (London Scottish), D Cummin (Gloucester), R R W Maclean (Gloucester), W L Renwick (London Scottish) (*capt*); R I Cramb (Harlequins), S Jardine (South Glamorgan Inst); D F Milne (Heriot's FP), B W Gilchrist (Rosslyn Park), A P Burnell (London Scottish), C A Gray (Nottingham), D F Cronin (Bath), G A E Buchanan-Smith (London Scottish), R I Wainwright (Cambridge U), A C Murray (Waterloo)
Scorers *Tries:* Renwick, Jardine   *Conversion:* Glasgow   *Penalty Goals:* Glasgow (2)   *Dropped Goal:* Cramb
Referee K W McCartney (Hawick)

17 December, Bellsland, Kilmarnock
Glasgow 13 (3PG 1T)   **North and Midlands 11** (1PG 2T)

Glasgow: D N Barrett (West of Scotland); M D F Duncan (West of Scotland) (*capt*), S W McAslan (Glasgow Acads), A C McGuffie (Ayr), D A Stark (Ayr); E R J Stewart (Kilmarnock), E D McCorkindale (Glasgow High/Kelvinside); G Graham (Stirling County), K D McKenzie (Stirling County), G B Robertson (Stirling County), D S Munro (Glasgow High/Kelvinside), R T Pirrie (Glasgow Acads), F D Wallace (Glasgow High/Kelvinside), K Young (Kilmarnock), H M Parker (Wigtownshire)   *Replacement* S A Baird (Glasgow Acads) for Wallace
Scorers *Try:* Stark   *Penalty Goals:* Barrett (3)
North and Midlands: H A Murray (Heriot's FP); B Ireland (Stirling County), B Edwards (Boroughmuir), J W Thomson (Kirkcaldy), M Cross (Dunfermline); C G MacGregory (Gordonians), M J de G Allingham (Heriot's FP); A D G Mackenzie (Highland), M W Scott (Dunfermline), J L Scobbie (Glasgow Acads), B H Bell (Highland) (*capt*), I T Rankin (Howe of Fife), J Bryce (Heriot's FP), D M McIvor (Edinburgh Acads), H J Edwards (Boroughmuir)
Scorers *Tries:* Ireland, Cross   *Penalty Goal:* Thomson
Referee J M Fleming (Boroughmuir)

24 December, Duffus Park, Cupar
North and Midlands 7 (1DG 1T)   **Edinburgh 16** (4PG 1T)

North and Midlands: G Spowart (Dundee HSFP); B Ireland (Stirling County), B Edwards (Boroughmuir), J W Thomson (Kirkcaldy), M Cross (Dunfermline); C G MacGregor (Gordonians), M J de G Allingham (Heriot's FP); A D G Mackenzie (Highland), M W Scott (Dunfermline), J L Scobbie (Glasgow Acads), B H Bell (Highland) (*capt*),

I T Rankin (Howe of Fife), J Bryce (Heriot's FP), D M McIvor (Edinburgh Acads), H J Edwards (Boroughmuir)
Scorer *Try:* MacGregor   *Dropped Goal:* MacGregor
Edinburgh: S B Douglas (Boroughmuir); P D Steven (Heriot's FP), S Hastings (Watsonians), S R P Lineen (Boroughmuir), M R DeBusk (Boroughmuir); D S Wyllie (Stewart's-Melville FP), M S Robertson (Boroughmuir); D M B Sole (Edinburgh Acads), C B Brown (Boroughmuir), I G Milne (Heriot's FP) (*capt*), J D Price (Boroughmuir) J F Richardson (Edinburgh Acads), J H Calder (Stewart's-Melville FP), F Calder (Stewart's-Melville FP), K P Rafferty (Heriot's FP)
Scorers *Try:* Rafferty   *Penalty Goals:* Steven (4)
Referee J Johnston (Dalziel HSFP)

24 December, Old Anniesland, Glasgow
Glasgow 10 (2PG 1T)   **South 26** (2G 2PG 2T)

Glasgow: D N Barrett (West of Scotland); R A Gilmour (Ayr), A C McGuffie (Ayr), S W McAslan (Glasgow Acads) (*capt*), D A Stark (Ayr); E R J Stewart (Kilmarnock), E D McCorkindale (Glasgow High/Kelvinside); G Graham (Stirling County), K D McKenzie (Stirling County), G B Robertson (Stirling County), D S Munro (Glasgow High/Kelvinside), R T Pirrie (Glasgow Acads), F D Wallace (Glasgow High/Kelvinside), K Young (Kilmarnock), D Millar (West of Scotland)   *Replacement* R Cairney (Glasgow Acads) for Young
Scorers *Try:* Gilmour   *Penalty Goals:* Barrett (2)
South: P W Dods (Gala); A G Stanger (Hawick), M Wright (Kelso), G R T Baird (Kelso), D R Robeson (Kelso); C M Chalmers (Melrose), G Armstrong (Jedforest); N A McIlroy (Jedforest), J A Hay (Hawick), G M McGuinness (Hawick), A J Campbell (Hawick), R S Graham (Hawick), C Millar (Kelso), G R Marshall (Selkirk), J Jeffrey (Kelso) (*capt*)
Scorers *Tries:* Robeson (2), Dods, Stanger   *Conversions:* Dods (2)   *Penalty Goals:* Dods (2)
Referee R J Megson (Edinburgh Wanderers)

31 December, Murrayfield
Anglo-Scots 32 (1G 6PG 2T)   **Glasgow 21** (7PG)

Anglo-Scots: I C Glasgow (Cambridge U); T J Exeter (Moseley), D Cummin (Gloucester), R R W Maclean (Gloucester), W L Renwick (London Scottish) (*capt*); R I Cramb (Harlequins), S Jardine (South Glamorgan Inst); D F Milne (Heriot's FP), B W Gilchrist (Rosslyn Park), D J D Butcher (London Scottish), C A Gray (Nottingham), D F Cronin (Bath), G A E Buchanan-Smith (London Scottish), R I Wainwright (Cambridge U), A C Murray (Waterloo)   *Replacements* R Howe (London Scottish) for Murray; C Campbell (Sale) for Renwick
Scorers *Tries:* Glasgow, Exeter, Cummin   *Conversion:* Glasgow   *Penalty Goals:* Glasgow (6)
Glasgow: D N Barrett (West of Scotland); R A Gilmour (Ayr), A C McGuffie (Ayr), I C Jardine (Stirling County), D A Stark (Ayr); E R J Stewart (Kilmarnock), E D McCorkindale (Glasgow High/Kelvinside); S A Baird (Glasgow Acads), K D McKenzie (Stirling County), G B Robertson (Stirling County), D S Munro (Glasgow High/Kelvinside), R T Pirrie (Glasgow Acads), F D Wallace (Glasgow High/Kelvinside) (*capt*), G T Mackay (Glasgow Acads), D Millar (West of Scotland)
Scorer *Penalty Goals:* Barrett (7)
Referee A P Thomson (Lancashire)

31 December, Netherdale, Galashiels
South 7 (1PG 1T)   **Edinburgh 29** (3G 1PG 2T)

South: P W Dods (Gala); A G Stanger (Hawick), M Wright (Kelso) G R T Baird (Kelso), D R Robeson (Kelso); C M Chalmers (Melrose), G Armstrong (Jedforest); G M McGuinness (Hawick), J A Hay (Hawick), K S Sudlow (Melrose), A J Campbell (Hawick), I A M Paxton (Selkirk), R E Paxton (Kelso), G R Marshall (Selkirk), J Jeffrey (Kelso) (*capt*)
Edinburgh: S B Douglas (Boroughmuir); P D Steven (Heriot's FP), S Hastings (Watsonians), S R P Lineen (Boroughmuir), M R DeBusk (Boroughmuir); D S Wyllie (Stewart's-Melville FP), J M Scott (Stewart's-Melville FP); D M B Sole (Edinburgh Acads), K S Milne (Heriot's FP), I G Milne (Heriot's FP) (*capt*), J D Price (Boroughmuir), J F Richardson (Edinburgh Acads), J H Calder (Stewart's-Melville FP), F Calder (Stewart's-Melville FP), K P Rafferty (Heriot's FP)
Scorers *Tries:* penalty tries (2), Steven, DeBusk, Scott   *Conversions:* Steven (3)   *Penalty Goal:* Steven
Referee F A Howard (Lancashire)

SCOTTISH INTERNATIONAL PLAYERS
(up to 30 April 1989)

ABBREVIATIONS

A – Australia; *E* – England; *F* – France; *I* – Ireland; *NSW* – New South Wales; *NZ* – New Zealand; *R* – Romania; *SA* – South Africa; *W* – Wales; *Z* – Zimbabwe; (C) – Centenary match v England at Murrayfield, 1971 (non-championship); P – Scotland v President's Overseas XV at Murrayfield in SRU's Centenary season, 1972-73; (R) Replacement. Entries in square brackets [ ] indicate appearances in the World Cup.

Note: Years given for Five Nations' matches are for second half of season; eg 1972 means season 1971-72. Years for all other matches refer to the actual year of the match. When a series has taken place, figures have been used to denote the particular matches in which players have featured. Thus 1981 *NZ* 1, 2 indicates that a player appeared in the first and second Tests of the series. The abandoned game with Ireland at Belfast in 1885 is now included as a cap-match.

Abercrombie, C H (United Services) 1910 *I*, *E*, 1911 *F*, *W*, 1913 *I*, *W*
Abercrombie, J G (Edinburgh U) 1949 *F*, *W*, *I*, 1950 *F*, *W*, *I*, *E*
Agnew, W C C (Stewart's Coll FP) 1930 *W*, *I*
Ainslie, R (Edinburgh Inst FP) 1879 *I*, *E*, 1880 *I*, *E*, 1881 *E*, 1882 *I*, *E*
Ainslie, T (Edinburgh Inst FP) 1881 *E*, 1882 *I*, *E*, 1883 *W*, *I*, *E*, 1884 *W*, *I*, *E*, 1885 *W*, *I*, *E*
Aitchison, G R (Edinburgh Wands) 1883 *I*
Aitchison, T G (Gala) 1929 *W*, *I*, *E*
Aitken, A I (Edinburgh Inst FP) 1889 *I*
Aitken, G G (Oxford U) 1924 *W*, *I*, *E*, 1925 *F*, *W*, *I*, *E*, 1929 *F*
Aitken, J (Gala) 1977 *E*, *I*, *F*, 1981 *F*, *W*, *E*, *I*, *NZ* 1,2, *R*, *A*, 1982 *E*, *I*, *F*, *W*, 1983 *F*, *W*, *E*, *NZ*, 1984 *W*, *E*, *I*, *F*, *R*
Aitken, R (London Scottish) 1947 *W*
Allan, B (Glasgow Acads) 1881 *I*
Allan, J L (Melrose) 1952 *F*, *W*, *I*, 1953 *W*
Allan, J L F (Cambridge U) 1957 *I*, *E*
Allan, J W (Melrose) 1927 *F*, 1928 *I*, 1929 *F*, *W*, *I*, *E*, 1930 *F*, *E*, 1931 *F*, *W*, *I*, *E*, 1932 *SA*, *W*, *I*, 1934 *I*, *E*
Allan, R C (Hutchesons' GSFP) 1969 *I*
Allardice, W D (Aberdeen GSFP) 1948 *A*, *F*, *W*, *I*, 1949 *F*, *W*, *I*, *E*
Allen, H W (Glasgow Acads) 1873 *E*
Anderson, A H (Glasgow Acads) 1894 *I*
Anderson, D G (London Scottish) 1889 *I*, 1890 *W*, *I*, *E*, 1891 *W*, *I*, 1892 *W*, *E*
Anderson, E (Stewart's Coll FP) 1947 *I*, *E*
Anderson, J W (W of Scotland) 1872 *E*
Anderson, T (Merchiston) 1882 *I*
Angus, A W (Watsonians) 1909 *W*, 1910 *F*, *W*, *E*, 1911 *W*, *I*, 1912 *F*, *W*, *I*, *E*, *SA*, 1913 *F*, *W*, 1914 *E*, 1920 *F*, *W*, *I*, *E*
Anton, P A (St Andrew's U) 1873 *E*
Armstrong, G (Jedforest) 1988 *A*, 1989 *W*, *E*, *I*, *F*
Arneil, R J (Edinburgh Acads, Leicester and Northampton) 1968 *I*, *E*, *A*, 1969 *F*, *W*, *I*, *E*, *SA*, 1970 *F*, *W*, *I*, *E*, *A*, 1971 *F*, *W*, *I*, *E* (2[1C]), 1972 *F*, *W*, *E*, 1973 *NZ*
Arthur, A (Glasgow Acads) 1875 *E*, 1876 *E*
Arthur, J W (Glasgow Acads) 1871 *E*, 1872 *E*
Asher, A G G (Oxford U) 1882 *I*, 1884 *W*, *I*, *E*, 1885 *W*, 1886 *I*, *E*
Auld, W (W of Scotland) 1889 *W*, 1890 *W*
Auldjo, L J (Abertay) 1878 *E*

Bain, D McL (Oxford U) 1911 *E*, 1912 *F*, *W*, *E*, *SA*, 1913 *F*, *W*, *I*, *E*, 1914 *W*, *I*
Baird, G R T (Kelso) 1981 *A*, 1982 *E*, *I*, *F*, *W*, *A* 1,2, 1983 *I*, *F*, *W*, *E*, *NZ*, 1984 *W*, *E*, *I*, *F*, *A*, 1985 *I*, *W*, *E*, 1986 *W*, *E*, *I*, *R*, 1987 *E*, 1988 *I*
Balfour, A (Watsonians) 1896 *W*, *I*, *E*, 1897 *E*
Balfour, L M (Edinburgh Acads) 1872 *E*
Bannerman, E M (Edinburgh Acads) 1872 *E*, 1873 *E*
Bannerman, J M (Glasgow HSFP) 1921 *F*, *W*, *I*, *E*, 1922 *F*, *W*, *I*, *E*, 1923 *F*, *W*, *I*, *E*, 1924 *F*, *W*, *I*, *E*, 1925 *F*, *W*, *I*, *E*, 1926 *F*, *W*, *I*, *E*, 1927 *F*, *W*, *I*, *E*, *NSW*, 1928 *F*, *W*, *I*, *E*, 1929 *F*, *W*, *I*, *E*
Barnes, I A (Hawick) 1972 *W*, 1974 *F* (R), 1975 *E* (R), *NZ*, 1977 *I*, *F*, *W*

Barrie, R W (Hawick) 1936 *E*
Bearne, K R F (Cambridge U, London Scottish) 1960 *F*, *W*
Beattie, J A (Hawick) 1929 *F*, *W*, 1930 *W*, 1931 *F*, *W*, *I*, *E*, 1932 *SA*, *W*, *I*, *E*, 1933 *W*, *E*, *I*, 1934 *I*, *E*, 1935 *W*, *I*, *E*, *NZ*, 1936 *W*, *I*, *E*
Beattie, J R (Glasgow Acads) 1980 *I*, *F*, *W*, *E*, 1981 *F*, *W*, *E*, *I*, 1983 *F*, *W*, *E*, *NZ*, 1984 *E* (R), *R*, *A*, 1985 *I*, 1986 *F*, *W*, *E*, *I*, *R*, 1987 *F*, *W*, *E*
Bedell-Sivright, D R (Cambridge U, Edinburgh U) 1900 *W*, 1901 *W*, *I*, *E*, 1902 *W*, *I*, *E*, 1903 *W*, *I*, 1904 *W*, *I*, *E*, 1905 *NZ*, 1906 *W*, *I*, *E*, *SA*, 1907 *W*, *I*, *E*, 1908 *W*, *I*
Bedell-Sivright, J V (Cambridge U) 1902 *W*
Begbie, T A (Edinburgh Wands) 1881 *I*, *E*
Bell, D L (Watsonians) 1975 *I*, *F*, *W*, *E*
Bell, J A (Clydesdale) 1901 *W*, *I*, *E*, 1902 *W*, *I*, *E*
Bell, L H I (Edinburgh Acads) 1900 *E*, 1904 *W*, *I*
Berkeley, W V (Oxford U) 1926 *F*, 1929 *F*, *W*, *I*
Berry, C W (Fettesian-Lorettonians) 1884 *I*, *E*, 1885 *I*, *I* 1, 1887 *I*, *W*, *E*, 1888 *W*, *I*
Bertram, D M (Watsonians) 1922 *F*, *W*, *I*, *E*, 1923 *F*, *W*, *I*, *E*, 1924 *W*, *I*, *E*
Biggar, A G (London Scottish) 1969 *SA*, 1970 *F*, *I*, *E*, *A*, 1971 *F*, *W*, *I*, *E* (2[1C]), 1972 *F*, *W*
Biggar, M A (London Scottish) 1975 *I*, *F*, *W*, *E*, 1976 *W*, *E*, *I*, 1977 *I*, *F*, *W*, 1978 *I*, *F*, *W*, *E*, *NZ*, 1979 *W*, *E*, *I*, *F*, *NZ*, 1980 *I*, *F*, *W*, *E*
Birkett, G A (Harlequins, London Scottish) 1975 *NZ*
Bishop, J M (Glasgow Acads) 1893 *I*
Bisset, A A (RIE Coll) 1904 *W*
Black, A W (Edinburgh U) 1947 *F*, *W*, 1948 *E*, 1950 *W*, *I*, *E*
Black, W P (Glasgow HSFP) 1948 *F*, *W*, *I*, *E*, 1951 *E*
Blackadder, W F (W of Scotland) 1938 *E*
Blaikie, C F (Heriot's FP) 1963 *I*, *E*, 1966 *E*, 1968 *A*, 1969 *F*, *W*, *I*, *E*
Blair, P C B (Cambridge U) 1912 *SA*, 1913 *F*, *W*, *I*, *E*
Bolton, W H (W of Scotland) 1876 *E*
Borthwick, J B (Stewart's Coll FP) 1938 *W*, *I*
Bos, F H ten (Oxford U, London Scottish) 1959 *E*, 1960 *F*, *W*, *SA*, 1961 *F*, *SA*, *W*, *I*, *E*, 1962 *F*, *W*, *I*, *E*, 1963 *F*, *W*, *I*, *E*
Boswell, J D (W of Scotland) 1889 *W*, *I*, 1890 *W*, *I*, *E*, 1891 *W*, *I*, *E*, 1892 *W*, *I*, *E*, 1893 *I*, *E*, 1894 *I*, *E*
Bowie, T C (Watsonians) 1913 *I*, *E*, 1914 *I*, *E*
Boyd, G M (Glasgow HSFP) 1926 *E*
Boyd, J L (United Services) 1912 *E*, *SA*
Boyle, A C W (London Scottish) 1963 *F*, *W*, *I*
Boyle, A H W (St Thomas's Hospital, London Scottish) 1966 *A*, 1967 *F*, *NZ*, 1968 *F*, *W*, *I*
Brash, J C (Cambridge U) 1961 *E*
Breakey, R W (Gosforth) 1978 *E*
Brewis, N T (Edinburgh Inst FP) 1876 *E*, 1878 *E*, 1879 *I*, *E*, 1880 *I*, *E*
Brewster, A K (Stewart's-Melville FP) 1977 *E*, 1980 *I*, *F*, 1986 *E*, *I*, *F*
Brown, A H (Heriot's FP) 1928 *E*, 1929 *F*, *W*
Brown, A R (Gala) 1971 *E* (2[1C]), 1972 *F*, *W*, *E*
Brown, C H C (Dunfermline) 1929 *E*
Brown, D I (Cambridge U) 1933 *W*, *E*, *I*
Brown, G L (W of Scotland) 1969 *SA*, 1970 *F*, *W* (R),

I, E, A, 1971 *F, W, I, E* (2[1C]), 1972 *F, W, E, NZ*, 1973 *E* (R), *P*, 1974 *W, E, I, F*, 1975 *I, F, W, E, A*, 1976 *F, W, E, I*

Brown, J A (Glasgow Acads) 1908 *W, I*

Brown, J B (Glasgow Acads) 1879 *I, E*, 1880 *I, E*, 1881 *I, E*, 1882 *I, E*, 1883 *W, I, E*, 1884 *W, I, E*, 1885 *I*1,2, 1886 *W, I, E*

Brown, P C (W of Scotland, Gala) 1964 *F, NZ, W, I, E*, 1965 *I, E, SA*, 1966 *A*, 1969 *I, E*, 1970 *W, E*, 1971 *F, W, I, E* (2[1C]), 1972 *F, W, E, NZ*, 1973 *F, W, I, E, P*

Brown, T G (Heriot's FP) 1929 *W*

Brown, W D (Glasgow Acads) 1871 *E*, 1872 *E*, 1873 *E*, 1874 *E*, 1875 *E*

Brown, W S (Edinburgh Inst FP) 1880, *I, E*, 1882 *I, E*, 1883 *W,E*

Browning, A (Glasgow HSFP) 1920 *I*, 1922 *F, W, I*, 1923 *W, I, E*

Bruce, C R (Glasgow Acads) 1947 *F, W, I, E*, 1949 *F, W, I, E*

Bruce, N S (Blackheath, Army and London Scottish) 1958 *F, A, I, E*, 1959 *F, W, I, E*, 1960 *F, W, I, E, SA*, 1961 *F, SA, W, I, E*, 1962 *F, W, I, E*, 1963 *F, W, I, E*, 1964 *F, NZ, W, I, E*

Bruce, R M (Gordonians) 1947 *A*, 1948 *F, W, I*

Bruce-Lockhart, J H (London Scottish) 1913 *W*, 1920 *E*

Bruce-Lockhart, L (London Scottish) 1948 *E*, 1950 *F, W*, 1953 *I, E*

Bruce-Lockhart, R B (Cambridge U and London Scottish) 1937 *I*, 1939 *I, E*

Bryce, C C (Glasgow Acads) 1873 *E*, 1874 *E*

Bryce, R D H (W of Scotland) 1973 *I* (R)

Bryce, W E (Selkirk) 1922 *W, I, E*, 1923 *F, W, I, E*, 1924 *F, W, I, E*

Brydon, W R C (Heriot's FP) 1939 *W*

Buchanan, A (Royal HSFP) 1871 *E*

Buchanan, F G (Kelvinside Acads and Oxford U) 1910 *E*, 1911 *F, W*

Buchanan, J C R (Stewart's Coll FP) 1921 *W, I, E*, 1922 *W, I, E*, 1923 *F, W, I, E*, 1924 *F, W, I, E*, 1925 *F, I*

Bucher, A M (Edinburgh Acads) 1897 *E*

Budge, G M (Edinburgh Wands) 1950 *F, W, I, E*

Bullmore, H H (Edinburgh U) 1902 *I*

Burnell, A P (London Scottish) 1989 *E, I, F*

Burnet, P J (London Scottish and Edinburgh Acads) 1960 *SA*

Burnet, W (Hawick) 1912 *E*

Burnet, W A (W of Scotland) 1934 *W*, 1935 *W, I, E*, *NZ*, 1936 *W, I, E*

Burnett, J N (Heriot's FP) 1980 *I, F, W, E*

Burrell, G (Gala) 1950 *F, W, I*, 1951 *SA*

Cairns, A G (Watsonians) 1903 *W, I, E*, 1904 *W, I, E*, 1905 *W, I, E*, 1906 *W, I, E*

Calder, F (Stewart's-Melville FP) 1986, *F, W, E, I, R*, 1987 *I, F, W, E*, [*F, Z, R, NZ*], 1988 *I, F, W, E*, 1989 *W, E, I, F*

Calder, J H (Stewart's-Melville FP) 1981 *F, W, E, I*, *NZ* 1,2, *R, A*, 1982 *E, I, F, W, A* 1,2, 1983 *I, F, W, E*, *NZ*, 1984 *W, E, I, F, A*, 1985 *I, F, W*

Callander, G J (Kelso) 1984 *R*, 1988 *I, F, W, E, A*

Cameron, A (Glasgow HSFP) 1948 *W*, 1950 *I, E*, 1951 *F, W, I, E, SA*, 1953 *I, E*, 1955 *F, W, I, E*, 1956 *F, W, I*

Cameron, A D (Hillhead HSFP) 1951 *F*, 1954 *F, W*

Cameron, A W (Watsonians) 1887 *W*, 1893 *W*, 1894 *I*

Cameron, D (Glasgow HSFP) 1953 *I, E*, 1954 *F, NZ*, *I, E*

Cameron, N W (Glasgow U) 1952 *E*, 1953 *F, W*

Campbell, A J (Hawick) 1984 *I, F, R*, 1985 *I, F, W, E*, 1986 *F, W, E, I, R*, 1988 *F, W, A*

Campbell, G T (London Scottish) 1892 *W, I, E*, 1893 *I, E*, 1894 *W, I, E*, 1895 *W, I, E*, 1896 *W, I, E*, 1897 *I*, 1899 *I*, 1900 *E*

Campbell, H H (Cambridge U, London Scottish) 1947 *I, E*, 1948 *I, E*

Campbell, J A (W of Scotland) 1878 *E*, 1879 *I, E*, 1881 *I, E*

Campbell, J A (Cambridge U) 1900 *I*

Campbell, N M (London Scottish) 1956 *F, W*

Campbell-Lamerton, J R E (London Scottish) 1986 *F*, 1987 [*Z, R*(R)]

Campbell-Lamerton, M J (Halifax, Army, London

Scottish) 1961 *F, SA, W, I*, 1962 *F, W, I, E*, 1963 *F, W, I, E*, 1964 *I, E*, 1965 *F, W, I, E, SA*, 1966 *F, W, I, E*

Carmichael, A B (W of Scotland) 1967 *I, NZ*, 1968 *F, W, I, E, A*, 1969 *F, W, I, E, SA*, 1970 *F, W, I, E, A*, 1971 *F, W, I, E* (2[1C]), 1972 *F, W, E, NZ*, 1973 *F, W, I, E, P*, 1974 *W, I, F*, 1975 *I, F, W, E, NZ, A*, 1976 *F, W, E, I*, 1977 *E, I, F* (R), *F, W*, 1978 *I*

Carmichael, J H (Watsonians) 1921 *F, W, I*

Carrick, J S (Glasgow Acads) 1876 *E*, 1877 *E*

Cassels, D Y (W of Scotland) 1880 *E*, 1881 *I*, 1882 *I*, *E*, 1883 *W, I, E*

Cathcart, C W (Edinburgh U) 1872 *E*, 1873 *E*, 1876 *E*

Cawkwell, G L (Oxford U) 1947 *F*

Chalmers, C M (Melrose) 1989 *W, E, I, F*

Chalmers, T (Glasgow Acads) 1871 *E*, 1872 *E*, 1873 *E*, 1874 *E*, 1875 *E*, 1876 *E*

Chambers, H F T (Edinburgh U) 1888 *W, I*, 1889 *W, I*

Charters, R G (Hawick) 1955 *W, I, E*

Chisholm, D H (Melrose) 1964 *I, E*, 1965 *E, SA*, 1966 *F, I, E, A*, 1967 *F, W, NZ*, 1968 *F, W, I*

Chisholm, R W T (Melrose) 1955 *I, E*, 1956 *F, W, I*, *E*, 1958 *F, W, A, I*, 1960 *SA*

Church, W C (Glasgow Acads) 1906 *W*

Clark, R L (Edinburgh Wands, Royal Navy) 1972 *F, W, E, NZ*, 1973 *F, W, I, E, P*

Clauss, P R A (Oxford U) 1891 *W, I, E*, 1892 *W, E*, 1895 *I*

Clay, A T (Edinburgh Acads) 1886 *W, I, E*, 1887 *I, W*, *E*, 1888 *W*

Clunies-Ross, A (St Andrews U) 1871 *E*

Coltman, S (Hawick) 1948 *I*, 1949 *F, W, I, E*

Colville, A G (Merchistonians, Blackheath) 1871 *E*, 1872 *E*

Connell, G C (Trinity Acads and London Scottish) 1968 *E, A*, 1969 *F, E*, 1970 *F*

Cooper, M McG (Oxford U) 1936 *W, I*

Cordial, I F (Edinburgh Wands) 1952 *F, W, I, E*

Cotter, J L (Hillhead HSFP) 1934 *I, E*

Cottington, G S (Kelso) 1934 *I, E*, 1935 *W, I*, 1936 *E*, 1937 *I, E*, 1963 *F, W, I, E*

Coughtrie, S (Edinburgh Acads) 1959 *F, W, I, E*, 1962 *W, I, E*, 1963 *F, W, I, E*

Couper, J H (W of Scotland) 1896 *W, I*, 1899 *I*

Coutts, F H (Melrose, Army) 1947 *W, I, E*

Coutts, I D F (Old Alleynians) 1951 *F*, 1952 *E*

Cowan, R C (Selkirk) 1961 *F*, 1962 *F, W, I, E*

Cowie, W L K (Edinburgh Wands) 1953 *E*

Cownie, W B (Watsonians) 1893 *W, I, E*, 1894 *W, I, E*, 1895 *W, I, E*

Crabbie, G E (Edinburgh Acads) 1904 *W*

Crabbie, J E (Edinburgh Acads, Oxford U) 1900 *W*, 1902 *I*, 1903 *W, I*, 1904 *E*, 1905 *W*

Craig, J B (Heriot's FP) 1939 *W*

Cramb, R I (Harlequins) 1987 [*R*(R)], 1988 *I, F, A*

Cranston, A G (Hawick) 1976 *W, E, I*, 1977 *E, W*, 1978 *F* (R), *W, E, NZ*, 1981 *NZ* 1,2

Crawford, J A (Army, London Scottish) 1934 *I*

Crawford, W H (United Services, RN) 1938 *W, I, E*, 1939 *W, E*

Crichton-Miller, D (Gloucester) 1931 *W, I, E*

Crole, G B (Oxford U) 1920 *F, W, I, E*

Cronin, D F (Bath) 1988 *I, F, W, E, A*, 1989 *W, E, I, F*

Cross, M (Merchistonians) 1875 *E*, 1876 *E*, 1877 *I, E*, 1878 *E*, 1879 *I, E*, 1880 *I, E*

Cross, W (Merchistonians) 1871 *E*, 1872 *E*

Cumming, R S (Aberdeen U) 1921 *F, W*

Cunningham, G (Oxford U) 1908 *W, I*, 1909 *W, E*, 1910 *F, I, E*, 1911 *E*

Cunningham, R F (Gala) 1978 *NZ*, 1979 *W, E*

Currie, L R (Dunfermline) 1947 *A*, 1948 *F, W, I*, 1949 *F, W, I, E*

Cuthbertson, W (Kilmarnock, Harlequins) 1980 *I*, 1981 *W, E, I, NZ* 1,2, *R, A*, 1982 *E, I, F, W, A* 1,2, 1983 *I, F, W, NZ*, 1984 *W, E, A*

Dalgleish, A (Gala) 1890 *W, E*, 1891 *W, I*, 1892 *W*, 1893 *W*, 1894 *W, I*

Dalgleish, K J (Edinburgh Wands, Cambridge U) 1951 *I, E*, 1953 *F, W*

Dallas, J D (Watsonians) 1903 *E*

Davidson, J A (London Scottish, Edinburgh Wands) 1959 *E*, 1960 *I, E*

Davidson, J N G (Edinburgh U) 1952 *F, W, I, E*, 1953 *F, W*, 1954 *F*

Davidson, J P (RIE Coll) 1873 *E*, 1874 *E*
Davidson, R S (Royal HSFP) 1893 *E*
Davies, D S (Hawick) 1922 *F*, *W*, *I*, *E*, 1923 *F*, *W*, *I*, *E*, 1924 *F*, *E*, 1925 *W*, *I*, *E*, 1926 *F*, *W*, *I*, *E*, 1927 *F*, *W*, *I*
Dawson, J C (Glasgow Acads) 1947 *A*, 1948 *F*, *W*, 1949 *F*, *W*, *I*, 1950 *F*, *W*, *I*, *E*, 1951 *F*, *W*, *I*, *E*, *SA*, 1952 *F*, *W*, *I*, *E*, 1953 *E*
Deans, C T (Hawick) 1978 *F*, *W*, *E*, *NZ*, 1979 *W*, *E*, *I*, *F*, *NZ*, 1980 *I*, *F*, 1981 *F*, *W*, *E*, *I*, *NZ* 1,2, *R*, *A*, 1982 *E*, *I*, *F*, *W*, *A* 1,2, 1983 *I*, *F*, *W*, *E*, *NZ*, 1984 *W*, *E*, *I*, *F*, *A*, 1985 *I*, *F*, *W*, *E*, 1986 *F*, *W*, *E*, *I*, *R*, 1987 *I*, *F*, *W*, *E*, [*F*, *Z*, *R*, *NZ*]
Deans, D T (Hawick) 1968 *E*
Deas, D W (Heriot's FP) 1947 *F*, *W*
Dick, L G (Loughborough Colls, Jordanhill, Swansea) 1972 *W* (R), *E*, 1974 *W*, *E*, *I*, *F*, 1975 *I*, *F*, *W*, *E*, *NZ*, *A*, 1976 *F*, 1977 *E*
Dick, R C S (Cambridge U, Guy's Hospital) 1934 *W*, *I*, *E*, 1935 *W*, *I*, *E*, *NZ*, 1936 *W*, *I*, *E*, 1937 *W*, 1938 *W*, *I*, *E*
Dickson, G (Gala) 1978 *NZ*, 1979 *W*, *E*, *I*, *F*, *NZ*, 1980 *W*, 1981 *F*, 1982 *W* (R)
Dickson, M R (Edinburgh U) 1905 *I*
Dickson, W M (Blackheath, Oxford U) 1912 *F*, *W*, *E*, *SA*, 1913 *F*, *W*, *I*
Dobson, J (Glasgow Acads) 1911 *E*, 1912 *F*, *W*, *I*, *E*, *SA*
Dobson, J D (Glasgow Acads) 1910 *I*
Dobson, W G (Heriot's FP) 1922 *W*, *I*, *E*
Docherty, J T (Glasgow HSFP) 1955 *F*, *W*, 1956 *E*, 1958 *F*, *W*, *A*, *I*, *E*
Dods, F P (Edinburgh Acads) 1901 *I*
Dods, J H (Edinburgh Acads) 1895 *W*, *I*, *E*, 1896 *W*, *I*, *E*, 1897 *I*, *E*
Dods, P W (Gala) 1983 *I*, *F*, *W*, *E*, *NZ*, 1984 *W*, *E*, *I*, *F*, *R*, *A*, 1985 *I*, *F*, *W*, *E*, 1989 *W*, *E*, *I*, *F*
Donald, D G (Oxford U) 1914 *W*, *I*
Donald, R L H (Glasgow HSFP) 1921 *W*, *I*, *E*
Donaldson, W P (Oxford U, W of Scotland) 1893 *I*, 1894 *I*, 1895 *E*, 1896 *I*, *E*, 1899 *I*
Don-Wauchope, A R (Fettesian-Lorettonians) 1881 *E*, 1882 *E*, 1883 *W*, 1884 *W*, *I*, *E*, 1885 *W*, *I*1,2, 1886 *W*, *I*, *E*, 1888 *I*
Don-Wauchope, P H (Fettesian-Lorettonians) 1885 *I*1,2, 1886 *W*, 1887 *I*, *W*, *E*
Dorward, A F (Cambridge U, Gala) 1950 *F*, 1951 *SA*, 1952 *W*, *I*, *E*, 1953 *F*, *W*, *E*, 1955 *F*, 1956 *I*, *E*, 1957 *F*, *W*, *I*, *E*
Dorward, T F (Gala) 1938 *W*, *I*, *E*, 1939 *I*, *E*
Douglas, G (Jedforest) 1921 *W*
Douglas, J (Stewart's Coll FP) 1961 *F*, *SA*, *W*, *I*, *E*, 1962 *F*, *W*, *I*, *E*, 1963 *F*, *W*, *I*
Douty, P S (London Scottish) 1927 *NSW*, 1928 *F*, *W*
Drew, D (Glasgow Acads) 1871 *E*, 1876 *E*
Druitt, W A H (London Scottish) 1936 *W*, *I*, *E*
Drummond, A H (Kelvinside Acads) 1938 *W*, *I*
Drummond, C W (Melrose) 1947 *F*, *W*, *I*, *E*, 1948 *F*, *I*, *E*, 1950 *F*, *W*, *I*, *E*
Drybrough, A S (Edinburgh Wands, Merchistonians) 1902 *I*, 1903 *I*
Dryden, R H (Watsonians) 1937 *E*
Drysdale, D (Heriot's FP) 1923 *F*, *W*, *I*, *E*, 1924 *F*, *W*, *I*, *E*, 1925 *F*, *W*, *I*, *E*, 1926 *F*, *W*, *I*, *E*, 1927 *F*, *W*, *I*, *E*, *NSW*, 1928 *F*, *W*, *I*, *E*, 1929 *F*
Duff, P L (Glasgow Acads) 1936 *W*, *I*, 1938 *W*, *I*, *E*, 1939 *W*
Duffy, H (Jedforest) 1955 *F*
Duke, A (Royal HSFP) 1888 *W*, *I*, 1889 *W*, *I*, 1890 *W*, *I*, 1891 *W*, *I*
Duncan, A W (Edinburgh U) 1901 *W*, *I*, *E*, 1902 *W*, *I*, *E*
Duncan, D D (Oxford U) 1920 *F*, *W*, *I*, *E*
Duncan, M D F (W of Scotland) 1986 *F*, *W*, *E*, *R*, 1987 *I*, *F*, *W*, *E*, [*F*, *Z*, *R*, *NZ*], 1988 *I*, *F*, *W*, *E*, *A*, 1989 *W*
Duncan, M M (Fettesian-Lorettonians) 1888 *W*
Dunlop, J W (W of Scotland) 1875 *E*
Dunlop, Q (W of Scotland) 1971 *E* (2[1C])
Dykes, A S (Glasgow Acads) 1932 *E*
Dykes, J C (Glasgow Acads) 1922 *F*, *E*, 1924 *I*, 1925 *F*, *W*, *I*, 1926 *F*, *W*, *I*, *E*, 1927 *F*, *W*, *I*, *E*, *NSW*, 1928 *F*, *I*, 1929 *F*, *W*, *I*
Dykes, J M (Clydesdale, Glasgow HSFP) 1898 *I*, *E*, 1899 *W*, *E*, 1900 *W*, *I*, 1901 *W*, *I*, *E*, 1902 *E*

Edwards, D B (Heriot's FP) 1960 *I*, *E*, *SA*
Elgie, M K (London Scottish) 1954 *NZ*, *I*, *E*, *W*, 1955 *F*, *W*, *I*, *E*
Elliot, C (Langholm) 1958 *E*, 1959 *F*, 1960 *F*, 1963 *E*, 1964 *F*, *NZ*, *W*, *I*, *E*, 1965 *F*, *W*, *I*
Elliot, M (Hawick) 1895 *W*, 1896 *E*, 1897 *I*, *E*, 1898 *I*, *E*
Elliot, T (Gala) 1905 *E*
Elliot, T (Gala) 1955 *W*, *I*, *E*, 1956 *F*, *W*, *I*, *E*, 1957 *F*, *W*, *I*, *E*, 1958 *W*, *A*, *I*
Elliot, T G (Langholm) 1968 *W*, *A*, 1969 *F*, *W*, 1970 *E*
Elliot, W I D (Edinburgh Acads) 1947 *F*, *W*, *E*, *A*, 1948 *F*, *W*, *I*, *E*, 1949 *F*, *W*, *I*, *E*, 1950 *F*, *W*, *I*, *E*, 1951 *F*, *W*, *I*, *E*, *SA*, 1952 *F*, *W*, *I*, *E*, 1954 *NZ*, *I*, *E*, *W*
Emslie, W D (Royal HSFP) 1930 *F*, 1932 *I*
Evans, H L (Edinburgh U) 1885 *I*1,2
Ewart, E N (Glasgow Acads) 1879 *E*, 1880 *I*, *E*

Fahmy, Dr E C (Abertillery) 1920 *F*, *W*, *I*, *E*
Fasson, F H (London Scottish, Edinburgh Wands) 1900 *W*, 1901 *W*, *I*, 1902 *W*, *E*
Fell, A N (Edinburgh U) 1901 *W*, *I*, *E*, 1902 *W*, *E*, 1903 *W*, *E*
Ferguson, J H (Gala) 1928 *W*
Ferguson, W G (Royal HSFP) 1927 *NSW*, 1928 *F*, *W*, *I*, *E*
Fergusson, E A J (Oxford U) 1954 *F*, *NZ*, *I*, *E*, *W*
Finlay, A B (Edinburgh Acads) 1875 *E*
Finlay, J F (Edinburgh Acads) 1871 *E*, 1872 *E*, 1874 *E*, 1875 *E*
Finlay, N J (Edinburgh Acads) 1875 *E*, 1876 *E*, 1878 *E*, 1879 *I*, *E*, 1880 *I*, *E*, 1881 *I*, *E*
Finlay, R (Watsonians) 1948 *E*
Fisher, A T (Waterloo, Watsonians) 1947 *I*, *E*
Fisher, C D (Waterloo) 1975 *NZ*, *A*, 1976 *W*, *E*, *I*
Fisher, D (W of Scotland) 1893 *I*
Fisher, J P (Royal HSFP, London Scottish) 1963 *E*, 1964 *F*, *NZ*, *W*, *I*, *E*, 1965 *F*, *W*, *I*, *E*, *SA*, 1966 *F*, *W*, *I*, *E*, *A*, 1967 *F*, *W*, *I*, *E*, *NZ*, 1968 *F*, *W*, *I*, *E*
Fleming, C J N (Edinburgh Wands) 1896 *I*, *E*, 1897 *I*
Fleming, G R (Glasgow Acads) 1875 *E*, 1876 *E*
Fletcher, H N (Edinburgh U) 1904 *E*, 1905 *W*
Flett, A B (Edinburgh U) 1901 *W*, *I*, *E*, 1902 *W*, *I*
Forbes, J L (Watsonians) 1905 *W*, 1906 *I*, *E*
Ford, D St C (United Services, RN) 1930 *I*, *E*, 1931 *E*, 1932 *W*, *I*, *E*
Ford, J R (Gala) 1893 *I*
Forrest, J E (Glasgow Acads) 1932 *SA*, 1935 *E*, *NZ*
Forrest, J G S (Cambridge U) 1938 *W*, *I*, *E*
Forrest, W T (Hawick) 1903 *W*, *I*, *E*, 1904 *W*, *I*, *E*, 1905 *W*, *I*
Forsayth, H H (Oxford U) 1921 *F*, *W*, *I*, *E*, 1922 *W*, *I*, *E*
Forsyth, I W (Stewart's Coll FP) 1972 *NZ*, 1973 *F*, *W*, *I*, *E*, *P*
Forsyth, J (Edinburgh U) 1871 *E*
Foster, R A (Hawick) 1930 *W*, 1932 *SA*, *I*, *E*
Fox, J (Gala) 1952 *F*, *W*, *I*, *E*
Frame, J N M (Edinburgh U, Gala) 1967 *NZ*, 1968 *F*, *W*, *I*, *E*, 1969 *W*, *I*, *E*, *SA*, 1970 *F*, *W*, *I*, *E*, *A*, 1971 *F*, *W*, *I*, *E* (2[1C]), 1972 *F*, *W*, *E*, 1973 *P* (R)
France, C (Kelvinside Acads) 1903 *I*
Fraser, C F P (Glasgow U) 1888 *W*, 1889 *W*
Fraser, J W (Edinburgh Inst FP) 1881 *E*
Fraser, R (Cambridge U) 1911 *F*, *W*, *I*, *E*
French, J (Glasgow Acads) 1886 *W*, 1887 *I*, *W*, *E*
Frew, A (Edinburgh U) 1901 *W*, *I*, *E*
Frew, G M (Glasgow HSFP) 1906 *SA*, 1907 *W*, *I*, *E*, 1908 *W*, *I*, *E*, 1909 *W*, *I*, *E*, 1910 *F*, *W*, *I*, 1911 *I*, *E*
Friebe, J P (Glasgow HSFP) 1952 *E*
Fulton, A K (Edinburgh U, Dollar Acads) 1952 *F*, 1954 *F*
Fyfe, K C (Cambridge U, Sale, London Scottish) 1933 *W*, *E*, 1934 *E*, 1935 *W*, *I*, *E*, *NZ*, 1936 *W*, *E*, 1939 *I*

Gallie, G H (Edinburgh Acads) 1939 *W*
Gallie, R A (Glasgow Acads) 1920 *F*, *W*, *I*, *E*, 1921 *F*, *W*, *I*, *E*
Gammell, W B B (Edinburgh Wands) 1977 *I*, *F*, *W*, 1978 *W*, *E*
Geddes, I C (London Scottish) 1906 *SA*, 1907 *W*, *I*, *E*, 1908 *W*, *I*
Geddes, K I (London Scottish) 1947 *F*, *W*, *I*, *E*

Gedge, H T S (Oxford U, London Scottish, Edinburgh Wands) 1894 *W, I, E,* 1896 *E,* 1899 *W, E*
Gedge, P M S (Edinburgh Wands) 1933 *I*
Gemmill, R (Glasgow HSFP) 1950 *F, W, I, E,* 1951 *F, W, I*
Gibson, W R (Royal HSFP) 1891 *I, E,* 1892 *W, I, E,* 1893 *W, I, E,* 1894 *W, I, E,* 1895 *W, I, E*
Gilbert-Smith, D S (London Scottish) 1952 *E*
Gilchrist, J (Glasgow Acads) 1925 *F*
Gill, A D (Gala) 1973 *P,* 1974 *W, E, I, F*
Gillespie, J I (Edinburgh Acads) 1899 *E,* 1900 *W, E,* 1901 *W, I, E,* 1902 *W, I,* 1904 *I, E*
Gillies, A C (Watsonians) 1924 *W, I, E,* 1925 *F, W, E,* 1926 *F, W,* 1927 *F, W, E*
Gilray, C M (Oxford U, London Scottish) 1908 *E,* 1909 *W, E,* 1912 *I*
Glasgow, R J C (Dunfermline) 1962 *F, W, I, E,* 1963 *I, E,* 1964 *I, E,* 1965 *W, I*
Glen, W S (Edinburgh Wands) 1955 *W*
Gloag, L G (Cambridge U) 1949 *F, W, I, E*
Goodfellow, J (Langholm) 1928 *W, I, E*
Goodhue, F W J (London Scottish) 1890 *W, I, E,* 1891 *W, I, E,* 1892 *W, I, E*
Gordon, R (Edinburgh Wands) 1951 *W,* 1952 *F, W, I, E,* 1953 *W*
Gordon, R E (Royal Artillery) 1913 *F, W, I*
Gordon, R J (London Scottish) 1982 *A* 1,2
Gore, A C (London Scottish) 1882 *I*
Gossman, B M (W of Scotland) 1980 *W,* 1983 *F, W*
Gossman, J S (W of Scotland) 1980 *E* (R)
Gowans, J J (Cambridge U, London Scottish) 1893 *W,* 1894 *W, E,* 1895 *W, I, E,* 1896 *I, E*
Gowland, G C (London Scottish) 1908 *W,* 1909 *W, E,* 1910 *F, W, I, E*
Gracie, A L (Harlequins) 1921 *F, W, I, E,* 1922 *F, W, I, E,* 1923 *F, W, I, E,* 1924 *F*
Graham, I N (Edinburgh Acads) 1939 *I, E*
Graham, J (Kelso) 1926 *I, E,* 1927 *F, W, I, E, NSW,* 1928 *F, W, I, E,* 1930 *I, E,* 1932 *SA, W*
Graham, J H S (Edinburgh Acads) 1876 *E,* 1877 *I, E,* 1878 *E,* 1879 *I, E,* 1880 *I, E,* 1881 *I, E*
Grant, D (Hawick) 1965 *F, E, SA,* 1966 *F, W, I, E, A,* 1967 *F, W, I, E, NZ,* 1968 *F*
Grant, D M (East Midlands) 1911 *W, I*
Grant, M L (Harlequins) 1955 *F,* 1956 *F, W,* 1957 *F*
Grant, T O (Hawick) 1960 *I, E, SA,* 1964 *F, NZ, W*
Grant, W St C (Craigmount) 1873 *E,* 1874 *E*
Gray, C A (Nottingham) 1989 *W, E, I, F*
Gray, D (W of Scotland) 1978 *E,* 1979 *I, F, NZ,* 1980 *I, F, W, E,* 1981 *F*
Gray, G L (Gala) 1935 *NZ,* 1937 *W, I, E*
Gray, T (Northampton, Heriot's FP) 1950 *E,* 1951 *F, E*
Greenlees, H D (Leicester) 1927 *NSW,* 1928 *F, W,* 1929 *I, E,* 1930 *E*
Greenlees, J R C (Cambridge U, Kelvinside Acads) 1900 *I,* 1902 *W, I, E,* 1903 *W, I, E*
Greenwood, J T (Dunfermline and Perthshire Acads) 1952 *F,* 1955 *F, W, I, E,* 1956 *F, W, I, E,* 1957 *F, W, E,* 1958 *F, W, A, I, E,* 1959 *F, W, I*
Greig, A (Glasgow HSFP) 1911 *I*
Greig, L L (Glasgow Acads, United Services) 1905 *NZ,* 1906 *SA,* 1907 *W,* 1908 *W, I*
Greig, R C (Glasgow Acads) 1893 *W,* 1897 *I*
Grieve, C F (Oxford U) 1935 *W,* 1936 *E*
Grieve, R M (Kelso) 1935 *W, I, E, NZ,* 1936 *W, I, E*
Gunn, A W (Royal HSFP) 1912 *F, W, I, SA,* 1913 *F*

Hamilton, A S (Headingley) 1914 *W,* 1920 *F*
Hamilton, H M (W of Scotland) 1874 *E,* 1875 *E*
Hannah, R S M (W of Scotland) 1971 *I*
Harrower, P R (London Scottish) 1885 *W*
Hart, J G M (London Scottish) 1951 *SA*
Hart, T M (Glasgow U) 1930 *W, I*
Hart, W (Melrose) 1960 *SA*
Harvey, L (Greenock Wands) 1899 *I*
Hastie, A J (Melrose) 1961 *W, I, E,* 1964 *I, E,* 1965 *E, SA,* 1966 *F, W, I, E, A,* 1967 *F, W, I, NZ,* 1968 *F, W*
Hastie, I R (Kelso) 1955 *F,* 1958 *F, E,* 1959 *F, W, I*
Hastie, J D H (Melrose) 1938 *W, I, E*
Hastings, A G (Cambridge U, Watsonians, London Scottish) 1986 *F, W, E, I, R,* 1987 *I, F, W, E, [F, Z, R, NZ],* 1988 *I, F, W, E, A*
Hastings, S (Watsonians) 1986 *F, W, E, I, R,* 1987 *I,*

F, W, [R], 1988 *I, F, W, A,* 1989 *W, E, I, F*
Hay, B H (Boroughmuir) 1975 *NZ, A,* 1976 *F,* 1978 *I, F, W, E, NZ,* 1979 *W, E, I, F, NZ,* 1980 *I, F, W, E,* 1981 *F, W, E, I, NZ* 1,2
Hay-Gordon, J R (Edinburgh Acads) 1875 *E,* 1877 *I, E*
Hegarty, C B (Hawick) 1978 *I, F, W, E*
Hegarty, J J (Hawick) 1951 *F,* 1953 *F, W, I, E,* 1955 *F*
Henderson, B C (Edinburgh Wands) 1963 *E,* 1964 *F, I, E,* 1965 *F, W, I, E,* 1966 *F, W, I, E*
Henderson, F W (London Scottish) 1900 *W, I*
Henderson, I C (Edinburgh Acads) 1939 *I, E,* 1947 *F, W, E, A,* 1948 *I, E*
Henderson, J H (Oxford U, Richmond) 1953 *F, W, I, E,* 1954 *F, NZ, I, E, W*
Henderson, J M (Edinburgh Acads) 1933 *W, E, I*
Henderson, J Y M (Watsonians) 1911 *E*
Henderson, M M (Dunfermline) 1937 *W, I, E*
Henderson, N F (London Scottish) 1892 *I*
Henderson, R G (Newcastle Northern) 1924 *I, E*
Hendrie, K G P (Heriot's FP) 1924 *F, W, I*
Hendry, T L (Clydesdale) 1893 *W, I, E,* 1895 *I*
Henriksen, E H (Royal HSFP) 1953 *I*
Hepburn, D P (Woodford) 1947 *A,* 1948 *F, W, I, E,* 1949 *F, W, I, E*
Heron, G (Glasgow Acads) 1874 *E,* 1875 *E*
Hill, C C P (St Andrew's U) 1912 *F, I*
Hinshelwood, A J W (London Scottish) 1966 *F, W, I, E, A,* 1967 *F, W, I, E, NZ,* 1968 *F, W, I, E, A,* 1969 *F, W, I, SA,* 1970 *F, W*
Hodgson, C G (London Scottish) 1968 *I, E*
Hogg, C G (Boroughmuir) 1978 *F* (R), *W* (R)
Holms, W F (RIE Coll) 1886 *W, E,* 1887 *I, E,* 1889 *W, I*
Horsburgh, G B (London Scottish) 1937 *W, I, E,* 1938 *W, I, E,* 1939 *W, I, E*
Howie, D D (Kirkcaldy) 1912 *F, W, I, E, SA,* 1913 *F, W*
Howie, R A (Kirkcaldy) 1924 *F, W, I, E,* 1925 *W, I, E*
Hoyer-Millar, G C (Oxford U) 1953 *I*
Huggan, J L (London Scottish) 1914 *E*
Hume, J (Royal HSFP) 1912 *F,* 1920 *F,* 1921 *F, W, I, E,* 1922 *F*
Hume, J W G (Oxford U, Edinburgh Wands) 1928 *I,* 1930 *F*
Hunter, F (Edinburgh U) 1882 *I*
Hunter, I G (Selkirk) 1984 *I* (R), 1985 *F* (R), *W, E*
Hunter, J M (Cambridge U) 1947 *F*
Hunter, M D (Glasgow High) 1974 *F*
Hunter, W J (Hawick) 1964 *F, NZ, W,* 1967 *F, W, I, E*
Hutchison, W R (Glasgow HSFP) 1911 *E*
Hutton, A H M (Dunfermline) 1932 *I*
Hutton, J E (Harlequins) 1930 *E,* 1931 *F*

Inglis, H M (Edinburgh Acads) 1951 *F, W, I, E, SA,* 1952 *W, I*
Inglis, J M (Selkirk) 1952 *E*
Inglis, W M (Cambridge U, Royal Engineers) 1937 *W, I, E,* 1938 *W, I, E*
Innes, J R S (Aberdeen GSFP) 1939 *W, I, E,* 1947 *A,* 1948 *F, W, I, E*
Ireland, J C H (Glasgow HSFP) 1925 *W, I, E,* 1926 *F, W, I, E,* 1927 *F, W, I, E*
Irvine, A R (Heriot's FP) 1972 *NZ,* 1973 *F, W, I, E, P,* 1974 *W, E, I, F,* 1975 *I, F, W, E, NZ, A,* 1976 *F, W, E, I,* 1977 *E, I, F, W,* 1978 *I, F, E, NZ,* 1979 *W, E, I, F, NZ,* 1980 *I, F, W, E,* 1981 *F, W, E, I, NZ* 1,2, *R, A,* 1982 *E, I, F, W, A* 1,2
Irvine, D R (Edinburgh Acads) 1878 *E,* 1879 *I, E*
Irvine, R W (Edinburgh Acads) 1871 *E,* 1872 *E,* 1873 *E,* 1874 *E,* 1875 *E,* 1876 *E,* 1877 *I, E,* 1878 *E,* 1879 *I, E,* 1880 *I, E*
Irvine, T W (Edinburgh Acads) 1885 *I* 1,2, 1886 *W, I, E,* 1887 *I, W, E,* 1888 *W, I,* 1889 *I*

Jackson, K L T (Oxford U) 1933 *W, E, I,* 1934 *W*
Jackson, T G H (Army) 1947 *F, W, E, A,* 1948 *F, W, I, E,* 1949 *F, W, I, E*
Jackson, W D (Hawick) 1964 *I,* 1965 *E, SA,* 1968 *A,* 1969 *F, W, I, E*
Jamieson, J (W of Scotland) 1883 *W, I, E,* 1884 *W, I, E,* 1885 *W, I* 1,2
Jeffrey, J (Kelso) 1984 *A,* 1985 *I, E,* 1986 *F, W, E, I, R,* 1987 *I, F, W, E, [F, Z, R],* 1988 *I, W, A,* 1989 *W, E, I, F*

Johnston, D I (Watsonians) 1979 NZ, 1980 I, F, W, E, 1981 R, A, 1982 E, I, F, W, A 1,2, 1983 I, F, W, NZ, 1984 W, E, I, F, R, 1986 F, W, E, I, R
Johnston, H H (Edinburgh Collegian FP) 1877 I, E
Johnston, J (Melrose) 1951 SA, 1952 F, W, I, E
Johnston, W C (Glasgow HSFP) 1922 F
Johnston, W G S (Cambridge U) 1935 W, I, 1937 W, I, E
Junor, J E (Glasgow Acads) 1876 E, 1877 I, E, 1878 E, 1879 E, 1881 I

Keddie, R R (Watsonians) 1967 NZ
Keith, G J (Wasps) 1968 F, W
Keller, D H (London Scottish) 1949 F, W, I, E, 1950 F, W, I
Kelly, R F (Watsonians) 1927 NSW, 1928 F, W, E
Kemp, J W Y (Glasgow HSFP) 1954 W, 1955 F, W, I, E, 1956 F, W, I, E, 1957 F, W, I, E, 1958 F, W, A, I, E, 1959 F, W, I, E, 1960 F, W, I, E, SA
Kennedy, A E (Watsonians) 1983 NZ, 1984 W, E, A
Kennedy, F (Stewart's Coll FP) 1920 F, W, I, E, 1921 E
Kennedy, N (W of Scotland) 1903 W, I, E
Ker, A B M (Kelso) 1988 W, E
Ker, H T (Glasgow Acads) 1887 I, W, E, 1888 I, 1889 W, 1890 I, E
Kerr, D S (Heriot's FP) 1923 F, W, 1924 F, 1926 I, E, 1927 W, I, E, 1928 I, E
Kerr, G C (Old Dunelmians, Edinburgh Wands) 1898 I, E, 1899 I, W, E, 1900 W, I, E
Kerr, J M (Heriot's FP) 1935 NZ, 1936 I, E, 1937 W, I
Kerr, W (London Scottish) 1953 E
Kidston, D W (Glasgow Acads) 1883 W, E
Kidston, W H (W of Scotland) 1874 E
Kilgour, I J (RMC Sandhurst) 1921 F
King, J H F (Selkirk) 1953 F, W, E, 1954 E
Kininmonth, P W (Oxford U, Richmond) 1949 F, W, I, E, 1950 F, W, I, E, 1951 F, W, I, E, SA, 1952 F, W, I, 1954 F, NZ, I, E, W
Kinnear, R M (Heriot's FP) 1926 F, W, I
Knox, J (Kelvinside Acads) 1903 W, I, E
Kyle, W E (Hawick) 1902 W, I, E, 1903 W, I, E, 1904 W, I, E, 1905 W, I, E, NZ, 1906 W, I, E, 1908 E, 1909 W, I, E, 1910 W

Laidlaw, A S (Hawick) 1897 I
Laidlaw, F A L (Melrose) 1965 F, W, I, E, SA, 1966 F, W, I, E, A, 1967 F, W, I, E, NZ, 1968 F, W, I, A, 1969 F, W, I, E, SA, 1970 F, W, I, E, A, 1971 F, W, I
Laidlaw, R J (Jedforest) 1980 I, F, W, E, 1981 F, W, E, I, NZ 1,2, R, A, 1982 E, I, F, W, A 1,2, 1983 I, F, W, E, NZ, 1984 W, E, I, F, R, A, 1985 I, F, 1986 F, W, E, I, R, 1987 I, F, W, E, [F, R, NZ], 1988 I, F, W, E
Laing, A D (Royal HSFP) 1914 W, I, E, 1920 F, W, I, 1921 F
Lambie, I K (Watsonians) 1978 NZ (R), 1979 W, E, NZ
Lambie, L B (Glasgow HSFP) 1934 W, I, E, 1935 W, I, E, NZ
Lamond, G A W (Kelvinside Acads) 1899 W, E, 1905 E
Lang, D (Paisley) 1876 E, 1877 I
Langrish, R W (London Scottish) 1930 F, 1931 F, W, I
Lauder, W (Neath) 1969 I, E, SA, 1970 F, W, I, A, 1973 F, 1974 W, E, I, F, 1975 I, F, NZ, A, 1976 F, 1977 E
Laughland, I H P (London Scottish) 1959 F, 1960 F, W, I, E, 1961 SA, W, I, E, 1962 F, W, I, E, 1963 F, W, I, 1964 F, NZ, W, I, E, 1965 F, W, I, E, SA, 1966 F, W, I, E, 1967 E
Lawrie, J R (Melrose) 1922 F, W, I, E, 1923 F, W, I, E, 1924 F, I, E
Lawrie, K G (Gala) 1980 F (R), W, E
Lawson, A J M (Edinburgh Wands, London Scottish) 1972 F (R), E, 1973 F, 1974 W, E, 1976 E, I, 1977 E, 1978 NZ, 1979 W, E, I, F, NZ, 1980 W (R)
Lawther, T H B (Old Millhillians) 1932 SA, W
Ledingham, G A (Aberdeen GSFP) 1913 F
Lees, J B (Gala) 1947 I, A, 1948 F, W, E
Leggatt, H T O (Watsonians) 1891 W, I, E, 1892 W, I, 1893 W, E, 1894 I, E
Lely, W G (Cambridge U, London Scottish) 1909 I
Leslie, D G (Dundee HSFP, W of Scotland, Gala) 1975 I, F, W, E, NZ, A, 1976 F, W, E, I, 1978 NZ, 1980 E, 1981 W, E, I, NZ 1,2, R, A, 1982 E, 1983 I, F, W, E,

1984 W, E, I, F, R, 1985 F, W, E
Liddell, E H (Edinburgh U) 1922 F, W, I, 1923 F, W, I, E
Lind, H (Dunfermline) 1928 I, 1931 F, W, I, E, 1932 SA, W, E, 1933 W, E, I, 1934 W, I, E, 1935 I, 1936 E
Lindsay, A B (London Hospital) 1910 I, 1911 I
Lindsay, G C (London Scottish) 1884 W, 1885 I 1, 1887 W, E
Lindsay-Watson, R H (Hawick) 1909 I
Lineen, S R P (Boroughmuir) 1989 W, E, I, F
Little, A W (Hawick) 1905 W
Logan, W R (Edinburgh U, Edinburgh Wands) 1931 E, 1932 SA, W, I, 1933 W, E, I, 1934 W, I, E, 1935 W, I, E, NZ, 1936 W, I, E, 1937 W, I, E
Lorraine, H D B (Oxford U) 1933 W, E, I
Loudoun-Shand, E G (Oxford U) 1913 E
Lowe, J D (Heriot's FP) 1934 W
Lumsden, I J M (Bath, Watsonians) 1947 F, W, A, 1949 F, W, I, E
Lyall, G G (Gala) 1947 A, 1948 F, W, I, E
Lyall, W J C (Edinburgh Acads) 1871 E

Mabon, J T (Jedforest) 1898 I, E, 1899 I, 1900 I
Macarthur, J P (Waterloo) 1932 E
MacCallum, J C (Watsonians) 1905 E, NZ, 1906 W, I, E, SA, 1907 W, I, E, 1908 W, I, E, 1909 W, I, E, 1910 F, W, I, E, 1911 F, I, E, 1912 F, W, I, E
McClung, T (Edinburgh Acads) 1956 I, E, 1957 W, I, E, 1959 F, W, I, 1960 W
McClure, G B (W of Scotland) 1873 E
McClure, J H (W of Scotland) 1872 E
McCowan, D (W of Scotland) 1880 I, E, 1881 I, E, 1882 I, E, 1883 I, E, 1884 I, E
McCowat, R H (Glasgow Acads) 1905 I
McCrae, I G (Gordonians) 1967 E, 1968 I, 1969 F (R), W, 1972 F, NZ
McCrow, J W S (Edinburgh Acads) 1921 I
McDonald, C (Jedforest) 1947 A
Macdonald, D C (Edinburgh U) 1953 F, W, 1958 I, E
Macdonald, D S M (Oxford U, London Scottish, W of Scotland) 1977 E, I, F, W, 1978 I, W, E
Macdonald, J D (London Scottish, Army) 1966 F, W, I, E, 1967 F, W, I, E
Macdonald, J M (Edinburgh Wands) 1911 W
Macdonald, J S (Edinburgh U) 1903 E, 1904 W, I, E, 1905 W
Macdonald, K R (Stewart's Coll FP) 1956 F, W, I, 1957 W, I, E
Macdonald, R (Edinburgh U) 1950 F, W, I, E
McDonald, W A (Glasgow U) 1889 W, 1892 I, E
Macdonald, W G (London Scottish) 1969 I (R)
Macdougall, J B (Greenock Wands, Wakefield) 1913 F, 1914 I, 1921 F, I, E
McEwan, M C (Edinburgh Acads) 1886 E, 1887 I, W, E, 1888 W, I, 1889 W, I, 1890 W, I, E, 1891 W, I, E, 1892 E
MacEwan, N A (Gala, Highland) 1971 F, W, I, E (2[1C]), 1972 F, W, E, NZ, 1973 F, W, I, E, P, 1974 W, E, I, F, 1975 W, E
McEwan, W M C (Edinburgh Acads) 1894 W, E, 1895 W, E, 1896 W, I, E, 1897 I, E, 1898 I, E, 1899 I, W, E, 1900 W, E
MacEwen, R K G (Cambridge U, London Scottish) 1954 F, NZ, I, W, 1956 F, W, I, E, 1957 F, W, I, E, 1958 W
Macfarlan, D J (London Scottish) 1883 W, 1884 W, I, E, 1886 W, I, 1887 I, 1888 I
McFarlane, J L H (Edinburgh U) 1871 E, 1872 E, 1873 E
McGaughey, S K (Hawick) 1984 R
McGeechan, I R (Headingley) 1972 NZ, 1973 F, W, I, E, P, 1974 W, E, I, F, 1975 I, F, W, E, NZ, A, 1976 F, W, E, I, 1977 E, I, F, W, 1978 I, F, W, NZ, 1979 W, E, I, F
McGlashan, T P L (Royal HSFP) 1947 F, I, E, 1954 F, NZ, I, E, W
MacGregor, D G (Watsonians, Pontypridd) 1907 W, I, E
MacGregor, G (Cambridge U) 1890 W, I, E, 1891 W, I, E, 1893 I, E, 1894 W, I, E, 1896 E
MacGregor, I A A (Hillhead HSFP, Llanelli) 1955 I, E, 1956 F, W, I, E, 1957 F, W, I
MacGregor, J R (Edinburgh U) 1909 I

McGuinness, G M (W of Scotland) 1982 *A* 1,2, 1983 *I*, 1985 *I, F, W, E*
McHarg, A F (W of Scotland, London Scottish) 1968 *I, E, A*, 1969 *F, W, I, E*, 1971 *F, W, I, E* (2(1C)), 1972 *F, E, NZ*, 1973 *F, W, I, E, P*, 1974 *W, E, I, F*, 1975 *I, F, W, E, NZ, A*, 1976 *F, W, E, I*, 1977 *E, I, F, W*, 1978 *I, F, W, NZ*, 1979 *W, E*
McIndoe, F (Glasgow Acads) 1886 *W, I*
MacIntyre, I (Edinburgh Wands) 1890 *W, I, E*, 1891 *W, I, E*
Mackay, E B (Glasgow Acads) 1920 *W*, 1922 *E*
McKeating, E (Heriot's FP) 1957 *F, W*, 1961 *SA, W, I, E*
Mckendrick, J G (W of Scotland) 1889 *I*
Mackenzie, A D G (Selkirk) 1984 *A*
Mackenzie, C J G (United Services) 1921 *E*
Mackenzie, D D (Edinburgh U) 1947 *W, I, E*, 1948 *F, W, I*
Mackenzie, D K A (Edinburgh, Wands) 1939 *I, E*
Mackenzie, J M (Edinburgh U) 1905 *NZ*, 1909 *W, I, E*, 1910 *W, I, E*, 1911 *W, I*
Mackenzie, R C (Glasgow Acads) 1877 *I, E*, 1881 *I, E*
Mackie, G Y (Highland) 1975 *A*, 1976 *F, W*, 1978 *F*
MacKinnon, A (London Scottish) 1898 *I, E*, 1899 *I, W, E*, 1900 *E*
Mackintosh, C E W C (London Scottish) 1924 *F*
Mackintosh, H S (Glasgow U, W of Scotland) 1929 *F, W, I, E*, 1930 *F, W, I, E*, 1931 *F, W, I, E*, 1932 *SA, W, I, E*
MacLachlan, L P (Oxford U, London Scottish) 1954 *NZ, I, E, W*
Maclagan, W E (Edinburgh Acads) 1878 *E*, 1879 *I, E*, 1880 *I, E*, 1881 *I, E*, 1882 *I, E*, 1883 *W, I, E*, 1884 *W, I, E*, 1885 *W, I*1,2, 1887 *I, W, E*, 1888 *W, I*, 1890 *W, I, E*
McLaren, A (Durham County) 1931 *F*
McLaren, E (London Scottish, Royal HSFP) 1923 *F, W, I, E*, 1924 *F*
McLauchlan, J (Jordanhill) 1969 *E, SA*, 1970 *F, W*, 1971 *F, W, I, E* (2[1C]), 1972 *F, W, E, NZ*, 1973 *F, W, I, E, P*, 1974 *W, E, I, F*, 1975 *I, F, W, E, NZ, A*, 1976 *F, W, E, I*, 1977 *W*, 1978 *I, F, W, E, NZ*, 1979 *W, E, I, F, NZ*
McLean, D I (Royal HSFP) 1947 *I, E*
Maclennan, W D (Watsonians) 1947 *F, I*
MacLeod, D A (Glasgow U) 1886 *I, E*
MacLeod, G (Edinburgh Acads) 1878 *E*, 1882 *I*
McLeod, H F (Hawick) 1954 *F, NZ, I, E, W*, 1955 *F, W, I, E*, 1956 *W, I, E*, 1957 *F, W, I, E*, 1958 *F, W, A, I, E*, 1959 *F, W, I, E*, 1960 *F, W, I, E, SA*, 1961 *F, SA, W, I, E*, 1962 *F, W, I, E*
MacLeod, K G (Cambridge U) 1905 *NZ*, 1906 *W, I, E, SA*, 1907 *W, I, E*, 1908 *I, E*
MacLeod, L M (Cambridge U) 1904 *W, I, E*, 1905 *W, I, NZ*
Macleod, W M (Fettesian-Lorettonians, Edinburgh Wands) 1886 *W, I*
McMillan, K H D (Sale) 1953 *F, W, I, E*
MacMillan, R G (London Scottish) 1887 *W, I, E*, 1890 *W, I, E*, 1891 *W, E*, 1892 *W, I, E*, 1893 *W, E*, 1894 *W, I, E*, 1895 *W, I, E*, 1897 *I, E*
MacMyn, D J (Cambridge U, London Scottish) 1925 *F, W, I, E*, 1926 *F, W, I, E*, 1927 *E, NSW*, 1928 *F*
McNeil, A S B (Watsonians) 1935 *I*
McPartlin, J J (Harlequins, Oxford U) 1960 *F, W*, 1962 *F, W, I, E*
Macphail, J A R (Edinburgh Acads) 1949 *E*, 1951 *SA*
Macpherson, D G (London Hospital) 1910 *I, E*
Macpherson, G P S (Oxford U, Edinburgh Acads) 1922 *F, W, I, E*, 1924 *W, E*, 1925 *F, W, E*, 1927 *F, W*, 1928 *F, W, E*, 1929 *I, E*, 1930 *F, W, I, E*, 1931 *W*, 1932 *SA, E*
Macpherson, N C (Newport, Mon) 1920 *W, I, E*, 1921 *F, E*, 1923 *I, E*
McQueen, S B (Waterloo) 1923 *F, W, I, E*
Macrae, D J (St Andrews U) 1937 *W, I, E*, 1938 *W, I, E*, 1939 *W, I, E*
Madsen, D F (Gosforth) 1974 *W, E, I, F*, 1975 *I, F, W, E* 1976 *F, I, F, W*, 1978 *I*
Mair, N G R (Edinburgh U) 1951 *F, W, I, E*
Maitland, G (Edinburgh Inst FP) 1885 *W, I*2
Maitland, R (Edinburgh Inst FP) 1881 *E*, 1882 *I, E*, 1884 *W*, 1885 *W*

Maitland, R P (Royal Artillery) 1872 *E*
Malcolm, A G (Glasgow U) 1888 *I*
Marsh, J (Edinburgh Inst FP) 1889 *W, I*
Marshall, A (Edinburgh Acads) 1875 *E*
Marshall, G R (Selkirk) 1988 *A* (R)
Marshall, J C (London Scottish) 1954 *F, NZ, I, E, W*
Marshall, K W (Edinburgh Acads) 1934 *W, I, E*, 1935 *W, I, E*, 1936 *W*, 1937 *E*
Marshall, T R (Edinburgh Acads) 1871 *E*, 1872 *E*, 1873 *E*, 1874 *E*
Marshall, W (Edinburgh Acads) 1872 *E*
Martin, H (Edinburgh Acads, Oxford U) 1908 *W, I, E*, 1909 *W, E*
Masters, W H (Edinburgh Inst FP) 1879 *I*, 1880 *I, E*
Maxwell, F T (Royal Engineers) 1872 *E*
Maxwell, G H H P (Edinburgh Acads, RAF, London Scottish) 1913 *I, E*, 1914 *W, I, E*, 1920 *W, E*, 1921 *F, W, I, E*, 1922 *F, E*
Maxwell, J M (Langholm) 1957 *I*
Mein, J (Edinburgh Acads) 1871 *E*, 1872 *E*, 1873 *E*, 1874 *E*, 1875 *E*
Melville, C L (Army) 1937 *W, I, E*
Menzies, H F (W of Scotland) 1893 *W, I*, 1894 *W, E*
Methuen, A (London Scottish) 1889 *W, I*
Michie, E J S (Aberdeen U, Aberdeen GSFP) 1954 *F, NZ, I, E*, 1955 *W, I, E*, 1956 *F, W, I, E*, 1957 *F, W, I, E*
Millar, J N (W of Scotland) 1892 *W, I, E*, 1893 *W*, 1895 *I, E*
Millar, R K (London Scottish) 1924 *I*
Millican, J G (Edinburgh U) 1973 *W, I, E*
Milne, C J B (Fettesian-Lorettonians, W of Scotland) 1886 *W, I, E*
Milne, I G (Heriot's FP, Harlequins) 1979 *I, F, NZ*, 1980 *I, F*, 1981 *NZ* 1,2, *R, A*, 1982 *E, I, F, W, A* 1,2, 1983 *I, F, W, E, NZ*, 1984 *W, E, I, F, A*, 1985 *F, W, E*, 1986 *F, W, E, I, R*, 1987 *I, F, W, E*, [F, Z, NZ], 1988 *A*, 1989 *W*
Milne, K S (Heriot's F P) 1989 *W, E, I, F*
Milne, W M (Glasgow Acads) 1904 *I, E*, 1905 *W, I*
Milroy, E (Watsonians) 1910 *W*, 1911 *E*, 1912 *W, I, E, SA*, 1913 *F, W, I, E*, 1914 *I, E*
Mitchell, G W E (Edinburgh Wands) 1967 *NZ*, 1968 *F, W*
Mitchell, J G (W of Scotland) 1885 *W, I*1,2
Moncreiff, F J (Edinburgh Acads) 1871 *E*, 1872 *E*, 1873 *E*
Monteith, H G (Cambridge U, London Scottish) 1905 *E*, 1906 *W, I, E, SA*, 1907 *W, I*, 1908 *E*
Monypenny, D B (London Scottish) 1899 *I, W, E*
Moodie, A R (St Andrew's U) 1909 *E*, 1910 *F*, 1911 *F*
Morgan, D W (Stewart's-Melville FP) 1973 *W, I, E, P*, 1974 *I, F*, 1975 *I, F, W, E, NZ, A*, 1976 *F, W*, 1977 *I, F, W*, 1978 *I, F, W, E*
Morrison, M C (Royal HSFP) 1896 *W, I, E*, 1897 *I, E*, 1898 *I, E*, 1899 *I, W, E*, 1900 *W, E*, 1901 *W, I, E*, 1902 *W, I, E*, 1903 *W, I*, 1904 *W, I, E*
Morrison, R H (Edinburgh U) 1886 *W, I, E*
Morrison, W H (Edinburgh Acads) 1900 *W*
Morton, D S (W of Scotland) 1887 *I, W, E*, 1888 *W, I*, 1889 *W, I*, 1890 *W, I*
Mowat, J G (Glasgow Acads) 1883 *W, E*
Muir, D E (Heriot's FP) 1950 *F, W, I, E*, 1952 *W, I, E*
Munnoch, N M (Watsonians) 1952 *F, W, I*
Munro, P (Oxford, London Scottish) 1905 *W, I, E, NZ*, 1906 *W, I, E, SA*, 1907 *I, E*, 1911 *F, W, I*
Munro, R (St Andrews U) 1871 *E*
Munro, S (Ayr, W of Scotland) 1980 *I, F*, 1981 *F, W, E, I, NZ* 1,2, *R*, 1984 *W*
Munro, W H (Glasgow HSFP) 1947 *I, E*
Murdoch, W C W (Hillhead HSFP) 1935 *E, NZ*, 1936 *W, I*, 1939 *E*, 1948 *F, W, I, E*
Murray, G M (Glasgow Acads) 1921 *I*, 1926 *W*
Murray, H M (Glasgow U) 1936 *W, I*
Murray, K T (Hawick) 1985 *I, F, W*
Murray, R O (Cambridge U) 1935 *W, E*
Murray, W A K (London Scottish) 1920 *F, I*, 1921 *F*
Napier, H M (W of Scotland) 1877 *I, E*, 1878 *E*, 1879 *I, E*
Neill, J B (Edinburgh Acads) 1963 *E*, 1964 *F, NZ, W, I, E*, 1965 *F*
Neill, R M (Edinburgh Acads) 1901 *E*, 1902 *I*

Neilson, G T (W of Scotland) 1891 *W, I, E*, 1892 *W, E*, 1893 *W*, 1894 *W, I*, 1895 *W, I, E*, 1896 *W, I, E*
Neilson, J A (Glasgow Acads) 1878 *E*, 1879 *E*
Neilson, R T (W of Scotland) 1898 *I, E*, 1899 *I, W*, 1900 *I, E*
Neilson, T (W of Scotland) 1874 *E*
Neilson, W (Merchiston, Cambridge U, London Scottish) 1891 *W, E*, 1892 *W, I, E*, 1893 *I, E*, 1894 *E*, 1895 *W, I, E*, 1896 *I*, 1897 *I, E*
Neilson, W G (Merchistonians) 1894 *E*
Nelson, J B (Glasgow Acads) 1925 *F, W, I, E*, 1926 *F, W, I, E*, 1927 *F, W, I, E*, 1928 *I, E*, 1929 *F, W, I, E*, 1930 *F, W, I, E*, 1931 *F, W, I*
Nelson, T A (Oxford U) 1898 *E*
Nichol, J A (Royal HSFP) 1955 *W, I, E*
Nimmo, C S (Watsonians) 1920 *E*

Ogilvy, C (Hawick) 1911 *I, E*, 1912 *I*
Oliver, G H (Hawick) 1987 *[Z]*
Oliver, G K (Gala) 1970 *A*
Orr, C E (W of Scotland) 1887 *I, E, W*, 1888 *W, I*, 1889 *W, I*, 1890 *W, I, E*, 1891 *W, I, E*, 1892 *W, I, E*
Orr, H J (London Scottish) 1903 *W, I, E*, 1904 *W, I*
Orr, J E (W of Scotland) 1889 *I*, 1890 *W, I, E*, 1891 *W, I, E*, 1892 *W, I, E*, 1893 *I, E*
Orr, J H (Edinburgh City Police) 1947 *F, W*
Osler, F L (Edinburgh U) 1911 *F, W*

Park, J (Royal HSFP) 1934 *W*
Paterson, D S (Gala) 1964, 1970 *I, E, A*, 1971 *F, W, I, E* (2[1C]), 1972 *W*
Paterson, G Q (Edinburgh Acads) 1876 *E*
Paterson, J R (Birkenhead Park) 1924 *F, W, I, E*, 1926 *F, W, I, E*, 1927 *F, W, I, E, NSW*, 1928 *F, W, I, E*, 1929 *F, W, I, E*
Patterson, D (Hawick) 1896 *W*
Pattullo, G L (Panmure) 1920 *F, W, I, E*
Paxton, I A M (Selkirk) 1981 *NZ* 1,2, *R, A*, 1982 *E, I, F, W, A* 1,2, 1983 *I, E, NZ*, 1984 *W, E, I, F*, 1985 *I* (R), *F, W, E*, 1986 *W, E, I, R*, 1987 *I, F, W, E, [F, Z, R, NZ]*, 1988 *I, E, A*
Paxton, R E (Kelso) 1982 *I, A* 2 (R)
Pearson, J (Watsonians) 1909 *I, E*, 1910 *F, W, I, E*, 1911 *F*, 1912 *F, W, SA*, 1913 *I, E*
Pender, I M (London Scottish) 1914 *E*
Pender, N E K (Hawick) 1977 *I*, 1978 *F, W, E*
Penman, W M (RAF) 1939 *I*
Peterkin, W A (Edinburgh U) 1881 *E*, 1883 *I*, 1884 *W, I, E*, 1885 *W, I*1,2
Petrie, A G (Royal HSFP) 1873 *E*, 1874 *E*, 1875 *E*, 1876 *E*, 1877 *I, E*, 1878 *E*, 1879 *I, E*, 1880 *I, E*
Philp, A (Edinburgh Inst FP) 1882 *E*
Pocock, E I (Edinburgh Wands) 1877 *I, E*
Pollock, J A (Gosforth) 1982 *W*, 1983 *E, NZ*, 1984 *E* (R), *I, F, R*, 1985 *F*
Polson, A H (Gala) 1930 *E*
Purdie, W (Jedforest) 1939 *W, I, E*
Purves, A B H L (London Scottish) 1906 *W, I, E, SA*, 1907 *W, I, E*, 1908 *W, I, E*
Purves, W D C L (London Scottish) 1912 *F, W, I, SA*, 1913 *I, E*

Rea, C W W (W of Scotland, Headingley) 1968 *A*, 1969 *F, W, I, SA*, 1970 *F, W, I, A*, 1971 *F, W, E* (2[1C])
Reid, C (Edinburgh Acads) 1881 *I, E*, 1882 *I, E*, 1883 *W, I, E*, 1884 *W, I, E*, 1885 *W, I*1,2, 1886 *W, I, E*, 1887 *I, W, E*, 1888 *W, I*
Reid, J (Edinburgh Wands) 1874 *E*, 1875 *E*, 1876 *E*, 1877 *I, E*
Reid, J M (Edinburgh Acads) 1898 *I, E*, 1899 *I*
Reid, M F (Loretto) 1883 *I, E*
Reid-Kerr, J (Greenock Wand) 1909 *E*
Ralph, W K L (Stewart's Coll FP) 1955 *F, W, I, E*
Renny-Tailyour, H W (Royal Engineers) 1872 *E*
Renwick, J M (Hawick) 1972 *F, W, E, NZ*, 1973 *F*, 1974 *W, E, I, F*, 1975 *I, F, W, E, NZ, A*, 1976 *F, W, E*(R), 1977 *I, F, W*, 1978 *I, F, W, E, NZ*, 1979 *W, E, I, F, NZ*, 1980 *I, F, W, E*, 1981 *F, W, E, I, NZ* 1,2, *R, A*, 1982 *E, I, F, W*, 1983 *I, F, W*, 1984 *R*
Renwick, W N (London Scottish, Edinburgh Wands) 1938 *E*, 1939 *W*
Ritchie, G (Merchistonians) 1871 *E*
Ritchie, G F (Dundee HSFP) 1932 *E*

Ritchie, J M (Watsonians) 1933 *W, E, I*, 1934 *W, I, E*
Ritchie, W T (Cambridge U) 1905 *I, E*
Robb, G H (Glasgow U) 1881 *I*, 1885 *W*
Roberts, G (Watsonians) 1938 *W, I, E*, 1939 *W, E*
Robertson, A H (W of Scotland) 1871 *E*
Robertson, A W (Edinburgh Acads) 1897 *E*
Robertson, D (Edinburgh Acads) 1875 *E*
Robertson, D D (Cambridge U) 1893 *W*
Robertson, I (London Scottish, Watsonians) 1968 *E*, 1969 *E, SA*, 1970 *F, W, I, E, A*
Robertson, I P M (Watsonians) 1910 *F*
Robertson, J (Clydesdale) 1908 *E*
Robertson, K W (Melrose) 1978 *NZ*, 1979 *W, E, I, F, NZ*, 1980 *W, E*, 1981 *F, W, E, I, R, A*, 1982 *E, I, F, A* 1,2, 1983 *I, F, W, E*, 1984 *E, I, F, R, A*, 1985 *I, F, W, E*, 1986 *I*, 1987 *F* (R), *W, E, [F, Z, NZ]*, 1988 *E, A*, 1989 *E, I, F*
Robertson, L (London Scottish, United Services) 1908 *E*, 1911 *W*, 1912 *W, I, E, SA*, 1913 *W, I, E*
Robertson, M A (Gala) 1958 *F*
Robertson, R D (London Scottish) 1912 *F*
Robson, A (Hawick) 1954 *F*, 1955 *F, W, I, E*, 1956 *F, W, I, E*, 1957 *F, W, I, E*, 1958 *W, A, I, E*, 1959 *F, W, I, E*, 1960 *F*
Rodd, J A T (United Services, RN, London Scottish) 1958 *F, W, A, I, E*, 1960 *F, W*, 1962 *F*, 1964 *F, NZ, W*, 1965 *F, W, I*
Rogerson, J (Kelvinside Acads) 1894 *W*
Roland, E T (Edinburgh Acads) 1884 *I, E*
Rollo, D M D (Howe of Fife) 1959 *E*, 1960 *F, W, I, E, SA*, 1961 *F, SA, W, I, E*, 1962 *F, W, E*, 1963 *F, W, I, E*, 1964 *F, NZ, W, I, E*, 1965 *F, W, I, E, SA*, 1966 *F, W, I, E, A*, 1967 *F, W, E, NZ*, 1968 *F, W, I*
Rose, D M (Jedforest) 1951 *F, W, I, E, SA*, 1953 *F, W*
Ross, A (Kilmarnock) 1924 *F, W*
Ross, A (Royal HSFP) 1905 *W, I, E*, 1909 *W, I*
Ross, A R (Edinburgh U) 1911 *W*, 1914 *W, I, E*
Ross, E J (London Scottish) 1904 *W*
Ross, G T (Watsonians) 1954 *NZ, I, E, W*
Ross, I A (Hillhead HSFP) 1951 *F, W, I, E*
Ross, J (London Scottish) 1901 *W, I, E*, 1902 *W*, 1903 *E*
Ross, K I (Boroughmuir FP) 1961 *SA, W, I, E*, 1962 *F, W, I, E*, 1963 *F, W, E*
Ross, W A (Hillhead HSFP) 1937 *W, E*
Rottenburg, H (Cambridge U, London Scottish) 1899 *W, E*, 1900 *W, I, E*
Roughead, W N (Edinburgh Acads, London Scottish) 1927 *NSW*, 1928 *F, W, I, E*, 1930 *I, E*, 1931 *F, W, I, E*, 1932 *W*
Rowan, N A (Boroughmuir) 1980 *W, E*, 1981 *F, W, E, I*, 1984 *R*, 1985 *I*, 1987 *[R]*, 1988 *I, F, W, E*
Rowand, R (Glasgow HSFP) 1930 *F, W*, 1932 *E*, 1933 *W, E, I*, 1934 *W*
Roy, A (Waterloo) 1938 *W, I, E*, 1939 *W, I, E*
Russell, W L (Glasgow Acads) 1905 *NZ*, 1906 *W, I, E*
Rutherford, J Y (Selkirk) 1979 *W, E, I, F, NZ*, 1980 *I, F, E*, 1981 *F, W, E, I, NZ* 1,2, *A*, 1982 *E, I, F, W*, *A* 1,2, 1983 *E, NZ*, 1984 *W, E, I, F, R*, 1985 *I, F, W, E*, 1986 *F, W, E, I, R*, 1987 *I, F, W, E, [F]*

Sampson, R W F (London Scottish) 1939 *W*, 1947 *W*
Sanderson, G A (Royal HSFP) 1907 *W, I, E*, 1908 *I*
Sanderson, J L P (Edinburgh Acads) 1873 *E*
Schulze, D G (London Scottish) 1905 *E*, 1907 *I, E*, 1908 *W, I, E*, 1909 *W, I, E*, 1910 *W, I, E*, 1911 *W*
Scobie, R M (Royal Military Coll) 1914 *W, I, E*
Scotland, K J F (Heriot's FP, Cambridge U, Leicester) 1957 *F, W, I, E*, 1958 *E*, 1959 *F, W, I, E*, 1960 *F, W, I, E*, 1961 *F, SA, W, I, E*, 1962 *F, W, I, E*, 1963 *F, W, I, E*, 1965 *F*
Scott, D M (Langholm, Watsonians) 1950 *I, E*, 1951 *W, I, E, SA*, 1952 *F, W, I*, 1953 *F*
Scott, J M B (Edinburgh Acads) 1907 *E*, 1908 *W, I, E*, 1909 *W, I, E*, 1910 *F, W, I, E*, 1911 *F, W, I*, 1912 *W, I, E, SA*, 1913 *W, I, E*
Scott, J S (St Andrews U) 1950 *E*
Scott, J W (Stewart's Coll FP) 1925 *F, W, I, E*, 1926 *F, W, I, E*, 1927 *F, W, I, E, NSW*, 1928 *F, W, E, NZ*, 1929 *E*, 1930 *F*
Scott, R (Hawick) 1898 *I*, 1900 *I, E*
Scott, T (Langholm, Hawick) 1896 *W*, 1897 *I, E*, 1898 *I, E*, 1899 *I, W, E*, 1900 *W, I, E*

Scott, T M (Hawick) 1893 *E*, 1895 *W*, *I*, *E*, 1896 *W*, *E*, 1897 *I*, *E*, 1898 *I*, *E*, 1900 *W*, *I*
Scott, W P (W of Scotland) 1900 *I*, *E*, 1902 *I*, *E*, 1903 *W*, *I*, *E*, 1904 *W*, *I*, *E*, 1905 *W*, *I*, *E*, *NZ*, 1906 *W*, *I*, *E*, *SA*, 1907 *W*, *I*, *E*
Scoular, J G (Cambridge U) 1905 *NZ*, 1906 *W*, *I*, *E*, *SA*
Selby, J A R (Watsonians) 1920 *W*, *I*
Shackleton, J A P (London Scottish) 1959 *E*, 1963 *F*, *W*, 1964 *NZ*, *W*, 1965 *I*, *SA*
Sharp, G (Stewart's FP, Army) 1960 *F*, 1964 *F*, *NZ*, *W*
Shaw, G D (Sale) 1935 *NZ*, 1936 *W*, 1937 *W*, *I*, *E*, 1939 *I*
Shaw, I (Glasgow HSFP) 1937 *I*
Shaw, J N (Edinburgh Acads) 1921 *W*, *I*
Shaw, R W (Glasgow HSFP) 1934 *W*, *I*, *E*, 1935 *W*, *I*, *E*, *NZ*, 1936 *W*, *I*, *E*, 1937 *W*, *I*, *E*, 1938 *W*, *I*, *E*, 1939 *W*, *I*, *E*
Shedden, D (W of Scotland) 1972 *NZ*, 1973 *F*, *W*, *I*, *E*, *P*, 1976 *W*, *E*, *I*, 1977 *I*, *F*, *W*, 1978 *I*, *F*, *W*
Shillinglaw, R B (Gala, Army) 1960 *I*, *E*, *SA*, 1961 *F*, *SA*
Simmers, B M (Glasgow Acads) 1965 *F*, *W*, 1966 *A*, 1967 *F*, *W*, *I*, 1971 *F* (R)
Simmers, W M (Glasgow Acads) 1926 *W*, *I*, *E*, 1927 *F*, *W*, *I*, *E*, *NSW*, 1928 *F*, *W*, *I*, *E*, 1929 *F*, *W*, *I*, *E*, 1930 *F*, *W*, *I*, *E*, 1931 *F*, *W*, *I*, *E*, 1932 *SA*, *W*, *I*, *E*
Simpson, J W (Royal HSFP) 1893 *I*, *E*, 1894 *W*, *I*, *E*, 1895 *W*, *I*, *E*, 1896 *W*, *I*, 1897 *E*, 1899 *W*, *E*
Simpson, R S (Glasgow Acads) 1923 *I*
Simson, E D (Edinburgh U, London Scottish) 1902 *E*, 1903 *W*, *I*, *E*, 1904 *W*, *I*, *E*, 1905 *W*, *I*, *E*, *NZ*, 1906 *W*, *I*, *E*, 1907 *W*, *I*, *E*
Simson, J T (Watsonians) 1905 *NZ*, 1909 *W*, *I*, *E*, 1910 *F*, *W*, 1911 *I*
Simson, R F (London Scottish) 1911 *E*
Sloan, A T (Edinburgh Acads) 1914 *W*, 1920 *F*, *W*, *I*, *E*, 1921 *F*, *W*, *I*, *E*
Sloan, D A (Edinburgh Acads, London Scottish) 1950 *F*, *W*, *E*, 1951 *W*, *I*, *E*, 1953 *F*
Sloan, T (Glasgow Acads, Oxford U) 1905 *NZ*, 1906 *W*, *SA*, 1907 *W*, *E*, 1908 *W*, 1909 *I*
Smeaton, P W (Edinburgh Acads) 1881 *I*, 1883 *I*, *E*
Smith, A R (Oxford U) 1895 *W*, *I*, *E*, 1896 *W*, *I*, 1897 *I*, *E*, 1898 *I*, *E*, 1900 *I*, *E*
Smith, A R (Cambridge U, Gosforth, Ebbw Vale, Edinburgh Wands) 1955 *W*, *I*, *E*, 1956 *F*, *W*, *I*, *E*, 1957 *F*, *W*, *I*, *E*, 1958 *F*, *W*, *A*, *I*, 1959 *F*, *W*, *I*, *E*, 1960 *F*, *W*, *I*, *E*, *SA*, 1961 *F*, *SA*, *W*, *I*, *E*, 1962 *F*, *W*, *I*, *E*
Smith, D W C (London Scottish) 1949 *F*, *W*, *I*, *E*, 1950 *F*, *W*, *I*, 1953 *I*
Smith, E R (Edinburgh Acads) 1879 *I*
Smith, G K (Kelso) 1957 *I*, *E*, 1958 *F*, *W*, *A*, 1959 *F*, *W*, *I*, *E*, 1960 *F*, *W*, *I*, *E*, 1961 *F*, *SA*, *W*, *I*, *E*
Smith, H O (Watsonians) 1895 *W*, 1896 *W*, *I*, *E*, 1898 *I*, *E*, 1899 *W*, *I*, *E*, 1900 *E*, 1902 *E*
Smith, I S (Oxford U, Edinburgh U) 1924 *W*, *I*, *E*, 1925 *F*, *W*, *I*, *E*, 1926 *F*, *W*, *I*, *E*, 1927 *F*, *I*, *E*, 1929 *F*, *W*, *I*, *E*, 1930 *F*, *W*, *I*, 1931 *F*, *W*, *I*, *E*, 1932 *SA*, *W*, *I*, *E*, 1933 *W*, *E*, *I*
Smith, I S G (London Scottish) 1969 *SA*, 1970 *F*, *W*, *I*, *E*, 1971 *F*, *W*, *I*
Smith, M A (London Scottish) 1970 *W*, *I*, *E*, *A*
Smith, R T (Kelso) 1929 *F*, *W*, *I*, *E*, 1930 *F*, *W*, *I*
Smith, S H (Glasgow Acads) 1877 *I*, 1878 *E*
Smith, T J (Gala) 1983 *E*, *NZ*, 1985 *I*, *F*
Sole, D M B (Bath, Edinburgh Acads) 1986 *F*, *W*, 1987 *I*, *F*, *W*, *E*, [*F*, *Z*, *R*, *NZ*], 1988 *I*, *F*, *W*, *E*, *A*, 1989 *W*, *E*, *I*, *F*
Somerville, D (Edinburgh Inst FP) 1879 *I*, 1882 *I*, 1883 *W*, *I*, *E*, 1884 *W*
Speirs, L M (Watsonians) 1906 *SA*, 1907 *W*, *I*, *E*, 1908 *W*, *I*, *E*, 1910 *F*, *W*, *E*
Spence, K M (Oxford U) 1953 *I*
Spencer, E (Clydedale) 1898 *I*
Stagg, P K (Sale) 1965 *F*, *W*, *E*, *SA*, 1966 *F*, *W*, *I*, *E*, *A*, 1967 *F*, *W*, *I*, *E*, *NZ*, 1968 *F*, *W*, *I*, *E*, *A*, 1969 *F*, *W*, *I* (R), *SA*, 1970 *F*, *W*, *I*, *E*, *A*
Steele, W C C (Langholm, Bedford, RAF, London Scottish) 1969 *E*, 1971 *F*, *W*, *I*, *E* (2(1C)), 1972 *F*, *W*, *E*, *NZ*, 1973 *F*, *W*, *I*, *E*, 1975 *I*, *F*, *W*, *E*, *NZ* (R), 1976 *W*, *E*, *I*, 1977 *E*
Stephen, A E (W of Scotland) 1885 *W*, 1886 *I*

Steven, P D (Heriot's FP) 1984 *A*, 1985 *F*, *W*, *E*
Steven, R (Edinburgh Wands) 1962 *I*
Stevenson, A K (Glasgow Acads) 1922 *F*, 1923 *F*, *W*, *E*
Stevenson, A M (Glasgow U) 1911 *F*
Stevenson, G D (Hawick) 1956 *E*, 1957 *F*, 1958 *F*, *W*, *A*, *I*, *E*, 1959 *W*, *I*, *E*, 1960 *W*, *I*, *E*, *SA*, 1961 *F*, *SA*, *W*, *I*, *E*, 1963 *F*, *W*, *I*, 1964 *E*, 1965 *F*
Stevenson, H J (Edinburgh Acads) 1888 *W*, *I*, 1889 *W*, *I*, 1890 *W*, *I*, *E*, 1891 *W*, *I*, *E*, 1892 *W*, *I*, *E*, 1893 *I*, *E*
Stevenson, L E (Edinburgh U) 1888 *W*
Stevenson, R C (London Scottish) 1897 *I*, *E*, 1898 *E*, 1899 *I*, *W*, *E*
Stevenson, R C (St Andrews U) 1910 *F*, *I*, *E*, 1911 *F*, *W*, *I*
Stevenson, W H (Glasgow Acads) 1925 *F*
Stewart, A K (Edinburgh U) 1874 *E*, 1876 *E*
Stewart, A M (Edinburgh Acads) 1914 *W*
Stewart, C A R (W of Scotland) 1880 *I*, *E*
Stewart, C E B (Kelso) 1960 *W*, 1961 *F*
Stewart, J (Glasgow HSFP) 1930 *F*
Stewart, J L (Edinburgh Acads) 1921 *I*
Stewart, M S (Stewart's Coll FP) 1932 *SA*, *W*, *I*, 1933 *W*, *E*, *I*, 1934 *W*, *I*, *E*
Stewart, W A (London Hospital) 1913 *F*, *W*, *I*, 1914 *W*
Steyn, S S L (Oxford U) 1911 *E*, 1912 *I*
Strachan, G M (Jordanhill) 1971 *E* (C)(R), 1973 *W*, *I*, *E*, *P*
Stronach, R S (Glasgow Acads) 1901 *W*, *E*, 1905 *W*, *I*, *E*
Stuart, C D (W of Scotland) 1909 *I*, 1910 *F*, *W*, *I*, *E*, 1911 *I*, *E*
Stuart, L M (Glasgow HSFP) 1923 *F*, *W*, *I*, *E*, 1924 *F*, 1928 *E*, 1930 *I*, *E*
Suddon, N (Hawick) 1965 *W*, *I*, *E*, *SA*, 1966 *A*, 1968 *E*, *A*, 1969 *F*, *W*, *I*, 1970 *I*, *E*, *A*
Sutherland, W R (Hawick) 1910 *W*, *E*, 1911 *F*, *E*, 1912 *F*, *W*, *E*, *SA*, 1913 *W*, *I*, *E*, 1914 *W*
Swan, J S (Army, London Scottish, Leicester) 1953 *E*, 1954 *F*, *NZ*, *I*, *E*, *W*, 1955 *F*, *W*, *I*, *E*, 1956 *F*, *W*, *I*, *E*, 1957 *F*, *W*, 1958 *F*
Swan, M W (Oxford U, London Scottish) 1958 *F*, *W*, *A*, *I*, *E*, 1959 *F*, *W*, *I*
Sweet, J B (Glasgow HSFP) 1913 *E*, 1914 *I*
Symington, A W (Cambridge U) 1914 *W*, *E*

Tait, A V (Kelso) 1987 [*F*(R), *Z*, *R*, *NZ*], 1988 *I*, *F*, *W*, *E*
Tait, J G (Edinburgh Acads) 1880 *I*, 1885 *I2*
Tait, P W (Royal HSFP) 1935 *E*
Taylor, E G (Oxford U) 1927 *W*, *NSW*
Taylor, R C (Kelvinside-West) 1951 *W*, *I*, *E*, *SA*
Telfer, C M (Hawick) 1968 *A*, 1969 *F*, *W*, *I*, *E*, 1972 *F*, *W*, *E*, 1973 *W*, *I*, *E*, *P*, 1974 *W*, *E*, *I*, 1975 *A*, 1976 *F*
Telfer, J W (Melrose) 1964 *F*, *NZ*, *W*, *I*, *E*, 1965 *F*, *W*, *I*, 1966 *F*, *W*, *I*, *E*, 1967 *W*, *I*, *E*, 1968 *E*, *A*, 1969 *F*, *W*, *I*, *E*, *SA*, 1970 *F*, *W*, *I*
Tennent, J M (W of Scotland) 1909 *W*, *I*, *E*, 1910 *F*, *W*, *E*
Thom, D A (London Scottish) 1934 *W*, 1935 *W*, *I*, *E*, *NZ*
Thom, G (Kirkcaldy) 1920 *F*, *W*, *I*, *E*
Thom, J R (Watsonians) 1933 *W*, *E*, *I*
Thomson, A E (United Services) 1921 *F*, *W*, *E*
Thomson, A M (St Andrews U) 1949 *I*
Thomson, B E (Oxford U) 1953 *F*, *W*, *I*
Thomson, I H M (Heriot's FP, Army) 1951 *W*, *I*, 1952 *F*, *W*, *I*, 1953 *I*, *E*
Thomson, J S (Glasgow Acads) 1871 *E*
Thomson, R H (London Scottish) 1960 *I*, *E*, *SA*, 1961 *F*, *SA*, *W*, *I*, *E*, 1963 *F*, *W*, *I*, *E*, 1964 *F*, *NZ*, *W*
Thomson, W H (W of Scotland) 1906 *SA*
Thomson, W J (W of Scotland) 1899 *W*, *E*, 1900 *W*
Timms, A B (Edinburgh U, Edinburgh Wands) 1896 *W*, 1900 *W*, *I*, 1901 *W*, *I*, *E*, 1902 *W*, *I*, *E*, 1903 *W*, *E*, 1904 *I*, *E*, 1905 *I*, *E*
Tod, H B (Gala) 1911 *F*
Tod, J (Watsonians) 1884 *W*, *I*, *E*, 1885 *W*, *I1,2*, 1886 *W*, *I*, *E*
Todd, J K (Glasgow Acads) 1874 *E*, 1875 *E*
Tolmie, J M (Glasgow HSFP) 1922 *E*
Tomes, A J (Hawick) 1976 *E*, *I*, 1977 *E*, 1978 *I*, *F*, *W*, *E*, *NZ*, 1979 *W*, *E*, *I*, *F*, *NZ*, 1980 *F*, *W*, *E*, 1981 *F*, *W*, *E*, *I*, *NZ* 1,2, *R*, *A*, 1982 *E*, *I*, *F*, *W*, *A* 1,2, 1983 *I*, *F*,

W, 1984 *W*, *E*, *I*, *F*, *R*, *A*, 1985 *W*, *E*, 1987 *I*, *F*, *E* (R), [*F*, *Z*, *R*, *NZ*]

Torrie, T J (Edinburgh Acads) 1877 *E*

Tukalo, I (Selkirk) 1985 *I*, 1987 *I*, *F*, *W*, *E*, [*F*, *Z*, *R*, *NZ*], 1988 *F*, *W*, *E*, *A*, 1989 *W*, *E*, *I*, *F*

Turk, A S (Langholm) 1971 *E* (R)

Turnbull, D J (Hawick) 1987 [*NZ*], 1988 *F*, *E*

Turnbull, F O (Kelso) 1951 *F*, *SA*

Turnbull, G O (W of Scotland) 1896 *I*, *E*, 1897 *I*, *E*, 1904 *W*

Turnbull, P (Edinburgh Acads) 1901 *W*, *I*, *E*, 1902 *W*, *I*, *E*

Turner, F H (Oxford U, Liverpool) 1911 *F*, *W*, *I*, *E*, 1912 *F*, *W*, *I*, *E*, *SA*, 1913 *F*, *W*, *I*, *E*, 1914 *I*, *E*

Turner, J W C (Gala) 1966 *W*, *A*, 1967 *F*, *W*, *I*, *E*, *NZ*, 1968 *F*, *W*, *I*, *E*, *A*, 1969 *F*, 1970 *E*, *A*, 1971 *F*, *W*, *I*, *E* (2[1C])

Usher, C M (United Services, Edinburgh Wands) 1912 *E*, 1913 *F*, *W*, *I*, *E*, 1914 *E*, 1920 *F*, *W*, *I*, *E*, 1921 *W*, *E*, 1922 *F*, *W*, *I*, *E*

Valentine, A R (RNAS, Anthorn) 1953 *F*, *W*, *I*

Valentine, D D (Hawick) 1947 *I*, *E*

Veitch, J P (Royal HSFP) 1882 *E*, 1883 *I*, 1884 *W*, *I*, *E*, 1885 *I*1,2, 1886 *E*

Villar, C (Edinburgh Wands) 1876 *E*, 1877 *I*, *E*

Waddell, G H (London Scottish, Cambridge U) 1957 *E*, 1958 *F*, *W*, *A*, *I*, *E*, 1959 *F*, *W*, *I*, *E*, 1960 *I*, *E*, *SA*, 1961 *F*, 1962 *F*, *W*, *I*, *E*

Waddell, H (Glasgow Acads) 1924 *F*, *W*, *I*, *E*, 1925 *I*, *E*, 1926 *F*, *W*, *I*, *E*, 1927 *F*, *W*, *I*, *E*, 1930 *W*

Wade, A L (London Scottish) 1908 *E*

Walker, A (W of Scotland) 1881 *I*, 1882 *E*, 1883 *W*, *I*, *E*

Walker, A W (Cambridge U, Birkenhead Park) 1931 *F*, *W*, *I*, *E*, 1932 *I*

Walker, J G (W of Scotland) 1882 *E*, 1883 *W*

Walker, M (Oxford U) 1952 *F*

Wallace, A C (Oxford U) 1923 *F*, 1924 *F*, *W*, *E*, 1925 *F*, *W*, *I*, *E*, 1926 *F*

Wallace, W M (Cambridge U) 1913 *E*, 1914 *W*, *I*, *E*

Walls, W A (Glasgow Acads) 1882 *E*, 1883 *W*, *I*, *E*, 1884 *W*, *I*, *E*, 1886 *W*, *I*, *E*

Walter, M W (London Scottish) 1906 *I*, *E*, *SA*, 1907 *W*, *I*, 1908 *W*, *I*, 1910 *I*

Warren, J R (Glasgow Acads) 1914 *I*

Warren, R C (Glasgow Acads) 1922 *W*, *I*, 1930 *W*, *I*, *E*

Waters, F H (Cambridge U, London Scottish) 1930 *F*, *W*, *I*, *E*, 1932 *SA*, *W*, *I*

Waters, J A (Selkirk) 1933 *W*, *E*, *I*, 1934 *W*, *I*, *E*, 1935 *W*, *I*, *E*, *NZ*, 1936 *W*, *I*, *E*, 1937 *W*, *I*, *E*

Waters, J B (Cambridge U) 1904 *I*, *E*

Watherston, J G (Edinburgh Wands) 1934 *I*, *E*

Watherston, W R A (London Scottish) 1963 *F*, *W*, *I*

Watson, D H (Glasgow Acads) 1876 *E*, 1877 *I*, *E*

Watson, W S (Boroughmuir) 1974 *W*, *E*, *I*, *F*, 1975 *NZ*, 1977 *I*, *F*, *W*, 1979 *I*, *F*

Watt, A G M (Edinburgh Acads) 1947 *F*, *W*, *I*, *A*, 1948 *F*, *W*

Weatherstone, T G (Stewart's Coll FP) 1952 *E*, 1953 *I*, *E*, 1954 *F*, *NZ*, *I*, *E*, *W*, 1955 *F*, 1958 *W*, *A*, *I*, *E*, 1959 *W*, *I*, *E*

Welsh, R (Watsonians) 1895 *W*, *I*, *E*, 1896 *W*

Welsh, R B (Hawick) 1967 *I*, *E*

Welsh, W B (Hawick) 1927 *NSW*, 1928 *F*, *W*, *I*, 1929 *I*, *E*, 1930 *F*, *W*, *I*, *E*, 1931 *F*, *W*, *I*, *E*, 1932 *SA*, *W*, *I*, *E*, 1933 *W*, *E*, *I*

Welsh, W H (Edinburgh U) 1900 *I*, *E*, 1901 *W*, *I*, *E*, 1902 *W*, *I*, *E*

Wemyss, A (Gala, Edinburgh Wands) 1914 *W*, *I*, 1920 *F*, *E*, 1922 *F*, *W*, *I*

West, L (Edinburgh U, West Hartlepool) 1903 *W*, *I*, *E*, 1905 *I*, *E*, *NZ*, 1906 *W*, *I*, *E*

Weston, V G (Kelvinside Acads) 1936 *I*, *E*

White, D B (Gala, London Scottish) 1982 *F*, *W*, *A* 1,2, 1987 *W*, *E*, [*F*, *R*, *NZ*], 1988 *I*, *F*, *W*, *E*, *A*, 1989 *W*, *E*, *I*, *F*

White, D M (Kelvinside Acads) 1963 *F*, *W*, *I*, *E*

White, T B (Edinburgh Acads) 1888 *W*, *I*, 1889 *W*

Whittington, T P (Merchistonians) 1873 *E*

Whitworth, R J E (London Scottish) 1936 *I*

Whyte, D J (Edinburgh Wands) 1965 *W*, *I*, *E*, *SA*, 1966 *F*, *W*, *I*, *E*, *A*, 1967 *F*, *W*, *I*, *E*

Will, J G (Cambridge U) 1912 *F*, *W*, *I*, *E*, 1914 *W*, *I*, *E*

Wilson, A W (Dunfermline) 1931 *F*, *I*, *E*

Wilson, G A (Oxford U) 1949 *F*, *W*, *E*

Wilson, G R (Royal HSFP) 1886 *E*, 1890 *W*, *I*, *E*, 1891 *I*

Wilson, J H (Watsonians) 1953 *I*

Wilson, J S (St Andrews U) 1931 *F*, *W*, *I*, *E*, 1932 *E*

Wilson, J S (United Services, London Scottish) 1908 *I*, 1909 *W*

Wilson, R (London Scottish) 1976 *E*, *I*, 1977 *E*, *I*, *F*, 1978 *I*, *F*, 1981 *R*, 1983 *I*

Wilson, R L (Gala) 1951 *F*, *W*, *I*, *E*, *SA*, 1953 *F*, *W*, *E*

Wilson, R W (W of Scotland) 1873 *E*, 1874 *E*

Wilson, S (Oxford U, London Scottish) 1964 *F*, *NZ*, *W*, *I*, *E*, 1965 *W*, *I*, *E*, *SA*, 1966 *F*, *W*, *I*, *A*, 1967 *F*, *W*, *I*, *E*, *NZ*, 1968 *F*, *W*, *I*, *E*

Wood, A (Royal HSFP) 1873 *E*, 1874 *E*, 1875 *E*

Wood, G (Gala) 1931 *W*, *I*, 1932 *W*, *I*, *E*

Woodburn, J C (Kelvinside Acads) 1892 *I*

Woodrow, A N (Glasgow Acads) 1887 *I*, *W*, *E*

Wotherspoon, W (W of Scotland) 1891 *I*, 1892 *I*, 1893 *W*, *E*, 1894 *W*, *I*, *E*

Wright, F A (Edinburgh Acads) 1932 *E*

Wright, H B (Watsonians) 1894 *W*

Wright, K M (London Scottish) 1929 *F*, *W*, *I*, *E*

Wright, R W J (Edinburgh Acads) 1973 *F*

Wright, S T H (Stewart's Coll FP) 1949 *E*

Wright, T (Hawick) 1947 *A*

Wyllie, D S (Stewart's-Melville FP) 1984 *A*, 1985 *W* (R), *E*, 1987 *I*, *F*, [*F*, *Z*, *R*, *NZ*]

Young, A H (Edinburgh Acads) 1874 *E*

Young, E T (Glasgow Acads) 1914 *E*

Young, R G (Watsonians) 1970 *W*

Young, T E B (Durham) 1911 *F*

Young, W B (Cambridge U, London Scottish) 1937 *W*, *I*, *E*, 1938 *W*, *I*, *E*, 1939 *W*, *I*, *E*, 1948 *E*

SCOTTISH INTERNATIONAL RECORDS

Both team and individual records are for official Scotland international matches, up to 30 April 1989.

TEAM RECORDS

Highest score
60 v Zimbabwe (60-21) 1987 Wellington
v individual countries
24 v Australia (24-15) 1981 Murrayfield
33 v England (33-6) 1986 Murrayfield
31 v France (31-3) 1912 Inverleith
37 v Ireland (37-21) 1989 Murrayfield
25 v N Zealand (25-25) 1983 Murrayfield
55 v Romania (55-28) 1987 Dunedin
10 v S Africa (10-18) 1960 Port Elizabeth
35 v Wales (35-10) 1924 Inverleith
60 v Zimbabwe (60-21) 1987 Wellington

Biggest winning points margin
39 v Zimbabwe (60-21) 1987 Wellington
v individual countries
 9 v Australia (24-15) 1981 Murrayfield
27 v England (33-6) 1986 Murrayfield
28 v France (31-3) 1912 Inverleith
23 v Ireland (32-9) 1984 Dublin
No win v N Zealand
27 v Romania (55-28) 1987 Dunedin
 6 v S Africa (6-0) 1906 Glasgow
25 v Wales (35-10) 1924 Inverleith
39 v Zimbabwe (60-21) 1987 Wellington

Highest score by opposing team
44 S Africa (0-44) 1951 Murrayfield
by individual countries
37 Australia (12-37) 1984 Murrayfield
30 England (18-30) 1980 Murrayfield
28 France (22-28) 1987 Parc des Princes
26 Ireland (8-26) 1953 Murrayfield
40 N Zealand (15-40) 1981 Auckland
28 Romania $\begin{cases} \text{(22-28) 1984 Bucharest} \\ \text{(55-28) 1987 Dunedin} \end{cases}$
44 S Africa (0-44) 1951 Murrayfield
35 Wales (12-35) 1972 Cardiff
21 Zimbabwe (60-21) 1987 Wellington

Biggest losing points margin
44 v S Africa (0-44) 1951 Murrayfield
v individual countries
25 v Australia (12-37) 1984 Murrayfield

20 v England (6-26) 1977 Twickenham
20 v France (3-23) 1977 Parc des Princes
21 v Ireland (0-21) 1950 Dublin
27 v N Zealand (3-30) 1987 Christchurch
 6 v Romania (22-28) 1984 Bucharest
44 v S Africa (0-44) 1951 Murrayfield
23 v Wales (12-35) 1972 Cardiff
No defeat v Zimbabwe

Most tries by Scotland in an international
12 v Wales 1887 Raeburn Place (Edinburgh)

Most tries against Scotland in an international
9 by S Africa (0-44) 1951 Murrayfield

Most points by Scotland in International Championship in a season – 86
in season 1983-84

Most tries by Scotland in International Championship in a season – 17
in season 1924-25

INDIVIDUAL RECORDS

Most capped player
J M Renwick 52 1972-84
C T Deans 52 1978-87
in individual positions
Full-back
A R Irvine 47(51)[1] 1972-82
Wing
A R Smith 33 1955-62
Centre
J M Renwick 51(52)[2] 1972-84
Fly-half
J Y Rutherford 42 1979-87

Scrum-half
R J Laidlaw 47 1980-88
Prop
A B Carmichael 50 1967-78
Hooker
C T Deans 52 1978-87
Lock
A J Tomes 48 1976-87
Flanker
W I D Elliot 29 1947-54
No 8
I A M Paxton 27(36)[3] 1981-88
[1]*Irvine played 4 matches as a wing*
[2]*Renwick played once, as a replacement, on the wing*
[3]*Paxton played 9 matches as a lock*

Longest international career
W C W Murdoch 14 seasons 1935-48

Most internationals as captain
J McLauchlan 19 1973-79

Most points in internationals – 273
A R Irvine (51 matches) 1972-82

**Most points in International
Championship in a season – 52**
A G Hastings (4 matches) 1985-86

Most points in an international – 27
A G Hastings v Romania 1987
    Dunedin

Most tries in internationals – 24
I S Smith (32 matches) 1924-33

**Most tries in International
Championship in a season – 8**
I S Smith (4 matches) 1924-25

Most tries in an international – 5
G C Lindsay v Wales 1887 Raeburn Place
(Edinburgh)

Most conversions in internationals – 30
A G Hastings (18 matches) 1986-88

**Most conversions in International
Championship in a season – 8**
P W Dods (4 matches) 1983-84

Most conversions in an international – 8
A G Hastings v Zimbabwe 1987 Wellington
A G Hastings v Romania 1987 Dunedin

Most dropped goals in internationals – 12
J Y Rutherford (42 matches) 1972-82

Most penalty goals in internationals – 61
A R Irvine (51 matches) 1972-82

**Most penalty goals in International
Championship in a season – 14**
A G Hastings (4 matches) 1985-86

Most points on overseas tour – 56
W Lauder (5 appearances) Australia 1970
A R Irvine (4 appearances) N Zealand
1981
*C D R Mair scored 100 points in the Far East in 1977, but
this was not on a major tour*

Most points in a tour match – 24
D W Morgan v Wellington 1975
    Wellington, (NZ)
A R Irvine v King Country 1981
    Taumarunui, (NZ)
A R Irvine v Wairarapa-Bush 1981
    Masterton, (NZ)
*P W Dods scored 43 points v Alberta in 1985, but this was
not on a major tour*

Most tries in a tour match – 3
A R Smith v Eastern Transvaal 1960
    Springs, (SA)
*K R F Bearne scored 5 tries v Ontario U in 1964, A J W
Hinshelwood scored 5 v Quebec in 1964, and D E W
Leckie scored 5 v Goshawks (Zimbabwe) in 1988, but these
were not on a major tour*

NO SUBSTANTIAL IMPROVEMENTS

THE 1988-89 SEASON IN IRELAND

Sean Diffley *Irish Independent*

After the gloomy 1988 international season, in which six tries were conceded at Twickenham, Ireland's fortunes in 1989 improved only marginally. The third consecutive victory over Wales at Cardiff was not to be sneezed at, but grasping at straws is par for the Irish course at the moment. Irish wins in Wales over the century have not been noted for their frequency but the Irish were realistic enough to accept that this slice of history owed more to Welsh shortcomings than Irish capabilities. But all round, there was a bit more resolve in the Irish defence in the matches in 1989. France got a rare fright when they trailed the Irish at Lansdowne Road; until their backs took the match by the scruff of the neck, there was the prospect of the shock of the season.

England, though clearly the better side, had to fight hard for their win at Lansdowne Road, something that had hardly been necessary the previous season. The Scots at Murrayfield were also very much the superior side. However, despite the obvious deficiencies of the Irish pack, the backs – in particular Brendan Mullin and Paul Dean – still contrived to weave some excellent moves and score tries in the most entertaining match of the series. The Irish sighed for what might have been: if only the forwards had held their own, if only the backs had been given slicker possession and better protection throughout the series.

It was Jimmy Davidson's second season as the Irish team coach and, despite the travails, he managed to retain a remarkable spirit of optimism. He contended that Ireland were back on the rails; that midfield defensive deficiencies had been remedied successfully; that fewer tries were being conceded. He let it be known that his plans were long term, aimed at the 1991 World Cup tournament, and that he didn't expect substantial improvements overnight. But Davidson received his share of fierce criticism during the season, most notably from the former coach, Mick Doyle, who, in his inimitable racy style, poured scorn on Davidson's preoccupation with theory. Doyle found much support for his idea that Davidson's technical approach was totally out of sympathy with the traditional Irish style.

There were other criticisms levelled, too, at Davidson and his fellow selectors. The recall of centre David Irwin may have sealed up the midfield defence but it seemed oddly out of character with the natural attacking, open style of play of the rest of the backs – half-backs Aherne and Dean, centre Mullin and wings Crossan and Kiernan. And the quality of leadership displayed by that excellent flanker, Philip Matthews, also came much into question. Early in the season Matthews was being hailed as a possible Lions captain and he led the Barbarians

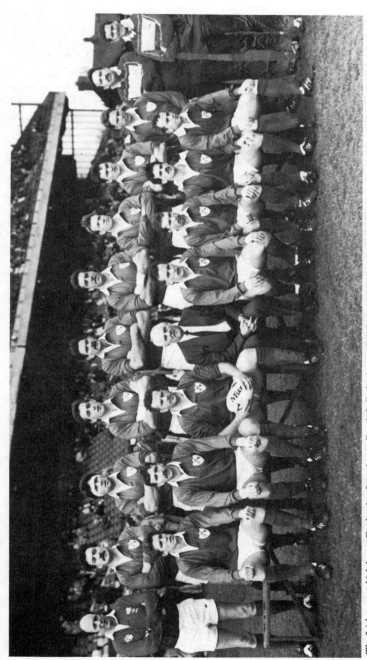

The Irish team which lost to England at Lansdowne Road. L-R, back row: L J Peard (WRU, referee) J J McCoy, T P J Clancy, N P Mannion, W A Anderson, D G Lenihan, P T J O'Hara, S J Smith, F J Dunlea, C Norling (touch-judge), W Jones (touch-judge); front row: B J Mullin, D G Irwin, P M Matthews (capt), T J Kiernan (president, IRFU), M J Kiernan, P M Dean, P P Haycock, L F P Aherne.

against the Australians in late November. However, not only did Matthews fail to win a Lions place for the Australian tour, but in early May he heard the devastating news that he had been relieved of the Irish captaincy for the tour of Canada and the USA in August and September. Incredibly, the selectors and the coach opted for David Irwin instead.

The one constructive move in Irish rugby came when the Irish Rugby Football Union inaugurated the National League. Ireland, until the Union's move, was the only International Board country without a national competition. For many years there had been calls, particularly from respected former players like Mike Gibson and Fergus Slattery, for an All-Ireland league, but many senior clubs, jealous of their status and fearful of losing caste in a promotion-relegation league, opposed the moves tooth and nail. In 1985 a format was proposed but the clubs were lukewarm. So the IRFU decided on a new format for the league, only to find in 1989 that the clubs wanted the original format. There was more than a suspicion that the clubs were more interested in being difficult, rather than being constructive. In the end, and to their great credit, the IRFU imposed the form the new league will take when it begins in season 1990-91. Two divisions of elite clubs will be invited to take part because of their recent records in their provincial leagues.

Ulster, once again, won the Inter-provincial Championship in fine style. Ballymena, cup and league winners in Ulster, was the club of the year. Brendan Mullin was selected by the Irish Rugby Writers as the player of the year.

WINNERS OF PROVINCIAL TOURNAMENTS
LEINSTER
Senior Cup: Lansdowne **Senior League:** St Mary's College **Schools Senior Cup:** Blackrock College **Schools Junior Cup:** Blackrock College
ULSTER
Senior Cup: Ballymena **Senior League:** Ballymena **Schools Senior Cup:** Methodist College **Schools Medallion:** Coleraine Academical
MUNSTER
Senior Cup: Constitution **Senior League:** Shannon **Schools Senior Cup:** Crescent **Schools Junior Cup:** St Munchins
CONNACHT
Senior Cup: University Cóllege, Galway **Senior League:** Corinthians **Schools Senior Cup:** Garbally **Schools Junior Cup:** Sligo Grammar School

INTER-PROVINCIAL TOURNAMENT 1988
22 October, Lansdowne Road

Leinster 23 (5PG 2T) **Munster 12** (4PG)
Leinster: F Dunlea (Lansdowne); J Sexton (Lansdowne), B J Mullin (London Irish), V Cunningham (St Mary's Coll), P Haycock (Terenure Coll); P M Dean (St Mary's Coll), F Aherne (Lansdowne); N Popplewell (Greystones), N Kearney (Old Wesley), D Fitzgerald (Lansdowne), N Francis (London Irish), B Rigney (Bective Rangers), C Pim (Old Wesley), D Fanning (St Mary's Coll), P Kenny (Wanderers)
Scorers *Tries:* Sexton, Mullin *Penalty Goals:* Cunningham (5)
Munster: P P Danaher (Garryowen); K Murphy (Cork Const), M J Kiernan (Dolphin), M Finn (Cork Const), N Barry (Garryowen); R P Keyes (Cork Const), M T Bradley (Cork Const); R Bevan (Highfield), T Kingston (Dolphin), P Clohessy (Young Munster), F Kearney (Sunday's Well), D G Lenihan (Cork Const), P T O'Hara (Sunday's Well), B Spillane (Bohemians), P Horgan (Garryowen)
Scorer *Penalty Goals:* Kiernan (4)
Referee S R Hilditch (Ulster)

22 October, Ravenhill, Belfast

Ulster 16 (1G 2PG 1T) **Connacht 3** (1PG)
Ulster: P Rainey (Ballymena); K Hooks (Bangor), D G Irwin (Instonians), J A Hewitt (London Irish), K D Crossan (Instonians); P Russell (Instonians), R Brady (Ballymena); M Reynolds (Malone), J McDonald (Malone), J J McCoy (Bangor), P Johns (Gosforth), W A Anderson (Dungannon), D McBride (Malone), P M Matthews (Wanderers), D Whittle (London Irish)
Scorers *Tries:* Irwin, Russell *Conversion:* Rainey *Penalty Goals:* Rainey (2)
Connacht: H O'Toole (Corinthians); F O'Flynn (Corinthians), M Cosgrave (Wanderers), J Daly (Corinthians), J Staples (London Irish); C Cruess-Callaghan (Old Belvedere), T Connelly (Corinthians); T Clancy (Lansdowne), J Riordan (UC Galway), D Henshaw (Athlone), M Moylett (Shannon), A Higgins (UC Galway), P Culhane (Corinthians), N Mannion (Corinthians), S Craven (Terenure Coll)
Scorer *Penalty Goal:* Cruess-Callaghan
Referee O E Doyle (Leinster)

12 November, Ravenhill, Belfast

Ulster 18 (1G 3PG 1DG) **Leinster 17** (1G 1PG 2T)
Ulster: C Wilkinson (Malone); T M Ringland (Ballymena), D G Irwin (Instonians), J A Hewitt (London Irish), K D Crossan (Instonians); P Russell (Instonians), R Brady (Ballymena); M Reynolds (Malone), J McDonald (Malone), J J McCoy (Bangor), C Morrison (Malone), J Rogers (Bangor), D McBride (Malone), W A Anderson (Dungannon), D Whittle (London Irish)
Scorers *Try:* Crossan *Conversion:* Russell *Penalty Goals:* Russell (3) *Dropped Goal:* Russell
Leinster: F Dunlea (Lansdowne); J Sexton (Lansdowne), B J Mullin (London Irish), V Cunningham (St Mary's Coll), P Purcell (Lansdowne); P M Dean (St Mary's Coll), F Aherne (Lansdowne); N Popplewell (Greystones), N Kearney (Old Wesley), D Fitzgerald (Lansdowne), M Gibson (London Irish), B Rigney (Bective Rangers), C Pim (Old Wesley), D Fanning (St Mary's Coll), P Kenny (Wanderers)
Scorers *Tries:* Sexton (2), Popplewell *Conversion:* Cunningham *Penalty Goal:* Cunningham
Referee B Smith (Munster)

12 November, Musgrave Park, Cork

Munster 25 (3G 1PG 1T) **Connacht 10** (2PG 1T)
Munster: P P Danaher (Garryowen); K Murphy (Cork Const), M J Kiernan (Dolphin), P Cross (Young Munster), P Murray (Shannon); N Barry (Garryowen), M T Bradley (Cork Const); R Bevan (Highfield), P Derham (Cork Const), P Clohessy (Young Munster), F Kearney (Sunday's Well), D G Lenihan (Cork Const), P T O'Hara (Sunday's Well), B Spillane (Bohemians), M Galwey (Shannon)
Scorers *Tries:* Murray, Danaher, Cross, Spillane *Conversions:* Kiernan (2), Barry *Penalty Goal:* Kiernan
Connacht: J Staples (London Irish); F O'Flynn (Corinthians), M Cosgrave (Wanderers), C Dunne (Blackrock Coll), E Guerin (Galwegians); C Cruess-Callaghan (Old Belvedere), S O'Beirne (St Mary's Coll); T Clancy (Lansdowne), J Riordan (UC Galway), D Henshaw (Athlone), M Moylett (Shannon), A Higgins (UC Galway), C Lydon (Bective Rangers), N Mannion (Corinthians), J B O'Driscoll (Liverpool SH)
Scorers *Try:* O'Driscoll *Penalty Goals:* O'Beirne (2)
Referee D I Templeton (Ulster)

3 December, Thomond Park, Limerick

Munster 9 (3PG) **Ulster 12** (3T)
Munster: P P Danaher (Garryowen); K Murphy (Cork Const), M J Kiernan (Dolphin), M Finn (Cork Const), P Murray (Shannon); R P Keyes (Cork Const), M T Bradley (Cork Const); R Bevan (Highfield), P Derham (Cork Const), P Clohessy (Young Munster), M Galwey (Shannon), D G Lenihan (Cork Const), P T O'Hara (Sunday's Well), N O'Donovan (Shannon), B Spillane (Bohemians)
Scorer *Penalty Goals:* Kiernan (3)
Ulster: P Rainey (Ballymena); K Hooks (Bangor), D G Irwin (Instonians), J A Hewitt (London Irish), K D Crossan (Instonians); P Russell (Instonians), R Brady (Ballymena); M Reynolds (Malone), J McDonald (Malone), J J McCoy (Bangor), P Johns (Gosforth), J J Rogers (Bangor), D McBride (Malone), W A Anderson (Dungannon), P M Matthews (Wanderers)
Scorers *Tries:* Crossan, Matthews, Hooks
Referee R Beamish (Leinster)

3 December, Galway

Connacht 11 (1PG 2T) **Leinster 10** (1G 1T)
Connacht: J Staples (London Irish); F O'Flynn (Corinthians), M Cosgrave (Wanderers), R Hernen (St Mary's Coll), E Guerin (Galwegians); C Cruess-Callaghan (Old Belvedere), S O'Beirne (St Mary's Coll); T Clancy (Lansdowne), J Riordan (UC Galway), D Henshaw (Athlone), M Moylett (Shannon), A Higgins (UC Galway), P Culhane (Corinthians), N Mannion (Corinthians), S Craven (Terenure Coll)
Scorers *Tries:* O'Riordan, Mannion *Penalty Goal:* O'Beirne
Leinster: F Dunlea (Lansdowne); J Sexton (Lansdowne), B J Mullin (London Irish), V Cunningham (St Mary's Coll), N Farren (Old Wesley); P M Dean (St Mary's Coll), F Aherne (Lansdowne); N Popplewell (Greystones), N Kearney (Old Wesley), D Fitzgerald (Lansdowne), N Francis (London Irish), B Rigney (Bective Rangers), C Pim (Old Wesley), D Fanning (St Mary's Coll), P Kenny (Wanderers)
Scorers *Tries:* Aherne, Fanning *Conversion:* Farren
Referee D I Templeton (Ulster)

IRISH INTERNATIONAL PLAYERS
(up to 30 April 1989)

ABBREVIATIONS

A – Australia; *C* – Canada; *E* – England; *F* – France; *It* – Italy; *M* – Maoris; *NSW* – New South Wales; *NZ* – New Zealand; *S* – Scotland; *SA* – South Africa; *P* – Ireland v IRFU President's XV at Lansdowne Road in IRFU centenary season, 1974-75; *R* – Romania; *Tg* – Tonga; *W* – Wales; *WS* – Western Samoa; (R) – Replacement. Entries in square brackets [ ] indicate appearances in the World Cup. NIFC – North of Ireland Football Club; CIYMS – Church of Ireland Young Men's Society; KCH – King's College Hospital

Note: Years given for Five Nations' matches are for second half of season; eg 1972 means season 1971-72. Years for all other matches refer to the actual year of the match. When a series has taken place, figures have been used to denote the particular matches in which players have featured. Thus 1981 *SA* 2 indicates that a player appeared in the second Test of the series. The abandoned game with Scotland at Belfast in 1885 is now included as a cap-match.

NB – The second of Ireland's two matches against France in 1972 was a non-championship match

Abraham, M (Bective Rangers) 1912 *E, S, W, SA*, 1914 *W*
Adams, C (Old Wesley) 1908 *E*, 1909 *E, F*, 1910 *F*, 1911 *E, S, W, F*, 1912 *S, W, SA*, 1913 *W, F*, 1914 *F, E, S*
Agar, R D (Malone) 1947 *F, E, S, W*, 1948 *F*, 1949 *S, W*, 1950 *F, E, W*
Agnew, P J (CIYMS) 1974 *F* (R), 1976 *A*
Ahearne, T (Queen's Coll, Cork) 1899 *E*
Aherne, L F P (Dolphin, Lansdowne) 1988 *E* 2, *WS, It*, 1989 *F, W, E, S*
Alexander, R (NIFC, Police Union) 1936 *E, S, W*, 1937 *E, S, W*, 1938 *E, S*, 1939 *E, S, W*
Allen, C E (Derry, Liverpool) 1900 *E, S, W*, 1901 *E, S, W*, 1903 *S, W*, 1904 *E, S, W*, 1905 *E, S, W, NZ*, 1906 *E, S, W, SA*, 1907 *S, W*
Allen, G G (Derry, Liverpool) 1896 *E, S, W*, 1897 *E, S*, 1898 *E, S*, 1899 *E, W*
Allen, T C (NIFC) 1885 *E, S* 1
Allen, W S (Wanderers) 1875 *E*
Allison, J B (Edinburgh U) 1899 *E, S*, 1900 *E, S, W*, 1901 *E, S, W*, 1902 *E, S, W*, 1903 *S*
Anderson, F E (Queen's U, Belfast, NIFC) 1953 *F, E, S, W*, 1954 *NZ, F, E, S, W*, 1955 *F, E, S, W*
Anderson, H J (Old Wesley) 1903 *E, S*, 1906 *E, S*
Anderson, W A (Dungannon) 1984 *A*, 1985 *S, F, W, E*, 1986 *F, S, R*, 1987 *E, S, F, W*, *[W, C, Tg, A]*, 1988 *S, F, W, E* 1,2, 1989 *F, W, E*
Andrews, G (NIFC) 1875 *E*, 1876 *E*
Andrews, H W (NIFC) 1888 *M*, 1889 *S, W*
Archer, A M (Dublin U, NIFC) 1879 *S*
Arigho, J E (Lansdowne) 1928 *F, E, W*, 1929 *F, E, S, W*, 1930 *F, E, S, W*, 1931 *F, E, S, W, SA*
Armstrong, W K (NIFC) 1960 *SA*, 1961 *E*
Arnott, D T (Lansdowne) 1876 *E*
Ash, W H (NIFC) 1875 *E*, 1876 *E*, 1877 *S*
Aston, H R (Dublin U) 1908 *E, W*
Atkins, A P (Bective Rangers) 1924 *F*
Atkinson, J M (NIFC) 1927 *F, NSW*
Atkinson, J R (Dublin U) 1882 *W, S*

Bagot, J C (Dublin U, Lansdowne) 1879 *S, E*, 1880 *E, S*, 1881 *S*
Bailey, A H (UC Dublin, Lansdowne) 1934 *W*, 1935 *E, S, W, NZ*, 1936 *E, S, W*, 1937 *E, S, W*, 1938 *E, S*
Bailey, N (Northampton) 1952 *E*
Bardon, M E (Bohemians) 1934 *E*
Barlow, M (Wanderers) 1875 *E*
Barnes, R J (Dublin U, Armagh) 1933 *W*
Barr, A (Methodist Coll, Belfast) 1898 *W*, 1899 *S*, 1901 *E, S, W*
Beamish, C E St J (RAF, Leicester) 1933 *W, S*, 1934 *S, W*, 1935 *E, S, W, NZ*, 1936 *E, S, W*, 1938 *W*
Beamish, G R (RAF, Leicester) 1925 *E, S, W*, 1928 *F, E, S, W*, 1929 *F, E, S, W*, 1930 *F, S, W*, 1931 *F, E, S, W, SA*, 1932 *E, S, W*, 1933 *E, W, S*
Beatty, W J (NIFC, Richmond) 1910 *F*, 1912 *F, W*
Becker, V A (Lansdowne) 1974 *F, W*
Beckett, G G P (Dublin U) 1908 *E, S, W*

Bell, R J (NIFC) 1875 *E*, 1876 *E*
Bell, W E (Belfast Collegians) 1953 *F, E, S, W*
Bennett, F (Belfast Collegians) 1913 *S*
Bent, G C (Dublin U) 1882 *W, E*
Berkery, P J (Lansdowne) 1954 *W*, 1955 *W*, 1956 *S, W*, 1957 *F, E, S, W*, 1958 *A, E, S*
Bermingham, J J C (Blackrock Coll) 1921 *E, S, W, F*
Blackham, J C (Queen's Coll, Cork) 1909 *S, W, F*, 1910 *E, S, W*
Blake-Knox, S E F (NIFC) 1976 *E, S*, 1977 *F* (R)
Blayney, J J (Wanderers) 1950 *S*
Bond, A T W (Derry) 1894 *S, W*
Bornemann, W W (Wanderers) 1960 *E, S, W, SA*
Bowen, D St J (Cork Const) 1977 *W, E, S*
Boyd, C A (Dublin U) 1900 *S*, 1901 *S, W*
Boyle, C V (Dublin U) 1935 *NZ*, 1936 *E, S, W*, 1937 *E, S, W*, 1938 *W*, 1939 *W*
Brabazon, H M (Dublin U) 1884 *E*, 1885 *S* 1, 1886 *E*
Bradley, M J (Dolphin) 1920 *W, F*, 1922 *E, S, W, F*, 1923 *E, S, W, F*, 1925 *F, S, W*, 1926 *F, E, S, W*, 1927 *F, W*
Bradley, M T (Cork Constitution) 1984 *A*, 1985 *S, F, W, E*, 1986 *F, S, R*, 1987 *E, S, F*, *[W, C, Tg, A]*, 1988 *S, F, W, E* 1
Bradshaw, G (Belfast Collegians) 1903 *W*
Bradshaw, R M (Wanderers) 1885 *E, S* 1,2
Brady, A M (UC Dublin, Malone) 1966 *S*, 1968 *E, S, W*
Brady, J A (Wanderers) 1976 *E, S*
Brady, J (CIYMS) 1951 *S, W*, 1953 *F, E, S, W*, 1954 *W*, 1956 *W*, 1957 *F, E, S, W*
Bramwell, T (NIFC) 1928 *F*
Brand, T N (NIFC) 1924 *NZ*
Brennan, J I (CIYMS) 1957 *S, W*
Bresnihan, F P K (UC Dublin, Lansdowne, London Irish) 1966 *E, W*, 1967 *A1, E, S, W, F*, 1968 *F, E, S, W, A*, 1969 *F, E, S, W*, 1970 *SA, F, E, S, W*, 1971 *F, E, S, W*
Brett, J T (Monkstown) 1914 *W*
Bristow, J R (NIFC) 1879 *E*
Brophy, N H (Blackrock Coll, UC Dublin, London Irish) 1957 *F, E*, 1959 *E, S, W, F*, 1960 *F, SA*, 1961 *S, W*, 1962 *E, S, W*, 1963 *E, W*, 1967 *E, S, W, F, A2*
Brown, E L (Instonians) 1958 *F*
Brown, G S (Monkstown, United Services) 1912 *S, W, SA*
Brown, H (Windsor) 1877 *E*
Brown, T (Windsor) 1877 *E, S*
Brown, W H (Dublin U) 1899 *E*
Brown, W J (Malone) 1970 *SA, F, S, W*
Brown, W S (Dublin U) 1893 *S, W*, 1894 *E, S, W*
Browne, A W (Dublin U) 1951 *SA*
Browne, D (Blackrock Coll) 1920 *F*
Browne, H C (United Services and RN) 1929 *E, S, W*
Browne, W F (United Services and Army) 1925 *E, S, W*, 1926 *S, W*, 1927 *F, E, S, W, NSW*, 1928 *E, S*
Browning, D R (Wanderers) 1881 *E, S*
Bruce, S A M (NIFC) 1883 *E, S*, 1884 *E*
Brunker, A A (Lansdowne) 1895 *E, W*

Bryant, C H (Cardiff) 1920 E, S
Buchanan, A McM (Dublin U) 1926 E, S, W, 1927 S, W, NSW
Buchanan, J W B (Dublin U) 1882 S, 1884 E, S
Buckley, J H (Sunday's Well) 1973 E, S
Bulger, L Q (Lansdowne) 1896 E, S, W, 1897 E, S, 1898 E, S, W
Bulger, M J (Dublin U) 1888 M
Burges, J H (Rosslyn Park) 1950 F, E
Burgess, R B (Dublin U) 1912 SA
Burkitt, J C S (Queen's Coll, Cork) 1881 E
Burns, I J (Wanderers) 1980 E (R)
Butler, L G (Blackrock Coll) 1960 W
Butler, N (Bective Rangers) 1920 E
Byers, R M (NIFC) 1928 S, W, 1929 E, S, W
Byrne, E M J (Blackrock Coll) 1977 S, F, 1978 F, W, E, NZ
Byrne, N F (UC Dublin) 1962 F
Byrne, S J (UC Dublin, Lansdowne) 1953 S, W, 1955 F
Byron, W G (NIFC) 1896 E, S, W, 1897 E, S, 1898 E, S, W, 1899 E, S, W

Caddell, E D (Dublin U, Wanderers) 1904 S, 1905 E, S, W, NZ, 1906 E, S, W, SA, 1907 E, S, 1908 S, W
Cagney, S J (London Irish) 1925 W, 1926 F, E, S, W, 1927 F, 1928 E, S, W, 1929 F, E, S, W
Callan, C P (Lansdowne) 1947 F, E, S, W, 1948 F, E, S, W, 1949 F, E
Cameron, E D (Bective Rangers) 1891 S, W
Campbell, C E (Old Wesley) 1970 SA
Campbell, E F (Monkstown) 1899 S, W, 1900 E, W
Campbell, S B B (Derry) 1911 E, S, W, F, 1912 F, E, S, W, SA, 1913 E, S, F
Campbell, S O (Old Belvedere) 1976 A, 1979 A 1,2, 1980 E, S, F, W, 1981 F, W, E, S, SA1, 1982 W, E, S, F, 1983 S, F, W, E, 1984 F, W
Canniffe, D M (Lansdowne) 1976 W, E
Cantrell, J L (UC Dublin, Blackrock Coll) 1976 A, F, W, E, S, 1981 S, SA 1,2, A
Carpendale, M J (Monkstown) 1886 S, 1887 W, 1888 W, S
Carr, N J (Ards) 1985 S, F, W, E, 1986 W, E, S, R, 1987 E, S, W
Carroll, C (Bective Rangers) 1930 F
Carroll, R (Lansdowne) 1947 F, 1950 S, W
Casement, B N (Dublin U) 1875 E, 1876 E, 1879 E
Casement, F (Dublin U) 1906 E, S, W
Casey, J C (Young Munster) 1930 S, 1932 E
Casey, P J (UC Dublin, Lansdowne) 1963 F, E, S, W, NZ, 1964 E, S, W, F, 1965 F, E, S
Chambers, J (Dublin U) 1886 E, S, 1887 E, S, W
Chambers, R R (Instonians) 1951 F, E, S, W, 1952 F, W
Clancy, T P J (Lansdowne) 1988 W, E 1,2, WS, It, 1989 F, W, E, S
Clarke, J A B (Bective Rangers) 1922 S, W, F, 1923 F, 1924 E, S, W
Clegg, R J (Bangor) 1973 F, 1975 E, S, F, W
Clifford, J T (Young Munster) 1949 F, E, S, W, 1950 F, E, S, W, 1951 F, E, SA, 1952 F, S, W
Clinch, A D (Dublin U, Wanderers) 1892 S, 1893 W, 1895 E, S, W, 1896 E, S, W, 1897 E, S
Clinch, J D (Wanderers, Dublin U) 1923 W, 1924 F, E, S, W, NZ, 1925 F, E, S, 1926 E, S, W, 1927 F, 1928 F, E, S, W, 1929 F, E, S, W, 1930 F, E, S, W, 1931 F, E, S, W, SA
Clune, J J (Blackrock Coll) 1912 SA, 1913 W, F, 1914 F, E, W
Coffey, J J (Lansdowne) 1900 E, 1901 W, 1902 E, S, W, 1903 E, S, W, 1905 E, S, W, NZ, 1906 E, S, W, SA, 1907 E, 1908 W, 1910 F
Cogan, W St J (Queen's Coll, Cork) 1907 E, S
Collier, S R (Queen's Coll, Belfast) 1883 S
Collins, P C (Lansdowne) 1987 [C]
Collis, W R F (KCH, Harlequins) 1924 F, W, NZ, 1925 F, E, S, 1926 F
Collis, W S (Wanderers) 1884 W
Collopy, G (Bective Rangers) 1891 S, 1892 S
Collopy, R (Bective Rangers) 1923 E, S, W, F, 1924 F, E, S, W, NZ, 1925 F, E, S, W
Collopy, W P (Bective Rangers) 1914 F, E, S, W, 1921 E, S, W, F, 1922 E, S, W, F, 1923 S, W, F, 1924 F, E, S, W
Combe, A (NIFC) 1875 E
Condon, H C (London Irish) 1984 S (R)

Cook, H G (Lansdowne) 1884 W
Coote, P B (RAF, Leicester) 1933 S
Corcoran, J C (London Irish) 1947 A, 1948 F
Corken, T S (Belfast Collegians) 1937 E, S, W
Corley, H H (Dublin U, Wanderers) 1902 E, S, W, 1903 E, S, W, 1904 E, S
Cormac, H S T (Clontarf) 1921 E, S, W
Costello, P (Bective Rangers) 1960 F
Cotton, J (Wanderers) 1889 W
Coulter, H H (Queen's U, Belfast) 1920 E, S, W
Courtney, A W (UC Dublin) 1920 S, W, F, 1921 E, S, W, F
Cox, H L (Dublin U) 1875 E, 1876 E, 1877 E, S
Craig, R G (Queen's U, Belfast) 1938 S, W
Crawford, E C (Dublin U) 1885 E, S 1
Crawford, W E (Lansdowne) 1920 E, S, W, F, 1921 E, S, W, F, 1922 E, S, 1923 E, S, W, F, 1924 F, E, W, NZ, 1925 F, E, S, W, 1926 F, E, S, W, 1927 F, E, S, W
Crean, T J (Wanderers) 1894 E, S, W, 1895 E, S, W, 1896 E, S, W
Crichton, R Y (Dublin U) 1920 E, S, W, F, 1921 F, 1922 E, 1923 W, F, 1924 F, E, S, W, NZ, 1925 E, S
Croker, E W D (Limerick) 1878 E
Cromey, G E (Queen's U, Belfast) 1937 E, S, W, 1938 E, S, W, 1939 E, S, W
Cronyn, A P (Dublin U, Lansdowne) 1875 E, 1876 E, 1880 S
Crossan, K D (Instonians) 1982 S, 1984 F, W, E, S, 1985 S, F, W, E, 1986 E, S, R, 1987 E, S, F, W, [W, C, Tg, A], 1988 S, F, W, E 1, WS, It, 1989 W, S
Crowe, J F (UC Dublin) 1974 NZ
Crowe, L (Old Belvedere) 1950 E, S, W
Crowe, M P (Lansdowne) 1929 W, 1930 E, S, W, 1931 F, S, W, SA, 1932 S, W, 1933 W, S, 1934 E
Crowe, P M (Blackrock Coll) 1935 E, 1938 E
Cullen, T J (UC Dublin) 1949 F
Cullen, W J (Monkstown and Manchester) 1920 E
Culliton, M G (Wanderers) 1959 E, S, W, F, 1960 E, S, W, F, SA, 1961 E, S, W, F, 1962 S, F, 1964 E, S, W, F
Cummins, W E A (Queen's Coll, Cork) 1879 S, 1881 E, 1882 E
Cunningham, D McC (NIFC) 1923 E, S, W, 1925 F, E, W
Cunningham, M J (UC Cork) 1955 F, E, S, W, 1956 F, S, W
Cunningham, V J G (St Mary's Coll) 1988 E 2, It
Cunningham, W A (Lansdowne) 1920 W, 1921 E, S, W, F, 1922 E, S, 1923 S, W
Cuppaidge, J L (Dublin U) 1879 E, 1880 E, S
Currell, J (NIFC) 1877 S
Curtis, A B (Oxford U) 1950 F, E, S
Cuscaden, W A (Dublin U, Bray) 1876 E
Cussen, D J (Dublin U) 1921 E, S, W, F, 1922 E, 1923 E, S, W, F, 1926 F, E, S, W, 1927 F, E

Daly, J C (London Irish) 1947 F, E, S, W, 1948 E, S, W
Daly, M J (Harlequins) 1938 E
Danaher, P P (Lansdowne, Garryowen) 1988 S, F, W, WS, It, 1989 F
Dargan, M J (Old Belvedere) 1952 S, W
Davidson, C T (NIFC) 1921 F
Davidson, I G (NIFC) 1899 E, 1900 S, W, 1901 E, S, W, 1902 E, S, W
Davidson, J C (Dungannon) 1969 F, E, S, W, 1973 NZ, 1976 NZ
Davies, F E (Lansdowne) 1892 S, W, 1893 E, S, W
Davis, J L (Monkstown) 1898 E, S
Davis, W J N (Edinburgh U, Bessbrook) 1890 S, W, E, 1891 E, S, W, 1892 E, S, 1895 S
Davison, W (Belfast Academy) 1887 W
Davy, E O'D (UC Dublin, Lansdowne) 1925 W, 1926 F, E, S, W, 1927 F, E, S, W, NSW, 1928 F, E, S, W, 1929 F, E, S, W, 1930 F, E, S, W, 1931 F, E, S, W, SA, 1932 E, S, 1933 E, W, S, 1934 E
Dawson, A R (Wanderers) 1958 A, E, S, W, F, 1959 E, S, W, F, 1960 F, SA, 1961 E, S, W, F, SA, 1962 S, F, W, 1963 E, W, F, NZ, 1964 E, S, F
Dean, P M (St Mary's Coll) 1981 SA 1,2, A, 1982 W, E, S, F, 1984 A, 1985 S, F, W, E, 1986 F, W, 1987 E, S, F, W, [W, A], 1988 S, F, W, E1,2, WS, It, 1989 F, W, E, S
Deane, E C (Monkstown) 1909 E
Deering, M J (Bective Rangers) 1929 W

209

Deering, S J (Bective Rangers) 1935 *E, S, W, NZ*, 1936 *E, S, W*, 1937 *E, S*
Deering, S M (Garryowen, St Mary's Coll) 1974 *W*, 1976 *F, W, E, S*, 1977 *W, E*, 1978 *NZ*
de Lacy, H (Harlequins) 1948 *E, S*
Delaney, M G (Bective Rangers) 1895 *W*
Dennison, S P (Garryowen) 1973 *F*, 1975 *E, S*
Dick, C J (Ballymena) 1961 *W, F, SA*, 1962 *W*, 1963 *F, E, S, W*
Dick, J S (Queen's U, Belfast) 1962 *E*
Dick, J S (Queen's Coll, Cork) 1887 *E, S, W*
Dickson, J A N (Dublin U) 1920 *E, W, F*
Doherty, A E (Old Wesley) 1974 *P* (R)
Doherty, W D (Guy's Hospital) 1920 *E, S, W*, 1921 *E, S, W, F*
Donaldson, J A (Belfast Collegians) 1958 *A, E, S, W*
Donovan, T M (Queen's Coll, Cork) 1889 *S*
Dooley, J F (Galwegians) 1959 *E, S, W*
Doran, B R W (Lansdowne) 1900 *S, W*, 1901 *E, S, W*, 1902 *E, S, W*
Doran, E F (Lansdowne) 1890 *S, W*
Doran, G P (Lansdowne) 1899 *S, W*, 1900 *E, S*, 1902 *S, W*, 1903 *W*, 1904 *E*
Douglas, A C (Instonians) 1923 *F*, 1924 *E, S*, 1927 *NSW*, 1928 *S*
Downing, A J (Dublin U) 1882 *W*
Dowse, J C A (Monkstown) 1914 *F, S, W*
Doyle, J A P (Greystones) 1984 *E, S*
Doyle, J T (Bective Rangers) 1935 *W*
Doyle, M G (Blackrock Coll, UC Dublin, Cambridge U, Edinburgh Wands) 1965 *F, E, S, W, SA*, 1966 *F, E, S, W*, 1967 *A* 1, *E, S, W, F, A* 2, 1968 *F, E, S, W, A*
Doyle, T J (Wanderers) 1968 *E, S, W*
Duggan, A T A (Lansdowne) 1963 *NZ*, 1964 *F*, 1966 *W*, 1967 *A* 1, *S, W, A* 2, 1968 *F, E, S, W*, 1969 *F, E, S, W*, 1970 *SA, F, E, S, W*, 1971 *F, E, S, W*, 1972 *F* 2
Duggan, W (UC Cork) 1920 *S, W*
Duggan, W P (Blackrock Coll) 1975 *E, S, F, W*, 1976 *A, F, W, S, NZ*, 1977 *W, E, S, F*, 1978 *S, F, W, E, NZ*, 1979 *E, S, A* 1,2, 1980 *F*, 1981 *F, W, E, S, SA* 1,2, *A*, 1982 *W, E, S*, 1983 *S, F, W, E*, 1984 *F, W, E, S*
Duncan, W R (Malone) 1984 *W, E*
Dunlea, F J (Lansdowne) 1989 *W, E, S*
Dunlop, R (Dublin U) 1889 *W*, 1890 *S, W, E*, 1891 *E, S, W*, 1892 *E, S*, 1893 *W*, 1894 *W*
Dunn, P E F (Bective Rangers) 1923 *S*
Dunn, T B (NIFC) 1935 *NZ*
Dunne, M J (Lansdowne) 1929 *F, E, S*, 1930 *F, E, S, W*, 1932 *E, S, W*, 1933 *E, W, S*, 1934 *E, S, W*
Dwyer, P J (UC Dublin) 1962 *W*, 1963 *F, NZ*, 1964 *S, W*

Edwards, H G (Dublin U) 1877 *E*, 1878 *E*
Edwards, R W (Malone) 1904 *W*
Edwards, T (Lansdowne) 1888 *M*, 1890 *S, W, E*, 1892 *W*, 1893 *E*
Edwards, W V (Malone) 1912 *F, E*
Egan, J D (Bective Rangers) 1922 *S*
Egan, J T (Cork Constitution) 1931 *F, E, SA*
Egan, M S (Garryowen) 1893 *E*, 1895 *S*
Ekin, W (Queen's Coll, Belfast) 1888 *W, S*
Elliott, W R J (Bangor) 1979 *S*
English, M A F (Lansdowne, Limerick Bohemians) 1958 *W, F*, 1959 *E, S, F*, 1960 *E, S*, 1961 *S, W, F*, 1962 *F, W*, 1963 *E, S, W, NZ*
Ennis, F N G (Wanderers) 1979 *A* 1 (R)
Ensor, A H (Wanderers) 1973 *W, F*, 1974 *F, W, E, S, P, NZ*, 1975 *E, S, F, W*, 1976 *A, F, W, E, NZ*, 1977 *E*, 1978 *S, F, W, E*
Entrican, J C (Queen's U, Belfast) 1931 *S*

Fagan, G L (Kingstown School) 1878 *E*
Fagan, W B C (Wanderers) 1956 *F, E, S*
Farrell, J L (Bective Rangers) 1926 *F, E, S, W*, 1927 *F, E, S, W, NSW*, 1928 *F, E, S, W*, 1929 *F, E, S, W*, 1930 *F, E, S, W*, 1931 *F, E, S, W, SA*, 1932 *E, S, W*
Feddis, N (Lansdowne) 1956 *E*
Feighery, C F P (Lansdowne) 1972 *F* 1, *E, F2*
Feighery, T A O (St Mary's Coll) 1977 *W, E*
Ferris, H H (Queen's Coll, Belfast) 1901 *W*
Ferris, J H (Queen's Coll, Belfast) 1900 *E, S, W*
Finlay, J E (Queen's Coll, Belfast) 1913 *E, S, W*, 1920 *E, S, W*

Finlay, W (NIFC) 1876 *E*, 1877 *E, S*, 1878 *E*, 1879 *S, E*, 1880 *S*, 1882 *S*
Finn, M C (UC Cork, Cork Constitution) 1979 *E*, 1982 *W, E, S, F*, 1983 *S, F, W, E*, 1984 *E, S, A*, 1986 *F, W*
Finn, R G A (UC Dublin) 1977 *F*
Fitzgerald, C C (Glasgow U, Dungannon) 1902 *E*, 1903 *E, S*
Fitzgerald, C F (St Mary's Coll) 1979 *A* 1,2, 1980 *E, S, F, W*, 1982 *W, E, S, F*, 1983 *S, F, W, E*, 1984 *F, W, A*, 1985 *S, F, W, E*, 1986 *F, W, E, S*
Fitzgerald, D C (Lansdowne) 1984 *E, S*, 1986 *W, E, S, R*, 1987 *E, S, F, W*, [*W, C, A*], 1988 *S, F, W, E* 1
Fitzgerald, J (Wanderers) 1884 *W*
Fitzgerald, J J (Young Munster) 1988 *S, F*
Fitzpatrick, M P (Wanderers) 1978 *S*, 1980 *S, F, W*, 1981 *F, W, E, S, A*, 1985 *F* (R)
Fletcher, W W (Kingstown) 1882 *W, S*, 1883 *E*
Flood, R S (Dublin U) 1925 *W*
Flynn, M K (Wanderers) 1959 *F*, 1960 *F*, 1962 *E, S, F, W*, 1964 *E, S, W, F*, 1965 *F, E, S, W, SA*, 1966 *F, E, S*, 1972 *F* 1, *E, F* 2, 1973 *NZ*
Fogarty, T (Garryowen) 1891 *W*
Foley, B O (Shannon) 1976 *F, E*, 1977 *W* (R), 1980 *F, W*, 1981 *F, E, S, SA* 1,2, *A*
Forbes, R E (Malone) 1907 *E*
Forrest, A J (Wanderers) 1880 *E, S*, 1881 *E, S*, 1882 *W, E*, 1883 *E*, 1885 *S* 2
Forrest, E G (Wanderers) 1888 *M*, 1889 *S, W*, 1890 *S, E*, 1891 *E*, 1893 *S*, 1894 *E, S, W*, 1895 *W*, 1897 *E, S*
Forrest, H (Wanderers) 1893 *S, W*
Fortune, J J (Clontarf) 1963 *NZ*, 1964 *E*
Foster, A R (Derry) 1910 *E, S, F*, 1911 *E, S, W, F*, 1912 *F, E, S, W*, 1914 *E, S, W*, 1921 *E, S, W*
Francis, N P T (Blackrock Coll, London Irish) 1987 [*Tg, A*], 1988 *WS, It*, 1989 *S*
Franks, J G (Dublin U) 1898 *E, S, W*
Frazer, E F (Bective Rangers) 1891 *S*, 1892 *S*
Freer, A E (Lansdowne) 1901 *E, S, W*
Fulton, J (NIFC) 1895 *S, W*, 1896 *E*, 1897 *E*, 1898 *W*, 1899 *E*, 1900 *W*, 1901 *E*, 1902 *E, S, W*, 1903 *E, S, W*, 1904 *E, S*

Gaffikin, W (Windsor) 1875 *E*
Gage, J H (Queen's U, Belfast) 1926 *S, W*, 1927 *S, W*
Galbraith, E (Dublin U) 1875 *E*
Galbraith, H T (Belfast Acad) 1890 *W*
Galbraith, R (Dublin U) 1875 *E*, 1876 *E*, 1877 *E*
Ganly, J B (Monkstown) 1927 *F, E, S, W, NSW*, 1928 *F, E, S, W*, 1929 *F, S*, 1930 *F*
Gardiner, F (NIFC) 1900 *E, S*, 1901 *E, W*, 1902 *E, S, W*, 1903 *E, W*, 1904 *E, S, W*, 1906 *E, S, W*, 1907 *S, W*, 1908 *S, W*, 1909 *E, S, F*
Gardiner, J B (NIFC) 1923 *E, S, W, F*, 1924 *F, E, S, W, NZ*, 1925 *F, E, S, W*
Gardiner, S (Belfast Albion) 1893 *E, S*
Gardiner, W (NIFC) 1892 *E, S*, 1893 *E, S, W*, 1894 *E, S, W*, 1895 *E, S, W*, 1896 *E, S, W*, 1897 *E, S*, 1898 *W*
Garry, M G (Bective Rangers) 1909 *E, S, W, F*, 1911 *E, S, W*
Gaston, J T (Dublin U) 1954 *NZ, F, E, S, W*, 1955 *W*, 1956 *F, E*
Gavin, T J (Moseley, London Irish) 1949 *F, E*
Gibson, C M H (Cambridge U, NIFC) 1964 *E, S, W, F*, 1965 *F, E, S, W, SA*, 1966 *F, E, S, W*, 1967 *A* 1, *E, S, W, F, A* 2, 1968 *E, S, W, A*, 1969 *E, S, W*, 1970 *SA, F, E, S, W*, 1971 *F, E, S, W*, 1972 *F* 1, *E, F* 2, 1973 *NZ, E, S, W, F*, 1974 *W, E, S, P*, 1975 *E, S, F, W*, 1976 *A, F, W, E, S, NZ*, 1977 *W, E, S, F*, 1978 *F, W, E, NZ*, 1979 *S, A* 1,2
Gibson, M E (Lansdowne, London Irish) 1979 *F, W, E, S*, 1981 *W* (R), 1986 *R*, 1988 *S, F, W, E* 2
Gifford, H P (Wanderers) 1890 *S*
Gillespie, J C (Dublin U) 1922 *W, F*
Gilpin, F G (Queen's U, Belfast) 1962 *E, S, F*
Glass, D C (Belfast Collegians) 1958 *F*, 1960 *W*, 1961 *W, SA*
Glennon, J J (Skerries) 1980 *E, S*, 1987 *E, S, F*, [*W* (R)]
Godfrey, R P (UC Dublin) 1954 *S, W*
Goodall, K G (City of Derry and Newcastle U) 1967 *A* 1, *E, S, W, F, A* 2, 1968 *F, E, S, W, A*, 1969 *F, E, S*, 1970 *SA, F, E, S, W*
Gordon, A (Dublin U) 1884 *S*

Gordon, T G (NIFC) 1877 *E*, *S*, 1878 *E*
Gotto, R P C (NIFC) 1906 *SA*
Goulding, W J (Cork) 1879 *S*
Grace, T O (UC Dublin, St Mary's Coll) 1972 *F* 1, *E*,
1973 *NZ*, *E*, *S*, *W*, 1974 *E*, *S*, *P*, *NZ*, 1975 *E*, *S*, *F*, *W*,
1976 *A*, *F*, *W*, *E*, *S*, *NZ*, 1977 *W*, *E*, *S*, *F*, 1978 *S*
Graham, R I (Dublin U) 1911 *F*
Grant, E L (CIYMS) 1971 *F*, *E*, *S*, *W*
Grant, P J (Bective Rangers) 1894 *S*, *W*
Graves, C R A (Wanderers) 1934 *E*, *S*, *W*, 1935 *E*, *S*,
W, *NZ*, 1936 *E*, *S*, *W*, 1937 *E*, *S*, 1938 *E*, *S*, *W*
Gray, R D (Old Wesley) 1923 *E*, *S*, 1925 *F*, 1926 *F*
Greene, E H (Dublin U, Kingstown) 1882 *W*, 1884 *W*,
1885 *E*, *S* 2, 1886 *E*
Greer, R (Kingstown) 1876 *E*
Greeves, T J (NIFC) 1907 *E*, *S*, *W*, 1909 *W*, *F*
Gregg, R J (Queen's U, Belfast) 1953 *F*, *E*, *S*, *W*, 1954
F, *E*, *S*
Griffin, C S (London Irish) 1951 *F*, *E*
Griffin, J L (Wanderers) 1949 *S*, *W*
Griffiths, W (Limerick) 1878 *E*
Grimshaw, C (Queen's U, Belfast) 1969 *E* (R)
Guerin, B N (Galwegians) 1956 *S*
Gwynn, A P (Dublin U) 1895 *W*
Gwynn, L H (Dublin U) 1893 *S*, 1894 *E*, *S*, *W*, 1897 *S*,
1898 *E*, *S*

Hakin, R F (CIYMS) 1976 *W*, *S*, *NZ*, 1977 *W*, *E*, *F*
Hall, R O N (Dublin U) 1884 *W*
Hall, W H (Instonians) 1923 *E*, *S*, *W*, *F*, 1924 *F*, *S*
Hallaran, C F G T (Royal Navy) 1921 *E*, *S*, *W*, 1922 *E*,
S, *W*, 1923 *E*, *F*, 1924 *F*, *E*, *S*, *W*, 1925 *F*, 1926 *F*, *E*
Halpin, T (Garryowen) 1909 *S*, *W*, *F*, 1910 *E*, *S*, *W*,
1911 *E*, *S*, *W*, *F*, 1912 *F*, *E*, *S*
Hamilton, A J (Lansdowne) 1884 *W*
Hamilton, R L (NIFC) 1926 *F*
Hamilton, R W (Wanderers) 1893 *W*
Hamilton, W J (Dublin U) 1877 *E*
Hamlet, G T (Old Wesley) 1902 *E*, *S*, *W*, 1903 *E*, *S*,
W, 1904 *S*, *W*, 1905 *E*, *S*, *W*, *NZ*, 1906 *SA*, 1907 *E*, *S*,
W, 1908 *E*, *S*, *W*, 1909 *E*, *S*, *W*, *F*, 1910 *E*, *S*, *F*, 1911
E, *S*, *W*, *F*
Hanrahan, C J (Dolphin) 1926 *S*, *W*, 1927 *E*, *S*, *W*,
NSW, 1928 *F*, *E*, *S*, 1929 *F*, *E*, *S*, *W*, 1930 *F*, *E*, *S*, *W*,
1931 *F*, 1932 *S*, *W*
Harbison, H T (Bective Rangers) 1984 *W* (R), *E*, *S*,
1986 *R*, 1987 *E*, *S*, *F*, *W*
Hardy, G G (Bective Rangers) 1962 *S*
Harman, G R A (Dublin U) 1899 *E*, *W*
Harper, J (Instonians) 1947 *F*, *E*, *S*
Harpur, T G (Dublin U) 1908 *E*, *S*, *W*
Harrison, T (Cork) 1879 *S*, 1880 *S*, 1881 *E*
Harvey, F M W (Wanderers) 1907 *W*, 1911 *F*
Harvey, G A D (Wanderers) 1903 *E*, *S*, 1904 *W*, 1905
E, *S*
Harvey, T A (Dublin U) 1900 *W*, 1901 *S*, *W*, 1902 *E*,
S, *W*, 1903 *E*, *W*
Haycock, P P (Terenure Coll) 1989 *E*
Headon, T A (UC Dublin) 1939 *S*, *W*
Healey, P (Limerick) 1901 *E*, *S*, *W*, 1902 *E*, *S*, *W*,
1903 *E*, *S*, *W*, 1904 *S*
Heffernan, M R (Cork Constitution) 1911 *E*, *S*, *W*, *F*
Hemphill, R (Dublin U) 1912 *F*, *E*, *S*, *W*
Henderson, N J (Queen's U, Belfast, NIFC) 1949 *S*,
W, 1950 *F*, 1951 *F*, *E*, *S*, *W*, *SA*, 1952 *F*, *S*, *W*, *E*, 1953
F, *E*, *S*, *W*, 1954 *NZ*, *F*, *E*, *S*, *W*, 1955 *F*, *E*, *S*, *W*,
1956 *S*, *W*, 1957 *F*, *E*, *S*, *W*, 1958 *A*, *E*, *S*, *W*, *F*, 1959
E, *S*, *W*, *F*
Henebrey, G J (Garryowen) 1906 *E*, *S*, *W*, *SA*, 1909
W, *F*
Heron, A G (Queen's Coll, Belfast) 1901 *E*
Heron, J (NIFC) 1877 *S*, 1879 *E*
Heron, W T (NIFC) 1880 *E*, *S*
Herrick, R W (Dublin U) 1886 *S*
Heuston, F S (Kingstown) 1882 *W*, 1883 *E*, *S*
Hewitt, D (Queen's U, Belfast, Instonians) 1958 *A*, *E*,
S, *F*, 1959 *S*, *W*, *F*, 1960 *E*, *S*, *W*, *F*, 1961 *E*, *S*, *W*, *F*,
1962 *S*, *F*, 1965 *W*
Hewitt, F S (Instonians) 1924 *W*, *NZ*, 1925 *F*, *E*, *S*,
1926 *E*, 1927 *E*, *S*, *W*
Hewitt, J A (NIFC) 1981 *SA* 1 (R), 2 (R)
Hewitt, T R (Queen's U, Belfast) 1924 *W*, *NZ*, 1925 *F*,
E, *S*, 1926 *F*, *E*, *S*, *W*

Hewitt, V A (Instonians) 1935 *S*, *W*, *NZ*, 1936 *E*, *S*, *W*
Hewitt, W J (Instonians) 1954 *E*, 1956 *S*, 1959 *W*, 1961
SA
Hewson, F T (Wanderers) 1875 *E*
Hickie, D J (St Mary's Coll) 1971 *F*, *E*, *S*, *W*, 1972 *F* 1,
E
Higgins, J A D (Civil Service) 1947 *S*, *W*, *A*, 1948 *F*, *S*, *W*
Higgins, W W (NIFC) 1884 *E*, *S*
Hillary, M F (UC Dublin) 1952 *E*
Hingerty, D J (UC Dublin) 1947 *F*, *E*, *S*, *W*
Hinton, W P (Old Wesley) 1907 *W*, 1908 *E*, *S*, *W*, 1909
E, *S*, 1910 *E*, *S*, *W*, *F*, 1911 *E*, *S*, *W*, 1912 *F*, *E*, *W*
Hipwell, M L (Terenure Coll) 1962 *E*, *S*, 1968 *F*, *A*,
1969 *F* (R), *S* (R), *W*, 1971 *F*, *E*, *S*, *W*, 1972 *F* 2
Hobbs, T H M (Dublin U) 1884 *S*, 1885 *E*
Hobson, E W (Dublin U) 1876 *E*
Hogg, W (Dublin U) 1885 *S* 2
Holland, J J (Wanderers) 1981 *SA* 1,2, 1986 *W*
Holmes, G W (Dublin U) 1912 *SA*, 1913 *E*, *S*
Holmes, L J (Lisburn) 1889 *S*, *W*
Hooks, K J (Queen's U, Belfast) 1981 *S*
Horan, A K (Blackheath) 1920 *E*, *W*
Houston, K J (Oxford U, London Irish) 1961 *SA*, 1964
S, *W*, 1965 *F*, *SA*
Hughes, R W (NIFC) 1878 *E*, 1880 *E*, *S*, 1881 *S*, 1882
E, *S*, 1883 *E*, *S*, 1884 *E*, *S*, 1885 *E*, 1886 *E*
Hunt, E W F de Vere (Army, Rosslyn Park) 1930 *F*,
1932 *E*, *S*, *W*, 1933 *E*
Hunter, D V (Dublin U) 1885 *S* 2
Hunter, L (Civil Service) 1968 *W*, *A*
Hunter, W R (CIYMS) 1962 *E*, *S*, *W*, *F*, 1963 *F*, *E*, *S*,
1966 *F*, *E*, *S*
Hutton, S A (Malone) 1967 *S*, *W*, *F*, *A* 2

Ireland, J (Windsor) 1876 *E*, 1877 *E*
Irvine, H A S (Collegians) 1901 *S*
Irwin, D G (Queen's U, Belfast, Instonians) 1980 *F*, *W*,
1981 *F*, *W*, *E*, *S*, *SA* 1,2, *A*, 1982 *W*, 1983 *S*, *F*, *W*, *E*,
1984 *F*, *W*, 1987 [*Tg*, *A*(R)], 1989 *F*, *W*, *E*, *S*
Irwin, J W S (NIFC) 1938 *E*, *S*, 1939 *E*, *S*, *W*
Irwin, S T (Queen's Coll, Belfast) 1900 *E*, *S*, *W*, 1901
E, *W*, 1902 *E*, *S*, *W*, 1903 *S*

Jack, H W (UC Cork) 1914 *S*, *W*, 1921 *W*
Jackson, A R V (Wanderers) 1911 *E*, *S*, *W*, *F*, 1913 *W*,
F, 1914 *F*, *E*, *S*
Jackson, F (NIFC) 1923 *E*
Jackson, H W (Dublin U) 1877 *E*
Jameson, J S (Lansdowne) 1888 *M*, 1889 *S*, *W*, 1891
W, 1892 *E*, *W*, 1893 *S*
Jeffares, E W (Wanderers) 1913 *E*, *S*
Johnston, J (Belfast Acad) 1881 *S*, 1882 *S*, 1884 *S*, 1885
S 1,2, 1886 *E*, 1887 *E*, *S*, *W*
Johnston, M (Dublin U) 1880 *E*, *S*, 1881 *E*, *S*, 1882 *E*,
1884 *E*, *S*, 1886 *E*
Johnston, R (Wanderers) 1893 *E*, *W*
Johnston, R W (Dublin U) 1890 *S*, *W*, *E*
Johnston, T J (Queen's Coll, Belfast) 1892 *E*, *S*, *W*,
1893 *E*, *S*, 1895 *E*
Johnstone, W E (Dublin U) 1884 *W*
Johnstone-Smyth, T R (Lansdowne) 1882 *E*

Kavanagh, J R (UC Dublin, Wanderers) 1953 *F*, *E*, *S*,
W, 1954 *NZ*, *S*, *W*, 1955 *F*, *E*, 1956 *E*, *S*, *W*, 1957 *F*,
E, *S*, *W*, 1958 *A*, *E*, *S*, *W*, 1959 *E*, *S*, *W*, *F*, 1960 *E*, *S*,
W, *F*, *SA*, 1961 *E*, *S*, *W*, *F*, *SA*, 1962 *F*
Kavanagh, P J (UC Dublin, Wanderers) 1952 *E*, 1955
W
Keane, M I (Lansdowne) 1974 *F*, *W*, *E*, *S*, *P*, *NZ*,
1975 *E*, *S*, *F*, *W*, 1976 *A*, *F*, *W*, *E*, *S*, *NZ*, 1977 *W*, *E*,
S, *F*, 1978 *S*, *F*, *W*, *E*, *NZ*, 1979 *F*, *W*, *E*, *S*, *A* 1,2,
1980 *E*, *S*, *F*, *W*, 1981 *F*, *W*, *E*, *S*, 1982 *W*, *E*, *S*, *F*,
1983 *S*, *F*, *W*, *E*, 1984 *F*, *W*, *E*, *S*
Kearney, R K (Wanderers) 1982 *F*, 1984 *A*, 1986 *F*, *W*
Keeffe, E (Sunday's Well) 1947 *F*, *E*, *S*, *W*, *A*, 1948 *F*
Kelly, H C (NIFC) 1877 *E*, *S*, 1878 *E*, 1879 *S*, 1880 *E*, *S*
Kelly, J C (UC Dublin) 1962 *F*, *W*, 1963 *F*, *E*, *S*, *W*,
NZ, 1964 *E*, *S*, *W*, *F*
Kelly, S (Lansdowne) 1954 *S*, *W*, 1955 *S*, 1960 *W*, *F*
Kelly, W (Wanderers) 1884 *S*
Kennedy, A G (Belfast Collegians) 1956 *F*
Kennedy, A P (London Irish) 1986 *W*, *E*
Kennedy, F (Wanderers) 1880 *E*, 1881 *E*, 1882 *W*

Kennedy, F A (Wanderers) 1904 *E, W*
Kennedy, H (Bradford) 1938 *S, W*
Kennedy, J M (Wanderers) 1882 *W*, 1884 *W*
Kennedy, K W (Queen's U, Belfast, London Irish)
1965 *F, E, S, W, SA*, 1966 *F, E, W*, 1967 *A* 1, *E, S, W*,
F, A 2, 1968 *F, A*, 1969 *F, E, S, W*, 1970 *SA, F, E, S*,
W, 1971 *F, E, S, W*, 1972 *F* 1, *E, F* 2, 1973 *NZ, E, S*,
W, F, 1974 *F, W, E, S, P, NZ*, 1975 *F, W*
Kennedy, T J (St Mary's Coll) 1978 *NZ*, 1979 *F, W, E*
(R), *A* 1,2, 1980 *E, S, F, W*, 1981 *SA* 1,2, *A*
Keogh, F S (Bective Rangers) 1964 *W, F*
Keon, J J (Limerick) 1879 *E*
Keyes, R P (Cork Constitution) 1986 *E*
Kidd, F W (Dublin U, Lansdowne) 1877 *E, S*, 1878 *E*
Kiely, M D (Lansdowne) 1962 *W*, 1963 *F, E, S, W*
Kiernan, M J (Dolphin, Lansdowne) 1982 *W* (R), *E, S*,
F, 1983 *S, F, W, E*, 1984 *E, S, A*, 1985 *S, F, W, E*,
1986 *F, W, E, S, R*, 1987 *E, S, F, W*, [*W, C, A*], 1988
S, F, W, E 1,2, *WS*, 1989 *F, W, E, S*
Kiernan, T J (UC Cork, Cork Const) 1960 *E, S, W*,
F,SA, 1961 *E, S, W, F, SA*, 1962 *E, W*, 1963 *F, S, W*,
NZ, 1964 *E, S*, 1965 *F, E, S, W, SA*, 1966 *F, E, S, W*,
1967 *A* 1, *E, S, W, F, A* 2, 1968 *F, E, S, W, A*, 1969 *F*,
E, S, W, 1970 *SA, F, E, S, W*, 1971 *F*, 1972 *F* 1, *E, F*
2, 1973 *NZ, E, S*
Killeen, G V (Garryowen) 1912 *E, S, W*, 1913 *E, S, W*,
F, 1914 *E, S, W*
King, H (Dublin U) 1883 *E, S*
Kingston, T J (Dolphin) 1987 [*W, Tg, A*], 1988 *S, F*,
W, E 1
Knox, J H (Dublin U, Lansdowne) 1904 *W*, 1905 *E, S*,
W, NZ, 1906 *E, S, W*, 1907 *W*, 1908 *S*
Kyle, J W (Queen's U, Belfast, NIFC) 1947 *F, E, S*,
W, A, 1948 *F, E, S, W*, 1949 *F, E, S, W*, 1950 *F, E, S*,
W, 1951 *F, E, S, W, SA*, 1952 *F, S, W, E*, 1953 *F, E*,
S, W, 1954 *NZ, F*, 1955 *F, E, W*, 1956 *F, E, S, W*,
1957 *F, E, S, W*, 1958 *A, E, S*

Lambert, N H (Lansdowne) 1934 *S, W*
Lamont, R A (Instonians) 1965 *F, E, SA*, 1966 *F, E, S*,
W, 1970 *SA, F, E, S, W*
Landers, M F (Cork Const) 1904 *W*, 1905 *E, S, W, NZ*
Lane, D (UC Cork) 1934 *S, W*, 1935 *E, S*
Lane, M F (UC Cork) 1947 *W*, 1949 *F, E, S, W*, 1950
F, E, S, W, 1951 *F, S, W, SA*, 1952 *F, S*, 1953 *F, E*
Lane, P (Old Crescent) 1964 *W*
Langan, D J (Clontarf) 1934 *W*
Langbroek, J A (Blackrock Coll) 1987 [*Tg*]
Lavery, P (London Irish) 1974 *W*, 1976 *W*
Lawler, P J (Clontarf) 1951 *S, SA*, 1952 *F, S, W, E*,
1953 *F*, 1954 *NZ, E, S*, 1956 *F, E*
Lawlor, P J (Bective Rangers) 1935 *E, S, W*, 1937 *E, S, W*
Leahy, M W (UC Cork) 1964 *W*
Lee, S (NIFC) 1891 *E, S, W*, 1892 *E, S, W*, 1893 *E, S*,
W, 1894 *E, S, W*, 1895 *E, S, W*, 1896 *E, S, W*, 1897 *E*,
1898 *E*
Le Fanu, V C (Cambridge U, Lansdowne) 1886 *E, S*, 1887
E, W, 1888 *S*, 1889 *W*, 1890 *E*, 1891 *E*, 1892 *E, S, W*
Lenihan, D G (UC Cork, Cork Const) 1981 *A*, 1982 *W*,
E, S, F, 1983 *S, F, W, E*, 1984 *F, W, E, S, A*, 1985 *S*,
F, W, E, 1986 *F, W, E, S, R*, 1987 *E, S, F, W*, [*W, C*,
Tg, A], 1988 *S, F, W, E* 1,2, *WS, It*, 1989 *F, W, E, S*
L'Estrange, L P F (Dublin U) 1962 *E*
Levis, F H (Wanderers) 1884 *E*
Lightfoot, E J (Lansdowne) 1931 *F, E, S, W, SA*, 1932
E, S, W, 1933 *E, W, S*
Lindsay, H (Dublin U, Armagh) 1893 *E, S, W*, 1894 *E*,
S, W, 1895 *E*, 1896 *E, S, W*, 1898 *E, S, W*
Little, T J (Bective Rangers) 1898 *W*, 1899 *S, W*, 1900
S, W, 1901 *E, S*
Lloyd, R A (Dublin U, Liverpool) 1910 *E, S*, 1911 *E*,
S, W, F, 1912 *F, E, S, W, SA*, 1913 *E, S, W, F*, 1914
F, E, 1920 *E, F*
Lydon, C T J (Galwegians) 1956 *S*
Lyle, R K (Dublin U) 1910 *W, F*
Lyle, T R (Dublin U) 1885 *E, S* 1,2, 1886 *E*, 1887 *E, S*,
Lynch, J F (St Mary's Coll) 1971 *F, E, S, W*, 1972 *F* 1,
E, F 2, 1973 *NZ, E, S, W*, 1974 *F, W, E, S, P, NZ*
Lynch, L (Lansdowne) 1956 *S*
Lytle, J H (NIFC) 1894 *E, S, W*, 1895 *W*, 1896 *E, S*,
W, 1897 *E, S*, 1898 *E, S*, 1899 *S*
Lytle, J N (NIFC) 1888 *M*, 1889 *W*, 1890 *E*, 1891 *E, S*,
1894 *E, S, W*

Lyttle, V J (Collegians, Bedford) 1938 *E*, 1939 *E, S*

McAllan, G H (Dungannon) 1896 *S, W*
Macaulay, J (Limerick) 1887 *E, S*
McBride, W D (Malone) 1988 *W, E* 1, *WS, It*, 1989 *S*
McBride, W J (Ballymena) 1962 *E, S, F, W*, 1963 *F*,
E, S, W, NZ, 1964 *E, S, F*, 1965 *F, E, S, W, SA*, 1966
F, E, S, W, 1967 *A* 1, *E, S, W, F, A* 2, 1968 *F, E, S, W*,
A, 1969 *F, E, S, W*, 1970 *SA, F, E, S, W*, 1971 *F, E, S*,
W, 1972 *F* 1, *E, F* 2, 1973 *NZ, E, S, W, F*, 1974 *F, W*,
E, S, P, NZ, 1975 *E, S, F, W*
McCall, B W (London Irish) 1985 *F* (R), 1986 *E, S*
McCallan, B (Ballymena) 1960 *E, S*
McCarten, R J (London Irish) 1961 *E, W, F*
McCarthy, E A (Kingstown) 1882 *W*
McCarthy, J S (Dolphin) 1948 *F, E, S, W*, 1949 *F, E*,
S, W, 1950 *W*, 1951 *F, E, S, W, SA*, 1952 *F, S, W, E*,
1953 *F, E, S*, 1954 *NZ, F, E, S, W*, 1955 *F, E*
MacCarthy, St G (Dublin U) 1882 *W*
McCarthy, T (Cork) 1898 *W*
McClelland, T A (Queen's U, Belfast) 1921 *E, S, W*,
F, 1922 *E, W, F*, 1923 *E, S, W, F*, 1924 *F, E, S, W, NZ*
McClenahan, R O (Instonians) 1923 *E, S, W*
McClinton, A N (NIFC) 1910 *W, F*
McCombe, W McM (Dublin U, Bangor) 1968 *F*, 1975
E, S, F, W
McConnell, A A (Collegians) 1947 *A*, 1948 *F, E, S, W*,
1949 *F, E*
McConnell, G (Derry, Edinburgh U) 1912 *F, E*, 1913
W, F
McConnell, J W (Lansdowne) 1913 *S*
McCormac, F M (Wanderers) 1909 *W*, 1910 *W, F*
McCormick, W J (Wanderers) 1930 *E*
McCoull, H C (Belfast Albion) 1895 *E, S, W*, 1899 *E*
McCourt, D (Queen's U, Belfast) 1947 *A*
McCoy, J J (Dungannon, Bangor, Ballymena) 1984 *W*,
A, 1985 *S, F, W, E*, 1986 *F*, 1987 [*Tg*], 1988 *E* 2, *WS*,
It, 1989 *F, W, E, S*
McCracken, H (NIFC) 1954 *W*
McDermott, S J (London Irish) 1955 *S, W*
Macdonald, J A (Methodist Coll, Belfast) 1875 *E*, 1876
E, 1877 *S*, 1878 *E*, 1879 *S*, 1880 *E*, 1881 *S*, 1882 *E, S*,
1883 *E, S*, 1884 *E, S*
McDonald, J P (Malone) 1987 [*C*]
McDonnell, A C (Dublin U) 1889 *W*, 1890 *S, W*, 1891 *E*
McDowell, J C (Instonians) 1924 *F, NZ*
McFarland, B A T (Derry) 1920 *S, W, F*, 1922 *W*
McGann, B J (Lansdowne) 1969 *F, E, S, W*, 1970 *SA*,
F, E, S, W, 1971 *F, E, S, W*, 1972 *F* 1, *E, F* 2,1973
NZ, E, S, W, 1976 *F, W, E, S, NZ*
McGown, T M (NIFC) 1899 *E, S*, 1901 *S*
McGrath, D G (UC Dublin, Cork Const) 1984 *S*, 1987
[*W, C, Tg, A*]
McGrath, N F (Oxford U, London Irish) 1934 *W*
McGrath, P J (UC Cork) 1965 *E, S, W, SA*, 1966 *F, E*,
S, W, 1967 *A* 1, *A* 2
McGrath, R J M (Wanderers) 1977 *W, E, F* (R), 1981
SA 1,2, *A*, 1982 *W, E, S, F*, 1983 *S, F, W, E*, 1984 *F*,
W
McGrath, T (Garryowen) 1956 *W*, 1958 *F*, 1960 *E, S*,
W, F, 1961 *SA*
McGuire, E P (UC Galway) 1963 *E, S, W, NZ*, 1964 *E*,
S, W, F
MacHale, S (Lansdowne) 1965 *F, E, S, W, SA*, 1966
F, E, S, W, 1967 *S, W, F*
McIldowie, G (Malone) 1906 *SA*, 1910 *E, S, W*
McIlrath, J A (Ballymena) 1976 *A, F, NZ*, 1977 *W, E*
McIlwaine, E H (NIFC) 1895 *S, W*
McIlwaine, E N (NIFC) 1875 *E*, 1876 *E*
McIlwaine, J E (NIFC) 1897 *E, S*, 1898 *E, S, W*, 1899
E, W
McIntosh, L M (Dublin U) 1884 *S*
MacIvor, C V (Dublin U) 1912 *F, E, S, W*, 1913 *E, S, F*
McKay, J W (Queen's U, Belfast) 1947 *F, E, S, W, A*,
1948 *F, E, S, W*, 1949 *F, E, S, W*, 1950 *F, E, S, W*,
1951 *F, E, S, W, SA*, 1952 *F*
McKee, W D (NIFC) 1947 *A*, 1948 *F, E, S, W*, 1949
F, E, S, W, 1950 *F, E*, 1951 *SA*
McKelvey, J M (Queen's U, Belfast) 1956 *F, E*
McKibbin, A R (Instonians, London Irish) 1977 *W, E*,
S, 1978 *S, F, E, NZ*, 1979 *F, W, E, S*, 1980 *E, S*
McKibbin, C H (Instonians) 1976 *S* (R)

McKibbin, D (Instonians) 1950 *F, E, S, W*, 1951 *F, E, S, W*
McKibbin, H R (Queen's U, Belfast) 1938 *W*, 1939 *E, S, W*
McKinney, S A (Dungannon) 1972 *F* 1, *E, F* 2, 1973 *W, F*, 1974 *F, E, S, P, NZ*, 1975 *E, S*, 1976 *A, F, W, E, S, NZ*, 1977 *W, E, S*, 1978 *S* (R), *F, W, E*
McLaughlin, J H (Derry) 1887 *E, S*, 1888 *W, S*
McLean, R E (Dublin U) 1881 *S*, 1882 *W, E, S*, 1883 *E, S*, 1884 *E, S*, 1885 *E, S* 1
Maclear, B (Cork County, Monkstown) 1905 *E, S, W, NZ*, 1906 *E, S, W, SA*, 1907 *E, S, W*
McLennan, A C (Wanderers) 1977 *F*, 1978 *S, F, W, E, NZ*, 1979 *F, W, E, S*, 1980 *E, F*, 1981 *F, W, E, S, SA* 1,2
McLoughlin, F M (Northern) 1976 *A*
McLoughlin, G A J (Shannon) 1979 *F, W, E, S, A* 1,2, 1980 *E*, 1981 *SA* 1,2, 1982 *W, E, S, F*, 1983 *S, F, W, E*, 1984 *F*
McLoughlin, R J (UC Dublin, Blackrock Coll, Gosforth) 1962 *E, S, F*, 1963 *E, S, W, NZ*, 1964 *E, S*, 1965 *F, E, S, W, SA*, 1966 *F, E, S, W*, 1971 *F, E, S, W*, 1972 *F* 1, *E, F* 2, 1973 *NZ, E, S, W, F*, 1974 *F, W, E, S, P, NZ*, 1975 *E, S, F, W*
McMahon, L B (Blackrock Coll, UC Dublin) 1931 *E, SA*, 1933 *E*, 1934 *E*, 1936 *E, S, W*, 1937 *E, S, W*, 1938 *E, S*
McMaster, A W (Ballymena) 1972 *F* 1, *E, F* 2, 1973 *NZ, E, S, W, F*, 1974 *F, E, S, P*, 1975 *F, W*, 1976 *A, F, W, NZ*
McMordie, J (Queen's Coll, Belfast) 1886 *S*
McMorrow, A (Garryowen) 1951 *W*
McMullen, A R (Cork) 1881 *E, S*
McNamara, V (UC Cork) 1914 *E, S, W*
McNaughton, P P (Greystones) 1978 *S, F, W, E*, 1979 *F, W, E, S, A* 1,2, 1980 *E, S, F, W*, 1981 *F*
MacNeill, H P (Dublin U, Oxford U, Blackrock Coll, London Irish) 1981 *F, W, E, S, A*, 1982 *W, E, S, F*, 1983 *S, F, W, E*, 1984 *F, W, E, S, A*, 1985 *S, F, W, E*, 1986 *F, W, E, S, R*, 1987 *E, S, F, W*, [*W, C, Tg, A*], 1988 *S*(R), *E* 1,2
MacSweeney, D A (Blackrock Coll) 1955 *S*
McVicker, H (Army, Richmond) 1927 *E, S, W, NSW*, 1928 *F*
McVicker, J (Collegians) 1924 *F, E, S, W, NZ*, 1925 *F, E, S, W*, 1926 *F, E, S, W*, 1927 *F, E, S, W, NSW*, 1928 *W*, 1930 *F*
McVicker, S (Queen's U, Belfast) 1922 *E, S, W, F*
Madden, M N (Sunday's Well) 1955 *E, S, W*
Magee, J T (Bective Rangers) 1895 *E, S*
Magee, A M (Louis) (Bective Rangers, London Irish) 1895 *E, S, W*, 1896 *E, S, W*, 1897 *E, S*, 1898 *E, S, W*, 1899 *E, S, W*, 1900 *E, S, W*, 1901 *E, S, W*, 1902 *E, S, W*, 1903 *E, S, W*, 1904 *W*
Maginiss, R M (Dublin U) 1875 *E*, 1876 *E*
Magrath, R M (Cork Constitution) 1909 *S*
Maguire, J F (Cork) 1884 *S*
Mahony, J (Dolphin) 1923 *E*
Malcolmson, G L (RAF, NIFC) 1935 *NZ*, 1936 *E, S, W*, 1937 *E, S, W*
Mannion N P (Corinthians) 1988 *WS, It*, 1989 *F, W, E, S*
Marshall, B D E (Queen's U, Belfast) 1963 *E*
Massey-Westropp, R H (Limerick, Monkstown) 1886 *E*
Matier, R N (NIFC) 1878 *E*, 1879 *S*
Matthews, P M (Ards, Wanderers) 1984 *A*, 1985 *S, F, W, E*, 1986 *R*, 1987 *E, S, F, W*, [*W, Tg, A*], 1988 *S, F, W, E* 1,2, *WS, It*, 1989 *F, W, E, S*
Mattsson, J (Wanderers) 1948 *E*
Mayne, R B (Queen's U, Belfast) 1937 *W*, 1938 *E, W*, 1939 *E, S, W*
Mayne, R H (Belfast Academy) 1888 *W, S*
Mayne, T (NIFC) 1921 *E, S, F*
Mays, K M A (UC Dublin) 1973 *NZ, E, S, W*
Meares, A W D (Dublin U) 1899 *S, W*, 1900 *E, W*
Megaw, J (Richmond, Instonians) 1934 *W*, 1938 *E*
Millar, A (Kingstown) 1880 *E, S*, 1883 *E*
Millar, H J (Monkstown) 1904 *W*, 1905 *E, S, W*
Millar, S (Ballymena) 1958 *F*, 1959 *E, S, W, F*, 1960 *E, S, W, F, SA*, 1961 *E, S, W, SA*, 1962 *E, S, F*, 1963 *F, E, S, W*, 1964 *F*, 1968 *F, E, S, W, A*, 1969 *F, E, S, W*, 1970 *SA, F, E, S, W*
Millar, W H J (Queen's U, Belfast) 1951 *E, S, W*, 1952 *S, W*

Miller, F H (Wanderers) 1886 *S*
Milliken, R A (Bangor) 1973 *E, S, W, F*, 1974 *F, W, E, S, P, NZ*, 1975 *E, S, F, W*
Millin, T J (Dublin U) 1925 *W*
Minch, J B (Bective Rangers) 1912 *SA*, 1913 *E, S*, 1914 *E, S*
Moffat, J (Belfast Academy) 1888 *W, S, M*, 1889 *S*, 1890 *S, W*, 1891 *S*
Moffatt, J E (Old Wesley) 1904 *S*, 1905 *E, S, W*
Moffett, J W (Ballymena) 1961 *E, S*
Molloy, M G (UC Galway, London Irish) 1966 *F, E*, 1967 *A* 1, *E, S, W, F, A* 2, 1968 *F, E, S, W, A*, 1969 *F, E, S, W*, 1970 *F, E, S, W*, 1971 *F, E, S, W*, 1973 *F*, 1976 *A*
Moloney, J J (St Mary's Coll) 1972 *F* 1, *E, F* 2, 1973 *NZ, E, S, W, F*, 1974 *F, W, E, S, P, NZ*, 1975 *E, S, F, W*, 1976 *S*, 1978 *S, F, W, E*, 1979 *A* 1,2, 1980 *S, W*
Moloney, L A (Garryowen) 1976 *W* (R), *S*, 1978 *S* (R), *NZ*
Molony, J U (UC Dublin) 1950 *S*
Monteith, J D E (Queen's U, Belfast) 1947 *E, S, W*
Montgomery, A (NIFC) 1895 *S*
Montgomery, F P (Queen's U, Belfast) 1914 *E, S, W*
Montgomery, R (Cambridge U) 1887 *E, S, W*, 1891 *E*, 1892 *W*
Moore, C M (Dublin U) 1887 *S*, 1888 *W, S*
Moore, D F (Wanderers) 1883 *E, S*, 1884 *E, W*
Moore, F W (Wanderers) 1884 *W*, 1885 *E, S* 2, 1886 *S*
Moore, H (Windsor) 1876 *E*, 1877 *S*
Moore, H (Queen's U, Belfast) 1910 *S*, 1911 *W, F*, 1912 *F, E, S, W, SA*
Moore, T A P (Highfield) 1967 *A* 2, 1973 *NZ, E, S, W, F*, 1974 *F, W, E, S, P, NZ*
Moore, W D (Queen's Coll, Belfast) 1878 *E*
Moran, F G (Clontarf) 1936 *E*, 1937 *E, S, W*, 1938 *S, W*, 1939 *E, S, W*
Morell, H B (Dublin U) 1881 *E, S*, 1882 *W, E*
Morgan, G J (Clontarf) 1934 *E, S, W*, 1935 *E, S, W*, 1936 *E, S, W*, 1937 *E, S, W*, 1938 *E, S, W*, 1939 *E, S, W*
Moriarty, C C H (Monkstown) 1899 *W*
Moroney, J C M (Garryowen) 1968 *W, A*, 1969 *F, E, S, W*
Moroney, R J M (Lansdowne) 1984 *F, W*, 1985 *F*
Moroney, T A (UC Dublin) 1964 *W*, 1967 *A* 1, *E*
Morphy, E McG (Dublin U) 1908 *E*
Morris, D P (Bective Rangers) 1931 *W*, 1932 *E*, 1935 *E, S, W, NZ*
Morrow, J W R (Queen's Coll, Belfast) 1882 *S*, 1883 *E, S*, 1884 *E, W*, 1885 *S* 1,2, 1886 *E, S*, 1888 *S*
Morrow R D (Bangor) 1986 *F, E, S*
Mortell, M (Bective Rangers, Dolphin) 1953 *F, E, S, W*, 1954 *NZ, F, E, S, W*
Morton, W A (Dublin U) 1888 *S*
Moyers, L W (Dublin U) 1884 *W*
Moylett, M M F (Shannon) 1988 *E* 1
Mulcahy, W A (UC Dublin, Bective Rangers, Bohemians) 1958 *A, E, S, W, F*, 1959 *E, S, W, F*, 1960 *E, S, W, SA*, 1961 *E, S, W, SA*, 1962 *E, S, F*, 1963 *F, E, S, W, NZ*, 1964 *E, S, W, F*, 1965 *F, E, S, W, SA*
Mullan, B (Clontarf) 1947 *F, E, S, W*, 1948 *F, E, S, W*
Mullane, J P (Limerick Bohemians) 1928 *W*, 1929 *F*
Mullen, K D (Old Belvedere) 1947 *F, E, S, W, A*, 1948 *F, E, S, W*, 1949 *F, E, S, W*, 1950 *F, E, S, W*, 1951 *F, E, S, W, SA*, 1952 *F, S, W*
Mulligan, A A (Wanderers) 1956 *F, E*, 1957 *F, E, S, W*, 1958 *A, E, S, F*, 1959 *E, S, W, F*, 1960 *E, S, W, F, SA*, 1961 *W, F, SA*
Mullin, B J (Dublin U, Oxford U, Blackrock Coll, London Irish) 1984 *A*, 1985 *S, W, E*, 1986 *F, W, E, S, R*, 1987 *E, S, F, W*, [*W, C, Tg, A*], 1988 *S, F, W, E* 1,2, *WS, It*, 1989 *F, W, E, S*
Murphy, C J (Lansdowne) 1939 *E, S, W*, 1947 *F, E*
Murphy, J G M W (London Irish) 1951 *SA*, 1952 *S, W*, *E*, 1954 *NZ*, 1958 *W*
Murphy, J J (Greystones) 1981 *SA* 1, 1982 *W* (R), 1984 *S*
Murphy, N A A (Cork Constitution) 1958 *A, E, S, W, F*, 1959 *E, S, W, F*, 1960 *E, S, W, F, SA*, 1961 *E, S, W*, 1962 *E*, 1963 *NZ*, 1964 *E, S, W, F*, 1965 *F, E, S, W, SA*, 1966 *F, E, S, W*, 1967 *A* 1, *E, S, W, F*, 1969 *F, E, S, W*
Murphy, N F (Cork Constitution) 1930 *E, W*, 1931 *F*,

E, S, W, SA, 1932 *E, S, W,* 1933 *E*
Murphy-O'Connor, J (Bective Rangers) 1954 *E*
Murray, H W (Dublin) 1877 *S,* 1878 *E,* 1879 *E*
Murray, J B (UC Dublin) 1963 *F*
Murray, P F (Wanderers) 1927 *F,* 1929 *F, E, S,* 1930
F, E, S, W, 1931 *F, E, S, W, SA,* 1932 *E, S, W,* 1933
E, W, S
Murtagh, C W (Portadown) 1977 *S*
Myles, J (Dublin U) 1875 *E*

Nash, L C (Queen's Coll, Cork) 1889 *S,* 1890 *W, E,*
1891 *E, S, W*
Neely, M R (Collegians) 1947 *F, E, S, W*
Neill, H J (NIFC) 1885 *E, S* 1,2, 1886 *S,* 1887 *E, S, W,*
1888 *W, S*
Neill, J McF (Instonians) 1926 *F*
Nelson, J E (Malone) 1947 *A,* 1948 *E, S, W,* 1949 *F, E,*
S, W, 1950 *F, E, S, W,* 1951 *F, E, W,* 1954 *F*
Nelson, R (Queen's Coll, Belfast) 1882 *E, S,* 1883 *S,*
1886 *S*
Nesdale, T J (Garryowen) 1961 *F*
Neville, W C (Dublin U) 1879 *S, E*
Nicholson, P C (Dublin U) 1900 *E, S, W*
Norton, G W (Bective Rangers) 1949 *F, E, S, W,* 1950
F, E, S, W, 1951 *F, E, S*
Notley, J R (Wanderers) 1952 *F, S*

O'Brien, B (Derry) 1893 *S, W*
O'Brien, B A P (Shannon) 1968 *F, E, S*
O'Brien, D J (London Irish, Cardiff, Old Belvedere)
1948 *E, S, W,* 1949 *F, E, S, W,* 1950 *F, E, S, W,* 1951
F, E, S, W, SA, 1952 *F, S, W, E*
O'Brien, K A (Broughton Park) 1980 *E,* 1981 *SA* 1
(R), 2
O'Brien-Butler, P E (Monkstown) 1897 *S,* 1898 *E, S,*
1899 *S, W,* 1900 *E*
O'Callaghan, C T (Carlow) 1910 *W, F,* 1911 *E, S, W,*
F, 1912 *F*
O'Callaghan, M P (Sunday's Well) 1962 *W,* 1964 *E, F*
O' Callaghan, P (Dolphin) 1967 *A* 1, *E, A* 2, 1968 *F, E,*
S, W, 1969 *F, E, S, W,* 1970 *SA, F, E, S, W,* 1976 *F,*
W, E, S, NZ
O'Connell, P (Bective Rangers) 1913 *W, F,* 1914 *F, E,*
S, W
O'Connell, W J (Lansdowne) 1955 *F*
O'Connor, H S (Dublin U) 1957 *F, E, S, W*
O'Connor, J (Garryowen) 1895 *S*
O'Connor, J H (Bective Rangers) 1888 *M,* 1890 *S, W,*
E, 1891 *E, S,* 1892 *E, W,* 1893 *E, S,* 1894 *E, S, W,* 1895
E, 1896 *E, S, W*
O'Connor, J J (Garryowen) 1909 *F*
O'Connor, J J (UC Cork) 1933 *S,* 1934 *E, S, W,* 1935
E, S, W, NZ, 1936 *S, W,* 1938 *S*
O'Connor, P J (Lansdowne) 1887 *W*
Odbert, R V M (RAF) 1928 *F*
O'Donnell, R C (St Mary's Coll) 1979 *A* 1,2, 1980 *S, F,*
W
O'Donoghue, P J (Bective Rangers) 1955 *F, E, S, W,*
1956 *W,* 1957 *F, E,* 1958 *A, E, S, W*
O'Driscoll, B J (Manchester) 1971 *F* (R), *E, S, W*
O'Driscoll, J B (London Irish, Manchester) 1978 *S,*
1979 *A* 1,2, 1980 *E, S, F, W,* 1981 *F, W, E, S, SA* 1,2,
A, 1982 *W, E, S, F,* 1983 *S, F, W, E,* 1984 *F, W, E, S*
O'Flanagan, K P (London Irish) 1947 *A*
O'Flanagan, M (Lansdowne) 1948 *S*
O'Hanlon, B (Dolphin) 1947 *E, S, W,* 1948 *F, E, S, W,*
1949 *F, E, S, W,* 1950 *F*
O'Hara, P T J (Sunday's Well) 1988 *WS* (R), 1989 *F,*
W, E
O'Leary, A (Cork Constitution) 1952 *S, W, E*
O'Loughlin, D B (UC Cork) 1938 *E, S, W,* 1939 *E, S, W*
O'Meara, J A (UC Cork, Dolphin) 1951 *F, E, S, W,*
SA, 1952 *F, S, W, E,* 1953 *F, E, S, W,* 1954 *NZ, F, E,*
S, 1955 *F, E,* 1956 *S, W,* 1958 *W*
O'Neill, H O'H (Queen's U, Belfast, UC Cork) 1930 *E,*
S, W, 1933 *E, S, W*
O'Neill, J B (Queen's U, Belfast) 1920 *S*
O'Neill, W A (UC Dublin, Wanderers) 1952 *E,* 1953 *F,*
E, S, W, 1954 *NZ*
O'Reilly, A J F (Old Belvedere, Leicester) 1955 *F, E,*
S, W, 1956 *F, E, S, W,* 1957 *F, E, S, W,* 1958 *A, E, S,*
W, F, 1959 *E, S, W, F,* 1960 *E,* 1961 *E, F, SA,* 1963
F, S, W, 1970 *E*

Orr, P A (Old Wesley) 1976 *F, W, E, S, NZ,* 1977 *W,*
E, S, F, 1978 *S, F, W, E, NZ,* 1979 *F, W, E, S, A* 1,2,
1980 *E, S, F, W,* 1981 *F, W, E, S, SA* 1,2, *A,* 1982 *W,*
E, S, F, 1983 *S, F, W, E,* 1984 *F, W, E, S, A,* 1985 *S,*
F, W, E, 1986 *F, S, R,* 1987 *E, S, F, W,* [*W, C, A*]
O'Sullivan, A C (Dublin U) 1882 *S*
O'Sullivan, J M (Limerick) 1884 *S,* 1887 *S*
O'Sullivan, P J A (Galwegians) 1957 *F, E, S, W,* 1959 *E, S,*
W, F, 1960 *SA,* 1961 *E, S,* 1962 *F, W,* 1963 *F, NZ*
O'Sullivan, W (Queen's Coll, Cork) 1895 *S*
Owens, R H (Dublin U) 1922 *E, S*

Parfrey, P (UC Cork) 1974 *NZ*
Parke, J C (Monkstown) 1903 *W,* 1904 *E, S, W,* 1905
W, NZ, 1906 *E, S, W, SA,* 1907 *E, S, W,* 1908 *E, S, W,*
1909 *E, S, W, F*
Parr, J S (Wanderers) 1914 *F, E, S, W*
Patterson, C S (Instonians) 1978 *NZ,* 1979 *F, W, E, S,*
A 1,2, 1980 *E, S, F, W*
Patterson, R d'A (Wanderers) 1912 *F, S, W, SA,* 1913
E, S, W, F
Payne, C T (NIFC) 1926 *E,* 1927 *F, E, S, NSW,* 1928
F, E, S, W, 1929 *F, E, W,* 1930 *F, E, S, W*
Pedlow, A C (CIYMS) 1953 *W,* 1954 *NZ, F, E,* 1955
F, E, S, W, 1956 *F, E, S, W,* 1957 *F, E, S, W,* 1958 *A,*
E, S, W, F, 1959 *E,* 1960 *E, S, W, F, SA,* 1961 *S,* 1962
W, 1963 *F*
Pedlow, J (Bessbrook) 1882 *S,* 1884 *W*
Pedlow, R (Bessbrook) 1891 *W*
Pedlow, T B (Queen's Coll, Belfast) 1889 *S, W*
Peel, T (Limerick) 1892 *E, S, W*
Peirce, W (Cork) 1881 *E*
Phipps, G C (Army) 1950 *E, W,* 1952 *F, W, E*
Pike, T O (Lansdowne) 1927 *E, S, W, NSW,* 1928 *F,*
E, S, W
Pike, V J (Lansdowne) 1931 *E, S, W, SA,* 1932 *E, S,*
W, 1933 *E, W, S,* 1934 *E, S, W*
Pike, W W (Kingstown) 1879 *E,* 1881 *E, S,* 1882 *E,*
1883 *S*
Pinion, G (Belfast Collegians) 1909 *E, S, W, F*
Piper, O J S (Cork Constitution) 1909 *E, S, W, F,* 1910
E, S, W, F
Polden, S E (Clontarf) 1913 *W, F,* 1914 *F,* 1920 *F*
Popham, I (Cork Constitution) 1922 *S, W, F,* 1923 *F*
Potterton, H N (Wanderers) 1920 *W*
Pratt, R H (Dublin U) 1933 *E, W, S,* 1934 *E, S*
Price, A H (Dublin U) 1920 *S, F*
Pringle, J C (NIFC) 1902 *S, W*
Purcell, N M (Lansdowne) 1921 *E, S, W, F*
Purdon, H (NIFC) 1879 *S, E,* 1880 *E,* 1881 *E, S*
Purdon, W B (Queen's Coll, Belfast) 1906 *E, S, W*
Purser, F C (Dublin U) 1898 *E, S, W*

Quinlan, S V J (Blackrock Coll) 1956 *F, E, W,* 1958 *W*
Quinn, B T (Old Belvedere) 1947 *F*
Quinn, F P (Old Belvedere) 1981 *F, W, E*
Quinn, J P (Dublin U) 1910 *E, S,* 1911 *E, S, W, F,*
1912 *E, S, W,* 1913 *E, W, F,* 1914 *F, E, S*
Quinn, K (Old Belvedere) 1947 *F, A,* 1953 *F, E, S*
Quinn, M A M (Lansdowne) 1973 *F,* 1974 *F, W, E, S,*
P, NZ, 1977 *S, F,* 1981 *SA* 2
Quirke, J M T (Blackrock Coll) 1962 *E, S,* 1968 *S*

Rambaut, D F (Dublin U) 1887 *E, S, W,* 1888 *W*
Rea, H H (Edinburgh U) 1967 *A* 1, 1969 *F*
Read, H M (Dublin U) 1910 *E, S,* 1911 *E, S, W, F,*
1912 *F, E, S, W, SA,* 1913 *E, S*
Rearden, J V (Cork Constitution) 1934 *E, S*
Reid, C (NIFC) 1899 *S, W,* 1900 *E,* 1903 *W*
Reid, J L (Richmond) 1934 *S, W*
Reid, P J (Garryowen) 1947 *A,* 1948 *F, E, W*
Reid, T E (Garryowen) 1953 *E, S, W,* 1954 *F, NZ,*
1955 *E, S,* 1956 *F, E,* 1957 *F, E, S, W*
Reidy, C J (London Irish) 1937 *W*
Reidy, G F (Dolphin, Lansdowne) 1953 *W,* 1954 *F, E,*
S, W
Richey, H A (Dublin U) 1889 *W,* 1890 *S*
Ridgeway, E C (Wanderers) 1932 *S, W,* 1935 *E, S, W*
Ringland, T M (Queen's U, Belfast, Ballymena) 1981
A, 1982 *W, E, F,* 1983 *S, F, W, E,* 1984 *F, W, E, S, A,*
1985 *S, F, W, E,* 1986 *F, W, E, S, R,* 1987 *E, S, F, W,*
[*W, C, Tg, A*], 1988 *S, F, W, E* 1
Riordan, W F (Cork Constitution) 1910 *E*

Ritchie, J S (London Irish) 1956 *F, E*
Robb, C G (Queen's Coll, Belfast) 1904 *E, S, W*, 1905 *NZ*, 1906 *S*
Robbie, J C (Dublin U, Greystones) 1976 *A, F, NZ*, 1977 *S, F*, 1981 *F, W, E, S*
Robinson, T T H (Wanderers) 1904 *E, S*, 1905 *E, S, W, NZ*, 1906 *SA*, 1907 *E, S, W*
Roche, J (Wanderers) 1890 *S, W, E*, 1891 *E, S, W*, 1892 *W*
Roche, R E (UC Galway) 1955 *E, S*, 1957 *S, W*
Roche, W J (UC Cork) 1920 *E, S, F*
Roddy, P J (Bective Rangers) 1920 *S, F*
Roe, R (Lansdowne) 1952 *E*, 1953 *F, E, S, W*, 1954 *F, E, S, W*, 1955 *F, E, S, W*, 1956 *F, E, S, W*, 1957 *F, E, S, W*
Rooke, C V (Dublin U) 1891 *E, W*, 1892 *E, S, W*, 1893 *E, S, W*, 1894 *E, S, W*, 1895 *E, S, W*, 1896 *E, S, W*, 1897 *E, S*
Ross, D J (Belfast Academy) 1884 *E*, 1885 *S* 1,2, 1886 *E, S*
Ross, G R P (CIYMS) 1955 *W*
Ross, J F (NIFC) 1886 *S*
Ross, J P (Lansdowne) 1885 *E, S* 1,2, 1886 *E, S*
Ross, N G (Malone) 1927 *F, E*
Ross, W McC (Queen's U, Belfast) 1932 *E, S, W*, 1933 *E, W, S*, 1934 *E, S*, 1935 *NZ*
Russell, J (UC Cork) 1931 *F, E, S, W, SA*, 1933 *E, W, S*, 1934 *E, S, W*, 1935 *E, S, W*, 1936 *E, S, W*, 1937 *E, S*
Rutherford, W G (Tipperary) 1884 *E, S*, 1885 *E, S* 1, 1886 *E*, 1888 *W*
Ryan, E (Dolphin) 1937 *W*, 1938 *E, S*
Ryan, J (Rockwell Coll) 1897 *E*, 1898 *E, S, W*, 1899 *E, S, W*, 1900 *S, W*, 1901 *E, S, W*, 1902 *E*, 1904 *E*
Ryan, J G (UC Dublin) 1939 *E, S, W*
Ryan, M (Rockwell Coll) 1897 *E, S*, 1898 *E, S, W*, 1899 *E, S, W*, 1900 *E, S, W*, 1901 *E, S, W*, 1903 *E*, 1904 *E, S*

Sayers, H J M (Lansdowne) 1935 *E, S, W*, 1936 *E, S, W*, 1938 *W, E, S, W*
Schute, F (Wanderers) 1878 *E*, 1879 *E*
Schute, F G (Dublin U) 1912 *SA*, 1913 *E, S*
Scott, D (Malone) 1961 *F, SA*, 1962 *S*
Scott, R D (Queen's U, Belfast) 1967 *E, F*, 1968 *F, E, S*
Scovell, R H (Kingstown) 1883 *E*, 1884 *E*
Scriven, G (Dublin U) 1879 *S, E*, 1880 *E, S*, 1881 *E*, 1882 *S*, 1883 *E, S*
Sealy, J (Dublin U) 1896 *E, S, W*, 1897 *S*, 1899 *E, S, W*, 1900 *E, S*
Sexton, J F (Dublin U, Lansdowne) 1988 *E* 2, *WS, It*, 1989 *F*
Sexton, W J (Garryowen) 1984 *A*, 1988 *S, E* 2
Shanahan, T (Lansdowne) 1885 *E, S* 1,2, 1886 *E*, 1888 *S, W*
Shaw, G M (Windsor) 1877 *S*
Sheehan, M D (London Irish) 1932 *E*
Sherry, B F (Terenure Coll) 1967 *A* 1, *E, S, A* 2, 1968 *F, E*
Sherry, M J A (Lansdowne) 1975 *F, W*
Siggins, J A E (Belfast Collegians) 1931 *F, E, S, W, SA*, 1932 *E, S, W*, 1933 *E, W, S*, 1934 *E, S, W*, 1935 *E, S, W, NZ*, 1936 *E, S, W*, 1937 *E, S, W*
Slattery, J F (UC Dublin, Blackrock Coll) 1970 *SA, F, E, S, W*, 1971 *F, E, S, W*, 1972 *F* 1, *E, F*, 2, 1973 *NZ, E, S, W, F*, 1974 *F, W, E, S, P, NZ*, 1975 *E, S, F, W*, 1976 *A*, 1977 *S, F*, 1978 *S, F, W, E, NZ*, 1979 *F, W, E, S, A* 1,2, 1980 *E, S, F, W*, 1981 *F, W, E, S, A, SA* 1,2, *A*, 1982 *W, E, S, F*, 1983 *S, F, W*, 1984 *F*
Smartt, F N B (Dublin U) 1908 *E, S*, 1909 *E*
Smith, J H (London Irish) 1951 *F, E, S, W, SA*, 1952 *F, S, W, E*, 1954 *NZ, W, F*
Smith, R E (Lansdowne) 1892 *E*
Smith, S J (Ballymena) 1988 *E* 2, *WS, It*, 1989 *F, W, E, S*
Smithwick, F F S (Monkstown) 1898 *S, W*
Smyth, J T (Queen's U, Belfast) 1920 *F*
Smyth, P J (Belfast Collegians) 1911 *E, S, F*
Smyth, R S (Dublin U) 1903 *E, S*, 1904 *E*
Smyth, T (Malone, Newport) 1908 *E, S, W*, 1909 *E, S, W* 1910 *E, S, W, F*, 1911 *E, S, W*, 1912 *E*
Smyth, W S (Belfast Collegians) 1910 *W, F*, 1920 *E*
Solomons, B A H (Dublin U) 1908 *E, S, W*, 1909 *E, S, W, F*, 1910 *E, S, W*

Spain, A W (UC Dublin) 1924 *NZ*
Sparrow, W (Dublin U) 1893 *W*, 1894 *E*
Spillane, B J (Bohemians) 1985 *S, F, W, E*, 1986 *F, W, E*, 1987 *F, W*, [*W, C, A*(R)], 1989 *E* (R)
Spring, D E (Dublin U) 1978 *S, NZ*, 1979 *S*, 1980 *S, F, W*, 1981 *W*
Spring, R M (Lansdowne) 1979 *F, W, E*
Spunner, H F (Wanderers) 1881 *E, S*, 1884 *W*
Stack, C R R (Dublin U) 1889 *S*
Stack, G H (Dublin U) 1875 *E*
Steele, H W (Ballymena) 1976 *E*, 1977 *F*, 1978 *F, W, E*, 1979 *F, W, E, A* 1,2
Stephenson, G V (Queen's U, Belfast, London Hosp) 1920 *F*, 1921 *E, S, W, F*, 1922 *E, S, W, F*, 1923 *E, S, W, F*, 1924 *F, E, S, W, NZ*, 1925 *F, E, S, W*, 1926 *F, E, S, W*, 1927 *F, E, S, W, NSW*, 1928 *F, E, S, W*, 1929 *F, E, W*, 1930 *F, E, S, W*
Stephenson, H W V (United Services) 1922 *S, W, F*, 1924 *F, E, S, W, NZ*, 1925 *F, E, S, W*, 1927 *NSW*, 1928 *E*
Stevenson, J (Dungannon) 1888 *M*, 1889 *S*
Stevenson, J B (Instonians) 1958 *A, E, S, W, F*
Stevenson, R (Dungannon) 1887 *E, S, W*, 1888 *M*, 1889 *S, W*, 1890 *S, W, E*, 1891 *W*, 1892 *W*, 1893 *E, S, W*
Stevenson, T H (Belfast Acad) 1895 *E, W*, 1896 *E, S, W*, 1897 *E, S*
Stewart, A L (NIFC) 1913 *W, F*, 1914 *F*
Stewart, W J (Queen's U, Belfast, NIFC) 1922 *F*, 1924 *S*, 1928 *F, E, S, W*, 1929 *F, E, S, W*
Stoker, E W (Wanderers) 1888 *W, S*
Stoker, F O (Wanderers) 1886 *S*, 1888 *W, M*, 1889 *S*, 1891 *W*
Stokes, O S (Cork Bankers) 1882 *E*, 1884 *E*
Stokes, P (Garryowen) 1913 *E, S*, 1914 *F*, 1920 *E, S, W, F*, 1921 *E, S, F*, 1922 *W, F*
Stokes, R D (Queen's Coll, Cork) 1891 *S, W*
Strathdee, E (Queen's U, Belfast) 1947 *E, S, W, A*, 1948 *W, F*, 1949 *E, S, W*
Stuart, C P (Clontarf) 1912 *SA*
Stuart, I M B (Dublin U) 1924 *E, S*
Sugars, H S (Dublin U) 1905 *NZ*, 1906 *SA*, 1907 *S*
Sugden, M (Wanderers) 1925 *F, E, S, W*, 1926 *F, E, S, W*, 1927 *E, S, W, NSW*, 1928 *F, E, S, W*, 1929 *F, E, S, W*, 1930 *F, E, S, W*, 1931 *F, E, S, W*
Sullivan, D B (UC Dublin) 1922 *E, S, W, F*
Sweeney, J A (Blackrock Coll) 1907 *E, S, W*
Symes, G R (Monkstown) 1895 *E*
Synge, J S (Lansdowne) 1929 *S*

Taggart, T (Dublin U) 1887 *W*
Taylor, A S (Queen's Coll, Belfast) 1910 *E, S, W*, 1912 *F*
Taylor, D R (Queen's Coll, Belfast) 1903 *E*
Taylor, J (Belfast Collegians) 1914 *E, S, W*
Taylor, J W (NIFC) 1879 *S*, 1880 *E, S*, 1881 *S*, 1882 *E, S*, 1883 *E, S*
Tector, W R (Wanderers) 1955 *F, E, S*
Tedford, A (Malone) 1902 *E, S, W*, 1903 *E, S, W*, 1904 *E, S, W*, 1905 *E, S, W, NZ*, 1906 *E, S, W, SA*, 1907 *E, S, W*, 1908 *E, S, W*
Teehan, C (UC Cork) 1939 *E, S, W*
Thompson, C (Belfast Collegians) 1907 *E, S*, 1908 *E, S, W*, 1909 *E, S, W, F*, 1910 *E, S, W, F*
Thompson, J A (Queen's Coll, Belfast) 1885 *S* 1,2
Thompson, J K S (Dublin U) 1921 *W*, 1922 *E, S, F*, 1923 *E, S, W, F*
Thompson, R G (Lansdowne) 1882 *W*
Thompson, R H (Instonians) 1951 *SA*, 1952 *F*, 1954 *NZ, F, E, S, W*, 1955 *F, S, W*, 1956 *W*
Thornhill, T (Wanderers) 1892 *E, S, W*, 1893 *E*
Thrift, H (Dublin U) 1904 *W*, 1905 *E, S, W, NZ*, 1906 *E, W, SA*, 1907 *E, S, W*, 1908 *E, S, W*, 1909 *E, S, W, F*
Tierney, D (UC Cork) 1938 *S, W*, 1939 *E*
Tillie, C R (Dublin U) 1887 *E, S*, 1888 *W, S*
Todd, A W P (Dublin U) 1913 *W, F*, 1914 *F*
Torrens, J D (Bohemians) 1938 *W*, 1939 *E, S, W*
Tucker, C C (Shannon) 1979 *F, W*, 1980 *F* (R)
Tuke, B B (Bective Rangers) 1890 *E*, 1891 *E, S*, 1892 *E*, 1894 *E, S, W*, 1895 *E, S*
Turley, N (Blackrock Coll) 1962 *E*
Tydings, J J (Young Munster) 1968 *A*
Tyrrell, W (Queen's U, Belfast) 1910 *F*, 1913 *E, S, W, F*, 1914 *F, E, S, W*

Uprichard, R J H (Harlequins, RAF) 1950 *S, W*

Waide, S L (Oxford U, NIFC) 1932 *E, S, W*, 1933 *E, W*
Waites, J (Bective Rangers) 1886 *S*, 1888 *M*, 1889 *W*, 1890 *S, W, E*, 1891 *E*
Waldron, O C (Oxford U, London Irish) 1966 *S, W*, 1968 *A*
Walker, S (Instonians) 1934 *E, S*, 1935 *E, S, W, NZ*, 1936 *E, S, W*, 1937 *E, S, W*, 1938 *E, S, W*
Walkington, D B (NIFC) 1887 *E, W*, 1888 *W*, 1890 *W*, *E*, 1891 *E, S, W*
Walkington, R B (NIFC) 1875 *E*, 1876 *E*, 1877 *E, S*, 1878 *E*, 1879 *S*, 1880 *E, S*, 1882 *E, S*
Wall, H (Dolphin) 1965 *S, W*
Wallace, Jas (Wanderers) 1904 *E, S*
Wallace, Jos (Wanderers) 1903 *S, W*, 1904 *E, S, W*, 1905 *E, S, W, NZ*, 1906 *W*
Wallace, T H (Cardiff) 1920 *E, S, W*
Wallis, A K (Wanderers) 1892 *E, S, W*, 1893 *E, W*
Wallis, C O'N (Old Cranleighans, Wanderers) 1935 *NZ*
Wallis, T G (Wanderers) 1921 *F*, 1922 *E, S, W, F*
Wallis, W A (Wanderers) 1880 *S*, 1881 *E, S*, 1882 *W*, 1883 *S*
Walmsley, G (Bective Rangers) 1894 *E*
Walpole, A (Dublin U) 1888 *S, M*
Walsh, E J (Lansdowne) 1887 *E, S, W*, 1892 *E, S, W*, 1893 *E*
Walsh, H D (Dublin U) 1875 *E*, 1876 *E*
Walsh, J C (UC Cork, Sunday's Well) 1960 *S, SA*, 1961 *E, S, F, SA*, 1963 *E, S, W, NZ*, 1964 *E, S, W, F*, 1965 *F, S, W, SA*, 1966 *F, S, W*, 1967 *E, S, W, F, A 2*
Ward, A J P (Garryowen, St Mary's Coll, Greystones) 1978 *S, F, W, E, NZ*, 1979 *F, W, E, S*, 1981 *W, E, S, A*, 1983 *E* (R), 1984 *E, S*, 1986 *S*, 1987 [*C, Tg*]
Warren, J P (Kingstown) 1883 *E*
Warren, R G (Lansdowne) 1884 *W*, 1885 *E, S* 1,2, 1886 *E*, 1887 *S, W*, 1888 *W, S, M*, 1889 *S, W*, 1890 *S, W, E*

Watson, R (Wanderers) 1912 *SA*
Wells, H G (Bective Rangers) 1891 *S, W*, 1894 *E, S*
Westby, A J (Dublin U) 1876 *E*
Wheeler, G H (Queen's Coll, Belfast) 1884 *S*, 1885 *E*
Wheeler, J R (Queen's U, Belfast) 1922 *E, S, W, F*, 1924 *E*
Whelan, P C (Garryowen) 1975 *E, S*, 1976 *NZ*, 1977 *W, E, S, F*, 1978 *S, F, W, E, NZ*, 1979 *F, W, E, S*, 1981 *F, W, E*
White, M (Queen's Coll, Cork) 1906 *E, S, W, SA*, 1907 *E, W*
Whitestone, A M (Dublin U) 1877 *E*, 1879 *S, E*, 1880 *E*, 1883 *S*
Whittle, D (Bangor) 1988 *F*
Wilkinson, R W (Wanderers) 1947 *A*
Williamson, F W (Dolphin) 1930 *E, S, W*
Willis, W J (Lansdowne) 1879 *E*
Wilson, F (CIYMS) 1977 *W, E, S*
Wilson, H G (Glasgow U, Malone) 1905 *E, S, W, NZ*, 1906 *E, S, W, SA*, 1907 *E, S, W*, 1908 *E, S, W*, 1909 *E, S, W*, 1910 *W*
Wilson, W H (Bray) 1877 *E, S*
Withers, H H C (Army, Blackheath) 1931 *F, E, S, W, SA*
Wolfe, E J (Armagh) 1882 *E*
Wood, G H (Dublin U) 1913 *W*, 1914 *F*
Wood, B G M (Garryowen) 1954 *E, S*, 1956 *F, E, S, W*, 1957 *F, E, S, W*, 1958 *A, E, S, W, F*, 1959 *E, S, W, F*, 1960 *E, S, W, F, SA*, 1961 *E, S, W, F, SA*
Woods, D C (Bessbrook) 1888 *M*, 1889 *S*
Wright, R A (Monkstown) 1912 *S*

Yeates, R A (Dublin U) 1889 *S, W*
Young, J (UC Cork) 1913 *E*
Young, R M (Collegians) 1965 *F, E, S, W, SA*, 1966 *F, E, S, W*, 1967 *W, F*, 1968 *W, A*, 1969 *F, E, S, W*, 1970 *SA, F, E, S, W*, 1971 *F, E, S, W*

IRISH INTERNATIONAL RECORDS

Both team and individual records are for official Ireland international matches up to 30 April 1989.

TEAM RECORDS

Highest score
60 v Romania (60-0) 1986 Dublin
v individual countries
27 v Australia (27-12) 1979 Brisbane
46 v Canada (46-19) 1987 Dunedin
26 v England (26-21) 1974 Twickenham
25 v France { (25-5) 1911 Cork
{ (25-6) 1975 Dublin
31 v Italy (31-15) 1988 Dublin
10 v N Zealand (10-10) 1973 Dublin
60 v Romania (60-0) 1986 Dublin
15 v S Africa (15-23) 1981 Cape Town
26 v Scotland (26-8) 1953 Murrayfield
32 v Tonga (32-9) 1987 Brisbane
21 v Wales { (21-24) 1979 Cardiff
{ (21-7) 1980 Dublin
{ (21-9) 1985 Cardiff
49 v W Samoa (49-22) 1988 Dublin

Biggest winning points margin
60 v Romania (60-0) 1986 Dublin
v individual countries
15 v Australia (27-12) 1979 Brisbane
27 v Canada (46-19) 1987 Dunedin
22 v England (22-0) 1947 Dublin
24 v France (24-0) 1913 Cork
16 v Italy (31-15) 1988 Dublin
No win v N Zealand
60 v Romania (60-0) 1986 Dublin
3 v S Africa (9-6) 1965 Dublin
21 v Scotland (21-0) 1950 Dublin
23 v Tonga (32-9) 1987 Brisbane
16 v Wales (19-3) 1925 Belfast
27 v W Samoa (49-22) 1988 Dublin

Highest score by opposing team
38 S Africa (0-38) 1912 Dublin
by individual countries
33 Australia (15-33) 1987 Sydney
19 Canada (46-19) 1987 Dunedin
36 England (14-36) 1938 Dublin
29 France (9-29) 1986 Paris
15 v Italy (31-15) 1988 Dublin
17 N Zealand (9-17) 1935 Dublin
0 Romania (60-0) 1986 Dublin

38 S Africa (0-38) 1912 Dublin
37 Scotland (21-37) 1989 Murrayfield
9 Tonga (32-9) 1987 Brisbane
34 Wales (9-34) 1976 Dublin
22 v W Samoa (49-22) 1988 Dublin

Biggest losing points margin
38 v S Africa (0-38) 1912 Dublin
v individual countries
18 v Australia (15-33) 1987 Sydney
32 v England (3-35) 1988 Twickenham
23 v France (3-26) 1976 Paris
15 v N Zealand (0-15) 1905 Dublin
38 v S Africa (0-38) 1912 Dublin
23 v Scotland (9-32) 1984 Dublin
29 v Wales (0-29) 1907 Cardiff
No defeats v Canada, Italy, Romania, Tonga or W Samoa

Most tries by Ireland in an international
10 v Romania (60-0) 1986 Dublin

Most tries against Ireland in an international
10 by S Africa (0-38) 1912 Dublin

Most points by Ireland in International Championship in a season – 71
in season 1982-83

Most tries by Ireland in International Championship in a season – 12
in seasons 1927-28 and 1952-53

INDIVIDUAL RECORDS

Most capped player
C M H Gibson   69   1964-79
in individual positions
Full-back
T J Kiernan   54   1960-73
Wing
T M Ringland   34   1981-88

217

Centre
C M H Gibson   40(69)[1]   1964-79
Fly-half
J W Kyle   46   1947-58
Scrum-half
M Sugden   28   1925-31
Prop
P A Orr   58   1976-87
Hooker
K W Kennedy   45   1965-75
Lock
W J McBride   63   1962-75
Flanker
J F Slattery   61   1970-84
No 8
W P Duggan   39(41)[2]   1975-84

[1]*Gibson won 40 caps as a centre, 25 at fly-half and 4 as a wing. G V Stephenson, 42 caps, won 37 as a centre and 5 on the wing. N J Henderson, 40 caps, won 35 as a centre and 5 at full-back*
[2]*Duggan won 39 caps at No 8 and 2 as a flanker*

Longest international career
A J F O'Reilly 16 seasons 1955-70
C M H Gibson 16 seasons 1964-79
Gibson's career ended during a Southern Hemisphere season

Most internationals as captain
T J Kiernan   24   1963-73

Most points in internationals – 263
M J Kiernan (37 matches) 1982-89

Most points in International Championship in a season – 52
S O Campbell (4 matches) 1982-83

Most points in an international – 21
S O Campbell v Scotland 1982 Dublin
S O Campbell v England 1983 Dublin

Most tries in internationals – 14
G V Stephenson (42 matches) 1920-30

Most tries in International Championship in a season – 5
J E Arigho (3 matches) 1927-28

Most tries in an international – 3
R Montgomery v Wales 1887 Birkenhead
J P Quinn v France 1913 Cork

E O'D Davy v Scotland 1930 Murrayfield
S J Byrne v Scotland 1953 Murrayfield
K D Crossan v Romania 1986 Dublin
B J Mullin v Tonga 1987 Brisbane

Most conversions in internationals – 39
M J Kiernan (37 matches) 1982-89

Most conversions in International Championship in a season – 7
R A Lloyd (4 matches) 1912-13

Most conversions in an international – 7
M J Kiernan v Romania 1986 Dublin

Most dropped goals in internationals – 7
R A Lloyd (19 matches) 1910-20
S O Campbell (22 matches) 1976-84

Most penalty goals in internationals – 54
S O Campbell (22 matches) 1976-84

Most penalty goals in International Championship in a season – 14
S O Campbell (4 matches) 1982-83

Most points for Ireland on overseas tour – 60
S O Campbell (5 appearances) 1979 Australia
M J Kiernan scored 65 points in Japan 1985, but this was not on a major tour

Most points in any match on tour – 19
A J P Ward v Australian Capital Territory 1979 Canberra
S O Campbell v Australia 1979 Brisbane
M J Kiernan scored 25 points in the second match against Japan 1985, but this was not on a major tour

Most tries in any match on tour – 3
A T A Duggan v Victoria 1967 Melbourne
J F Slattery v SA President's XV 1981 East London
M J Kiernan v Gold Cup XV 1981 Oudtshoorn, SA
T M Ringland scored 3 tries v Japan at Osaka 1985, but this was not on a major tour

WALES SAVE A WHITEWASH

THE 1988-89 SEASON IN WALES

John Billot *Western Mail*

There was unexpected sourness mixed with solace as Wales saved the season from becoming a total disaster by defeating England in their final match at the Arms Park. The nation was stunned by the angry gesticulations of the Welsh captain, Paul Thorburn, to the television cameras as he ran from the field after the final whistle. Never had such an exhibition been witnessed and the WRU and Thorburn eventually expressed their regret for the incidents that followed the match.

In view of the seriousness of the incident, many were surprised that Thorburn retained the captaincy of the national side for the B-type tour to Canada in May and June, but Wales coach John Ryan expressed the view: 'The controversy may well make him a better captain. He did a fine job throughout the season and has apologised for his actions'. Thorburn was not chosen for the Lions' tour to Australia, which was a surprise in view of his displays throughout the season, during which he passed Phil Bennett's record aggregate for Wales of 166 points and finished the season with 199.

It was a dismal season for Wales at international level and their true pride and passion was not evident until the final match. Then, England had no answer to the cold fury of a team facing the humiliation of defeat on their home ground by England for the first time since 1963 and a first-ever whitewash in the International Championship.

The horrendous experience of the tour to New Zealand in summer 1988, when both Tests resulted in record defeats, left a scar that was a stark reminder of failure throughout the following season. The Triple Crown champions of a year earlier became a team of vastly diminished confidence: there was no dynamic drive from the back row and unsettled half-back partnerships meant lack of tactical control. The selectors struggled to find a successful blend and once again players became disenchanted with a lack of communication. There is a growing demand in Wales for a more positive team management system. Jeff Squire, the former Wales captain, joined the selection committee to serve with R H Williams, Rod Morgan, David Richards and Ryan. Welsh rugby suffered a great loss with the sudden death of Mr Morgan, aged 59, in April. He was a dedicated administrator and a dominating influence on the WRU.

The rugby league's chequebook took a toll of Welsh talent. Jonathan Davies, the Welsh captain, went to Widnes after the defeat by Romania, enticed by a record four-year deal of some £200,000. Paul Moriarty, the former Wales back row forward, also signed for Widnes for a record fee for a forward of £100,000. David Bishop, Adrian Hadley, Jonathan

The Welsh team which lost to Scotland at Murrayfield. L-R, back row: W H Hall, J D M Wakeford, H Williams-Jones, M H J Douglas, A Clement, R Diplock (all replacements); standing: D J Bryant, K Moseley, M A Jones, P T Davies, N G Davies, D Young; seated: J A Devereux, C Davies, R Phillips, M R Hall, P H Thorburn (capt), B Bowen, J L Griffiths, M Griffiths, I J Watkins.

Griffiths and Mike Carrington also went to league. It was suggested that the loss of Jonathan Davies, particularly after his poor tactical kicking against Romania, would benefit Wales by broadening their options. Alas, this proved an unrealistic hope. By the time the final match of the Championship arrived, Wales had won just one of eight successive games, that against the Western Samoans at the Arms Park.

'We were too loose', admitted Ryan, the first uncapped player to be appointed national coach, after the disappointing performance against the Samoans in November. Against Romania the Welsh display was mechanically uninventive. Thorburn took over from Jonathan Davies, becoming the 100th player to captain Wales in a full-cap international match, but his side slumped at Murrayfield. 'Some of our players panicked', he said. Some Welsh spectators probably panicked too, as Wales trailed 19-0 at half-time! There was a spirited rally in the second half, but the omens for the rest of the season were grim.

Ireland were fortunate to win in Cardiff: referee Roger Quittenton missed David Irwin's knock-on that permitted the winning score. Yet the general view was that Wales should have capitalised on their creative play and made the game safe long before the fateful blunder at the end. There was never any question of Wales winning in Paris, so it was on to the England match and a final chance for Wales to salvage something from the wreck. England, unbeaten, were full of confidence, but at long last the Welsh team responded with fighting defiance. Robert Jones box-kicked to build platforms and turn the defence while Robert Norster was a giant in command of the line-out. The lion-hearted Phil Davies surged at the England forwards and Wales triumphed yet again in a match that has become a special symbol for Welshmen.

Ray Williams resigned as WRU secretary on 2 September 1988 in a dispute over his salary, severing a 21-year association with the Union. He was then appointed Director of the 1991 World Cup tournament, while another famous Welsh rugby personality, Keith Rowlands, took over as full-time secretary of the International Board. The new secretary of the WRU is Mr David East. The WRU set up a special investigative panel under the chairmanship of progressive-minded elder statesman Hermas Evans. The six-man team includes three law graduates from outside the WRU in Alan Meredith, a former Swansea scrum-half; Denis Gethin, formerly a full-back with Cardiff; and retired top referee Corris Thomas of Cardiff. Their brief is to redraft the WRU constitution and to make significant recommendations. Accommodation at the Cardiff Arms Park National Ground was reduced to 58,000 by the conversion of the south enclosure into an all-seating area, a move that was completed ready for the first home match of the home internationals.

It was a notable season for Neath as they won the Schweppes Cup, defeating holders Llanelli in the final, and regained the Western Mail Welsh Club Championship title. They lost only four games and set world records for points (1,914), and tries (345). Llanelli won the

Whitbread Merit Table title while Newbridge celebrated their Centenary season with third place in both tables, a notable home victory over Neath, 19-18, a place in the semi-final stage of the Schweppes Cup and an international cap for their talented outside half, Paul Turner.

Only 14 players were sent off in major matches in Wales, which represented a significant improvement on 27 the previous season. Undoubtedly the sin-bin experiment introduced by the WRU helped in this direction, though some top referees still remained sceptical. There was some justification for the claims that the sin-bin would be used by referees to opt out of sending players off when Mr Les Peard put Neath's Mark Jones in the sin-bin for stamping in the Schweppes Cup final. As there had already been an earlier outbreak of fighting and a warning to the captains, the Neath No 8 should have been sent off.

WESTERN MAIL CLUB CHAMPIONSHIP 1988-89

	W	D	L	F	A	Avge
Neath	33	0	4	1423	384	89.18
Llanelli	34	0	7	1260	670	82.92
Newbridge	31	2	6	838	525	82.05
Bridgend	32	0	11	904	583	74.41
Pontypridd	27	1	10	1034	514	72.36
Swansea	28	0	13	874	657	68.29
Cardiff	19	4	13	780	694	58.33
Abertillery	22	0	17	754	600	56.41
Maesteg	22	3	17	732	695	55.95
Newport	22	1	20	934	889	52.32
Ebbw Vale	20	1	22	646	886	47.67
Pontypool	18	0	23	706	805	43.90
Glam Wands	17	1	22	760	696	43.75
S W Police	13	1	24	650	741	35.52
Cross Keys	11	2	24	449	874	32.43
Aberavon	10	1	29	537	835	26.25
Tredegar	9	0	27	430	873	25.00
London Welsh	7	2	24	470	868	24.24
Penarth	4	0	30	375	1124	11.76

WHITBREAD WELSH MERIT TABLE 1988-89

	W	D	L	F	A	Avge
Llanelli	23	0	2	796	388	92.00
Neath	24	0	4	1069	276	85.71
Newbridge	23	1	4	673	390	83.92
Bridgend	25	0	6	645	377	80.64
Pontypridd	23	1	7	905	407	75.80
Swansea	15	0	9	500	371	62.49
Cardiff	11	2	7	411	384	60.00
Abertillery	16	0	13	542	494	55.17
Maesteg	14	3	15	470	516	48.43
Newport	13	0	16	595	602	44.82
Pontypool	14	0	18	527	627	43.75
Ebbw Vale	14	0	18	438	688	43.75
S W Police	8	0	18	433	566	30.76
Glam Wands	8	0	20	436	511	28.57
Cross Keys	7	2	22	349	756	25.80
Aberavon	7	1	23	378	660	24.19
Tredegar	4	0	21	283	685	16.00
Penarth	1	0	24	253	958	4.00

SNELLING SEVENS 1988-89

27 August 1988, Rodney Parade, Newport

Preliminary round: Tredegar 12, Penarth 8; Bridgend 16, Cardiff 6
First round: Llanelli 20, Neath 6; Maesteg 16, Abertillery 4; Pontypridd 12, Cross Keys 8; Glamorgan Wanderers 10, Newbridge 0; Aberavon 28, Newport 10; Pontypool 12, Swansea 4; South Wales Police 24, Ebbw Vale 0; Bridgend 30, Tredegar 9
Second round: Llanelli 24, Bridgend 4; Maesteg 16, Pontypridd 15; Aberavon 14, Glamorgan Wanderers 6; South Wales Police 20, Pontypool 6
Semi-finals: Llanelli 24, Maesteg 6; South Wales Police 18, Aberavon 12
Final: Llanelli 40, South Wales Police 4

Teams in the Final
Llanelli: I G Evans; N Davies, J Davies, S Bowling; G Jones, D Fox, P T Davies (*capt*)
South Wales Police: A Hughes (*capt*); D Jones, S Davies, D Harrett; M Hembury, D Roberts, N Jones
Referee R O P Jones (Swansea)

SCHWEPPES CHALLENGE CUP 1988-89

John Billot *Western Mail*

6 May, Cardiff Arms Park
Neath 14 (1G 2T)   **Llanelli 13** (2PG 1DG 1T)

Neath's victory in front of a record Welsh club match attendance of 58,000 will be remembered for the controversy surrounding the decision of referee Les Peard to send Mark Jones, the Neath No 8, to the sin-bin some ten minutes before half-time. To most people it appeared a straightforward case of sending-off. Jones, scorer of the first of the three tries that set his side on the road to the Cup after the long wait since their success in the inaugural season of 1971-72, stamped on Laurence Delaney's head. Mr Peard, who had already called both captains together for a general warning after an outbreak of fighting 15 minutes after the start, defended his action, stressing that it had not been a sending-off offence. Two stitches for Delaney represented a sin-bin punishment. How many stitches for an early bath? It was a blunder by Mr Peard, and even the Neath captain, Kevin Phillips, admitted that Jones was very fortunate to be allowed to return.

Neath's forward drive into the rucks, which typifies their successful game plan, and the high chipping into the box by Chris Bridges, chosen as the outstanding player of the match, were the match-winning factors. The ball-winning consistency of the young Gareth Llewelyn in the middle line was also an unexpected setback for Llanelli.

The lead swung six times. Stephens dropped a goal, but Mark Jones surged over for a try to put Neath 4-3 ahead. Stephens' penalty goal was followed by a Brian Williams try which stole back the lead for Neath at 8-6. Ieuan Evans went over wide out after the ball had been swept right across field by Carwyn Davies, putting Llanelli 10-8 in front. But Bridges dropped another high ball out of the sun and Paul Williams dived as it bounced in-goal. Thorburn converted and Stephens' second penalty goal was not enough to save the Scarlets.

Neath: P H Thorburn; C Higgs, C Laity, A Bateman, A Edmunds; P Williams, C Bridges; B Williams, K H Phillips (*capt*), J Pugh, H Richards, G Llewelyn, P Pugh, M Jones, D F Pickering
Scorers *Tries:* Jones, B Williams, P Williams   *Conversion:* Thorburn
Llanelli: S Bowling; I C Evans, N G Davies, D Setaro, C Davies; C Stephens; J Griffiths; A Buchanan, E James, L Delaney, P S May, R Cornelius, G Jones, P T Davies (*capt*), I Jones *Replacement* E Lewis for G Jones (80 mins)
Scorers *Try:* Evans   *Penalty Goals:* Stephens (2)   *Dropped Goal:* Stephens
Referee L J Peard (Castleton)

Newbridge, celebrating their centenary season, were by no means overawed at the prospect of facing Llanelli in the semi-finals. Their response to the challenge, indeed, was stimulating and the Scarlets found themselves under totally unexpected pressure late in the game before they emerged shaken but successful at 26-24. It was the first time a semi-final tie had been staged at the Arms Park, the WRU switching it from the Cardiff club ground in order to provide live television coverage. The major clubs all refused permission for live TV from their grounds. If Paul Turner, the Newbridge outside half, had not blundered in taking a couple of audacious quick drop-outs that went tragically wrong, his side might well have stolen a sensational victory.

In the other semi-final, Neath never really imposed the domination that marked their consistent success throughout the season, and ill-chosen options allowed Cardiff to remain in contention longer than they should have at St Helen's. Yet Cardiff could not create a try and went out 19-12. It was an all-ticket event, restricted to just over 11,000 because of ground reconstruction. A week later, Cardiff inflicted a surprise defeat on the Gnoll club 20-12 at the Arms Park, but it was small consolation for the result that really mattered.

Inevitably, the giant-killing deeds of village teams colour the Cup canvas and Llanharan once again made a praiseworthy contribution, reaching the quarter-final stage for the second successive year. They put out South Wales Police in the fifth round and hopes were high that, with ground advantage, they would surprise a Cardiff side that were enduring one of their least successful post-war seasons. We all remembered how the villagers had rocked the great club at the Arms Park before Cardiff scraped an 18-14 win in the fifth round two years earlier.

The fifth round saw ugly scenes in Llanelli's victory over Pontypridd at Sardis Road, which resulted in Llanelli breaking off fixtures with the home club. Television recordings were used to show some unsavoury incidents, including the punch from behind by Mac Knowles that felled Russell Cornelius, the Llanelli lock. He was detained in hospital overnight. The cameras also revealed savage stamping acts by players on both sides. Pontypridd took disciplinary action by dropping two of their forwards for a short period. The Llanelli team left the ground immediately after the match without participating in the customary hospitality.

Another small club to enjoy a particularly pleasing Cup triumph was Glynneath. Maesteg went there in the fourth round, failed to put over eight penalty attempts, and went out 15-13. Glynneath's famous rugby club president, folk singer Max Boyce, was on stage at Cardiff's New Theatre, killing the giant during the matinee performance of Jack and the Beanstalk, in which he played the title role, while his team were eliminating Maesteg. Every time he killed the giant after that, Max would mutter under his breath, 'That's Maesteg again!' Another twist to this match was that the Glynneath coach and inspiring No 8 was a former Maesteg star, Baden Evans. However, his team were not able to repeat the feat and Bridgend won 42-9 in the fifth round.

Three major clubs were dismissed from the tournament in the third round, including Swansea, who had never before failed in their first tie of the season. They were well beaten 18-8 away to Glamorgan Wanderers. Blackwood triumphed 27-7 at Penarth while Blaina were 26-10 winners at Tredegar. Pontypool scraped through 10-9 at Vardre at this stage as Shaun White chased after a penalty kick that rebounded from the post straight into his arms. But Pontypool's luck ran out after that because they had unwittingly fielded a cup-tied player – Wayne Terry had appeared for Llanhilleth in a previous round. Pontypool accepted their disqualification, but urged that the Cup regulations be reviewed.

RESULTS

Third Round
Aberaman 35, Bridgend Sports Club 6; Aberavon Quins 29, Kidwelly 6; Abercarn 15, Gilfach Goch 3; Beddau 0, Felinfoel 6; Blaenau Gwent 26, Amman United 27; Bridgend 39, Neath Athletic 4; Cefn Cribbwr 6, St Peter's 7; Cross Keys 16, Cwmbran 6; Ebbw Vale 46, Cefn Coed 16; Glamorgan Wanderers 18, Swansea 8; Glynneath 17, Merthyr 7; Hirwaun 20, Cowbridge 0; Llandovery 3, Abertillery 4; Llanharan 40, Penygraig 0; Llantrisant 7, Maesteg 25; Neath 46, Caerphilly 0; Newbridge 49, Mold 6; Newport 35, Llangennech 6; Penarth 7, Blackwood 27; Pembroke Dock Quins 0, Pencoed 4; Pontyberem 3, Llanelli 39; Pontypool United 19, Abercynon 3; Pontypridd 40, Tylorstown 9; Pyle 9, Cardiff 25; Senghenydd 9, Aberavon 16; Seven Sisters 9, Carmarthen Athletic 15; South Wales Police 9, Nantyffyllon 6; Taffs Well 17, Maesteg Celtic 10; Tonyrefail 10, Trimsaran 7; Tredegar 10, Blaina 26; Vardre 9, *Pontypool 10; Waunarlwydd 15, Bedwas 9
*Pontypool were disqualified for fielding an ineligible player

Fourth Round
Aberavon Quins 19, Aberavon 6; Abercarn 3, Neath 33; Abertillery 15, Pencoed 4; Cardiff 54, Amman United 0; Carmarthen Athletic 6, Llanharan 30; Cross Keys 0, Pontypridd 38; Ebbw Vale 10, Aberaman 3; Felinfoel 6, Bridgend 21; Glamorgan Wanderers 25, Waunarlwydd 3; Glynneath 15, Maesteg 13; Hirwaun 4, Newport 40; Newbridge 36, Blackwood 3; Pontypool United 3, Llanelli 65; St Peter's 11, South Wales Police 12; Tonyrefail 6, Blaina 12; Vardre 23, *Taffs Well 23
*Winners on 'most tries' rule

Fifth Round
Cardiff 24, Aberavon Quins 15; Ebbw Vale 6, Abertillery 17; Glamorgan Wanderers 18, Taffs Well 4; Glynneath 9, Bridgend 42; Llanharan 17, South Wales Police 10; Neath 47, Blaina 12; Newport 3, Newbridge 7; Pontypridd 11, Llanelli 26

Sixth Round
Glamorgan Wanderers 0, Neath 38; Llanelli 22, Bridgend 13; Llanharan 13, Cardiff 25; Newbridge 12, Abertillery 9

Semi-finals
Llanelli 26 Newbridge 24
    (at Cardiff Arms Park)
Neath 19 Cardiff 12
    (at Swansea)

FINAL (at Cardiff Arms Park)
Neath 14 Llanelli 13

Previous finals
(all at Cardiff, National Ground)
1972 Neath 15 Llanelli 9
1973 Llanelli 30 Cardiff 7
1974 Llanelli 12 Aberavon 10
1975 Llanelli 15 Aberavon 6
1976 Llanelli 15 Swansea 4
1977 Newport 16 Cardiff 15
1978 Swansea 13 Newport 9
1979 Bridgend 18 Pontypridd 12
1980 Bridgend 15 Swansea 9
1981 Cardiff 14 Bridgend 6
1982* Cardiff 12 Bridgend 12
1983 Pontypool 18 Swansea 6
1984 Cardiff 24 Neath 19
1985 Llanelli 15 Cardiff 14
1986 Cardiff 28 Newport 21
1987 Cardiff 16 Swansea 15
1988 Llanelli 28 Neath 13
*Winners on 'most tries' rule

WELSH INTERNATIONAL PLAYERS
(up to 30 April 1989)

ABBREVIATIONS

A – Australia; *C* – Canada; *E* – England; *F* – France; *Fj* – Fiji; *I* – Ireland; *M* – Maoris; *NSW* – New South Wales; *NZ* – New Zealand; *NZA* – New Zealand Army; *R* – Romania; *S* – Scotland; *SA* – South Africa; *Tg* – Tonga; *US* – United States; *WS* – Western Samoa; (R) – Replacement. Entries in square brackets [ ] indicate appearances in the World Cup.

Note: Years given for Five Nations' matches are for second half of season; eg 1972 means season 1971-72. Years for all other matches refer to the actual year of the match. When a series has taken place, figures have been used to denote the particular matches in which players have featured. Thus 1969 *NZ* 2 indicates that a player appeared in the second Test of the series.

Ackerman, R A (Newport, London Welsh) 1980 *NZ*, 1981 *E, S, A*, 1982 *I, F, E, S*, 1983 *S, I, F, R*, 1984 *S, I, F, E, A*, 1985 *S, I, F, E, Fj*
Alexander, E P (Llandovery Coll, Cambridge U) 1885 *S*, 1886 *E, S*, 1887 *E, I*
Alexander, W H (Llwynypia) 1898 *I, E*, 1899 *E, S, I*, 1901 *S, I*
Allen, C P (Oxford U, Beaumaris) 1884 *E, S*
Andrews, F (Pontypool) 1912 *SA*, 1913 *E, S, I*
Andrews, F G (Swansea) 1884 *E, S*
Andrews, G E (Newport) 1926 *E, S*, 1927 *E, F, I*
Anthony, L (Neath) 1948 *E, S, F*
Arnold, W R(Swansea) 1903 *S*
Arthur, C S (Cardiff) 1888 *I, M*, 1891 *E*
Arthur, T (Neath) 1927 *S, F, I*, 1929 *E, S, F, I*, 1930 *E, S, I, F*, 1931 *E, S, F, I, SA*, 1933 *E, S*
Ashton, C(Aberavon) 1959 *E, S, I*, 1960 *E, S, I*, 1962 *I*
Attewell, S L (Newport) 1921 *E, S, F*

Badger, O (Llanelli) 1895 *E, S, I*, 1896 *E*
Baker, A (Neath) 1921 *I*, 1923 *E, S, F, I*
Baker, A M (Newport) 1909 *S, F*, 1910 *S*
Bancroft, J (Swansea) 1909 *E, S, I, F*, 1910 *F, E, S, I*, 1911 *E, F, I*, 1912 *E, S, I*, 1913 *I*, 1914 *E, S, F*
Bancroft, W J (Swansea) 1890 *S, E, I*, 1891 *E, S, I*, 1892 *E, S, I*, 1893 *E, S, I*, 1894 *E, S, I*, 1895 *E, S, I*, 1896 *E, S, I*, 1897 *E*, 1898 *I, E*, 1899 *E, S, I*, 1900 *E, S, I*, 1901 *E, S, I*
Barlow, T M (Cardiff) 1884 *I*
Barrell, R (Cardiff) 1929 *S, F, I*, 1933 *I*
Bartlett, J D (Llanelli) 1927 *S*, 1928 *E, S*
Bassett, A (Cardiff) 1934 *I*, 1935 *E, S, I*, 1938 *E, S*
Bassett, J A (Penarth) 1929 *E, S, F, I*, 1930 *E, S, I*, 1931 *E, S, F, I, SA*, 1932 *E, S, I*
Bayliss, G (Pontypool) 1933 *S*
Bebb, D I E (Carmarthen TC, Swansea) 1959 *E, S, I, F*, 1960 *E, S, I, F, SA*, 1961 *E, S, I, F*, 1962 *E, S, F, I*, 1963 *E, F, NZ*, 1964 *E, S, F, SA*, 1965 *E, S, I, F*, 1966 *F, A*, 1967 *S, I, F, E*
Beckingham, G (Cardiff) 1953 *E, S*, 1958 *F*
Bennett, I (Aberavon) 1937 *I*
Bennett, P (Cardiff Harlequins) 1891 *E, S*, 1892 *S, I*
Bennett, P (Llanelli) 1969 *F* (R), 1970 *SA, S, F*, 1972 *S* (R), *NZ*, 1973 *E, S, I, F, A*, 1974 *S, I, F, E*, 1975 *S* (R), *I*, 1976 *E, S, I, F*, 1977 *I, F, E, S*, 1978 *E, S, I, F*
Bergiers, R T E (Cardiff Coll of Ed, Llanelli) 1972 *E, S, F, NZ*, 1973 *E, S, I, F, A*, 1974 *E*, 1975 *I*
Bevan, G W (Llanelli) 1947 *E*
Bevan, J A (Cambridge U) 1881 *E*
Bevan, J C (Cardiff, Cardiff Coll of Ed) 1971 *E, S, I, F*, 1972 *E, S, F, NZ*, 1973 *E, S*
Bevan, J D (Aberavon) 1975 *F, E, S, A*
Bevan, S (Swansea) 1904 *I*
Beynon, B (Swansea) 1920 *E, S*
Beynon, G E (Swansea) 1925 *F, I*
Biggs, N W (Cardiff) 1888 *M*, 1889 *I*, 1892 *I*, 1893 *E, S, I*, 1894 *E, I*
Biggs, S H (Cardiff) 1895 *E, S*, 1896 *S*, 1897 *E*, 1898 *I, E*, 1899 *S, I*, 1900 *I*
Birch, J (Neath) 1911 *S, F*
Birt, F W (Newport) 1911 *E, S*, 1912 *E, S, I, SA*, 1913 *E*
Bishop, D J (Pontypool) 1984 *A*
Bishop, E H (Swansea) 1889 *S*

Blackmore, J H (Abertillery) 1909 *E*
Blackmore, S W (Cardiff) 1987 *I*, [*Tg*(R), *C, A*]
Blake, J (Cardiff) 1899 *E, S, I*, 1900 *E, S, I*, 1901 *E, S, I*
Blakemore, R E (Newport) 1947 *E*
Bland, A F (Cardiff) 1887 *E, S, I*, 1888 *S, I, M*, 1890 *S, E, I*
Blyth, L (Swansea) 1951 *SA*, 1952 *E, S*
Blyth, W R (Swansea) 1974 *E*, 1975 *S* (R), 1980 *F, E, S, I*
Boon, R W (Cardiff) 1930 *S, F*, 1931 *E, S, F, I, SA*, 1932 *E, S, I*, 1933 *E, I*
Booth, J (Pontymister) 1898 *I*
Boots, J G (Newport) 1898 *I, E*, 1899 *I*, 1900 *E, S, I*, 1901 *E, S, I*, 1902 *E, S, I*, 1903 *E, S, I*, 1904 *E*
Boucher, A W (Newport) 1892 *E, S, I*, 1893 *E, S, I*, 1894 *E*, 1895 *E, S, I*, 1896 *E, I*, 1897 *E*
Bowcott, H M (Cardiff, Cambridge U) 1929 *S, F, I*, 1930 *E*, 1931 *E, S*, 1933 *E, I*
Bowdler, F A (Cross Keys) 1927 *NSW*, 1928 *E, S, I, F*, 1929 *E, S, F, I*, 1930 *E*, 1931 *SA*, 1932 *E, S, I*, 1933 *I*
Bowen, B (S Wales Police, Swansea) 1983 *R*, 1984 *S, I, F, E*, 1985 *Fj*, 1986 *E, S, I, F, Fj, Tg, WS*, 1987 [*C, E, NZ*], *US*, 1988 *E, S, I, F, WS*, 1989 *S, I*
Bowen, C A (Llanelli) 1896 *E, S, I*, 1897 *E*
Bowen D H (Llanelli) 1883 *E*, 1886 *E, S*, 1887 *E*
Bowen, G E (Swansea) 1887 *S, I*, 1888 *S, I*
Bowen, W (Swansea) 1921 *S, F*, 1922 *E, S, I, F*
Bowen, Wm A (Swansea) 1886 *E, S*, 1887 *E, S, I*, 1888 *M*, 1889 *S, I*, 1890 *S, E, I*, 1891 *E, S*
Brace, D O (Llanelli, Oxford U) 1956 *E, S, I, F*, 1957 *E*, 1960 *S, I, F*, 1961 *I*
Braddock, K J (Newbridge) 1966 *A*, 1967 *S, I*
Bradshaw, K (Bridgend) 1964 *E, S, I, F, SA*, 1966 *E, S, I, F*
Brewer, T J (Newport) 1950 *E*, 1955 *E, S*
Brice, A B (Aberavon) 1899 *E, S, I*, 1900 *E, S, I*, 1901 *E, S, I*, 1902 *E, S, I*, 1903 *E, S, I*, 1904 *E, S, I*
Bridie, R H (Newport) 1882 *I*
Britton, G R (Newport) 1961 *S*
Broughton, A S (Treorchy) 1927 *NSW*, 1929 *S*
Brown, A (Newport) 1921 *I*
Brown, J (Cardiff) 1925 *I*
Brown, J A (Cardiff) 1907 *E, S, I*, 1908 *E, S, F*, 1909 *E*
Brown, M (Pontypool) 1983 *R*, 1986 *E, S, Fj*(R), *Tg, WS*
Bryant, D J (Bridgend) 1988 *NZ* 1,2, *WS*, R, 1989 *S, I, F, E*
Buchanan, A (Llanelli) 1987 [*Tg, E, NZ, A*], 1988 *I*
Burcher, D H (Newport) 1977 *I, F, E, S*
Burgess, R C (Ebbw Vale) 1977 *I, F, E, S*, 1981 *I, F*, 1982 *F, E, S*
Burnett, R (Newport) 1953 *E*
Burns, J (Cardiff) 1927 *F, I*
Bush, P F (Cardiff) 1905 *NZ*, 1906 *E, SA*, 1907 *I*, 1908 *E, S*, 1910 *S, I*
Butler, E T (Pontypool) 1980 *F, E, S, I, NZ* (R), 1982 *S*, 1983 *E, S, I, F, R*, 1984 *S, I, F, E, A*

Cale, W R (Newbridge, Pontypool) 1949 *E, S, I*, 1950 *E, S, I, F*
Cattell, A (Llanelli) 1883 *E, S*
Challinor, C (Neath) 1939 *E*
Clapp, T J S (Newport) 1882 *I*, 1883 *E, S*, 1884 *E, S, I*, 1885 *E, S*, 1886 *S*, 1887 *E, S, I*, 1888 *S, I*

Clare, J (Cardiff) 1883 *E*
Clark, S S (Neath) 1882 *I*, 1887 *I*
Cleaver, W B (Cardiff) 1947 *E, S, F, I, A*, 1948 *E, S, F, I*, 1949 *I*, 1950 *E, S, I, F*
Clegg, B G (Swansea) 1979 *F*
Clement, A (Swansea) 1987 *US*(R), 1988 *E, NZ* 1, *WS*(R), *R*
Clement, W H (Llanelli) 1937 *E, S, I*, 1938 *E, S, I*
Cobner, T J (Pontypool) 1974 *S, I, F, E*, 1975 *F, E, S, I, A*, 1976 *E, S*, 1977 *F, E, S*, 1978 *E, S, I, F, A* 1
Coldrick, A P (Newport) 1911 *E, S, I*, 1912 *E, S, F*
Coleman, E (Newport) 1949 *E, S, I*
Coles, F C (Pontypool) 1960 *S, I, F*
Collins, J (Aberavon) 1958 *A, E, S, F*, 1959 *E, S, I, F*, 1960 *E*, 1961 *F*
Collins, R G (S Wales Police, Cardiff) 1987 *E* (R), *I*, [*I, E, NZ*], *US*, 1988 *E, S, I, F, R*
Collins, T (Mountain Ash) 1923 *I*
Conway-Rees, J (Llanelli) 1892 *S*, 1893 *E*, 1894 *E*
Cook, T (Cardiff) 1949 *S, I*
Cope, W (Cardiff, Blackheath) 1896 *S*
Cornish, F H (Cardiff) 1897 *E*, 1898 *I, E*, 1899 *I*
Cornish, R A (Cardiff) 1923 *E, S*, 1924 *E*, 1925 *E, S, F*, 1926 *E, S, I, F*
Coslett, K (Aberavon) 1962 *E, S, F*
Cowey, B T V (Welch Regt, Newport) 1934 *E, S, I*, 1935 *E*
Cresswell, B (Newport) 1960 *E, S, I, F*
Cummins, W (Treorchy) 1922 *E, S, I, F*
Cunningham, L J (Aberavon) 1960 *E, S, I, F*, 1962 *E, S, F, I*, 1963 *NZ*, 1964 *E, S, I, F, SA*

Dacey, M (Swansea) 1983 *E, S, I, F, R*, 1984 *S, I, F, E, A*, 1986 *Fj, Tg, WS*, 1987 *F* (R), [*Tg*]
Daniel, D J (Llanelli) 1891 *S*, 1894 *E, S, I*, 1898 *I, E*, 1899 *E, I*
Daniel, L T D (Newport) 1970 *S*
Daniels, P C T (Cardiff) 1981 *A*, 1982 *I*
Darbishire, G (Bangor) 1881 *E*
Dauncey, F H (Newport) 1896 *E, S, I*
Davey, E C (Swansea) 1930 *F*, 1931 *E, S, F, I, SA*, 1932 *E, S, I*, 1933 *E, S*, 1934 *E, S, I*, 1935 *E, S, I, NZ*, 1936 *S*, 1937 *E, I*, 1938 *E, I*
David, R J (Cardiff) 1907 *I*
David, T P (Llanelli, Pontypridd) 1973 *F, A*, 1976 *I, F*
Davidge, G D (Newport) 1959 *F*, 1960 *S, I, F, SA*, 1961 *E, S, I*, 1962 *F*
Davies, A C (London Welsh) 1889 *I*
Davies, A E (Llanelli) 1984 *A*
Davies, B (Llanelli) 1895 *E*, 1896 *E*
Davies, C (Cardiff) 1947 *S, F, I, A*, 1948 *E, S, F, I*, 1949 *F*, 1950 *E, S, I, F*, 1951 *E, S, I*
Davies C (Llanelli) 1988 *WS*, 1989 *S, I* (R), *F*
Davies, C H A (Llanelli, Cardiff) 1957 *I*, 1958 *A, E, S, I*, 1960 *SA*, 1961 *E*
Davies, C L (Cardiff) 1956 *E, S, I*
Davies, C R (Bedford, RAF) 1934 *E*
Davies, D (Bridgend) 1921 *I*, 1925 *I*
Davies, D B (Llanelli) 1907 *E*
Davies, D B (Llanelli) 1962 *I*, 1963 *E, S*
Davies, D G (Cardiff) 1923 *E, S*
Davies, D H (Neath) 1904 *S*
Davies, D H (Aberavon) 1924 *E*
Davies, D I (Swansea) 1939 *E*
Davies, D J (Neath) 1962 *I*
Davies, D M (Somerset Police) 1950 *E, S, I, F*, 1951 *E, S, I, F, SA*, 1952 *E, S, I, F*, 1953 *I, F, NZ*, 1954 *E*
Davies, E (Aberavon) 1947 *A*, 1948 *I*
Davies, E (Maesteg) 1919 *NZA*
Davies, E G (Cardiff) 1912 *E, F*
Davies, G (Swansea) 1900 *E, S, I*, 1901 *E, S, I*, 1905 *E, S, I*
Davies, G (Cambridge U, Pontypridd) 1947 *S, A*, 1948 *E, S, F, I*, 1949 *E, S, F*, 1951 *E, S*
Davies, G (Llanelli) 1921 *F, I*, 1925 *F*
Davies, G (Cardiff) 1928 *F*, 1929 *E*, 1930 *S*
Davies, H (Swansea) 1898 *I, E*, 1901 *S, I*
Davies, H (Swansea, Llanelli) 1939 *S, I*, 1947 *E, S, F, I*
Davies, H (Neath) 1912 *E, S*
Davies, H (Bridgend) 1984 *S, I, F, E*
Davies, H J (Cambridge U, Aberavon) 1959 *E, S*
Davies, H J (Newport) 1924 *S*
Davies, I T (Llanelli) 1914 *S, F, I*

Davies, J (Neath, Llanelli) 1985 *E, Fj*, 1986 *E, S, I, F, Fj, Tg, WS*, 1987 *F, E, S, I*, [*I, Tg*(R), *C, E, NZ, A*], 1988 *E, S, I, F, NZ*1,2, *WS, R*
Davies, Rev J A (Swansea) 1913 *S, F, I*, 1914 *E, S, F, I*
Davies, J H (Aberavon) 1923 *I*
Davies, L (Swansea) 1939 *S, I*
Davies, L (Bridgend) 1966 *E, S, I*
Davies, L M (Llanelli) 1954 *F, S*, 1955 *I*
Davies, M (Swansea) 1981 *A*, 1982 *I*, 1985 *Fj*
Davies, M J (Blackheath) 1939 *S, I*
Davies, N G (London Welsh) 1955 *E*
Davies, N G (Llanelli) 1988 *NZ*2, *WS*, 1989 *S, I*
Davies, P T (Llanelli) 1985 *E, Fj*, 1986 *E, S, I, F, Fj, Tg, WS*, 1987 *F, E, I*, [*Tg, C, NZ*], 1988 *WS, R*, 1989 *S, I, F, E*
Davies, R H (Oxford U, London Welsh) 1957 *S, I, F*, 1958 *A*, 1962 *E, S*
Davies, S (Treherbert) 1923 *I*
Davies, T G R (Cardiff, London Welsh) 1966 *A*, 1967 *S, I, F, E*, 1968 *E, S*, 1969 *S, I, F, NZ* 1,2, *A*, 1971 *E, S, I, F*, 1972 *E, S, F, NZ*, 1973 *E, S, I, F, A*, 1974 *S, F, E*, 1975 *F, E, S, I*, 1976 *E, S, I, F*, 1977 *I, F, E, S*, 1978 *E, S, I, A* 1,2
Davies, T J (Devonport Services, Swansea, Llanelli) 1953 *E, S, I, F*, 1957 *E, S, I, F*, 1958 *A, E, S, F*, 1959 *E, S, I, F*, 1960 *E, SA*, 1961 *E, S, F*
Davies, T M (London Welsh, Swansea) 1969 *S, I, F, E, NZ* 1,2, *A*, 1970 *SA, S, E, I, F*, 1971 *E, S, I, F*, 1972 *E, S, F, NZ*, 1973 *E, S, I, F, A*, 1974 *S, I, F, E*, 1975 *F, E, S, I, A*, 1976 *E, S, I, F*
Davies, W (Cardiff) 1896 *S*
Davies, W (Swansea) 1931 *SA*, 1932 *E, S, I*
Davies, W A (Aberavon) 1912 *S, I*
Davies, W G (Cardiff) 1978 *A* 1,2, *NZ*, 1979 *S, I, F, E*, 1980 *F, E, S, NZ*, 1981 *E, S, A*, 1982 *I, F, E, S*, 1985 *S, I, F*
Davies, W T H (Swansea) 1936 *I*, 1937 *E, I*, 1939 *E, S, I*
Davis, C E (Newbridge) 1978 *A* 2, 1981 *E, S*
Davis, W E N (Cardiff) 1939 *E, S, I*
Dawes, S J (London Welsh) 1964 *I, F, SA*, 1965 *E, S, I, F*, 1966 *A*, 1968 *I, F*, 1969 *E, NZ* 2, *A*, 1970 *SA, S, E, I, F*, 1971 *E, S, I, F*
Day, H C (Newport) 1930 *S, I, F*, 1931 *E, S*
Day, H T (Newport) 1892 *I*, 1893 *E, S*, 1894 *S, I*
Day, T B (Swansea) 1931 *E, S, F, I, SA*, 1932 *E, S, I*, 1934 *S, I*, 1935 *E, S, I*
Deacon, J T (Swansea) 1891 *I*, 1892 *E, S, I*
Delahay, W J (Bridgend) 1922 *E, S, I, F*, 1923 *E, S, F, I*, 1924 *NZ*, 1925 *E, S, F, I*, 1926 *E, S, I, F*, 1927 *S*
Delaney, L (Llanelli) 1989 *I, F, E*
Devereux, D (Neath) 1958 *A, E, S*
Devereux, J A (S Glamorgan Inst, Bridgend) 1986 *E, S, I, F, Fj, Tg, WS*, 1987 *F, E, S, I*, [*I, C, E, NZ, A*], 1988 *NZ*1,2, *R*, 1989 *S, I*
Diplock, R (Bridgend) 1988 *R*
Dobson, G (Cardiff) 1900 *S*
Dobson, T (Cardiff) 1898 *I, E*, 1899 *E, S*
Donovan, A J (Swansea) 1978 *A* 2, 1981 *I* (R), *A*, 1982 *E, S*
Donovan, R (S Wales Police) 1983 *F* (R)
Douglas, M H J (Llanelli) 1984 *S, I, F*
Douglas, W M (Cardiff) 1886 *E, S*, 1887 *E, S*
Dowell, W H (Newport) 1907 *E, S, I*, 1908 *E, S, F, I*
Dyke, J C M (Penarth) 1906 *SA*
Dyke, L M (Penarth, Cardiff) 1910 *I*, 1911 *S, F, I*

Edwards, A B (London Welsh, Army) 1955 *E, S*
Edwards, B O (Newport) 1951 *I*
Edwards, D (Glynneath) 1921 *E*
Edwards, G O (Cardiff, Cardiff Coll of Ed) 1967 *F, E, NZ*, 1968 *E, S, I, F*, 1969 *S, I, F, E, NZ* 1,2, *A*, 1970 *SA, S, E, I, F*, 1971 *E, S, I, F*, 1972 *E, S, F, NZ*, 1973 *E, S, I, F, A*, 1974 *S, I, F, E*, 1975 *F, E, S, I, A*, 1976 *E, S, I, F*, 1977 *I, F, E, S, I, F*
Eidman, I H (Cardiff) 1983 *S, R*, 1984 *I, F, E, A*, 1985 *S, I, Fj*, 1986 *E, S, I, F*
Elliott, J E (Cardiff) 1894 *I*, 1898 *I, E*
Elsey, W J (Cardiff) 1895 *E*
Emyr, Arthur (see Jones, A E)
Evans, A C (Pontypool) 1924 *E, I, F*
Evans, B (Swansea) 1933 *S*
Evans, B (Llanelli) 1933 *E, S*, 1936 *E, S, I*, 1937 *E*

227

Evans, B S (Llanelli) 1920 E, 1922 E, S, I, F
Evans, C (Pontypool) 1960 E
Evans, D (Penygraig) 1896 S, I, 1897 E, 1898 E
Evans, D B (Swansea) 1926 E
Evans, D D (Cheshire, Cardiff U) 1934 E
Evans, D P (Llanelli) 1960 SA
Evans, D W (Cardiff) 1889 S, I, 1890 E, I, 1891 E
Evans, D W (Oxford U, Cardiff) 1989 F, E
Evans, E (Llanelli) 1937 E, 1939 S, I
Evans, F (Llanelli) 1921 S
Evans, G (Cardiff) 1947 E, S, F, I, A, 1948 E, S, F, I, 1949 E, S, I
Evans, G (Maesteg) 1981 S (R), I, F, A, 1982 I, F, E, S, 1983 F, R
Evans, G L (Newport) 1977 F (R), 1978 F, A 2 (R)
Evans, I (London Welsh) 1934 S, I
Evans, I (Swansea) 1922 E, S, I, F
Evans, I C (Llanelli) 1987 F, E, S, I, [I, C, E, NZ, A], 1988 E, S, I, F, NZ1,2 1989 I, F, S
Evans, J (Llanelli) 1896 S, I, 1897 E
Evans, J (Blaina) 1904 E
Evans, J (Pontypool) 1907 E, S, I
Evans, J D (Cardiff) 1958 I, F
Evans, J E (Llanelli) 1924 S
Evans, J R (Newport) 1934 E
Evans, O J (Cardiff) 1887 E, S, 1888 S, I
Evans, P D (Llanelli) 1951 E, F
Evans, R (Cardiff) 1889 S
Evans, R (Bridgend) 1963 S, I, F
Evans, R T (Newport) 1947 F, I, 1950 E, S, I, F, 1951 E, S, I, F
Evans, S (Swansea, Neath) 1985 F, E, 1986 Fj, Tg, WS, 1987 F, E, [I, Tg]
Evans, T (Swansea) 1924 I
Evans, T G (London Welsh) 1970 SA, S, E, I, 1972 E, S, F
Evans, T H (Llanelli) 1906 I, 1907 E, S, I, 1908 I, A, 1909 E, S, F, I, 1910 F, E, S, I, 1911 E, S, F, I
Evans, T P (Swansea) 1975 F, E, S, I, A, 1976 E, S, I, F, 1977 I
Evans, V (Neath) 1954 I, F, S
Evans, W (Llanelli) 1958 A
Evans, W F (Rhymney) 1882 I, 1883 S
Evans, W G (Brynmawr) 1911 I
Evans, W H (Llwynypia) 1914 E, S, F, I
Evans, W J (Pontypool) 1947 S
Evans, W R (Bridgend) 1958 A, E, S, I, F, 1960 SA, 1961 E, S, I, F, 1962 E, S, I
Everson, W A (Newport) 1926 S

Faulkner, A G (Pontypool) 1975 F, E, S, I, A, 1976 E, S, I, F, 1978 E, S, I, F, A 1,2, NZ, 1979 S, I, F
Faull, J (Swansea) 1957 I, F, 1958 A, E, S, I, F, 1959 E, S, I, 1960 E, F
Fauvel, T J (Aberavon) 1988 NZ1(R)
Fear, A G (Newport) 1934 S, I, 1935 S, I
Fender, N H (Cardiff) 1930 I, F, 1931 E, S, F, I
Fenwick, S P (Bridgend) 1975 F, E, S, A, 1976 E, S, I, F, 1977 I, F, E, S, 1978 E, S, I, F, A 1,2, NZ, 1979 S, I, F, E, 1980 F, E, S, I, NZ, 1981 E, S
Finch, E (Llanelli) 1924 F, NZ, 1925 F, I, 1926 F, 1927 NSW, 1928 I
Finlayson, A A J (Cardiff) 1974 I, F, E
Fitzgerald, D (Cardiff) 1894 S, I
Ford, F J V (Welch Regt, Newport) 1939 E
Ford, I (Newport) 1959 E, S
Forward, A (Pontypool, Mon Police) 1951 S, SA, 1952 E, S, I, F
Fowler, I J (Llanelli) 1919 NZA
Francis, D G (Llanelli) 1919 NZA 1924 S
Francis, P (Maesteg) 1987 S

Gabe, R T (Cardiff, Llanelli) 1901 I, 1902 E, S, I, 1903 E, S, I, 1904 E, S, I, 1905 E, S, I, NZ, 1906 E, I, SA, 1907 E, S, I, 1908 E, S, F, I
Gale, N R (Swansea, Llanelli) 1960 I, 1963 E, S, I, NZ, 1964 E, S, I, F, SA, 1965 E, S, I, F, 1966 E, S, I, F, A, 1967 E, NZ, 1968 E, 1969 NZ 1 (R), 2, A
Gallacher, I S (Llanelli) 1970 F
Garrett, R M (Penarth) 1888 M, 1889 S, 1890 S, E, I, 1891 S, I, 1892 E
Geen, W P (Oxford U, Newport) 1912 SA, 1913 E, I
George, E E (Pontypridd, Cardiff) 1895 S, I, 1896 E

Gething, G I (Neath) 1913 F
Gibbs, R A (Cardiff) 1906 S, I, 1907 E, S, 1908 E, S, F, I, 1910 F, E, S, I, 1911 E, S, F, I
Giles, R (Aberavon) 1983 R, 1985 Fj (R), 1987 [C]
Girling, B E (Cardiff) 1881 E
Goldsworthy, S J (Swansea) 1884 I, 1885 E, S
Gore, J H (Blaina) 1924 I, F, NZ, 1925 E
Gore, W (Newbridge) 1947 S, F, I
Gould, A J (Newport) 1885 E, S, 1886 E, S, 1887 E, S, I, 1888 S, 1889 I, 1890 S, E, I, 1892 E, S, I, 1893 E, S, I, 1894 E, S, 1895 E, S, I, 1896 E, S, I, 1897 E
Gould, G H (Newport) 1892 I, 1893 S, I
Gould, R (Newport) 1882 I, 1883 E, S, 1884 E, S, I, 1885 E, S, 1886 E, 1887 E, S
Graham, T C (Newport) 1890 I, 1891 S, I, 1892 E, S, 1893 E, S, I, 1894 E, S, 1895 E, S
Gravell, R W R (Llanelli) 1975 F, E, S, I, A, 1976 S, I, F, 1978 E, S, I, F, A 1,2, NZ, 1979 S, I, 1981 I, F, 1982 F, E, S
Gray, A J (London Welsh) 1968 E, S
Greenslade, D (Newport) 1962 S
Greville, H G (Llanelli) 1947 A
Griffin, Dr J (Edinburgh U) 1883 S
Griffiths, C (Llanelli) 1979 E (R)
Griffiths, D (Llanelli) 1888 M, 1889 I
Griffiths, G (Llanelli) 1889 I
Griffiths, G M (Cardiff) 1953 E, S, I, F, NZ, 1954 I, F, S, 1955 I, F, 1957 E, S
Griffiths, J L (Llanelli) 1988 NZ2, 1989 S
Griffiths, M (Bridgend) 1988 WS, R, 1989 S, I, F, E
Griffiths, V M (Newport) 1924 S, I, F
Gronow, B (Bridgend) 1910 F, E, S, I
Gwilliam, J A (Cambridge U, Newport) 1947 A, 1948 I, 1949 E, S, I, F, 1950 E, S, I, F, 1951 E, S, I, SA, 1952 E, S, I, F, 1953 E, I, F, NZ, 1954 E, S
Gwynn, D (Swansea) 1883 E, 1887 S, 1890 E, I, 1891 E, S
Gwynn, W H (Swansea) 1884 E, S, I, 1885 E, S

Hadley, A M (Cardiff) 1983 R, 1984 S, I, F, E, 1985 F, E, Fj, 1986 E, S, I, F, Fj, Tg, 1987 S (R), I, [I, Tg, C, E, NZ, A], US, 1988 E, S, I, F
Hall, I (Aberavon) 1967 NZ, 1970 SA, S, E, 1971 S, 1974 S, I, F
Hall, M R (Cambridge U, Bridgend) 1988 NZ1(R),2, WS, R, 1989 S, I, F, E
Hall, W H (Bridgend) 1988 WS
Hancock, F E (Cardiff) 1884 I, 1885 E, S, 1886 S
Hannan, J (Newport) 1888 M, 1889 S, I, 1890 S, E, I, 1891 E, 1892 E, S, I, 1893 E, S, I, 1894 E, S, I, 1895 E, S, I
Harding, A F (London Welsh) 1902 E, S, I, 1903 E, S, I, 1904 E, S, I, 1905 E, S, I, NZ, 1906 E, S, I, 1907 I, 1908 E, S
Harding, G F (Newport) 1881 E, 1882 I, 1883 E, S
Harding, T (Newport) 1888 M, 1889 S, I
Harding, W R (Swansea, Cambridge U) 1923 E, S, F, I, 1924 I, F, NZ, 1925 F, I, 1926 E, I, F, 1927 E, S, F, I, 1928 E
Harris, D J E (Pontypridd, Cardiff) 1959 I, F, 1960 S, I, F, SA, 1961 E, S, I, F
Harris, T (Aberavon) 1927 NSW
Hathway, G F (Newport) 1924 I, F
Havard, Rev W T (Llanelli) 1919 NZA
Hawkins, F (Pontypridd) 1912 I, F
Hayward, D (Newbridge) 1949 E, F, 1950 E, S, I, F, 1951 E, S, I, F, SA, 1952 E, S, I, F
Hayward, D J (Cardiff) 1963 E, NZ, 1964 S, I, F, SA
Hayward, G (Swansea) 1908 S, F, I, A, 1909 E
Hellings, R (Llwynypia) 1897 E, 1898 I, E, 1899 S, I, 1900 E, I, 1901 E, S
Herrerá, R C (Cross Keys) 1925 S, F, I, 1926 E, S, I, F, 1927 E
Hiams, H (Swansea) 1912 I, F
Hickman, A (Neath) 1930 E, 1933 S
Hiddlestone, D D (Neath) 1922 E, S, I, F, 1924 NZ
Hill, A F (Cardiff) 1885 S, 1886 E, S, 1888 S, I, M, 1889 S, 1890 S, I, 1893 E, S, I, 1894 E, S, I
Hinam, S (Cardiff) 1925 I, 1926 E, S, I, F
Hinton, J T (Cardiff) 1884 I
Hirst, G L (Newport) 1912 S, 1913 S, 1914 E, S, F, I
Hodder, W (Pontypool) 1921 E, S, F
Hodges, J J (Newport) 1899 E, S, I, 1900 E, S, I, 1901

E, S, 1902 *E, S, I*, 1903 *E, S, I*, 1904 *E, S*, 1905 *E, S, I*,
NZ, 1906 *E, S, I*
Hodgson, G T R (Neath) 1962 *I*, 1963 *E, S, I, F, NZ*,
1964 *E, S, I, F, SA*, 1966 *S, I, F*, 1967 *I*
Hollingdale, H (Swansea) 1912 *SA*, 1913 *E*
Hollingdale, T H (Neath) 1927 *NSW*, 1928 *E, S, I, F*,
1930 *E*
Holmes, T D (Cardiff) 1978 *A* 2, *NZ*, 1979 *S, I, F, E*,
1980 *F, E, S, I, NZ*, 1981 *A*, 1982 *I, F, E*, 1983 *E, S, I*,
F, 1984 *E*, 1985 *S, I, F, E, Fj*
Hopkin, W H (Newport) 1937 *S*
Hopkins, K (Cardiff, Swansea) 1985 *E*, 1987 *F, E, S*,
[*Tg, C*(R)], *US*
Hopkins, P L (Swansea) 1908 *A*, 1909 *E, I*, 1910 *E*
Hopkins, R (Maesteg) 1970 *E* (R)
Hopkins, T (Swansea) 1926 *E, S, I, F*
Hopkins, W J (Aberavon) 1925 *E, S*
Howells, B (Llanelli) 1934 *E*
Howells, W G (Llanelli) 1957 *E, S, I, F*
Howells, W H (Swansea) 1888 *S, I*
Hughes, D (Newbridge) 1967 *NZ*, 1969 *NZ* 2, 1970
SA, S, E, I
Hughes, G (Penarth) 1934 *E, S, I*
Hughes, H (Cardiff) 1887 *S*, 1889 *S*
Hughes, K (Cambridge U, London Welsh) 1970 *I*,
1973 *A*, 1974 *S*
Hullin, W (Cardiff) 1967 *S*
Hurrell, J (Newport) 1959 *F*
Hutchinson, F (Neath) 1894 *I*, 1896 *S, I*
Huxtable, R (Swansea) 1920 *F, I*
Huzzey, H V P (Cardiff) 1898 *I, E*, 1899 *E, S, I*
Hybart, A J (Cardiff) 1887 *E*

Ingledew, H M (Cardiff) 1890 *I*, 1891 *E, S*
Isaacs, I (Cardiff) 1933 *E, S*

Jackson, T H (Swansea) 1895 *E*
James, B (Bridgend) 1968 *E*
James, C R (Llanelli) 1958 *A, F*
James, D (Swansea) 1891 *I*, 1892 *S, I*, 1899 *E*
James, D R (Treorchy) 1931 *F, I*
James, E (Swansea) 1890 *S*, 1891 *I*, 1892 *S, I*, 1899 *E*
James, M (Cardiff) 1947 *A*, 1948 *E, S, F, I*
James, T O (Aberavon) 1935 *I*, 1937 *S*
James, W J (Aberavon) 1983 *E, S, I, F, R*, 1984 *S*,
1985 *S, I, F, E, Fj*, 1986 *E, S, I, F, Fj, Tg, WS*, 1987
E, S, I
James, W P (Aberavon) 1925 *E, S*
Jarman, H (Newport) 1910 *E, S, I*, 1911 *E*
Jarrett, K S (Newport) 1967 *E*, 1968 *E, S*, 1969 *S, I, F*,
E, NZ 1,2, *A*
Jeffery, J J (Cardiff Coll of Ed, Newport) 1967 *NZ*
Jenkin, A M (Swansea) 1895 *I*, 1896 *E*
Jenkins, A (Llanelli) 1920 *E, S, F, I*, 1921 *S, F*, 1922
F, 1923 *E, S, F, I*, 1924 *NZ*, 1928 *S, I*
Jenkins, D M (Treorchy) 1926 *E, S, I, F*
Jenkins, D R (Swansea) 1927 *NSW*, 1929 *E*
Jenkins, E (Newport) 1910 *S, I*
Jenkins, E M (Aberavon) 1927 *S, F, I, NSW*, 1928 *E,
S, I, F*, 1929 *F*, 1930 *E, S, I, F*, 1931 *E, S, F, I, SA*,
1932 *E, S, I*
Jenkins, J C (London Welsh) 1906 *SA*
Jenkins, J L (Aberavon) 1923 *S, F*
Jenkins, L H (Mon TC, Newport) 1954 *I*, 1956 *E, S, I*,
F
Jenkins, V G J (Oxford U, Bridgend, London Welsh)
1933 *E, I*, 1934 *S, I*, 1935 *E, S, NZ*, 1936 *E, S, I*, 1937
E, 1938 *E, S*, 1939 *E*
Jenkins, W (Cardiff) 1912 *I, F*, 1913 *S, I*
John, A (Llanelli) 1925 *I*, 1928 *E, S, I*
John, B (Llanelli, Cardiff) 1966 *A*, 1967 *S, NZ*, 1968 *E,
S, I, F*, 1969 *S, I, F, E, NZ* 1,2, *A*, 1970 *SA, S, E, I*,
1971 *E, S, I, F*, 1972 *E, S, F*
John D E (Llanelli) 1923 *F, I*, 1928 *E, S, I*
John, E R (Neath) 1950 *E, S, I, F*, 1951 *E, S, I, F, SA*,
1952 *E, S, I, F*, 1953 *E, S, I, F, NZ*, 1954 *E*
John, G (St Luke's Coll, Exeter) 1954 *E, F*
John, J H (Swansea) 1926 *E, S, I, F*, 1927 *E, S, F, I*
Johnson, T A (Cardiff) 1921 *E, F, I*, 1923 *E, S, F*,
1924 *E, S, NZ*, 1925 *E, S, F*
Johnson, W D (Swansea) 1953 *E*
Jones, A E (known as Emyr) (Swansea) 1989 *E*
Jones, A H (Cardiff) 1933 *E, S*

Jones, B (Abertillery) 1914 *E, S, F, I*
Jones, Bert (Llanelli) 1934 *S, I*
Jones, Bob (Llwynypia) 1901 *I*
Jones, B J (Newport) 1960 *I, F*
Jones, B Lewis (Devonport Services, Llanelli) 1950 *E,
S, I, F*, 1951 *E, S, SA*, 1952 *E, I, F*
Jones, C W (Cambridge U, Cardiff) 1934 *E, S, I*, 1935
E, S, I, NZ, 1936 *E, S, I*, 1938 *E, S, I*
Jones, C W (Bridgend) 1920 *E, S, F*
Jones, D (Neath) 1927 *NSW*
Jones, D (Aberavon) 1897 *E*
Jones, D (Swansea) 1947 *E, F, I*, 1949 *E, S, I, F*
Jones, D (Treherbert) 1902 *E, S, I*, 1903 *E, S, I*, 1905
E, S, I, NZ, 1906 *E, S, SA*
Jones, D (Newport) 1926 *E, S, I, F*, 1927 *E*
Jones, D (Llanelli) 1948 *E*
Jones, D K (Llanelli, Cardiff) 1962 *E, S, F, I*, 1963 *E,
F, NZ*, 1964 *E, S, SA*, 1966 *E, S, I, F*
Jones, D P (Pontypool) 1907 *I*
Jones, E L (Llanelli) 1930 *F*, 1933 *E, S, I*, 1935 *E*
Jones, Elvet L (Llanelli) 1939 *S*
Jones, G (Ebbw Vale) 1963 *S, I, F*
Jones, G (Llanelli) 1988 *NZ*2, 1989 *F, E*
Jones, G G (Cardiff) 1930 *S*, 1933 *I*
Jones, H (Penygraig) 1902 *S, I*
Jones, H (Neath) 1904 *I*
Jones, H (Neath) 1929 *E, S*
Jones, H (Swansea) 1930 *I, F*
Jones, Iorwerth (Llanelli) 1927 *NSW*, 1928 *E, S, I, F*
Jones, I C (London Welsh) 1968 *I*
Jones, Ivor E (Llanelli) 1924 *E, S*, 1927 *S, F, I, NSW*,
1928 *E, S, I, F*, 1929 *E, S, F, I*, 1930 *E, S*
Jones, J (Aberavon) 1901 *E*
Jones, J (Swansea) 1924 *F*
Jones, Jim (Aberavon) 1919 *NZA*, 1920 *E, S*, 1921 *S,
F, I*
Jones, J A (Cardiff) 1883 *S*
Jones, J P (Tuan) (Pontypool) 1913 *S*
Jones, J P (Pontypool) 1908 *A*, 1909 *E, S, F, I*, 1910 *F,
E*, 1912 *E, F*, 1913 *F, I*, 1920 *F, I*, 1921 *E*
Jones, K D (Cardiff) 1960 *SA*, 1961 *E, S, I*, 1962 *E, F*,
1963 *E, S, I, NZ*
Jones, K J (Newport) 1947 *E, S, F, I, A*, 1948 *E, S, F*,
1, 1949 *E, S, I, F*, 1950 *E, S, I, F*, 1951 *E, S, I, F, SA*,
1952 *E, S, I, F*, 1953 *E, S, I, F, NZ*, 1954 *E, I, F, S*,
1955 *E, S, I, F*, 1956 *E, S, I, F*, 1957 *S*
Jones, K W J (Oxford U, London Welsh) 1934 *E*
Jones, M A (Neath) 1987 *S*, 1988 *NZ*2(R), 1989 *S, I,
F, E*
Jones, P (Newport) 1912 *SA*, 1913 *E, S, F*, 1914 *E, S,
F, I*
Jones, P B (Newport) 1921 *S*
Jones, R (Swansea) 1901 *I*, 1902 *E*, 1904 *E, S*, 1905
E, 1908 *F, I, A*, 1909 *E, S, F, I*, 1910 *F, E*
Jones, R (London Welsh) 1929 *E*
Jones, R (Northampton) 1926 *E, S, F*
Jones, R (Swansea) 1927 *NSW*, 1928 *F*
Jones, R B (Cambridge U) 1933 *E, S*
Jones, R E (Coventry) 1967 *F, E*, 1968 *S, I, F*
Jones, R N (Swansea) 1986 *E, S, I, F, Fj, Tg, WS* 1987
F, E, S, I, [*I, Tg, E, NZ, A*], *US*, 1988 *E, S, I, F,
NZ*1, *WS, R*, 1989 *I, F, E*
Jones, S T (Pontypool) 1983 *S, I, F, R*, 1984 *S*, 1988
*E, S, F, NZ*1,2
Jones, Tom (Newport) 1922 *E, S, I, F*, 1924 *E, S*
Jones, T B (Newport) 1882 *I*, 1883 *E, S*, 1884 *S*, 1885
E, S
Jones, W (Cardiff) 1898 *I, E*
Jones, W (Mountain Ash) 1905 *I*
Jones, W I (Llanelli, Cambridge U) 1925 *E, S, F, I*
Jones, W J (Llanelli) 1924 *I*
Jones, W K (Cardiff) 1967 *NZ*, 1968 *E, S, I, F*
Jones-Davies, T E (London Welsh) 1930 *E, I*, 1931 *E,
S*

Jordan, H M (Newport) 1885 *E, S*, 1889 *S*
Joseph, W (Swansea) 1902 *E, S, I*, 1903 *E, S, I*, 1904
E, S, 1905 *E, S, I, NZ*, 1906 *E, S, I, SA*
Jowett, W F (Swansea) 1903 *E*
Judd, S (Cardiff) 1953 *E, S, I, F, NZ*, 1954 *E, F, S*,
1955 *E, S*
Judson, J H (Llanelli) 1883 *E, S*

Kedzlie, Q D (Cardiff) 1888 *S, I*

Keen, L (Aberavon) 1980 *F, E, S, I*
Knill, F M D (Cardiff) 1976 *F* (R)

Lane, S M (Cardiff) 1978 *A* 1 (R), 2, 1979 *I* (R), 1980 *S, I*
Lang, J (Llanelli) 1931 *F, I,* 1934 *S, I,* 1935 *E, S, I, NZ,* 1936 *E, S, I,* 1937 *E*
Lawrence, S (Bridgend) 1925 *S, I,* 1926 *S, I, F,* 1927 *E*
Law, V J (Newport) 1939 *I*
Legge, W G (Newport) 1937 *I,* 1938 *I*
Leleu, J (London Welsh, Swansea) 1959 *E, S,* 1960 *F, SA*
Lemon, A (Neath) 1929 *I,* 1930 *S, I, F,* 1931 *E, S, F, I, SA,* 1932 *E, S, I,* 1933 *I*
Lewis, A J L (Ebbw Vale) 1970 *F,* 1971 *E, I, F,* 1972 *E, S, F,* 1973 *E, S, I, F*
Lewis, A R (Abertillery) 1966 *E, S, I, F, A,* 1967 *I*
Lewis, B R (Swansea, Cambridge U) 1912 *I,* 1913 *I*
Lewis, C P (Llandovery Coll) 1882 *I,* 1883 *E, S,* 1884 *E, S*
Lewis, D H (Cardiff) 1886 *E, S*
Lewis, E J (Llandovery) 1881 *E*
Lewis, G W (Richmond) 1960 *E, S*
Lewis, H (Swansea) 1913 *S, F, I,* 1914 *E*
Lewis, J G (Llanelli) 1887 *I*
Lewis, J M C (Cardiff, Cambridge U) 1912 *E,* 1913 *S, F, I,* 1914 *E, S, F, I,* 1921 *I,* 1923 *E, S*
Lewis, J R (S Glam Inst, Cardiff) 1981 *E, S, I, F,* 1982 *F, E, S*
Lewis, M (Treorchy) 1913 *F*
Lewis, P I (Llanelli) 1984 *A,* 1985 *S, I, F, E,* 1986 *E, S, I*
Lewis, T W (Cardiff) 1926 *E,* 1927 *E, S*
Lewis, W (Llanelli) 1925 *F*
Lewis, W H (London Welsh, Cambridge U) 1926 *I,* 1927 *E, F, I, NSW,* 1928 *F*
Llewellyn, P D (Swansea) 1973 *I, F, A,* 1974 *S, E*
Llewellyn, W (Llwynypia) 1899 *E, S, I,* 1900 *E, S, I,* 1901 *E, S, I,* 1902 *E, S, I,* 1903 *I,* 1904 *E, S, I,* 1905 *E, S, I, NZ*
Llewellyn, D B (Newport, Llanelli) 1970 *SA, S, E, I, F,* 1971 *E, S, I, F,* 1972 *E, S, F, NZ*
Lloyd, D J (Bridgend) 1966 *E, S, I, F, A,* 1967 *S, I, F, E,* 1968 *S, I, F,* 1969 *S, I, F, E, NZ* 1, *A,* 1970 *F,* 1972 *E, S, F,* 1973 *E, S*
Lloyd, E (Llanelli) 1895 *S*
Lloyd, G L (Newport) 1896 *I,* 1899 *S, I,* 1900 *E, S,* 1901 *E, S,* 1902 *S, I,* 1903 *E, S, I*
Lloyd, P (Llanelli) 1890 *S, E,* 1891 *E, I*
Lloyd, R A (Pontypool) 1913 *S, F, I,* 1914 *E, S, F, I*
Lloyd, T (Maesteg) 1953 *I, F*
Lloyd, T C (Neath) 1909 *F,* 1913 *F, I,* 1914 *E, S, F, I*
Lockwood, T W (Newport) 1887 *E, S, I*
Long, E C (Swansea) 1936 *E, S, I,* 1937 *E, S,* 1939 *S, I*
Lyne, H S (Newport) 1883 *S,* 1884 *E, S, I,* 1885 *E*

McCall, B E W (Welch Regt, Newport) 1936 *E, S, I*
McCarley, A (Neath) 1938 *E, S, I*
McCutcheon, W M (Swansea) 1891 *S,* 1892 *E, S,* 1893 *E, S, I,* 1894 *E*
Maddock, H T (London Welsh) 1906 *E, S, I,* 1907 *E, S,* 1910 *F*
Maddocks, K (Neath) 1957 *E*
Main, D R (London Welsh) 1959 *E, S, I, F*
Mainwaring, H J (Swansea) 1961 *F*
Mainwaring, W T (Aberavon) 1967 *S, I, F, E, NZ,* 1968 *E*
Major, W C (Maesteg) 1949 *F,* 1950 *S*
Male, B O (Cardiff) 1921 *F,* 1923 *S,* 1924 *S, I,* 1927 *E, S, F, I,* 1928 *S, I, F*
Manfield, L (Mountain Ash, Cardiff) 1939 *S, I,* 1947 *A,* 1948 *E, S, F, I*
Mann, B B (Cardiff) 1881 *E*
Mantle, J T (Loughborough Colls, Newport) 1964 *E, SA*
Margrave, F L (Llanelli) 1884 *E, S*
Marsden-Jones, D (Cardiff) 1921 *E,* 1924 *NZ*
Martin, A J (Aberavon) 1973 *A,* 1974 *S, I,* 1975 *F, E, S, I, A,* 1976 *E, S, I, F,* 1977 *I, F, E, S,* 1978 *E, S, I, F, A* 1,2, *NZ,* 1979 *S, I, F, E,* 1980 *F, E, S, I, NZ,* 1981 *I, F*
Martin, W J (Newport) 1912 *I, F,* 1919 *NZA*
Mason, J (Pontypridd) 1988 *NZ2*(R)

Mathews, Rev A A (Lampeter) 1886 *S*
Mathias, R (Llanelli) 1970 *F*
Matthews, C (Bridgend) 1939 *I*
Matthews, J (Cardiff) 1947 *E, A,* 1948 *E, S, F,* 1949 *E, S, I, F,* 1950 *E, S, I, F,* 1951 *E, S, I, F*
May, P S (Llanelli) 1988 *E, S, I, F, NZ*1,2
Meredith, A (Devonport Services) 1949 *E, S, I*
Meredith, B V (St Luke's Coll, London Welsh, Newport) 1954 *I, F, S,* 1955 *E, S, I, F,* 1956 *E, S, I, F,* 1957 *E, S, I, F,* 1958 *A, E, S, I,* 1959 *E, S, I, F,* 1960 *E, S, F, SA,* 1961 *E, S, I,* 1962 *E, S, F, I*
Meredith, C C (Neath) 1953 *S, NZ,* 1954 *E, I, F, S,* 1955 *E, S, I, F,* 1956 *E, I,* 1957 *E, S*
Meredith, J (Swansea) 1888 *S, I,* 1890 *S, E*
Merry, A E (Pill Harriers) 1912 *I, F*
Michael, G (Swansea) 1923 *E, S, F*
Michaelson, R C B (Aberavon, Cambridge U) 1963 *E*
Miller, F (Mountain Ash) 1896 *I,* 1900 *E, S, I,* 1901 *E, S, I*
Mills, F M (Swansea, Cardiff) 1892 *E, S, I,* 1893 *E, S, I,* 1894 *E, S, I,* 1895 *E, S, I,* 1896 *E*
Moore, W J (Bridgend) 1933 *I*
Morgan, C H (Llanelli) 1957 *I, F*
Morgan, C I (Cardiff) 1951 *I, F, SA,* 1952 *E, S, I,* 1953 *S, I, F, NZ,* 1954 *E, I, S,* 1955 *E, S, I, F,* 1956 *E, S, I, F,* 1957 *E, S, I, F,* 1958 *E, S, I, F*
Morgan, D (Swansea) 1885 *S,* 1886 *E, S,* 1887 *E, S, I,* 1889 *I*
Morgan, D (Llanelli) 1895 *I,* 1896 *E*
Morgan, D R R (Llanelli) 1962 *E, S, F, I,* 1963 *E, S, I, F, NZ*
Morgan, E (Llanelli) 1920 *I,* 1921 *E, S, F*
Morgan, Edgar (Swansea) 1914 *E, S, F, I*
Morgan, E T (London Welsh) 1902 *E, S, I,* 1903 *I,* 1904 *E, S, I,* 1905 *E, S, I, NZ,* 1906 *E, S, I, SA,* 1908 *F*
Morgan, F L (Llanelli) 1938 *E, S, I,* 1939 *E*
Morgan, H J (Abertillery) 1958 *E, S, I, F,* 1959 *I, F,* 1960 *E,* 1961 *E, S, I, F,* 1962 *E, S, F, I,* 1963 *S, I, F,* 1965 *E, S, I, F,* 1966 *E, S, I, F, A*
Morgan, H P (Newport) 1956 *E, S, I, F*
Morgan, I (Swansea) 1908 *A,* 1909 *E, S, F, I,* 1910 *F, E, S, I,* 1911 *E, F, I,* 1912 *S*
Morgan, J L (Llanelli) 1912 *SA,* 1913 *E*
Morgan, M E (Swansea) 1938 *E, S, I,* 1939 *E*
Morgan, N (Newport) 1960 *S, I, F*
Morgan, P E J (Aberavon) 1961 *E, S, F*
Morgan, P J (Llanelli) 1980 *S* (R), *I, NZ* (R), 1981 *I*
Morgan, R (Newport) 1984 *S*
Morgan, T (Llanelli) 1889 *I*
Morgan, W G (Cambridge U) 1927 *F, I,* 1929 *E, S, F, I,* 1930 *I, F*
Morgan, W L (Cardiff) 1910 *S*
Moriarty, R D (Swansea) 1981 *A,* 1982 *I, F, E, S,* 1983 *E,* 1984 *S, I, F, E,* 1985 *S, I, F,* 1986 *Fj, Tg, WS,* 1987 *[I, Tg, C(R), E, NZ, A]*
Moriarty, W P (Swansea) 1986 *I, F, Fj, Tg, WS,* 1987 *F, E, S, I, [I, Tg, C, E, NZ, A],* 1988 *E, S, I, F, NZ*1
Morley, J C (Newport) 1929 *E, S, F, I,* 1930 *E, I,* 1931 *E, S, F, I, SA,* 1932 *E, S, I*
Morris, G L (Swansea) 1882 *I,* 1883 *E, S,* 1884 *E, S,* 1910 *F*
Morris, H T (Cardiff) 1951 *F,* 1955 *I, F*
Morris, J (Swansea) 1924 *E, S*
Morris, M S (S Wales Police) 1985 *S, I, F*
Morris, R R (Swansea, Bristol) 1933 *S,* 1937 *S*
Morris, S (Cross Keys) 1920 *E, S, F, I,* 1922 *E, S, I, F,* 1923 *E, S, F, I,* 1924 *E, S, F, NZ,* 1925 *E, S, F*
Morris, W (Abertillery) 1919 *NZA,* 1920 *F,* 1921 *I*
Morris, W (Llanelli) 1896 *S, I,* 1897 *E*
Morris, W D (Neath) 1967 *F, E,* 1968 *E, S, I, F,* 1969 *S, I, F, E, NZ* 1,2, *A,* 1970 *SA, S, E, I, F,* 1971 *E, S, I, F,* 1972 *E, S, F, NZ,* 1973 *E, S, I, A,* 1974 *S, I, F, E*
Morris, W J (Newport) 1965 *S,* 1966 *F*
Morris, W J (Pontypool) 1963 *S, I*
Moseley, K (Pontypool) 1988 *NZ2, R,* 1989 *S, I*
Murphy, C D (Cross Keys) 1935 *E, S, I*

Nash, D (Ebbw Vale) 1960 *SA,* 1961 *E, S, I, F,* 1962 *F*
Newman, C H (Newport) 1881 *E,* 1882 *I,* 1883 *E, S,* 1884 *E, S,* 1885 *E, S,* 1886 *E,* 1887 *E*
Nicholas, D L (Llanelli) 1981 *E, S, I, F*
Nicholas, T J (Cardiff) 1919 *NZA*
Nicholl, C B (Cambridge U, Llanelli) 1891 *I,* 1892 *E,*

S, I, 1893 *E, S, I*, 1894 *E, S*, 1895 *E, S, I*, 1896 *E, S, I*
Nicholl, D W (Llanelli) 1894 *I*
Nicholls, E G (Cardiff) 1896 *S, I*, 1897 *E*, 1898 *I, E,* 1899 *E, S, I*, 1900 *S, I*, 1901 *E, S, I*, 1902 *E, S, I*, 1903 *I*, 1904 *E*, 1905 *I, NZ*, 1906 *E, S, I, SA*
Nicholls, F E (Cardiff Harlequins) 1892 *I*
Nicholls, H (Cardiff) 1958 *I*
Nicholls, S H (Cardiff) 1888 *M*, 1889 *S, I*, 1891 *S*
Norris, C H (Cardiff) 1963 *F*, 1966 *F*
Norster, R L (Cardiff) 1982 *S*, 1983 *E, S, I, F*, 1984 *S, I, F, E, A*, 1985 *S, I, F, E, Fj*, 1986 *Fj, Tg, WS*, 1987 *F, E, S, I*, [*I, C, E*], *US*, 1988 *E, S, I, F, NZ*1, *WS*, 1989 *F, E*
Norton, W B (Cardiff)) 1882 *I*, 1883 *E, S*, 1884 *E, S, I*

O'Connor, A (Aberavon) 1960 *SA*, 1961 *E, S*, 1962 *F, I*
O'Connor, R (Aberavon) 1957 *E*
O'Neill, W (Cardiff) 1904 *S, I*, 1905 *E, S, I*, 1907 *E, I*, 1908 *E, S, F, I*
O'Shea, J P (Cardiff) 1967 *S, I*, 1968 *S, I, F*
Oliver, G (Pontypool) 1920 *E, S, F, I*
Osborne, W T (Mountain Ash) 1902 *E, S, I*, 1903 *E, S, I*
Ould, W J (Cardiff) 1924 *E, S*
Owen, A (Swansea) 1924 *E*
Owen, G D (Newport) 1955 *I, F*, 1956 *E, S, I, F*
Owen, R M (Swansea) 1901 *I*, 1902 *E, S, I*, 1903 *E, S, I*, 1904 *E, S, I*, 1905 *E, S, I, NZ*, 1906 *E, S, I, SA*, 1907 *E, S*, 1908 *F, I, A*, 1909 *E, S, F, I*, 1910 *F, E*, 1911 *E, S, F, I*, 1912 *E, S*

Packer, H (Newport) 1891 *E*, 1895 *S, I*, 1896 *E, S, I*, 1897 *E*
Palmer, F (Swansea) 1922 *E, S, I*
Parfitt, F C (Newport) 1893 *E, S, I*, 1894 *E, S, I*, 1895 *S*, 1896 *S, I*
Parker, D (Swansea) 1924 *I, F, NZ*, 1925 *E, S, F, I*, 1929 *F, I*, 1930 *E*
Parker, T (Swansea) 1919 *NZA*, 1920 *E, S, I*, 1921 *E, S, F, I*, 1922 *E, S, I, F*, 1923 *E, S, F*
Parker, W (Swansea) 1899 *E, S*
Parsons, G W (Newport) 1947 *E*
Pascoe, D (Bridgend) 1923 *F, I*
Pask, A E I (Abertillery) 1961 *F*, 1962 *E, S, F, I*, 1963 *E, S, I, F, NZ*, 1964 *E, S, I, F, SA*, 1965 *E, S, I, F*, 1966 *E, S, I, F, A*, 1967 *S, I*
Payne, G W (Army, Pontypridd) 1960 *E, S, I*
Payne, H (Swansea) 1935 *NZ*
Peacock, H (Newport) 1929 *S, F, I*, 1930 *S, I, F*
Peake, E (Chepstow) 1881 *E*
Pearce, G P (Bridgend) 1981 *I, F*, 1982 *I* (R)
Pearson, T W (Cardiff, Newport) 1891 *E, I*, 1892 *E, S*, 1894 *S, I*, 1895 *E, S, I*, 1897 *E*, 1898 *I, E*, 1903 *E*
Pegge, E V (Neath) 1891 *E*
Perkins, S J (Pontypool) 1983 *S, I, F, R*, 1984 *S, I, F, E, A*, 1985 *S, I, F, E, Fj*, 1986 *E, S, I, F*, 1987 [*C, E, A*]
Perrett, F L (Neath) 1912 *SA*, 1913 *E, S, F, I*
Perrins, V C (Newport) 1970 *SA, S*
Perry, W (Neath) 1911 *E*
Phillips, A J (Cardiff) 1979 *E*, 1980 *F, E, S, I, NZ*, 1981 *E, S, I, F, A*, 1982 *I, F, E, S*, 1987 [*C, E, A*]
Phillips, B (Aberavon) 1925 *E, S, F, I*, 1926 *E*
Phillips, D H (Swansea) 1952 *F*
Phillips, H P (Newport) 1892 *E*, 1893 *E, S, I*, 1894 *E, S*
Phillips, H T (Newport) 1927 *E, S, F, I, NSW*, 1928 *E, S, I, F*
Phillips, K H (Neath) 1987 *F*, [*I, Tg, NZ*], *US*, 1988 *E, NZ*1
Phillips, L A (Newport) 1900 *E, S, I*, 1901 *S*
Phillips, R (Neath) 1987 *US*, 1988 *E, S, I, F, NZ*1,2, *WS*, 1989 *S, I*
Phillips, W D (Cardiff) 1881 *E*, 1882 *I*, 1884 *E, S, I*
Pickering, D F (Llanelli) 1983 *E, S, I, F, R*, 1984 *S, I, F, E, A*, 1985 *S, I, F, E, Fj*, 1986 *E, S, I, F, Fj*, 1987 *F, E, S*
Plummer, R C S (Newport) 1912 *S, I, F, SA*, 1913 *E*
Pook, T (Newport) 1895 *S*
Powell, G (Ebbw Vale) 1957 *I, F*
Powell, J (Cardiff) 1906 *I*
Powell, J (Cardiff) 1923 *I*
Powell, R W (Newport) 1888 *S, I*
Powell, W C (London Welsh) 1926 *S, I, F*, 1927 *E, F,*

I, 1928 *S, I, F*, 1929 *E, S, F, I*, 1930 *S, I, F*, 1931 *E, S, F, I, SA*, 1932 *E, S, I*, 1935 *E, S, I*
Powell, W J (Cardiff) 1920 *E, S, F, I*
Price, B (Newport) 1961 *I, F*, 1962 *E, S*, 1963 *E, S, F, NZ*, 1964 *E, S, I, F, SA*, 1965 *E, S, I, F*, 1966 *E, S, I, F, A*, 1967 *S, I, F, E*, 1969 *S, I, F, NZ* 1,2, *A*
Price, G (Pontypool) 1975 *F, E, S, I, A*, 1976 *E, S, I, F*, 1977 *I, F, E, S*, 1978 *E, S, I, F, A* 1,2, *NZ*, 1979 *S, I, F, E*, 1980 *F, E, S, I, NZ*, 1981 *E, S, I, F, A*, 1982 *I, F, E, S*, 1983 *E, I, F*
Price, M J (Pontypool, RAF) 1959 *E, S, I, F*, 1960 *E, S, I, F*, 1962 *E*
Price, R E (Weston) 1939 *S, I*
Price, T G (Llanelli) 1965 *E, S, I, F*, 1966 *E, A*, 1967 *S, F*
Priday, A J (Cardiff) 1958 *I*, 1961 *I*
Pritchard, C (Pontypool) 1928 *E, S, I, F*, 1929 *E, S, F, I*
Pritchard, C C (Newport, Pontypool) 1904 *S, I*, 1905 *NZ*, 1906 *E, S*
Pritchard, C M (Newport) 1904 *I*, 1905 *E, S, NZ*, 1906 *E, S, I, SA*, 1907 *E, S, I*, 1908 *E*, 1910 *F, E*
Prosser, D R (Neath) 1934 *S, I*
Prosser, G (Neath) 1934 *E, S, I*, 1935 *NZ*
Prosser, J (Cardiff) 1921 *I*
Prosser, T R (Pontypool) 1956 *S, F*, 1957 *E, S, I, F*, 1958 *A, E, S, I, F*, 1959 *E, S, I, F*, 1960 *E, S, I, F, SA*, 1961 *I, F*
Prothero, G J (Bridgend) 1964 *S, I, F*, 1965 *E, S, I, F*, 1966 *E, S, I, F*
Pryce-Jenkins, T J (London Welsh) 1888 *S, I*
Pugh, C (Maesteg) 1924 *E, S, I, F, NZ*, 1925 *E, S*
Pugh, J D (Neath) 1987 *US*, 1988 *S*(R)
Pugsley, J (Cardiff) 1910 *E, S, I*, 1911 *E, S, F, I*
Pullman, J J (Neath) 1910 *F*
Purdon, F T (Newport) 1881 *E*, 1882 *I*, 1883 *E, S*

Quinnell, D L (Llanelli) 1972 *F* (R), *NZ*, 1973 *E, S, A*, 1974 *S, F*, 1975 *E* (R), 1977 *I* (R), *F, E, S*, 1978 *E, S, I, F, A* 1, *NZ*, 1979 *S, I, F, E*, 1980 *NZ*

Radford, W J (Newport) 1923 *I*
Ralph, A R (Newport) 1931 *F, I, SA*, 1932 *E, S, I*
Ramsey, S H (Treorchy) 1896 *E*, 1904 *E*
Randell, R (Aberavon) 1924 *I, F*
Raybould, W H (London Welsh, Cambridge U, Newport) 1967 *S, I, F, E, NZ*, 1968 *I, F*, 1970 *SA, E, I, F* (R)
Rees, Aaron (Maesteg) 1919 *NZA*
Rees, Alan (Maesteg) 1962 *E, S, F*
Rees, A M (London Welsh) 1934 *E*, 1935 *E, S, I, NZ*, 1936 *E, S, I*, 1937 *E, S, I*, 1938 *E, S*
Rees, B I (London Welsh) 1967 *S, I, F*
Rees, C F W (London Welsh) 1974 *I*, 1975 *A*, 1978 *NZ*, 1981 *F, A*, 1982 *I, F, E, S*, 1983 *E, S, I, F*
Rees, D (Swansea) 1968 *S, I, F*
Rees, Dan (Swansea) 1900 *E*, 1903 *E, S*, 1905 *E, S*
Rees, E B (Swansea) 1919 *NZA*
Rees, H (Cardiff) 1937 *S, I*, 1938 *E, S, I*
Rees, H E (Neath) 1979 *S, I, F, E*, 1980 *F, E, S, I, NZ*, 1983 *E, S, I, F*
Rees, J (Swansea) 1920 *E, S, F, I*, 1921 *E, S, I*, 1922 *E*, 1923 *E, F, I*, 1924 *E*
Rees, J I (Swansea) 1934 *E, S, I*, 1935 *S, NZ*, 1936 *E, S, I*, 1937 *E, S, I*, 1938 *E, S, I*
Rees, L M (Cardiff) 1933 *I*
Rees, P (Llanelli) 1947 *F, I*
Rees, P M (Newport) 1961 *E, S, I*, 1964 *I*
Rees, T (Newport) 1935 *S, I, NZ*, 1936 *E, S, I*, 1937 *E, S*
Rees, T A (Llandovery) 1881 *E*
Rees, T E (London Welsh) 1926 *I, F*, 1927 *NSW*, 1928 *E*
Rees-Jones, G R (Oxford U, London Welsh) 1934 *E, S*, 1935 *I, NZ*, 1936 *E*
Reeves, F (Cross Keys) 1920 *F, I*, 1921 *E*
Rhapps, J (Penygraig) 1897 *E*
Rice-Evans, W (Swansea) 1890 *S*, 1891 *E, S*
Richards, C (Pontypool) 1922 *E, S, I, F*, 1924 *I*
Richards, D S (Swansea) 1979 *F, E*, 1980 *F, E, S, I, NZ*, 1981 *E, S, I, F*, 1982 *I, F*, 1983 *E, S, I, R* (R)
Richards, E S (Swansea) 1885 *E*, 1887 *S*

231

Richards, G (Cardiff) 1927 S
Richards, H D (Neath) 1986 Tg(R), 1987 [Tg, E(R), NZ]
Richards, I (Cardiff) 1925 E, S, F
Richards, K H L (Bridgend) 1960 SA, 1961 E, S, I, F
Richards, M C R (Cardiff) 1968 I, F, 1969 S, I, F, E, NZ 1,2, A
Richards, R (Aberavon) 1913 S, F, I
Richards, R (Cross Keys) 1956 F
Richards, T L (Maesteg) 1923 I
Richardson, S J (Aberavon) 1978 A 2 (R), 1979 E
Rickards, A R (Cardiff) 1924 F
Ring, J (Aberavon) 1921 E
Ring, M G (Cardiff, Pontypool) 1983 E, 1984 A, 1985 S, I, F, 1987 I, [I, Tg, A], US, 1988 E, S, I, F, NZ 1,2
Ringer, P (Ebbw Vale, Llanelli) 1978 NZ, 1979 S, I, F, E, 1980 F, E, NZ
Roberts, C (Neath) 1958 I, F
Roberts, D E A (London Welsh) 1930 E
Roberts, E (Llanelli) 1886 E, 1887 I
Roberts, E J (Llanelli) 1888 S, I, 1889 I
Roberts, G J (Cardiff) 1985 F (R), E, 1987 [I, Tg, C, E, A]
Roberts, H M (Cardiff) 1960 SA, 1961 E, S, I, F, 1962 S, F, 1963 I
Roberts, J (Cardiff) 1927 E, S, F, I, NSW, 1928 E, S, I, F, 1929 E, S, F, I
Roberts, M G (London Welsh) 1971 E, S, I, F, 1973 I, F, 1975 S, 1979 E
Roberts, T (Newport, Risca) 1921 S, F, I, 1922 E, S, I, F, 1923 E, S
Roberts, W (Cardiff) 1929 E
Robins, J D (Birkenhead Park) 1950 E, S, I, F, 1951 E, S, I, F, 1953 E, I, F
Robins, R J (Pontypridd) 1953 S, 1954 F, S, 1955 E, S, I, F, 1956 E, F, 1957 E, S, I, F
Robinson, I R (Cardiff) 1974 F, E
Rocyn-Jones, D N (Cambridge U) 1925 I
Roderick, W B (Llanelli) 1884 I
Rosser, M A (Penarth) 1924 S, F
Rowland, E M (Lampeter) 1885 E
Rowlands, C F (Aberavon) 1926 I
Rowlands, D C T (Pontypool) 1963 E, S, I, F, NZ, 1964 E, S, I, F, SA, 1965 E, S, I, F
Rowlands, G (RAF, Cardiff) 1953 NZ, 1954 E, F, 1956 F
Rowlands, K A (Cardiff) 1962 F, I, 1963 I, 1965 I, F
Rowles, G R (Penarth) 1892 E
Russell, S (London Welsh), 1987 US

Samuel, D (Swansea) 1891 I, 1893 I
Samuel, F (Mountain Ash) 1922 S, I, F
Samuel, J (Swansea) 1891 I
Scourfield, T (Torquay) 1930 F
Scrine, G F (Swansea) 1899 E, S, 1901 I
Shanklin, J L (London Welsh) 1970 F, 1972 NZ, 1973 I, F
Shaw, G (Neath) 1972 NZ, 1973 E, S, I, F, A, 1974 S, I, F, E, 1977 I, F
Shaw, T W (Newbridge) 1983 R
Shea, J (Newport) 1919 NZA, 1920 E, S, 1921 E
Shell, R C (Aberavon) 1973 A (R)
Simpson, H J (Cardiff) 1884 E, S, I
Skrimshire, R T (Newport) 1899 E, S, I
Skym, A (Llanelli) 1928 E, S, I, F, 1930 E, S, I, F, 1931 E, S, F, I, SA, 1932 E, S, I, 1933 E, S, I, 1935 E
Smith, J S (Cardiff) 1884 E, I, 1885 E
Sparks, B (Neath) 1954 I, 1955 E, F, 1956 E, S, I, 1957 S
Spiller, W J (Cardiff) 1910 S, I, 1911 E, S, F, I, 1912 E, F, SA, 1913 E
Squire, J (Newport, Pontypool) 1977 I, F, 1978 E, S, I, F, A 1, NZ, 1979 S, I, F, E, 1980 F, E, S, I, NZ, 1981 E, S, I, F, A, 1982 I, F, E, 1983 E, S, I, F
Stadden, W J W (Cardiff) 1884 I, 1886 E, S, 1887 I, 1888 S, M, 1890 S, E
Stephens, G (Neath) 1912 E, S, I, F, SA, 1913 E, S, F, I, 1919 NZA
Stephens, I (Bridgend) 1981 E, S, I, F, A, 1982 I, F, E, S, 1984 I, F, E, A
Stephens, Rev J G (Llanelli) 1922 E, S, I, F
Stephens, J R G (Neath) 1947 E, S, F, I, 1948 I, 1949 S, I, F, 1951 F, SA, 1952 E, S, I, F, 1953 E, S, I, F,

NZ, 1954 E, I, 1955 E, S, I, F, 1956 S, I, F, 1957 E, S, I, F
Stock, A (Newport) 1924 F, NZ, 1926 E, S
Stone, P (Llanelli) 1949 F
Strand-Jones, J (Llanelli) 1902 E, S, I, 1903 E, S
Summers, R H B (Haverfordwest) 1881 E
Sutton, S (Pontypool, S Wales Police) 1982 F, E, 1987 F, E, S, I, [C, NZ(R), A]
Sweet-Escott, R B (Cardiff) 1891 S, 1894 I, 1895 I

Tamplin, W E (Cardiff) 1947 S, F, I, A, 1948 E, S, F
Tanner, H (Swansea, Cardiff) 1935 NZ, 1936 E, S, I, 1937 E, S, I, 1938 E, S, I, 1939 E, S, I, 1947 E, S, F, I, 1948 E, S, F, I, 1949 E, S, I, F
Tarr, D J (Swansea, Royal Navy) 1935 NZ
Taylor, A R (Cross Keys) 1937 I, 1938 I, 1939 E
Taylor, C G (Ruabon) 1884 E, S, I, 1885 E, S, 1886 E, S, 1887 E, I
Taylor, J (London Welsh) 1967 S, I, F, E, NZ, 1968 I, F, 1969 S, I, F, E, NZ 1, A, 1970 F, 1971 E, S, I, F, 1972 E, S, F, NZ, 1973 E, S, I, F
Thomas, A (Newport) 1963 NZ, 1964 E
Thomas, A G (Swansea, Cardiff) 1952 E, S, I, F, 1953 S, I, F, 1954 E, I, F, 1955 S, I, F
Thomas, Bob (Swansea) 1900 E, S, I, 1901 E
Thomas, Brian E (Neath, Cambridge U) 1963 E, S, I, F, NZ, 1964 E, S, I, F, SA, 1965 E, 1966 E, S, I, 1967 NZ, 1969 S, I, F, E, NZ 1,2
Thomas, C (Bridgend) 1925 E, S
Thomas, C J (Newport) 1888 I, M, 1889 S, I, 1890 S, E, I, 1891 E, I
Thomas, D (Aberavon) 1961 I
Thomas, D (Llanelli) 1954 I
Thomas, Dick (Mountain Ash) 1906 SA, 1908 F, I, 1909 S
Thomas, D J (Swansea) 1904 E, 1908 A, 1910 E, S, I, 1911 E, S, F, I, 1912 E
Thomas, D J (Swansea) 1930 S, I, 1932 E, S, I, 1933 E, S, 1934 E, 1935 E, S, I
Thomas, D L (Neath) 1937 E
Thomas, D R (Neath) 1904 S, I, 1909 S, F, I, 1910 F
Thomas, G (Llanelli) 1923 E, S, F, I
Thomas, G (Newport) 1888 M, 1890 I, 1891 S
Thomas, H (Llanelli) 1912 F
Thomas, H (Neath) 1936 E, S, I, 1937 E, S, I
Thomas, H W (Swansea) 1912 SA, 1913 E
Thomas, I (Bryncethin) 1924 E
Thomas, L C (Cardiff) 1885 E, S
Thomas, M C (Newport, Devonport Services) 1949 F, 1950 E, S, I, F, 1951 E, S, I, F, SA, 1952 E, S, I, F, 1953 E, 1956 E, S, I, F, 1957 E, S, 1958 E, S, I, F, 1959 I, F
Thomas, M G (St Bart's Hospital) 1919 NZA, 1921 S, F, I, 1923 F, 1924 E
Thomas, R (Pontypool) 1909 F, I, 1911 S, F, 1912 E, S, SA, 1913 E
Thomas, R C C (Swansea) 1949 F, 1952 I, F, 1953 S, I, F, NZ, 1954 E, I, F, S, 1955 S, I, 1956 E, S, I, 1957 F, 1958 A, E, S, I, F, 1959 E, S, I, F
Thomas, R L (London Welsh) 1889 S, I, 1890 I, 1891 E, S, I, 1892 E
Thomas, S (Llanelli) 1890 S, E, 1891 I
Thomas, W D (Llanelli) 1966 A, 1968 S, I, F, 1969 E, NZ 2, A, 1970 SA, S, E, I, F, 1971 E, S, I, F, 1972 E, S, F, NZ, 1973 E, S, I, F, 1974 E
Thomas, W G (Llanelli, Waterloo, Swansea) 1927 E, S, F, I, 1929 E, 1931 E, S, SA, 1932 E, S, I, 1933 E, S, I
Thomas, W H (Llandovery Coll, Cambridge U) 1885 S, 1886 E, S, 1887 E, S, 1888 S, I, 1890 E, I, 1891 S, I
Thomas, W J (Cardiff) 1961 F, 1963 F
Thomas, W L (Newport) 1894 S, 1895 E, I
Thomas, W T (Abertillery) 1930 E
Thompson, J F (Cross Keys) 1923 E
Thorburn, P H (Neath) 1985 F, E, Fj, 1986 E, S, I, F, 1987 F, [I, Tg, C, E, NZ, A], US, 1988 S, I, F, WS, R(R), 1989 S, I, F, I
Titley, M H (Bridgend, Swansea) 1983 R, 1984 S, I, F, E, A, 1985 S, I, Fj, 1986 F, Fj, Tg, WS
Towers, W H (Swansea) 1887 I, 1888 M
Travers, G (Pill Harriers) 1903 E, S, I, 1905 E, S, I, NZ, 1906 E, S, I, SA, 1907 E, S, I, 1908 E, S, F, I, A, 1909 E, S, I, 1911 S, F, I

Travers, W H (Newport) 1937 S, I, 1938 E, S, I, 1939 E, S, I, 1949 E, S, I, F
Treharne, E (Pontypridd) 1881 E, 1883 E
Trew, W J (Swansea) 1900 E, S, I, 1901 E, S, 1903 S, 1905 S, 1906 S, 1907 E, S, 1908 E, S, F, I, A, 1909 E, S, F, I, 1910 F, E, S, 1911 E, S, F, I, 1912 S, 1913 S, F
Trott, R F (Cardiff) 1948 E, S, F, I, 1949 E, S, I, F
Truman, W H (Llanelli) 1934 E, 1935 E
Trump, L C (Newport) 1912 E, S, I, F
Turnbull, B R (Cardiff) 1925 I, 1927 E, S, 1928 E, F, 1930 S
Turnbull, M J L (Cardiff) 1933 E, I
Turner, P (Newbridge) 1989 I(R), F, E

Uzzell, H (Newport) 1912 E, S, I, F, 1913 S, F, I, 1914 E, S, F, I, 1920 E, S, F, I
Uzzell, J R (Newport) 1963 NZ, 1965 E, S, I, F

Vickery, W (Aberavon) 1938 E, S, I, 1939 E
Vile, T H (Newport) 1908 E, S, 1910 I, 1912 I, F, SA, 1913 E, 1921 S
Vincent, H C (Bangor) 1882 I

Wakeford, J D M (S Wales Police) 1988 WS, R
Waldron, R (Neath) 1965 E, S, I, F
Waller, P D (Newport) 1908 A, 1909 E, S, F, I, 1910 F
Walters, N (Llanelli) 1902 E
Wanbon, R (Aberavon) 1968 E
Ward, W (Cross Keys) 1934 S, I
Warlow, J (Llanelli) 1962 I
Waters D R (Newport) 1986 E, S, I, F
Watkins, D (Newport) 1963 E, S, I, F, NZ, 1964 E, S, I, F, SA, 1965 E, S, I, F, 1966 E, S, I, F, 1967 I, F, E
Watkins, E (Neath) 1924 E, S, I, F
Watkins, E (Blaina) 1926 S, I, F
Watkins, E (Cardiff) 1935 NZ, 1937 S, I, 1938 E, S, I, 1939 E, S
Watkins, H (Llanelli) 1904 S, I, 1905 E, S, I, 1906 E
Watkins, I J (Ebbw Vale) 1988 E(R), S, I, F, NZ2, R, 1989 S, I, F, E
Watkins, L (Oxford U, Llandaff) 1881 E
Watkins, M J (Newport) 1984 I, F, E, A
Watkins, S J (Newport, Cardiff) 1964 S, I, F, 1965 E, S, I, F, 1966 E, S, I, F, A, 1967 S, I, F, E, NZ, 1968 E, S, 1969 S, I, F, E, NZ 1, 1970 E, I
Watkins, W R (Newport) 1959 F
Watts, D (Maesteg) 1914 E, S, F, I
Watts, J (Llanelli) 1907 E, S, I, 1908 E, S, F, I, A, 1909 S, F, I
Watts, W (Llanelli) 1914 E
Watts, W H (Newport) 1892 E, S, I, 1893 E, S, I, 1894 E, S, I, 1895 E, I, 1896 E
Weaver, D (Swansea) 1964 E
Webb, J (Abertillery) 1907 S, 1908 E, S, F, I, A, 1909 E, S, F, I, 1910 F, E, S, I, 1911 E, S, F, I, 1912 E, S
Webb, J E (Newport) 1888 M, 1889 S
Webbe, G M C (Bridgend) 1986 Tg (R), WS, 1987 F, E, S, [Tg], US, 1988 F(R), NZ1, R
Webster, R E (Swansea) 1987 [A]
Wells, G T (Cardiff) 1955 E, S, 1957 I, F, 1958 A, E, S
Westacott, D (Cardiff) 1906 I
Wetter, H (Newport) 1912 SA, 1913 E
Wetter, J J (Newport) 1914 S, F, I, 1920 E, S, F, I, 1921 E, 1924 I, NZ
Wheel, G A D (Swansea) 1974 I, E (R), 1975 F, E, I, A, 1976 E, S, I, F, 1977 I, E, S, 1978 E, S, I, F, A 1,2, NZ, 1979 S, I, 1980 F, E, S, I, 1981 E, S, I, F, A, 1982 I
Wheeler, P J (Aberavon) 1967 NZ, 1968 E
Whitefoot, J (Cardiff) 1984 A (R), 1985 S, I, F, E, Fj, 1986 E, S, I, F, Fj, Tg, WS, 1987 F, E, S, I, [I, C]
Whitfield, J (Newport) 1919 NZA, 1920 E, S, F, I, 1921 E, 1922 E, S, I, F, 1924 S, I
Whitson, G K (Newport) 1956 F, 1960 S, I
Williams, B (Llanelli) 1920 S, F, I
Williams, B L (Cardiff) 1947 E, S, F, I, A, 1948 E, S, F, I, 1949 E, S, I, 1951 I, SA, 1952 S, 1953 E, S, I, F, NZ, 1954 S, 1955 E
Williams, C (Llanelli) 1924 NZ, 1925 E
Williams, C (Aberavon, Swansea) 1977 E, S, 1980 F, E, S, I, NZ, 1983 E

Williams, C D (Cardiff, Neath) 1955 F, 1956 F
Williams, D (Ebbw Vale) 1963 E, S, I, F, 1964 E, S, I, F, SA, 1965 E, S, I, F, 1966 E, S, I, A, 1967 F, E, NZ, 1968 E, 1969 S, I, F, E, NZ 1,2, A, 1970 SA, S, E, I, 1971 E, S, I, F
Williams, D B (Newport, Swansea) 1978 A 1, 1981 E, S
Williams, E (Neath) 1924 NZ, 1925 F
Williams, E (Aberavon) 1925 E, S
Williams, F L (Cardiff) 1929 S, F, I, 1930 E, S, I, F, 1931 F, I, SA, 1932 E, S, I, 1933 I
Williams G (Aberavon) 1936 E, S, I
Williams G (London Welsh) 1950 I, F, 1951 E, S, I, F, SA, 1952 E, S, I, F, 1953 NZ, 1954 E
Williams, G (Bridgend) 1981 I, F, 1982 E (R), S
Williams, G P (Bridgend) 1980 NZ, 1981 E, S, A, 1982 I
Williams, J (Blaina) 1920 E, S, F, I, 1921 S, F, I
Williams, J F (London Welsh) 1905 I, NZ, 1906 S, SA
Williams, J J (Llanelli) 1973 F (R), A, 1974 S, I, F, E, 1975 F, E, S, I, A, 1976 E, S, I, F, 1977 I, F, E, S, 1978 E, S, I, F, A 1,2, NZ, 1979 S, I, F, E
Williams, J L (Cardiff) 1906 SA, 1907 E, S, I, 1908 E, S, I, A, 1909 E, S, F, I, 1910 I, 1911 E, S, F, I
Williams, J P R (London Welsh, Bridgend) 1969 S, I, F, E, NZ 1,2, A, 1970 SA, S, E, I, F, 1971 E, S, I, F, 1972 E, S, F, NZ, 1973 E, S, I, F, A, 1974 S, I, F, 1975 F, E, S, I, A, 1976 E, S, I, F, 1977 I, F, E, S, 1978 E, S, I, F, A 1,2, NZ, 1979 S, I, F, E, 1980 NZ, 1981 E, S
Williams, L (Llanelli, Cardiff) 1947 E, S, F, I, A, 1948 I, 1949 E
Williams, L H (Cardiff) 1957 S, I, F, 1958 E, S, I, F, 1959 E, S, I, 1961 F, 1962 E, S
Williams, M (Newport) 1923 F
Williams, O (Llanelli) 1947 E, S, A, 1948 E, S, F, I
Williams, R (Llanelli) 1954 S, 1957 F, 1958 A
Williams, R D G (Newport) 1881 E
Williams, R F (Cardiff) 1912 SA, 1913 E, S, 1914 I
Williams, R H (Llanelli) 1954 I, F, S, 1955 S, I, F, 1956 E, S, I, 1957 E, S, I, F, 1958 A, E, S, I, F, 1959 E, S, I, F, 1960 E
Williams, S (Llanelli) 1947 E, S, F, I, 1948 S, F
Williams, S A (Aberavon) 1939 E, S, I
Williams, T (Pontypridd) 1882 I
Williams, T (Swansea) 1888 S, I
Williams, T (Swansea) 1912 I, 1913 F, 1914 E, S, F, I
Williams, Tudor (Swansea) 1921 F
Williams, T G (Cross Keys) 1935 S, I, NZ, 1936 E, S, I, 1937 S
Williams, W A (Crumlin) 1927 E, S, F, I
Williams, W A (Newport) 1952 I, F, 1953 E
Williams, W E O (Cardiff) 1887 S, I, 1889 S, 1890 S, E
Williams, W H (Pontymister) 1900 E, S, I, 1901 E
Williams, W O G (Swansea, Devonport Services) 1951 F, SA, 1952 E, S, I, F, 1953 E, S, I, F, NZ, 1954 E, I, F, S, 1955 E, S, I, F, 1956 E, S, I
Williams, W M J (Neath) 1974 I, F
Williams-Jones, H (S Wales Police) 1989 S(R)
Willis, W R (Cardiff) 1950 E, S, I, F, 1951 E, S, I, F, SA, 1952 E, S, 1953 S, NZ, 1954 E, I, F, S, 1955 E, S, I, F
Wiltshire, M L (Aberavon) 1967 NZ, 1968 E, S, F
Windsor, R W (Pontypool) 1973 A, 1974 S, I, F, E, 1975 F, E, S, I, A, 1976 E, S, I, F, 1977 I, F, E, S, 1978 E, S, I, F, A 1,2, NZ, 1979 S, I, F
Winfield, H B (Cardiff) 1903 I, 1904 E, S, I, 1905 NZ, 1906 E, S, I, 1907 S, I, 1908 E, S, F, I, A
Winmill, S (Cross Keys) 1921 E, S, F, I
Wintle, R V (London Welsh) 1988 WS(R)
Wooller, W (Sale, Cambridge U, Cardiff) 1933 E, S, I, 1935 E, S, I, NZ, 1936 E, S, I, 1937 E, S, I, 1938 S, I, 1939 E, S, I
Wyatt, M A (Swansea) 1983 E, S, I, F, 1984 A, 1985 S, I, 1987 E, S, I

Young, D (Swansea, Cardiff) 1987 [E, NZ], US, 1988 E, S, I, F, NZ 1,2 WS, R, 1989 S
Young, G A (Cardiff) 1886 E, S
Young, J (Harrogate, RAF, London Welsh) 1968 S, I, F, 1969 S, I, F, E, NZ 1, 1970 E, I, F, 1971 E, S, I, F, 1972 E, S, F, NZ, 1973 E, S, I, F

233

WELSH INTERNATIONAL RECORDS

Both team and individual records are for official Welsh international matches up to 30 April 1989.

TEAM RECORDS

Highest score
49 v France (49-14) 1910 Swansea
v individual countries
28 v Australia (28-3) 1975 Cardiff
40 v Canada (40-9) 1987 Invercargill
34 v England (34-21) 1967 Cardiff
49 v France (49-14) 1910 Swansea
40 v Fiji (40-3) 1985 Cardiff
34 v Ireland (34-9) 1976 Dublin
16 v N Zealand (16-19) 1972 Cardiff
9 v Romania (9-15) 1988 Cardiff
35 v Scotland (35-12) 1972 Cardiff
6 v S Africa (6-6) 1970 Cardiff
29 v Tonga (29-16) 1987 Palmerston North
46 v United States (46-0) 1987 Cardiff
32 v W Samoa (32-14) 1986 Apia

Biggest winning points margin
46 v United States (46-0) 1987 Cardiff
v individual countries
25 v Australia (28-3) 1975 Cardiff
31 v Canada (40-9) 1987 Invercargill
25 v England (25-0) 1905 Cardiff
42 v France (47-5) 1909 Colombes
37 v Fiji (40-3) 1985 Cardiff
29 v Ireland (29-0) 1907 Cardiff
5 v N Zealand (13-8) 1953 Cardiff
23 v Scotland (35-12) 1972 Cardiff
13 v Tonga (29-16) 1987 Palmerston North
46 v United States (46-0) 1987 Cardiff
22 v W Samoa (28-6) 1988 Cardiff
No wins v Romania or South Africa

Highest score by opposing team
54 N Zealand (9-54) 1988 Auckland
v individual countries
28 Australia (9-28) 1984 Cardiff
9 Canada (40-9) 1987 Invercargill
25 England (0-25) 1896 Blackheath
31 France (12-31) 1989 Paris
15 Fiji (22-15) 1986 Suva
21 Ireland { (24-21) 1979 Cardiff
{ (7-21) 1980 Dublin
{ (9-21) 1985 Cardiff
54 N Zealand (9-54) 1988 Auckland
24 Romania (6-24) 1983 Bucharest
35 Scotland (10-35) 1924 Inverleith
24 S Africa (3-24) 1964 Durban
16 Tonga (29-16) 1987 Palmerston North
0 United States (46-0) 1987 Cardiff
14 W Samoa (32-14) 1986 Apia

Biggest losing points margin
49 v N Zealand (3-52) 1988 Christchurch
v individual countries
19 v Australia (9-28) 1984 Cardiff
25 v England (0-25) 1896 Blackheath
19 v France (12-31) 1989 Paris
16 v Ireland (3-19) 1925 Belfast
49 v N Zealand (3-52) 1988 Christchurch
18 v Romania (6-24) 1983 Bucharest
25 v Scotland (10-35) 1924 Inverleith
21 v S Africa (3-24) 1964 Durban
No defeats v Canada, Fiji, Tonga, United States or Western Samoa

Most tries by Wales in an international
11 v France (47-5) 1909 Colombes

Most tries against Wales in an international
13 by England 1881 Blackheath

Most points by Wales in International Championship in a season – 102
in season 1975-76

Most tries by Wales in International Championship in a season – 21
in season 1909-10

INDIVIDUAL RECORDS

Most capped player
J P R Williams 55 1969-81
in individual positions
Full-back
J P R Williams 54(55)[1] 1969-81
Wing
K J Jones 44[2] 1947-57
Centre
S P Fenwick 30 1975-81

234

Fly-half
C I Morgan 29[3] 1951-58
Scrum-half
G O Edwards 53 1967-78
Prop
G Price 41 1975-83
Hooker
B V Meredith 34 1954-62
Lock
A J Martin 34 1973-81
R L Norster 34 1982-89
Flanker
W D Morris 32(34)[4] 1967-74
No 8
T M Davies 38 1969-76
[1]*Williams won one cap as a flanker*
[2]*T G R Davies, 46 caps, won 35 as a wing, 11 as a centre*
[3]*P Bennett, 29 caps, played 25 times as a fly-half*
[4]*Morris won his first two caps as a No 8*

Longest international career
W J Trew
14 seasons 1899-1900 to 1912-13
T H Vile
14 seasons 1907-08 to 1920-21
H Tanner
14 seasons 1935-36 to 1948-49

Most internationals as captain
A J Gould 18 1889-97

Most points in internationals – 199
P H Thorburn (24 matches) 1985-89

Most points in International Championship in a season – 52
P H Thorburn (4 matches) 1985-86

Most points in an international – 19
J Bancroft v France 1910 Swansea
K S Jarrett v England 1967 Cardiff
P Bennett v Ireland 1976 Dublin

Most tries in internationals – 20
G O Edwards (53 matches) 1967-78
T G R Davies (46 matches) 1966-78

Most tries in International Championship in a season – 6
R A Gibbs (4 matches) 1907-08
M C R Richards (4 matches) 1968-69

Most tries in an international – 4
W M Llewellyn* v England 1899 Swansea
R A Gibbs v France 1908 Cardiff
M C R Richards v England 1969 Cardiff
I C Evans v Canada 1987 Invercargill
**on first appearance*

Most conversions in internationals – 38
J Bancroft (18 matches) 1909-1914

Most conversions in International Championship in a season – 11
J Bancroft (4 matches) 1908-09

Most conversions in an international – 8
J Bancroft v France 1910 Swansea

Most dropped goals in internationals – 13
J Davies (27 matches) 1985-88

Most penalty goals in internationals – 45
P H Thorburn (24 matches) 1985-89

Most penalty goals in International Championship in a season – 16
P H Thorburn (4 matches) 1985-86

Most points on overseas tour – 55
S P Fenwick (7 matches) Australia 1978
P Bennett scored 63 points in the Far East in 1975, but this was not on a major tour

Most points in a tour match – 21
J Davies v Hawke's Bay 1988 Napier, NZ
P Bennett scored 34 points v Japan in Tokyo in 1975, but this was not on a major tour

Most tries in a tour match – 3
M C R Richards v Otago 1969 Dunedin, NZ
Several others have scored 3 in matches on non-major tours

QUALIFIED SUCCESS

THE 1988-89 SEASON IN FRANCE
Bob Donahue *International Herald Tribune*

This was a season of success and occasional brilliance, but also of doubt. The contrast between bright and dark was sharpest in Dublin in January, but it was apparent throughout the season. On 21 May, in Valence, a French XV full of candidates for the impending tour of New Zealand was embarrassed by the Soviet Union, who led 10-0 after 24 minutes and 16-12 in the fourth quarter, although penalty goals by Jean-Baptiste Lafond preserved first place in the FIRA Championship. This difficult 18-16 victory did not bode well for the battle against the Kiwis under tour manager Jacques Fouroux, Daniel Dubroca (coach) and Henri Fourès, especially as the squad lacked an established front five, an experienced breakaway and a proven goal-kicker.

In contrast, the club final a week later was stunning. Supporters of the country's two wealthiest clubs filled the Parc des Princes, with the President of the Republic attending. It was a reward for two outstanding coaches, Daniel Herrero of Toulon and Pierre Villepreux (with Jean-Claude Skréla and Guy Novès) of Toulouse, and a grand farewell to first-class rugby for Jérôme Gallion, Didier Codorniou and the international referee Guy Maurette. Most of all, it was simply a great match – one that will live on in legend, as *L'Equipe* dared to put it. Serge Laïrle, the veteran Toulouse loose-head, galloped over for a try in the first minute in a raid launched by Albert Cigagna at the line-out that followed Toulon's kick-off. Toulon drew level at 9-9 after 20 minutes. Twelve minutes later came the high point of the season.

Feigning to kick to touch from behind his 22-metre line on the left, Philippe Rougé-Thomas observed that Toulon's backs were concentrated in front of him, leaving the right side of the field open. So he tapped the penalty and Cigagna fed Codorniou, who drew two defenders and put Denis Charvet through for a 70-metre dash to the right corner. From 15-9 at the interval, the score went to 18-12. Toulouse were champions for the tenth time since 1912 and for the third time since 1985. The skills, commitment and self-control of the two packs were worthy of a Test match. The two Toulouse tries, both from rehearsed moves, were flashes of intelligence and attacking craft that illuminated a titanic combat. Charvet, who accounted for 59 of the 151 points scored by Toulouse in their five knock-out matches, was finally admitted (along with Rougé-Thomas) to the tour squad for New Zealand.

Names in the news during the season included Francis Sénégas, president of the Languedoc Committee, who became secretary-general of the FFR after the re-election of President Albert Ferrasse to a sixth four-year term in December. Guy Maurette was named assistant treasurer of the FFR. Raoul Barrière and André Leymat joined Fouroux's

The French team before the match against Ireland at Lansdowne Road. L-R, back row: P Ondarts, C Portolan, P Marocco, L Rodriguez, M Cecillon, A Carminati, J Condom, G Bourguignon; front row: J-B Lafond, P Sella, S Blanco, P Berbizier (capt), F Mesnel, M Andrieu, P Lagisquet

coaching staff. Pierre Villepreux's advisory role in the England camp was seen by most Frenchmen as agreeably flattering to France, but the Ferrasse circle grumbled. Scotland's John Rutherford also visited Villepreux at Toulouse. Fouroux failed to persuade Ferrasse to admit Peter FitzSimons, an Australian lock with Brive, into the French national squad. Daniel and Jean-Philippe Revallier, father and son, played together in first division matches for Graulhet. Jean-Baptiste Lafond's first match at Twickenham recalled the appearance there in 1922 of his grandfather André, also on the wing. In another family of wings, Jean-Michel Rancoule, in his third victorious club final for Toulouse, equalled the achievement of his father Henri for Lourdes.

After the laborious 16-12 defeat of Romania in November, Christian Darrouy was proud that it had taken a player of the class of Serge Blanco to equal his French international career record of 23 tries set up in 1967. (Blanco went on to score four more tries in the International Championship.) Earlier that month, against Argentina, Philippe Sella scored his 21st international try. Philippe Dintrans and Laurent Rodriguez were the captains for the two Tests against Argentina, in which France scored nine tries and conceded none.

Then, in Dublin, the French revival made one wonder whether a team had ever before recovered from a 0-15 deficit to win an international match. Against Wales in Paris the backs shone again. Then England dealt a historic blow to French prestige, leading Robert Paparemborde to warn that 'this team is finished', and Henri Nayrou wrote that England had perhaps taken over the torch of European leadership from France. Whereupon, the Scots, who had held England at Twickenham, were thoroughly outplayed in Paris, and Finlay Calder judged the French side to be as good as ever. Thanks to the Welsh victory over England, France finished in first place for the fourth consecutive year – something no British Isles country has ever achieved in the International Championship – which, despite the Russians, put the team in good heart for the difficult journey to New Zealand.

FRENCH CLUB CHAMPIONSHIP FINAL 1989
27 May, Parc des Princes

Toulouse 18 (2G 2PG)   **Toulon 12** (3PG 1DG)

Toulouse: J Dupuy; J-M Rancoule, D Codorniou, D Charvet, D Berty; P Rougé-Thomas, J Cazalbou; S Laïrle, P Soula, C Portolan, G Miorin, J-M Cadieu, T Maset, A Cigagna (*capt*), K Janik *Replacements* H Leconte for Maset (68 mins); G Portolan for Laïrle (72 mins)
Scorers *Tries:* Laïrle, Charvet   *Conversions:* Dupuy (2)   *Penalty Goals:* Charvet, Dupuy
Toulon: J Bianchi; E Fourniols, P Trémouille, A Carbonel, P Jehl; C Cauvy, J Gallion; M Diaz (*capt*), J-M Casalini, Y Braendlin, Y Roux, J-C Orso, E Champ, E Melville, J-F Tordo *Replacements* J-L Raibaut for Casalini (76 mins); J-P Alarcon for Orso (79 mins)
Scorers *Penalty Goals:* Bianchi (3)   *Dropped Goal:* Cauvy
Referee G Maurette (Limousin)

FRENCH INTERNATIONAL PLAYERS
(up to 30 April 1989)

ABBREVIATIONS

A – Australia; *Arg* – Argentina; *B* – British Forces Teams; *Cz* – Czechoslovakia; *E* – England; *Fj* – Fiji; *G* – Germany; *I* – Ireland; *It* – Italy; *J* – Japan; *K* – New Zealand Services; *M* – Maoris; *NSW* – New South Wales; *NZ* – New Zealand; *R* – Romania; *S* – Scotland; *SA* – South Africa; *US* – United States of America; *W* – Wales; *Z* – Zimbabwe; (R) – Replacement. Entries in square brackets [ ] indicate appearances in the World Cup

Club Abbreviations: ASF-Association Sportive Française; BEC-Bordeaux Etudiants Club; CASG-Club Athlétique des Sports Généraux; PUC-Paris Université Club; RCF-Racing Club de France; SB-Stade Bordelais; SBUC-Stade Bordelais Université Club; SCUF-Sporting Club Universitaire de France; SF-Stade Français; SOE-Stade Olympien des Etudiants; TOEC-Toulouse Olympique Employés Club.

Note: Years given for Five Nations' matches are for second half of season, eg 1972 refers to season 1971-72. Years for all other matches refer to the actual year of the match. When a series has taken place, or more than one match has been played against a country in the same year, figures have been used to denote the particular matches in which players have featured. Thus 1967 *SA* 2,4 indicates that a player appeared in the second and fourth Tests of the 1967 series against South Africa. This list includes only those players who have appeared in FFR International Matches '*donnant droit au titre d'international*'.

Abadie, A (Pau) 1964 *I*
Abadie, A (Graulhet) 1965 *R*, 1967 *SA* 1, 3, 4, *NZ*, 1968 *S, I*
Abadie, L (Tarbes) 1963 *R*
Aguerre, R (Biarritz O) 1979 *S*
Aguilar, D (Pau) 1937 *G*
Aguirre, J-M (Bagnères) 1971 *A* 2, 1972 *S*, 1973 *W, I, J, R*, 1974 *I, W, Arg* 2, *R, SA* 1, 1976 *W* (R), *E, US, A* 2, *R*, 1977 *W, E, S, I, Arg* 1, 2, *NZ* 1, 2, *R*, 1978 *E, S, I, W, R*, 1979 *I, W, E, S, NZ* 1, 2, *R*, 1980 *W, I*
Ainciart, E (Bayonne) 1933 *G*, 1934 *G*, 1935 *G*, 1937 *G*, *It*, 1938 *G* 1
Albaladejo, P (Dax) 1954 *E, It*, 1960 *W, I, It, R*, 1961 *S, SA, E, W, I, NZ* 1, 2, *A*, 1962 *S, E, W, I*, 1963 *S, I, E, W, It*, 1964 *S, NZ, W, It, I, SA, Fj*
Alvarez, A-J (Tyrosse) 1945 *B* 2, 1946 *B, I, K, W*, 1947 *S, I, W, E*, 1948 *I, A, S, W, E*, 1949 *I, E, W*, 1951 *S, E, W*
Amand, H (SF) 1906 *NZ*
Ambert, A (Toulouse) 1930 *S, I, E, G, W*
Amestoy, J-B (Mont-de-Marsan) 1964 *NZ, E*
André, G (RCF) 1913 *SA, E, W, I*, 1914 *I, W, E*
Andrieu, M (Nîmes) 1986 *Arg* 2, *NZ* 1, *R* 2, *NZ* 2, 1987 [*R, Z*], *R*, 1988 *E, S, I, W, Arg* 1, 2, 3, 4, *R*, 1989 *I, W, E, S*
Anduran, J (SCUF) 1910 *W*
Araou, R (Narbonne) 1924 *R*
Arcalis, R (Brive) 1950 *S, I*, 1951 *I, E, W*
Arino, M (Agen) 1962 *R*
Aristouy, P (Pau) 1948 *S*, 1949 *Arg* 2, 1950 *S, I, E, W*
Armary, L (Lourdes) 1987 [*R ´, R*, 1988 *S, I, W, Arg* 3, 4, *R*, 1989 *W, S*
Arnal, J-M (RCF) 1914 *I, W*
Arnaudet, M (Lourdes) 1964 *I*, 1967 *It, W*
Arotca, R (Bayonne) 1938 *R*
Arrieta, J (SF) 1953 *E, W*
Arthapignet, P (Tarbes) 1988 *Arg* 4 (R)
Astre, R (Béziers) 1971 *R*, 1972 *I* 1, 1973 *E* (R), 1975 *E, S, I, SA* 1, 2, *Arg* 2, 1976 *A* 2, *R*
Augé, J (Dax) 1929 *S, W*
Augras, L (Agen) 1931 *I, S, W*
Averous, J-L (La Voulte) 1975 *S, I, SA* 1, 2, 1976 *I, W, E, US, A* 1, 2, *R*, 1977 *W, E, S, I, Arg* 1, *R*, 1978 *E, S, I*, 1979 *NZ* 1, 2, 1980 *E, S*, 1981 *A* 2
Azarete, J-L (Dax, St Jean-de-Luz) 1969 *W, R*, 1970 *S, I, W, R*, 1971 *S, I, E, SA* 1, 2, *A* 1, 1972 *E, W, I* 2, *A* 1, *R*, 1973 *NZ, W, I, R*, 1974 *I, R, SA* 1, 2, 1975 *W*

Bader, E (Primevères) 1926 *M*, 1927 *I, S*
Badin, C (Chalon) 1973 *W, I*, 1975 *Arg* 1
Baillette, M (Perpignan) 1925 *I, NZ, S*, 1926 *W, M*, 1927 *I, W, G* 2, 1929 *G*, 1930 *S, I, E, G*, 1931 *I, S, E*, 1932 *G*
Baladie, G (Agen) 1945 *B* 1, 2, *W*, 1946 *B, I, K*
Ballarin, J (Tarbes) 1924 *E*, 1925 *NZ, S*
Baquet, J (Toulouse) 1921 *I*

Barbazanges, A (Roanne) 1932 *G*, 1933 *G*
Barrau, M (Beaumont, Toulouse) 1971 *S, E, W*, 1972 *E, W, A* 1, 2, 1973 *S, NZ, E, I, J, R*, 1974 *I, S*
Barrère, P (Toulon) 1929 *G*, 1931 *W*
Barrière, R (Béziers) 1960 *R*
Barthe, E (SBUC) 1925 *W, E*
Barthe, J (Lourdes) 1954 *Arg* 1, 2, 1955 *S*, 1956 *I, W, It, E, Cz*, 1957 *S, I, E, W, R* 1, 2, 1958 *S, E, A, W, It, I, SA* 1, 2, 1959 *S, E, It, W*
Basauri, R (Albi) 1954 *Arg* 1
Bascou, P (Bayonne) 1914 *E*
Basquet, G (Agen) 1945 *W*, 1946 *B, I, K, W*, 1947 *S, I, W, E*, 1948 *I, A, S, W, E*, 1949 *S, I, E, W, Arg* 1, 1950 *S, I, E, W*, 1951 *S, I, E, W*, 1952 *S, I, SA, W, E, I*
Bastiat, J-P (Dax) 1969 *R*, 1970 *S, I, W*, 1971 *S, I, SA* 2, 1972 *S, A* 1, 1973 *E*, 1974 *Arg* 1, 2, *SA* 2, 1975 *W, Arg* 1, 2, *R*, 1976 *S, I, W, E, A* 1, 2, *R*, 1977 *W, E, S, I*, 1978 *E, S, I, W*
Baudry, N (Montferrand) 1949 *S, I, W, Arg* 1, 2
Baulon, R (Vienne, Bayonne) 1954 *S, NZ, W, E, It*, 1955 *I, E, W, It*, 1956 *S, I, W, It, E, Cz*, 1957 *S, I, It*
Baux, J-P (Lannemezan) 1968 *NZ* 1, 2, *SA* 1, 2
Bavozet, J (Lyon) 1911 *S, E, W*
Bayard, J (Toulouse) 1923 *S, W, E*, 1924 *W, R, US*
Bayardon, J (Chalon) 1964 *S, NZ, E*
Beaurin, C (SF) 1907 *E*, 1908 *E*
Bégu, J (Dax) 1982 *Arg* 2 (R), 1984 *E, S*
Béguerie, C (Agen) 1979 *NZ* 1
Beguet, L (RCF) 1922 *I*, 1923 *S, W, E, I*, 1924 *S, I, E, R, US*
Behoteguy, A (Bayonne, Cognac) 1923 *E*, 1924 *S, I, E, W, R, US*, 1926 *E*, 1927 *E, G* 1, 2, 1928 *NSW, I, E, G*, 1929 *S, W, E*
Behoteguy, H (RCF, Cognac) 1923 *W*, 1928 *NSW, I, E, G, W*
Belascain, C (Bayonne) 1977 *R*, 1978 *E, S, I, W, R*, 1979 *I, W, E, S*, 1982 *W, E, S, I*, 1983 *E, S, I, W*
Belletante, G (Nantes) 1951 *I, E, W*
Bénésis, R (Narbonne) 1969 *W, R*, 1970 *S, I, W, E, R*, 1971 *S, I, E, W, A* 2, *R*, 1972 *S, I* 1, *E, W, I* 2, *A* 1, *R*, 1973 *NZ, E, W, I, J, R*, 1974 *W, I, E, S*
Benetière, J (Roanne) 1954 *It, Arg* 1
Berbizier, P (Lourdes, Agen) 1981 *S, I, W, E, NZ* 1, 2, 1982 *I, R*, 1983 *S, I*, 1984 *S* (R), *NZ* 1, 2, 1985 *Arg* 1, 2, 1986 *S, I, W, E, R, Arg* 1, *A, NZ* 1, *R* 2, *NZ* 2, 3, 1987 *W, E, S, I*, [*S, R, Fj, A, NZ*], *R*, 1988 *E, S, I, W, Arg* 1, 2, 1989 *I, W, E, S*
Berejnoi, J-C (Tulle) 1963 *R*, 1964 *S, W, It, I, SA, Fj, R*, 1965 *S, I, E, W, It, R*, 1966 *S, I, E, W, It, R*, 1967 *S, A, E, It, W, I, R*
Berges, B (Toulouse) 1926 *I*
Berges-Cau, R (Lourdes) 1976 *E* (R)
Bergeze, F (Bayonne) 1936 *G* 2, 1937 *G, It*, 1938 *G* 1, *R, G* 2
Bergougnan, Y (Toulouse) 1945 *B* 1, *W*, 1946 *B, I, K, W*, 1947 *S, I, W, E*, 1948 *S, W, E*, 1949 *S, E, Arg* 1, 2

239

Bernard, R (Bergerac) 1951 *S, I, E, W*
Bernon, J (Lourdes) 1922 *I*, 1923 *S*
Bérot, J-L (Toulouse) 1968 *NZ* 3, *A*, 1969 *S, I*, 1970 *E, R*, 1971 *S, I, E, W, SA* 1, 2, *A* 1, 2, *R*, 1972 *S, I* 1, *E, W, A* 1, 1974 *I*
Bérot, P (Agen), 1986 *R* 2, *NZ* 2, 3, 1987 *W, E, S, I, R*, 1988 *E, S, I, Arg* 1, 2, 3, 4, *R*, 1989 *S*
Bertrand, P (Bourg) 1951 *I, E, W*, 1953 *S, I, E, W, It*
Bertranne, R (Bagnères) 1971 *E, W, SA* 2, *A* 1, 2, 1972 *S, I* 1, 1973 *NZ, E, J, R*, 1974 *I, W, E, S, Arg* 1, 2, *R, SA* 1, 2, 1975 *W, E, S, I, SA* 1, 2, *Arg* 1, 2, *R*, 1976 *S, I, W, E, US, A* 1, 2, *R*, 1977 *W, E, S, I, Arg* 1, 2, *NZ* 1, 2, *R*, 1978 *E, S, I, W, R*, 1979 *I, W, E, S, R*, 1980 *W, E, S, I, SA, R*, 1981 *S, I, W, E, R, NZ* 1, 2
Besset, E (Grenoble) 1924 *S*
Besset, L (SCUF) 1914 *W, E*
Besson, M (CASG) 1924 *I*, 1925 *I, E*, 1926 *S, W*, 1927 *I*
Besson, P (Brive) 1963 *S, I, E*, 1965 *R*, 1968 *SA* 1
Bianchi, J (Toulon) 1986 *Arg* 1
Bichendaritz, J (Biarritz O) 1954 *It, Arg* 1, 2
Bidart, L (La Rochelle) 1953 *W*
Biemouret, P (Agen) 1969 *E, W*, 1970 *I, W, E*, 1971 *W, SA* 1, 2, *A* 1, 1972 *E, W, I* 2, *A* 2, *R*, 1973 *S, NZ, E, W, I*
Biénès, R (Cognac) 1950 *S, I, E, W*, 1951 *S, I, E, W*, 1952 *S, I, SA, W, E, It*, 1953 *S, I, E*, 1954 *S, I, NZ, W, E, Arg* 1, 2, 1956 *S, I, W, It, E*
Bigot, C (Quillan) 1930 *S, E*, 1931 *I, S*
Bilbao, L (St Jean de Luz) 1978 *I*, 1979 *I*
Billac, E (Bayonne) 1920 *S, E, W, I, US*, 1921 *S, W*, 1922 *W*, 1923 *E*
Billière, M (Toulouse) 1968 *NZ* 3
Bioussa, A (Toulouse) 1924 *W, US*, 1925 *I, NZ, S, E*, 1926 *S, I, E*, 1928 *E, G, W*, 1929 *I, S, W, E*, 1930 *S, I, E, G, W*
Bioussa, C (Toulouse) 1913 *W, I*, 1914 *I*
Biraben, M (Dax) 1920 *W, I, US*, 1921 *S, W, E, I*, 1922 *S, E, I*
Blain, A (Carcassonne) 1934 *G*
Blanco, S (Biarritz O) 1980 *SA, R*, 1981 *S, W, E, A* 1, 2, *R, NZ* 1, 2, 1982 *W, E, S, I, R, Arg* 1, 2, 1983 *E, S, I, W*, 1984 *I, W, E, S, NZ* 1, 2, *R*, 1985 *E, S, I, W, Arg* 1, 2, 1986 *S, I, W, E, R* 1, *Arg* 2, *A, NZ* 1, *R* 2, *NZ* 2, 3, 1987 *W, E, S, I, [S, R, Fj, A, NZ], R*, 1988 *E, S, I, W, Arg* 1, 2, 3, 4, *R*, 1989 *I, W, E, S*
Blond, J (SF) 1935 *G*, 1936 *G* 2, 1937 *G*, 1938 *G* 1, *R, G* 2
Boffelli, V (Aurillac) 1971 *A* 2, *R*, 1972 *S, I* 1, 1973 *J, R*, 1974 *I, W, E, S, Arg* 1, 2, *R, SA* 1, 2, 1975 *W, S I*
Bonal, J-M (Toulouse) 1968 *E, W, Cz, NZ* 2, 3, *SA* 1, 2, *R*, 1969 *S, I, E, R*, 1970 *W, E*
Bonamy, R (SB) 1928 *NSW, I*
Boniface, A (Mont-de-Marsan) 1954 *I, NZ, W, E, It, Arg* 1, 2, 1955 *S, I*, 1956 *S, I, W, It, Cz*, 1957 *S, I, W, R* 2, 1958 *S, E*, 1959 *E*, 1961 *NZ* 1, 3, *A, R*, 1962 *E, W, I, It, R*, 1963 *S, I, E, W, It, R*, 1964 *S, NZ, E, W, It*, 1965 *W, It, R*, 1966 *S, I, E, W*
Boniface, G (Mont-de-Marsan) 1960 *W, I, It, R, Arg* 1, 2, 3, 1961 *S, SA, E, W, It, I, NZ* 1, 2, 3, *R*, 1962 *R*, 1963 *S, I, E, W, It, R*, 1964 *S, I, E, W*, 1965 *S, I, E, W, It, R*, 1966 *S, I, E, W*
Bonnes, E (Narbonne) 1924 *W, R, US*
Bonneval, E (Toulouse) 1984 *NZ* 2 (R), 1985 *W, Arg* 1, 1986 *W, E, R* 1, *Arg* 1, 2, *A, R* 2, *NZ* 2, 3, 1987 *W, E, S, I, [Z]*, 1988 *E*
Bonnus, F (Toulon) 1950 *S, I, E, W*
Bonnus, M (Toulon) 1937 *It*, 1938 *G* 1, *R, G* 2, 1940 *B*
Bontemps, D (La Rochelle) 1968 *SA* 2
Borchard, G (RCF) 1908 *E*, 1909 *E, W, I*, 1911 *I*
Borde, F (RCF) 1920 *I, US*, 1921 *S, W, E*, 1922 *S, W*, 1923 *S, I*, 1924 *E*, 1925 *I*, 1926 *E*
Bordenave, L (Toulon) 1948 *A, S, W, E*, 1949 *S*
Boubee, J (Tarbes) 1921 *S, E, I*, 1922 *E, W*, 1923 *E, I*, 1925 *NZ, S*
Boudreau, R (SCUF) 1910 *W, S*
Bouguyon, G (Grenoble) 1961 *SA, E, W, It, I, NZ* 1, 2, 3, *A*
Boujet, C (Grenoble) 1968 *NZ* 2, *A* (R), *SA* 1
Bouquet, J (Bourgoin, Vienne) 1954 *S*, 1955 *E*, 1956 *S, I, W, It, E, Cz*, 1957 *S, E, W, R* 2, 1958 *S, E*, 1959 *S, It, W, I*, 1960 *S, E, W, I, R*, 1961 *S, SA, E, W, It, I, R*, 1962 *S, E, W, I*
Bourdeu, J R (Lourdes) 1952 *S, I, SA, W, E, It*, 1953 *S, I, E*

Bourgarel, R (Toulouse) 1969 *R*, 1970 *S, I, E, R*, 1971 *W, SA* 1, 2, 1973 *S*
Bourguignon, G (Narbonne) 1988 *Arg* 3, 1989 *I, E*
Bousquet, A (Béziers) 1921 *E, I*, 1924 *R*
Bousquet, R (Albi) 1926 *M*, 1927 *I, S, W, E, G* 1, 1929 *W, E*, 1930 *W*
Boyau, M (SBUC) 1912 *I, S, W, E*, 1913 *W, I*
Boyer, P (Toulon) 1935 *G*
Branca, G (SF) 1928 *S*, 1929 *I, S*
Branlat, A (RCF) 1906 *NZ, E*, 1908 *W*
Brejassou, R (Tarbes) 1952 *S, I, SA, W, E*, 1953 *W, E*, 1954 *S, I, NZ*, 1955 *S, I, E, W, It*
Brethes, R (St Sever) 1960 *Arg* 2
Bringeon, A (Biarritz O) 1925 *W*
Brun, G (Vienne) 1950 *E, W*, 1951 *S, E, W*, 1952 *S, I, SA, W, E, It*, 1953 *E, W, It*
Bruneau, M (SBUC) 1910 *W, E*, 1913 *SA, E*
Brunet, Y (Perpignan) 1975 *SA* 1, 1977 *Arg* 1
Buchet, E (Nice) 1980 *R*, 1982 *E, R* (R), *Arg* 1, 2
Buisson, H (Béziers) 1931 *E, G*
Buonomo, Y (Béziers) 1971 *A* 2, *R*, 1972 *I* 1
Burgun, M (RCF) 1909 *I*, 1910 *W, S, I*, 1911 *S, E*, 1912 *I, S*, 1913 *S, E*, 1914 *E*
Bustaffa, D (Carcassonne) 1977 *Arg* 1, 2, *NZ* 1, 2, 1978 *W, R*, 1980 *W, E, S, A, R*
Buzy, C-E (Lourdes) 1946 *K, W*, 1947 *S, I, W, E*, 1948 *I, A, S, W, E*, 1949 *S, I, E, W, Arg* 1, 2

Cabanier, J-M (Montauban) 1963 *R*, 1964 *S, Fj*, 1965 *S, I, W, It, R*, 1966 *S, I, E, W, It, R*, 1967 *S, A, E, It, W, I, SA* 1, 3, *NZ, R*, 1968 *S, I*
Cabrol, H (Béziers) 1972 *A* 1 (R), *A* 2, 1973 *J*, 1974 *SA* 2
Cadenat, J (SCUF) 1910 *S, E*, 1911 *W, I*, 1912 *W, E*, 1913 *I*
Cahuc, F (St Girons) 1922 *S*
Cals, R (RCF) 1938 *G* 1
Calvo, G (Lourdes) 1961 *NZ* 1, 3
Camberabero, D (La Voulte, Béziers) 1982 *R, Arg* 1, 2, 1983 *E, W*, 1987 *[R(R), Z, Fj(R), A, NZ]*, 1988 *I*
Camberabero, G (La Voulte) 1961 *NZ* 3, 1962 *R*, 1964 *R*, 1967 *A, E, It, W, I, SA* 1, 3, 4, 1968 *S, E, W*
Camberabero, L (La Voulte) 1964 *R*, 1965 *S, I*, 1966 *E, W*, 1967 *A, E, It, W, I*, 1968 *S, E, W*
Cambré, T (Oloron) 1920 *E, W, I, US*
Camel, A (Toulouse) 1928 *S, NSW, I, E, G, W*, 1929 *W, E, G*, 1930 *S, I, E, G, W*, 1935 *G*
Camel, M (Toulouse) 1929 *S, W, E*
Camicas, F (Tarbes) 1927 *G* 2, 1928 *S, I, E, G, W*, 1929 *I, S, W, E*
Camo, E (Villeneuve) 1931 *I, S, W, E, G*, 1932 *G*
Campaes, A (Lourdes) 1965 *W*, 1967 *NZ*, 1968 *S, I, E, W, Cz, NZ* 1, 2, *A*, 1969 *S, W*, 1972 *R*, 1973 *NZ*
Cantoni, J (Béziers) 1970 *W, R*, 1971 *S, I, E, W, SA* 1, 2, *A* 1, *R*, 1972 *S, I* 1, 1973 *S, NZ, W, I*, 1975 *W* (R)
Capdouze, J (Pau) 1964 *SA, Fj, R*, 1965 *S, I, E*
Capendeguy, J-M (Begles) 1967 *NZ, R*
Capitani, P (Toulon) 1954 *Arg* 1, 2
Capmau, J-L (Toulouse) 1914 *E*
Carabignac, J (Agen) 1951 *S, I*, 1952 *SA, W, E*, 1953 *S, I*
Carbonne, J (Perpignan) 1927 *W*
Carminati, A (Béziers) 1986 *R* 2, *NZ* 2, 1987 *[R, Z]*, 1988 *I, W, Arg* 1, 2, 1989 *I, W, S*
Caron, D (Lyon O, Castres) 1947 *E*, 1948 *I, A, W, E*, 1949 *S, I, E, W, Arg* 1
Carpentier, M (Lourdes) 1980 *E, SA, R*, 1981 *S, I, A* 1, 1982 *E, S*
Carrère, C (Toulon) 1966 *R*, 1967 *S, A, E, W, I, SA* 1, 3, 4, *NZ, R*, 1968 *S, I, E, W, Cz, NZ* 3, *A, R*, 1969 *S, I*, 1970 *S, I, W, E*, 1971 *E, W*
Carrère, J (Vichy, Toulon) 1956 *S*, 1957 *E, W, R* 2, 1958 *S, SA* 1, 2, 1959 *I*
Carrère, M (Mont-de-Marsan) 1953 *E, It*
Casaux, L (Tarbes) 1959 *I, It*, 1962 *S*
Cassagne, P (Pau) 1957 *It*
Cassayet, A (Tarbes, Narbonne) 1920 *S, E, W, US*, 1921 *W, E, I*, 1922 *S, E, W*, 1923 *S, W, E, I*, 1924 *S, E, W, R, US*, 1925 *I, NZ, S, W*, 1926 *S, I, E, W, M*, 1927 *I, S, W*
Cassiède, M (Dax) 1961 *NZ* 3, *A, R*
Castets, J (Toulon) 1923 *W, E, I*
Caujolle, J (Tarbes) 1909 *E*, 1913 *SA, E*, 1914 *W, E*

240

Caunègre, R (SB) 1938 R, G 2
Caussade, A (Lourdes) 1978 R, 1979 I, W, E, NZ 1, 2, R, 1980 W, E, S, 1981 S (R), I
Caussarieu, G (Pau) 1929 I
Cayrefourcq, E (Tarbes) 1921 E
Cazals, P (Mont-de-Marsan) 1961 NZ 1, A, R
Cazenave, A (Pau) 1927 E, G 1, 1928 S, NSW, G
Cazenave, F (RCF) 1950 E, 1952 S, 1954 I, NZ, W, E
Cecillon, M (Bourgoin) 1988 I, W, Arg 2, 3, 4, R, 1989 I, E
Celaya, M (Biarritz O, SBUC) 1953 E, W, It, 1954 I, E, It, Arg 1, 2, 1955 S, I, E, W, It, 1956 S, I, W, It, E, Cz, 1957 S, I, E, W, R 2, 1958 S, E, A, W, It, 1959 S, E, 1960 S, E, W, I, R, Arg 1, 2, 3, 1961 S, SA, E, W, It, I, NZ 1, 2, 3, A, R
Celhay, M (Bayonne) 1935 G, 1936 G 1, 1937 G, It, 1938 G 1, 1940 B
Cessieux, N (Lyon) 1906 NZ
Cester, E (TOEC, Valence) 1966 S, I, E, 1967 W, 1968 S, I, E, W, Cz, NZ 1, 3, A, SA 1, 2, R, 1969 S, I, E, W, 1970 S, I, W, E, 1971 A 1, 1972 R, 1973 S, NZ, W, I, J, R, 1974 I, W, E, S
Chaban-Delmas, J (CASG) 1945 B 2
Chabowski, H (Nice, Bourgoin) 1985 Arg 2 1986 R 2, NZ 2
Chadebech, P (Brive) 1982 R, Arg 1, 2, 1986 S, I
Champ, E (Toulon) 1985 Arg 1, 2, 1986 I, W, E, R 1, Arg 1, 2, A, NZ 1, R 2, NZ 2, 3, 1987 W, E, S, I, [S, R, Fj, A, NZ], R, 1988 E, S, Arg 1, 3, 4, R, 1989 W, S
Chapuy, L (SF) 1926 S
Charpentier, G (SF) 1911 E, 1912 W, E
Charton, P (Montferrand) 1940 B
Charvet, D (Toulouse) 1986 W, E, R 1, Arg 1, A, NZ 1, 3, 1987 W, E, S, I, [S, R, Z, Fj, A, NZ], R, 1989 E(R)
Chassagne, J (Montferrand) 1938 G 1
Chatau, A (Bayonne) 1913 SA
Chaud, E (Toulon) 1932 G, 1934 G, 1935 G
Chenevay, C (Grenoble) 1968 SA 1
Chevallier, B (Montferrand) 1952 S, I, SA, W, E, It, 1953 E, W, It, 1954 S, I, NZ, W, Arg 1, 1955 S, I, E, W, It, 1956 S, I, W, It, E, Cz, 1957 S
Chiberry, J (Chambéry) 1955 It
Chilo, A (RCF) 1920 S, W, 1925 I, NZ
Cholley, G (Castres) 1975 E, S, I, SA 1, 2, Arg 1, 2, R, 1976 S, I, W, E, A 1, 2, R, 1977 W, E, S, I, Arg 1, 2, NZ 1, 2, R, 1978 E, S, I, W, R, 1979 I, S
Choy, J (Narbonne) 1930 S, I, E, G, W, 1931 I, 1933 G, 1934 G, 1935 G, 1936 G 2
Cimarosti, J (Castres) 1976 US (R)
Clady, A (Lezignan) 1929 G, 1931 I, S, E, G
Clarrac, H (St Girons) 1938 G 1
Claudel, R (Lyon) 1932 G, 1934 G
Clauzel, F (Béziers) 1924 E, W, 1925 W
Clave, J (Agen) 1936 G 2, 1938 R, G 2
Claverie, H (Lourdes) 1954 NZ, W
Clement, G (RCF) 1931 W
Clement, J (RCF) 1921 S, W, E, 1922 S, E, W, I, 1923 S, W, I
Clemente, M (Oloron) 1978 R, 1980 S, I
Cluchague, L (Biarritz O) 1924 S, 1925 E
Coderc, J (Chalon) 1932 G, 1933 G, 1934 G, 1935 G, 1936 G 1
Codorniou, D (Narbonne) 1979 NZ 1, 2, R, 1980 W, E, S, I, 1981 S, W, E, A 2, 1983 E, S, I, W, A 1, 2, R, 1984 I, W, E, S, NZ 1, 2, R, 1985 E, S, I, W, Arg 1, 2
Cognet, L (Montferrand) 1932 G, 1936 G 1, 2, 1937 G, It
Colombier, J (St Junien) 1952 SA, W, E
Colomine, G (Narbonne) 1979 NZ 1
Combe, J (SF) 1910 S, E, I, 1911 S
Combes, G (Fumel) 1945 B 2
Communeau, M (SF) 1906 NZ, E, 1907 E, 1908 E, W, 1909 E, W, I, 1910 S, E, I, 1911 S, E, I, 1912 I, S, W, E, 1913 SA, E, W
Condom, J (Boucau, Biarritz) 1982 R, 1983 E, S, I, W, A 1, 2, R, 1984 I, W, E, S, NZ 1, 2, R, 1985 E, S, I, W, Arg 1, 2, 1986 S, I, W, E, R 1, Arg 1, 2, NZ 1, R 2, NZ 2, 3, 1987 W, E, S, I, [S, R, Z, A, NZ], R, 1988 E, S, W, Arg 1, 2, 3, 4, R, 1989 I, W, E, S
Conilh de Beyssac, J (SBUC) 1912 I, S, 1914 I, W, E
Constant, G (Perpignan) 1920 W
Coscolla, G (Béziers) 1921 S, W
Costantino, J (Montferrand) 1973 R

Costes, F (Montferrand) 1979 E, S, NZ 1, 2, R, 1980 W, I
Coulon, E (Grenoble) 1928 S
Crabos, R (RCF) 1920 S, E, W, I, US, 1921 S, W, E, I, 1922 S, E, W, I, 1923 S, I, 1924 S, I
Crampagne, J (Begles) 1967 SA 4
Crancee, R (Lourdes) 1960 Arg 3, 1961 S
Crauste, M (RCF, Lourdes) 1957 R 1, 2, 1958 S, E, A, W, It, I, 1959 E, It, W, I, 1960 S, E, W, I, It, R, Arg 1, 3, 1961 S, SA, E, W, It, I, NZ 1, 2, 3, A, R, 1962 S, E, W, I, It, R, 1963 S, I, E, W, It, R, 1964 S, NZ, E, W, It, I, SA, Fj, R, 1965 S, I, E, W, It, R, 1966 S, I, E, W, It
Cremaschi, M (Lourdes) 1980 R, 1981 R, NZ 1, 2, 1982 W, S, 1983 A 1, 2, R, 1984 I, W
Crichton, W H (Le Havre) 1906 NZ, E
Cristina, J (Montferrand) 1979 R
Cussac, P (Biarritz O) 1934 G
Cutzach, A (Quillan) 1929 G

Daguerre, F (Biarritz O) 1936 G 1
Daguerre, J (CASG) 1933 G
Dalmaso, M (Mont-de-Marsan) 1988 R(R)
Danion, J (Toulon) 1924 I
Danos, P (Toulon, Béziers) 1954 Arg 1, 2, 1957 R 2, 1958 S, E, W, It, I, SA 1, 2, 1959 S, E, It, W, I, 1960 S, E
Darbos, P (Dax) 1969 R
Darracq, R (Dax) 1957 It
Darrieussecq, A (Biarritz O) 1973 E
Darrieussecq, J (Mont-de-Marsan) 1933 It
Darrouy, C (Mont-de-Marsan) 1957 I, E, W, It, R 1, 1959 E, 1961 R, 1963 S, I, E, W, It, 1964 NZ, E, W, It, I, SA, Fj, R, 1965 S, I, E, W, It, R, 1966 S, I, E, W, It, R, 1967 S, A, E, It, W, I, SA 1, 2, 4
Daudignon, G (SF) 1928 S
Dauga, B (Mont-de-Marsan) 1964 S, NZ, E, W, It, SA, Fj, R, 1965 S, I, E, W, It, R, 1966 S, I, E, W, It, R, 1967 S, A, E, It, W, I, SA 1, 2, 3, 4, NZ, R, 1968 S, I, NZ 1, 2, 3, A, SA 1, 2, R, 1969 S, I, E, R, 1970 S, I, W, E, R, 1971 S, I, E, W, SA 1, 2, A 1, 2, R, 1972 S, I 1, W
Dauger, J (Bayonne) 1945 B 1, 2, 1953 S
Daulouede, P (Tyrosse) 1937 G, It, 1938 G 1, 1940 B
Decamps, P (RCF) 1911 S
Dedet, J (SF) 1910 S, E, I, 1911 W, I, 1912 S, 1913 E, I
Dedeyn, P (RCF) 1906 NZ
Dedieu, P (Béziers) 1963 E, It, 1964 W, It, I, SA, Fj, R, 1965 S, I, E, W
De Gregorio, J (Grenoble) 1960 S, E, W, I, It, R, Arg 1, 2, 1961 S, SA, E, W, It, I, 1962 S, E, W, 1963 S, W, It, 1964 NZ, E
Dehez, J-L (Agen) 1967 SA 2, 1969 R
De Jouvencel, E (SF) 1909 W, I
De Laborderie, M (RCF) 1921 I, 1922 I, 1925 W, E
Delage, C (Agen) 1983 S, I
De Malherbe, H (CASG) 1932 G, 1933 G
De Malmann, R (RCF) 1908 E, W, 1909 E, W, I, 1910 E, I
De Muizon, J J (SF) 1910 I
Delaigue, A (Toulon) 1973 J, R
Delque, A (Toulouse) 1937 It, 1938 G 1, R, G 2
Descamps, (SB) 1927 G 2
Desclaux, F (RCF) 1949 Arg 1, 2, 1953 It
Desclaux, J (Perpignan) 1934 G, 1935 G, 1936 G 1, 2, 1937 G, It, 1938 G 1, R, G 2, 1945 B 1
Desnoyer, L (Brive) 1974 R
Destarac, L (Tarbes) 1926 S, I, E, W, M, 1927 W, E, G 1, 2
Desvouges, R (SF) 1914 W
Detrez, P-E (Nîmes) 1983 A 2 (R), 1986 Arg 1 (R), 2, A (R), NZ 1
Devergie, T (Nîmes) 1988 R
Deygas, M (Vienne) 1937 It
Dintrans, P (Tarbes) 1979 NZ 1, 2, R, 1980 E, S, I, SA, R, 1981 S, I, W, E, A 1, 2, R, NZ 1, 2, 1982 W, E, S, I, R, Arg 1, 2, 1983 E, S, I, W, A 1, 2, R, 1984 I, W, E, S, NZ 1, 2, R, 1985 E, S, I, W, Arg 1, 2, 1987 [R], 1988 Arg 1, 2, 3, 1989 W, E, S
Dizabo, P (Tyrosse) 1948 A, S, E, 1949 S, I, E, W, Arg 2, 1950 S, I, 1960 Arg 1, 2, 3
Domec, A (Carcassonne) 1929 W
Domec, H (Lourdes) 1953 W, It, 1954 S, I, NZ, W, E,

It, 1955 *S, I, E, W*, 1956 *I, W, It*, 1958 *E, A, W, It, I*
Domenech, A (Vichy, Brive) 1954 *W, E, It*, 1955 *S, I,
E, W*, 1956 *S, I, W, It, E, Cz*, 1957 *S, I, E, W, It, R* 1,
2, 1958 *S, E, It*, 1959 *It*, 1960 *S, E, W, I, It, R, Arg* 1, 2,
3, 1961 *S, SA, E, W, It, I, NZ* 1, 2, 3, *A, R*, 1962 *S, E,
W, I, It, R*, 1963 *W, It*
Domercq, J (Bayonne) 1912 *I, S*
Dorot, J (RCF) 1935 *G*
Dospital, P (Bayonne) 1977 *R*, 1980 *I*, 1981 *S, I, W, E*,
1982 *I, R, Arg* 1, 2, 1983 *E, S, I, W*, 1984 *E, S, NZ* 1,2,
R, 1985 *E, S, I, W, Arg* 1
Dourthe, C (Dax) 1966 *R*, 1967 *S, A, E, W, I, SA* 1, 2,
3, *NZ*, 1968 *W, NZ* 3, *SA* 1, 2, 1969 *W*, 1971 *SA* 2 (R),
R, 1972 *I* 1, 2, *A* 1, 2, *R*, 1973 *S, NZ, E*, 1974 *I, Arg* 1,
2, *SA* 1, 2, 1975 *W, E, S*
Dousseau, E (Angoulême) 1938 *R*
Droitecourt, M (Montferrand) 1972 *R*, 1973 *NZ* (R),
E, 1974 *E, S, Arg* 1, *SA* 2, 1975 *SA* 1, 2, *Arg* 1, 2, *R*,
1976 *S, I, W, A* 1, 1977 *Arg* 2
Dubertrand, A (Montferrand) 1971 *A* 2, *R*, 1972 *I* 2,
1974 *I, W, E, SA* 2, 1975 *Arg* 1, 2, *R*, 1976 *S, US*
Dubois, D (Begles) 1971 *S*
Dubroca, D (Agen) 1979 *NZ* 2, 1981 *NZ* 2 (R), 1982 *E,
S*, 1984 *W, E, S*, 1985 *Arg* 2, 1986 *S, I, W, E, R* 1, *Arg*
2, *A, NZ* 1, *R* 2, *NZ* 2, 3, 1987 *W, E, S, I, [S, Z, Fj, A,
NZ]*, *R*, 1988 *E, S, I, W*
Duche, A (Limoges) 1929 *G*
Duclos, A (Lourdes) 1931 *S*
Ducousso, J (Tarbes) 1925 *S, W, E*
Dufau, G (RCF) 1948 *I, A*, 1949 *I, W*, 1950 *S, E, W*,
1951 *S, I, E, W*, 1952 *SA, W*, 1953 *S, I, E, W*, 1954 *S,
I, NZ, W, E, It*, 1955 *S, I, E, W, It*, 1956 *S, I, W, It*,
1957 *S, I, E, W, It, R* 1
Dufau, J (Biarritz) 1912 *I, S, W, E*
Duffaut, Y (Agen) 1954 *Arg* 1, 2
Dufour, R (Tarbes) 1911 *W*
Dufourcq, J (SBUC) 1906 *NZ, E*, 1907 *E*, 1908 *W*
Duhard, Y (Bagnères) 1980 *E*
Duhau, J (SF) 1928 *I*, 1930 *I, G*, 1931 *I, S, W*, 1933 *G*
Dulaurens, C (Toulouse) 1926 *I*, 1928 *S*, 1929 *W*
Duluc, A (Béziers) 1934 *G*
Du Manoir, Y LeP (RCF) 1925 *I, NZ, S, W, E*, 1926
S, 1927 *I, S*
Dupont, C (Lourdes) 1923 *S, W, I*, 1924 *S, I, W, R,
US*, 1925 *S*, 1927 *E, G* 1, 2, 1928 *NSW, G, W*, 1929 *I*
Dupont, J-L (Agen) 1983 *S*
Dupont, L (RCF) 1934 *G*, 1935 *G*, 1936 *G* 1, 2, 1938 *R,
G* 2
Dupouy, A (SB) 1924 *W, R*
Duprat, B (Bayonne) 1966 *E, W, It, R*, 1967 *S, A, E,
SA* 2, 3, 1968 *S, I*, 1972 *E, W, I* 2, *A* 1
Dupré, P (RCF) 1909 *W*
Dupuy, J (Tarbes) 1956 *S, I, W, It, E, Cz*, 1957 *S, I, E,
W, It, R* 2, 1958 *S, I, E, SA* 1, 2, 1959 *S, E, It, W, I*, 1960
W, I, It, Arg 1, 3, 1961 *S, SA, E, NZ* 2, *R*, 1962 *S, E,
W, I, It*, 1963 *W, It, R*, 1964 *S*
Du Souich, C J (SCUF) 1911 *W, I*
Dutin, B (Mont-de-Marsan) 1968 *NZ* 2, *A, SA* 2, *R*
Dutour, F X (Toulouse) 1911 *E, I*, 1912 *S, W, E*, 1913
S
Dutrain, H (Toulouse) 1945 *W*, 1946 *B, I*, 1947 *E*,
1949 *I, E, W, Arg* 1
Dutrey, J (Lourdes) 1940 *B*
Duval, R (SF) 1908 *E, W*, 1909 *E*, 1911 *E, W, I*

Echave, L (Agen) 1961 *S*
Elissalde, E (Bayonne) 1936 *G* 2, 1940 *B*
Elissalde, J-P (La Rochelle) 1980 *SA, R*, 1981 *A* 1, 2, *R*
Erbani, D (Agen) 1981 *A* 1, 2, *NZ* 1, 2, 1982 *Arg* 1, 2,
1983 *S* (R), *I, W, A* 1, 2, *R*, 1984 *W, E, R*, 1985 *E,
W*(R), *Arg* 2, 1986 *S, I, W, E, R* 1, *Arg* 2, *NZ* 1, 2 (R),
3, 1987 *W, E, S, I, [S, R, Fj, A, NZ]*, 1988 *E, S*, 1989
I(R), *W, E, S*
Escaffre, P (Narbonne) 1933 *G*, 1934 *G*
Escommier, M (Montelimar) 1955 *It*
Esponda, J-M (RCF) 1967 *SA* 1, 2, *R*, 1968 *NZ* 1, 2,
SA 2, *R*, 1969 *S, I* (R), *E*
Estève, A (Béziers) 1971 *SA* 1, 1972 *I* 1, *E, W, I* 2, *A* 2,
R, 1973 *S, NZ, E, I*, 1974 *I, W, E, S, R, SA* 1, 2, 1975
W, E
Estève, P (Narbonne, Lavelanet) 1982 *R, Arg* 1, 2,
1983 *E, S, I, W, A* 1, 2, *R*, 1984 *I, W, E, S, NZ* 1,2, *R*,
1985 *E, S, I, W*, 1986 *S, I*, 1987 *[S, Z]*

Etcheberry, J (Rochefort, Cognac) 1923 *W, I*, 1924 *S,
I, E, W, R, US*, 1926 *S, I, E, M*, 1927 *I, S, W, G* 2
Etchenique, J (Biarritz O) 1974 *R, SA* 1, 1975 *E, Arg* 2
Etchepare, A (Bayonne) 1922 *I*
Etcheverry, M (Pau) 1971 *S, I*
Eutrope, A (SCUF) 1913 *I*

Fabre, E (Toulouse) 1937 *It*, 1938 *G* 1, 2
Fabre, J (Toulouse) 1963 *S, I, E, W, It*, 1964 *S, NZ, E*
Fabre, L (Lezignan) 1930 *G*
Fabre, M (Béziers) 1981 *A* 1, *R, NZ* 1, 2, 1982 *I, R*
Failliot, P (RCF) 1911 *S, W, I*, 1912 *I, S, E*, 1913 *E, W*
Fargues, G (Dax) 1923 *I*
Faure, F (Tarbes) 1914 *I, W, E*
Fauvel, J-P (Tulle) 1980 *R*
Favre, M (Lyon) 1913 *E, W*
Ferrand, L (Chalon) 1940 *B*
Ferrien, R (Tarbes) 1950 *S, I, E, W*
Finat, R (CASG) 1932 *G*, 1933 *G*
Fite, R (Brive) 1963 *W, It*
Forestier, J (SCUF) 1912 *W*
Forgues, F (Bayonne) 1911 *S, E, W*, 1912 *I, W, E*,
1913 *S, SA, W*, 1914 *I, E*
Fort, J (Agen) 1967 *It, W, I, SA* 1, 2, 3, 4
Fourcade, G (BEC) 1909 *E, W*
Foures, H (Toulouse) 1951 *S, I, E, W*
Fournet, F (Montferrand) 1950 *W*
Fouroux, J (La Voulte) 1972 *I* 2, *R*, 1974 *W, E, Arg* 1,
2, *R, SA* 1, 2, 1975 *W, Arg* 1, *R*, 1976 *S, I, W, E, US, A*
1, 1977 *W, E, S, I, Arg* 1, *NZ* 1, 2, *R*
Franquenelle, A (Vaugirard) 1911 *S*, 1913 *W, I*
Furcade, R (Perpignan) 1952 *S*

Gabernet, S (Toulouse) 1980 *E, S*, 1981 *S, I, W, E, A*
1, 2, *R, NZ* 1, 2, 1982 *I*, 1983 *A* 2, *R*
Gachassin, J (Lourdes) 1961 *S, I*, 1963 *R*, 1964 *S, NZ,
E, W, It, I, SA, Fj, R*, 1965 *S, I, E, W, It, R*, 1966 *S, I,
E, W*, 1967 *S, A, It, W, I, NZ*, 1968 *I, E*, 1969 *S, I*
Galau, H (Toulouse) 1924 *S, I, E, W, US*
Galia, J (Quillan) 1927 *E, G* 1, 2, 1928 *S, NSW, I, E,
W*, 1929 *I, E, G*, 1930 *S, I, E, G, W*, 1931 *S, W, E, G*
Gallion, J (Toulon) 1978 *E, S, I, W*, 1979 *I, W, E, S,
NZ* 2, *R*, 1980 *W, E, S, I*, 1983 *A* 1, 2, *R*, 1984 *I, W, E,
S, R* 1985 *E, S, I, W*, 1986 *Arg* 2
Galy, J (Perpignan) 1953 *W*
Garuet, J-P (Lourdes) 1983 *A* 1, 2, *R*, 1984 *I, NZ* 1,2,
R, 1985 *E, S, I, W, Arg* 1, 1986 *S, I, W, E, R* 1, *Arg* 1,
NZ 1, *R* 2, *NZ* 2, 3, 1987 *W, E, S, I, [S, R, Fj, A, NZ]*,
1988 *E, S, Arg* 1,2, *R*, 1989 *E*(R), *S*
Gasc, J (Graulhet) 1977 *NZ* 2
Gasparotto, G (Montferrand) 1976 *A* 2, *R*
Gauby, G (Perpignan) 1956 *Cz*
Gaudermen, R (RCF) 1906 *E*
Gayraud, W (Toulouse) 1920 *I*
Geneste, R (BEC) 1945 *B* 1, 1949 *Arg* 2
Gensanne, R (Béziers) 1962 *S, E, W, I, It, R*, 1963 *S*
Gerald, G (RCF) 1927 *E, G* 2, 1928 *S, I, E, W*,
G, 1930 *S, I, E, G, W*, 1931 *I, S, E, G*
Gerintes, G (CASG) 1924 *R*, 1925 *I*, 1926 *W*
Geschwind, P (RCF) 1936 *G* 1, 2
Giacardy, M (SBUC) 1907 *E*
Gommes, J (RCF) 1909 *I*
Gonnet, C-A (Albi) 1921 *E, I*, 1922 *E, W*, 1924 *S, E*,
1926 *S, I, E, W, M*, 1927 *I, S, W, E, G* 1
Got, R (Perpignan) 1920 *I, US*, 1921 *S, W*, 1922 *S, E,
W, I*, 1924 *I, E, W, R, US*
Gourdon, J-F (RCF, Bagnères) 1974 *S, Arg* 1, 2, *R, SA*
1, 2, 1975 *W, E, S, I, R*, 1976 *S, I, W, E*, 1978 *E, S*,
1979 *W, E, S, R*, 1980 *I*
Goyard, A (Lyon U) 1936 *G* 1, 2, 1937 *G, It*, 1938 *G* 1,
R, G 2
Graciet, R (SBUC) 1926 *I, W*, 1927 *S, G* 1, 1929 *E*,
1930 *W*
Gratton, J (Agen) 1984 *NZ* 2, *R*, 1985 *E, S, I, W, Arg*
1, 2, 1986 *S, NZ* 1
Graule, V (Arl Perpignan) 1926 *I, E, W*, 1927 *S, W*,
1931 *G*
Greffe, M (Grenoble) 1968 *W, Cz, NZ* 1, 2, *SA* 1
Griffard, J (Lyon U) 1932 *G*, 1933 *G*, 1934 *G*
Gruarin, A (Toulon) 1964 *W, It, I, SA, Fj, R*, 1965 *S,
I, E, W, It*, 1966 *S, I, E, W, It, R*, 1967 *S, A, E, It, W,
I, NZ*, 1968 *S, I*
Guelorget, P (RCF) 1931 *E, G*

FRENCH INTERNATIONAL PLAYERS

Guichemerre, A (Dax) 1920 *E*, 1921 *E, I*, 1923 *S*
Guilbert, A (Toulon) 1975 *E, S, I, SA* 1, 2, 1976 *A* 1, 1977 *Arg* 1, 2, *NZ* 1, 2, *R*, 1979 *I, W, E*
Guillemin, P (RCF) 1908 *E, W*, 1909 *E, I*, 1910 *W, S, E, I*, 1911 *S, E, W*
Guilleux, P (Agen) 1952 *SA, It*
Guiral, M (Agen) 1931 *G*, 1932 *G*, 1933 *G*

Haget, A (PUC) 1953 *E*, 1954 *I, NZ, E, Arg* 2, 1955 *E, W, It*, 1957 *I, E, It, R* 1, 1958 *It, SA* 2
Haget, F (Agen, Biarritz O) 1974 *Arg* 1, 2, 1975 *SA* 2, *Arg* 1, 2, *R*, 1976 *S*, 1978 *S, I, W, R*, 1979 *I, W, E, S, NZ* 1, 2, *R*, 1980 *W, S, I*, 1984 *S, NZ* 1,2, *R*, 1985 *E, S, I*, 1986 *S, I, W, E, R* 1, *Arg* 1, *A, NZ* 1, 1987 *S, I*, [*R, Fj*]
Haget, H (CASG) 1928 *S*, 1930 *G*
Halet, (Strasbourg) 1925 *NZ, S, W*
Harize, D (Cahors, Toulouse) 1975 *SA* 1, 2, 1976 *A* 1, 2, *R*, 1977 *W, E, S, I*
Hauc, J (Toulon) 1928 *E, G*, 1929 *I, S, G*
Hauser, M (Lourdes) 1969 *E*
Hedembaigt, M (Bayonne) 1913 *S, SA*, 1914 *W*
Herice, D (Begles) 1950 *I*
Herrero, A (Toulon) 1963 *R*, 1964 *NZ, E, W, It, I, SA, Fj, R*, 1965 *S, I, E, W*, 1966 *W, It, R*, 1967 *S, A, E, It, I, R*
Herrero, B (Nice) 1983 *I*, 1986 *Arg* 1
Hiquet, J-C (Agen) 1964 *E*
Hoche, M (PUC) 1957 *I, E, W, It, R* 1
Hondagne, M (Tarbes) 1988 *Arg* 2 (R)
Hortoland, J-P (Béziers) 1971 *A* 2
Houblain, H (SCUF) 1909 *E*, 1910 *W*
Houdet, R (SF) 1927 *S, W, G* 1, 1928 *G, W*, 1929 *I, S, E*, 1930 *S, E*
Hourdebaigt, (SBUC) 1909 *I*, 1910 *W, S, E, I*
Hubert, A (ASF) 1906 *E*, 1907 *E*, 1908 *E, W*, 1909 *E, W, I*
Hutin, R (CASG) 1927 *I, S, W*

Icard, J (SF) 1909 *E, W*
Iguiniz, E (Bayonne) 1914 *E*
Ihingoué, D (BEC) 1912 *I, S*
Imbernon, J-F (Perpignan) 1976 *I, W, E, US, A* 1, 1977 *W, E, S, I, Arg* 1, 2, *NZ* 1, 2, 1978 *E, R*, 1979 *I*, 1981 *S, I, W, E*, 1982 *I*, 1983 *I, W*
Iraçabal, J (Bayonne) 1968 *NZ* 1, 2, *SA* 1, 1969 *S, I, W, R*, 1970 *S, I, W, E, R*, 1971 *W, SA* 1, 2, *A* 1, 1972 *E, W, I* 2, *A* 2, *R*, 1973 *S, NZ, E, W, I, J*, 1974 *I, W, E, S, Arg* 1, 2, *SA* 2 (R)
Isaac, H (RCF) 1907 *E*, 1908 *E*
Ithurra, E (Biarritz O) 1936 *G* 1, 2, 1937 *G*

Janeczek, T (Tarbes) 1982 *Arg* 1, 2
Janik, K (Toulouse) 1987 *R*
Jarasse, A (Brive) 1945 *B* 1
Jardel, J (SB) 1928 *I, E*
Jauréguy, A (RCF, Toulouse, SF) 1920 *S, E, W, I, US*, 1922 *S, W*, 1923 *S, W, E, I*, 1924 *S, W, R, US*, 1925 *I, NZ*, 1926 *S, E, W, M*, 1927 *I, E*, 1928 *S, NSW, E, G, W*, 1929 *I, S, E*
Jauréguy, P (Toulouse) 1913 *S, SA, W, I*
Jeangrand, M-H (Tarbes) 1921 *I*
Jeanjean, P (Toulon) 1948 *I*
Jérôme, G (SF) 1906 *NZ, E*
Joinel, J-L (Brive) 1977 *NZ* 1, 1978 *R*, 1979 *I, W, E, S, NZ* 1, 2, *R*, 1980 *W, S, I, SA*, 1981 *S, I, W, E, R*, *NZ* 1, 2, 1982 *E, S, I, R*, 1983 *E, S, I, W, A* 1, 2, *R*, 1984 *I, W, E, S, NZ* 1,2, 1985 *S, I, W, Arg* 1, 1986 *S, I, W, E, R* 1, *Arg* 1, 2, *A*, 1987 [*Z*]
Jol, M (Biarritz O) 1947 *S, I, W, E*, 1949 *S, I, E, W, Arg* 1, 2
Junquas, L (Tyrosse) 1945 *B* 1, 2, *W*, 1946 *B, I, K, W*, 1947 *S, I, W, E*, 1948 *S, W*

Kaczorowksi, D (Le Creusot) 1974 *I* (R)
Kaempf, A (St Jean-de-Luz) 1946 *B*

Labadie, P (Bayonne) 1952 *S, I, SA, W, E, It*, 1953 *S, I, It*, 1954 *S, I, NZ, W, E, Arg* 2, 1955 *S, I, E, W*, 1956 *I*, 1957 *I*
Labarthete, R (Pau) 1952 *S*
Labazuy, A (Lourdes) 1952 *I*, 1954 *S, W*, 1956 *E*, 1958

A, W, I, 1959 *S, E, It, W*
Laborde, C (RCF) 1962 *It, R*, 1963 *R*, 1964 *SA*, 1965 *E*
Lacans, P (Béziers) 1980 *SA*, 1981 *W, E, A* 2, *R*, 1982 *W*
Lacassagne, H (SBUC) 1906 *NZ*, 1907 *E*
Lacaussade, R (Begles) 1948 *A, S*
Lacaze, C (Lourdes, Angoulême) 1961 *NZ* 2, 3, *A, R*, 1962 *E, W, I, It*, 1963 *W, R*, 1964 *S, NZ, E*, 1965 *It, R*, 1966 *S, I, E, W, It, R*, 1967 *S, E, SA* 1, 3, 4, *R*, 1968 *S, E, W, Cz, NZ* 1, 1969 *E*
Lacaze, H (Périgueux) 1928 *I, G, W*, 1929 *I, W*
Lacaze, P (Lourdes) 1958 *SA* 1, 2, 1959 *S, E, It, W, I*
Lacazedieu, C (Dax) 1923 *W, I*, 1928 *NSW, I*, 1929 *S*
Lacome, M (Pau) 1960 *Arg* 2
Lacoste, R (Tarbes) 1914 *I, W, E*
Lacrampe, F (Béziers) 1949 *Arg* 2
Lacroix, P (Mont-de-Marsan, Agen) 1958 *A*, 1960 *W, I, It, R, Arg* 1, 2, 3, 1961 *S, SA, E, W, I, NZ* 1, 2, 3, *A, R*, 1962 *S, E, W, I, R*, 1963 *S, I, E, W*
Lafarge, Y (Montferrand) 1978 *R*, 1979 *NZ* 1, 1981 *I* (R)
Laffond, A (Bayonne) 1922 *E*
Laffont, H (Narbonne) 1926 *W*
Lafitte, R (SCUF) 1910 *W, S*
Lafond, J-B (RCF) 1983 *A* 1, 1985 *Arg* 1, 2, 1986 *S, I, W, E, R* 1, 1987 *I* (R), 1988 *W*, 1989 *I, W, E*
Lagisquet, P (Bayonne) 1983 *A* 1, 2, *R*, 1984 *I, W, NZ* 1, 2, 1986 *R* 1 (R), *Arg* 1, 2, *A, NZ* 1, 1987 [*S, R, Fj, A, NZ*], *R*, 1988 *S, I, W, Arg*1, 2, 3, 4, *R*, 1989 *I, W, E, S*
Lagrange, J-C (RCF) 1966 *It*
Lalande, M (RCF) 1923 *S, W, I*
Lane, G (RCF) 1906 *NZ, E*, 1907 *E*, 1908 *E, W*, 1909 *E, W, I*, 1910 *W, E*, 1911 *S, W*, 1912 *I, W, E*, 1913 *S*
Laporte, G (Graulhet) 1981 *I, W, E, R, NZ* 1, 2, 1986 *S, I, W, E, R* 1, *Arg* 1, *A* (R), 1987 [*R, Z*(R), *Fj*]
Larreguy, P (Bayonne) 1954 *It*
Larribeau, J (Périgueux) 1912 *I, S, W, E*, 1913 *S*, 1914 *I, E*
Larrieu, J (Tarbes) 1920 *I, US*, 1921 *W*, 1923 *S, W, E, I*
Larrieu, M (SB) 1927 *G* 2
Larrue, H (Carmaux) 1960 *W, I, It, R, Arg* 1, 2, 3
Lasâosa, P (Dax) 1950 *I*, 1952 *S, I, E, It*, 1955 *It*
Lassegue, J-B (Toulouse) 1946 *W*, 1947 *S, I, W*, 1948 *W*, 1949 *I, E, W*
Lasserre, F (René) (Bayonne, Cognac, Grenoble) 1914 *I*, 1920 *S*, 1921 *S, W, I*, 1922 *S, E, W, I*, 1923 *W, E*, 1924 *S, I, R, US*
Lasserre, J-C (Dax) 1963 *It*, 1964 *S, NZ, E, W, It, I, Fj*, 1965 *W, It, R*, 1966 *R*, 1967 *S*
Lasserre, M (Agen) 1967 *SA* 2, 3, 1968 *E, W, Cz, NZ* 3, *A, SA* 1, 2, 1969 *S, I, E*, 1970 *E*, 1971 *E, W*
Laterrade, G (Tarbes) 1910 *E, I*, 1911 *S, E, I*
Laudouar, J (Soustons, SBUC) 1961 *NZ* 1, 2, *R*, 1962 *I, R*
Lauga, P (Vichy) 1950 *S, I, E, W*
Laurent, A (Biarritz O) 1925 *NZ, S, W, E*, 1926 *W*
Laurent, J (Bayonne) 1920 *S, E, W*
Laurent, M (Auch) 1932 *G*, 1933 *G*, 1934 *G*, 1935 *G*, 1936 *G* 1
Lavail, G (Perpignan) 1937 *G*, 1940 *B*
Lavaud, R (Carcassonne) 1914 *I, W*
Lavergne, P (Limoges) 1950 *S*
Lavigne, B (Agen) 1984 *R*, 1985 *E*
Lavigne, J (Dax) 1920 *E, W*
Lazies, H (Auch) 1954 *Arg* 2, 1955 *It*, 1956 *E*, 1957 *S*
Le Bourhis, R (La Rochelle) 1961 *R*
Lecointre, M (Nantes) 1952 *It*
Le Droff, J (Auch) 1963 *It*, 1964 *S, NZ, E*, 1970 *E, R*, 1971 *S, I*
Lefevre, R (Brive) 1961 *NZ* 2
Lefort, J-B (Biarritz O) 1938 *G* 1
Le Goff, R (Métro) 1938 *R, G* 2
Legrain, M (SF) 1909 *I*, 1910 *I*, 1911 *S, E, W, I*, 1913 *S, SA, E, I*, 1914 *I, W*
Lenient, J-J (Vichy) 1967 *R*
Lepatey, J (Mazamet) 1954 *It*, 1955 *S, I, E, W*
Lepatey, L (Mazamet) 1924 *S, I, E*
Lescarboura, J-P (Dax) 1982 *W, E, S, I*, 1983 *A* 1, 2, *R*, 1984 *I, W, E, S, NZ* 1,2, *R*, 1985 *E, S, I, W, Arg* 1, 2, 1986 *Arg* 2, *A, NZ* 1, *R*, *NZ* 2, 1988 *S, W*
Lesieur, E (SF) 1906 *E*, 1908 *E*, 1909 *W*, 1910 *S, E, I*, 1911 *E, I*, 1912 *W*

243

Leuvielle, M (SBUC) 1908 W, 1913 S, SA, E, W, 1914 W, E
Levasseur, R (SF) 1925 W, E
Levee, H (RCF) 1906 NZ
Lewis, E W (Le Havre) 1906 E
Libaros, G (Tarbes) 1936 G 1, 1940 B
Lira, M (La Voulte) 1962 R, 1963 I, E, W, It, R, 1964 W, It, I, SA, 1965 S, I, R
Llary, (Carcassonne) 1926 S
Lobies, J (RCF) 1921 S, W, E
Lombard, F (Narbonne) 1934 G, 1937 It
Lombarteix, R (Montferrand) 1938 R, G 2
Londios, J (Montauban) 1967 SA 3
Lorieux, A (Grenoble, Aix) 1981 A 1, R, NZ 1, 2, 1982 W, 1983 A 2, R, 1984 I, W, E, 1985 Arg 1, 2 (R), 1986 R 2, NZ 2, 3, 1987 W, E, [S, Z, Fj, A, NZ], 1988 S, I, W, Arg1, 2, 4, 1989 W
Loury, A (RCF) 1927 E, G 1, 2, 1928 S, NSW, I
Loustau, M (Dax) 1923 E
Lubin-Lebrère, M-F (Toulouse) 1914 I, W, E, 1920 S, E, W, I, US, 1921 S, 1922 S, E, W, 1924 W, US, 1925 I
Lubrano, A (Béziers) 1972 A 2, 1973 S
Lux, J-P (Tyrosse, Dax) 1967 E, It, W, I, SA 1, 2, 4, R, 1968 I, E, Cz, NZ 3, A, SA 1, 2, 1969 S, I, E, 1970 S, I, W, E, R, 1971 S, I, E, W, A 1, 2, 1972 S, I 1, E, W, I 2, A 1, 2, R, 1973 S, NZ, E, 1974 I, W, E, S, Arg 1, 2, 1975 W

Maclos, P (SF) 1906 E, 1907 E
Magnanou, C (RCF) 1923 E, 1925 W, E, 1926 S, 1929 S, W, 1930 S, I, E, W
Magnol, L (Toulouse) 1928 S, 1929 S, W, E
Magois, H (La Rochelle) 1968 SA 1, 2, R
Majerus, R (SF) 1928 W, 1929 I, S, 1930 S, I, E, G, W
Malbet, J-C (Agen) 1967 SA 2, 4
Maleig, A (Oloron) 1979 W, E, NZ 2, 1980 W, E, SA, R
Malquier, Y (Narbonne) 1979 S
Manterola, T (Lourdes) 1955 It, 1957 R 1
Mantoulan, C (Pau) 1959 I
Marcet, J (Albi) 1925 I, NZ, S, W, E, 1926 I, E
Marchal, J-F (Lourdes) 1979 S, R, 1980 W, S, I
Marchand, R (Poitiers) 1920 S, W
Marocco, P (Montferrand) 1986 S, I, W, E, R 1, Arg 1, 2, A, 1988 Arg 4, 1989 I
Marot, A (Brive) 1969 R, 1970 S, I, W, 1971 SA 1, 1972 I 2, 1976 A 1
Marquesuzaa, A (RCF) 1958 It, SA 1, 2, 1959 S, E, It, W, 1960 S, E, Arg 1
Marracq, H (Pau) 1961 R
Martin, C (Lyon) 1909 I, 1910 W, S
Martin, H (SBUC) 1907 E, 1908 W
Martin, J-L (Béziers) 1971 A 2, R, 1972 S, I 1
Martin, L (Pau) 1948 I, A, S, W, E, 1950 S
Martine, R (Lourdes) 1952 S, I, It, 1953 It, 1954 S, I, NZ, W, E, It, Arg 2, 1955 S, I, W, 1958 A, W, It, I, SA 1, 2, 1960 S, E, Arg 3, 1961 S, It
Martinez, G (Toulouse) 1982 W, E, S, Arg 1, 2, 1983 E, W
Mas, F (Béziers) 1962 R, 1963 S, I, E, W
Maso, J (Perpignan, Narbonne) 1966 It, R, 1967 S, R, 1968 S, W, Cz, NZ 1, 2, 3, A, R, 1969 S, I, W, 1971 SA 1, 2, R, 1972 E, W, A 2, 1973 W, I, J, R
Massare, J (PUC) 1945 B 1, 2, W, 1946 B, I, W
Masse, A (SBUC) 1908 W, 1909 E, W, 1910 W, S, E, I
Masse, H (Grenoble) 1937 G
Matheu, J (Agen) 1945 W, 1946 B, I, K, W, 1947 S, I, W, E, 1948 I, A, S, W, E, 1949 S, I, E, W, Arg 1, 2, 1950 E, W, 1951 S, I
Mauduy, G (Périgueux) 1957 It, R 1, 2, 1958 S, E, 1961 W, It
Mauran, J (Castres) 1952 SA, W, E, It, 1953 I, E
Mauriat, P (Lyon) 1907 E, 1908 E, W, 1909 W, I, 1910 W, S, E, I, 1911 S, E, W, I, 1912 I, S, 1913 S, SA, W, I
Maurin, G (ASF) 1906 E
Maury, A (Toulouse) 1925 I, NZ, S, W, E, 1926 S, I, E
Maysonnie, A (Toulouse) 1908 E, W, 1910 W
Menrath, R (SCUF) 1910 W
Menthiller, Y (Romans) 1964 W, It, SA, R, 1965 E
Meret, F (Tarbes) 1940 B
Mericq, S (Agen) 1959 I, 1960 S, E, W, 1961 I
Merquey, J (Toulon) 1950 S, I, E, W
Mesnel, F (RCF) 1986 NZ 2 (R), 3, 1987 W, E, S, I,

[S, Z, Fj, A, NZ], R, 1988 E, Arg1, 2, 3, 4, R, 1989 I, W, E, S
Mesny, P (RCF, Grenoble) 1979 NZ 1, 2, 1980 SA, R, 1981 I, W (R), A 1, 2, R, NZ 1, 2, 1982 I, Arg 1, 2
Meyer, G-S (Périgueux) 1960 S, E, It, R, Arg 2
Meynard, J (Cognac) 1954 Arg 1, 1956 Cz
Mias, L (Mazamet) 1951 S, I, E, W, 1952 I, SA, W, E, It, 1953 S, I, W, It, 1954 S, I, NZ, W, 1957 R 2, 1958 S, E, A, W, I, SA 1, 2, 1959 S, It, W, I
Milliand, P (Grenoble) 1936 G 2, 1937 G, It
Minjat, R (Lyon) 1945 B 1
Mir, J-H (Lourdes) 1967 R, 1968 I
Mir, J-P (Lourdes) 1967 A
Modin, R (Brive) 1987 [Z]
Moga, A-M-A (Begles) 1945 B 1, 2, W, 1946 B, I, K, W, 1947 S, I, W, E, 1948 I, A, S, W, E, 1949 S, I, E, W, Arg 1, 2
Mommejat, B (Cahors, Albi) 1958 It, I, SA 1, 2, 1959 S, E, It, W, I, 1960 S, E, I, R, 1962 S, E, W, I, It, R, 1963 S, I, W
Moncla, F (RCF, Pau) 1956 Cz, 1957 I, E, W, It, R, 1, 1958 SA 1, 2, 1959 S, E, It, W, I, 1960 S, E, W, I, It, R, Arg 1, 2, 3, 1961 S, SA, E, W, It, I, NZ 1, 2, 3
Monie, R (Perpignan) 1956 Cz, 1957 E
Monier, R (SBUC) 1911 I, 1912 S
Monniot, M (RCF) 1912 W, E
Montade, A (Perpignan) 1925 I, NZ, S, W, 1926 W
Moraitis, B (Toulon) 1969 E, W
Morel, A (Grenoble) 1954 Arg 2
Morere, J (Toulouse) 1927 E, G 1, 1928 S, NSW
Mouiq, P (Toulouse) 1911 S, E, W, I, 1912 I, E, 1913 S, SA, E
Moure, H (SCUF) 1908 E
Moureu, P (Béziers) 1920 I, US, 1921 W, E, I, 1922 S, W, I, 1923 S, W, E, I, 1924 S, I, E, W, 1925 E
Mournet, A (Bagnères) 1981 A 1 (R)
Mouronval, F (SF) 1909 I
Muhr, A H (RCF) 1906 NZ, E, 1907 E
Murillo, G (Dijon) 1954 It, Arg 1

Namur, R (Toulon) 1931 E, G
Noble, J-C (La Voulte) 1968 E, W, Cz, NZ 3, A, R
Normand, A (Toulouse) 1957 R 1
Novès, G (Toulouse) 1977 NZ 1, 2, R, 1978 W, R, 1979 I, W

Olive, D (Montferrand) 1951 I, 1952 I
Ondarts, P (Biarritz O) 1986 NZ 3, 1987 W, E, S, I, [S, Z, Fj, A, NZ], R, 1988 E, I, W, Arg1, 2, 3, 4, R, 1989 I, W, E
Orso, J-C (Nice, Toulon) 1982 Arg 1, 2, 1983 E, S, A 1, 1984 E (R), S, NZ 1, 1985 I (R), W, 1988 I
Othats, J (Dax) 1960 Arg 2, 3

Paco, A (Béziers) 1974 Arg 1, 2, R, SA 1, 2, 1975 W, E, Arg 1, 2, R, 1976 S, I, W, E, US, A 1, 2, R, 1977 W, E, S, I, NZ 1, 2, R, 1978 E, S, I, W, R, 1979 I, W, E, S, 1980 W
Palat, J (Perpignan) 1938 G 2
Palmié, M (Béziers) 1975 SA 1, 2, Arg 1, 2, R, 1976 S, I, W, E, US, 1977 W, E, S, I, Arg 1, 2, NZ 1, 2, R, 1978 E, S, I, W
Paoli, R (SF) 1911 I, 1912 I, S
Paparemborde, R (Pau) 1975 SA 1, 2, Arg 1, 2, R, 1976 S, I, W, E, US, A 1, 2, R, 1977 W, E, S, I, Arg 1, NZ 1, 2, 1978 E, S, I, W, R, 1979 I, W, E, S, NZ 1, 2, R, 1980 W, E, S, SA, R, 1981 S, I, W, A 1, 2, R, NZ 1, 2, 1982 W, I, R, Arg 1, 2, 1983 E, S, I, W
Pardo, L (Hendaye) 1924 I, E
Pardo, L (Bayonne) 1980 SA, R, 1981 S, I, W, E, A 1, 1982 W, E, S, 1983 A 1 (R), 1985 S, I, Arg 2
Pargade, J-H (Lyon U) 1953 It
Paries, L (Biarritz O) 1968 SA 2, R, 1970 S, I, W, 1975 E, S, I
Pascalin, P (Mont-de-Marsan) 1950 I, E, W, 1951 S, I, E, W
Pascarel, J-R (TOEC) 1912 W, E, 1913 S, SA, E, I
Pascot, J (Perpignan) 1922 S, E, I, 1923 S, 1926 I, 1927 G 2
Paul, R (Montferrand) 1940 B
Pauthe, G (Graulhet) 1956 E
Pebeyre, E-J (Fumel, Brive) 1945 W, 1946 I, K, W, 1947 S, I, W, E

244

Pebeyre, M (Vichy, Montferrand) 1970 *E, R*, 1971 *I, SA* 1, 2, *A* 1, 1973 *W*
Pecune, J (Tarbes) 1974 *W, E, S*, 1975 *Arg* 1, 2, *R*, 1976*I, W, E, US*
Pedeutour, P (Begles) 1980 *I*
Pellissier, L (RCF) 1928 *NSW, I, E, G, W*
Peron, P (RCF) 1975 *SA* 1, 2
Perrier, P (Bayonne) 1982 *W, E, S, I* (R)
Pesteil, J-P (Béziers) 1975 *SA* 1, 1976 *A* 2, *R*
Petit, C (Lorrain) 1931 *W*
Peyrelade, H (Tarbes) 1940 *B*
Peyroutou, (Périgueux) 1911 *S, E*
Phliponneau, J-F (Montferrand) 1973 *W, I*
Piazza, A (Montauban) 1968 *NZ* 1, *A*
Picard, T (Montferrand) 1985 *Arg* 2, 1986 *R* 1 (R), *Arg* 2
Pierrot, G (Pau) 1914 *I, W, E*
Pilon, J (Périgueux) 1949 *E*, 1950 *E*
Piqué, J (Pau) 1961 *NZ* 2, 3, *A*, 1962 *S, It*, 1964 *NZ, E, W, It, I, SA, Fj, R*, 1965 *S, I, E, W, It*
Piquemal, M (Tarbes) 1927 *I, S*, 1929 *I, G*, 1930 *S, I, E, G, W*
Piquiral, E (RCF) 1924 *S, I, E, W, R, US*, 1925 *E*, 1926 *S, I, E, W, M*, 1927 *I, S, W, E, G* 1, 2, 1928 *E*
Piteu, R (Pau) 1921 *S, W, E, I*, 1922 *S, E, W, I*, 1923 *E*, 1924 *E*, 1925 *I, NZ, W, E*, 1926 *E*
Plantefol, A (RCF) 1967 *SA* 2, 3, 4, *NZ, R*, 1968 *E, W, Cz, NZ* 2, 1969 *E, W*
Plantey, S (RCF) 1961 *A*, 1962 *It*
Podevin, G (SF) 1913 *W, I*
Poeydebasque, F (Bayonne) 1914 *I, W*
Poirier, A (SCUF) 1907 *E*
Pomathios, M (Agen, Lyon U, Bourg) 1948 *I, A, S, W, E*, 1949 *S, I, E, W, Arg* 1, 2, 1950 *S, I, W*, 1951 *S, I, E, W*, 1952 *W, E*, 1953 *S, I, W*, 1954 *S*
Pons, P (Toulouse) 1920 *S, E, W*, 1921 *S, W*, 1922 *S*
Porra, M (Lyon) 1931 *I*
Porthault, A (RCF) 1951 *S, E, W*, 1952 *I*, 1953 *S, I, It*
Portolan, C (Toulouse) 1986 *A*, 1989 *I, E*
Potel, A (Begles) 1932 *G*
Prat, J (Lourdes) 1945 *B* 1, 2, *W*, 1946 *B, I, K, W*, 1947 *S, I, W, E*, 1948 *I, A, S, W, E*, 1949 *S, I, E, W, Arg* 1, 2, 1950 *S, I, E, W*, 1951 *S, E, W*, 1952 *S, I, SA, W, E, It*, 1953 *S, I, E, W, It*, 1954 *S, I, NZ, W, E, It*, 1955 *S, I, E, W, It*
Prat, M (Lourdes) 1951 *I*, 1952 *S, I, SA, W, E*, 1953 *S, I, E*, 1954 *I, NZ, W, E, It*, 1955 *S, I, E, W, It*, 1956 *I, W, It, Cz*, 1957 *S, I, W, It, R* 1, 1958 *A, W, I*
Prevost, A (Albi) 1926 *M*, 1927 *I, S, W*
Prin-Clary, J (Cavaillon, Brive) 1945 *B* 1, 2, *W*, 1946 *B, I, K, W*, 1947 *S, I, W*
Puech, L (Toulouse) 1920 *S, E, I*, 1921 *E, I*
Puget, M (Toulouse) 1961 *It*, 1966 *S, I, It*, 1967 *SA* 1, 3, 4, *NZ*, 1968 *Cz, NZ* 1, 2, *SA* 1, 2, *R*, 1969 *E, R*, 1970 *W*
Puig, A (Perpignan) 1926 *S, E*
Pujol, A (SOE Toulouse) 1906 *NZ*

Quaglio, A (Mazamet) 1957 *R* 2, 1958 *S, E, A, W, I, SA* 1, 2, 1959 *S, E, It, W, I*
Quilis, A (Narbonne) 1967 *SA* 1, 4, *NZ*, 1970 *R*, 1971 *I*

Ramis, R (Perpignan) 1922 *E, I*, 1923 *W*
Rancoule, H (Lourdes, Toulon, Tarbes) 1955 *E, W, It*, 1958 *A, W, It, I, SA* 1, 1959 *S, It, W*, 1960 *I, It, R, Arg* 1, 2, 1961 *SA, E, W, It, NZ* 1, 2, 1962 *S, E, W, I, It*
Rapin, A (SBUC) 1938 *R*
Raymond, F (Toulouse) 1925 *S*, 1927 *W*, 1928 *I*
Raynal, F (Perpignan) 1935 *G*, 1936 *G* 1, 2, 1937 *G, It*
Raynaud, F (Carcassonne) 1933 *G*
Razat, J-P (Agen) 1962 *R*, 1963 *S, I, R*
Rebujent, R (RCF) 1963 *E*
Revallier, D (Graulhet) 1981 *S, I, W, E, A* 1, 2, *R, NZ* 1, 2, 1982 *W, S, I, R, Arg* 1
Revillon, J (RCF) 1926 *I, E*, 1927 *S*
Ribère, E (Perpignan, Quillan) 1924 *I*, 1925 *I, NZ, S*, 1926 *S, I, W, M*, 1927 *I, S, W, E, G* 1, 2, 1928 *S, NSW, I, E, G, W*, 1929 *I, E, G*, 1930 *S, I, E, W*, 1931 *I, S, W, E, G*, 1932 *G*, 1933 *G*
Rives, J-P (Toulouse, RCF) 1975 *E, S, I, Arg* 1, 2, *R*, 1976 *S, I, W, E, US, A* 1, 2, *R*, 1977 *W, E, S, I, Arg* 1, 2, *R*, 1978 *E, S, I, W, R*, 1979 *I, W, E, S, NZ* 1, 2, *R*, 1980 *W, E, S, I, SA*, 1981 *S, I, W, E, A* 2, 1982 *W, E,*

S, I, R, 1983 *E, S, I, W, A* 1, 2, *R*, 1984 *I, W, E, S*
Rochon, A (Montferrand) 1936 *G* 1
Rodrigo, M (Mauléon) 1931 *I, W*
Rodriguez, L (Mont-de-Marsan, Montferrand, Dax) 1981 *A* 1, 2, *R, NZ* 1, 2, 1982 *W, E, S, I, R*, 1983 *E, S*, 1984 *I, NZ* 1, 2, *R*, 1985 *E, S, I, W* 1986 *Arg* 1, *A, R* 2, *NZ* 2, 3, 1987 *W, E, S, I, [S, Z, Fj, A, NZ], R*, 1988 *E, S, I, W, Arg* 1, 2, 3, 4, *R*, 1989 *I, E, S*
Rogé, L (Béziers) 1952 *It*, 1953 *E, W, It*, 1954 *S, Arg* 1, 2, 1955 *S, I*, 1956 *W, It, E*, 1957 *S*, 1960 *S, E*
Rollet, J (Bayonne) 1960 *Arg* 3, 1961 *NZ* 3, *A*, 1962 *It*, 1963 *I*
Romero, H (Montauban) 1962 *S, E, W, I, It, R*, 1963 *E*
Romeu, J-P (Montferrand) 1972 *R*, 1973 *S, NZ, E, W, I, R*, 1974 *W, E, S, Arg* 1, 2, *R, SA* 1, 2 (R), 1975 *W, SA* 2, *Arg* 1, 2, *R*, 1976 *S, I, W, E, US*, 1977 *W, E, S, I, Arg* 1, 2, *NZ* 1, 2, *R*
Roques, A (Cahors) 1958 *A, W, It, I, SA* 1, 2, 1959 *S, E, W, I*, 1960 *S, E, W, I, It, Arg* 1, 2, 3, 1961 *S, SA, E, W, It, I*, 1962 *S, E, W, I, It*, 1963 *S*
Roques, J-C (Brive) 1966 *S, I, It, R*
Rossignol, J-C (Brive) 1972 *A* 2
Rouan, J (Narbonne) 1953 *S, I*
Roucaries, G (Perpignan) 1956 *S*
Rouffia, L (Narbonne) 1945 *B* 2, *W*, 1946 *W*, 1948 *I*
Rougerie, J (Montferrand) 1973 *J*
Roujas, F (Tarbes) 1910 *I*
Rousie, M (Villeneuve) 1931 *S, G*, 1932 *G*, 1933 *G*
Rousset, G (Béziers) 1975 *SA* 1, 1976 *US*
Ruiz, A (Tarbes) 1968 *SA* 2, *R*
Rupert, J-J (Tyrosse) 1963 *R*, 1964 *S, Fj*, 1965 *E, W, It*, 1966 *S, I, E, W, It*, 1967 *It, R*, 1968 *S*

Sagot, P (SF) 1906 *NZ*, 1908 *E*, 1909 *W*
Sahuc, A (Métro) 1945 *B* 1, 2
Sahuc, F (Toulouse) 1936 *G* 2
Saisset, O (Béziers) 1971 *R*, 1972 *S, I* 1, *A* 1, 2, 1973 *S, NZ, E, W, I, J, R*, 1974 *I, Arg* 2, *SA* 1, 2, 1975 *W* *A* 1, 1982 *Arg* 2
Salas, P (Narbonne) 1979 *NZ* 1, 2, *R*, 1980 *W, E*, 1981 *A* 1, 1982 *Arg* 2
Salinie, R (Perpignan) 1923 *E*
Sallefranque, M (Dax) 1981 *A* 2, 1982 *W, E, S*
Salut, J (TOEC) 1966 *R*, 1967 *S*, 1968 *I, E, Cz, NZ* 1, 1969 *I*
Samatan, R (Agen) 1930 *S, I, E, G, W*, 1931 *I, S, W, E, G*
Sanac, A (Perpignan) 1952 *It*, 1953 *S, I*, 1954 *E*, 1956 *Cz*, 1957 *S, I, E, W, It*
Sangalli, F (Narbonne) 1975 *I, SA* 1, 2, 1976 *S, A* 1, 2, *R*, 1977 *W, E, S, I, Arg* 1, 2, *NZ* 1, 2
Sanz, H (Narbonne) 1988 *Arg* 3, 4, *R*
Sappa, M (Nice) 1973 *J, R*, 1977 *R*
Sarrade, R (Pau) 1929 *I*
Saux, J-P (Pau) 1960 *W, It, Arg* 1, 2, 1961 *SA, E, W, It, I, NZ* 1, 2, 3, *A*, 1962 *S, E, W, I, It*, 1963 *S, I, E, It*
Savitsky, M (La Voulte) 1969 *R*
Savy, M (Montferrand) 1931 *I, S, W, E*, 1936 *G* 1
Sayrou, J (Perpignan) 1926 *W, M*, 1928 *E, G, W*, 1929 *S, W, E, G*
Scohy, R (BEC) 1931 *S, W, E, G*
Sébedio, J (Tarbes) 1913 *S, E*, 1914 *I*, 1920 *S, I, US*, 1922 *S, E*, 1923 *S*
Seguier, N (Béziers) 1973 *J, R*
Sella, P (Agen) 1982 *R, Arg* 1, 2, 1983 *E, S, I, W, A* 1, 2, *R*, 1984 *I, W, E, S, NZ* 1, 2, *R*, 1985 *E, S, I, W, Arg* 1, 2, 1986 *S, I, W, E, R* 1, *Arg* 1, 2, *A, NZ* 1, *R* 2, *NZ* 2, 3, 1987 *W, E, S, I, [S, R, Z(R), Fj, A, NZ]*, 1988 *E, S, I, W, Arg* 1, 2, 3, 4, *R*, 1989 *I, W, E, S*
Semmartin, J (SCUF) 1913 *W, I*
Senal, G (Béziers) 1974 *Arg* 1, 2, *R, SA* 1, 2, 1975 *W*
Sentilles, J (Tarbes) 1912 *W, E*, 1913 *S, SA*
Serin, L (Béziers) 1928 *E*, 1929 *W, E, G*, 1930 *S, I, E, G, W*, 1931 *I, W, E*
Serre, P (Perpignan) 1920 *S, E*
Serrière, P (RCF) 1986 *A*, 1987 *R*, 1988 *E*
Servole, L (Toulon) 1931 *I, S, W, E, G*, 1934 *G*, 1935 *G*
Sicart, N (Perpignan) 1922 *I*
Sillières, J (Tarbes) 1968 *R*, 1970 *S, I*, 1971 *S, I, E*, 1972 *E, I*
Siman, M (Montferrand) 1948 *E*, 1949 *S, I, E, W*

245

Sitjar, M (Agen) 1964 *W, It, I, R*, 1965 *It, R*, 1967 *A, E, It, W, I, SA* 1, 2
Skréla, J-C (Toulouse) 1971 *SA* 2, *A* 1, 2, 1972 *I* 1 (R), *E, W, I* 2, *A* 1, 1973 *W, J, R*, 1974 *W, E, S, Arg* 1, *R*, 1975 *W* (R), *E, S, I, SA* 1, 2, *Arg* 1, 2, *R*, 1976 *S, I, W, E, US, A* 1, 2, *R*, 1977 *W, E, S, I, Arg* 1, 2, *NZ* 1, 2, *R*, 1978 *E, S, I, W*
Soler, M (Quillan) 1929 *G*
Soro, R (Lourdes, Romans) 1945 *B* 1, 2, *W*, 1946 *B, I, K*, 1947 *S, I, W, E*, 1948 *I, A, S, W, E*, 1949 *S, I, E, W, Arg* 1, 2
Sorrondo, L-M (Montauban) 1946 *K*, 1947 *S, I, W, E*, 1948 *I*
Soulié, E (CASG) 1920 *E, I, US*, 1921 *S, E, I*, 1922 *E, W, I*
Sourgens, J (Begles) 1926 *M*
Spanghero, C (Narbonne) 1971 *E, W, SA* 1, 2, *A* 1, 2, *R*, 1972 *S, E, W, I* 2, *A* 1, 2, 1974 *I, W, E, S, R, SA* 1, 1975 *E, S, I*
Spanghero, W (Narbonne) 1964 *SA, Fj, R*, 1965 *S, I, E, W, It, R*, 1966 *S, I, E, W, It, R*, 1967 *S, A, E, SA* 1, 2, 3, 4, *NZ*, 1968 *S, I, E, W, NZ* 1, 2, 3, *A, SA* 1, 2, *R*, 1969 *S, I, W*, 1970 *R*, 1971 *E, W, SA* 1, 1972 *E, I* 2, *A* 1, 2, *R*, 1973 *S, NZ, E, W, I*
Stener, G (PUC) 1956 *S, I, E*, 1958 *SA* 1, 2
Struxiano, P (Toulouse) 1913 *W, I*, 1920 *S, E, W, I, US*
Sutra, G (Narbonne) 1967 *SA* 2, 1969 *W*, 1970 *S, I*
Swierczinski, C (Begles) 1969 *E*, 1977 *Arg* 2

Taffary, M (RCF) 1975 *W, E, S, I*
Taillantou, J (Pau) 1930 *I, G, W*
Tarricq, P (Lourdes) 1958 *A, W, It, I*
Tavernier, H (Toulouse) 1913 *I*
Terreau, M-M (Bourg) 1945 *W*, 1946 *B, I, K, W*, 1947 *S, I, W, E*, 1948 *I, A, W, E*, 1949 *S, Arg* 1, 2, 1951 *S*
Theuriet, A (SCUF) 1909 *E, W*, 1910 *S*, 1911 *W*, 1913 *E*
Thevenot, M (SCUF) 1910 *W, E, I*
Thierry, R (RCF) 1920 *S, E, W, US*
Thiers, P (Montferrand) 1936 *G* 1, 2, 1937 *G, It*, 1938 *G* 1, 2, 1940 *B*, 1945 *B* 1, 2
Thil, P (Nantes) 1912 *W, E*, 1913 *S, SA, E, W*
Tignol, P (Toulouse) 1953 *S, I*
Tolot, J-L (Agen) 1987 [Z]
Torreilles, S (Perpignan) 1956 *S*
Tourte, R (St Girons) 1940 *B*
Trillo, J (Begles) 1967 *SA* 3, 4, *NZ, R*, 1968 *S, I, NZ* 1,

2, 3, *A*, 1969 *I, E, W, R*, 1970 *E, R*, 1971 *S, I, SA* 1, 2, *A* 1, 2, 1972 *S, A* 1, 2, *R*, 1973 *S, E*
Triviaux, R (Cognac) 1931 *E, G*
Tucoo-Chala, M (PUC) 1940 *B*

Ugartemendia, J-L (St Jean-de-Luz) 1975 *S, I*

Vaills, G (Perpignan) 1928 *NSW*, 1929 *G*
Vallot, C (SCUF) 1912 *S*
Vannier, M (RCF, Chalon) 1953 *W*, 1954 *S, I, Arg* 1, 2, 1955 *S, I, E, W, It*, 1956 *S, I, W, It, E*, 1957 *S, I, E, W, It, R* 1, 2, 1958 *S, E, A, W, It, I*, 1960 *S, E, W, I, It, R, Arg* 1, 3, 1961 *SA, E, W, It, I, NZ* 1, *A*
Vaquer, F (Perpignan) 1921 *S, W*, 1922 *W*
Vaquerin, A (Béziers) 1971 *R*, 1972 *S, I* 1, *A* 1, 1973 *S*, 1974 *W, E, S, Arg* 1, 2, *R, SA* 1, 2, 1975 *W, E, S, I*, 1976 *US, A* 1 (R), 2, *R*, 1977 *Arg* 2, 1979 *W, E*, 1980 *S, I*
Vareilles, C (SF) 1907 *E*, 1908 *E, W*, 1910 *S, E*
Varenne, F (RCF) 1952 *S*
Varvier, T (RCF) 1906 *E*, 1909 *E, W*, 1911 *E, W*, 1912 *I*
Vassal, G (Carcassonne) 1938 *R, G* 2
Vaysse, J (Albi) 1924 *US*, 1926 *M*
Vellat, E (Grenoble) 1927 *I, E, G* 1, 2, 1928 *NSW*
Verger, A (SF) 1927 *W, E, G* 1, 1928 *I, E, G, W*
Verges, (SF) 1906 *NZ, E*, 1907 *E*
Viard, G (Narbonne) 1969 *W*, 1970 *S, R*, 1971 *S, I*
Vigerie, M (Agen) 1931 *W*
Vigier, R (Montferrand) 1956 *S, W, It, E, Cz*, 1957 *S, E, W, It, R* 1, 2, 1958 *S, E, A, W, It, I, SA* 1, 2, 1959 *S, E, It, W, I*
Vigneau, A (Bayonne) 1935 *G*
Vignes, C (RCF) 1957 *R* 1, 2, 1958 *S, E*
Villa, E (Tarbes) 1926 *M*
Villagra, J (Vienne) 1945 *B* 2
Villepreux, P (Toulouse) 1967 *It, I, SA* 2, *NZ*, 1968 *I, Cz, NZ* 1, 2, 3, *A*, 1969 *S, I, E, W, R*, 1970 *S, I, W, E, R*, 1971 *S, I, E, W, A* 1, 2, *R*, 1972 *S, I* 1, *E, W, I* 2, *A* 1, 2
Viviès, B (Agen) 1978 *E, S, I, W*, 1980 *SA, R*, 1981 *S, A* 1, 1983 *A* 1 (R)
Volot, M (SF) 1945 *W*, 1946 *B, I, K, W*

Wolff, J-P (Béziers) 1980 *SA, R*, 1981 *A* 2, 1982 *E*

Yachvili, M (Tulle, Brive) 1968 *E, W, Cz, NZ* 3, *A, R*, 1969 *S, I, R*, 1971 *E, SA* 1, 2, *A* 1, 1972 *R*, 1975 *SA* 2

Zago, F (Montauban) 1963 *I, E*

FRENCH INTERNATIONAL RECORDS

Both team and individual records are for official French international matches, up to 30 April 1989.

TEAM RECORDS

Highest score
70 v Zimbabwe (70-12) 1987 Auckland
v individual countries
37 v Argentina (37-3) 1960 Buenos Aires
34 v Australia (34-6) 1976 Parc des Princes
28 v Czechoslovakia (28-3) 1956 Toulouse
37 v England (37-12) 1972 Colombes
31 v Fiji (31-16) 1987 Auckland
38 v Germany (38-17) 1933 Parc des Princes
29 v Ireland (29-9) 1986 Parc des Princes
60 v Italy (60-13) 1967 Toulon
30 v Japan (30-18) 1973 Bordeaux
24 v N Zealand (24-19) 1979 Auckland
59 v Romania (59-3) 1924 Colombes
28 v Scotland (28-22) 1987 Parc des Princes
25 v S Africa (25-38) 1975 Bloemfontein
33 v United States (33-14) 1976 Chicago
31 v Wales (31-12) 1989 Parc des Princes
70 v Zimbabwe (70-12) 1987 Auckland

Biggest winning points margin
58 v Zimbabwe (70-12) 1987 Auckland
v individual countries
34 v Argentina (37-3) 1960 Buenos Aires
28 v Australia (34-6) 1976 Parc des Princes
25 v Czechoslovakia (28-3) 1956 Toulouse
25 v England (37-12) 1972 Colombes
18 v Fiji (21-3) 1964 Colombes
34 v Germany (34-0) 1931 Colombes
23 v Ireland (26-3) 1976 Parc des Princes
47 v Italy (60-13) 1967 Toulon
12 v Japan (30-18) 1973 Bordeaux
13 v N Zealand (16-3) 1986 Nantes
56 v Romania (59-3) 1924 Colombes
20 v Scotland (23-3) 1977 Parc des Princes
5 v S Africa (19-14) 1967 Johannesburg
19 v United States (33-14) 1976 Chicago
19 v Wales (31-12) 1989 Parc des Princes
58 v Zimbabwe (70-12) 1987 Auckland

Highest score by opposing team
49 Wales (14-49) 1910 Swansea
S Africa beat 'France' 55-6 at Parc des Princes on 3 January 1907, but it is not regarded as an official international match

by individual countries
27 Argentina (31-27) 1974 Buenos Aires
27 Australia (14-27) 1986 Sydney
6 Czechoslovakia (19-6) 1968 Prague
41 England (13-41) 1907 Richmond
16 Fiji (31-16) 1987 Auckland
17 Germany { (16-17) 1927 Frankfurt
{ (38-17) 1933 Parc des Princes
25 Ireland { (5-25) 1911 Cork
{ (6-25) 1975 Dublin
13 Italy (60-13) 1967 Toulon
18 Japan (30-18) 1973 Bordeaux
38 New Zealand (8-38) 1906 Parc des Princes
15 Romania   on several occasions
31 Scotland (3-31) 1912 Inverleith
38 South Africa { (5-38) 1913 Bordeaux
{ (25-38) 1975 Bloemfontein
17 United States (3-17) 1924 Colombes
49 Wales (14-49) 1910 Swansea
12 Zimbabwe (70-12) 1987 Auckland

Biggest losing points margin
42 v Wales (5-47) 1909 Colombes
The 6-55 defeat by S Africa in Paris in 1907 is regarded as unofficial
v individual countries
12 v Argentina (6-18) 1988 Buenos Aires
13 v Australia (14-27) 1986 Sydney
37 v England (0-37) 1911 Twickenham
3 v Germany (0-3) 1938 Frankfurt
24 v Ireland (0-24) 1913 Cork
30 v N Zealand (8-38) 1906 Parc des Princes
15 v Romania (0-15) 1980 Bucharest
28 v Scotland (3-31) 1912 Inverleith
33 v S Africa (5-38) 1913 Bordeaux
14 v United States (3-17) 1924 Colombes
42 v Wales (5-47) 1909 Colombes
No defeats v Czechoslovakia, Fiji, Italy, Japan or Zimbabwe

Most tries by France in an international
13 v Romania (59-3) 1924 Paris

247

Most tries against France in an international
11 by Wales (5-47) 1909 Colombes

Most points by France in International Championship in a season – 98
in season 1985-86

Most tries by France in International Championship in a season – 13
in seasons 1975-76 and 1985-86

INDIVIDUAL RECORDS

Most capped player
R Bertranne 69 1971-81
in individual positions
Full-back
S Blanco 56(68)[1] 1980-89
Wing
C Darrouy 40[2] 1957-67
Centre
R Bertranne 52(69)[3] 1971-81
P Sella 52(58)[3] 1982-89
Fly-half
J-P Romeu 33(34)[4] 1972-77
Scrum-half
P Berbizier 46 1981-89
Prop
R Paparemborde 55 1975-83
Hooker
P Dintrans 49 1979-89
Lock
J Condom 54[5] 1982-89
Flanker
J-P Rives 59[5] 1975-84
No 8
G Basquet 33[5] 1945-52
[1]*S Blanco has won 12 caps as a wing*
[2]*J Dupuy, 40 caps, played once in the centre and 39 times on the wing*
[3]*Bertranne played 17 times on the wing, and Sella has played 6 times as a wing*
[4]*Romeu was capped once as a replacement full-back*
[5]*B Dauga and M Crauste, 63 caps each, are France's most-capped forwards. Dauga was capped as a lock and No 8; Crauste as flanker and No 8*

Longest international career
F Haget 14 seasons 1974-87

Most internationals as captain
J-P Rives 34 1978-84

Most points in internationals – 265
J-P Romeu (34 matches) 1972-77

Most points in International Championship in a season – 54
J-P Lescarboura (4 matches) 1983-84

Most points in an international – 30
D Camberabero v Zimbabwe 1987
  Auckland

Most tries in internationals – 27
S Blanco (68 matches) 1980-89

Most tries in International Championship in a season – 5
P Estève (4 matches) 1982-83
E Bonneval (4 matches) 1986-87

Most tries in an international – 4
A Jauréguy v Romania 1924 Colombes
M Celhay v Italy 1937 Parc des Princes

Most conversions in internationals – 45
M Vannier (43 matches) 1953-61

Most conversions in International Championship in a season – 7
P Villepreux (4 matches) 1971-72

Most conversions in an international – 9
G Camberabero v Italy 1967 Toulon
D Camberabero v Zimbabwe 1987
  Auckland
Father and son

Most dropped goals in internationals – 15
J-P Lescarboura (27 matches) 1982-88

Most penalty goals in internationals – 56
J-P Romeu (34 matches) 1972-77

Most penalty goals in international Championship in a season – 10
J-P Lescarboura (4 matches) 1983-84

Most points on overseas tour – 71
J-P Romeu (7 matches) 1975 South Africa

Most points in any match on tour – 19
J L Dehez v SW Districts 1967
    George (SA)
P Estève scored 32 points against East Japan in 1984, but this was not on a major tour

Most tries in a tour match – 4
R Bertranne v W Transvaal 1971
    Potchefstroom (SA)
M Bruel v Australian Capital Territory
    1981 Canberra (Aus)
P Estève scored 8 tries v East Japan in 1984, but this was not on a major tour

Pierre Berbizier, now the most capped French scrum-half of all time, whips the ball away against Wales in Paris.

A SEASON STAINED BY STRIFE

THE 1988 SEASON IN SOUTH AFRICA
Reg Sweet

It was a moot point whether or not South African rugby, moving into its Centenary year, was confronting its 100th major problem at the same time. All manner of appropriate celebrations were planned; but a variety of stumbling blocks remained as we went to press.

Talks with other nations on the continent, known as the African Initiative, begun by Dr Danie Craven and Dr Louis Luyt, looked likely at one stage to precipitate a major schism within the executive of the SA Rugby Board itself. Dr Craven knew, even before he travelled, that he would have to perform a delicate balancing act.

But Craven certainly does not lack moral fibre. He stood before his Board and said: 'This might be the last thing I am able to do for my country', before adding unequivocably, 'and if my head must roll, it will roll'. He then made it clear that the process of racial integration in rugby, a road along which the SA Board has travelled some distance, must be accelerated at all levels, including that of schools. Non-white schools are already incorporated in the annual Craven Week schools festival, and the SA Board has dismissed two executive members in the past year for not supporting its integration drive.

However, the African Initiative brought to light a couple of major figures on the executive who, it was thought, would be strongly opposed to 'going too far' and were moving towards a head-on clash with Craven. Prof Fritz Eloff and Steve Strydom were mentioned in this context. The problem was exacerbated because African National Congress members were involved in the talks. Craven made it clear that if politicians were present, this was merely coincidental. He also said, subsequently, that he would not be parleying with any bodies whose policies incorporated violence as a cornerstone.

Dr Craven had put his cards on the table. He insisted upon maintaining contact with SARU, the organisation of Mr Ibrahim Patel, which is not part of the SARB, and that talks aimed at 'establishing a single, non-racial controlling body for rugby in South Africa' would take place. The opposition faded away and, in a gesture of complete support, the Board executive backed the Craven African Initiative to the hilt.

Externally, the Board went ahead with its plan for an alliance between African and South American rugby countries, to be known as the Gondwana Rugby Union. It is hoped that this will eventually include all the Southern Hemisphere countries. The proposed name baffled many in the rugby world: Gondwana is simply the name given by geologists to the once-single land mass of Africa and South America. The idea was for an alliance arranged broadly along the lines of that between the four Home Unions and France in the International Championship. It was announced from Santiago in Chile that rugby chiefs from South Africa, Argentina, Chile, Uruguay, Paraguay and Brazil had agreed on the Gondwana concept. Dr Craven then resigned as chairman.

Nothing stressed the frustrations of the season more pointedly than the bitter disappointment when, just before the start of the visit by a promised World XV in August and September 1988, the tour was officially abandoned. This non-starter rekindled the activities of those who believe that the IRB will no longer back any reasonable South African request, and see 'rebel' tours and professionalism as the only way out. At the time of writing, there remained a chance that an IRB-backed International XV would play in South Africa as part of the SA Board's Centenary celebrations during 1989. There were also firm reports that an Australian side was 'ready and willing' to come. As so often, though, nothing was certain.

Northern Transvaal were in the news again when they axed Naas Botha for one match following a running disagreement between Botha and his home union over his lucrative contract in Italy. He has now declared that he is severing his connection with South African rugby. In any event, Botha once again dominated the Currie Cup final, in which Northern Transvaal defeated Western Province 19-18, scoring 15 of his team's points with the boot.

The SA Board voted to increase Section A of the Currie Cup to eight teams in the 1989 season, thus ensuring that Free State, who had lost the promotion/relegation matches, retained their place in the premier competition. When activists exploded a limpet mine just outside Johannesburg's Ellis Park Stadium as the crowds were leaving a Currie Cup match, two spectators were killed and many others injured. It was the final, tragic and futile end to a season stained by strife.

CURRIE CUP

Section A

	P	W	D	L	F	A	Pts
Northern Transvaal	12	11	0	1	328	188	22
Western Province	12	10	0	2	379	156	20
South West Africa	12	6	0	6	254	269	12
Transvaal	12	5	0	7	251	253	10
Natal	12	4	0	8	225	292	8
Eastern Province	12	3	0	9	216	332	6
Free State	12	3	0	9	200	363	6

Section B

	P	W	D	L	F	A	Pts
Northern Orange Free State	10	8	1	1	265	125	17
Western Transvaal	10	7	1	2	375	135	15
Griqualand West	10	7	0	3	187	128	14
Vaal Triangle	10	5	0	5	176	120	10
Eastern Transvaal	10	2	0	8	181	242	4
Eastern Orange Free State	10	0	0	10	79	513	0

Currie Cup final: *Northern Transvaal 19, Western Province 18;* **Lion Cup final:** *Northern Transvaal 12, Western Province 24;* **Yardley Cup final:** *Transvaal 15, Natal 21;* **Toyota National Club Championship final:** *Despatch 13, Pretoria University 12.*

SOUTH AFRICAN INTERNATIONAL PLAYERS *(up to 30 April 1989)*

ABBREVIATIONS

A – Australia; *BI* – British Isles teams; *Cv* – New Zealand Cavaliers; *E* – England; *F* – France; *I* – Ireland; *NZ* – New Zealand; *S* – Scotland; *S Am* – South America; *US* – United States of America; *W* – Wales; *Wld* – World Invitation XV; (R) – Replacement

PROVINCIAL ABBREVIATIONS

Bor – Border; Bol – Boland; EP – Eastern Province; GW – Griqualand West; N – Natal; NT – Northern Transvaal; OFS – Orange Free State; R – Rhodesia; SET – South East Transvaal; SWA – South West Africa; SWD – South West Districts; Tvl – Transvaal; WP – Western Province; WT – Western Transvaal; Z-R – Zimbabwe-Rhodesia

Note: When a series has taken place, figures denote the particular matches in which players featured. Thus 1968 *BI* 1,2,4 indicates that a player appeared in the first, second and fourth Tests of the 1968 series against the British Isles.

Ackermann, D S P (WP) 1955 *BI* 2,3,4, 1956 *A* 1,2, *NZ* 1,3, 1958 *F* 2
Albertyn, P K (SWD) 1924 *BI* 1,2,3,4
Alexander, E (GW) 1891 *BI* 1,2
Allen, P B (EP) 1960 *S*
Allport, P (WP) 1910 *BI* 2,3
Anderson, J A (WP) 1903 *BI* 3
Anderson, J H (WP) 1896 *BI* 1,3,4
Andrew, J B (Tvl) 1896 *BI* 2
Antelme, M J G (Tvl) 1960 *NZ* 1,2,3,4, 1960-61 *F*
Apsey, J T (WP) 1933 *A* 4,5, 1938 *BI* 2
Ashley, S (WP) 1903 *BI* 2
Aston, F T D (Tvl) 1896 *BI* 1,2,3,4
Aucamp, J (WT) 1924 *BI* 1,2

Baard, A P (WP) 1960-61 *I*
Babrow, L (WP) 1937 *A* 1,2, *NZ* 1,2,3
Barnard, A S (EP) 1984 *S Am* 1,2, 1986 *Cv* 1,2
Barnard, J H (Tvl) 1965 *S*, *A* 1,2, *NZ* 3,4
Barnard, R W (Tvl) 1970 *NZ* 2(R)
Barnard, W H M (NT) 1949 *NZ* 4, 1951-52 *W*
Barry, J (WP) 1903 *BI* 1,2,3
Bartmann, W J (Tvl) 1986 *Cv* 1,2,3,4
Bastard, W E (N) 1937 *A* 1, *NZ* 1,2,3, 1938 *BI* 1,3
Bates, A J (WT) 1969-70 *E*, 1970 *NZ* 1,2, 1972 *E*
Bayvel, P C R (Tvl) 1974 *BI* 2,4, *F* 1,2, 1975 *F* 1,2, 1976 *NZ* 1,2,3,4
Beck, J J (WP) 1981 *NZ* 2(R), 3(R), *US*
Bedford, T P (N) 1963 *A* 1,2,3,4, 1964 *W*, *F*, 1965 *I*, *A* 1,2, 1968 *BI* 1,2,3,4, *F* 1,2, 1969 *A* 1,2,3,4, 1969-70 *S*, *E*, *I*, *W*, 1971 *F* 1,2
Bekker, H J (WP) 1981 *NZ* 1,3
Bekker, H P J (NT) 1951-52 *E*, *F*, 1953 *A* 1,2,3,4, 1955 *BI* 2,3,4, 1956 *A* 1,2, *NZ* 1,2,3,4
Bekker, M J (NT) 1960 *S*
Bekker, R P (NT) 1953 *A* 3,4
Bergh, W F (SWD) 1931-32 *W*, *I*, *E*, *S*, 1933 *A* 1, 2,3,4,5, 1937 *A* 1,2, *NZ* 1,2,3, 1938 *BI* 1,2,3
Bestbier, A (OFS) 1974 *F* 2(R)
Bester, J L A (WP) 1938 *BI* 2,3
Bester, J J N (WP) 1924 *BI* 2,4
Beswick, A M (Bor) 1896 *BI* 2,3,4
Bezuidenhoudt, C E (NT) 1962 *BI* 2,3,4
Bezuidenhoudt, N S E (NT) 1972 *E*, 1974 *BI* 2,3,4, *F* 1,2, 1975 *F* 1,2, 1977 Wld
Bierman, J (Tvl) 1931-32 *I*
Bisset, W M (WP) 1891 *BI* 1,3
Blair, R (WP) 1977 Wld
Bosch, G R (Tvl) 1974 *BI* 2, *F* 1,2, 1975 *F* 1,2, 1976 *NZ* 1,2,3,4
Bosman, N J S (Tvl) 1924 *BI* 2,3,4
Botha, D S (NT) 1981 *NZ* 1
Botha, H E (NT) 1980 *S Am* 1,2, *BI* 1,2,3,4, *S Am* 3,4, *F*, 1981 *I* 1,2, *NZ* 1,2,3, *US*, 1982 *S Am* 1,2,3,4, 1986 *Cv* 1,2,3,4
Botha, J (Tvl) 1903 *BI* 3
Botha, J P F (NT) 1962 *BI* 2,3,4
Botha, P H (Tvl) 1965 *A* 1,2
Boyes, H C (GW) 1891 *BI* 1,2

Brand, G H (WP) 1928 *NZ* 2,3, 1931-32 *W*, *I*, *E*, *S*, 1933 *A* 1,2,3,4,5, 1937 *A* 1,2, *NZ* 2,3, 1938 *BI* 1
Bredenkamp, M (GW) 1896 *BI* 1,3
Breedt, J C (Tvl) 1986 *Cv* 1,2,3,4
Brewis, J D (NT) 1949 *NZ* 1,2,3,4, 1951-52 *S*, *I*, *W*, *E*, *F*, 1953 *A* 1
Briers, T P D (WP) 1955 *BI* 1,2,3,4, 1956 *NZ* 2,3,4
Brink, D J (WP) 1906 *S*, *W*, *E*,
Brooks, D (Bor) 1906 *S*
Brown, C (WP) 1903 *BI* 1,2,3
Brynard, G S (WP) 1965 *A* 1, *NZ* 1,2,3,4, 1968 *BI* 3,4
Buchler, J U (Tvl) 1951-52 *S*, *I*, *W*, *E*, *F*, 1953 *A* 1,2,3,4, 1956 *A* 2
Burdett, A F (WP) 1906 *S*, *I*
Burger, M B (NT) 1980 *BI* 2(R), *S Am* 3, 1981 *US* (R)
Burger, S W P (WP) 1984 *E* 1,2, 1986 *Cv* 1,2,3,4
Burger, W A G (Bor) 1906 *S*, *I*, *W*, 1910 *BI* 2

Carelse, G (EP) 1964 *W*, *F*, 1965 *I*, *S*, 1967 *F* 1,2,3, 1968 *F* 1,2, 1969 *A* 1,2,3,4, 1969-70 *S*
Carlson, R A (WP) 1972 *E*
Carolin, H W (WP) 1903 *BI* 3, 1906 *S*, *I*
Castens, H H (WP) 1891 *BI* 1
Chignell, T W (WP) 1891 *BI* 3
Cilliers, G D (OFS) 1963 *A* 1,3,4
Claassen, J T (WT) 1955 *BI* 1,2,3,4, 1956 *A* 1,2, *NZ* 1,2,3,4, 1958 *F* 1,2, 1960 *S*, *NZ* 1,2,3, 1960-61 *W*, *I*, *E*, *S*, *F*, 1961 *I*, *A* 1,2, 1962 *BI* 1,2,3,4
Claassen, W (N) 1981 *I* 1,2, *NZ* 2,3, *US*, 1982 *S Am* 1,2
Clarke, W H (Tvl) 1933 *A* 3
Clarkson, W A (N) 1921 *NZ* 1,2, 1924 *BI* 1
Cloete, H A (WP) 1896 *BI* 4
Cockrell, C H (WP) 1969-70 *S*, *I*, *W*
Cockrell, R J (WP) 1974 *F* 1,2, 1975 *F* 1,2, 1976 *NZ* 1,2, 1977 Wld, 1981 *NZ* 1,2(R),3, *US*
Coetzee, J H H (WP) 1974 *BI* 1, 1975 *F* 2(R), 1976 *NZ* 1,2,3,4
Cope, D (Tvl) 1896 *BI* 2
Cotty, W (GW) 1896 *BI* 3
Crampton, G (GW) 1903 *BI* 2
Craven, D H (WP) 1931-32 *W*, *I*, *S*, 1933 *A* 1,2,3,4,5, 1937 *A* 1,2, *NZ* 1,2,3, 1938 *BI* 1,2,3
Cronje, P A (Tvl) 1971 *F* 1,2, *A* 1,2,3, 1974 *BI* 3,4
Crosby, J H (Tvl) 1896 *BI* 2
Crosby, N J (Tvl) 1910 *BI* 1,3
Currie, C (GW) 1903 *BI* 2

D'Alton, G (WP) 1933 *A* 1
Daneel, G M (WP) 1928 *NZ* 1,2,3,4, 1931-32 *W*, *I*, *E*, *S*
Daneel, H J (WP) 1906 *S*, *I*, *W*, *E*
Davidson, M (EP) 1910 *BI* 1
De Bruyn, J (OFS) 1974 *BI* 3
De Jongh, H P K (WP) 1928 *NZ* 3
De Klerk, I J (Tvl) 1969-70 *E*, *I*, *W*
De Klerk, K B H (Tvl) 1974 *BI* 1,2,3(R), 1975 *F* 1,2, 1976 *NZ* 2(R),3,4, 1980 *S Am* 1,2, *BI* 2, 1981 *I* 1,2
De Kock, A (GW) 1891 *BI* 2
De Kock, J S (WP) 1921 *NZ* 3, 1924 *BI* 3

Delport, W H (EP) 1951-52 *S, I, W, E, F*, 1953 *A* 1,2,3,4
De Melker, S C (GW) 1903 *BI* 2, 1906 *E*
Devenish, C (GW) 1896 *BI* 2
Devenish, G St L (Tvl) 1896 *BI* 2
Devenish, M (Tvl) 1891 *BI* 1
De Villiers, D I (Tvl) 1910 *BI* 1,2,3
De Villiers, D J (WP, Bol) 1962 *BI* 2,3, 1965 *I, NZ* 1,3,4, 1967 *F* 1,2,3,4, 1968 *BI* 1,2,3,4, *F* 1,2, 1969 *A* 1,4, 1969-70 *E, I, W*, 1970 *NZ* 1,2,3,4
De Villiers, H A (WP) 1906 *S, W, E*
De Villiers, H O (WP) 1967 *F* 1,2,3,4, 1968 *F* 1,2, 1969 *A* 1,2,3,4, 1969-70 *S, E, I, W*
De Villiers, P du P (WP) 1928 *NZ* 1,3,4, 1931-32 *E*, 1933 *A* 4, 1937 *A* 1,2, *NZ* 1
Devine, D (Tvl) 1924 *BI* 3, 1928 *NZ* 2
De Vos, D J J (WP) 1965 *S*, 1969 *A* 3, 1969-70 *S*
De Waal, A N (WP) 1967 *F* 1,2,3,4
De Waal, P (WP) 1896 *BI* 4
De Wet, A E (WP) 1969 *A* 3,4, 1969-70 *E*
De Wet, P (WP) 1938 *BI* 1,2,3
Dinkelmann, E E (NT) 1951-52 *S, I, E, F*, 1953 *A* 1,2
Dirksen, C W (NT) 1963 *A* 4, 1964 *W*, 1965 *I, S*, 1967 *F* 1,2,3,4, 1968 *BI* 1,2
Dobbin, F J (GW) 1903 *BI* 1,2, 1906 *S, W, E*, 1910 *BI* 1, 1912-13 *S, I, W*
Dobie, J A R (Tvl) 1928 *NZ* 2
Dormehl, P J (WP) 1896 *BI* 3,4
Douglass, F W (EP) 1896 *BI* 1
Dryburgh, R G (WP) 1955 *BI* 2,3,4, 1956 *A* 2, *NZ* 1,4, 1960 *NZ* 1,2
Duff, B (WP) 1891 *BI* 1,2,3
Duffy, B A (Bor) 1928 *NZ* 1
Du Plessis, C J (WP) 1982 *S Am* 1,2, 1984 *E* 1,2, *S Am* 1,2, 1986 *Cv* 1,2,3,4
Du Plessis, D C (NT) 1977 Wld, 1980 *S Am* 2
Du Plessis, F (Tvl) 1949 *NZ* 1,2,3
Du Plessis, M (WP) 1971 *A* 1,2,3, 1974 *BI* 1,2, *F* 1,2, 1975 *F* 1,2, 1976 *NZ* 1,2,3,4, 1977 Wld, 1980 *S Am* 1,2, *BI* 1,2,3,4, *S Am* 4, *F*
Du Plessis, M J (WP) 1984 *S Am* 1,2, 1986 *Cv* 1,2,3,4
Du Plessis, N J (WT) 1921 *NZ* 2,3, 1924 *BI* 1,2,3
Du Plessis, P G (NT) 1972 *E*
Du Plessis, T D (NT) 1980 *S Am* 1,2
Du Plessis, W (WP) 1980 *S Am* 1,2, *BI* 1,2,3,4, *S Am* 3,4, *F*, 1981 *NZ* 1,2,3, 1982 *S Am* 1,2
Du Plooy, A J J (EP) 1955 *BI* 1
Du Preez, F C H (NT) 1960-61 *E, S*, 1961 *A* 1,2, 1962 *BI* 1,2,3,4, 1963 *A* 1, 1964 *W, F*, 1965 *A* 1,2, *NZ* 1,2,3,4, 1967 *F* 4, 1968 *BI* 1,2,3,4, *F* 1,2, 1969 *A* 1,2, 1969-70 *S, I, W*, 1970 *NZ* 1,2,3,4, 1971 *F* 1,2, *A* 1,2,3
Du Preez, J G H (WP) 1956 *NZ* 1
Du Rand, J A (R, NT) 1949 *NZ* 2,3, 1951-52 *S, I, W, E, F*, 1953 *A* 1,2,3,4, 1955 *BI* 1,2,3,4, 1956 *A* 1,2, *NZ* 1,2,3,4
Du Toit, A F (WP) 1928 *NZ* 3,4
Du Toit, B A (Tvl) 1938 *BI* 1,2,3
Du Toit, P A (NT) 1949 *NZ* 2,3,4, 1951-52 *S, I, W, E, F*
Du Toit, P G (WP) 1981 *NZ* 1, 1982 *S Am* 1,2, 1984 *E* 1,2
Du Toit, P S (WP) 1958 *F* 1,2, 1960 *NZ* 1,2,3,4, 1960-61 *W, I, E, S, F*, 1961 *I, A* 1,2
Duvenhage, F P (GW) 1949 *NZ* 1,3

Edwards, P (NT) 1980 *S Am* 1,2
Ellis, J H (SWA) 1965 *NZ* 1,2,3,4, 1967 *F* 1,2,3,4, 1968 *BI* 1,2,3,4, *F* 1,2, 1969 *A* 1,2,3,4, 1969-70 *S, I, W*, 1970 *NZ* 1,2,3,4, 1971 *F* 1,2, *A* 1,2,3, 1972 *E*, 1974 *BI* 1,2,3,4, *F* 1,2, 1976 *NZ* 1
Ellis, M (Tvl) 1921 *NZ* 2,3, 1924 *BI* 1,2,3,4
Engelbrecht, J P (WP) 1960 *S*, 1960-61 *W, I, E, S, F*, 1961 *A* 1,2, 1962 *BI* 2,3,4, 1963 *A* 2,3, 1964 *W, F*, 1965 *I, S, A* 1,2, *NZ* 1,2,3,4, 1967 *F* 1,2,3,4, 1968 *BI* 1,2, *F* 1,2, 1969 *A* 1,2
Erasmus, F S (NT) 1986 *Cv* 3,4
Etlinger, T E (WP) 1896 *BI* 4

Ferreira, C (OFS) 1986 *Cv* 1,2
Ferreira, P S (WP) 1984 *S Am* 1,2
Ferris, H H (Tvl) 1903 *BI* 3
Forbes, H H (Tvl) 1896 *BI* 2
Fourie, C (EP) 1974 *F* 1,2, 1975 *F* 1,2
Fourie, T T (SET) 1974 *BI* 3

Fourie, W L (SWA) 1958 *F* 1,2
Francis, J A J (Tvl) 1912-13 *S, I, W, E, F*
Frederickson, C A (Tvl) 1974 *BI* 2, 1980 *S Am* 1,2
Frew, A (Tvl) 1903 *BI* 1
Froneman, D C (OFS) 1977 Wld
Froneman, I L (Bor) 1933 *A* 1
Fry, S P (WP) 1951-52 *S, I, W, E, F*, 1953 *A* 1,2,3,4, 1955 *BI* 1,2,3,4

Gage, J H (OFS) 1933 *A* 1
Gainsford, J L (WP) 1960 *S, NZ* 1,2,3,4, 1960-61 *W, I, E, S, F*, 1961 *A* 1,2, 1962 *BI* 1,2,3,4, 1963 *A* 1,2,3,4, 1964 *W, F*, 1965 *I, S, A* 1,2, *NZ* 1,2,3,4, 1967 *F* 1,2,3
Geel, P J (OFS) 1949 *NZ* 3
Geere, V (Tvl) 1933 *A* 1,2,3,4,5
Geffin, A O (Tvl) 1949 *NZ* 1,2,3,4, 1951-52 *S, I, W*
Geldenhuys, S B (NT) 1981 *NZ* 2,3, *US*, 1982 *S Am* 1,2
Gentles, T A (WP) 1955 *BI* 1,2,4, 1956 *NZ* 2,3, 1958 *F* 2
Geraghty, E M (Bor) 1949 *NZ* 4
Gerber, D M (EP) 1980 *S Am* 3,4, *F*, 1981 *I* 1,2, *NZ* 1,2,3, *US*, 1982 *S Am* 1,2, 1984 *E* 1,2, *S Am* 1,2, 1986 *Cv* 1,2,3,4
Gerber, M C (EP) 1958 *F* 1,2, 1960 *S*
Gericke, F W (Tvl) 1960 *S*
Germishuys, J S (OFS, Tvl) 1974 *BI* 2, 1976 *NZ* 1,2,3,4, 1977 Wld, 1980 *S Am* 1,2, *BI* 1,2,3,4, *S Am* 3,4, *F*, 1981 *I* 1,2, *NZ* 2,3, *US*
Gibbs, B (GW) 1903 *BI* 2
Goosen, C P (OFS) 1965 *NZ* 2
Gorton, H C (Tvl) 1896 *BI* 1
Gould, R L (N) 1968 *BI* 1,2,3,4
Gray, B G (WP) 1931-32 *W, E, S*, 1933 *A* 5
Greenwood, C M (WP) 1961 *I*
Greyling, P J (OFS) 1967 *F* 1,2,3,4, 1968 *BI* 1, *F* 1,2, 1969 *A* 1,2,3,4, 1969-70 *S, E, I, W*, 1970 *NZ* 1,2,3,4, 1971 *F* 1,2, *A* 1,2,3, 1972 *E*
Grobler, C J (OFS) 1974 *BI* 4, 1975 *F* 1,2
Guthrie, F H (WP) 1891 *BI* 1,3, 1896 *BI* 1

Hahn, C H L (Tvl) 1910 *BI* 1,2,3
Hamilton, F (EP) 1891 *BI* 1
Harris, T A (Tvl) 1937 *NZ* 2,3, 1938 *BI* 1,2,3
Hartley, A J (WP) 1891 *BI* 3
Hattingh, L B (OFS) 1933 *A* 2
Heatlie, B H (WP) 1891 *BI* 2,3, 1896 *BI* 1,4, 1903 *BI* 1,3
Hepburn, T (WP) 1896 *BI* 4
Heunis, J W (NT) 1981 *NZ* 3(R), *US*, 1982 *S Am* 1,2, 1984 *E* 1,2, *S Am* 1,2, 1986 *Cv* 1,2,3,4
Hill, R A (R) 1960-61 *W, I*, 1961 *I, A* 1,2, 1962 *BI* 4, 1963 *A* 3
Hirsch, J G (EP) 1906 *I*, 1910 *BI* 1
Hobson, T E C (WP) 1903 *BI* 3
Hoffman, R S (Bol) 1953 *A* 3
Holton, D N (EP) 1960 *S*
Hopwood, D J (WP) 1960 *S, NZ* 3,4, 1960-61 *W, E, S, F*, 1961 *I, A* 1,2, 1962 *BI* 1,2,3,4, 1963 *A* 1,2,4, 1964 *W, F*, 1965 *S, NZ* 3,4
Howe, B F (Bor) 1956 *NZ* 1,4
Howe-Browne, N R F G (WP) 1910 *BI* 1,2,3

Immelman, J H (WP) 1912-13 *F*

Jackson, D C (WP) 1906 *I, W, E*
Jackson, J S (WP) 1903 *BI* 2
Jansen, E (OFS) 1981 *NZ* 1
Jansen, J S (OFS) 1970 *NZ* 1,2,3,4, 1971 *F* 1,2, *A* 1,2,3, 1972 *E*
Jennings, C B (Bor) 1937 *NZ* 1
Johnstone, P G A (WP) 1951-52 *S, I, W, E, F*, 1956 *A* 1, *NZ* 1,2,4
Jones, C H (Tvl) 1903 *BI* 1,2
Jones, P S T (WP) 1896 *BI* 1,3,4
Jordaan, R P (NT) 1949 *NZ* 1,2,3,4
Joubert, S J (WP) 1906 *I, W, E*

Kahts, W J H (NT) 1980 *BI* 1,2,3, *S Am* 3,4, *F*, 1981 *I* 1,2, *NZ* 2, 1982 *S Am* 1,2
Kaminer, J (Tvl) 1958 *F* 2
Kelly, E W (GW) 1896 *BI* 3
Kenyon, B J (Bor) 1949 *NZ* 4
Kipling, H G (GW) 1931-32 *W, I, E, S*, 1933 *A* 1,2,3,4,5

Kirkpatrick, A I (GW) 1953 *A* 2, 1956 *NZ* 2, 1958 *F* 1, 1960 *S, NZ* 1,2,3,4, 1960-61 *W, I, E, S, F*
Knight, A S (Tvl) 1912-13 *S, I, W, E, F*
Koch, A C (Bol) 1949 *NZ* 2,3,4, 1951-52 *S, I, W, E, F*, 1953 *A* 1,2,4, 1955 *BI* 1,2,3,4, 1956 *A* 1, *NZ* 2,3, 1958 *F* 1,2, 1960 *NZ* 1,2
Koch, H V (WP) 1949 *NZ* 1,2,3,4
Kotze, G J M (WP) 1967 *F* 1,2,3,4
Krantz, E F W (OFS) 1976 *NZ* 1, 1981 *I* 1
Krige, J D (WP) 1903 *BI* 1,3, 1906 *S, I, W*
Kritzinger, J L (Tvl) 1974 *BI* 3,4, *F* 1,2, 1975 *F* 1,2, 1976 *NZ* 4
Kroon, C M (EP) 1955 *BI* 1
Kruger, P E (Tvl) 1986 *Cv* 3,4
Kruger, T L (Tvl) 1921 *NZ* 1,2, 1924 *BI* 1,2,3,4, 1928 *NZ* 1,2
Kuhn, S P (Tvl) 1960 *NZ* 3,4, 1960-61 *W, I, E, S, F*, 1961, *I, A* 1,2, 1962 *BI* 1,2,3,4, 1963 *A* 1,2,3, 1965 *I, S*

La Grange, J B (WP) 1924 *BI* 3,4
Larard, A (Tvl) 1896 *BI* 2,4
Lategan, M T (WP) 1949 *NZ* 1,2,3,4, 1951-52 *S, I, W, E, F*, 1953 *A* 1,2
Lawless, M J (WP) 1964 *F*, 1969-70 *E* (R), *I, W*
Ledger, S H (GW) 1912-13 *S, I, E, F*
Le Roux, M (OFS) 1980 *BI* 1,2,3,4, *S Am* 3,4, *F*, 1981 *I* 1
Le Roux, P A (WP) 1906 *I, W, E*
Little, E M M (GW) 1891 *BI* 1,3
Lochner, G P (WP) 1955 *BI* 3, 1956 *A* 1,2, *NZ* 1,2,3,4, 1958 *F* 1,2
Lochner, G P (EP) 1937 *NZ* 3, 1938 *BI* 1,2
Lockyear, R J (GW) 1960 *NZ* 1,2,3,4, 1960-61 *I, F*
Lombard, A C (EP) 1910 *BI* 2
Lotz, J W (Tvl) 1937 *A* 1,2, *NZ* 1,2,3, 1938 *BI* 1,2,3
Loubser, J A (WP) 1903 *BI* 3, 1906 *S, I, W, E*, 1910 *BI* 1,3
Lourens, M J (NT) 1968 *BI* 2,3,4
Louw, J S (Tvl) 1891 *BI* 1,2,3
Louw, M J (Tvl) 1971 *A* 2,3
Louw, M M (WP) 1928 *NZ* 3,4, 1931-32 *W, I, E, S*, 1933 *A* 1,2,3,4,5, 1937 *A* 1,2, *NZ* 2,3, 1938 *BI* 1,2,3
Louw, R J (WP) 1980 *S Am* 1,2, *BI* 1,2,3,4, *S Am* 3,4, *F* 1981 *I* 1,2, *NZ* 1,3, 1982 *S Am* 1,2, 1984 *E* 1,2, *S Am* 1,2
Louw, S C (WP) 1933 *A* 1,2,3,4,5, 1937 *A* 1, *NZ* 1,2,3, 1938 *BI* 1,2,3
Luyt, F P (WP) 1910 *BI* 1,2,3, 1912-13 *S, I, W, E*
Luyt, J D (EP) 1912-13 *S, W, E, F*
Luyt, R R (WP) 1910 *BI* 2,3, 1912-13 *S, I, W, E, F*
Lyons, D (EP) 1896 *BI* 1
Lyster, P J (N) 1933 *A* 2,5, 1937 *NZ* 1

MacDonald, A W (R) 1965 *A* 1, *NZ* 1,2,3,4
Macdonald, D A (WP) 1974 *BI* 2
Malan, A S (Tvl) 1960 *NZ* 1,2,3,4, 1960-61 *W, I, E, S, F*, 1962 *BI* 1, 1963 *A* 1,2,3, 1964 *W*, 1965 *I, S*
Malan, E (NT) 1980 *BI* 3(R),4
Malan, G F (WP) 1958 *F* 2, 1960 *NZ* 1,3,4, 1960-61 *E, S, F*, 1962 *BI* 1,2,3, 1963 *A* 1,2,4, 1964 *W*, 1965 *A* 1,2, *NZ* 1,2
Malan, P (Tvl) 1949 *NZ* 4
Mallett, N V H (WP) 1984 *S Am* 1,2
Mans, W J (WP) 1965 *I, S*
Marais, F P (Bol) 1949 *NZ* 1,2, 1951-52 *S*, 1953 *A* 1,2
Marais, J F K (WP) 1963 *A* 3, 1964 *W, F*, 1965 *I, S, A* 2, 1968 *BI* 1,2,3,4, *F* 1,2, 1969 *A* 1,2,3,4, 1969-70 *S, E, I, W*, 1970 *NZ* 1,2,3,4, 1971 *F* 1,2, *A* 1,2,3, 1974 *BI* 1,2,3,4, *F* 1,2
Maré, D S (Tvl) 1906 *S*
Marsberg, A F W (GW) 1906 *S, W, E*
Marsberg, P A (GW) 1910 *BI* 1
Martheze, W C (GW) 1903 *BI* 2, 1906 *I, W*
Martin, H J (Tvl) 1937 *A* 2
McCallum, I D (WP) 1970 *NZ* 1,2,3,4, 1971 *F* 1,2, *A* 1,2,3, 1974 *BI* 1,2
McCallum, R J (WP) 1974 *BI* 1
McCulloch, J D (GW) 1912-13 *E, F*
McDonald, J A J (WP) 1931-32 *W, I, E, S*
McEwan, W M C (Tvl) 1903 *BI* 1,3
McHardy, E E (OFS) 1912-13 *S, I, W, E, F*
McKendrick, J A (WP) 1891 *BI* 3
Mellett, T (GW) 1896 *BI* 2

Mellish, F W (WP) 1921 *NZ* 1,3, 1924 *BI* 1,2,3,4
Merry, J (EP) 1891 *BI* 1
Metcalf, H D (Bor) 1903 *BI* 2
Meyer, C du P (WP) 1921 *NZ* 1,2,3
Meyer, P J (GW) 1896 *BI* 1
Michau, J M (Tvl) 1921 *NZ* 1
Michau, J P (WP) 1921 *NZ* 1,2,3
Millar, W A (WP) 1906 *E*, 1910 *BI* 2,3, 1912-13 *I, W, F*
Mills, W J (WP) 1910 *BI* 2
Moll, T (Tvl) 1910 *BI* 2
Montini, P E (WP) 1956 *A* 1,2
Moolman, L C (NT) 1977 *Wld*, 1980 *S Am* 1,2, *BI* 1,2,3,4, *S Am* 3,4, *F*, 1981 *I* 1,2, *NZ* 1,2,3, *US*, 1982 *S Am* 1,2, 1984 *S Am* 1,2, 1986 *Cv* 1,2,3,4
Mordt, R H (Z-R, NT) 1980 *S Am* 1,2, *BI* 1,2,3,4, *S Am* 3,4, *F*, 1981 *I* 2, *NZ* 1,2,3, *US*, 1982 *S Am* 1,2, 1984 *S Am* 1,2
Morkel, A O (Tvl) 1903 *BI* 1
Morkel, D F T (Tvl) 1906 *I, E*, 1910 *BI* 1,3, 1912-13 *S, I, W, E, F*
Morkel, H J (WP) 1921 *NZ* 1
Morkel, H W (WP) 1921 *NZ* 1,2
Morkel, J A (WP) 1921 *NZ* 2,3
Morkel, J W H (WP) 1912-13 *S, I, W, E, F*
Morkel, P G (WP) 1912-13 *S, I, W, E, F*, 1921 *NZ* 1,2,3
Morkel, P K (WP) 1928 *NZ* 4
Morkel, W H (WP) 1910 *BI* 3, 1912-13 *S, I, W, E, F*, 1921 *NZ* 1,2,3
Morkel, W S (Tvl), 1906 *S, I, W, E*
Moss, C (N) 1949 *NZ* 1,2,3,4
Mostert, P J (WP) 1921 *NZ* 1,2,3, 1924 *BI* 1,2,4, 1928 *NZ* 1,2,3,4, 1931-32 *W, I, E, S*
Muller, G H (WP) 1969 *A* 3,4, 1969-70 *S, W*, 1970 *NZ* 1,2,3,4, 1971 *F* 1,2, 1972 *E*, 1974 *BI* 1,3,4
Muller, H L (OFS) 1986 *Cv* 4 (R)
Muller, H S V (Tvl) 1949 *NZ* 1,2,3,4, 1951-52 *S, I, W, E, F*, 1953 *A* 1,2,3,4
Myburgh, F R (EP) 1896 *BI* 1
Myburgh, J L (NT) 1962 *BI* 1, 1963 *A* 4, 1964 *W, F*, 1968 *BI* 1,2,3, *F* 1,2, 1969 *A* 1,2,3,4, 1969-70 *E, I, W*, 1970 *NZ* 3,4
Myburgh, W H (WT) 1924 *BI* 1

Naude, J P (WP) 1963 *A* 4, 1965 *A* 1,2, *NZ* 1,3,4, 1967 *F* 1,2,3,4, 1968 *BI* 1,2,3,4
Neethling, J B (WP) 1967 *F* 1,2,3,4, 1968 *BI* 4, 1969-70 *S*, 1970 *NZ* 1,2
Nel, J A (Tvl) 1960 *NZ* 1,2, 1963 *A* 1,2, 1965 *A* 2, *NZ* 1,2,3,4, 1970 *NZ* 3,4
Nel, J J (WP) 1956 *A* 1,2, *NZ* 1,2,3,4, 1958 *F* 1,2
Nel, P A R O (Tvl) 1903 *BI* 1,2,3
Nel, P J (N) 1928 *NZ* 1,2,3,4, 1931-32 *W, I, E, S*, 1933 *A* 1,3,4,5, 1937 *A* 1,2, *NZ* 2,3
Nimb, C F (WP) 1961 *I*
Nomis, S H (Tvl) 1967 *F* 4, 1968 *BI* 1,2,3,4, *F* 1,2, 1969 *A* 1,2,3,4, 1969-70 *S, E, I, W*, 1970 *NZ* 1,2,3,4, 1971 *F* 1,2, *A* 1,2,3, 1972 *E*
Nykamp, J L (Tvl) 1933 *A* 1

Ochse, J K (WP) 1951-52 *I, W, E, F*, 1953 *A* 1,2,4
Oelofse, J S A (Tvl) 1953 *A* 1,2,3,4
Oliver, J F (Tvl) 1928 *NZ* 3,4
Olivier, E (WP) 1967 *F* 1,2,3,4, 1968 *BI* 1,2,3,4, *F* 1,2, 1969 *A* 1,2,3,4, 1969-70 *S, E*,
Olver, E (EP) 1896 *BI* 1
Oosthuizen, J J (WP) 1974 *BI* 1, *F* 1,2, 1975 *F* 1,2, 1976 *NZ* 1,2,3,4
Oosthuizen, O W (NT, Tvl) 1981 *I* 1(R),2, *NZ* 2,3, *US*, 1982 *S Am* 1,2, 1984 *E* 1,2
Osler, B L (WP) 1924 *BI* 1,2,3,4, 1928 *NZ* 1,2,3,4, 1931-32 *W, I, E, S*, 1933 *A* 1,2,3,4,5
Osler, S G (WP) 1928 *NZ* 1
Oxlee, K (N) 1960 *NZ* 1,2,3,4, 1960-61 *W, I, S*, 1961 *A* 1,2, 1962 *BI* 1,2,3,4, 1963 *A* 1,2,4, 1964 *W*, 1965 *NZ* 1,2

Parker, W H (EP) 1965 *A* 1,2
Partridge, J E C (Tvl) 1903 *BI* 1
Payn, C (N) 1924 *BI* 1,2
Pelser, H J M (Tvl) 1958 *F* 1, 1960 *NZ* 1,2,3,4, 1960-61 *W, I, F*, 1961 *I, A* 1,2
Pfaff, B D (WP) 1956 *A* 1

Pickard, J A J (WP) 1953 A 3,4, 1956 NZ 2, 1958 F 2
Pienaar, Z M J (OFS) 1980 S Am 2(R), BI 1,2,3,4, S Am 3,4, F, 1981 I 1,2, NZ 1,2,3
Pitzer, G (NT) 1967 F 1,2,3,4, 1968 BI 1,2,3,4, F 1,2, 1969 A 3,4
Pope, C F (WP) 1974 BI 1,2,3,4, 1975 F 1,2, 1976 NZ 2,3,4
Potgieter, H J (OFS) 1928 NZ 1,2
Potgieter, H L (OFS) 1977 Wld
Powell, A W (GW) 1896 BI 3
Powell, J M (GW) 1891 BI 2, 1896 BI 3, 1903 BI 1,2
Prentis, R B (Tvl) 1980 S Am 1,2, BI 1,2,3,4, S Am 3,4, F, 1981 I 1,2
Pretorius, N F (Tvl) 1928 NZ 1,2,3,4
Prinsloo, J (Tvl) 1958 F 1,2
Prinsloo, J (NT) 1963 A 3
Prinsloo, J P (Tvl) 1928 NZ 1
Putter, D J (WT) 1963 A 1,2,4

Raaff, J W E (GW) 1903 BI 1,2, 1906 S, W, E, 1910 BI 1
Ras, W J de Wet (OFS) 1976 NZ 1(R), 1980 S Am 2(R)
Reid, A (WP) 1903 BI 3
Reid, B C (Bor) 1933 A 4
Reinach, J (OFS) 1986 Cv 1,2,3,4
Rens, I J (Tvl) 1953 A 3,4
Retief, D F (NT) 1955 BI 1,2,4, 1956 A 1,2, NZ 1,2,3,4
Reynecke, H J (WP) 1910 BI 3
Richards, A R (WP) 1891 BI 1,2,3
Riley, N M (ET) 1963 A 3
Riordan, C E (Tvl) 1910 BI 1,2
Robertson, I W (R) 1974 F 1,2, 1976 NZ 1,2,4
Rogers, C D (Tvl) 1984 E 1,2, S Am 1,2
Roos, G D (WP) 1910 BI 2,3
Roos, P J (WP) 1903 BI 3, 1906 I, W, E,
Rosenberg, W (Tvl) 1955 BI 2,3,4, 1956 NZ 3, 1958 F 1
Rossouw, D H (WP) 1953 A 3,4
Rousseau, W P (WP) 1928 NZ 3,4
Roux, F du T (WP) 1960-61 W, 1961 A 1,2, 1962 BI 1,2,3,4, 1963 A 2, 1965 A 1,2, NZ 1,2,3,4, 1968 BI 3,4, F 1,2, 1969 A 1,2,3,4, 1969-70 I, 1970 NZ 1,2,3,4
Roux, O A (NT) 1969-70 E, I, W, 1972 E, 1974 BI 3,4

Samuels, T A (GW) 1896 BI 2,3,4
Sauermann, J T (Tvl) 1971 F 1,2, A 1, 1972 E, 1974 BI 1
Schlebusch, J J J (OFS) 1974 BI 3,4, 1975 F 2
Schmidt, L U (NT) 1958 F 2, 1962 BI 2
Schmidt, U L (NT) 1986 Cv 1,2,3,4
Schoeman, J (WP) 1963 A 3,4, 1965 I, S, A 1, NZ 1,2
Scholtz, H H (WP) 1921 NZ 1,2
Scott, P (Tvl) 1896 BI 1,2,3,4
Sendin, W D (GW) 1921 NZ 2
Serfontein, D J (WP) 1980 BI 1,2,3,4, S Am 3,4, F, 1981 I 1,2, NZ 1,2,3, US, 1982 S Am 1,2, 1984 E 1,2, S Am 1,2
Shand, R (GW) 1891 BI 2,3
Sheriff, A R (Tvl) 1938 BI 1,2,3
Shum, E H (Tvl) 1912-13 E
Sinclair, D J (Tvl) 1955 BI 1,2,3,4
Sinclair, J H (Tvl) 1903 BI 1
Skene, A L (WP) 1958 F 2
Slater, J T (EP) 1924 BI 3,4, 1928 NZ 1
Smal, G P (WP) 1986 Cv 1,2,3,4
Smith, C M (OFS) 1963 A 3,4, 1964 W, F, 1965 A 1,2, NZ 2
Smith, C W (GW) 1891 BI 2, 1896 BI 2,3
Smith, D (GW) 1891 BI 2
Smith, D J (Z-R) 1980 BI 1,2,3,4
Smith, G A C (EP) 1938 BI 3
Smollan, F C (Tvl) 1933 A 3,4,5
Snedden, R C (GW) 1891 BI 2
Snyman, D S L (WP) 1972 E, 1974 BI 1,2(R), F 1,2, 1975 F 1,2, 1976 NZ 2,3, 1977 Wld
Snyman, J C P (OFS) 1974 BI 2,3,4
Sonnekus, G H H (OFS) 1974 BI 3, 1984 E 1,2
Spies, J J (NT) 1970 NZ 1,2,3,4
Stander, J C J (OFS) 1974 BI 4(R), 1976 NZ 1,2,3,4
Stapelberg, W P (NT) 1974 F 1,2
Starke, J J (WP) 1956 NZ 4
Starke, K T (WP) 1924 BI 1,2,3,4
Steenekamp, J G A (Tvl) 1958 F 1

Stegmann, A C (WP) 1906 S, I
Stegmann, J A (Tvl) 1912-13 S, I, W, E, F
Stewart, D A (WP) 1960 S, 1960-61 E, S, F, 1961 I, 1963 A 1,3,4, 1964 W, F, 1965 I
Stofberg, M T S (OFS, NT, WP) 1976 NZ 2,3, 1977 Wld, 1980 S Am 1,2, BI 1,2,3,4, S Am 3,4, F, 1981 I 1,2, NZ 1,2, US, 1982 S Am 1,2, 1984 E 1,2
Strachan, L C (Tvl) 1931-32 E, S, 1937 A 1,2, NZ 1,2,3, 1938 BI 1,2,3
Strauss, J A (WP) 1984 S Am 1,2
Strauss, J H P (Tvl) 1976 NZ 3,4, 1980 S Am 1
Strauss, S S F (GW) 1921 NZ 3
Strydom, C F (OFS) 1955 BI 3, 1956 A 1,2, NZ 1,4, 1958 F 1
Strydom, L J (NT) 1949 NZ 1,2
Suter, M R (N) 1965 I, S
Swart, J J N (SWA) 1955 BI 1

Taberer, W S (GW) 1896 BI 2
Taylor, O B (N) 1962 BI 1
Theunissen, D J (GW) 1896 BI 3
Thompson, G (WP) 1912-13 S, I, W
Tindall, J C (WP) 1924 BI 1, 1928 NZ 1,2,3,4
Tobias, E G (SARF, Bol) 1981 I 1,2, 1984 E 1,2, S Am 1,2
Tod, N S (N) 1928 NZ 2
Townsend, W H (N) 1921 NZ 1
Trenery, W (GW) 1891 BI 2
Truter, D R (WP) 1924 BI 2,4
Truter, J T (N) 1963 A 1, 1964 F, 1965 A 2
Turner, F G (EP) 1933 A 1,2,3, 1937 A 1,2, NZ 1,2,3, 1938 BI 1,2,3
Twigge, R J (NT) 1960 S

Ulyate, C A (Tvl) 1955 BI 1,2,3,4, 1956 NZ 1,2,3
Uys, P de W (NT) 1960-61 W, E, S, 1961 I, A 1,2, 1962 BI 1,4, 1963 A 1,2, 1969 A 1(R),2
Van Aswegen, H J (WP) 1981 NZ 1
Van Broekhuizen, H D (WP) 1896 BI 4
Van Buuren, M C (Tvl) 1891 BI 1
Van De Vyver, D F (WP) 1937 A 2
Van Den Berg, D S (N) 1975 F 1,2, 1976 NZ 1,2
Van Den Berg, M A (WP) 1937 A 1, NZ 1,2,3
Van Der Merwe, A J (Bol) 1955 BI 2,3,4, 1956 A 1,2, NZ 1,2,3,4, 1958 F 1, 1960 S, NZ 2
Van Der Merwe, A V (WP) 1931-32 W
Van Der Merwe, B S (NT) 1949 NZ 1
Van Der Merwe, H S (NT) 1960 NZ 4, 1963 A 2,3,4, 1964 F
Van Der Merwe, J P (WP) 1969-70 W
Van Der Merwe, P R (SWD, WT) 1981 NZ 2,3, US, 1986 Cv 1,2
Vanderplank, B E (N) 1924 BI 3,4
Van Der Schyff, J H (GW) 1949 NZ 1,2,3,4, 1955 BI 1
Van Der Watt, A E (WP) 1969-70 S (R), E, I
Van Der Westhuizen, J C (WP) 1928 NZ 2,3,4, 1931-32 I
Van Der Westhuizen, J H (WP) 1931-32 I, E, S
Van Druten, N J V (Tvl) 1924 BI 1,2,3,4, 1928 NZ 1,2,3,4
Van Heerden, A J (Tvl) 1921 NZ 1,3
Van Heerden, J L (NT, Tvl) 1974 BI 3,4, F 1,2, 1975 F 1,2, 1976 NZ 1,2,3,4, 1977 Wld, 1980 BI 1,3,4, S Am 3,4, F
Van Jaarsveld, C J (Tvl) 1949 NZ 1
Van Jaarsveldt, D C (R) 1960 S
Van Niekerk, J A (WP) 1928 NZ 4
Van Reenen, G L (WP) 1937 A 2, NZ 1
Van Reenen, C G (WP) 1891 BI 3, 1896 BI 1,4
Van Renen, W (WP) 1903 BI 1,3
Van Rooyen, G W (Tvl) 1921 NZ 2,3
Van Ryneveld, R C B (WP) 1910 BI 2,3
Van Schoor, R A M (R) 1949 NZ 2,3,4, 1951-52 S, I, W, E, F, 1953 A 1,2,3,4
Van Vollenhoven, K T (NT) 1955 BI 1,2,3,4, 1956 A 1,2, NZ 3
Van Wyk, C J (Tvl) 1951-52 S, I, W, E, F, 1953 A 1,2,3,4, 1955 BI 1
Van Wyk, J F B (NT) 1970 NZ 1,2,3,4, 1971 F 1,2, A 1,2,3, 1972 E, 1974 BI 1,3,4, 1976 NZ 3,4
Van Wyk, S P (WP) 1928 NZ 1,2

Van Zyl, B P (WP) 1961 *I*
Van Zyl, C G P (OFS) 1965 *NZ* 1,2,3,4
Van Zyl, G H (WP) 1958 *F* 1, 1960 *S, NZ* 1,2,3,4, 1960-61 *W, I, E, S, F*, 1961 *I, A* 1,2, 1962 *BI* 1,3,4
Van Zyl, H J (Tvl) 1960 *NZ* 1,2,3,4, 1960-61 *I, E, S*, 1961 *I, A* 1,2
Van Zyl, P J (Bol) 1961 *I*
Veldsman, P E (WP) 1977 *Wld*
Venter, F D (Tvl) 1931-32 *W, S*, 1933 *A* 3
Versfeld, C (WP) 1891 *BI* 3
Versfeld, M (WP) 1891 *BI* 1,2,3
Vigne, J T (Tvl) 1891 *BI* 1,2,3
Viljoen, J F (GW) 1971 *F* 1,2, *A* 1,2,3, 1972 *E*
Viljoen, J T (N) 1971 *A* 1,2,3
Villet, J V (WP) 1984 *E* 1,2
Visagie, P J (GW) 1967 *F* 1,2,3,4, 1968 *BI* 1,2,3,4, *F* 1,2, 1969 *A* 1,2,3,4, 1969-70 *S, E*, 1970 *NZ* 1,2,3,4, 1971 *F* 1,2, *A* 1,2,3
Visagie, R G (OFS) 1984 *E* 1,2, *S Am* 1,2
Visser, J de V (WP) 1981 *NZ* 2, *US*
Visser, P J (Tvl) 1933 *A* 2
Viviers, S S (OFS) 1956 *A* 1,2, *NZ* 2,3,4
Vogel, M L (OFS) 1974 *BI* 2(R)

Wagenaar, C (NT) 1977 *Wld*
Wahl, J J (WP) 1949 *NZ* 1

Walker, A P (N) 1921 *NZ* 1,3, 1924 *BI* 1,2,3,4
Walker, H N (OFS) 1953 *A* 3, 1956 *A* 2, *NZ* 1,4
Walker, H W (Tvl) 1910 *BI* 1,2,3
Walton, D C (N) 1964 *F*, 1965 *I, S, NZ* 3,4, 1969 *A* 1,2, 1969-70 *E*
Waring, F W (WP) 1931-32 *I, E*, 1933 *A* 1,2,3,4,5
Wessels, J J (WP) 1896 *BI* 1,2,3
Whipp, P J M (WP) 1974 *BI* 1,2, 1975 *F* 1, 1976 *NZ* 1,3,4, 1980 *S Am* 1,2
White, J (Bor) 1931-32 *W*, 1933 *A* 1,2,3,4,5, 1937 *A* 1,2, *NZ* 1,2
Williams, A E (GW) 1910 *BI* 1
Williams, A P (WP) 1984 *E* 1,2
Williams, D O (WP) 1937 *A* 1,2, *NZ* 1,2,3, 1938 *BI* 1,2,3
Williams, J G (NT) 1971 *F* 1,2, *A* 1,2,3, 1972 *E*, 1974 *BI* 1,2,4, *F* 1,2, 1976 *NZ* 1,2
Wilson, L G (WP) 1960 *NZ* 3,4, 1960-61 *W, I, E, F*, 1961 *I, A* 1,2, 1962 *BI* 1,2,3,4, 1963 *A* 1,2,3,4, 1964 *W, F*, 1965 *I, S, A* 1,2, *NZ* 1,2,3,4
Wolmarans, B J (OFS) 1977 *Wld*
Wright, G D (EP) 1986 *Cv* 3,4
Wyness, M R K (WP) 1962 *BI* 1,2,3,4, 1963 *A* 2

Zeller, W C (N) 1921 *NZ* 2,3
Zimerman, M (WP) 1931-32 *W, I, E, S*

SOUTH AFRICAN INTERNATIONAL RECORDS

Both team and individual records are for official South African international matches, up to 30 April 1989.

TEAM RECORDS

Highest score
50 v S America (50-18) 1982 Pretoria
v individual countries
30 v Australia (30-11) 1969 Johannesburg
34 v B Isles (34-14) 1962 Bloemfontein
35 v England (35-9) 1984 Johannesburg
38 v France $\left\{\begin{array}{l}(38\text{-}5) \ 1913 \text{ Bordeaux} \\ (38\text{-}25) \ 1975 \text{ Bloemfontein}\end{array}\right.$
38 v Ireland (38-0) 1912 Dublin
24 v N Zealand (24-12) 1981 Wellington
33 v NZ Cavaliers (33-18) 1986 Pretoria
50 v S America (50-18) 1982 Pretoria
44 v Scotland (44-0) 1951 Murrayfield
38 v United States (38-7) 1981 New York
24 v Wales (24-3) 1964 Durban

Biggest winning points margin
44 v Scotland (44-0) 1951 Murrayfield
v individual countries
25 v Australia (28-3) 1961 Johannesburg
20 v B Isles (34-14) 1962 Bloemfontein
26 v England (35-9) 1984 Johannesburg
33 v France (38-5) 1913 Bordeaux
38 v Ireland (38-0) 1912 Dublin
17 v N Zealand (17-0) 1928 Durban
15 v NZ Cavaliers (33-18) 1986 Pretoria
32 v S America (50-18) 1982 Pretoria
44 v Scotland (44-0) 1951 Murrayfield
31 v United States (38-7) 1981 New York
21 v Wales (24-3) 1964 Durban

Highest score by opposing team
28 B Isles (9-28) 1974 Pretoria
by individual countries
21 Australia (6-21) 1933 Durban
28 B Isles (9-28) 1974 Pretoria
18 England (9-18) 1972 Johannesburg
25 France (38-25) 1975 Bloemfontein
15 Ireland (23-15) 1981 Cape Town
25 N Zealand (22-25) 1981 Auckland
19 NZ Cavaliers (18-19) 1986 Durban
21 S America (12-21) 1982 Bloemfontein
10 Scotland (18-10) 1960 Port Elizabeth
7 United States (38-7) 1981 New York
6 Wales (6-6) 1970 Cardiff

Biggest losing points margin
19 v B Isles (9-28) 1974 Pretoria
v individual countries
15 v Australia (6-21) 1933 Durban
19 v B Isles (9-28) 1974 Pretoria
9 v England (9-18) 1972 Johannesburg
5 v France (14-19) 1967 Johannesburg
3 v Ireland (6-9) 1965 Dublin
17 v N Zealand (3-20) 1965 Auckland
1 v NZ Cavaliers (18-19) 1986 Durban
9 v S America (12-21) 1982 Bloemfontein
6 v Scotland (0-6) 1906 Glasgow
No defeats v United States or Wales

Most tries by South Africa in an international
10 v Ireland (38-0) 1912 Dublin

Most tries against South Africa in an international
$5\left\{\begin{array}{l}\text{by B Isles (22-23) 1955 Johannesburg} \\ \text{by N Zealand (3-20) 1965 Auckland} \\ \text{by B Isles (9-28) 1974 Pretoria}\end{array}\right.$

Most points on overseas tour (all matches)
753 in Australia/N Zealand (26 matches) 1937

Most tries on overseas tour (all matches)
161 in Australia/N Zealand (26 matches) 1937

INDIVIDUAL RECORDS

Most capped player
F C H du Preez $\left.\begin{array}{l}\text{F C H du Preez} \\ \text{J H Ellis}\end{array}\right\} 38 \left\{\begin{array}{l}1960\text{-}71 \\ 1965\text{-}76\end{array}\right.$
in individual positions
Full-back
L G Wilson   27   1960-65
Wing
J P Engelbrecht   33   1960-69

257

Centre
J L Gainsford   33   1960-67
Fly-half
P J Visagie   25   1967-71
Scrum-half
D J de Villiers   25   1962-70
Prop
J F K Marais   35   1963-74
Hooker
G F Malan   18   1958-65
Lock
F C H du Preez   31(38)[1]   1960-71
Flanker
J H Ellis   38   1965-76
No 8
D J Hopwood   22[2]   1960-65

[1] *du Preez won 7 caps as a flanker*
[2] *T P Bedford, 25 caps, won 19 at No 8 and 6 as a flanker*

Longest international career
J M Powell   13 seasons   1891-1903
B H Heatlie   13 seasons   1891-1903

Most internationals as captain
D J de Villiers   22   1965-70

Most points in internationals – 242
H E Botha (21 matches) 1980-86

Most points in an international – 22
G R Bosch v France 1975 Pretoria

Most tries in internationals – 15
D M Gerber (19 matches) 1980-86

Most tries in an international – 3
E E McHardy v Ireland 1912 Dublin
J A Stegmann v Ireland 1912 Dublin
K T van Vollenhoven v B Isles
   1955 Cape Town
H J van Zyl v Australia 1961 Johannesburg
R H Mordt v New Zealand 1981 Auckland
R H Mordt v United States
   1981 New York
D M Gerber v S America 1982 Pretoria
D M Gerber v England 1984 Johannesburg

Most conversions in internationals – 41
H E Botha (21 matches) 1980-86

Most conversions in an international – 7
A Geffin v Scotland 1951 Murrayfield

Most dropped goals in internationals – 14
H E Botha (21 matches) 1980-86

Most penalty goals in internationals – 38
H E Botha (21 matches) 1980-86

Most points in international series – 69
H E Botha (4 appearances) v
   NZ Cavaliers 1986

**Most points in international series
on tour – 35**
H E Botha (3 appearances)
   1981 N Zealand

**Most tries in international series
on tour – 6**
E E McHardy (5 appearances) 1912-13
   B Isles/France

Most points on overseas tour – 190
G H Brand (20 appearances) 1937
   Australia/N Zealand

Most tries on overseas tour – 22
J A Loubser (20 appearances) 1906-07
   B Isles/France

Most points in a tour match – 35
W J de Wet Ras v British Schools OB
   1980 Montevideo

Most tries in a tour match – 6
R G Dryburgh v Queensland 1956
   Brisbane

SUBTLE CHANGES BRING RUNAWAY SUCCESS

THE 1988 SEASON IN NEW ZEALAND
Donald Cameron *New Zealand Herald*

The awesome development of All Black strength in the late 1980s soared to even greater heights. Winning the first World Cup in 1987, which seemed to be a peak, has in fact turned out to be a launching pad from which the All Blacks have propelled themselves further upward. Wales were brushed aside in two home Tests, 52-3 and 54-9. Soon afterwards the All Blacks journeyed to Australia. They won the first Test handily, drew the second and then, to compensate for that hiccup, the All Black juggernaut fell upon the Wallabies in the third Test.

One of the most influential men of recent years in New Zealand rugby, John Hart, who brought the Auckland style of play, and most of the personnel, to the All Blacks was not involved. He had failed in his bid in December 1987 to become the All Black coach and refused to work as a selector. This opened up one of the more interesting questions in modern New Zealand rugby: would Alex Wyllie, he of the grizzled countenance and sometimes old-fashioned methods, be able to switch his talents to guiding an All Black side with very modern ways of thinking? He answered the question emphatically when he assumed the role of All Black coach without any trouble at all.

There were subtle changes in the All Black manner and method. David Kirk, the World Cup-winning half-back, had departed for Oxford, and with him went some of the public relations polish. His replacement as All Black captain, Wayne Shelford, is a forward with the same hard, uncompromising attitude that Wyllie himself brought to his rugby. Both Wyllie and Shelford, at home against Wales and on tour in Australia, handled the public relations aspect very tidily. However, this was not surprising – the All Blacks were winning.

The second Test draw at Ballymore, and a key Ranfurly Shield match between Auckland, the holders, and Otago, the challengers, offered just a hint that some of the All Black armour is starting to wear a little. The Wallabies caught the All Blacks off-balance in the second Test, and kept them there. In the end Grant Fox, in yet another record-breaking season, had perhaps his only failure of the year when he missed a reasonable conversion attempt which would have won the match. But the Wallabies had shown that a basically sound team which tackles well, and has some attacking skill and ambition of its own, can worry a side as apparently impregnable as the All Blacks.

The Auckland side, filled with All Blacks, comfortably won their early matches in defence of the Ranfurly Shield but, as the injuries mounted and the season became longer and longer, Auckland, like the

All Blacks, became vulnerable. The tough tackling of Otago unsettled the Auckland machine. Otago grabbed one try-scoring chance and had they gained another they would have led 23-12 and might well have gone on to win, but they missed that vital second try by a yard or two and Auckland recovered to emerge 27-17 victors. By the end of the winter, injury and other commitments had cut Auckland's ration of All Blacks down to nine, but they still completed yet another marvellous season, emerging unbeaten in the First Division of the National Championship and, most important of all, winning all eight Ranfurly Shield matches, breaking the old record of 25 consecutive challenges held by Auckland (1960-63) and Canterbury (1982-85). Having lost only Steve McDowell, the All Black prop, who has returned to the Bay of Plenty, Auckland should maintain their hold on the Shield.

It was a generous gesture when Auckland took the Shield on tour to King Country, Taranaki and Hawke's Bay. This gave the challenging unions the benefit of playing on their home ground and of taking the match proceeds. This was last done by Hawke's Bay 62 years ago.

1988 ended with reconciliation between the New Zealand Rugby Football Union and John Hart. It had previously been thought that Hart could never be happy with a minor role and would return only when there was the prospect of unseating or replacing Alex Wyllie as coach. However, Hart swallowed his pride and accepted a place on the All Black selection panel with Wyllie and Lane Penn (causing Earl Kirton to be tossed aside after one year), even though Wyllie is in charge for the home Tests against France, Argentina and Australia, and will still be there for the tour of Wales and Ireland at the end of 1989.

NATIONAL CHAMPIONSHIP
First Division

	P	W	D	L	F	A	Pts
Auckland	10	10	0	0	321	114	40
Wellington	10	8	0	2	304	161	34
Otago	10	8	0	2	316	154	32
North Harbour	10	5	1	4	227	187	24
North Auckland	10	5	0	5	237	202	22
Canterbury	10	5	0	5	180	197	22
Counties	10	4	1	5	160	208	19
Waikato	10	4	0	6	174	248	18
Taranaki	10	2	0	8	173	268	14
Bay of Plenty	10	1	0	9	182	282	6
Manawatu	10	1	0	9	84	337	5

Second Division

	P	W	D	L	F	A	Pts
Hawke's Bay	7	7	0	0	225	113	28
Marlborough	7	6	0	1	160	113	24
Wairarapa-Bush	7	5	0	2	197	136	21
Southland	7	3	0	4	141	132	13
Poverty Bay	7	3	0	4	109	135	12
King Country	7	2	0	5	99	128	10
Mid-Canterbury	7	1	0	6	80	153	7
S Canterbury	7	1	0	6	92	193	5

RANFURLY SHIELD
Auckland 28, King Country 0; Auckland 41, Taranaki 13; Auckland 43, North Auckland 15; Auckland 62, Hawke's Bay 9; Auckland 39, North Harbour 12; Auckland 59, Manawatu 3; Auckland 27, Otago 17; Auckland 31, Canterbury 10

NEW ZEALAND INTERNATIONAL PLAYERS (*up to 30 April 1989*)

ABBREVIATIONS

A – Australia; *Arg* – Argentina; *AW* – Anglo-Welsh; *BI* – British Isles teams; *E* – England; *F* – France; *Fj* – Fiji; *I* – Ireland; *It* – Italy; *R* – Romania; *S* – Scotland; *SA* – South Africa; *US* – United States of America; *W* – Wales; (R) – Replacement. Entries in square brackets [ ] indicate appearances in the Rugby World Cup

Note: When a series has taken place, figures denote the particular matches in which players featured. Thus 1959 *BI* 2,4 indicates that a player appeared in the second and fourth Tests of the 1959 series against the British Isles.

Abbott, H L (Taranaki) 1906 *F*
Aitken, G G (Wellington) 1921 *SA* 1,2
Allen, F R (Auckland) 1946 *A* 1,2, 1947 *A* 1,2, 1949 *SA* 1,2
Allen, N H (Counties) 1980 *A* 3, *W*
Alley, G T (Canterbury) 1928 *SA* 1,2,3
Anderson, A (Canterbury) 1983 *S, E*, 1984 *A* 1,2,3, 1987 [*Fj*]
Anderson, B L (Wairarapa-Bush) 1986 *A* 1
Archer, W R (Otago, Southland) 1955 *A* 1,2, 1956 *SA* 1,3
Argus, W G (Canterbury) 1946 *A* 1,2, 1947 *A* 1,2
Arnold, D A (Canterbury) 1963 *I, W*, 1964 *E, F*
Arnold, K D (Waikato) 1947 *A* 1,2
Ashby, D L (Southland) 1958 *A* 2
Asher, A A (Auckland) 1903 *A*
Ashworth, B G (Auckland) 1978 *A* 1,2
Ashworth, J C (Canterbury, Hawke's Bay) 1978 *A* 1,2,3, 1980 *A* 1,2,3, 1981 *SA* 1,2,3, 1982 *A* 1,2, 1983 *BI* 1,2,3,4, A, 1984 *F* 1,2, *A* 1,2,3, 1985 *E* 1,2, *A*
Atkinson, H (West Coast) 1913 *A* 1
Avery, H E (Wellington) 1910 *A* 1,2,3

Badeley, C E O (Auckland) 1921 *SA* 1,2
Baird, J A S (Otago) 1913 *A* 2
Ball, N (Wellington) 1931 *A*, 1932 *A* 2,3, 1935 *W*, 1936 *E*
Barrett, J (Auckland) 1913 *A* 2,3
Barry, E F (Wellington) 1934 *A* 2
Batty, G B (Wellington, Bay of Plenty) 1972 *W, S*, 1973 *E, I, F, E*, 1974 *A* 1,3, *I*, 1975 *S*, 1976 *SA* 1,2,3,4, 1977 *BI* 1
Batty, W (Auckland) 1930 *BI* 1,3,4, 1931 *A*
Beatty, G E (Taranaki) 1950 *BI* 1
Bell, R H (Otago) 1951 *A* 3, 1952 *A* 1,2
Belliss, E A (Wanganui) 1921 *SA* 1,2,3
Bennet, R (Otago) 1905 *A*
Berghan, T (Otago) 1938 *A* 1,2,3
Berry, M J (Wairarapa-Bush) 1986 *A* 3(R)
Bevan, V D (Wellington) 1949 *A* 1,2, 1950 *BI* 1,2,3,4
Birtwistle, W M (Canterbury) 1965 *SA* 1,2,3,4, 1967 *E, W, S*
Black, J E (Canterbury) 1977 *F* 1, 1979 *A*, 1980 *A* 3
Black, N W (Auckland) 1949 *SA* 3
Black, R S (Otago) 1914 *A* 1
Blake, A W (Wairarapa) 1949 *A* 1
Boggs, E G (Auckland) 1946 *A* 2, 1949 *SA* 1
Bond, J G (Canterbury) 1949 *A* 2
Booth, E E (Otago) 1906 *F*, 1907 *A* 1,3
Boroevich, K G (Wellington) 1986 *F* 1, *A* 1, *F* 3(R)
Botica, F M (North Harbour) 1986 *F* 1, *A* 1,2,3, *F* 2,3
Bowden, N J G (Taranaki) 1952 *A* 2
Bowers, R G (Wellington) 1954 *I, F*
Bowman, A W (Hawke's Bay) 1938 *A* 1,2,3
Braid, G J (Bay of Plenty) 1983 *S, E*
Bremner, S G (Auckland, Canterbury) 1952 *A* 2, 1956 *SA* 2
Brewer, M R (Otago) 1986 *F* 1, *A* 1,2,3, *F* 2,3, 1988 *A* 1
Briscoe, K C (Taranaki) 1959 *BI* 2, 1960 *SA* 1,2,3,4, 1963 *I, W*, 1964 *E, S*
Brooke, Z V (Auckland) 1987 [*Arg*]
Brooke-Cowden, M (Auckland) 1986 *F* 1, *A* 1, 1987 [*W*]
Brown, C (Taranaki) 1913 *A* 2
Brown, R H (Taranaki) 1955 *A* 3, 1956 *SA* 1,2,3,4, 1957 *A* 1,2, 1958 *A* 1,2,3, 1959 *BI* 1,3, 1961 *F* 1,2,3, 1962 *A* 1
Brownlie, C J (Hawke's Bay) 1924 *W*, 1925 *E, F*

Brownlie, M J (Hawke's Bay) 1924 *I, W*, 1925 *E, F*, 1928 *SA* 1,2,3,4
Bruce, J A (Auckland) 1914 *A* 1,2
Bruce, O D (Canterbury) 1976 *SA* 1,2,4, 1977 *BI* 2,3,4, *F* 1,2, 1978 *A* 1,2, *I, W, E, S*
Bryers, R F (King Country) 1949 *A* 1
Budd, T A (Southland) 1946 *A* 2, 1949 *A* 2
Bullock-Douglas, G A H (Wanganui) 1932 *A* 1,2,3, 1934 *A* 1,2
Burgess, G A J (Auckland) 1981 *SA* 2
Burgess, G F (Southland) 1905 *A*
Burgess, R E (Manawatu) 1971 *BI* 1,2,3, 1972 *A* 3, *W*, 1973 *I, F*
Burke, P S (Taranaki) 1955 *A* 1, 1957 *A* 1,2
Burns, P J (Canterbury) 1908 *AW* 2, 1910 *A* 1,2,3, 1913 *A* 3
Bush, R G (Otago) 1931 *A*
Bush, W K (Canterbury) 1974 *A* 1,2, 1975 *S*, 1976 *I, SA* 2,4, 1977 *BI* 2,3,4(R), 1978 *I, W*, 1979 *A*
Buxton, J B (Canterbury) 1955 *A* 3, 1956 *SA* 1

Cain, M J (Taranaki) 1913 *US*, 1914 *A* 1,2,3
Callesen, J A (Manawatu) 1974 *A* 1,2,3, 1975 *S*
Cameron, D (Taranaki) 1908 *AW* 1,2,3
Cameron, L M (Manawatu) 1980 *A* 3, 1981 *SA* 1(R),2,3, *R* 1,2,3
Carleton, S R (Canterbury) 1928 *SA* 1,2,3, 1929 *A* 1,2,3
Carrington, K R (Auckland) 1971 *BI* 1,3,4
Casey, S T (Otago) 1905 *S, I, E, W*, 1907 *A* 1,2,3, 1908 *AW* 1
Catley, E H (Waikato) 1946 *A* 1, 1947 *A* 1,2, 1949 *SA* 1,2,3,4
Caughey, T H C (Auckland) 1932 *A* 1,3, 1934 *A* 1,2, 1935 *S, I*, 1936 *E*, *A*1, 1937 *SA* 3
Caulton, R W (Wellington) 1959 *BI* 2,3,4, 1960 *SA* 1,4, 1961 *F* 2, 1963 *E* 1,2, *I, W*, 1964 *E, S, F, A* 1,2,3
Cherrington, N P (North Auckland) 1950 *BI* 1
Christian, D L (Auckland) 1949 *SA* 4
Clamp, M (Wellington) 1984 *A*2,3
Clark, D W (Otago) 1964 *A* 1,2
Clark, W H (Wellington) 1953 *W*, 1954 *I, E, S*, 1955 *A* 1,2, 1956 *SA* 2,3,4
Clarke, A H (Auckland) 1958 *A* 3, 1959 *BI* 4, 1960 *SA* 1
Clarke, D B (Waikato) 1956 *SA* 3,4, 1957 *A* 1,2, 1958 *A* 1,3, 1959 *BI* 1,2,3,4, 1960 *SA* 1,2,3,4, 1961 *F* 1,2,3, 1962 *A* 1,2,3,4,5, 1963 *E* 1,2, *I, W*, 1964 *E, S, F, A*2,3
Clarke, I J (Waikato) 1953 *W*, 1955 *A* 1,2,3, 1956 *SA* 1,2,3,4, 1957 *A* 1,2, 1958 *A* 1,3, 1959 *BI* 1,2, 1960 *SA* 2,4, 1961 *F* 1,2,3, 1962 *A* 1,2,3, 1963 *E* 1,2
Clarke, R L (Taranaki) 1932 *A* 2,3
Cobden, D G (Canterbury) 1937 *SA* 1
Cockerill, M S (Taranaki) 1951 *A* 1,2,3
Cockroft, E A P (South Canterbury) 1913 *A* 3, 1914 *A* 2,3
Codlin, B W (Counties) 1980 *A* 1,2,3
Collins, A H (Taranaki) 1932 *A* 2,3, 1934 *A* 1
Collins, J L (Poverty Bay) 1964 *A* 1, 1965 *SA* 1,4
Colman, J T H (Taranaki) 1907 *A* 1,2, 1908 *AW* 1,3
Connor, D M (Auckland) 1961 *F* 1,2,3, 1962 *A* 1,2,3, 4,5, 1963 *E* 1,2, 1964 *A* 2,3
Conway, R J (Otago, Bay of Plenty) 1959 *BI* 2,3,4, 1960 *SA* 1,3,4, 1965 *SA* 1,2,3,4
Cooke, A E (Auckland, Wellington) 1924 *I, W*, 1925 *E, F*, 1930 *BI* 1,2,3,4
Cooke, R J (Canterbury) 1903 *A*
Cooper, G J L (Auckland) 1986 *F* 1, *A* 1,2

261

Corner, M M N (Auckland) 1930 *BI* 2,3,4, 1931 *A*, 1934 *A* 1, 1936 *E*
Cossey, R R (Counties) 1958 *A* 1
Cottrell, A I (Canterbury) 1929 *A* 1,2,3, 1930 *BI* 1,2, 3,4, 1931 *A*, 1932 *A* 1,2,3
Cottrell, W D (Canterbury) 1968 *A* 1,2, *F* 2,3, 1970 *SA* 1, 1971 *BI* 1,2,3,4
Couch, M B R (Wairarapa) 1947 *A* 1, 1949 *A* 1,2
Coughlan, T D (South Canterbury) 1958 *A* 1
Creighton, J N (Canterbury) 1962 *A* 4
Crichton, S (Wellington) 1983 *S, E*
Cross, T (Canterbury) 1904 *BI*, 1905 *A*
Crowley, K J (Taranaki) 1985 *E* 1,2, *A, Arg* 1,2, 1986 *A* 3, *F* 2,3, 1987 *[Arg]*
Crowley, P J B (Auckland) 1949 *SA* 3,4, 1950 *BI* 1,2,3,4
Cummings, W (Canterbury) 1913 *A* 2,3
Cundy, R T (Wairarapa) 1929 *A* 2(R)
Cunningham, G R (Auckland) 1979 *A, S, E*, 1980 *A* 1,2
Cunningham, W (Auckland) 1905 *S, I*, 1906 *F*, 1907 *A* 1,2,3, 1908 *AW* 1,2,3
Cupples, L F (Bay of Plenty) 1924 *I, W*
Currie, C J (Canterbury) 1978 *I, W*
Cuthill, J E (Otago) 1913 *A* 1, *US*

Dalley, W C (Canterbury) 1924 *I*, 1928 *SA* 1,2,3,4
Dalton, A G (Counties) 1977 *F* 2, 1978 *A* 1,2,3, *I, W, E, S*, 1979 *F* 1,2, *S*, 1981 *S* 1,2, *SA* 1,2,3, *R, F* 1,2, 1982 *A* 1,2,3, 1983 *BI* 1,2,3,4, *A*, 1984 *F* 1,2, *A* 1,2,3, 1985 *E* 1,2, *A*
Dalton, D (Hawke's Bay) 1935 *I, W*, 1936 *A* 1,2, 1937 *SA* 1,2,3, 1938 *A* 1,2
Dalton, R A (Wellington) 1947 *A* 1,2
Dalzell, G N (Canterbury) 1953 *W*, 1954 *I, E, S, F*
Davie, M G (Canterbury) 1983 *E* (R)
Davies, W A (Auckland, Otago) 1960 *SA* 4, 1962 *A* 4,5
Davis, K (Auckland) 1952 *A* 2, 1953 *W*, 1954 *I, E, S, F*, 1955 *A* 2, 1958 *A* 1,2,3
Davis, L J (Canterbury) 1976 *I*, 1977 *BI* 3,4
Davis, W L (Hawke's Bay) 1967 *A, E, W, F, S*, 1968 *A* 1,2, *F* 1, 1969 *W* 1,2, 1970 *SA* 2
Deans, I B (Canterbury) 1988 *W* 1,2, *A* 1,2,3
Deans, R G (Canterbury) 1905 *S, I, E, W*, 1908 *AW* 3
Deans, R M (Canterbury) 1983 *S, E*, 1984 *A* 1(R),2,3
Delamore, G W (Wellington) 1949 *SA* 4
Dewar, H (Taranaki) 1913 *A* 1, *US*
Diack, E S (Otago) 1959 *BI* 2
Dick, J (Auckland) 1937 *SA* 1,2, 1938 *A* 3
Dick, M J (Auckland) 1963 *I, W*, 1964 *E, S, F*, 1965 *SA* 3, 1966 *BI* 4, 1967 *A, E, W, F*, 1969 *W* 1,2, 1970 *SA* 1,4
Dixon, M J (Canterbury) 1954 *I, E, S, F*, 1956 *SA* 1,2,3,4, 1957 *A* 1,2
Dobson, R L (Auckland) 1949 *A* 1
Dodd, E H (Wellington) 1905 *A*
Donald, A J (Wanganui) 1983 *S, E*, 1984 *F* 1,2, *A* 1,2,3
Donald, J G (Wairarapa) 1921 *SA* 1,2
Donald, Q (Wairarapa) 1924 *I, W*, 1925 *E, F*
Donaldson, M W (Manawatu) 1977 *F* 1,2, 1978 *A* 1, 2,3, *I, E, S*, 1979 *F* 1,2, *A, S* (R), 1981 *SA* 3(R)
Dougan, J P (Wellington) 1972 *A* 1, 1973 *E*
Downing, A J (Auckland) 1913 *A* 1, *US*, 1914 *A* 1,2,3
Drake, J A (Auckland) 1986 *F* 2,3, 1987 *[Fj, Arg, S, W, F], A*
Duff, R H (Canterbury) 1951 *A* 1,2,3, 1952 *A* 1,2, 1955 *A* 2,3, 1956 *SA* 1,2,3,4
Duncan, J (Otago) 1903 *A*
Duncan, M G (Hawke's Bay) 1971 *BI* 3(R), 4
Duncan, W D (Otago) 1921 *SA* 1,2,3
Dunn, E J (North Auckland) 1979 *S*, 1981 *S* 1
Dunn, I T W (North Auckland) 1983 *BI* 1,4, *A*
Dunn, J M (Auckland) 1946 *A* 1

Earl, A T (Canterbury) 1986 *F* 1, *A* 1, *F* 3(R), 1987 *[Arg]*
Eastgate, B P (Canterbury) 1952 *A* 1,2, 1954 *S*
Elliott, K G (Wellington) 1946 *A* 1,2
Elsom, A E G (Canterbury) 1952 *A* 1,2, 1953 *W*, 1955 *A* 1,2,3
Elvidge, R R (Otago) 1946 *A* 1,2, 1949 *SA* 1,2,3,4, 1950 *BI* 1,2,3
Erceg, C P (Auckland) 1951 *A* 1,2,3, 1952 *A* 1

Evans, D A (Hawke's Bay) 1910 *A* 2
Eveleigh, K A (Manawatu) 1976 *SA* 2,4, 1977 *BI* 1,2

Fanning, A H N (Canterbury) 1913 *A* 3
Fanning, B J (Canterbury) 1903 *A*, 1904 *BI*
Farrell, C P (Auckland) 1977 *BI* 1,2
Fawcett, C L (Auckland) 1976 *SA* 2,3
Fea, W R (Otago) 1921 *SA* 3
Finlay, B E L (Manawatu) 1959 *BI* 1
Finlay, J (Manawatu) 1946 *A* 1
Finlayson, I (North Auckland) 1928 *SA* 1,2,3,4, 1930 *BI* 1,2
Fitzgerald, J T (Wellington) 1952 *A* 1
Fitzpatrick, B B J (Wellington) 1953 *W*, 1954 *I, F*
Fitzpatrick, S B T (Auckland) 1986 *F* 1, *A* 1, *F* 2,3, 1987 *[It, Fj, Arg, S, W, F], A*, 1988 *W* 1,2, *A* 1,2,3
Fleming, J K (Wellington) 1979 *S, E*, 1980 *A* 1,2,3
Fletcher, C J C (North Auckland) 1921 *SA* 3
Fogarty, R (Taranaki) 1921 *SA* 1,3
Ford, B R (Marlborough) 1977 *BI* 3,4, 1978 *I*, 1979 *E*
Fox, G J (Auckland) 1985 *Arg* 1, 1987 *[It, Fj, Arg, S, W, F], A*, 1988 *W* 1,2, *A* 1,2,3
Francis, A R H (Auckland) 1905 *A*, 1907 *A* 1,2,3, 1908 *AW* 1,2,3, 1910 *A* 1,2,3
Francis, W C (Wellington) 1913 *A* 2,3, 1914 *A* 1,2,3
Fraser, B G (Wellington) 1979 *S, E*, 1980 *A* 3, *W*, 1981 *S* 1,2, *SA* 1,2,3, *R, F* 1, 2, 1982 *A* 1,2,3, 1983 *BI* 1,2,3,4, *A, S, E*, 1984 *A* 1
Frazer, H F (Hawke's Bay) 1946 *A* 1,2, 1947 *A* 1,2, 1949 *SA* 2
Fryer, F C (Canterbury) 1907 *A* 1,2,3, 1908 *AW* 2
Fuller, W B (Canterbury) 1910 *A* 1,2
Furlong, B D M (Hawke's Bay) 1970 *SA* 4

Gallagher, J A (Wellington) 1987 *[It, Fj, S, W, F], A*, 1988 *W* 1,2, *A* 1,2,3
Gallaher, D (Auckland) 1903 *A*, 1904 *BI*, 1905 *S, E, W*, 1906 *F*
Gard, P C (North Otago) 1971 *BI* 4
Gardiner, A J (Taranaki) 1974 *A* 3
Geddes, J H (Southland) 1929 *A* 1
Geddes, W McK (Auckland) 1913 *A* 2
Gemmell, B McL (Auckland) 1974 *A* 1,2
George, V L (Southland) 1938 *A* 1,2,3
Gilbert, G D M (West Coast) 1935 *S, I, W*, 1936 *E*
Gillespie, C T (Wellington) 1913 *A* 2
Gillespie, W D (Otago) 1958 *A* 3
Gillett, G A (Canterbury, Auckland) 1905 *S, I, E, W*, 1907 *A* 2,3, 1908 *AW* 1,3
Gillies, C C (Otago) 1936 *A* 2
Gilray, C M (Otago) 1905 *A*
Glasgow, F T (Taranaki, Southland) 1905 *S, I, E, W*, 1906 *F*, 1908 *AW* 3
Glenn, W S (Taranaki) 1904 *BI*, 1906 *F*
Goddard, M P (South Canterbury) 1946 *A* 2, 1947 *A* 1,2, 1949 *SA* 3,4
Going, S M (North Auckland) 1967 *A, F*, 1968 *F* 3, 1969 *W* 1,2, 1970 *SA* 1(R), 4, 1971 *BI* 1,2,3,4, 1972 *A* 1,2,3, *W, S*, 1973 *E, I, F, E*, 1974 *I*, 1975 *S*, 1976 *I* (R), *SA* 1,2,3,4, 1977 *BI* 1,2
Graham, D J (Canterbury) 1958 *A* 1,2, 1960 *SA* 2,3, 1961 *F* 1,2,3, 1962 *A* 1,2,3,4,5, 1963 *E* 1,2, *I, W*, 1964 *E, S, F, A* 1,2,3
Graham, J B (Otago) 1913 *US*, 1914 *A* 1,3
Graham, W G (Otago) 1979 *F* 1(R)
Grant, L A (South Canterbury) 1947 *A* 1,2, 1949 *SA* 1,2
Gray, G D (Canterbury) 1908 *AW* 2, 1913 *A* 1, *US*
Gray, K F (Wellington) 1963 *I, W*, 1964 *E, S, F, A* 1,2,3, 1965 *SA* 1,2,3,4, 1966 *BI* 1,2,3,4, 1967 *W, F, S*, 1968 *A* 1, *F* 2,3, 1969 *W* 1,2
Gray, W N (Bay of Plenty) 1955 *A* 2,3, 1956 *SA* 1,2,3,4
Green, C I (Canterbury) 1983 *S*(R), *E*, 1984 *A* 1,2,3, 1985 *E* 1,2, *A, Arg* 1,2, 1986 *A* 2,3, *F* 2,3, 1987 *[It, Fj, S, W, F], A*
Grenside, B A (Hawke's Bay) 1928 *SA* 1,2,3,4, 1929 *A* 2,3
Griffiths, J L (Wellington) 1934 *A* 2, 1935 *S, I, W*, 1936 *A* 1,2, 1938 *A* 3
Guy, R A (North Auckland) 1971 *BI* 1,2,3,4

Haden, A M (Auckland) 1977 *BI* 1,2,3,4, *F* 1,2, 1978 *A* 1,2,3, *I, W, E, S*, 1979 *F* 1,2, *A, S, E*, 1980 *A* 1,2,3,

W, 1981 S 2, SA 1,2,3, R, F 1,2, 1982 A 1,2,3, 1983 BI 1,2,3,4, A, 1984 F 1,2, 1985 Arg 1,2
Hadley, S (Auckland) 1928 SA 1,2,3,4
Hadley, W E (Auckland) 1934 A 1,2, 1935 S, I, W, 1936 E, A 1,2
Haig, J S (Otago) 1946 A 1,2
Haig, L S (Otago) 1950 BI 2,3,4, 1951 A 1,2,3, 1953 W, 1954 E, S
Hales, D A (Canterbury) 1972 A 1,2,3, W
Hamilton, D C (Southland) 1908 AW 2
Hammond, I A (Marlborough) 1952 A 2
Harper, E T (Canterbury) 1904 BI, 1906 F
Harris, P C (Manawatu) 1976 SA 3
Hart, A H (Taranaki) 1924 I
Hart, G F (Canterbury) 1930 BI 1,2,3,4, 1931 A, 1934 A 1, 1935 S, I, W, 1936 A 1,2
Harvey, B A (Wairarapa-Bush) 1986 F 1
Harvey, I H (Wairarapa) 1928 SA 4
Harvey, L R (Otago) 1949 SA 1,2,3,4, 1950 BI 1,2,3,4
Harvey, P (Canterbury) 1904 BI
Hasell, C N (Canterbury) 1913 A 2,3
Hayward, H O (Auckland) 1908 AW 3
Hazlett, E J (Southland) 1966 BI 1,2,3,4, 1967 A, E
Hazlett, W E (Southland) 1928 SA 1,2,3,4, 1930 BI 1,2,3,4
Heeps, T R (Wellington) 1962 A 1,2,3,4,5
Heke, W R (North Auckland) 1929 A 1,2,3
Hemi, R C (Waikato) 1953 W, 1954 I, E, S, F, 1955 A 1,2,3, 1956 SA 1,3,4, 1957 A 1,2, 1959 BI 1,3,4
Henderson, P (Wanganui) 1949 SA 1,2,3,4, 1950 BI 2,3,4
Herewini, M A (Auckland) 1962 A 5, 1963 I, 1964 S, F, 1965 SA 4, 1966 BI 1,2,3,4, 1967 A
Hewson, A R (Wellington) 1981 S 1,2, SA 1,2,3, R, F 1,2, 1982 A 1,2,3, 1983 BI 1,2,3,4, A, 1984 F 1,2, A 1 A 1
Higginson, G (Canterbury, Hawke's Bay) 1980 W, 1981 S 1, SA 1, 1982 A 1,2, 1983 A
Hill, S F (Canterbury) 1955 A 3, 1956 SA 1,3,4, 1957 A 1,2, 1958 A 3, 1959 BI 1,2,3,4
Hines, G R (Waikato) 1980 A 3
Hobbs, M J B (Canterbury) 1983 BI 1,2,3,4, A, S, E, 1984 F 1,2, A 1,2,3, 1985 E 1,2, A, Arg 1,2, 1986 A 2,3, F 2,3
Holder, E C (Buller) 1934 A 2
Hook, L S (Auckland) 1929 A 1,2,3
Hooper, J A (Canterbury) 1937 SA 1,2,3
Hopkinson, A E (Canterbury) 1967 S, 1968 A 2, F 1,2,3, 1969 W 2, 1970 SA 1,2,3
Hore, J (Otago) 1930 BI 2,3,4, 1932 A 1,2,3, 1934 A 1,2, 1935 S, 1936 E
Horsley, R H (Wellington) 1960 SA 2,3,4
Hotop, J (Canterbury) 1952 A 1,2, 1955 A 3
Hughes, A M (Auckland) 1949 A 1,2, 1950 BI 1,2,3,4
Hughes, E (Southland, Wellington) 1907 A 1,2,3, 1908 AW 1, 1921 SA 1,2
Hunter, B A (Otago) 1971 BI 1,2,3
Hunter, J (Taranaki) 1905 S, I, E, W, 1906 F, 1907 A 1,2,3, 1908 AW 1,2,3
Hurst, I A (Canterbury) 1973 I, F, E, 1974 A 1,2

Ifwersen, K D (Auckland) 1921 SA 3
Innes, G D (Canterbury) 1932 A 2
Irvine, I B (North Auckland) 1952 A 1
Irvine, J G (Otago) 1914 A 1,2,3
Irvine, W R (Hawke's Bay, Wairarapa) 1924 I, W, 1925 E, F, 1930 BI 1
Irwin, M W (Otago) 1955 A 1,2, 1956 SA 1, 1958 A 2, 1959 BI 3,4, 1960 SA 1

Jackson, E S (Hawke's Bay) 1936 A 1,2, 1937 SA 1,2,3, 1938 A 3
Jaffray, J L (Otago, South Canterbury) 1972 A 2, 1975 S, 1976 I, SA 1, 1977 BI 2, 1979 F 1,2
Jarden, R A (Wellington) 1951 A 1,2, 1952 A 1,2, 1953 W, 1954 I, E, S, F, 1955 A 1,2,3, 1956 SA 1,2,3,4
Jefferd, A C R (East Coast) 1981 S 1,2, SA 1
Jessep, E M (Wellington) 1931 A, 1932 A 1
Johnson, L M (Wellington) 1928 SA 1,2,3,4
Johnston, W (Otago) 1907 A 1,2,3
Johnstone, B R (Auckland) 1976 SA 2, 1977 BI 1,2, F 1,2, 1978 I, W, E, S, 1979 F 1,2, S, E
Johnstone, P (Otago) 1949 SA 2,4, 1950 BI 1,2,3,4, 1951 A 1,2,3

Jones, M G (North Auckland) 1973 E
Jones, M N (Auckland) 1987 [It, Fj, S, F], A, 1988 W 1,2, A 2,3
Jones, P F H (North Auckland) 1954 E, S, 1955 A 1,2, 1956 SA 3,4, 1958 A 1,2,3, 1959 BI 1, 1960 SA 1
Joseph, H T (Canterbury) 1971 BI 2,3

Karam, J F (Wellington, Horowhenua) 1972 W, S, 1973 E, I, F, 1974 A 1,2,3, I, 1975 S
Katene, T (Wellington) 1955 A 2
Kearney, J C (Otago) 1947 A 2, 1949 SA 1,2,3
Kelly, J W (Auckland) 1949 A 1,2
Kember, G F (Wellington) 1970 SA 4
Ketels, R C (Counties) 1980 W, 1981 S 1,2, R, F 1
Kiernan, H A D (Auckland) 1903 A
Kilby, F D (Wellington) 1932 A 1,2,3, 1934 A 2
Killeen, B A (Auckland) 1936 A 1
King, R R (West Coast) 1934 A 2, 1935 S, I, W, 1936 E, A 1,2, 1937 SA 1,2,3, 1938 A 1,2,3
Kingstone, C N (Taranaki) 1921 SA 1,2,3
Kirk, D E (Auckland) 1985 E 1,2, A, Arg 1, 1986 F 1, A 1,2,3, F 2,3, 1987 [It, Fj, Arg, S, W, F], A
Kirkpatrick, I A (Canterbury, Poverty Bay) 1967 F, 1968 A 1(R), 2, F 1,2,3, 1969 W 1,2, 1970 SA 1,2,3,4, 1971 BI 1,2,3,4, 1972 A 1,2,3, W, S, 1973 E, I, F, E, 1974 A 1,2,3, I 1975 S, 1976 I, SA 1,2,3,4, 1977 BI 1,2,3,4
Kirton, E W (Otago) 1967 E, W, F, S, 1968 A 1,2, F 1,2,3, 1969 W 1,2, 1970 SA 2,3
Kirwan, J J (Auckland) 1984 F 1,2, 1985 E 1,2, A, Arg 1,2, 1986 F 1, A 1,2,3, F 2,3, 1987 [It, Fj, Arg, S, W, F], A, 1988 W 1,2 A 1,2,3
Kivell, A L (Taranaki) 1929 A 2,3
Knight, A (Auckland) 1934 A 1
Knight, G A (Manawatu) 1977 F 1,2, 1978 A 1,2,3, E, S, 1979 F 1,2, A, 1980 A 1,2,3, W, 1981 S 1,2, SA 1,3, 1982 A 1,2,3, 1983 BI 1,2,3,4, A, 1984 F 1,2, A 1,2,3, 1985 E 1,2, A, 1986 A 2,3
Knight, L G (Poverty Bay) 1977 BI 1,2,3,4, F 1,2 1982 A 3
Koteka, T T (Waikato) 1981 F 2, 1982 A 3
Kreft, A J (Otago) 1968 A 2

Laidlaw, C R (Otago, Canterbury) 1964 F, A 1, 1965 SA 1,2,3,4, 1966 BI 1,2,3,4, 1967 E, W, S, 1968 A 1,2, F 1,2, 1970 SA 1,2,3
Laidlaw, K F (Southland) 1960 SA 2,3,4
Lambert, K K (Manawatu) 1972 S(R), 1973 E, I, F, E, 1974 I, 1976 SA 1,3,4, 1977 BI 1,4
Lambourn, A (Wellington) 1934 A 1,2, 1935 S, I, W, 1936 E, 1937 SA 1,2,3, 1938 A 3
Le Lievre, J M (Canterbury) 1962 A 4
Lendrum, R N (Counties) 1973 E
Leslie, A R (Wellington) 1974 A 1,2,3, I, 1975 S, 1976 I, SA 1,2,3,4
Leys, E T (Wellington) 1929 A 3
Lilburne, H T (Canterbury, Wellington) 1928 SA 3,4, 1929 A 1,2,3, 1930 BI 1,4, 1931 A, 1932 A 1, 1934 A 2
Lindsay, D F (Otago) 1928 SA 1,2,3
Lineen, T R (Auckland) 1957 A 1,2, 1958 A 1,2,3, 1959 BI 1,2,3,4, 1960 SA 1,2,3
Lister, T N (South Canterbury) 1968 A 1,2, F 1, 1969 W 1,2, 1970 SA 1,4, 1971 BI 4
Little, P F (Auckland) 1961 F 2,3, 1962 A 2,3,5, 1963 I, W, 1964 E, S, F
Loader, C J (Wellington) 1954 I, E, S, F
Lochore, B J (Wairarapa) 1964 E, S, 1965 SA 1,2,3,4, 1966 BI 1,2,3,4, 1967 A, E, W, F, S, 1968 A 1, F 2,3, 1969 W 1,2, 1970 SA 1,2,3,4, 1971 BI 3
Loe, R W (Waikato) 1987 [It, Arg], 1988 W 1,2, A 1,2,3
Long, A J (Auckland) 1903 A
Loveridge, D S (Taranaki) 1978 W, 1979 S, E, 1980 A 1,2,3, W, 1981 S 1,2, SA 1,2,3, R, F 1,2, 1982 A 1,2,3, 1983 BI 1,2,3,4, A, 1985 Arg 2
Lucas, F W (Auckland) 1924 I, 1925 F, 1928 SA 4, 1930 BI 1,2,3,4
Lunn, W A (Otago) 1949 A 1,2
Lynch, T W (South Canterbury) 1913 A 1, 1914 A 1,2,3
Lynch, T W (Canterbury) 1951 A 1,2,3

McAtamney, F S (Otago) 1956 SA 2
McCahill, B J (Auckland) 1987 [Arg, S(R), W(R)]

McCaw, W A (Southland) 1951 *A* 1,2,3, 1953 *W*, 1954 *F*
McCool, M J (Wairarapa-Bush) 1979 *A*
McCormick, W F (Canterbury) 1965 *SA* 4, 1967 *E, W, F, S*, 1968 *A* 1,2, *F* 1,2,3, 1969 *W* 1,2, 1970 *SA* 1,2,3, 1971 *BI* 1
McCullough, J F (Taranaki) 1959 *BI* 2,3,4
McDonald, A (Otago) 1905 *S, I, E, W*, 1907 *A* 1, 1908 *AW* 1, 1913 *A* 1, *US*
Macdonald, H H (Canterbury, North Auckland) 1972 *W, S*, 1973 *E, I, F, E*, 1974 *I*, 1975 *S*, 1976 *I, SA* 1,2,3
McDowell, S C (Auckland) 1985 *Arg* 1,2, 1986 *A* 2,3, *F* 2,3, 1987 [*It, Fj, S, W, F*], *A*, 1988 *W* 1,2, *A* 1,2,3
McEldowney, J T (Taranaki) 1977 *BI* 3,4
MacEwan, I N (Wellington) 1956 *SA* 2, 1957 *A* 1,2, 1958 *A* 1,2,3, 1959 *BI* 1,2,3, 1960 *SA* 1,2,3,4, 1961 *F* 1,2,3, 1962 *A* 1,2,3,4
McGrattan, B (Wellington) 1983 *S, E*, 1985 *Arg* 1,2, 1986 *F* 1, *A* 1
McGregor, A J (Auckland) 1913 *A* 1, *US*
McGregor, D (Canterbury, Southland) 1903 *A*, 1904 *BI*, 1905 *E, W*
McGregor, N P (Canterbury) 1924 *W*, 1925 *E*
McGregor, R W (Auckland) 1903 *A*, 1904 *BI*
McHugh, M J (Auckland) 1946 *A* 1,2, 1949 *SA* 3
McIntosh, D N (Wellington) 1956 *SA* 1,2, 1957 *A* 1,2
McKay, D W (Auckland) 1961 *F* 1,2,3, 1963 *E* 1,2
McKechnie, B J (Southland) 1977 *F* 1,2, 1978 *A* 2(R),3, *W*(R), *E, S*, 1979 *A*, 1981 *SA* 1(R), *F* 1
McKellar, G F (Wellington) 1910 *A* 1,2,3
McKenzie, R J (Wellington) 1913 *A* 1, *US*, 1914 *A* 2,3
McKenzie, R McC (Manawatu) 1934 *A* 1, 1935 *S*, 1936 *A* 1, 1937 *SA* 1,2,3, 1938 *A* 1,2,3
McLachlan, J S (Auckland) 1974 *A* 2
McLaren, H C (Waikato) 1952 *A* 1
McLean, A L (Bay of Plenty) 1921 *SA* 2,3
McLean, H F (Wellington, Auckland) 1930 *BI* 3,4, 1932 *A* 1,2,3, 1934 *A* 1, 1935 *I, W*, 1936 *E*
McLean, J K (King Country, Auckland) 1947 *A* 1, 1949 *A* 2
McLeod, B E (Counties) 1964 *A* 1,2,3, 1965 *SA* 1,2,3,4, 1966 *BI* 1,2,3,4, 1967 *E, W, F, S*, 1968 *A* 1,2, *F* 1,2,3, 1969 *W* 1,2, 1970 *SA* 1,2
McMinn, A F (Wairarapa, Manawatu) 1903 *A*, 1905 *A*
McMinn, F A (Manawatu) 1904 *BI*
McMullen, R F (Auckland) 1957 *A* 1,2, 1958 *A* 1,2,3, 1959 *BI* 1,2,3, 1960 *SA* 2,3,4
McNab, J R (Otago) 1949 *SA* 1,2,3, 1950 *BI* 1,2,3
McNaughton, A M (Bay of Plenty) 1971 *BI* 1,2,3
McNeece, J (Southland) 1913 *A* 2,3, 1914 *A* 1,2,3
McPhail, B E (Canterbury) 1959 *BI* 1,4
Macpherson, D G (Otago) 1905 *A*
MacPherson, G L (Otago) 1986 *F* 1
MacRae, I R (Hawke's Bay) 1966 *BI* 1,2,3,4, 1967 *A, E, W, F, S*, 1968 *F* 1,2, 1969 *W* 1,2, 1970 *SA* 1,2,3,4
McRae, J A (Southland) 1946 *A* 1(R),2
McWilliams, R G (Auckland) 1928 *SA* 2,3,4, 1929 *A* 1,2,3, 1930 *BI* 1,2,3,4
Mackrell, W H C (Auckland) 1906 *F*
Macky, J V (Auckland) 1913 *A* 2
Maguire, J R (Auckland) 1910 *A* 1,2,3
Mahoney, A (Bush) 1935 *S, I, W*, 1936 *E*
Mains, L W (Otago) 1971 *BI* 2,3,4, 1976 *I*
Major, J (Taranaki) 1967 *A*
Manchester, J E (Canterbury) 1932 *A* 1,2,3, 1934 *A* 1,2, 1935 *S, I, W*, 1936 *E*
Mason, D F (Wellington) 1947 *A* 2(R)
Masters, R R (Canterbury) 1924 *I, W*, 1925 *E, F*
Mataira, H K (Hawke's Bay) 1934 *A* 2
Matheson, J D (Otago) 1972 *A* 1,2,3, *W, S*
Max, D S (Nelson) 1931 *A*, 1934 *A* 1,2
Meads, C E (King Country) 1957 *A* 1,2, 1958 *A* 1,2,3, 1959 *BI* 2,3,4, 1960 *SA* 1,2,3,4, 1961 *F* 1,2,3, 1962 *A* 1,2,3,5, 1963 *E* 1,2, *I, W*, 1964 *E, S, F, A* 1,2,3, 1965 *SA* 1,2,3,4, 1966 *BI* 1,2,3,4, 1967 *A, E, W, F, S*, 1968 *A* 1,2, *F* 1,2,3, 1969 *W* 1,2, 1970 *SA* 3,4, 1971 *BI* 1,2,3,4
Meads, S T (King Country) 1961 *F* 1, 1962 *A* 4,5, 1963 *I*, 1964 *A* 1,2,3, 1965 *SA* 1,2,3,4, 1966 *BI* 1,2,3,4
Meates, K F (Canterbury) 1952 *A* 1,2
Meates, W A (Otago) 1949 *SA* 2,3,4, 1950 *BI* 1,2,3,4
Metcalfe, T C (Southland) 1931 *A*, 1932 *A* 1
Mexted, G G (Wellington) 1950 *BI* 4

Mexted, M G (Wellington) 1979 *S, E*, 1980 *A* 1,2,3, *W*, 1981 *S* 1,2, *SA* 1,2,3, *R, F* 1,2, 1982 *A* 1,2,3, 1983 *BI* 1,2,3,4, *A, S, E*, 1984 *F* 1,2, *A* 1,2,3, 1985 *E* 1,2, *A, Arg* 1,2
Mill, J J (Hawke's Bay, Wairarapa) 1924 *W*, 1925 *E, F*, 1930 *BI* 1
Milliken, H M (Canterbury) 1938 *A* 1,2,3
Milner, H P (Wanganui) 1970 *SA* 3
Mitchell, N A (Southland, Otago) 1935 *S, I, W*, 1936 *E, A* 2, 1937 *SA* 3, 1938 *A* 1,2
Mitchell, T W (Canterbury) 1976 *SA* 4(R)
Mitchell, W J (Canterbury) 1910 *A* 2,3
Mitchinson, F E (Wellington) 1907 *A* 1,2,3, 1908 *AW* 1,2,3, 1910 *A* 1,2,3, 1913 *A* 1(R), *US*
Moffitt, J E (Wellington) 1921 *SA* 1,2,3
Moore, G J T (Otago) 1949 *A* 1
Moreton, R C (Canterbury) 1962 *A* 3,4, 1964 *A* 1,2,3, 1965 *SA* 2,3
Morgan, J E (North Auckland) 1974 *A* 3, *I*, 1976 *SA* 2,3,4
Morris, T J (Nelson Bays) 1972 *A* 1,2,3
Morrison, T C (South Canterbury) 1938 *A* 1,2,3
Morrison, T G (Otago) 1973 *E*(R)
Morrissey, P J (Canterbury) 1962 *A* 3,4,5
Mourie, G N K (Taranaki) 1977 *BI*, 3,4, *F* 1,2, 1978 *I, W, E, S*, 1979 *F* 1,2, *A, S, E*, 1980 *W*, 1981 *S* 1,2, *F* 1,2, 1982 *A* 1,2,3
Muller, B L (Taranaki) 1967 *A, E, W, F*, 1968 *A* 1, *F* 1, 1969 *W* 1, 1970 *SA* 1,2,3,4, 1971 *BI* 1,2,3,4
Mumm, W J (Buller) 1949 *A* 1
Murdoch, K (Otago) 1970 *SA* 4, 1972 *A* 3, *W*
Murdoch, P H (Auckland) 1964 *A* 2,3, 1965 *SA* 1,2,3
Murray, H V (Canterbury) 1913 *A* 1, *US*, 1914 *A* 2,3
Murray, P C (Wanganui) 1908 *AW* 2
Myers, R G (Waikato) 1978 *A* 3
Mynott, H J (Taranaki) 1905 *I, W*, 1906 *F*, 1907 *A* 1,2,3, 1910 *A* 1,3

Nathan, W J (Auckland) 1962 *A* 1,2,3,4,5, 1963 *E* 1,2, *W*, 1964 *F*, 1966 *BI* 1,2,3,4, 1967 *A*
Nelson, K A (Otago) 1962 *A* 4,5
Nepia, G (Hawke's Bay, East Coast) 1924 *I, W*, 1925 *E, F*, 1929 *A* 1, 1930 *BI* 1,2,3,4
Nesbit, S R (Auckland) 1960 *SA* 2,3
Newton, F (Canterbury) 1905 *E, W*, 1906 *F*
Nicholls, H E (Wellington) 1921 *SA* 1
Nicholls, M F (Wellington) 1921 *SA* 1,2,3, 1924 *I, W*, 1925 *E, F*, 1928 *SA* 4, 1930 *BI* 2,3
Nicholson, G W (Auckland) 1903 *A*, 1904 *BI*, 1907 *A* 2,3
Norton, R W (Canterbury) 1971 *BI* 1,2,3,4, 1972 *A* 1,2,3, *W, S*, 1973 *E, I, F, E*, 1974 *A* 1,2,3, *I*, 1975 *S*, 1976 *I, SA* 1,2,3,4, 1977 *BI* 1,2,3,4

O'Brien, J G (Auckland) 1914 *A* 1
O'Callaghan, M W (Manawatu) 1968 *F* 1,2,3
O'Callaghan, T R (Wellington) 1949 *A* 2
O'Donnell, D H (Wellington) 1949 *A* 2
Old, G H (Manawatu) 1981 *SA* 3, *R*(R), 1982 *A* 1(R)
O'Leary, M J (Auckland) 1910 *A* 1,3, 1913 *A* 2,3
Oliver, C J (Canterbury) 1929 *A* 1,2,3, 1934 *A* 1, 1935 *S, I, W*, 1936 *E*
Oliver, D J (Wellington) 1930 *BI* 1,2
Oliver, D O (Otago) 1954 *I, F*
Oliver, F J (Southland, Otago, Manawatu) 1976 *SA* 4, 1977 *BI* 1,2,3,4, *F* 1,2, 1978 *A* 1,2,3, *I, W, E, S*, 1979 *F* 1,2, 1981 *SA* 2
Orr, R W (Otago) 1949 *A* 1
Osborne, W M (Wanganui) 1975 *S*, 1976 *SA* 2(R), 4(R), 1977 *BI* 1,2,3,4, *F* 1(R), 2, 1978 *I, W, E, S*, 1980 *W*, 1982 *A* 1,3
O'Sullivan, J M (Taranaki) 1905 *S, I, E, W*, 1907 *A* 3
O'Sullivan, T P A (Taranaki) 1960 *SA* 1, 1961 *F* 1, 1962 *A* 1,2

Page, J R (Wellington) 1931 *A*, 1932 *A* 1,2,3, 1934 *A* 1,2
Palmer, B P (Auckland) 1929 *A* 2, 1932 *A* 2,3
Parker, J H (Canterbury) 1924 *I, W*, 1925 *E*
Parkhill, A A (Otago) 1937 *SA* 1,2,3, 1938 *A* 1,2,3
Parkinson, R M (Poverty Bay) 1972 *A* 1,2,3, *W, S*, 1973 *E, E*
Paterson, A M (Otago) 1908 *AW* 2,3, 1910 *A* 1,2,3

Paton, H (Otago) 1910 *A* 1,3
Phillips, W J (King Country) 1937 *SA* 2, 1938 *A* 1,2
Pickering, E A R (Waikato) 1958 *A* 2, 1959 *BI* 1,4
Pierce, M J (Wellington) 1985 *E* 1,2, *A*, *Arg* 1, 1986 *A* 2,3, *F* 2,3, 1987 [*It, Arg, S, W, F*], *A*, 1988 *W* 1,2, *A* 1,2,3
Pokere, S T (Southland, Auckland) 1981 *SA* 3, 1982 *A* 1,2,3, 1983 *BI* 1,2,3,4, *A, S, E*, 1984 *F* 1,2, *A* 2,3, 1985 *E* 1,2, *A*
Pollock, H R (Wellington) 1932 *A* 1,2,3, 1936 *A* 1,2
Porter, C G (Wellington) 1925 *F*, 1929 *A* 2,3, 1930 *BI* 1,2,3,4
Procter, A C (Otago) 1932 *A* 1
Purdue, C A (Southland) 1905 *A*
Purdue, E (Southland) 1905 *A*
Purdue, G B (Southland) 1931 *A*, 1932 *A* 1,2,3
Purvis, N A (Otago) 1976 *I*

Quaid, C E (Otago) 1938 *A* 1,2

Rangi, R E (Auckland) 1964 *A* 2,3, 1965 *SA* 1,2,3,4, 1966 *BI* 1,2,3,4
Rankin, J G (Canterbury) 1936 *A* 1,2, 1937 *SA* 2
Reedy, W J (Wellington) 1908 *AW* 2,3
Reid, A R (Waikato) 1952 *A* 1, 1956 *SA* 3,4, 1957 *A* 1,2
Reid, H R (Bay of Plenty) 1980 *A* 1,2, *W*, 1983 *S, E*, 1985 *Arg* 1,2, 1986 *A* 2,3
Reid, K H (Wairarapa) 1929 *A* 1,3
Reid, S T (Hawke's Bay) 1935 *S, I, W*, 1936 *E, A* 1,2, 1937 *SA* 1,2,3
Reside, W B (Wairarapa) 1929 *A* 1
Rhind, P K (Canterbury) 1946 *A* 1,2
Richardson, J (Otago, Southland) 1921 *SA* 1,2,3, 1924 *I, W*, 1925 *E, F*
Rickit, H (Waikato) 1981 *S* 1,2
Ridland, A J (Southland) 1910 *A* 1,2,3
Roberts, E J (Wellington) 1914 *A* 1,2,3, 1921 *SA* 2,3
Roberts, F (Wellington) 1905 *S, I, E, W*, 1907 *A* 1,2,3, 1908 *AW* 1,3, 1910 *A* 1,2,3
Roberts, R W (Taranaki) 1913 *A* 1, *US*, 1914 *A* 1,2,3
Robertson, B J (Counties) 1972 *A* 1,3, *S*, 1973 *E, I, F* 1974 *A* 1,2,3, *I*, 1976 *I, SA* 1,2,3,4, 1977 *BI* 1,3,4, *F* 1,2, 1978 *A* 1,2,3, *W, E, S*, 1979 *F* 1,2, *A*, 1980 *A* 2,3, *W*, 1981 *S* 1,2
Robertson, D J (Otago) 1974 *A* 1,2,3, *I*, 1975 *S*, 1976 *I, SA* 1,3,4, 1977 *BI* 1
Robilliard, A C C (Canterbury) 1928 *SA* 1,2,3,4
Robinson, C E (Southland) 1951 *A* 1,2,3, 1952 *A* 1,2
Rollerson, D L (Manawatu) 1980 *W*, 1981 *S* 2, *SA* 1,2,3, *R, F* 1(R), 2
Roper, R A (Taranaki) 1949 *A* 2, 1950 *BI* 1,2,3,4
Rowley, H C B (Wanganui) 1949 *A* 2
Rutledge, L M (Southland) 1978 *A* 1,2,3, *I, W, E, S*, 1979 *F* 1,2, *A*, 1980 *A* 1,2,3
Ryan, J (Wellington) 1910 *A* 2, 1914 *A* 1,2,3

Sadler, B S (Wellington) 1935 *S, I, W*, 1936 *A* 1,2
Salmon, J L B (Wellington) 1981 *R, F* 1, 2(R)
Savage, L T (Canterbury) 1949 *SA* 1,2,4
Saxton, C K (South Canterbury) 1938 *A* 1,2,3
Schuster, J N (Wellington) 1988 *A* 1,2,3
Scott, R W H (Auckland) 1946 *A* 1,2, 1947 *A* 1,2, 1949 *SA* 1,2,3,4, 1950 *BI* 1,2,3,4, 1953 *W*, 1954 *I, E, S, F*
Scown, A I (Taranaki) 1972 *A* 1,2,3, *W*(R), *S*
Scrimshaw, G (Canterbury) 1928 *SA* 1
Seear, G A (Otago) 1977 *F* 1,2, 1978 *A* 1,2,3, *I, W, E, S*, 1979 *F* 1,2, *A*
Seeling, C E (Auckland) 1904 *BI*, 1905 *S, I, E, W*, 1906 *F*, 1907 *A* 1,2, 1908 *AW* 1,2,3
Sellars, G M V (Auckland) 1913 *A* 1, *US*
Shaw, M W (Manawatu, Hawke's Bay) 1980 *A* 1,2,3(R), *W*, 1981 *S* 1,2, *SA* 1,2, 1981 *R, F* 1,2, 1982 *A* 1,2,3, 1983 *BI* 1,2,3,4, *A, S, E*, 1984 *F* 1,2, *A* 1, 1985 *E* 1,2, *A, Arg* 1,2, 1986 *A* 3
Shelford, F N K (Bay of Plenty) 1981 *SA* 3, *R*, 1984 *A* 2,3
Shelford, W T (North Harbour) 1986 *F* 2,3, 1987 [*It, Fj, S, W, F*], *A*, 1988 *W* 1,2, *A* 1,2,3
Siddells, S K (Wellington) 1921 *SA* 3
Simon, H J (Otago) 1937 *SA* 1,2,3
Simpson, J G (Auckland) 1947 *A* 1,2, 1949 *SA* 1,2,3,4, 1950 *BI* 1,2,3
Simpson, V L J (Canterbury) 1985 *Arg* 1,2

Sims, G S (Otago) 1972 *A* 2
Skeen, J R (Auckland) 1952 *A* 2
Skinner, K L (Otago, Counties) 1949 *SA* 1,2,3,4, 1950 *BI* 1,2,3,4, 1951 *A* 1,2,3, 1952 *A* 1,2, 1953 *W*, 1954 *I, E, S, F*, 1956 *SA* 3,4
Skudder, G R (Waikato) 1969 *W* 2
Sloane, P H (North Auckland) 1979 *E*
Smith, A E (Taranaki) 1969 *W* 1,2, 1970 *SA* 1
Smith, B W (Waikato) 1984 *F* 1,2, *A* 1
Smith, G W (Auckland) 1905 *S, I*
Smith, I S T (Otago, North Otago) 1964 *A* 1,2,3, 1965 *SA* 1,2,4, 1966 *BI* 1,2,3
Smith, J B (North Auckland) 1946 *A* 1, 1947 *A* 2, 1949 *A* 1,2
Smith, R M (Canterbury) 1955 *A* 1
Smith, W E (Nelson) 1905 *A*
Smith, W R (Canterbury) 1980 *A* 1, 1982 *A* 1,2,3, 1983 *BI* 2,3, *S, E*, 1984 *F* 1,2, *A* 1,2,3, 1985 *E* 1,2, *A, Arg* 2
Snow, E M (Nelson) 1929 *A* 1,2,3
Solomon, F (Auckland) 1931 *A*, 1932 *A* 2,3
Sonntag, W T C (Otago) 1929 *A* 1,2,3
Speight, M W (Waikato) 1986 *A* 1
Spencer, J C (Wellington) 1905 *A*, 1907 *A* 1(R)
Spiers, J E (Counties) 1979 *S, E*, 1981 *R, F* 1,2
Spillane, A P (South Canterbury) 1913 *A* 2,3
Stanley, J T (Auckland) 1986 *F* 1, *A* 1,2,3, *F* 2,3, 1987 [*It, Fj, Arg, S, W, F*], *A*, 1988 *W* 1,2, *A* 1,2,3
Stead, J W (Southland) 1904 *BI*, 1905 *S, I, E*, 1906 *F*, 1908 *AW* 1,3
Steel, A G (Canterbury) 1966 *BI* 1,2,3,4, 1967 *A, F, S*, 1968 *A* 1,2
Steel, J (West Coast) 1921 *SA* 1,2,3, 1924 *W*, 1925 *E, F*
Steele, L B (Wellington) 1951 *A* 1,2,3
Steere, E R G (Hawke's Bay) 1930 *BI* 1,2,3,4, 1931 *A*, 1932 *A* 1
Stephens, O G (Wellington) 1968 *F* 3
Stevens, I N (Wellington) 1972 *S*, 1973 *E*, 1974 *A* 3
Stewart, A J (Canterbury, South Canterbury) 1963 *E* 1,2, *I, W*, 1964 *E, S, F, A* 3
Stewart, J D (Auckland) 1913 *A* 2,3
Stewart, K W (Southland) 1973 *E*, 1974 *A* 1,2,3, *I*, 1975 *S*, 1976 *I, SA* 1,3, 1979 *S, E*, 1981 *SA* 1,2
Stewart, R T (South Canterbury, Canterbury) 1928 *SA* 1,2,3,4, 1930 *BI* 2
Stohr, L B (Taranaki) 1910 *A* 1,2,3
Stone, A M (Waikato, Bay of Plenty) 1981 *F* 1,2, 1983 *BI* 3(R), 1984 *A* 3, 1986 *F* 1, *A* 1,3, *F* 2,3
Storey, P W (South Canterbury) 1921 *SA* 1,2
Strahan, S C (Manawatu) 1967 *A, E, W, F, S*, 1968 *A* 1,2, *F* 1,2,3, 1970 *SA* 1,2,3, 1972 *A* 1,2,3, 1973 *E*
Strang, W A (South Canterbury) 1928 *SA* 1,2, 1930 *BI* 3,4, 1931 *A*
Stringfellow, J C (Wairarapa) 1929 *A* 1(R),3
Stuart, K C (Canterbury) 1955 *A* 1
Stuart, R C (Canterbury) 1949 *A* 1,2, 1953 *W*, 1954 *I, E, S, F*
Stuart, R L (Hawke's Bay) 1977 *F* 1(R)
Sullivan, J L (Taranaki) 1937 *SA* 1,2,3, 1938 *A* 1,2,3
Sutherland, A R (Marlborough) 1970 *SA* 2,4, 1971 *BI* 1, 1972 *A* 1,2,3, *W*, 1973 *E, I, F*
Svenson, K S (Wellington) 1924 *I, W*, 1925 *E, F*
Swain, J P (Hawke's Bay) 1928 *SA* 1,2,3,4

Tanner, J M (Auckland) 1950 *BI* 4, 1951 *A* 1,2,3, 1953 *W*
Tanner, K J (Canterbury) 1974 *A* 1,2,3, *I*, 1975 *S*, 1976 *I, SA* 1
Taylor, H M (Canterbury) 1913 *A* 1, *US*, 1914 *A* 1,2,3
Taylor, J M (Otago) 1937 *SA* 1,2,3, 1938 *A* 1,2,3
Taylor, M B (Waikato) 1979 *F* 1,2, *A, S, E*, 1980 *A* 1,2
Taylor, N M (Bay of Plenty, Hawke's Bay) 1977 *BI* 2,4(R) *F* 1,2, 1978 *A* 1,2,3, *I*, 1982 *A* 2
Taylor, R (Taranaki) 1913 *A* 2,3
Taylor, W T (Canterbury) 1983 *BI* 1,2,3,4, *A, S*, 1984 *F* 1,2, *A* 1,2, 1985 *E* 1,2, *A, Arg* 1,2, 1986 *A* 2, 1987 [*It, Fj, S, W, F*], *A*, 1988 *W* 2
Tetzlaff, P L (Auckland) 1947 *A* 1,2
Thimbleby, N W (Hawke's Bay) 1970 *SA* 3
Thomas, B T (Auckland, Wellington) 1962 *A* 5, 1964 *A* 1,2,3
Thomson, H D (Wellington) 1908 *AW* 1
Thorne, G S (Auckland) 1968 *A* 1,2, *F* 1,2,3, 1969 *W* 1, 1970 *SA* 1,2,3,4
Thornton, N H (Auckland) 1947 *A* 1,2, 1949 *SA* 1

Tilyard, J T (Wellington) 1913 *A* 3
Tindill, E W T (Wellington) 1936 *E*
Townsend, L J (Otago) 1955 *A* 1,3
Tremain, K R (Canterbury, Hawke's Bay) 1959 *BI* 2,3,4, 1960 *SA* 1,2,3,4, 1961 *F* 2,3, 1962 *A* 1,2,3, 1963 *E* 1,2, *I*, *W*, 1964 *E*, *S*, *F*, *A* 1,2,3, 1965 *SA* 1,2,3,4, 1966 *BI* 1,2,3,4, 1967 *A*, *E*, *W*, *S*, 1968 *A* 1, *F* 1,2,3
Trevathan, D (Otago) 1937 *SA* 1,2,3
Tuck, J M (Waikato) 1929 *A* 1,2,3
Turtill, H S (Canterbury) 1905 *A*
Twigden, T M (Auckland) 1980 *A* 2,3
Tyler, G A (Auckland) 1903 *A*, 1904 *BI*, 1905 *S*, *I*, *E*, *W*, 1906 *F*

Udy, D K (Wairarapa) 1903 *A*
Urbahn, R J (Taranaki) 1959 *BI* 1,3,4
Urlich, R A (Auckland) 1970 *SA* 3,4
Uttley, I N (Wellington) 1963 *E* 1,2

Vincent, P B (Canterbury) 1956 *SA* 1,2
Vodanovich, I M H (Wellington) 1955 *A* 1,2,3

Wallace, W J (Wellington) 1903 *A*, 1904 *BI*, 1905 *S*, *I*, *E*, *W*, 1906 *F*, 1907 *A* 1,2,3, 1908 *AW* 2
Walsh, P T (Counties) 1955 *A* 1,2,3, 1956 *SA* 1,2,4, 1957 *A* 1,2, 1958 *A* 1,2,3, 1959 *BI* 1, 1963 *E* 2
Ward, R H (Southland) 1936 *A* 2, 1937 *SA* 1,3
Waterman, A C (North Auckland) 1929 *A* 1,2
Watkins, E L (Wellington) 1905 *A*
Watt, B A (Canterbury) 1962 *A* 1,4, 1963 *E* 1,2, *W*, 1964 *E*, *S*, *A* 1
Watt, J M (Otago) 1936 *A* 1,2
Watt, J R (Wellington) 1958 *A* 2, 1960 *SA* 1,2,3,4, 1961 *F* 1,3, 1962 *A* 1,2
Watts, M G (Taranaki) 1979 *F* 1,2, 1980 *A* 1,2,3(R)
Webb, D S (North Auckland) 1959 *BI* 2
Wells, J (Wellington) 1936 *A* 1,2
West, A H (Taranaki) 1921 *SA* 2,3
Whetton, A J (Auckland) 1984 *A* 1(R), 3(R), 1985 *A*(R), *Arg* 1(R), 1986 *A* 2, 1987 [*It*, *Fj*, *Arg*, *S*, *W*, *F*], *A*, 1988 *W* 1,2, *A* 1,2,3
Whetton, G W (Auckland) 1981 *SA* 3, *R*, *F* 1,2, 1982 *A* 3, 1983 *BI* 1,2,3,4, 1984 *F* 1,2, *A* 1,2,3, 1985 *E* 1,2, *A*, *Arg* 2, 1986 *A* 2,3, *F* 2,3 1987 [*It*, *Fj*, *Arg*, *S*, *W*, *F*], *A*, 1988 *W* 1,2, *A* 1,2,3
Whineray, W J (Canterbury, Waikato, Auckland) 1957 *A* 1,2, 1958 *A* 1,2,3, 1959 *BI* 1,2,3,4, 1960 *SA* 1,2,3,4,

1961 *F* 1,2,3, 1962 *A* 1,2,3,4,5, 1963 *E* 1,2, *I*, *W*, 1964 *E*, *S*, *F*, 1965 *SA* 1,2,3,4
White, A (Southland) 1921 *SA* 1, 1924 *I*, 1925 *E*, *F*
White, H L (Auckland) 1954 *I*, *E*, *F*, 1955 *A* 3
White, R A (Poverty Bay) 1949 *A* 1,2, 1950 *BI* 1,2,3,4, 1951 *A* 1,2,3, 1952 *A* 1,2, 1953 *W*, 1954 *I*, *E*, *S*, *F*, 1955 *A* 1,2,3, 1956 *SA* 1,2,3,4
White, R M (Wellington) 1946 *A* 1,2, 1947 *A* 1,2
Whiting, G J (King Country) 1972 *A* 1,2, *S*, 1973 *E*, *I*, *F*
Whiting, P J (Auckland) 1971 *BI* 1,2,4, 1972 *A* 1,2,3, *W*, *S*, 1973 *E*, *I*, *F*, 1974 *A* 1,2,3, *I*, 1976 *I*, *SA* 1,2,3,4
Williams, B G (Auckland) 1970 *SA* 1,2,3,4, 1971 *BI* 1,2,4, 1972 *A* 1,2,3, *W*, *S*, 1973 *E*, *I*, *F*, *E*, 1974 *A* 1,2,3, *I*, 1975 *S*, 1976 *I*, *SA* 1,2,3,4, 1977 *BI* 1,2,3,4, *F* 1, 1978 *A* 1,2,3, *I*(R), *W*, *E*, *S*
Williams, G C (Wellington) 1967 *E*, *W*, *F*, *S*, 1968 *A* 2
Williams, P (Otago) 1913 *A* 1
Williment, M (Wellington) 1964 *A* 1, 1965 *SA* 1,2,3, 1966 *BI* 1,2,3,4, 1967 *A*
Willocks, C (Otago) 1946 *A* 1,2, 1949 *SA* 1,3,4
Wilson, B W (Otago) 1977 *BI* 3,4, 1978 *A* 1,2,3, 1979 *F* 1,2, *A*
Wilson, D D (Canterbury) 1954 *E*, *S*
Wilson, H W (Otago) 1949 *A* 1, 1950 *BI* 4, 1951 *A* 1,2,3
Wilson, N A (Wellington) 1908 *AW* 1,2, 1910 *A* 1,2,3, 1913 *A* 2,3, 1914 *A* 1,2,3
Wilson, N L (Otago) 1951 *A* 1,2,3
Wilson, R G (Canterbury) 1979 *S*, *E*
Wilson, S S (Wellington) 1977 *F* 1,2, 1978 *A* 1,2,3, *I*, *W*, *E*, *S*, 1979 *F* 1,2, *A*, *S*, *E*, 1980 *A* 1, *W*, 1981 *S* 1,2, *SA* 1,2,3, *R*, *F* 1,2, 1982 *A* 1,2,3, 1983 *BI* 1,2,3,4, *A*, *S*, *E*
Wolfe, T N (Wellington, Taranaki) 1961 *F* 1,2,3, 1962 *A* 2,3, 1963 *E* 1
Wood, M E (Canterbury, Auckland) 1903 *A*, 1904 *BI*
Woodman, F A (North Auckland) 1981 *SA* 1,2, *F* 2
Wrigley, E (Wairarapa) 1905 *A*
Wright, T J (Auckland) 1986 *F* 1, *A* 1, 1987 [*Arg*], 1988 *W* 1,2, *A* 1,2,3
Wylie, J T (Auckland) 1913 *A* 1, *US*
Wyllie, A J (Canterbury) 1970 *SA* 2,3, 1971 *BI* 2,3,4, 1972 *W*, *S*, 1973 *E*, *I*, *F*, *E*

Yates, V M (North Auckland) 1961 *F* 1,2,3
Young, D (Canterbury) 1956 *SA* 2, 1958 *A* 1,2,3, 1960 *SA* 1,2,3,4, 1961 *F* 1,2,3, 1962 *A* 1,2,3,5, 1963 *E* 1,2, *I*, *W*, 1964 *E*, *S*, *F*

NEW ZEALAND INTERNATIONAL RECORDS

Both team and individual records are for official New Zealand international matches, up to 30 April 1989.

TEAM RECORDS

Highest score
74 v Fiji (74-13) 1987 Christchurch
v individual countries
46 v Argentina (46-15) 1987 Wellington
38 v Australia (38-3) 1972 Auckland
38 v British Isles (38-6) 1983 Auckland
42 v England (42-15) 1985 Wellington
74 v Fiji (74-13) 1987 Christchurch
38 v France (38-8) 1906 Paris
17 v Ireland (17-9) 1935 Dublin
70 v Italy (70-6) 1987 Auckland
14 v Romania (14-6) 1981 Bucharest
25 v S Africa (25-22) 1981 Auckland
40 v Scotland (40-15) 1981 Auckland
51 v United States (51-3) 1913 Berkeley
54 v Wales (54-9) 1988 Auckland

Biggest winning points margin
64 v Italy (70-6) 1987 Auckland
v individual countries
31 v Argentina (46-15) 1987 Wellington
35 v Australia (38-3) 1972 Auckland
32 v B Isles (38-6) 1983 Auckland
27 v England (42-15) 1985 Wellington
61 v Fiji (74-13) 1987 Christchurch
30 v France (38-8) 1906 Paris
15 v Ireland (15-0) 1905 Dublin
64 v Italy (70-6) 1987 Auckland
8 v Romania (14-6) 1981 Bucharest
17 v S Africa (20-3) 1965 Auckland
27 v Scotland (30-3) 1987 Christchurch
48 v United States (51-3) 1913 Berkeley
49 v Wales (52-3) 1988 Christchurch

Highest score by opposing team
30 Australia (16-30) 1978 Auckland
by individual countries
21 Argentina (21-21) 1985 Buenos Aires
30 Australia (16-30) 1978 Auckland
17 B Isles (18-17) 1959 Dunedin
16 England (10-16) 1973 Auckland
13 Fiji (74-13) 1987 Christchurch
24 France (19-24) 1979 Auckland
10 Ireland (10-10) 1973 Dublin
6 Italy (70-6) 1987 Auckland
6 Romania (14-6) 1981 Bucharest
24 S Africa (12-24) 1981 Wellington
25 Scotland (25-25) 1983 Edinburgh
3 United States (51-3) 1913 Berkeley
16 Wales (19-16) 1972 Cardiff

Biggest losing points margin
17 v S Africa (0-17) 1928 Durban
v individual countries
16 v Australia (10-26) 1980 Sydney
10 v B Isles (3-13) 1971 Wellington
13 v England (0-13) 1936 Twickenham
13 v France (3-16) 1986 Nantes
17 v S Africa (0-17) 1928 Durban
5 v Wales (8-13) 1953 Cardiff
No defeats v Argentina, Fiji, Ireland, Italy, Romania, Scotland or United States

Most tries by New Zealand in an international
13 v United States (51-3) 1913 Berkeley

Most tries against New Zealand in an international
5 by ⎰ S Africa (6-17) 1937 Auckland
      ⎱ Australia (16-30) 1978 Auckland

Most points on overseas tour (all matches)
868 in B Isles/France (33 matches) 1905-06

Most tries on overseas tour (all matches)
215 in B Isles/France (33 matches) 1905-06

INDIVIDUAL RECORDS

Most capped player
C E Meads   55   1957-71
in individual positions
Full-back
D B Clarke   31   1956-64
Wing
B G Williams   36(38)[1]   1970-78
Centre (includes 2nd five-eighth)
B J Robertson   34   1972-81
1st five-eighth
W R Smith   17   1980-85
Scrum-half
S M Going   29   1967-77
Prop
G A Knight   36   1977-86
Hooker
A G Dalton   35   1977-85
Lock
C E Meads   48(55)[2]   1957-71
Flanker
K R Tremain   36(38)[3]   1959-68
I A Kirkpatrick   36(39)[4]   1967-77
No 8
M G Mexted   34   1979-85

[1] *Williams won 2 caps as a centre*
[2] *Meads won 5 caps as a flanker, 2 as a No 8*
[3] *Tremain won 2 caps as a No 8*
[4] *Kirkpatrick won 3 caps as a No 8*

Longest international career
E Hughes   15 seasons   1907-21
C E Meads   15 seasons   1957-71

Most internationals as captain
W J Whineray   30   1958-65

Most points in internationals – 214
G J Fox (13 matches) 1985-88

Most points in an international – 26
A R Hewson v Australia 1982 Auckland
G J Fox v Fiji 1987 Christchurch

Most tries in internationals – 22
J J Kirwan (25 matches) 1984-88

Most tries in an international – 4
D McGregor v England 1905 Crystal Palace

C I Green v Fiji 1987 Christchurch
J A Gallagher v Fiji 1987 Christchurch
J J Kirwan v Wales 1988 Christchurch

Most conversions in internationals – 53
G J Fox (13 matches) 1985-88

Most conversions in an international – 10
G J Fox v Fiji 1987 Christchurch

Most dropped goals in internationals – 5
D B Clarke (31 matches) 1956-64

Most penalty goals in internationals – 43
A R Hewson (19 matches) 1981-84

Most points in international series – 46
A R Hewson (4 appearances) v B Isles 1983

Most points in international series on tour – 37
G J Fox (3 appearances) 1988
Australia

Most tries in international series on tour – 5
K Svenson (4 appearances) 1924-25
B Isles/France
Svenson scored in each match of the international series

Most points on tour – 230
W J Wallace (25 appearances) 1905-06
B Isles/France

Most tries on tour – 42
J Hunter (23 appearances) 1905-06
B Isles/France

Most points in a tour match – 43
R M Deans v South Australia 1984
Adelaide

Most tries in a tour match – 8
T R Heeps v Northern NSW 1962
Quirindi

PROSPERING UNDER NEW LEADERSHIP

THE 1988 SEASON IN AUSTRALIA
Greg Campbell *The Australian*

The 1988 Australian rugby season began as the previous 12 months had finished – with controversy. Alan Jones was sacked as national coach and the financial problems surrounding the Concord Oval development in Sydney continued. But by the end of the season Australian rugby had recovered in many areas under a variety of new leaders, its playing results were mixed and the future appeared brighter. In one single year not only did Australia acquire a new coach in Bob Dwyer, but a new president in Mr Joe French, a new captain in Nick Farr-Jones and a new executive director in former international referee Bob Fordham.

Encouragingly, the bitter division between the New South Wales Rugby Union and the Sydney Rugby Union over the Sydney competition structure was finally healed late in the year when common sense ultimately prevailed. Furthermore, the Federal Government announced that rugby would be admitted, on a decentralised basis, to the Australian Institute of Sport. Up to 40 young players, aged between 17 and 21, would receive fully funded Government scholarships. These announcements were most important as they provided much-needed stability and incentive to the code, which continues to resist the threat posed by rugby league. But another, potentially serious, threat emerged late in the year when Luke Hyde, a colts player with the Warringah club, won the right to sue international referee Brian Kinsey and the Sydney Rugby Referees Association after a collapsed scrum in a match against Gordon in 1986 left him quadriplegic. The decision, granted in the New South Wales Supreme Court, could have far-reaching consequences for Australian sport.

The decision to remove Alan Jones as national coach, after four successful years which included a Grand Slam of Test victories in the United Kingdom and Ireland and a Bledisloe Cup series victory over New Zealand, was most controversial. Many felt, despite the disappointments of 1987, that Jones deserved another year while others held that Jones had been in command too long and it was time for a change. A key factor in Jones' overthrow was that a majority of Wallaby players pressed for the change. But it must be stated that Jones' marvellous coaching record and contribution to Australian rugby remains without peer.

There was, therefore, much pressure on Dwyer when he took office again for the first time since 1983. He began with instant success when Australia won the Cathay Pacific-Hong Kong Bank Invitation Sevens, but a week later his team was eliminated by Scotland in the International Sevens in Sydney. Dwyer, working slowly to alter Australia's playing strategy, was fortunate to have a warm-up match when a national XV defeated a star-studded World XV 42–38 prior to the Test series with England. The 2–0 series win over England provided Australia with its first Test victories in five internationals. While the wins, 22–16 and 28–8 respectively, were much enjoyed, Australia failed to play convincingly, which did not bode well for the impending arrival of New Zealand. The faults in the Australian team, on which England failed to capitalise, were brutally exposed by the All Blacks, who retained the Bledisloe Cup by winning the first Test 32–7 and the third 30–9, the second Test being drawn 19–19. Unfortunately, the series was marred by some curious refereeing.

Despite losing the series, the Wallabies headed for England, Scotland and Italy with high hopes of a clean sweep of the internationals. But the team were not sufficiently prepared for the first international against England and were beaten 28–19 in a spectacular match. Once the Australians arrived in Scotland, however, a new-found determination and polish was evident and Scotland paid heavily for the earlier Twickenham loss when they were punished 32–13. It was then a matter of retaining pride in the final international of the tour with a handsome 55–6 win over Italy. By the end of the year, Australia were playing sparkling rugby as evidenced by their wins over the Scots and the 40–22 victory over the Barbarians. Their back play, with David Campese in exceptional form, thrilled crowds everywhere.

During the year ten players won their first caps. They were Rob Lawton, David Carter, James Grant, Brad Burke, Tim Gavin, Peter Kay, Lloyd Walker, Brad Girvan, Scott Gourley and Acura Niuqila. Flanker Simon Poidevin announced his retirement from Test rugby but was enticed back to play against the All Blacks, and so took his Test tally to 50, making him the first Australian to reach this milestone. Campese's six Test tries on the Wallaby tour, which took his tally to 32, saw him consolidate his position as the world record try-scorer.

Rugby ties with South Africa were again a major issue. Farr-Jones, Campese, Poidevin, Ian Williams, Michael Lynagh and Steve Cutler were all invited by the South African Rugby Board to join a World Invitation team to tour the republic in August 1988. But the tour failed to happen when other national unions refused to allow selected players to tour. The Federal Government released a report, *Race and Rugby in South Africa,* which re-affirmed its stand that there should be no sporting links with the republic.

Queensland lost their stranglehold on inter-state rugby when New South Wales won both fixtures, 37–15 and 27–18. This was not a fitting end to the long and distinguished coaching career at state level of former Wallaby coach Bob Templeton. On the domestic scene the Sydney club Randwick again dominated. They qualified for their 13th successive grand final and won their second title in successive years when beating Warringah 26–13. They also captured the Australian club championship by defeating the Brisbane club, Brothers, 27–9.

AUSTRALIAN INTERNATIONAL PLAYERS (*up to 30 April 1989*)

ABBREVIATIONS

Arg – Argentina; *BI* – British Isles teams; *C* – Canada; *E* – England; *F* – France; *Fj* – Fiji; *I* – Ireland; *It* – Italy; *J* – Japan; *M* – Maoris; *NZ* – New Zealand; *S* – Scotland; *SA* – South Africa; *SK* – South Korea; *Tg* – Tonga; *US* – United States of America; *W* – Wales; (R) – Replacement (2[1R]) denotes two appearances, one as a replacement; (T) – Tour to Northern Hemisphere; (ST) – Short tour to Northern Hemisphere. Entries in square brackets [ ] indicate appearances in the Rugby World Cup
N.B. In the summer of 1986, the ARU retrospectively granted full Australian Test status to the five international matches played by the 1927-28 touring team to Europe

Abrahams, A M F (New South Wales) 1967 *NZ*, 1968 *NZ*, 1969 *W*
Adams, N J (New South Wales) 1955 *NZ*
Adamson, R W (New South Wales) 1912 *US*
Allan, T (New South Wales) 1946 *NZ* (2), *M*, 1947 *NZ*, 1947-48 (T) *S, I, W, E, F*, 1949 *M* (3), *NZ* (2)
Anlezark, E A (New South Wales) 1905 *NZ*
Austin, L R (New South Wales) 1963 *E*

Baker, R L (New South Wales) 1904 *BI* (2)
Baker, W H (New South Wales) 1914 *NZ* (3)
Ballesty, J P (New South Wales) 1968 *NZ* (2), *F*, 1968-69 (ST) *I, S*, 1969 *W, SA* (3)
Bannon D P (New South Wales) 1946 *M*
Barker, H S (New South Wales) 1952 *Fj* (2), *NZ* (2), 1953 *SA*, 1954 *Fj* (2)
Barnett, J T (New South Wales) 1907 *NZ* (3), 1908-09 (T), *W, E*
Barry, M J (Queensland) 1971 *SA*
Barton, R F D (New South Wales) 1899 *BI*
Batch, P G (Queensland) 1975-76 (T), *S, W, E*, 1976 *Fj* (3), 1976-77 (ST) *F* (2), 1978 *W* (2), *NZ* (3), 1979 *Arg*
Batterham, R P (New South Wales) 1967 *NZ*, 1970 *S*
Battishall, B R (New South Wales) 1973-74 (ST) *E*
Baxter, A J (New South Wales) 1949 *M* (3), *NZ* (2), 1951 *NZ* (2), 1952 *NZ* (2)
Baxter, T J (Queensland) 1958 *NZ*
Beith, B McN (New South Wales) 1914 *NZ*
Bell, K R (Queensland) 1968-69 (ST) *S*
Bennett, W G (Queensland) 1931 *M*, 1933 *SA* (3)
Bermingham, J V (Queensland) 1934 *NZ* (2), 1937 *SA*
Berne, J E (New South Wales) 1975-76 (T) *S*
Besomo, K S (New South Wales) 1979 *I*
Betts, T N (Queensland) 1951 *NZ* (2), 1954 *Fj*
Biilmann, R R (New South Wales) 1933 *SA* (4)
Birt, R (Queensland) 1914 *NZ*
Black, J W (New South Wales) 1985 *C* (2), *NZ, Fj*
Blackwood, J G (New South Wales) 1927-28 (T) *I, W, S, E, F*
Blair, M R (New South Wales) 1927-28 (T) *F*, 1931 *M, NZ*
Bland, G V (New South Wales) 1932 *NZ* (3), 1933 *SA* (4)
Blomley, J (New South Wales) 1949 *M* (3), *NZ* (2), 1950 *BI* (2)
Boland, S B (Queensland) 1899 *BI* (2), 1903 *NZ*
Bonis, E T (Queensland) 1929 *NZ* (3), 1930 *BI*, 1931 *M, NZ*, 1932 *NZ* (3), 1933 *SA* (5), 1934 *NZ* (2), 1936 *NZ* (2), *M*, 1937 *SA*, 1938 *NZ*
Bosler, J M (New South Wales) 1953 *SA*
Bouffler, R G (New South Wales) 1899 *BI*
Bourke, T K (Queensland) 1947 *NZ*
Bowers, A J (New South Wales) 1927-28 (T) *I*
Boyce, E S (New South Wales) 1962 *NZ* (2), 1964 *NZ* (3), 1965 *SA* (2), 1966-67 (T) *W, S, E, I, F*, 1967 *I*
Boyce, J S (New South Wales) 1962 *NZ* (2), 1963 *E, SA* (4), 1964 *NZ* (2), 1965 *SA* (2)
Boyd, A (New South Wales) 1899 *BI*
Boyd, A F McC (Queensland) 1958 *M*
Brass, J E (New South Wales) 1966 *BI*, 1966-67 (T) *W, S, E, I, F*, 1967 *I, NZ*, 1968 *NZ, F*, 1968-69 (ST) *I, S*
Breckenridge, J W (New South Wales) 1927-28 (T) *I, W, S, E, F*, 1929 *NZ* (3), 1930 *BI*
Bridle, O L (Victoria) 1931 *M*, 1932 *NZ* (3), 1933 *SA* (3), 1934 *NZ* (2), 1936 *NZ* (2), *M*

Broad, E G (Queensland) 1949 *M*
Brockhoff, J D (New South Wales) 1949 *M* (2), *NZ* (2), 1950 *BI* (2), 1951 *NZ* (2)
Brown, B R (Queensland) 1972 *NZ* (2)
Brown, J V (New South Wales) 1956 *SA* (2), 1957 *NZ* (2), 1957-58 (T) *W, I, E, S, F*
Brown, R C (New South Wales) 1975 *E* (2)
Brown, S W (New South Wales) 1953 *SA* (3)
Buchan, A J (New South Wales) 1946 *NZ* (2), 1947 *NZ* (2), 1947-48 (T) *S, I, W, E, F*, 1949 *M*
Burdon, A (New South Wales) 1903 *NZ*, 1904 *BI* (2), 1905 *NZ*
Burge, A B (New South Wales) 1907 *NZ*, 1908-09 (T) *W*
Burge, P H (New South Wales) 1907 *NZ* (3)
Burke, B T (New South Wales) 1988 (ST) *S* (R)
Burke, C T (New South Wales) 1946 *NZ*, 1947 *NZ* (2), 1947-48 (T), *S, I, W, E, F*, 1949 *M* (2), 1950 *BI* (2), 1951 *NZ* (3), 1953 *SA* (3), 1954 *Fj*, 1955 *NZ* (3), 1956 *SA* (2)
Burke, M P (New South Wales) 1984 (T) *E* (R), *I*, 1985 *C* (2), *NZ, Fj* (2), 1986 *It* (R), *F, Arg* (2), *NZ* (3), 1987 *SK, [US, J, I, F, W], NZ, Arg* (2)
Burnet, D R (New South Wales) 1972 *F* (2), *NZ* (3), *Fj*
Butler, O F (New South Wales) 1969 *SA* (2), 1970 *S*, 1971 *SA* (2), 1971-72 (ST) *F* (2)

Calcraft, W J (New South Wales) 1985 *C*, 1986 *It, Arg*
Cameron, A S (New South Wales) 1951 *NZ* (3), 1952 *Fj* (2), *NZ* (2), 1953 *SA* (4), 1954 *Fj* (2), 1955 *NZ* (3), 1956 *SA* (2), 1957 *NZ*, 1957-58 (T) *I*
Campbell, J D (New South Wales) 1910 *NZ* (3)
Campbell, W A (Queensland) 1984 *Fj*, 1986 *It, F, Arg* (2), *NZ* (3), 1987 *SK, [E, US, J*(R), *I, F], NZ*, 1988 (ST) *E*
Campese, D I (Australian Capital Territory, New South Wales) 1982 *NZ* (3), 1983 *US, Arg* (2), *NZ*, 1983 (ST) *It, F* (2), 1984 *Fj, NZ* (3), 1984 (T) *E, I, W, S*, 1985 *Fj* (2), 1986 *It, F, Arg* (2), *NZ* (3), 1987 *[E, US, J, I, F, W], NZ*, 1988 *E* (2), *NZ* (3), 1988 (ST) *E, S, It*
Canniffe, W D (Queensland) 1907 *NZ*
Carberry, C M (New South Wales, Queensland) 1973 *Tg*, 1973-74 (ST) *E*, 1975-76 (T) *I, US*, 1976 *Fj* (3), 1981 *F* (2), 1981-82 (T) *I, W, S, E*
Cardy, A M (New South Wales) 1966 *BI* (2), 1966-67 (T) *W, S, E, I, F*, 1968 *NZ* (2)
Carew, P J (Queensland) 1899 *BI* (4)
Carmichael, P P (Queensland) 1904 *BI*, 1907 *NZ*, 1908-09 (T) *W, E*
Carpenter, M G (Victoria) 1938 *NZ* (2)
Carr, E T A (New South Wales) 1913 *NZ* (3), 1914 *NZ* (3)
Carroll, D B (New South Wales) 1908-09 (T) *W*, 1912 *US*
Carroll, J C (New South Wales) 1953 *SA*
Carroll, J H (New South Wales) 1958 *M* (2), *NZ* (3), 1959 *BI* (2)
Carson, J (New South Wales) 1899 *BI*
Carson, P J (New South Wales) 1979 *NZ*, 1980 *NZ*
Carter, D G (New South Wales) 1988 *E* (2), *NZ*
Casey, T V (New South Wales) 1963 *SA* (3), 1964 *NZ* (3)
Catchpole, K W (New South Wales) 1961 *Fj* (3), *SA* (2), *F*, 1962 *NZ* (3), 1963 *SA* (3), 1964 *NZ* (3), 1965 *SA* (2), 1966 *BI* (2), 1966-67 (T) *W, S, E, I, F*, 1967 *I, NZ*, 1968 *NZ*

Cawsey, R M (New South Wales) 1949 *M, NZ* (2)
Cerutti, W H (New South Wales) 1929 *NZ* (3), 1930 *BI*, 1931 *M, NZ*, 1932 *NZ* (3), 1933 *SA* (5), 1936 *M*, 1937 *SA* (2)
Challoner, R L (New South Wales) 1899 *BI*
Chapman, G A (New South Wales) 1962 *NZ* (3)
Clark, J G (Queensland) 1931 *M, NZ*, 1932 *NZ* (2), 1933 *SA*
Clarken, J C (New South Wales) 1905 *NZ*, 1910 *NZ* (3)
Cleary, M A (New South Wales) 1961 *Fj* (3), *SA* (2), *F*
Clements, P (New South Wales) 1982 *NZ*
Clifford, M (New South Wales) 1938 *NZ*
Cobb, W G (New South Wales) 1899 *BI* (2)
Cocks, M R (New South Wales and Queensland) 1972 *F* (2), *NZ* (2), *Fj*, 1973 *Tg* (2), 1973-74 (ST) *W, E*, 1975 *J*
Codey, D (NSW Country, Queensland) 1983 *Arg*, 1984 (T) *E, W, S*, 1985 *C, NZ*, 1986 *F, Arg*, 1987 [*US, J, F*(R), *W*], *NZ*
Cody, E W (New South Wales) 1913 *NZ* (3)
Coker, T (Queensland) 1987 [*E, US, F, W*]
Colbert, R (New South Wales) 1952 *Fj, NZ* (2), 1953 *SA* (3)
Cole, J W (New South Wales) 1968 *NZ* (2), *F*, 1968-69 (ST), *I, S*, 1969 *W, SA* (4), 1970 *S*, 1971 *SA* (3), 1971-72 (ST) *F* (2), 1972 *NZ* (3), 1973 *Tg* (2), 1974 *NZ* (3)
Collins, P K (New South Wales) 1937 *SA*, 1938 *NZ* (2)
Colton, A J (Queensland) 1899 *BI* (2)
Colton, T (Queensland) 1904 *BI* (2)
Connor, D M (Queensland) 1957-58 (T) *W, I, E, S, F*, 1958 *M* (2), *NZ* (3), 1959 *BI* (2)
Cook, M T (Queensland) 1986 *F*, 1987 *SK*, [*J*], 1988 *E* (2), *NZ* (3), 1988 (ST) *E, S, It*
Cooke, B P (Queensland) 1979 *I*
Cooke, G M (Queensland) 1932 *NZ* (3), 1933 *SA* (3), 1946 *NZ*, 1947 *NZ*, 1947-48 (T) *S, I, W, E, F*
Coolican, J E (New South Wales) 1982 *NZ*, 1983 (ST) *It, F* (2)
Corfe, A C (Queensland) 1899 *BI*
Cornelsen, G (New South Wales) 1974 *NZ* (2), 1975 *J*, 1975-76 (T) *S, W, E*, 1976-77 (ST) *F* (2), 1978 *W* (2), *NZ* (3), 1979 *I* (2), *NZ, Arg* (2), 1980 *NZ* (3), 1981-82 (T) *I, W, S, E*
Cornes, J R (Queensland) 1972 *Fj*
Cornforth, R G W (New South Wales) 1947 *NZ*, 1950 *BI*
Costello, P P S (Queensland) 1950 *BI*
Cottrell, N V (Queensland) 1949 *M* (3), *NZ* (2), 1950 *BI* (2), 1951 *NZ* (3), 1952 *Fj* (2), *NZ* (2)
Cowper, D L (Victoria) 1931 *NZ*, 1932 *NZ* (3), 1933 *SA* (5)
Cox, B P (New South Wales) 1952 *Fj* (2), *NZ* (2), 1954 *Fj*, 1955 *NZ*, 1956 *SA*, 1957 *NZ* (2)
Cox, M H (New South Wales) 1981-82 (T) *W, S*
Cox, P A (New South Wales) 1979 *Arg* (2), 1980 *Fj, NZ* (2), 1981-82 (T) *W* (R), *S*, 1982 *S* (2), *NZ* (3), 1984 *Fj, NZ* (3)
Craig, R R (New South Wales) 1908-09 (T) *W*
Cremin, J F (New South Wales) 1946 *NZ* (2), 1947 *NZ*
Crittle, C P (New South Wales) 1962 *NZ* (2), 1963 *SA* (3), 1964 *NZ* (3), 1965 *SA* (2), 1966 *BI* (2), 1966-67 (T) *S, E, I*
Cross, J R (New South Wales) 1955 *NZ* (3)
Cross, K A (New South Wales) 1949 *M, NZ* (2), 1950 *BI* (2), 1951 *NZ* (2), 1952 *NZ*, 1953 *SA* (4), 1954 *Fj* (2), 1955 *NZ*, 1956 *SA* (2), 1957 *NZ* (2)
Crossman, O C (New South Wales) 1929 *NZ*, 1930 *BI*
Crowe, P J (New South Wales) 1976-77 (ST) *F*, 1978 *W* (2), 1979 *I, NZ, Arg*
Curley, T G P (New South Wales) 1957 *NZ* (2), 1957-58 (T) *W, I, E, S, F*, 1958 *M, NZ* (3)
Curran, D J (New South Wales) 1980 *NZ*, 1981 *F* (2), 1981-82 (T) *W*, 1983 *Arg*
Currie, E W (Queensland) 1899 *BI*
Cutler, S A G (New South Wales) 1982 *NZ* (R), 1984 *NZ* (3), 1984 (T) *E, I, W, S*, 1985 *C* (2), *NZ, Fj* (2), 1986 *It, F, NZ* (3), 1987 *SK*, [*E, J, I, F, W*], *NZ, Arg* (2), 1988 *E* (2), *NZ* (3), 1988 (ST), *E, S, It*

D'Arcy, A M (Queensland) 1980 *Fj, NZ*, 1981 *F* (2), 1981-82 (T) *I, W, S, E*, 1982 *S* (2)
Darveniza, P (New South Wales) 1969 *W, SA* (3)
Davidson, R A L (New South Wales) 1952 *Fj* (2), *NZ*

(2), 1953 *SA*, 1957 *NZ* (2), 1957-58 (T) *W, I, E, S, F, 1958 *M*
Davis, C C (New South Wales) 1949 *NZ*, 1951 *NZ* (3)
Davis, E H (Victoria) 1947-48 (T) *S, W*, 1949 *M* (2)
Davis, G V (New South Wales) 1963 *E, SA* (4), 1964 *NZ* (3), 1965 *SA*, 1966 *BI* (2), 1966-67 (T) *W, S, E, I, F*, 1967 *I, NZ*, 1968 *NZ* (2), *F*, 1968-69 (ST) *I, S*, 1969 *W, SA* (4), 1970 *S*, 1971 *SA* (3), 1971-72 (ST) *F* (2), 1972 *F* (2), *NZ* (3)
Davis, G W G (New South Wales) 1955 *NZ* (2)
Davis, R A (New South Wales) 1974 *NZ* (3)
Davis, W (New South Wales) 1899 *BI* (3)
Dawson, W L (New South Wales) 1946 *NZ* (2)
Diett, L J (New South Wales) 1959 *BI* (2)
Dix, W (New South Wales) 1907 *NZ* (3), 1908-09 (T) *E*
Dixon, E J (Queensland) 1904 *BI*
Donald, K J (Queensland) 1957 *NZ*, 1957-58 (T) *W, I, E, S*, 1958 *M* (2), 1959 *BI* (2)
Dore, E (Queensland) 1904 *BI*
Dore, M J (Queensland) 1905 *NZ*
Dorr, R W (Victoria) 1936 *M*, 1937 *SA*
Douglas, J A (Victoria) 1962 *NZ* (3)
Dowse, J H (New South Wales) 1961 *Fj* (2), *SA* (2)
Dunbar, A R (New South Wales) 1910 *NZ* (3), 1912 *US*
Dunlop, E E (Victoria) 1932 *NZ*, 1934 *NZ*
Dunn, P K (New South Wales) 1958 *NZ* (3), 1959 *BI* (2)
Dunworth, D A (Queensland) 1971-72 (ST) *F* (2), 1972 *F* (2), 1976 *Fj*
Dwyer, L J (New South Wales) 1910 *NZ* (3), 1912 *US*, 1913 *NZ*, 1914 *NZ* (3)

Eastes, C C (New South Wales) 1946 *NZ* (2), 1947 *NZ* (2), 1949 *M* (2)
Ella, G A (New South Wales) 1982 *NZ* (2), 1983 (ST) *F* (2), 1988 *E, NZ*
Ella, G J (New South Wales) 1982 *S*, 1983 (ST) *It*, 1985 *C* (R), *Fj*
Ella, M G (New South Wales) 1980 *NZ* (3), 1981 *F*, 1981-82 (T) *S, E*, 1982 *S, NZ* (3), 1983 *US, Arg* (2), *NZ*, 1983 (ST) *It, F* (2), 1984 *Fj, NZ* (3), 1984 (T) *E, I, W, S*
Ellem, M A (New South Wales) 1976 *Fj* (R)
Elliott, F M (New South Wales) 1957 *NZ*
Ellis, C S (New South Wales) 1899 *BI* (4)
Ellis, K J (New South Wales) 1958 *NZ* (3), 1959 *BI* (2)
Ellwood, B J (New South Wales) 1958 *NZ* (3), 1961 *Fj* (2), *SA, F*, 1962 *NZ* (5), 1963 *SA* (4), 1964 *NZ*, 1965 *SA* (2), 1966 *BI*
Emanuel, D M (New South Wales) 1957 *NZ*, 1957-58 (T) *W, I, E, S, F*, 1958 *M* (3)
Emery, N A (New South Wales) 1947 *NZ*, 1947-48 (T) *S, I, W, E, F*, 1949 *M* (2), *NZ* (2)
Evans, L J (Queensland) 1903 *NZ*, 1904 *BI* (2)
Evans, W T (Queensland) 1899 *BI* (2)

Fahey, E J (New South Wales) 1912 *US*, 1913 *NZ* (2), 1914 *NZ*
Fairfax, R L (New South Wales) 1971-72 (ST) *F* (2), 1972 *F* (2), *NZ, Fj* 1973-74 (ST) *W, E*
Farmer, E H (Queensland) 1910 *NZ*
Farr-Jones, N C (New South Wales) 1984 (T) *E, I, W, S*, 1985 *C* (2), *NZ, Fj* (2), 1986 *It, F, Arg* (2), *NZ* (3), 1987 *SK*, [*E, I, F, W*(R)], *NZ, Arg*, 1988 *E* (2), *NZ* (3), 1988 (ST) *E, S, It*
Fay, G (New South Wales) 1971 *SA*, 1972 *NZ* (3), 1973 *Tg* (2), 1973-74 (ST) *W, E*, 1974 *NZ* (3), 1975 *E* (2), *J*, 1975-76 (T) *S, W, I, US*, 1978 *W* (2), *NZ* (3), 1979 *I*
Fenwicke, P T (New South Wales) 1957 *NZ*, 1957-58 (T) *W, I, E*, 1959 *BI* (2)
Fihelly, J A (Queensland) 1907 *NZ* (2[1R])
Finlay, A N (New South Wales) 1927-28 (T) *I, W, S, E, F*, 1929 *NZ* (3), 1930 *BI*
Finley, F G (New South Wales) 1904 *BI*
Finnane, S C (New South Wales) 1975 *E, J* (2), 1975-76 (T) *E*, 1978 *W* (2)
Flanagan, P (Queensland) 1907 *NZ* (2)
Flynn, J P (Queensland) 1914 *NZ* (2)
Fogarty, J R (Queensland) 1949 *M* (2)
Forbes, C F (Queensland) 1953 *SA* (3), 1954 *Fj*, 1956 *SA* (2)
Ford, B (Queensland) 1957 *NZ*
Ford, E E (New South Wales) 1927-28 (T), *I, W, S, E, F*, 1929 *NZ* (2)

Ford, J A (New South Wales) 1927-28 (T), *I, W, S, E,* 1929 *NZ* (3), 1930 *BI*
Forman, T R (New South Wales) 1968-69 (ST) *I, S,* 1969 *W, SA* (4)
Fox, C L (New South Wales) 1927-28 (T) *F*
Fox, O G (New South Wales) 1957-58 (T) *F*
Francis, E (Queensland) 1914 *NZ* (2)
Frawley, D (Queensland, New South Wales) 1986 *Arg* (R), 1987 *Arg* (2), 1988 *E* (2), *NZ* (3), 1988 (ST) *S, It*
Freedman, J E (New South Wales) 1962 *NZ* (3), 1963 *SA*
Freeman, E (New South Wales) 1946 *NZ* (R), *M*
Freney, M E (Queensland) 1972 *NZ* (3), 1973 *Tg,* 1973-74 (ST) *W, E,* (R)
Furness, D C (New South Wales) 1946 *M*
Futter, F C (New South Wales) 1904 *BI*

Gardner, J M (Queensland) 1987 *Arg,* 1988 *E, NZ,* 1988 (ST) *E*
Gardner, W C (New South Wales) 1950 *BI*
Garner, R L (New South Wales) 1949 *NZ* (2)
Gavin, K A (New South Wales) 1908-09 (T) *E*
Gavin, T B (New South Wales) 1988 *NZ* (2), 1988 (ST) *S, It* (R)
Gelling, A M (New South Wales) 1972 *NZ, Fj*
George, H W (New South Wales) 1910 *NZ* (3), 1912 *US,* 1913 *NZ* (2), 1914 *NZ* (2)
Gibbons, E de C (New South Wales) 1936 *NZ* (2) *M*
Gibbs, P R (Victoria) 1966-67 (T) *S*
Gilbert, H (New South Wales) 1910 *NZ* (3)
Girvan, B (Australian Capital Territory) 1988 (ST) *E*
Gordon, G C (New South Wales) 1929 *NZ*
Gordon, K M (New South Wales) 1950 *BI* (2)
Gould, R G (Queensland) 1980 *NZ* (3), 1981-82 (T) *I, W, S,* 1982 *S, NZ* (3), 1983 *US, Arg,* 1983 (ST) *F* (2), 1984 *NZ* (3), 1984 (T) *E, I, W, S,* 1985 *NZ,* 1986 *It,* 1987 *SK, [E]*
Gourley, S R (Eastwood) 1988 (ST) *S, It*
Graham, C S (Queensland) 1899 *BI*
Graham, R (New South Wales) 1973 *Tg* (2), 1973-74 (ST), *W, E,* 1974 *NZ* (2), 1975 *E, J* (2), 1975-76 (T) *S, W, I, US,* 1976 *Fj* (3), 1976-77 (ST) *F* (2)
Gralton, A S I (Queensland) 1899 *BI* (2), 1903 *NZ*
Grant, J C (New South Wales) 1988 *E, NZ* (2), 1988 (ST) *E*
Graves, R H (New South Wales) 1907 *NZ* (R)
Greatorex, E N (New South Wales) 1927-28 (T) *E, F*
Gregory, S C (Queensland) 1968 *NZ, F,* 1968-69 (ST) *I, S,* 1969 *SA* (2), 1971 *SA* (2), 1971-72 (ST) *F* (2) 1972 *F* (2), 1973 *Tg* (2), 1973-74 (ST) *W, E*
Grey, G O (New South Wales) 1972 *F* (R), *NZ* (3), *Fj* (R)
Griffin, T S (New South Wales) 1907 *NZ* (2), 1908-09 (T) *W,* 1910 *NZ* (2), 1912 *US*
Grigg, P C (Queensland) 1980 *NZ,* 1982 *S, NZ* (3), 1983 *Arg, NZ,* 1984 *Fj,* 1984 (T) *W, S,* 1985 *C* (2), *NZ, Fj* (2), 1986 *Arg* (2), *NZ* (2), 1987 *SK, [E, J, I, F, W]*
Grimmond, D N (New South Wales) 1964 *NZ*
Gudsell, K E (New South Wales) 1951 *NZ* (2)
Guerassimoff, J (Queensland) 1963 *SA* (3), 1964 *NZ* (3), 1965 *SA,* 1966 *NZ* (2), 1966-67 (T) *E, I, F*
Gunther, W J (New South Wales) 1957 *NZ*

Hall, D (Queensland) 1980 *Fj, NZ* (3), 1981 *F* (2), 1982 *S* (2), *NZ* (2), 1983 *US, Arg* (2), *NZ,* 1983 (ST) *It*
Hamalainen, H A (Queensland) 1929 *NZ* (3)
Hamilton, B G (New South Wales) 1946 *M*
Hammand, C A (New South Wales) 1908-09 (T), *W, E*
Hammon, J D C (Victoria) 1937 *SA*
Handy, C B (Queensland) 1978 *NZ,* 1979 *NZ, Arg* (2), 1980 *NZ* (2)
Hanley, R G (Queensland) 1983 *US* (R), 1983 (ST) *It* (R)
Hardcastle, P A (New South Wales) 1946 *NZ* (2), *M,* 1947 *NZ,* 1949 *M*
Hardcastle, W R (New South Wales) 1899 *BI,* 1903 *NZ*
Harding, M A (New South Wales) 1983 (ST) *It*
Hartill, M N (New South Wales) 1986 *NZ* (3), 1987 *SK, [J], Arg,* 1988 *NZ* (2), 1988 (ST) *E, It*
Harvey, P B (Queensland) 1949 *M* (2)
Harvey, R M (New South Wales) 1957-58 (T) *F,* 1958 *M*
Hatherell, W I (Queensland) 1952 *Fj* (2)
Hauser, R G (Queensland) 1975 *J* (2[1R]), 1975-76

(T) *W* (R), *E, I, US,* 1976 *Fj* (3), 1976-77 (ST) *F* (2), 1978 *W* (2), 1979 *I* (2)
Hawker, M J (New South Wales) 1980 *Fj, NZ* (3), 1981 *F* (2), 1981-82 (T) *I, W, E,* 1982 *S* (2), *NZ* (3), 1983 *US, Arg* (2), *NZ,* 1983 (ST) *It, F* (2), 1984 *NZ* (3), 1987 *NZ*
Hawthorne, P F (New South Wales) 1962 *NZ* (3), 1963 *E, SA* (4), 1964 *NZ* (3), 1965 *SA* (2), 1966 *BI* (2), 1966-67 (T) *W, E, I, F,* 1967 *I, NZ*
Hayes, E S (Queensland) 1934 *NZ* (2), 1938 *NZ* (3)
Heinrich, E L (New South Wales) 1961 *Fj* (3), *SA, F,* 1962 *NZ* (3), 1963 *E, SA*
Heinrich, V W (New South Wales) 1954 *Fj* (2)
Heming, R J (New South Wales) 1961 *Fj* (2), *SA* (2), *F,* 1962 *NZ* (4), 1963 *SA* (3), 1964 *NZ* (3), 1965 *SA* (2), 1966 *BI* (2), 1966-67 (T) *W, F*
Hemingway, W H (New South Wales) 1931 *M, NZ,* 1932 *NZ*
Henry, A R (Queensland) 1899 *BI*
Herbert, A (Queensland) 1987 *SK*(R), *[F*(R)]
Herd, H V (New South Wales) 1931 *M*
Hickey, J (New South Wales) 1908-09 (T) *W, E*
Hillhouse, D W (Queensland) 1975-76 (T) *S, E,* 1976 *Fj* (3), 1976-77 (ST) *F* (2), 1978 *W* (2), 1983 *US, Arg* (2), *NZ,* 1983 (ST) *It, F* (2)
Hills, E F (Victoria) 1950 *BI* (2)
Hindmarsh, J A (Queensland) 1904 *BI*
Hindmarsh, J C (New South Wales) 1975 *J,* 1975-76 (T) *S, W, US,* 1976 *Fj* (3), 1976-77 (ST) *F* (2)
Hipwell, J N B (New South Wales) 1968 *NZ* (2[1R]), *F,* 1968-69 (ST) *I, S,* 1969 *W, SA* (4), 1970 *S,* 1971 *SA* (2), 1971-72 (ST) *F* (2), 1972 *F* (2), 1973 *Tg,* 1973-74 (ST) *W, E,* 1974 *NZ* (3), 1975 *E* (2), *J,* 1975-76 (T) *S, W,* 1978 *NZ* (3), 1981 *F* (2), 1981-82 (T) *I, W, E*
Hirschberg, W A (New South Wales) 1905 *NZ*
Hodgins, C H (New South Wales) 1910 *NZ* (3)
Hodgson, A J (New South Wales) 1933 *SA* (3), 1934 *NZ,* 1936 *NZ* (2), *M,* 1937 *SA,* 1938 *NZ* (3)
Holt, N C (Queensland) 1984 *Fj*
Honan, B D (Queensland) 1968 *NZ* (2[1R]), *F,* 1968-69 (ST) *I, S,* 1969 *SA* (4)
Honan, R E (Queensland) 1964 *NZ* (2)
Horodam, D J (Queensland) 1913 *NZ* (2)
Horsley, G R (Queensland) 1954 *Fj*
Horton, P A (New South Wales) 1974 *NZ* (3), 1975 *E* (2), *J* (2), 1975-76 (T) *S, W, E,* 1976-77 (ST) *F* (2), 1978 *W* (2), *NZ* (3), 1979 *NZ, Arg*
How, R A (New South Wales) 1967 *I*
Howard, J (Queensland) 1938 *NZ* (2)
Howard, J L (New South Wales) 1970 *S,* 1971 *SA,* 1972 *NZ, F,* 1973 *Tg* (2), 1973-74 (ST) *W*
Howell, M L (New South Wales) 1946 *NZ* (R), 1947 *NZ,* 1947-48 (T) *S, I, W*
Hughes, B D (New South Wales) 1913 *NZ* (2)
Hughes, J C (New South Wales) 1907 *NZ* (2)
Hughes, N McL (New South Wales) 1953 *SA* (4), 1955 *NZ* (3), 1956 *SA* (2), 1957-58 (T) *W, I, E, S, F*
Hutchinson, E E (New South Wales) 1937 *SA* (2)
Hutchinson, F E (New South Wales) 1936 *NZ* (2), 1938 *NZ* (2)

Ide, W P J (Queensland) 1938 *NZ* (2)
Ives, W N (New South Wales) 1929 *NZ*

James, P M (Queensland) 1958 *M* (2)
James, S L (New South Wales) 1987 *SK*(R), *[E*(R)], *NZ, Arg* (2), 1988 *NZ* (R)
Jessep, E M (Victoria) 1934 *NZ* (2)
Johnson, A P (New South Wales) 1946 *NZ, M*
Johnson, B B (New South Wales) 1952 *Fj* (2), *NZ* (2), 1953 *SA* (3), 1955 *NZ* (2)
Johnson, P G (New South Wales) 1959 *BI* (2), 1961 *Fj* (3), *SA* (2), *F,* 1962 *NZ* (5), 1963 *E, SA* (4), 1964 *NZ* (3), 1965 *SA* (2), 1966 *BI* (2), 1966-67 (T) *W, S, E, I, F,* 1967 *I, NZ,* 1968 *NZ* (2), *F,* 1968-69 (ST) *I, S,* 1970 *S,* 1971 *SA* (2), 1971-72 (ST) *F* (2)
Jones, G G (Queensland) 1952 *Fj* (2), 1953 *SA* (4), 1954 *Fj* (2), 1955 *NZ* (3), 1956 *SA*
Jones, H (New South Wales) 1913 *NZ* (3)
Jones, P A (New South Wales) 1963 *E, SA*
Joyce, J E (New South Wales) 1903 *NZ*
Judd, H A (New South Wales) 1903 *NZ,* 1904 *BI* (3), 1905 *NZ*

Judd, P B (New South Wales) 1927-28 (T) *I, W, S, E,* 1931 *M, NZ*

Kassulke, N (Queensland) 1985 *C* (2)
Kay, A R (Victoria) 1958 *NZ,* 1959 *BI*
Kay, P (New South Wales) 1988 *E*
Kearney, K H (New South Wales) 1947 *NZ* (2), 1947-48 (T) *S, I, W, E, F*
Kelaher, J D (New South Wales) 1933 *SA* (5), 1934 *NZ* (2), 1936 *NZ* (2), *M,* 1937 *SA* (2), 1938 *NZ*
Kelleher, R J (Queensland) 1969 *SA* (2)
Keller, D H (New South Wales) 1947 *NZ,* 1947-48 (T) *S, I, W, E, F*
Kelly, A J (New South Wales) 1899 *BI*
Kelly, R L F (New South Wales) 1936 *NZ* (2), *M,* 1937 *SA* (2), 1938 *NZ* (2)
Kent, A (Queensland) 1912 *US*
Kerr, F R (Victoria) 1938 *NZ*
King, S C (New South Wales) 1927-28 (T) *W, S, E, F,* 1929 *NZ* (3), 1930 *BI,* 1932 *NZ* (2)
Knight, M (New South Wales) 1978 *W* (2), *NZ*
Knight, S O (New South Wales) 1969 *SA* (2), 1970 *S,* 1971 *SA* (3)
Knox, D J (New South Wales) 1985 *Fj* (2)
Kraefft, D F (New South Wales) 1947 *NZ,* 1947-48 (T) *S, I, W, E, F*
Kreutzer, S D (Queensland) 1914 *NZ*

Lambie, J K (New South Wales) 1974 *NZ* (3), 1975-76 (T) *W*
Lane, T A (Queensland) 1985 *C* (2), *NZ*
Lang, C W P (Victoria) 1938 *NZ* (2)
Larkin, E R (New South Wales) 1903 *NZ*
Larkin, K K (Queensland) 1958 *M* (2)
Latimer, N B (New South Wales) 1957 *NZ*
Lawton, R (Queensland) 1988 *E, NZ* (2[1R]), 1988 (ST) *S*
Lawton, T (Queensland) 1927-28 (T) *I,W,S,E,F,* 1929 *NZ* (3), 1930 *BI,* 1932 *NZ* (2)
Lawton, T A (Queensland) 1983 (ST) *F* (2[1R]), 1984 *Fj, NZ* (3), 1984 (T) *E, I, W, S,* 1985 *C* (2), *NZ, Fj,* 1986 *It, F, Arg* (2), *NZ* (3), 1987 *SK,* [*E, US, I, F, W*], *NZ, Arg* (2), 1988 *E* (2), *NZ* (3), 1988 (ST) *E, S, It*
Leeds, A J (New South Wales) 1986 *NZ,* 1987 [*US, W*], *NZ, Arg* (2), 1988 *E* (2), *NZ* (3), 1988 (ST) *E, S, It*
Lenehan, J K (New South Wales) 1957-58 (T) *W, E, S, F,* 1958 *M* (3), 1959 *BI* (2), 1961 *SA* (2), *F,* 1962 *NZ* (4), 1965 *SA* (2), 1966-67 (T) *W, S, E, I, F,* 1967 *I*
L'Estrange, R D (Queensland) 1971-72 (ST) *F* (2), 1972 *NZ* (3), 1973 *Tg* (2), 1973-74 (ST) *W, E,* 1974 *NZ* (3), 1975-76 (T) *S, W, I, US*
Lewis, L S (Queensland) 1934 *NZ* (2), 1936 *NZ,* 1938 *NZ*
Lidbury, S (New South Wales) 1987 *Arg,* 1988 *E*
Lillicrap, C A (Queensland) 1985 *Fj,* 1987 [*US, I, F, W*]
Lindsay, R T G (Queensland) 1932 *NZ*
Lisle, R J (New South Wales) 1961 *Fj* (3), *SA*
Livermore, A E (Queensland) 1946 *NZ, M*
Loane, M E (Queensland) 1973 *Tg* (2), 1974 *NZ,* 1975 *E* (2), *J,* 1975-76 (T) *E, I,* 1976 *Fj* (3), 1976-77 (ST) *F* (2), 1978 *W* (2), 1979 *I* (2), *NZ, Arg* (2), 1981 *F* (2), 1981-82 (T) *I, W, S, E,* 1982 *S* (2)
Logan, D L (New South Wales) 1958 *M*
Loudon, R B (New South Wales) 1929 *NZ,* 1933 *SA* (4), 1934 *NZ*
Love, E W (New South Wales) 1932 *NZ* (3)
Lowth, D R (New South Wales) 1958 *NZ*
Lucas, B C (Queensland) 1905 *NZ*
Lucas, P W (New South Wales) 1982 *NZ* (3)
Lutge, D (New South Wales) 1903 *NZ,* 1904 *BI* (3)
Lynagh, M P (Queensland) 1984 *Fj,* 1984 (T) *E, I, W, S,* 1985 *C* (2), *NZ,* 1986 *It, F, Arg* (2), *NZ* (3), 1987 [*E, US, J, I, F, W*], *Arg* (2), 1988 *E* (2), *NZ* (2[1R]), 1988 (ST) *E, S, It*

McArthur, M (New South Wales) 1908-09 (T) *E*
McBain, M I (Queensland) 1983 (ST) *It, F,* 1985 *Fj,* 1986 *It* (R), 1987 [*J*], 1988 *E* (R)
MacBride, J W T (New South Wales) 1946 *NZ* (2), *M,* 1947 *NZ* (2), 1947-48 (T) *S, I, W, E, F*

McCabe, A J M (New South Wales) 1908-09 (T) *E*
McCarthy, F J C (Queensland) 1950 *BI*
McCowan, R H (Queensland) 1899 *BI* (3)
McCue, P A (New South Wales) 1907 *NZ* (2), 1908-09 (T) *W, E*
McDermott, L C (Queensland) 1962 *NZ* (2)
McDonald, B S (New South Wales) 1969 *SA,* 1970 *S*
McDonald, J C (Queensland) 1938 *NZ* (2)
Macdougall, D G (New South Wales) 1961 *Fj, SA*
Macdougall, S G (New South Wales and Australian Capital Territory) 1971 *SA,* 1973-74 (ST) *E,* 1974 *NZ* (3), 1975 *E* (2), 1975-76 (T) *E*
McGhie, G H (Queensland) 1929 *NZ* (2), 1930 *BI*
McGill, A N (New South Wales) 1968 *NZ* (2), *F,* 1969 *W, SA* (4), 1970 *S,* 1971 *SA* (3), 1971-72 (ST) *F* (2), 1972 *F* (2), *NZ* (3), 1973 *Tg* (2)
McIntyre, A J (Queensland) 1982 *NZ* (3), 1983 (ST) *F* (2), 1984 *Fj, NZ* (3), 1984 (T) *E, I, W, S,* 1985 *C* (2), *NZ, Fj* (2), 1986 *It, F, Arg* (2), 1987 [*E, US, I, F, W*], *NZ, Arg,* 1988 *E* (2), *NZ* (3), 1988 (ST) *E, S, It*
McKid, W A (New South Wales) 1975-76 (T) *E,* 1976 *Fj,* 1978 *NZ* (2), 1979 *I* (2)
McKinnon, A (Queensland) 1904 *BI*
McKivat, C H (New South Wales) 1907 *NZ* (2), 1908-09 (T) *W, E*
McLaughlin, R E M (New South Wales) 1936 *NZ* (2)
McLean, A D (Queensland) 1933 *SA* (5), 1934 *NZ* (2), 1936 *NZ* (2), *M*
McLean, J D (Queensland) 1904 *BI* (2), 1905 *NZ*
McLean, J J (Queensland) 1971 *SA* (2), 1971-72 (ST) *F* (2), 1972 *F* (2), *NZ* (3), *Fj,* 1973-74 (ST) *W, E,* 1974 *NZ*
McLean, P E (Queensland) 1974 *NZ* (3), 1975 *J* (2), 1975-76 (T) *S, W, E, I,* 1976 *Fj* (3), 1976-77 (ST) *F* (2), 1978 *W* (2), *NZ,* 1979 *I* (2), *NZ, Arg* (2), 1980 *Fj,* 1981 *F* (2), 1981-82 (T) *I, W, S, E,* 1982 *S*
McLean, P W (Queensland) 1978 *NZ* (3), 1979 *I* (2), *NZ, Arg* (2), 1980 *Fj* (R), *NZ,* 1981-82 (T) *I, W, S, E,* 1982 *S* (2)
McLean, R A (New South Wales) 1971 *SA* (3), 1971-72 (ST) *F* (2)
McLean, W M (Queensland) 1946 *NZ* (2), *M,* 1947 *NZ* (2)
McMahon, M J (Queensland) 1913 *NZ*
McMaster, R E (Queensland) 1946 *NZ* (2), *M,* 1947 *NZ* (2), 1947-48 (T) *I, W*
MacMillan, D I (Queensland) 1950 *BI* (2)
McMullen, K V (New South Wales) 1962 *NZ* (2), 1963 *E, SA*
McShane, J M S (New South Wales) 1937 *SA* (2)
Mackney, W A R (New South Wales) 1933 *SA* (2), 1934 *NZ* (2)
Magrath, E (New South Wales) 1961 *Fj, SA, F*
Malcolm, S J (New South Wales) 1927-28 (T) *S, E, F,* 1929 *NZ* (3), 1930 *BI,* 1931 *NZ,* 1932 *NZ* (3), 1933 *SA* (2), 1934 *NZ* (2)
Malone, J H (New South Wales) 1936 *NZ* (2), *M,* 1937 *SA*
Malouf, B P (New South Wales) 1982 *NZ*
Mandible, E F (New South Wales) 1907 *NZ* (2), 1908-09 (T) *W*
Manning, J (New South Wales) 1904 *BI*
Manning, R C S (Queensland) 1967 *NZ*
Mansfield, B W (New South Wales) 1975 *J*
Marks, H (New South Wales) 1899 *BI* (2)
Marks, R J P (Queensland) 1962 *NZ* (2), 1963 *E, SA* (3), 1964 *NZ* (3), 1965 *SA* (2), 1966-67 (T) *W, S, E, I, F,* 1967 *I*
Marshall, J S (New South Wales) 1949 *M*
Martin, M C (New South Wales) 1980 *Fj, NZ* (2), 1981 *F* (2), 1981-82 (T) *W* (R)
Massey-Westropp, M (New South Wales) 1914 *NZ*
Mathers, M J (New South Wales) 1980 *Fj, NZ* (R)
Maund, J W (New South Wales) 1903 *NZ*
Meadows, J E C (Victoria, Queensland) 1974 *NZ,* 1975-76 (T) *S, W, I, US,* 1976 *Fj* (2), 1976-77 (ST) *F* (2), 1978 *NZ* (3), 1979 *I* (2), 1981-82 (T) *I, S, E,* 1982 *NZ* (2), 1983 *US, Arg, NZ*
Meadows, R W (New South Wales) 1958 *M* (3), *NZ* (3)
Meagher, F W (New South Wales) 1927-28 (T) *I,W*
Meibusch, J H (Queensland) 1904 *BI*
Meibusch, L S (Queensland) 1912 *US*
Melrose, T C (New South Wales) 1978 *NZ,* 1979 *I* (2),

NZ, Arg (2)
Messenger, H H (New South Wales) 1907 *NZ* (2)
Middleton, S A (New South Wales) 1908-09 (T) *E*, 1910 *NZ* (3)
Miller, A R (New South Wales) 1952 *Fj* (2), *NZ* (2), 1953 *SA* (4), 1954 *Fj* (2), 1955 *NZ* (3), 1956 *SA* (2), 1957 *NZ* (2), 1957-58 (T) *W, E, S, F*, 1958 *M* (3), 1959 *BI* (2), 1961 *Fj* (3), *SA, F* 1962 *NZ* (2), 1966 *BI* (2), 1966-67 (T) *W, S, I, F*, 1967 *I, NZ*
Miller, J M (New South Wales) 1962 *NZ*, 1963 *E, SA*, 1966-67 (T) *W, S, E*
Miller, J S (Queensland) 1986 *NZ* (2), 1987 *SK*, [*US, I, F*], *NZ, Arg* (2), 1988 *E* (2), *NZ* (2), 1988 (ST) *E, S, It*
Miller, S W J (New South Wales) 1899 *BI*
Monaghan, L E (New South Wales) 1973-74 (ST) *E*, 1974 *NZ* (3), 1975 *E* (2), 1975-76 (T) *S, W, E, I, US*, 1976-77 (ST) *F*, 1978 *W* (2), *NZ* 1979 *I* (2)
Monti, C I A (Queensland) 1938 *NZ*
Moon, B J (Queensland) 1978 *NZ* (2), 1979 *I* (2), *NZ*, *Arg* (2), 1980 *Fj, NZ* (3), 1981 *F* (2), 1981-82 (T) *I, W, S, E*, 1982 *S* (2), 1983 *US*, *Arg* (2), *NZ*, 1983 (ST) *It, F* (2), 1984 *Fj, NZ* (3), 1984 (T) *E*, 1986 *It, F*, *Arg* (2)
Mooney, T P (Queensland) 1954 *Fj* (2)
Moran, H M (New South Wales) 1908-09 (T) *W*
Morrissey, W (Queensland) 1914 *NZ*
Morton, A R (New South Wales) 1957 *NZ* (2), 1957-58 (T) *F*, 1958 *M* (3), 1959 *BI* (2)
Mossop, R P (New South Wales) 1949 *NZ* (2), 1950 *BI* (2), 1951 *NZ*
Moutray, I E (New South Wales) 1963 *SA*
Murphy, P J (Queensland) 1910 *NZ* (3), 1913 *NZ* (3), 1914 *NZ* (3)
Murphy, W (Queensland) 1912 *US*

Nicholson, F C (Queensland) 1904 *BI*
Nicholson, F V (Queensland) 1903 *NZ*, 1904 *BI*
Niuqila, A S (New South Wales) 1988 (ST) *S, It*

O'Brien, F W H (New South Wales) 1937 *SA*, 1938 *NZ*
O'Connor, M D (Australian Capital Territory, Queensland) 1979 *Arg* (2), 1980 *Fj, NZ* (3), 1981 *F* (2), 1981-82 (T) *I, E*, 1982 *S* (2)
O'Donnell, C (New South Wales) 1913 *NZ* (2)
O'Donnell, I C (New South Wales) 1899 *BI* (2)
O'Donnell, J M (New South Wales) 1899 *BI*
O'Gorman, J F (New South Wales) 1961 *Fj, SA* (2), *F*, 1962 *NZ*, 1963 *E, SA* (4), 1965 *SA* (2), 1966-67 (T) *W, S, E, I, F*, 1967 *I*
O'Neill, D J (Queensland) 1964 *NZ* (2)
O'Neill, J M (Queensland) 1952 *NZ* (2), 1956 *SA* (2)
Osborne, D H (Victoria) 1975 *E* (2), *J*
Outterside, R (New South Wales) 1959 *BI* (2)
Oxenham, A McE (Queensland) 1904 *BI*, 1907 *NZ*
Oxlade, A M (Queensland) 1904 *BI* (2), 1905 *NZ*, 1907 *NZ*
Oxlade, B D (Queensland) 1938 *NZ* (3)

Palfreyman, J R L (New South Wales) 1929 *NZ*, 1930 *BI*, 1931 *NZ*, 1932 *NZ*
Papworth, B (New South Wales) 1985 *Fj* (2), 1986 *It*, *Arg* (2), *NZ* (3), 1987 [*E, US, J*(R), *I, F*], *NZ, Arg* (2)
Parker, A J (Queensland) 1983 *Arg* (2[1R]), *NZ*
Parkinson, C E (Queensland) 1907 *NZ*
Pashley, J J (New South Wales) 1954 *Fj* (2), 1958 *M* (3)
Pauling, T P (New South Wales) 1936 *NZ*, 1937 *SA*
Pearse, G K (New South Wales) 1975-76 (T) *W* (R), *I, US*, 1976 *Fj* (3), 1978 *NZ* (3)
Penman, A P (New South Wales) 1905 *NZ*
Perrin, P D (Queensland) 1962 *NZ*
Perrin, T D (New South Wales) 1931 *M, NZ*
Phelps, R (New South Wales) 1955 *NZ* (2), 1956 *SA* (2), 1957 *NZ* (2), 1957-58 (T) *W, I, E, S, F*, 1958 *M, NZ* (3), 1961 *Fj* (3), *SA* (2), *F*, 1962 *NZ* (2)
Phipps, J A (New South Wales) 1953 *SA* (4), 1954 *Fj* (2), 1955 *NZ* (2), 1956 *SA* (2)
Phipps, P J (New South Wales) 1955 *NZ*
Pilecki, S J (Queensland) 1978 *W* (2), *NZ* (2), 1979 *I* (2), *NZ, Arg* (2), 1980 *Fj, NZ* (2), 1982 *S* (2), 1983 *US, Arg* (2), *NZ*
Piper, B J C (New South Wales) 1946 *NZ* (2), *M*, 1947 *NZ*, 1947-48 (T) *S, I, W, E, F*, 1949 *M* (3)
Poidevin, S P (New South Wales) 1980 *Fj, NZ* (3),

1981 *F* (2), 1981-82 (T) *I, W, S, E*, 1982 *NZ* (3), 1983 *US, Arg* (2), *NZ*, 1983 (ST) *It, F* (2), 1984 *Fj, NZ* (3), 1984 (T), *E, I, W, S*, 1985 *C* (2), *NZ, Fj* (2), 1986 *It, F*, *Arg* (2), *NZ* (3), 1987 *SK*, [*E, J, I, F, W*], *Arg*, 1988 *NZ* (3)
Pope, A M (Queensland) 1968 *NZ* (R)
Potter, R T (Queensland) 1961 *Fj*
Potts, J M (New South Wales) 1957 *NZ* (2), 1957-58 (T) *W, I*, 1959 *BI*
Prentice, C W (New South Wales) 1914 *NZ*
Prentice, W S (New South Wales) 1908-09 (T) *E*, 1910 *NZ* (3), 1912 *US*
Price, R A (New South Wales) 1974 *NZ* (3), 1975 *E* (2), *J* (2), 1975-76 (T) *US*
Primmer, C J (Queensland) 1951 *NZ* (2)
Proctor, I J (New South Wales) 1967 *NZ*
Prosser, R B (New South Wales) 1966-67 (T) *E, I*, 1967 *I, NZ*, 1968 *NZ* (2), *F*, 1968-69 (ST) *I, S*, 1969 *W, SA* (4), 1971 *SA* (3), 1971-72 (ST) *F* (2), 1972 *F* (2), *NZ* (3), *Fj*
Pugh, G H (New South Wales) 1912 *US*
Purcell, M P (Queensland) 1966-67 (T) *W, S*, 1967 *I*
Purkis, E M (New South Wales) 1957-58 (T) *S*, 1958 *M*

Ramalli, C (New South Wales) 1938 *NZ* (2)
Ramsay, K M (New South Wales) 1936 *M*, 1937 *SA*, 1938 *NZ* (2)
Rankin, R (New South Wales) 1936 *NZ* (2), *M*, 1937 *SA* (2), 1938 *NZ* (2)
Rathie, D S (Queensland) 1972 *F* (2)
Redwood, C (Queensland) 1903 *NZ*, 1904 *BI* (3)
Reid, T W (New South Wales) 1961 *Fj* (3), *SA*, 1962 *NZ*
Reilly, N P (Queensland) 1968 *NZ* (2), *F*, 1968-69 (ST) *I, S*, 1969 *W, SA* (4)
Reynolds, L J (New South Wales) 1910 *NZ* (2[1R])
Reynolds, R J (New South Wales) 1984 *Fj, NZ* (3), 1985 *Fj* (2), 1986 *Arg* (2), *NZ*, 1987 [*J*]
Richards, E W (Queensland) 1904 *BI* (2), 1905 *NZ*, 1907 *NZ*
Richards, G (New South Wales) 1978 *NZ* (2[1R]), 1981 *F*
Richards, T J (Queensland) 1908-09 (T) *W, E*, 1912 *US*
Richards, V S (New South Wales) 1936 *NZ* (2[1R]), *M*, 1937 *SA*, 1938 *NZ*
Richardson, G C (Queensland) 1971 *SA* (3), 1972 *NZ* (2), *Fj*, 1973 *Tg* (2), 1973-74 (ST) *W*
Riley, S A (New South Wales) 1903 *NZ*
Roberts, B T (New South Wales) 1956 *SA*
Roberts, H F (Queensland) 1961 *Fj* (2), *SA, F*
Robertson, I J (New South Wales) 1975 *J* (2)
Roche, C (Queensland) 1982 *S* (2), *NZ* (3), 1983 *US*, *Arg* (2), *NZ*, 1983 (ST) *It, F* (2), 1984 *Fj, NZ* (3), 1984 (T) *I*
Rodriguez, E E (New South Wales) 1984 *Fj, NZ* (3), 1984 (T) *E, I, W, S*, 1985 *C* (2), *NZ, Fj*, 1986 *It, F, Arg* (2), *NZ* (3), 1987 *SK*, [*E, J, W*(R)], *NZ, Arg* (2)
Rose, H A (New South Wales) 1967 *I, NZ*, 1968 *NZ* (2), *F*, 1968-69 (ST) *I, S*, 1969 *W, SA* (4), 1970 *S*
Rosenblum, R G (New South Wales) 1969 *SA* (2), 1970 *S*
Rosewell, J S H (New South Wales) 1907 *NZ* (2)
Ross, A W (New South Wales) 1927-28 (T) *I, W, S, E, F*, 1929 *NZ*, 1930 *BI*, 1931 *M, NZ*, 1932 *NZ* (2), 1933 *SA*, 1934 *NZ* (2)
Ross, W S (Queensland) 1979 *I* (2), *Arg*, 1980 *Fj, NZ* (3), 1982 *S* (2), 1983 *US, Arg* (2), *NZ*
Rothwell, P R (New South Wales) 1951 *NZ* (3), 1952 *Fj*
Row, F L (New South Wales) 1899 *BI* (3)
Row, N E (New South Wales) 1907 *NZ* (2), 1908-09 (T) *E*, 1910 *NZ* (3)
Rowles, P G (New South Wales) 1972 *Fj*, 1973-74 (ST) *E*
Roxburgh, J R (New South Wales) 1968 *NZ* (2), *F*, 1969 *SA* (4), 1970 *S*
Ruebner, G (New South Wales) 1966 *BI* (2)
Russell, C J (New South Wales) 1907 *NZ* (3), 1908-09 (T) *W, E*
Ryan, J R (New South Wales) 1975 *J*, 1975-76 (T) *I, US*, 1976 *Fj* (3)
Ryan, K J (Queensland) 1957-58 (T) *E*, 1958 *M, NZ* (3)
Ryan, P F (New South Wales) 1963 *E, SA* 1966 *BI* (2)

Sampson, J H (New South Wales) 1899 *BI*
Sayle, J L (New South Wales) 1967 *NZ*
Schulte, B G (Queensland) 1946 *NZ, M*
Scott, P R I (New South Wales) 1962 *NZ* (2)
Shambrook, G G (Queensland) 1976 *Fj* (2)
Shaw, A A (Queensland) 1973-74 (ST) *W, E,* 1975 *E* (2), *J,* 1975-76 (T) *S, W, E, I, US,* 1976 *Fj* (3), 1976-77 (ST) *F* (2), 1978 *W* (2), *NZ* (3), 1979 *I* (2), *NZ, Arg* (2), 1980 *Fj, NZ* (3), 1981 *F* (2), 1981-82 (T) *I, W, S,* 1982 *S* (2)
Shaw, G A (New South Wales) 1969 *W, SA* (R), 1970 *S,* 1971 *SA* (3), 1971-72 (ST) *F* (2), 1973-74 (ST) *W, E,* 1974 *NZ* (3), 1975 *E* (2), *J* (2), 1975-76 (T) *W, E, I, US,* 1976 *Fj* (3), 1976-77 (ST) *F* (2), 1979 *NZ*
Sheehan, W B J (New South Wales) 1927-28 (T) *W, S*
Shehadie, N M (New South Wales) 1947 *NZ,* 1947-48 (T) *E, F,* 1949 *M* (3), *NZ* (2), 1950 *BI* (2), 1951 *NZ* (3), 1952 *Fj* (2), *NZ,* 1953 *SA* (4), 1954 *Fj* (2), 1955 *NZ* (3), 1956 *SA* (2), 1957 *NZ,* 1957-58 (T) *W, I*
Sheil, A G R (Queensland) 1956 *SA*
Shepherd, D J (Victoria) 1964 *NZ,* 1965 *SA* (2), 1966 *BI* (2)
Simpson, R J (New South Wales) 1913 *NZ*
Skinner, A J (New South Wales) 1969 *W, SA,* 1970 *S*
Slack, A G (Queensland) 1978 *W* (2), *NZ* (2), 1979 *NZ, Arg* (2), 1980 *Fj,* 1981-82 (T) *I, W, S, E,* 1982 *S, NZ,* 1983 *US, Arg* (2), *NZ,* 1983 (ST) *It,* 1984 *Fj, NZ* (3), 1984 (T) *E, I, W, S,* 1986 *It, F, NZ* (3), 1987 *SK, [E, US, J, I, F, W]*
Slater, S H (New South Wales) 1910 *NZ*
Smith, B (Queensland) 1987 *SK, [US, J, I*(R), *W], Arg*
Smith, F B (New South Wales) 1905 *NZ,* 1907 *NZ* (3)
Smith, L M (New South Wales) 1905 *NZ*
Smith, P V (New South Wales) 1967 *NZ,* 1968 *NZ* (2), *F,* 1968-69 (ST) *I, S,* 1969 *W, SA*
Smith, R A (New South Wales) 1971 *SA* (2), 1972 *F* (2), *NZ* (3[1R]), *Fj,* 1975 *E* (2), *J* (2), 1975-76 (T) *S, W, E, I, US,* 1976 *Fj* (3), 1976-77 (ST) *F* (2)
Solomon, H J (New South Wales) 1949 *M, NZ,* 1950 *BI* (2), 1951 *NZ* (2), 1952 *Fj* (2), *NZ* (2), 1953 *SA* (3), 1955 *NZ*
Spragg, S A (New South Wales) 1899 *BI* (4)
Stapleton, E T (New South Wales) 1951 *NZ* (3), 1952 *Fj* (2), *NZ* (2), 1953 *SA* (4), 1954 *Fj,* 1955 *NZ* (3), 1958 *NZ*
Steggall, J C (Queensland) 1931 *M, NZ,* 1932 *NZ* (3), 1933 *SA* (5)
Stegman, T R (New South Wales) 1973 *Tg* (2)
Stephens, O G (New South Wales) 1973 *Tg* (2), 1973-74 (ST) *W,* 1974 *NZ* (2)
Stewart, A A (New South Wales) 1979 *NZ, Arg* (2)
Stone, A H (New South Wales) 1937 *SA,* 1938 *NZ* (2)
Stone, C G (New South Wales) 1938 *NZ*
Stone, J M (New South Wales) 1946 *M, NZ*
Storey, G P (New South Wales) 1927-28 (T) *I, W, S, E, F,* 1929 *NZ* (R), 1930 *BI*
Storey, K P (New South Wales) 1936 *NZ*
Storey, N J D (New South Wales) 1962 *NZ*
Strachan, D J (New South Wales) 1955 *NZ* (2)
Street, N O (New South Wales) 1899 *BI*
Streeter, S F (New South Wales) 1978 *NZ*
Stuart, R (New South Wales) 1910 *NZ* (2)
Stumbles, B D (New South Wales) 1972 *NZ* (3[1R]), *Fj*
Sturtridge, G S (Victoria) 1929 *NZ,* 1932 *NZ* (3), 1933 *SA* (5)
Sullivan, P D (New South Wales) 1971 *SA* (3), 1971-72 (ST) *F* (2), 1972 *F* (2), *NZ* (2), *Fj,* 1973 *Tg* (2), 1973-74 (ST) *W*
Summons, A J (New South Wales) 1957-58 (T) *W, I, E, S,* 1958 *M, NZ* (3), 1959 *BI* (2)
Suttor, D C (New South Wales) 1913 *NZ* (3)
Swannell, B I (New South Wales) 1905 *NZ*
Sweeney, T L (Queensland) 1953 *SA*

Taafe, B S (New South Wales) 1969 *SA,* 1972 *F* (2)
Tancred, A J (New South Wales) 1927-28 (T) *I, W, S*
Tancred, J L (New South Wales) 1927-28 (T) *F*
Tanner, W H (Queensland) 1899 *BI* (2)
Tasker, W G (New South Wales) 1913 *NZ* (3), 1914 *NZ* (3)
Tate, M J (New South Wales) 1951 *NZ,* 1952 *Fj* (2),

NZ (2), 1953 *SA,* 1954 *Fj* (2)
Taylor, D A (Queensland) 1968 *NZ* (2), *F,* 1968-69 (ST) *I, S*
Taylor, J I (New South Wales) 1971 *SA,* 1972 *F* (2), *Fj* 1967 *I, NZ*
Teitzel, R G (Queensland) 1966-67 (T) *W, S, E, I, F,* 1967 *I, NZ*
Thompson, E G (Queensland) 1929 *NZ* (3), 1930 *BI*
Thompson, F (New South Wales) 1913 *NZ* (3), 1914 *NZ* (2)
Thompson, J (Queensland) 1914 *NZ* (2)
Thompson, P D (Queensland) 1950 *BI*
Thompson, R J (Western Australia) 1971 *SA,* 1971-72 (ST) *F* (R), 1972 *Fj*
Thornett, J E (New South Wales) 1955 *NZ* (3), 1956 *SA* (2), 1957-58 (T) *W, I, S, F,* 1958 *M* (2), *NZ* (2), 1959 *BI* (2), 1961 *Fj* (2), *SA* (2), *F,* 1962 *NZ* (4), 1963 *E, SA* (4), 1964 *NZ* (3), 1965 *SA* (2), 1966 *BI* (2), 1966-67 (T) *F*
Thornett, R N (New South Wales) 1961 *Fj* (3), *SA* (2), *F,* 1962 *NZ* (5)
Thorpe, A C (New South Wales) 1929 *NZ* (R)
Timbury, F R V (Queensland) 1910 *NZ* (2)
Tindall, E N (New South Wales) 1973 *Tg*
Tolhurst, H A (New South Wales) 1931 *M, NZ*
Tonkin, A E J (New South Wales) 1947-48 (T) *S, I, W, E, F,* 1950 *BI*
Tooth, R M (New South Wales) 1951 *NZ* (3), 1954 *Fj* (2), 1955 *NZ* (3), 1957 *NZ* (2)
Towers, C H T (New South Wales) 1927-28 (T) *I, E, F,* 1929 *NZ* (2), 1930 *BI,* 1931 *M, NZ,* 1934 *NZ* (2), 1937 *SA* (2)
Trivett, R K (Queensland) 1966 *BI* (2)
Turnbull, A (Victoria) 1961 *Fj*
Turnbull, R V (New South Wales) 1968-69 (ST) *I*
Tuynman, S N (New South Wales) 1983 (ST) *F* (2), 1984 (T) *E, I, W, S,* 1985 *C* (2), *NZ, Fj* (2), 1986 *It, F, Arg* (2), *NZ* (3), 1987 *SK, [E, US, J, I, W], NZ, Arg* (2[1R]), 1988 (ST) *E, It*
Tweedale, E (New South Wales) 1946 *NZ* (2), 1947 *NZ,* 1947-48 (T) *S, I, E, F,* 1949 *M* (3)

Vaughan, D (New South Wales) 1983 *US, Arg,* 1983 (ST) *It, F* (2)
Vaughan, G N (Victoria) 1957-58 (T) *E, S, F,* 1958 *M* (3)
Verge, A (New South Wales) 1904 *BI* (2)

Walden, R J (New South Wales) 1934 *NZ,* 1936 *NZ* (2), *M*
Walker, A K (New South Wales) 1947 *NZ,* 1947-48 (T) *E, F,* 1950 *BI* (2)
Walker, A S B (New South Wales) 1912 *US*
Walker, L F (New South Wales) 1988 *NZ* (2), 1988 (ST) *S, It*
Walker, L R (New South Wales) 1982 *NZ* (2)
Wallace, A C (New South Wales) 1927-28 (T) *I, W, S, E, F*
Wallach, C (New South Wales) 1913 *NZ* (2), 1914 *NZ* (3)
Walsh, J J (New South Wales) 1953 *SA* (4)
Walsh, P B (New South Wales) 1904 *BI* (3)
Walsham, K P (New South Wales) 1962 *NZ,* 1963 *E*
Ward, P G (New South Wales) 1899 *BI* (4)
Ward, T (Queensland) 1899 *BI*
Watson, G W (Queensland) 1907 *NZ*
Watson, W T (New South Wales) 1912 *US,* 1913 *NZ* (3), 1914 *NZ*
Weatherstone, L J (Australian Capital Territory) 1975 *E* (2), *J* (2), 1975-76 (T) *S* (R), *E, I*
Webb, W (New South Wales) 1899 *BI* (2)
Wells, B G (New South Wales) 1958 *M*
Westfield, R E (New South Wales) 1929 *NZ* (2)
White, C J B (New South Wales) 1899 *BI,* 1903 *NZ,* 1904 *BI*
White, J M (New South Wales) 1904 *BI*
White, J P L (New South Wales) 1958 *NZ* (3), 1961 *Fj* (3), *SA* (2), *F,* 1962 *NZ* (5), 1963 *E, SA* (4), 1964 *NZ* (3), 1965 *SA* (2)
White, M C (Queensland) 1931 *M, NZ,* 1932 *NZ* (2), 1933 *SA* (5)
White, S W (New South Wales) 1956 *SA* (2), 1957-58 (T) *I, E, S,* 1958 *M* (2)
White, W G S (Queensland) 1933 *SA* (5), 1934 *NZ* (2), 1936 *NZ* (2), *M*

White, W J (New South Wales) 1932 *NZ*
Wickham, S M (New South Wales) 1903 *NZ*, 1904 *BI* (3), 1905 *NZ*
Williams, D (Queensland) 1913 *NZ*, 1914 *NZ* (3)
Williams, I M (New South Wales) 1987 *Arg* (2), 1988 *E* (2), *NZ* (3)
Williams, J L (New South Wales) 1963 *SA* (3)
Williams, S A (New South Wales) 1980 *Fj, NZ* (2), 1981 *F* (2), 1981-82 (T) *E*, 1982 *NZ* (3), 1983 *US, Arg* (2[1R]), *NZ*, 1983 (ST) *It, F* (2), 1984 *NZ* (3), 1984 (T) *E, I, W, S*, 1985 *C* (2), *NZ, Fj* (2)
Wilson, B J (New South Wales) 1949 *NZ* (2)
Wilson, C R (Queensland) 1957 *NZ*, 1958 *NZ* (3)
Wilson, V W (Queensland) 1937 *SA* (2), 1938 *NZ* (3)
Windon, C J (New South Wales) 1946 *NZ* (2), 1947

NZ, 1947-48 (T) *S, I, W, E, F*, 1949 *M* (3), *NZ* (2), 1951 *NZ* (3), 1952 *Fj* (2), *NZ* (2)
Windon, K S (New South Wales) 1937 *SA* (2), 1946 *M*
Windsor, J C (Queensland) 1947 *NZ*
Winning, K C (Queensland) 1951 *NZ*
Wogan, L W (New South Wales) 1913 *NZ* (3), 1914 *NZ* (3)
Wood, F (New South Wales) 1907 *NZ* (3), 1910 *NZ* (3), 1913 *NZ* (3), 1914 *NZ* (3)
Wood, R N (Queensland) 1972 *Fj*
Woods, H F (New South Wales) 1927-28 (T) *I, W, S, E*
Wright, K J (New South Wales) 1975 *E* (2), *J*, 1975-76 (T) *US*, 1976-77 (ST) *F* (2), 1978 *NZ* (3)

Yanz, K (New South Wales) 1957-58 (T) *F*

AUSTRALIAN INTERNATIONAL RECORDS

Both team and individual records are for official Australian international matches, up to 30 April 1989.

TEAM RECORDS

Highest score
65 v South Korea (65-18) 1987 Brisbane
v individual countries
39 v Argentina (39-19) 1986 Brisbane
13 v British Isles (13-3) 1899 Sydney
59 v Canada (59-3) 1985 Sydney
30 v England (30-21) 1975 Brisbane
52 v Fiji (52-28) 1985 Brisbane
27 v France (27-14) 1986 Sydney
33 v Ireland (33-15) 1987 Sydney
55 v Italy (55-6) 1988 Rome
50 v Japan (50-25) 1975 Brisbane
30 v N Zealand (30-16) 1978 Auckland
37 v Scotland (37-12) 1984 Murrayfield
21 v South Africa (21-6) 1933 Durban
65 v South Korea (65-18) 1987 Brisbane
30 v Tonga (30-12) 1973 Sydney
49 v United States (49-3) 1983 Sydney
28 v Wales (28-9) 1984 Cardiff

Biggest winning points margin
56 v Canada (59-3) 1985 Sydney
v individual countries
26 v Argentina (26-0) 1986 Sydney
10 v British Isles (13-3) 1899 Sydney
56 v Canada (59-3) 1985 Sydney
20 v England (28-8) 1988 Sydney
13 v France (27-14) 1986 Sydney
18 v Ireland (33-15) 1987 Sydney
49 v Italy (55-6) 1988 Rome
30 v Japan (37-7) 1975 Sydney
16 v N Zealand (26-10) 1980 Sydney
25 v Scotland (37-12) 1984 Murrayfield
15 v South Africa (21-6) 1933 Durban
47 v South Korea (65-18) 1987 Brisbane
18 v Tonga (30-12) 1973 Sydney
46 v United States (49-3) 1983 Sydney
19 v Wales (28-9) 1984 Cardiff

Highest score by opposing team
38 { N Zealand (13-38) 1936 Dunedin
     { N Zealand (3-38) 1972 Auckland
by individual countries
27 Argentina (19-27) 1987 Buenos Aires
31 British Isles (0-31) 1966 Brisbane
15 Canada (43-15) 1985 Brisbane

28 England (19-28) 1988 Twickenham
28 Fiji (52-28) 1985 Brisbane
34 France (6-34) 1976 Paris
27 Ireland (12-27) 1979 Brisbane
18 Italy (39-18) 1986 Brisbane
25 Japan (50-25) 1975 Brisbane
38 { N Zealand (13-38) 1936 Dunedin
     { N Zealand (3-38) 1972 Auckland
24 Scotland (15-24) 1981 Murrayfield
30 South Africa (11-30) 1969 Johannesburg
18 South Korea (65-18) 1987 Brisbane
16 Tonga (11-16) 1973 Brisbane
12 United States (47-12) 1987 Brisbane
28 Wales (3-28) 1975 Cardiff

Biggest losing points margin
35 v N Zealand (3-38) 1972 Auckland
v individual countries
15 v Argentina (3-18) 1983 Brisbane
31 v British Isles (0-31) 1966 Brisbane
17 v England { (3-20) 1973 Twickenham
              { (6-23) 1976 Twickenham
2 v Fiji { (15-17) 1952 Sydney
          { (16-18) 1954 Sydney
28 v France (6-34) 1976 Paris
15 v Ireland (12-27) 1979 Brisbane
35 v New Zealand (3-38) 1972 Auckland
9 v Scotland (15-24) 1981 Murrayfield
25 v South Africa (3-28) 1961 Johannesburg
5 v Tonga (11-16) 1973 Brisbane
25 v Wales (3-28) 1975 Cardiff
No defeats v Canada, Italy, Japan, South Korea or United States.

Most tries by Australia in an international
13 v South Korea (65-18) 1987 Brisbane

Most tries against Australia in an international
9 by New Zealand (13-38) 1936 Dunedin

Most points on overseas tour (all matches)
500 in B Isles/France (35 matches) 1947-48

Most tries on overseas tour (all matches)
115 in B Isles/France (35 matches) 1947-48

INDIVIDUAL RECORDS

Most capped player
S P Poidevin 50 1980-88
in individual positions
Full-back
R G Gould 25 1980-87
Wing
B J Moon 35[1] 1978-86
Centre
A G Slack 39 1978-87
Fly-half
M G Ella 25 1980-84
Scrum-half
J N B Hipwell 36 1968-82
Prop
A J McIntyre 37 1982-88
Hooker
P G Johnson 42 1959-71
Lock
S A G Cutler 35 1982-88
Flanker
S P Poidevin 50 1980-88
No 8
M E Loane 26[2] 1973-82
[1]*Campese, 42 caps, has won 31 as a wing and 11 as a full-back*
[2]*Loane won 28 caps altogether, gaining two as a flanker*

Longest international career
G M Cooke 16 seasons 1932-1947/8
A R Miller 16 seasons 1952-1967
Cooke's career ended during a Northern hemisphere season

Most internationals as captain
J E Thornett 16   1962-67
G V Davis   16   1969-72

Most points in internationals – 385
M P Lynagh (30 matches) 1984-88

Most points in an international – 23
M P Lynagh v Canada 1985 Sydney
M P Lynagh v France 1986 Sydney
M P Lynagh v Argentina 1986 Brisbane
M P Lynagh v Italy 1988 Rome

Most tries in internationals – 32
D I Campese (42 matches) 1982-88

Most tries in an international – 4
G Cornelsen v N Zealand 1978 Auckland
D I Campese v United States 1983 Sydney

Most conversions in internationals – 70
M P Lynagh (30 matches) 1984-88

Most conversions in an international – 8
M P Lynagh v Italy 1988 Rome

Most dropped goals in internationals – 9
P F Hawthorne (21 matches) 1962-67

Most penalty goals in internationals – 69
M P Lynagh (30 matches) 1984-88

Most points in international series on tour – 42
M P Lynagh (4 appearances) 1984
B Isles

Most tries in international series on tour – 4
G Cornelsen (3 appearances) 1978
N Zealand
M G Ella (4 appearances) 1984
B Isles
Ella scored in each match of the international series

Most points on overseas tour – 154
P E McLean (18 appearances) B Isles
1975-76

Most tries on overseas tour – 23
C J Russell B Isles 1908-09

Most points in a tour match – 26
A J Leeds v Buller 1986 Westport

Most tries in a tour match – 6
J S Boyce v Wairarapa (NZ) 1962
Masterton

LEADING CAP-WINNERS
(up to 30 April 1989)

ENGLAND

A Neary	43
J V Pullin	42
P J Wheeler	41
D J Duckham	36
G S Pearce	35
D P Rogers	34
W B Beaumont	34
J P Scott	34
P W Dodge	32
R Underwood	32
W W Wakefield	31
F E Cotton	31
M A C Slemen	31
E Evans	30
R Cove-Smith	29
C R Jacobs	29
M P Weston	29
P J Squires	29
P J Winterbottom	29
J Butterfield	28
S J Smith	28
W A Dooley	28
A T Voyce	27
J S Tucker	27
J Carleton	26
C N Lowe	25
J D Currie	25
M S Phillips	25
C B Stevens	25
W H Hare	25
M J Colclough	25
C R Andrew	25
R E G Jeeps	24
P J Larter	24
A G Ripley	24
J MacG K Kendall-Carpenter	23
R W D Marques	23
R M Uttley	23
W J A Davies	22
P E Judd	22
C W Ralston	22

P J Dixon	22
P A G Rendall	22
J G G Birkett	21
H G Periton	21
C R Woodward	21
G H Davies	21
P B Jackson	20
N E Horton	20

SCOTLAND

J M Renwick	52
C T Deans	52
A R Irvine	51
A B Carmichael	50
A J Tomes	48
R J Laidlaw	47
A F McHarg	44
K W Robertson	44
J McLauchlan	43
J Y Rutherford	42
I G Milne	42
H F McLeod	40
D M D Rollo	40
J MacD Bannerman	37
I A M Paxton	36
A R Smith	33
I S Smith	32
F A L Laidlaw	32
I R McGeechan	32
D G Leslie	32
N S Bruce	31
I H P Laughland	31
G L Brown	30
W I D Elliot	29
W M Simmers	28
P K Stagg	28
J W Y Kemp	27
K J F Scotland	27
P C Brown	27
J H Calder	27
D I Johnston	27

G R T Baird	27
W E Maclagan	26
D Drysdale	26
J C McCallum	26
G P S Macpherson	26
J B Nelson	25
J P Fisher	25
J R Beattie	25
J W Telfer	25
G D Stevenson	24
M A Biggar	24
J Aitken	24
M C Morrison	23
J A Beattie	23
M J Campbell-Lamerton	23
J N M Frame	23
W C C Steele	23
B H Hay	23
D R Bedell-Sivright	22
A Robson	22
S Wilson	22
R J Arneil	22
J Jeffrey	22
C Reid	21
R G MacMillan	21
W P Scott	21
W E Kyle	21
J M B Scott	21
J R Paterson	21
W B Welsh	21
P W Kininmonth	21
A J W Hinshelwood	21
D W Morgan	21
W Cuthbertson	21
F Calder	21
D S Davies	20
J C Dykes	20
W R Logan	20
J C Dawson	20
J T Greenwood	20
J W C Turner	20
N A MacEwan	20

IRELAND

C M H Gibson	69
W J McBride	63

J F Slattery	61
P A Orr	58
T J Kiernan	54
M I Keane	51
J W Kyle	46
K W Kennedy	45
G V Stephenson	42
D G Lenihan	42
N A A Murphy	41
W P Duggan	41
N J Henderson	40
R J McLoughlin	40
S Millar	37
H P MacNeill	37
M J Kiernan	37
J R Kavanagh	35
W A Mulcahy	35
E O'D Davy	34
T M Ringland	34
P M Dean	32
A C Pedlow	30
G T Hamlet	30
W E Crawford	30
J D Clinch	30
J L Farrell	29
B G M Wood	29
A J F O'Reilly	29
M Sugden	28
J S McCarthy	28
K D Crossan	28
B J Mullin	28
A M Magee	27
A R Dawson	27
M G Molloy	27
J J Moloney	27
J C Walsh	26
R M Young	26
J B O'Driscoll	26
G R Beamish	25
K D Mullen	25
F P K Bresnihan	25
A T A Duggan	25
B J McGann	25
T O Grace	25
S A McKinney	25
C F Fitzgerald	25

J A E Siggins	24	J Squire	29
P M Matthews	24	R W Windsor	28
W A Anderson	24	A J Gould	27
A Tedford	23	W C Powell	27
J W McKay	23	M C Thomas	27
F Gardiner	22	H J Morgan	27
J A O'Meara	22	A M Hadley	27
A A Mulligan	22	J Davies	27
M K Flynn	22	R N Jones	27
A H Ensor	22	R C C Thomas	26
S O Campbell	22	A E I Pask	26
M T Bradley	22	S J Watkins	26
D G Irwin	22	J Taylor	26
C E Allen	21	G Travers	25
R Roe	21	H Tanner	25
P O'Callaghan	21	B John	25
J C Parke	20	N R Gale	25
J McVicker	20	W D Thomas	25
C J Hanrahan	20	T D Holmes	25
D J O'Brien	20	E Gwyn Nicholls	24
N H Brophy	20	R T Gabe	24
M G Doyle	20	D J Lloyd	24
		B Bowen	24
WALES		P H Thorburn	24
J P R Williams	55	J J Hodges	23
G O Edwards	53	E C Davey	23
T G R Davies	46	J A Gwilliam	23
K J Jones	44	R H Williams	23
G Price	41	J Young	23
T M Davies	38	D L Quinnell	23
D Williams	36	R W R Gravell	23
R M Owen	35	D F Pickering	23
B V Meredith	34	T R Prosser	22
D I E Bebb	34	B L Williams	22
W D Morris	34	W O G Williams	22
A J Martin	34	S J Dawes	22
R L Norster	34	R A Ackerman	22
W J Bancroft	33	R D Moriarty	22
B Price	32	T J Davies	21
J R G Stephens	32	E M Jenkins	21
G A D Wheel	32	B Thomas	21
J J Williams	30	W R Willis	21
S P Fenwick	30	D Watkins	21
W J Trew	29	W G Davies	21
C I Morgan	29	W J James	21
P Bennett	29	P T Davies	21

J A Devereux	21	D Dubroca	33
W P Moriarty	21	J Gachassin	32
W Llewellyn	20	J-P Bastiat	32
A F Harding	20	A Cassayet	31
J Webb	20	A Jauréguy	31
A Skym	20	M Prat	31
		F Moncla	31

FRANCE

		G Cholley	31
R Bertranne	69	D Codorniou	31
S Blanco	68	E Champ	31
M Crauste	63	P Albaladéjo	30
B Dauga	63	A Roques	30
J-P Rives	59	R Bénésis	30
P Sella	58	P Lagisquet	30
R Paparemborde	55	R Biénès	29
J Condom	54	L Mias	29
A Domenech	52	A Lorieux	29
J Prat	51	J Trillo	28
W Spanghéro	51	H Rancoule	27
J-L Joinel	51	P Lacroix	27
M Celaya	50	J-C Berejnoi	27
P Dintrans	49	C Carrère	27
A Boniface	48	J Fouroux	27
J-P Lux	47	J Gallion	27
L Rodriguez	47	J-P Lescarboura	27
J-C Skréla	46	B Chevallier	26
P Berbizier	46	J Barthe	26
M Vannier	43	J-M Cabanier	26
D Erbani	42	A Gruarin	26
J Dupuy	40	J-L Azarète	26
C Darrouy	40	A Vaquerin	26
F Haget	40	R Martine	25
J-M Aguirre	39	J Maso	25
G Dufau	38	J-L Averous	25
J-P Garuet	38	P Estève	25
G Boniface	35		

E Cester	35

SOUTH AFRICA

A Paco	35	F C H Du Preez	38
E Ribère	34	J H Ellis	38
J Bouquet	34	J F K Marais	35
P Villepreux	34	J P Engelbrecht	33
J Iraçabal	34	J L Gainsford	33
J-P Romeu	34	J T Claassen	28
G Basquet	33	F du T Roux	27
C Lacaze	33	L G Wilson	27
C Dourthe	33	T P Bedford	25

D J de Villiers	25
P J F Greyling	25
S H Nomis	25
P J Visagie	25
L C Moolman	24
D J Hopwood	22
A C Koch	22
M Du Plessis	22
J A du Rand	21
M T S Stofberg	21
H E Botha	21
J S Germishuys	20

NEW ZEALAND

C E Meads	55
A M Haden	41
I A Kirkpatrick	39
K R Tremain	38
B G Williams	38
G A Knight	36
A G Dalton	35
B J Robertson	34
S S Wilson	34
M G Mexted	34
G W Whetton	34
W J Whineray	32
D B Clarke	31
M W Shaw	30
S M Going	29
R W Norton	27
B J Lochore	25
J J Kirwan	25
B E McLeod	24
K F Gray	24
I J Clarke	24
J C Ashworth	24
D S Loveridge	24
W T Taylor	24
R A White	23
B G Fraser	23
D J Graham	22
D Young	22
G N K Mourie	21
M J B Hobbs	21
K L Skinner	20

C R Laidlaw	20
I N MacEwan	20
P J Whiting	20
C I Green	20

AUSTRALIA

S P Poidevin	50
P G Johnson	42
D I Campese	42
A R Miller	41
G V Davis	39
A G Slack	39
T A Lawton	38
J E Thornett	37
A J McIntyre	37
J N B Hipwell	36
A A Shaw	36
B J Moon	35
S A G Cutler	35
N C Farr-Jones	31
N M Shehadie	30
P E McLean	30
M P Lynagh	30
S N Tuynman	29
M E Loane	28
S A Williams	28
K W Catchpole	27
G A Shaw	27
C T Burke	26
E E Rodriguez	26
R B Prosser	25
G Cornelsen	25
M G Ella	25
R G Gould	25
P C Grigg	25
M J Hawker	25
J K Lenehan	24
J P L White	24
J W Cole	24
G Fay	24
R Phelps	23
M P Burke	23
R A Smith	22
J E C Meadows	22
E T Bonis	21

P F Hawthorne	21	A S Cameron	20
R J Heming	21	B J Ellwood	20
A N McGill	21	C J Windon	20

WORLD'S LEADING CAP-WINNERS
(up to 30 April 1989)

For purposes of comparison, the following list includes appearances for individual countries in major international matches.

C M H Gibson (Ireland)	69	J Condom (France)	54
R Bertranne (France)	69	G O Edwards (Wales)	53
S Blanco (France)	68	A Domenech (France)	52
M Crauste (France)	63	J M Renwick (Scotland)	52
W J McBride (Ireland)	63	C T Deans (Scotland)	52
B Dauga (France)	63	J Prat (France)	51
J F Slattery (Ireland)	61	W Spanghero (France)	51
J-P Rives (France)	59	A R Irvine (Scotland)	51
P A Orr (Ireland)	58	M I Keane (Ireland)	51
P Sella (France)	58	J-L Joinel (France)	51
C E Meads (New Zealand)	55	M Celaya (France)	50
J P R Williams (Wales)	55	A B Carmichael (Scotland)	50
R Paparemborde (France)	55	S P Poidevin (Australia)	50
T J Kiernan (Ireland)	54		

The following list incorporates appearances by home countries' players for British Isles teams (the Lions) in International matches against New Zealand, Australia and South Africa (up to 30 April 1989). The number of Lions' appearances is shown in brackets.

C M H Gibson (Ireland)	81 (12)	J Condom (France)	54
W J McBride (Ireland)	80 (17)	J M Renwick (Scotland)	53 (1)
R Bertranne (France)	69	G Price (Wales)	53 (12)
S Blanco (France)	68	A Domenech (France)	52
J F Slattery (Ireland)	65 (4)	C T Deans (Scotland)	52
G O Edwards (Wales)	63 (10)	J W Kyle (Ireland)	52 (6)
J P R Williams (Wales)	63 (8)	M I Keane (Ireland)	52 (1)
M Crauste (France)	63	J Prat (France)	51
B Dauga (France)	63	W Spanghero (France)	51
A R Irvine (Scotland)	60 (9)	T G R Davies (Wales)	51 (5)
T J Kiernan (Ireland)	59 (5)	J McLauchlan (Scotland)	51 (8)
J-P Rives (France)	59	J-L Joinel (France)	51
P A Orr (Ireland)	59 (1)	M Celaya (France)	50
P Sella (France)	58	A B Carmichael (Scotland)	50
C E Meads (New Zealand)	55	S P Poidevin (Australia)	50
R Paparemborde (France)	55		

Most appearances for the Lions are by W J McBride 17, R E G Jeeps (England) 13, C M H Gibson 12, G Price 12, and A J F O'Reilly (Ireland), R H Williams (Wales), and G O Edwards 10 each, up to 30 April 1989.

INTERNATIONAL REFEREES 1988-89

Leading Referees

Up to 30 April 1989, in major international matches. These include all matches for which full members of the International Board have awarded caps, and also all matches played in the World Cup final stages.

12 or more internationals

K D Kelleher	Ireland	23	D I H Burnett	Ireland	15
D G Walters	Wales	23	C H Gadney	England	15
M Joseph	Wales	22	J B Anderson	Scotland	14
R C Williams	Ireland	21	I David	Wales	14
A M Hosie	Scotland	19	Dr I R Vanderfield	Australia	14
Capt M J Dowling	Ireland	18	R G Byres	Australia	13
A E Freethy	Wales	18	K V J Fitzgerald	Australia	13
C Norling	Wales	18	J P Murphy	New Zealand	13
R C Quittenton	England	18	N R Sanson	Scotland	13
J R West	Ireland	18	R F Johnson	England	12
D P D'Arcy	Ireland	17	T D Schofield	Wales	12
F Palmade	France	17	T H Vile	Wales	12
B S Cumberlege	England	16	W Williams	England	12

Major international match appearances 1988-89

Matches controlled between 30 April 1988 and 30 April 1989

1988

NZ v W(2)	G Maurette (France)
A v E(2)	D J Bishop (New Zealand)
Fj v E	K V J Fitzgerald (Australia)
Arg v F(2)	O E Doyle (Ireland)
A v NZ	F A Howard (England)
A v NZ(2)	J B Anderson (Scotland)
I v WS	W D Bevan (Wales)
E v A	D J Bishop (New Zealand)
F v Arg(2)	*A McNeil (Australia)
W v WS	O E Doyle (Ireland)
S v A	D J Bishop (New Zealand)
R v F	C Norling (Wales)
It v A	*D Robin (France)
W v R	*I M Bullerwell (England)
I v It	R J Megson (Scotland)

1989

S v W	*J-C Doulcet (France)
I v F	J B Anderson (Scotland)
E v S	G Maurette (France)
W v I	R C Quittenton (England)
F v W	J M Fleming (Scotland)
I v E	*L J Peard (Wales)
S v I	K V J Fitzgerald (Australia)
E v F	S R Hilditch (Ireland)
F v S	O E Doyle (Ireland)
W v E	K V J Fitzgerald (Australia)

* Denotes debut in a major international

Referees dismissing players in a major international

A E Freethy	E v NZ	1925	C Norling	F v I	1984
K D Kelleher	S v NZ	1967	K V J Fitzgerald	NZ v W	1987
R T Burnett	A v E	1975	F A Howard	A v W	1987
W M Cooney	A v Fj	1976	K V J Fitzgerald	Fj v E	1988
N R Sanson (two)	W v I	1977	O E Doyle	Arg v F	1988
D I H Burnett	E v W	1980			

INTERNATIONAL REFEREES

The list which follows shows referees who have controlled major internationals (i.e. games for which a member country of the IB has awarded caps, or an official World Cup match) since 1876, when referees were first appointed, up to 30 April, 1989.

ABBREVIATIONS

A – Australia; *Arg* – Argentina; *AW* – Anglo-Welsh; *B* – British Forces' XV; *BI* – British Isles; *C* – Canada; *Cv* – New Zealand Cavaliers; *Cz* – Czechoslovakia; *E* – England; *F* – France; *Fj* – Fiji; *GB* – Great Britain; *G* – Germany; *I* – Ireland; *It* – Italy; *J* – Japan; *K* – New Zealand Kiwis; *M* – New Zealand Maoris; *NZ* – New Zealand; *NZA* – New Zealand Army; *P* – President's XV; *R* – Romania; *S* – Scotland; *SA* – South Africa; *SAm* – South America; *SK* – South Korea; *Tg* – Tonga; *US* – United States of America; *W* – Wales; *Wld* – World XV; *WS* – Western Samoa; *Z* – Zimbabwe; (C) – Special Centenary Match; (R) – Replacement. Entries in square brackets [ ] indicate matches in the World Cup.

Ackermann, C J (South Africa) 1953 *SA v A* (2), 1955 *SA v BI*, 1958 *SA v F*
Acton, W H (Ireland) 1926 *W v E, E v S*
Alderson, F H R (England) 1903 *S v I*
Allan, M A (Scotland) 1931 *I v W, I v SA*, 1933 *E v I, I v W*, 1934 *I v E*, 1935 *E v I, I v W*, 1936 *I v E*, 1937 *I v W*, 1947 *I v E*, 1948 *I v W*
Allen, J W (Ireland) 1906 *W v S, S v E*
Anderson, C (Scotland) 1928 *I v F*
Anderson, J B (Scotland) 1981 *W v E, I v A*, 1982 *R v F*, 1983 *I v E, A v NZ*, 1984 *E v W*, 1986 *W v F, NZ v A*, 1987 [*A v US, A v I, F v A*], 1988 *A v NZ* (2), 1989 *I v F*
Anderson, J H (South Africa) 1903 *SA v GB*
Angus, A W (Scotland) 1924 *W v E*, 1927 *I v A*
Ashmore, H L (England) 1890 *S v I*, 1891 *S v W*, 1892 *S v I*, 1894 *I v S*, 1895 *S v I*
Austin, A W C (Scotland) 1952 *W v F*, 1953 *I v E*, 1954 *I v W*
Austry, R (France) 1972 *E v I*

Badger, Dr (England) 1900 *I v S*
Baise, M (South Africa) 1967 *SA v F* (2), 1968 *SA v BI* (2), 1969 *SA v A*, 1974 *SA v BI* (2)
Baise, S (South Africa) 1969 *SA v A*
Barnes, P (Australia) 1938 *A v NZ*
Baxter, J (England) 1913 *F v S, S v I*, 1914 *I v S*, 1920 *S v I*, 1921 *W v S, I v S*, 1923 *W v S*, 1925 *W v S, I v W*
Bean, A S (England) 1939 *W v S*, 1945 *W v F*, 1946 *F v W*, 1947 *F v W, W v A*, 1948 *S v F, W v F*, 1949 *S v I*
Beattie, R A (Scotland) 1937 *E v W*, 1938 *W v E*, 1945 *B v F*, 1947 *W v E, I v A*, 1948 *E v W*, 1949 *I v E*, 1950 *E v I, I v W*
Beattie, W H (Australia) 1899 *A v GB*, 1904 *A v GB*
Bell, T (Ireland) 1932 *S v W*, 1933 *E v W*
Bevan, W D (Wales) 1985 *E v R*, 1986 *F v E, NZ v A* (2), 1987 [*NZ v Fj, F v Z*], *A v NZ*, 1988 *I v WS*
Beves, G (South Africa) 1896 *SA v GB*
Bezuidenhout, G P (South Africa) 1976 *SA v NZ* (3)
Bishop, D J (New Zealand) 1986 *Fj v W, R v F, I v R*, 1987 [*W v Tg, W v C*], 1988 *A v E* (2), *E v A, S v A*
Bissett, W M (South Africa) 1896 *SA v GB*
Bonnet, J-P (France) 1979 *W v E*, 1980 *S v E, SA v BI* (2), 1981 *I v E, Arg v E* (2), 1982 *W v S*
Bott, J G (England) 1931 *W v S*, 1933 *W v S*
Boundy, L M (England) 1955 *S v I*, 1956 *W v S*, 1957 *F v S, I v F, S v I, R v F*, 1958 *S v F*, 1959 *S v I*, 1961 *S v SA*
Bowden, G (Scotland) 1910 *F v E*
Bowen, D H (Wales) 1905 *E v S*
Bradburn, T J (England) 1928 *F v A*, 1929 *F v G*
Bressy, Y (France) 1988 *W v S*
Brook, P G (England) 1963 *F v W*, 1964 *W v S*, 1965 *W v I, I v SA*, 1966 *F v I, It v F, R v F*
Brown, A (Australia) 1907 *A v NZ*
Brown, D A (England) 1960 *I v W, It v F*
Brunton, J (England) 1924 *W v NZ*
Buchanan, A (Scotland) 1877 *I v S*, 1880 *S v I*
Bullerwell, I M (England) 1988 *W v R*
Burmeister, R D (South Africa) 1949 *SA v NZ* (2), 1953 *SA v A*, 1955 *SA v BI* (2), 1960 *SA v NZ* (2), 1961 *SA v A*

Burnand, F W (England) 1890 *I v W*
Burnet, W (Scotland) 1932 *I v E*, 1934 *W v I*
Burnett, D I H (Ireland) 1977 *W v E*, 1979 *F v W*, 1980 *E v W*, 1981 *S v W, E v S*, 1982 *W v F, F v Arg*, 1983 *E v F*, 1984 *S v E, A v NZ*, 1985 *E v F, NZ v A*, 1986 *S v F*, 1987 [*S v Z, NZ v S*]
Burnett, R T (Australia) 1973 *A v Tg*, 1974 *A v NZ*, 1975 *A v E, A v J*, 1978 *A v W*
Burrell, G (Scotland) 1958 *E v I*, 1959 *W v I*
Burrell, R P (Scotland) 1966 *I v W*, 1967 *I v F, F v NZ*, 1969 *I v E, F v W*
Butt, C C (Australia) 1914 *A v NZ*
Byres, R G (Australia) 1976 *A v Fj*, 1978 *A v W*, 1979 *A v I* (2), *A v NZ*, 1980 *A v NZ*, 1981 *NZ v S*, 1982 *A v S* (2), 1983 *NZ v BI* (2), 1984 *I v W, W v F*

Calitz, M (South Africa) 1961 *SA v I*
Calmet, R (France) 1970 *E v W*
Calver, E W (England) 1914 *F v I*
Camardon, J (Argentina) 1960 *Arg v F*
Campbell, A (New Zealand) 1908 *NZ v AW* (2)
Carlson, R V (South Africa) 1962 *SA v BI*
Cartwright, V H (England) 1906 *I v S*, 1909 *S v I*, 1910 *I v S, F v I*, 1911 *S v I*
Castens, H H (South Africa) 1891 *SA v GB*
Chambers, J (Ireland) 1888 *W v S, I v M*, 1890 *S v E*, 1891 *E v S*
Chapman, W S (Australia) 1938 *A v NZ* (2)
Charman, R (England) 1919 *W v NZA*
Chevrier, G (France) 1980 *I v S*
Chiene, Dr J (Scotland) 1879 *I v S*
Clark, K H (Ireland) 1973 *E v F*, 1974 *S v F*, 1976 *F v E*
Cochrane, C B (Australia) 1907 *A v NZ*
Coffey, J J (Ireland) 1912 *S v F*
Coles, P (England) 1903 *W v I*, 1905 *S v I*
Collett, C K (Australia) 1981 *NZ v S*
Combe, A (Ireland) 1876 *I v E*
Cook, H G (Ireland) 1886 *S v E*
Cooney, R C (Australia) 1929 *A v NZ*, 1930 *A v BI*, 1932 *A v NZ*, 1934 *A v NZ*
Cooney, W M (Australia) 1972 *A v F*, 1975 *A v E, A v J*, 1976 *A v Fj*
Cooper, Dr P F (England) 1952 *I v W*, 1953 *S v W, W v I, F v It*, *W v NZ*, 1954 *I v NZ, W v S, It v F*, 1956 *F v I, W v F*, 1957 *F v W*
Corley, H H (Ireland) 1906 *S v SA*, 1908 *S v E*
Corr, W S (Australia) 1899 *A v GB* (2)
Costello, J (Fiji) 1972 *Fj v A*
Craven, W S D (England) 1920 *F v W*
Crawford, S H (Ireland) 1913 *W v E, S v W*, 1920 *S v W*, 1921 *S v E*
Cross, W (Scotland) 1877 *S v E*
Crowe, K J (Australia) 1965 *A v SA*, 1966 *A v BI*, 1968 *A v NZ*, 1974 *A v Fj*
Cumberlege, B S (England) 1926 *S v I, W v I*, 1927 *S v F, I v S, I v W*, 1928 *F v I, S v F, I v S*, 1930 *I v F, S v I*, 1931 *I v S*, 1932 *S v SA, S v I*, 1933 *I v S*, 1934 *S v I*
Cunningham, J G (Scotland) 1913 *W v I*, 1921 *F v I*
Cuny, Dr A (France) 1976 *W v S*
Curnow, J (Canada) 1976 *US v F*
Currey, F I (England) 1887 *S v W*

Dallas, J D (Scotland) 1905 *W v NZ*, 1908 *I v W*, 1909 *W v E, I v E*, 1910 *E v W, I v W*, 1911 *I v E*, 1912 *I v W*
D'Arcy, D P (Ireland) 1967 *E v F, E v S, F v W, F v R*, 1968 *E v W, S v E, F v SA*, 1969 *E v F, W v E*, 1970 *W v S*, 1971 *W v E*, 1973 *F v NZ, F v W, F v R*, 1975 *E v S, F v Arg, W v A*
David, I (Wales) 1938 *E v S*, 1939 *S v E*, 1947 *E v S*, 1952 *S v F, I v S, E v I*, 1953 *S v I*, 1954 *S v F, E v NZ, S v NZ, F v NZ, F v E*, 1955 *I v F*, 1956 *F v E*
Davidson, I G (Ireland) 1911 *S v W*
Day, H L V (England) 1934 *S v W*
Day, P W (South Africa) 1903 *SA v GB*
Dedet, L (France) 1906 *F v NZ, F v E*
De Bruyn, C J (South Africa) 1969 *SA v A*, 1974 *SA v BI* (2)
Delany, M G (Ireland) 1899 *S v W*, 1900 *S v E*
Dickie, A I (Scotland) 1954 *F v I, E v I, W v F*, 1955 *I v E, W v I*, 1956 *E v I, I v W*, 1957 *W v E, I v E*, 1958 *W v A, W v F*
Dodds, J (Ireland) 1898 *S v E*
Domercq, G (France) 1972 *S v NZ*, 1973 *W v E*, 1976 *E v W*, 1977 *S v W*, 1978 *I v W*
Donaldson, S (Ireland) 1937 *S v E*
Donaldson, W P (Scotland) 1903 *SA v GB*
Don Wauchope, A R (Scotland) 1889 *W v I*, 1890 *E v I*, 1893 *I v E*
Doocey, T F (New Zealand) 1976 *NZ v I*, 1983 *E v S, F v W*
Douglas, W M (Wales) 1891 *I v E*, 1894 *E v I*, 1896 *S v E*, 1903 *E v S*
Doulcet, J-C (France) 1989 *S v W*
Dowling, M J (Ireland) 1947 *S v W*, 1950 *W v S, S v E*, *W v F*, 1951 *W v E, S v W, F v W, E v S, S v SA*, 1952 *W v S, F v SA, S v E*, 1953 *W v E, E v S, S v SA*, 1954 *E v W*, 1955 *S v W*, 1956 *S v F, S v E*
Downes, A D (New Zealand) 1913 *NZ v A*
Doyle, O E (Ireland) 1984 *W v S, R v S, W v A*, 1987 *E v S*, 1988 *F v E, Arg v F* (2), *W v WS*, 1989 *F v S*
Drennan, V (Ireland) 1914 *W v S*
Duffy, B (New Zealand) 1977 *NZ v BI*
Duncan, J (New Zealand) 1908 *NZ v AW*
Durand, C (France) 1969 *E v S*, 1970 *I v S*, 1971 *E v S*

Elliott, H B (England) 1955 *F v S, F v It*, 1956 *I v S*
Engelbrecht, Dr G K (South Africa) 1964 *SA v W*
Evans, F T (New Zealand) 1904 *NZ v GB*
Evans, G (England) 1905 *E v NZ*, 1908 *W v A*
Evans, W J (Wales) 1958 *I v A, F v E*

Farquhar, A B (New Zealand) 1961 *NZ v F* (3), 1962 *NZ v A* (2), 1964 *NZ v A*
Faull, J W (Wales) 1936 *E v NZ, S v I*, 1937 *E v I*
Ferguson, C F (Australia) 1963 *A v E*, 1965 *A v SA*, 1968 *A v F*, 1969 *A v W*, 1971 *A v SA* (2)
Ferguson, P (Australia) 1914 *A v NZ*
Findlay, D G (Scotland) 1895 *I v E*, 1896 *E v W, E v I*, 1897 *I v E*, 1898 *E v I*, 1899 *I v E*, 1900 *E v I*, 1901 *I v E*
Findlay, J C (Scotland) 1902 *I v W*, 1903 *I v E*, 1904 *E v W, I v W*, 1905 *I v W*, 1911 *I v F*
Finlay, A K (Australia) 1961 *A v Fj*, 1962 *A v NZ*
Fitzgerald, K V J (Australia) 1985 *I v F, W v I, NZ v E* (2), *Arg v NZ* (2), 1987 [*I v W, E v US, NZ v W, NZ v F*], 1988 *Fj v E*, 1989 *S v I, W v E*
Fleming, G R (Scotland) 1879 *S v E*
Fleming, J M (Scotland) 1985 *I v E*, 1986 *A v Arg* (2), 1987 *E v F*, [*A v J, Fj v Arg*], *F v R*, 1989 *F v W*
Fleury, A L (New Zealand) 1959 *NZ v BI*
Fong, A S (New Zealand) 1946 *NZ v A*, 1950 *NZ v BI*
Fordham, R J (Australia) 1986 *E v W, F v I, Arg v F* (2), 1987 [*NZ v It, F v R*]
Fornès, E (Argentina) 1954 *Arg v F* (2)
Forsyth, R A (New Zealand) 1958 *NZ v A*
Frames, P R (South Africa) 1891 *SA v GB*
Francis, R C (New Zealand) 1984 *E v A, I v A*, 1985 *Arg v F* (2), 1986 *W v S, S v E, WS v W*
Freeman, W L (Ireland) 1932 *E v SA*
Freethy, A E (Wales) 1923 *F v E*, 1924 *E v F, I v NZ, F v US*, 1925 *E v NZ, I v S, S v E, F v E*, 1926 *E v F*, 1927 *F v E*, 1928 *I v E, E v F*, 1929 *E v I, F v E*, 1930 *I v E, E v F*, 1931 *E v I, F v E*
Fright, W H (New Zealand) 1956 *NZ v SA* (2)
Frood, J (New Zealand) 1952 *NZ v A*

Fry, H A (England) 1945 *F v B*
Furness, D C (Australia) 1952 *A v Fj* (2), 1954 *A v Fj*

Gadney, C H (England) 1935 *S v NZ, W v NZ*, 1936 *S v W, W v I*, 1937 *W v S, I v S*, 1938 *S v W, S v I*, 1939 *I v S*, 1940 *F v B*, 1946 *F v B*, 1947 *F v S, S v I*, 1948 *F v A, I v S*
Games, J (Wales) 1909 *E v A*, 1913 *E v F*, 1914 *F v E*
Gardiner, F (Ireland) 1912 *S v E*
Gardner, J A (Scotland) 1884 *E v W*, 1887 *W v I*
Garling, A F (Australia) 1981 *A v NZ* (2)
Garrard, W G (New Zealand) 1899 *A v GB*
Gilchrist, N R (New Zealand) 1936 *M v A*
Gillespie, J I (Scotland) 1907 *W v E*, 1911 *W v E*
Gillies, C R (New Zealand) 1958 *NZ v A* (2), 1959 *NZ v BI* (2)
Gilliland, R W (Ireland) 1964 *It v F*, 1965 *S v W, E v F*, *F v W, F v R*, 1966 *E v W*, 1967 *F v A*
Gillmore, W N (England) 1956 *F v Cz*, 1958 *I v S, It v F*
Glasgow, O B (Ireland) 1953 *F v S, F v W*, 1954 *S v E*, 1955 *W v E, F v W*
Goulding, W J (Ireland) 1882 *I v W*
Gourlay, I W (South Africa) 1976 *SA v NZ*
Gouws, Dr J (South Africa) 1977 *SA v Wld*
Greenlees, Dr J R C (Scotland) 1913 *I v E*, 1914 *E v W*
Grierson, T F E (Scotland) 1970 *I v SA*, 1971 *F v R*, 1972 *F v I*, 1973 *W v I*, 1975 *E v F*
Griffin, Dr (South Africa) 1891 *SA v GB*
Griffiths, A A (New Zealand) 1946 *M v A*, 1952 *NZ v A*
Guillemard, A G (England) 1877 *E v I*, 1878 *E v S*, 1879 *E v I*, 1880 *E v S*, 1881 *E v I, E v W*
Gurdon, E T (England) 1898 *I v S*, 1899 *S v I*

Hamilton, F M (Ireland) 1902 *S v E*
Harland, R W (Ireland) 1922 *E v W*, 1925 *W v F*, 1926 *F v W*, 1928 *E v W, S v W, F v W*, 1929 *E v W*, 1931 *W v F*
Harnett, G H (England) 1896 *W v S*, 1901 *S v I, W v I*
Harris, G A (Ireland) 1910 *S v F*
Harrison, G L (New Zealand) 1980 *Fj v A*, 1981 *A v F*, 1983 *A v US, F v A* (2), 1984 *Fj v A*
Harrison, H C (England) 1922 *F v S*
Hartley, A (England) 1900 *W v S*
Haslett, F W (Ireland) 1934 *W v E, E v S*, 1935 *E v W, W v S*, 1936 *W v E*
Haydon, N V (Australia) 1957 *A v NZ*
Helliwell, D (England) 1926 *S v W*, 1927 *W v A*, 1929 *W v S*, 1930 *F v S, W v I, G v F, F v W*
Herbert, D (Wales) 1883 *W v E*
Herck, M (Romania) 1938 *F v G*
High, C J (England) 1987 *F v W, W v US*
Hilditch, S R (Ireland) 1984 *S v A*, 1985 *W v Fj*, 1987 [*R v Z, S v R*], 1988 *E v W*, 1989 *E v F*
Hill, A (England) 1902 *I v S*
Hill, E D (New Zealand) 1949 *NZ v A*
Hill, G R (England) 1883 *S v W*, 1884 *S v I, W v I*, 1885 *S v W*, 1886 *S v I*, 1887 *W v E, I v S*, 1888 *I v W*, 1889 *E v M*, 1891 *I v S*, 1893 *I v S*
Hill, W W (Australia) 1913 *US v NZ*
Hinton, W P (Ireland) 1921 *S v F*
Hodgson, J (England) 1892 *W v S*
Hofmeyr, E W (South Africa) 1949 *SA v NZ* (2), 1961 *SA v A*, 1963 *SA v A*
Hollander, S (New Zealand) 1930 *NZ v BI* (3), 1931 *NZ v A*
Hollis, M (England) 1931 *F v G*
Holmes, E (England) 1931 *W v SA*, 1932 *W v I*
Holmes, E B (England) 1892 *I v W*, 1894 *W v S*, 1895 *S v W, W v I*, 1896 *I v S, I v W*, 1897 *S v I*
Horak, A T (South Africa) 1938 *SA v BI*
Hosie, A M (Scotland) 1973 *I v E*, 1974 *F v I*, 1975 *W v E*, 1976 *I v F, F v A*, 1977 *F v W, I v F*, 1979 *W v I, I v E*, 1980 *W v F, F v I*, 1981 *E v F, R v NZ*, 1982 *E v I, NZ v A* (2), 1983 *I v F, E v NZ*, 1984 *F v E*
Hourquet, R (France) 1983 *S v NZ*, 1984 *E v I, SA v E* (2), *SA v SAm* (2), 1985 *S v W*, 1987 *I v E*, [*E v F, W v E*], 1988 *I v E*
Howard, F A (England) 1984 *I v S*, 1986 *I v W, A v F*, *NZ v F*, 1987 [*F v S, I v C, A v W*], 1988 *W v F, A v NZ*
Hughes, D M (Wales) 1965 *F v It*, 1966 *S v F, I v S*, 1967 *I v E, S v I*
Hughes, J (England) 1935 *I v S*

Hughes, P E (England) 1977 *F v R*, 1978 *I v S*
Humphreys, W H (England) 1893 *S v W*, *W v I*

Ireland, J C H (Scotland) 1938 *I v E*, *W v I*, 1939 *E v W*, *E v I*, *I v W*
Irving, A L C (Australia) 1934 *A v NZ*, 1937 *A v SA*

Jackson, W H (England) 1926 *F v M*, 1927 *W v S*, *W v F*, *F v G*, *G v F*
Jamison, G A (Ireland) 1972 *W v S*
Jardine, A (Scotland) 1906 *E v W*
Jeffares, R W (Ireland) 1930 *W v E*, *E v S*, 1931 *S v F*, 1935 *S v E*, *I v NZ*
Jeffares, R W (Sen) (Ireland) 1901 *S v W*, *E v S*, 1902 *E v W*, 1909 *S v W*
Jeffreys, M (England) 1920 *F v US*
Johns, E A (Wales) 1911 *E v F*
Johnson, R F (England) 1969 *F v R*, 1970 *F v I*, *E v W* (R), 1971 *W v I*, 1972 *I v F*, *W v NZ*, 1973 *I v F*, 1974 *W v S*, *I v NZ*, *F v SA*, 1975 *S v I*, *S v A*
Jones, A O (England) 1906 *W v SA*, 1907 *S v I*, 1911 *F v S*, 1912 *F v I*, *W v F*
Jones, T (Wales) 1947 *E v F*, 1948 *E v I*, *F v E*, 1949 *E v F*, 1950 *S v F*, 1951 *I v E*
Jones, W (Wales) 1984 *S v F*, *NZ v F* (2), 1988 *S v E*
Jones, W K M (Wales) 1968 *I v A*, 1970 *F v E*, 1971 *S v I*
Joseph, M (Wales) 1966 *S v A*, 1967 *I v A*, 1968 *I v S*, *E v I*, *F v F*, 1969 *S v I*, *S v SA*, 1970 *S v E*, 1971 *I v E*, *S v E* (C), 1972 *S v F*, *S v E*, 1973 *I v NZ*, *S v P* (C), *F v J*, 1974 *E v I*, 1975 *F v Arg*, 1976 *E v A*, *F v A*, 1977 *E v S*, *S v I*, *F v S*
Joynson, D C (Wales) 1955 *E v S*

Keenan, H (England) 1962 *I t v F*, 1963 *I v NZ*
Kelleher, J C (Wales) 1973 *E v S*, 1974 *F v E*, 1976 *R v F*, 1977 *E v F*
Kelleher, K D (Ireland) 1960 *W v S*, 1961 *W v E*, *E v S*, 1962 *S v E*, *W v F*, 1963 *W v E*, *F v It*, 1964 *E v W*, *R v F*, 1965 *F v S*, *W v E*, 1966 *S v E*, *W v F*, *W v A*, 1967 *E v A*, *F v S*, *S v W*, *S v NZ*, 1968 *S v F*, 1969 *S v W*, *E v SA*, 1970 *W v F*, 1971 *F v S*
Kelly, H C (Ireland) 1881 *I v S*, 1883 *I v S*, *S v E*, 1885 *S v I*
Kemsley, H B (South Africa) 1896 *SA v GB*
Kennedy, G H B (Ireland) 1905 *S v W*, 1910 *W v S*, *S v E*
Kennedy, W (Ireland) 1905 *S v NZ*
Kilner, W F B (Australia) 1937 *A v SA*
King, J S (New Zealand) 1937 *NZ v SA* (2)
King, M H R (England) 1961 *S v I*
Kinsey, B (Australia) 1986 *Tg v W*
Knox, J (Argentina) 1949 *Arg v F*
Krembs, M (Germany) 1938 *G v F*

Lacroix, M (Belgium) 1962 *R v F*
Laidlaw, H B (Scotland) 1963 *I v E*, 1964 *W v F*, 1965 *I v E*, 1968 *F v E*, *W v F*
Lamb, G C (England) 1968 *F v I*, *W v S*, *F v SA*, 1969 *F v S*, *I v F*, 1970 *S v F*, *W v SA*, *I v W*, *R v F*, 1971 *I v F*, *F v A*
Lambert, N H (Ireland) 1947 *S v A*, 1948 *E v A*, *S v E*, 1949 *W v E*, *S v W*, *E v S*, *F v W*, 1950 *E v W*, *F v E*, 1951 *W v SA*, 1952 *E v W*
Lang, J S (Scotland) 1884 *I v E*
Larkin, F A (Australia) 1932 *A v NZ*
Lathwell, H G (England) 1946 *I v F*
Lawrence, K H (New Zealand) 1985 *A v C* (2), 1986 *A v It*, 1987 *F v S*, *S v W*, *[F j v It, A v E]*, *Arg v A* (2)
Lawrie, A A (Scotland) 1924 *I v F*, 1925 *E v W*, 1926 *I v F*
Lee, S (Ireland) 1904 *S v E*
Lefevre, C (Ireland) 1905 *W v E*, 1907 *S v W*
Lewis, C P (Wales) 1885 *W v E*
Lewis, E M (Wales) 1971 *F v A*
Lewis, M S (Wales) 1975 *F v S*, 1976 *I v S*
Lewis, R (Wales) 1970 *E v I*, 1971 *E v F*, 1972 *F v I*, 1973 *S v I*, *E v A*, 1974 *Arg v F* (2)
Lieprand, M (Germany) 1934 *G v F*
Llewellyn, A (Wales) 1906 *E v I*
Llewellyn, V S (Wales) 1951 *E v F*
Llewellyn, W J (Wales) 1926 *F v S*, *I v E*, 1927 *S v A*
Lloyd, D M (Wales) 1975 *I v F*, 1976 *S v E*

Lloyd, R A (Ireland) 1922 *S v W*, *E v S*
Louw, L L (South Africa) 1953 *SA v A*
Luff, A C (England) 1963 *W v I*, 1964 *I v S*, *I v W*
Lyle, T R (Ireland) 1887 *E v S*
Lyne, H S (Wales) 1885 *E v I*

Macassey, L E (New Zealand) 1937 *NZ v SA*
McAllister, E (Ireland) 1889 *S v W*, 1890 *W v S*
McAuley, C J (New Zealand) 1962 *NZ v A*
McDavitt, P A (New Zealand) 1972 *NZ v A*, 1975 *NZ v S*, 1977 *NZ v BI*
McEwan, M C (Scotland) 1892 *E v W*
McGill, J (Scotland) 1925 *F v I*, 1929 *I v W*
McGowan, J B (Ireland) 1923 *W v F*, 1924 *S v W*
McKenzie, E (New Zealand) 1921 *NZ v SA*
McKenzie, H J (New Zealand) 1936 *NZ v A*
MacLaren, J S (Ireland) 1884 *W v S*, 1888 *S v I*
McMahon, D C J (Scotland) 1961 *W v I*, 1963 *E v F*, 1964 *E v NZ*, 1967 *E v NZ*, *W v E*, 1969 *W v I*
McMullen, R F (New Zealand) 1973 *NZ v E*
McNeil, A (Australia) 1988 *F v Arg* (2)
Magee, J T (Ireland) 1897 *W v S*, *E v S*, 1898 *E v W*, 1899 *E v S*
Magrath, R M (Ireland) 1928 *F v S*
Mailhan, L (France) 1933 *F v G*, 1935 *F v G*, 1937 *F v G*
Malan, Dr W C (South Africa) 1970 *SA v NZ*, 1971 *SA v F* (2)
Marie, B (France) 1960 *Arg v F* (2), 1965 *F v W* (R), 1966 *E v I*
Marsh, F W (England) 1907 *W v I*
Martelli, E (Ireland) 1903 *S v W*
Martin, N B (Australia) 1910 *A v NZ* (2)
Matheson, A M (New Zealand) 1946 *NZ v A*
Maurette, G (France) 1987 *W v I*, *[J v US, I v Tg]*, 1988 *NZ v W* (2), 1989 *E v S*
Mayne, A V (Australia) 1929 *A v NZ* (2), 1932 *A v NZ*
Megson, R J (Scotland) 1987 *W v E*, 1988 *I v W*, *I v It*
Miles, J H (England) 1913 *F v W*, *I v F*, 1914 *W v F*
Millar, D H (New Zealand) 1965 *NZ v SA*, 1968 *NZ v F*, 1977 *NZ v BI* (2), 1978 *NZ v A* (3)
Millar, W A (South Africa) 1924 *SA v BI* (2)
Mitchell, R (Ireland) 1955 *E v F*, 1956 *E v W*, 1957 *E v S*
Moffat, F J C (Scotland) 1932 *W v E*
Moffitt, J (New Zealand) 1936 *NZ v A*
Moolman, Dr J (South Africa) 1972 *SA v E*
Moore, D F (Ireland) 1886 *E v W*, *W v S*
Moore, T W (Australia) 1947 *A v NZ*, 1950 *A v BI*, 1951 *A v NZ*, 1954 *A v Fj*, 1956 *A v SA*
Morgan, C E (Australia) 1907 *A v NZ*, 1910 *A v NZ*
Morgan, K (Wales) 1967 *F v It*
Morrison, D (USA) 1981 *US v SA*
Mortimer, J (England) 1888 *W v M*
Morton, D S (Scotland) 1893 *W v E*
Muller, F (South Africa) 1982 *SA v SAm*, 1988 *S v F*, *F v I*
Mullock, R (Wales) 1886 *I v E*
Muntz, J (France) 1924 *F v R*
Murdoch, W C W (Scotland) 1951 *W v I*, *I v SA*, 1952 *E v SA*, *F v E*
Murphy, J P (New Zealand) 1959 *NZ v BI*, 1963 *NZ v E*, 1964 *NZ v A* (2), 1965 *NZ v SA* (3), 1966 *NZ v BI* (3), 1968 *NZ v F*, 1969 *NZ v W* (2)
Myburgh, P A (South Africa) 1962 *SA v BI*, 1963 *SA v A* (3)

Neilson, A E (New Zealand) 1921 *NZ v SA* (2)
Neser, V H (South Africa) 1924 *SA v BI*, 1928 *SA v NZ* (4), 1933 *SA v A* (4)
Neville, Dr W C (Ireland) 1882 *I v E*
Nicholls, E G (Wales) 1909 *E v S*
Nicholls, F (England) 1904 *W v S*
Nicholson, G W (New Zealand) 1913 *NZ v A*
Noon, O (Argentina) 1949 *Arg v F*
Norling, C (Wales) 1978 *I v NZ*, 1979 *E v S*, 1980 *F v E*, 1981 *I v F*, *NZ v SA* (2), *F v NZ*, 1982 *I v S*, 1983 *A v Arg* (2), 1984 *F v I*, 1985 *E v S*, 1986 *E v I*, 1987 *I v F*, *[C v Tg, F v Fj]*, 1988 *E v I*, *R v F*
Nugent, G P (Ireland) 1880 *I v E*

Oakley, L D (South Africa) 1924 *SA v BI*
O'Callaghan, B J (Australia) 1959 *A v BI*
O'Leary, J (Australia) 1958 *A v M*

289

Palmade, F (France) 1973 *F v S* (R), *S v W*, 1974 *I v S*, 1975 *I v E*, 1977 *I v E*, 1978 *E v I*, 1979 *S v W*, 1980 *SA v BI* (2), 1981 *W v I*, *SA v I* (2), 1982 *E v W*, 1983 *NZ v BI* (2), 1985 *W v E*, 1986 *I v S*
Parfitt, V J (Wales) 1953 *E v F*, 1954 *I v S*
Parkes, Dr N M (England) 1958 *W v S*, *F v A*, *I v W*, *F v I*, 1959 *F v It*, *F v W*, 1960 *W v F*, 1961 *F v W*, 1962 *W v S*, *I v S*
Parkinson, F G M (New Zealand) 1955 *NZ v A*, 1956 *NZ v SA* (2)
Paton, R J (New Zealand) 1931 *M v A*
Pattinson, K A (England) 1973 *F v S*, *W v A*, 1974 *I v W*, *R v F*, 1975 *F v W*, 1976 *S v F*
Pattisson, A S (Scotland) 1883 *E v I*
Pauling, T G (Australia) 1904 *A v GB* (2), 1914 *A v NZ*
Pearce, T N (England) 1948 *F v I*, *W v S*, 1949 *F v S*, *I v F*, *W v I*, 1950 *F v I*, *I v S*, 1951 *F v S*, *I v F*, *S v I*, 1952 *F v I*
Peard, L J (Wales) 1989 *I v E*
Petrie, A G (Scotland) 1882 *S v I*
Phillips, T H (Wales) 1936 *E v S*
Phillips, W D (Wales) 1887 *I v E*, 1889 *I v S*
Pontin, A C (USA) 1976 *US v A*
Potter-Irwin, F C (England) 1909 *W v I*, 1911 *W v I*, 1912 *W v S*, *I v S*, *S v SA*, *I v SA*, *W v SA*, 1920 *F v S*, *W v I*
Pozzi, S (Italy) 1957 *F v R*, 1960 *R v F*
Pretorius, N F (South Africa) 1938 *SA v BI*
Price, F G (Wales) 1963 *I v F*
Prideaux, L (England) 1980 *W v S*, *I v W*, *SAm v SA* (2), 1981 *S v I*, *NZ v SA*, 1985 *F v S*
Priest, T E (England) 1952 *It v F*, 1953 *I v F*
Pring, J P G (New Zealand) 1966 *NZ v BI*, 1967 *NZ v A*, 1968 *NZ v F*, 1971 *NZ v BI* (4), 1972 *NZ v A*
Purcell, N M (Ireland) 1927 *S v E*

Quittenton, R C (England) 1977 *Arg v F* (2), 1978 *W v NZ*, 1979 *I v F*, *F v S*, *S v NZ*, 1981 *S v A*, 1982 *NZ v A*, 1983 *S v W*, *F v R*, 1984 *A v NZ* (2), 1986 *R v S*, 1987 *S v I*, [*Arg v It*, *NZ v Arg*], 1988 *I v S*, 1989 *W v I*

Rainie, R D (Scotland) 1890 *E v W*, 1891 *W v E*, 1894 *I v W*
Rea, M D M (Ireland) 1978 *R v F*, 1981 *S v R*, 1982 *F v E*
Reading, L S (England) 1912 *US v A*
Reilly, J R (Australia) 1972 *A v F*
Richards, A (Wales) 1980 *R v F*, 1981 *A v F*, 1982 *E v A*, 1983 *F v S*
Richards, A R (South Africa) 1896 *SA v GB*
Robbertse, P (South Africa) 1967 *SA v F*, 1969 *SA v A*, 1970 *SA v NZ* (2)
Roberts, E (Wales) 1924 *F v S*
Roberts, R A (England) 1924 *F v W*
Robertson, W A (Scotland) 1920 *E v F*, *I v E*
Robin, D (France) 1988 *It v A*
Robinson, H L (Ireland) 1882 *E v S*
Robson, C F (New Zealand) 1963 *NZ v E*
Roca, J (France) 1937 *F v It*
Rowlands, K (Wales) 1980 *SA v SAm* (2), 1981 *F v S*, 1982 *S v E*, 1986 *SA v Cv* (4)
Rowsell, A (England) 1891 *W v I*
Royds, P M R (England) 1921 *W v F*, 1923 *F v I*
Rutherford, C F (Scotland) 1908 *F v E*
Rutter, A (England) 1876 *E v S*

St Guilhem, J (France) 1974 *S v E*, 1975 *W v I*
Sanson, N R (Scotland) 1974 *W v F*, *F v SA*, 1975 *I v P*(C), *SA v F* (2), *F v R*, 1976 *I v A*, *I v W*, 1977 *W v I*, 1978 *F v E*, *E v W*, *E v NZ*, 1979 *E v NZ*
Schoeman, J P J (South Africa) 1968 *SA v BI*
Schofield, T D (Wales) 1907 *E v S*, 1908 *E v I*, 1910 *E v I*, 1911 *E v S*, 1912 *E v I*, *F v E*, 1913 *E v S*, 1914 *E v I*, *S v E*, 1920 *E v S*, 1921 *E v I*, 1922 *S v I*
Schwoenberg, M (Germany) 1938 *R v F*
Scott, J M B (Scotland) 1923 *E v W*
Scott, R L (Scotland) 1927 *F v I*, *E v W*
Scriven, G (Ireland) 1884 *E v S*
Short, J A (Scotland) 1979 *F v R*, 1982 *I v W*
Simpson, J W (Scotland) 1906 *I v W*
Simpson, R L (New Zealand) 1913 *NZ v A*

Slabber, M J (South Africa) 1955 *SA v BI*, 1960 *SA v NZ*
Smith, J A (Scotland) 1892 *E v I*, 1894 *E v W*, 1895 *W v E*
Stanton, R W (South Africa) 1910 *SA v GB* (3)
Steyn, M (Germany) 1932 *G v F*
Strasheim, Dr E A (South Africa) 1958 *SA v F*, 1960 *SA v S*, *SA v NZ*, 1962 *SA v BI* (2), 1964 *SA v F*, 1967 *SA v F*, 1968 *SA v BI*
Strasheim, Dr J J (South Africa) 1938 *SA v BI*
Strydom, S (South Africa) 1979 *Arg v A* (2), 1982 *SA v SAm*, 1985 *S v I*, *F v W*, 1986 *F v NZ* (2)
Sturrock, J C (Scotland) 1921 *E v W*, *F v E*, 1922 *W v I*
Sullivan, G (New Zealand) 1950 *NZ v BI*
Sutherland, F E (New Zealand) 1930 *NZ v BI*
Swainston, E (England) 1878 *I v E*

Tagnini, S (Italy) 1968 *Cz v F*
Taylor, A R (New Zealand) 1965 *NZ v SA* (R), 1972 *NZ v A*
Taylor, J A S (Scotland) 1957 *W v I*, 1960 *E v W*, *F v E*, *W v SA*, 1961 *F v It*, 1962 *E v W*, *F v I*, *I v W*
Tennent, J M (Scotland) 1920 *I v F*, 1921 *I v W*, 1922 *W v E*, *E v F*, *I v F*, *I v E*, 1923 *I v W*
Thomas, C (Wales) 1979 *S v I*, 1980 *E v I*
Thomas, C G P (Wales) 1977 *F v NZ*, 1978 *S v F*, *F v I*
Tierney, A T (Australia) 1957 *A v NZ*, 1958 *A v M*, 1959 *A v BI*
Tindill, E W T (New Zealand) 1950 *NZ v BI* (2), 1955 *NZ v A*
Titcomb, M H (England) 1966 *W v S*, 1967 *W v I*, *W v NZ*, 1968 *I v W*, *S v A*, 1971 *S v W*, *E v P* (C), 1972 *W v F*
Tolhurst, H A (Australia) 1951 *A v NZ* (2)
Tomalin, L C (Australia) 1947 *A v NZ*, 1949 *A v M* (2) 1950 *A v BI*
Treharne, G J (Wales) 1960 *I v SA*, 1961 *E v SA*, *I v E*, *I v F*, 1963 *S v I*
Trigg, J A F (England) 1981 *F v R*, 1982 *S v F*, 1983 *W v I*
Tulloch, J T (Scotland) 1906 *I v SA*, *E v SA*, 1907 *I v E*, 1908 *E v W*, 1912 *E v W*, 1913 *E v SA*, 1914 *I v W*, 1920 *W v E*, 1924 *W v I*
Turnbull, A (Scotland) 1898 *I v W*, 1899 *W v E*, *W v I*, 1900 *E v W*, *I v W*, 1901 *W v E*

Vanderfield, Dr I R (Australia) 1956 *A v SA*, 1958 *A v M*, 1961 *A v Fj* (2), *A v F*, 1962 *A v NZ*, 1966 *A v BI*, 1967 *A v I*, 1968 *A v NZ*, 1970 *A v S*, 1971 *A v SA*, 1973 *A v Tg*, 1974 *A v NZ* (2)
Van der Horst, A W (South Africa) 1933 *SA v A*
Van der Moerve, M (Germany) 1936 *G v F*
Vile, T H (Wales) 1923 *S v F*, *E v I*, *I v S*, *S v E*, 1924 *I v E*, *S v I*, *E v S*, 1925 *E v I*, 1927 *E v I*, 1928, *E v A*, *E v S*, 1931 *F v I*

Waldron, C A (Australia) 1986 *F v R*, 1987 *A v SK*
Waldron, H (England) 1957 *F v It*
Walsh, L (New Zealand) 1949 *NZ v A*
Walters, D G (Wales) 1959 *F v S*, *I v E*, *E v S*, *I v F*, 1960 *S v F*, *E v I*, *I v S*, *F v I*, 1961 *F v SA*, *E v F*, 1962 *E v I*, *F v E*, 1963 *E v S*, *F v R*, 1964 *E v I*, *F v E*, *F v I*, *F v Fj*, 1965 *I v F*, *S v I*, *E v S*, *S v SA*, 1966 *F v E*
Warden, G (England) 1946 *F v K*
Warren, R G (Ireland) 1892 *S v E*
Warren, T H H (Scotland) 1928 *W v I*
Watson, D H (Scotland) 1881 *S v E*
Waugh, Dr R (Australia) 1903 *A v NZ*
Welsby, A (England) 1976 *F v I*, 1978 *W v F*, 1981 *F v W*, 1982 *F v I*
Welsh, R (Scotland) 1902 *E v I*, 1903 *W v E*, 1905 *I v E*
West, J R (Ireland) 1974 *E v W*, 1975 *S v W*, 1976 *W v F*, 1977 *F v NZ*, 1978 *W v S*, *S v E*, *S v NZ*, 1979 *E v F*, *NZ v F* (2), 1980 *S v F*, *NZ v W*, 1981 *F v NZ*, *W v A*, 1982 *F v Arg*, 1983 *W v E*, 1984 *R v F*
Wheeler, De E de C (Ireland) 1925 *S v F*
Wheeler, Dr J R (Ireland) 1929 *S v E*, 1930 *S v W*, 1931 *E v W*, *S v E*, 1932 *E v S*, 1933 *S v E*
Whittaker, J B G (England) 1947 *I v F*, *W v I*
Wiesse, M (Germany) 1936 *G v F*
Wilkins, H E B (England) 1925 *F v NZ*, 1928 *G v F*, 1929 *W v F*

Wilkins, W H (Wales) 1893 *E v S*, 1894 *S v E*, 1895 *E v S*
Williams, J (New Zealand) 1905 *NZ v A*
Williams, R C (Ireland) 1957 *S v W*, *E v F*, 1958 *E v W*, *E v A*, *S v A*, *S v E*, 1959 *W v E*, *S v W*, *E v F*, 1960 *S v E*, 1961 *F v S*, *S v E*, 1962 *S v F*, 1963 *F v S*, *S v W*, *W v NZ*, 1964 *S v F*, *S v NZ*, *F v NZ*, *S v E*
Williams, T (Wales) 1904 *E v I*
Williams, W (England) 1904 *I v S*, 1905 *W v I*, 1907 *E v F*, 1908 *W v S*, *I v S*, *W v F*, 1909 *E v F*, *F v W*, *I v F*, 1910 *W v F*, 1911 *F v W*, 1913 *F v SA*
Wolstenholme, B H (New Zealand) 1955 *NZ v A*
Woolley, A (South Africa) 1970 *SA v NZ*
Wyllie, W D (Australia) 1949 *A v M*

Yché, J-C (France) 1983 *S v I*, *R v W*, *It v A*, 1985 *A v Fj* (2)
Young, J (Scotland) 1971 *F v W*, 1972 *E v W*, *R v F*, 1973 *E v NZ*

A distinguished gathering of international referees at the International Referees' Dinner held in Dublin in February, 1989. L-R, standing: R F Johnson (England), J R West (Ireland), C Norling (Wales), S R Hilditch (Ireland), D P D'Arcy (Ireland), M D M Rea (Ireland), A Welsby (England), R W Gilliland (Ireland), P G Brook (England); seated: D I H Burnett (Ireland), W Jones (Wales), K D Kelleher (Ireland), L J Peard (Wales), J A F Trigg (England), N H Lambert (Ireland), R Mitchell (Ireland), O E Doyle (Ireland).

INTERNATIONAL MATCH APPEARANCES FOR BRITISH ISLES TEAMS (*up to 30 April 1989*)

From 1910 onwards, when British Isles teams first became officially representative of the Four Home Unions. (*Uncapped when first selected to play in a Test match for the British Isles.)

ABBREVIATIONS

A – Australia; *NZ* – New Zealand; *SA* – South Africa; (R) – Replacement.

CLUB ABBREVIATIONS

NIFC – North of Ireland Football Club; CIYMS – Church of Ireland Young Men's Society

Note: When a series has taken place, figures have been used to denote the particular matches in which players have featured. Thus 1962 *SA* 1,4 indicates that a player appeared in the first and fourth Tests of a series.

Aarvold, C D (Cambridge U, Blackheath and England) 1930 *NZ* 1,2,3,4, *A*
Ackerman, R A (L Welsh and Wales) 1983 *NZ* 1,4(R)
Alexander, R (NIFC and Ireland) 1938 *SA* 1,2,3
Arneil, R J (Edinburgh Acads and Scotland) 1968 *SA* 1,2,3,4
Ashcroft, A (Waterloo and England) 1959 *A* 1, *NZ* 2

Bainbridge, S J (Gosforth and England) 1983 *NZ* 3,4
Baird, G R T (Kelso and Scotland) 1983 *NZ* 1,2,3,4
Baker, A M (Newport and Wales) 1910 *SA* 3
Baker, D G S (Old Merchant Taylors' and England) 1955 *SA* 3,4
Bassett, J (Penarth and Wales) 1930 *NZ* 1,2,3,4, *A*
Beamish, G R (Leicester, RAF and Ireland) 1930 *NZ* 1,2,3,4, *A*
Beattie, J R (Glasgow Acads and Scotland) 1983 *NZ* 2(R)
Beaumont, W B (Fylde and England) 1977 *NZ* 2,3,4, 1980 *SA* 1,2,3,4
Bebb, D I E (Swansea and Wales) 1962 *SA* 2,3, 1966 *A* 1,2, *NZ* 1,2,3,4
Bennett, P (Llanelli and Wales) 1974 *SA* 1,2,3,4, 1977 *NZ* 1,2,3,4
Bevan, J C (Cardiff Coll of Ed, Cardiff and Wales) 1971 *NZ* 1
Black, A W (Edinburgh U and Scotland) 1950 *NZ* 1,2
Black, B H (Oxford U, Blackheath and England) 1930 *NZ* 1,2,3,4, *A*
Blakiston, A F (Northampton and England) 1924 *SA* 1,2,3,4
Bowcott, H M (Cambridge U, Cardiff and Wales) 1930 *NZ* 1,2,3,4, *A*
Boyle, C V (Dublin U and Ireland) 1938 *SA* 2,3
Brand, T N (NIFC and *Ireland) 1924 *SA* 1,2
Bresnihan, F P K (UC Dublin and Ireland) 1968 *SA* 1,2,4
Brophy, N H (UC Dublin and Ireland) 1962 *SA* 1,4
Brown, G L (W of Scotland and Scotland) 1971 *NZ* 3,4, 1974 *SA* 1,2,3, 1977 *NZ* 2,3,4
Budge, G M (Edinburgh Wands and Scotland) 1950 *NZ* 4
Burcher, D H (Newport and Wales) 1977 *NZ* 3
Butterfield, J (Northampton and England) 1955 *SA* 1,2,3,4

Calder, J H (Stewart's-Melville FP and Scotland) 1983 *NZ* 3
Cameron, A (Glasgow HSFP and Scotland) 1955 *SA* 1,2
Campbell, S O (Old Belvedere and Ireland) 1980 *SA* 2(R), 3,4, 1983 *NZ* 1,2,3,4
Campbell-Lamerton, M J (Halifax, Army and Scotland) 1962 *SA* 1,2,3,4, 1966 *A* 1,2, *NZ* 1,3
Carleton, J (Orrell and England) 1980 *SA* 1,2,4, 1983 *NZ* 2,3,4
Cleaver, W B (Cardiff and Wales) 1950 *NZ* 1,2,3
Clifford, T (Young Munster and Ireland) 1950 *NZ* 1,2,3, *A* 1,2
Cobner, T J (Pontypool and Wales) 1977 *NZ* 1,2,3

Colclough, M J (Angoulême and England) 1980 *SA* 1,2,3,4, 1983 *NZ* 1,2,3,4
Connell, G C (Trinity Acads and Scotland) 1968 *SA* 4
Cotton, F E (Loughborough Colls, Coventry and England) 1974 *SA* 1,2,3,4, 1977 *NZ* 2,3,4
Coulman, M J (Moseley and England) 1968 *SA* 3
Cove-Smith, R (Old Merchant Taylors' and England) 1924 *SA* 1,2,3,4
Cowan, R C (Selkirk and Scotland) 1962 *SA* 4
Cromey, G E (Queen's U, Belfast and Ireland) 1938 *SA* 3
Cunningham, W A (Lansdowne and Ireland) 1924 *SA* 3

Dancer, G T (Bedford) 1938 *SA* 1,2,3
Davies, C (Cardiff and Wales) 1950 *NZ* 4
Davies, D M (Somerset Police and Wales) 1950 *NZ* 3,4, *A* 1
Davies, D S (Hawick and Scotland) 1924 *SA* 1,2,3,4
Davies, H J (Newport and Wales) 1924 *SA* 2
Davies, T G R (Cardiff, London Welsh and Wales) 1968 *SA* 3, 1971 *NZ* 1,2,3,4
Davies, T J (Llanelli and Wales) 1959 *NZ* 2,4
Davies, T M (London Welsh, Swansea and Wales) 1971 *NZ* 1,2,3,4, 1974 *SA* 1,2,3,4
Davies, W G (Cardiff and Wales) 1980 *SA* 2
Davies, W P C (Harlequins and England) 1955 *SA* 1,2,3
Dawes, S J (London Welsh and Wales) 1971 *NZ* 1,2,3,4
Dawson, A R (Wanderers and Ireland) 1959 *A* 1,2, *NZ* 1,2,3,4
Dixon, P J (Harlequins and England) 1971 *NZ* 1,2,4
Dodge, P W (Leicester and England) 1980 *SA* 3,4
Doyle, M G (Blackrock Coll and Ireland) 1968 *SA* 1
Drysdale, D (Heriot's FP and Scotland) 1924 *SA* 1,2,3,4
Duckham, D J (Coventry and England) 1971 *NZ* 2,3,4
Duggan, W P (Blackrock Coll and Ireland) 1977 *NZ* 1,2,3,4
Duff, P L (Glasgow Acads and Scotland) 1938 *SA* 2,3

Edwards, G O (Cardiff and Wales) 1968 *SA* 1,2, 1971 *NZ* 1,2,3,4, 1974 *SA* 1,2,3,4
Evans, G (Maesteg and Wales) 1983 *NZ* 3,4
Evans, G L (Newport and Wales) 1977 *NZ* 2,3,4
Evans, R T (Newport and Wales) 1950 *NZ* 1,2,3,4, *A* 1,2
Evans, T P (Swansea and Wales) 1977 *NZ* 1
Evans, W R (Cardiff and Wales) 1959 *A* 2, *NZ* 1,2,3

Farrell, J L (Bective Rangers and Ireland) 1930 *NZ* 1,2,3,4, *A*
Faull, J (Swansea and Wales) 1959 *A* 1, *NZ* 1,3,4
Fenwick, S P (Bridgend and Wales) 1977 *NZ* 1,2,3,4
Fitzgerald, C F (St Mary's Coll and Ireland) 1983 *NZ* 1,2,3,4
Foster, A R (Queen's U, Belfast and Ireland) 1910 *SA* 1,2

Gibson, C M H (Cambridge U, NIFC and Ireland) 1966, *NZ* 1,2,3,4, 1968 *SA* 1(R),2,3,4, 1971 *NZ* 1,2,3,4

Giles, J L (Coventry and England) 1938 *SA* 1,3

Gravell, R W R (Llanelli and Wales) 1980 *SA* 1 (R),2,3,4

Graves, C R A (Wanderers and Ireland) 1938 *SA* 1,3

Greenwood, J T (Dunfermline and Scotland) 1955 *SA* 1,2,3,4

Grieve, C F (Oxford U and Scotland) 1938 *SA* 2,3

Griffiths, G M (Cardiff and Wales) 1955 *SA* 2,3,4

Griffiths, V M (Newport and Wales) 1924 *SA* 3,4

Handford, F G (Manchester and England) 1910 *SA* 1,2,3

Harding, W R (Cambridge U, Swansea and Wales) 1924 *SA* 2,3,4

Harris, S W (Blackheath and England) 1924 *SA* 3,4

Hay, B H (Boroughmuir and Scotland) 1980 *SA* 2,3,4

Hayward, D J (Newbridge and Wales) 1950 *NZ* 1,2,3

Henderson, N J (Queen's U, Belfast, NIFC and Ireland) 1950 *NZ* 3

Henderson, R G (Northern and Scotland) 1924 *SA* 3,4

Hendrie K G P (Heriot's FP and Scotland) 1924 *SA* 2

Hewitt, D (Queen's U, Belfast, Instonians and Ireland) 1959 *A* 1,2, *NZ* 1,3,4, 1962 *SA* 4

Higgins, R (Liverpool and England) 1955 *SA* 1

Hinshelwood, A J W (London Scottish and Scotland) 1966 *NZ* 2,4, 1968 *SA* 3

Hodgson, J McD (Northern and *England) 1930 *NZ* 1,3

Holmes, T D (Cardiff and Wales) 1983 *NZ* 1

Hopkins, R (Maesteg and Wales) 1971 *NZ* 1(R)

Horrocks-Taylor, J P (Leicester and England) 1959 *NZ* 3

Horton, A L (Blackheath and England) 1968 *SA* 2,3,4

Howard, W G (Old Birkonians) 1938 *SA* 1

Howie, R A (Kirkcaldy and Scotland) 1924 *SA* 1,2,3,4

Irvine, A R (Heriot's FP and Scotland) 1974 *SA* 3,4, 1977 *NZ* 1,2,3,4, 1980 *SA* 2,3,4

Irwin, D G (Instonians and Ireland) 1983 *NZ* 1,2,4

Isherwood, G A M (Old Alleynians, Sale) 1910 *SA* 1,2,3

Jackson, P B (Coventry and England) 1959 *A* 1,2, *NZ* 1,3,4

Jarman, H (Newport and Wales) 1910 *SA* 1,2,3,

Jeeps, R E G (Northampton and *England) 1955 *SA* 1,2,3,4, 1959 *A* 1,2, *NZ* 1,2,3, 1962 *SA* 1,2,3,4

Jenkins, V G J (Oxford U, London Welsh and Wales) 1938 *SA* 1

John, B (Cardiff and Wales) 1968 *SA* 1, 1971 *NZ* 1,2,3,4

John, E R (Neath and Wales) 1950 *NZ* 1,2,3,4, *A* 1,2

Jones, B L (Devonport Services, Llanelli and Wales) 1950 *NZ* 4, *A* 1,2

Jones, D K (Llanelli, Cardiff and Wales) 1962 *SA* 1,2,3, 1966 *A* 1,2, *NZ* 1

Jones, E L (Llanelli and *Wales) 1938 *SA* 1,3

Jones, Ivor (Llanelli and Wales) 1930 *NZ* 1,2,3,4, *A* 2,4,

Jones, J P (Newport and Wales) 1910 *SA* 1,2,3

Jones, K D (Cardiff and Wales) 1962 *SA* 1,2,3,4

Jones, K J (Newport and Wales) 1950 *NZ* 1,2,4

Jones, S T (Pontypool and Wales) 1983 *NZ* 2,3,4

Keane, M I (Lansdowne and Ireland) 1977 *NZ* 1

Kennedy, K W (CIYMS, London Irish and Ireland) 1966 *A* 1,2, *NZ* 1,4

Kiernan, M J (Dolphin and Ireland) 1983 *NZ* 2,3,4

Kiernan, T J (Cork Const and Ireland) 1962 *SA* 3, 1968 *SA* 1,2,3,4

Kinnear, R M (Heriot's FP and *Scotland) 1924 *SA* 1,2,3,4

Kininmonth, P W (Oxford U, Richmond and Scotland) 1950 *NZ* 1,2,4

Kyle, J W (Queen's U, Belfast, NIFC and Ireland) 1950 *NZ* 1,2,3,4, *A* 1,2

Laidlaw, F A L (Melrose and Scotland) 1966 *NZ* 2,3

Laidlaw, R J (Jedforest and Scotland) 1983 *NZ* 1(R), 2,3,4

Lamont, R A (Instonians and Ireland) 1966 *NZ* 1,2,3,4

Lane, M F (UC Cork and Ireland) 1950 *NZ* 4, *A* 2

Larter, P J (Northampton, RAF and England) 1968 *SA* 2

Lewis, A R (Abertillery and Wales) 1966 *NZ* 2,3,4

Lynch, J F (St Mary's Coll and Ireland) 1971 *NZ* 1,2,3,4

McBride, W J (Ballymena and Ireland) 1962 *SA* 3,4, 1966 *NZ* 2,3,4, 1968 *SA* 1,2,3,4, 1971 *NZ* 1,2,3,4, 1974 *SA* 1,2,3,4

Macdonald, R (Edinburgh U and Scotland) 1950 *NZ* 1, *A* 2

McFadyean, C W (Moseley and England) 1966 *NZ* 1,2,3,4

McGeechan, I R (Headingley and Scotland) 1974 *SA* 1,2,3,4, 1977 *NZ* 1,2,3(R),4

McKay, J W (Queen's U, Belfast and Ireland) 1950 *NZ* 1,2,3,4, *A* 1,2

McKibbin, H R (Queen's U, Belfast and Ireland) 1938 *SA* 1,2,3

McLauchlan, J (Jordanhill and Scotland) 1971 *NZ* 1,2,3,4, 1974 *SA* 1,2,3,4

McLeod, H F (Hawick and Scotland) 1959 *A* 1,2, *NZ* 1,2,3,4

McLoughlin, R J (Gosforth, Blackrock Coll and Ireland) 1966 *A* 1,2, *NZ* 4

MacNeill, H P (Oxford U and Ireland) 1983 *NZ* 1, 2,4(R)

Macpherson, N C (Newport and Scotland) 1924 *SA* 1,2,3,4

Macrae, D J (St Andrew's U and Scotland) 1938 *SA* 1

McVicker, J (Collegians and Ireland) 1924 *SA* 1,3,4

Marques, R W D (Harlequins and England) 1959 *A* 2, *NZ* 2

Marsden-Jones, D (London Welsh and Wales) 1924 *SA* 1,2

Martin, A J (Aberavon and Wales) 1977 *NZ* 1

Martindale, S A (Kendal and England) 1930 *A*

Matthews, J (Cardiff and Wales) 1950 *NZ* 1,2,3,4, *A* 1,2

Maxwell, R B (Birkenhead Park) 1924 *SA* 1

Mayne, R B (Queen's U, Belfast and Ireland) 1938 *SA* 1,2,3

Meredith, B V (Newport and Wales) 1955 *SA* 1,2,3,4, 1962 *SA* 1,2,3,4

Meredith, C C (Neath and Wales) 1955 *SA* 1,2,3,4

Millar, S (Ballymena and Ireland) 1959 *A* 1,2, *NZ* 2, 1962 *SA* 1,2,3,4, 1968 *SA* 1,2

Milliken, R A (Bangor and Ireland) 1974 *SA* 1,2,3,4

Morgan, C I (Cardiff and Wales) 1955 *SA* 1,2,3,4

Morgan, D W (Stewart's-Melville FP and Scotland) 1977 *NZ* 3(R),4

Morgan, G J (Clontarf and Ireland) 1938 *SA* 3

Morgan, H J (Abertillery and Wales) 1959 *NZ* 3,4, 1962 *SA* 2,3

Morgan, M E (Swansea and Wales) 1938 *SA* 1,2

Morley, J C (Newport and Wales) 1930 *NZ* 1,2,3

Mulcahy, W A (UC Dublin and Ireland) 1959 *A* 1, *NZ* 4, 1962 *SA* 1,2,3,4

Mullen, K D (Old Belvedere and Ireland) 1950 *NZ* 1,2, *A* 2

Mulligan, A A (Wanderers, London Irish and Ireland) 1959 *NZ* 4

Murphy, N A A (Cork Const and Ireland) 1959 *A* 2, *NZ* 1,2,4, 1966 *A* 1,2, *NZ* 2,3

Murray, P F (Wanderers and Ireland) 1930 *NZ* 1,2,4, *A*

Neale, M E (Bristol, Blackheath and *England) 1910 *SA* 1,2,3

Neary, A (Broughton Park and England) 1977 *NZ* 4

Nelson, J E (Malone and Ireland) 1950 *NZ* 3,4, *A* 1,2

Nicholson, B E (Harlequins and England) 1938 *SA* 2

Norris, C H (Cardiff and Wales) 1966 *NZ* 1,2,3

Norster, R L (Cardiff and Wales) 1983 *NZ* 1,2

Novis, A L (Blackheath and England) 1930 *NZ* 2,4, *A*

O'Donnell, R C (St Mary's Coll and Ireland) 1980 *SA* 1

O'Driscoll, J B (London Irish and Ireland) 1980 *SA* 1,2,3,4, 1983 *NZ* 2,4

O'Neill, H O'H (Queen's U, Belfast and Ireland) 1930 *NZ* 1,2,3,4, *A*

293

O'Reilly, A J F (Old Belvedere and Ireland) 1955 *SA* 1,2,3,4, 1959 *A* 1,2, *NZ* 1,2,3,4
Orr, P A (Old Wesley and Ireland) 1977 *NZ* 1
O'Shea, J P (Cardiff and Wales) 1968 *SA* 1

Parker, D (Swansea and Wales) 1930 *NZ* 1,2,3,4, *A*
Pask, A E I (Abertillery and Wales) 1962 *SA* 1,2,3, 1966 *A* 1,2, *NZ* 1,3,4
Patterson, C S (Instonians and Ireland) 1980 *SA* 1,2,3
Patterson, W M (Sale and *England) 1959 *NZ* 2
Paxton, I A M (Selkirk and Scotland) 1983 *NZ* 1,2,3,4
Pedlow, A C (CIYMS and Ireland) 1955 *SA* 1,4
Pillman, C H (Blackheath and England) 1910 *SA* 2,3
Piper, O J S (Cork Const and Ireland) 1910 *SA* 1
Poole, H (Cardiff) 1930 *NZ* 3
Preece, I (Coventry and England) 1950 *NZ* 1
Prentice, F D (Leicester and England) 1930 *NZ* 2, *A*
Price, B (Newport and Wales) 1966 *A* 1,2, *NZ* 1,4
Price, G (Pontypool and Wales) 1977 *NZ* 1,2,3,4, 1980 *SA* 1,2,3,4, 1983 *NZ* 1,2,3,4
Price, M J (Pontypool and Wales) 1959 *A* 1,2, *NZ* 1,2,3
Prosser, T R (Pontypool and Wales) 1959 *NZ* 4
Pullin, J V (Bristol and England) 1968 *SA* 2,3,4, 1971 *NZ* 1,2,3,4

Quinnell, D L (Llanelli and *Wales) 1971 *NZ* 3, 1977 *NZ* 2,3, 1980 *SA* 1,2

Ralston, C W (Richmond and England) 1974 *SA* 4
Rees, H E (Neath and *Wales) 1977 *NZ* 4
Reeve, J S R (Harlequins and England) 1930 *NZ* 1,3,4, *A*
Reid, T E (Garryowen and Ireland) 1955 *SA* 2,3
Renwick, J M (Hawick and Scotland) 1980 *SA* 1
Rew, H (Blackheath, Army and England) 1930 *NZ* 1,2,3,4
Reynolds, F J (Old Cranleighans and England) 1938 *SA* 1,2
Richards, D S (Swansea and Wales) 1980 *SA* 1
Richards, M C R (Cardiff and Wales) 1968 *SA* 1,3,4
Richards, T J (Bristol and Australia) 1910 *SA* 1,2
Rimmer, G (Waterloo and England) 1950 *NZ* 3
Ringland, T M (Ballymena and Ireland) 1983 *NZ* 1
Risman, A B W (Loughborough Colls and England) 1959 *A* 1,2, *NZ* 1,4
Robbie, J C (Greystones and Ireland) 1980 *SA* 4
Robins, J D (Birkenhead Park and Wales) 1950 *NZ* 1,2,3, *A* 1,2
Robins, R J (Pontypridd and Wales) 1955 *SA* 1,2,3,4
Rogers, D P (Bedford and England) 1962 *SA* 1,4
Rowlands, K A (Cardiff and Wales) 1962 *SA* 1,2,4
Rutherford, D (Gloucester and England) 1966 *A* 1
Rutherford, J Y (Selkirk and Scotland) 1983 *NZ* 3

Savage, K F (Northampton and England) 1968 *SA* 1,2,3,4
Scotland, K J F (Cambridge U, Heriot's FP and Scotland) 1959 *A* 1,2, *NZ* 1,3,4
Sharp, R A W (Oxford U, Redruth and England) 1962 *SA* 3,4
Slattery, J F (Blackrock Coll and Ireland) 1974 *SA* 1,2,3,4
Slemen, M A C (Liverpool and England) 1980 *SA* 1
Smith, A R (Edinburgh Wands, London Scottish and Scotland) 1962 *SA* 1,2,3
Smith, D F (Richmond and England) 1910 *SA* 1,2,3
Smith, D W C (London Scottish and Scotland) 1950 *A* 1
Smith, G K (Kelso and Scotland) 1959 *A* 1,2, *NZ* 1,3
Smith, I S (Oxford U, London Scottish and Scotland) 1924 *SA* 1,2
Smyth, T (Malone, Newport and Ireland) 1910 *SA* 2,3
Spong, R S (Old Millhillians and England) 1930 *NZ* 1,2,3,4, *A*
Spoors, J A (Bristol) 1910 *SA* 1,2,3
Squire, J (Newport, Pontypool and Wales) 1977 *NZ* 4, 1980 *SA* 1,2,3,4, 1983 *NZ* 1
Squires, P J (Harrogate and England) 1977 *NZ* 1
Stagg, P K (Oxford U, Sale and Scotland) 1968 *SA* 1,3,4
Steele, W C C (Bedford, RAF and Scotland) 1974 *SA* 1,2

Stephens, I (Bridgend and Wales) 1983 *NZ* 1
Stephens, J R G (Neath and Wales) 1950 *A* 1,2
Stevenson, R C (St Andrew's U and Scotland) 1910 *SA* 1,2,3

Tanner, H (Swansea and Wales) 1938 *SA* 2
Taylor, A R (Cross Keys and Wales) 1938 *SA* 1,2
Taylor, J (London Welsh and Wales) 1971 *NZ* 1,2,3,4
Taylor, R B (Northampton and England) 1968 *SA* 1,2,3,4
Telfer, J W (Melrose and Scotland) 1966 *A* 1,2, *NZ* 1,2,4, 1968 *SA* 2,3,4
Thomas, M C (Devonport Services, Newport and Wales) 1950 *NZ* 2,3, *A* 1, 1959 *NZ* 2
Thomas, R C C (Swansea and Wales) 1955 *SA* 3,4
Thomas, W D (Llanelli and *Wales) 1966 *NZ* 2,3, 1968 *SA* 3(R),4, 1971 *NZ* 1,2
Thompson, R H (Instonians, London Irish and Ireland) 1955 *SA* 1,2,4
Travers, W H (Newport and Wales) 1938 *SA* 2,3
Tucker, C C (Shannon and Ireland) 1980 *SA* 3,4
Turner, J W C (Gala and Scotland) 1968 *SA* 1,2,3,4

Unwin, E J (Rosslyn Park, Army and England) 1938 *SA* 1,2
Uttley, R M (Gosforth and England) 1974 *SA* 1,2,3,4

Voyce, A T (Gloucester and England) 1924 *SA* 3,4

Waddell, G H (Cambridge U, London Scottish and Scotland) 1962 *SA* 1,2
Waddell, H (Glasgow Acads and Scotland) 1924 *SA* 1,2,4
Walker, S (Instonians and Ireland) 1938 *SA* 1,2,3
Wallace, W (Percy Park) 1924 *SA* 1
Waller, P D (Newport and Wales) 1910 *SA* 1,2,3
Ward, A J P (Garryowen and Ireland) 1980 *SA* 1
Waters, J A (Selkirk and Scotland) 1938 *SA* 3
Watkins, D (Newport and Wales) 1966 *A* 1,2, *NZ* 1,2,3,4
Watkins, S J (Newport and Wales) 1966 *A* 1,2, *NZ* 3
Webb, J (Abertillery and Wales) 1910 *SA* 1,2,3
Welsh, W B (Hawick and Scotland) 1930 *NZ* 4
Weston, M P (Richmond, Durham City and England) 1962 *SA* 1,2,3,4, 1966 *A* 1,2
Wheeler, P J (Leicester and England) 1977 *NZ* 2,3,4, 1980 *SA* 1,2,3,4
Whitley, H (Northern and *England) 1924 *SA* 1,3,4
Willcox, J G (Oxford U, Harlequins and England) 1962 *SA* 1,2,4
Williams, B L (Cardiff and Wales) 1950 *NZ* 2,3,4, *A* 1,2
Williams, C (Swansea and Wales) 1980 *SA* 1,2,3,4
Williams, D (Ebbw Vale and Wales) 1966 *A* 1,2, *NZ* 1,2,4
Williams, D B (Cardiff and *Wales) 1977 *NZ* 1,2,3
Williams, J J (Llanelli and Wales) 1974 *SA* 1,2,3,4, 1977 *NZ* 1,2,3
Williams, J P R (London Welsh and Wales) 1971 *NZ* 1,2,3,4, 1974 *SA* 1,2,3,4
Williams, R H (Llanelli and Wales) 1955 *SA* 1,2,3,4, 1959 *A* 1,2, *NZ* 1,2,3,4
Williams, S H (Newport and *England) 1910 *SA* 1,2,3
Williams, W O G (Swansea and Wales) 1955 *SA* 1,2,3,4
Willis, W R (Cardiff and Wales) 1950 *NZ* 4, *A* 1,2
Windsor, R W (Pontypool and Wales) 1974 *SA* 1,2,3,4, 1977 *NZ* 1
Winterbottom, P J (Headingley and England) 1983 *NZ* 1,2,3,4
Wilson, S (London Scottish and Scotland) 1966 *A* 2, *NZ* 1,2,3,4
Wood, B G M (Garryowen and Ireland) 1959 *NZ* 1,3
Wood, K B (Leicester) 1910 *SA* 1,3
Woodward, C R (Leicester and England) 1980 *SA* 2,3

Young, A T (Cambridge U, Blackheath and England) 1924 *SA* 2
Young, J (Harrogate, RAF and Wales) 1968 *SA* 1
Young, J R C (Oxford U, Harlequins and England) 1959 *NZ* 2
Young, R M (Queen's U, Belfast, Collegians and Ireland) 1966 *A* 1,2, *NZ* 1, 1968 *SA* 3

RESULTS OF BRITISH ISLES MATCHES
(*up to 30 April 1989*)

From 1910 onwards – the tour to South Africa in that year was the first fully representative one in which the Four Home Unions cooperated.

v SOUTH AFRICA

Played 30   British Isles won 8, South Africa won 18, Drawn 4

1910 *1* Johannesburg
South Africa 1G 3T (14)
to 1DG 2T (10)

2 Port Elizabeth
British Isles 1G 1T (8) to 1T (3)

3 Cape Town
South Africa 3G 1PG 1T (21) to 1G (5)
South Africa won series 2-1

1924 *1* Durban
South Africa 1DG 1T (7) to 1T (3)

2 Johannesburg
South Africa 1G 1PG 3T (17) to 0

3 Port Elizabeth
Drawn 1T (3) each

4 Cape Town
South Africa 1DG 4T (16) to 1PG 2T (9)
South Africa won series 3-0, with 1 draw

1938 *1* Johannesburg
South Africa 4G 2PG (26)
to 4PG (12)

2 Port Elizabeth
South Africa 2G 2PG 1T (19)
to 1T (3)

3 Cape Town
British Isles 1G 1PG 1DG 3T (21)
to 2G 1PG 1T (16)
South Africa won series 2-1

1955 *1* Johannesburg
British Isles 4G 1T (23) to 2G 2PG 2T (22)

2 Cape Town
South Africa 2G 5T (25)
to 1PG 2T (9)

3 Pretoria
British Isles 1PG 1DG 1T (9)
to 2PG (6)

4 Port Elizabeth
South Africa 2G 1DG 3T (22)
to 1G 1T (8)
Series drawn 2-2

1962 *1* Johannesburg
Drawn 1T (3) each

2 Durban
South Africa 1PG (3) to 0

3 Cape Town
South Africa 1G 1PG (8) to 1DG (3)

4 Bloemfontein
South Africa 5G 2PG 1T (34)
to 1G 1PG 2T (14)
South Africa won series 3-0, with 1 draw

1968 *1* Pretoria
South Africa 2G 4PG 1T (25)
to 1G 5PG (20)

2 Port Elizabeth
Drawn 2PG (6) each

3 Cape Town
South Africa 1G 2PG (11) to 2PG (6)

4 Johannesburg
South Africa 2G 1DG 2T (19) to 2PG (6)
South Africa won series 3-0, with 1 draw

1974 *1* Cape Town
British Isles 3PG 1DG (12) to 1DG (3)

2 Pretoria
British Isles 1G 1PG 1DG 4T (28)
to 2PG 1DG (9)

3 Port Elizabeth
British Isles 1G 2PG 2DG 2T (26)
to 3PG (9)

4 Johannesburg
Drawn British Isles 1G 1PG 1T (13)
South Africa 3PG 1T (13)
British Isles won series 3-0, with 1 draw

1980 *1* Cape Town
South Africa 3G 2T (26)
to 5PG 1DG 1T (22)

2 Bloemfontein
South Africa 2G 2PG 2T (26)
to 1G 3PG 1T (19)

3 Port Elizabeth
South Africa 1G 1PG 1DG (12)
to 2PG 1T (10)

4 Pretoria
British Isles 1G 1PG 2T (17)
to 3PG 1T (13)
South Africa won series 3-1

v NEW ZEALAND

Played 28   British Isles won 5, New Zealand won 21, Drawn 2

1930 *1* Dunedin
British Isles 2T (6) to 1T (3)

2 Christchurch
New Zealand 2G 1GM (13) to 2G (10)

3 Auckland
New Zealand 1G 1DG 2T (15)
to 2G (10)

4 Wellington
New Zealand 2G 4T (22) to 1G 1PG (8)
New Zealand won series 3-1

1950 *1* Dunedin
Drawn 2T 1PG (9) each

2 Christchurch
New Zealand 1G 1T (8) to 0

3 Wellington
New Zealand 1PG 1T (6) to 1PG (3)

4 Auckland
New Zealand 1G 1DG 1T (11)
to 1G 1PG (8)
New Zealand won series 3-0, with 1 draw

1959 *1* Dunedin
New Zealand 6PG (18)
to 1G 1PG 3T (17)

2 Wellington
New Zealand 1G 2T (11) to 1G 1PG (8)

3 Christchurch
New Zealand 2G 1PG 1DG 2T (22)
to 1G 1PG (8)

4 Auckland
British Isles 3T (9) to 2PG (6)
New Zealand won series 3-1

1966 *1* Dunedin
New Zealand 1G 2PG 1DG 2T (20)
to 1PG (3)

2 Wellington
New Zealand 2G 1PG 1T (16)
to 3PG 1DG (12)

3 Christchurch
New Zealand 2G 2PG 1T (19) to 2T (6)

4 Auckland
New Zealand 3G 1PG 1DG 1T (24)
to 1G 1PG 1T (11)
New Zealand won series 4-0

1971 *1* Dunedin
British Isles 2PG 1T (9) to 1PG (3)

2 Christchurch
New Zealand 2G 1PG 3T (22)
to 1PG 1DG 2T (12)

3 Wellington
British Isles 2G 1DG (13) to 1T (3)

4 Auckland
Drawn British Isles 1G 2PG 1DG (14)
New Zealand 1G 2PG 1T (14)
British Isles won series 2-1, with 1 draw

1977 *1* Wellington
New Zealand 2G 1T (16) to 4PG (12)

2 Christchurch
British Isles 3PG 1T (13) to 3PG (9)

3 Dunedin
New Zealand 1G 2PG 1DG 1T (19)
to 1PG 1T (7)

4 Auckland
New Zealand 2PG 1T (10) to 1G 1PG (9)
New Zealand won series 3-1

1983 *1* Christchurch
New Zealand 3PG 1DG 1T (16)
to 3PG 1DG (12)

2 Wellington
New Zealand 1G 1PG (9) to 0

3 Dunedin
New Zealand 1G 3PG (15) to 2T (8)

4 Auckland
New Zealand 4G 2PG 2T (38) to 2PG (6)
New Zealand won series 4-0

v AUSTRALIA
Played 7   British Isles won 6, Australia won 1, Drawn 0

1930 Sydney
Australia 2T (6) to 1G (5)

1950 *1* Brisbane
British Isles 2G 2PG 1DG (19)
to 2PG (6)

2 Sydney
British Isles 3G 1PG 2T (24) to 1T (3)
British Isles won series 2-0

1959 *1* Brisbane
British Isles 1G 2PG 1DG 1T (17)
to 2PG (6)

2 Sydney
British Isles 3G 1PG 2T (24) to 1PG (3)
British Isles won series 2-0

1966 *1* Sydney
British Isles 1G 1PG 1T (11)
to 1G 1PG (8)

2 Brisbane
British Isles 5G 1PG 1DG (31) to 0
British Isles won series 2-0

BRITISH ISLES RECORDS
(*up to 30 April 1989*)

From 1910 onwards – the tour to South Africa in that year was the first fully representative one in which the Four Home Unions cooperated.

TEAM RECORDS

Highest score
31 v Australia (31-0) 1966 Brisbane
v individual countries
28 v S Africa (28-9) 1974 Pretoria
17 v New Zealand (17-18) 1959 Dunedin
31 v Australia (31-0) 1966 Brisbane

Biggest winning points margin
31 v Australia (31-0) 1966 Brisbane
v individual countries
19 v S Africa (28-9) 1974 Pretoria
10 v New Zealand (13-3) 1971 Wellington
31 v Australia (31-0) 1966 Brisbane

Highest score by opposing team
38 New Zealand (6-38) 1983 Auckland
by individual countries
34 S Africa (14-34) 1962 Bloemfontein
38 New Zealand (6-38) 1983 Auckland
8 Australia (11-8) 1966 Sydney
Australia scored 13pts against the 1899 tourists (13-3) at Sydney

Biggest losing points margin
32 v New Zealand (6-38) 1983 Auckland
v individual countries
20 v S Africa (14-34) 1962 Bloemfontein
32 v New Zealand (6-38) 1983 Auckland
1 v Australia (5-6) 1930 Sydney
Australia beat the 1899 tourists by ten points (13-3) at Sydney

Most tries by B Isles in an international
{ v Australia (24-3) 1950 Sydney
v S Africa (23-22) 1955 Johannesburg
5 { v Australia (24-3) 1959 Sydney
v Australia (31-0) 1966 Brisbane
v S Africa (28-9) 1974 Pretoria

Most tries against B Isles in an international
7 by South Africa (9-25) 1955 Cape Town

Most points on overseas tour (all matches)
842 in Australia, New Zealand and Canada (33 matches) 1959
(includes 582 points in 25 matches in New Zealand)

Most tries on overseas tour (all matches)
165 in Australia, New Zealand and Canada (33 matches) 1959
(includes 113 tries in 25 matches in New Zealand)

INDIVIDUAL RECORDS
Most capped player
W J McBride 17 1962-74
in individual positions
Full-back
J P R Williams 8[1] 1971-74
Wing
A J F O'Reilly 9[2] 1955-59
Centre
C M H Gibson 8[3] 1966-71
Fly-half
P Bennett 8 1974-77
Scrum-half
R E G Jeeps 13 1955-62
Prop
G Price 12 1977-83
Hooker
B V Meredith 8 1955-62
Lock
W J McBride 17 1962-74
Flanker
N A A Murphy 8 1959-66
No 8
T M Davies 8[4] 1971-74

[1] *A R Irvine, 9 Tests, played 7 times at full-back and twice as a wing*
[2] *O'Reilly, 10 Tests in all, played once as a centre*
[3] *Gibson, 12 Tests in all, played 4 times as a fly-half. I R McGeechan, 8 Tests, played 7 times as a centre and once, as a replacement, on the wing*
[4] *Both A E I Pask and J W Telfer (8 Tests each), played 4 Tests at No 8 and 4 Tests at flanker*

Longest international career
W J McBride   13 seasons   1962-74

Most internationals as captain – 6
A R Dawson 1959

Most points in internationals – 44
P Bennett (8 appearances) 1974-77

Most points in an international – 18
A J P Ward v S Africa 1980 Cape Town

Most tries in internationals – 6
A J F O'Reilly (10 appearances) 1955-59

Most tries in an international – 2
C D Aarvold v New Zealand 1930
   Christchurch
J E Nelson v Australia 1950 Sydney
M J Price v Australia 1959 Sydney
M J Price v New Zealand 1959 Dunedin
D K Jones v Australia 1966 Brisbane
T G R Davies v New Zealand 1971
   Christchurch
J J Williams v S Africa 1974 Pretoria
J J Williams v S Africa 1974 Port Elizabeth

Most conversions in internationals – 6
S Wilson (5 matches) 1966

Most conversions in an international – 5
S Wilson v Australia 1966 Brisbane

Most dropped goals in internationals–2
D Watkins (6 matches) 1966
B John (5 matches) 1968-71
P Bennett (8 matches) 1974-77
*P F Bush also dropped 2 goals in tests played by British
teams prior to 1910*

Most penalty goals in internationals – 11
T J Kiernan (5 matches) 1962-68

**Most points for B Isles on overseas tour
– 188**
B John (17 appearances) 1971 Australia/
   N Zealand
(includes 180 points in 16 appearances in
   N Zealand)

**Most tries for B Isles on overseas tour
– 22***
A J F O'Reilly (23 appearances) 1959
   Australia/N Zealand/Canada
(includes 17* tries in 17 appearances in
   N Zealand)
Includes one penalty try

**Most points for B Isles in international
series – 35**
T J Kiernan (4 appearances) 1968 S Africa

**Most tries for B Isles in international
series – 4**
J J Williams (4 appearances) 1974 S Africa

**Most points for B Isles in any match on
tour – 37**
A G B Old v South Western Districts
   1974 Mossel Bay, SA

**Most tries for B Isles in any match on
tour – 6**
D J Duckham v West Coast-Buller 1971
   Greymouth NZ
J J Williams v South Western Districts
   1974 Mossel Bay, SA
(A R Irvine scored 5 tries from full-back
   v King Country-Wanganui 1977
   Taumarunui, NZ)

WORLD INTERNATIONAL RECORDS

Both team and individual records are for official International matches played by full members of the International Board, up to 30 April 1989.

TEAM RECORDS

Highest score – 74
New Zealand (74-13) v Fiji 1987
Christchurch

Biggest winning margin – 64
New Zealand (70-6) v Italy 1987 Auckland

Most tries in an international – 13
England v Wales 1881 Blackheath
New Zealand v United States 1913 Berkeley
France v Romania 1924 Paris
France v Zimbabwe 1987 Auckland

Most conversions in an international – 10
New Zealand v Fiji 1987 Christchurch

Most penalty goals in an international – 7
South Africa v France 1975 Pretoria

Most consecutive international victories – 17
New Zealand between 1965 and 1969

Most points in an international series – 106
New Zealand v Wales (2 matches) 1988 in New Zealand

Most tries in an international series – 18
New Zealand v Wales (2 matches) 1988 in New Zealand

Most points in Five Nations Championship in a season – 102
Wales 1975-76

Most tries in Five Nations Championship in a season – 21
Wales 1909-10

Most points on an overseas tour (all matches) – 868
New Zealand to B Isles/France (33 matches) 1905-06

Most tries on an overseas tour (all matches) – 215
New Zealand to B Isles/France (33 matches) 1905-06

Biggest win on a major tour (all matches)
117-6 New Zealand v S Australia 1974 Adelaide

INDIVIDUAL RECORDS
including appearances for British Isles, shown in brackets

Most capped player
C M H Gibson (Ireland) 81(12)[1] 1964-79
in individual positions
Full-back
J P R Williams (Wales) 62(8)[2] 1969-81
Wing
K J Jones (Wales) 47(3)[3] 1947-57
Centre (includes 2nd five-eighth)
R Bertranne (France) 52[4] 1971-81
J M Renwick (Scotland) 52(1)[4] 1972-84
P Sella (France) 52[4] 1982-89
Fly-half (includes 1st five-eighth)
J W Kyle (Ireland) 52(6) 1947-58
Scrum-half
G O Edwards (Wales) 63(10) 1967-78
Prop
P A Orr (Ireland) 59(1) 1976-87
Hooker
C T Deans (Scotland) 52 1978-87
Lock
W J McBride (Ireland) 80(17) 1962-75
Flanker
J F Slattery (Ireland) 65(4) 1970-84
No 8
T M Davies (Wales) 46(8) 1969-76
[1]*Gibson played 48 of his matches at centre, 29 at fly-half, and 4 on the wing.*

[2]*Williams won 63 caps in all, but was chosen once for Wales as a flanker.*
[3]*T G R Davies (Wales), 51(5), won 39 caps as a wing, 12 as a centre.*
[4]*Bertranne won 69 caps in all, 17 as a wing; Sella has won 58 caps in all, 6 as a wing; and Renwick won 53 caps in all, one as a replacement wing.*

Most consecutive internationals for a country – 53
G O Edwards (Wales) 1967-78

Most internationals as captain – 34
J-P Rives (France) 1979-84

Most points in internationals – 385
M P Lynagh (Australia) (30 matches) 1984-88

Most points in an international – 30
D Camberabero (France) v Zimbabwe 1987 Auckland

Most tries in internationals – 32
D I Campese (Australia) (42 matches) 1982-88

Most tries in an international – 5
G C Lindsay (Scotland) v Wales 1887 Edinburgh
D Lambert (England) v France 1907 (Richmond)

Most conversions in internationals – 70
M P Lynagh (Australia) (30 matches) 1984-88

Most conversions in an international – 10
G J Fox (New Zealand) v Fiji 1987 Christchurch

Most dropped goals in internationals – 15
J-P Lescarboura (France) (27 matches) 1982-88

Most dropped goals in an international – 3
P Albaladejo (France) v Ireland 1960 Paris
P F Hawthorne (Australia) v England 1967 Twickenham

H E Botha (South Africa) v S America 1980 Durban
H E Botha (South Africa) v Ireland 1981 Durban
J-P Lescarboura (France) v England 1985 Twickenham
J-P Lescarboura (France) v New Zealand 1986 Christchurch

Most penalty goals in internationals – 69
M P Lynagh (Australia) 30 matches 1984-88

Most penalty goals in an international – 6
D B Clarke (NZ) v B Isles 1959 Dunedin
G R Bosch (SA) v France 1975 Pretoria
J-M Aguirre (France) v Argentina 1977 Buenos Aires
G Evans (Wales) v France 1982 Cardiff
S O Campbell (Ireland) v Scotland 1982 Dublin
⋆K J Crowley (NZ) v England 1985 Christchurch
C R Andrew (England) v Wales 1986 Twickenham
⋆ A G Hastings (Scotland) v France 1986 Murrayfield
M P Lynagh (Australia) v France 1986 Sydney
G J Fox (NZ) v Argentina 1987 Wellington
G J Fox (NZ) v Scotland 1987 Christchurch
M P Lynagh (Australia) v England 1988 Brisbane
⋆*on international debut*

Fastest player to 100 points in internationals
G J Fox (New Zealand) in his 6th match

Fastest player to 200 points in internationals
G J Fox (New Zealand) in his 13th match

Most points in Five Nations Championship in a season – 54
J-P Lescarboura (France) (4 appearances) 1983-84

Most tries in Five Nations Championship in a season – 8
C N Lowe (England) (4 appearances) 1913-14

I S Smith (Scotland) (4 appearances)
1924-25

**Tries in each Five Nations
Championship matches**
H C Catcheside (England) 1923-24
A C Wallace (Scotland) 1924-25
P Estève (France) 1982-83
P Sella (France) 1985-86

**Most penalty goals in Five Nations
Championship in a season – 16**
P H Thorburn (Wales) (4 appearances)
1985-86

**Most conversions in Five Nations
Championship in a season – 11**
J Bancroft (Wales) (4 appearances)
1908-09

**Most dropped goals in Five Nations
Championship in a season – 5**
G Camberabero (France) (3 appearances)
1966-67
J-P Lescarboura (France) dropped a goal in each Championship match 1983-84, a feat never performed before.

Most points on an overseas tour – 230
W J Wallace (NZ) (25 appearances) in
B Isles/France 1905-06

Most tries on an overseas tour – 42
J Hunter (NZ) (23 appearances) in
B Isles/France 1905-06

Most points in any match on tour – 43
R M Deans (NZ) v South Australia 1984
Adelaide

Most tries in any match on tour – 8
T R Heeps (NZ) v Northern NSW 1962
P Estève scored 8 for France v East Japan in 1984, but this was not on a major tour

PARTNERSHIP RECORDS
Centre threequarters
B J Mullin and M J Kiernan (Ireland) 20
Half-backs
J Y Rutherford and R J Laidlaw
(Scotland) 35
Front row
R Paparemborde, A Paco and G Cholley
(France) 21
Second row
A J Martin and G A D Wheel (Wales) 27
Back row
J Matheu, G Basquet and J Prat (France) 22

INTERNATIONAL TOURS
(up to 30 April 1989)
*Indicates replacement during tour, throughout this section

BRITISH ISLES TEAMS TO AUSTRALIA AND NEW ZEALAND

1888

Full record

in Australia	Played 16	Won 14	Lost 0	Drawn 2	Points for 210	Against 65
in New Zealand	Played 19	Won 13	Lost 2	Drawn 4	Points for 82	Against 33

Players
Full-backs: J T Haslam (Batley), A G Paul (Swinton)
Threequarters: H C Speakman (Runcorn), Dr H Brooks (Edinburgh U, Durham), J Anderton (Salford), A E Stoddart (Blackheath)
Half-backs: W Bumby (Swinton), J Nolan (Rochdale Hornets), W Burnett (Hawick)
Forwards: C Mathers (Bramley), S Williams (Salford), T Banks (Swinton), R L Seddon (Swinton), H Eagles (Swinton), A J Stuart (Dewsbury), W H Thomas (Cambridge U), T Kent (Salford), A P Penketh (Douglas, IOM), R Burnett (Hawick), A J Laing (Hawick), Dr J Smith (Edinburgh U), J P Clowes (Halifax)
Captains †R L Seddon, A E Stoddart **Managers** A Shaw, A Shrewsbury

†*Stoddart took over as captain after Seddon had been drowned in Australia*

1899 (Australia only)

Full record	Played 21	Won 18	Lost 3	Drawn 0	Points for 333	Against 90
International record	Played 4	Won 3	Lost 1			

International details				
Jun 24	Australia 13	British Isles 3	(Sydney)
Jul 22	Australia 0	British Isles 11	(Brisbane)
Aug 5	Australia 10	British Isles 11	(Sydney)
Aug 12	Australia 0	British Isles 13	(Sydney)

Players
Full-backs: E Martelli (Dublin U), C E K Thompson (Lancashire)
Threequarters: A B Timms (Edinburgh U), E T Nicholson (Birkenhead Park), A M Bucher (Edinburgh Acads), E G Nicholls (Cardiff), G P Doran (Lansdowne)
Half-backs: Rev M Mullineux (Blackheath), G Cookson (Manchester), C Y Adamson (Durham)
Forwards: F M Stout (Gloucester), J W Jarman (Bristol), H G S Gray (Scottish Trials), G R Gibson (Northern), W Judkins (Coventry), F C Belson (Bath), J S Francomb (Manchester), B I Swannell (Northampton), G V Evers (Moseley), T M W McGown (N of Ireland), A Ayre-Smith (Guy's Hospital)
Captain and Manager Rev M Mullineux

1904

Full record

in Australia	Played 14	Won 14	Lost 0	Drawn 0	Points for 265	Against 51
in New Zealand	Played 5	Won 2	Lost 2	Drawn 1	Points for 22	Against 33

International record

v Australia	Played 3	Won 3
v New Zealand	Played 1	Lost 1

International details

v Australia	Jul 2	Australia	0	British Isles 17	(Sydney)
	Jul 23	Australia	3	British Isles 17	(Brisbane)
	Jul 30	Australia	0	British Isles 16	(Sydney)
v New Zealand	Aug 13	New Zealand 9		British Isles 3	(Wellington)

Players

Full-back: C F Stanger-Leathes (Northern)
Threequarters: J L Fisher (Hull and E Riding), R T Gabe (Cardiff),
W F Jowett (Swansea), W Llewellyn (Llwynypia and Newport),
E Morgan (London Welsh and Guy's Hospital), P F McEvedy (Guy's Hospital),
A B O'Brien (Guy's Hospital)
Half-backs: P F Bush (Cardiff), F C Hulme (Birkenhead Park), T H Vile (Newport)
Forwards: D R Bedell-Sivright (Cambridge U), T S Bevan (Swansea),
S N Crowther (Lennox), J T Sharland (Streatham), D D Dobson (Oxford U),
C D Patterson (Malone), R W Edwards (Malone), A F Harding (Cardiff, London
Welsh), B S Massey (Hull and E Riding), R J Rogers (Bath), F McK Saunders (Guy's
Hospital), D H Traill (Guy's Hospital), B I Swannell (Northampton)
Captain D R Bedell-Sivright   **Manager** A B O'Brien

1908 (Anglo-Welsh)

Full record

in Australia	Played 9	Won 7	Lost 2	Drawn 0	Points for 139	Against 48
in New Zealand	Played 17	Won 9	Lost 7	Drawn 1	Points for 184	Against 153

International record

v New Zealand	Played 3	Lost 2	Drawn 1

International details

	Jun 6	New Zealand 32	British Isles 5	(Dunedin)
	Jun 27	New Zealand 3	British Isles 3	(Wellington)
	Jul 25	New Zealand 29	British Isles 0	(Auckland)

Players

Full-backs: J C M Dyke (Cardiff), E J Jackett (Falmouth, Leicester)
Threequarters: F E Chapman (Westoe, West Hartlepool), R A Gibbs (Cardiff),
J L Williams (Cardiff), R B Griffiths (Newport), J P 'Ponty' Jones (Pontypool,
London Welsh), J P 'Tuan' Jones (Guy's Hospital), Dr P F McEvedy (Guy's Hospital),
H H Vassall (Oxford U, Blackheath)
Half-backs: J Davey (Redruth), H Laxon (Cambridge U), W L Morgan (Cardiff),
G L Williams (Liverpool)
Forwards: H Archer (Guy's Hospital), R Dibble (Bridgwater and Albion),
P J Down (Bristol), G V Kyrke (Marlborough Nomads), R K Green (Neath),
E Morgan (Swansea), L S Thomas (Penarth), A F Harding (Cardiff, London Welsh),
J F Williams (London Welsh), G R Hind (Guy's Hospital), F S Jackson (Leicester),
W L Oldham (Coventry), J A S Ritson (Northern), T W Smith (Leicester)
Captain A F Harding   **Manager** G H Harnett

1930

Full record

in New Zealand	Played 21	Won 15	Lost 6	Drawn 0	Points for 420	Against 205
in Australia	Played 7	Won 5	Lost 2	Drawn 0	Points for 204	Against 113

International record

v New Zealand	Played 4	Won 1	Lost 3
v Australia	Played 1	Lost 1	

International details

v New Zealand	Jun 21	New Zealand 3	British Isles 6	(Dunedin)
	Jul 5	New Zealand 13	British Isles 10	(Christchurch)
	Jul 26	New Zealand 15	British Isles 10	(Auckland)

	Aug 9	New Zealand 22	British Isles 8	(Wellington)
v Australia	Aug 30	Australia 6	British Isles 5	(Sydney)

Players

Full-backs: J Bassett (Penarth), W G McG Bonner (Bradford)
Threequarters: C D Aarvold (Cambridge U and Blackheath), J S R Reeve (Harlequins),
J C Morley (Newport), A L Novis (Blackheath and Army),
R Jennings (Redruth), H M Bowcott (Cambridge U and Cardiff),
T E Jones-Davies (London Welsh), P F Murray (Wanderers)
Half-backs: R S Spong (Old Millhillians), W H Sobey (Old Millhillians),
T C Knowles (Birkenhead Park), H Poole (Cardiff)
Forwards: F D Prentice (Leicester), H Rew (Blackheath and Army), D Parker
(Swansea), W B Welsh (Hawick), B H Black (Oxford U and Blackheath),
M J Dunne (Lansdowne), G R Beamish (Leicester and RAF), J L Farrell (Bective
Rangers), J McD Hodgson (Northern), H O'H O'Neill (Queen's U, Belfast),
Ivor Jones (Llanelli), H Wilkinson (Halifax), S A Martindale (Kendal),
D A Kendrew (Woodford, Leicester and Army), H C S Jones (Manchester)
Captain F D Prentice **Manager** J Baxter

1950

Full record

in New Zealand	Played 23	Won 17	Lost 5	Drawn 1	Points for 420	Against 162
in Australia	Played 6	Won 5	Lost 1	Drawn 0	Points for 150	Against 52

International record

v New Zealand	Played 4	Lost 3	Drawn 1
v Australia	Played 2	Won 2	

International details

v New Zealand	May 27	New Zealand 9	British Isles 9	(Dunedin)
	Jun 10	New Zealand 8	British Isles 0	(Christchurch)
	Jul 1	New Zealand 6	British Isles 3	(Wellington)
	Jul 29	New Zealand 11	British Isles 8	(Auckland)
v Australia	Aug 19	Australia 6	British Isles 19	(Brisbane)
	Aug 26	Australia 3	British Isles 24	(Sydney)

Players

Full-backs: G W Norton (Bective Rangers), W B Cleaver (Cardiff),
B Lewis Jones* (Devonport Services and Llanelli)
Threequarters: D W C Smith (London Scottish), M F Lane (U C Cork),
K J Jones (Newport), M C Thomas (Devonport Services and Newport),
B L Williams (Cardiff), J Matthews (Cardiff), N J Henderson (Queen's U, Belfast),
R Macdonald (Edinburgh U)
Half-backs: J W Kyle (Queen's U, Belfast), I Preece (Coventry), W R Willis (Cardiff),
G Rimmer (Waterloo), A W Black (Edinburgh U)
Forwards: V G Roberts (Penryn), J S McCarthy (Dolphin), R T Evans (Newport),
J W McKay (Queen's U, Belfast), J R G Stephens (Neath), E R John (Neath),
P W Kininmonth (Oxford U and Richmond), J E Nelson (Malone),
D J Hayward (Newbridge), J D Robins (Birkenhead Park), T Clifford (Young Munster),
C Davies (Cardiff), G M Budge (Edinburgh Wanderers), D M Davies (Somerset Police),
Dr K D Mullen (Old Belvedere)
Captain Dr K D Mullen **Manager** Surgeon-Captain (D) L B Osborne (RN)
Assistant Manager E L Savage

1959

Full record

in Australia	Played 6	Won 5	Lost 1	Drawn 0	Points for 174	Against 70
in New Zealand	Played 25	Won 20	Lost 5	Drawn 0	Points for 582	Against 266

International record

v Australia	Played 2	Won 2	
v New Zealand	Played 4	Won 1	Lost 3

International details

v Australia	Jun 6	Australia	6	British Isles	17	(Brisbane)
	Jun 13	Australia	3	British Isles	24	(Sydney)
v New Zealand	Jul 18	New Zealand	18	British Isles	17	(Dunedin)
	Aug 15	New Zealand	11	British Isles	8	(Wellington)
	Aug 29	New Zealand	22	British Isles	8	(Christchurch)
	Sep 19	New Zealand	6	British Isles	9	(Auckland)

Players

Full-backs: T J Davies (Llanelli), K J F Scotland (Cambridge U)
Threequarters: J R C Young (Oxford U), P B Jackson (Coventry),
A J F O'Reilly (Old Belvedere), N H Brophy (UC Dublin), M J Price (Pontypool),
W M Patterson* (Sale), D Hewitt (Queen's U, Belfast), J Butterfield (Northampton),
M C Thomas (Newport), G H Waddell (Cambridge U)
Half-backs: J P Horrocks-Taylor* (Leicester), A B W Risman (Manchester U),
M A F English (Limerick Bohemians), R E G Jeeps (Northampton),
S Coughtrie (Edinburgh Acads), A A Mulligan* (Wanderers, London Irish)
Forwards: B V Meredith (Newport), R Prosser (Pontypool), A R Dawson (Wanderers),
H F McLeod (Hawick), G K Smith (Kelso), S Millar (Ballymena),
B G M Wood (Garryowen), R H Williams (Llanelli), W A Mulcahy (UC Dublin),
W R Evans (Cardiff), R W D Marques (Harlequins), A Ashcroft (Waterloo),
N A A Murphy (Cork Constitution), H J Morgan (Abertillery), J Faull (Swansea)
Captain A R Dawson   **Manager** A Wilson   **Assistant Manager** O B Glasgow

---

1966

Full record

in Australia	Played 8	Won 7	Lost 0	Drawn 1	Points for 202	Against 48
in New Zealand	Played 25	Won 15	Lost 8	Drawn 2	Points for 300	Against 281

International record

v Australia	Played 2	Won 2
v New Zealand	Played 4	Lost 4

International details

v Australia	May 28	Australia	8	British Isles	11	(Sydney)
	Jun 4	Australia	0	British Isles	31	(Brisbane)
v New Zealand	Jul 16	New Zealand	20	British Isles	3	(Dunedin)
	Aug 6	New Zealand	16	British Isles	12	(Wellington)
	Aug 27	New Zealand	19	British Isles	6	(Christchurch)
	Sep 10	New Zealand	24	British Isles	11	(Auckland)

Players

Full-backs: D Rutherford (Gloucester), S Wilson (London Scottish), T G Price* (Llanelli)
Threequarters: D I E Bebb (Swansea), A J W Hinshelwood (London Scottish),
K F Savage (Northampton), S J Watkins (Newport), D K Jones (Cardiff),
F P K Bresnihan* (UC Dublin), M P Weston (Durham City),
C W McFadyean (Moseley), J C Walsh (Sunday's Well)
Half-backs: C M H Gibson (Cambridge U), D Watkins (Newport),
A R Lewis (Abertillery), R M Young (Queen's U, Belfast)
Forwards: R A Lamont (Instonians), A E I Pask (Abertillery),
N A A Murphy (Cork Constitution), D Grant (Hawick), G J Prothero (Bridgend),
J W Telfer (Melrose), W J McBride (Ballymena), M J Campbell-Lamerton
(London Scottish), W D Thomas (Llanelli), B Price (Newport), R J McLoughlin
(Gosforth), D L Powell (Northampton), C H Norris (Cardiff), D Williams
(Ebbw Vale), K W Kennedy (CIYMS), F A L Laidlaw (Melrose)

305

Captain M J Campbell-Lamerton   **Manager** D J O'Brien
Assistant Manager J D Robins

1971

Full record
in Australia   Played 2   Won 1   Lost 1   Drawn 0   Points for 25   Against 27
in New Zealand   Played 24 Won 22 Lost 1 Drawn 1 Points for 555 Against 204
International record
v New Zealand   Played 4   Won 2   Lost 1   Drawn 1
International details

v New Zealand	Jun 26	New Zealand 3	British Isles 9	(Dunedin)
	Jul 10	New Zealand 22	British Isles 12	(Christchurch)
	Jul 31	New Zealand 3	British Isles 13	(Wellington)
	Aug 14	New Zealand 14	British Isles 14	(Auckland)

Players
Full-backs: R Hiller (Harlequins), J P R Williams (London Welsh)
Threequarters: D J Duckham (Coventry), A G Biggar (London Scottish), T G R Davies (London Welsh), J C Bevan (Cardiff Coll of Education), A J Lewis (Ebbw Vale), J S Spencer (Headingley), S J Dawes (London Welsh), C W W Rea (Headingley)
Half-backs: C M H Gibson (North of Ireland), B John (Cardiff), G O Edwards (Cardiff), R Hopkins (Maesteg)
Forwards: T M Davies (London Welsh), P J Dixon (Harlequins), J Taylor (London Welsh), J F Slattery (U C Dublin), M L Hipwell (Terenure Coll), D L Quinnell (Llanelli), R J Arneil* (Leicester), W D Thomas (Llanelli), W J McBride (Ballymena), M G Roberts (London Welsh), G L Brown (West of Scotland), T G Evans* (London Welsh), A B Carmichael (West of Scotland), R J McLoughlin (Blackrock Coll), J McLauchlan (Jordanhill Coll), J F Lynch (St Mary's Coll), C B Stevens* (Harlequins and Penzance-Newlyn), J V Pullin (Bristol), F A L Laidlaw (Melrose)
Captain S J Dawes   **Manager** Dr D W C Smith   **Assistant Manager** C R James

1977 (New Zealand and Fiji only)

Full record   Played 26   Won 21   Lost 5   Drawn 0   Points for 607   Against 320
in New Zealand Played 25 Won 21 Lost 4 Drawn 0 Points for 586 Against 295
in Fiji   Played 1   Won 0   Lost 1   Drawn 0   Points for 21   Against 25
International record
v New Zealand   Played 4   Won 1   Lost 3
International details

v New Zealand	Jun 18	New Zealand 16	British Isles 12	(Wellington)
	Jul 9	New Zealand 9	British Isles 13	(Christchurch)
	Jul 30	New Zealand 19	British Isles 7	(Dunedin)
	Aug 13	New Zealand 10	British Isles 9	(Auckland)

Players
Full-backs: A R Irvine (Heriot's FP), B H Hay (Boroughmuir)
Threequarters: P J Squires (Harrogate), H E Rees (Neath), J J Williams (Llanelli), G L Evans (Newport), C M H Gibson (North of Ireland FC), S P Fenwick (Bridgend), D H Burcher (Newport), I R McGeechan (Headingley)
Half-backs: P Bennett (Llanelli), J D Bevan (Aberavon), D W Morgan (Stewart's Melville FP), D B Williams (Cardiff), A D Lewis* (Cambridge U & London Welsh)
Forwards: W P Duggan (Blackrock Coll), J Squire (Newport), T J Cobner (Pontypool), T P Evans (Swansea), A Neary (Broughton Park), D L Quinnell (Llanelli), G L Brown (West of Scotland), N E Horton (Moseley), A J Martin (Aberavon), M I Keane (Lansdowne), W B Beaumont* (Fylde), F E Cotton (Sale), P A Orr (Old Wesley), G Price (Pontypool), C Williams (Aberavon), A G Faulkner* (Pontypool), R W Windsor (Pontypool), P J Wheeler (Leicester)
Captain P Bennett   **Manager** G Burrell   **Assistant Manager** S J Dawes

1983 (New Zealand only)

Full record	Played 18 Won 12 Lost 6 Drawn 0 Points for 478 Against 276
International record	Played 4 Lost 4

International details

Jun 4	New Zealand 16	British Isles 12	(Christchurch)
Jun 18	New Zealand 9	British Isles 0	(Wellington)
Jul 2	New Zealand 15	British Isles 8	(Dunedin)
Jul 16	New Zealand 38	British Isles 6	(Auckland)

Players

Full-backs: H P MacNeill (Oxford U), W H Hare (Leicester), G Evans (Maesteg)
Threequarters: J Carleton (Orrell), G R T Baird (Kelso), T M Ringland (Ballymena), D G Irwin (Instonians), M J Kiernan (Dolphin), R A Ackerman (London Welsh), C R Woodward (Leicester)
Half-backs: S O Campbell (Old Belvedere), J Y Rutherford (Selkirk), T D Holmes (Cardiff), R J Laidlaw (Jedforest), N D Melville★ (Wasps), S J Smith★ (Sale)
Forwards: S T Jones (Pontypool), I Stephens (Bridgend), G A J McLoughlin★ (Shannon), G Price (Pontypool), I G Milne (Heriot's FP), C T Deans (Hawick), C F Fitzgerald (St Mary's Coll), S B Boyle (Gloucester), R L Norster (Cardiff), M J Colclough (Angoulême), D G Lenihan★ (Cork Const), S J Bainbridge (Gosforth), J H Calder (Stewart's-Melville FP), J B O'Driscoll (London Irish), P J Winterbottom (Headingley), J Squire (Pontypool), N C Jeavons★ (Moseley), J R Beattie (Glasgow Acads), I A M Paxton (Selkirk), E T Butler★ (Pontypool)
Captain C F Fitzgerald **Manager** W J McBride **Assistant Manager** J W Telfer

BRITISH ISLES TEAMS TO SOUTH AFRICA

1891

Full record	Played 19 Won 19 Lost 0 Drawn 0 Points for 224 Against 1
International record	Played 3 Won 3

International details

Jul 30	South Africa 0	British Isles 4	(Port Elizabeth)
Aug 29	South Africa 0	British Isles 3	(Kimberley)
Sep 5	South Africa 0	British Isles 4	(Cape Town)

Players

Full-backs: W G Mitchell (Cambridge U and Richmond), E Bromet (Cambridge U)
Threequarters: P R Clauss (Oxford U), R L Aston (Cambridge U), W E Maclagan (London Scottish)
Half-backs: H Marshall (Blackheath), B G Roscoe (Lancashire), A Rotherham (Cambridge U), W Wotherspoon (Cambridge U)
Forwards: W E Bromet (Oxford U), J H Gould (Old Leysians), J Hammond (Cambridge U), P F Hancock (Somerset), W J Jackson (Gloucester), R G MacMillan (London Scottish), E Mayfield (Cambridge U), C P Simpson (Cambridge U), A A Surtees (Cambridge U), R Thompson (Cambridge U), W H Thorman (Cambridge U), T Whittaker (Lancashire)
Captain W E Maclagan **Manager** E H Ash

1896

Full record	Played 21 Won 19 Lost 1 Drawn 1 Points for 310 Against 45
International record	Played 4 Won 3 Lost 1

International details

Jul 30	South Africa 0	British Isles 8	(Port Elizabeth)
Aug 22	South Africa 8	British Isles 17	(Johannesburg)
Aug 29	South Africa 3	British Isles 9	(Kimberley)
Sep 5	South Africa 5	British Isles 0	(Cape Town)

Players
Full-back: J F Byrne (Moseley)
Threequarters: C A Boyd (Dublin U), J T Magee (Bective Rangers),
L Q Bulger (Dublin U and Lansdowne), C O Robinson (Northumberland),
O G Mackie (Cambridge U and Wakefield Trinity)
Half-backs: Rev M Mullineux (Blackheath), S P Bell (Cambridge U),
L M Magee (Bective Rangers and London Irish)
Forwards: J Hammond (Blackheath and Cambridge U), T J Crean (Dublin Wands),
A W D Meares (Dublin U), R Johnston (Dublin Wands), A D Clinch (Dublin U),
J Sealy (Dublin U), W J Carey (Oxford U), P F Hancock (Blackheath and Somerset),
W Mortimer (Marlborough Nomads), A F Todd (Blackheath),
R C Mullins (Oxford U), G W Lee* (Rockcliff)
Captain J Hammond   **Manager** R Walker

1903

Full record	Played 22 Won 11 Lost 8 Drawn 3 Points for 231 Against 138			
International record	Played 3 Lost 1 Drawn 2			
International details	Aug 26	South Africa 10	British Isles 10	(Johannesburg)
	Sep 5	South Africa 0	British Isles 0	(Kimberley)
	Sep 12	South Africa 8	British Isles 0	(Cape Town)

Players
Full-backs: E M Harrison (Guy's Hospital)
Threequarters: A E Hind (Cambridge U), I G Davidson (North of Ireland),
G F Collett (Gloucestershire), R T Skrimshire (Newport and Blackheath),
E F Walker (Lennox)
Half-backs: L L Greig (United Services), J I Gillespie (Edinburgh Acads),
R M Neill (Edinburgh Acads), P S Hancock (Richmond)
Forwards: M C Morrison (Royal HSFP), W P Scott (West of Scotland),
D R Bedell-Sivright (Cambridge U), W T C Cave (Cambridge U),
J C Hosack (Edinburgh Wands), A Tedford (Malone), R S Smyth (Dublin U),
Joseph Wallace (Dublin Wands), James Wallace (Dublin Wands),
F M Stout (Richmond), T A Gibson (Cambridge U)
Captain M C Morrison   **Manager** J Hammond

1910

Full record	Played 24 Won 13 Lost 8 Drawn 3 Points for 290 Against 236			
International record	Played 3 Won 1 Lost 2			
International details	Aug 6	South Africa 14	British Isles 10	(Kimberley)
	Aug 27	South Africa 3	British Isles 8	(Port Elizabeth)
	Sep 3	South Africa 21	British Isles 5	(Cape Town)

Players
Full-backs: S H Williams (Newport)
Threequarters: A Melville Baker (Newport), R C S Plummer (Newport),
M E Neale (Bristol), A R Foster (Derry), C G Timms (Edinburgh U),
J P Jones (Pontypool and Newport), J A Spoors (Bristol), K B Wood (Leicester)
Half-backs: N F Humphreys (Tynedale), A N McClinton (North of Ireland),
G A M Isherwood (Cheshire, Sale and Old Alleynians), E Milroy* (Watsonians)
Forwards: Dr T Smyth (Newport), W Tyrrell (Queen's U, Belfast),
D F Smith (Richmond), P D Waller (Newport), J Reid-Kerr (Greenock Wands),
R Stevenson (St Andrew's U), L M Speirs (Watsonians), E O'D Crean (Liverpool),
H Jarman (Newport), O J S Piper (Cork Constitution),
Dr W A Roberston (Edinburgh U and Hartlepool Rovers), C H Pillman
(Blackheath), W J Ashby (Queen's Coll, Cork), F G Handford* (Kersal),
T J Richards* (Bristol), J Webb* (Abertillery)
Captain Dr T Smyth   **Managers** W Cail and Walter E Rees

1924

Full record   Played 21   Won 9   Lost 9   Drawn 3   Points for 175   Against 155
International record   Played 4   Lost 3   Drawn 1
International details   Aug 16   South Africa 7   British Isles 3   (Durban)
                                    Aug 23   South Africa 17   British Isles 0   (Johannesburg)
                                    Sep 13   South Africa 3   British Isles 3   (Port Elizabeth)
                                    Sep 20   South Africa 16   British Isles 9   (Cape Town)

Players

Full-backs: D Drysdale (Heriot's FP), W F Gaisford (St Bart's Hospital),
T E Holliday (Aspatria)
Threequarters: R Harding (Swansea), I S Smith (Oxford U), S W Harris
(Blackheath), W Wallace (Percy Park), R M Kinnear (Heriot's FP), J H Bordass
(Cambridge U), R B Maxwell (Birkenhead Park)
Half-backs: H J Davies* (Newport), V M Griffiths (Newport), H Waddell
(Glasgow Acads), W A Cunningham* (Lansdowne), A T Young (Blackheath),
H Whitley (Northern)
Forwards: Dr R Cove-Smith (Old Merchant Taylors), A F Blakiston (Blackheath),
A T Voyce (Gloucester), N C Macpherson (Newport), R G Henderson (Northern),
K G P Hendrie (Heriot's FP), D S Davies (Hawick), R A Howie (Kirkcaldy),
A Ross (Kilmarnock), J D Clinch (Dublin U), Dr W J Roche (UC Cork, Newport),
J McVicker (Belfast Collegians), D Marsden-Jones (Cardiff and London Welsh),
M J Bradley (Dolphin), T N Brand (North of Ireland)
Captain Dr R Cove-Smith   **Manager**   H Packer

1938

Full record   Played 23   Won 17   Lost 6   Drawn 0   Points for 407   Against 272
International record   Played 3   Won 1   Lost 2
International details   Aug 6   South Africa 26   British Isles 12   (Johannesburg)
                                    Sep 3   South Africa 19   British Isles 3   (Port Elizabeth)
                                    Sep 10   South Africa 16   British Isles 21   (Cape Town)

Players

Full-backs: V G J Jenkins (London Welsh), C F Grieve (Oxford U)
Threequarters: E J Unwin (Rosslyn Park), W H Clement (Llanelli), E L Jones
(Llanelli), C V Boyle (Dublin U), R Leyland (Waterloo), D J Macrae
(St Andrews U), H R McKibbin (Queen's U, Belfast), B E Nicholson
(Old Whitgiftians and Harlequins)
Half-backs: F J Reynolds (Old Cranleighans), G E Cromey (Queen's U, Belfast),
J L Giles (Coventry), H Tanner (Swansea), G J Morgan (Clontarf)
Forwards: S Walker (Belfast Instonians), M E Morgan (Swansea), W G Howard
(Old Birkonians), W H Travers (Newport), C R A Graves (Dublin Wands),
R B Mayne (Queen's U), G T Dancer (Bedford), S R Couchman
(Old Cranleighans), A G Purchas (Coventry), J A Waters (Selkirk), P L Duff
(Glasgow Acads), I Williams (Cardiff), A R Taylor (Cross Keys), R Alexander
(North of Ireland)
Captain   S Walker   **Manager** Col B C Hartley   **Assistant Manager** H A Haigh-Smith

1955

Full record   Played 24   Won 18   Lost 5   Drawn 1   Points for 418   Against 271
International record   Played 4   Won 2   Lost 2
International details   Aug 6   South Africa 22   British Isles 23   (Johannesburg)
                                    Aug 20   South Africa 25   British Isles 9   (Cape Town)
                                    Sep 3   South Africa 6   British Isles 9   (Pretoria)
                                    Sep 24   South Africa 22   British Isles 8   (Port Elizabeth)

Players
Full-backs: A Cameron (Glasgow HSFP), A G Thomas (Llanelli)
Threequarters: A R Smith (Cambridge U), F D Sykes (Northampton),
H Morris (Cardiff), A C Pedlow (Queen's U, Belfast), J Butterfield
(Northampton), W P C Davies (Harlequins), A J F O'Reilly (Old Belvedere),
J P Quinn (New Brighton), G Griffiths* (Cardiff)
Half-backs: C I Morgan (Cardiff), D G S Baker (Old Merchant Taylors),
J E Williams (Old Millhillians), R E G Jeeps (Northampton), T Lloyd (Maesteg)
Forwards: R H Thompson (Instonians), C C Meredith (Neath),
B V Meredith (Newport), H F McLeod (Hawick), W O Williams (Swansea),
R Roe (Lansdowne), T Elliot (Gala), E J S Michie (Aberdeen U),
T E Reid (Garryowen), R H Williams (Llanelli), J T Greenwood (Dunfermline),
R J Robins (Pontypridd), R Higgins (Liverpool), D S Wilson
(Metropolitan Police), R C C Thomas (Swansea)
Captain R H Thompson   **Manager** J A E Siggins   **Assistant Manager** D E Davies

1962

Full record	Played 24	Won 15	Lost 5	Drawn 4	Points for 351	Against 208
International record	Played 4	Lost 3	Drawn 1			
International details	Jun 23	South Africa 3	British Isles 3	(Johannesburg)		
	Jul 21	South Africa 3	British Isles 0	(Durban)		
	Aug 4	South Africa 8	British Isles 3	(Cape Town)		
	Aug 25	South Africa 34	British Isles 14	(Bloemfontein)		

Players
Full-backs: T J Kiernan (UC Cork), J G Willcox (Oxford U)
Threequarters: N H Brophy (Blackrock), D I E Bebb (Swansea), R C Cowan (Selkirk),
A R Smith (Edinburgh Wands), J M Dee (Hartlepool Rovers), W R Hunter (CIYMS),
M P Weston (Durham City), D K Jones (Llanelli), D Hewitt (Queen's U, Belfast)
Half-backs: R A W Sharp (Oxford U), R E G Jeeps (Northampton),
G H Waddell (London Scottish), A O'Connor (Aberavon),
H J C Brown* (RAF, Blackheath)
Forwards: S Millar (Ballymena), K D Jones (Cardiff), D M D Rollo (Howe of Fife),
T P Wright (Blackheath), B V Meredith (Newport), A E I Pask (Abertillery),
S A M Hodgson (Durham City), M J Campbell-Lamerton (Army, Halifax),
W J McBride (Ballymena), W A Mulcahy (Bohemians), K A Rowlands (Cardiff),
H J Morgan (Abertillery), D P Rogers (Bedford), J Douglas (Stewart's Coll FP),
D Nash (Ebbw Vale), H O Godwin* (Coventry), G D Davidge* (Newport)
Captain A R Smith   **Manager** Instructor-Commander D B Vaughan RN
Assistant Manager H R McKibbin

1968

Full record	Played 20	Won 15	Lost 4	Drawn 1	Points for 377	Against 181
International record	Played 4	Lost 3	Drawn 1			
International details	Jun 8	South Africa 25	British Isles 20	(Pretoria)		
	Jun 22	South Africa 6	British Isles 6	(Port Elizabeth)		
	Jul 13	South Africa 11	British Isles 6	(Cape Town)		
	Jul 27	South Africa 19	British Isles 6	(Johannesburg)		

Players
Full-backs: T J Kiernan (Cork Constitution), R Hiller (Harlequins)
Threequarters: A J W Hinshelwood (London Scottish), W K Jones (Cardiff),
M C R Richards (Cardiff), K F Savage (Northampton), F P K Bresnihan (UC Dublin),
T G R Davies (Cardiff), K S Jarrett (Newport), W H Raybould (London Welsh),
J W C Turner (Gala)
Half-backs: C M H Gibson (North of Ireland), B John (Cardiff), G O Edwards
(Cardiff), R M Young (Queen's U, Belfast), G C Connell* (London Scottish)

Forwards: A L Horton (Blackheath), M J Coulman (Moseley), S Millar (Ballymena),
J P O'Shea (Cardiff), P J Larter (Northampton), W J McBride (Ballymena),
P K Stagg (Sale), W D Thomas (Llanelli), J V Pullin (Bristol), J Young (Harrogate),
M G Doyle (Blackrock Coll), J Taylor (London Welsh), K G Goodall* (City of Derry),
R J Arneil (Edinburgh Acads), R B Taylor (Northampton), J W Telfer (Melrose),
B R West* (Northampton)
Captain T J Kiernan **Manager** D K Brooks **Assistant Manager** A R Dawson

1974

Full record	Played 22 Won 21 Lost 0 Drawn 1 Points for 729 Against 207		
International record	Played 4 Won 3 Drawn 1		
International details	Jun 8	South Africa 3	British Isles 12	(Cape Town)
	Jun 22	South Africa 9	British Isles 28	(Pretoria)
	Jul 13	South Africa 9	British Isles 26	(Port Elizabeth)
	Jul 27	South Africa 13	British Isles 13	(Johannesburg)

Players
Full-backs: A R Irvine (Heriot's FP), J P R Williams (London Welsh)
Threequarters: T O Grace (St Mary's Coll, Dublin), C F W Rees (London Welsh),
W C C Steele (Bedford and RAF), J J Williams (Llanelli), A J Morley* (Bristol),
R T E Bergiers (Llanelli), G W Evans (Coventry), I R McGeechan (Headingley),
R A Milliken (Bangor, N Ireland)
Half-backs: P Bennett (Llanelli), A G B Old (Leicester),
C M H Gibson* (North of Ireland FC), G O Edwards (Cardiff),
J J Moloney (St Mary's Coll, Dublin)
Forwards: T M Davies (Swansea), A G Ripley (Rosslyn Park), T P David (Llanelli),
S A McKinney (Dungannon), A Neary (Broughton Park), J F Slattery (Blackrock Coll),
G L Brown (West of Scotland), W J McBride (Ballymena), C W Ralston (Richmond),
R M Uttley (Gosforth), M A Burton (Gloucester), A B Carmichael (West of Scotland),
F E Cotton (Coventry), J McLauchlan (Jordanhill), K W Kennedy (London Irish),
R W Windsor (Pontypool)
Captain W J McBride **Manager** A G Thomas **Assistant Manager** S Millar

1980

Full record	Played 18 Won 15 Lost 3 Drawn 0 Points for 401 Against 244		
International record	Played 4 Won 1 Lost 3		
International details	May 31	South Africa 26	British Isles 22	(Cape Town)
	Jun 14	South Africa 19	British Isles 19	(Bloemfontein)
	Jun 28	South Africa 12	British Isles 10	(Port Elizabeth)
	Jul 12	South Africa 13	British Isles 17	(Pretoria)

Players
Full-backs: B H Hay (Boroughmuir), R C O'Donnell (St Mary's Coll, Dublin),
A R Irvine* (Heriot's FP)
Threequarters: J Carleton (Orrell), H E Rees (Neath), M A C Slemen (Liverpool),
P Morgan (Llanelli), R W R Gravell (Llanelli), J M Renwick (Hawick),
D S Richards (Swansea), C R Woodward (Leicester), P W Dodge* (Leicester)
Half-backs: S O Campbell (Old Belvedere), W G Davies (Cardiff),
A J P Ward* (Garryowen), T D Holmes (Cardiff), C S Patterson (Instonians),
J C Robbie* (Greystones), S J Smith* (Sale)
Forwards: J R Beattie (Glasgow Acads), D L Quinnell (Llanelli), S M Lane (Cardiff),
J B O'Driscoll (London Irish), J Squire (Pontypool), C C Tucker (Shannon),
G P Williams* (Bridgend), W B Beaumont (Fylde), M J Colclough (Angoulême),
A J Martin (Aberavon), A J Tomes (Hawick), P J Blakeway (Gloucester),

G Price (Pontypool), F E Cotton (Sale), C Williams (Swansea), I Stephens* (Bridgend),
P A Orr* (Old Wesley), A J Phillips (Cardiff), P J Wheeler (Leicester)
Captain W B Beaumont   **Manager** S Millar   **Assistant Manager** N A A Murphy

NEW ZEALAND TO BRITISH ISLES AND FRANCE

1888-89 (The Maoris)

Full record	Played 74	Won 49	Lost 20	Drawn 5	Points for 394	Against 188
International record	Played 3	Won 1	Lost 2			
International details	Dec 1	Ireland	4	Maoris 13	(Dublin)
	Dec 22	Wales	5	Maoris 0	(Swansea)
	Feb 16	England	7	Maoris 0	(Blackheath)

Players
Backs: W Elliot (Grafton), D R Gage (Poneke), C Goldsmith (Te Aute Coll),
E Ihimaira (Te Aute Coll), P Keogh (Kaikorai), H H Lee (Riverton),
C Madigan (Grafton), E McCausland (Gordon), F Warbrick (Tauranga),
J A Warbrick (Hawke's Bay), W Warbrick (Matata), H J Wynyard (North Shore),
W T Wynyard (North Shore)
Forwards: W Anderson (Hokianga), T R Ellison (Poneke), Wi Karauria (Nelson),
R Maynard (North Shore), Wiri Nehua (Te Aute Coll), T Rene (Nelson),
D Stewart (Thames), R G Taiaroa (Dunedin), Alfred Warbrick (Matata),
Arthur Warbrick (Matata), A Webster (Hokianga), G A Williams (Poneke),
G Wynyard (North Shore)
Captain J A Warbrick   **Managers** J R Scott and T Eyton

1905-06

Full record	Played 33	Won 32	Lost 1	Drawn 0	Points for 868	Against 47
in B Isles	Played 32	Won 31	Lost 1	Drawn 0	Points for 830	Against 39
in France	Played 1	Won 1	Lost 0	Drawn 0	Points for 38	Against 8
International record	Played 5	Won 4	Lost 1			
International details	Nov 18	Scotland 7	New Zealand 12	(Inverleith)
	Nov 25	Ireland 0	New Zealand 15	(Dublin)
	Dec 2	England 0	New Zealand 15	(Crystal Palace)
	Dec 16	Wales 3	New Zealand 0	(Cardiff)
	Jan 1	France 8	New Zealand 38	(Parc des Princes)

Players
Full-backs: G A Gillett (Canterbury), W J Wallace (Wellington)
Threequarters: H L Abbott (Taranaki), E E Booth (Otago), R G Deans (Canterbury),
E T Harper (Canterbury), D McGregor (Wellington), G W Smith (Auckland),
H D Thomson (Wanganui)
Five-eighths: J Hunter (Taranaki), H J Mynott (Taranaki), J W Stead (Southland)
Scrum-half: F Roberts (Wellington)
Forwards: S Casey (Otago), J Corbett (West Coast), W Cunningham (Auckland),
D Gallaher (Auckland), F T Glasgow (Taranaki), W S Glenn (Taranaki),
W Johnston (Otago), W H Mackrell (Auckland), A McDonald (Otago),
F Newton (Canterbury), G W Nicholson (Auckland), J M O'Sullivan (Taranaki),
C E Seeling (Auckland), G A Tyler (Auckland)
Captain D Gallaher   **Manager** G H Dixon

1924-25

Full record	Played 30	Won 30	Lost 0	Drawn 0	Points for 721	Against 112
in B Isles	Played 28	Won 28	Lost 0	Drawn 0	Points for 654	Against 98
in France	Played 2	Won 2	Lost 0	Drawn 0	Points for 67	Against 14
International record	Played 4	Won 4				

International details

Nov 1	Ireland	0	New Zealand	6	(Dublin)
Nov 29	Wales	0	New Zealand	19	(Swansea)
Jan 3	England	11	New Zealand	17	(Twickenham)
Jan 18	France	6	New Zealand	30	(Toulouse)

Players

Full-back: G Nepia (Hawke's Bay)
Threequarters: H W Brown (Taranaki), A H Hart (Taranaki), F W Lucas (Auckland),
A C C Robilliard (Canterbury), J Steel (West Coast), K S Svenson (Wellington)
Five-eighths: C E O Badeley (Auckland), A E Cooke (Auckland),
N P McGregor (Canterbury), M F Nicholls (Wellington), L Paewai (Hawke's Bay)
Scrum-halves: W C Dalley (Canterbury), J J Mill (Hawke's Bay)
Forwards: C J Brownlie (Hawke's Bay), M J Brownlie (Hawke's Bay),
L F Cupples (Bay of Plenty), Q Donald (Wairarapa), I H Harvey (Wairarapa),
W R Irvine (Hawke's Bay), R R Masters (Canterbury), B V McCleary (Canterbury),
H G Munro (Otago), J H Parker (Canterbury), C G Porter (Wellington),
J Richardson (Southland), R T Stewart (South Canterbury), A H West (Taranaki),
A White (Southland)
Captain C G Porter   **Manager** S S M Dean

1926-27 (The Maoris)

Full record	Played 31	Won 22	Lost 7	Drawn 2	Points for 459	Against 194
in England						
and Wales	Played 16	Won 8	Lost 6	Drawn 2	Points for 126	Against 113
in France	Played 15	Won 14	Lost 1	Drawn 0	Points for 333	Against 81

International record   Played 1   Won 1
International details   Dec 26   France 3   Maoris 12   (Paris, Colombes)
Players

Full-backs: R Pelham (Auckland), H Phillips (Marlborough)
Threequarters: W P Barclay (Hawke's Bay), A C Falwasser (Taranaki),
L R Grace (Hawke's Bay), W Lockwood (East Coast), E Love (Wellington),
W Potaka (Wanganui), T P Robinson (Canterbury)
Five-eighths: J R Bell (Southland), J H MacDonald (Marlborough),
M Mete (Manawhenua), D Wi Neera (Wellington)
Scrum-halves: H Kingi (Wanganui), W H Shortland (Hawke's Bay)
Forwards: A Crawford (East Coast), T Dennis (Poverty Bay), J Gemmell (Hawke's Bay),
S W Gemmell (Hawke's Bay), P Haupapa (Bay of Plenty), J Manihera (Canterbury),
T Manning (South Canterbury), Rev P Matene (North Auckland),
O S Olsen (North Auckland), W Rika (North Auckland), J Stewart (Otago),
D Tatana (Manawhenua), W H Wilson (Hawke's Bay)
Captain W P Barclay   **Managers** W T Parata and H Harris

1935-36 (British Isles only)

Full record	Played 28	Won 24	Lost 3	Drawn 1	Points for 431	Against 180

International record   Played 4   Won 2   Lost 2
International details

Nov 23	Scotland	8	New Zealand	18	(Murrayfield)
Dec 7	Ireland	9	New Zealand	17	(Dublin)
Dec 21	Wales	13	New Zealand	12	(Cardiff)
Jan 4	England	13	New Zealand	0	(Twickenham)

Players

Full-back: G D M Gilbert (West Coast)
Threequarters: N Ball (Wellington), H M Brown (Auckland),
T H C Caughey (Auckland), G F Hart (Canterbury), N A Mitchell (Southland),
C J Oliver (Canterbury)
Five-eighths: J L Griffiths (Wellington), J R Page (Wellington), D Solomon (Auckland),
E W T Tindill (Wellington)

Scrum-halves: M M N Corner (Auckland), B S Sadler (Wellington)
Forwards: G T Adkins (South Canterbury), J J Best (Marlborough),
W R Collins (Hawke's Bay), D Dalton (Hawke's Bay), W E Hadley (Auckland),
J Hore (Otago), R R King (West Coast), A Lambourn (Wellington),
A Mahoney (Bush), J E Manchester (Canterbury), R M McKenzie (Manawatu),
H F McLean (Auckland), C S Pepper (Auckland), S T Reid (Hawke's Bay),
F H Vorrath (Otago), J G Wynyard (Waikato)
Captain J E Manchester   **Manager** V R S Meredith

1953-54

Full record	Played 31	Won 25	Lost 4	Drawn 2	Points for 446	Against 129
in B Isles	Played 29	Won 25	Lost 2	Drawn 2	Points for 438	Against 115
in France	Played 2	Won 0	Lost 2	Drawn 0	Points for 8	Against 14
International record	Played 5	Won 3	Lost 2			
International details	Dec 19	Wales 13	New Zealand 8	(Cardiff)		
	Jan 9	Ireland 3	New Zealand 14	(Dublin)		
	Jan 30	England 0	New Zealand 5	(Twickenham)		
	Feb 13	Scotland 0	New Zealand 3	(Murrayfield)		
	Feb 27	France 3	New Zealand 0	(Paris, Colombes)		

Players
Full-backs: J W Kelly (Auckland), R W H Scott (Auckland)
Threequarters: M J Dixon (Canterbury), A E G Elsom (Canterbury),
W S S Freebairn (Manawatu), R A Jarden (Wellington), J T Fitzgerald (Wellington),
J M Tanner (Auckland)
Five-eighths: B B J Fitzpatrick (Wellington), C J Loader (Wellington),
D D Wilson (Canterbury), R G Bowers (Wellington), L S Haig (Otago)
Scrum-halves: V D Bevan (Wellington), K Davis (Auckland)
Forwards: W A McCaw (Southland), R C Stuart (Canterbury),
W H Clark (Wellington), P F Jones (North Auckland), R J O'Dea (Thames Valley),
O D Oliver (Otago), K P Bagley (Manawatu), G N Dalzell (Canterbury),
R A White (Poverty Bay), I J Clarke (Waikato), B P Eastgate (Canterbury),
K L Skinner (Otago), H L White (Auckland), R C Hemi (Waikato),
C A Woods (Southland)
Captain R C Stuart   **Manager** N Millard   **Assistant Manager** A E Marslin

1963-64

Full record	Played 34	Won 32	Lost 1	Drawn 1	Points for 568	Against 153
in B Isles	Played 30	Won 28	Lost 1	Drawn 1	Points for 508	Against 137
in France	Played 4	Won 4	Lost 0	Drawn 0	Points for 60	Against 16
International record	Played 5	Won 4	Drawn 1			
International details	Dec 7	Ireland 5	New Zealand 6	(Dublin)		
	Dec 21	Wales 0	New Zealand 6	(Cardiff)		
	Jan 4	England 0	New Zealand 14	(Twickenham)		
	Jan 18	Scotland 0	New Zealand 0	(Murrayfield)		
	Feb 8	France 3	New Zealand 12	(Paris, Colombes)		

Players
Full-back: D B Clarke (Waikato)
Threequarters: R W Caulton (Wellington), W L Davis (Hawke's Bay),
M J Dick (Auckland), I S T Smith (Otago), P F Little (Auckland),
I R MacRae (Hawke's Bay)
Five-eighths: D A Arnold (Canterbury), P T Walsh (Counties),
M A Herewini (Auckland), E W Kirton (Otago), B A Watt (Canterbury)
Scrum-halves: K C Briscoe (Taranaki), C R Laidlaw (Otago)
Forwards: I J Clarke (Waikato), K F Gray (Wellington), J M Le Lievre (Canterbury),

W J Whineray (Auckland), D Young (Canterbury), J Major (Taranaki),
R H Horsley (Manawatu), C E Meads (King Country), A J Stewart (Canterbury),
S T Meads (King Country), K E Barry (Thames Valley), D J Graham (Canterbury),
W J Nathan (Auckland), K R Tremain (Hawke's Bay), B J Lochore (Wairarapa),
K A Nelson (Otago)
Captain W J Whineray   **Manager** F D Kilby   **Assistant Manager** N J McPhail

1967

Full record	Played 15	Won 14	Lost 0	Drawn 1	Points for 294	Against 129
in B Isles	Played 11	Won 10	Lost 0	Drawn 1	Points for 207	Against 78
in France	Played 4	Won 4	Lost 0	Drawn 0	Points for 87	Against 51
International record	Played 4	Won 4				
International details	Nov 4	England 11	New Zealand 23	(Twickenham)		
	Nov 11	Wales 6	New Zealand 13	(Cardiff)		
	Nov 25	France 15	New Zealand 21	(Paris, Colombes)		
	Dec 2	Scotland 3	New Zealand 14	(Murrayfield)		

Players
Full-back: W F McCormick (Canterbury)
Threequarters: M J Dick (Auckland), W M Birtwistle (Waikato), A G Steel (Canterbury),
P H Clarke (Marlborough), G S Thorne (Auckland), W L Davis (Hawke's Bay)
Five-eighths: I R MacRae (Hawke's Bay), G F Kember (Wellington),
W D Cottrell (Canterbury), E W Kirton (Otago), M A Herewini (Auckland)
Scrum-halves: C R Laidlaw (Otago), S M Going (North Auckland)
Forwards: B J Lochore (Wairarapa), I A Kirkpatrick (Canterbury),
W J Nathan (Auckland), K R Tremain (Hawke's Bay), G C Williams (Wellington),
M C Wills (Taranaki), C E Meads (King Country), A G Jennings (Bay of Plenty),
S C Strahan (Manawatu), A E Smith (Taranaki), A E Hopkinson (Canterbury),
E J Hazlett (Southland), B L Muller (Taranaki), K F Gray (Wellington),
B E McLeod (Counties), J Major (Taranaki)
Captain B J Lochore   **Manager** C K Saxton   **Assistant Manager** F R Allen

1972-73

Full record	Played 30	Won 23	Lost 5	Drawn 2	Points for 568	Against 254
in Britain and						
Ireland	Played 26	Won 20	Lost 4	Drawn 2	Points for 521	Against 227
in France	Played 4	Won 3	Lost 1	Drawn 0	Points for 47	Against 27
International record	Played 5	Won 3	Lost 1	Drawn 1		
International details	Dec 2	Wales 16	New Zealand 19	(Cardiff)		
	Dec 16	Scotland 9	New Zealand 14	(Murrayfield)		
	Jan 6	England 0	New Zealand 9	(Twickenham)		
	Jan 20	Ireland 10	New Zealand 10	(Dublin)		
	Feb 10	France 13	New Zealand 6	(Parc des Princes)		

Players
Full-backs: J F Karam (Wellington), T J Morris (Nelson-Bays)
Threequarters: B G Williams (Auckland), G B Batty (Wellington),
D A Hales (Canterbury), G R Skudder (Waikato), B J Robertson (Counties),
I A Hurst (Canterbury)
Five-eighths: R M Parkinson (Poverty Bay), M Sayers (Wellington),
R E Burgess (Manawatu), I N Stevens (Wellington)
Scrum-halves: S M Going (North Auckland), G L Colling (Otago)
Forwards: A R Sutherland (Marlborough), A J Wyllie (Canterbury),
B Holmes (North Auckland), I A Kirkpatrick (Poverty Bay), K W Stewart (Southland),
A I Scown (Taranaki), H H Macdonald (Canterbury), I M Eliason (Taranaki),
A M Haden (Auckland), P J Whiting (Auckland), K Murdoch (Otago),

J D Matheson (Otago), K K Lambert (Manawatu), G J Whiting (King Country),
R A Urlich (Auckland), R W Norton (Canterbury), L A Clark* (Otago),
A L R McNicol* (Wanganui)
Captain I A Kirkpatrick   **Manager** E L Todd   **Assistant Manager** R H Duff

1974 (to Ireland and UK)

Full record	Played 8	Won 7	Lost 0	Drawn 1	Points for 127 Against 50
in Ireland	Played 6	Won 6	Lost 0	Drawn 0	Points for 102 Against 34
International record	Played 1	Won 1			
International details	Nov 23	Ireland 6	New Zealand 15	(Dublin)	

Players
Full-backs: J F Karam (Wellington), K T Going (North Auckland)
Threequarters: T W Mitchell (Canterbury), B G Williams (Auckland),
G Batty (Wellington), B J Robertson (Counties), I A Hurst (Canterbury),
J E Morgan (North Auckland), G M Kane (Waikato)
Half-backs: D J Robertson (Otago), O D Bruce (Canterbury),
S M Going (North Auckland), I N Stevens (Wellington)
Forwards: A R Leslie (Wellington), L G Knight (Auckland),
I A Kirkpatrick (Poverty Bay), K W Stewart (Southland), K A Eveleigh (Manawatu),
P J Whiting (Auckland), H H Macdonald (Canterbury), J A Callesen (Manawatu),
K J Tanner (Canterbury), A J Gardiner (Taranaki), W K Bush (Canterbury),
K K Lambert (Manawatu), R W Norton (Canterbury), G M Crossman (Bay of Plenty)
Captain A R Leslie   **Manager** N H Stanley   **Assistant Manager** J J Stewart

1977 (France only, except for one match in Italy)

Full record	Played 9	Won 8	Lost 1	Drawn 0	Points for 216 Against 86
in Italy	Played 1	Won 1	Lost 0	Drawn 0	Points for 17 Against 9
in France	Played 8	Won 7	Lost 1	Drawn 0	Points for 199 Against 77
International record	Played 2	Won 1	Lost 1		
International details	Nov 11	France 18	New Zealand 13	(Toulouse)	
	Nov 19	France 3	New Zealand 15	(Parc des Princes)	

Players
Full-back: B W Wilson (Otago)
Threequarters: B G Williams (Auckland), B R Ford (Marlborough),
B J Robertson (Counties), S S Wilson (Wellington), N M Taylor (Bay of Plenty),
W M Osborne (Wanganui), B Hegarty* (Wellington & Biarritz)
Half-backs: O D Bruce (Canterbury), B J McKechnie (Southland),
M W Donaldson (Manawatu), K M Green (Waikato)
Forwards: G N K Mourie (Taranaki), K A Eveleigh (Manawatu),
L G Knight (Poverty Bay), G A Seear (Otago), R G Myers (Waikato),
R L Stuart (Hawke's Bay), F J Oliver (Southland), A M Haden (Auckland),
G A Knight (Manawatu), B R Johnstone (Auckland), J C Ashworth (Canterbury),
J T McEldowney (Taranaki), A G Dalton (Counties), J E Black (Canterbury)
Captain G N K Mourie   **Manager** R M Don   **Assistant Manager** J Gleeson

1978 (no matches in France)

Full record	Played 18	Won 17	Lost 1	Drawn 0	Points for 364 Against 147
International record	Played 4	Won 4			
International details	Nov 4	Ireland 6	New Zealand 10	(Dublin)	
	Nov 11	Wales 12	New Zealand 13	(Cardiff)	
	Nov 25	England 6	New Zealand 16	(Twickenham)	
	Dec 9	Scotland 9	New Zealand 18	(Murrayfield)	

Players
Full-backs: C J Currie (Canterbury), B J McKechnie (Southland),

R G Wilson* (Canterbury)
Threequarters: B R Ford (Marlborough), B G Williams (Auckland),
S S Wilson (Wellington), R Kururangi (Counties), B J Robertson (Counties),
Five-eighths: J L Jaffray (Otago), W M Osborne (Wanganui), N M Taylor
(Bay of Plenty), O D Bruce (Canterbury), E J Dunn (North Auckland),
Scrum-halves: M W Donaldson (Manawatu), D S Loveridge (Taranaki)
Forwards: G A Seear (Otago), A A McGregor (Southland), G N K Mourie (Taranaki),
B G Ashworth (Auckland), L M Rutledge (Southland), W G Graham (Otago),
A M Haden (Auckland), F J Oliver (Otago), J K Loveday (Manawatu),
J K Fleming (Wellington), W K Bush (Canterbury), J C Ashworth (Canterbury),
G A Knight (Manawatu), B R Johnstone (Auckland), A G Dalton (Counties),
J E Black (Canterbury)
Captain G N K Mourie   **Manager** R W Thomas   **Assistant Manager** J Gleeson

1979 (to England and Scotland only, except for one match in Italy)

Full record	Played 11	Won 10	Lost 1	Drawn 0	Points for 192	Against 95
International record (in UK)		Played 2	Won 2			
International details	Nov 10	Scotland 6	New Zealand 20	(Murrayfield)		
	Nov 24	England 9	New Zealand 10	(Twickenham)		

Players
Full-backs: R G Wilson (Canterbury), A R Hewson (Wellington)
Threequarters: S S Wilson (Wellington), B R Ford (Marlborough),
B G Fraser (Wellington), G R Cunningham (Auckland), T M Twigden (Auckland)
Five-eighths: K J Keane (Canterbury), E Dunn (North Auckland),
M B Taylor (Waikato)
Scrum-halves: M W Donaldson (Manawatu), D S Loveridge (Taranaki)
Forwards: M G Mexted (Wellington), G N K Mourie (Taranaki),
K W Stewart (Southland), M Burgoyne (North Auckland), V E Stewart (Canterbury),
A M Haden (Auckland), J K Fleming (Wellington), B R Johnstone (Auckland),
B A Thompson (Canterbury), R C Ketels (Counties), J E Speirs (Counties),
A G Dalton (Counties), P H Sloane (North Auckland)
Captain G N K Mourie   **Manager** R W Thomas   **Assistant Manager** E A Watson

1980 (to Wales only, except for two matches in North America)

Full record	Played 7	Won 7	Lost 0	Drawn 0	Points for 197	Against 41
in Wales	Played 5	Won 5	Points for 101	Against 25		
International record	Played 1	Won 1				
International details	Nov 1	Wales 3	New Zealand 23	(Cardiff)		

Players
Full-backs: B W Codlin (Counties), D L Rollerson (Manawatu)
Threequarters: S S Wilson (Wellington), B G Fraser (Wellington),
F A Woodman (North Auckland), B J Robertson (Counties)
Five-eighths: W M Osborne (Wanganui), M B Taylor (Waikato), N H Allen (Counties)
Scrum-halves: M W Donaldson (Manawatu), D S Loveridge (Taranaki)
Forwards: G H Old (Manawatu), M G Mexted (Wellington), G N K Mourie (Taranaki),
G R Hines (Waikato), M W Shaw (Manawatu), G Higginson (Canterbury),
F J Oliver (Manawatu), A M Haden (Auckland), R C Ketels (Counties),
G A Knight (Manawatu), J E Speirs (Counties), J C Ashworth (Canterbury),
H R Reid (Bay of Plenty), A G Dalton (Counties)
Captain G N K Mourie   **Manager** R A Harper   **Assistant Manager** E A Watson

1981 (to France only, except for two matches in Romania)

Full record	Played 10	Won 8	Lost 1	Drawn 1	Points for 170	Against 108

in Romania	Played 2	Won 2	Lost 0	Drawn 0	Points for 39	Against 15
in France	Played 8	Won 6	Lost 1	Drawn 1	Points for 131	Against 93

International record

v Romania	Played 1	Won 1
v France	Played 2	Won 2

International details

v Romania	Oct 24	Romania 6	New Zealand 14	(Bucharest)
v France	Nov 14	France 9	New Zealand 13	(Toulouse)
	Nov 21	France 6	New Zealand 18	(Parc des Princes)

Players
Full-back: A R Hewson (Wellington)
Threequarters: B G Fraser (Wellington), S S Wilson (Wellington),
F A Woodman (North Auckland), J L B Salmon (Wellington), A M Stone (Waikato),
L M Cameron (Manawatu)
Five-eighths: S T Pokere (Southland), D L Rollerson (Manawatu),
B J McKechnie (Southland), J Boe* (Waikato)
Scrum-halves: D S Loveridge (Taranaki), A Donald (Wanganui)
Forwards: M G Mexted (Wellington), G H Old (Manawatu), G N K Mourie (Taranaki),
F K Shelford (Bay of Plenty), M W Shaw (Manawatu), B Morrissey* (Waikato),
A M Haden (Auckland), G W Whetton (Auckland), J Ross (Mid-Canterbury),
R C Ketels (Counties), W Neville (North Auckland), J E Spiers (Counties),
P T Koteka (Waikato), H R Reid (Bay of Plenty), A G Dalton (Counties)
Captain G N K Mourie   **Manager** P Gill   **Assistant Manager** P Burke

1983 (to England and Scotland only)

Full record	Played 8	Won 5	Lost 2	Drawn 1	Points for 162	Against 116
International record	Played 2	Lost 1	Drawn 1			

International details	Nov 12	Scotland 25	New Zealand 25	(Murrayfield)
	Nov 19	England 15	New Zealand 9	(Twickenham)

Players
Full-backs: K J Crowley (Taranaki), R M Deans (Canterbury)
Threequarters: S S Wilson (Wellington), B G Fraser (Wellington), B W Smith (Waikato),
C I Green (Canterbury), S T Pokere (Southland), W T Taylor (Canterbury)
Half-backs: I T Dunn (North Auckland), W R Smith (Canterbury),
A J Donald (Wanganui), D E Kirk (Otago)
Forwards: K G Boroevich (King Country), S A Crichton (Wellington),
M G Davie (Canterbury), B McGrattan (Wellington), H R Reid (Bay of Plenty),
B H Wilson (Counties), A Anderson (Canterbury), G J Braid (Bay of Plenty),
A G Robinson (North Auckland), M J Hobbs (Canterbury), M W Shaw (Manawatu),
F N K Shelford (Hawke's Bay), M G Mexted (Wellington), G H Old (Manawatu)
Captain S S Wilson   **Manager** P W Mitchell   **Assistant Manager** D B Rope

1986 (to France only)

Full record	Played 8	Won 7	Lost 1	Drawn 0	Points for 218	Against 87
International record	Played 2	Won 1	Lost 1			

International details	Nov 8	France 7	New Zealand 19	(Toulouse)
	Nov 15	France 16	New Zealand 3	(Nantes)

Players
Full-backs: K J Crowley (Taranaki), J A Gallagher (Wellington)
Threequarters: J J Kirwan (Auckland), C I Green (Canterbury), T J Wright (Auckland),
M J Berry (Wairarapa-Bush), J T Stanley (Auckland), A M Stone (Bay of Plenty)
Half-backs: F M Botica (North Harbour), G J Fox (Auckland), D J Kenny (Otago),
D E Kirk (Auckland)
Forwards: K G Boroevich (Wellington), J A Drake (Auckland), S C McDowell (Auckland),

S B T Fitzpatrick(Auckland), H R Reid (Bay of Plenty), G W Whetton (Auckland),
M W Speight (Waikato), M J Pierce (Wellington), A T Earl (Canterbury), M J B Hobbs
(Canterbury), M W Shaw (Hawke's Bay), M Brooke-Cowden (Auckland), M R Brewer
(Otago), W T Shelford (North Harbour)
Captain M J B Hobbs **Manager** R A Guy **Assistant Manager** B J Lochore

NEW ZEALAND TO SOUTH AFRICA
1928

Full record	Played 22 Won 16 Lost 5 Drawn 1 Points for 339 Against 144

International record Played 4 Won 2 Lost 2

International details	Jun 30	South Africa 17	New Zealand 0	(Durban)
	Jul 21	South Africa 6	New Zealand 7	(Johannesburg)
	Aug 18	South Africa 11	New Zealand 6	(Port Elizabeth)
	Sep 1	South Africa 5	New Zealand 13	(Cape Town)

Players
Full-back: H T Lilburne (Canterbury)
Threequarters: S R Carleton (Canterbury), B A Grenside (Hawke's Bay),
D F Lindsay (Otago), F W Lucas (Auckland), A C C Robilliard (Canterbury),
C A Rushbrook (Wellington), T R Sheen (Auckland)
Five-eighths: L M Johnson (Wellington), N P McGregor (Canterbury),
M F Nicholls (Wellington), W A Strang (South Canterbury)
Scrum-halves: W C Dalley (Canterbury), F D Kilby (Wellington)
Forwards: G T Alley (Canterbury), C J Brownlie (Hawke's Bay),
M J Brownlie (Hawke's Bay), J T Burrows (Canterbury),
I H Finlayson (North Auckland), S Hadley (Auckland), I H Harvey (Wairarapa),
W E Hazlett (Southland), J Hore (Otago), R G McWilliams (Auckland),
G Scrimshaw (Canterbury), E M Snow (Nelson), R T Stewart (South Canterbury),
J P Swain (Hawke's Bay), E P Ward (Taranaki)
Captain M J Brownlie **Manager** W F Hornig

1949

Full record	Played 24 Won 14 Lost 7 Drawn 3 Points for 230 Against 146

International record Played 4 Lost 4

International details	Jul 16	South Africa 15	New Zealand 11	(Cape Town)
	Aug 13	South Africa 12	New Zealand 6	(Johannesburg)
	Sep 3	South Africa 9	New Zealand 3	(Durban)
	Sep 17	South Africa 11	New Zealand 8	(Port Elizabeth)

Players
Full-backs: J W Goddard (South Canterbury), R W H Scott (Auckland)
Threequarters: E G Boggs (Auckland), I J Botting (Otago), P Henderson (Wanganui),
W A Meates (Otago), Dr R R Elvidge (Otago), M P Goddard (South Canterbury)
Five-eighths: F R Allen (Auckland), K E Gudsell (Wanganui), N W Black (Auckland),
G W Delamore (Wellington), J C Kearney (Otago)
Scrum-halves: W J Conrad (Waikato), L T Savage (Canterbury)
Forwards: L A Grant (South Canterbury), N H Thornton (Auckland),
P J B Crowley (Auckland), P Johnstone (Otago), J R McNab (Otago),
H F Frazer (Hawke's Bay), L R Harvey (Otago), M J McHugh (Auckland),
C Willocks (Otago), D L Christian (Auckland), R A Dalton (Otago),
J G Simpson (Auckland), K L Skinner (Otago), E H Catley (Waikato),
N L Wilson (Otago)
Captain F R Allen **Manager** J H Parker **Assistant Manager** A McDonald

1960

Full record	Played 26	Won 20	Lost 4	Drawn 2	Points for 441	Against 164

International record   Played 4   Won 1   Lost 2   Drawn 1

International details	Jun 25	South Africa 13	New Zealand 0	(Johannesburg)
	Jul 23	South Africa 3	New Zealand 11	(Cape Town)
	Aug 13	South Africa 11	New Zealand 11	(Bloemfontein)
	Aug 27	South Africa 8	New Zealand 3	(Port Elizabeth)

Players

Full-backs: D B Clarke (Waikato), W A Davies (Auckland)

Threequarters: D H Cameron (Mid-Canterbury), R W Caulton (Wellington),
K F Laidlaw (Southland), R F McMullen (Auckland), T P A O'Sullivan (Taranaki),
J R Watt (Wellington)

Five-eighths: S G Bremner (Canterbury), A H Clarke (Auckland),
T R Lineen (Auckland), S R Nesbit (Auckland)

Scrum-halves: K C Briscoe (Taranaki), R J Urbahn (Taranaki)

Forwards: E J Anderson (Bay of Plenty), R J Boon* (Taranaki),
Dr H C Burry (Canterbury), I J Clarke (Waikato), R J Conway (Otago),
W D Gillespie (Otago), D J Graham (Canterbury), R C Hemi (Waikato),
R H Horsley (Wellington), M W Irwin (Otago), P F Jones (North Auckland),
I N MacEwan (Wellington), C E Meads (King Country), E A R Pickering (Waikato),
K R Tremain (Canterbury), W J Whineray (Auckland), D Young (Canterbury)

Captain W J Whineray   **Manager** T H Pearce   **Assistant Manager** J L Sullivan

1970

Full record	Played 24	Won 21	Lost 3	Drawn 0	Points for 687	Against 228

International record   Played 4   Won 1   Lost 3

International details	Jul 25	South Africa 17	New Zealand 6	(Pretoria)
	Aug 8	South Africa 8	New Zealand 9	(Cape Town)
	Aug 29	South Africa 14	New Zealand 3	(Port Elizabeth)
	Sep 12	South Africa 20	New Zealand 17	(Johannesburg)

Players

Full-back: W F McCormick (Canterbury)

Threequarters: M J Dick (Auckland), B A Hunter (Otago), B G Williams (Auckland),
G S Thorne (Auckland), W L Davis (Hawke's Bay), H P Milner (Wanganui)

Five-eighths: I R MacRae (Hawke's Bay), W D Cottrell (Canterbury),
E W Kirton (Otago), B D M Furlong (Hawke's Bay), G F Kember (Wellington)

Scrum-halves: C R Laidlaw (Otago), S M Going (North Auckland)

Forwards: B J Lochore (Wairarapa), A R Sutherland (Marlborough),
I A Kirkpatrick (Poverty Bay), A J Wyllie (Canterbury), T N Lister
(South Canterbury), B Holmes (North Auckland), C E Meads (King Country),
S C Strahan (Manawatu), A E Smith (Taranaki), J F Burns (Canterbury), B L Muller
(Taranaki), K Murdoch (Otago), A E Hopkinson (Canterbury), N W Thimbleby
(Hawke's Bay), B E McLeod (Counties), R A Urlich (Auckland)

Captain B J Lochore   **Manager** R L Burk   **Assistant Manager** I M H Vodanovich

1976

Full record	Played 24	Won 18	Lost 6	Drawn 0	Points for 610	Against 291

International record   Played 4   Won 1   Lost 3

International details	Jul 24	South Africa 16	New Zealand 7	(Durban)
	Aug 14	South Africa 9	New Zealand 15	(Bloemfontein)
	Sep 4	South Africa 15	New Zealand 10	(Cape Town)
	Sep 18	South Africa 15	New Zealand 14	(Johannesburg)

Players

Full-backs: L W Mains (Otago), C L Fawcett (Auckland)

Threequarters: B G Williams (Auckland), N A Purvis (Otago), B J Robertson (Counties), W M Osborne (Wanganui), G B Batty (Bay of Plenty), T W Mitchell (Canterbury)
Five-eighths: J E Morgan (North Auckland), J L Jaffray (Otago), D J Robertson (Otago), O D Bruce (Canterbury)
Scrum-halves: L J Davis (Canterbury), S M Going (North Auckland)
Forwards: A R Leslie (Wellington), A R Sutherland (Marlborough), K A Eveleigh (Manawatu), L G Knight (Poverty Bay), I A Kirkpatrick (Poverty Bay), K W Stewart (Southland), P J Whiting (Auckland), G A Seear (Otago), F J Oliver (Southland), H H Macdonald (North Auckland), K K Lambert (Manawatu), W K Bush (Canterbury), K J Tanner (Canterbury), B R Johnstone (Auckland), P C Harris* (Manawatu), R W Norton (Canterbury), G M Crossman (Bay of Plenty)
Captain A R Leslie   **Manager** N H Stanley   **Assistant Manager** J J Stewart

SOUTH AFRICA TO BRITISH ISLES AND FRANCE

1906-07 (British Isles only)

Full record	Played 28	Won 25	Lost 2	Drawn 1	Points for 553	Against 79
International record	Played 4	Won 2	Lost 1	Drawn 1		
International details	Nov 17	Scotland 6	South Africa 0	(Glasgow)		
	Nov 24	Ireland 12	South Africa 15	(Belfast)		
	Dec 1	Wales 0	South Africa 11	(Swansea)		
	Dec 8	England 3	South Africa 3	(Crystal Palace)		

Players
Full-backs: A R Burmeister (WP), A F Marsberg (GW), S Joubert* (WP)
Threequarters: A C Stegmann (WP), J A Loubser (WP), J le Roux (WP), A Morkel (TVL), J D Krige (WP), H A de Villiers (WP), J G Hirsch (EP), S C de Melker (GW)
Half-backs: H W Carolin (WP), F J Dobbin (GW), D C Jackson (WP), D Mare (WP)
Forwards: P J Roos (WP), W A Burger (B), D Brooks (B), W A Neill (B), H J Daneel (WP), P A le Roux (WP), D J Brink (WP), W C Martheze (GW), J W E Raaff (GW), W S Morkel (TVL), D F T Morkel (TVL), H G Reid (TVL), W A Millar (WP), A F Burdett (WP)
Captain P J Roos   **Manager** J C Carden

1912-13

Full record	Played 27	Won 24	Lost 3	Drawn 0	Points for 441	Against 101
in B Isles	Played 26	Won 23	Lost 3	Drawn 0	Points for 403	Against 96
in France	Played 1	Won 1	Lost 0	Drawn 0	Points for 38	Against 5
International record	Played 5	Won 5				
International details	Nov 23	Scotland 0	South Africa 16	(Inverleith)		
	Nov 30	Ireland 0	South Africa 38	(Dublin)		
	Dec 14	Wales 0	South Africa 3	(Cardiff)		
	Jan 4	England 3	South Africa 9	(Twickenham)		
	Jan 11	France 5	South Africa 38	(Bordeaux)		

Players
Full-backs: P G Morkel (WP), J J Meintjies (GW)
Threequarters: J Stegmann (WP), A van der Hoff (TVL), E E McHardy (OFS), W J Mills (WP), R R Luyt (WP), G M Wrentmore (WP), W A Krige (WP), J Morkel (WP)
Half-backs: J D McCulloch (GW), F P Luyt (WP), J Immelman (WP), F J Dobbin (GW)
Forwards: E H Shum (TVL), D F T Morkel (TVL), T F van Vuuren (EP), G Thompson (WP), A S Knight (TVL), S N Cronje (TVL), E T Delaney (GW), W H Morkel (WP), S H Ledger (GW), L H Louw (WP), J A J Francis (TVL), J S Braine (GW), W A Millar (WP), J D Luyt (EP)
Captain W A Millar   **Manager** M Honnet

1931-32 (British Isles only)

Full record	Played 26	Won 23	Lost 1	Drawn 2	Points for 407	Against 124
International record	Played 4	Won 4			
International details	Dec 5	Wales	3	South Africa 8	(Swansea)
	Dec 19	Ireland	3	South Africa 8	(Dublin)
	Jan 2	England	0	South Africa 7	(Twickenham)
	Jan 16	Scotland	3	South Africa 6	(Murrayfield)

Players
Full-backs: J C Tindall (WP), G H Brand (WP)
Threequarters: J van Niekerk (WP), M Zimerman (WP), J H van der Westhuizen (WP),
F D Venter (TVL), J C van der Westhuizen (WP), B G Gray (WP), F W Waring (WP),
J White (B), D O Williams* (Villagers)
Half-backs: B L Osler (WP), M G Francis (OFS), P de Villiers (WP),
D H Craven (Stellenbosch U)
Forwards: M M Louw (WP), S R du Toit (WP), A van der Merwe (Worcester),
S C Louw (WP), P J Mostert (WP), A J McDonald (WP), L C Strachan (TVL),
J N Bierman (TVL), H G Kipling (GW), G M Daneel (TVL), V Geere (TVL),
P J Nel (N), W F Bergh (SWD), H M Forrest (TVL), J B Dold (EP)
Captain B L Osler   **Manager** T B Pienaar

1951-52

Full record	Played 31	Won 30	Lost 1	Drawn 0	Points for 562	Against 167
in B Isles	Played 27	Won 26	Lost 1	Drawn 0	Points for 499	Against 143
in France	Played 4	Won 4	Lost 0	Drawn 0	Points for 63	Against 24
International record	Played 5	Won 5			
International details	Nov 24	Scotland	0	South Africa 44	(Murrayfield)
	Dec 8	Ireland	5	South Africa 17	(Dublin)
	Dec 22	Wales	3	South Africa 6	(Cardiff)
	Jan 5	England	3	South Africa 8	(Twickenham)
	Feb 16	France	3	South Africa 25	(Paris, Colombes)

Players
Full-backs: J Buchler (TVL), A C Keevy (E TVL)
Threequarters: J K Ochse (WP), F P Marais (Boland), M J Saunders (B),
P Johnstone (WP), M T Lategan (WP), R A M van Schoor (R), D J Sinclair (TVL),
S S Viviers (OFS)
Half-backs: J D Brewis (N TVL), D J Fry (WP), J S Oelofse (TVL),
P A du Toit (N TVL)
Forwards: P W Wessels (OFS), W H Delport (EP), A C Koch (Boland), A Geffin
(TVL), H P J Bekker (N TVL), F E van der Ryst (TVL), E E Dinkelmann
(N TVL), J A Pickard (WP), G Dannhauser (TVL), W H M Barnard (GW),
S P Fry (WP), C J van Wyk (TVL), B Myburgh (E TVL), J A du Rand (R),
B J Kenyon (B), H S Muller (TVL)
Captain B J Kenyon   **Manager** F W Mellish   **Assistant Manager** Dr D H Craven

1960-61

Full record	Played 34	Won 31	Lost 1	Drawn 2	Points for 567	Against 132
in B Isles	Played 30	Won 28	Lost 1	Drawn 1	Points for 476	Against 110
in France	Played 4	Won 3	Lost 0	Drawn 1	Points for 91	Against 22
International record	Played 5	Won 4	Drawn 1		
International details	Dec 3	Wales	0	South Africa 3	(Cardiff)
	Dec 17	Ireland	3	South Africa 8	(Dublin)
	Jan 7	England	0	South Africa 5	(Twickenham)
	Jan 21	Scotland	5	South Africa 12	(Murrayfield)
	Feb 18	France	0	South Africa 0	(Paris, Colombes)

Players
Full-backs: L G Wilson (WP), G J Wentzel (EP)
Threequarters: H J van Zyl (TVL), M J G Antelme (TVL), J P Engelbrecht (WP),
F du T Roux (WP), B P van Zyl* (WP), A I Kirkpatrick (GW), J L Gainsford (WP),
D A Stewart (WP), B B van Niekerk (OFS)
Half-backs: K Oxlee (N), C F Nimb (WP), R J Lockyear (GW), P de W Uys (N TVL)
Forwards: P S du Toit (WP), S P Kuhn (TVL), J L Myburgh (N TVL),
D N Holton (EP), G F Malan (WP), R A Hill (R), R G Johns* (WP),
A S Malan (TVL), J T Claassen (W TVL), H S van der Merwe (N TVL),
P J van Zyl (Boland), H J M Pelser (TVL), G H van Zyl (WP), J P F Botha (N TVL),
F C H du Preez (N TVL), D J Hopwood (WP), A P Baard (WP)
Captain A S Malan **Manager** W F Bergh **Assistant Manager** M M (Boy) Louw

1965 (Ireland and Scotland only)

Full record	Played 5	Won 0	Lost 4	Drawn 1	Points for 37	Against 53
International record	Played 2	Lost 2				
International details	Apr 10	Ireland	9	South Africa 6	(Dublin)	
	Apr 17	Scotland	8	South Africa 5	(Murrayfield)	

Players
Full-back: L G Wilson (WP)
Threequarters: C D Cilliers (OFS), C W Dirksen (N TVL), J P Engelbrecht (WP),
J L Gainsford (WP), W J Mans (WP), D A Stewart (WP)
Half-backs: J H Barnard (TVL), K Oxlee (N), S C Conradie* (WP),
D J de Villiers (WP), D J J de Vos (WP)
Forwards: S P Kuhn (TVL), J F K Marais (WP), J B Neethling (WP), D C Walton (N),
J W Wessels (OFS), G Carelse (EP), F C H du Preez (N TVL), A S Malan (TVL),
J Schoeman (WP), M R Suter (N), T P Bedford (N), D J Hopwood (WP)
Captain A S Malan **Manager** B M Medway **Assistant Manager** M M Louw

1968 (France only)

Full record	Played 6	Won 5	Lost 1	Drawn 0	Points for 84	Against 43
International record	Played 2	Won 2				
International details	Nov 9	France	9	South Africa 12	(Bordeaux)	
	Nov 16	France	11	South Africa 16	(Paris, Colombes)	

Players
Full-backs: H O de Villiers (WP), R L Gould (N)
Threequarters: J P Engelbrecht (WP), S H Nomis (TVL), E Olivier (WP),
F du T Roux (WP), O A Roux (N TVL)
Half-backs: P J Visagie (GW), M A Menter (N TVL), D J de Villiers (WP),
P de W Uys (N TVL)
Forwards: J F K Marais (WP), J L Myburgh (N TVL), J B Neethling (WP), G Pitzer
(N TVL), D C Walton (N), F C H du Preez (N TVL), J P Naude (WP), G Carelse (EP),
J H Ellis (SWA), P J F Greyling (OFS), M J Lourens (N TVL), T P Bedford (N)
Captain D J de Villiers **Manager** F C Eloff **Assistant Manager** J T Claassen

1969-70 (British Isles only)

Full record	Played 24	Won 15	Lost 5	Drawn 4	Points for 323	Against 157
International record	Played 4	Lost 2	Drawn 2			
International details	Dec 6	Scotland	6	South Africa 3	(Murrayfield)	
	Dec 20	England	11	South Africa 8	(Twickenham)	
	Jan 10	Ireland	8	South Africa 8	(Dublin)	
	Jan 24	Wales	6	South Africa 6	(Cardiff)	

Players
Full-backs: H O de Villiers (WP), P J Durand (WP)

Threequarters: R N Grobler (N TVL), G H Muller (WP), S H Nomis (TVL),
A E van der Watt (WP), E Olivier (WP), O A Roux (N TVL),
J P van der Merwe (WP), P J van der Schyff (W TVL), F du T Roux* (GW)
Half-backs: M J Lawless (WP), P J Visagie (GW), D J de Villiers (Boland),
D J J de Vos (W TVL)
Forwards: J L Myburgh (N TVL), J B Neethling (WP), J F K Marais (EP),
R Potgieter (N TVL), G Carelse (EP), A E de Wet (WP), F C H du Preez
(N TVL), G Pitzer (N TVL), D C Walton (N), M C J van Rensburg (N),
A J Bates (W TVL), J H Ellis (SWA), P J F Greyling (TVL), P I van Deventer (GW),
T P Bedford (N), M W Jennings (Boland), I J de Klerk* (TVL),
C H Cockrell* (WP), R Barnard* (TVL)
Captain D J de Villiers   **Manager** C A J Bornman   **Assistant Manager** A S Malan

1974 (France only)

Full record	Played 9	Won 8	Lost 1	Drawn 0	Points for 170	Against 74
International record	Played 2	Won 2				
International details	Nov 23	France 4	South Africa 13	(Toulouse)		
	Nov 30	France 8	South Africa 10	(Paris, Parc des Princes)		

Players
Full-backs: I W Robertson (R), D S L Snyman (WP)
Threequarters: C Fourie (EP), W P Stapelberg (N TVL), C F Pope (WP),
P J M Whipp (WP), J J Oosthuizen (WP), J A van Staden (N TVL)
Half-backs: J C P Snyman (OFS), G R Bosch (TVL), P C R Bayvel (TVL),
R J McCallum (WP)
Forwards: M du Plessis (WP), J L Kritzinger (TVL), J H Ellis (SWA),
T T Fourie (SE TVL), C J Grobler (OFS), J L van Heerden (N TVL),
J G Williams (N TVL), K B H De Klerk (TVL), J De Bruyn (OFS),
J F K Marais (EP), N S E Bezuidenhoudt (N TVL), J C J Stander (OFS),
D S van Den Berg (N), A Bestbier (OFS), R J Cockrell (WP)
Captain J F K Marais   **Managers** J Z le Roux
Assistant Managers J T Claassen and A I Kirkpatrick*

SOUTH AFRICA TO AUSTRALIA AND NEW ZEALAND

1921

Full record						
in Australia	Played 4	Won 4	Lost 0	Drawn 0	Points for 83	Against 38
in New Zealand	Played 19	Won 15	Lost 2	Drawn 2	Points for 244	Against 81
International record						
v New Zealand	Played 3	Won 1	Lost 1	Drawn 1		
International details	Aug 13	New Zealand 13	South Africa 5	(Dunedin)		
	Aug 27	New Zealand 5	South Africa 9	(Auckland)		
	Sep 17	New Zealand 0	South Africa 0	(Wellington)		

Players
Full-backs: P G Morkel (WP), I B de Villiers (TVL)
Threequarters: A J van Heerden (TVL), W C Zeller (N), J S Weepner (WP),
Henry Morkel (WP), W D Sendin (GW), W A Clarkson (N), S S Strauss (GW),
C du P Meyer (WP)
Half-backs: J S de Kock (WP), J C Tindall (WP), J P Michau (WP),
W H Townsend (N)
Forwards: T B Pienaar (WP), W H (Boy) Morkel (WP), M Ellis (TVL),
N J du Plessis (W TVL), G W van Rooyen (TVL), J M Michau (TVL),
T L Kruger (TVL), A P Walker (N), Royal Morkel (WP), F W Mellish (WP),

Harry Morkel (WP), J S Olivier (WP), L B Siedle (N), P J Mostert (WP),
H H Scholtz (WP)
Captain T B Pienaar   **Manager** H C Bennett

1937

Full record

in Australia	Played 9	Won 8	Lost 1	Drawn 0	Points for 342	Against 65
in New Zealand	Played 17	Won 16	Lost 1	Drawn 0	Points for 411	Against 104

International record

in Australia	Played 2	Won 2
in New Zealand	Played 3	Won 2	Lost 1

International details

v Australia	Jun 26	Australia	5	South Africa 9	(Sydney)
	Jul 17	Australia	17	South Africa 26	(Sydney)
v New Zealand	Aug 14	New Zealand	13	South Africa 7	(Wellington)
	Sep 4	New Zealand	6	South Africa 13	(Christchurch)
	Sep 25	New Zealand	6	South Africa 17	(Auckland)

Players

Full-backs: G H Brand (WP), F G Turner (TVL)
Threequarters: D O Williams (WP), P J Lyster (N), J A Broodryk (TVL),
A D Lawton (WP), L Babrow (WP), J L A Bester (Gardens), S R Hofmeyr (WP),
J White (B), G P Lochner (EP)
Half-backs: D F van de Vyver (WP), T A Harris (TVL), D H Craven (EP),
P du P de Villiers (WP)
Forwards: W E Bastard (N), W G Bergh (TVL), B A du Toit (TVL), C B Jennings (B),
J W Lotz (TVL), M M Louw (WP), S C Louw (TVL), H J Martin (TVL),
P J Nel (N), A R Sheriff (TVL), L C Strachan (TVL), M A van den Berg (WP),
G L van Reenen (WP), H H Watt (WP)
Captain P J Nel   **Manager** P W Day   **Assistant Manager** A de Villiers

1956

Full record

in Australia	Played 6	Won 6	Lost 0	Drawn 0	Points for 150	Against 26
in New Zealand	Played 23	Won 16	Lost 6	Drawn 1	Points for 370	Against 177

International record

in Australia	Played 2	Won 2
in New Zealand	Played 4	Won 1	Lost 3

International details

v Australia	May 26	Australia	0	South Africa 9	(Sydney)
	Jun 2	Australia	0	South Africa 9	(Brisbane)
v New Zealand	Jul 14	New Zealand	10	South Africa 6	(Dunedin)
	Aug 4	New Zealand	3	South Africa 8	(Wellington)
	Aug 18	New Zealand	17	South Africa 10	(Christchurch)
	Sep 1	New Zealand	11	South Africa 5	(Auckland)

Players

Full-backs: J U Buchler (TVL), S S Viviers (OFS)
Threequarters: K T van Vollenhoven (N TVL), P G Johnstone (TVL),
R G Dryburgh (N), J du Preez (WP), T P Briers* (WP), W Rosenberg (TVL),
P E Montini (WP), A I Kirkpatrick (GW), J J Nel (WP)
Half-backs: C A Ulyate (TVL), B F Howe (B), B D Pfaff (WP), T A Gentles (WP),
C F Strydom (OFS)
Forwards: H P J Bekker (N TVL), A C Koch (Boland), P S du Toit (WP),
H N Walker (W TV), A J van der Merwe (Boland), M Hanekom (Boland),
J A du Rand (N TVL), J T Claassen (W TVL), C J de Nysschen (N), J A J Pickard (WP),

C J van Wyk (TVL), D S P Ackermann (WP), C J De Wilzem (OFS),
G P Lochner (WPI), D F Retief (N TVL), J J Starke* (Stellenbosch)
Captain S S Viviers **Manager** Dr D H Craven **Assistant Manager** D J de Villiers

1965

Full record
in Australia   Played 6   Won 3   Lost 3   Drawn 0   Points for 184   Against 53
in New Zealand   Played 24 Won 19 Lost 5   Drawn 0   Points for 485   Against 232
International record
v Australia   Played 2   Lost 2
v New Zealand   Played 4   Won 1   Lost 3
International details
v Australia   Jun 19   Australia   18   South Africa 11   (Sydney)
                 Jun 26   Australia   12   South Africa 8   (Brisbane)
v New Zealand   Jul 31   New Zealand 6   South Africa 3   (Wellington)
                 Aug 21   New Zealand 13   South Africa 0   (Dunedin)
                 Sep 4   New Zealand 16   South Africa 19   (Christchurch)
                 Sep 18   New Zealand 20   South Africa 3   (Auckland)

Players
Full-backs: L G Wilson (WP), C G Mulder (E TVL)
Threequarters: J P Engelbrecht (WP), F du T Roux (GW), J L Gainsford (WP),
E Olivier* (WP), G Brynard (WP), J T Truter (N), S H Nomis (TVL),
W J Mans (WP), C J C Cronje (E TVL)
Half-backs: K Oxlee (N), J H Barnard (TVL), D J de Villiers (WP), C M Smith (OFS)
Forwards: D J Hopwood (WP), J A Nel (W TVL), J Schoeman (WP),
F C H du Preez (N TVL), J P Naude (WP), J H Ellis (SWA), A W MacDonald (Rho),
G F Malan (TVL), C P van Zyl (OFS), D C Walton (N), C P Goosen (OFS),
T P Bedford (N), L J Slabber* (OFS), P H Botha (TVL), A Janson (WP),
W H Parker (EP), J F Marais (EP)
Captain D J de Villiers **Manager** J F Louw **Assistant Manager** H S (Hennie) Muller

1971 (Australia only)

Full record   Played 13 Won 13 Lost 0   Drawn 0   Points for 396   Against 102
International record Played 3   Won 3
International details Jul 17   Australia 11   South Africa 19   (Sydney)
                           Jul 31   Australia 6   South Africa 14   (Brisbane)
                           Aug 7   Australia 6   South Africa 18   (Sydney)

Players
Full-backs: I D McCallum (WP), O A Roux (N TVL)
Threequarters: G H Muller (WP), S H Nomis (TVL), J T Viljoen (N),
P A Cronje (TVL), J S Jansen (OFS), P S Swanson (TVL), A E van der Watt* (WP)
Half-backs: P J Visagie (GW), D S L Snyman (WP), J F Viljoen (GW),
D J J de Vos (W TVL)
Forwards: J F K Marais (EP), M J Louw (TVL), J T Sauermann (TVL),
J F B van Wyk (N TVL), R W Barnard (TVL), F C H du Preez (N TVL),
J J Spies (N TVL), J G Williams (N TVL), J H Ellis (SWA), P J F Greyling (TVL),
M J Lourens (N TVL), T P Bedford (N), M du Plessis (WP), A J Bates* (W TVL),
Captain J F K Marais **Manager** G P Lochner **Assistant Manager** J T Claassen

1981 (New Zealand only, except for three matches in USA)

Full record   Played 17 Won 14 Lost 2 Drawn 1 Points for 535   Against 190
in New Zealand   Played 14 Won 11 Lost 2 Drawn 1 Points for 410   Against 171
in USA   Played 3   Won 3   Lost 0 Drawn 0 Points for 125   Against 19

International record

v New Zealand   Played 3   Won 1   Lost 2
v USA   Played 1   Won 1

International details

v New Zealand   Aug 15   New Zealand 14   South Africa 9   (Christchurch)
                 Aug 29   New Zealand 12   South Africa 24   (Wellington)
                 Sep 12   New Zealand 25   South Africa 22   (Auckland)
v USA   Sep 26   USA   7   South Africa 38   (Glenville, NY)

Players

Full-backs: Z M J Pienaar (OFS), J W Heunis (N TVL)

Threequarters: J S Germishuys (TVL), D S Botha (N TVL) E F W Krantz (OFS),
R H Mordt (TVL), C J du Plessis (WP), W du Plessis (WP), E G Tobias (Boland),
D M Gerber (EP)

Half-backs: H E Botha (N TVL), J J Beck (WP), D J Serfontein (WP),
B J Wolmarans (OFS), G Visagie* (Natal)

Forwards: W Claassen (Natal), J H Marais (N TVL), M B Burger (N TVL),
S B Geldenhuys (N TVL), E Jansen (OFS), R J Louw (WP), H J Bekker (WP),
L C Moolman (N TVL), M T S Stofberg (N TVL), J de V Visser (WP), P G du Toit (WP),
O W Oosthuizen (N TVL), H J van Aswegen (WP), P R van der Merwe (S W Districts),
R J Cockrell (WP), W J H Kahts (N TVL), S Povey* (WP)

Captain W Claassen   **Manager** J T Claassen

Assistant Managers C M Smith, A Williams

AUSTRALIA TO BRITISH ISLES AND FRANCE

1908-09 (England and Wales only)

Full record	Played 31 Won 25 Lost 5 Drawn 1 Points for 438 Against 149
International record	Played 2 Won 1 Lost 1
International details	Dec 12 Wales 9 Australia 6 (Cardiff)
	Jan 9 England 3 Australia 9 (Blackheath)

Players

Full-backs: P P Carmichael (Queensland), W Dix (Armidale)

Threequarters: C Russell (Newtown), F B Smith (Central West), H Daly (Central West),
D B Carroll (St George), J Hickey (Glebe), E Mandible (Sydney),
E Parkinson (Queensland)

Five-eighths: W Prentice (West Suburbs), A J McCabe (Sydney),
J M Stevenson (Northern)

Scrum-halves: F Wood (Glebe), C H McKivat (Glebe)

Forwards: Dr H M Moran (Newcastle), T S Griffen (Glebe), S A Middleton (Glebe),
E McIntyre (Central West), K Gavin* (Central West), P A McCue (Newtown),
J T Barnett (Newtown), P H Burge (S Sydney), A B Burge* (S Sydney),
C E Murnin (Eastern Suburbs), N E Row (Eastern Suburbs),
M McArthur (Eastern Suburbs), P Flanagan (Queensland), T J Richards (Queensland),
C H McMurtrie (Orange), R R Craig (Balmain), C A Hammand (University)

Captain Dr H M Moran   **Manager** J McMahon   **Assistant Manager** S Wickham

1927-28 (Known as 'The Waratahs')

Full record	Played 31 Won 24 Lost 5 Drawn 2 Points for 432 Against 207
in B Isles	Played 28 Won 22 Lost 4 Drawn 2 Points for 400 Against 177
in France	Played 3 Won 2 Lost 1 Drawn 0 Points for 32 Against 30
International record	Played 5 Won 3 Lost 2
International details	Nov 12 Ireland 3 Australia 5 (Dublin)
	Nov 26 Wales 8 Australia 18 (Cardiff)
	Dec 17 Scotland 10 Australia 8 (Murrayfield)

Jan 7   England 18   Australia 11 (Twickenham)
Jan 22   France   8   Australia 11 (Paris, Colombes)

Players
Full-back: A W Ross (Sydney U)
Threequarters: E E Ford (Glebe-Balmain), A C Wallace (University and
Glebe-Balmain), A J A Bowers (Randwick), G C Gordon (YMCA), W H Mann
(University), C H T Towers (Randwick), W B J Sheehan (University),
S C King (Western Suburbs), J B Egan (Eastern Suburbs)
Half-backs: T Lawton (Western Suburbs), S J Malcolm (Newcastle),
F W Meagher (Randwick), J L Duncan (Randwick)
Forwards: J A Ford (Glebe-Balmain), A J Tancred (Glebe-Balmain),
J W Breckenridge (Glebe-Balmain), E N Greatorex (YMCA), A N Finlay (University),
G P Storey (Western Suburbs), G Bland (Manly), E J Thorn (Manly),
C L Fox (North Sydney), B Judd (Randwick), M R Blair (Western Suburbs),
J G Blackwood (Eastern Suburbs), H F Woods (YMCA), K Tarleton (YMCA),
J L Tancred (Glebe-Balmain)
Captain A C Wallace   **Manager** E Gordon Shaw

1947-48

Full record	Played 35	Won 29	Lost 6	Drawn 0	Points for 500	Against 243
in B Isles	Played 30	Won 25	Lost 5	Drawn 0	Points for 429	Against 197
in France	Played 5	Won 4	Lost 1	Drawn 0	Points for 71	Against 46
International record	Played 5	Won 3	Lost 2			
International details	Nov 22	Scotland 7	Australia 16	(Murrayfield)		
	Dec 6	Ireland 3	Australia 16	(Dublin)		
	Dec 20	Wales 6	Australia 0	(Cardiff)		
	Jan 3	England 0	Australia 11	(Twickenham)		
	Jan 11	France 13	Australia 6	(Paris, Colombes)		

Players
Full-backs: B J C Piper (NSW), C J Windsor (Queensland)
Threequarters: C C Eastes (NSW), A E J Tonkin (NSW), J W T MacBride (NSW),
T K Bourke (Queensland), T Allan (NSW), M L Howell (NSW), A K Walker (NSW)
Five-eighths: J F Cremin (NSW), N A Emery (NSW), E G Broad (Queensland)
Scrum-halves: C T Burke (NSW), R M Cawsey (NSW)
Forwards: W M McLean (Queensland), A J Buchan (NSW), C J Windon (NSW),
J O Stenmark (NSW), K C Winning (Queensland), J G Fuller (NSW),
G M Cooke (Queensland), P A Hardcastle (NSW), D F Kraefft (NSW),
N Shehadie (NSW), R E McMaster (Queensland), E Tweedale (NSW),
D H Keller (NSW), E H Davis (Victoria), K H Kearney (NSW), W L Dawson (NSW)
Captain W M McLean   **Manager** A J Tancred   **Assistant Manager** J Noseda

1957-58

Full record	Played 34	Won 16	Lost 15	Drawn 3	Points for 285	Against 244
in B Isles	Played 30	Won 14	Lost 13	Drawn 3	Points for 248	Against 203
in France	Played 4	Won 2	Lost 2	Drawn 0	Points for 37	Against 41
International record	Played 5	Lost 5				
International details	Jan 4	Wales 9	Australia 3	(Cardiff)		
	Jan 18	Ireland 9	Australia 6	(Dublin)		
	Feb 1	England 9	Australia 6	(Twickenham)		
	Feb 15	Scotland 12	Australia 8	(Murrayfield)		
	Mar 9	France 19	Australia 0	(Paris, Colombes)		

Players
Full-backs: T G Curley (NSW), J K Lenehan (NSW)
Threequarters: K J Donald (Queensland), R Phelps (NSW), A R Morton (NSW),

O G Fox (NSW), J A Phipps (NSW), G D Bailey (NSW), J M Potts (NSW),
S W White (NSW)
Half-backs: R Harvey (NSW), A Summons (NSW), D Logan (NSW),
D M Connor (Queensland)
Forwards: R A L Davidson (NSW), P T Fenwicke (NSW), N M Hughes (NSW),
W J Gunther (NSW), J E Thornett (NSW), K Yanz (NSW), E M Purkis (NSW),
A R Miller (NSW), A S Cameron (NSW), D M Emanuel (NSW), S Scotts (NSW),
N Shehadie (NSW), G N Vaughan (Victoria), K J Ryan (Queensland),
J V Brown (NSW), R Meadows (NSW)
Captain R A L Davidson **Manager** T H McClenaghan
Assistant Manager D L Cowper

1966-67

Full record	Played 34	Won 17	Lost 14	Drawn 3	Points for 348	Against 322
in B Isles	Played 30	Won 15	Lost 13	Drawn 2	Points for 303	Against 280
in France	Played 4	Won 2	Lost 1	Drawn 1	Points for 45	Against 42

International record	Played 5	Won 2	Lost 3		
International details	Dec 3	Wales	11	Australia 14	(Cardiff)
	Dec 17	Scotland	11	Australia 5	(Murrayfield)
	Jan 7	England	11	Australia 23	(Twickenham)
	Jan 21	Ireland	15	Australia 8	(Dublin)
	Feb 11	France	20	Australia 14	(Paris, Colombes)

Players
Full-backs: J K Lenehan (NSW), P F Ryan (NSW)
Threequarters: E S Boyce (NSW), P V Smith (NSW), R Webb (Victoria)
R J Marks (Queensland), J E Brass (NSW), A M Cardy (NSW), J A Francis (NSW)
Five-eighths: P R Gibbs (Victoria), A M C Moore (NSW), P F Hawthorne (NSW)
Scrum-halves: J N B Hipwell (NSW), K W Catchpole (NSW)
Forwards: J E Thornett (NSW), R Cullen (Queensland), R B Prosser (NSW),
R G Teitzel (Queensland), R J Heming (NSW), R D Tulloch (Victoria),
J O'Gorman (NSW), G V Davis (NSW), C P Crittle (NSW), P G Johnson (NSW),
A R Miller (NSW), J M Miller (NSW), D A O'Callaghan (NSW),
D A Taylor (Queensland), M P Purcell (Queensland), J Guerassimoff (Queensland),
R Taylor* (NSW)
Captain J E Thornett **Manager** R E M McLaughlin **Assistant Manager** A S Roper

1968 (Ireland and Scotland only)

Full record	Played 5	Won 2	Lost 3	Drawn 0	Points for 38	Against 40

International record	Played 2	Lost 2		
International details	Oct 26	Ireland 10	Australia 3	(Dublin)
	Nov 2	Scotland 9	Australia 3	(Murrayfield)

Players
Full-back: A N McGill (NSW)
Threequarters: T R Forman (NSW), R P Batterham (NSW), J W Cole (NSW),
B D Honan (Queensland), A M Pope (Queensland), P V Smith (NSW),
J E Brass (NSW)
Five-eighth: J P Ballesty (NSW)
Scrum-halves: M J Barry (Queensland), J N B Hipwell (NSW)
Forwards: P G Johnson (NSW), P Darveniza (NSW), R B Prosser (NSW),
R V Turnbull (NSW), N P Reilly (Queensland), S C Gregory (Queensland),
K R Bell (Queensland), A J Skinner (NSW), D A Taylor (Queensland),
H A Rose (NSW), G V Davis (NSW)
Captain P G Johnson **Manager** J H Lord **Assistant Manager** D M Connor

1971 (France only)

Full record   Played 8   Won 4   Lost 4   Drawn 0   Points for 110   Against 101
International record   Played 2   Won 1   Lost 1
International details   Nov 20   France 11   Australia 13   (Toulouse)
                           Nov 27   France 18   Australia 9   (Paris, Colombes)

Players
Full-back: A N McGill (NSW)
Threequarters: J W Cole (NSW), R P Batterham (NSW), L Monaghan (NSW),
J J McLean (Queensland), D L'Estrange (Queensland), D Rathie (Queensland),
G A Shaw (NSW)
Half-backs: G C Richardson (Queensland), R L Fairfax (NSW), J N B Hipwell (NSW),
G Grey (NSW)
Forwards: G V Davis (NSW), M Flynn (Queensland), P D Sullivan (NSW),
R McLean (NSW), O Butler (NSW), S Gregory (Queensland), B Stumbles (NSW),
R Smith (NSW), D Dunworth (Queensland), R B Prosser (NSW),
B Brown (Queensland), P G Johnson (NSW), R Thompson (WA)
Captain G V Davis   **Manager** J French   **Assistant Manager** R I Templeton

1973 (England and Wales only)

Full record   Played 8   Won 2   Lost 5   Drawn 1   Points for 85   Against 131
International record   Played 2   Lost 2
International details   Nov 10   Wales   24   Australia 0   (Cardiff)
                           Nov 17   England 20   Australia 3   (Twickenham)

Players
Full-backs: A N McGill (NSW), R L Fairfax (NSW) (utility back)
Threequarters: L E Monaghan (NSW), O Stephens (NSW), J J McLean (Queensland),
D R Burnet (NSW), R D L'Estrange (Queensland), G A Shaw (NSW)
Half-backs: G C Richardson (Queensland), P G Rowles (NSW), J N B Hipwell (NSW),
R G Hauser (South Australia)
Forwards: K G McCurrach (NSW), A A Shaw (Queensland), P D Sullivan (NSW),
B R Battishall (NSW), M R Cocks (Queensland), G Fay (NSW), R A Smith (NSW),
S C Gregory (NSW), J L Howard (NSW), R Graham (NSW), S G Macdougall (NSW),
M E Freney (Queensland), C M Carberry (NSW)
Captain P D Sullivan   **Manager** J E Freedman   **Assistant Manager** R I Templeton

1975-76 (including one match in USA)

Full record   Played 26   Won 19   Lost 6   Drawn 1   Points for 496   Against 349
   in B Isles   Played 25   Won 18   Lost 6   Drawn 1   Points for 472   Against 337
   in USA   Played 1   Won 1   Lost 0   Drawn 0   Points for 24   Against 12
International record   Played 5   Won 2   Lost 3
International details   Dec 6   Scotland 10   Australia 3   (Murrayfield)
                           Dec 20   Wales   28   Australia 3   (Cardiff)
                           Jan 3   England 23   Australia 6   (Twickenham)
                           Jan 17   Ireland 10   Australia 20   (Dublin)
                           Jan 31   USA   12   Australia 24   (Los Angeles)

Players
Full-back: M A Fitzgerald (NSW)
Threequarters: J R Ryan (NSW), L E Monaghan (NSW), P G Batch (Queensland),
L J Weatherstone (ACT), G A Shaw (NSW), W A McKid (NSW),
R D L'Estrange (Queensland), J Berne (NSW)
Half-backs: K J Wright (NSW), P E McLean (Queensland), J C Hindmarsh (NSW),
J N B Hipwell (NSW), R G Hauser (Queensland), G O Grey★ (NSW)
Forwards: A A Shaw (Queensland), M E Loane (Queensland), R A Price (NSW),

G K Pearse (NSW), J K Lambie (NSW), G Cornelsen (NSW), R A Smith (NSW),
B W Mansfield (NSW), D W Hillhouse (Queensland), G S Eisenhauer (NSW[C]),
G Fay* (NSW), J E C Meadows (Victoria), S G Macdougall (ACT),
S C Finnane (NSW), R Graham (NSW), P A Horton (NSW), C M Carberry (NSW)
Captain J N B Hipwell **Manager** R V Turnbull **Assistant Manager** J D Brockhoff

1976 (France only, except for one match in Italy)

Full record						
Full record	Played 10	Won 4	Lost 6	Drawn 0	Points for 114	Against 163
in France	Played 9	Won 3	Lost 6	Drawn 0	Points for 98	Against 148
in Italy	Played 1	Won 1	Lost 0	Drawn 0	Points for 16	Against 15
International record	Played 2	Lost 2				
International details	Oct 24	France 18	Australia 15	(Bordeaux)		
	Oct 30	France 34	Australia 6	(Paris, Parc des Princes)		

Players
Full-back: P E McLean (Queensland)
Threequarters: P G Batch (Queensland), L E Monaghan (NSW), J R Ryan (NSW),
P J Crowe (NSW), G A Shaw (NSW), W A McKid (NSW),
G G Shambrook (Queensland)
Half-backs: K J Wright (NSW), J C Hindmarsh (NSW), R G Hauser (Queensland),
G O Grey (NSW)
Forwards: M E Loane (Queensland), A A Shaw (Queensland), G Cornelsen (NSW),
G K Pearse (NSW), B R Battishall (NSW), R A Smith (NSW), D W Hillhouse
(Queensland), G S Eisenhauer (NSW), K S Besomo (NSW), R Graham (NSW),
S C Finnane (NS), J E C Meadows (Victoria), D A Dunworth (Queensland),
C M Carberry (NSW), P A Horton (NSW), A M Gelling* (NSW)
Captain G A Shaw **Manager** J G Bain **Assistant Manager** R I Templeton

1981-82

Full record						
Full record	Played 23	Won 16	Lost 6	Drawn 1	Points for 431	Against 219
International record	Played 4	Won 1	Lost 3			
International details	Nov 21	Ireland 12	Australia 16	(Dublin)		
	Dec 5	Wales 18	Australia 13	(Cardiff)		
	Dec 19	Scotland 24	Australia 15	(Murrayfield)		
	Jan 2	England 15	Australia 11	(Twickenham)		

Players
Full-backs: R G Gould (Queensland), G J Ella (NSW)
Threequarters: B J Moon (Queensland), M C Martin (NSW), P C Grigg (Queensland),
G A Ella (NSW), A G Slack (Queensland), M D O'Connor (Queensland),
M H Cox (NSW), M J Hawker (NSW)
Half-backs: P E McLean (Queensland), M G Ella (NSW), J N B Hipwell (NSW),
A J Parker (Queensland), P A Cox* (NSW)
Forwards: M E Loane (Queensland), D Hall (Queensland), A A Shaw (Queensland),
C Roche (Queensland), S P Poidevin (NSW), G Cornelsen (NSW), P W Lucas (NSW),
S A Williams (NSW), M J Mathers (NSW), P W McLean (Queensland), S J Pilecki
(Queensland), J E C Meadows (Victoria), A M D'Arcy (Queensland), D J Curran
(NSW), B P Malouf (NSW), C M Carberry (Queensland), L R Walker* (NSW)
Captain A A Shaw **Manager** Sir Nicholas Shehadie, OBE
Assistant Manager R I Templeton

1983 (to France only, except for two matches in Italy)

Full record						
Full record	Played 11	Won 6	Lost 3	Drawn 2	Points for 190	Against 157
in Italy	Played 2	Won 2	Lost 0	Drawn 0	Points for 55	Against 7
in France	Played 9	Won 4	Lost 3	Drawn 2	Points for 135	Against 150
International record	Played 3	Won 1	Lost 1	Drawn 1		

International details	Oct 22	Italy	7	Australia 29	(Rovigo)
	Nov 13	France	15	Australia 15	(Clermont-Ferrand)
	Nov 19	France	15	Australia 6	(Parc des Princes)

Players

Full-backs: G J Ella (NSW), R G Gould (Queensland)
Threequarters: D I Campese (ACT), R G Hanley (Queensland), B J Moon (Queensland),
G A Ella (NSW), M J Hawker (NSW), A G Slack (Queensland)
Half-backs: M G Ella (NSW), A J Parker (Queensland), D Vaughan (NSW),
M Lynagh (Queensland), T A Lane* (Queensland)
Forwards: J E Coolican (NSW), O B Hall (NSW), M A Harding (NSW),
A J McIntyre (Queensland), T A Lawton (Queensland), M I McBain (Queensland),
S A G Cutler (NSW), D W Hillhouse (Queensland), N C Holt (Queensland),
S A Williams (NSW), J S Miller (Queensland), S P Poidevin (NSW),
C Roche (Queensland), D Hall (Queensland), S N Tuynman (NSW), R Crerar* (NSW)
Captain M G Ella **Manager** Dr C R Wilson **Assistant Manager** R Dwyer

1984

Full record	Played 18	Won 13	Lost 4		Drawn 1	Points for 400	Against 232
International record	Played 4	Won 4					
International details	Nov 3	England	3	Australia 19	(Twickenham)		
	Nov 10	Ireland	9	Australia 16	(Dublin)		
	Nov 24	Wales	9	Australia 28	(Cardiff)		
	Dec 8	Scotland	12	Australia 37	(Murrayfield)		

Players

Full-back: R G Gould (Queensland)
Threequarters: D I Campese (ACT), P C Grigg (Queensland), B J Moon (Queensland),
R G Hanley (Queensland), J W Black (NSW), M P Burke (NSW), T A Lane
(Queensland), M J Hawker (NSW), A G Slack (Queensland), I M Williams* (NSW)
Half-backs: M G Ella (NSW), M P Lynagh (Queensland), P A Cox (NSW),
N C Farr-Jones (NSW)
Forwards: C A Lillicrap (Queensland), A J McIntyre (Queensland), S Pilecki
(Queensland), E E Rodriguez (NSW), G H Burrow* (NSW), T A Lawton (Queensland),
M I McBain (Queensland), S A Williams (NSW), W A Campbell (Queensland),
N G Holt (Queensland), S A G Cutler, (NSW), C Roche (Queensland), W J Calcraft
(NSW), D Codey (Queensland), S P Poidevin (NSW), R J Reynolds (NSW), S N
Tuynman (NSW)
Captain A G Slack **Manager** Dr C R Wilson **Assistant Manager** A B Jones

1988 (to England, Scotland, Wales and Italy)

Full record	Played 15	Won 11	Lost 4	Drawn 0	Points for 438	Against 236
in Britain	Played 13	Won 9	Lost 4	Drawn 0	Points for 357	Against 212
in Italy	Played 2	Won 2	Lost 0	Drawn 0	Points for 81	Against 24
International record	Played 3	Won 2		Lost 1		
International details	Nov 5	England 28	Australia 19	(Twickenham)		
	Nov 19	Scotland 13	Australia 32	(Murrayfield)		
	Dec 3	Italy 6	Australia 55	(Rome)		

Players

Full-back: A J Leeds (NSW)
Threequarters: D I Campese (NSW), P V Carozza (Queensland), M T Cook (Queensland),
P Cornish (ACT), B Girvan (ACT), J C Grant (NSW), A S Niuqila (NSW), R C Toombs
(Queensland), L F Walker (NSW)
Half-backs: M P Lynagh* (Queensland), S L James (NSW), D J Knox (NSW),
B T Burke (NSW), N C Farr-Jones (NSW)
Forwards: M N Hartill (NSW), R Lawton (Queensland), A J McIntyre (Queensland),

E J A McKenzie (NSW), M I McBain (Queensland), T A Lawton (Queensland),
W A Campbell (Queensland), S A G Cutler (NSW), D Frawley (NSW), T B Gavin
(NSW), R J McCall (Queensland), D G Carter (NSW), J M Gardner (Queensland),
S R Gourley (Eastwood), J S Miller (Queensland), S N Tuynman (NSW)
Captain N C Farr-Jones **Manager** A J Conway **Coach** R S F Dwyer

AUSTRALIA TO SOUTH AFRICA
1933

Full record	Played 23 Won 12 Lost 10 Drawn 1 Points for 299 Against 195
International record	Played 5 Won 2 Lost 3

International details				
Jul 8	South Africa 17	Australia 3	(Cape Town)
Jul 22	South Africa 6	Australia 21	(Durban)
Aug 12	South Africa 12	Australia 3	(Johannesburg)
Aug 26	South Africa 11	Australia 0	(Port Elizabeth)
Sep 2	South Africa 4	Australia 15	(Bloemfontein)

Players
Full-backs: Dr A W Ross (NSW), F G McPhillips (NSW)
Threequarters: W J Warlow (Queensland), B A Grace (NSW), A D McLean
(Queensland), J Kelaher (NSW), J B Young (NSW), Dr G S Sturtridge (Victoria),
D L Cowper (Victoria), J C Steggall (Queensland)
Half-backs: R R Biilmann (NSW), C N Campbell (NSW), S J Malcolm (NSW),
W G Bennett (Queensland)
Forwards: O L Bridle (Victoria), J B T Doneley (Queensland), G M Cooke
(Queensland), W A Mackney (NSW), W Ritter (Queensland), W G S White
(Queensland), A J Hodgson (NSW), E Love (NSW), J G Clark (Queensland),
G Bland (NSW), R B Loudon (NSW), M C White (Queensland), M F Morton (NSW),
W H Cerutti (NSW), E T Bonis (Queensland)
Captain A W Ross **Manager** Dr W F Mathews

1953

Full record	Played 27 Won 16 Lost 10 Drawn 1 Points for 450 Against 413
International record	Played 4 Won 1 Lost 3

International details				
Aug 22	South Africa 25	Australia 3	(Johannesburg)
Sep 5	South Africa 14	Australia 18	(Cape Town)
Sep 19	South Africa 18	Australia 8	(Durban)
Sep 26	South Africa 22	Australia 9	(Port Elizabeth)

Players
Full-backs: T Sweeney (Queensland), R Colbert (NSW)
Threequarters: E Stapleton (NSW), G Jones (Queensland), S W White (NSW),
G Horsley (Queensland), H S Barker (NSW), J Blomley (NSW), H J Solomon (NSW),
J A Phipps (NSW)
Half-backs: S W Brown (NSW), M Tate (NSW), C T Burke (NSW), J Bosler (NSW)
Forwards: N Shehadie (NSW), E Morey (NSW), A S Cameron (NSW),
A R Miller (NSW), C F Forbes (Queensland), R A L Davidson (NSW),
J C Carroll (NSW), F M Elliott (NSW), J J Walsh (NSW), J Bain (NSW),
K A Cross (NSW), R Outterside (NSW), C Windon (NSW), D Brockhoff (NSW),
B B Johnson (NSW), N McL Hughes (NSW)
Captain H J Solomon **Manager** J W Breckenridge **Assistant Manager** A C Wallace

1961 (Short)

Full record	Played 6 Won 3 Lost 2 Drawn 1 Points for 90 Against 80
International record	Played 2 Lost 2

International details				
Aug 5	South Africa 28	Australia 3	(Johannesburg)
Aug 12	South Africa 23	Australia 11	(Port Elizabeth)

Players
Full-back: J Lenehan (NSW)
Threequarters: M Cleary (NSW), E Magrath (NSW), R Phelps (NSW),
B Ellwood (NSW), J Lisle (NSW)
Half-backs: J Dowse (NSW), H Roberts (Queensland), O Edwards (Queensland),
K Catchpole (NSW)
Forwards: T Reid (NSW), E Heinrich (NSW), J O'Gorman (NSW), R Heming (NSW),
J Thornett (NSW), R Thornett (NSW), G Macdougall (NSW), A Miller (NSW),
J White (NSW), D McDeed (NSW), P Johnson (NSW)
Captain K Catchpole **Manager** B J Halvorsen

1963

Full record	Played 24 Won 15 Lost 8 Drawn 1 Points for 303 Against 233
International record	Played 4 Won 2 Lost 2

International details				
	Jul 13	South Africa 14	Australia 3	(Pretoria)
	Aug 10	South Africa 5	Australia 9	(Cape Town)
	Aug 24	South Africa 9	Australia 11	(Johannesburg)
	Sep 7	South Africa 22	Australia 6	(Port Elizabeth)

Players
Full-backs: T Casey (NSW), P Ryan (NSW)
Threequarters: K Walsham (NSW), J Williams (NSW), J Boyce (NSW),
J Wolfe (Queensland), R Marks (Queensland), I Moutray (NSW), P Jones (NSW),
B Ellwood (NSW)
Half-backs: P Hawthorne (NSW), J Klem (NSW), K Catchpole (NSW),
K McMullen (NSW)
Forwards: J Guerassimoff (Queensland), D O'Neill (Queensland), G Davis (NSW),
D Shepherd (Victoria), E Heinrich (NSW), J O'Gorman (NSW), R Heming (NSW),
J M Miller (NSW), P Crittle (NSW), J Thornett (NSW), J White (NSW),
L Austin (NSW), J Freedman (NSW), B Bailey (NSW), P Johnson (NSW),
M Jenkinson (NSW)
Captain J Thornett **Manager** R E M McLaughlin **Assistant Manager** A S Roper

1969

Full record	Played 26 Won 15 Lost 11 Drawn 0 Points for 465 Against 353
International record	Played 4 Lost 4

International details				
	Aug 2	South Africa 30	Australia 11	(Johannesburg)
	Aug 16	South Africa 16	Australia 9	(Durban)
	Sep 6	South Africa 11	Australia 3	(Cape Town)
	Sep 20	South Africa 19	Australia 8	(Bloemfontein)

Players
Full-backs: A N McGill (NSW), B A Weir (NSW)
Threequarters: T R Forman (NSW), R P Batterham (NSW), J W Cole (NSW),
P D Moore (Queensland), S O Knight (NSW), P V Smith (NSW),
B D Honan (Queensland), G A Shaw (NSW)
Half-backs: J P Ballesty (NSW), R G Rosenblum (NSW), J N B Hipwell (NSW),
M J Barry (Queensland)
Forwards: J R Roxburgh (NSW), J L Howard (NSW), R B Prosser (NSW),
S S Sullivan (Queensland), B S Taafe (NSW), P Darveniza (NSW),
S C Gregory (Queensland), A M Abrahams (NSW), N P Reilly (Queensland),
O F Butler (NSW), G V Davis (NSW), M R Cocks (NSW), B McDonald (NSW),
R J Kelleher (Queensland), H A Rose (NSW), A J Skinner (NSW),
R Wood* (Queensland)
Captain G V Davis **Manager** C C Eastes **Assistant Manager** D M Connor

ENGLAND TO AUSTRALIA, NEW ZEALAND AND FIJI

1963 (New Zealand and Australia only)

Full record

in New Zealand	Played 5	Won 1	Lost 4	Drawn 0	Points for 45	Against 73
in Australia	Played 1	Won 0	Lost 1	Drawn 0	Points for 9	Against 18

International record

v New Zealand	Played 2	Lost 2
v Australia	Played 1	Lost 1

International details	May 25	New Zealand 21	England 11	(Auckland)
	Jun 1	New Zealand 9	England 6	(Christchurch)
	Jun 4	Australia 18	England 9	(Sydney)

Players

Full-back: R W Hosen (Northampton)
Threequarters: M S Phillips (Fylde), F D Sykes (Northampton),
M P Weston (Durham City), J C Gibson (United Services), J M Ranson (Rosslyn Park),
J M Dee (Hartlepool Rovers)
Half-backs: R F Read (Harlequins), J P Horrocks-Taylor (Leicester),
T C Wintle (St Mary's Hospital), S J S Clarke (Cambridge U)
Forwards: P E Judd (Coventry), J E Highton (United Services),
C R Jacobs (Northampton), H O Godwin (Coventry), J D Thorne (Bristol),
J E Owen (Coventry), T A Pargetter (Coventry), A M Davis (Torquay Athletic),
D P Rogers (Bedford), D G Perry (Bedford), B J Wightman (Coventry),
V R Marriott (Harlequins)
Captain M P Weston   **Manager** J T W Berry
Assistant Manager M R Steele-Bodger

1973 (Fiji and New Zealand only)

Full record

in Fiji	Played 1	Won 1	Lost 0	Drawn 0	Points for 13	Against 12
in New Zealand	Played 4	Won 1	Lost 3	Drawn 0	Points for 47	Against 60

International record

v New Zealand	Played 1	Won 1

International details	Sep 15	New Zealand 10	England 16	(Auckland)

Players

Full-backs: P A Rossborough (Coventry), A M Jorden (Blackheath)
Threequarters: D J Duckham (Coventry), P M Knight (Bristol), P J Squires (Harrogate),
J P A G Janion (Richmond), G W Evans (Coventry), P S Preece (Coventry)
Half-backs: A G B Old (Leicester), M J Cooper (Moseley), S J Smith (Sale),
J G Webster (Moseley)
Forwards: M A Burton (Gloucester), C B Stevens (Penzance-Newlyn),
F E Cotton (Loughborough Colls and Coventry), J V Pullin (Bristol), J White (Bristol),
C W Ralston (Richmond), N O Martin (Bedford), R M Uttley (Gosforth),
R M Wilkinson (Cambridge U and Bedford), P J Hendy (St Ives),
A Neary (Broughton Park), J A Watkins (Gloucester), A G Ripley (Rosslyn Park)
Captain J V Pullin   **Manager** D L Sanders   **Assistant Manager** J Elders

1975 (Australia only)

Full record	Played 8	Won 4	Lost 4	Drawn 0	Points for 217	Against 110
International record	Played 2	Lost 2				
International details	May 24	Australia 16	England 9	(Sydney)		
	May 31	Australia 30	England 21	(Brisbane)		

Players
Full-backs: P E Butler (Gloucester), A J Hignell (Cambridge U)
Threequarters: P J Squires (Harrogate), A J Morley (Bristol), D M Wyatt (Bedford),
P S Preece (Coventry), K Smith (Roundhay), A W Maxwell (New Brighton),
J P A G Janion* (Richmond)
Half-backs: W N Bennett (Bedford), A J Wordsworth (Cambridge U),
A G B Old* (Middlesbrough), W B Ashton (Orrell), P Kingston (Gloucester),
I N Orum* (Roundhay)
Forwards: A G Ripley (Rosslyn Park), D M Rollitt (Bristol), A Neary (Broughton Park),
S R Callum (Upper Clapton), P J Dixon* (Gosforth), R M Uttley (Gosforth),
W B Beaumont (Fylde), R M Wilkinson (Bedford), N D Mantell (Rosslyn Park),
F E Cotton (Coventry), M A Burton (Gloucester), P J Blakeway (Gloucester),
B G Nelmes* (Cardiff), J V Pullin (Bristol), J A G D Raphael (Northampton)
Captain A Neary   **Manager** A O Lewis   **Assistant Manager** J Burgess

1985 (New Zealand only)

Full record	Played 7	Won 4	Lost 3	Drawn 0	Points for 146	Against 123
International record	Played 2	Lost 2				

International details	Jun 1	New Zealand 18	England 13	(Christchurch)
	Jun8	New Zealand 42	England 15	(Wellington)

Players
Full-backs: C R Martin (Bath), I R Metcalfe (Moseley).
Threequarters: M E Harrison (Wakefield), S T Smith (Wasps), J M Goodwin (Moseley),
P W Dodge (Leicester), J L B Salmon (Harlequins), B Barley (Wakefield)
Half-backs: G H Davies (Wasps), S Barnes (Bristol), R J Hill (Bath),
N D Melville (Wasps)
Forwards: R P Huntsman (Headingley), M Preedy (Gloucester), G S Pearce
(Northampton), A Sheppard (Bristol), S E Brain (Coventry), A W Simpson (Sale),
W A Dooley (Preston Grasshoppers), J Orwin (Gloucester, RAF), S Bainbridge
(Gosforth), D H Cooke (Harlequins), G W Rees (Nottingham), J P Hall (Bath),
M C Teague (Gloucester), R Hesford (Bristol)
Captain P W Dodge   **Manager** W G D Morgan   **Assistant Manager** M J Green

1988 (Australia and Fiji only)

Full record	Played 9	Won 6	Lost 3	Drawn 0	Points for 203	Against 136
in Australia	Played 8	Won 5	Lost 3	Drawn 0	Points for 178	Against 124
in Fiji	Played 1	Won 1	Lost 0	Drawn 0	Points for 25	Against 12
International record						
v Australia	Played 2	Lost 2				
v Fiji	Played 1	Won 1				

International details				
v Australia	May 29	Australia 22	England 16	(Brisbane)
	Jun 12	Australia 28	England 8	(Sydney)
v Fiji	Jun 17	Fiji 12	England 25	(Suva)

Players
Full-backs: R Adamson (Wakefield), J M Webb (Bristol)
Threequarters: R Underwood (Leicester & RAF), J Bentley (Sale), B J Evans
(Leicester), B Barley (Wakefield), S J Halliday (Bath), J R B Buckton (Saracens),
T Buttimore* (Leicester), W D C Carling* (Harlequins & Army)
Half-backs: S Barnes (Bath), C R Andrew (Wasps), S Robson (Moseley), R M Harding
(Bristol)

Forwards: P A G Rendall (Wasps), G J Chilcott (Bath), J A Probyn (Wasps), G S Pearce (Northampton), B C Moore (Nottingham), R G R Dawe (Bath), N C Redman (Bath), J Orwin (Bedford), W A Dooley (Preston Grasshoppers), R A Robinson (Bath), D W Egerton (Bath), G W Rees (Nottingham), M G Skinner (Harlequins), D Richards (Leicester)

Captain J Orwin **Manager** G Cooke **Coaches** A B C Davies & D Robinson

ENGLAND TO SOUTH AFRICA
1972

Full record	Played 7	Won 6	Lost 0	Drawn 1	Points for 166	Against 58

International record Played 1 Won 1

International details Jun 3 South Africa 9 England 18 (Johannesburg)

Players

Full-backs: S A Doble (Moseley), D F Whibley (Leicester)
Threequarters: P M Knight (Bristol), A A Richards (Fylde), J P A G Janion (Bedford), A J Morley (Bristol), J S Spencer (Headingley), P S Preece (Coventry)
Half-backs: A G B Old (Middlesbrough), T Palmer (Gloucester), L E Weston (West of Scotland), J B Webster (Mosley), S J Smith* (Loughborough Colls)
Forwards: M A Burton (Gloucester), F E Cotton (Loughborough Colls), C B Stevens (Harlequins and Penzance-Newlyn), J V Pullin (Bristol), A V Boddy (Metropolitan Police), P J Larter (RAF and Northampton), C W Ralston (Richmond), D E J Watt (Bristol), T A Cowell (Rugby), A Neary (Broughton Park), J A Watkins (Gloucester), J Barton (Coventry), A G Ripley (Rosslyn Park)

Captain J V Pullin **Manager** A O Lewis **Assistant Manager** J Elders

1984

Full record	Played 7	Won 4	Lost 2	Drawn 1	Points for 156	Against 145

International record Played 2 Lost 2

International details	Jun 2	South Africa 33	England 15	(Port Elizabeth)
	Jun 9	South Africa 35	England 9	(Johannesburg)

Players

Full-backs: W H Hare (Leicester), N C Stringer (Wasps)
Threequarters: M D Bailey (Cambridge U), A H Swift (Swansea), D M Trick (Bath), P W Dodge (Leicester), J A Palmer (Bath), S B Burnhill (Loughborough U), B Barley* (Wakefield), G H Davies (Wasps)
Half-backs: J P Horton (Bath), N G Youngs (Leicester), R J Hill (Bath)
Forwards: P J Blakeway (Gloucester), G S Pearce (Northampton), M Preedy (Gloucester), P A G Rendall (Wasps), S G F Mills (Gloucester), S E Brain (Coventry), J P Scott (Cardiff), D A Cusani (Orrell), J H Fidler (Gloucester), G W Rees (Nottingham), P J Winterbottom (Headingley), J P Hall (Bath), C J S Butcher (Harlequins), M C Teague (Gloucester)

Captain J P Scott **Manager** C R Jacobs **Assistant Managers** W G D Morgan and J R H Greenwood

SCOTLAND TO SOUTH AFRICA
1960

Full record	Played 3	Won 2	Lost 1	Drawn 0	Points for 61	Against 45

International record Played 1 Lost 1

International details Apr 30 South Africa 18 Scotland 10 (Port Elizabeth)

Players

Full-back: R W T Chisholm (Melrose)

Threequarters: A R Smith (Cambridge U, Edinburgh Wands),
R H Thomson (London Scottish), R C Cowan (Selkirk), G D Stevenson (Hawick),
T McClung (Edinburgh Acads), P J Burnet (London Scottish)
Half-backs: G H Waddell (London Scottish), R B Shillinglaw (Gala and Army),
A J Hastie (Melrose)
Forwards: H F McLeod (Hawick), J B Neill (Edinburgh Acads),
D M D Rollo (Howe of Fife), N S Bruce (Blackheath), T O Grant (Hawick),
J W Y Kemp (Glasgow HSFP), F H ten Bos (Oxford U, London Scottish),
W Hart (Melrose), D B Edwards (Heriot's FP), R M Tollervey (Heriot's FP),
C E B Stewart (Kelso)
Captain G H Waddell   **Managers** R W Shaw and C W Drummond

SCOTLAND TO AUSTRALIA

1970

Full record	Played 6 Won 3 Lost 3 Drawn 0 Points for 109 Against 94
International record	Played 1 Lost 1
International details	Jun 6 Australia 23 Scotland 3 (Sydney)

Players
Full-back: I S G Smith (London Scottish)
Threequarters: M A Smith (London Scottish), J N M Frame (Gala), J W C Turner (Gala),
C W Rea (West of Scotland), A G Biggar (London Scottish), A D Gill (Gala)
Half-backs: I Robertson (Watsonians), C M Telfer (Hawick), D S Paterson (Gala),
G C Connell (London Scottish)
Forwards: F A L Laidlaw (Melrose), D T Deans (Hawick), N Suddon (Hawick),
J McLauchlan (Jordanhill Coll), A B Carmichael (West of Scotland), P K Stagg (Sale),
G L Brown (West of Scotland), P C Brown (Gala), T G Elliott (Langholm),
W Lauder (Neath), G K Oliver (Gala), R J Arneil (Leicester)
Captain F A L Laidlaw   **Managers** H S P Monro and G Burrell

1982

Full record	Played 9 Won 6 Lost 3 Drawn 0 Points for 220 Against 113
International record	Played 2 Won 1 Lost 1
International details	Jul 4 Australia 7 Scotland 12 (Brisbane)
	Jul 10 Australia 33 Scotland 9 (Sydney)

Players
Full-backs: P W Dods (Gala), A R Irvine (Heriot's FP)
Threequarters: G R T Baird (Kelso), J A Pollock (Gosforth), R J Gordon (London
Scottish), D I Johnston (Watsonians), K W Robertson (Melrose), C J Williamson
(West of Scotland)
Half-backs: B M Gossman (West of Scotland), J Y Rutherford (Selkirk), I G Hunter
(Selkirk), R J Laidlaw (Jedforest)
Forwards: J Aitken (Gala), G M McGuinness (West of Scotland), I G Milne (Heriot's FP),
N A Rowan (Boroughmuir), R F Cunningham (Bath), C T Deans (Hawick),
W Cuthbertson (Kilmarnock), I D McKie (Sale), A J Tomes (Hawick), F Calder
(Stewart's Melville FP), J H Calder (Stewart's Melville FP), I A M Paxton (Selkirk),
D B White (Gala), R E Paxton (Kelso), John Calder* (Stewart's Melville FP)
Captain A R Irvine   **Manager** I A A MacGregor   **Assistant Manager** J W Telfer

SCOTLAND TO NEW ZEALAND

1975

Full record	Played 7 Won 4 Lost 3 Drawn 0 Points for 157 Against 104

International record   Played 1   Lost 1
International details   Jun 14   New Zealand 24   Scotland 0   (Auckland)
Players
Full-backs: A R Irvine (Heriot's FP), B H Hay (Boroughmuir)
Threequarters: W C C Steele (RAF and London Scottish), L G Dick (Jordanhill),
J N M Frame (Gala), D L Bell (Watsonians), G A Birkett (Harlequins),
J M Renwick (Hawick)
Half-backs: I R McGeechan (Headingley), C M Telfer (Hawick),
A J M Lawson (London Scottish), D W Morgan (Stewart's Melville FP)
Forwards: D G Leslie (Dundee HSFP), G Y Mackie (Highland),
W S Watson (Boroughmuir), W Lauder (Neath), M A Biggar (London Scottish),
A J Tomes (Hawick), I A Barnes (Hawick), A F McHarg (London Scottish),
N A K Pender (Hawick), A B Carmichael (West of Scotland),
J McLauchlan (Jordanhill), D F Madsen (Gosforth), C D Fisher (Waterloo)
Captain J McLauchlan   **Manager** G Burrell   **Assistant Manager** W Dickinson

1981

Full record   Played 8   Won 5   Lost 3   Drawn 0   Points for 189   Against 125
International record   Played 2   Lost 2
International details   Jun 13   New Zealand 11   Scotland 4   (Dunedin)
                            Jun 20   New Zealand 40   Scotland 15   (Auckland)
Players
Full-backs: A R Irvine (Heriot's FP), P W Dods (Gala)
Threequarters: S Munro (Ayr), B H Hay (Boroughmuir), G R T Baird (Kelso),
R W Breakey (Gosforth), A G Cranston (Hawick), J M Renwick (Hawick)
Half-backs: J Y Rutherford (Selkirk), R Wilson (London Scottish), R J Laidlaw
(Jedforest), I G Hunter (Selkirk), A J M Lawson* (London Scottish, Heriot's FP)
Forwards: D B White (Gala), I A M Paxton (Selkirk), P M Lillington* (Durham U),
J H Calder (Stewart's Melville FP), G Dickson (Gala), D G Leslie (Gala),
W Cuthbertson (Kilmarnock), T J Smith (Gala), A J Tomes (Hawick), J Aitken (Gala),
G M McGuinness (West of Scotland), I G Milne (Heriot's FP),
N A Rowan (Boroughmuir), C T Deans (Hawick), K G Lawrie (Gala)
Captain A R Irvine   **Manager** G K Smith   **Assistant Manager** J W Telfer

IRELAND TO SOUTH AFRICA
1961

Full record   Played 4   Won 3   Lost 1   Drawn 0   Points for 59   Against 36
International record   Played 1   Lost 1
International details   May 13   South Africa 24   Ireland 8   (Cape Town)
Players
Full-back: T J Kiernan (UC Cork, Cork Constitution)
Threequarters: A J F O'Reilly (Old Belvedere, Leicester), N H Brophy (UC Dublin),
J C Walsh (UC Cork, Sunday's Well), K J Houston (London Irish, Oxford U),
W J Hewitt (Instonians), J F Dooley (Galwegians)
Half-backs: W G Tormey (UC Dublin), D C Glass (Belfast Collegians),
A A Mulligan (Cambridge U, London Irish), T J Cleary (Limerick)
Forwards: S Millar (Ballymena), B G M Wood (Garryowen), J N Thomas (Blackrock),
A R Dawson (Wanderers), J S Dick (Queen's U, Belfast),
W A Mulcahy (UC Dublin, Bective Rangers), M G Culliton (Wanderers),
C J Dick (Ballymena), N A A Murphy (Cork Constitution), D Scott (Malone),
J R Kavanagh (UC Dublin, Wanderers), T McGrath (Garryowen)
Captain A R Dawson   **Manager** N F Murphy   **Assistant Manager** T A O'Reilly

1981

Full record	Played 7 Won 3 Lost 4 Drawn 0 Points for 207 Against 90
International record	Played 2 Lost 2
International details	May 30 South Africa 23 Ireland 15 (Cape Town)
	Jun 6 South Africa 12 Ireland 10 (Durban)

Players

Full-backs: J J Murphy (Greystones), K A O'Brien (Broughton Park)
Threequarters: K D Crossan (Instonians), T J Kennedy (St Mary's Coll),
M J Kiernan (Dolphin), A C McLennan (Wanderers), J A Hewitt (North of Ireland FC),
A W Irwin (Queen's U, Belfast), D G Irwin (Queen's U, Belfast)
Half-backs: S O Campbell (Old Belvedere), P M Dean (St Mary's Coll),
M A M Quinn* (Lansdowne), J C Robbie (Greystones), R J M McGrath (Wanderers),
J B O'Connor* (Palmerston)
Forwards: W P Duggan (Blackrock Coll), R K Kearney (Wanderers), J F Slattery
(Blackrock Coll), J B O'Driscoll (London Irish), A F O'Leary (Cork Constitution),
B O Foley (Shannon), J J Holland (Wanderers), G H Wallace (Old Wesley),
D C Fitzgerald (Dublin U), G A J McLoughlin (Shannon), P A Orr (Old Wesley),
J L Cantrell (Blackrock Coll), H T Harbison (UC Dublin)
Captain J F Slattery **Manager** P F Madigan **Assistant Manager** T J Kiernan

IRELAND TO AUSTRALIA

1967

Full record	Played 6 Won 4 Lost 2 Drawn 0 Points for 119 Against 80
International record	Played 1 Won 1
International details	May 13 Australia 5 Ireland 11 (Sydney)

Players

Full-backs: T J Kiernan (Cork Constitution)
Threequarters: A T A Duggan (Lansdowne), F P K Bresnihan (UC Dublin),
J C Walsh (UC Cork), N H Brophy (UC Dublin), P J McGrath (UC Cork),
J B Murray (UC Dublin)
Half-backs: C M H Gibson (NIFC), B F Sherry (Terenure), L Hall (UC Cork)
Forwards: S A Hutton (Malone), K W Kennedy (London Irish), S MacHale
(Lansdowne), P O'Callaghan (Dolphin), W J McBride (Ballymena), M G Molloy
(UC Galway), K G Goodall (City of Derry), T A Moore (Highfield),
M G Doyle (UC Dublin), L G Butler (Blackrock), J M Flynn (Wanderers),
D J Hickie (St Mary's College)
Captain T J Kiernan **Manager** E O'D Davy **Assistant Manager** D McKibbin

1979

Full record	Played 8 Won 7 Lost 1 Drawn 0 Points for 184 Against 75
International record	Played 2 Won 2
International details	Jun 3 Australia 12 Ireland 27 (Brisbane)
	Jun 16 Australia 3 Ireland 9 (Sydney)

Players

Full-backs: F N G Ennis (Wanderers), R C O'Donnell (St Mary's Coll)
Threequarters: C M H Gibson (North of Ireland FC), T J Kennedy (St Mary's Coll),
A C McLennan (Wanderers), P A J Andreucetti (St Mary's Coll), D G Irwin
(Queen's U, Belfast), P P McNaughton (Greystones)
Half-backs: S O Campbell (Old Belvedere), A J P Ward (Garryowen), J J Moloney
(St Mary's Coll), C S Patterson (Instonians)
Forwards: W P Duggan (Blackrock Coll), C D Cantillon (Cork Constitution),

A J McLean (Ballymena), J B O'Driscoll (London Irish), J F Slattery (Blackrock Coll), B O Foley (Shannon), M I Keane (Lansdowne), H W Steele (Ballymena), E M J Byrne (Blackrock Coll), M P Fitzpatrick* (Wanderers), G A J McLoughlin (Shannon), P A Orr (Old Wesley), C F Fitzgerald (St Mary's Coll), P C Whelan (Garryowen)
Captain J F Slattery **Manager** J F Coffey **Assistant Manager** N A A Murphy

IRELAND TO NEW ZEALAND AND FIJI
1976

Full record	Played 8	Won 5	Lost 3	Drawn 0	Points for 96	Against 68
in New Zealand	Played 7	Won 4	Lost 3	Drawn 0	Points for 88	Against 68
in Fiji	Played 1	Won 1	Lost 0	Drawn 0	Points for 8	Against 0

International record Played 1 Lost 1
International details Jun 5   New Zealand 11   Ireland 3   (Wellington)
Players
Full-backs: A H Ensor (Wanderers), L A Moloney (Garryowen)
Threequarters: T O Grace (St Mary's Coll), A W McMaster (Ballymena), J A Brady (Wanderers), C M H Gibson (North of Ireland FC), J A McIlrath (Ballymena)
Half-backs: B J McGann (Cork Constitution), M A Quinn (Lansdowne), D M Canniffe (Lansdowne), J C Robbie (Dublin U), R J M McGrath* (Wanderers)
Forwards: W P Duggan (Blackrock Coll), H W Steele (Ballymena), S A McKinney (Dungannon), S M Deering (Garryowen), J C Davidson* (Dungannon), R F Hakin (CIYMS), M I Keane (Lansdowne), B O Foley (Shannon), E J O'Rafferty (Wanderers), T A O Feighery (St Mary's Coll), P O'Callaghan (Dolphin), P A Orr (Old Wesley), R J Clegg (Bangor), J L Cantrell (UC Dublin), P C Whelan (Garryowen)
Captain T O Grace **Manager** K J Quilligan **Assistant Manager** T W Meates

WALES TO SOUTH AFRICA
1964

Full record	Played 4	Won 2	Lost 2	Drawn 0	Points for 43	Against 58

International record Played 1 Lost 1
International details May 23   South Africa 24   Wales 3   (Durban)
Players
Full-backs: G T R Hodgson (Neath), H J Davies (London Welsh)
Threequarters: D I Bebb (Carmarthen TC, Swansea), S J Watkins (Newport), P M Rees (Newport), K Bradshaw (Bridgend), D K Jones (London Welsh, Cardiff), S J Dawes (London Welsh)
Half-backs: D Watkins (Newport), M Young (Bridgend), D C T Rowlands (Pontypool), A R Lewis (Abertillery)
Forwards: L J Cunningham (Aberavon), D Williams (Ebbw Vale), R G Waldron (Neath), N R Gale (Llanelli), J Isaacs (Swansea), B E Thomas (Neath), B Price (Newport), J T Mantle (Loughborough Colls), D J Hayward (Cardiff), H J Morgan (Abertillery), G J Prothero (Bridgend), A E I Pask (Abertillery)
Captain D C T Rowlands **Manager** D J Phillips
Assistant Manager Alun G Thomas

WALES TO AUSTRALIA, NEW ZEALAND AND FIJI
1969

Full record
in New Zealand	Played 5	Won 2	Lost 2	Drawn 1	Points for 62	Against 76

| in Australia | Played 1 | Won 1 | Lost 0 | Drawn 0 | Points for 19 | Against 16 |
| in Fiji | Played 1 | Won 1 | Lost 0 | Drawn 0 | Points for 31 | Against 11 |

International record

| v New Zealand | Played 2 | Lost 2 |
| v Australia | Played 1 | Won 1 |

International details

v New Zealand	May 31	New Zealand 19	Wales 0	(Christchurch)
	Jun 14	New Zealand 33	Wales 12	(Auckland)
v Australia	Jun 21	Australia 16	Wales 19	(Sydney)

Players

Full-back: J P R Williams (London Welsh)
Threequarters: S J Watkins (Newport), A P Skirving (Newport),
M C R Richards (Cardiff), S J Dawes (London Welsh), T G R Davies (Cardiff),
K S Jarrett (Newport)
Half-backs: B John (Cardiff), P Bennett (Llanelli), G O Edwards (Cardiff),
R Hopkins (Maesteg)
Forwards: T M Davies (London Welsh), D Hughes (Newbridge), W D Morris (Neath),
J Taylor (London Welsh), B Price (Newport), B E Thomas (Neath),
W D Thomas (Llanelli), D B Llewelyn (Newport), D J Lloyd (Bridgend),
D Williams (Ebbw Vale), N R Gale (Llanelli), J Young (Harrogate),
V C Perrins* (Newport)
Captain B Price   **Manager** H C Rogers   **Assistant Manager** D C T Rowlands

---

1978 (Australia only)

Full record	Played 9	Won 5	Lost 4	Drawn 0	Points for 227	Against 106
International record	Played 2	Lost 2				
International details	Jun 11	Australia 18	Wales 8	(Brisbane)		
	Jun 17	Australia 19	Wales 17	(Sydney)		

Players

Full-back: J P R Williams (Bridgend)
Threequarters: T G R Davies (Cardiff), G L Evans (Newport), J J Williams (Llanelli),
P C T Daniels (Cardiff), A J Donovan (Swansea), S P Fenwick (Bridgend),
R W R Gravell (Llanelli)
Half-backs: W G Davies (Cardiff), D S Richards (Swansea), T D Holmes (Cardiff),
D B Williams (Newport)
Forwards: C Davis (Newbridge), D L Quinnell (Llanelli), J Squire (Newport),
T J Cobner (Pontypool), S M Lane (Cardiff), B G Clegg (Swansea), A J Martin
(Aberavon), G A D Wheel (Swansea), A G Faulkner (Pontypool), G Price (Pontypool),
S J Richardson (Aberavon), M J Watkins (Cardiff), R W Windsor (Pontypool)
Captain T J Cobner   **Manager** D C T Rowlands   **Assistant Manager** S J Dawes

---

1988 (New Zealand only)

Full record	Played 8	Won 2	Lost 5	Drawn 1	Points for 135	Against 243
International record	Played 2	Lost 2				
International details	May 28	New Zealand 52	Wales 3	(Christchurch)		
	Jun 11	New Zealand 54	Wales 9	(Auckland)		

Players

Full-backs: A Clement (Swansea), S Bowling (Llanelli), J Mason* (Pontypridd)
Threequarters: I C Evans (Llanelli), G M C Webbe (Bridgend), C Davies (Llanelli),
J A Devereux (Bridgend), B Bowen (S Wales Police), M R Hall (Cambridge Univ &
Bridgend), M G Ring (Pontypool), N G Davies (Llanelli)
Half-backs: J Davies (Llanelli), R N Jones (Swansea), J L Griffiths (Llanelli)

Forwards: S T Jones (Pontypool), D A Buchanan (Llanelli), D Young (Swansea), J D Pugh (Neath), M Pugh* (S Wales Police), I J Watkins (Ebbw Vale), K H Phillips (Neath), R L Norster (Cardiff), P S May (Llanelli), K Moseley (Pontypool), S Sutton* (S Wales Police), R Phillips (Neath), W P Moriarty (Swansea), R G Collins (S Wales Police), G Jones* (Llanelli), T Fauvel (Aberavon), D J Bryant (Bridgend), M A Jones* (Neath)
Captain B Bowen   **Manager** R Morgan   **Coach** A J Gray

FRANCE TO SOUTH AFRICA
1958

Full record	Played 10	Won 5	Lost 3	Drawn 2	Points for 137	Against 124
International record	Played 2	Won 1	Drawn 1			
International details	Jul 26	South Africa 3	France 3	(Cape Town)		
	Aug 16	South Africa 5	France 9	(Johannesburg)		

Players
Full-backs: M Vannier (Racing Club de France), P Lacaze (FC Lourdais)
Threequarters: J Dupuy (S Tarbais), H Rancoule (FC Lourdais), J Lepatey (SC Mazamet), L Rogé (AS Béziers), A Marquesuzaa (Racing Club de France), G Stener (Paris U), L Casaux (S Tarbais)
Half-backs: R Martine (FC Lourdais), A Haget (Paris UC), P Danos (AS Béziers), P Lacroix (S Montois)
Forwards: J Barthe (FC Lourdais), M Celaya (Biarritz), J Carrère (RC Toulonnais), L Mias (SC Mazamet), B Mommejat (S Cadurcien), R Baulon (A Bayonnais), F Moncla (Racing Club de France), L Echavé (SU Agen), A Roques (S Cadurcien), R Barrière (AS Béziers), A Quaglio (SC Mazamet), R Vigier (AS Montferrand), A Fremaux (Paris U), J de Gregorio (FC Grenoble)
Captain M Celaya   **Manager** S Saulnier   **Assistant Manager** M Laurent

1964

Full record	Played 6	Won 5	Lost 1	Drawn 0	Points for 117	Against 55
International record	Played 1	Won 1				
International details	Jul 25	South Africa 6	France 8	(Springs)		

Players
Full-back: P Dedieu (AS Béziers)
Threequarters: J Gachassin (FC Lourdais), C Darrouy (S Montois), M Arnaudet (FC Lourdais), R Halçaren (FC Lourdais), J Dupuy (S Tarbais), J Piqué (S Paloise)
Half-backs: P Albaladejo (US Dacquoise), J Capdouze (S Paloise), J-C Hiquet (SU Agen), J-C Lasserre (US Dax), C Laborde (RCF)
Forwards: W Spanghero (RC Narbonne), M Crauste (FC Lourdais), M Lira (La Voulte S), M Sitjar (SU Agen), J-J Rupert (US Tyrosse), B Dauga (S Montois), E Cester (Toulouse OEC), A Herrero (RC Toulonnais), A Gruarin (RC Toulonnais), J C Berejnoi (SC Tulle), M Etcheverry (S Paloise), Y Menthiller (US Romans), J M Cabanier (US Montauban)
Captain M Crauste   **Manager** S Saulnier   **Assistant Manager** J Prat

1967

Full record	Played 13	Won 8	Lost 4	Drawn 1	Points for 209	Against 161
International record	Played 4	Won 1	Lost 2	Drawn 1		
International details	Jul 15	South Africa 26	France 3	(Durban)		
	Jul 22	South Africa 16	France 3	(Bloemfontein)		
	Jul 29	South Africa 14	France 19	(Johannesburg)		
	Aug 12	South Africa 6	France 6	(Cape Town)		

Players
Full-backs: C Lacaze (SC Angoulême), P Villepreux (S Toulousain),
J Crampagne (CA Beglais)
Threequarters: C Darrouy (S Montois), J Londios (US Montauban),
B Duprat (A Bayonnais), J-P Lux (US Tyrosse), C Dourthe (US Dax),
J Trillo (CA Beglais), J Saby (SC Graulhet), J-P Mir (FC Lourdais)
Half-backs: G Camberabero (La Voulte S), J-L Dehez (SU Agen),
J-C Roques (CA Brive), M Puget (CA Brive), G Sutra (RC Narbonne)
Forwards: A Abadie (SC Graulhet), J-M Esponda (Racing Club de France),
M Lasserre (SU Agen), B Cardebat (US Montauban), J-M Cabanier (US Montauban),
J-C Malbet (SU Agen), B Dauga (S Montois), W Spanghero (RC Narbonne).
J Fort (SU Agen), A Plantefol (Racing Club de France), C Carrère (RC Toulonnais),
M Sitjar (SU Agen), A Quilis (RC Narbonne), G Viard (RC Narbonne)
Captain C Darrouy **Manager** M Laurent **Assistant Manager** A Garrigues

1971

Full record   Played 9   Won 7   Lost 1   Drawn 1   Points for 228   Against 92
International record   Played 2   Lost 1   Drawn 1
International details   Jun 12   South Africa 22   France 9   (Bloemfontein)
                             Jun 19   South Africa 8   France 8   (Durban)
Players
Full-back: P Villepreux (S Toulousain)
Threequarters: R Bertranne (S Bagnerais), R Bourgarel (S Toulousain),
J Cantoni (AS Béziers), C Dourthe (US Dax), A Marot (CA Brive),
J Maso (RC Narbonne), J Sillières (S Tarbais), J Trillo (CA Beglais)
Half-backs: M Barrau (S Beaumontois), J-L Berot (S Toulousain),
G Pardiès★ (SU Agen), M Pebeyre (AS Montferrand)
Forwards: J-L Azarète (St Jean-de-Luz Ol), J-P Bastiat (US Dax),
P Biemouret (SU Agen), C Carrère (RC Toulonnais), B Dauga (S Montois),
A Estève (AS Béziers), M Etcheverry (S Paloise), J Iraçabal (A Bayonnais),
M Lasserre (SU Agen), J le Droff (FC Auch), J-C Skrela (S Toulousain),
C Spanghero (RC Narbonne), W Spanghero (RC Narbonne),
C Swierczinski (CA Beglais), M Yachvili (CA Brive)
Captain C Carrère **Manager** E Pebeyre
Assistant Managers F Cazenave and M Celaya

1975

Full record   Played 11   Won 6   Lost 4   Drawn 1   Points for 282   Against 190
International record   Played 2   Lost 2
International details   Jun 21   South Africa 38   France 25   (Bloemfontein)
                             Jun 28   South Africa 33   France 18   (Pretoria)
Players
Full-backs: J M Aguirre (S Bagnerais), M Droitecourt (AS Montferrand)
Threequarters: J-C Amade (Biarritz Ol), J-L Averous (La Voulte Sp),
D Harize (S Cahors), M Dupey (FC Auch), C Badin (CA Brive),
R Bertranne (S Bagnerais), J-M Etchenique (Biarritz Ol), F Sangalli (RC Narbonne)
Half-backs: J-P Romeu (AS Montferrand), J P Pesteil (AS Béziers),
R Astre (AS Béziers), J Fouroux (La Voulte Sp)
Forwards: Y Brunet (USA Perpignan), J Costantino (AS Montferrand),
D Revallier (UA Gaillac), R Paparemborde (S Paloise), B Forestier (CA Beglais),
G Cholley (Castres Ol), J-P Decrae (Racing Club de France), F Haget (SU Agen),
A Guilbert (RC Toulon), M Julian (Castres Ol), M Yachvili (CA Brive),
J-C Skréla (S Toulousain), P Peron (Racing Club de France), S Lassoujade (SU Agen),
G Rousset (AS Béziers), J-L Joinel (CA Brive), M Palmie★ (AS Béziers)

Captains (joint) R Astre and J Fouroux   **Manager** M Batigne
Assistant Managers M Celaya and F Cazenave

1980

Full record	Played 4	Won 3	Lost 1	Drawn 0	Points for 90	Against 95
International record	Played 1	Lost 1				

International details   Nov 8   South Africa 37   France 15   (Pretoria)

Players

Full-backs: S Gabernet (Toulouse), S Blanco (Biarritz)

Threequarters: D Bustaffa (Carcassonne), C Martinez (Béziers), J-C Castagnet (Pau), L Pardo (Bayonne), R Bertranne (Bagnères), P Mesny (Grenoble)

Half-backs: B Viviès (Agen), P Fort (Béziers), J Gallion (Toulon), J-P Elissalde (La Rochelle)

Forwards: J-L Joinel (Brive), M Carpentier (Lourdes), T Sinico (Valence), J-P Rives (Toulouse), P Lacans (Béziers), J-P Wolff (Béziers), A Maleig (Tarbes), J-P Fauvel (SC de Tulle), D Dubroca (Agen), R Paparemborde (Pau), P Dospital (Bayonne), B Herrero (Nice), P Dintrans (Tarbes)

Captain J-P Rives   **Manager** Y Noe   **Assistant Managers** M Celaya, J Piqué

FRANCE TO AUSTRALIA AND NEW ZEALAND
1961

Full record						
in New Zealand	Played 13	Won 6	Lost 7	Drawn 0	Points for 150	Against 149
in Australia	Played 2	Won 2	Lost 0	Drawn 0	Points for 30	Against 20
International record						
v New Zealand	Played 3	Lost 3				
v Australia	Played 1	Won 1				

International details

v New Zealand	Jul 22	New Zealand	13	France	6	(Auckland)
	Aug 5	New Zealand	5	France	3	(Wellington)
	Aug 19	New Zealand	32	France	3	(Christchurch)
v Australia	Aug 26	Australia	8	France	15	(Sydney)

Players

Full-backs: M Vannier (RC Chalon), J Meynard (US Cognac)

Threequarters: S Plantey (Racing Club de France), G Boniface (S Montois), H Rancoule (RC Toulon), J Dupuy (S Tarbais), G Calvo (FC Lourdais), J Piqué (S Paloise), J Bouquet (CS Vienne), A Boniface (S Montois)

Half-backs: C Lacaze (FC Lourdais), G Camberabero (La Voulte S), P Albaladejo (US Dacquoise), P Lacroix (SU Agen), L Camberabero (La Voulte S), J Serin (SC Mazamet)

Forwards: M Celaya (S Bordelais), S Meyer (CA Perigueux), R Lefèvre (CA Brive), M Crauste (FC Lourdais), F Moncla (S Paloise), C Vidal (SC Mazamet), M Cassiede (US Dax), J P Saux (S Paloise), A Domenech (CA Brive), A Bianco (FC Auch), G Bouguyon (FC Grenoble) P Cazals (S Montois), J Laudouar (AS Soustons), J Rollet (A Bayonnais)

Captain F Moncla   **Manager** M Laurent   **Assistant Manager** G Basquet

1968

Full record						
in New Zealand	Played 12	Won 8	Lost 4	Drawn 0	Points for 154	Against 120
in Australia	Played 2	Won 1	Lost 1	Drawn 0	Points for 41	Against 22

International record

v New Zealand   Played 3   Lost 3
v Australia   Played 1   Lost 1

International details

v New Zealand	Jul 13	New Zealand	12	France	9	(Christchurch)
	Jul 27	New Zealand	9	France	3	(Wellington)
	Aug 10	New Zealand	19	France	12	(Auckland)
v Australia	Aug 17	Australia	11	France	10	(Sydney)

Players

Full-backs: P Villepreux (S Toulousain), C Lacaze (Angoulême)
Threequarters: A Campaes (FC Lourdais), J M Bonal (S Toulousain),
P Besson (CA Brive), A Piazza (US Montauban), J-P Lux (US Tyrosse),
C Dourthe (US Dax), J Trillo (CA Beglais), J Maso (US Perpignan)
Half-backs: J Andrieu (SC Graulhet), C Boujet (Grenoble), J-L Berot (S Toulousain),
M Puget (CA Brive)
Forwards: M Greffe (Grenoble), W Spanghero (RC Narbonne),
M Billiere (S Toulousain), J Salut (Toulouse, OEC), C Carrère (RC Toulonnais),
B Dutin (Mont de Marsan), C Chenevay (Grenoble), B Dauga (Mont de Marsan),
A Plantefol (SU Agen), E Cester (Toulouse OEC), J-M Esponda (US Perpignan),
M Lasserre (SU Agen), J-C Noble (La Voulte S), J Iraçabal (A Bayonnais),
M Yachvili (SC Tulle), J-P Baux (CA Lannemezan)
Captain C Carrère   **Manager** J-C Bourrier   **Assistant Manager** A Garrigues

1972 (Australia only)

Full record	Played 9	Won 8	Lost 0	Drawn 1	Points for 254	Against 122
International record	Played 2	Won 1	Drawn 1			
International details	Jun 17	Australia 14	France 14	(Sydney)		
	Jun 25	Australia 15	France 16	(Brisbane)		

Players

Full-backs: P Villepreux (S Toulousain), H Cabrol (AS Béziers)
Threequarters: B Duprat (A Bayonnais), J Cantoni (AS Béziers), G Lavagne
(AS Béziers), J Trillo (CA Beglais), C Dourthe (US Dax), J-P Lux (US Dax),
J Maso (RC Narbonne)
Half-backs: J-L Berot (S Toulousain), A Marot (CA Briviste), M Barrau (S Beaumontois)
J Fouroux (La Voulte Sp)
Forwards: J-C Skrela (S Toulousain), P Biemouret (SU Agen), O Saisset (AS Béziers),
W Spanghero (RC Narbonne), B Vinsonneau (US Dax), C Spanghero (RC Narbonne),
J-P Bastiat (US Dax), A Estève (AS Béziers), J Iraçabal (A Bayonnais),
J-L Azarète (St Jean de Luz), A Vaquerin (AS Béziers), J-C Rossignol (CA Briviste),
A Lubrano (AS Béziers), R Bénésis (SU Agen)
Captain W Spanghero   **Manager** R Dasse
Assistant Managers M Celaya and F Cazenave

1979 (New Zealand only, except one match in Fiji)

Full record	Played 9	Won 6	Lost 3	Drawn 0	Points for 168	Against 116
in New Zealand	Played 8	Won 5	Lost 3	Drawn 0	Points for 155	Against 112
International record (in NZ)						
	Played 2	Won 1	Lost 1			
International details	Jul 7	New Zealand 23	France 9	(Christchurch)		
	Jul 14	New Zealand 19	France 24	(Auckland)		

Players

Full-backs: J-M Aguirre (Bagnères), S Blanco (Biarritz)
Threequarters: F Costes (Montferrand), J-L Averous (La Voulte), D Bustaffa

(Carcassonne), D Codorniou (Narbonne), P Mesny* (Racing Club de France),
M Duffranc (Tyrosse), L Pardo (Tarbes)
Half-backs: A Caussade (Lourdes), G Laporte (Graulhet), J Gallion (Toulon),
Y Laffarge (Montferrand)
Forwards: Y Malquier (Narbonne), C Beguerie (Agen), J-L Joinel (Brive),
J-P Rives (Toulouse), F Haget (Biarritz), P Salas (Narbonne), J-F Marchal (Lourdes),
A Maleig (Oloron), G Colomine (Narbonne), D Dubroca (Agen), R Paparemborde (Pau),
P Dintrans (Tarbes), J-F Perche (Bourg)
Captain J-P Rives **Manager** Y Noé **Assistant Managers** F Cazenave, J Desclaux

1981 (Australia only)

Full record Played 9 Won 6 Lost 3 Drawn 0 Points for 189 Against 112
International record Played 2 Lost 2
International details Jul 5 Australia 17 France 15 (Brisbane)
Jul 11 Australia 24 France 14 (Sydney)
Players
Full-backs: S Gabernet (Toulouse), S Blanco (Biarritz)
Threequarters: M Bruel (Pau), M Fabre (Béziers), J-L Averous (La Voulte),
P Chadebech (Brive), D Codorniou (Narbonne), P Mesny (Grenoble),
L Pardo (Bayonne)
Half-backs: B Viviès (Agen), M Sallefranque (Dax), P Berbizier (Lourdes),
J-P Elissalde (La Rochelle), A Mournet* (Bagnères)
Forwards: M Carpentier (Lourdes), D Erbani (Agen), J-P Rives (Toulouse),
P Lacans (Béziers), L Rodriguez (Mont-de-Marsan), O Derghali (Bagnères),
D Revallier (Graulhet), A Lorieux (Grenoble), P Salas (Narbonne),
R Paparemborde (Pau), M Crémaschi (Lourdes), J-P Wolff (Béziers),
J-L Dupont (Agen), P Dintrans (Tarbes)
Captain J-P Rives **Manager** Y Noé **Assistant Managers** J Fouroux, J Piqué

1984 (New Zealand only)

Full record Played 8 Won 6 Lost 2 Drawn 0 Points for 224 Against 138
International record Played 2 Lost 2
International details Jun 16 New Zealand 10 France 9 (Christchurch)
Jun 23 New Zealand 31 France 18 (Auckland)
Players
Full-backs: S Blanco (Biarritz), B Viviès (Agen)
Threequarters: P Estève (Narbonne), P Lagisquet (Bayonne), M Andrieu (Nîmes),
L Pardo (Montferrand), D Codorniou (Narbonne), P Sella (Agen), E Bonneval
(Toulouse)
Half-backs: J-P Lescarboura (Dax), G Laporte (Graulhet), P Berbizier (Lourdes),
H Sanz (Graulhet)
Forwards: P Dospital (Bayonne), J-P Garuet (Lourdes), P-E Detrez (Nîmes), D Dubroca
(Agen), B Herrero (Nice), P Dintrans (Tarbes), A Lorieux (Grenoble), F Haget
(Biarritz), J Condom (Boucau), P Lacans (Béziers), L Rodriguez (Mont-de-Marsan),
J-C Orso (Nice), J-L Joinel (Brive), J Grattan (Agen)
Captain P Dintrans **Manager** Y Noé **Assistant Manager** J Fouroux

1986 (including three matches in Argentina)

Full record
in Argentina Played 3 Won 2 Lost 1 Drawn 0 Points for 80 Against 48
in Australia Played 3 Won 1 Lost 1 Drawn 1 Points for 80 Against 54
in New Zealand Played 2 Won 1 Lost 1 Drawn 0 Points for 39 Against 37

International record

v Argentina	Played 2	Won 1	Lost 1	
v Australia	Played 1	Lost 1		
v New Zealand	Played 1	Lost 1		

International details

v Argentina	May 31	Argentina	15	France 13	(Buenos Aires)
	Jun 7	Argentina	9	France 22	(Buenos Aires)
v Australia	Jun 21	Australia	27	France 14	(Sydney)
v New Zealand	Jun 28	New Zealand	18	France 9	(Christchurch)

Players

Full-backs: J Bianchi (Toulon), S Blanco (Biarritz)

Threequarters: M Andrieu (Nîmes), P Bérot (Agen), E Bonneval (Toulouse), P Lagisquet (Bayonne), P Chadebach (Brive), P Sella (Agen), J-B Lafond (RCF), D Charvet (Toulouse)

Half-backs: J-P Lescarboura (Dax), G Laporte (Graulhet), J Gallion (Toulon), P Berbizier (Agen), R Modin* (Brive)

Forwards: P-E Detrez (Nîmes), J-P Garuet (Lourdes), P Marocco (Montferrand), C Portolan (Toulouse), D Dubroca (Agen), B Herrero (Toulon), J Condom (Boucau), F Haget (Biarritz), J-C Orso (Nice), T Picard (Montferrand), P Serrière (RCF), M Cecillon (Bourgoin), E Champ (Toulon), D Erbani (Agen), J Gratton (Agen), J-L Joinel (Brive), L Rodriguez (Mont-de-Marsan)

Captain D Dubroca   **Manager** Y Noé   **Assistant Manager** J Fouroux

TOP 50 SCORERS 1988-89

Peter Jackson *Daily Mail*

As if to prove that he could have gone on forever, Dusty Hare kicked more goals in his farewell season than ever before, topping 400 points in a season for the first time in a career the like of which will probably never be seen again. Along the way he raised his world record points total beyond 7,000, as if he hadn't put it out of human reach years earlier. Only Hare could finish with a match kicking average almost as high as his batting average in his last year in county cricket with Nottinghamshire.

Chris Howard followed him home, breaking Rugby's points record for the second time in successive seasons. Murry Walker had the distinction of being the highest-placed Scot. Paul Thorburn, not for the first time, led the Welsh challenge.

Two more Welsh players, both uncapped, ran in more tries than anyone else in British senior rugby last season. Gerald Cordle's hat-trick in Cardiff's closing match at Llanelli took him clear of Alun Edmunds.

The figures are based on all first-class fixtures. They include Cup ties, County Championship, Barbarian, representative and international matches up to the official end of the English season.

POINTS
444 – Dusty Hare (Leicester); **403** – Chris Howard (Rugby); **393** – Murry Walker (Boroughmuir); **363** – Callum McDonald (Stirling County), Paul Thorburn (Neath); **348** – Byron Hayward (Abertillery); **342** – Tim Smith (Gloucester); **330** – Jeff Bird (Maesteg/ Llanelli); **318** – Simon Hodgkinson (Nottingham); **315** – Peter Hewitt (Heriot's FP); **314** – Simon Irving (Headingley); **299** – Stuart Barnes (Bath); **298** – Paul Turner (Newbridge); **297** – Andy Kennedy (Saracens); **291** – Gary Abraham (Newport); **287** – Peter Dods (Gala); **285** – Arwel Parry (Bridgend), Ian Ramsey (Melrose); **278** – Ian Aitcheson (Waterloo); **277** – Robin Goodliffe (Sheffield); **274** – Andy Phillips (Pontypridd); **272** – Colin Gass (Hawick); **269** – Steve Burnage (Fylde); **266** – Brian Bolderson (Glamorgan Wanderers); **261** – Carl Arntzen (Moseley); **257** – Dave Barrett (West of Scotland); **254** – Andrew Ker (Kelso); **251** – Alistair Donaldson (Currie); **245** – Brian Mullen (London Irish); **242** – Colin Stephens (Llanelli), Paul Williams (Neath); **241** – Kevin O'Brien (Broughton Park); **239** – David Pears (Sale); **230** – Simon Hogg (Bristol); **227** – Gregor McKechnie (Jedforest); **225** – Rodney Pow (Selkirk); **222** – Colin Parker (Blackheath), Rob Andrew (Wasps); **221** – Andy Finnie (Bedford); **215** – Andy Atkinson (Wakefield), Stuart Thresher (Harlequins); **212** – John Graves (Rosslyn Park); **211** – Bruce Gibson (Dalziel); **209** – Andy Higgin (Vale of Lune); **205** – Paul Clark (Gosforth); **197** – Finlay Duncan (Edinburgh Wanderers); **195** – Robbie Stewart (Kilmarnock); **194** – Mike Rayer (Cardiff); **185** – Jonathan Mason (Pontypridd); **184** – Jon Webb (Bristol)

TRIES
36 – Gerald Cordle (Cardiff); **33** – Alun Edmunds (Neath); **30** – Neil Summers (Headingley); **28** – Eddie Saunders (Rugby), Jeremy Guscott (Bath); **27** – Alex Moore (Edinburgh Acads); **26** – Derek Stark (Ayr), Mark Jones (Neath); **25** – Mark Moncrieff (Gala); **24** – Steve Ford (Cardiff); **23** – David Kennell (Headingley), Colin Laity (Neath),

David Fairclough (Sheffield); **22** – Chris Bridges (Neath), Frank Packman (Northampton), Peter Hewitt (Heriot's FP), Douglas Robeson (Kelso); **21** – Steve Bowling (Llanelli), Audley Lumsden (Bath), Steve Brown (Broughton Park), David Cooke (West Hartlepool), Steve Walkin (Plymouth Albion), Tony Stanger (Hawick), Tony Swift (Bath), Colin McCartney (Boroughmuir); **20** – Damien Griffiths (Newport), Jonathan Griffiths (Llanelli), Nigel Heslop (Orrell), Peter Cooley (Waterloo), Scott Forrester (Currie), Peter Steven (Heriot's FP), Shaun White (Pontypool); **19** – Chris Howard (Rugby), Bleddyn Taylor (Swansea), Jim Mallinder (Roundhay), Gary Walker (Roundhay), John Thomas (Newport), Nick Price (Gloucester), Barry Evans (Leicester), Mark Bailey (Wasps); **18** – Paul Thorburn (Neath), Mike de Busk (Boroughmuir), Brian Ireland (Stirling County), Brendan Hanavan (Fylde), Chris Sever (Broughton Park), Chris Phillips (Newbridge), Chris Huish (Pontypool), Paul Williams (Neath), Andrew Hughes (South Wales Police), Murry Walker (Boroughmuir), Euan Gillies (Watsonians), Paul Collings (Bristol)

Dusty Hare, whose 444 points in his retirement season took his world record career total to an incredible 7,191 points.

CLUBS SECTION

(Records of most capped players are complete up to 30 April 1989)

ENGLAND

Bath

Year of formation 1865
Grounds Recreation Ground, London Road, Bath   Tel: Bath (0225) 25192;
Horse Show Ground, London Road, Bath   Tel: Bath (0225) 330365
Colours Blue, white, and black
Most capped player J P Hall (England) 18 caps
Captain 1988-89 S Barnes
1st XV 1988-89   P42   W35   D2   L5   F1263   A511
Courage Leagues Div 1 1st   **Pilkington Cup** *Winners* beat Leicester 10-6 (final)
Top scorer S Barnes (265)   **Most tries** J C Guscott (25)

League Record in 1988-89

Date	Venue	Opponents	Result	Scorers
10 Sep	(A)	Harlequins	W 26-9	*T:* Swift, Guscott, Hall, Dawe *C:* Barnes (2) *PG:* Barnes (2)
24 Sep	(H)	Gloucester	W 19-9	*T:* Guscott, Egerton, Morrison *C:* Barnes (2) *PG:* Barnes
8 Oct	(A)	Rosslyn Park	W 19-6	*T:* Guscott, Swift, Chilcott *C:* Barnes (2) *PG:* Barnes
22 Oct	(H)	Bristol	W 16-9	*T:* Hill *PG:* Barnes (3) *DG:* Barnes
12 Nov	(A)	Moseley	W 38-0	*T:* Guscott (3), Hall (2), Egerton, Robinson, Lumsden *C:* Guscott (3)
19 Nov	(H)	Orrell	W 36-12	*T:* Guscott (2), Trevaskis, Sagoe, Lumsden *C:* Barnes (2) *PG:* Barnes (4)
26 Nov	(H)	Wasps	W 16-6	*T:* Morrison, Pen try *C:* Barnes *PG:* Barnes (2)
14 Jan	(A)	Liverp'l St H	W 21-7	*T:* Guscott (2), Egerton (2) *C:* Barnes *PG:* Barnes
11 Mar	(H)	Nottingham	W 22-16	*T:* Egerton, Lumsden *C:* Barnes *PG:* Barnes (3), *DG:* Barnes
8 Apr	(H)	Waterloo	W 38-9	*T:* Cronin (2), Simpson, Hill, Hoskin, Swift, Halliday, Westcott *C:* Barnes (2), Halliday
22 Apr	(A)	Leicester	L 12-15	*T:* Bamsey, Deane, Maslen

Bedford

Year of formation 1886
Ground Goldington Road, Bedford   Tel: Bedford (0234) 59160/54619
Colours Wide hoops in Oxford and Cambridge blues
Most capped player D P Rogers (England) 34 caps
Captain 1988-89 J Orwin
1st XV 1988-89   P40   W19   D2   L19   F649   A696
Courage Leagues Div 2 2nd *promoted*   **Pilkington Cup** Lost 3-6 to Nottingham
(3rd round)   **Top scorer** A Finnie (221)   **Most tries** K Canning (9)

League Record in 1988-89

Date	Venue	Opponents	Result	Scorers
10 Sep	(A)	Gosforth	W 17-16	*T:* Twigton, Bygraves *PG:* Gabriel *DG:* Cunningham, Finnie

David Egerton, the Bath No 8, grounds the ball for a try in the win over Nottingham, which clinched the Courage Division 1 title.

24 Sep	(H)	L Scottish	W 9–6	*T:* Harris *C:* Finnie *PG:* Finnie
8 Oct	(A)	Headingley	D 7–7	*T:* Cunningham *PG:* Finnie
22 Oct	(H)	L Irish	L 15–21	*PG:* Finnie (5)
12 Nov	(H)	Coventry	W 19–9	*T:* Gabriel, Batty *C:* Finnie *PG:* Finnie (3)
19 Nov	(A)	Saracens	L 10–50	*T:* Colleran (2) *C:* Finnie
26 Nov	(A)	Northampton	L 3–42	*DG:* Vaudin
14 Jan	(H)	Richmond	W 15–3	*T:* Skingsley, Niven *C:* Vaudin (2) *PG:* Vaudin
11 Mar	(A)	Blackheath	W 13–12	*T:* Canning *PG:* Finnie (3)
8 Apr	(H)	L Welsh	W 18–6	*T:* Harris *C:* Vaudin *PG:* Vaudin (3), Greed
22 Apr	(A)	Sale	D 15–15	*T:* Greed *C:* Finnie *PG:* Finnie (2) *DG:* Vaudin

Blackheath

Year of formation 1858
Ground Rectory Field, Blackheath, London SE3   Tel: 01-858 1578/3677
Colours Red and black hoops
Most capped player C N Lowe (England) 25 caps
Captain 1988-89 T Fenby
1st XV 1988-89 P33 W17 D1 L15 F581 A358
Courage Leagues Div 2 8th   **Pilkington Cup** Lost 6-13 to Waterloo (3rd round)
Top scorer C Parker (223)   **Most tries** D Craig (8)

League Record in 1988–89

Date	Venue	Opponents	Result	Scorers
10 Sep	(A)	L Welsh	D 15–15	*T:* Vaughan *C:* Parker *PG:* Parker (3)
24 Sep	(H)	Gosforth	W 34–10	*T:* Vaughan, Parker, Alcorn, Swain, Aris, Annous *C:* Parker (2) PG: Parker *DG:* King
8 Oct	(A)	L Scottish	L 3–6	*PG:* Parker
22 Oct	(H)	Headingley	W 21–3	*T:* Annous *C:* Parker *PG:* Parker (4) *DG:* King
12 Nov	(H)	Richmond	W 31–3	*T:* Scott, Harris, Vaughan, Rutter *C:* Parker (3) *PG:* Parker (2) *DG:* King
19 Nov	(A)	Coventry	L 12–18	*T:* Craig *C:* Parker *DG:* King (2)
26 Nov	(H)	Saracens	L 12–24	*PG:* Parker (3) *DG:* King
14 Jan	(A)	Northampton	L 7–15	*T:* Scott *PG:* Harris
11 Mar	(H)	Bedford	L 12–13	*T:* Parker, King *C:* Parker (2)
8 Apr	(H)	Sale	L 12–16	*T:* Scott *C:* Pound *PG:* Pound (2)
22 Apr	(A)	L Irish	W 22–21	*T:* Pound, Craig *C:* Pound *PG:* Pound (2) *DG:* King (2)

Bristol

Year of formation 1888
Ground Memorial Ground, Filton Avenue, Horfield, Bristol BS7 0AG
Tel: Bristol (0272) 514448
Colours Blue and white
Most capped player J V Pullin (England) 42 caps
Captain 1988-89 A F Dun
1st XV 1988-89 P45 W30 D2 L13 F1138 A556
Courage Leagues Div 1 7th   **Pilkington Cup** Lost 12-14 to Bath (quarter-final)
Top scorer S Hogg (228)   **Most tries** P Collings (18)

League Record in 1988–89

Date	Venue	Opponents	Result	Scorers
10 Sep	(H)	Orrell	W 15–6	*T:* Hone *C:* Webb *PG:* Webb (2) *DG:* Hogg

24 Sep	(A)	Nottingham	L	6–10	*PG:* Webb (2)
8 Oct	(H)	Moseley	W	18–0	*T:* Carr, Knibbs, Phillips *PG:* Webb (2)
22 Oct	(A)	Bath	L	9–16	*PG:* Hogg (2), Webb
12 Nov	(H)	Harlequins	W	18–6	*T:* Duggan (2) *C:* Webb, Hogg *PG:* Hogg (2)
19 Nov	(A)	Gloucester	W	11–10	*T:* Webb (2) *PG:* Hogg
26 Nov	(A)	Rosslyn Park	L	16–18	*T:* Phillips *PG:* Webb (4)
14 Jan	(H)	Waterloo	W	14–3	*T:* Jeffery (2) *PG:* Hogg *DG:* Hogg
11 Mar	(A)	Leicester	L	12–13	*T:* Essien *C:* Webb *PG:* Webb *DG:* Hogg
8 Apr	(A)	Wasps	L	19–21	*T:* Stiff, Collings, Woodman *C:* Hogg (2) *PG:* Hogg
22 Apr	(H)	Liverp'l St H	W	50–14	*T:* Davis (2), Dun (2), Knibbs, Hogg, Palmer, Whitehead, Collings *C:* Sorrell (3), Hogg *PG:* Hogg (2)

Coventry

Year of formation 1874
Ground Coundon Road, Coventry Tel: Coventry (0203) 591274
Colours Navy and white hoops, navy shorts
Most capped player D J Duckham (England) 36 caps
Captain 1988-89 M Fairn
1st XV 1988-89 P40 W13 D1 L26 F528 A817
Courage Leagues Div 2 5th **Pilkington Cup** Lost 7-12 to Plymouth Albion (2nd round)
Top scorer M Fairn (136) **Most tries** L McKenzie (15)

League Record in 1988–89

Date	Venue	Opponents	Result		Scorers
10 Sep	(A)	L Irish	W	29–6	*T:* Rowlands (3), Parton, Lakey, Travers *C:* Fairn *PG:* Thomas
24 Sep	(H)	Sale	W	7–3	*T:* Travers *PG:* Fairn
8 Oct	(A)	L Welsh	W	21–14	*T:* Lakey, Parton, Hall *PG:* Fairn (3)
22 Oct	(H)	Gosforth	W	19–12	*T:* Gulliver, McKenzie, Travers *C:* Thomas (2) *DG:* Lakey
12 Nov	(A)	Bedford	L	9–19	*PG:* Thomas (2) *DG:* Lakey
19 Nov	(H)	Blackheath	W	18–12	*T:* Thomas, Travers, Parton *PG:* Fairn (2)
26 Nov	(A)	Richmond	L	3–12	*PG:* Fairn
14 Jan	(H)	Saracens	L	6–13	*T:* Medford *C:* Fairn
11 Mar	(H)	Northampton	W	22–10	*T:* Graham, Hickey, McKenzie *C:* Fairn (2) *PG:* Fairn *DG:* Lakey
8 Apr	(H)	Headingley	L	7–18	*T:* Tandy *DG:* Lakey
22 Apr	(A)	L Scottish	L	9–24	*T:* McKenzie *C:* Fairn *PG:* Fairn

Gloucester

Year of formation 1873
Ground Kingsholm, Kingsholm Road, Gloucester GL1 3AX
Tel: Gloucester (0452) 20901 (office) 28385 (club)
Colours Cherry and white
Most capped player A T Voyce (England) 27 caps
Captain 1988-89 M Hannaford
1st XV 1988-89 P44 W34 D1 L9 F1028 A525
Courage Leagues Div 1 2nd **Pilkington Cup** Lost 3-6 to Bath (semi-finals)
Top scorer T Smith (345) **Most tries** N Price (19)

League Record in 1988–89

Date	Venue	Opponents	Result	Scorers
10 Sep	(H)	Moseley	W 37–9	*T:* Cummins (2), Maclean, Hamlin, Teague *C:* Smith (4) *PG:* Smith (3)
24 Sep	(A)	Bath	L 9–19	*PG:* Smith (3)
8 Oct	(H)	Wasps	W 19–3	*T:* Scrivens, Cummins *C:* Smith *PG:* Smith (3)
22 Oct	(A)	Liverp'l St H	W 31–9	*T:* Mann (2), Hamlin (2), Mogg *C:* Smith (4) *PG:* Smith
12 Nov	(A)	Rosslyn Park	W 26–8	*T:* Pascall, Mogg, Gadd, Teague *C:* Marment (2) *PG:* Marment (2)
19 Nov	(H)	Bristol	L 10–11	*T:* Hamlin, Teague *C:* Smith
26 Nov	(A)	Waterloo	D 15–15	*T:* Hamlin *C:* Smith *PG:* Smith (3)
14 Jan	(H)	Leicester	W 28–0	*T:* Breeze (2), Hamlin, Teague, Dunn, Hannaford, Price
11 Mar	(A)	Harlequins	L 11–26	*T:* Breeze (2) *PG:* Smith
8 Apr	(A)	Orrell	W 16–6	*T:* Smith, Price *C:* Smith *PG:* Smith (2)
22 Apr	(H)	Nottingham	W 13–6	*T:* Dunn *PG:* Smith (3)

Gosforth

Year of formation 1877
Ground New Ground, Great North Road, Gosforth, Newcastle upon Tyne NE3 2DT
Tel: Newcastle (0632) 856915
Colours Green and white hoops, white shorts, green and white hooped stockings
Most capped player R J McLoughlin (Ireland) 40 caps
Captain 1988-89 G Smallwood
1st XV 1988-89 P40 W21 D1 L18 F732 A652
Courage Leagues Div 2 10th **Pilkington Cup** Lost 9-29 to Wakefield (3rd round)
Top scorer P Clark (201) **Most tries** D Walker (17)

League Record in 1988–89

Date	Venue	Opponents	Result	Scorers
10 Sep	(H)	Bedford	L 16–17	*T:* Briggs, Moffat *C:* Henderson *PG:* Henderson (2)
24 Sep	(A)	Blackheath	L 10–34	*T:* Henderson, Pen try *C:* Chandler
8 Oct	(H)	Richmond	W 16–4	*T:* Briggs *PG:* Henderson (4)
22 Oct	(A)	Coventry	L 12–19	*T:* Edwards *C:* Henderson *PG:* Henderson (2)
12 Nov	(H)	L Welsh	W 34–26	*T:* Cooper, Clark, Edwards, Clegg *C:* Clark (3) *PG:* Clark (3) *DG:* Clark
19 Nov	(A)	L Irish	L 7–35	*T:* Flowers *PG:* Clark
26 Nov	(H)	L Scottish	W 16–14	*T:* Walker (2) *C:* Clark *PG:* Clark (2)
14 Jan	(H)	Headingley	W 29–14	*T:* Smallwood (2), Curry, Johns *C:* Clark (2) *PG:* Clark (3)
11 Mar	(A)	Sale	L 15–23	*T:* Westgarth *C:* Clark *PG:* Clark (3)
8 Apr	(A)	Northampton	L 12–13	*T:* Johns, Elliott *C:* Clegg (2)
22 Apr	(H)	Saracens	L 9–47	*T:* Walker *C:* Medhurst *PG:* Medhurst

Harlequins

Year of formation 1866
Grounds Stoop Memorial Ground, Craneford Way, Twickenham, Middlesex and RFU Ground, Twickenham Tel: 01-892 0822 (Stoop)
Colours Light blue, magenta, chocolate, French grey, black and light green
Most capped player W W Wakefield (England) 31 caps

Captain 1988-89 J Olver
1st XV 1988-89   P31   W17   D1   L13   F561   A497
Courage Leagues Div 1 8th   **Pilkington Cup** Lost 7-16 to Leicester (semi-finals)
Top scorer S Thresher (139)   **Most tries** J Eagle (7)

League Record in 1988–89

Date	Venue	Opponents	Result	Scorers
10 Sep	(H)	Bath	L 9–26	T: Harriman C: Salmon PG: Thresher
24 Sep	(A)	Wasps	L 15–23	PG: Rose (4) DG: Cramb
8 Oct	(H)	Liverp'l St H	W 15–6	T: Langhorn C: Thresher PG: Thresher (3)
22 Oct	(A)	Orrell	L 15–16	T: Skinner, Carling C: Rose (2) PG: Rose
12 Nov	(A)	Bristol	L 6–18	PG: Thresher (2)
19 Nov	(H)	Waterloo	L 23–24	T: Salmon (2), Johnston C: Thresher PG: Thresher (3)
26 Nov	(A)	Leicester	W 31–21	T: Thompson, Ackford, Skinner, Moon C: Thresher (3) PG: Thresher (2) DG: Cramb
14 Jan	(A)	Rosslyn Park	W 16–12	T: Eagle (2) C: Thresher PG: Thresher (2)
11 Mar	(H)	Gloucester	W 26–11	T: Thresher (2), Eagle, Salmon, Glenister C: Thresher, Salmon (2)
8 Apr	(A)	Nottingham	L 0–12	
22 Apr	(H)	Moseley	W 38–15	T: Butcher, Cleary (2), Skinner (2), Eagle, Mullins C: Thresher (5)

Headingley

Year of formation 1878
Ground Bridge Road, Kirkstall, Leeds 5   Tel: Leeds (0532) 755029
Colours Green, black and white jerseys, blue shorts
Most capped player I R McGeechan (Scotland) 32 caps
Captain 1988-89 P Huntsman
1st XV 1988-89   P44   W28   D2   L14   F999   A562
Courage Leagues Div 2 7th   **Pilkington Cup** Lost 7-10 to Wakefield (2nd round)
Top scorer S Irving (313)   **Most tries** N Summers (30)

League Record in 1988–89

Date	Venue	Opponents	Result	Scorers
10 Sep	(H)	Saracens	L 3–7	PG: Howarth
24 Sep	(A)	Northampton	L 7–19	T: Kennell PG: Howarth
8 Oct	(H)	Bedford	D 7–7	T: Summers PG: Kirk
22 Oct	(A)	Blackheath	L 3–21	PG: Appleson
12 Nov	(H)	L Irish	W 48–9	T: Tweed (2), Kennell (2), Hargreaves, Swales, Irving C: Irving (7) PG: Irving (2)
19 Nov	(A)	Sale	W 24–15	T: Atkinson, Kennell, Pepper, Irving, Summers C: Irving (2)
26 Nov	(H)	L Welsh	W 24–0	T: Hargreaves, Pepper, Atkinson C: Irving (3) PG: Irving (2)
14 Jan	(A)	Gosforth	L 14–29	T: Kennell (3) C: Irving
11 Mar	(H)	L Scottish	W 22–10	T: Irving, Kennell, Johnston C: Irving (2) PG: Irving (2)
8 Apr	(A)	Coventry	W 18–7	T: Sellar, Lumley, Hargreaves C: Irving (3)
22 Apr	(H)	Richmond	L 9–12	PG: Irving (3)

Leicester

Year of formation 1880
Ground The Clubhouse, Aylestone Road, Leicester LE2 7LF
Tel: Leicester (0533) 540276

Colours Scarlet, green and white
Most capped player P J Wheeler (England) 41 caps
Captain 1988-89 P W Dodge
1st XV 1988-89 P38 W28 D1 L9 F918 A573
Courage Leagues Div 1 6th **Pilkington Cup** Lost 6-10 to Bath (final)
Top scorer W H Hare (438) (*club record*) **Most tries** B Evans (19)

League Record in 1988–89

Date	Venue	Opponents	Result	Scorers
10 Sep	(H)	Wasps	W 15–6	*PG:* Hare (5)
24 Sep	(A)	Liverp'l St H	W 23–12	*T:* Reed, Richards, Thornley, Underwood *C:* Hare (2) *PG:* Hare
8 Oct	(H)	Orrell	L 15–27	*PG:* Hare (5)
22 Oct	(A)	Nottingham	D 12–12	*T:* Evans *C:* Hare *PG:* Hare (2)
12 Nov	(A)	Waterloo	W 34–22	*T:* Richards (2), Redfern, Cusworth, Evans, Kardooni, *C:* Harris (2) *PG:* Harris *DG:* Cusworth
19 Nov	(H)	Rosslyn Park	W 28–15	*T:* Hare, Underwood *C:* Hare *PG:* Hare (6)
26 Nov	(H)	Harlequins	L 21–31	*T:* Hare, Kardooni, Underwood *C:* Hare (3) *PG:* Hare
14 Jan	(A)	Gloucester	L 0–28	
11 Mar	(H)	Bristol	W 13–12	*T:* Evans *PG:* Hare (2) *DG:* Cusworth
8 Apr	(A)	Moseley	L 13–22	*T:* Grant *PG:* Hare (3)
22 Apr	(H)	Bath	W 15–12	*T:* McDonald *C:* Harris *PG:* Liley (3)

Liverpool St Helens

Year of formation 1986 (On amalgamation of Liverpool – founded 1857 – and St Helens)
Ground Moss Lane, Windle, St Helens Tel: St Helens (0744) 25708
Colours Red, blue and black horizontal stripes, white shorts
Most capped player M A C Slemen (England) 31 caps
Captain 1988-89 B Wellens
1st XV 1988-89 P37 W13 D3 L21 F546 A657
Courage Leagues Div 1 12th *relegated* **Pilkington Cup** Lost 6-37 to Leicester (3rd round)
Top scorer A Askew (138) **Most tries** B Hanavan (14)

League Record in 1988–89

Date	Venue	Opponents	Result	Scorers
10 Sep	(A)	Waterloo	W 12–6	*T:* Hanavan *C:* Bruchez *PG:* Bruchez (2)
24 Sep	(H)	Leicester	L 12–23	*T:* Buckton *C:* Bruchez *PG:* Bruchez (2)
8 Oct	(A)	Harlequins	L 6–15	*PG:* Askew (2)
22 Oct	(H)	Gloucester	L 9–31	*T:* Jones *C:* Askew *PG:* Askew
12 Nov	(A)	Orrell	L 4–20	*T:* Davies
19 Nov	(H)	Nottingham	L 15–22	*T:* Pen try *C:* Askew *PG:* Askew (3)
26 Nov	(A)	Moseley	L 15–18	*PG:* Askew (5)
14 Jan	(H)	Bath	L 7–21	*T:* Rabbitt *PG:* Askew
11 Mar	(A)	Wasps	L 10–16	*T:* Hanavan *PG:* Wellens *DG:* Mallalieu
8 Apr	(H)	Rosslyn Park	L 12–32	*PG:* Askew (4)
22 Apr	(A)	Bristol	L 14–50	*T:* Hanavan, Hamer *PG:* Askew *DG:* Mallalieu

Dewi Morris, pictured winning his first cap against Australia, could not prevent Liverpool St Helens slipping down into Division 2.

London Irish

Year of formation 1898
Ground The Avenue, Sunbury-on-Thames, Middlesex Tel: 0932 783034
Colours Emerald green jerseys, white shorts
Most capped player K W Kennedy (Ireland) 45 caps
Captain 1988-89 D Fitzgerald
1st XV 1988-89 P34 W18 D2 L4 F761 A662
Courage Leagues Div 2 6th **Pilkington Cup** Lost 16-45 to Bristol (4th round)
Top scorer B Mullen (245) **Most tries** S Geoghegan (19)

League Record in 1988–89

Date	Venue	Opponents	Result	Scorers
10 Sep	(H)	Coventry	L 6–29	T: Marty C: Mullen
24 Sep	(A)	Saracens	L 3–20	PG: Mullen
8 Oct	(H)	Northampton	W 18–10	T: Fitzgerald C: Mullen PG: Mullen (4)
22 Oct	(A)	Bedford	W 21–15	T: Fitzgerald, Rollandi, Davidson PG: Mullen (3)
12 Nov	(A)	Headingley	L 9–48	T: Geoghegan C: Mullen PG: Mullen
19 Nov	(H)	Gosforth	W 35–7	T: Collins (2), Mullin (2), Hewitt, Staples C: Mullen (4) DG: Mullen
26 Nov	(H)	Sale	D 18–18	T: Stevens C: Mullen PG: Mullen (4)
14 Jan	(A)	L Scottish	W 21–16	PG: Mullen (5) DG: Kuhn (2)
11 Mar	(H)	L Welsh	W 24–19	T: Collins, Geoghegan (2), Staples C: Bell PG: Bell DG: Bell
8 Apr	(A)	Richmond	D 18–18	PG: Mullen (4) DG: Mullen (2)
22 Apr	(H)	Blackheath	L 21–22	T: Geoghegan (2), Francis PG: Mullen (3)

London Scottish

Year of formation 1878
Ground Richmond Athletic Ground, Richmond, Surrey Tel: 01940 0397
Colours Blue jerseys, red lion on left breast, white shorts, red stockings
Most capped player A F McHarg (Scotland) 44 caps
Captain 1988-89 G Hastings
1st XV 1988-89 P31 W13 D3 L15 F458 A464
Courage Leagues Div 2 11th *relegated* **Pilkington Cup** Lost 6-22 to Harlequins (4th round)
Top scorer G Hastings (96) **Most tries** D Millard, A Campbell (7)

League Record in 1988–89

Date	Venue	Opponents	Result	Scorers
10 Sep	(H)	Northampton	D 3–3	PG: Hastings
24 Sep	(A)	Bedford	L 6–9	PG: Hastings, Chesworth
8 Oct	(H)	Blackheath	W 6–3	T: Howe C: Mitchell
22 Oct	(A)	Richmond	W 32–12	T: Grecian (2), Morrison, Campbell, Pen try C: Russell (2), Hastings PG: Russell (2)
12 Nov	(H)	Sale	L 16–17	T: Campbell PG: Hastings (4)
19 Nov	(A)	L Welsh	L 10–29	T: Grecian, Buchanan C: Russell
26 Nov	(A)	Gosforth	L 14–16	T: Corbett, Howe PG: Grecian DG: Grecian
14 Jan	(H)	L Irish	L 16–21	T: Corbett PG: Glasgow (4)
11 Mar	(A)	Headingley	L 10–22	T: Richardson PG: Grecian, Glasgow
8 Apr	(A)	Saracens	L 9–19	PG: Hastings (3)
22 Apr	(H)	Coventry	W 24–9	T: Hastings, Renwick C: Hastings (2) PG: Hastings (4)

London Welsh

Year of formation 1885
Ground Old Deer Park, Kew Road, Richmond, Surrey Tel: 01-940 2520
Colours Scarlet jerseys and white shorts
Most capped player J P R Williams (Wales) 55 caps
Captain 1988-89 M M J Douglas
1st XV 1988-89 P35 W8 D2 L25 F502 A898
Courage Leagues Div 2 12th *relegated* **Pilkington Cup** Lost 9-24 to Berry Hill
(2nd round)
Top scorer C Cormack (113) **Most tries** G Leleu, J Walters (9)

League Record in 1988–89

Date	Venue	Opponents	Result	Scorers
10 Sep	(H)	Blackheath	D 15–15	*T:* Leleu *C:* Humphreys *PG:* Humphreys (3)
24 Sep	(A)	Richmond	L 3–14	*PG:* Humphreys
8 Oct	(H)	Coventry	L 14–21	*T:* Williams, Evans *PG:* Thomas (2)
22 Oct	(A)	Saracens	L 4–37	*T:* Leleu
12 Nov	(A)	Gosforth	L 26–34	*T:* Douglas (2), Waldron (2), Nairne, Griffiths *C:* Nairne
19 Nov	(H)	L Scottish	W 29–10	*T:* Wintle, Roblin, Evans, Smith, Williams *C:* Nairne (3) *PG:* Nairne
26 Nov	(A)	Headingley	L 0–24	
14 Jan	(H)	Sale	L 9–16	*PG:* Humphreys (3)
11 Mar	(A)	L Irish	L 19–24	*T:* Douglas, Leleu (2) *C:* Cormack (2) *PG:* Cormack
8 Apr	(A)	Bedford	L 6–18	*PG:* Cormack (2)
22 Apr	(H)	Northampton	L 0–22	

Moseley

Year of formation 1873
Ground The Reddings, Reddings Road, Moseley, Birmingham B13 81W
Tel: Birmingham (021) 449 2149
Colours Black and red
Most capped player N E Horton (England) 20 caps
Captain 1988-89 S Robson
1st XV 1988-89 P43 W21 D1 L21 F766 A837
Courage Leagues Div 1 10th **Pilkington Cup** Lost 3-6 to Aspatria (3rd round)
Top scorer C Arntzen (258) **Most tries** P Shillingford (15)

League Record in 1988–89

Date	Venue	Opponents	Result	Scorers
10 Sep	(A)	Gloucester	L 9–37	*PG:* Jones (3)
24 Sep	(H)	Rosslyn Park	L 7–13	*T:* Smith *PG:* Jones
8 Oct	(A)	Bristol	L 0–18	
22 Oct	(H)	Waterloo	W 13–6	*T:* Parsons, Shillingford *C:* Arntzen *PG:* Arntzen
12 Nov	(H)	Bath	L 0–38	
19 Nov	(A)	Wasps	L 10–39	*T:* Smith *PG:* Arntzen (2) *DG:* Johnson
26 Nov	(H)	Liverp'l St H	W 18–15	*T:* Barr, James *C:* Arntzen (2) *PG:* Arntzen (2)
14 Jan	(A)	Nottingham	L 9–13	*T:* Pen try *C:* Arntzen *PG:* Arntzen
11 Mar	(H)	Orrell	L 10–12	*T:* Shillingford *PG:* Arntzen (2)

8 Apr	(H)	Leicester	W 22–13	*T:* Shillingford, Suckling, Robson
				C: Arntzen (2) *PG:* Arntzen (2)
22 Apr	(A)	Harlequins	L 15–38	*T:* Shillingford, Smith *C:* Arntzen (2)
				PG: Arntzen

Northampton

Year of formation 1880
Ground Franklins Gardens, Northampton   Tel: Northampton (0604) 51543
Colours Black, green and gold
Most capped player G S Pearce (England) 31 caps
Captain 1988-89 G S Pearce
1st XV 1988-89 P40 W19 D1 L20 F733 A637
Courage Leagues Div 2 3rd   **Pilkington Cup** Lost 0-6 to Richmond (3rd round)
Top scorer J Steele (154)   **Most tries** F Packman (22)

League Record in 1988–89

Date	Venue	Opponents	Result	Scorers
10 Sep	(A)	L Scottish	D 3–3	*PG:* Steele
24 Sep	(H)	Headingley	W 19–7	*T:* Thame, Steele, Packman, Alston
				PG: Steele
8 Oct	(A)	L Irish	L 10–18	*T:* Steele *PG:* Steele *DG:* Steele
22 Oct	(H)	Sale	W 15–12	*T:* Burns, Tebbutt, Charles *PG:* Moss
12 Nov	(H)	Saracens	L 4–32	*T:* Charles
19 Nov	(A)	Richmond	L 12–15	*T:* Packman, Thame *C:* Steele (2)
26 Nov	(H)	Bedford	W 42–3	*T:* Charles (2), Tebbutt (2), Pearce, Packman, Ebsworth *C:* Ebsworth (4) *PG:* Ebsworth, Steele
14 Jan	(H)	Blackheath	W 15–7	*T:* Thorneycroft, Elkington, Packman *PG:* Moss
11 Mar	(A)	Coventry	L 10–22	*T:* Charles, Dyte *C:* Larkin
8 Apr	(H)	Gosforth	W 13–12	*T:* Packman *PG:* Steele (2), Moss
22 Apr	(A)	L Welsh	W 22–0	*T:* Packman, Carr, Elkington, Glenn *C:* Steele (2), Moss

Nottingham

Year of formation 1877
Ground Ireland Avenue, Beeston, Nottingham   Tel: Nottingham (0602) 254238
Colours White jerseys, green shorts
Most capped player G W Rees (England) 18 caps
Captain 1988-89 B C Moore
1st XV 1988-89 P43 W25 D3 L15 F825 A522
Courage Leagues Div 1 4th   **Pilkington Cup** Lost 9-15 to Harlequins (quarter-final)
Top scorer S Hodgkinson (257)   **Most tries** R Byrom (12)

League Record in 1988–89

Date	Venue	Opponents	Result	Scorers
10 Sep	(A)	Rosslyn Park	W 18–9	*T:* Rees *C:* Hodgkinson
				PG: Hodgkinson (3) *DG:* Hodgkinson
24 Sep	(H)	Bristol	W 10–6	*T:* Johnson, Hodgkinson *C:* Hodgkinson
8 Oct	(A)	Waterloo	W 18–9	*PG:* Hodgkinson (5) *DG:* Hodgkinson
22 Oct	(H)	Leicester	D 12–12	*PG:* Hodgkinson (4)
12 Nov	(H)	Wasps	L 9–15	*PG:* Hodgkinson (2) *DG:* Hodgkinson

19 Nov	(A)	Liverp'l St H	W 22–15	*T:* Kaye, Moore, Cook *C:* Hodgkinson (2)
				PG: Hodgkinson (2)
26 Nov	(A)	Orrell	L 6–12	*PG:* Hodgkinson *DG:* Hodgkinson
14 Jan	(H)	Moseley	W 13–9	*T:* Byrom *PG:* Hodgkinson (2)
				DG: Hodgkinson
11 Mar	(A)	Bath	L 16–22	*T:* Johnson, Hackney *C:* Sutton
				PG: Hartley (2)
8 Apr	(H)	Harlequins	W 12–0	*T:* Byrom *C:* Hodgkinson
				PG: Hodgkinson (2)
22 Apr	(A)	Gloucester	L 6–13	*PG:* Hodgkinson *DG:* Hodgkinson

Orrell

Year of formation 1927
Ground Edge Hall Road, Orrell, nr Wigan, Greater Manchester, Lancs WN5 8TL
Tel: Upholland (0695) 623193
Colours Amber and black hoops, black shorts and stockings
Most capped player J Carleton (England) 25 caps
Captain 1988-89 S Langford
1st XV 1988-89 P44 W29 D2 L13 F956 A546
Courage Leagues Div 1 5th **Pilkington Cup** Lost 13-7 to Bristol (3rd round)
Top scorer G Ainscough (148) **Most tries** N Heslop (20)

League Record in 1988–89

Date	Venue	Opponents	Result	Scorers
10 Sep	(A)	Bristol	L 6–15	*PG:* Langford, Ainscough
24 Sep	(H)	Waterloo	W 15–12	*T:* Halsall *C:* Ainscough
				PG: Ainscough (2), Langford
8 Oct	(A)	Leicester	W 27–15	*T:* Kimmins, Wilkinson, ap Dafydd
				C: Langford (3) *PG:* Langford (3)
22 Oct	(H)	Harlequins	W 16–15	*T:* Cleary, Heslop *C:* Ainscough
				PG: Ainscough (2)
12 Nov	(H)	Liverp'l St H	W 20–4	*T:* ap Dafydd (2) *PG:* Ainscough (3),
				Langford
19 Nov	(A)	Bath	L 12–36	*PG:* Ainscough (3), Langford
26 Nov	(H)	Nottingham	W 12–6	*T:* Winstanley *C:* Langford *PG:* Ainscough
				DG: Ainscough
14 Jan	(H)	Wasps	D 9–9	*T:* Heslop *C:* Langford *PG:* Strett
11 Mar	(A)	Moseley	W 12–10	*T:* Halsall *C:* Ainscough *PG:* Ainscough,
				Langford
8 Apr	(H)	Gloucester	L 6–16	*T:* Heslop *C:* Langford
22 Apr	(A)	Rosslyn Park	L 13–19	*T:* Cleary *PG:* Ainscough (2) *DG:* Strett

Richmond

Year of formation 1861
Ground Athletic Ground, Richmond, Surrey Tel: 01-940 0397
Colours Old gold, red and black
Most capped player C W Ralston (England) 22 caps
Captain 1988-89 J Cullen
1st XV 1988-89 P31 W13 D2 L16 F419 A553
Courage Leagues Div 2 9th **Pilkington Cup** Lost 9-12 to Nottingham (4th round)
Top scorer M Livesey (182) **Most tries** R Rydon (7)

League Record in 1988–89

Date	Venue	Opponents	Result	Scorers
10 Sep	(A)	Sale	L 9–50	*T:* Seccombe *C:* Livesey *PG:* Livesey

24 Sep	(H)	L Welsh	W 14–3	T: Seccombe, Catt PG: Breddy (2)
8 Oct	(A)	Gosforth	L 4–16	T: Catt
22 Oct	(H)	L Scottish	L 12–32	PG: Livesey (4)
12 Nov	(A)	Blackheath	L 3–31	PG: Livesey
19 Nov	(H)	Northampton	W 15–12	PG: Livesey (2) DG: Livesey (3)
26 Nov	(H)	Coventry	W 12–3	T: Seccombe C: Livesey PG: Livesey (2)
14 Jan	(A)	Bedford	L 3–15	PG: Livesey
11 Mar	(H)	Saracens	L 10–27	T: Morrish, Rydon C: Livesey
8 Apr	(H)	L Irish	D 18–18	PG: Livesey (6)
22 Apr	(A)	Headingley	W 12–9	T: Fallow C: Livesey PG: Livesey (2)

Rosslyn Park

Year of formation 1879
Ground Priory Lane, Upper Richmond Road, Roehampton, London SW15
Tel: 01-876 1879
Colours Red and white hoops
Most capped player A G Ripley (England) 24 caps
Captain 1988-89 T Brooks
1st XV 1988-89 P35   W20   D0   L15   F710   A561
Courage Leagues Div 1 9th   **Pilkington Cup** Lost 9-23 to Leicester (4th round)
Top scorer J Graves (212)   **Most tries** S Hunter (16)

League Record in 1988–89

Date	Venue	Opponents	Result	Scorers
10 Sep	(H)	Nottingham	L 9–18	PG: Graves (3)
24 Sep	(A)	Moseley	W 13–7	T: Williams, Brooks C: Graves PG: Graves
8 Oct	(H)	Bath	L 6–19	PG: Graves (2)
22 Oct	(A)	Wasps	L 16–39	T: Hunter, Wyles, Smith C: Graves (2)
12 Nov	(H)	Gloucester	L 8–26	T: Dear, Summers
19 Nov	(A)	Leicester	L 15–28	T: Smith C: Graves PG: Graves (3)
26 Nov	(H)	Bristol	W 18–16	T: Williams, Hunter C: Graves (2) PG: Graves (2)
14 Jan	(H)	Harlequins	L 12–16	T: Williams C: Graves PG: Graves (2)
11 Mar	(A)	Waterloo	W 24–14	T: Crawford, Hunter C: Graves (2) PG: Graves (3) DG: Jermyn
8 Apr	(A)	Liverp'l St H	W 32–12	T: McCauley, Woodhouse, Brooker, Hyde, Crawford C: Graves (3) PG: Graves (2)
22 Apr	(H)	Orrell	W 19–13	T: Curtis, Crawford C: Gray PG: Gray (3)

Sale

Year of formation 1861
Ground Heywood Road, Brooklands, Sale, Cheshire   Tel: 061 973 6348
Colours Blue and white hoops, blue shorts, blue stockings
Most capped player F E Cotton (England) 31 caps
Captain 1988-89 A Simpson
1st XV 1988-89 P39   W20   D4   L15   F784   A560
Courage Leagues Div 2 4th   **Pilkington Cup** Lost 10-19 to Durham City (2nd round)
Top scorer D Pears (171)   **Most tries** G Powell (11)

League Record in 1988–89

Date	Venue	Opponents	Result	Scorers
10 Sep	(H)	Richmond	W 50–3	T: Gittens (2), Powell (2), Simpson, Bentley, Macfarlane, Stansfield C: Jenion (6) PG: Jenion (2)

24 Sep	(A)	Coventry	L 3–7	*PG:* Bentley
8 Oct	(H)	Saracens	L 10–12	*T:* Duggart *PG:* Pears (2)
22 Oct	(A)	Northampton	L 12–15	*PG:* Jenion (3) *DG:* Jee
12 Nov	(A)	L Scottish	W 17–16	*T:* Campbell, Pears *PG:* Pears (3)
19 Nov	(H)	Headingley	L 15–24	*PG:* Pears (5)
26 Nov	(A)	L Irish	D 18–18	*T:* Pears *C:* Pears *PG:* Pears (4)
14 Jan	(A)	L Welsh	W 16–9	*T:* Lowther, Crompton *C:* Pears *PG:* Pears (2)
11 Mar	(H)	Gosforth	W 23–15	*T:* Kenrick, Pears *PG:* Pears (5)
8 Apr	(A)	Blackheath	W 16–12	*T:* Fitton *PG:* Pears (4)
22 Apr	(H)	Bedford	D 15–15	*T:* Baldwin *C:* Pears *PG:* Pears *DG:* Pears (2)

Saracens

Year of formation 1876
Ground Bramley Sports Ground, Green Road, Southgate, London N14
Tel: 01-449 3770
Colours Black jerseys with red star and crescent, black shorts, red stockings
Most capped player V S Harding (England) 6 caps
Captain 1988-89 F Steadman
1st XV 1988-89 P34 W25 D1 L8 F722 A448
Courage Leagues Div 2 1st *promoted* **Pilkington Cup** Lost 0-6 to London Scottish (3rd round)
Top scorer A Kennedy (297) **Most tries** S Robinson, D McLagen (15)

League Record in 1988–89

Date	Venue	Opponents	Result	Scorers
10 Sep	(A)	Headingley	W 7–3	*T:* McLagen *PG:* Kennedy
24 Sep	(H)	L Irish	W 20–3	*T:* McLagen (2), Steadman *C:* Kennedy *PG:* Kennedy (2)
8 Oct	(A)	Sale	W 12–10	*T:* Lindley *C:* McLagen *PG:* McLagen (2)
22 Oct	(H)	L Welsh	W 37–4	*T:* Kennedy (2), Roberts, Holmes, Robinson, McFarland *C:* Kennedy (2) *PG:* Kennedy (3)
12 Nov	(A)	Northampton	W 32–4	*T:* Kennedy (2), Buckton, Smith *C:* Kennedy (2) *PG:* Kennedy (4)
19 Nov	(H)	Bedford	W 50–10	*T:* Steadman (2), Buckton, McLagen, McFarland, Smith, Robinson *C:* Kennedy (5) *PG:* Kennedy (4)
26 Nov	(A)	Blackheath	W 24–12	*T:* Kennedy, McLagen *C:* Kennedy (2) *PG:* Kennedy (4)
14 Jan	(H)	Coventry	W 13–6	*T:* Holmes *PG:* Kennedy (2) *DG:* Holmes
11 Mar	(A)	Richmond	W 27–10	*T:* McLagen (2) *C:* Kennedy (2) *PG:* Kennedy (5)
8 Apr	(H)	L Scottish	W 19–9	*T:* Steadman *PG:* Kennedy (5)
22 Apr	(A)	Gosforth	W 47–9	*T:* Smith (3), Steadman (2), Robinson (2), Given, Phillips *C:* Robinson (4) *PG:* Robinson

Wasps

Year of formation 1867
Ground Repton Avenue (off Rugby Avenue), Sudbury (Wembley), Middlesex
Tel: 01-902 4220
Colours Black jerseys with golden wasp on left breast, black shorts, black stockings with gold hoop on turnover
Most capped player R M Uttley (England) 23 caps
Captain 1988-89 R A P Lozowski
1st XV 1988-89 P35 W20 D2 L13 F791 A560
Courage Leagues Div 1 3rd **Pilkington Cup** Lost 18-22 to Leicester (quarter-final)
Top scorer C R Andrew (178) **Most tries** M D Bailey (15)

David Pegler gets a pass away playing for England B against Australia. Pegler has now stepped down after a highly-successful stint as captain of Wasps.

League Record in 1988–89

Date	Venue	Opponents	Result	Scorers
10 Sep	(A)	Leicester	L 6–15	*PG:* Richardson *DG:* Andrew
24 Sep	(H)	Harlequins	W 23–15	*T:* Andrew, Bailey, Clough *C:* Andrew *PG:* Andrew (3)
8 Oct	(A)	Gloucester	L 3–19	*PG:* Andrew
22 Oct	(H)	Rosslyn Park	W 39–16	*T:* Davies, Smith, Ellison, Pilgrim, Andrew *C:* Andrew (5) *PG:* Andrew (3)
12 Nov	(A)	Nottingham	W 15–9	*PG:* Andrew (5)
19 Nov	(H)	Moseley	W 39–10	*T:* Bailey (3), Rigby, Ellison, Clough *C:* Andrew (3), Pilgrim (2), O'Leary *DG:* Andrew
26 Nov	(A)	Bath	W 6–16	*PG:* Pilgrim (2)
14 Jan	(A)	Orrell	D 9–9	*PG:* Andrew (3)
11 Mar	(H)	Liverp'l St H	W 16–10	*T:* Oti, Ellison *C:* Andrew *PG:* Andrew (2)
8 Apr	(H)	Bristol	W 21–19	*T:* Pilgrim, Oti, Simms *PG:* Andrew (3)
22 Apr	(A)	Waterloo	W 29–0	*T:* Simms (2), Smith, Rose, Oti *C:* Andrew (3) *PG:* Andrew

Waterloo

Year of formation 1882
Ground St Anthony's Road, Blundellsands, Liverpool L23 8TW   Tel: 051 924 4552
Colours Green, red and white hoops
Most capped player H G Periton (England) 21 caps
Captain 1988-89 S Gallagher
1st XV 1988-89 P40 W24 D1 L15 F914 A579
Courage Leagues Div 1 11th *relegated* **Pilkington Cup** Lost 19-16 to Gloucester (4th round)
Top scorer I Aitchison (252) **Most tries** P Cooley (20)

League Record in 1988–89

Date	Venue	Opponents	Result	Scorers
10 Sep	(H)	Liverp'l St H	L 6–12	*PG:* Aitchison (2)
24 Sep	(A)	Orrell	L 12–15	*PG:* Aitchison (4)
8 Oct	(H)	Nottingham	L 9–18	*PG:* Aitchison (3)
22 Oct	(A)	Moseley	L 6–13	*PG:* Aitchison (2)
12 Nov	(H)	Leicester	L 22–34	*T:* Murray, Cooley *C:* Aitchison *PG:* Aitchison (3) *DG:* Aitchison
19 Nov	(A)	Harlequins	W 24–23	*T:* Cooley, Bracegirdle, Jenkins *C:* Aitchison (3) *PG:* Aitchison (2)
26 Nov	(H)	Gloucester	D 15–15	*PG:* Aitchison (5)
14 Jan	(A)	Bristol	L 3–14	*PG:* Aitchison
11 Mar	(H)	Rosslyn Park	L 14–24	*T:* Greenhalgh, Cooley *PG:* Carfoot, Tickle
8 Apr	(A)	Bath	L 9–38	*T:* Cooley *C:* Angell *PG:* Angell
22 Apr	(H)	Wasps	L 0–29	

SCOTLAND

Ayr

Year of formation 1897
Ground Millbrae, Alloway, Ayr   Tel: Alloway (0292) 41944
Colours Pink and black
Most capped player S Munro (Scotland) 10 caps
Captain 1988-89 G G Steel
1st XV 1988-89 P36   W19   D1   L16   F711   A548
Schweppes/SRU Div 1 11th   **Top scorer** A C McGuffie (146)
Most tries D A Stark (18)

Boroughmuir

Year of formation 1919 (Boroughmuir FP until 1974)
Ground Meggetland, Colinton Road, Edinburgh EH14 IAS
Tel: Edinburgh (031) 443 7571
Colours Navy blue and emerald green
Most capped player B H Hay (Scotland) 23 caps
Captain 1988-89 B Edwards
1st XV 1988-89 P36   W28   D2   L6   F969   A407
Schweppes/SRU Div 1 joint 1st *2nd on points difference*   **Top scorer** M Walker (317)
Most tries C J Macartney (21)

Corstorphine

Year of formation Reformed in 1950
Ground Union Park, Carrick Knowe Parkway, Corstorphine, Edinburgh
Tel: Edinburgh (031) 334 8063
Colours Navy blue and scarlet quarters
Captain 1988-89 G B Liddle
1st XV 1988-89 P30   W11   D3   L16   F478   A525
Schweppes/SRU Div 2 joint 9th   **Top scorer** G B Liddle (162)
Most tries D R T Gill (13)

Currie

Year of formation 1970
Ground Malleny Park, Balerno, Edinburgh EH14 5HA   Tel: Edinburgh (031) 449 2432
Colours Amber and black
Captain 1988-89 P Farrer
1st XV 1988-89 P31   W21   D0   L10   F691   A407
Schweppes/SRU Div 2 3rd   **Top scorer** A Donaldson (251)
Most tries S Forrester (18)

Dalziel High School FP

Year of formation 1925
Ground Cleland Estate   Tel: 0698 860000
Colours Black, blue and navy
Captain 1988-89 C Westmorland
1st XV 1988-89 P34   W17   D1   L16   F564   A491
Schweppes/SRU Div 2 joint 9th   **Top scorer** B W Gibson (199)
Most tries B W Gibson (7)

Sean Lineen, the New Zealand born centre who won selection for Scotland on the strength of his inspirational performances at club level for Boroughmuir.

Dunfermline

Year of formation 1904
Ground McKane Park, Dunfermline, Fife
Colours Royal blue and white
Most capped player J T Greenwood (Scotland) 20 caps
Captain 1988-89 I Michie
1st XV 1988-89 P27 W9 D0 L18 F312 A588
Schweppes/SRU Div 2 12th   **Top scorer** N Sharp (53)   **Most tries** S Morman (6)

Edinburgh Academicals

Year of formation 1857
Ground Raeburn Place, Edinburgh   Tel: Edinburgh (031) 332 1070
Colours Blue and white stripes
Most capped player W I D Elliot (Scotland) 29 caps
Captain 1988-89 J F Richardson
1st XV 1988-89 P34 W19 D3 L12 F698 A430
Schweppes/SRU Div 1 joint 4th   **Top scorer** S A D Burns (147)
Most tries A Moore (27)

Edinburgh Wanderers

Year of formation 1868
Ground Murrayfield, Edinburgh EH12 5PJ
Colours Red and black
Most capped player A R Smith (Scotland) 33 caps
Captain 1988-89 G W M Hamilton
1st XV 1988-89 P37 W21 D2 L14 F715 A586
Schweppes/SRU Div 2 5th   **Top scorer** F Duncan (170)   **Most tries** E S Gillies (18)

Gala

Year of formation 1875
Ground Netherdale, Galashiels   Tel: Galashiels (0896) 3811
Colours Maroon
Most capped player P C Brown (Scotland) 27 caps
Captain 1988-89 K R Macaulay
Ist XV 1988-89 P32 W23 D0 L9 F807 A346
Schweppes/SRU Div 2 2nd *promoted*   **Top scorer** P W Dods (172)
Most tries M Moncrieff (25)

Glasgow Academicals

Year of formation 1867
Ground New Anniesland, Helensburgh Drive, Glasgow   Tel: (041) 959 1323
Colours Navy blue and white
Most capped player W M Simmers (Scotland) 28 caps
Captain 1988-89 G T MacGregor
1st XV 1988-89 P31 W10 D1 L20 F457 A532
Schweppes/SRU Div 1 13th *relegated*   **Top scorer** D C Cameron (163)
Most tries G T MacGregor (8)

Glasgow High/Kelvinside

Year of formation 1982 (on amalgamation of Glasgow HS FP and Kelvinside Academicals)
Ground Old Anniesland, Crow Road, Glasgow   Tel: Glasgow (041) 959 1154
Colours Chocolate and gold
Most capped player None (Prior to amalgamation J M Bannerman (Glasgow High) was capped 37 times and D M White (Kelvinside) 4 times – both for Scotland)
Captain 1988-89 F D Wallace
1st XV 1988-89   P27   W13   D1   L13   F498   A416
Schweppes/SRU Div 1 12th   **Top scorer** G Breckenridge (143)
Most tries J D M Wilson (12)

Hawick

Year of formation 1873
Ground Mansfield Park, Mansfield Road, Hawick   Tel: Hawick (0450) 74291
Colours Green
Most capped player J M Renwick (Scotland) 52 caps
Captain 1988-89 K T Murray
1st XV 1988-89   P34   W23   D0   L11   F701   A418
Schweppes/SRU Div 1 joint 1st *3rd on points difference*   **Top scorer** C W Gass (272)
Most tries A G Stanger (14)

Heriot's FP

Year of formation 1890
Ground Goldenacre, Inverleith Row, Edinburgh
Tel: Edinburgh (031) 552 5925 (pavilion); 552 4097 (groundsman)
Colours Blue and white horizontal stripes
Most capped player A R Irvine (Scotland) 51 caps
Captain 1988-89 K P Rafferty
1st XV 1988-89   P31   W21   D1   L9   F772   A475
Schweppes/SRU Div 1 joint 4th   **Top scorer** P J Hewitt (303)
Most tries P J Hewitt (22)

Hillhead/Jordanhill

Year of formation 1988 (on amalgamation of Hillhead and Jordanhill)
Ground Hughenden, 32 Hughenden Road, Glasgow G12
Colours Chocolate, navy and gold
Most capped player None (before amalgamation J McLauchlan (Jordanhill) was capped 43 times and W C W Murdoch and I A A MacGregor (Hillhead) 9 times – all for Scotland)
Captain 1988-89 S G Morgan
1st XV 1988-89   P30   W12   D1   L17   F460   A584
Schweppes/SRU Div 2 8th   **Top scorer** A S Robertson (94)
Most tries S Lapping (12)

Howe of Fife

Year of formation 1922
Ground Duffus Park, Cupar; clubhouse 15 Provost's Wynd, Cupar
Tel: Cupar (0334) 52819
Colours Blue and white hoops
Most capped player D M D Rollo (Scotland) 40 caps

Captain 1988-89 C Douglas
1st XV 1988-89   P35   W10   D1   L24   F432   A655
Schweppes/SRU Div 2 14th *relegated*   **Top scorer** M Stevens (173)
Most tries J Stewart (14)

Jedforest

Year of formation 1885
Ground Riverside Park, Jedburgh   Tel: Jedburgh (0835) 62232 and 62855
Colours Royal blue
Most capped player R J Laidlaw (Scotland) 47 caps
Captain 1988-89 J Raeburn
1st XV 1988-89   P32   W22   D2   L8   F786   A445
Schweppes/SRU Div 2 6th   **Top scorer** G J McKechnie (224)
Most tries R M Kirkpatrick (15)

Kelso

Year of formation 1876
Ground Poynder Park, Kelso, Roxburghshire   Tel: Kelso (0573) 24300 and 23773
Colours Black and white
Most capped player G R T Baird (Scotland) 27 caps
Captain 1988-89 J Jeffrey
1st XV 1988-89   P32   W21   D0   L11   F763   A349
Schweppes/SRU Div 1 *winners*   **Top scorer** A B M Ker (254)
Most tries D R Robeson (16)

Kilmarnock

Year of formation 1868
Ground Bellsland, Queens Drive, Kilmarnock   Tel: Kilmarnock (0563) 22314
Colours White with red hoop surmounted by white Maltese cross
Most capped player W Cuthbertson (Scotland) 22 caps
Captain 1988-89 B G Yates
1st XV 1988-89   P34   W19   D0   L15   F541   A466
Schweppes/SRU Div 2 4th   **Top scorer** E R J Stewart (171)
Most tries B G Yates (12)

Langholm

Year of formation 1872
Ground Milntown, Langholm, Dumfriesshire   Tel: Langholm (054) 80386
Colours Crimson and blue
Most capped player C Elliot (Scotland) 12 caps
Captain 1988-89 D Glendinning
1st XV 1988-89   P28   W4   D4   L20   F243   A677
Schweppes/SRU Div 2 11th   **Top scorer** C Turk (110)   **Most tries** D Glendinning (7)

Melrose

Year of formation 1877
Ground Greenyards, Melrose   Tel: Melrose (089682) 2559 and 2993
Colours Yellow and black
Most capped player K W Robertson (Scotland) 40 caps
Captain 1988-89 I J Ramsey

1st XV 1988-89 P31 W21 D0 L10 F725 A378
Schweppes/SRU Div 1 10th **Top scorer** I J Ramsey (285)
Most tries A A Purves (16)

Musselburgh

Year of formation 1921
Ground Stoneyhill, Stoneyhill Farm Road, Musselburgh
Tel: Edinburgh (031) 665 3435
Colours Navy blue with narrow white hoops
Captain 1988-89 A J G Johnston
1st XV 1988-89 P31 W16 D2 L13 F473 A494
Schweppes/SRU Div 2 7th **Top scorer** C Livingstone (139) **Most tries** N Smith (8)

Portobello FP

Year of formation Reformed in 1954
Ground Cavalry Park, Duddingston Road West, Edinburgh
Tel: Edinburgh (031) 661 4554
Colours Navy blue and old gold hoops
Captain 1988-89 I T Boyter
1st XV 1988-89 P29 W8 D1 L20 F345 A497
Schweppes/SRU Div 2 13th *relegated* **Top scorer** M Gorman (100)
Most tries A T I Denham (11)

Preston Lodge

Year of formation 1929
Ground Pennypit Park, Prestonpans, East Lothian Tel: Edinburgh (031) 661 4554
Colours Black with maroon and white hoops
Captain 1988-89 S B Love
1st XV 1988-89 P28 W18 D0 L10 F442 A270
Schweppes/SRU Div 2 6th **Top scorer** B Palmer (141)
Most tries S Mackay, S Payne (9)

Selkirk

Year of formation 1907
Ground Philiphaugh, Selkirk Tel: Selkirk (0750) 20403
Colours Navy blue
Most capped player J Y Rutherford (Scotland) 42 caps
Captain 1988-89 G W Craig
1st XV 1988-89 P33 W21 D1 L11 F586 A393
Schweppes/SRU Div 1 7th **Top scorer** R L Pow (225) **Most tries** R L Pow (14)

Stewart's-Melville FP

Year of formation 1973 (on amalgamation of Daniel Stewart's College FP and Melville College FP)
Ground Inverleith, Ferry Road, Edinburgh EH5 2DW Tel: Edinburgh (031) 522 1515
Colours Scarlet with broad black bands divided by narrow gold bands
Most capped player J H Calder (Scotland) 27 caps
Captain 1988-89 J M Scott
1st XV 1988-89 P35 W16 D1 L18 F511 A731
Schweppes/SRU Div 1 joint 8th **Top scorer** C St J Spence (108)
Most tries M Lowes (13)

Stirling County

Year of formation 1904
Ground Bridgehaugh Park, Stirling   Tel: Stirling (0786) 74827
Colours Red, white and black
Most capped player Dr W Welsh (Scotland) 8 caps
Captain 1988-89 J S Hamilton
1st XV 1988-89 P34 W30 D1 L3 F959 A353
Schweppes/SRU Div 2 *winners promoted* **Top scorer** C T MacDonald (349)
Most tries B Ireland (17)

Watsonians

Year of formation 1875
Ground Myreside, Edinburgh   Tel: Edinburgh (031) 447 1395
Colours Maroon
Most capped player D I Johnston (Scotland) 27 caps
Captain 1988-89 S Hastings
1st XV 1988-89 P29 W3 D0 L26 F282 A935
Schweppes/SRU Div 1 14th *relegated* **Top scorer** C A M Hunter (82)
Most tries S Hastings (8)

West of Scotland

Year of formation 1865
Ground Burnbrae, Glasgow Road, Milngavie, Glasgow G62 6HX
Tel: Glasgow (041) 956 2891 and 956 1960
Colours Red and yellow hoops
Most capped player A B Carmichael (Scotland) 50 caps
Captain 1988-89 D R Livingston
1st XV 1988-89 P32 W15 D1 L16 F477 A567
Schweppes/SRU Div 1 joint 8th **Top scorer** D N Barrett (215)
Most tries D G Ross, F Stott (8)

WALES

Aberavon

Year of formation 1876
Ground Talbot Athletic Ground, Manor Street, Port Talbot, West Glamorgan
Tel: Port Talbot (0639) 882427/886038
Colours Red and black hoops, white shorts, and red stockings
Most capped player A J Martin (Wales) 34 caps
Captain 1988-89 W J James/G Matthews
1st XV 1988-89 P46   W14   D1   L31   F663   A894
Western Mail Championship 16th   **Whitbread Merit Table** 16th
WRU Schweppes Cup Lost 6-19 to Aberavon Quins (4th round)
Top scorer N Forrester (95)   **Most tries** P Middleton, J Hopkins (9 each)

Abertillery

Year of formation 1884
Ground The Park, Abertillery, Gwent   Tel: Abertillery (0495) 212226
Colours Green and white hoops
Most capped player H J Morgan (Wales) 27 caps
Captain 1988-89 W Evans
1st XV 1988-89 P50   W30   D0   L20   F1022   A693
Western Mail Championship 8th   **Whitbread Merit Table** 8th
WRU Schweppes Cup Lost 9-12 to Newbridge (6th round)
Top scorer B Hayward (359) *record*   **Most tries** S Nunnerley (16)

Bridgend

Year of formation 1878
Ground Brewery Field, Tondu Road, Bridgend, Mid-Glamorgan
Tel: Bridgend (0656) 59032
Colours Blue and white stripes
Most capped player J P R Williams (Wales) 55 caps
Captain 1988-89 J Morgan
1st XV 1988-89 P53   W40   D1   L12   F1243   A673
Western Mail Championship 4th   **Whitbread Merit Table** 4th
WRU Schweppes Cup Lost 13-22 to Llanelli (6th round)
Top scorer A Parry (299)   **Most tries** K Ellis (19)

Cardiff

Year of formation 1876
Ground Cardiff Arms Park, Westgate Street, Cardiff   Tel: Cardiff (0222) 383546
Colours Cambridge blue and black
Most capped player G O Edwards (Wales) 53 caps
Captain 1988-89 R L Norster
1st XV 1988-89 P44   W26   D4   L14   F1075   A773
Western Mail Championship 7th   **Whitbread Merit Table** 7th
WRU Schweppes Cup Lost 12-19 to Neath (semi-final)
Top scorer M Rayer (215)   **Most tries** G Cordle (38)

Cross Keys

Year of formation 1885
Ground Pandy Park, Cross Keys, Gwent   Tel: Cross Keys (0495) 270289

Colours Black and white hoops
Most capped player S Morris (Wales) 19 caps
Captain 1988-89 G Johnston
1st XV 1988-89 P50 W22 D2 L26 F715 A1018
Western Mail Championship 15th **Whitbread Merit Table** 15th
WRU Schweppes Cup Lost 0-38 to Pontypridd (4th round)
Top scorer C Thomas (101) **Most tries** S Nutt (16)

Ebbw Vale

Year of formation 1880
Ground Eugene Cross Park, Ebbw Vale   Tel: Ebbw Vale (0495) 302157/302995
Colours Red, white, and green hoops
Most capped player Denzil Williams (Wales) 36 caps
Captain 1988-89 N Robinson
1st XV 1988-89 P48 W23 D2 L23 F737 A939
Western Mail Championship 11th **Whitbread Merit Table** 12th
WRU Schweppes Cup Lost 6-17 to Abertillery (5th round)
Top scorer M Davies (94) **Most tries** I Jeffreys (16)

Glamorgan Wanderers

Year of formation 1893
Ground The Memorial Ground, Stirling Road, Ely, Cardiff   Tel: Cardiff (0222) 591039
Colours Cambridge blue, black and white
Captain 1988-89 P Prickett
1st XV 1988-89 P49 W25 D1 L23 F968 A785
Western Mail Championship 13th **Whitbread Merit Table** 14th
WRU Schweppes Cup Lost 0-38 to Neath (6th round)
Top scorer B Bolderson (279) **Most tries** C Norman (17)

Llanelli

Year of formation 1872
Ground Stradey Park, Llanelli, Dyfed   Tel: Llanelli (0554) 774060
Colours Scarlet jerseys with white collars, club crest on left breast
Most capped player J J Williams (Wales) 30 caps
Captain 1988-89 P T Davies
1st XV 1988-89 P50 W41 D0 L9 F1578 A780
Western Mail Championship 2nd **Whitbread Merit Table** 1st
WRU Schweppes Cup Lost 13-14 to Neath (final)
Top scorer C Stephens (216) **Most tries** S Bowling (22)

Maesteg

Year of formation 1882
Ground Llynvi Road, Maesteg, Mid-Glamorgan   Tel: Maesteg (0656) 732283
Colours Black and amber
Most capped player G Evans (Wales) 10 caps
Captain 1988-89 C Davey
1st XV 1988-89 P50 W27 D3 L20 F903 A766
Western Mail Championship 9th **Whitbread Merit Table** 9th
WRU Schweppes Cup Lost 13-15 to Glynneath (4th round)
Top scorer J Bird (311) **Most tries** M Owens (13)

Nigel Davies, pictured playing for Wales against Scotland, had an outstanding season for Llanelli.

Neath

Year of formation 1871
Ground The Gnoll, Gnoll Park Road, Neath, West Glamorgan   Tel: Neath (0639) 4420
Colours Black with white Maltese cross
Most capped player W D Morris (Wales) 34 caps
Captain 1988-89 K H Phillips
1st XV 1988-89   P50   W46   D0   L4   F1917   A471
Western Mail Championship 1st   **Whitbread Merit Table** 2nd
WRU Schweppes Cup *Winners*   **Top scorer** P H Thorburn (319)
Most tries A Edmunds (39)

Newbridge

Year of formation 1890
Ground Welfare Ground, Bridge Street, Newbridge, Gwent   Tel: Newbridge (0495) 243247
Colours Blue and black hoops (alternate, red)
Most capped player D Hayward (Wales) 15 caps
Captain 1988-89 S Griffiths   *Centenary season*
1st XV 1988-89   P48   W38   D2   L8   F1197   A625
Western Mail Championship 3rd   **Whitbread Merit Table** 3rd
WRU Schweppes Cup Lost 24-26 to Llanelli (semi-final)   **Top scorer** P Turner (330)
Most tries C Phillips (18)

Newport

Year of formation 1874
Ground Rodney Parade, Newport, Gwent   Tel: Newport (0633) 58193
Colours Black and amber
Most capped player K J Jones (Wales) 44 caps
Captain 1988-89 G George
1st XV 1988-89   P49   W27   D1   L21   F1066   A927
Western Mail Championship 10th   **Whitbread Merit Table** 10th
WRU Schweppes Cup Lost 3-7 to Newbridge (5th round)
Top scorer G Abraham (301)   **Most tries** J Thomas (21)

Penarth

Year of formation 1880
Ground Athletic Grounds, Lavernock Road, Penarth, South Glamorgan
Tel: Penarth (0222) 708402
Colours Royal blue (alternative with white hoops)
Most capped player J Bassett (Wales) 15 caps
Captain 1988-89 M Owen/C Lewis
1st XV 1988-89   P44   W9   D0   L35   F519   A1348
Western Mail Championship 19th   **Whitbread Merit Table** 18th
WRU Schweppes Cup Lost 7-27 to Blackwood (3rd round)
Top scorer P Elias (79)   **Most tries** M Owen (12)

Pontypool

Year of formation 1901
Ground Pontypool Park, Pontypool   Tel: Pontypool (0495) 3492 (ground) 2524 (HQ)
Colours Red, white, and black hoops

Most capped player G Price (Wales) 41 caps
Captain 1988-89 M Brown
1st XV 1988-89   P48   W24   D1   L23   F886   A853
Western Mail Championship 12th   **Whitbread Merit Table** 11th
WRU Schweppes Cup Disqualified for fielding ineligible player in 10-9 win over Vardre in (3rd round)   **Top scorer** D Wright (142)   **Most tries** S White (24)

Pontypridd

Year of formation 1876
Ground Sardis Road Ground, Pwllgwaun, Pontypridd   Tel: Pontypridd (0433) 405006
Colours Black and white hoops
Most capped player R J Robins (Wales) 13 caps
Captain 1988-89 C Jones
1st XV 1988-89   P45   W33   D1   L11   F1280   A596
Western Mail Championship 5th   **Whitbread Merit Table** 5th
WRU Schweppes Cup Lost 11-26 to Llanelli (5th round)
Top scorer A Phillips (326)   **Most tries** M Jones (18)

South Wales Police

Year of formation 1969
Ground Police Recreation Ground, Waterton Cross, Bridgend, Mid-Glamorgan
Tel: Bridgend (0656) 55555 ext 218/Bridgend 4481
Colours Red jerseys, white shorts, royal blue stockings
Most capped player Bleddyn Bowen (Wales) 21 caps
Captain 1988-89 M Pugh
1st XV 1988-89   P51   W24   D1   L26   F964   A919
Western Mail Championship 14th   **Whitbread Merit Table** 13th
WRU Schweppes Cup Lost 10-17 to Llanharan (5th round)
Top scorer A Hughes (156)   **Most tries** A Hughes (20)

Swansea

Year of formation 1874
Ground St Helen's Ground, Swansea, West Glamorgan
Tel: Swansea (0792) 464918/466593
Colours All white
Most capped player T M Davies (Wales) 38 caps
Captain 1988-89 R D Moriarty
1st XV 1988-89   P44   W30   D0   L14   F1110   A701
Western Mail Championship 6th   **Whitbread Merit Table** 6th
WRU Schweppes Cup Lost 8-18 to Glamorgan Wanderers (3rd round)
Top scorer M Wyatt (164)   **Most tries** B Taylor (19)

Tredegar

Year of formation 1899
Ground Tredegar Recreation Ground, Park Hill, Tredegar, Gwent
Tel: Tredegar (0495) 2879
Colours Red, black and white
Captain 1988-89 H Evans
1st XV 1988-89   P48   W16   D1   L31   F627   A1032
Western Mail Championship 17th   **Whitbread Merit Table** 17th
WRU Schweppes Cup Lost 10-26 to Blaina (3rd round)
Top scorer S Williams (156)   **Most tries** N Hunt (12)

IRELAND

Ards

Year of formation 1878 (reformed 1928)
Ground Lansdowne Road, Newtownards   Tel: Newtownards 813961
Colours Black with white collar, black shorts
Most capped player N J Carr (Ireland) 11 caps
Ulster Senior Cup Lost 9-33 to Ballymena (2nd round)
Ulster Senior League Section 1 7th (bottom)

Ballymena

Year of formation 1922
Ground Eaton Park, Ballymena   Tel: Ballymena 6746
Colours Black jerseys, white shorts, black stockings with white turnover
Most capped player W J McBride (Ireland) 63 caps
Captain 1988-89 A R Brady
Ulster Senior Cup *Winners* beat Bangor 25-3 (final)
Ulster Senior League Section 1 *Winners*

Bangor

Year of formation 1885
Ground Upritchard Park, Bloomfield Road South, Bangor, Co Down, N Ireland
Colours Old gold, royal blue and black
Most capped player R A Milliken (Ireland) 14 caps
Captain 1988-89 D Morrow
Ulster Senior Cup Lost 25-3 to Ballymena (final)
Ulster Senior League Section 1 5th

Bective Rangers

Year of formation 1881
Ground Donnybrook, Dublin 4   Tel: Dublin 693894
Colours Red, green and white striped jerseys, white shorts
Most capped player J L Farrell (Ireland) 29 caps
Captain 1988-89 C Lydon
Leinster Senior Cup Lost 14-24 to Lansdowne (2nd round *replay*)
Leinster Senior League Div 1 8th

Blackrock College

Year of formation 1882
Ground Stradbrook Road, Blackrock   Tel: Dublin 805697
Colours Narrow royal blue and white striped jerseys, navy shorts, navy stockings
Most capped player J F Slattery (Ireland) 61 caps
Captain 1988-89 J Langbroek
Leinster Senior Cup Lost 12-20 to Wanderers (1st round)
Leinster Senior League Div 2 1st

Bohemians

Year of formation 1922
Ground Thomond Park, Limerick   Tel: Limerick 51877
Colours Red and white
Most capped player M A F English (Ireland) 16 caps
Captain 1988-89 B Hurley
Munster Senior Cup Lost 0-19 to Young Munster (1st round)
Munster Senior League 10th

CIYMS

Year of formation 1922
Ground Circular Road, Belfast   Tel: Belfast 768225/760120
Colours Black and white hooped jerseys, black shorts, blue stockings
Most capped player A C Pedlow (Ireland) 30 caps
Captain 1988-89 L McCallan
Ulster Senior Cup Lost 9-12 to Ards (1st round)
Ulster Senior League Section 1 5th

Clontarf

Year of formation 1876
Ground Castle Avenue, Clontarf, Dublin   Tel: Dublin 336214
Colours Red and blue jerseys, white shorts, red and blue striped stockings
Most capped player G J Morgan (Ireland) 19 caps
Captain 1988-89 A R Foley
Leinster Senior Cup Lost 12-16 to Terenure Coll (2nd round *replay*)
Leinster Senior League Div 2 3rd

Collegians

Year of formation 1890
Ground Deramore Park, Belfast, N Ireland   Tel: Belfast 665943
Colours White and maroon, navy stockings with maroon tops
Most capped player J McVicker (Ireland) 20 caps
Ulster Senior Cup Lost 9-46 to Ballymena (semi-final)
Ulster Senior League Section 2 5th

Constitution FC

Year of formation 1892
Ground Temple Hill, Ballintemple, Cork   Tel: Cork 32563
Colours White, black and blue
Most capped player T J Kiernan (Ireland) 54 caps
Captain 1988-89 M T Bradley
Munster Senior Cup *Winners* beat Shannon 13-12 (final)
Munster Senior League 2nd

Corinthians

Year of formation 1932
Ground Corinthian Park, Tuam Road, Galway
Colours Blue, black and white

Captain 1988-89 M O'Toole
Connacht Senior Cup Lost 9-15 to UC Galway (semi-final)
Connacht Senior League *Winners*

De La Salle Palmerston

Year of formation 1985 (on amalgamation of De La Salle and Palmerston)
Ground Kilternan, Co Dublin   Tel: Dublin 953650/953550
Colours Green, white, wine and black jerseys, black shorts
Captain 1988-89 A O'Connor
Leinster Senior Cup Lost 3-15 to Clontarf (1st round)
Leinster Senior League Div 2 6th

Dolphin

Year of formation 1902
Ground Musgrave Park, Cork   Tel: Cork 22069
Colours Navy blue
Most capped player M J Kiernan (Ireland) 32 caps
Captain 1988-89 T Kingston
Munster Senior Cup Lost 11-12 to Shannon (semi-final)
Munster Senior League 8th

Dublin University

Year of formation 1854
Ground College Park, Trinity College, Dublin 2   Tel: 778423
Colours White jerseys and shorts, black stockings with red bands
Most capped player J D Clinch (Ireland) 30 caps
Captain 1988-89 D Sheehan
Leinster Senior Cup Lost 3-19 to Old Belvedere (2nd round)
Leinster Senior League Div 1 7th

Dungannon

Year of formation 1873
Ground Stevenson Park, Dungannon, N Ireland   Tel: Dungannon 22387
Colours Royal blue and white hoops, white shorts
Most capped player S A McKinney (Ireland) 25 caps
Captain 1988-89 W Anderson
Ulster Senior Cup Lost 7-13 to Bangor (2nd round)
Ulster Senior League Section 2 *Winners*

Galwegians

Year of formation 1922
Ground Glenina, Galway, Co Galway   Tel: Galway (091) 62484
Colours Sky blue jerseys, white shorts, sky blue stockings with black tops
Most capped player P J A O'Sullivan (Ireland) 15 caps
Captain 1988-89 F Kinneen
Connacht Senior Cup Lost 7-13 to UC Galway (final)
Connacht Senior League 3rd

Garryowen

Year of formation 1884
Ground Dooradoyle, Limerick   Tel: Limerick 46094
Colours Light blue jerseys with white star on breast
Most capped player B G M Wood (Ireland) 29 caps
Captain 1988-89 D Duggan
Munster Senior Cup Lost 0-7 to Dolphin (1st round *replay*)
Munster Senior League 3rd

Greystones

Year of formation 1937
Ground Hickey Park, Greystones   Tel: Dublin 874640
Colours Green and white hooped jerseys, white shorts, green stockings
Most capped player A J P Ward (Ireland) 19 caps
Captain 1988-89 T Morley
Leinster Senior Cup Lost 6-17 to Terenure Coll (1st round *replay*)
Leinster Senior League Div 1 3rd

Instonians

Year of formation 1919
Ground Shane Park, Stockmans Lane, Belfast BT9 7JD   Tel: Belfast 660629
Colours Yellow, black and purple
Most capped player D Hewitt (Ireland) 18 caps
Captain 1988-89 D Spratt
Ulster Senior Cup Lost 9-25 to Bangor (semi-final)
Ulster Senior League Section 1 4th

Lansdowne

Year of formation 1872
Ground Lansdowne Road, Dublin 4   Tel: Dublin 689292/689300
Colours Red, yellow and black
Most capped player M I Keane (Ireland) 51 caps
Captain 1988-89 G Dilger
Leinster Senior Cup *Winners*
Leinster Senior League Div 1 6th

Malone

Year of formation 1892
Ground Gibson Park Avenue, Cregagh Road, Belfast BT6 9GL
Tel: Belfast 57819/51312 (office)
Colours White shirts, blue shorts, red stockings
Most capped player W E Crawford (Ireland) 30 caps
Captain 1988-89 C Patterson
Ulster Senior Cup Lost 9-13 to Collegians (2nd round)
Ulster Senior League Section 1 2nd

Monkstown

Year of formation 1883
Ground Sydney Parade, Dublin 4   Tel: Dublin 691794
Colours Royal blue and gold

Most capped player J C Parke (Ireland) 20 caps
Captain 1988-89 D Dent
Leinster Senior Cup Lost 6-10 to Lansdowne (1st round)
Leinster Senior League Div 2 2nd

North of Ireland (NIFC)

Year of formation 1859
Ground Shaftesbury Avenue, Belfast BT7 2ES   Tel: Belfast 21096/23342
Colours Red, black and blue jerseys, navy shorts, black stockings with red, black and blue turnover
Most capped player C M H Gibson (Ireland) 69 caps
Captain 1988-89 G Hamilton
Ulster Senior Cup Lost 12-17 to Malone (2nd round)
Ulster Senior League Section 1 3rd

Old Belvedere

Year of formation 1930
Ground Anglesea Road, Ballsbridge, Dublin 4   Tel: Dublin 689748
Colours Black and white hooped jerseys, black shorts
Most capped player A J F O'Reilly (Ireland) 29 caps
Captain 1988-89 C Cruess-Callaghan
Leinster Senior Cup Lost 16-19 to Lansdowne (semi-final)
Leinster Senior League Div 2 4th

Old Wesley

Year of formation 1891
Ground Donnybrook, Dublin 4   Tel: Dublin 689149
Colours White jerseys with red and white band, white shorts
Most capped player P A Orr (Ireland) 58 caps
Captain 1988-89 N Farren
Leinster Senior Cup Lost 3-18 to Bective Rangers (1st round)
Leinster Senior League Div 1 2nd

Queen's University, Belfast

Year of formation 1869
Ground Upper Malone Playing Fields, Upper Malone Road, Belfast
Tel: Belfast 611662
Colours Royal blue jerseys, white shorts, green, blue and black stockings
Most capped player J W Kyle (Ireland) 46 caps
Captain 1988-89 B Murray
Ulster Senior Cup Lost 4-16 to Instonians (2nd round)
Ulster Senior League Section 2 4th

St Mary's College

Year of formation 1900
Ground Templeville Road, Dublin 6   Tel: Dublin 900440
Colours Royal blue jerseys with white star, white shorts, royal blue stockings
Most capped player J J Moloney (Ireland) 27 caps
Captain 1988-89 R Hernan
Leinster Senior Cup Lost 3-6 to Terenure Coll (semi-final)
Leinster Senior League Div 1 *Winners*

Shannon

Year of formation 1884
Ground Gortatoger, Parteen, Co Clare
Colours Black and blue
Most capped player G A J McLoughlin (Ireland) 18 caps
Captain 1988-89 S Minihan
Munster Senior Cup Lost 12-13 to Constitution (final)
Munster Senior League *Winners*

Sunday's Well

Year of formation 1924
Ground Musgrave Park, Cork   Tel: Cork 25926
Colours Red, white and green
Most capped player J C Walsh (Ireland) 25 caps
Captain 1988-89 D O'Leary
Munster Senior Cup Lost 4-12 to Dolphin (2nd round)
Munster Senior League 6th

Terenure College

Year of formation 1941
Ground Lakelands Park, Terenure, Dublin 6   Tel: Dublin 907572
Colours Purple, black and white
Most capped player M L Hipwell (Ireland) 12 caps
Captain 1988-89 R O'Brien
Leinster Senior Cup Lost 0-29 to Lansdowne (final)
Leinster Senior League Div 2 5th

University College, Dublin

Year of formation 1910
Ground University College Dublin, Belfield, Dublin 4   Tel: Dublin 693616
Colours St Patrick's blue jerseys, white shorts, navy blue stockings with St Patrick's blue tops
Most capped player J F Slattery (Ireland) 61 caps
Captain 1988-89 J Connolly
Leinster Senior Cup Lost 3-19 to Old Belvedere (2nd round)
Leinster Senior League Div2 5th

Wanderers

Year of formation 1870
Ground Lansdowne Road, Dublin 4   Tel: Dublin 689277
Junior ground Merrion Road, Dublin   Tel: Dublin 693227/695272
Colours Blue, black and white hooped jerseys, navy shorts, black stockings with blue and white turnover
Most capped player J R Kavanagh (Ireland) 35 caps
Captain 1988-89 A Kelly
Leinster Senior Cup Lost 9-13 to St Mary's Coll (2nd round)
Leinster Senior League Div 1 4th

FIXTURES 1989-90

Venues and fixtures are understood to be correct at the time of going to press, but are subject to alteration. We would like to thank all those who have assisted in the compilation of this list, especially those at the various headquarters of the Home Unions. Additional thanks go to Peter Jackson and John Jeavons-Fellows for help with Courage Leagues fixtures, and we are once again especially grateful to the clubs who have given permission for us to use their fixture lists.

Friday, 1 September

Glynneath v Cardiff

Saturday, 2 September

Yorkshire v Ulster (Hull)
Connacht v Glasgow Dist
Blackrock Rugby Festival
Collegians RFC Tournament
Aberavon v Glamorgan Wands
Bath v Pontypool
Blackheath v Fylde
Bridgend v Tredegar
Bristol v Cardiff
Broughton Park v Birkenhead Park
Coleraine v Howe of Fife
Cork Const v Clontarf
Coventry v Newport
De La Salle/Palmerston v Sunday's Well
Dolphin v Bohemians
Dundee HSFP v Edinburgh Wands
Dungannon v Highfield
Ebbw Vale v Newbridge
Exeter v Public School Wands
Falmouth v Redruth
Glasgow High/Kelvinside v Glasgow Acads
Gosforth v Roundhay
Haddington v Watsonians
Halifax v Nuneaton
Hartlepool Rovers v Huddersfield
Headingley v Abertillery
Jedforest v Melrose
Kilmarnock v Ayr
Llanelli v Rosslyn Park
Lydney v Penarth
Malone v Greystones
Manchester v Wigan
Morley v Middlesbrough
Nantes v Plymouth Albion
Neath v Moseley
Northampton v Harlequins
Northern v Liverpool St Helens
Nottingham v Hawick
Old Belvedere v Wanderers
Orrell v London Irish
Oxford v Esher
Rugby v Askeans

Sale v Kendal
Stewart's-Melville FP v Trinity Acads
Stirling County v Wigton
Swansea v Gloucester
SW Police v London Welsh
Terenure Coll v CIYMS
Wasps v Maesteg
Waterloo v West Hartlepool
Waterpark v Monkstown
West of Scotland v Vale of Lune
Wrexham v Preston Grasshoppers

Sunday, 3 September

Northern Sevens
North Shields v Neath

Monday, 4 September

Munster v Glasgow Dist (Limerick)
Redruth v Truro

Tuesday, 5 September

Boroughmuir v Howe of Fife
Edinburgh Wands v Portobello
Glasgow Acads v Clarkston
Glasgow High/Kelvinside v Kilmarnock
Greenock Wands v Ayr
Hawick v Langholm
Stirling County v Perthshire
Waterloo v Wirral XV

Wednesday, 6 September

Abertillery v Llanelli
Canton v SW Police
Cefn Cribbwr v Aberavon
Dolphin v Sunday's Well
Gilfach Goch v Pontypridd
Glamorgan Wands v Cardiff
Nantyffyllon v Maesteg
Newport v Pill Harriers

Pontypool v Talywain
Selkirk v Jedforest
St Mary's Coll v Greystones
Tredegar Ironsides v Tredegar

Thursday, 7 September

Trinity Acads v Preston Lodge

Saturday, 9 September

RFU Leagues
Division 1
Orrell v Bristol
Moseley v Gloucester
Bath v Harlequins
Wasps v Leicester
Nottingham v Rosslyn Park
Bedford v Saracens
Division 2
Liverpool St Helens v Gosforth
Waterloo v Headingley
Coventry v London Irish
Northampton v Plymouth Albion
Blackheath v Rugby
Richmond v Sale
Division 3
Sheffield v Exeter
Askeans v Fylde
Nuneaton v Roundhay
West Hartlepool v Lydney
Wakefield v London Scottish
Vale of Lune v London Welsh
Area North
Kendal v Broughton Park
Stoke v Lichfield
Stourbridge v Morley
Walsall v Northern
Winnington Park v Durham City
Area South
Basingstoke v Camborne
Met Police v Havant
Redruth v Clifton
Southend v Salisbury
Sudbury v Cheltenham

Academy v Terenure Coll
Ards v Instonians
Ayr v Edinburgh Academy
Cardiff v Neath
Clontarf v Monkstown
Collegians v Selkirk
De La Salle/Palmerston v Dolphin
Dungannon v Portadown
Gala v Jedforest
Glamorgan Wands v Abertillery
Glasgow Acads v Hutcheson's
Glasgow High/Kelvinside v Dalziel
Greystones v Cork Const

Hawick v Ballymena
Highfield v Old Wesley
Kilmarnock v Howe of Fife
Langholm v Melrose
Lansdowne v Swansea
Llanelli v Aberavon
Maesteg v SW Police
Malone v St Mary's Coll
Newbridge v Bridgend
Newport v Penarth
Pontypool v Ebbw Vale
Pontypridd v Cross Keys
Skerries v Bangor
Stewart's-Melville FP v Edinburgh Wands
Stirling County v Preston Lodge
Wanderers v Queen's U, Belfast
Watsonians v Kelso
West of Scotland v Boroughmuir

Sunday, 10 September

Sunday's Well v Thomond

Tuesday, 12 September

Cornwall v Devon (St Austell)
Dorset/Wilts v Somerset
Ebbw Vale v Moseley
Glasgow Acads v Kilmarnock
Hutcheson's v Stirling County
Kelso v Hawick
Otley v Headingley
Selkirk v Melrose

Wednesday, 13 September

Buckinghamshire v Sussex
Bedford v Waterpark
Gilfach Goch v Maesteg
Halifax v Huddersfield
Highfield v Sunday's Well
New Brighton v Liverpool St Helens
Newport v Pontypool
Newquay Hornets v Camborne
Portadown v Instonians
Sale v Broughton Park

Saturday, 16 September

Connacht v Scottish North/Midlands
(Galway)
Munster v Pontypool
RFU Cup: *1st Round*
WRU Cup: *1st Round*
(*English and Welsh fixtures subject to re-arrangement*)
Aberavon v Newbridge

Abertillery v Bedford
Ayr v City of Derry
Ballymena v Galwegians
Bangor v Garryowen
Bective Rangers v Old Wesley
Birkenhead Park v Kendal
Blackheath v Waterloo
Bridgend v Saracens
Camborne v Devonport Services
CIYMS v Edinburgh Acads
Collegians v Dolphin
Coventry v Cardiff
Edinburgh Wands v Trinity Acads
Falmouth v Paignton
Gloucester v Pontypridd
Gosforth v Headingley
Hawick v Gateshead Fell
Heriot's FP v Lansdowne
Hillhead v Glasgow Acads
Jedforest v Langholm
Kirkcaldy v Howe of Fife
Leicester v Northampton
Liverpool St Helens v Wasps
Llanelli v Harlequins
Maesteg v Glamorgan Wands
Manchester v Halifax
Melrose v Kelso
Middlesbrough v Rugby
Monkstown v Young Munster
Moseley v Bath
Neath v Newport
Old Crescent v Dungannon
Preston Grasshoppers v Huddersfield
Preston Lodge v Watsonians
Rosslyn Park v Richmond
Sale v Nottingham
Stewart's-Melville FP v NIFC
Stirling County v
    Glasgow High/Kelvinside
Sunday's Well v Waterpark
Swansea v Bristol
SW Police v Tredegar
Terenure Coll v London Irish
Totnes v Plymouth Albion
Wanderers v Corinthians
Waterloo v Orrell
West Park v Birkenhead Park

Sunday, 17 September

Galway v Scottish North/Midlands
(Galway)
Wasps v President's XV

Monday, 18 September

Plymouth Albion v Devonport Services

Tuesday, 19 September

Somerset v Dorset/Wilts
Camborne v Falmouth
Narberth v Neath
Monkstown v De La Salle/Palmerston
Taibach v Aberavon

Wednesday, 20 September

Hampshire v Royal Navy
Bective Rangers v Wanderers
Cork Const v Sunday's Well
Cross Keys v SW Police
Dolphin v Cork Counties
Ebbw Vale v Penarth
Glynneath v Maesteg
Llanelli v Bridgend
Old Wesley v St Mary's Coll

Saturday, 23 September

RFU Leagues
Division 1
Gloucester v Bath
Leicester v Bedford
Rosslyn Park v Moseley
Bristol v Nottingham
Harlequins v Wasps
Saracens v Orrell
Division 2
Plymouth Albion v Liverpool St Helens
Gosforth v Blackheath
Sale v Coventry
Headingley v Northampton
Rugby v Richmond
London Irish v Waterloo
Division 3
Exeter v Askeans
Fylde v Nuneaton
London Welsh v Sheffield
London Scottish v Vale of Lune
Lydney v Wakefield
Roundhay v West Hartlepool
Area North
Durham City v Stourbridge
Lichfield v Winnington Park
Morley v Kendal
Northern v Stoke
Preston Grasshoppers v Walsall
Area South
Cheltenham v Basingstoke
Clifton v Met Police
Havant v Sudbury
Maidstone v Southend
Salisbury v Redruth

SRU Leagues
Division 1
Boroughmuir v West of Scotland

Glasgow High/Kelvinside v Kelso
Hawick v Melrose
Heriot's FP v Edinburgh Acads
Jedforest v Ayr
Selkirk v Gala
Stirling County v Stewart's-Melville FP
Division 2
Corstorphine v Edinburgh Wands
Dalziel HSFP v Dunfermline
Gordonians v Preston Lodge
Hillhead/Jordanhill v Langholm
Kirkcaldy v Currie
Musselburgh v Kilmarnock
Watsonians v Glasgow Acads

Leinster v Llanelli
Blackrock Coll v Bangor
Cardiff v Aberavon
CIYMS v Old Wesley
Collegians v Ballymena
Dolphin v Clontarf
Ebbw Vale v SW Police
Greystones v Sunday's Well
Maesteg v Abertillery
Malone v De La Salle/Palmerston
Old Belvedere v Instonians
Newbridge v Glamorgan Wands
Newport v Swansea
NIFC v Portadown
Penarth v Tredegar
Pontypool v Bridgend
Pontypridd v Neath

Sunday, 24 September

Lansdowne v Dublin U
St Mary's Coll v Cork Const
Wanderers v Skerries

Monday, 25 September

Cornwall v Crawshay's Welsh XV
(Camborne)
Llanelli Youth v Welsh Youth
Hawick v Glasgow High/Kelvinside

Tuesday, 26 September

RFU County Championship
Midland Division
Notts, Lincs & Derbys v Warwickshire
Staffordshire v Leicestershire

Moseley v Coventry
Northampton v London Welsh
Old Wesley v Old Belvedere
Tredegar v Aberavon
UC Dublin v Terenure Coll

Wednesday, 27 September

Bath v SW Police
Blaenavon v Pontypool
Bridgend v Central Glam Dist RU
Bristol v Met Police
Cambridge U v Cambridge City
Ebbw Vale v Llanelli
Gloucester v Exeter
Lydney v Maesteg
Morley v Sale
Orrell v Kendal
Pontypridd v Cardiff
Wasps v London Irish

Saturday, 30 September

RFU County Championship
Northern Division
Cheshire v Cumbria (New Brighton)
Northumberland v Lancashire
(Northern)
Yorkshire v Durham
South & South-West Division
Cornwall v Berkshire (Redruth)
Gloucestershire v Dorset/Wilts
Oxfordshire v Devon
Somerset v Buckinghamshire (Taunton)

SRU Leagues
Division 1
Ayr v Boroughmuir
Gala v Stirling County
Hawick v Jedforest
Kelso v Heriot's FP
Melrose v Selkirk
Stewart's-Melville FP v Edinburgh Acads
West of Scotland v
    Glasgow High/Kelvinside
Division 2
Dalziel HSFP v Corstorphine
Dunfermline v Watsonians
Edinburgh Wands v Musselburgh
Glasgow Acads v Hillhead/Jordanhill
Kilmarnock v Gordonians
Langholm v Currie
Preston Lodge v Kirkcaldy

Aberavon v SW Police
Aspatria v Preston Grasshoppers
Bedford v Wasps
Blackheath v Pontypridd
Blackrock Coll v Dolphin
Bohemians v Instonians
Bridgend v Cross Keys
Cambridge U v Northampton
Cardiff v Moseley
City of Derry v Dungannon
Clifton v Plymouth Albion
Corinthians v Academy
Coventry v Bristol

De La Salle/Palmerston v Collegians
Durham City v Gosforth
Exeter v Saracens
Galwegians v Monkstown
Gloucester v Pontypool
Greystones v Ballymena
Harlequins v London Irish
Kendal v Middlesbrough
Lansdowne v UC Dublin
Liverpool St Helens v Wakefield
Llanelli v Leicester
London Welsh v Newport
Malone v Young Munster
Met Police v Askeans
Morley v Fylde
Neath v Bath
Nottingham v Ebbw Vale
Old Wesley v Bangor
Penarth v Newbridge
Portadown v Ballina
Richmond v Orrell
Rosslyn Park v Abertillery
Roundhay v Broughton Park
Shannon v Old Belvedere
Sheffield v Sale
Swansea v Maesteg
Sunday's Well v CIYMS
Tredegar v Glamorgan Wands
Vale of Lune v Waterloo
Wanderers v Highfield

Sunday, 1 October

Rugby Sevens (Rugby School)
Cork Const v Terenure Coll
Falmouth v Penryn
St Ives v Camborne

Tuesday, 3 October

RFU County Championship
Northern Division
Durham v Northumberland
Lancashire v Cumbria
Yorkshire v Cheshire
Midland Division
Leicestershire v N Midlands (Leicester)
Warwickshire v E Midlands

Maesteg v S Glam Inst
Moseley v HM Prison Service
Weston-super-Mare v Bristol

Wednesday, 4 October

FRANCE v BRITISH ISLES (Paris)
Bath v Royal Navy
Bedford v Loughborough Students

Cambridge U v St Mary's Hosp
Ebbw Vale v Tredegar
Met Police v Wasps
Nuneaton v Coventry
Pontypool v Swansea
SW Police v Bridgend

Saturday, 7 October

RFU County Championship
Northern Division
Cheshire v Northumberland (Wilmslow)
Durham v Lancashire
Yorkshire v Cumbria
South & South-West Division
Berkshire v Gloucestershire (Reading)
Buckinghamshire v Oxfordshire
(Aylesbury)
Cornwall v Dorset/Wilts (Redruth)
Devon v Somerset (Exeter)

SRU Leagues
Division 1
Edinburgh Acads v Kelso
Gala v Melrose
Glasgow High/Kelvinside v Ayr
Heriot's FP v West of Scotland
Jedforest v Stewart's-Melville FP
Selkirk v Boroughmuir
Stirling County v Hawick
Division 2
Corstorphine v Langholm
Currie v Preston Lodge
Glasgow Acads v Dunfermline
Gordonians v Edinburgh Wands
Hillhead/Jordanhill v Dalziel HSFP
Kirkcaldy v Kilmarnock
Watsonians v Musselburgh

Aberavon v Bath
Abertillery v Plymouth Albion
Ards v Collegians
Bective Rangers v De La Salle/Palmerston
Bridgend v Ebbw Vale
City of Derry v Academy
CIYMS v Ballymena
Cork Const v Shannon
Cross Keys v Penarth
Dolphin v Old Crescent
Dungannon v NIFC
Fylde v Bedford
Glamorgan Wands v Exeter
Gosforth v Broughton Park
Greystones v Old Wesley
Harlequins v Swansea
Leicester v Coventry
Liverpool St Helens v Cambridge U
Llanelli v Neath
London Irish v Bristol
Maesteg v Pontypool

Malone v Instonians
Manchester v Huddersfield
Middlesbrough v Sheffield
Monkstown v St Mary's Coll
Morley v Headingley
Newport v Cardiff
Northampton v Nottingham
Orrell v Birkenhead Park
Otley v Vale of Lune
Oxford U v UC Cork
Pontypridd v Richmond
Preston Grasshoppers v Hull ER
Queen's U, Belfast v Portadown
Rosslyn Park v London Welsh
Sale v Moseley
Saracens v Newbridge
Stroud v Met Police
Sunday's Well v Athlone
Terenure Coll v Lansdowne
Torquay Ath v SW Police
UC Dublin v Young Munster
Wakefield v Harrogate
Wasps v Blackheath
Waterloo v Wanderers
West Hartlepool v Kendal
Winnington Park v Halifax
Wrexham v Tredegar

Bath v Rosslyn Park
Nottingham v Saracens
Division 2
Richmond v Gosforth
Liverpool St Helens v Headingley
Northampton v London Irish
Blackheath v Plymouth Albion
Coventry v Rugby
Waterloo v Sale
Division 3
Nuneaton v Exeter
West Hartlepool v Fylde
Wakefield v Roundhay
Vale of Lune v Lydney
Sheffield v London Scottish
Askeans v London Welsh
Area North
Broughton Park v Morley
Kendal v Durham City
Stoke v Preston Grasshoppers
Stourbridge v Lichfield
Winnington Park v Northern
Area South
Basingstoke v Havant
Camborne v Cheltenham
Met Police v Salisbury
Redruth v Maidstone
Sudbury v Clifton

Tuesday, 10 October

Newport v Barbarians
Penarth v Aberavon
Tredegar v Pontypridd

Wednesday, 11 October

French Selection v Fijians (Nîmes)
Cardiff v Bridgend
Ebbw Vale v Gloucester
Maesteg v Cross Keys
Newbridge v Abertillery
Pontypool v Monmouthshire RU
SW Police v Pembrokeshire
Wasps v Loughborough Students

Saturday, 14 October

Cardiff v New Zealanders
French Selection v Fijians (Bergerac)
Connacht v Ulster
Munster v Leinster

RFU Leagues
Division 1
Moseley v Bristol
Wasps v Gloucester
Bedford v Harlequins
Orrell v Leicester

SRU Leagues
Division 1
Ayr v Gala
Boroughmuir v Jedforest
Hawick v Edinburgh Acads
Melrose v West of Scotland
Stewart's-Melville FP v Heriot's FP
Selkirk v Glasgow High/Kelvinside
Stirling County v Kelso
Division 2
Dalziel HSFP v Currie
Dunfermline v Kilmarnock
Edinburgh Wands v Glasgow Acads
Hillhead/Jordanhill v Preston Lodge
Langholm v Kirkcaldy
Musselburgh v Corstorphine
Watsonians v Gordonians

Ards v Academy
Ballymena v Dublin U
Bohemians v Old Wesley
Bridgend v Cambridge U
CIYMS v De La Salle/Palmerston
Clontarf v Terenure Coll
Collegians v Bangor
Dolphin v Wanderers
Ebbw Vale v Pontypridd
Galwegians v Dungannon
Greystones v NIFC
Maesteg v Aberavon
Malone v Portadown
Neath v Glamorgan Wands
Shannon v Skerries

Swansea v Llanelli
SW Police v Penarth
Tredegar v Abertillery

Sunday, 15 October

Oxford U v International XV
Athlone v Monkstown
Garryowen v UC Dublin
Newport v Newbridge
Waterpark v Sunday's Well

Tuesday, 17 October

RFU County Championship
Northern Division
Cheshire v Lancashire (Birkenhead Park)
Cumbria v Durham
Northumberland v Yorkshire
  (Percy Park)
Midland Division
E Midlands v Notts, Lincs & Derbys
N Midlands v Staffordshire (Moseley)

Roundhay v Headingley

Wednesday, 18 October

Pontypool v New Zealanders
French Selection v Fijians
  (Basque Coast)
French Selection v Australians
  (Toulouse)
Aberavon v Pontypridd
Bath v Exeter U
Bedford v Cambridge U
Glamorgan Wands v Bristol
Harlequins v Askeans
Llanelli v Newport
Met Police v Richmond
Orrell v Broughton Park
Rosslyn Park v Loughborough Students

Friday, 20 October

Leicester v Bay of Plenty

Saturday, 21 October

Swansea v New Zealanders
French Selection v Australians (Béziers)
Connacht v Munster
Leinster v Ulster
Anglo-Scots v Richmond (Richmond)

RFU County Championship
Northern Division
Cumbria v Northumberland
Durham v Cheshire
Lancashire v Yorkshire
South & South-West Division
Devon v Buckinghamshire
Dorset/Wilts v Berkshire
Gloucestershire v Cornwall
Oxfordshire v Somerset
WRU Cup: *2nd round*
(*Welsh fixtures subject to rearrangement*)

SRU Leagues
Division 1
Ayr v Stewart's-Melville FP
Boroughmuir v Gala
Edinburgh Acads v Stirling County
Glasgow High/Kelvinside v Jedforest
Heriot's FP v Hawick
Kelso v Melrose
West of Scotland v Selkirk
Division 2
Currie v Hillhead/Jordanhill
Edinburgh Wands v Langholm
Gordonians v Corstorphine
Kilmarnock v Watsonians
Kirkcaldy v Dalziel HSFP
Musselburgh v Glasgow Acads
Preston Lodge v Dunfermline

Aberavon v Moseley
Academy v Highfield
Ballina v CIYMS
Blackheath v Vale of Lune
Bristol v Northampton
Broughton Park v Nuneaton
Cambridge U v Rosslyn Park
Cardiff v Wasps
Collegians v Clontarf
Corinthians v Portadown
Coventry v Bridgend
De La Salle/Palmerston v Ballymena
Exeter v Clifton
Fylde v Hartlepool Rovers
Gloucester v Newport
Gosforth v Orrell
Harlequins v London Scottish
Headingley v Sheffield
Kendal v Roundhay
Lansdowne v Instonians
London Irish v Bedford
London Welsh v Llanelli
Lydney v Abertillery
Met Police v Loughborough Students
Monkstown v Sunday's Well
Morley v Birkenhead Park
Neath v Sale
Oxford U v Richmond
Plymouth Albion v Maesteg
Pontypridd v Newbridge
Preston Grasshoppers v Manchester

Redruth v Falmouth
Saracens v Ebbw Vale
Skerries v Queen's U, Belfast
SW Police v Glamorgan Wands
Wakefield v Otley
Wanderers v Ards
Waterloo v Pontypool
Young Munster v Greystones

Sunday, 22 October

French Barbarians v Fijians
  (Bordeaux)
Bangor v St Mary's Coll
Bohemians V Dolphin
Galwegians v Cork Const
Old Wesley v Dublin U
Terenure Coll v Shannon
UC Dublin v Malone

Monday, 23 October

Glynneath v Aberavon

Tuesday, 24 October

Glasgow Dist v Fijians
Newport v Glamorgan Wands
Oxford U v Leicester

Wednesday, 25 October

Neath v New Zealanders
French Selection v Australians (Toulon)
Ebbw Vale v S Glam Inst
Maesteg v Penarth
Pontypool v Cardiff
SW Police v Bridgend

Thursday, 26 October

Bridgend v Bay of Plenty

Friday, 27 October

Howe of Fife v Edinburgh Wands
West of Scotland v Clarkston

Saturday, 28 October

SCOTLAND v FIJI (Murrayfield)
Llanelli v New Zealanders
French Selection v Australians (Grenoble)

Leinster v Connacht
Ulster v Munster

RFU Leagues
Division 1
Bristol v Bath
Gloucester v Bedford
Saracens v Moseley
Leicester v Nottingham
Harlequins v Orrell
Rosslyn Park v Wasps
Division 2
London Irish v Liverpool St Helens
Headingley v Blackheath
Gosforth v Coventry
Sale v Northampton
Plymouth Albion v Richmond
Rugby v Waterloo
Division 3
London Scottish v Askeans
London Welsh v Nuneaton
Lydney v Sheffield
Roundhay v Vale of Lune
Fylde v Wakefield
Exeter v West Hartlepool
Area North
Durham City v Broughton Park
Lichfield v Kendal
Northern v Stourbridge
Preston Grasshoppers v Winnington Park
Walsall v Stoke
Area South
Clifton v Basingstoke
Havant v Camborne
Maidstone v Met Police
Salisbury v Sudbury
Southend v Redruth

Abertillery v Pontypridd
Athlone v Academy
Bridgend v Aberavon
Cardiff v Cambridge U
Collegians v Bohemians
Cross Keys v Ebbw Vale
Dolphin v St Mary's Coll
Dungannon v Clontarf
Gala v Hawick
Glasgow Acads v Melrose
Kilmarnock v Stirling County
Malone v CIYMS
Musselburgh v Glasgow High/Kelvinside
Neath v Swansea
Newbridge v Maesteg
Portadown v Shannon
Queen's U, Belfast v Bective Rangers
Royal High v Preston Lodge
Stewart's-Melville FP v Jedforest
SW Police v Pontypool
Sunday's Well v Dublin U
Tredegar v Penarth
UC Cork v Old Wesley
Watsonians v Edinburgh U

Sunday, 29 October

De La Salle/Palmerston v UC Galway
Greystones v Blackrock Coll
Old Belvedere v Lansdowne
Terenure Coll v Young Munster
UC Dublin v Galwegians

Monday, 30 October

Monkstown v Wanderers

Tuesday, 31 October

Newport v New Zealanders
French Selection v Australians
  (Clermont-Ferrand)
RFU County Championship
Midland Division: Semi-final Play-offs
Ebbw Vale v Glamorgan Wands
Moseley v Sheffield
Northampton v Oxford U
Swansea v Tredegar

Wednesday, 1 November

Abertillery v Pontypool
Bridgend v Pontypridd
Hartlepool Rovers v Durham U
Maesteg v Mid Districts RU

Friday, 3 November

Cross Keys v Aberavon
Ebbw Vale v Cheltenham
Wrexham v Birkenhead Park

Saturday, 4 November

WALES v NEW ZEALAND (Cardiff)
FRANCE v AUSTRALIA (Strasbourg)
ENGLAND v FIJI (Twickenham)
RFU Cup: *2nd round*
(*English fixtures subject to rearrangement*)

SRU Leagues
Division 1
Gala v Glasgow High/Kelvinside
Hawick v Ayr
Jedforest v West of Scotland
Melrose v Edinburgh Acads
Selkirk v Kelso
Stewart's-Melville FP v Boroughmuir

Stirling County v Heriot's FP
Division 2
Corstorphine v Kilmarnock
Dalziel HSFP v Edinburgh Wands
Dunfermline v Currie
Glasgow Acads v Gordonians
Hillhead/Jordanhill v Kirkcaldy
Langholm v Musselburgh
Watsonians v Preston Lodge

Ballymena v Wanderers
Bath v Llanelli
Bedford v Oxford U
Bradford/Bingley v Broughton Park
Bristol v Bridgend
Cambridge U v Harlequins
Clontarf v Greystones
Collegians v Malone
De La Salle/Palmerston v
  Bective Rangers
Dublin U v Monkstown
Dungannon v Blackrock Coll
Glamorgan Wands v Rosslyn Park
Gloucester v Newbridge
Halifax v Roundhay
Hayle v Falmouth
Instonians v Armagh
Kendal v Sheffield
Lansdowne v Dolphin
Leicester v Cardiff
Middlesbrough v Wakefield
Moseley v Newport
Old Belvedere v UC Dublin
Old Crescent v Cork Const
Old Wesley v Skerries
Orrell v Harrogate
Penarth v Stroud
Preston Grasshoppers v New Brighton
Redruth v Camborne
Sheffield v Otley
Sunday's Well v Garryowen
SW Police v Abertillery
Terenure Coll v St Mary's Coll
Vale of Lune v Saracens
Wilmslow v Hartlepool Rovers

Sunday, 5 November

London Division v Ulster
  (London Irish)
Corinthians v Shannon
Falmouth v St Bart's Hosp

Tuesday, 7 November

French Selection v Australians (Paris)
Gloucester v SW Police
Leicester v Cambridge U

Wednesday, 8 November

Leinster v New Zealanders
Aberavon v Ebbw Vale
Cardiff v Oxford U
Cross Keys v Newport
Pontypool v Neath
Pontypridd v Mid Dist RU
S Glam Inst v Penarth

Thursday, 9 November

Ulster v New Zealand Under-21

Saturday, 11 November

FRANCE v AUSTRALIA (Lille)
Munster v New Zealanders (Cork)

RFU Leagues
Division 1
Harlequins v Bristol
Bath v Moseley
Wasps v Nottingham
Bedford v Orrell
Gloucester v Rosslyn Park
Leicester v Saracens
Division 2
Coventry v Liverpool St Helens
Richmond v Blackheath
Rugby v Gosforth
London Irish v Headingley
Sale v Plymouth Albion
Waterloo v Northampton
Division 3
Wakefield v Askeans
Lydney v Exeter
Roundhay v Fylde
West Hartlepool v Nuneaton
London Scottish v London Welsh
Vale of Lune v Sheffield
Area North
Broughton Park v Lichfield
Kendal v Northern
Morley v Durham City
Stourbridge v Preston Grasshoppers
Winnington Park v Walsall
Area South
Basingstoke v Salisbury
Camborne v Clifton
Cheltenham v Havant
Met Police v Southend
Sudbury v Maidstone

SRU Leagues
Division 1
Ayr v Stirling County
Boroughmuir v Hawick
Edinburgh Acads v Selkirk

Glasgow High/Kelvinside v
  Stewart's-Melville FP
Heriot's FP v Melrose
Kelso v Jedforest
West of Scotland v Gala
Division 2
Currie v Watsonians
Edinburgh Wands v Hillhead/Jordanhill
Gordonians v Langholm
Kilmarnock v Glasgow Acads
Kirkcaldy v Dunfermline
Musselburgh v Dalziel HSFP
Preston Lodge v Corstorphine

Abertillery v Maesteg
Academy v Queen's U, Belfast
Armagh v Ards
Ballymena v Malone
Blackrock Coll v Lansdowne
Cardiff v Ebbw Vale
Collegians v Dungannon
De La Salle/Palmerston v Skerries
Instonians v Bangor
Llanelli v Swansea
Monkstown v Greystones
Neath v Bridgend
Newport v Aberavon
NIFC v CIYMS
Penarth v Glamorgan Wands
Pontypool v Cross Keys
Pontypridd v SW Police
Portadown v City of Derry
St Mary's Coll v Old Wesley
Tredegar v Newbridge
UC Dublin v Clontarf
Wanderers v Terenure Coll

Sunday, 12 November

Bohemians v Sunday's Well

Tuesday, 14 November

Connacht v New Zealanders
Cambridge U v Richmond

Wednesday, 15 November

Rosslyn Park v Oxford U

Friday, 17 November

Bangor v Old Belvedere
Portadown v CIYMS

Saturday, 18 November

IRELAND v NEW ZEALAND
(Lansdowne Road)

RFU Leagues
Division 1
Orrell v Bath
Bristol v Gloucester
Saracens v Harlequins
Rosslyn Park v Leicester
Nottingham v Bedford
Moseley v Wasps
Division 2
Blackheath v Coventry
Gosforth v London Irish
Plymouth Albion v Rugby
Northampton v Richmond
Headingley v Sale
Liverpool St Helens v Waterloo
Division 3
Exeter v Roundhay
London Welsh v Lydney
Fylde v London Scottish
Askeans v Vale of Lune
Nuneaton v Wakefield
Sheffield v West Hartlepool
Area North
Lichfield v Morley
Northern v Broughton Park
Preston Grasshoppers v Kendal
Stoke v Winnington Park
Walsall v Stourbridge
Area South
Clifton v Cheltenham
Maidstone v Basingstoke
Redruth v Met Police
Salisbury v Camborne
Southend v Sudbury

SRU Leagues
Division 1
Gala v Kelso
Hawick v Glasgow High/Kelvinside
Jedforest v Edinburgh Acads
Melrose v Ayr
Selkirk v Heriot's FP
Stewart's-Melville FP v West of Scotland
Stirling County v Boroughmuir
Division 2
Corstorphine v Currie
Dalziel HSFP v Gordonians
Dunfermline v Edinburgh Wands
Glasgow Acads v Preston Lodge
Hillhead/Jordanhill v Musselburgh
Langholm v Kilmarnock
Watsonians v Kirkcaldy

WRU Cup: *3rd round*
(*Welsh fixtures subject to rearrangement*)
Bective Rangers v Sunday's Well
Clontarf v Malone

Lansdowne v UC Cork
Loughborough Students v Cambridge U
Monkstown v Dungannon
Old Wesley v Cork Const
Portadown v CIYMS
St Mary's Coll v Collegians
Wanderers v NIFC

Sunday, 19 November

Greystones v Garryowen
Shannon v Highfield
Terenure Coll v Queen's U, Belfast
UC Dublin v St Mary's Coll

Tuesday, 21 November

Ulster v New Zealanders
S Glam Inst v Neath
Swansea v Bridgend

Wednesday, 22 November

Oxford U v Major R V Stanley's XV
Abertillery v Newport
Maesteg v Llanelli
Newbridge v SW Police

Friday, 24 November

Ebbw Vale v Swansea
Newport v Pontypridd

Saturday, 25 November

Barbarians v New Zealanders
(Twickenham)
Glasgow Dist v Edinburgh Dist
**South of Scotland v Scottish
North/Midlands**

RFU Leagues
Division 1
Wasps v Bath
Harlequins v Leicester
Bedford v Moseley
Nottingham v Orrell
Bristol v Rosslyn Park
Gloucester v Saracens
Division 2
Waterloo v Blackheath
Plymouth Albion v Gosforth
Rugby v Headingley

Sale v London Irish
Liverpool St Helens v Northampton
Coventry v Richmond
Division 3
Exeter v Fylde
Vale of Lune v Nuneaton
Roundhay v London Welsh
Askeans v Sheffield
Lydney v London Scottish
Wakefield v West Hartlepool
Area North
Broughton Park v Preston Grasshoppers
Durham City v Lichfield
Kendal v Walsall
Morley v Northern
Stourbridge v Stoke
Area South
Basingstoke v Southend
Camborne v Maidstone
Cheltenham v Salisbury
Havant v Clifton
Sudbury v Redruth

Aberavon v Pontypool
Ballymena v Stewart's-Melville FP
Bangor v Dublin U
Bridgend v Newbridge
Cambridge U v Neath
CIYMS v UC Dublin
Clarkston v Preston Lodge
Collegians v Corinthians
Currie v Hawick
Dalziel HSFP v Ayr
De La Salle/Palmerston v Portadown
Garryowen v Dolphin
Glasgow Acads v Watsonians
Glasgow High/Kelvinside v
    Edinburgh Acads
Howe of Fife v Leith Acads
Instonians v Bective Rangers
Jedforest v Otley
Llanelli v Cardiff
Maesteg v Tredegar
Malone v Ards
Melrose v Langholm
Penarth v SW Police
Queen's U, Belfast v UC Galway
Skerries v Academy
Stirling County v Edinburgh Acads
Sunday's Well v Old Crescent
Torquay Ath v Abertillery
Watsonians v Gala
West of Scotland v Musselburgh

Sunday, 26 November

Cork Const v Bohemians
Greystones v St Mary's Coll
Lansdowne v Wanderers
Old Wesley v Monkstown

Terenure Coll v Blackrock Coll
Young Munster v Shannon

Monday, 27 November

Oxford U v Scottish Students

Tuesday, 28 November

RFU County Championship
Midland Division: Final Play-off
Nottingham v Loughborough Students
Tredegar v Newport
Wakefield v Moseley

Wednesday, 29 November

RFU County Championship
London Division
Middlesex v Kent
Surrey v E Counties
Sussex v Hampshire (Brighton)

Cambridge U v
    M R Steele-Bodger's XV
Aberavon v Abertillery
Bedford v Bedfordshire
Bridgend v S Glam Inst
Ebbw Vale v Lydney
Met Police v Rosslyn Park
Newbridge v Neath
Pontypool v SW Police
Pontypridd v Penarth

Saturday, 2 December

RFU Divisional Championship
Midland Division v
    London Division (Coventry)
South & South-West Division v
    Northern Division

Anglo-Scots v South of Scotland
Edinburgh Dist v
    Scottish North/Midlands
Abertillery v Saracens
Ards v Ayr
Bath v London Scottish
Bangor v CIYMS
Bohemians v Ballymena
Boroughmuir v Stirling County
Bridgwater Albion v Falmouth
Camborne v Penryn
Cardiff v Swansea
Cheltenham v Exeter

Collegians v Academy
Cork Const v Sunday's Well
Corstorphine v Glasgow High/Kelvinside
Cross Keys v Newbridge
De La Salle/Palmerston v Clontarf
Dolphin v Shannon
Dunfermline v Melrose
Ebbw Vale v Maesteg
Gala v Preston Lodge
Gloucester v Leicester
Halifax v Kendal
Harlequins v Blackheath
Hartlepool Rovers v Morley
Instonians v NIFC
Irish Civil Service v Monkstown
Langholm v Jedforest
London Irish v Met Police
London Welsh v Aberavon
Malone v Dungannon
Manchester v Manchester U
Middlesbrough v Huddersfield
Moseley v Bridgend
Neath v Orrell
Newport v Bristol
Northampton v Llanelli
Penarth v Lydney
Plymouth Albion v Tredegar
Pontypool v Glamorgan Wands
Pontypridd v Sale
Portadown v Armagh
Queen's U, Belfast v City of Derry
Richmond v Nottingham
Rosslyn Park v Rugby
Roundhay v Liverpool St Helens
Selkirk v Hawick
Stewart's-Melville FP v Kilmarnock
Terenure Coll v Greystones
Torquay Ath v Wasps
Tredegar v Plymouth
Truro v Redruth
Vale of Lune v Harrogate
Wanderers v Coventry
Watsonians v Edinburgh Wands
West Hartlepool v Waterloo
West of Scotland v Glasgow Acads
Wrexham v Broughton Park

Sunday, 3 December

Lansdowne v Garryowen
Wellington v Wasps

Tuesday, 5 December

Edinburgh Wands v Boroughmuir
Glenrothes v Howe of Fife
Neath v Cross Keys
Rugby v Moseley

Wednesday, 6 December

RFU County Championship
London Division
Hampshire v E Counties
 (US Portsmouth)
Hertfordshire v Middlesex
 (Croxley Green)
Sussex v Surrey (Crawley)
Aberavon v Central Glam Dist RU
Bedford v RAF
Glynneath v SW Police
Llanelli v Pontypool
Pontypridd v S Glam Inst
Rosslyn Park v Exeter U
UC Dublin v Dublin U

Friday, 8 December

Stirling County v Clarkston

Saturday, 9 December

SCOTLAND v ROMANIA
 (Murrayfield)
Scotland B v Ireland B (Murrayfield)

RFU Divisional Championship
London Division v
 South & South-West Division
 (Imber Court)
Midland Division v Northern Division
 (Moseley)

Academy v Portadown
Askeans v Clifton
Bangor v Malone
Bath v Richmond
Birkenhead Park v Durham City
Blackheath v Leicester
Blackrock Coll v Monkstown
Boroughmuir v Stewart's-Melville FP
Bridgend v Neath
Bristol v Moseley
Broughton Park v Liverpool St Helens
Cardiff v London Welsh
Cheltenham v Abertillery
City of Derry v Ards
CIYMS v Dungannon
Collegians v Armagh
Cork Const v Highfield
Coventry v Nottingham
Dunfermline v West of Scotland
Falmouth v Truro
Glamorgan Wands v Newport
Glasgow Acads v Howe of Fife
Gosforth v Wakefield
Greystones v Lansdowne
Harlequins v Bedford

Hawick v Fylde
Headingley v Wasps
Jedforest v Watsonians
Kendal v Harrogate
Leith Acads v Edinburgh Wands
Llanelli v Ebbw Vale
Melrose v Tynedale
New Brighton v Halifax
NIFC v Ballymena
Northampton v Aberavon
Orrell v Northern
Old Wesley v Terenure Coll
Penarth v Pontypool
Penzance-Newlyn v Camborne
Plymouth Albion v Gloucester
Pontypridd v Maesteg
Preston Lodge v Haddington
Redruth v Hayle
Roundhay v Huddersfield
Shannon v Waterpark
Sheffield v Preston Grasshoppers
Swansea v Newbridge
Sunday's Well v Dolphin
SW Police v Exeter
Tredegar v S Glam Inst
UC Cork v Queen's U, Belfast
Wanderers v St Mary's Coll
Waterloo v London Irish
West Hartlepool v Sale
Wrexham v Manchester

Tuesday, 12 December

Oxford U v Cambridge U (Twickenham)
Nottingham v RAF

Wednesday, 13 December

Royal Navy v Cornwall (Devonport)

RFU County Championship
London Division
E Counties v Sussex (Grange Road)
Kent v Hertfordshire
Surrey v Hampshire

U of Ulster v Queen's U, Belfast

Saturday, 16 December

Ireland Trial (Lansdowne Road)

RFU Divisional Championship
Northern Division v London Division
South & South-West Division
 v Midland Division

Anglo-Scots v Edinburgh Dist
Scottish North/Midlands
 v Glasgow Dist
Cornwall v Russians
WRU Cup: 4th round
(Welsh fixtures subject to rearrangement)
Ballymena v St Mary's Coll
Bedford v Rosslyn Park
Blackrock Coll v CIYMS
Collegians v Old Belvedere
De La Salle/Palmerston v Bangor
Dungannon v Terenure Coll
Edinburgh Wands v
 Glasgow High/Kelvinside
Exeter v Plymouth Albion
Gala v Gosforth
Gloucester v Coventry
Gordonians v Howe of Fife
Greystones v Shannon
Halifax v Broughton Park
Harrogate v West Hartlepool
Heriot's FP v Glasgow Acads
Jedforest v Kelso
Leicester v Richmond
Lichfield v Roundhay
Liverpool St Helens v
 Preston Grasshoppers
London Scottish v Birkenhead Park
London Welsh v Bath
Maesteg v Cheltenham
Malone v Monkstown
Melrose v Hawick
Met Police v Blackheath
NIFC v Lansdowne
Nottingham v Bristol
Old Wesley v Dolphin
Orrell v Otley
Penzance-Newlyn v Falmouth
Portadown v Sunday's Well
Portobello v Stirling County
Preston Lodge v Stewart's-Melville FP
Queen's U, Belfast v Lansdowne
Redruth v Penryn
Rugby v Harlequins
Sale v Headingley
Sheffield v Hartlepool Rovers
Torquay Ath v Tredegar
Tynedale v West of Scotland
UC Dublin v Bective Rangers
US Portsmouth v Askeans
Vale of Lune v London Irish
Wanderers v Young Munster
Wasps v Northampton
Waterloo v Moseley
Watsonians v Edinburgh Acads

Tuesday, 19 December

Devonport Services v Exeter
Neath v Maesteg

Wednesday, 20 December

RFU County Championship
London Division: Final Play-off

Friday, 22 December

Bedford v Met Police
Headingley v Nottingham
Northampton v Nuneaton

Saturday, 23 December

England B v Soviet Union (Twickenham)
Scottish North/Midlands v Anglo-Scots
South of Scotland v Glasgow Dist
Aberavon v Maesteg
Ards v CIYMS
Askeans v Maidstone
Ayr v Clarkston
Bangor v Portadown
Bath v Blackheath
Birkenhead Park v Liverpool St Helens
Bridgend v Cardiff
Bristol v Llanelli
Broughton Park v Vale of Lune
City of Derry v Ballymena
Collegians v Instonians
Cork Const v UC Dublin
Cross Keys v Tredegar
Davenport v Manchester
De La Salle/Palmerston v Old Wesley
Ebbw Vale v Coventry
Edinburgh Acads v Edinburgh Wands
Exeter v Taunton
Fylde v Waterloo
Glasgow Acads v Currie
Gosforth v Middlesbrough
Harlequins v Richmond
Hartlepool Rovers v Hawick
Hayle v Camborne
Howe of Fife v Madras FP
Huddersfield v Sheffield
Jedforest v Glasgow High/Kelvinside
Keighley v Halifax
Kendal v Melrose
London Welsh v Welsh Students
Morley v Bradford/Bingley
Moseley v Swansea
Newport v Gloucester
Old Crescent v Shannon
Plymouth Albion v SW Police
Pontypool v Abertillery
Portobello v Watsonians
Preston Grasshoppers v Rugby
Preston Lodge v Heriot's FP
Redruth v Newquay Hornets
Roundhay v Orrell

Saracens v Sale
Stewart's-Melville FP v Haddington
Stirling County v Dunfermline
Sunday's Well v UC Cork
Wasps v Rosslyn Park

Tuesday, 26 December

Abertillery v Ebbw Vale
Bedford v Old Paulines
Academy v President's XV
Armagh v Portadown
Bath v Clifton
Birkenhead Park v Waterloo
Bradford/Bingley v Halifax
Bristol v Weston-super-Mare
Broughton Park v Sale
Camborne v Redruth
Cardiff v Pontypridd
Collegians v Exiles
Cork Const v UC Cork
Coventry v Moseley
Dungannon v Ballymena
Exeter v Torquay Ath
Glasgow High/Kelvinside v
  Glasgow Acads
Greystones v Firbolgs
Harrogate v Roundhay
Instonians v Campbellians
Jedforest v Hawick
Liverpool St Helens v Wrexham
Llanelli v London Welsh
Maesteg v Bridgend
Melrose v Gala
Neath v Aberavon
Newbridge v Newport
Northern v Gosforth
Old Penarthians v Penarth
Otley v Morley
Penryn v Falmouth
Pontypool v Tredegar
Preston Grasshoppers v Fylde
Swansea v SW Police
Vale of Lune v Kendal
West Hartlepool v Hartlepool Rovers
Wilmslow v Manchester

Wednesday, 27 December

Leicester v Barbarians
Skibbereen v Sunday's Well

Saturday, 30 December

Edinburgh Dist v South of Scotland
Glasgow Dist v South of Scotland
Abertillery v Neath

Ayr v Kilmarnock
Barnstaple v Exeter
Bedford v Blackheath
Blackrock Coll v Ballymena
Bridgend v Gloucester
Camborne v Truro
City of Derry v Malone
Collegians v CIYMS
Coventry v Pontypridd
Cross Keys v Pontypool
Dolphin v Corinthians
Dundee HSFP v Glasgow Acads
Ebbw Vale v Aberavon
Edinburgh Wands v Jedforest
Falmouth v St Ives
Gala v Stewart's-Melville FP
Galwegians v Lansdowne
Glamorgan Wands v SW Police
Gosforth v Boroughmuir
Harlequins v Cardiff
Hartlepool Rovers v Hartlepool
Hawick v Kirkcaldy
Heriot's FP v Watsonians
Highfield v Shannon
Huddersfield v Otley
Hull ER v Sheffield
Leicester v Nuneaton
London Welsh v Wasps
Lydney v Tredegar
Manchester v Winnington Park
Melrose v Aspatria
Monkstown v Bective Rangers
Moseley v Llanelli
Musselburgh v Preston Lodge
New Brighton v Birkenhead Park
Northampton v Cheltenham
Nottingham v Newport
Old Wesley v Clontarf
Orrell v Liverpool St Helens
Penarth v Maesteg
Perthshire v Howe of Fife
Plymouth Albion v Newbridge
Preston Grasshoppers v Vale of Lune
Sale v Fylde
St Mary's Coll v Dungannon
Stirling County v West of Scotland
Swansea v Bath
Terenure Coll v Garryowen
Wanderers v Cork Const
Waterloo v Broughton Park
West Hartlepool v Middlesbrough
West of Scotland v Stirling County

Monday, 1 January 1990

Ards v Malone
Bristol v Clifton
Broughton Park v Wigan
Collegians v Queen's U, Belfast
Gloucester v Moseley

Greystones v Old Belvedere
Hawick v Heriot's FP
Highfield v Sunday's Well
Llanelli v Swansea
Novocastrians v Gosforth
Pontypridd v Aberavon
Portadown v President's XV
Richmond v London Welsh
Roundhegians v Roundhay
Sale v Birkenhead Park
Sidcup v Askeans

Tuesday, 2 January

Glasgow High/Kelvinside v Melrose
Stirling County v Kirkcaldy

Wednesday, 3 January

Pontypool v Lydney

Saturday, 6 January

Scotland Trial (Murrayfield)
Aberavon v Swansea
Abertillery v Glamorgan Wands
Ayr v Dunfermline
Ballymena v Old Wesley
Bangor v Greystones
Birkenhead Park v Fylde
Blackheath v London Scottish
Blackrock Coll v Cork Const
Broughton Park v New Brighton
Cardiff v Bath
Chester v Halifax
CIYMS v Lansdowne
Collegians v Wanderers
Cross Keys v Pontypridd
De La Salle/Palmerston v Bohemians
Dungannon v UC Dublin
Edinburgh Wands v West of Scotland
Glasgow Acads v Dalziel HSFP
Headingley v Leicester
Howe of Fife v Panmure
Instonians v St Mary's Coll
Jedforest v Gateshead Fell
Langholm v Hawick
Liverpool St Helens v Otley
Llanelli v Coventry
London Welsh v Bristol
Malone v Queen's U, Belfast
Manchester v Widnes
Melrose v Musselburgh
Met Police v US Portsmouth
Middlesbrough v Northern
Moseley v Newbridge
Neath v Ebbw Vale

Newport v Bridgend
Northampton v Bective Rangers
Nottingham v London Irish
Nuneaton v Pontypool
Old Crescent v Monkstown
Orrell v Morley
Oxford v Lydney
Penzance-Newlyn v Redruth
Plymouth Albion v Rosslyn Park
Preston Grasshoppers v Roundhay
Sale v Waterloo
Sheffield v Bradford/Bingley
Skerries v Dolphin
Stewart's-Melville FP v
   Glasgow High/Kelvinside
Sunday's Well v Clontarf
SW Police v Richmond
Terenure Coll v Highfield
Tredegar v Maesteg
Vale of Lune v Hartlepool Rovers
Wakefield v Bedford
Wasps v Harlequins
Watsonians v Stirling County

Tuesday, 9 January

Tredegar v S Glam Inst

Wednesday, 10 January

RAF v Civil Service (RAF Halton)
Ebbw Vale v Newport

Saturday, 13 January

RFU Leagues
Division 1
Saracens v Bristol
Leicester v Gloucester
Bath v Bedford
Moseley v Nottingham
Wasps v Orrell
Harlequins v Rosslyn Park
Division 2
Richmond v Liverpool St Helens
Headingley v Gosforth
London Irish v Plymouth Albion
Sale v Rugby
Blackheath v Northampton
Coventry v Waterloo
Division 3
West Hartlepool v Askeans
London Scottish v Exeter
London Welsh v Fylde
Lydney v Roundhay
Nuneaton v Sheffield
Wakefield v Vale of Lune

Area North
Northern v Durham City
Preston Grasshoppers v Morley
Stoke v Kendal
Walsall v Broughton Park
Winnington Park v Stourbridge
Area South
Maidstone v Cheltenham
Met Police v Sudbury
Redruth v Basingstoke
Salisbury v Havant
Southend v Camborne

SRU Leagues
Division 1
Ayr v Selkirk
Boroughmuir v Melrose
Edinburgh Acads v Gala
Glasgow High/Kelvinside v
   Stirling County
Heriot's FP v Jedforest
Kelso v Stewart's-Melville FP
West of Scotland v Hawick
Division 2
Currie v Glasgow Acads
Edinburgh Wands v Watsonians
Gordonians v Hillhead/Jordanhill
Kilmarnock v Dalziel HSFP
Kirkcaldy v Corstorphine
Musselburgh v Dunfermline
Preston Lodge v Langholm

Aberavon v Cardiff
Ards v Queen's U, Belfast
Armagh v Academy
Ballymena v Instonians
Bohemians v Shannon
Bridgend v Abertillery
CIYMS v Malone
De La Salle/Palmerston v Dublin U
Dolphin v Cork Const
Dungannon v Bangor
Greystones v Wanderers
Lansdowne v St Mary's Coll
Maesteg v Ebbw Vale
Neath v Llanelli
Old Wesley v Blackrock Coll
Penarth v Cross Keys
Pontypridd v Pontypool
Portadown v Collegians
Swansea v Newport
SW Police v Newbridge
Terenure Coll v Monkstown
UC Dublin v Waterpark
Young Munster v Sunday's Well

Tuesday, 16 January

Edinburgh Wands v Edinburgh U
Neath v Newbridge
Plymouth Albion v RAF

Wednesday, 17 January

Surrey v Royal Navy
Cardiff v Bridgend
Cross Keys v S Glam Inst
Glynneath v Swansea
Newport v Newport Dist RU

Friday, 19 January

Bangor v Ards
Bath v Met Police
Bedford v Leicester
Bristol v Begles
Glamorgan Wands v Pontypridd
London Irish v Terenure Coll
Northampton v Moseley
Penarth v Abertillery
Rosslyn Park v Old Wesley
SW Police v Ebbw Vale
Tredegar v Wrexham

Saturday, 20 January

ENGLAND v IRELAND
(Twickenham)
WALES v FRANCE (Cardiff)
Birkenhead Park v Wilmslow
Blackheath v Gloucester
Boroughmuir v Middlesbrough
Bridgwater Albion v Redruth
Cambridge U v Durham U
Glasgow Acads v Ayr
Glasgow High/Kelvinside v
    West of Scotland
Gosforth v Hawick
Greystones v Athlone
Halifax v West Hartlepool
Harrogate v Headingley
Hartlepool Rovers v Broughton Park
Kendal v New Brighton
London Welsh v Neath
Malone v Ballymena
Melrose v Stewart's-Melville FP
Morley v Vale of Lune
Newton Abbot v Falmouth
Nottingham v Wasps
Old Belvedere v Queen's U, Belfast
Orrell v Sale
Oxford U v Dublin U
Penryn v Camborne
Portadown v Monkstown
Preston Lodge v Howe of Fife
Richmond v Sheffield
Selkirk v Watsonians
Shannon v Lansdowne
Stirling County v Edinburgh Wands
St Mary's Hosp v Askeans
UC Galway v Dolphin

US Portsmouth v Oxford
Waterloo v Liverpool St Helens
Weston-super-Mare v Plymouth Albion
Widnes v Preston Grasshoppers
Young Munster v
    De La Salle/Palmerston

Sunday, 21 January

France B v Scotland B
Blackrock Coll v UC Dublin
Newbridge v Coventry
Skerries v Sunday's Well
Wanderers v Dublin U

Monday, 22 January

Exeter v Exeter U
Pontypool v Penarth

Wednesday, 24 January

Cambridge U v RAF
Combined London OB v Oxford U

Saturday, 27 January

WRU Cup: *5th round*
RFU Cup: *3rd round*
(*English and Welsh fixtures subject to
    rearrangement*)

SRU Leagues
Division 1
Ayr v Heriot's FP
Boroughmuir v
    Glasgow High/Kelvinside
Hawick v Kelso
Jedforest v Selkirk
Melrose v Stirling County
Stewart's-Melville FP v Gala
West of Scotland v Edinburgh Acads
Division 2
Corstorphine v Watsonians
Dalziel HSFP v Preston Lodge
Dunfermline v Hillhead/Jordanhill
Edinburgh Wands v Kirkcaldy
Kilmarnock v Currie
Langholm v Glasgow Acads
Musselburgh v Gordonians

Abertillery v Cross Keys
Academy v Ards
Askeans v Oxford
Ballymena v Dungannon

Bective Rangers v Shannon
Blackrock Coll v Greystones
Camborne v Hayle
City of Derry v Collegians
Dolphin v Young Munster
Halifax v Stoke
Hartlepool Rovers v Northern
Instonians v CIYMS
Lichfield v Birkenhead Park
Liverpool St Helens v Vale of Lune
London Welsh v Gosforth
Lydney v SW Police
Manchester v Hull ER
Met Police v Maesteg
Monkstown v Lansdowne
NIFC v Bangor
Old Belvedere v De La Salle/Palmerston
Old Crescent v Sunday's Well
Otley v Broughton Park
Penarth v Clifton
Portadown v Malone
Preston Grasshoppers v Waterloo
Queen's U, Belfast v Armagh
Redruth v St Ives
Roundhay v Middlesbrough
Rugby v Swansea
Sheffield v UC Dublin
St Mary's Coll v Terenure Coll
Tredegar v Barnstaple
Wanderers v Old Wesley
Waterpark v Cork Const
Weston-super-Mare v Falmouth

Wednesday, 31 January

Aberavon v S Glam Inst
Cambridge U v Royal Navy
Glamorgan Wands v Bridgend
Oxford U v RAF
Plymouth Albion v Exeter U
Swansea v Penarth

Friday, 2 February

Ayr v London Scottish
Bangor v Queen's U, Belfast
Bath v Newport
Bedford v Rugby
Cambridge U v Nuneaton
Clontarf v West of Scotland
Gloucester v Bristol
Monkstown v Royal High
Northampton v Leicester
Old Belvedere v Watsonians
Old Wesley v Kelso
Portadown v Ballymena
RCF v Rosslyn Park
UC Dublin v UC Cork
Wanderers v Hawick

Saturday, 3 February

IRELAND v SCOTLAND
(Lansdowne Road)
FRANCE v ENGLAND (Paris)
Abertillery v S Glam Inst
Barnstaple v Penarth
Blackheath v Exeter
Bridgend v Llanelli
Broughton Park v Wakefield
Cheltenham v Oxford
Cork Const v Instonians (Dublin)
Dublin U v Collegians
Ebbw Vale v Cardiff
Falmouth v Camborne
Haddington v Melrose
Glasgow High/Kelvinside v Currie
Harlequins v London Welsh
Harrogate v Sheffield
Hayle v Redruth
Jedforest v Boroughmuir
Lansdowne v Old Crescent
Maesteg v London Irish
Manchester v Aspatria
Morley v Halifax
Neath v Pontypool
Newbridge v Aberavon
Nottingham v Liverpool St Helens
Old Wesley v Edinburgh Acads
Orrell v London Scottish
Plymouth Albion v Bridgwater Albion
Pontypridd v Swansea
Preston Grasshoppers v Wilmslow
Richmond v Moseley
Sale v Wasps
Saracens v Met Police
Stewart's-Melville FP v Glasgow Acads
St Mary's Coll v Shannon
Sunderland v Hartlepool Rovers
SW Police v Cross Keys
Tredegar v Berry Hill
Vale of Lune v Headingley
Wanderers v Hawick
Waterloo v Coventry
West Hartlepool v Gosforth

Sunday, 4 February

Garryowen v De La Salle/Palmerston
Greystones v Highfield
Sunday's Well v Galwegians
Terenure Coll v Skerries

Tuesday, 6 February

Cambridge U v Army
Cross Keys v Bridgend
Llanelli v S Glam Inst

Old Belvedere v Terenure Coll
Pontypridd v Tredegar
Royal Navy v Oxford U

Saturday, 10 February

RFU Cup: *4th round*
(*English fixtures subject to rearrangement*)

SRU Leagues
Division 1
Edinburgh Acads v Ayr
Gala v Hawick
Heriot's FP v Boroughmuir
Kelso v West of Scotland
Melrose v Glasgow High/Kelvinside
Selkirk v Stewart's-Melville FP
Stirling County v Jedforest
Division 2
Currie v Edinburgh Wands
Dunfermline v Gordonians
Glasgow Acads v Dalziel HSFP
Hillhead/Jordanhill v Corstorphine
Kirkcaldy v Musselburgh
Preston Lodge v Kilmarnock
Watsonians v Langholm

Aberavon v Blackheath
Ards v Portadown
Armagh v City of Derry
Bangor v Ballymena
Bath v Rugby
Blackrock Coll v Wanderers
Broughton Park v Harrogate
Cardiff v Newport
City of Derry v CIYMS
Collegians v Queen's U, Belfast
Cork Const v Garryowen
Cross Keys v Maesteg
Dolphin v UC Cork
Dungannon v Instonians
Ebbw Vale v Richmond
Exeter v Maidstone
Falmouth v Taunton
Glamorgan Wands v Newbridge
Glynneath v Penarth
Lansdowne v Old Wesley
Liverpool St Helens v Orrell
London Scottish v Coventry
London Welsh v Bridgend
Malone v NIFC
Morley v Roundhay
Moseley v Bedford
Nottingham v Pontypridd
Nuneaton v Abertillery
Plymouth Albion v Tredegar
Pontypool v Llanelli
Preston Grasshoppers v
   Loughborough Students
Queen's U, Belfast v Greystones

Redruth v Penzance-Newlyn
Rosslyn Park v Sale
Shannon v Sunday's Well
Sheffield v Gosforth
Swansea v Neath
SW Police v Northampton
Torquay Ath v Camborne
UC Dublin v De La Salle/Palmerston
Vale of Lune v Met Police
Wakefield v Hartlepool Rovers
Wasps v Waterloo

Sunday, 11 February

Dorset/Wilts v Southern Universities

Tuesday, 13 February

Edinburgh Wands v Heriot's FP
Leicester v RAF
Nottingham v Nuneaton

Wednesday, 14 February

Cambridge U v Luddites
Cwmbran v Pontypool
Glamorgan Wands v Aberavon
Llanelli v Cross Keys
Newport v Abertillery
Oxford U v Army
Pontypridd v Lydney
Rosslyn Park v W London Inst

Friday, 16 February

Askeans v Tredegar
Bridgwater Albion v Exeter
Coventry v Northampton
Met Police v Birkenhead Park
Moseley v Leicester
Penarth v Ebbw Vale
Wasps v Neath
Wrexham v SW Police

Saturday, 17 February

ENGLAND v WALES (Twickenham)
SCOTLAND v FRANCE (Murrayfield)
Ards v Old Wesley
Bath v Gloucester
Bedford v London Scottish
Blackheath v Wakefield
Broughton Park v Rugby

Cambridge U v Vale of Lune
CIYMS v Portadown
Collegians v NIFC
De La Salle/Palmerston v St Mary's Coll
Dungannon v Wanderers
Durham City v Hartlepool Rovers
Edinburgh Wands v Royal High
Glasgow Acads v Stirling County
Gosforth v Nottingham
Greystones v Instonians
Lansdowne v Ballymena
Liverpool St Helens v Fylde
London Welsh v Cardiff
Malone v Bangor
Manchester v Kendal
Musselburgh v Jedforest
Otley v Preston Grasshoppers
Oxford v Oxford U
Preston Lodge v Selkirk
Queen's U, Belfast v UC Dublin
Richmond v Bristol
Roundhay v Gala
Sale v Hawick
Saracens v Waterloo
Shannon v Monkstown
Sheffield v Halifax
Sunday's Well v Highfield
Terenure Coll v Galwegians
Truro v Camborne
UC Cork v Cork Const
Waterpark v Dolphin
Watsonians v Stewart's-Melville FP
West Hartlepool v Morley

Sunday, 18 February

Harlequins v Headingley
London Irish v Rosslyn Park

Tuesday, 20 February

Old Belvedere v Monkstown

Wednesday, 21 February

Civil Service v Royal Navy (Chiswick)
Army v Met Police
Cambridge U v Penguins
Lydney v RAF
Oxford U v Anti-Assassins

Saturday, 24 February

RFU Cup: *Quarter-finals*

WRU Cup: *Quarter-finals*
(*English and Welsh fixtures subject to rearrangement*)

SRU Leagues
Division 1
Ayr v Kelso
Boroughmuir v Edinburgh Acads
Glasgow High/Kelvinside v Heriot's FP
Hawick v Selkirk
Jedforest v Gala
Stewart's-Melville FP v Melrose
Stirling County v West of Scotland
Division 2
Corstorphine v Glasgow Acads
Dalziel HSFP v Watsonians
Edinburgh Wands v Preston Lodge
Gordonians v Kirkcaldy
Hillhead/Jordanhill v Kilmarnock
Langholm v Dunfermline
Musselburgh v Currie

Abertillery v Aberavon
Academy v De La Salle/Palmerston
Ballymena v Terenure Coll
Bangor v Lansdowne
Bedford v Coventry
Bridgend v Rosslyn Park
Broughton Park v Sheffield
City of Derry v Portadown
Clontarf v CIYMS
Camborne v Penzance-Newlyn
Corinthians v Sunday's Well
Dolphin v Old Belvedere
Dublin U v Queen's U, Belfast
Ebbw Vale v Cross Keys
Exeter v Bath
Gloucester v Liverpool St Helens
Greystones v Dungannon
Halifax v Northern
Huddersfield v Kendal
Instonians v Blackrock Coll
Leicester v London Welsh
Lichfield v Askeans
London Irish v Pontypool
Met Police v London Scottish
Middlesbrough v Durham City
Monkstown v Highfield
Morley v Wakefield
Moseley v Headingley
Newbridge v Penarth
Northampton v Fylde
Nottingham v Blackheath
Old Wesley v Collegians
Penryn v Redruth
Plymouth Albion v Nuneaton
Pontypridd v Rosslyn Park
Richmond v Maesteg
Rosslyn Park v London Scottish
Roundhay v Sale
Rugby v Cambridge U
Shannon v UC Cork

Skerries v Malone
St Ives v Falmouth
Swansea v Saracens
SW Police v Torquay Ath
UC Galway v UC Dublin
Vale of Lune v Gosforth
Wanderers v Irish Army
Waterloo v Harlequins
West Hartlepool v Orrell
Weston-super-Mare v Tredegar
West Park v Preston Grasshoppers
Young Munster v Cork Const

Sunday, 25 February

Athlone v Shannon

Tuesday, 27 February

Halifax v Wakefield
Nuneaton v Moseley

Wednesday, 28 February

Bridgend v Newport
Cambridge U v Anti-Assassins
Clifton v Bath
Ebbw Vale v Neath
Met Police v Royal Navy
Pontypool v S Glam Inst
Rosslyn Park v UWIST
Roundhay v RAF
Sale v Loughborough Students
Swansea U v Oxford U
SW Police v Swansea

Thursday, 1 March

Kilmarnock v Glasgow High/Kelvinside

Friday, 2 March

Aberavon v Nottingham
Abertillery v Blaina
Bath v Plymouth Albion
Exeter v Devon/Cornwall Police
Howe of Fife v West of Scotland
Maesteg v Cardiff
Musselburgh v Stewart's-Melville FP
Northampton v Gloucester
Pontypool v Boroughmuir
Pontypridd v Bristol
Rugby v Leicester

Saturday, 3 March

WALES v SCOTLAND (Cardiff)
FRANCE v IRELAND (Paris)
RFU County Championship: *Semi-finals*
Askeans v Stourbridge
Ayr v Watsonians
Bangor v Wanderers
Bath v Plymouth Albion
Birkenhead Park v Vale of Lune
Blackheath v Rosslyn Park
Bohemians v Greystones
Blackrock Coll v Shannon
Bradford/Bingley v Cambridge U
Camborne v Taunton
CIYMS v Bective Rangers
Cork Const v Monkstown
Devonport Services v Redruth
De La Salle/Palmerston v Corinthians
Dolphin v Galwegians
Dungannon v Ards
Edinburgh Wands v Gala
Falmouth v Barnstaple
Fylde v Met Police
Gosforth v Harlequins
Halifax v Wrexham
Hawick v Roundhay
Headingley v Orrell
Huddersfield v Broughton Park
Instonians v Malone
Jedforest v Kendal
Kelso v Middlesbrough
Liverpool St Helens v West Hartlepool
London Irish v Moseley
London Welsh v Saracens
Melrose v Currie
Morley v Sheffield
Old Wesley v Garryowen
Preston Grasshoppers v Wakefield
Sale v Northern
Skerries v Lansdowne
Stoke v Manchester
Wasps v Coventry
Waterloo v Bedford
Waterpark v Portadown

Sunday, 4 March

Sunday's Well v UC Galway
Terenure Coll v UC Dublin

Tuesday, 6 March

Cambridge U v Crawshay's Welsh XV
Clifton v RAF
Leicester v Loughborough Students
Neath v SW Police

Wednesday, 7 March

E Midlands v Barbarians
  (Northampton)
Bridgend v Swansea
Newbridge v S Glam Inst
Newport v Ebbw Vale
Oxford U v Oxfordshire
Pontypridd v Abertillery

Saturday, 10 March

Army v Royal Navy (Twickenham)

RFU Leagues
Division 1
Nottingham v Bath
Gloucester v Harlequins
Bristol v Leicester
Orrell v Moseley
Bedford v Wasps
Rosslyn Park v Saracens
Division 2
Liverpool St Helens v Blackheath
Northampton v Coventry
Plymouth Albion v Headingley
Rugby v London Irish
Waterloo v Richmond
Gosforth v Sale
Division 3
Fylde v Lydney
Askeans v Nuneaton
Roundhay v London Scottish
Exeter v London Welsh
Sheffield v Wakefield
Vale of Lune v West Hartlepool
Area North
Broughton Park v Stoke
Durham City v Preston Grasshoppers
Kendal v Winnington Park
Lichfield v Northern
Morley v Walsall
Area South
Basingstoke v Met Police
Camborne v Redruth
Cheltenham v Southend
Clifton v Salisbury
Havant v Maidstone

SRU Leagues
Division 1
Edinburgh Acads v
  Glasgow High/Kelvinside
Gala v Heriot's FP
Kelso v Boroughmuir
Melrose v Jedforest
Selkirk v Stirling County
Stewart's-Melville FP v Hawick
West of Scotland v Ayr

Division 2
Currie v Gordonians
Dunfermline v Corstorphine
Glasgow Acads v Kirkcaldy
Kilmarnock v Edinburgh Wands
Langholm v Dalziel HSFP
Preston Lodge v Musselburgh
Watsonians v Hillhead/Jordanhill

Aberavon v Bridgend
Abertillery v SW Police
Cardiff v Pontypool
Cambridge U v Kyoto U
Cork Const v Lansdowne
Glamorgan Wands v Tredegar
Maesteg v Neath
Newbridge v Pontypridd
Newport v Llanelli
Penarth v S Glam Inst
Shannon v Old Wesley
St Mary's Coll v Monkstown
Sunday's Well v Dolphin
Swansea v Ebbw Vale
Terenure Coll v Bective Rangers
Wanderers v Garryowen

Sunday, 11 March

UC Dublin v Greystones

Tuesday, 13 March

Northampton v Met Police
Moseley v Abertillery
Penarth v Neath

Wednesday, 14 March

UAU Final (Twickenham)
Dorset/Wilts v Royal Navy
Cardiff v S Glam Inst
Cross Keys v Swansea
Ebbw Vale v Bath
Glamorgan Wands v Pontypool
Llanelli v SW Police

Friday, 16 March

Boroughmuir v Fylde
Bristol v Plymouth Albion
Kelso v Ballymena
Moseley v Northampton
Nottingham v Leicester
West of Scotland v Sheffield

Saturday, 17 March

SCOTLAND v ENGLAND
(Murrayfield)
Athlone v Dolphin
Bangor v City of Derry
Bath v Newbridge
Bedford v Gosforth
Bridgend v Glamorgan Wands
Camborne v Exeter
Coventry v Harlequins
Dungannon v Collegians
Edinburgh Wands v Glasgow Acads
Gala v Howe of Fife (Edinburgh)
Garryowen v Shannon
Glasgow High/Kelvinside v Hutcheson's
Gloucester v Llanelli
Halifax v Liverpool St Helens
Hawick v London Scottish
Hull ER v Broughton Park
Instonians v Skerries
Kendal v Gosforth
Maesteg v London Welsh
Middlesbrough v Met Police
Morley v Malone
Neath v Abertillery
Newport v Cross Keys
Old Crescent v Portadown
Penarth v Cheltenham
Pontypool v Aberavon
Richmond v Wasps
Roundhay v Northern
Royal High v Stewart's-Melville FP
Sale v Orrell
Saracens v Blackheath
Selkirk v Rosslyn Park
Stirling County v Heriot's FP
Swansea v Cardiff
SW Police v S Glam Inst
Tredegar v Lydney
Truro v Falmouth
Vale of Lune v Rugby
Wakefield v Waterloo
Watsonians v Dunfermline
Weston-super-Mare v Redruth

Sunday, 18 March

Bective Rangers v Lansdowne
Cork Const v NIFC
Monkstown v UC Galway
Old Wesley v UC Dublin
Terenure Coll v De La Salle/Palmerston
Wanderers v Blackrock Coll

Tuesday, 20 March

Northampton v RAF
Tredegar v SW Police
408

Wednesday, 21 March

Scottish Schools Cup Final
(Murrayfield)
Abertillery v Bridgend
Llanelli v Newbridge
Lydney v S Glam Inst
Penarth v Cardiff
Pontypool v Newport

Friday, 23 March

Ebbw Vale v Bridgend
Glynneath v Pontypridd
Greystones v Neath
Old Belvedere v Cork Const

Saturday, 24 March

IRELAND v WALES
(Lansdowne Road)
Royal Navy v Royal Air Force
(Twickenham)
Scotland Under-18 v Scotland Schools
(18 Group) (Murrayfield)
RFU Cup: *Semi-finals*

Bedford v Nottingham
Blackheath v Orrell
Blaydon v Halifax
Bradford/Bingley v Roundhay
Broughton Park v Middlesbrough
Corstorphine v Howe of Fife
Dalziel HSFP v West of Scotland
Edinburgh Acads v Gosforth
Edinburgh Wands v Ayr
Glasgow Acads v Portobello
Hartlepool Rovers v Selkirk
Headingley v Rosslyn Park
Highland v Glasgow High/Kelvinside
Jedforest v Preston Lodge
Leicester v Sale
Liverpool St Helens v Aspatria
London Scottish v Wasps
London Welsh v Moseley
Maesteg v Coventry
Manchester v West Park
Monkstown v Bangor
Northampton v Bath
Northern v Melrose
Nuneaton v Morley
Old Wesley v Queen's U, Belfast
Otley v W Hartlepool
Plymouth Albion v Penarth
Rugby v Birkenhead Park
Sheffield v Durham City
Sidcup v Oxford
St Ives v Redruth

Stewart's-Melville FP v Kelso
SW Police v Met Police
Stirling County v Haddington
Tynedale v Hawick
Waterloo v Vale of Lune
Watsonians v Boroughmuir

Sunday, 25 March

Athlone v De La Salle/Palmerston
Old Wesley v UC Galway
Shannon v Galwegians
Terenure Coll v Lansdowne
Wanderers v UC Dublin

Monday, 26 March

Cardiff v Bristol

Tuesday, 27 March

Glamorgan Wands v Maesteg
Neath v Pontypridd
Penarth v Newport

Wednesday, 28 March

Bridgend v Pontypool
Cheltenham v Tredegar
Cross Keys v Abertillery
Glynneath v Llanelli
SW Police v Aberavon

Saturday, 31 March

Army v Royal Air Force (Twickenham)

RFU Leagues
Division 1
Saracens v Bath
Rosslyn Park v Bedford
Leicester v Moseley
Harlequins v Nottingham
Gloucester v Orrell
Bristol v Wasps
Division 2
Rugby v Liverpool St Helens
Sale v Blackheath
Headingley v Coventry
Gosforth v Northampton
London Irish v Richmond
Plymouth Albion v Waterloo

Division 3
Lydney v Askeans
London Scottish v Nuneaton
Roundhay v Sheffield
Fylde v Vale of Lune
Exeter v Wakefield
London Welsh v West Hartlepool
Area North
Preston Grasshoppers v Lichfield
Stoke v Morley
Stourbridge v Kendal
Walsall v Durham City
Winnington Park v Broughton Park
Area South
Maidstone v Clifton
Met Police v Camborne
Redruth v Cheltenham
Southend v Havant
Sudbury v Basingstoke

Aberavon v Newport
Abertillery v Swansea
Cardiff v Llanelli
CIYMS v Collegians
Glamorgan Wands v Penarth
Glasgow High/Kelvinside v
    London Scottish
Gordonians v Stirling County
Hawick v Boroughmuir
Heriot's FP v Ayr
Howe of Fife v Musselburgh
Jedforest v Currie
Kirkcaldy v West of Scotland
Monkstown v Ballinasloe
Pontypool v Maesteg
Pontypridd v Ebbw Vale
Selkirk v Glasgow Acads
S Glam Inst v SW Police
Tredegar v Neath
Watsonians v Melrose

Sunday, 1 April

Bective Rangers v Greystones

Tuesday, 3 April

Exeter v Bristol
Tredegar v Pontypool

Wednesday, 4 April

Coventry v Nuneaton
Newport v Bath
Swansea v S Glam Inst
SW Police v Maesteg

Saturday, 7 April

RFU County Championship: *Final*
 (Twickenham)
WRU Cup: *Semi-finals*
Aberavon v Llanelli
Abertillery v Tredegar
Bath v Bridgend
Blackheath v Nuneaton
Bristol v Harlequins
Broughton Park v Met Police
Camborne v St Ives
Cardiff v Nottingham
Coventry v Pontypool
Fylde v Orrell
Hartlepool Rovers v Novocastrians
Headingley v Bedford
Instonians v Glasgow High/Kelvinside
Kendal v Edinburgh Wands
Leicester v London Scottish
London Welsh v Swansea
Maesteg v Rosslyn Park
Middlesbrough v New Brighton
Monkstown v CIYMS
Morley v Harrogate
Neath v Gloucester
Newbridge v Ebbw Vale
Newport v Moseley
Northern v Otley
Penarth v Pontypridd
Portadown v Skerries
Plymouth Albion v Cheltenham
Rosslyn Park v Northampton
Sale v Wakefield
Sheffield v Liverpool St Helens
Stourbridge v Birkenhead Park
SW Police v Lydney
Wasps v Gosforth
Waterloo v Roundhay

Tuesday, 10 April

Brynamman v Neath

Wednesday, 11 April

Llanelli v Maesteg
Mountain Ash v Pontypridd
Richmond v Bedford
Rugby v Coventry

Friday, 13 April

Penarth v Public Schools Wands
Birkenhead Park v Wasps
Redruth v St Mary's Hosp
Sale v Preston Grasshoppers

Saturday, 14 April

Cardiff v Barbarians
Aberavon v London Welsh
Ballymena v Leicester
Bath v Bristol
Bedford v Sheffield
Bridgend v Maesteg
Broughton Park v Manchester
Ebbw Vale v Abertillery
Gosforth v Fylde
Halifax v Preston Grasshoppers
Hartlepool Rovers v Kendal
Liverpool St Helens v Morley
Llanelli v Northampton
Maidstone v Blackheath
Malone v Collegians
Neath v Coventry
Newbridge v Tredegar
NIFC v West of Scotland
Nottingham v Moseley
Orrell v Wakefield
Plymouth Albion v Askeans
Pontypool v Newport
Rugby v Met Police
Sale v Vale of Lune
Swansea v Rosslyn Park
SW Police v Pontypridd
Torquay Ath v Exeter
Waterloo v Wasps
Wrexham v Roundhay

Monday, 16 April

Swansea v Barbarians
Aberavon v Neath
Abertillery v Newbridge
Bath v Cheltenham
Bristol v Glamorgan Wands
Broughton Park v Davenport
Coventry v Headingley
Gloucester v Birkenhead Park
Maesteg v Maesteg Celtic
Moseley v Liverpool St Helens
New Brighton v Wasps
Newport v London Welsh
Northampton v Bedford
Nottingham v Fylde
Orrell v Waterloo
Plymouth Albion v Torquay Ath
Pontypool v Nuneaton
Pontypridd v Bridgend
Tredegar v Ebbw Vale
Vale of Lune v Northern

Wednesday, 18 April

England Students v Scotland Under-21

Saturday, 21 April

Belfast Collegians Centenary Match
Barnstaple v Redruth
Birkenhead Park v London Welsh
Bradford/Bingley v Kendal
Bristol v Newport
Coventry v SW Police
Durham City v Halifax
Glamorgan Wands v Bedford
Gloucester v Sale
Hartlepool Rovers v Edinburgh Wands
Headingley v Fylde
Instonians v City of Derry
Leicester v Gosforth
Llanelli v Bath
Met Police v Abertillery
Monkstown v Corinthians
Neath v Cardiff
New Brighton v Manchester
Nottingham v Northampton
Orrell v Vale of Lune
Pontypool v Pontypridd
Preston Grasshoppers v Davenport
Richmond v Newbridge
Rosslyn Park v Harlequins
Saracens v Liverpool St Helens
Sheffield v Winnington Park
Sidcup v Blackheath
Swansea v Aberavon
Torquay Ath v Penarth
Tredegar v Cross Keys
Wasps v Moseley
Waterloo v Morley
West of Scotland v Broughton Park

Sunday, 22 April

Brixham v Penarth

Tuesday, 24 April

Glynneath v Neath

Wednesday, 25 April

SRU Youth Leagues Final
  (Murrayfield)
Bedwas v Cardiff
Ebbw Vale v Pontypool
Gilfach Goch v Bridgend
Glamorgan Wands v Swansea
Maesteg v Newbridge

Saturday, 28 April

Scotland v Wales (Under-21)
Munster Cup Final
Ulster Cup Final

RFU Leagues
Division 1
Bedford v Bristol
Nottingham v Gloucester
Moseley v Harlequins
Bath v Leicester
Orrell v Rosslyn Park
Wasps v Saracens
Division 2
Waterloo v Gosforth
Richmond v Headingley
Blackheath v London Irish
Coventry v Plymouth Albion
Northampton v Rugby
Liverpool St Helens v Sale
Division 3
Vale of Lune v Exeter
Sheffield v Fylde
Askeans v Roundhay
Nuneaton v Lydney
West Hartlepool v London Scottish
Wakefield v London Welsh
Area North
Broughton Park v Stourbridge
Durham City v Stoke
Lichfield v Walsall
Morley v Winnington Park
Northern v Preston Grasshoppers
Area South
Camborne v Sudbury
Cheltenham v Met Police
Clifton v Southend
Havant v Redruth
Salisbury v Maidstone

Aberavon v Cross Keys
Abertillery v Penarth
Bridgend v SW Police
Cardiff v Newbridge
Glamorgan Wands v Ebbw Vale
Llanelli v Wrexham
Maesteg v Pontypridd
Newport v Neath
Swansea v Pontypool
West of Scotland v Instonians

Monday, 30 April

Pontypridd v Glamorgan Wands

Saturday, 5 May

RFU Cup Final (Twickenham)
WRU Cup Final (Cardiff)
Camborne Sevens (Camborne RFC)
Fylde v Broughton Park
Hartlepool Rovers v RF Oakes' XV

Saturday, 12 May

Middlesex Sevens (Twickenham)

Thursday, 24 May

FRANCE v ROMANIA

Saturday, 26 May

French Clubs Cup Final
  (Parc des Princes)

MAJOR TOURS

NEW ZEALANDERS TO BRITAIN AND IRELAND 1989

October

14	**Cardiff**
18	**Pontypool**
21	**Swansea**
25	**Neath**
28	**Llanelli**
31	**Newport**

November

4	**WALES** (Cardiff)
8	**Leinster** (Dublin)
11	**Munster** (Cork)
14	**Connacht** (Galway)
18	**IRELAND** (Lansdowne Road)
21	**Ulster** (Belfast)
25	**Barbarians** (Twickenham)

AUSTRALIANS TO FRANCE 1989

October

18	**French Selection** (Toulouse)
21	**French Selection** (Béziers)
25	**French Selection** (Toulon)
28	**French Selection** (Grenoble)
31	**French Selection** (Clermont-Ferrand)

November

4	**FRANCE** (Strasbourg)
7	**French Selection** (Paris)
11	**FRANCE** (Lille)

FIJIANS TO FRANCE, SCOTLAND AND ENGLAND 1989

October

11	**French Selection** (Nîmes)
14	**French Selection** (Bergerac)
18	**French Selection** (Basque Coast)
22	**French Barbarians** (Bordeaux)
24	**Glasgow District** (Glasgow)
28	**SCOTLAND** (Murrayfield)

November

4	**ENGLAND** (Twickenham)

COUNTY CHAMPIONSHIP FIXTURES 1989-90

NORTHERN DIVISION

September

30 **Cheshire v Cumbria**
  (New Brighton)
  Northumberland v Lancashire
  (Northern)
  Yorkshire v Durham

October

3 **Durham v Northumberland**
  Lancashire v Cumbria
  Yorkshire v Cheshire
7 **Cheshire v Northumberland**
  (Wilmslow)
  Durham v Lancashire
  Yorkshire v Cumbria
17 **Cheshire v Lancashire**
  (Birkenhead Park)
  Cumbria v Durham
  Northumberland v Yorkshire
  (Percy Park)
21 **Cumbria v Northumberland**
  Durham v Cheshire
  Lancashire v Yorkshire

MIDLAND DIVISION

Group A
September

26 **Staffordshire v Leicestershire**

October

3 **Leicestershire v North Midlands**
  (Leicester)
17 **North Midlands v Staffordshire**
  (Moseley)

Group B
September

26 **Notts, Lincs & Derbys v**
  Warwickshire (Leicester)

October

3 **Warwickshire v East Midlands**
17 **East Midlands v Notts,**
  Lincs & Derbys
31 **Semi-finals:**
  Winners Group A v
  Runners-up Group B
  Winners Group B v
  Runners-up Group A

November

28 **Final play-off**

SOUTH & SOUTH-WEST DIVISION

Division 1
September

30 **Cornwall v Berkshire**
  (Redruth)
  Gloucestershire v Dorset/Wilts

October

7 **Berkshire v Gloucestershire**
  (Reading)
  Cornwall v Dorset/Wilts (Redruth)
21 **Dorset/Wilts v Berkshire**
  Gloucestershire v Cornwall
  (Cheltenham)

Division 2
September

30 **Oxfordshire v Devon**
  Somerset v Buckinghamshire
  (Taunton)

October

7   **Buckinghamshire v Oxfordshire**
     (Aylesbury)
     Devon v Somerset (Exeter)
21   **Devon v Buckinghamshire**
     Oxfordshire v Somerset

LONDON DIVISION

Group A
November

29   **Middlesex v Kent**

December

6   **Hertfordshire v Middlesex**
     (Croxley Green)
13   **Kent v Hertfordshire**

Group B
November

29   **Surrey v Eastern Counties**
     Sussex v Hampshire (Brighton)

December

6   **Hampshire v Eastern Counties**
     (US Portsmouth)
     Sussex v Surrey (Crawley)
13   **Eastern Counties v Sussex**
     (Grange Road)
     Surrey v Hampshire
20   **Final play-off:**
     Winners Group A v
     Winners Group B

March

3   **County Championship Semi-finals**

April

7   **County Championship Final**
     (Twickenham)

MAJOR FIXTURES IN BRITAIN, IRELAND AND FRANCE 1989-90

October 1989

4　**FRANCE v BRITISH ISLES**
(Paris)

28　**SCOTLAND v FIJI** (Murrayfield)

November

4　**WALES v NEW ZEALAND**
(Cardiff)
ENGLAND v FIJI (Twickenham)
FRANCE v AUSTRALIA
(Strasbourg)

11　**FRANCE v AUSTRALIA**
(Lille)

18　**IRELAND v NEW ZEALAND**
(Lansdowne Road)

25　**Barbarians v New Zealanders**
(Twickenham)

December

2　**RFU Divisional Championship**

9　**SCOTLAND v ROMANIA**
(Murrayfield)
Scotland B v Ireland B (Murrayfield)
RFU Divisional Championship

12　**Oxford U v Cambridge U**
(Twickenham)

16　**Ireland Trial** (Lansdowne Road)
RFU Divisional Championship

January 1990

6　**Scotland Trial** (Murrayfield)

20　**ENGLAND v IRELAND**
(Twickenham)
WALES v FRANCE
(Cardiff)

21　**France B v Scotland B**

February

3　**IRELAND v SCOTLAND**
(Lansdowne Road)
FRANCE v ENGLAND (Paris)

17　**ENGLAND v WALES**
(Twickenham)
SCOTLAND v FRANCE
(Murrayfield)

March

3　**WALES v SCOTLAND**
(Cardiff)
FRANCE v IRELAND (Paris)
RFU County Championship Semi-finals

10　**Army v Royal Navy** (Twickenham)

14　**UAU Final** (Twickenham)

17　**SCOTLAND v ENGLAND**
(Murrayfield)

24　**IRELAND v WALES**
(Lansdowne Road)
Royal Navy v Royal Air Force
(Twickenham)

31　**Army v Royal Air Force**
(Twickenham)

April

7　**RFU County Championship Final**
(Twickenham)

May

5　**RFU Cup Final** (Twickenham)
WRU Cup Final (Cardiff)

12　**Middlesex Sevens** (Twickenham)

24　**FRANCE v ROMANIA**

26　**French Clubs Cup Final** (Paris)